Investigations Operations Manual 2003

- Department of Health & Human Services
- Food & Drug Administration
- Office of Regulatory Affairs
- Office of Regional Operations
- Division of Field Investigations

Foreword 2003

The *Investigations Operations Manual* (IOM) is the primary source of guidance regarding Agency policy and procedures for field investigators and inspectors. This extends to all individuals who perform field investigational activities in support of the Agency's public mission. Accordingly, it directs the conduct of all fundamental field investigational activities. Adherence to this manual is paramount to assure quality, consistency, and efficiency in field operations. Since the IOM is the primary source of policy, the specific information in this manual is supplemented, not superseded, by other manuals and field guidance documents. Recognizing that this manual may not cover all situations or variables arising from field operations, any significant departures from IOM established procedures must have the concurrence of district management with appropriate documentation as needed.

In its role of protecting the public health, ORA developed a vision, a mission statement and specific core values. These are depicted in the pages immediately following this "Foreword".

There are many changes and additions to the Year 2003 IOM. We have revised instructions regarding release of information. As much as possible we have updated the FACTS screen shots used as examples so they are from the current release of FACTS. We have finally included the Import for Exports instructions in 501.7 and 602. We've also added updated information on photo identification and submission when taking digital photographs for evidentiary purposes. We continue to field a number of questions that can be answered by referral to the Data Codes Manual such as definitions for operation codes. That manual, while not up-to-date for FACTS, still contains agency policy. As much as possible, without re-creating the Data Codes Manual in the IOM, we have tried to provide information relative to code definitions and how/when to use various codes in preparing C/Rs and the EI Record. Please take time to review sections of the IOM that apply to your work.

Since December 1996, the IOM has been posted to ORA's Internet Home Page, http://www.fda.gov/ora/inspect ref/iom/iomtc.html. The entire IOM is available there, with all graphics included. Future updates to the IOM will be done periodically during the year to this on-line version. Hard copy publication will be done yearly. Remember, whether reviewing the "hard copy" or the "on-line' version of the IOM, the most recent version is the document of record.

We are committed to the continual improvement of the quality and usefulness of the IOM. Suggestions for the 2004 edition of the IOM or recommended changes, deletions, editions for updates to the IOM may be sent to the Division of Field Investigations (HFC-130), 5600 Fishers Lane, Rockville, MD 20857 or via e-mail to Director, DFI. You can also send e-mail for the IOM to IOM@ORA.FDA.GOV. If you are recommending a change or revision, please use the IOM Change Request Form available from the web site and included in the IOM as Appendix H.

John M.Taylor, III, Associate Commissioner for Regulatory Affairs

FDA/Office of Regulatory Affairs

NOTE: This manual is reference material for investigators and other FDA personnel. The document does not bind FDA and does not confer any rights, privileges, benefits or immunities for or on any person(s).

ORA VISION

We are an empowered, flexible public health team that is customer oriented and results driven to produce high quality work and develop innovative ways to leverage resources. We focus on assuring compliance of FDA regulated products to achieve consumer protection.

ORA MISSION

Achieve effective and efficient compliance of regulated products through high quality, science-based work that results in maximizing consumer protection.

ORA CORE VALUES

- We value our people.

- We are a public health agency with law enforcement responsibilities.

- There are many knowledgeable, dedicated people in government agencies and industry.

- Properly trained, empowered employees who are held accountable can produce high quality work.

- Outcomes are important.

- The changes are here to stay - Government Reinvention makes common sense and can be applied to make ORA a more effective organization - we are under a mandate to change.

- Most of industry shares the same goal as FDA - to produce safe and effective products.

- Corrective action is our goal through the most efficient means - using more stringent actions for those who will not comply.

- We can achieve compliance not only with enforcement actions, but also with tools such as: workshops, meetings, and joint problem solving.

- We must recognize that we must prioritize what we do, considering the needs and expectations of our customers. Everyone contributes to the solution.

CONTENTS 2003

CHAPTER 1 - ADMINISTRATION

CONTENTS

SUBCHAPTER 110 - TRAVEL

All official travel must be authorized and approved with a valid travel order (T.O.). Emergency travel can be approved and the travel order prepared and authorized after the fact. "After the fact" travel orders (T.O.s) should be utilized on a very limited basis.

The federal travel regulations contained in 41 CFR 301, Department of Health and Human Services (DHHS) Travel Manual, and the Food and Drug Administration (FDA) supplements thereto, govern official travel. Become familiar with these documents. All material contained in the Investigations Operations Manual (IOM) must be used in conjunction with, and subject to, federal travel regulations. Additional travel information can be obtained from the Office of Financial Management (OFM) Intranet home page http://intranet.fda.gov/ofm/default.htm.

For foreign travel, be aware that there are differences in reporting requirements and reimbursable expenses. See the Guide to International Inspections and Travel, Chapter 1, Subchapter 110 - Travel, for specifics.

Effective March 1, 2000, federal employees must put most official travel-related charges on government-issued credit cards, with exceptions only for expenses that are either relatively minor or inconvenient for credit card usage such as parking, local transportation, tips, phone calls, and certain expenses for which credit cards are not accepted.

FDA selected Carlson-Wagonlit as the Agency-wide Travel Management Center. Carlson-Wagonlit operates from one central reservation center located in San Antonio, Texas. This reservation center has the capability to book airline tickets, hotel reservations, and car rentals via telephone, facsimile (fax), and through their on-line web reservation system. You are encouraged to use the "online" method when making reservations because of the flexibility associated with this service. The system incorporates Federal Government travel policies which include the city pair airfare contract program and Federal Travel Regulations and is structured to require justification if you want to deviate from General Services Administration's (GSA) regulations. A policy has been established with the FDA so that your government-issued credit card will be your primary method of billing and payment when you book flights, make hotel reservations, or reserve a rental car. Additional information can be obtained by contacting your Administrative Officer (AO) or visiting OFM's website at http://intranet.fda.gov/ofm/default.htm.

111   COMMON CARRIER

Request round-trip tickets when it can be expected you will use them. This reduces paperwork costs, even though there may be no savings on the tickets themselves.

You should cancel reserved tickets if you will not be using them. Failure to do so may result in charges levied by the carrier. Note the date and time of your cancellation, and the name or code number of the agent that you advised. Unused tickets must be returned to your AO or Travel Management Center.

Requirements which authorize you to use cash payments for procurement of common carrier transportation and related expenses, in lieu of your government-issued credit card, or centrally billed account, are specified in 41 CFR 301-72.200 and 301-51.100. Cash payments are generally permitted:

1.   To obtain passenger transportation services, in an emergency, for any amount when authorized by your District Director (DD) and documented on your T.O. Otherwise, cash and personal credit cards may not be used for transportation expenses exceeding $100.00.

2.   To pay air excess baggage charges up to $15.00 for each leg of a trip.

When cash is used, claim a reimbursement on your travel voucher and submit your ticket stubs or other appropriate receipts. You must also explain the circumstances for using cash on your travel voucher. See IOM 117 for mandatory statements required on a travel voucher.

111.1 Air

It is FDA's policy to require all travelers to use coach class service for official travel. A contract air carrier must be used unless one of three approved exceptions is met and your DD approves another carrier. See your fiscal clerk for further information. Justification for use of non-contract carriers must be approved on the T. O. by the Regional Food and Drug Director (RFDD), DD or AO, or on the voucher, if "after the fact."

The Deputy Commissioner for Management and Systems must authorize First Class travel. The use of first class travel must be pre-approved, and such approval will not be granted, even for medical reasons, unless business class is not available.

Frequent traveler benefits accumulated while traveling on official business may not be used to upgrade to first-class air accommodations, although such benefits may be used to upgrade to premium, other than first-class, accommodations. You are allowed to retain all frequent traveler benefits, including frequent flyer miles, earned on official government travel for your personal use.

111.2 Auto Rental

GSA and the Department of Defense (DOD) both provide employees with a nationwide commercial auto rental program. The Federal Travel Directory, published monthly on floppy diskette, contains a list of vehicle leasing companies participating in this program. Agency policy dictates leasing the least expensive auto to satisfy the transportation requirements.

Commercial auto rental is available when specifically authorized by a special or blanket T.O. You will be reimbursed for rental expense when it is properly vouchered and your receipt is attached to your travel voucher.

Optional Collision Damage Insurance known as CDW will not be reimbursed. Participating rental companies have agreed to settle any claim for damages with the FDA. It is important to note that only damages incident to official travel will be covered by this agreement. If an investigation shows your vehicle damage or personal injury was the result of your unauthorized use of a rental vehicle, you may be personally liable for all related costs. See IOM 112.3 - Liability.

CDW is required for foreign travel and will be reimbursed. See the Guide to International Inspections and Travel, 111.5 – Auto Rental.

111.3 Taxi

Reimbursement for the use of taxicabs will only be allowed when authorized on your T.O. Allowable tips are 15% of the reimbursable fare. Receipts are required for fares over $75.00.

You will be reimbursed for the usual cab and/or airport limousine fares plus tip from your home/office to the common carrier terminal on the day you depart on an official overnight trip, and upon your return. In lieu of cab, you may use your personal car at a mileage rate not to exceed the cab fare plus tip. See your administrative personnel for current mileage rates, the maximum allowable taxicab fares, and other pertinent details.

111.4 Accident Insurance

The government will not pay or reimburse you if you purchase accident insurance. Obtaining accident insurance is at your expense since you are covered while on official business by workmen's compensation insurance. See IOM 111.2 for payment of insurance on rental cars.

Many insurance policies will not cover you if you perform any duties connected with your job while on an interstate transportation carrier. This could affect you if you perform on-board inspections under the Interstate Travel Sanitation Program during a trip.

111.5 Gainsharing

The Government Employees Incentive Awards Act, 5 USC Paragraphs 4501-4507, authorizes an agency to pay a cash award for "efficiency" or "economy". FDA in conjunction with the National Treasury Employees Union (NTEU) implemented a Gainsharing Travel Savings Program which rewards you if you save the FDA money while you are on temporary travel (TDY). Your participation is optional. The Agency's gainsharing policy as well as filing instructions for gainsharing claims can be found by accessing OFM's website: http://intranet.fda.gov/ofm/default.htm.

112 GOVERNMENT FURNISHED VEHICLES (GFVs)

GFVs are provided for official purposes only. The term "official purpose" shall be interpreted strictly, and not construed to mean mingling of official business with non-official business. Using a GFV for sightseeing, personal business, personal convenience or preference will be construed as unauthorized use of a GFV. The distance involved in any such misuse is irrelevant. The following is an excerpt from the DHHS Travel Manual Appendix A 1-2.6a., dated May 31, 1988 which further defines official purpose:

"Use of Government-furnished Vehicles."

a. "Use limited to official purposes - When a Government furnished vehicle is used by an employee for official travel, its use shall be limited to official purposes (31 U.S.C. 638a) which include transportation between places where the employee's presence is required incident to official business; between such places and places of temporary lodging when public transportation is unavailable or its use is impractical; and between either of the above places and suitable eating places, drug stores, barber shops, places of worship, cleaning establishments, and similar places necessary for the sustenance, comfort, or health of the employee in order to foster the continued efficient performance of Government business."

You are responsible at all times for the proper care, operation, maintenance, and protection of a GFV. If you willfully or knowingly use or authorize the use of a GFV for other than official purposes, you are subject to suspension or removal.

112.1 Interagency Motor Pool

GFVs for district operations are furnished by the regional GSA motor pool. Be guided by the district operating procedures in effect for the appropriate regional pool.

Vehicle Operation - You are required to have a valid state, District of Columbia, or commonwealth operator's permit for the type vehicle to be operated, and a valid DHHS identification document (i.e. Agency ID card, credentials, building pass, etc.).

Each district has working arrangements for the repair and maintenance of vehicles, either with GSA contractors or the GSA motor pool. It is your responsibility to adhere to those safety and maintenance checks. Do not operate cars known to be mechanically unsafe. Handle emergency repairs in travel status in accordance with your District and GSA motor pool procedures.

Purchase gas and oil for your GFV with GSA Credit Cards. Make emergency purchases with cash only when the GSA Credit Card is refused. Your receipts are required by the GSA motor pool. Provide for the safe and proper overnight storage of GFVs while you are in travel status, and put the charges on your travel voucher.

You are responsible for all traffic violations, including parking fines, you incur during the use and operation of a GFV. See DHHS Material Management Manual Section 103-38-052.1.

Allowance - While on official business, you may be reimbursed for parking fees or overnight storage charges. Put these charges on your travel voucher. Receipts are required when available.

Bridge, ferry and road tolls may be paid in cash. Put these charges on your travel voucher. Receipts are only required for amounts over $75.00.

3

112.2 Accidents

Immediate Action - Render first aid. If you are injured, obtain emergency treatment.

Information to be obtained: (1) description of vehicles involved, including license numbers, (2) name, address and other pertinent information about drivers and owners of other vehicles, (3) names, addresses and signed statements of witnesses, (4) names, official affiliation of investigating police officers, (5) photographs of the scene and the damage, (6) make no statements as to responsibility for the accident, except to your supervisor or investigating official.

Reporting - Report the accident to the police after rendering emergency first aid to the injured. Telephone your supervisor and the chief of the motor pool from which the vehicle is assigned, unless your supervisor advises you the district will handle it.

1.   Complete SF 91, Operator's Report of Motor Vehicle Accident. If there are witnesses, prepare SF-94, Statement of Witness. Submit these promptly with a narrative report of all circumstances. Report the actual damage done to all parties, vehicles or property involved.

2.   File reports to comply with all local and state laws dealing with accident reporting. Keep copies of all reports made and attach them to the federal accident report.

3.   Check with your own insurance carrier for their requirements.

4.   Immediately submit to your supervisor any notice, summons, legal paper or claim, which may subsequently arise from the accident.

5.   Check with your district safety officer to determine if additional reports or information are needed.

112.3 Liability

The Federal Drivers Act (28 U.S.C. 2679(a)-(e)) was enacted to protect government drivers from personal liability while driving within the scope of their employment. This means you must be on official business to be covered. It relieves you from the burden of acquiring private automobile liability insurance for driving while on the job.

The government's exclusive liability provided by this Act is predicated on its status as employer, without regard to whether the vehicle involved is government owned or privately owned.

112.4 Use of a GFV Between Your Residence and Place of Employment

Use of government owned or leased autos between your residence and place of employment is approved by the Secretary, DHHS, for certain job series as stated in FDA Staff Manual Guide (SMG) 2173.1. The use of a DHHS-16 "Request To Use Government Furnished Vehicle For Transportation Between Domicile and Place of Employment" is no longer required, however, local management may continue to use the form or establish a verbal approval process, if desired. The Daily Log of Government Vehicle (Form FDA-3369) must be maintained by all approved persons using a GFV, assuring that all items indicated on the form are completed for each trip. The DHHS now requires that each person taking a GFV home, in order to perform field work, must indicate in Column 10 on the Form 3369, the location of their residence. The Daily Log must be kept for at least a period of three years and must be available for audit purposes. The use of Form DHHS-17 "Quarterly Report on Use of Government-Owned or Leased Vehicles Between Domicile and Place of Employment" is no longer required.

112.5 Care and Custody of U.S. Vehicles

GSA has issued instructions on the use and protection of U.S. Government vehicles, Government National Credit Cards, and car keys. The parts of these instructions applicable to you while the car is in your custody are:

1.   The car should be locked when parked in public areas, in private lots, or in open government parking areas.

2.   The operator is responsible for the keys and the credit card. They should be removed from the vehicle and carried whenever the vehicle is parked.

3.   The keys and credit card are returned to the motor pool office when the vehicle is returned. These items should be kept in a safe place at the office if the vehicle is stored at other than a motor pool location.

4.   The credit card must be removed when a vehicle is left at a garage or service station and the keys remain with the garage or station attendant.

5.   The credit card may only be used to purchase fuel and lubricants or other items listed on the back of the card for the vehicle identified, and not used for other vehicles.

6.   Before signing a service ticket, check for accuracy. Be sure the imprinted address is legible, and write the vehicle mileage (odometer reading) on the ticket.

7.   The use of tobacco products is prohibited in government-owned or commercial, leased vehicles

113   PRIVATELY OWNED VEHICLE (POV)

On official business, you may use your POV instead of a GFV, if authorized. However, reimbursement for mileage will not exceed the cost of using a GFV. You should carry a set of government accident reporting forms whenever you use your POV for official business. See IOM 112.2 for accident reporting requirements.

Allowances - In general, the mileage allowance is in lieu of all expenses of operating your POV, except tolls. Unless otherwise authorized, reimbursement is limited to the cost of travel by common carrier. Standard highway guide mileage may be used in lieu of odometer readings for direct travel from one town to another. Explain any extra mileage on your travel voucher.

113.1 Accidents

The Federal Employee's Compensation Act (Workmen's Compensation) protects employees against losses due to personal injuries received while operating POVs on official business.

Under the Federal Driver's Act [28 U.S.C. 2679(a)-(e)], you are immune from any civil liability to other parties for property damage, personal injury, or death resulting from operation of a vehicle within the scope of your employment. This immunity applies whether the vehicle involved is a GFV or POV. The government would defend any such claim or suit, and would pay any damage award to the injured party.

If an accident was caused by your negligent operation of a vehicle, and your vehicle is damaged, the cost of repairing your vehicle will not be paid for by the government. You should look to your own private insurance carrier for reimbursement, payable under the terms of your own automobile insurance policy. You are protected from liability by the Federal Drivers Act. See IOM 112.3 for further information on this.

If the accident is determined not to have been caused by your negligence, the provisions of the Military Personnel and Civilian Employees Claims Act (31 U.S.C. 240-243) would be applicable. Under this Act, you would be reimbursed for the deductible portion of the repair not covered by your own automobile insurance policy, up to a maximum of $250.00 deductible. (You may also collect from the other party's insurance.) Form DHHS-481, Employee Claim for Loss or Damage to Personal Property, should be obtained from, completed, and submitted to the Personal Property Management Section (HFA-225) Room 9-82, Parklawn Building, 5600 Fishers Lane, Rockville, MD 20857, with evidence establishing that the use of a POV was authorized for official purposes and that the accident was not caused by your negligence.

Employee Liability - see IOM 112.3.

Reporting - Report vehicle accidents as instructed in IOM 112.2.

114   PER DIEM AND SUBSISTENCE

Subsistence is the cost of lodging, meals, tips, and the miscellaneous expenses you incur while in travel status. Per Diem is based on the actual cost of lodging, plus a set amount for "Meals and Incidental Expenses" (M&IE), not to exceed the maximum rate for the prescribed city or area. Note: For domestic travel only, report lodging taxes separate from lodging expenses and claim them in the "Other" column on your travel voucher. Foreign travel taxes still remain a part of your lodging expenses.

Lodging expenses should be paid using your government-issued credit card, when possible. The credit card bill will be mailed directly to you. It is your responsibility to pay the bill on time. The FDA will reimburse late charges on your bill only when you can show the late payment was due to late reimbursement of funds by the FDA.

Accurately record all of your expenditures. Document the date of your departure from each point where your duty is performed. Be guided by your district's policy for where to record this information, e.g. in an administrative diary, etc. If your district permits entry of this information in a regulatory diary, be certain that administrative information can be readily distinguished from regulatory entries.

Administrative Notes - Your regulatory notes (See IOM 190) should not contain notes of a purely administrative nature (documentation of travel, expenses [tolls, sample costs, etc.], fiscal data, mileage, etc.) These administrative notes can be documented in some kind of an administrative diary. They do not need to be kept in a permanent record other than the completed Travel Voucher, Claim for Reimbursement for Expenditures on Official Business, Receipt for Samples, etc. Follow your district's requirements for maintaining this information.

114.1   Per Diem Rates

Consult your supervisor or administrative personnel for specific rates for specific locations.

Per Diem commences when you depart your home, office, or other point of departure, and terminates when you return to your home, office, or other point. This applies whether you are traveling by auto or by common carrier. See IOM Exhibit 110-D.

The M&IE Allowance is 3/4 of the daily rate on the first and last day of travel when overnight travel is involved, and the full daily rate for each intervening day.

1.   M&IE may apply where there is no overnight lodging. However, M&IE will not be allowed for periods of time less than twelve hours.

Your work time plus your total commute time must be greater than twelve hours for you to be eligible for M&IE.

114.2   Hospitalized In Travel Status

If, while you are in travel status, you become hospitalized by illness or injury not due to your own misconduct, your per diem continues (even if covered by your health insurance carrier) provided you do not receive hospitalization (or reimbursement therefore) under any Federal statute such as Workmen's Compensation, VA, or military hospital.

Your per diem is calculated on the lodgings-plus system, not to exceed the per diem rate allowed. Check with your district supervisor or administrative personnel.

115   CHANGE OF OFFICIAL STATION

The complexity of regulations pertaining to allowable expenses, per diem, advance trips to seek housing, etc. necessitate consultation with your supervisor or administrative personnel.

116   ADVANCE OF FUNDS

You will use your government-issued credit card to obtain a cash advance from an ATM machine, for official government business only. Make sure your T.O. contains a statement that you are authorized to use an ATM to obtain cash advances and the amount authorized. ATM cash advances may be used to purchase samples.

117   CLAIMS FOR REIMBURSEMENT

Submit your claim for reimbursement after each trip unless instructed otherwise by your supervisor. Submit expenses for special travel orders promptly (within 5 days) after each trip. If local travel only, submit expenses on an SF 1164, "Claim for Reimbursement for Expenditures on Official Business." Claim expenses for all other travel on an SF 1012, "Travel Voucher." (See IOM Exhibit 110-D.)

Preparation of Claim on Travel Voucher - Clerical procedures vary from district to district, so consult your supervisor or administrative office for instructions. State all items in chronological order. Show your mode of transportation and if accompanied, the names of the other travelers.

Show your date of departure and return to your official duty station, and when periods of leave commence and end. Show all points where costs are incurred.

Mandatory Statements Required on Travel Voucher - See IOM Exhibit 110-B for allowable expenses, receipts required, etc.

1.   Leave Taken in Travel Status - If you take any type of leave while in travel status, include a statement on your travel voucher that you apprised your timekeeper of the amount and type of leave taken. The timekeeper must initial your voucher to show that the leave has been recorded.

Reimbursable Expenses - Explain the necessity for unusual expenditures such as rental equipment, stenographic services and emergency charges (See IOM Exhibit 110-B). The following cash purchases are reimbursable when accompanied by necessary receipts (see Documentation below):

1.   Travel costs such as road and bridge tolls, storage and parking for government cars, and handling of official (not personal) baggage.

2.   Costs for samples and the necessary casual labor charges for their collection and packing. (See IOM 405.1(d) Official Samples.)

3.   Telephone and telegraph expenses. Document that the use was for official purposes. For local telephone calls, show the number of calls only and the total cost each day.

4.   Emergency purchases (flashlights, batteries, photographic film, jars, or dry ice for samples, etc.)

5.   Coveralls or lab coat laundry while in travel status

6.   Personal laundry while in travel status within continental U.S. (CONUS) for four or more consecutive nights

Documentation - Except for samples, all cash payments should be supported by itemized invoices or receipts signed by vendor, if possible. If you are unable to furnish receipts when submitting your voucher, explain that on the voucher.

Receipts for registration fees at meetings are required regardless of the amount. See IOM Exhibit 110-D and IOM 111 for receipts required for cash expenditures for transportation and IOM Exhibit 110-B.

118   TELEPHONE COMMUNICATIONS

Commercial – Local, official telephone calls are reimbursable. When placing an official call from a non-government phone, use your government-issued calling card, call collect if permitted by your District's policy, or call commercially and claim reimbursement on your travel voucher.

Commercial calls from hotels or motels should be made using your government-issued calling card, whenever possible. If not possible, they should be claimed on your travel voucher and be supported by the phone bill. Calls made using a personal credit card or similar billing arrangements should be claimed on your travel voucher if a receipt is available at the time of voucher preparation. Otherwise, a follow-up petty cash voucher should be submitted, supported by a copy of your itemized phone bill, and certification the charge was for official government business.

Calls To Residence - FDA has established the following guidelines under which an employee in travel status for more than one night within the U.S. may be reimbursed for telephone calls home:

1. Calls should be made as economically as possible.

2. Calls should be made on the FTS network when possible. If not possible, calls should be made using your government-issued calling card. Telephone calls made with government-issued calling cards are automatically billed to the FDA. You are reimbursed through the voucher system when a surcharge is imposed for credit card calls from the traveler's motel/hotel room. Refer to Staff Manual Guide 2343.2 to determine the maximum allowable reimbursement for telephone calls home.

Districts that have differing union-negotiated agreements regarding telephone calls home while in travel status should be guided by those agreements.

119   ITINERARIES

Since situations arise which necessitate contacting you while in travel status, provide your supervisor with a travel itinerary listing where and how you can be reached.

SUBCHAPTER 120 - LEAVE

Annual, compensatory, and sick leave is charged in one-quarter hour increments. Prior approval must be obtained from your supervisor for all leave, whenever possible. If this is not possible, advise your supervisor within the first hour of your workday when you will not be on duty. Questions relating to leave should be directed to your immediate supervisor.

If it is necessary for you to take leave while in travel status, notify your supervisor immediately. Include a specific statement on your travel voucher that you did so.

Refer to the NTEU Collective Bargaining Agreement dated 10/1/99 or the agreement negotiated at your local site for additional information regarding leave issues.

120.1 Family and Medical Leave

Under the Family and Medical Leave Act of 1993 (FMLA), covered employees are entitled to a total of twelve administrative workweeks of leave without pay (LWOP) during any twelve month period for: birth and care of new-borns, the care of a spouse, child, or parent — with a serious health condition, adoption or foster care, or a serious health condition.

You may substitute annual and/or sick leave, if appropriate, for unpaid leave under FMLA.

120.2 Leave for Organ Donation

You are entitled to paid leave (excused absence) each calendar year (in addition to annual and sick leave) to serve as a bone marrow donor or organ donor. Consult your AO for the specific number of days of paid leave allowed for the different donation programs.

120.3 Voluntary Leave Transfer Program

If affected by a medical or family medical emergency, you may make written application to become a leave recipient. The approval/disapproval of an application will be based on the determination that your absence from duty is, or is expected to be, at least 24 hours of unpaid leave.

120.4 EASE

EASE (Enterprise Administrative Support Environment) is the agency's automated administrative system. Every employee can view their own official and operational data in the CORE module, update their location data, and view their timekeeping records in the ETA (EASE Time and Attendance) module, which includes leave balances and timecards.

To access the system, ORA headquarters employees should contact either Terri Ausfresser (301) 1827-1201 or Michele Berger (301) 827-1452 for an EASE password. Field employees should contact their Regional/District EASE Lead AO for assistance in determining their EASE Regional Automated Data Processing (ADP) Coordinator. A security statement must be completed and retained by the Information Systems Security Officer (ISSO). The EASE Helpdesk can be reached at (301) 998-6777 for user support. Additional information about EASE is available on FDA's Intranet.

121 ANNUAL LEAVE

Rate of Accrual

Length of Service	Hrs/Pay Period
Less than 3 years	4
3-14 years	6
15 or more years	8

Maximum Accumulation - Unused annual leave can accumulate up to 240 hours. (Under special circumstances some employees may have more than 240 hours) Annual leave in excess of 240 hours at the beginning of the first pay period of the new leave year is lost. If loss is due to administrative error, emergencies (exigencies) of public business, or sickness of the employee, and leave has been approved prior to the beginning of the third pay period before the end of the leave year, restoration may be requested.

Taking Annual Leave - As soon as you enter on duty you may use annual leave as accrued. Request annual leave from your supervisor by completing an SF 71- "Application for Leave," or other methods "he/she approves."

Advanced Annual Leave - You may be granted all annual leave that will accrue up to the end of the last pay period of the leave year, except that annual leave may not be advanced to the following:

1. To a temporary employee beyond the date set for the expiration of his temporary appointment, or the end of the leave year, whichever is earlier.

2. To any employee if there is likelihood they will retire or be separated from the service before the date when they will have earned the leave.

122 SICK LEAVE

Rate of Accrual - Each employee earns four hours of sick leave each pay period. There is no maximum limit on accumulation of sick leave. Sick Leave may be authorized for the following reasons:

1. Inability to work - Sick leave may be taken when you are unable to work because of sickness or injury. Consult your supervisor for leave options covering on-the-job injury. If in travel status, consult your supervisor.

2. Medical Treatment - for medical, dental, or optical examination or treatment.

3. Contagious Disease - (a) when a member of your family has a contagious disease and requires your care and attendance. A contagious disease is one ruled by health authorities having jurisdiction as subject to quarantine or requiring isolation of the patient; (b) when your presence on duty would jeopardize the health of others because of exposure to a contagious disease.

4. Adoption and adoption-related activities

5. Care for a family member with a serious health condition. Most employees may use a total of up to 12 administrative workweeks of sick leave each leave year to care for a family member with a serious health condition. The employee must, however, maintain a sick leave balance of 80 hours.

6. Care for a family member as a result of a physical or mental illness, injury, pregnancy, childbirth, or medical, dental, or optical examination or treatment. Under the Family Friendly Leave Act, FFLA, an employee is entitled to up to 40 hours of sick leave to care for a family member. An additional 64 hours of sick leave may be used if an employee's leave balance is over 80 hours. The 104 hours of sick leave available for family care counts toward the 12 administrative workweeks mentioned in number 5.

7. Bereavement - Make arrangements necessitated by the death of a family member or to attend a funeral of a family member.

Supporting Evidence – Any grant of sick leave in excess of three working days must be supported by a medical certificate or other evidence administratively acceptable. Advanced Sick Leave not to exceed thirty days may be advanced in cases of serious disability or ailments.

Advanced sick leave may be granted during a period of absence for maternity reasons when it is expected the employee will return to duty, and is supported by a medical certificate.

123   COMPENSATORY TIME OFF

Compensatory (Comp) time off is absence from duty for the equivalent of approved overtime previously worked.

Employees must use compensatory leave by the end of the eighth pay period after the pay period in which it is earned. If not used by this time, it automatically reverts to pay as described in this section.

Employee Option - Employees whose rate of basic pay is less than the maximum step for the GS-10 grade may elect to take compensatory time off in lieu of pay for authorized overtime.

Supervisory Option - For employees whose rate of basic pay is in excess of the maximum for GS-10, Step Ten, the district has the option of requesting compensatory time off in lieu of pay for authorized overtime. However, if premium pay is authorized, the basic pay rate of GS-10, Step One, will be the maximum amount used for premium pay computation.

124   MILITARY LEAVE

The reserve components of the Armed Forces are the U.S. Army and Air National Guards, the Army, Naval, Marine Corps, Coast Guard, and Air Reserves.

Each reservist of the Armed Forces or member of the National Guard is entitled to leave of absence from his/her duties without loss of pay, time, or efficiency rating for each day he/she is on active military duty. An eligible employee accrues fifteen days military leave (less for part-time employees) each fiscal year, and the military leave (not to exceed fifteen days) which is unused at the end of the prior fiscal year is carried forward for use in addition to the days which are credited at the beginning of a current fiscal year. This gives the full-time employee the potential of thirty days military leave during a fiscal year. Military leave is charged on a per hour basis. Employees will not be charged military leave for weekends and holidays that occur within the period of military leave.

The maximum amount of military leave that can be accrued and carried forward from fiscal year to fiscal year is fifteen days. It is the responsibility of the employee and their timekeeper to keep track of carried over military leave.

Military Aid to Enforce The Law - Each reservist or National Guardsman who is called to duty under certain conditions for the purpose of providing military aid to enforce the law is entitled to military leave up to twenty-two workdays (not including Saturday and Sunday) in a calendar year without loss of pay, time, or efficiency rating.

National Guard duty in cases of disaster such as floods, earthquakes, hurricanes, etc., is covered by this type military leave.

Certain activities are not eligible for military leave: (1) summer training for the Reserve Officers Training Corps, (2) temporary Coast Guard Reserve, (3) participation in parades by members of the State National Guard, (4) training with a State Guard or other state military organization which is not a part of the National Guard, and (5) Civil Air Patrol.

Time taken on a work day to travel to the place where training is to begin must be either annual leave or leave without pay, unless military training orders encompass the period of travel time required.

Taking Military Leave - Present your military orders to your immediate supervisor as early as possible.

Military Furlough - Military leave of absence with pay is to be distinguished from military furlough when an employee is ordered to extended active duty for general service with the Armed Forces without civilian compensation. However, if you are recalled to extended active duty from a reserve unit, the first fifteen days of this duty can be credited to military leave with pay. Check with your supervisor regarding re-employment rights.

125   COURT LEAVE

Authorized absence without charge to annual leave or loss of compensation is granted an employee for jury duty, or for attending court in a non-official capacity as a witness on behalf of the United States in a State or Federal Court. For leave purposes, municipal courts are considered state courts.

Jury Duty (Federal Court) - You will be granted leave without loss of pay or annual leave. You will receive no additional fee for jury duty.

Jury Duty (State Court) - You will be granted leave without loss of pay or annual leave. You must accept any fees you are paid and remit them to your district. You may exclude from that amount the portion paid which covers local mileage and meals. See your fiscal clerk.

Government Witness in Official Capacity - This is official duty status with no charge to leave.

Government Witness in Non-Official Capacity - You are paid your regular salary and carried on court leave.

Non-Government Witness - If you are not appearing on behalf of the government or in official capacity, you will be granted court leave to appear as a non-official witness on behalf of private parties if the Federal Government, the District of Columbia, or a state or local government is a party to the proceedings. You must turn in to your district any fees received. The only expense you are allowed to claim is mileage for use of a personally owned car.

If you are appearing as a non-official witness involving only private parties, you are required to take annual leave or leave without pay. You keep any fees received.

Upon completion of court leave, written evidence of court attendance must be submitted to your leave-approving official. See the Guide for Timekeeping and/or the Collective Bargaining Agreement, Article 19, Section 3A for more specifics.

126   LEAVE WITHOUT PAY (LWOP)

LWOP is a temporary non-pay status and absence from duty, which may, at administrative discretion, be granted upon your request.

Under the Family Medical Leave Act (FMLA), taking LWOP is an entitlement. You are entitled to take job protected, unpaid leave for up to a total of 12 work weeks in any 12 month period.

Extended LWOP has been authorized in the past for:

1.   Educational purposes, when the course of study or research is in line with a type of work being performed by the FDA.

2.   Certain types of service with non-federal public or private enterprise.

3.   Recovery from illness or disability that is not of a permanent or disqualifying nature, when continued employment or immediate return to employment would threaten impairment of employee's health or the health of other employees.

Absence Without Leave - Absence without leave is not to be confused with LWOP. Absence without leave is a non-pay status resulting from an Agency determination that it will not grant any type of leave (including LWOP) for a period of absence for which the employee did not obtain authorization.

127   ABSENCE FOR MATERNITY REASONS

Absence for maternity reasons is a period of approved absence for incapacitation related to pregnancy and confinement. It is chargeable to sick leave or a combination, as appropriate, of sick leave, annual leave, compensatory time, credit hours, time off awards, and LWOP under FMLA. Voluntary Leave Transfer Program (VLTP) may also be an option.

It is your responsibility to advise your supervisor as soon as your pregnancy is known, so that steps can be taken to protect your health and personnel adjustments can be made.

The length of absence from work will be determined by the employee, her physician, and her supervisor on a case by case basis. Advanced leave for absences for maternity reasons is generally governed by the same policies and procedures as for other absences. See IOM 122.

128   VOTING AND REGISTRATION LEAVE

When feasible, and without interfering seriously with operations, employees who desire to vote or register in any election or in referendums on a civic matter will be excused for a reasonable time for that purpose. When the polls are not open at least three hours either before or after an employee's regular hours of work, the employee will be excused for enough time to permit reporting for work three hours after the polls open or for leaving work three hours before the polls close, whichever requires lesser time off.

Example: If polls open at 6:30 AM and close at 6:30 PM, an employee who works 8:00 AM to 4:30 PM may be excused from 3:30 PM to 4:30 PM since this would be three hours before the polls close.

129   COMMISSIONED CORPS LEAVE

The following information is provided for general guidance concerning the leave policy of the PHS Commissioned Corps.

This is a synopsis of the regulations covering this type of leave and does not cover all necessary information. Information concerning the complete Commissioned Corps leave policy can be obtained from the district copy of the "Commissioned Corps Personnel Manual" and/or "A Supervisors Guide to the Commissioned Personnel System".

Annual Leave - An officer earns thirty days of annual leave a year, at a rate of 2 1/2 days per month. Annual leave is accrued on a calendar year basis, and an officer may carry forward sixty days of unused annual leave from one calendar year to another. Leave in excess of sixty days not used by December 31 is forfeited.

Annual leave should be requested and approved in advance on a PHS-1345 form – "Request and Authority for Leave of Absence." If this is not possible, e.g. because of an emergency, an officer should immediately notify his official superior of the reason for the absence and complete the PHS-1345 upon return to duty.

Annual leave is granted in full days. Absence for less than a full workday is considered station leave. Non-workdays (e.g. Saturdays, Sundays, Holidays) at the beginning, or end, of a period of annual leave are not chargeable against an officer's leave account. However, non-workdays that fall within a period of leave are chargeable against an officer's annual leave account. This includes legal holidays. A consecutive period of absence from duty may not be authorized in two or more parts to avoid charging non-workdays falling within the period of annual leave.

An officer's annual leave record is maintained by his/her designated timekeeper as the official record.

Sick Leave - There is no accrual of, or charge for, sick leave. It is granted as needed for an officer's illness. Absence because of illness of a member of the family may not be charged to sick leave.

An officer unable to report for duty because of personal illness must notify his official superior. Upon return to duty, a PHS-1345 must be completed. This form is used to request and grant sick leave, in addition to annual leave. If an officer is on sick leave for more than three days, the officer must record in the "Remarks" section of the PHS-1345, either "the nature of the illness or disability" or "the need for medical services". The leave granting authority may, at its discretion, require a medical certificate signed by the officer's attending physician.

Sick leave requests are forwarded to the Chief, Medical Branch, Division of Commissioned Personnel, Room 4C-06, 5600 Fishers Lane, Rockville, MD 20857.

Station Leave - If an officer is absent from duty for a period of less than one workday or on non-workdays (e.g. weekends, holidays, days which an officer is not scheduled for duty, see exceptions under Annual Leave, above), such absence is considered station leave and is not chargeable to annual leave.

If an officer desires to take station leave during regularly scheduled working hours, the absence must have advanced oral approval from the officer's official superior. An officer is automatically entitled to station leave during off-duty hours and on non-workdays, unless otherwise directed by the official superior. Therefore, station leave taken on non-workdays does not require the approval of the official superior. This is true, even if travel away from the vicinity of the duty station is contemplated, since there are no restrictions on an officer's travel while in leave status. An officer, however, is required to keep their official superior informed of their whereabouts when traveling away from the vicinity of the duty station.

Station leave may be granted for legitimate reasons, e.g., taking a family member to the doctor, personal business, etc. Normal practice is for station leave to be half day or less.

Additional information is available on the Internet. See http://dcp.psc.gov.

SUBCHAPTER 130 – DISCLOSURE OF OFFICIAL INFORMATION

You are not to release or divulge any information obtained during FDA investigative or inspectional operations. This includes information contained in diaries and field notes, except for official issuance of forms or documents to addressees. Do not release any originals or copies of reports, memos, diaries, forms (e.g.: FDA-483, 484, 464, etc.), or similar investigational documents to anyone outside the Agency without express concurrence of district or regional management and without following FDA's laws and procedures (21 CFR 20.85—federal, 21 CFR 20.88—state/local, 21 CFR 20.89—foreign, 21 CFR Part 20—Freedom of Information Act (FOIA), and 21 CFR Part 21—Privacy Act). See IOM 190. Procedures for release of Agency documents are established under the FOIA and the Privacy Act and are carried out by Agency and/or district information disclosure personnel e.g., FOI officers. If you are requested by anyone outside the Agency to release any of the aforementioned items or information, refer them to your district information disclosure personnel.

Material in FDA files not specifically exempted or not considered privileged under the laws enforced by the Agency shall be available to the public. See IOM 190 and 134.

131   SUBPOENA

If you are served a subpoena (commanding your appearance in court) or a subpoena duces tecum, (commanding the production of any record or testimony, or the giving of information relating to official FDA matters), immediately advise your supervisor. You will be instructed by your District officials as to the proper procedures and actions on your part in complying with the subpoena. See 21 CFR 20.1 and 20.2.

132   REQUESTS BY THE PUBLIC, INCLUDING TRADE

Be guided by IOM 134 on requests for information desired by the public under the Freedom of Information Act (FOIA). Refer to FDA's "Information Disclosure Manual"

(IDM) for procedures for sharing non-public information with federal, state, local, or foreign government officials. (See IOM 133).

In the case of complaints where a sample has been collected from the complainant, your District may inform the complainant of FDA's findings when an examination is actually made of the sample. When you collect a sample from a complainant, and he asks for analytical results, he may be told that the FDA will advise him by letter of the general nature of the findings. See IOM 408 and IOM 431.3 for cautions on collecting this type sample.

133   SHARING NON-PUBLIC INFORMATION WITH OTHER GOVERNMENT OFFICIALS

If you receive requests for non-public information from officials of other federal agencies or from state, local or foreign government officials, be guided by the current IDM published by the Division of Compliance Policy (DCP) (HFC-230). You may not share FDA non-public information with such officials without being authorized to do so under FDA's procedures.

The procedures contained in the IDM on disclosing information to the public or sharing non-public information with officials from other federal agencies, or from state, local, or foreign governments were formerly found in Chapter 8 of the FDA's Regulatory Procedures Manual (RPM). With the publication of the IDM, this material no longer appears in the RPM.

The most current IDM is available on the FDA Intranet by visiting the Office of Enforcement's website. Relevant sections on non-public disclosure may be found in the IDM, Section 4 as follows:

1)   Sharing Non-Public Information with Foreign Government Officials,

2)   Sharing Non-Public Information with Federal Government Officials,

3)   Sharing Non-Public Information with State and Local Government Officials

134   FREEDOM OF INFORMATION ACT

Public Law 89-487, the Public Information section of the Administrative Procedures Act, more commonly known as the FOIA, adopts a general rule that, except where specifically exempt, all documents in government files shall be made available to the public. There are various exemptions in certain areas, and it is these that mostly affect your operations in FDA. The regulations exempt certain information, such as trade secrets or names and titles of individuals against which no legal action is taken. Certain other material which the firm considers privileged information, and which FDA rules actually is privileged or confidential under the regulations, may also be exempted.

Procedures - Study and become familiar with the general provisions of the FOIA and the regulations in the Code of Federal Regulations (CFR) regarding the release of information to the public. In particular, study 21 CFR 20, 21 71.15, 171.1, 314.430, 431.70, 514.10, 514.11, 514.12 and others, all of which contain provisions regarding confidentiality in various FDA records and documents.   See also, the RPM, subchapter 8, "Freedom of Information Act" and the IDM.

In addition to the FOIA, various other Acts such as the Federal Food, Drug, and Cosmetic (FD&C) Act, the Public Health Services (PHS) Act, and 18 U.S.C. 1905 each contain information relating to the confidentiality of information in government files, and are of particular interest. Special care should be taken to protect the identity of informants. See IOM 518 for further guidance.

Requests for Documents - No field FDA employee has authority to deny any request for documents, no matter what form the request takes. Authority to deny requests rests with the Associate Commissioner for Public Affairs.

Each field and district office is responsible for the internal handling of requests. Information disclosure personnel, e.g. FOI Officers, designated by their respective RFDD's, are responsible for coordinating the implementation of the regulations, for development of procedures within their organization to handle requests, and for adherence to FDA's laws and procedures regarding the maintenance of confidentiality of non-public information. If you receive a request for information under the FOIA, advise the requester to write to the Food & Drug Administration, Freedom of Information Staff (HFI-35), 5600 Fishers Lane, Rockville, MD 20857.

135   INTERNAL FDA DOCUMENTS

Do not quote to non-FDA personnel information which is identified "For Official Use Only", unless so instructed by your supervisor.

Work Plans - Do not divulge district work planning operations without authority from your supervisor.

If you receive requests for internal documents or for parts of them, refer to IOM 134 and IOM 1017.

SUBCHAPTER 140 - SAFETY

Safety is a responsibility of FDA employees, their supervisors, and the Agency's management. These responsibilities include (1) the reporting of any hazards or suspected hazards, (2) taking the necessary safeguards to minimize the opportunity for safety problems. The Agency cannot permit employees or supervisors to disregard established or otherwise reasonable safety precautions and thereby place themselves and/or their fellow employees and/or the Agency's facilities at risk.

Physical resistance to FDA inspections and threats to, or assaults on, FDA employees engaged in their work are extremely rare, and the agency intends to keep them rare. If you receive physical resistance or threats, or if you sense the real possibility of an assault, disengage from the confrontation, get to safety, and call your supervisor immediately. Make careful and exact notes later of who said what to whom, who did what, and whether someone tried or succeeded in threatening, assaulting or taking information or equipment or samples from you. Your safety is more important to the United States than the inspection or the sample. Your supervisor can summon FDA's Office of Criminal

Investigations' (OCI) Special Agents, local police, or United States Marshals to accompany an inspection team if there is a reasonable fear of danger to the investigator.

If you are assaulted (either physically or put in fear by threats of physical violence), your supervisor can summon local police, United States Marshals, or contact OCI headquarters for assistance (301-294-4030). While OCI does not normally provide physical security in these cases, they will assist in threat evaluation based on specific facts and available data bases. OCI can also make contacts with local police and federal agencies based on previous liaison. Be careful in any descriptions you give or write of such events, just as you are in recording other evidence that may result in a court case. Make sure that any inspected facility where weapons are observed, or where threats or assaults occur, is identified in that facility's Central File jacket and to your supervisor, so that investigators or agents who follow you into that facility will be alert to those possibilities. For specific safety guidance related to inspections and interviews, see IOM 514.1 Hostile and Uncooperative Interviewees.

Be alert for problems associated with defective or misused equipment or supplies and their possible impact on patients and/or users. Contact your supervisor and/or the headquarters contacts listed in the applicable compliance program as necessary for assessment. The home district of the manufacturer should be notified of product misuse, so it may be brought to the manufacturer's attention for consideration of precautionary labeling or redesign of the product. Fully document these problems, to include the hazard and/or defect observed and whether user actions could be a contributing factor. Documentation should present sufficient data, such as photos and diagrams, to supplement a narrative describing the situation as well as the collection of samples.

When conducting an inspection or collecting a sample in a facility which requires donning personal protective equipment, guidance should be provided by the firm's management as follows:

1.   Information about the specific hazards that may be encountered

2.   The potential concentrations of these hazards

3.   The personnel protective equipment determined to protect against these hazards

The firm's management should be able to provide you with documentation showing how these hazards were determined, what the expected exposures are and how they relate to the Occupational Safety and Health Administration's (OSHA) Permissible Exposure Limit (PEL). It should also offer information about the personal protective equipment that will protect you against a hazardous exposure. If you have any doubts about the hazards or the equipment recommended or provided to protect against them, do not enter these areas. Your Regional Industrial Hygienist or the Office of Regulatory Affairs (ORA) Safety and Occupational Health Manager may be able to help you evaluate the information provided to you, or furnish information regarding the hazard and the recommended personal protective equipment.

If you do not have the specific personal protective equipment recommended by the firm's management, have your District furnish what you need. In some cases, the firm may be willing to provide the necessary personal protective equipment, however if respiratory protection is required, you should not wear any respiratory protection unless your District has a written Respiratory Protection Program and you have been certified by your District's Respiratory Protection Program Administrator as having currently met the requirements of this program. See IOM 141. It is ultimately your responsibility to ensure that you do not expose yourself to any hazard.

Disaster conditions present inherently dangerous situations. See IOM 940.

Operations in the radiological area also pose special dangers. See IOM 144.2. Obtain advice on protective measures from regional radiological health personnel.

141 PROTECTIVE EQUIPMENT

141.1 Eye Protection

Wear safety glasses during all inspectional activities in which there is a potential for physical or chemical injury to the eye. These glasses should, at a minimum, meet the American National Standard Z87.1-1989 standard for impact resistance. Guidance should be provided by the management of the facility being inspected as to additional eye protection required. Unvented goggles should be worn whenever there is the potential for a chemical splash or irritating mists. Additional eye protection may be required in facilities that use exposed high intensity UV lights for bacteriostatic purposes, tanning booth establishment inspections (Els), etc. Follow the manufacturer's recommendation regarding eye protection for any instrumentation generating light in the UV or higher energy wavelength range.

141.2 Hearing Protection

You should wear hearing protection in noisy areas. The OSHA PEL for employees exposed to noise ranges from 90 decibels for an 8-hour time-weighted average to 115 decibels for 15 or fewer minutes per day. However, risk factors for hearing loss include personal susceptibility, noise intensity, noise frequency, distance from the noise source, etc. The noise reduction rating is provided by the manufacturer of various earplugs and muffs, but also depends on the appropriate fit. The efficiency of muff type protectors is reduced when they are worn over the frames for eye-protective devices.

141.3 Protective Clothing

(1) Wear safety shoes on inspections, as required.
(2) Wear hard hats in hard hat designated areas
(3) Use appropriate gloves to avoid slivers and/or splinters when handling rough wooden cases or similar items. Use protective gloves when handling hot items or working around steam pipes, and when handling frozen products or working in freezers. Use protective gloves when handling lead pigs containing radioactive materials to

avoid hand contamination. If you are handling solvents, wear gloves that are impermeable to the solvent. Your regional industrial hygienist or the ORA Safety and Occupational Health Manager can provide guidance in the type of gloves to use for a particular solvent.

(4) Plan ahead for the clothing that may be required for a particular location or situation. Such clothing includes coveralls, lab coats, freezer coats, rubber or vinyl aprons, and disposable paper-like coveralls.

141.4 Respiratory Protection

If it is possible to perform an inspection without entering areas in which respiratory protection is mandated or recommended, do not enter these areas. If you determine it is necessary to enter an area in which you must wear a respirator, you must have documented evidence showing the requirements of the District Respiratory Protection Program have been met prior to wearing your respirator. Your District shall have a written Respiratory Protection Program, as delineated in the following paragraph.

In any workplace where respirators are necessary to protect the health of the employee, or whenever respirators are required by the employer, OSHA requires the employer to establish and implement a written respiratory protection program with worksite specific procedures according to the requirements in 29 CFR 1910.134. The program must include the following provisions:

(1) Procedures for selecting respirators for use in the workplace, and annual fit testing of each employee wearing the selected respirator(s);

(2) Medical evaluation of employees required to use a respirator prior to the employee's use of a respirator, and repeated as specified in the Respiratory Protection Program (a medical evaluation can be obtained by contacting your local Industrial Hygienist or Ann Stack, SERL. (404) 253-2214;

(3) Procedures for using respirators in routine and reasonably foreseeable emergency situations;

(4) Procedures for maintaining respirators;

(5) Training of employees in the hazards to which they are potentially exposed during routine and emergency situations, and in the proper use of respirators including limitations of their use and fit checking procedures each time the respirator is donned;

(6) Procedures for regularly evaluating the effectiveness of the program. OSHA requires each employer perform an evaluation of any workplace which may contain respiratory hazards. If these respiratory hazards cannot be removed through engineering controls, the employer must provide respirator protection. Do not enter any area you suspect may contain an unevaluated respiratory hazard. Your training should include a determination of the minimum respiratory protection for each type of inspection you may perform. Your regional Industrial Hygienist or the ORA Safety and Occupational Health Manager may be consulted for guidance in the type of respirator, type of cartridge or filter, and the useful life of the cartridge or filter.

The following list includes situations, which have been identified as having the potential for respiratory hazards:

(1)   Feed or drug plants where there is a possible inhalation hazard due to airborne particulates.

(2)   Fumigation or storage facilities where treated grain or produce is encountered, including trucks, vessels, railroad cars, fumigation chambers.

- Do not enter any structure or conveyance or sample any product that is being treated with the fumigants Methyl Bromide or Phosphine.
- Areas and/or products being treated with fumigants are required by Environmental Protection Agency (EPA) to be placarded, and the placards not removed until the treatment is complete (usually 12 hours to 4 or more days) and the areas and/or products are clear of fumigant gases (phosphine <0.3 ppm and methyl bromide <1 ppm).
- Self-contained breathing apparatus (SCBA) is generally the only respiratory protection gear approved for use in areas being fumigated. It is necessary to follow many other precautions when working around fumigants. See Note on Methyl Bromide and Phosphine at the end of this section for additional information.

(3)   Facilities using ozone, or where ozone is produced as a by-product of the manufacturing operation.

(4)   Facilities where sterilizers utilize ethylene oxide gas (EO) - See IOM 144.2 Factory Inspection

(5)   Grain elevators or other grain storage facilities that potentially contain aflatoxin in the dust.

(6)   Spice grinders and repackers that potentially produce airborne respiratory irritants such as pepper.

(7)   Any rodent-infested area. - See IOM 145.4 Hantavirus Associated Diseases

Note - Methyl Bromide and Phosphine

If a sampling area is suspected of having been fumigated with methyl bromide or phosphine, and has not been cleared according to the EPA requirements, contact your local industrial hygienist for guidance as to how to ensure that the area is safe to enter. Do not enter the area until it is appropriately aerated and tested. If entry is required using personal protective equipment, you local industrial hygienist can provide guidance to ensure you are using the appropriate respirator and cartridge, and any other protective equipment necessary based upon the fumigant concentration. See IOM 143.4, Asphyxiation Hazards, and IOM 144.2, Factory Inspections, for additional cautions related to fumigants.

142   AUTOMOBILE SAFETY

Automobile Condition - See IOM 165.

Prior to driving, check the following: (1) Tires, check for tread wear, etc.; (2) Mirrors, for proper adjustment; (3) Brakes; (4) Windshield; (5) Lights, headlight, turn signals and brake; (6) Gasoline & oil gauges; (7) Spare, jack, lug wrench, first aid kit, flares, etc.; (8) Fire extinguishers are no longer required in vehicles; (9) Seat belts must be used.

Ensure all volatile solvents, either in the sample collection kit or contained in a sampled material, are sealed to prevent contamination of the air in a closed vehicle. Be especially aware of the hazard of transporting dry ice in a closed vehicle. The concentration of carbon dioxide gas can cause drowsiness, or even an asphyxiation hazard, if the dry ice is carried in an unventilated vehicle. See Section 143.4 Asphyxiation Hazards.

143   SAMPLING

When you are collecting samples, always be alert for possible dangerous conditions (e.g., poisonous materials or fumes, flammable or caustic chemicals, high places, etc.)

143.1 Sample Fumigation and Preservation

Follow safety precautions when fumigating and/or preserving samples. Guidance is as follows:

1.   Whenever possible, freeze the sample. If freezing is not practical, contact your servicing laboratory for alternative fumigants and preservatives.

2.   When fumigants or preservatives are used, exercise care to limit your exposure to these chemicals. Contact your servicing laboratory for the appropriate precautions necessary with these chemicals.

3.   Material Safety Data Sheets (MSDS) for each of these chemicals must be available at each duty site (e.g., District office, resident posts), and can be obtained from your servicing laboratory. These sheets list the hazards involved with these chemicals and precautions to take for use. You must read and follow the instructions in the MSDS prior to using the chemical. If a measured amount of chemical fumigant or preservative is present at the time of shipping, enclose a copy of its MSDS with the shipped sample. Again, if you have any questions, contact your servicing laboratory.

4.   Avoid excessive heat and open flame.

5.   Use glass vials or jars with lined lids whenever possible. Depending on the type of fumigant used, some polypropylene containers can also be used.

143.2 Electrical Hazards

Many samples are collected in poorly lighted areas, or in older poorly wired buildings. Be alert for low hanging wires, bare, exposed, or worn wires, and broken or cracked electrical outlets.

When you are using portable power tools, etc., be extra cautious of the shock hazard. See Inspectors Technical Guide # 22 regarding Ground Fault Circuit Interrupters, and use one if feasible. Do not use flash units in dusty areas because of the possibility of explosion hazard. See IOM 523 for additional information.

143.3 Physical Hazards

Be alert for dangerous conditions on all sampling operations. If it is necessary to use a flame to sterilize sampling equipment, use extreme care.

All flammable liquids in your sampling kits must be in metal safety cans. See IOM 426.1

Care must be taken when handling sharp objects, e.g.; knives, syringes with needles, glass, etc. If it is necessary to sample such objects, take care in packing the sample to avoid injuring anyone who handles the sample later. Place them in a rigid container, e.g. glass jar, plastic box, etc. In addition, state in the Remarks or Flag Section of the Collection Report (C/R) (FDA-464) that a syringe & needle were collected as part of your sample.

1. Railcars
    a. When sampling, make sure doors are propped open to avoid accidental closing if the car is bumped while you are in it.
    b. Display a warning flag or similar device to alert others you are in the car. If possible, have a railroad yardman present.
    c. When entering the car make sure the ladder is secure.
    d. On hot days, or after a car has been fumigated, it should be aired out prior to entering, preferably by opening both doors.
    e. Observe "No Smoking" in rail cars.
    f. Don't crawl under railcars - go around them.
    g. Avoid any cables between the railroad tracks. These are often used to move cars on sidings. A cable snapping taut can kill or maim.
2. Grain Elevators
    a. Prior to use, make sure man lifts are operating properly.
    b. Make sure cross-rungs on ladders are safe.
    c. When stepping off ladders or man lifts, be sure the floor is actually a floor and not a bin covered with canvas, cardboard, or other temporary non-supportive cover.
    d. Make sure walkways between bins are sturdy.
    e. Use caution when sampling from high bins or tanks. Wet or icy conditions may prevail, so check these conditions.
    f. When brass grain bombs are used to collect bin samples, do not drop the bomb to the surface of the grain. This could cause sparks if it hits the bottom or side of a bin. Lower the bomb gently to the grain surface, then raise it four to five feet and let it fall to the grain surface to collect the sample. Do not use steel grain bombs; use only brass bombs for sampling.
3. Clothing
    a. Do not wear loose fitting clothes when collecting samples or conducting inspections, the clothes could catch on equipment or conveyor belts and lead to injuries.
    b. Do not carry notebooks, credentials, etc., in the outer pockets of your inspectional uniform because they could fall into the equipment.
    c. Steel mesh gloves should be worn when cutting portions from frozen products such as fish, etc.
4. Trucks – Make sure any truck you enter during sampling and/or inspection will remain stationary while you are in it.

143.4 Asphyxiation Hazards

1. Prior to entering closed areas, ascertain if they have been fumigated and, if so, air them out prior to entering.
2. When sampling or inspecting at rendering plants or fishmeal plants, be alert to possible hydrogen sulfide accumulations in dump pits and other areas. These fumes can be deadly.
3. Be alert and take proper safety precautions in plants, silos, bins, pits, and any closed areas where semi-solid buttermilk or other liquid dairy products, silage, or other bulk products are stored. If not properly stored, improperly handled, or decomposing, certain products can produce dangerous amounts of carbon dioxide, or other gases, or may deplete the oxygen supply in these areas.
4. When transporting dry ice or packages containing dry ice in your car, have some external ventilation (See IOM 144.2, 452.5, and 943 for additional dry ice cautions).
5. When sampling from the top of a grain elevator, do not jump down on top of grain. There may be a cavity caused by crusted grain which could break and result in your being buried in grain, or being in an atmosphere of fumigating gas.
6. Be alert when entering storage areas having controlled atmospheres, e.g., where oxygen has been replaced by carbon dioxide to prolong fruit storage, added sulfur dioxide for preservation purposes, etc. These areas must either be aerated prior to entering, or Oxygen Breathing Apparatus (OBA) must be used.

143.5 Radioactive Product Sampling

The sampling and viewing of radiopharmaceuticals may be accomplished working through a lead shield or viewing through lead glass and using protective clothing latex gloves and tongs to prevent exposure to "unnecessary" radiation.

143.6 Chemical Hazards

You may be assigned to collect samples of FDA regulated products involved in a wreck where chemicals pose a threat, or in areas of chemical spills or hazardous waste sites. In such instances, unprotected personnel are not permitted into hazardous zones. You will be permitted into those areas deemed safe, however, consult with the on-site DHHS Coordinator, usually an employee of the Agency For Toxic Substances and Disease Registry (ATSDR), to ascertain if any safety precautions are necessary on your part. Follow instructions provided. See IOM 322 for further information and for the address and phone numbers of the ATSDR contacts.

143.7 Carbadox Sampling

Concentrated Carbadox (above 95%) has a severe dust explosiveness rating, is a flammable solid, and is also carcinogenic. The only approved source of Carbadox in the US is "Mecadox 10", a medicated pre-mix at a 2.2% concentration.

High concentrations of Carbadox (up to 99%) have been found during investigations of illegal bulk drugs. Some have been falsely labeled as Mecadox. Carbadox, in its pure form, is a minute yellow crystal. It is considered dangerous. Do not collect physical samples of any bulk substance identified or represented as Carbadox or Mecadox. The Center for Veterinary Medicine (CVM) will take action on documentary samples.

If there is no labeling and/or a dealer refuses to identify any yellow powder, inform the dealer of the hazards of Carbadox. Contact your supervisor before collecting any samples of suspected Carbadox. If instructed to collect a sample, use extreme caution and proceed as follows: (1) Wear disposable gloves: (2) Use a respirator or other effective means to avoid breathing the dust. Paper masks are not adequate; (3) Use goggles; (4) Do not sample in drafty places; (5) Use only plastic bottles with plastic caps; (6) Collect only 1-2 oz. per sub; (7) Cover material collected with at least an equal amount of distilled or deionized water and gently mix. It is preferable to use too much water than not enough; (8) Note on collection report (CR) the approximate amount of water added to the bottle of suspect product; (9) Protect subs from excessive heat and do not store in the trunk of car in the sun; (10) Store in insulated cartons with ice, if necessary; (11) Flag the CR as to possible presence of Carbadox; (12) Notify the receiving laboratory of sample collection.

144   INSPECTIONS

Many firms pose safety hazards or problems. Some include: (1) Flying glass in bottling plants; (2) Explosion hazards from dust; (3) Man-lifts which do not operate properly; (4) Asphyxiation problems in rendering plants, fish meal plants, fumigated bins in elevators, fumigation chambers and any closed bins or areas; (5) Forklifts and other power equipment operated in the plant. Be alert for their presence and avoid being hit.

144.1 Man Lifts and Ladders

1. Many firms have either power or hand driven man lifts for movement between floors. Do not use the man lift if company policy forbids non-employees using them.

2. Before riding mechanical lifts, make sure safety equipment is installed and operating properly.

3. When riding power lifts, observe the following safety precautions: (a) Determine ahead of time what floors are serviced by the lift and at which floor you intend to get off; (b) Determine safety devices, and how they operate. Check lift for automatic cut off at the top or a safety stop cord; (c) Always face the belt when riding the lift; (d) Never carry excess equipment or items that protrude and could get caught between floors.

4. When using hand powered lifts, remember to: (a) Check the foot brake for proper operation; (b) Check if control rope is firmly fastened at the bottom; (c) If lift has a stop pin which must be removed prior to use or after use, determine how it is used and use it; (d) Check counterbalance of lift, and add or remove weights if necessary; (e) Never free-fall on the lift when descending; always keep descent in control by using the brake; (f) Use gloves to avoid rope burns or slivers from the hemp or metal pull ropes.

5. Never over-extend a ladder. If possible, have the bottom held by someone while you are using it. Use blocks on base of portable Grain Car Ladders to hold base away from car wall to provide foot space on ladder rungs.

6. Some mills and elevators have makeshift ladders. Extreme care should be exercised when using these.

144.2 Factory Inspection

Inspections of retorts require extra safety precautions. Be alert for live steam and other potentially dangerous heat sources. Do not enter a retort if your safety cannot be assured. When it is necessary to enter a retort, inform plant management. If firm has safety interlock switches, make sure they are engaged and locked. Have a second investigator or plant management stand outside the retort to assure nothing will happen.

When inspecting freezers, make sure doors cannot accidentally snap shut and lock you inside. Be alert to ammonia leaks while inspecting freezing and refrigerating operations. Note: ammonia under normal operating conditions retains its chemical stability and will not burn or support combustion. An ammonia leak in a freezer can cause explosions if proper air/ammonia mixtures are reached. It can be toxic if inhaled, and can cause eye and throat irritation. If an ammonia leak is discovered during an inspection, leave the area immediately and notify management of the leak. Warning: If an ammonia-contaminated area must be entered, a full-face mask or self-contained oxygen mask or a gas absorbing canister mask must be worn. Protective clothing is also necessary, if the ammonia concentration is high. If you are unable to obtain the use of the mask & protective clothing, then do not enter the area.

Use care when entering areas where large amounts of dry ice are used or stored. Be sure the area is adequately ventilated prior to entering. See IOM 143.4, 452.5 & 943 for additional cautions concerning use of dry ice.

When visiting facilities handling drug products, check with management to determine if any of the articles produced require special handling or protective equipment, such as respirators.

When conducting inspections of firm's using chemicals, pesticides, etc., ask to review the MSDS for the products involved to determine what, if any, safety precautions you must take. This could include the use of respirators or other safety equipment.

Ethylene Oxide (EO) - EO is a colorless gas or volatile liquid with a characteristic ether-like odor above 500 ppm. Unmonitored and inadequate ventilation will allow EO buildup of extremely high concentrations, especially in facilities utilizing malfunctioning or leaking equipment. Door gaskets, valves, and threaded fittings are typical areas where leaks have been observed. Additionally, exhaust vents from the sterilizer and the sterilizer room should not be located near air conditioning intake vents, or vented directly into work areas. If the odor of EO is detected, ventilation and containment are inadequate. Leave the area and report the problem to firm management.

OSHA standard regulating employee exposure to EO is presently 1 ppm over an 8-hour day. You should avoid all unnecessary and preventable exposure to it. This gas has toxic (including possible cancer and reproductive hazards), flammable and explosive properties, and must be used and handled with caution. Adhere to any procedures the firm has established for protection of personnel from over-exposure to EO. Where improper venting procedures or defective equipment are observed, take adequate precautions, i.e., do not enter potentially hazardous areas, and/or wear protective clothing and a respirator. Refer to IOM 141. 29 CFR 1910.134 contains basic requirements for proper selection, use, cleaning, and maintenance of respirators.

Ionizing Radiation - Each investigator who visits a manufacturer of radioactive products or tests ionizing radiation emitting products (e.g., diagnostic x-ray tests) must wear a Thermoluminescent Dosimeter (TLD) to estimate external exposure. These are available in each district; personal alarm dosimeters are also available. These can alert the investigator to high exposure areas during visits to manufacturing firms. Make an estimate of the time spent in areas where radiation is present, and estimate exposure during this time from your personal dosimeter. The estimate can be compared to the results from the TLD badges, which would be processed by Winchester Engineering & Analytical Center (WEAC). Contact WEAC for additional information concerning TLD badges.

Experience has shown there is a potential for internal exposure from inhalation of radioactive material, especially in the case of iodine isotopes. Ingestion of radioactive material from contaminated notebooks, workpads, etc. is also possible.

When you are inspecting radiation-emitting devices and substances, take every precaution to avoid undue exposure or contamination. Time, distance, and shielding are important when working around radioactive materials. Adhere to the firm's established safety procedures and precautions. Where employees are required to wear protective apparel, eyeglasses, or monitoring equipment, follow those procedures. Use protective gloves to avoid hand contamination when handling the lead pigs containing radioactive materials.

Monitoring devices must be used whenever exposure is possible. Monitoring equipment must be calibrated periodically in order to be accurate. There are a variety of meters that can be utilized for radiation protection. Film badges are usually used to determine accumulated amounts of radiation, and unless these are analyzed the exposure dosage is unknown. This will be done by WEAC. Dosimeters will provide a reading at the time of exposure.

145   MICROBIOLOGICAL HAZARDS

When processes involve potential for microbiological contamination, normal controls and procedures should contain or protect against any possible hazards. The procedures may include routine use of protective clothing and equipment. Precautions mentioned below concerning gowning, masks, gloves, etc., in this section, are also important in the event that accidents, spills or unexpected,

uncontrolled contamination occurs while you are in work areas. If contamination is known in advance to be uncontrolled or you must handle contaminated materials, do not enter an area or handle these materials without first consulting with your supervisor.

145.1 Animal Origin Products

Caution: It may be necessary to wear gowns, masks, rubber gloves, etc., when inspecting some of these work areas. Be guided by how the firm's employees dress for their work areas, and dress accordingly. Consult with the firm's management and your supervisor regarding dress and precautions to follow.

When inspecting manufacturers or collecting samples of animal origin products, be alert for possible routes of contamination that could lead to your injury or illness. Some possible vectors of disease exist in firms that process products, which use animal origin products as raw materials. Some include:

1.   Anthrax - Care must be taken during inspections of processors of bone meal, dicalcium phosphate and gelatin.

2.   Tularemia - Use caution when inspecting rabbit processors. Be careful of scratches from bone splinters. Use gloves for protection.

145.2 Viral and Other Biological Products

Take proper precautions to protect yourself. If necessary, consult your supervisor and/or district microbiological personnel. NOTE: Inspection of vaccine manufacturers may require inoculation in advance of the inspection to adequately protect the investigator. Contact the Center for Biologics Evaluation and Research (CBER), Division of Viral Products, HFM-445, for guidance.

Methods of transmission include: (1) Aerosols, which may be created by manufacturing operations (e.g., centrifugation, filling, etc.) or spills. Transmission may occur through inhalation; (2) Contact with contaminated objects, including equipment, animals, waste materials, reagents, file cabinets and doorknobs. Transmission can occur through ingestion, inhalation, or through broken skin.

Protective and preventive measures include:

1.   Precautions listed in IOM 145.1 and 145.3

2.   Do not touch. This means equipment, materials, reagents, animals, etc.

3.   Wear protective clothing. Evaluate the needs for gowns, caps, masks, gloves, and shoe coverings, and wear them where necessary.

Protective clothing worn in a work area where a virus or spore bearing microorganism is handled must not be worn into a work area for another product.

Leave all used protective clothing at the firm for proper disposal.

4.   Wash hands thoroughly after leaving each work area.

5.   Determine if the firm has established safety precautions and procedures, and follow them if adequate.

6.   If the firm is processing viruses or other potentially infectious biological agents during the inspection, deter-

mine if it is advisable to enter the work areas. Chances of infection through aerosols are reduced when there is no active processing.

7.   Females of childbearing age are advised not to inspect areas where the Rubella virus is actively processed unless immunity has been established. Infection during pregnancy may result in congenital abnormalities.

8.   Vaccines are available for your protection against some organisms (e.g., Rubella). For information on inoculations and physical examinations, refer to IOM 169.6.

Precaution - Blood and Plasma Inspections - Viral Hepatitis and Human Immunodeficiency Virus (HIV), the Acquired Immune Deficiency Syndrome (AIDS) virus - Be alert around blood banks or blood processing operations to the possible dangers of these and other infectious agents.

Keep in mind the following warnings:

1.   Do not touch. This means do not handle lab instruments, blood samples, containers or reagents in blood bank labs unless absolutely necessary. Wear lab coats with long sleeves. Disposable lab coats that are impervious to blood are best. These should be left in the laboratory area.

2.   Do not smoke, drink, eat or have meetings in the blood banks or in the testing areas for Hepatitis B Surface Antigen (HBsAg), HIV, or any other infectious agents.

3.   Consider blood samples, the antigen and antigen testing kits and other associated HIV, HBsAg, and other test reagents as potentially infectious.

4.   Consider the possibility of aerosol contamination if there is spilling or splashing of test reagents or blood samples.

5.   Use care when placing inspectional or personal equipment in lab areas. Wash hands thoroughly after these inspections. Hepatitis can be transmitted by hand to mouth.

6.   Use disposable gloves. Spills may be wiped with a 5% sodium hypochlorite solution and/or solutions such as Wescodyne or Betadine. Autoclaving is the preferred method (121°C/60 minutes) for sterilizing reagents, samples and equipment.

Note: When accidental spills, etc. occur in your presence, you are not required to participate in cleaning or disposing of materials. This is the firm's responsibility.

7.   Use scrupulous personal hygiene at all times in the blood bank and in the testing areas for HBsAg, HIV, and other infectious agents.

Precaution – Non-Clinical Laboratory Inspections - During inspections/investigations of sub-human primate facilities (e.g., Good Laboratory Practices (GLPs), non-clinical laboratory testing facilities, animal holding facilities, etc.) do not enter rooms housing sub-human primates. Monkeys normally housed in these facilities can carry "Herpes-B Virus", "Simian B Virus", or "monkey-virus". During inspections of this type, use the following guidance:

1.   Investigators shall not enter any rooms which hold or house subhuman primates. Bioresearch monitoring (BIMO) inspectional information should be derived from personnel interviews and record examinations conducted outside of the primate areas.

2.   All study records usually found in the monkey rooms (Standard Operating Procedures (SOPs); protocols; animal housing, feeding, handling, and care records; animal isolation and health records, room environmental records; dosing and animal I.D. records; animal daily observation records; equipment and room cleaning records, et al.) should be reviewed outside of the rooms.

3.   Although contact with subhuman primates in the course of an inspection is prohibited, information on animal room activities may be obtained through personnel interviews.

145.3 Bacteriological Problems

Take proper precautions to protect yourself. If necessary consult with your supervisor and/or district microbiological personnel. Possible routes of Salmonellosis include dust inhalation in dried milk and dried yeast plants. Thyroid processing plants may also be a source of this problem.

In no case should you taste any item implicated or suspect of causing injuries or illnesses (e.g., consumer complaint samples, etc.). Handle these with extra care since even minute portions of certain items may cause serious illness or even death (See IOM 912).

145.4 Hantavirus Associated Diseases

Rodents and other small mammals have been identified as the primary hosts for recognized hantaviruses. Infected rodents shed the virus in saliva, urine and feces. The time of this virus' survival in the environment is unknown.

Human infection may occur when contact is made with infected saliva or excreta, through inhalation of aerosol produced when the animals sneeze, or contaminated dust particles are stirred up. In addition, infection can also occur when dried contaminated materials are disturbed and directly introduced into broken skin or onto the conjunctivae.

Hantaviruses can present some or all of the following symptoms: fever, headache, muscle aches, nausea & vomiting, chills, dry cough, and shortness of breath.

Investigators/Inspectors may be subject to an increased risk of infection because of unpredictable or incidental contact with rodents or their habitations, i.e., entering various buildings, crawl spaces and other sites that may be rodent infested.

When encountering or suspecting rodent infested areas, the following protective and preventive measures are recommended:

1.   First and foremost, DO NOT HANDLE RODENTS - DEAD OR ALIVE.

2.   Be careful when moving items around, excessive dust may increase the risk.

3.   To prevent eye contamination, wear goggles or a full-face respirator.

4.   High-Efficiency Particulate Air (HEPA) filter masks or respirator cartridges are recommended to avoid inhalation of aerosols. Because of the minute size of the virus, dust masks will likely not filter out the organism.

5.   Wear coveralls, and handle and dispose of as infected material.

6.   Wear disposable latex or rubber gloves. Be careful to avoid hand contamination when removing gloves. Wash hands thoroughly after removal.

7.   In addition to these measures, follow any guidance issued by state health departments.

Anyone who develops a febrile or respiratory illness within 45 days of the last potential exposure should immediately seek medical attention. Inform the attending physician of the potential occupational risk of Hantavirus infection.

146   REPORTING

Automobile Accidents - See IOM 112.2 - Accidents, for procedures.

Injuries - If you are injured during the performance of official duties, report immediately to your supervisor. If medical aid is required, obtain it as soon as possible. Check with your supervisor on what accident report forms are required and procedures to be followed.

Note: Supervisors must refer to Chapter IV - Guide 8, Compensation for Injury, of the DHHS Personnel Guides for Supervisors concerning procedures to follow and forms to be filled out whenever an employee is injured.

SUBCHAPTER 160 - PUBLIC RELATIONS, ETHICS & CONDUCT

161   MASS MEDIA (Press, Radio, and TV)

Over the past few years, the inspectional and investigational activities of the FDA have received extensive coverage in the electronic and print media. Regional and District Directors are the spokespersons for FDA in their respective areas. However, investigators and inspectors are occasionally requested by the media to comment or provide information on their individual inspectional activities. Such requests include being interviewed and filmed during inspections, investigations and sample collections. If media representatives contact you, be courteous and helpful, but refer all requests for information, interviews and personal appearances to your supervisor. You may be permitted to appear on camera or be interviewed, but authorization must be gained in advance. Otherwise, your Regional or District office will handle the inquiry, or refer it to the Associate Commissioner for Public Affairs (HFI-20) at headquarters.

Do not solicit media interviews or on-camera appearances unless you are authorized. In those instances where media request you be interviewed or filmed, the request should be tactfully declined and referred to the district office. There may be occasions when management of a firm you are inspecting invites representatives from the news media to observe the inspectional process. Please see Section 504.3 for instructions on how to appropriately handle such events.

FDA publications, press releases and talk papers on a wide variety of subjects are available in your district, and are helpful in answering media and public inquiries. In addition, you should refer them to FDA's Internet Web site http://www.fda.gov. Talk papers, press releases, FDA publications, federal register announcements, etc. are on-line at this Web site.

162   NON-GOVERNMENT MEETINGS

Speakers and representation at meetings will be provided when such attendance is for official purposes, and consistent with the policies and best interest of FDA. As a public agency FDA must be responsive to public inquiries of all kinds.

Authorization - Attendance must be authorized in advance. Form DHHS 99 is required, unless the primary purpose of attendance is to officially explain, interpret or acquaint the public with FDA programs or activities.

Selectivity - Selection will not arbitrarily favor one sponsoring organization over another.

Fees - Acceptance of payment in cash or kind must be approved in advance. No such payment may be accepted when inspectional or administrative and/or a supervisory relationship exists between the employee and the non-federal organization offering to pay his/her expenses.

163   RECRUITING

When assigned recruiting duties, your primary objective is to attract outstanding people to work for FDA. During recruiting discussions, explain the function and duties of the FDA, with emphasis on the relationship between the duties and the requirement for the highest standards of conduct and integrity.

Colleges - Your attitude in your contacts with the college placement officers, faculty members, and the students themselves will play an important part in the success of this program. Various booklets, prepared by FDA, set forth the objectives of the FDA college recruitment program. Obtain copies from your district for use in your recruitment activities.

Professional Societies - Since many experienced professional and scientific personnel are members of professional societies and organizations, this is another excellent recruitment source.

Do not overlook recruitment opportunities offered by such groups, e.g., in setting up displays and exhibits in connection with national or regional meetings or conventions. You are also encouraged to join and be active in professional organizations, including attendance at conventions and meetings.

Community Relations - Consumer information material has been prepared for use by FDA. In presenting such material to local business, civic, industrial, educational, and professional groups, the employment opportunities offered by the FDA may be discussed.

Publicity – Most consumer oriented publicity is handled by FDA's Consumer Affairs Officers, and you may be requested to assist at times. Radio and television stations are required to devote a certain percentage of broadcast time to public service programs, announcements, and other features. Therefore, most stations are eager to run spot announcements and/or feature stories about FDA employees who have made significant contributions to the Agency's program. These are also readily accepted and used by newspapers throughout the country. This is particularly so when the person featured is a local resident.

Successful placement of physically or mentally handicapped persons, dedication of a new office building, awards ceremonies, etc., are other possibilities for development of news releases which could be used as recruitment tools. Be constantly alert, utilizing the recruitment potential of such situations as they present themselves, and alert your supervisor.

164   COMMUNITY ACTIVITIES

All FDA employees are encouraged to take part in normal community, civic, charitable, or religious activities. See your supervisor if you have any questions about conflict of interest limitations.

165   EQUIPMENT CARE, CUSTODY, AND LOSS

Care and custody

You are responsible for the proper care and custody of all government property entrusted to you. This includes:

1.   Storing government vehicles in protected off-street parking facilities, when possible.

2.   Keeping inspectional and investigational equipment securely locked in the trunk of the car while the car is under your direct control. Do not leave valuable equipment in the car's trunk while the car is in for servicing, unless you stay with the car. Do not leave electronic equipment, such as computers, in the trunk of the car for extended periods in extreme hot or cold weather conditions.

3.   Storing all property in safe, secure areas.

Your responsibility for government property in your custody is specified in the Supervisory Staff Manual Guide FDA 2620.2, Section 9.

165.2 Maintenance of Equipment

First-line maintenance rests with you as, the custodian of the items entrusted to you. You are expected to perform, or have performed, the normal maintenance such as checking oil, tires, battery, windshield wipers, etc. on the GFV you are using. Other equipment requires little or no maintenance as such, other than dusting, replacing batteries and bulbs, making minor adjustments, properly packing in carrying cases, and proper protection as necessary. Common sense, and handling the equipment as if it belonged to you, should suffice.

1.   Repairs - Any repairs needed, defects, or inoperative equipment observed, should be immediately reported to your supervisor.

When in travel status, necessary minor repairs to equipment may be obtained locally, if possible, and reimbursement claimed on your travel voucher. Major repairs should be cleared through your supervisor.

2.   Equipment Calibration – You are responsible to assure equipment assigned to you is calibrated for accuracy. This includes thermometers, pyrometers, balances, scales, stopwatches, etc. Keep a record of the calibration with each item requiring calibration. Calibration of certain

inspectional equipment can be done by your District laboratory.

Stopwatches may be calibrated using the atomic clock at the U.S. Naval Observatory in Washington D.C., using the commercial number at (202) 762-1401 or (202) 762-1069. Calibrate stopwatches at several different time intervals within the expected parameters of use. At least three runs should be made at each interval, then averaged for each interval and the correction factor, if any, entered on the record of calibration maintained with the watch. Calibration of your computer's internal clock can be obtained from the same source. Information and software is available on the U.S. Naval Observatory's Web. See http://tycho.usno.navy.mil/ctime.html.

165.3 Lost or Stolen Equipment

As soon as you discover any government property assigned to you or in your custody is missing, report it verbally to your supervisor. Normally, you must submit a form GSA-3155, "Offense/Incident Report". Your district should have these in stock. This form must be supplemented by a memorandum detailing the circumstances surrounding the loss, including the comprehensive steps you took to recover the items. The procedure is outlined in the Supervisory Staff Manual Guide FDA 2620.2, Section 9d.

Follow your district procedures for any additional requirements.

166   OFFICIAL CREDENTIALS, BADGE

Show your credentials to appropriate firm personnel during all non-undercover investigations, inspections, sample collections, recall effectiveness checks, etc.

1.   Delegated Authority - When you are issued the FDA official forms FDA-200 A&B, certain parts of the Commissioner's enforcement authority, as specified in 21 CFR 5.35, is re-delegated to you. You are expected to use this authority wisely and judiciously. See IOM 501 on cautions against Xeroxing or photocopying your credentials.

Your investigator badge, if you are issued one, is for use in certain situations to reinforce the official credentials when needed. Check your district Supervisory Staff Manual Guide, FDA 2280.3, 5b, for situations in which use of the badge may be appropriate.

2.   Qualifications for Credentials - FDA employees engaged in general inspectional and investigational operations are issued FDA-200 A&B credentials. By virtue of their position, these employees are recognized as qualified to perform the duties assigned.

FDA Official Credentials confer extensive inspectional authority on you. Exercise the utmost care of your badge and credentials. Carry them in a manner that will assure positive protection against loss. For example, do not carry them in the upper pockets of your clothing where they may fall out if you bend over. You may not only lose your credentials and badge, but they may, during inspections, fall into vats or machinery resulting in embarrassment and possible financial loss to you as well. Also, carrying your credentials and badge in the glove compartment of your car or leaving them in the pocket of an unattended coat or jacket are invitations to loss or theft.

3.   Lost or Stolen Credentials, Badge - The procedure for reporting loss or theft of credentials and/or badge is in the Supervisory Staff Manual Guide, SMG 2280.3. Notify your supervisor immediately, and submit a written report of the loss or theft to him. If instructed, report the loss or theft to local law enforcement authorities and request the police report identification number. Also ask that the number of the lost credentials/badge be entered into the National Crime Information Center (NCIC). Include this information in your report.

168   BUSINESS CARDS

In June 1999, the FDA determined it is proper to use general appropriation funds to purchase business cards for employees whose interactions with outside organizations further the agency's mission. Due to certain restrictions pertaining to the purchase of business cards, employees should consult with local management prior to purchasing such items, to ensure adherence to agency policy and procedures.

169   EMPLOYEE CONDUCT

As a government employee of the FDA, as few limits as possible are placed on your interests and activities. Nonetheless, certain limitations are necessary to protect the interest of the government. These constraints are briefly covered in the various subsections in this section. Study the Standards of Ethical Conduct for Employees of the Executive Branch, and consult with your supervisor if you have any questions or concerns in this regard. The Standards of Ethical Conduct for Employees of the Executive Branch can be found on FDA's intranet under the Office of Human Resources & Management Services' (OHRMS) ethics laws: http://www.usoge.gov/pages/laws_regs_fedreg_stats/oge_regs/5cfr2635.html.

As you work to advance the health and welfare of the public, seek to maintain the highest standards of ethical conduct. The essence of good government is the personal responsibility that each public servant feels for the public trust he/she holds. You are responsible for complying with the regulations, obtaining advice from your supervisor, personnel or AO, and when required, obtaining advanced approval for certain outside activities.

FDA employees must be persons of unrivalled integrity, and observe the highest standards of conduct. Because of FDA's special regulatory responsibility, its personnel must carry on the agency's business effectively, objectively, and without even the appearance of impropriety. Their actions must be unquestionable, and free of suspicion.

The Standards of Ethical Conduct for Employees of the Executive Branch (5 CFR Part 2635) gives concise details on what is expected, insofar as conduct is concerned. In addition, certain subparts, and Appendix A to Part 73 of the HHS Standards of Conduct, remain in effect. Additional information is also available on FDA's intranet.

169.1 Professional Stature

You are the eyes and ears of FDA, and to most of the public you are their only contact with FDA. Your actions may be the basis upon which they judge the entire FDA. The public expects exemplary behavior and conduct from the government employee. This responsibility applies to both on the job and off the job activities. As you inspect or appraise individuals, you are, in turn, being evaluated. Both the industries FDA regulates and the public-at-large are keenly aware of, and are quick to report, what they consider improper actions by government employees.

Integrity - This is steadfast adherence to a strict moral or ethical code. It characterizes a person of deep-seated honesty and dependability, with a devotion to accuracy, objectivity and fairness.

Employees may not use or permit others to use official information not available to the general public for gain or to advance a private interest.

You are expected to conduct yourself in a prudent manner, so that the work of the Agency is effectively accomplished. Your job is to gather and present the facts. Accuracy and objective observation are absolutely essential.

The Office of Internal Affairs (OIA), Office of the Commissioner (OC), is responsible for obtaining factual information for the FDA on any matter relating to allegations of misconduct, impropriety, conflict of interest, or other violations of Federal statutes by Agency personnel. If you uncover or suspect any such problems, report them to your supervisor. The District/Region will contact OIA. 21 CFR 19.21(b) requires the facts be forwarded to OIA, HF-9, in writing. OIA will maintain the anonymity of your complaint, if you so desire.

Under the Federal Managers' Financial Integrity Act, it is your duty to report any serious problems of waste, mismanagement, fraud or misuse of Government funds by any personnel from other agencies or government contractors. These problems should be reported to your supervisor, who will, in turn, notify the Division of Management Programs (HFA-320).

Attitude - Be dignified, tactful, courteous and diplomatic. Make your approach firm but not unresponsive. Do not display strong-arm tactics, an air of superiority, an attitude of special authority, or an over-bearing posture. Do not apologize or justify your request for necessary and authorized information.

Attire - Good public relations and practical common sense requires you dress appropriately for the activity in which you are engaged. Consult your supervisor for district policy on normal office attire.

Protective clothing is required for many inspectional tasks. The District provides coveralls or other clothing for this purpose. Failure to wear suitable attire, including head coverings, while the firm's employees are so attired, is indefensible. Plastic foot guards over street shoes are required, if walking on raw materials such as bulk grains, bagged material, etc. Prophylactic measures - to guard against the spread of disease may be required during certain investigations. See IOM 141 and IOM 519.

Prohibitions - Gifts, Luncheons, and Snacks - The Standards of Ethical Conduct for Employees of the Executive Branch, 5 CFR Part 2635, Subpart B, specifically provide that an employee shall not, directly or indirectly, solicit or accept a gift: (1) from a prohibited source; or (2) given because of the employee's official position. Notwithstanding any of the exceptions provided in Subpart B, an employee shall not (1) accept a gift in return for being influenced; (2) solicit or coerce the offering of a gift; or (3) accept gifts from the same or different sources on a basis so frequent that a reasonable person would be led to believe the employee is using his/her public office for private gain.

The Standards of Ethical Conduct for Employees of the Executive Branch cover many aspects governing employee conduct and provide that an employee shall avoid any action, whether or not specifically prohibited by the regulation which might result in or create the appearance of: (1) holding a conflicting financial interest; (2) loss of impartiality in performing official duties; or (3) using public office for private gain.

An area of concern for inspectional personnel is a setting where, during an establishment inspection, you have lunch with plant officials and/or personnel and find your lunch paid for by them, or there is no way you can pay for your portion of the luncheon.

It is always best for an employee to decline any gift, including meals, offered by a regulated company's staff. However, when circumstances arise where refusal is imprudent or impractical, such as finding your lunch paid for by the firm, be gracious, but make it clear the situation cannot be repeated. Always use your best judgment. Modest items of food and refreshment, such as soft drinks, coffee, and donuts offered as other than part of a meal, are excluded from consideration as gifts.

ORA's policy requires you do not use or consume a firm's products at any of the firm's facilities. This can be interpreted as acceptance a product is satisfactory and could embarrass the Agency, particularly in the event of a subsequent regulatory action against the firm.

Professional Personnel Contacts - During inspections and investigations, your activities often involve discussions, conferences, and interviews with professional people.

When dealing with top management officials and other professional persons, your presence may often be disruptive to their activities. Many times you may be squeezed into already crowded schedules and your interviews or investigations may, of necessity, be conducted in offices, waiting rooms, or other areas where customers, patients, or employees are present. If you find yourself in this type of situation, be aware your conversations or activities may be overheard by others.

If it is necessary to review records or conduct interviews, conduct your activities in a quiet and dignified manner. Always try to arrange with management for a private area for this work.

If the person becomes unreasonable, and it is impossible to continue the assignment, terminate the interview and consult your supervisor.

169.2 Outside Activity

Each FDA employee is encouraged to engage in outside activities which contribute to his technical or professional development, or advances the mission of FDA.

Standards Setting Activity - FDA encourages organizations to set standards of quality and safety, and to promote adherence to them. Since FDA considers such standards as supplemental to its own regulatory functions, its employees may, with limitations, be authorized to participate in such outside standards setting activities. These include such activities as: (1) development of standard performance requirements; (2) testing methodology; (3) manufacturing practices; (4) product standards; (5) scientific protocols; (6) compliance criteria; (7) ingredient specifications; (8) labeling; (9) other technical or policy criteria. For information and procedures to follow in obtaining approval for these activities see your district copy of the Staff Manual Guides, Guide Number 2125.1.

Outside Employment - Certain outside activities, paid or unpaid, unrelated to FDA's activities are permissible. Such employment must be approved. Outside jobs must not involve a real or apparent conflict of interest. They must not interfere with your efficiency, or require official time or use of official facilities or records. These limitations apply to all outside activities. In addition, you may not:

1.   Engage in any work that identifies the DHHS or FDA with any commercialization of products.

2.   Accept anything of value for helping a contractor in the procurement of a government contract.

3.   Represent the Department in dealing with a matter in which you have a conflicting interest.

4.   Be paid from outside sources for services in any matter "in which the United States has an interest."

5.   Accept, from the outside, pay for the performance of your official duties.

Political Activity - As a Federal employee you may vote as you please and express your opinion on political subjects. However you may not:

1.   Use your official authority or influence for the purpose of affecting the results of an election.

2.   Take an active part in political management of political campaigns. Consult your supervisor if there is any doubt in your mind regarding departmental regulations on activities prohibited by the Hatch Act.

Teaching, Speaking and Writing - The Standards of Ethical Conduct contain detailed information on teaching, writing and speaking. Please review them in detail if you are involved in outside activities of this nature. Employees may participate in these activities, however, advance approval is required and there are certain restrictions on accepting compensation for these activities.

Financial Interest - You may not have financial interests that conflict, or appear to conflict, with your responsibilities and duties as an FDA employee. You cannot engage, directly or indirectly, in financial transactions as a result of or primarily relying upon information obtained through your job. If you are required to file a Public or Confidential Financial Disclosure Report, you may not have substantial financial interest in industries regulated by FDA. See your supervisor if you have any reservation or question relative to financial interest or contact the Division of Management Programs, Ethics and Integrity Staff at 301-827-5511.

169.3 Financial Responsibility

You are expected to conduct your financial affairs in accordance with accepted standards of ethical business practice, and to pay your just debts promptly.

169.4 Gifts

Under Subpart C of the Standards of Ethical Conduct, guidance is provided on rules governing gifts between employees, including gifts to supervisors. On an occasional basis, such as a birthday or holiday, you may give an unsolicited gift valued at $10 or less to your supervisor. Also, you may give a gift to your supervisor to mark a special occasion such as his/her marriage, the birth of his/her child, and his/her retirement or transfer.

169.5 Attempted Bribery

Bribery is the practice of offering something, such as money or a favor, to a person in a position of trust to influence that person's views or conduct. Occasionally, FDA employees experience bribery attempts.

Bribery or attempted bribery of a Federal Officer is a crime (18 U.S.C. 201). If you are offered money or anything else of value, pursue the following course of action:

1.   Attempt to obtain a clarification of the offer (e.g., Ask questions like, "What is this for?").

2.   Do not accept or refuse the offer. Appear to vacillate, and keep the door open for future contact.

3.   Calmly terminate the exchange.

4.   As soon as possible, prepare detailed notes concerning what transpired.

5.   Contact your supervisor as soon as possible. The District should notify the OCI office immediately. See IOM 980. If OCI does not respond without delay, notify the Federal Bureau of Investigations (FBI). Experience has shown the FDA will initiate an active investigation at once. You should also advise OIA. You may be asked to assist the OCI/FBI and other investigative bodies by accepting proffered money as evidence, under controlled conditions. Do not participate in any such activity, or accept anything of value outside the controlled conditions of an undercover activity conducted by the FBI and/or other involved Federal law enforcement agencies.

169.6 Health and Hygiene

Inoculations - FDA provides operating field personnel with various inoculations for protection from infection or injury on the job.

The following schedules of shots are recommended:

1.   Domestic Work (a) Tetanus: Permanent immunity through the Tetanus Toxoid series followed by a booster dose every ten years; (b) Typhoid: No longer required even if working in a contaminated environment. Booster dose may be given every three years if desired and requested by employee; (c) Smallpox: No longer required in the U.S.; (d) Other: As required by your specific job.

Hepatitis B Vaccine: a synthetic vaccine has been developed and is available to those employees that may be exposed to the virus during the normal course of official duties. Contact your AO to arrange for this vaccination. Keep in mind a vaccination is not to be considered a substitute for good laboratory/field safety practices. This vaccine is specific for Hepatitis B virus (HBV) only, and not for other blood pathogens.

2.   Foreign Travel - Check with your supervisor well in advance of planned foreign travel as to specific requirements of the countries to be visited.

a.   Typhoid: recommended for travel to areas where typhoid fever is endemic.

b.   Cholera: a primary vaccination or a booster within six months is required for traveling to India and Korea. May also be required occasionally for other nations.

c.   Other: as required for specific country.

Physical Examinations - There is no requirement for periodic physical examinations. Even so, it is your responsibility to adhere to good personal hygiene and health practices.

If any firm management demands evidence of recent physical examination before permitting inspection, consult your supervisor. A mere request to examine your hands for sores, etc., is not unreasonable. However, do not accede to a physical examination.

169.7 Sexual Harassment

Sexual Harassment is a violation of Sec. 703 of Title VII of the Civil Rights Act of 1964. Unwelcome sexual advances and other verbal or physical conduct constitute sexual harassment when:

1.   Submission to such conduct is made, either explicitly or implicitly, a term or condition of an individual's employment,

2.   Submission to, or rejection of, such conduct by an individual is used as the basis for employment decisions affecting such an individual, or

3.   Such conduct has the purpose or effect of unreasonably interfering with an individual's work performance, or creating an intimidating, hostile, or offensive working environment.

In identifying sexual harassment, keep the following in mind: (1) the harasser's behavior must be unwelcome, (2) the gender of the harasser or the victim (whether opposite or same sex) does not lessen the legal relevance of a claim of sexual harassment, (3) even without suffering economic loss, (fired, demoted, denial of training) the mere fact the person is the recipient of unwelcome advances or working in a hostile environment makes the employee a victim of sexual harassment, (4) any person who is exposed to sexual harassment, regardless of whether he/she is the direct recipient, may be considered a victim.

FDA is responsible when an employee is sexually harassed, regardless of whether supervisors knew or should have known of the conduct.

Some actions a supervisor may take if sexual harassment complaints occur:

1.   Conduct an inquiry of the sexual harassment allegation, and determine the facts.

2.   Inform the alleged harasser(s) of the allegations.

3.   Warn the alleged harasser(s) sexual harassment is a violation of Federal law and will not be tolerated.

4.   Provide the alleged harasser(s) a copy of the FDA's sexual harassment policy and a copy of Sec. 703 of Title VII of the Civil Rights Act of 1964.

If the inquiry supports the victim's allegation(s) of sexual harassment, the supervisor should contact the Equal Employment Opportunity (EEO) office for guidance, and the Employee Relations Branch to determine if disciplinary action is warranted.

If a field employee is sexually harassed by a non-FDA employee during an inspection/investigation they should tell the individual to stop the harassing behavior, inform the individual's supervisor, and immediately notify their supervisor. If appropriate, the firm's management should be contacted by District management by phone, followed by correspondence informing them sexual harassment on the basis of sex is a violation Federal law. A copy of the FDA's sexual harassment policy should also be included. If the harassment continues contact FDA's EEO Office (HF-15) at 301-827-4848.

169.9 Disciplinary Action

Penalties for violation of the statutes covering employee conduct are prescribed by law. They range from suspension or dismissal to fine and/or imprisonment. Some laws specify prohibitions but leave the penalty to administrative action. In any such violation, FDA will take such disciplinary action as best meets the objectives of deterring similar offenses and maintaining high standards of employee conduct and public confidence.

SUBCHAPTER 170 - INTERDISTRICT ASSIGNMENTS

This subchapter defines the procedures for issuing assignments between districts and referring information between Districts and ORA headquarters. FDA has put a new data system in place, Field Accomplishments and Compliance Tracking System (FACTS), which includes the ability to generate assignments. This system should be used whenever possible to issue and manage all assignments. You received training on that process during your basic FACTS training. If you have any questions, contact your FACTS Lead User.

Issuance authority - FACTS is the preferred method to generate, issue, and manage assignments for all activities. Memorandums must be used when hard copy attachments accompany the assignment. If mail delay for memorandums is objectionable, overnight delivery is authorized. Use the telephone when urgency requires instant communication; however, all assignments must be entered into FACTS as soon as possible. The receiving District can use the "ad hoc" process in FACTS to generate the assignment in urgent situations. The EIR endorsement shall not be used to make assignments, although it may be an attachment to a written assignment. E-mail the receiving district of an assignment if there is any urgency.

Assignments, excluding recall audit checks, must be approved and signed or issued by a first line manager/team leader, compliance officer, those acting in these positions, or a higher level of management. Recall audit checks may be signed by the Recall and Emergency (R & E) Coordinator.

Assignments involving three or more districts, or requiring more than three working days to complete, shall be approved by the branch director or appropriate manager of the issuing district. Multiple district assignments need to be closely monitored by the issuing district to avoid unnecessary duplication of work.

Procedures - Each assignment shall contain the following details:

1.   Description of the problem and nature of the assignment, i.e., sample collection, records collection, inspection, etc.

2.   Full name, address and the FDA Establishment Identifier (FEI) number of the responsible firm. You may also provide the central file number (CFN) if known or available.

3.   Program Assignment Code (PAC).

4.   Product code and full description of product including lot number(s) and code(s).

5.   Home district code.

6.   Full name and address of the firm (or firms) and individual(s) to contact to accomplish the assignment

7.   Priority and requested completion date.

8.   Name, telephone number and mailing symbol of the contact person who can answer questions concerning the assignment and the person who should be notified of results.

9.   Where to send samples, records, reports, etc.

If all the data is contained in the FACTS fields, there may be no need for a separate memorandum.

Assignments for fieldwork are to be sent to the accomplishing district(s). Assignment memorandums, attachments, or other documents needed to complete the assignment should be sent to the appropriate branch director in the accomplishing district.

Copies of assignments which involve emergencies, danger to health situations or highly publicized investigations shall be sent via e-mail or Federal Express (FedEx) to the Emergency Operations Center, HFC-160 (301-443-1240). Completion and referrals - A copy of the Establishment Inspection Report (EIR), C/R, memorandum, etc., showing results should be sent to the person specified in the assignment, along with a copy of the assignment. When an assignment is completed, make sure the appropriate FACTS fields are updated/entered as necessary. Copies of responses to assignments that involve emergencies, danger to health situations, or highly publicized investigations shall also be sent to Emergency Operations Center, HFC-160.

In the case of samples going to a non-FDA laboratory or a Headquarters' laboratory, a copy of the assignment should be printed and attached to a copy of the C/R which is included in the FDA-525.

All documents relating to an assignment shall include the FACTS assignment and/or operation number.

SUBCHAPTER 180 - FIELD ACCOMPLISHMENTS AND COMPLIANCE TRACKING SYSTEM (FACTS)

The Field Accomplishments and Compliance Tracking System (FACTS) is FDA's automated system for field assignments, work results, firm information, consumer complaints, compliance actions, and time reporting. FACTS incorporates assignment management and work results for the following investigational activities: sample collections, establishment inspections, domestic investigations, and field examinations. FACTS also includes detailed information concerning analytical findings and compliance activities. All these data fields can be searched and viewed by any FACTS user.

FACTS has not changed the requirements for evidence development and documentation, identification of evidence or samples, submission procedures for records collected during inspections or investigations, timeframes for submission of potential regulatory actions, or many other activities you do. Be guided by outstanding policy and procedures in the IOM in these areas. Enter all information required by policy or procedure which may go beyond the "mandatory fields" to simply store information in FACTS. Consult the IOM, Compliance Program (CP) or Assignment for required information. FACTS does not replace hardcopy narrative reporting for things such as inspections, investigations, consumer complaint follow-up and others.

FDA has not developed a "user's manual" for FACTS. Be guided by the information you received during your FACTS training, information and instructions contained in the Data Codes Manual (DCM) and the IOM. FACTS on-line HELP is your first source of information on the functioning of FACTS and how to enter data. If additional help is necessary, users contact the local FACTS Lead Users.

Each Supervisory Investigator (SCSO), Investigator (CSO) and Inspector (CSI) has a FACTS "electronic signature". This signature is used to electronically sign sample collection, inspectional, and investigational reports in FACTS. It also provides the same legal basis for regulatory activities as a handwritten signature on a paper document. FACTS is designed to limit the ability of individuals, other than the person recording the information, to make changes to stored information, in many, but not all, cases.

You are responsible for reporting your activities and time on all reportable operations. FACTS is designed to capture all the necessary data formerly kept in the Program Oriented Data (PODS) and Manpower Utilization Systems (MUS). You are responsible for reviewing and updating information in FACTS in the "MAINTAIN FIRM" data area. This is the same information previously kept in the Official Establishment Inventory (OEI) data system. These updates should be completed when you enter data into any FACTS record or record your time for the assignment.

Since most assignments will be requested and managed within FACTS, you should check your FACTS "Inbox" at least daily.

SUBCHAPTER 181 - OPERATIONAL AND ADMINISTRATIVE SYSTEM FOR IMPORT SUPPORT (OASIS)

The Operational and Administrative System for Import Support (OASIS), is a national database on imports, enforcement activities and findings. OASIS is designed to accomplish the following objectives:
- Make a risk assessment of incoming entry data to identify those which must be reviewed by FDA personnel and allow the others to enter commerce without further action
- Increase the productivity of investigations' personnel in the field though automated interfaces with the FDA Centers, Brokers/Filers, and the U.S. Customs Service (USCS)
- Integrate OASIS with other ORA systems to provide for seamless linkage of import and domestic functions
- Improve screening of imports by providing suggestions for actions likely to result in discovery of violations
- Provide faster turn-around for processing of importer's entries and faster and more consistent response to discovered violations and import alerts
- Provide national and district uniformity in processing of entries
- Assist compliance personnel in tracking the status of suspected violative products and information related to these products
- Provide the ability to track the performance of Private Laboratories who submit analytical work to FDA for imported products
- Automate the generation of the Notices of Action sent to firms regarding actions taken by FDA
- Provide redundant electronic notification of cargo hold/detain/release/refusal statuses to the filers via the USCS interface
- Maintain a base of information for generation of reports at the district, regional, and national level
- Adjust the regulatory strategy and screening of products based upon national database of trade patterns and sample/examination results
- Respond to congressional and management needs for information on the effectiveness of FDA programs

The system not only supports FDA field personnel in carrying-out their day-to-day activities, but also provides headquarters personnel and program staff within the FDA Centers with vital information on FDA compliance programs and workforce accomplishments. By having national data on imports, enforcement activities and findings, FDA management is better able to spot emerging trends, identify emergency situations and alert all field personnel quickly, allocate resources more effectively, and effect greater uniformity in enforcement activities throughout the country.

Additional information about OASIS and guidance on its use can be found in IOM Chapter 6, Imports, and in the OASIS "Help" module.

SUBCHAPTER 190 - REGULATORY NOTES

190 OVERVIEW

Regulatory notes are the record of your daily investigatory efforts. They record your observations relevant to violations and active cases. They are the vital link between your findings and your subsequent testimony in court. Because of the data, which regulatory notes contain, such as information pertaining to open investigatory files, trade secrets, and personal information protected under the Privacy Act, they are confidential. Regulatory notes are government property. The notes cannot be released to anyone outside the Agency, except with the express permission of your management, and after following FDA's procedures. (See IOM 130)

See IOM 114 for guidance on administrative notes.

191 USES OF REGULATORY NOTES

Accurate regulatory notes are to refresh your memory when reporting certain important details of a sample collection, inspection, and investigation. Notes also support the principle of "presumption of regularity", i.e., in the absence of clear evidence to the contrary, courts presume public officers properly discharge their official duties. Regulatory notes are useful as a means to refute assertions by defendants, witnesses or others. Regulatory notes also aid in defending lawsuits against FDA agents. This has been an issue of significance in a number of regulatory cases in the Federal Sector.

192 REQUIREMENTS FOR REGULATORY NOTES

Regulatory notes should be made at the time of the event they represent. Regulatory notes must be original recordings of an activity, and may be handwritten (in ink) or electronic. Do not erase, edit or rewrite original notes. Any corrections should be identified.

Regulatory notes in electronic format must be authenticated to ensure document integrity. If electronic notes are utilized, adhere to agency directives and procedures to safeguard and file electronic notes. Positive identification of regulatory notes in electronic format is imperative. Regulatory notes can be printed, and each page initialed (handwritten initials) and dated by the Investigator. If this procedure is used, the original disk can be identified with the firm name, dates, and investigator's initials; placed in a FDA-525 envelope; and then sealed with an Official Seal, FDA-415a. NOTE: See IOM 522 -Exhibits, for guidance on the identification and storage of electronic data obtained from inspected firms, and used as exhibits for the EIR. Regulatory notes must be accurate, objective, factual, and free of personal feelings or conclusions.

193 REGULATORY ENTRIES

Regulatory notes should contain sufficient detail to refresh an investigator's memory regarding inspections, investigations and sample collections. They must include objectionable conditions, pertinent information about your activities during an operation, details of a sample collection, etc. If a checklist is used during an inspection, don't repeat that information in your regulatory notes. The checklist should be handled as part of the notes. Likewise, when relevant information is contained on an FDA form, or in an exhibit collected during an inspection, that information need not be repeated in your notes.

Regulatory notes should contain the substance of all significant discussions with people contacted during the activity; e.g., discussions of individual responsibility. When entering a direct quote in a notebook, such as a statement against self-interest, it is important the exact words be used to preserve the original intent of the individual and subject. Every quote of significance appearing in the final report should be in your regulatory notes since they are part of the source documents, which will support any regulatory or administrative action.

Regulatory notes should not contain purely administrative information. See IOM 114 for guidance on administrative notes.

194 FORMAT FOR REGULATORY NOTES

Your regulatory notes should always be kept in a bound notebook. The reason for this is the continuity and integrity provided by bound pages. Loose-leaf and spiral bindings allow easy removal of pages, an invitation to vigorous and heated cross-examination on the witness stand. Bound notebooks also prevent lost or misplaced pages.

Regulatory notes in electronic format are a valuable tool to expediting the conduct of an inspection. They may be stored on computer disk, but must be preserved in a manner that ensures data integrity.

Regulatory notes whether written or electronic are subject to audit at any time; must be available for review; and must, on demand, be surrendered to your supervisors or other authorized personnel. Regulatory notes should be identified with your name, telephone number, and address to facilitate their return if lost. Advancing technology may increase the preservation options available. District policy should be followed regarding the preservation of all regulatory notes.

195 RETENTION OF REGULATORY NOTES

Regulatory notes are to be appropriately identified with your name and the bracketing dates they cover before they are turned over for storage. Follow your District's policy regarding the maintenance of regulatory notes.

Based on your district's policy, regulatory notes (including computer disks) may be kept by you, filed with the final report, or kept by the district in a separate, designated file. At a minimum, regulatory notes must be retained for the same period of time as the inspection report, collection report or other investigational report, or until all court actions, including appeals, have been adjudicated.

If you leave FDA, or are transferred from your district, any regulatory notes in your possession must be identified and turned in to the district you are leaving. Districts are to retain regulatory notes as official records as outlined in the FDA Staff Manual Guide.

Regulatory notes prepared by headquarters' personnel during a field inspection/investigation are official records. Headquarters personnel are to follow their Center's policy regarding the retention of regulatory notes. In general, all regulatory notes should be maintained in the District or Center where the original report is filed.

EXHIBIT 110-B
ALLOWABLE EXPENSES CHART

Below is a table of allowable expense items and the requirements that must be met to assure reimbursement. Unless "xx" appears in one or more of the columns at the right, there are no special requirements for reimbursement.

EXPENSE ITEM	Specific authorization or approval	Receipt	Justification on voucher for any amount	Statement on voucher if over $25.00

A. BAGGAGE
1. Weight allowance on baggage transported free of charge by common carrier on ticket:
  a. **Rail.** Up to 150 lbs. (domestic)
  b. **Air**. Varies. Up to 70 lbs. per each of 2 bags within the continental U.S. on major trunk or regional carriers.
  c. **Steamship**. No specific limitation on baggage carried in traveler's stateroom.
There is no additional allowance for free transportation of baggage for infants.				

2. Excess Baggage Charges for government property Note: Where air coach or air tourist accommodations are used, transportation of baggage up to the weight carried free on first-class service is allowed	xx	xx	xx[1]	
3. Service Charge for checking baggage by checking agent where such charges for checking baggage in baggage rooms, or station or air terminal		xx	xx	
4. Storage Charges (e.g., when traveler stores baggage or equipment not needed during a portion of his trip		xx	xx[2]	
5. Transfer Charges - when necessary for official travel (e.g., when changing between stations where free transportation is not issued by common carrier.) CAUTION: Where the traveler's plans are changed he shall make sure that baggage that has been checked beyond the point where he leaves the train is stopped or transferred. If baggage cannot be intercepted or transferred and is carried to original destination on unused portion of ticket, the traveler shall give full explanation of facts when submitting unused portion of ticket. Failure to do so will result in any excess cost being charged to traveler.		xx	xx	
B. FEES OR TIPS 1. Parking Fees – charges for parking automobiles	xx	xx (over $75)		
2. Porter – allowable only at transportation terminals for handling Government property carried by travelers. Porter fees for personal property, brief cases, etc. are not allowed.			xx[3]	
3. Registration a. for attendance at local non-government sponsored meetings b. other	HHS-99			

EXHIBIT 110-B   INVESTIGATIONS OPERATIONS MANUAL

EXPENSE ITEM	Specific authorization or approval	Receipt	Justification on voucher for any amount	Statement on voucher if over $25.00

4. Exchange of Currency
  a. ALLOWED
    (1) fees for cashing U.S. Government checks or drafts reimbursing traveler for travel expenses only incurred in foreign countries
	xx	xx		

(2) commissions for conversion of currency in foreign countries	xx	xx[4]		
(3) Costs of traveler's checks, money orders, certified checks purchased in connection with official travel. Costs may not exceed amount needed to cover reimbursable expenses. b. NOT ALLOWED: exchange fees for cashing checks or drafts issued in payment of salary.	xx			
5. For Foreign Travel - Passports, visa fees, costs of photographs for passports and visas, costs of certificates of birth, health, identity, and of affidavits, and charges for inoculations not obtainable through a Federal dispensary	xx	xx		
6. Not Allowed - Gratuities (tips) to Government employees				
C. HIRE OF ROOM 1. ALLOWED: When necessary to engage a room in a hotel or other place to transact official business	xx	xx	xx[6]	
2. NOT ALLOWED: Hotel accommodations for personal use (cost included in subsistence allowance).				
D. PERSONAL SERVICES 1. Stenographic and typing services, guides, interpreters, drivers of vehicles, etc.	xx	xx	xx[5]	
2. Rental of typewriter	xx	xx	xx[5]	
E. POSTAGE Postage necessary for official airmail, foreign, or parcel post mail; and for official registered and special delivery mail.	xx	xx	xx[7]	
F. POST OFFICE BOX RENTAL Where necessary for official airmail, foreign, or parcel post mail; and for official registered and special delivery mail.	xx	xx	xx	
G. STEAMER CHAIRS, RUGS, CUSHIONS, ETC. For official steamship travel, expenses incident thereto at customary rates actually charged				

H. STREETCARS AND BUSES WHILE IN TRAVEL STATUS
  1. ALLOWED: Public transportation fares;
    a. from (or to) common carrier, or other terminals, to (or from) place of abode or place of business
    b. between place of abode and place of business, or between places of business
	xx	xx
		(over $75)
			xx[9]	

EXPENSE ITEM	Specific authorization or approval	Receipt	Justification on voucher for any amount	Statement on voucher if over $25.00
2. NOT ALLOWED: Public transportation fares between places where meals are taken, and places of business or places of lodging, except where nature and location of work at temporary duty station is such that suitable meals cannot be procured there - allowance will be made for transportation to the nearest available place for such meals.				

I. TAXICABS WHEN USED LOCALLY WHILE IN TRAVEL STATUS
1. USE ALLOWED:
  a. from (or to) common carrier or other terminal to (or from) place of abode or place of business.
  b. between place of abode and place of business, or between places of business, where cheaper mode of transportation is not available, or is impracticable to use.
	xx	xx (over $75)
		
		xx (over $75)
			xx[9]	

2. USE NOT ALLOWED: between places where meals are taken, and places of business, except where nature and locations of suitable meals cannot be procured there - allowance will be made for transportation to the nearest available place for such meals.	xx	xx (over $75)	xx[9]	
3. Fares and Tips (refer to IOM 111.3)		xx (over $75)		
J. CHARGES for limousine service plus taxicab tip rates between airport and limousine pick-up or discharge point.		xx (over $75)		
K. TELEGRAMS AND CABLEGRAMS 1. ALLOWED: Charges for telegrams, cablegrams, and radiograms on official business. (Note: traveler shall use government facilities where available. Where not available official messages may be sent collect via commercial facilities.		xx	xx[10]	
2. NOT ALLOWED: messages of a personal nature, including request for leave, information about salary check, expense voucher, hotel reservation, etc.; except that a request for hotel reservation incident to official business provided reference is made to official conference or official business involved is allowable.				
L. TELEPHONE CALLS 1. ALLOWED: charges for local and long distance calls when made on official business		xx[10] & xx[11]		
2. Personal calls - see IOM 118				
M. RECORDS - charges for copies of records furnished by State officials, such as Clerks of Courts, etc., when necessary for performance of official business		xx	xx[5]	
N. SHIPMENTS (FREIGHT OR EXPRESS) – See IOM 454		xx	xx[12]	

EXHIBIT 110-B   INVESTIGATIONS OPERATIONS MANUAL

EXPENSE ITEM	Specific authorization or approval	Receipt	Justification on voucher for any amount	Statement on voucher if over $25.00
O. EMERGENCY OR OTHER MISCELLANEOUS EXPENSES 1. Cash used in lieu of transportation request for passenger transportation and accommodations. 2. Purchase of emergency supplies. 3. Any other miscellaneous expenditures incurred by traveler in performance of official business, such as samples of drugs, cosmetics, etc. purchased by FDA inspectors and investigators.	xx xx	xx xx	xx[5]	
P. LAUNDRY EXPENSES - Effective November 1, 1999 reimbursement of laundry expenses is allowed for travel within the continental U.S. (CONUS)[13] when the traveler is in travel status for four or more consecutive nights and provides a receipt for all official laundry expenses. When a coin operated machine is used to launder clothing and a receipt can not be obtained, a statement must appear on the voucher to substantiate the claim.		xx		

FOOTNOTES:

1. Voucher must show weight of baggage when claim is the result of exceeding weight limitations and points between which moved
2. State that storage is solely on account of official business.
3. State that porter fee was for handling Government property carried by traveler.
4. Voucher shall show rate of conversion and commission charges.
5. Voucher shall show date of service, quantity, unit, and unit price.
6. In addition to information required in footnote #5, state necessity for hire of room.
7. State that postage was used for official mail.
8. (Omitted)
9. State necessity for daily travel.
10. For telegrams, cablegrams, and long distance telephone calls, show points between which service was rendered, date, amount paid on each and "official business".
11. For local telephone, calls show number of calls, rate per call, total amount expended each day, and "official business".
12. When government Bill of Lading is not used, explain circumstances.
13. Continental United States (CONUS) is defined as the 48 contiguous states and the District of Columbia.

TRAVEL VOUCHER *(Read Privacy Act Statement on the back)*	1. DEPARTMENT OR ESTABLISHMENT BUREAU DIVISION OR OFFICE ① FDA/SER/ATL/DO/IB	2. TYPE OF TRAVEL ☒ TEMPORARY DUTY ☐ PERMANENT CHANGE OF STATION	3. VOUCHER NO. 4. SCHEDULE NO.

5. **a. NAME** *(Last, first, middle initial)* ②
Rogers, Sidney H.

c. MAILING ADDRESS *(Include ZIP Code)* ③
60 Eighth St. NE
Atlanta, GA 30309

e. PRESENT DUTY STATION ④
Atlanta, GA

f. RESIDENCE *(City and State)* ⑤
Atlanta, GA

b. SOCIAL SECURITY NO. ⑥
444-44-4444

d. OFFICE TELEPHONE NO. ⑦
404-881-3151

6. PERIOD OF TRAVEL
a. FROM ⑧ 09/28/98   **b. TO** 10/02/98

7. TRAVEL AUTHORIZATION
a. NUMBER(S) ⑨   **b. DATE(S)** ⑩

10. CHECK NO.

11. PAID BY

8. TRAVEL ADVANCE
a. Outstanding ⑪   0.00
b. Amount to be applied   0.00
c. Amount due Government *(Attached)* ☐ Check ☐ Cash
D. Balance outstanding

9. CASH PAYMENT RECEIPT
a. DATE RECEIVED
b. AMOUNT RECEIVED $
c. PAYEE'S SIGNATURE

12. GOVERNMENT TRANSPORTATION REQUESTS, OR TRANSPORTATION TICKETS, IF PURCHASED WITH CASH *(List by number below and attach passenger coupon; if cash is used show claim on reverse side)*

I hereby assign the United States any right I may have against any parties in connection with reimbursable transportation charges described below, purchased under cash payment procedures (FPMR 101-7) ▶ Traveler's initials

	AGENT'S VALUATION OF TICKET (a)	ISSUING CARRIER (Initials) (b)	MODE CLASS OF SERVICE AND ACCOMMODATIONS (c)	DATE ISSUED (d)	POINTS OF TRAVEL	
					FROM (e)	TO (f)
A 0 612,080	154.50	EA	Y	09/23/98	ATL-Atlanta,	JAX-Jacksonv
	⑫	⑬	⑭	⑮	⑯	

COMMENTS: ㉕
Purpose of Travel (When Travel Manager is used to prepare travel voucher, the purpose of travel is not shown anywhere on the voucher. It is only documented on the travel order. The comments block can be used to state the purpose if necessary.) This travel voucher was created using Travel Manager 7.CB.

13. I certify that this voucher is true and correct to the best of my knowledge and belief, and that payment or credit has not been received by me. When applicable, per diem claimed is based on the average cost of lodging incurred during the period covered by this voucher.

TRAVELER SIGN HERE ▶ *Sidney H Rogers* ⑰   DATE ⑱   AMOUNT CLAIMED ▶   ⑲ 603.85

NOTE: Falsification of an item in an expense account works a forfeiture of claim (28 U.S.C. 2514) and may result in a fine of not more than $10,000 or imprisonment for not more than 5 years or both (18 U.S.C. 287, id. 1001).

14. This voucher is approved. Long distance phone calls, if any, are verified as necessary in the interest of the Government. *(NOTE: If long distance telephone calls are included, the approving official must have been authorized in writing by the head of the department or agency to so certify (31 U.S.C. 680a).)*

APPROVING OFFICIAL SIGN HERE ▶ ⑳   DATE

15. LAST PRECEDING VOUCHER PAID UNDER SAME TRAVEL AUTHORIZATION
a. VOUCHER NO   b. D.O. SYMBOL   c. MONTH & YEAR

16. THIS VOUCHER IS CERTIFIED CORRECT AND PROPER FOR PAYMENT
AUTHORIZED CERTIFYING OFFICIAL SIGN HERE ▶ ㉑   DATE

17. FOR FINANCE OFFICE USE ONLY COMPUTATION ㉒ $
a. DIFFERENCES, IF ANY *(Explain and show amount)*
b. TOTAL VERIFIED CORRECT FOR CHARGE TO APPROPRIATION   Certifier's initials $
c. APPLIED TO TRAVEL ADVANCE *(Appropriation symbol):* $
d. NET TO TRAVELER ▶ $

18. ACCOUNTING CLASSIFICATION

SCHEDULE OF EXPENSES AND AMOUNTS CLAIMED

Complete this information if this is a continuation sheet

PAGE 2 OF PAGES

TRAVEL AUTHORIZATION NO. ⑨ a ⑩

TRAVELER'S LAST NAME: Rogers

INSTRUCTIONS TO TRAVELER (Unlisted items are self-explanatory)

Col. (g) If the voucher includes per diem allowance for members of employee's immediate family, show dependent names, ages, and relationships to employee and marital status of children (juniors, information is shown or claimed (meals, lodging).)

(h) Show amount incurred for each meal, including tax and tips, and daily total meal cost.

(j) Show expenses such as laundry, cleaning and pressing of clothes, tips to bellboys, porters, etc. (other than for meals).

(k) Complete for per diem and actual expense travel.

(m) Show total subsistence expense incurred for actual personal travel.

(m) Show per diem amount, limited to maximum rate, or travel on actual expense, show the lesser of the amount from col. (j) or maximum rate.

(n) Show expense, such as taxicab fare, air fare (if purchased with cash), local or long distance telephone calls for Government business, car rental, miscellaneous other than subsistence, etc.

DATE 19 98 ㉓	DESCRIPTION (Departure/arrival, city, per diem conditions, or other exceptions) ㉔	BREAK-FAST	MEALS LUNCH	DINNER	TOTAL	MISCEL-LANEOUS SUBSIS-TENCE	LODGING	TOTAL SUBSISTENCE EXPENSE	MILEAGE NO. OF MILES ㉗	MILEAGE	SUBSISTENCE ㉘	OTHER
09/28	D-:RES: Atlanta,GA 25			Air fare								154.50
09/28	A-:JACKSONVILLE,FL			22.50			73.00	95.50			95.50	
09/28												61.90
09/29	Taxi-airport to hotel											21.30
09/29	Subsistence			30.00			73.00	103.00			103.00	
09/30	Subsistence Official Business						-					2.30
09/30	Subsistence			30.00			73.00	103.00			103.00	
10/01	Subsistence			30.00			73.00	103.00			103.00	
10/02	D-:JACKSONVILLE,FL											
10/02				Taxi-airport to res								6.90
10/02	A:RES: Atlanta,GA			Taxi-hotel to airport								3.45
10/02	Subsistence			22.50				22.50			22.50	
	SUBTOTALS									0.00	427.00	176.35
	TOTALS									0.00	427.00	176.35

㉖

Enter grand total of columns (l), (m) and (n), below and to item 11 on the front of this form

TOTAL AMOUNT CLAIMED ▶ 603.35 ㉙

STANDARD FORM 1012 BACK (10-77)

EXHIBIT 110-D
TRAVEL VOUCHER (SF-1012) PREPARATION INSTRUCTIONS

The numbers below correspond to the circled numbers on IOM Exhibit 110-D. Check with your supervisor for any additional requirements by your district. Travel vouchers should be legible and must be completed in ink.

1.   Location: Insert the name of the Department, Agency, & Center/Office or Field District Office.
2.   Payee's Name: Enter traveler's name exactly as it appears on Travel Order. (Commissioned Officers, also show rank.)
3.   Mailing Address: Show address to which payment would be mailed if applicable.
4.   Present Duty Station: Enter your official duty station such as District. In case travel is to new station as on transfer, enter new station.
5.   Residence: Enter your permanent residence.
6.   Social Security Number: Insert your number.
7.   Office Telephone No.: Enter number at which you can be reached.
8.   Period of Travel: Enter first and last dates of expenses covered by voucher.
9.   Authority No.: Enter Travel Order number from your travel order or obtain DO number from supervisor.
10. Authority Date: Enter date of TO. Obtain from your fiscal clerk for travel under district TO.
11. Travel Advance: Claim government-issued cash advances here. Don't claim federal credit card ATM withdrawals here.
12. Agent's Valuation of Ticket: Enter the total amount of travel and/or accommodation as shown on the TR.
13. Initials of Carrier Issuing Ticket: Show the initials of the carrier who issued the ticket.
14. Mode, Class of Service & Accommodation: Specify the type of transportation, i.e., rail air, bus; also type of accommodation used.
15. Date issued: Insert the date the ticket was issued.
16. Points of Travel: Enter point of origin and destination. If round trip, specify "& return".
17. Payee: Sign your name.
18. Date: Enter date you sign the voucher.
19. Amount Claimed: Enter the total amount of expenses for which gross reimbursement is claimed.
20. Approved: Your supervisor or other administrative official signs here to indicate administrative approval. If any expenses claimed require specific approval, e.g., taxi fares in excess of maximum or goods or services not specified on TO, the approval must be made by an official designated to authorize travel.
21. Last Preceding Voucher: If you submitted a previous voucher under the same TO, enter date submitted.
22. Accounting Classification: Your DO Fiscal Clerk normally enters this.

REVERSE SIDE OF VOUCHER

23. Date: Show date on which item of expense was incurred.
24. Time: Show date of departure from, and arrival at, official station or other place where official travel begins and ends. Other places visited while in travel status should be shown, but time of arrival is not necessary unless required by your district.
25. Description: State the general purpose of trip. (Note: Travel Manager computerized authorization/voucher program does not allow for placement of purpose on the reverse side of the voucher. If needed, the purpose can be placed in the comment section which prints on the front of the voucher.)

     Itemize chronologically all expenses for the period covered by voucher including per diem and lodging.
     Where a constructive cost is required, such as when your personal car is used in lieu of taxi or common carrier, provide specific flight or carrier schedules, times, and names of carriers. When allowable expenses are not to exceed constructive cost by common carrier, show the lesser of the actual cost or constructive cost in the "Amount Claimed" column.
a.   24 Hours or Less:
     No M&IE shall be allowed for domestic travel when the travel period is 12 hours or less in the same calendar day, or the employees workday plus 2 hours for employees who work a so-called non-standard workday.
     When the travel period (entire trip) for which per diem has been authorized is more than 12 hours, but does not exceed 24 hours, the per diem allowance for the trip will be ¾ of the applicable M&IE allowance for the temporary duty assignment location.
b.   Over 24 Hours:
     The M&IE Allowance is ¾ of the daily rate on first and last date of travel when overnight travel is involved and the full daily rate for each intervening day.
26. Instructions to Traveler: Self-explanatory.
27. Mileage Rate: Show rate per mile as authorized in the TO and the net mileage claimed. Any significant difference between mileage claimed and the Standard Highway Mileage should be explained.
28. Amount Claimed: Enter the amounts claimed opposite the specific description of items explained under "Description".
29. Grand Total: Enter the grand total to be carried forward to the face of the voucher. (Item 20)

NOTE:

1.   When reclaiming a portion of a previous voucher which was suspended, identify fully and attach a copy of the suspension notice.
2.   Lodging receipts are required. Submit Hotel Receipt with voucher.

CHAPTER 2 - ORGANIZATION

SUBCHAPTER 200 - ORGANIZATION OVERVIEW

A complete description of the FDA's organizational structure and its functional statement is found in various chapters of the Staff Manual Guides (SMG) which are available on FDA's Intranet Website see http://intranet.fda.gov/oc/oms/oirm/manuals/smg/smg.htm.

The FDA is a part of the Department of Health and Human Services (HHS). An appointed Commissioner who serves at the discretion of the President heads the agency.

There are approximately 9300 FDA employees.

The FDA is a team of dedicated professionals working to protect and promote the health of the American people.

FDA is responsible for ensuring:

Foods are safe, wholesome, and sanitary; human and veterinary drugs, biological products, and medical devices are safe and effective; cosmetics are safe; and electronic products that emit radiation are safe.

Regulated products are honestly, accurately, and informatively represented.

These products are in compliance with the law and FDA regulations; noncompliance is identified and corrected; and any unsafe or unlawful products are removed from the marketplace.

201   FDA PRINCIPLES

We strive to:

Enforce FDA laws and regulations, using all appropriate legal means.

Base regulatory decisions on a strong scientific and analytical base and the law; and understand, conduct, and apply excellent science and research.

Be a positive force in making safe and effective products available to the consumer, and focus special attention on rare and life-threatening diseases.

Provide clear standards of compliance to regulated industry, and advise industry on how to meet those standards.

Identify and effectively address critical public health problems arising from use of FDA-regulated products.

Increase FDA's effectiveness through collaboration and cooperation with state and local governments; domestic, foreign, and international agencies; industry; and academia.

Assist the media, consumer groups, and health professionals in providing accurate, current information about regulated products to the public.

Work consistently toward effective and efficient application or resources to our responsibilities,

Provide superior public service by developing, maintaining, and supporting a high-quality, diverse workforce.

Be honest, fair, and accountable in all our actions and decisions.

SUBCHAPTER 210 - OFFICE OF THE COMMISSIONER

210   IMMEDIATE OFFICE (OC)(HF-1)

The Commissioner of the Food and Drug Administration is Mark B. McClellan, M.D., Ph.D.

The Deputy Commissioner of the Food and Drug Administration is Lester M. Crawford, D.V.M., Ph.D.

The immediate staff offices within the OC are:
1.   Office of the Chief Council (GCF-1), Daniel Troy, Chief Counsel.
2.   Administrative Law Judge (HF-3) Daniel J. Davidson, ALJ
3.   Office of Equal Opportunity (HF-15) Anthony J. Kaminski, Acting Director
4.   Senior Advisor for Science (HF-1) Bernard A. Schwetz, D.V.M., Ph.D.

The immediate OC has approximately 147 employees.

In addition, the four offices listed below will be discussed separately.

211   OFFICE OF THE SENIOR ASSOCIATE COMMISSIONER (HF- 2)

The Office of the Senior Associate Commissioner is responsible for agency-level activities and decisions which affect agency-wide programs, projects, strategies and initiatives. Components under this office are:
1.   Office of Executive Secretariat (HF-40) Catherine P. Beck, Director
2.   Office of Public Affairs (HFI-1) Larry Bachorik, Interim Associate Commissioner
3.   Office of the Ombudsman, Steve Unger, Acting Chief Mediator & Ombudsman
4.   Office of Orphan Products Development (HF-35) Marlene E. Haffner, MD, Director
5.   Office of Internal Affairs (HF-9) Tommy L. Hampton, Special Agent in Charge

212   OFFICE OF POLICY, PLANNING, AND LEGISLATION (HF-22)

The Associate Commissioner for Policy, Planning and Legislation is William K. Hubbard.

The Acting Associate Commissioner for Policy is Margaret Dotzel.

This office is responsible for developing, coordinating, managing, and researching the policy of the agency and includes the following staffs:
1.   Office of Policy
Regulations Policy and Management Staff, Edwin V. Dutra, Director
Policy Development and Coordination Staff, Catherine Lorraine, Director
2.   Office of Planning
Planning Staff, Morris R. Bosin, Director
Evaluation Staff, Kathleen A. McEvoy, Director
Economics Staff, Lawrence Braslow, Director

3. Office of Legislation, Melinda Plaisier,
Interim Associate Commissioner
Michael A. Eck, Director
Congressional Affairs Staff I,
Congressional Affairs Staff II,
Jarilyn Dupont, Director
Congressional Affairs Staff III, Vacant, Director
The OPP&L has approximately 37 employees.

213 OFFICE OF MANAGEMENT AND SYSTEMS (HF-20)

This office is responsible for the planning and evaluation of agency activities and for the management of overall agency financial operations, human resources and management services, facilities, acquisitions and central services, plus information resources management.

The following offices are located in the Office of Management & Systems:
1. Office of Human Resources & Management Services (HFA-400), Mary L. Babcock, Director
2. Office of Information Resources Management (HFA-80), William M. Bristow, II, Chief Information Officer
3. Office of Financial Management (HFA-100) Donald J. Sauer, Acting Director
4. Office of Facilities, Acquisitions & Central Services (HFA-500), James L. Tidmore, Director

The Office of Management and Systems has approximately 616 employees

214 OFFICE OF INTERNATIONAL AND CONSTITUENT RELATIONS (HF-24)

The Deputy Commissioner for the Office of International and Constituent Relations (OICR) is Sharon Smith Holston. This office is responsible for special health issues, women's health, consumer affairs, and international programs.

The following offices are located in OICR:
1. Office of International Programs (HFG-1) Sharon Smith Holston, Acting Director
2. Office of Consumer Affairs (HFE-1) Patricia M. Kuntze, Acting Associate Commissioner
3. Office of Women's Health Audrey Sheppard, Acting Director
3. Office of Special Health Issues (HF-12) Theresa Toigo, R.Ph., MBA, Associate Commissioner

The OICR has approximately 82 employees.

SUBCHAPTER 220 - CENTER FOR BIOLOGICS EVALUATION AND RESEARCH (CBER)

220 OFFICE OF THE CENTER DIRECTOR

The CBER director is Jesse Goodman, M.D., M.P.H.

This center is responsible for administering the regulation of biological products under the biological product control provisions of the Public Health Services Act (PHS Act) and applicable provisions of the Federal Food Drug and Cosmetic Act (FD&C Act).

Establishes written and physical standards, conducts research, tests products submitted for release, approves licensing of biological manufacturers and biological products, and inspects licensed manufacturers' facilities for compliance with standards. Provides focus in FDA for coordination of the Acquired Immune Deficiency Syndrome (AIDS) program. Works to develop an AIDS vaccine, AIDS diagnostic tests and conducts other AIDS-related activities.

Plans and conducts research on the preparation, preservation, and safety of blood and blood products, the methods of testing safety, purity, potency and efficacy of such products of therapeutic use, and the immunological problems concerned with products, testing, and use of diagnostic reagents employed in grouping and typing blood.

In carrying out these functions, cooperates with other FDA components, other PHS organizations, governmental and international agencies, volunteer health organizations, universities, individual scientists, non-governmental laboratories and manufacturers of biological products.

Office of the Center Director is organized as follows:
1. Deputy Director (Operations), (HFM-2) Mark A. Elengold
2. Deputy Director (Medicine), (HFM-6).
3. Associate Director for Quality Assurance (HFM-4), Sheryl L. Lard-Whitford, Ph.D.
4. Associate Director for Policy (HFM-10), Diane Maloney. JD.
5. Associate Director for Review Management (HFM-25), Robert A. Yetter, Ph.D.
6. Associate Director for Research (HFM-20), Neil D. Goldman, Ph.D.
7. Associate Director for Medical and International Affairs, (HFM-30) Elaine C. Esber, M.D.
8. Senior Policy Advisor (HFM-1) Jill H. Warner, J.D.

The Center has seven Offices under the direction of the Center Director, which will be discussed below.

220.1 Office of Biostatistics and Epidemiology (OBE) (HFM-210) Susan S. Ellengerg, Ph.D., Director

This office provides oversight and resources for the review of biological products and is responsible for statistical and epidemiological services to the Center, including responsibility for the adverse event reporting system.

The Office of Biostatistics and Epidemiology is organized as follows:
1. Division of Biostatistics (HFM-217) Peter A. Lachenbruch, Ph.D, Director
2. Division of Epidemiology (HFM-220) M. Miles Braun, MD, MPH, Acting Director

221 OFFICE OF COMMUNICATION, TRAINING, AND MANUFACTURERS ASSISTANCE (OCTMA) (HFM-40) MARY T. MEYER, DIRECTOR

This office manages the Center's professional and management training program, career and staff development program, employee orientation program, and related employee development policies. Directs the Center's consumer and professional informational activities in coordination with the other Agency components.

Serves as a liaison with Center components to provide advice and assistance to manufacturers and scientific associations to promote their understanding and compliance with FDA regulations. The Office is responsible for all activities relating to the administration of the Center's central documentation room.

The Office has the following Divisions:
1. Division of Manufacturers Assistance and Training (HFM-42) Gail H. Sherman, Director
2. Division of Disclosure and Oversight Management (HFM-44) JoAnne C. Binkley, Director

222 OFFICE OF MANAGEMENT (OM) (HFM-100) DON R. PETERSON, DIRECTOR

This Office monitors the development and operation of planning systems for Center activities and resource allocations and advises the Center Director on Center administrative policies, guidelines, and information systems and services. Plans and directs Center operations for financial, personnel and administrative management services. Directs and counsels Center managers through program evaluation and technological forecasting. .

Functions as an advisor on contract and grant proposals. Office of Management is organized as follows:
1. Regulatory Information Management Staff (HFM-110) Roger D. Eastep, Director
2. Division of Management Services (HFM-115) Gerald L. Anderson, Director
3. Division of Planning, Evaluation and Budget (HFM-140) Nancy D. Williams, Director

22.1 Office of Information Technology Management (OITM) (HFM-160) Ron D. Connor, Director

This office manages the Center's microcomputer resources and LAN/WAN network architecture, provides oversight and management of CBER's automated information systems and acts as the liaison with Center activities and contract Information Technology vendors.

Develops, implements, and monitors ADP standards and policies for all Center Information Resource activities and maintains the Center-wide Information Resource security program for all legacy data and electronic access. Provides budget execution and contract monitoring of Information Technology resources.

The Office has the following Divisions:

1. Division of Information Technology Operations (HFM-165) Ginger Leo, Director
2. Division of Information Technology Development (HFM-170) John C. Chang, Director
3. Division of Information Technology Infrastructure (HFM-180) Vacant Director

223 OFFICE OF BLOOD RESEARCH AND REVIEW (OBRR) (HFM-300) JAY S. EPSTEIN, MD, DIRECTOR

OBRR develops policy and procedures governing the pre-market approval review and evaluation of biological blood products in keeping with the provisions of the PHS Act and applicable provisions of the FD&C Act.

Performs the investigational device exemption (IDE) review process for devices related to biological blood products and develops related policy of those products regulated by the Office. Reviews, evaluates and takes appropriate action on investigational new drug applications (INDs) related to biological blood products and amendments or supplements to these applications; product applications submitted by manufacturers of biological blood products, including labeling; and establishment license applications submitted by blood and plasma establishments.

Plans and conducts research related to the development, manufacture, and testing of biological blood products, including those related to AIDS and those prepared by genetic engineering and synthetic procedures. Develops and maintains a scientific base for establishing standards designed to ensure the continued safety, purity, potency, and effectiveness of biological blood products.

Plans and conducts research on the preparation, preservation, characteristics, action and safety of blood and blood products; the methods of evaluating safety, purity, potency and efficacy of such products; the therapeutic uses of such products; and the testing and use of diagnostic reagents employed in grouping and typing blood, and screening for markers of infectious diseases.

This office has the following Divisions
1. Division of Emerging and Transfusion Transmitted Diseases (HFM-310) Hira L. Nakhasi, Ph.D., Director
2. Division of Hematology (HFM-330) Mark J. Weinstein, Ph.D., Acting Director
3. Division of Blood Applications (HFM-370) Vacant, Director, Director

224 OFFICE OF VACCINES RESEARCH AND REVIEW (OVRR) (HFM-400) KAREN MIDTHUS, DIRECTOR

OVRR covers vaccines, allergenic products, antigen specific, immunomodulators, and diagnostic antigens.

Reviews, evaluates, and takes appropriate action on INDs related to vaccines and regulated products and amendments or supplements to these applications, including approval or disapproval of research plans and protocols, modifications and restrictions. Performs the IDE review process for devices related to vaccines and related products regulated by CBER. Develops all related policy and procedures governing pre-market approval review and evaluation of vaccines and related products in keeping with the provisions of the PHS Act and applicable provisions of the FD&C Act.

Plans and conducts research related to the development, manufacture, and testing of vaccines and related products, including those related to AIDS and those prepared by genetic engineering and synthetic products. Develops and maintains a scientific base for establishing standards designed to ensure continued safety, purity, potency and effectiveness of vaccines and related products.

In cooperation with other CBER components, tests products submitted for release by manufacturers; evaluates clinical experience and reports of adverse events as necessary; participates in inspection of manufacturing facilities; and takes appropriate action on recommendations concerning denial of license applications for products.

The divisions in this office are:
1. Division of Bacterial, Parasitic, and Allergenic Products (HFM-410)
   Drusilla L. Burns, PhD., Acting Director
2. Division of Viral Products (HFM-445)
   Peter Patriarca, MD, Director
3. Division of Vaccines & Related Products Applications (HFM-475)
   Karen L. Goldenthal, MD, Director

225   OFFICE OF THERAPEUTICS & RESEARCH REVIEW (OTRR) (HFM-500) JAY SIEGEL, MD, DIRECTOR

OTRR covers cytokines and analogous products, growth factors, thrombolytic products, enzymes, monoclonal antibodies and analogous products, and biological gene therapy products.

Develops policy and procedures governing the pre-market approval, review and evaluation of biological therapeutic products and, certain devices and drugs under the jurisdiction of the Office. in keeping with the provisions of the PHS Act and applicable provisions of the FD&C Act.

Reviews, evaluates and takes appropriate action on investigational new drug applications (INDs) related to therapeutic products and amendments or supplements to these applications, including approval or disapproval of research plans and protocols, modifications and restrictions; and, product applications submitted by manufacturers of biological therapeutic products and labeling.

Performs the investigational device exemption (IDE) review process for devices related to biological therapeutic products regulated by the Office, and develops related policy and reference standards.

Plans and conducts research related to the development, manufacture, testing and activities of therapeutic biological products, including those related to AIDS and those prepared by genetic engineering and synthetic procedures, in order to develop and maintain a scientific base for establishing standards designed to ensure the continued safety, purity, potency and effectiveness of biological therapeutic products.

In cooperation with other Center components, tests products submitted for release by manufacturers; evaluates clinical experience and reports of adverse events as necessary. Participates in inspection of manufacturing facilities.

Reviews, evaluates and takes appropriate action on recommendations concerning denial of license applications for products.

This office has the following Divisions:
1. Div. of Cellular and Gene Therapies (HFM-515)
   Philip D. Noguchi, MD, Director
2. Div. of Therapeutic Products (HFM-535)
   Vacant, Director
3. Div. of Monoclonal Antibodies (HFM-555)
   Kathryn E. Stein, PhD, Director
4. Div. of Clinical Trial Design and Analysis (HFM-570) Karen Weiss, MD, Director
5. Div. of Application Review and Policy (HFM-585)
   Glen D. Jones, Director

226   OFFICE OF COMPLIANCE AND BIOLOGICS QUALITY (HFM-600) STEVEN A. MASIELLO, DIRECTOR

OCBQ monitors the quality of marketed biological products through surveillance, inspections, compliance activities, application review, and lot release programs. Advises the Center Director and other Agency officials on FDA's regulatory compliance responsibilities for biological products. Reviews license applications and supplements to determine if the facilities are appropriate for the manufacturing activities. Participates in prelicense and annual inspections and on license application review committees.

Serves as the focal point for all CBER enforcement activities. Provides guidance to Headquarters and field personnel in the development of evidence to support enforcement actions for deviations from the applicable standards. Coordinates Center/field compliance activities, including planning activities and field assignments, with the exception of consumer affairs activities.

Manages the CBER biological product inspection program. Coordinates with other Center Offices and Agency components. Directs the Center's bioresearch monitoring and recall programs for biological products.

Develops biological product compliance and surveillance programs, coordinates field implementation, and advises other Center components on these programs. Evaluates, in coordination with appropriate Agency officials, firms' conformance with CGMP in producing biological products for procurement by Federal and State agencies.

Coordinates the Center's export program and serves as the Center's focal point for import and export issues.

Identifies and recommends appropriate action, in coordination with other FDA components, on the results of continuing surveillance and evaluation of advertising and clinical experience reports submitted by manufacturers and sponsors of products regulated by CBER.

Maintains a reference reagent program, and establishes written and reference standards for biological product establishments (except blood and plasma establishments). In coordination with other CBER components, tests products submitted for release by manufacturers.

This office has three Divisions:
1. Division of Case Management (HFM-610)
   Mary A. Malarkey, Director
2. Division of Inspections and Surveillance (HFM-650)
   Elaine Knowles Cole, Director
3. Division of Manufacturing and Product Quality (HFM-670) John A. Eltermann, Jr., Director

SUBCHAPTER 230 - CENTER FOR DRUG EVALUATION AND RESEARCH (CDER)

230   OFFICE OF THE CENTER DIRECTOR (HFD-1)

Janet Woodcock, M.D. is the CDER Director.

Dr. Murray Lumpkin is the Deputy Center Director for Review Management and the Deputy Center Director for Pharmaceutical Science is currently vacant.

James Morrison (HFD-100) is CDER's Ombudsman.

CDER is responsible for developing FDA policy with regard to safety, effectiveness, and labeling of all drug products for human use; reviewing and evaluating new drug applications (NDAs) and investigational new drug applications (INDs); and developing and implementing standards for the safety and effectiveness of all over-the-counter (OTC) drugs. CDER is responsible for monitoring the quality of marketed drug products; developing and promulgating guidelines on Current Good Manufacturing Practices; conducting research and developing scientific standards on the composition, quality, safety, and effectiveness of human drugs. CDER is responsible for collecting and evaluating information on the effects and use trends of marketed drug products; monitoring prescription drug advertising and promotional labeling; and analyzing data on accidental poisonings and disseminating toxicity and treatment information on household products and medicines.

There are four staffs under the immediate office of the Center Director:
1. Regulatory Policy Staff (HFD-7)
   Jane Axelrad, Acting Director
2. Executive Operations Staff (HFD-6)
   Deborah Henderson, Director
3. EEO Staff (HFD-8)
   Margaret Bell, Director
4. Project Management Program Staff (HFD-9)
   Jean Yager, Director

The Office of Medical Policy, Robert Temple, MD, Director operates directly under the Center Director. There are two divisions under this office:
1. Div. Of Marketing, Advertising and Communications (HFD-40), Norm Drezin, Acting Director
2. Division of Scientific Investigations (HFD-340), David Lepay, MD, PhD, Director

231   OFFICE OF MANAGEMENT (HFD-10) RUSSELL ABBOTT, DIRECTOR

The Office of Management monitors the development and operation of planning systems for resource allocations and information systems; manages studies designed to improve processes and resource allocations; advises the Center on contract and grant proposals; and provides coordination, receipt and distribution of initial drug applications.

There are two divisions and one staff under the Office of Management:
1. Strategic Planning Staff (HFD-10)
   Charlene Cherry, Director
2. Division of Planning, Evaluation, and Resource
3. Division of Management Services (HFD-60)
   Ruth Clements, Director

232   OFFICE OF INFORMATION TECHNOLOGY (HFD-070) RALPH LILLIE, DIRECTOR

The Office of Information Technology oversees CDER's installation, maintenance and development of computer systems and databases. There are two staffs and three divisions:
1. Quality Assurance Staff (HFD-070)
   Judy McIntyre, Director
2. Technology Support Services Staff (HFD-070)
   David Moss, Director
3. Division of Infrastructure Management and Services (HFD-072), Patrick David, Director
4. Division of Applications Development Services (HFD-072), Melissa Chapman, Director
5. Division of Data Management and Services (HFD-090), Greg Warzala, Director

233   OFFICE OF TRAINING AND COMMUNICATIONS (HFD-200) NANCY SMITH, Ph.D. DIRECTOR

The Office of Training and Communications prepares, develops, and coordinates Center and Agency responses to drug-related requests under the Freedom of Information Act, Privacy Act and other statues. The office provides leadership and direction for all Center internal and external communications; plans coordinates, and evaluates policies, procedures, and programs for the orientation and training of Center staff; and provides scientific and technical resources and other library services.

There is one staff and three divisions under the Office of Training and Communications:
1. Freedom of Information Staff (HFD-200)
   Director - Vacant
2. Division of Training and Development (HFD-220)
   Janice Newcomb, Director
3. Division of Communications Management (HFD-210), Ellen Shapiro, Director
4. Division of Medical Library (HFD-230)
   Carol Assoud, Acting Director

234 OFFICE OF COMPLIANCE (HFD-300), DIRECTOR - DAVID J. HOROWITZ

The Office of Compliance monitors the quality of marketed drugs through product testing, surveillance, and compliance programs; develops standards for drug industry practices, including Current Good Manufacturing Practice (CGMP) regulations, and ensures their uniform interpretation.

There are three divisions under the Office of Compliance as follows:

1. Division of New Drugs and Labeling Compliance (HFD-310), Director - Vacant
2. Division of Manufacturing and Product Quality (HFD-320, Director, Joseph C. Famulare
3. Division of Compliance Risk Management and Surveillance, (HFD-330), Director – Vacant

235 OFFICE OF PHARMACEUTICAL SCIENCE, (HFD-3) DEPUTY CENTER DIRECTOR FOR PHARMACEUTICAL SCIENCE DIRECTOR - VACANT

The Office of Pharmaceutical Science provides advice and information on pharmaceutical programs and issues; and oversees the development of standards for the safety and effectiveness of generic drugs. OPS oversees the review and evaluation of Abbreviated New Drug Applications (ANDAs), Abbreviated Antibiotic Drug Applications (AADAs), and their amendments or supplements, and determines approvability.

There are two staffs and four offices under the Office of Pharmaceutical Science

1. Product Quality Support Staff
   Vacant, Director
2. Operations Staff (HFD-358)
   Helen Winkle, Acting Director

235.1 Office of New Drug Chemistry (HFD-800) Yuan Yuan Chiu, Ph.D., Director

The Office of New Drug Chemistry manages the science issues of chemistry, microbiology, manufacturing and control reviews; and ensures consistency in new drug chemistry reviews; and manages the overall coordination for IND and NDA chemistry and microbiology review processes.

There are three divisions under the Office of New Drug Chemistry:

1. Division of New Drug Chemistry I (HFD-810)
   Charles Hoiberg, Ph.D., Director
2. Division of New Drug Chemistry II (HFD-820)
   John Gibbs, Ph.D., Director
3. Division of New Drug Chemistry III (HFD-830)
   Chi-Wan Chen, Ph.D., Director

235.2 Office of Generic Drugs (HFD-600), Gary Buehler, Acting Director

The Office of Generic Drugs oversees the development and implementation of standards for the safety and effectiveness of generic drugs; reviews and evaluates ANDAs and AADAs and the amendments or supplements, and determines approvability; and establishes bioequivalency specifications for drug products.

There are four divisions under the Office of Generic Drugs:

1. Division Of Labeling & Program Support (HFD-605) Jerry Philips, Director
2. Division of Chemistry I (HFD-620)
   Rashmikant Patel, Ph.D., Director
3. Division of Chemistry II (HFD-640)
   Frank Holcombe, Jr., Ph.D., Director
4. Division of Bioequivalence (HFD-650)
   Nicholas Fleischer, Ph.D., Director

235.3 Office of Testing and Research (HFD-900) James MacGregor, Ph.D., Director

The Office of Testing and Research conducts research and develops scientific standards on the composition, quality, safety, and effectiveness of human drug products.

There is one staff, one laboratory, and three divisions under the Office of Testing and Research:

1. Regulatory Research and Analysis Staff (HFD-901) Joseph Contrera, PhD, Director
2. Laboratory of Clinical Pharmacy (HFD-902)
   Jerry Collins, Ph.D., Director
3. Division of Product Quality Research (HFD-940) Karl Flora, Ph.D., Director
4. Division of Applied Pharmacology Research (HFD-910) Frank Sistare, Ph.D., Director
5. Division of Testing and Applied Analytical Development (HFD-920) Moheb Nasr, Ph.D., Director

235.4 Office of Clinical Pharmacology & Biopharmaceutics (HFD-850) Larry Lesko, PhD, Director

The Office of Clinical Pharmacology & Biopharmaceutics evaluates pharmacokinetic, pharmacodynamic, bioavailability, bioequivalence, and drug metabolism protocols and data in notices of claimed investigational exemption for INDs, NDAs, antibiotic applications, and their supplements and amendments.

There is one staff and three divisions under the Office of Clinical Pharmacology & Biopharmaceutics:

1. Pharmacometrics Staff (HFD-851)
   William Gillespie, Ph.D., Acting Director
2. Division of Pharmaceutical Evaluation I (HFD-860)
   Hank Malinowski, Ph.D., Director
3. Division of Pharmaceutical Evaluation II (HFD-870)
   Mei Ling Chen, Ph.D., Director

4. Division of Pharmaceutical Evaluation III
    (HFD-870) John Lazor, Ph.D. Acting Director

236 OFFICE OF REVIEW MANAGEMENT (HFD-20) MURRAY LUMPKIN, DEPUTY DIRECTOR

The Office of Review Management develops and implements the Center's review management and scientific policies, including user fee policies, pertaining to the drug review process.

There are three staffs and seven offices under the Office of Review Management:

1. Advisors and Consultants Staff (HFD-21)
    John Treacy, Director
2. Program Management Team (HFD-022)
    William Oswald, Team Leader
3. Reports and Data Management Team (HFD-023)
    Ann Myers, Team Leader
4. Pharmacology/Technology Staff (HFD-024)
    Joseph DeGeorge, Ph.D., Team Leader

236.1 Office of Drug Evaluation I (HFD-101) Robert Temple, MD

This office reviews notices of claimed investigational exemptions for new drugs (INDs) within classes of drugs regulated by this Office and recommends appropriate action with respect to safety and effectiveness of clinical trials. Evaluates for safety and effectiveness and approves new drug applications (NDAs) for products regulated by this Office, and evaluates supplements proposing changes in the conditions upon which NDA approvals are based.

There are three divisions in this Office as follows:

1. Division of Neuropharmacological Drug Products (HFD-120) Russ Katz, MD, Director
2. Division of Oncologic Drug Products (HFD-150) Robert Justice, MD, Director
3. Division of Cardio-Renal Drug Products (HFD-110) Raymond Lipicky, MD, Director

236.2 Office of Drug Evaluation II (HFD-102) John Jenkins, MD, Director

This office reviews notices of claimed investigational exemptions for new drugs (INDs) within classes of drugs regulated by this Office and recommends appropriate action with respect to safety and effectiveness of clinical trials. Evaluates for safety and effectiveness and approves new drug applications (NDAs) for products regulated by this Office, and evaluates supplements proposing changes in the conditions upon which NDA approvals are based.

There are three divisions in this Office as follows:

1. Division of Metabolic & Endocrine Drug Products (HFD-510) Solomon Sobel, MD, Director
2. Division of Pulmonary Drug Products (HFD-570) Robert Meyer, MD, Acting Director
3. Division of Reproductive and Urologic Drug Products (HFD-580) Lisa Rarick, MD, Director

236.3 Office of Drug Evaluation III (HFD-103) Florence Houn, MD, Director

The Office of Drug Evaluation III reviews notices of claimed investigational exemptions for new drugs (INDs) within classes of drugs regulated by this Office and recommends appropriate action with respect to safety and effectiveness of clinical trials. They evaluate for safety and effectiveness and approve new drug applications (NDAs) for products regulated by this Office, and evaluate supplements proposing changes in the conditions upon which NDA approvals are based.

There are three divisions in this office as follows:

1. Division of Gastrointestinal & Coagulation Drug Products (HFD-180) Lilia Talarico, MD, Director
2. Division of Anesthetic, Critical Care, & Addiction Drug Products (HFD-170) Cynthia McCormick, MD, Acting Director
3. Division of Medical Imaging & Radiopharmaceutical Drug Products (HFD-160) Patricia Love, MD, Director

236.4 Office of Drug Evaluation IV (HFD-104) Sandra Kweder, MD, Acting Director

The Office of Drug Evaluation IV reviews notices of claimed investigational exemptions for new drugs for (INDs) within classes of drugs regulated by this Office and recommends appropriate action with respect to safety and effectiveness of clinical trials. The office evaluates for safety and effectiveness and approves new drug applications (NDAs) for products regulated by this Office, and evaluates supplements proposing changes in the conditions upon which NDA approvals are based.

There are three divisions in this office as follows:

1. Division of Anti-Infective Drug Products (HFD-520) Gary Chikami. MD, Director
2. Division of Anti-Viral Drug Products (HFD-530) Heidi Jolson, MD, Acting Director
3. Division of Special Pathogen and Immunologic Drug Products (HFD-590) Mark Goldberg, MD, Director

236.5 Office of Drug Evaluation V (HFD-105) Robert DeLap, MD, Director

This office reviews notices of claimed investigational exemptions for new drugs (INDs) within classes of drugs regulated by this Office and recommends appropriate action with respect to safety and effectiveness of clinical trials. This office evaluates for safety and effectiveness and approves new drug applications (NDAs) for products regulated by this Office, and evaluates supplements proposing changes in the conditions upon which NDA approvals are based.

There are three divisions in this office as follows:

1. Division of Anti-Inflammatory, Analgesic & Ophthalmologic Drug Products (HFD-550) Director Vacant
2. Division of Dermatologic & Dental Drug Products (HFD- 540) Jonathan Wilkin, MD, Director

3.   Division of Over-the-Counter Drug Evaluation
(HFD-560) Charles Ganley, MD, Director

236.6 Office of Biostatistics (HFD-700)
Robert O'Neill, Ph.D., Director

The Office of Biostatistics conducts programs to collect and evaluate epidemiological and non-epidemiological information on drug and biological product usage, adverse reactions, poisonings, safety, quality, and effectiveness.

There is one staff and three divisions under the Office of Biostatistics:
1.   Quantitative Methods Research Staff (HFD-705)
Stella Machado, Ph.D., Director
2.   Division of Biometrics I (HFD-710)
George Chi, Ph.D., Director
3.   Division of Biometrics II (HFD-715)
S. Edward Nevius, Ph.D., Director
4.   Division of Biometrics III (HFD-720)
Mohammed Huque, Ph.D., Director

236.7 Office of Post Marketing Drug Risk Assessment (HFD-730)
Murray Lumpkin, Acting Director

This office is responsible for obtaining and evaluating post-market information on approved NDAs, ANDAs, INDs, etc.

There are two staffs and two divisions under the Office of Post Marketing Drug Risk Assessment:
1.   Extramural Program Staff (HFD-730)
Tom Conrad
2.   Information Technology Staff (HFD-730)
William Calvert
3.   Division of Drug Risk Evaluation I (HFD-730)
Peter Honig, MD, Director
4.   Division of Drug Risk Evaluation II (HFD-730)
Evelyn Rodriguez

SUBCHAPTER 240 - CENTER FOR DEVICES AND RADIOLOGICAL HEALTH (CDRH)

240   OFFICE OF THE CENTER DIRECTOR

David Feigal, MD is the Center Director of CDRH. Linda Kahan is the Deputy Center Director of CDRH. Lillian J. Gill is the Acting Senior Associate Director of CDRH.

The Center for Devices and Radiological Health (CDRH) develops and carries out a national program to assure the safety, effectiveness, and labeling of medical devices for human use. It reviews and evaluates medical device pre-market approval applications (PMA's), product development protocols (PDP's), exemption requests for investigational devices (IDE's), and premarket notifications [510(k)'s].

The Center provides technical and other nonfinancial assistance to small manufacturers of medical devices. CDRH develops and carries out a national program

designed to control unnecessary exposures of humans to, and assure the safe and efficacious use of, ionizing and non-ionizing radiation-emitting electronic products.

CDRH has about 1000 employees.

The Office of the Center Director, in addition to providing overall leadership and direction for the Center, provides advice and consultation to the Commissioner and other Agency officials on policy matters concerning radiological health and medical device activities. The office recommends changes in legislative authority to the Commissioner, establishes policy in the areas of education and communications, and formulates strategies for developing and disseminating educational and programmatic information to health professionals, consumers, and other government agencies. The office plans and coordinates the Center's equal employment opportunity programs.

241   OFFICE OF SYSTEMS AND MANAGEMENT (HFZ-2)
RUTH CLEMENTS, DIRECTOR

The Office of Systems and Management (OSM) advises the Center Director on all administrative and management matters, and plans, develops and implements Center management policies and programs concerning such areas as manpower and financial management, personnel management, contracts and grants. OSM also develops and applies evaluation techniques to measure the effectiveness of Center programs, and provides general information and technical publications support to the Center. Other functions include planning and coordinating all of the Center's scientific advisory committee management activities.

OSM also determines and implements Center strategy and utilization of information management resources. OSM designs administrative and scientific technical information systems in support of Center programs, designs and conducts educational programs for Center employees in data processing and management, and provides assistance to Center staff in accessing information necessary to carry out the Center's mission.

OSM is also responsible for carrying out the Center's FOI activities.

The Office of Systems and Management is comprised of the following:
1.   Integrity, Committee and Conference Management Staff - Communicates and coordinates ethics issues, FMFIA, committee management activities, serves as the Center's Intramural Research Integrity Officer, conference management program.
2.   Division of Management Operations - Provides advice and guidance to Center management on personnel, procurement, property, facilities, occupational health and safety. Implements Center management policies and/or programs.
3.   Division of Planning, Analysis and Finance - Develops and justifies budget, manages budget, develops and implements long-range and strategic planning, conducts evaluations, impact studies and research studies, and implements administrative policies for extramural research programs.
4.   Division of Information Dissemination - Provides infor-

mation dissemination services to Center and the public, develops and manages library science strategies and systems, provides advice, guidance and technical support to program officials on FOIA.

5. Division of Information Technology Management - Develops and implements information management strategies and policies, maintains ADP security plan, trains Center personnel and provides user assistance.

6. Program Management Staff – Provides administrative functions and computer support to the Office of Systems and Management.

242 OFFICE OF SCIENCE AND TECHNOLOGY (HFZ-100) LARRY KESSLER, Sc.D., DIRECTOR

The Office of Science and Technology (OST) provides scientific and laboratory support in response to program needs of other Center and Agency components. OST plans, develops, and implements Center research and testing programs, and protocols in the areas of physical science, life science, and engineering. OST develops, modifies, and calibrates scientific instruments and equipment for use in testing programs; plans, conducts or stimulates research on the human health effects of radiation and medical devices and provides scientific and engineering support for the review of medical devices and radiological product submissions. OST conducts research related to existing and emerging health technologies.

OST provides leadership and technical expertise to other Departmental components in applying health physics procedures and radiation protection principles to radiological emergencies and other public radiation instances, and provides technical services and health physics advice to the Center.

OST also conducts studies to assess or advance the practical application of radiation protection principles, and maintains liaison with national and international radiation protection organizations.

There are 5 divisions in the OST as follows:

1. Division of Management, Information and Support Services - Provides the following services for the office: administrative support, fabrication and engineering support, technical information and reading room information.

2. Division of Electronics & Computer Science - Provides electronics, engineering and imaging and computer science support for Center programs.

3. Division of Mechanics and Material Science - Develops and provides technical support for measurement methods and analytical procedures, conducts and/or supports research studies for safety thresholds, provides support to the device evaluation process.

4. Division of Physical Sciences - Plans and conducts laboratory and program activities in the physical science s and general engineering disciplines.

5. Division of Life Sciences - Plans, conducts, supports and evaluates research on the health effects of radiation and medical devices.

243 OFFICE OF HEALTH AND INDUSTRY PROGRAMS, (HFZ-200) LIREKA P. JOSEPH, Ph.D., DIRECTOR

The Office of Health and Industry Programs (OHIP) conducts and evaluates nationwide programs to prevent injuries and deaths resulting from misuse of medical devices. It applies Special Controls authorities specified in the Safe Medical Devices Act of 1990, as a means of assuring safe and effective use of medical devices. OHIP performs in-depth analyses of medical device adverse incident reports, often with the assistance of representatives of relevant health professional, manufacturer and consumer organizations. OHIP conducts and coordinates informational and training activities for these groups; provides training services to the Agency, and other federal, state and foreign government agencies and health-related missions; and participates in the development of national and international consensus standards and voluntary guidelines. In addition, OHIP establishes and maintains liaison with consumer and professional organizations, industry associations and groups, and foreign and domestic governmental organizations to promote Center program goals.

Other functions include coordinating the Center's cooperative activities with foreign government counterparts and international health organizations.

OHIP is the focal point for liaison with the Office of General Counsel and appropriate Agency components on FDA regulation development responsibilities relating to medical device and radiological health activities.

Provides expertise in communications technology in support of Center & FDA programs and the Staff College functions.

Staff College - Develops training courses for Center, sponsors seminars and lectures, performs needs assessments and develops training objectives.

Regulations Staff - Advises Center and Agency officials on FDA regulation development responsibilities.

Program Operations Staff - Provides administrative and computer support to the office, serves as the Center Consumer Affairs representative.

Division of Small Manufacturers, International and Consumer Assistance (DSMICA) - Provides technical and other non-financial assistance to small manufacturers.

Division of Device User Programs and Systems Analysis - Participates in the postmarket problem analysis and solution strategy activities, such as labeling and human factors guidance, to ensure user-related issues are addressed.

Division of Communication Media - Provides and maintains expertise in communications technology services and coordinates media and graphic arts services to the Center, FDA, and other Government agencies.

Division of Mammography Quality and Radiation Programs - Responsible for implementing the Mammography Quality Standards Act of 1992 and provides program planning and support activities for cooperative programs with other agencies which have radiological health responsibilities. Provides education and communication to mammography facilities and parties interested in mammography quality.

244 OFFICE OF COMPLIANCE (HFZ-300) TIM ULATOWSKI, DIRECTOR

The Office of Compliance (OC) develops, directs, coordinates, evaluates, and monitors compliance programs covering regulated industry. OC conducts electronic product field tests and inspections when necessary for regulatory purposes, and evaluates industry quality control and testing programs to assure compliance with regulations. OC provides advice to Agency field offices on, and manages Center activities relating to, legal actions, case development, and contested case assistance. OC coordinates field planning activities and issues all field assignments for the Center.

The Office of Compliance has five divisions as follows:

1. Division of Program Operations - Administrative functions for the office; clearinghouse for all assignments issued by the Center to the field; processing of Compliance Programs, Compliance Policy Guides; registration and listing program; certificates for export products.

2. Division Bioresearch Monitoring - Manages and coordinates the administrative and regulatory responsibilities of the Agency's Bioresearch Monitoring Program for medical devices.

The Enforcement divisions were created along product lines as follows:

3. Division of Enforcement I - in vitro diagnostics, diagnostics devices and general surgery devices

4. Division of Enforcement II - dental, ear, nose and throat; ophthalmic; urology, gastroenterology, general hospital, and obstetrics/gynecology.

5. Division of Enforcement III - cardiovascular and neurology devices; orthopedic, physical medicine, and anesthesiology devices; therapeutic radiographic devices and electronic products.

245 OFFICE OF DEVICE EVALUATION (HFZ-400), DANIEL SCHULTZ, M.D., Ph.D., DIRECTOR

The Office of Device Evaluation (ODE) plans, conducts, and coordinates appropriate Center actions regarding approval, denial, and withdrawal of approval of pre-market approval applications (PMA's), product development protocols (PDP's), and investigational device exemptions (IDE's). ODE makes substantially equivalent determinations for pre-market notification submissions [510(k)'s]; and monitors sponsors' conformance with requirements of all programs. ODE also coordinates Center Classification activities, reviews petitions for or initiates reclassification of medical devices, provides executive secretariat and other technical support to medical device advisory panels, and conducts continuing review, surveillance, and medical evaluation of the labeling clinical experience, and required reports submitted by sponsors of approved applications.

The Office of Device Evaluation is organized as follows:

1. Program Management Office - Provides administrative functions for the office.

2. Program Operations Staff - Advises Office officials on premarket approval application, investigational device exemptions, premarket notification activities and classification/reclassification activities.

The Divisions serve as the primary source for scientific and medical device expertise with regard to safety and effectiveness.

3. Division of General, Restorative and Neurological Devices - general and restorative devices and neurological devices.

4. Division of Clinical Laboratory Devices-clinical laboratory devices.

5. Division of Cardiovascular Devices - cardiovascular and respiratory.

6. Division of Ophthalmic and Ear, Nose and Throat Devices - ophthalmic devices and ear, nose, and throat.

7. Division of Reproductive, Abdominal, & Radiological Devices; radiology; obstetrics/gynecology; and gastroenterology/urology medical devices.

8. Division of Anesthesiology, General Hospital, Infection Control and Dental Devices - dental, infection control and general hospital devices.

246 OFFICE OF SURVEILLANCE AND BIOMETRICS (HFZ-500) SUSAN N. GARDNER, Ph.D., DIRECTOR

The Office of Surveillance and Biometrics (OSB) manages Center programs to collect, evaluate and disseminate medical device data, including information on injuries and other device related experiences. OSB also provides statistical, epidemiological, and biometrics services in support of the operating and administrative programs of the Center.

This office has a staff and three Divisions as follows:

1. Issues Management Staff - Directs and monitors the analysis, resolution and development and solution implementation of postmarket issues.

2. Division of Surveillance Systems - Serves as the office focal point in planning, developing, implementing, and maintaining databases and information systems.

3. Division of Postmarket Surveillance - Plans, evaluates, and coordinates all postmarket surveillance activities.

4. Division of Biostatistics - Provides statistical computational support activities for internal and external Center programs.

247 OFFICE OF IN VITRO DIAGNOSTICS (HFZ-440) STEVE GUTMAN, M.D., DIRECTOR

SUBCHAPTER 250 - CENTER FOR VETERINARY MEDICINE (CVM)

250 OFFICE OF THE CENTER DIRECTOR (HFV-1)

Stephen F. Sundlof, DVM, Ph.D., is the Center Director.
George A. Mitchell, DVM, is the Associate Director for Policy and Regulations. The Deputy Center Director is Linda K. Tollefson, DVM,Ph.D.

The Office of the Director is located at: MPN IV, 7519 Standish Place, Rockville, MD 20855 (301-827-2950).

CVM develops and recommends the veterinary medical policy of the Agency with respect to the safety and effectiveness of animal drugs, feeds, feed additives, veterinary medical devices (medical devices for animal use), and other veterinary medical products. CVM also ensures the food from these animals is safe before drugs are approved for marketing.

The Center evaluates, for animal safety and effectiveness, proposed and marketed animal drugs and feed additives and marketed veterinary medical devices. It coordinates, evaluates, and plans Agency inspectional, investigational and surveillance programs.

Additional information on CVM can be found on their website at: www.fda.gov/cvm.

There are four offices within CVM that help to accomplish the mission of the Center. Those offices are as follows:

251 OFFICE OF MANAGEMENT AND COMMUNICATION (HFV-10)

Robert W. Sauer is the Office Director. The Office is located at MPN IV. A contact phone number is 301-827-4410.

This office provides management oversight, administrative program and systems support for CVM. It is the CVM Freedom of Information focal point and provides educational information and material to both the consumer and industry. It also serves as liaison within FDA as well as with other government agencies.

The four staffs within this office are:

1. Administrative Staff (HFV-15)
   Barbara E. Leach, Director
2. Communications Staff (HFV-12)
   Jon W. Scheid, Director
3. Program Planning and Evaluation Staff (HFV-11)
   David L. Lynch, Acting Director
4. Information Resources Management Staff (HFV-16):
   Information Resources Support: Michele Koff
   Data Applications: Dr. Jerome J. McDonald

252 OFFICE OF NEW ANIMAL DRUG EVALUATION (HFV-100)

The Office Director is Dr. Claire M. Lathers. This Office is located at MPN II, 7500 Standish Place, Rockville, MD 20855. A contact phone number is: 301-827-1796.

This office is responsible for evaluating for animal safety and effectiveness new animal drugs in pharmaceutical dosage forms or feed delivered products. It evaluates the safety aspects of drug and food additive residues remaining in food produced for human consumption from animals given drugs or food additives. It also coordinates the development and implementation of regulations and policies pertaining to new drugs intended for animal use.

The five divisions in this office are:

1. Div. of Therapeutic Drugs for Non-Food Animals (HFV-110), Dr. Melanie R. Berson, DVM, Director
2. Div. of Biometrics & Production Drugs (HFV-120) Woodrow M. Knight, Ph.D., Director
3. Div. of Therapeutic Drugs for Food Animals (HFV-130), Steven V. Vaughn, DVM, Director
4. Div. of Manufacturing Technologies (HFV-140) William G. Marnane, Director
5. Div. of Human Food Safety (HFV-150) Dr. Mark Robinson, Ph.D., Director

253 OFFICE OF SURVEILLANCE AND COMPLIANCE (HFV-200)

The Acting Director for this office is Daniel G. McChesney, Ph.D. This office is located at MPN II. A contact phone number is 301-827-6644.

This office has the responsibility of maintaining the effectiveness of the animal drugs which have been approved and ensuring animals treated with drugs are safe for human consumption. It also maintains the safety and effectiveness of animal feeds, feed additives, veterinary medical devices, and other veterinary medical products.

The four divisions in this office are:

1. Division of Surveillance (HFV-210)
   William C. Keller, DVM, Director
2. Division of Animal Feeds (HFV-220)
   George Graber, Ph.D., Director
3. Division of Compliance (HFV-230)
   Gloria Dunnavan, Director
4. Division of Epidemiology (HFV-250)
   Charlotte Spires, Director

254 OFFICE OF RESEARCH (HFV-500)

The Director is Norris E. Alderson, Ph.D. This office is located at MOD II, 8401 Muikirk Road, Laurel, MD. A contact phone number is: 301-827-8010.

This office provides a focal point for all research activities in the Center. It serves as the liaison for intramural and extramural research. It evaluates and interprets results of scientific research, initiates and recommends action as appropriate to implement policy changes.

The three divisions in this office are:

1. Division of Residue Chemistry (HFV-510)
   Michael H. Thomas, Director
2. Division of Animal Research (HFV-520)
   Dr. David A. Frobish, Director
3. Division of Animal and Food Microbiology (HFV-530), Robert Walker, Ph.D., Director

SUBCHAPTER 260 - CENTER FOR FOOD SAFETY AND APPLIED NUTRITION (CFSAN)

260 OFFICE OF THE CENTER DIRECTOR

The majority of CFSAN's offices moved to a new building in College Park, MD. This address is 5100 Paint Branch Parkway, College Park, MD 20740-3835. Agency and Center on-line directories have been updated.

The CFSAN director is Joseph Levitt, J.D. The Center Director's Office consists of the Deputy Director, Janice F. Oliver; Director Food Safety Initiatives, Robert Brackett, Ph.D; Director Office of Regulations and Policy, L. Robert Lake; Director, Office of Constituent Operations, Catherine W. Carnevale, DVM; Director Office of Management Systems, Juanita Wills; and Director Office of Science, Robert L. Buchanan, Ph.D.

This Center develops FDA policy with respect to the safety, composition, quality (including nutrition), and labeling of foods, food additives, colors, and cosmetics.

CFSAN researches and develops standards on the safety and composition of foods, food additives, colors and cosmetics. CFSAN also conducts research to improve methodology and methods of detection of various contaminants for regulated products.

It develops and promulgates good manufacturing practice regulations (GMP's), model ordinances, compliance programs, reviews food and color additive applications and has other food related programs.

CFSAN has about 900 employees.

260.1 Food Safety Initiative (HFS-32) Robert Brackett, Ph.D. Director

This office provides guidance, oversight, and coordination to a variety of substantive activities in response to the President's Food Safety Initiative mandates. Serves as liaison to appropriate Federal, State, local and foreign governments, industry, consumer groups, and academia with regard to the Food Safety Initiative activities.

260.2 Office of Regulation and Policy (HFS-4), L. Robert Lake, Director

The Office of Regulations and Policy (ORP) coordinates the development and review of food regulations and policies and resolves food policy issues in collaboration with the Center Director and other members of the senior management team. ORP serves as the Center focal point and provides a centralized monitoring, coordinating, and advisory function for the Center on policies involving sensitive, controversial and complex food issues, including proposed regulations. ORP also advises Center officials on regulatory approaches and manages the planning of the Center's regulation development activities. There is one office staff, a Food Biotechnology Coordinator and one office under the Director of Regulation and Policy:

1. Office of Constituent Operations (HFS-550), Catherine Carnevele, DVM, Director, which provides oversight and direction of food and cosmetic-related international activities including international standard setting, bilateral and multilateral agreements and international relations and policies. OCO serves as the Center's stakeholder, outreach coordinator and focal point. This function is carried out by consumer education, industry outreach and international staffs. The Office runs an Outreach and Information Center with 24-hour phone lines providing information to CFSAN stakeholders. The Office

OCO also provides oversight over content of CFSAN's website and its efficient operations.
2. Regulations Coordination Staff
3. Food Biotechnology Coordinator

260.3 Office of Management Systems (HFS-650), Juanita Wills, Director

Advise the Center Director on administrative policies and guidelines and scientific and technical information systems. Plans and directs all operations related to budget, financial, personnel management, training, employee development, etc. Provides guidance for Center ADP systems and there purchase.

260.4 Office of Science (HFS-6) Robert L. Buchanan

Advises Center Director and CFSAN management team on scientific issues related to food safety and applied nutrition. Provides coordination and review on matters related to cross-cutting scientific issues involving multiple offices or disciplines. Develops centerwide management systems for effective planning, use and mobilization of CFSAN scientific resources. Serves as focal point for activities related to scientific collaborations, particularly scientific consortia in which CFSAN is a member (i.e. National Center for Food Safety and Technology, Joint Institute for Food Safety and Applied Nutrition, National Center for Natural Products Research.
Associate Senior Science Advisor: Patricia Hansen
Associate Senior Science Advisor for Research and Planning: V. Kelly Bunning
Advisory Committee Staff: Catherine DeRoever
Joint Institute for Food Safety and Applied Nutrition: Arthur J. Miller, Ph.D.
Staff College: George J. Jackson, Ph.D.
National Center for Food Safety and Technology: David Armstrong
Lead Scientist for Nutrition: Elizabeth Yetley
Lead Scientist for Epidemiology: Morris E. Potter, DVM

261 OFFICE OF THE DEPUTY DIRECTOR, JANICE F. OLIVER

This office advises and assists the Center Director and other key officials on Center programmatic matters. It provides direction, coordination and oversight for the programmatic activites of the center.

261.1 Associate Director For Operations, Arnold P. Borsetti, Ph.D.

Assists the Deputy Center Director in providing direction and oversight to CFSAN program functions.

261.2 EEO Office, Joan J. Jappa, Ph.D.

This office plans, develops and implements the Center's Affirmative Action and Equal Employment Opportunity Programs.

261.3 Executive Operations Staff, Catherine J. Bailey, Director

This office provides correspondence control for the Center; processes Agency public correspondence referred to the Center Director; develops and operates tracking systems designed to provide early warning and to resolve delays in controlled correspondence. It provides direct support to the Center Director and to the Deputy Center Director including briefing materials, background information for meetings and preparation and coordination of speeches. The staff manages the Center's Freedom of Information Act activities, coordinating responses with other Center technical, regulatory and policy units as well as developing direct responses and performs special Center wide assignments involving complex problems and issues related to Center programs, strategies and activities.

261.4 Office of Cosmetics and Colors (HFS-100), Linda Katz, Ph.D., Director

Serves as focal point for actions involving colors and cosmetics including, but not limited to scientific studies, toxicological studies, microbiological studies, etc. It also serves as reviewer of cosmetic and color petitions, legal actions involving these products and develops regulations, compliance policy, position papers, regulatory guidelines and advisory opinions.

261.5 Office of Nutritional Products, Labeling and Dietary Supplements (HFS-800), Christine J. Taylor, Ph.D., Director

Has the primary responsibility for all matters pertaining to food labeling, food standards, dietary supplements and special nutritionals, including infant formula and medical foods. The office develops regulations, compliance policy, position papers, regulatory guidelines, and advisory opinions for matters within the scope of the responsibility of the Office and establishes labeling requirements appropriate for such foods, in coordination with other Center components. Reviews proposed regulatory actions for policy consideration, and provides technical evaluation and necessary scientific support. Develops appropriate methods for food and dietary supplement analyses and, in cooperation with the Field, maintains the Center's analytical capability for labeling compliance. Provides expert advice and assistance to the Center Director, other key officials, and the field on policy issues, field programs, and responses to petitions, initiatives, and related activities within the scope of the responsibility of the Office. The Office of Nutritional Products, Labeling and Dietary Supplements has four divisions which are:

1. Division of Compliance and Enforcement (HFS-810), John B. Foret
2. Division of Standards and Labeling Regulations (HFS-820), Felicia B. Satchell
3. Division of Nutrition Science and Policy (HFS-830), Lynn A. Larsen

4. Division of Research and Applied Technology (HFS-840), Jeanne I. Rader

261.6 Office of Food Additive Safety (HFS-200), Alan M. Rulis, Ph.D., Director

Develops regulations, advisory opinions, guidelines, position papers, etc. related to safe uses of food additives, color additives, GRAS substances, prior sanctioned substances and bioengineered foods. Manages petition review process for food and color additives and notification processes for food contact substances, GRAS substances, and bioengineered foods. Reviews proposed regulatory actions.

261.7 Office of Plant and Dairy Foods and Beverages (HFS-300) Terry C. Troxell, Ph.D., Director

Develops regulations, compliance policy, position papers, regulatory guidelines, etc. on food production and packaging techniques including chemical and microbial issues of food safety. Assesses chemical and biological contaminants including pesticides and industrial chemicals in foods for safety. Reviews proposed regulatory actions.

261.8 Office of Seafood (HFS-400), Philip Spiller, Director

Develops regulations, compliance policy, regulatory guidelines, labeling requirements, etc. for seafood and related products. Manages voluntary and mandatory seafood safety programs and researches various seafood industries such as aquaculture, harvesting and processing. Administers the National Shellfish Sanitation Program. Reviews proposed regulatory actions.

The Office of Seafood has two Divisions which are:
1. Division of Programs and Enforcement Policy (HFS-415) - Mary I. Snyder, Director
2. Division of Applied Science and Technology (HFS-425) - George Hoskin, Director

261.9 Office of Applied Research and Safety Assessment (HFS-025), Thomas A. Cebula, Director

The Office of Applied Research and Safety Assessment (OARSA) recommends, develops, coordinates and conducts research in the areas of molecular biology, microbiology (virulence assessment), toxicology and nutrition to help meet the research needs of the Center's Program Offices. The Office also coordinates development of long-term research planning, in responsible program areas, with other Center and Agency components, and serves as the Center's principal research liaison with other agency centers and organizations outside the Agency. Within the molecular biology and microbial areas, OARSA scientists provide materials and training in gene probe methodology and conduct research on: the effects of microbes, their toxins and metabolic products using a variety of animal and in vitro models; identification of unknown microbial illness factors; and the mechanisms of gene activation. The toxicology divisions conduct research to determine the safety and health hazards of foods, nutritional supplements, food and color additives, chemical contaminants, cosmetic ingredients and natural toxicants, and the metabolites of these substances. The elucidation of toxicological effects is undertaken using a variety of short-term indicators, including tissue and cell culture methods, as well as through the conduct of standard regulatory toxicology studies.

261.10 Office of Compliance (HFS-600), Joseph Baca, Director

Serves as CFSAN's liaison and focal point with the field. Serves as Center's lead office for all communications between ORA/ORO/Emergency Operations Center, HFC-160 and CFSAN relating to emergency response. Coordinates Center's program office activities with the Office of Regional Operations in development of field programs and evaluates field accomplishments by providing feedback to Center management. Manages and provides guidance to the various cooperative programs such as shellfish, milk safety, food service, interstate travel sanitation and HACCP.

This Office has the following three divisions:
1. Division of Enforcement (HFS-605) Judith Gushee, Director
2. Division of Field Programs (HFS-615) Leslie Bluhm, Director
3. Division of Cooperative Programs (HFS-625) Faye Feldstein, Acting Director

261.11 Office of Scientific Analysis and Support (HFS-700) Kenneth J. Falci, Ph.D., Director

Provides scientific analysis and support to all CFSAN offices in carrying out their mission. This includes developing economic impact analyses for food and cosmetic regulations, conducting consumer attitude and behavior studies related to diet and disease, biotechnology, food labeling and claims, and infant feeding and food safety practices. Provides epidemiological reviews for microorganism risk assessment, acute health hazard evaluations, and estimates the burden of foodborne illness. Supports CFSAN research through assistance with experimental design, mathematical input and statistical analysis of experimental data. Conducts post-market surveillance and assesses adverse reactions to food products. Develops compliance and survey sampling plans. Assists international organizations such as the AOAC International and CODEX in the development of policy and criteria for review of analytical methods performance and in developing sampling plans to ensure fair and valid procedures are used when food is being tested for compliance with commodity standards. Provides pathology support to the in-house experimental studies for animal necropsies and processing and evaluation of animal tissues, in evaluating pathology data and

reviewing microslides provides to the Agency as part of industry submissions, and in assisting other FDA Centers with pathology issues when requested. Provides analytical support. Additionally, the Office contributes to the activities of the Health Hazard Evaluation Board, the Institutional Animal Care and Use Committee (IACUC), and Cancer Assessment and Quantitative Risk Assessment Committees.

This office has the following divisions:
1. Division of Mathematics - Foster D. McClure, Director Petition Review and Experimental Design Team Biometrics and Risk Assessment Team
2. Division of General Scientific Support - Prem N. Dua, DVM, Ph.D., Director
3. Division of Market Studies - Richard A. Williams, Jr., Ph.D., Director
4. CFSAN Adverse Events Reporting (CAERS) Staff

The Division of Market Studies has the following Teams:
A. Economics Team
B. Consumer Studies Team
C. Epidemiology Team

SUBCHAPTER 270 - OFFICE OF REGULATORY AFFAIRS

270 ASSOCIATE COMMISSIONER FOR REGULATORY AFFAIRS (HFC-1)

The Associate Commissioner for Regulatory Affairs (ACRA) is John M. Taylor, III and the Deputy Associate Commissioner for Regulatory Affairs is John Marzilli. The Assistant Commissioner for Regulatory Affairs is Steven Niedelman.

ORA is under the leadership of an Associate Commissioner known as the ACRA. This office is responsible for the activities and operations of the field headquarters staff and the field staff of FDA. The Regional Food and Drug Directors (RFDD's) report to this office.

This office advises and assists the Commissioner and other key officials on regulations and compliance oriented matters which have an impact on policy development and execution and long-range program goals.

There are currently about 620 employees in ORA headquarters and about 3490 employees in the ORA field organization. A phone directory for ORA is provided at the end of this chapter.

Immediate office of ORA:
Special Assistant to ACRA – Alyson Saben
Special Assistant for Import Policy – Benjamin England
Performance Results Staff Coordinator - Marie Urban
Equal Employment Opportunity Staff - Mary Davis
Senior Advisor for Clinical Science – Lori Love

271 ORA HEADQUARTERS ORGANIZATION

ORA consists of four individual offices which operate independently of each other. However, their functions are related and they support each other. A description of the function of each office is outlined below.

271.1 Office of Resource Management (ORM) (HFC-10), Malcolm L. Frazier, Director

ORM is basically responsible for the planning, management, and evaluation of the operations of the field offices. It is also responsible for the computer systems which handle the information generated by the field offices.

Monetary resources available to the field for day to day operations are budgeted and controlled by the Division of Management Operations. Funds are allocated as determined by actual needs of the field and headquarters units.

The training of personnel stationed in the field is also coordinated by the Division of Human Resource Development within this office.

The Deputy Director of ORM is James M. Strachan. Special Assistant to the Director is Richard Garwood.

ORM has the following divisions:

1.   Division of Management Operations (HFC-20)
     Director - Vacant
     Management Operations & Analysis Group
     Director - Vacant
     Financial & Program Analysis Group,
     Lee Swerock, Director
     Facilities Management Group,
     Randy Higgins, Director
2.   Office of Information Technology (HFC-30)
     Mark Gregory, Director
     Donald Chi, Deputy Director
     Hardware & Systems Software Branch,
     Paul Banas Director
     Statistical Systems & Minicomputer Appls. Branch,
     Carol Stone, Director
     Field Appls. & Microcomputer Support Branch,
     Director Vacant
3.   Division of Planning, Evaluation and
     Management (HFC-40), Susan C. Baer, Director
     Vacant, Deputy Director
     Program Planning & Workforce Mgmt. Branch,
     David Aken, Director
     Program Evaluation Branch
     John A. Lechus, Director
4.   Division of Human Resource Development
     (HFC-60), Gary German, Director
     Leona O'Reilly, Deputy Director
5.   Division of Personnel Operations
     Kimberly Carter, Director
6.   Commissioned Corps Liaison, Virginia Mahady

Also included within ORM is the FDA History Office: Wallace Janssen, Ronald Ottes, Suzanne White Junod, and John Swann.

271.2 Office of Regional Operations (ORO) (HFC-100) Deborah D. Ralston, Director

The Director of ORO is currently Deborah D. Ralston.

The Deputy Director is Steven Solomon, Ph.D. Special Assistant to the Director is Kara Lynch.

ORO coordinates and manages all Agency field operations and the Team Biologics Core Team on behalf of the ACRA; develops, issues, approves, or clears proposals and instructions affecting field activities; serves as the central point within the Agency through which headquarters offices obtain field support services.

It evaluates the overall management and capabilities of the Agency's field organization; initiates action to improve the management of field activities. Coordinates nationwide health fraud activities between the field, states, and Headquarters organizations. Coordinates field public affairs and information programs; distributes timely information to the field; coordinates activities with Agency counterpart organizations. Serves as the Agency focal point in developing and maintaining international regulatory policy and activities to assure the safety, efficacy, and wholesomeness of regulated imported products. Coordinates Agency procedures with Headquarters and field offices and is the primary contact with the U.S. Customs Service and others among those offices. Develops and/or recommends to the ACRA policy, program, and plans for applied research relating to Agency enforcement problems; coordinates such research efforts with appropriate agency components. Directs and coordinates the Agency's emergency preparedness and civil defense programs. Provides other Agency components with laboratory support in highly specialized areas.

ORO has the following components:

1.   **Emergency Operations Center (HFC-160)**
     Ellen Morrison, Director
     Conception Cruz, Deputy Director
     The Emergency Operations Center, was recently reorganized into the new Office of Crisis Management under the Office of the Commissioner. Future IOM updates will reflect this change. It coordinates and provides facts regarding epidemiological investigations and other potential imminent dangers to public health on a 24-hour, seven-day-a-week basis to Headquarters, regional and district staff.

     The Division Director and Deputy Director may be reached at (301) 827-5653, the 24 hour emergency line (301)443-1240 or on their direct lines (301) 827-5660 (Ellen Morrison) and (301)827-5655 (Dep. Director).

     Personnel assigned to the Emergency Operations Center:

Pete Cook	Emergency Coordinator	(301) 827-5630
Lara Davidson	Bioterrorism Coordinator	(301) 827-2170
Mark I. Fow, Ph.D.	Emergency Coordinator	(301) 827-5650
Sandra Hanson	Emergency Coordinator	(301) 827-5642
Vacant	Epidemiologist	(301) 827-2180
Israel Santiago	National Consumer Complaint and Emergency Operations Coordinator	(301) 827-5670

2.   **Division of Field Investigations (HFC-130)**
     Michael C. Rogers, Director (301) 827-5653

DFI provides coordination, direction, assistance, and management for the field's domestic and foreign investigative activities. It serves as the Agency focal point for Headquarters/field relationships on investigational and inspection problems, and programs and operations.

It develops and reviews investigative and inspectional procedures, training programs, and prepares and issues investigative and inspectional guidance manuals. The division provides the field investigative and engineering technical assistance and guidance for foreign inspections.

DFI has two branches: Domestic Operations Branch and International Operations Branch. The Division's deputy director manages ORA's National Experts.

Patricia Alcock Lefler is the Deputy Director. She can be reached at (301) 827-5653.

Gerald Miller is the Director of the Domestic Operations Branch. He can be reached at (301) 827-5653.

Rebecca Ramos Hackett is the Manager of the International Operations Branch. She may be reached at (301) 827-5653.

The following personnel within the Domestic Operations Branch are available to help you in various program related activities and may be reached at DFI's main number (301) 827-5653 or at the number below:

Charles Ahn	Computers/Computer Utilization, Human Drugs	(301) 827-5637
James Dunnie	Human Drugs, Veterinary Drugs	(301) 827-5652
Alan Gion	Medical Devices	(301) 827-5649
Gail Katz	Biologics	(301) 827-3357
Ruark Lanham	Foods	(301) 827-6691
Barbara Marcelletti	Foods, Seafood HACCP	(301) 827-5635
Diann Shaffer	Bioresearch Monitoring	(301) 827-1124
Christine Twohy	Biologics, Microbiology	(301) 827-5662

Personnel responsible for foreign inspections and trip planning in the International Operations Branch:

Linda Adams	Tech. Asst. Int'l Inspections	(301) 827-5648
Doreen Chin Quee	Tech Asst. Int'l Inspections	(301) 827-5632
Pattie Everett	Tech Asst. Int'l Inspections	(301) 827-5629
Cherae Frazier	Tech Asst. Int'l Inspections	(301) 827-5628
Atilla Kadar	BIMO Int'l Inspections	(301) 827-5647
MaryBet López	Drug Int'l Inspections	(301) 827-2975
Irma Rivera	Tech Asst. Intl. Inspections	(301) 827-5665
Janet Rowe	Tech. Asst. Int'l Inspections	(301) 827-5633
Patricia Simmons	Tech. Asst. Int'l Inspections	(301) 827-5668
Lourdes Valentin	Drug Int'l Inspections	(301) 827-5653
Joyce Watson	Biologics Int'l Inspections	(301) 827-5636

The National Experts assigned to DFI are:

Thomas Arista	DAL-DO Biotechnology NE	(214) 655-5308
Mary T. Carden,	NYK/BUF Biologics NE	(716) 551-4461
Karen A. Coleman	ATL-DO Devices NE	(404) 347-3218
Robert Coleman	ATL-DO Drugs/Bimo NE	(404) 347-3218
Debra Devlieger	SEA-DO Food/LACF NE	(206) 553-7001
Charles M. Edwards	PHI-DO Drugs/Bimo NE	(215) 597-0983
Mike Ellison	BLT-DO Food/LACF NE	(410) 749-0540
Brian Hendrickson	DET-DO Food/LACF NE	(317) 226-6500x12
Joan Loreng	PHI-DO Biologics NE	(215) 362-0740
David B. Wieneke	MIN-DO Food, Aseptic Processing, Dairy NE	(612) 334-4100
Norman Wong	SEA-DO Devices NE	(206) 483-4935

3.   **Division of Field Science (DFS) HFC-140**
Michael Olson, Director
Thomas Savage, Deputy Director
(301) 827-1232

DFS provides a focal point for all aspects of ORA Field Laboratories and serves as the Headquarters' scientific and technical staff. It manages FDA's overall field scientific resources to assure their coordinated, efficient, and effective use; provides coordination between field and center scientific programs, and develops and manages the Science Advisor Program and Department of Defense Shelflife Extension Program.

DFS manages field research programs and the applicability of new, complex, scientific instruments for field analyses and provides scientific and analytical expertise related to laboratory automation, analysis, process control and acquisition of automated data laboratory instruments. DFS manages the scientific aspects of the FACTS. The Division participates in the determination of long and short-range field scientific facility needs and in the formulation, delivery, and evaluation of training and career development plans for field scientists. Program contacts in DFS are:

a.   Carl Sciacchitano, Research Planning & Coordination Team Leader (301) 827-7606
b.   Larry D'Hoostelaere, CBER/CDRH programs contact
c.   Marsha Hayden, CFSAN programs contact
d.   Elise Murphy, CDER programs contact
e.   George Salem, CVM programs contact

4.   **Division of Federal-State Relations (DFSR)**
HFC-150 - Richard Barnes, Director
(301) 443-3360
Paul Raynes, Deputy Director

DFSR is the ORA headquarters focal point for interactions with the regional specialists located in every region, that comprise the Federal-State Cooperative Programs (SCP). The SCP are composed of three separate food safety programs, the Interstate Milk Shippers Program, the National Shellfish Sanitation Program and the Retail Food Protection Program. The authority for these programs is provided in the Public Health Service Act (42 USC 243).

FDA has signed Memoranda of Understanding (MOU's) with the Interstate Milk Shippers Conference and the Interstate Shellfish Sanitation Conference. These MOU's spell out FDA and state responsibilities that must be met to insure the uninterrupted shipment of these commodities between states. FDA has also signed an MOU with the Conference of Food Protection that will guide future federal-state cooperation in this program. See IOM Chapter 3 for an explanation of all MOU's.

Funding and position allocation for the Cooperative Programs is through the Center for Food Safety and Applied Nutrition (CFSAN) which makes allocations to ORA for the programs.

Regional Specialists are the first point of contact for the states for answers and explanations on any technical issues that arise. Several Cooperative Program Specialists are located in each Region and are available to answer questions and offer assistance and expertise when investigations involve these products.

- RETAIL FOOD PROTECTION PROGRAM (Retail Food Safety Program)
The primary objective of the Retail Food Safety Program is to prevent foodborne illness at the retail level of the food industry by directing activities toward promotion of effective state and regulatory programs. Regional Food Specialists (RFS) are responsible for state program evaluations, stan-

dardization of state officials, training and technical assistance to state programs. Interstate Travel Sanitation Program (ITP) Specialists, located in the Districts, receive training and standardization from the RFS. Regional Food Specialists may be asked for technical assistance on a variety of food safety and public health topics.

- INTERSTATE MILK SHIPPERS PROGRAM (Milk Safety Program)

The objectives of the Milk Safety Program activities are to provide assistance to the states in the prevention of food-borne and communicable diseases and in the adoption, implementation and enforcement of the uniform technical guidelines, administrative procedures and regulatory standards provided in the Pasteurized Milk Ordinance (PMO) and related documents. Regional Milk Specialists (RMS) provide technical assistance and training, conduct check-ratings (audits) and standardize state officials. The RMS's also evaluate state programs to measure state program effectiveness, provide advice on the program's strengths and weaknesses and make recommendations for improvements.

- NATIONAL SHELLFISH SANITATION PROGRAM (Shellfish Safety Program)

The objective of the Shellfish Safety Program is to prevent food-borne illness from the consumption of raw Molluscan shellfish, primarily oysters, clams and mussels. Food borne illnesses from these organisms include a variety of hazardous materials such as heavy metals, biological toxins, and pathogens. FDA provides oversight to 29 states and four foreign countries that are members in the National Shellfish Sanitation Program (NSSP). The NSSP provides for a system of controls, which follow the shellfish from their growing area through harvest, distribution and wholesale sale. FDA Regional Shellfish Specialists (RSS) evaluate state and foreign programs, and provide training and technical assistance regarding the current practice in shellfish control and related topics of environmental science and shellfish processing.

5.   **Division of Import Operations Policy (DIOP) HFC-170**
      Director Carl Nielsen
      Deputy Director, Joseph L. McCallion

This division provides direction, assistance, management and oversight of field import operations. Serves as Agency focal point for contact with U.S. Customs and other Federal Agencies regarding import activities. Develops and reviews agency import policies, procedures, programs, etc. and is responsible for issuing import informational directives (Import Alerts, Bulletins, etc.) and RPM, Chapter 9. DIOP is responsible for the maintenance of the Operational and Administrative System for Import Support (OASIS), including the coordination with program Centers to establish automated screening criteria.

Contact points within DIOP are:

a.   Systems Branch (HFC-171)
      Vacant, Director
b.   Operations and Policy Staff (HFC-172)
      Rotational Coordinator
c.   Customs Liaison (HFC-170)
      Vacant

271.3 Office of Enforcement (OE) - HFC-200 Vacant, Director

The Director of OE is vacant and the Deputy Director is vacant.

OE advises and assists the ACRA and other key officials on regulations and compliance policy matters which impact on policy development, implementation and long range goals. OE also coordinates, interprets, and evaluates the FDA's overall compliance efforts and, as necessary, establishes compliance policy and recommends policy to the ACRA.

OE also acts as liaison with other federal agencies on compliance matters, evaluates proposed legal actions, coordinates actions with the Office of Regional Operations (ORO) and the Office of Chief Counsel (OCC) and handles appeals of proposed compliance actions which are disapproved by the centers or OCC.

This office coordinates agency bioresearch monitoring activities and serves as Agency focal point for the Federal Medical Products Quality Assurance Program (GWQAP).

OE consists of the following elements:

1.   Division of Compliance Management and Operations & Recall Staff (HFC-210)
      Sandra Whetstone, Director
2.   Division of Compliance Policy (HFC-230)
      Lana Ogram, Director
3.   Division of Compliance Information & Quality Assurance Staff (HFC-240)
      Scott MacIntire, Director

271.4 Office of Criminal Investigations (OCI) (HFC-300) Terrell L. Vermillion, Director

This office advises and assists the ACRA and other key officials on regulations and criminal violations involving regulated activities and products.

OCI directs and conducts criminal investigative activities in coordination with FDA headquarters units and with other Federal, state and local law enforcement agencies. OCI is instrumental in implementing FDA criminal investigation policy, training, and coordination. OCI interfaces directly with Federal and local prosecutorial offices and participates in grand jury proceedings and judicial actions as required.

OCI has 170 employees in headquarters and the field.

272   ORA FIELD ORGANIZATION

The ORA field organization is divided into regional offices. The Regional Offices are under the control of Regional Food and Drug Directors (RFDD's) who report to the ACRA. There are currently five regional offices which are located as follows:

Northeast	New York, NY
Central	Philadelphia, PA
Southeast	Atlanta, GA
Southwest	Dallas, TX
Pacific	San Francisco, CA

Each regional office controls 2 to 7 district offices.

There are currently 20 district offices located in major cities around the country. IOM Appendix G shows the location of these district offices. The regional affiliation of these offices is also indicated in the Appendix.

Each district office (DO) is usually comprised of four branches or units as follows:

1.   Administrative Branch

2.   Compliance Branch

3.   Investigations Branch - some DO's may have 2 investigations sections, one for domestic products and one for imported products.

4.   Laboratory Branch – not all DO's have laboratories

Some districts have combined branches and some have gone to team based structures which are different from the traditional branch structure.

ORA HEADQUARTERS DIRECTORY

Associate Commissioner for Regulatory Affairs, (ACRA), 5600 Fishers Lane, Rockville, MD 20857

Emergency (after hours) Answering Service - Office of Crisis Management (301) 443-1240
John M. Taylor III, Associate Commissioner for Regulatory Affairs, Rm. 14-90, HFC-1 (301) 827-3101 FAX (301) 443-6591
Benjamin L. England, Regulatory Counsel to ACRA, HFC-1, (301) 827-2806 FAX (301) 827-0963
John Marzilli, Deputy Associate Commissioner, Rm. 14-90, HFC-2, (301) 827-3101 FAX 301-443-6591
Steven M. Niedelman, Assistant Commissioner for Regulatory Affairs, HFC-1, (301) 827-3101 FAX (301) 443-6591
Alyson L. Saben, Special Assistant to the ACRA, Rm. 14-90, HFC-1, (301) 827-3101 FAX (301) 443-6591
Amy R. Folden, Executive Assistant, Rm. 14-90, HFC-1, (301) 827-3101 FAX (301) 443-6591
Richard Baldwin, Senior Advisor for Regulatory Policy, Rm. 14-90, HFC-2, (301) 827-2682
Lori Love, Senior Advisor for Clinical Science, Rm. 12-A46 HFC-2, (301) 827-3684 FAX (301) 443-6591
Marie Urban, Director, Performance Results Staff, Rm. 13-93, HFC-2, (301) 827-0947 FAX (301) 827-0963
Mary Davis, Equal Opportunity Staff, Rm. 12A-05, HFC-15, (301) 827-2883 FAX (301) 480-7803

Office of Resource Management, (ORM), 5600 Fishers Lane, Rockville, MD 20857

Malcolm L. Frazier, Director ORM, Rm. 13-45, HFC-10, (301) 443-2175 FAX (301) 443-7270
James M. Strachan, Deputy Director ORM, Rm. 13-45, HFC-10, (301) 443-2175
CAPT Virginia Mahady, Commissioned Corps Liaison, HFC-10, HFC-10, Rm. 163, 109 Holton St., Winchester, MA 01890, (781) 729-5700 Ext. 702
George Bork, Labor Management Relations Specialist, Rm. 13-45, HFC-10, (301) 827-1643
Vacant, Dir. Div. of Management Operations, Rm. 12-69, HFC-20, (301) 827-2864 FAX (301) 443-7267
Lee Swerock, Dir., Financial Program & Analysis Group, Rm. 12-69, HFC-21, (301) 827-1206
Randy Higgins, Dir., Facilities Mgmt. Group, Rm. 12-69, HFC-21, (301) 827-1202
Karen Flanigan, Safety Management Officer, Rm. 12-69, HFC-21, (301) 827-1212
Ron Ottes, FDA History Office, Rm. 13-51, HFC-24, (301) 827-3758
John Swann, FDA History Office, Rm. 13-51, HFC-24, (301) 827-3756 FAX (301) 443-7270
Suzanne White Junod, FDA History Office, Rm. 13-51, HFC-24, (301) 827-3759 FAX (301) 443-7270
Mark Gregory, Director, Office of Information Technology, Rm. 7B-21, HFC-30, (301) 827-4090 FAX (301) 443-7270
Donald Chi, Dep. Dir. Office of Information Technology, Rm. 7B-21, HFC-30, (301) 827-1562 FAX (301) 443-0868
Paul Banas, Dir. Hardware and System Software Br., Rm. 12-74, HFC-31, (301) 827-1558
Carol Stone, Dir. Infrastructure Applications Br., Rm. 12-74, HFC-33, (301) 827-1561
Susan C. Baer, Dir. Planning, Evaluation & Management Div., Rm. 12-38, HFC-40, (301) 827-1626 FAX (301) 443-7212
Vacant, Deputy Dir. Planning, Evaluation and Management Br., Rm. 12-38, HFC-41, (301) 827-1629
Dave Aken, Dir. Prog. Planning & Workforce Management Br., Rm. 12-38 HFC-41, (301) 827-1638
John A. Lechus, Dir. Program Evaluation Br., Rm. 12-38, HFC-42, (301) 827-1637
Gary German, Dir. Div. of Human Resource Development, HFC-60, (301) 594-1710 FAX (301) 594-1966
Leona O'Reilly, Dep. Dir. Div. of Human Resource Development, HFC-60, (301) 594-2174 FAX (301) 594-1966
Kimberly Holden (Carter), Dir., Div. Of Personnel Operations, HFC-50, Rm. 7B-24, (301) 827-4074

Office of Regional Operations, (ORO), 5600 Fishers Lane, Rockville, MD 20857

Emergency (after hours) Answering Service (301) 443-1240
Deborah D. Ralston, Dir. ORO, Rm. 13-61, HFC-100, (301) 443-6230 FAX (301) 443-1778
Steven M. Solomon, DVM, Dep. Dir. ORO, Rm. 13-61, HFC-101, (301) 443-6230
Kara Lynch, Special Assistant to the Dir., Rm. 13-61, HFC-102,(301) 443-6230
Michael C. Rogers, Dir. Div. of Field Investigations, Rm. 13-64, HFC-130, (301) 827-5653 FAX (301) 443-3757
Patricia Alcock Lefler, Dep. Dir. Div. of Field Investigations, Rm. 13-64, HFC-130, (301) 827- 5653 FAX (301) 443-3757
Gerald W. Miller, Dir., Domestic Operations Branch, Rm. 13-64, HFC-130, (301) 827-5653 FAX (301) 443-3757
Rebecca Ramos Hackett, Manager, Internat'l Oper. Br., Rm. 13-71, HFC-130, (301) 827-3777 FAX (301) 827-6685
Michael Olson, Dir. Div. of Field Science, Rm. 12-41, HFC-140, (301) 827-1232 FAX (301) 827-4575
Thomas Savage, Dep. Dir. Field Science, Rm. 12-41, HFC-140, (301) 443-3320
Richard H. Barnes, Div. of Fed-State Rel, Rm. 12-07, HFC-150, (301) 827-2905 FAX (301) 443-2143
Paul Raynes, Dep. Dir. Div. of Fed-State Rel., Rm. 12-07 HFC-150, (301) 827-2910
Cynthia Leggett, Pub Affairs & Health Fraud, Rm. 12-17, HFC-110, (301) 827-2914 FAX (301) 443-2143
Carl R. Nielsen, Dir. Div. of Import Oper & Policy, HFC-170, (301) 443-6553 FAX (301) 594-0413
(Overnight/Express Mail to: 15800 Crabbs Branch Way, Suite 118, Rockville, MD 20855)
Joseph L. McCallion, Deputy Dir. Div. of Import Operations and Policy, HFC-170, (301) 594-1218 FAX (301) 594-3787
Vacant, Dir., Systems Branch, HFC-171, (301) 443-6553

Office of Enforcement, (OE), 1350 Piccard Dr., 4th Floor, Rockville, Md. 20850
(Regular Mail to: 5600 Fishers Lane, Rockville, MD 20857)
Vacant, Director OE, HFC-200, (301) 827-0421 FAX (301) 827-1222
Vacant, Deputy Director OE, HFC-201, (301) 594-4611 FAX (301) 594-4638
Donald Vasbinder, Special Assistant OE, HFC-201, (301) 827-0414 FAX (301) 827-1222
Sandra Whetstone, Dir. Div. of Compl Mgmt & Oper, HFC-210, (301) 827-0391 FAX (301) 827-0342
Lana Ogram, Dir. Div. of Compl Policy, HFC-230, (301) 827-0393 FAX (301) 827-0482
Scott MacIntire, Dir. Div. Comp Info & QA, HFC-240, (301) 827-0386 FAX (301) 827-0482

Office of Criminal Investigations, (OCI), HFC-300, 7500 Standish Place Suite 250 N., Rockville, MD 20855
Terrell L. Vermillion, Director, HFC-300, (301) 294-4030 FAX (301) 594-1971
Horace Coleman, Deputy Director, HFC-300, (301) 294-4030 FAX (301) 594-1971
James Dahl, Assistant Director (Special Programs), HFC-300, (301) 294-4030 FAX (301) 594-1971
Rodney V. Turner, Special Agent in Charge (SAIC), Investigative Operations Division, HFC-300, (301) 294-4030 FAX (301) 594-1971
Kathleen Martin-Weis, SAIC, Administrative Operations Division, HFC-300, (301) 294-4030 FAX (301) 827-1234

OCI, Chicago Field Office, HFH-530, 901 Warrenville Road, Suite 360, Lisle, IL 60532
Michael Cleary, SAIC, HFH-530 (630) 769-5520 FAX (630) 769-5550
(Covers IL, IN, MI, MN, ND, SD, WI)

OCI, Minneapolis Domicile, 21985 Keather Avenue North, Forest Lake, MN 55025
Kenneth Kulick, Special Agent (SA), (651) 433-5404 FAX (651) 433-4110

OCI, Kansas City Field Office, HFH-510, Three Pine Ridge Plaza, 10901 W. 84th Ter, Suite 201, Lenexa, KS 66214
Larry Sperl, Special Agent in Charge (SAIC), HFH-510 (913) 541-7400 FAX (913) 541-7421
(Covers AR, CO, IA, KS, MO, NE, NM, UT, WY)

OCI, Austin Resident Office, HFH-511, 9430 Research Blvd., Bldg 2, Ste 250, Echelon II, Austin, TX 78759
James Cook, Assistant Special Agent in Charge (ASAIC), HFH-511 (512) 349-2599 FAX (512) 349-2986
(Covers TX , OK)

OCI, Dallas Domicile, P.O. Box 270760, Flower Mound, TX 75022
Tommy Hennesy, Special Agent (SA), (214) 513-2779 FAX (214) 513-2779

OCI, Houston Domicile, P.O. Box 273406, Houston, TX 77277-3406
Douglas Mason, SA (713) 661-7164 FAX (713) 661-7164

OCI, San Antonio Domicile
Esteban Morales, SA, (210) 269-5649

OCI, Denver Domicile, P.O. Box 1538, Evergreen, CO 80437
Kim Heavey, SA, (303) 670-7332 FAX (303) 670-7150

OCI, Los Angeles Field Office, HFH-520, Fairway Professional Bldg., 201 Avenida Fabricante, Suite 200, San Clemente, CA 92672
George (Jud) Bohrer, SAIC, (949) 366-4600 FAX (949) 366-4627
(Covers AZ, NV, So.CA,)

OCI, San Francisco Resident Office, HFH-521, 1301 Clay St., Suite 260 South, Oakland, CA 94612-5201
David Bourne, RAIC, HFH-521 (510) 637-3480 FAX (510) 637-3483
(Covers AK, No. CA, HI, ID, MT, NV, OR, WA)

OCI, Seattle Domicile, 22833 Bothell-EVT HWY, #1285, Bothell, WA 98021-9365
DaLi Borden, SA (206) 262-2245 FAX (206) 402-0848

OCI, Phoenix Domicile, PMB 217, 4727 E. Bell Rd #45, Phoenix, AZ 85032
Robert Olexy, SA (602) 664-5658 FAX (602) 664-5688

OCI, Metropolitan Washington Field Office, HFH-550, 4041 Powder Mill Rd, Suite 200, Calverton, MD 20705
Kim Rice, SAIC, HFH-550, (301) 902-1500 FAX (301) 344-3465
(Covers DE, KY, MD, South NJ, OH, PA, VA, WV, Washington, DC)

OCI, Task Force Maryland, HFH-551, 11750 Beltsville Dr, 1st Floor, Suite 100, Beltsville, MD 20705
Charles Zielinski, ASAIC, HFH-551, (301) 344-0614 FAX (301) 344-0002

OCI, Delaware Domicile, DE, P.O. Box 1717, Hockessin, DE. 19707
George (Butch) Muller, SA (302) 239-3796 FAX (302) 239-3796

OCI Philadelphia Domicile, P.O. 39845, Philadelphia, PA 19106-9845
Glen McElravy, SA (215) 861-8315, FAX (215) 861-8593

OCI, Norfolk Domicile, 5203 Sandstone Court, Suffolk, VA 23435
Timothy Royster, SA

OCI, Miami Field Office, HFH-500, 865 SW 78th Ave., Suite 201, Plantation, FL 33324
David Bourne, SAIC, HFH-500, (954) 476-5400 FAX (954) 476-5435
(Covers AL, FL, LA, MS, TN)

OCI, Atlanta Resident Office, HFH-502, 401 W. Peachtree Street, Suite 1917, Atlanta, GA 30308
Leroy Wagner, Resident Agent in Charge (RAIC), HFH-502, (404) 253-2317 FAX (404) 253-2324
(Covers GA)

OCI, New Orleans Resident Office, HFH-503, 103 Northpark Blvd., Suite 210, Covington, LA 70433
Michael Niemiec, RAIC, (985) 871-5152 FAX (985) 871-6922
(Covers LA)

OCI, San Juan Resident Office, HFH-501, 525 FD Roosevelt Ave., Suite 1118, San Juan, PR 00918
Donald Pettit, RAIC, (787) 281-4863 FAX (787) 281-4865
(Covers PR, VI)

OCI Tampa Domicile, 2203 Lois Avenue, Suite 600, Tampa, FL 33607
Randy Matteson, SA, (813) 348-1900 Ext. 2063 FAX (813) 348-1871

OCI, Nashville Domicile, 330 Franklin Rd, Suite 135-A-108, Brentwood, TN 37027
Bob West, SA, (615) 377-7782 FAX (615) 790-0715

OCI, New York Field Office, HFH-540 10 Exchange Place, Suite 804, Jersey City, NJ 07302
George (Stu) Magee, SAIC, (201) 547-3851 FAX (201) 547-6309
(Covers CT, ME, NH, NoNJ, NY, RI, VT)

OCI, Boston Resident Office, HFH-541 3 Centennial Drive, 2nd Floor, Peabody, MA 09160
Mark Dragonetti, RAIC, HFH-541, (508) 531-5850 FAX (508) 531-7356
(Covers MA,)

OCI, Buffalo Domicile, 138 Delaware Ave., Rm. 563, Buffalo, NY 14202
James Husted, SA, (716) 551-4811 Ext. 825 FAX (716) 855-3341

ORA FIELD DIRECTORY

NORTHEAST REGION

NE Region, New York (NER-FO), 158-15 Liberty Ave., Jamaica, NY 11433
Emergency (after hours) answering service (718) 340-7000
Diana J. Kolaitis, Regional Food and Drug Dir., HFR-NE1, (718) 662- 5416 FAX (718) 662-5434
John P. Schrade, Director, State Programs Branch, HFR-NE16, 718-662-5634 FAX (718) 662-5434
Bruce I. Skolnick, Deputy RFDD, HFR-NE12, 718-662-5610
Dolores Lanzarone, Mgmt. Analyst, HFR-NE11, 718-662-5488
Helen Shum, Mgmt Analyst, HFR-NE11, 718-662-5615
Vacant, Small Business Rep., HFR-NE17, 718-662-5618 FAX (718) 662-5434
Ronald E. Bernacki, Rad. Health Rep., HFR-NE19, 718-662-5612
Jerrold H. Mulnick, Sr. Regional Shellfish Specialist, HFR-NE13, 718-662-5613
Elizabeth O'Malley, Regional Food Specialist, HFR-NE14, (718) 662-5621
Carl Ponticello, Regional Computer Center Dir., HFR-NE31, 718-662-5513

NE Region New England (NWE-FO), One Montvale Ave., Stoneham, MA 02180
Max Lager, Electro-Optics Specialist for NE Reg. HFR-NE25, (781) 596-7744 FAX (781) 596-7894
Raymond A. Duffill, Sr. Regional Food Specialist, HFR-NE26, (781)-596-7725
Martin Dowgert, Regional Shellfish Specialist, HFR-NE27, (781) 596-7801
Peter Koufopoulos, Regional Shellfish Specialist, HFR-NE27, (781) 596-7780
Mary Yebba, Regional Food Specialist, HFR-NE28, (781) 596-7788

NE Region Albany Office, One Winners Circle, Suite 110, Albany, NY 12205 FAX (518) 453-2443
Stephen E. Pierson, Sr. Regional Milk Specialist, HFR-NE3520, (518) 453-2341 Ext. 31
Robert Altobelli, Regional Milk Specialist, HFR-NE3520, (518) 453-2341 Ext. 32

Northeast Regional Laboratory (NRL), 158-15 Liberty Ave., Jamaica, NY 11433
Marleen M. Wekell, Ph.D., Dir. Northeast Regional Lab. (NRL), HFR-NE500, (718) 662-5450 FAX (718) 662-5439
Alfred C. King, Dir. Drug Chem. Br., HFR-NE560, (718) 340-7126
Keroline Simmonds, Dir. Food Chem. Br., HFR-NE580, (718) 340-7132
Marilyn Smith, Dir. Micro. Science Br., HFR-NE570, (718) 340-7133
Rona Stromberg, Asst. to NRL Director, HFR-NE525, (718) 662-5457
Melanie Bailey, Admin. Officer, HFR-NE530, (718) 662-5440

Winchester Engineering & Analytical Center (WEAC), 109 Holton St., Winchester, MA 01890
Martin J. Finkelson, Director, HFR-NE400, (781) 729-5700 Ext. 721, FAX (781) 729-3593
Laurence Coyne, Dir. Engineering Br., HFR-NE480, (781) 729-5700 Ext. 761
Vacant, Dir. Analytical Br., HFR-NE460, (781) 729-5700 Ext. 749
Edward B. Barrett, Admin. Officer, HFR-NE430, (781) 729-5700 Ext. 741

NEW ENGLAND DISTRICT, (NWE-DO), One Montvale Ave., 4th Floor, Stoneham, MA 02180
Main Number (781) 596-7700, Emergency (after hours) Answering Service (978) 939-2380
Gail T. Costello, District Director, HFR-NE200 (781) 596-7717 FAX (781) 596-7896
David K. Elder, LCDR., Dir. Comp. Branch, HFR-NE240, (781) 596-7795
Linda Muccioli, Dir. MPSB., HFR-NE230, (781) 596-7757
Vacant, Public Affairs Specialist, HFR-NE245, (781) 596-7730
Michael R. Kravchuk, Dir. Invest. Branch, HFR-NE250, (781) 596-7799 FAX (781) 596-7896
William Boivin, Supervisor, HFR-NE250, (781) 596-7783 FAX (781) 596-7896
Willis I. Cobb, Jr., Supervisor, HFR-NE2500, (207) 622-8268/64 FAX (207) 622-8273
Sylvia Craven, Supervisor, HFR-NE250, (781) 596-7718 FAX (781) 596-7896
Janice Gordon, Supervisor, HFR-NE2540, (802) 951-6240 FAX (802) 879-5217
Ellen Madigan, Supervisor, HFR-NE250, (781) 596-7753 FAX (781) 596-7896
Frank J. Mazzoni, Supervisor, HFR-NE250, (781) 596-7754 FAX (781) 596-7896
Stephen Souza, Supervisor, HFR-NE2530, (860) 240-4289/90 FAX (860) 240-4313
Dominic J. Veneziano, Supervisor, HFR-NE250, (781) 596-7785 FAX (781) 596-7896

Augusta R.P., 330 Civic Center Drive, Suite 1, Augusta, ME 04330
Willis I. Cobb, Jr., Supervisor, HFR-NE2500, (207) 622-8268/64 FAX (207) 622-8273

Boston Border Station, WTC-Seaport Blvd., Suite 125, Boston, MA 02210

Bridgeport R.P., 915 Lafayette Blvd., Rm. 110, Bridgeport, CT 06604
Eduardo Rodriguez, Acting Resident in Charge (RIC), HFR-NE2510, (203) 579-5822/3 FAX (203) 579-5822

Calais Border Station, PO & Federal Building, 50 North Street, Rm. 132, Calais, ME 04619
(Mail to: P.O. Box 421, Calais, ME 04619) Telephone: (207) 454-3070

Concord R.P., 2 Capital Plaza, 3rd Floor, Concord, NH 03301
(Mail to: P.O. Box 488, Concord, NH 03302)
Garry H. Stewart, Resident in Charge (RIC), HFR-NE2520, (603) 225-1511 FAX (603) 225-1457

Essex Junction R.P., 11 Lincoln St., Rm. 208, Essex Junction, VT 05453
(Mail to: P.O. Box 802, Essex Junction, VT 05453)
Janice Gordon, Supervisor, HFR-NE2540, (802) 951-6240 FAX (802) 879-5217

Hartford R.P., 135 High St., Rm. 371, Hartford, CT 06103
Stephen Souza, Supervisor, HFR-NE2530, (860) 240-4289/90 FAX (860) 240-4313

Highgate Border Station, 112 Meyers Road, Swanton, VT 05488

Houlton Border Station, USPS Building, 39 Court St., Houlton, ME 04730
(Mail to: P.O. Box 66, Houlton, ME 04730)
Telephone: (207) 521-0347

Providence, R.P., 2224 Pawtucket Ave, Suite 201, East Providence, RI 02914
Beth Griffin, Acting Resident in Charge (RIC), HFR-NE2560, (401) 528-5399/5284 FAX (401) 528-5526

Worcester, R.P., 120 Front St., Suite 680, Worcester, MA 01608
Michael Leal, Acting Resident in Charge (RIC), HFR-NE2570, (508) 793-0421 FAX (508) 793-0456
Joseph A. Raulinaitis, Public Affairs Specialist, (508) 793-0422

NEW YORK DISTRICT, (NYK-DO), 158-15 Liberty Ave., Jamaica, NY. 11433 (New York City Office)
Main Number and Emergency (after hours) Answering Service (718) 340-7000
Jerome G. Woyshner, District Director, HFR-NE100, (718) 340-7000 FAX (718) 662-5665, Ext. 5447
Edward W. Thomas, Dir. Domestic Compliance Br., HFR-NE140, (716) 551-4461 Ext. 3116 FAX (716) 551-4499
Dilcia Granville, Public Affairs Specialist, HFR-NE145, (718) 340-7000 Ext. 5445
Cindy Maciejewski, Admin. Officer, HFR-NE130, (718) 340-7000 Ext. 5499
Wanda Eng, Dir. Invest. Br. (Domestic), HFR-NE150, (718) 340-7000 Ext. 5586
Richard Ferfoglia, Supervisor (718) 340-7000 Ext. 5587
Arthur Ted Ogdahl, Import Program Manager, HFR-NE152, (718) 340-7000, Ext. 5461 FAX (718) 662-5662
Connie Gallagher, Supervisor Ext. (718) 340-7000 Ext. 5569

Buffalo Office, 300 Pearl St. Suite 100, Buffalo, NY 14202
Emergency (after hours) Answering Service (716) 551-4461
Edward W. Thomas, Dir. Domestic Compliance Br., HFR-NE350, (716) 551-4461 Ext. 3116 FAX (716) 551-4499
Cindy Maciejewski, Dir. MPSB, HFR-NE330 (716) 551-4461 Ext. 3102 FAX (716) 551-4470
Diana Monaco, Public Affairs Specialist, HFR-NE345, (716) 551-4461 Ext. 3118
Robert L. Hart, Dir. Import Operations Br., HFR-NE3500, (716) 551-4461 Ext. 3142 FAX (716) 551-3813
Kevin V. Murray, Supervisory Investigator, Import Branch, HFR-NE3500, Ext. 3129 FAX (716) 551-3813
Mark P. Prusak, Supervisory Investigator, Import Branch, HFR-NE3500, Ext. 3153 FAX (716) 551-3813
Raymond D. Kent, Supervisory Investigator, Domestic Investigations, HFR-NE350, (716) 551-4461 Ext. 3126

Albany R.P., One Winners Circle, Suite 110, Albany, NY 12205
Perry T. Nichols, Supervisor, HFR-NE3520, (518) 453-2314/2316 FAX (518) 453-2443

Alexandria Bay R.P., 46735 Interstate #81, Alexandria Bay, NY 13067
Donald G. Gordon, Supervisor, HFR-NE3565

Binghamton R.P., 15 Henry St, Rm. 324, Binghamton, NY 13901
(Mail to: PO Box 1093, Binghamton, NY 13902)
Steven J. Libal, Resident in Charge (RIC), HFR-NE3530, (607) 773-2752 FAX (607) 773-2608

Champlain R.P., 198 West Service Rd, Champlain, NY 12919-1348
(Mail to: c/o U.S. Customs, 198 W. Service Rd., Champlain, NY 12919)
Todd A. Manning, Supervisor, HFR-NE3535, (518) 298-8240 FAX (518) 298-5538

Long Island R.P., North Shore Atrium, 6800 Jericho Tnpke, Suite 109E, Syosset, NY 11791
Otto Vitillo, Supervisor HFR-NE1500, (516) 921-2035 FAX (516) 921-3025

Massena R.P., Port of Massena, Seaway International Bridge Plaza, Rooseveltown, NY 13683
HFR-NE3570

Newburgh R.P., 15 Governor Drive, Newburgh, NY 12550
Perry T. Nichols, Supervisor, HFR-NE3545, (845) 567-0324 FAX (845) 567-1821

Ogdensburg R.P., U.S. Bridge Plaza, Route 812, Ogdensburg, NY 13669
HFR-NE3575, (315) 393-1851

Port Elizabeth R.P., 1201 Corbin St., 2nd Floor, Elizabeth, NJ 07201
Anthony Tepedino, Supervisor, HFR-NE1520, (973) 645-2386/2389 FAX (732) 351-7954
Voice Message (732) 351-7931/7932

Rochester R.P. 100 State St. Room 820 (lower lobby) Rochester, NY 14614
Joseph Erdmann, Supervisor, HFR-NE3540, (585) 263-3140   FAX (585) 263-3138

Syracuse R.P., 250 S. Clinton, Suite 120, Syracuse, NY 13202
(Mail to: PO Box 7197, Syracuse, NY 13261-7197)
Joseph H. Erdmann, Supervisory Investigator, HFR-NE3550, (315) 448-7601 Ext. 13
Domestic Investigations FAX (315) 448-7604
Imports FAX (315) 448-7623

White Plains R.P., 300 Hamilton Ave., Rm. 309, White Plains, NY 10601
Perry T. Nichols, Supervisor, HFR-NE1510, (914) 682-6166 Ext. 17 FAX (914) 682-6170
Elizabeth M. Jacobson, Supervisor (914) 682-6166 Ext. 27 FAX (914) 682-6170

CENTRAL REGION

Central Region-Philadelphia (PHI-FO), 900 U.S. Customhouse, 200 Chestnut Street, Philadelphia, PA 19106
Main Number and Emergency (after hours) answering service (215) 597-4390
Susan M. Setterberg, Regional Food and Drug Dir., HFR-CE1, (215) 597-4390 FAX (215) 597-5798
Mary Womack, ARFDD, HFR-CE4 (513) 679-2700 Ext. 150 (CIN-DO)
Marie Falcone, Small Business Representative, HFR-CE5, (215) 597-4390 Ext. 4003
Lorraine Beaver, Management Analyst, HFR-CE11, (215) 597-4390 Ext. 4006
Rita F. LaRocca-Mahoney, Regional Training Officer, HFR-CE14, (215) 597-4390 Ext. 4004
Vacant, Regional Milk Program, HFR-CE15, (215) 597-4390 Ext. 4005
Susan Alba, Supervisor, Regional Computer Center, HFR-CE33, (215) 597-4390 Ext. 4103

Baltimore Regional Staff, 6000 Metro Drive, Suite 101, Baltimore, MD 21215
Alexander A. Ondis, Reg. Shellfish Specialist, HFR-CE250, (410) 779-5102

Central Region-Chicago (CHI-FO), 20 N. Michigan Ave., Room 510, Chicago, IL 60602
Andrew Bonanno, DRFDD, HFR-CE2, (312) 353-9400 Ext. 120 FAX (312) 886-1682
Shirley H. James, Program Analyst, HFR-CE23, (312) 353-9400 Ext. 113
Richard Nelson, Supervisor, Regional Computer Center, HFR-CE34, (312) 353-9400 Ext. 125

Vacant, Regional Radiological Health Rep., HFR-CE24, Ext. 129
Charles D. Price, Sr. Regional Milk Specialist, HFR-CE25, (312) 353-9400 Ext. 112
Vacant, Administrative Specialist, HFR-CE26, Ext. 122
Vacant, State Cooperative Programs Director, Ext. 123

Cincinnati Regional Staff, 6751 Steger Drive, Cincinnati, OH 45237
James E. Frye, Electro-Optics Specialist, (513) 679-2700 Ext. 100

Columbus Regional Staff, 1600 Watermark Dr., Suite 105, Columbus, OH 43215
Vacant, Supervisor, Regional Retail Food Program, HFR-CE4530, (614) 487-1273

Forensic Chemistry Center (FCC), 6751 Steger Drive, Cincinnati, OH 45237
Frederick L. Fricke Jr., Dir., HFR-CE500, (513) 679-2700, Ext. 180 FAX (513) 679-2761
R. Duane Satzger, Dir. Organic Branch, HFR-CE501, (513) 679-2700 Ext. 182
Karen A. Wolnik, Dir. Inorganic Branch, HFR-CE502, (513) 679-2700 Ext. 181

Gurnee Regional Staff, 501 N. Riverside Dr., Suite 203, Gurnee, IL 60031
John Powell, Reg. Food Service, HFR-CE25 (847) 249-8632 Ext. 27

Minneapolis Regional Staff, 212 3rd Ave. S., Minneapolis, MN 55401
John L. Kunkel, Director, Regional Computer Center, HFR-CE30, (612) 334-4100

Voorhees Regional Staff 1034 Laurel Oak Rd, Voorhees, NJ 08043
Gary J. Wolf, Regional Shellfish Specialist, (856) 757-5389

BALTIMORE DISTRICT (BLT-DO) 6000 Metro Drive, Suite 101, Baltimore, MD 21215
Main Number and Emergency (after hours) Answering Service (410) 779-5454
Lee Bowers, District Director, HFR-CE200, (410) 779-5424 FAX (410) 779-5707
Nathaniel R. Esaw, Assistant to DD, (410) 779-5450 FAX (410) 779-5707
Dennis C. Westhoff, Science Advisor, HFR-CE205, (410) 779-5454
Button Beck, Dir. Admin. Mgt. Branch, HFR-CE230, (410) 779-5406 FAX (410) 779-5707
Vacant, Dir. Compliance Branch, HFR-CE240, (410) 779-5412 FAX (410) 779-5703
Stephen R. King, Public Affairs Specialist, HFR-CE245, (410) 779-5426 FAX (410) 779-5707
Roberta F. Wagner, Dir. Investigations Br. HFR-CE250, (410) 779-5430 FAX (410) 779-5705
Marc J. Balzarini, Assistant to DIB, (410) 779-5432 FAX (410) 779-5705
Matthew M. Henciak, Supervisor, (410) 779-5438 FAX (410) 779-5705
Valerie H. Wright, Supervisor, (410) 779-5434 FAX (410) 779-5705

Regional Staff:
Alexander A. Ondis, Reg. Shellfish Specialist, HFR-CE250,   (410) 779-5102 FAX (410) 779-5705
Robert Hoffa, Supervisory ITS, (410) 779-5104 FAX (410) 779-5705
Gertrude Mortis, Chicago FASTeam (410) 779-5103 FAX (410) 779-5705

NY Personnel:
Shirley J. Edwards, Personnel Management Specialist   (410) 779-5101 FAX (410) 779-5712

Charleston R.P. (CHN-RP) 10 Hale St., Suite 201, Charleston, WV 25301
William D. Basset Jr., Resident in Charge (RIC), HFR-CE2530, (304) 347-5173 FAX (304) 347-5480

Dundalk Marine Terminal R.P. (DMT-RP) Dundalk Marine Terminal 2700 Broening Highway, Baltimore, MD 21222
Dean Cook, Supervisor, HFR-CE24A102A, (410) 631-0322/3, Ext. 11 FAX (410) 631-0332

Morgantown R.P. (MGN-RP) 75 High Street, Room 220, Morgantown, WV 26507
(Mail to: P.O. Box 900, Morgantown, WV 26507-7558)
William Warnick, Resident in Charge (RIC), HFR-CE2560, (304) 291-4410, FAX (304) 291-4960

Northern Virginia R.P. (covers Wash DC area) (NOVA-RP) 101 W. Broad Street, Suite 400
Falls Church, VA 22046-4200
Vacant, Supervisor, HFR-CE2535, (703) 235-8440, Ext. 507 FAX (703) 235-8292

Norfolk International Terminal R.P. (NIT-RP) Norfolk Intl. Terminal, 7737 Hampton Blvd., Whse. 4C, Room 206, Norfolk, VA 23505-1204
Linda Eason, Supervisor, HFR-CE2410, (757) 441-3787 Ext. 109 FAX 757-441-3709

Norfolk R.P., 200 Granby Mall, Room 821, Norfolk, VA 23510
Stephen C. Eason, Wilfred Darang, Thomas Hudson, CSOs, HFR-CE2540, (757) 441-3326/7 FAX (757) 441-3718

Richmond R.P., 10710 Midlothian Turnpike, Suite 424, Richmond, VA 23235
Karen S. Anthony, Supervisor, HFR-CE2545, (804) 379-1627/2357 Ext. 11 FAX (804) 379-2968

Roanoke R.P., 5162 Valley Point Pkwy, Suite 105, Roanoke, VA 24019
Dennis L. Doupnik, Resident in Charge (RIC), HFR-CE2550, (540) 265-6037/6040 FAX (540) 265-6036

Salisbury R.P., 129 E. Main Street, Salisbury, MD 21803-0587
(Mail to: P.O. Box 587, Salisbury, MD 21803)
Bruce C. Kovak, Resident In Charge (RIC), HFR-CE2555, (410) 749-0540 FAX (410) 860-1029

CHICAGO DISTRICT, (CHI-DO), 550 West Jackson Blvd., Suite 1500, South, Chicago, IL 60661
Main Number (312) 353-5863/Emergency (after hours) Answering Service (630) 978-5763
Main Number (312) 353-5863 FAX (312) 596-4170
Arlyn Baumgarten, District Director, HFR-CE600, (312) 596-4200 FAX (312) 596-4242
Virginia R. Connelly, Executive Officer, HFR-CE665, (312) 596-4210
Richard E. Harrison, Dir. Compliance Branch, HFR-CE640, (312) 596-4220
Darlene Bailey, Public Affairs Specialist, HFR-CE645, (312) 596-4205
Gerald Berg, Dir. Investigations Branch, HFR-CE650, (312) 596-4240
Roger J. Adams, Supervisor, HFR-CE6520, (217) 492-4095 FAX (217) 492-4103
Stephen D. Eich, Supervisor (Imports-O'Hare) (630) 860-1307 Ext. 15
Bradley J. Maunder, HFR-CE150, (312) 596-4224
Nicholas F. Lyons, HFR-CE150, (312) 596-4247
Larry Stringer, Supervisor, HFR-CE150, (312) 596-4245
Oenia Watkins, Administrative Officer, HFR-CE630, (312) 596-4230

Gurnee R.P., 501 N. Riverside Dr., Suite 203, Gurnee, IL 60031
Darrell E. Luedtke, Resident in Charge (RIC), HFR-CE6505, (847) 249-8632 Ext. 28 FAX (847) 249-0175

Hinsdale R.P., Suite 201, 908 N. Elm St., Hinsdale, IL 60521
Jeanne Morris, Resident in Charge (RIC), HFR-CE6512, (630) 323-2763 FAX (630) 323-7137

Mt. Vernon R.P., 105 S. Sixth St, Rm. 223, Mt. Vernon, IL 62864-1525
Wayne W. Grundstrom, Resident in Charge (RIC), HFR-CE6502, (618) 242-9124 FAX (618) 242-9567

O'Hare R.P., Import Office, 1000 Tower Lane, Suite 190, Bensenville, IL 60106
Stephen D. Eich, Supervisor, HFR-CE6521, (630) 860-1307 Ext. 15
Charles Spivey, Import Program Manager, HFR-CE6521, (630) 860-1028 Ext. 10 FAX (630) 860-1066

Peoria, R.P., 2918 Willow Knolls Road, Suite B, Peoria, IL 61614-1129
James Finn, Resident in Charge (RIC), HFR-CE6510, (309) 691-3192 FAX (309) 691-3669

Springfield R.P., 511 W. Capitol, Suite 205, Springfield, IL 62704
Mail to: PO Box 1120, Springfield, IL 62705)
Roger J. Adams, Supervisor, HFR-CE6520, (217) 492-4095 FAX (217) 492-4103

CINCINNATI DISTRICT, (CIN-DO), 6751 Steger Dr., Cincinnati, OH 45237-3097
Main Number/Emergency (after hours) Answering Service (513) 679-2700
Carol A. Heppe, District Director, HFR-CE400, (513) 679-2700 Ext. 116 FAX (513) 679-2771
Patricia L. Wolfzorn, Administrative Officer, HFR-CE430, (513) 679-2700 Ext. 102 FAX (513) 679-2771
Deborah A. Grelle, Dir. Compliance Br., HFR-CE440, (513) 679-2700 Ext. 160
Marilyn R. Zipkes, Public Affairs Specialist, HFR-CE445, (513) 679-2700 Ext. 110
Vacant, Dir. Investigations Branch, HFR-CE450, (513) 679-2700 Ext. 120 FAX (513) 679-2772
Guy W. Cartwright, Supervisor, HFR-CE4530, (614) 487-1273 Ext. 11 FAX (614) 487-9658

Robert W. Connatser, Supervisor HFR-CE 450, (513) 679-2700 Ext. 121 FAX (513) 679-2772
Steven P. Eastham, Supervisor, HFR-CE450, (513) 679-2700 Ext. 123   FAX (513) 679-2772
Susan C. Morgan, Supervisor, HFR-CE4525, (330) 273-1038 FAX (330) 225-7477
Stephen J. Rabe, Supervisor, HFR-CE450, (513) 679-2700 Ext. 122 FAX (513) 679-2772
James E. Frye, Electro Optics Specialist, (513) 679-2700 Ext. 100

Brunswick R.P., 3820 Center Rd, Brunswick, OH 44212-0838
Susan C.Morgan, Supervisor, HFR-CE4525, (330) 273-1038 FAX (330) 225-7477
Ruth E. Weisheit, Public Affairs Specialist, HFR-CE4525, (330) 273-1038 FAX (330) 225-7477

Columbus, R.P., 1600 Watermark Dr., Rm. 105, Columbus, OH 43215
Guy W. Cartwright, Supervisor, HFR-CE4530, (614) 487-1273 Ext. 11 FAX (614) 487-9658

Louisville R.P., 9600 Brownstone Rd., Suite 302, Louisville, KY 40241
Robert W. Hudson, Resident in Charge (RIC), HFR-CE4550, (502) 425-0069 FAX (502) 425-0450

Toledo R.P., 420 Madison Avenue, Suite 560, Toledo, OH 43604
Robert Rodriguez, Resident In Charge (RIC), HFR-CE4535, (419) 259-6347 FAX (419) 259-6211

DETROIT DISTRICT. (DET-DO), 300 River Place, Suite 5900, Detroit, MI 48207
Main Number: (313) 393-8100/Emergency (after hours) Answering Service (313) 343-5120
Joann M. Givens, District Director, HFR-CE700, (313) 393-8106 FAX (313) 393-8105
Keith J. Jasukaitis, Special Asst. to the District Director, HFR-CE700, (313) 393-8107
Evelyn DeNike, Public Affairs Specialist, HFR-CE745, (313) 393-8109
David M. Kaszubiski, Dir. Compliance Branch, HFR-CE740, (313) 393-8110
Brenda M. McCurdy, Dir. Laboratory, HFR-CE760, (313) 393-8203 FAX (313) 393-3224
Melanie S. Bourcier, Supervisory Administrative Specialist, HFR-CE730, (313) 393-8126
John P. Dempster, Dir. Investigations Branch, HFR-CE750, (313) 393-8141 FAX (313) 393-8139/8140
George A. Domingo, Asst. to DIB, HFR-CE750, (313) 393-8142
Nancy Bellamy, Supervisor, HFR-CE750, (313) 393-8143
Greta Budweg, Supervisor, Imports, HFR-CE750, (313) 393- 8190
Eric Joneson, Supervisor, HFR-CE750, (313) 393-8157
Anthony Taube, Supervisor, Imports, HFR-CE750, (313) 393-8176

Evansville R.P., Rm. 233, Federal Bldg., 101 NW M.L. King Blvd, Evansville, IN 47708-1951
Larry K. Austin, HFR-CE7545, (812) 465-6414 FAX (812) 465-6359

Fort Wayne R.P., 6528 Rockingham Drive, Fort Wayne, IN 46835
William R. Brubaker, HFR-CE7550, (260) 486-8593 FAX (SAME)

Grand Rapids R.P., 678 Front St., Suite 218, Grand Rapids, MI 49504
Frederic W. French, Supervisor, HFR-CE7555, (616) 233-9311 FAX (616) 233-9224

Indianapolis R.P., 101 West Ohio St., Suite 1300, Indianapolis, IN 46204-1994
Dennis R. Downer, Supervisor, HFR-CE7560, (317) 226-6500 Ext. 11 FAX (317) 226-6506
Andrew Paeng, Supervisor, HFR-CE7560, Ext. 19
Janet LeClair, Public Affairs Specialist, Ext. 13

Kalamazoo R.P., 410 W. Michigan Ave., Room B26, Kalamazoo, MI 49007-3746
William D. Tingley, (Acting) HFR-CE7565, (269) 345-3203 FAX (269) 345-8144

Port Huron Bluewater Bridge Import Station 2321 Pine Grove Ave. Suite 2114, Port Huron, MI 48060
(810) 985-8514 and (810) 985-8513 FAX (810) 985-8528
Greta Budweg, Supervisor, HFR-CE750, (313) 393-8190

Saginaw R.P., 1585 Tittabawassee Road, c/o Michigan Dept. of Agriculture, Saginaw, MI 48604-9445
Paige E. Wilson, HFR-CE7570, (989) 771-2073 FAX (989) 771-2073

South Bend R.P., Viridian Place, 2422 Viridian Drive, Suite 102, South Bend, IN 46628-4300
William Nelson, Resident in Charge (RIC), HFR-CE7575, (574) 288-7222 FAX (574) 288-0737

MINNEAPOLIS DISTRICT (MN-DO) 212 3rd Ave. South, Minneapolis, MN 55401
Main Number and Emergency (after hours) Answering Service (612) 334-4100
W. Charles Becoat, District Director, HFR-CE800, (612) 334-4100 FAX (612) 334-4134
C. Annette Byrne, Special Asst. to the District Director, HFR-CE800, (612) 334-4100
Cindy Grindahl, Admin. Officer, HFR-CE830, (612) 334-4100
David R. Yost, Dir. Compliance Branch, HFR-CE840, (612) 334-4100
Amy C. Johnson, Public Affairs Specialist, HFR-CE845, (612) 334-4100
Cheryl Bigham, Dir. Investigations Branch, HFR-CE850, (612) 334-4100 FAX (612) 334-4134
Calvin D. Baas, Ass't. to DIB, HFR-CE850, (612) 334-4100 FAX (612) 334-4134
Anthony Duran, Supervisor, HFR-CE850, (612) 334-4100 FAX (612) 334-4134
Carrie A. Hoffman, Supervisor, HFR-CE850, (612) 334-4100 FAX (612) 334-4134
Rhonda Mecl, Supervisor, HFR-CE850, (612) 334-4100 FAX (612) 334-4134
Constance L. Richard-Math, Supervisor, HFR-CE850, (612) 334-4100 FAX (612) 334-4134
Steven A. Skaar, Supervisor, HFR-CE850, (612) 334-4100 FAX (612) 334-4134
M. Edith Snyder, Supervisor, HFR-CE850, (612) 334-4100 FAX (612) 334-4134
Elizabeth Waltrip, Supervisor, HFR-CE850, (612) 334-4100 FAX (612) 334-4134
Richard Willey, Supervisory Investigator, HFR-CE8590, (414) 771-7167 FAX (414) 771-7512

International Falls, R.P., 200 4th St. West, International Falls, MN 55649
Jennifer A. Vollom, Investigator, HFR-CE8575

Dunseith R.P., 7972 26th Avenue NE, Willow City, ND 58534
Sharon M. Harold, Resident in Charge (RIC), HFR-CE8591, (701) 776-9038   FAX (701) 776-9039

Fargo, R.P., Rm. 453, 657 2nd Ave. North, Fargo, ND 58102
Darren D. Holaday, Resident in Charge (RIC), HFR-CE8592, (701) 239-5109 FAX (701) 239-5107

Pembina R.P. 10997 I-29 Customs, P.O. Box 349, Pembina, ND 58271
Jean M. Trimbo, Investigator, HFR-CE8593, (701) 825-0022 FAX (701) 825-0023

Green Bay R.P., Old Fort Square, Suite 202, 211 North Broadway, Green Bay, WI 54303
Jeffrey Hangartner, Resident in Charge (RIC), HFR-CE8580, (414) 433-3924 FAX (414) 433-3949

La Crosse R.P., 1627 Keller Court, Onalaska, WI 54650
William E. Keer, Resident in Charge (RIC), HFR-CE8596, (608) 785-9950 FAX (608) 785-9951

Madison, R.P., 700 Regent Street, Suite 202 Madison, WI 53715
Charles R. Cote, Resident in Charge (RIC), HFR-CE8585, (608) 264-5332 FAX (608) 264-5335

Milwaukee R.P., 2675 North Mayfair Road, Suite 200, Milwaukee, WI 53226-1305
Richard Willey, Supervisory Investigator, HFR-CE8590, (414) 771-7167 FAX (414) 771-7512
Stephen Davis, Public Affairs Specialist, (414) 771-7114

Sioux Falls R.P., 230 South Phillips Ave, Rm. 406, Sioux Falls, SD 57104
Howard A. Burmester, Resident in Charge (RIC), HFR-CE8594, (605) 330-4383 FAX (605) 330-4384

NEW JERSEY DISTRICT (NWJ-DO) Waterview Corp. Center, 10 Waterview Blvd., 3rd Floor, Parsippany, NJ 07054
Main Number and Emergency (after hours) Answering Service (973) 526-6000
Douglas I. Ellsworth, District Director HFR-CE300, (973) 526-6001 FAX (973) 526-6069
Kimberly Bailey, Admin. Officer, HFR-CE330, (973) 526-6023
Ray Abrahams, Dir. Compliance Branch, HFR-CE340, (973) 526-6002
Joan Lytle, Public Affairs Specialist, HFR-CE345, (973) 526-6035
Edward H. Wilkens, Dir., Prod Surv. Appr. Unit, HFR-CE320, (973) 526-6011
Diana Amador, Dir. Investigations Branch, HFR-CE350, (973) 526-6015
Mimi Roa Remache, Special Asst. to the DIB, HFR-CE350, (973) 526-6019 FAX (973) 526-6032
Cary Greene, Supervisor, HFR-CE350, (973) 526-6061
Lisa Harlan, Supervisor, HFR-CE350, (973) 526-6014
Shirley H. Isbill, Supervisor, HFR-CE3565, (732) 940-8946/8996 Ext. 13 FAX (732) 940-8936

Robert W. McCullough, Supervisory Investigator, HFR-CE3560, (856) 757-5389 FAX (856) 783-1513
Meyer Slobotsky, Supervisor, HFR-CE3565, (732) 940-8946/8996 Ext. 12 FAX (732) 940-8936
Toniette Williams, Supervisor, HFR-CE350, (973) 526-6018

North Brunswick R.P.,120 Center Dr., Bldg. C, North Brunswick, NJ 08902
Shirley H. Isbill, Supervisor, HFR-CE3565, (732) 940-8946/8996 Ext. 13 FAX (732) 940-8936
Meyer Slobotsky, Supervisor, HFR-CE3565, (732) 940-8946/8996 Ext. 12

Voorhees R.P., 1034 Laurel Oak Rd, Voorhees, NJ 08043
Robert W. McCullough, Supervisory Investigator, HFR-CE3560, (856) 757-5389 FAX (856) 783-1513
Gary J. Wolf, Regional Shellfish Specialist, (856) 757-5389

PHILADELPHIA DISTRICT OFFICE (PHI-DO), 900 US Customhouse, 2nd & Chestnut Sts., Philadelphia, PA 19106
Main Number and Emergency (after hours) Answering Service (215) 597-4390
Thomas D.Gardine, District Director, HFR-CE100, (215) 597-4390 Ext. 4200 FAX (215) 597-4660
Maryann B. Yates, Admin. Officer, HFR-CE130, Ext. 4300 FAX (215) 597-6649
Dorothy Miller, Dir. Compliance Br., HFR-CE140, Ext. 4410 FAX (215) 597-8212
Anitra D. Brown-Reed, Public Affairs Specialist, HFR-CE145, (215) 597-4390 Ext. 4202
Vacant, Dir. Science Br., HFR-CE160, Ext. 4600, FAX (215) 597-4660
Peter C. Baker, Dir. Investigations Br., HFR-CE150, (215) 597-4390 Ext. 4500 FAX (215) 597-0875
Ann L. deMarco, Asst. to DIB, HFR-CE150, (215) 597-4390 Ext. 4408, FAX (215) 597-0875
Steve L. Carter, Supervisor, HFR-CE 150, (215) 597-4390 Ext. 4520, FAX (215) 597-0875
Susan F. Laska, Supervisor, HFR-CE1500, (215) 362-0740/41 Ext. 21 FAX (215) 362-0510
Michael D. O'Meara, Supervisor, HFR-CE1505, (302) 573-6447 Ext. 11 FAX (302) 573-6398
LuAnn M. Pallas, Supervisor, HFR-CE1520, (717) 541-9924 Ext. 12 FAX (302) 573-6398
Alfred J. Puglia, Supervisor, HFR-CE150, (215) 597-4390 Ext. 4540 FAX (215) 597-0875
Daniel R. Tamariello, Supervisor, HFR-CE1515, (412) 644-3394 Ext. 16 FAX (412) 644-5496

Harrisburg R.P., 3605 Vartan Way, Suite 305, Harrisburg, PA 17110
LuAnn M. Pallas, Supervisor, HFR-CE1510 (717) 541-9924 Ext. 12 FAX (717) 541-9927

North Wales R.P., 1180 Welsh Road, Gwynedd Corporate Center, Suite 250, North Wales, PA 19454
Susan F. Laska, Supervisor, HFR-CE1500 (215) 362-0740/41 Ext. 21 FAX (215) 362-0510

Pittsburgh, R.P., 7 Parkway Center, Suite 250, Pittsburgh, PA 15220
Daniel R. Tammariello, Supervisor, HFR-CE1515 (412) 644-3394/95 Ext. 16 FAX (412) 644-5496

Scranton R.P., 235 N. Washington Ave., Suite 307, Scranton, PA. 18503
(Mail To: PO Box 828 Scranton, PA 18501)
LuAnn M. Pallas, Supervisor, HFR-CE1520 (570) 342-5699 FAX (570) 342-8058

Wilmington R.P., 920 King St., Suite 409, Wilmington, DE 19801
Michael D. O'Meara, Supervisor, HFR-CE1505 (302) 573-6447, Ext. 11 FAX (302) 573-6398

SOUTHEAST REGION

SE REGION, ATLANTA (ATL-FO), 60 Eight St. NE, Atlanta, GA 30309
Gary Dykstra, Regional Food and Drug Dir., HFR-SE1, (404) 253-1171 FAX (404) 253-1207
James A. Casey, Deputy Food and Drug Dir., HFR-SE1, (404) 253-1172
Vacant, Specialist, Asst. to RFDD, HFR-SE1, (404) 253-1177
Laurie Chase-Farmer, Special Asst. to RFDD, HFR-SE1, (404) 253-1175
Nikita Harris, Quality Program Specialist, HFR-SE12, (404) 253-1288
James C. Mac Laughlin, Regional Training Officer, HFR-SE14, (404) 253-1269
Chester Morris, Dir. State Programs Branch, HFR-SE12, (404) 253-1266
Dan Redditt, Sr. Regional Food Specialist, HFR-SE14, (404) 253-1265
Ralph T. Trout, Health Rep., HFR-SE150, (615) 781-5380 Ext.171
Vacant, Sr. Reg. Milk Specialist, HFR-SE14, (404) 253-1166
Marc B. Glatzer, Sr. Regional Shellfish, HFR-SE2580, (850) 942-8323
Vacant, Regional Small Business Rep., HFR-SE17, (404) 253-2238

Vacant, Electro-Optics Specialist, HFR-SE400, (504) 253-4508
Vacant, Dir., Regional Computer Center, HFR-SE4, (404) 253-1264

Southeast Regional Lab (SRL), 60 Eight St. NE, Atlanta, GA 30309

Gayle Lancette, Dir. of Science, HFR-SE600, (404) 253-1176 FAX (404) 253-1208
Perry Wilkes, Deputy Dir. of Science, HFR-SE600, (404) 253-2215
Curtis W. Edwards, Dir. Chemistry (Drugs, Filth, Decomposition) HFR-SE660, (404) 253-1178
Lurlene Dixon, Dir. Microbiology Br., HFR-SE670, (404) 253-1179
Evelyn Bonnin, Dir. Atlanta Center for Nutrient Analysis, HFR-SE680, (404) 253-1181
Vacant, Dir. Chemistry II (Pesticides, Mycotoxins, Additives), HFR-SE690, (404) 253-2262

ATLANTA DISTRICT, (ATL-DO), 60 Eight St. NE, Atlanta, GA 30309

Main number and Emergency (after hours) Answering Service (404) 253-1164
Mary H. Woleske, District Director, HFR-SE100, (404) 253-1161 FAX (404) 253-1202
Emilio Rodriguez, Dir., Mgmt & Prog Support Branch, HFR-SE130, (404) 253-1184 FAX (404) 253-1206
Barbara A. Wood, Dir. Compliance Branch, HFR-SE140, (404) 253-1274 FAX (404) 253-1163
JoAnn Pittman, Public Affairs Specialist, HFR-SE145, (404) 253-1272
Mary Lewis, Public Affairs Specialist, HFR-SE145, (919) 856-4456
Dawn L. Todd-Murrell, Dir. Investigations Branch, HFR-SE150, (404) 253-2242 FAX (404) 253-1205
Vincent M. Williams, Supervisor HFR-SE150, (404) 253-2240 FAX (404) 253-1205
Calvin Foulks, Supervisor HFR-SE150, (404) 253-2241 FAX (404) 253-1205
Mallory W. Lawrence, Supervisor HFR-SE150, (404) 253-2243 FAX (404) 253-1205
Sandra C. Lawrence, Supervisor HFR-SE150, (404) 253-2222 FAX (404) 253-1205
Vacant, Supervisor, HFR-SE150, (336) 292-9351
Fulton A. Varner, Supervisor HFR-SE150, (404) 253-2225
Andrew B. Bevill, Supervisor HFR-SE150, (404) 253-2218
Janice L. King, Supervisor HFR-SE150, (843) 746-2990

Asheville R.P., 44 Buck Shoals Rd, Unit A-1, Arden, NC 28704

R. Edward DeBerry, Resident in Charge (RIC), HFR-SE1525, (828) 684-3585 FAX (828) 684-4932

Charleston R.P., 4600 Goer Drive, Suite 106, North Charleston, SC 29406

(Mail to: PO Box 21077 Charleston, SC 29413)
Janice L. King, Supervisor, HFR-SE1505, (843) 746-2990 FAX (843) 746-2994

Charlotte R.P., 5701 Executive Center Dr., Suite 104, Charlotte, NC 28212

Eileen J. Bannerman, Resident in Charge (RIC), HFR-SE1510, (704) 344-6116 FAX (704) 344-6402

Columbia R.P., Varo Bldg., 1801 Assembly St., Rm. B-17, Columbia, SC 29201

Carol J. Blackwood, Resident in Charge (RIC), HFR-SE1515, (803) 765-5845 FAX (803) 765-5680

Greensboro R.P., 2302 W. Meadowview Rd., Suite 122, Greensboro, NC 27407

Vacant, Supervisor, HFR-SE150, (336) 292-9351 FAX (336) 855-6528

Greensboro R.P., 2302 w. Meadowview Rd., Suite 203, Greensboro, NC 27407

Joe A. Odom, Resident in Charge (RIC), HFR-SE150, (336) 333-5419 FAX (336) 333-5563

Greenville, N.C. R.P., 3110-D South Evans St., Greenville, NC 27835

Perry H. Gambrell, Resident In Charge (RIC), HFR-SE1536, (252) 758-0738 FAX (252) 758-5007

Greenville, S.C. R.P., 300 Executive Center Dr., Suite 200 B (B-129), Greenville, SC 29615

David Williams, Resident in Charge (RIC), HFR-SE1522, (864) 234-9966 FAX (864) 234-0806

Middle GA. R.P., 485 Milledgeville Road, Eatonton, GA. 31024

(Mail to: Food and Drug Administration, PO Box 767, Milledgeville, GA 31061)
Robert P. Neligan, Resident in Charge (RIC), HFR-SE1537, (706) 485-2725 FAX (706) 485-2725

Raleigh R.P., 310 New Bern Ave., Rm. 370, Raleigh, NC 28601

Vacant, Resident in Charge (RIC), HFR-SE1535, (919) 856-4474 FAX (919) 856-4776

Savannah R.P., 120 Barnard St., Rm. A301, Savannah, GA 31401
Janet Grey, Resident in Charge (RIC), HFR-SE1538, (912) 652-4106 FAX (912) 652-4231

Tifton, GA, R.P., Tift Adm. Bldg., 225 Tift Ave., Rm. 107, Tifton, GA 31794
B. Douglas Brogden, Resident in Charge (RIC) HFR-SE1537, (912) 382-5963 FAX (912) 386-9610

Wilmington, R.P., 2202 Burnett Blvd. C/O NC State Port Authority, Wilmington, NC 28401
Gary Coleman, Resident, (910) 251-8480 FAX (910) 251-8484
Randy Clarida, Resident, (910) 251-8480 FAX (910) 251-8484

FLORIDA DISTRICT (FLA-DO), 555 Winderley Place, Suite 200, Maitland, FL 32751
Main Number and Emergency (after hours) Answering Service (407) 475-4700
Emma R. Singleton, District Director, HFR-SE200, (407) 475-4701 FAX (407) 475-4768
Kendall W. Hester, Compliance Branch, HFR-SE240, (407) 475-4734 FAX (407) 475-4769
Johnny Cruz, Supervisory Administrative Specialist, HFR-SE230, (407) 475-4760 FAX (407) 475-4770
Lynne C. Isaacs, Public Affairs Specialist, HFR-SE245, (407) 475-4715 FAX (407) 475-4768
David J. Gallant, Dir., Investigations Branch, HFR-SE250, (407) 475-4710 FAX (407) 475-4768
Justin H. Price, Supervisor, Invest. Branch HFR-SE250, (407) 475-4710 FAX (407) 475-4768
Ronald T. Weber, Supervisor, Invest. Branch HFR-SE250, (407) 475-4724 FAX (407) 475-4768
Imports (407) 475-4755 FAX (407) 475-4768

Boca Raton-RP, Interstate Plaza, 1499 W Palmetto Park Rd Suite 110, Boca Raton, FL 33486
Keith S. Ehrlich, Supervisor, HFR-SE2590, (561) 338-7631 Ext. 11 FAX (561) 367-8685
Imports (561) 338-7631 Ext. 39 FAX (561) 367-8685

Jacksonville-RP, 6800 Southpoint Pkwy, Suite 502, Jacksonville, FL 32216
Harry R. Bringger, Resident in Charge (RIC), HFR-SE2570, (904) 281-1924 FAX (904) 281-1124
Imports (904) 281-1196

Miami-RP Imports Group, 6601 NW 25th St., Rm. 241, Miami, FL 33122
(Mail to: P.O. Box 592256, Miami, FL 33159-2256)
Kathleen M. Sinninger, Import Program Manager, HFR-SE2575, (305) 526-2800 Ext. 964 FAX (305) 526-2693
Facundo I. Bernal, Import Supervisor, HFR-SE2575, (305) 526-2800 Ext. 927
Bruce E. Taylor, Import Supervisor, HFR-SE2575, (305) 526-2800 Ext. 911

Miami-RP Domestics Investigations Group, 8600 NW 36th St., Suite 400, Miami, FL 33166
Vacant, Supervisor, HFR-SE2560, (305) 513-4417 Ext. 4832 FAX (786) 437-4866
Estella N. Brown, Public Affairs Specialist, (305) 526-2800 Ext. 930 FAX (305) 526-2693

Tallahassee-RP, Hobbs Fed. Bldg., Ste. 5022, 227 N. Bronough St., Tallahassee, FL 32301
Courtney A. Hunt, Resident in Charge (RIC), HFR-SE2580, (850) 942-8325 FAX (850) 942-8326

Tampa-RP, 3350 W. Buschwood Park Rd., Suite 170, Tampa, FL 33618
Leon L. Law, Supervisor, HFR-SE2585, (813) 228-2671 Ext. 20, FAX (813) 228-2046

Ft. Myers-RP, 2000 Main Street, Room 305, Ft. Myers, FL 33901
Keith Schwartz, Resident in Charge (RIC), HFR-SE2595, (239) 337-5681 FAX (239) 337-5691

NEW ORLEANS DISTRICT (NOL-DO), 6600 Plaza Drive, Suite 400, New Orleans, LA 70127
Main Number and Emergency (after hours) Answering Service, (504) 253-4500
Carl E. Draper, District Director, HFR-SE400, (504) 253-4501 FAX (504) 253-4504
Patricia K. Schafer, Compliance Branch Director, HFR-SE440, (504) 253-4515, FAX (504) 253-4520
Denise H. Collins, Supv. Admin. Specialist, HFR-SE430, (504) 253-4558, FAX (504) 253-4560
Stacy M. Below, Public Affairs Specialist, HFR-SE445, (504) 253-4506, FAX (504) 253-4507
F. Dwight Herd, Dir., Investigations Branch, HFR-SE450, (504) 253-4522, FAX (504) 253-4521
Vacant, Asst to DIB, HFR-SE450, (504) 253-4524
James W. Blakely, Supervisor, (JKS-RP), HFR-SE4570, (601) 965-4581, FAX (601) 965-4584
Joseph T. Goertz, Import Supervisor, HFR-SE450, (504) 253-4508, FAX (504) 253-4521

Tura L. King, Supervisor, HFR-SE450, (504) 253-4552
Michael W. Roosevelt, Supervisor, HFR-SE450, (504) 253-4525
Carolyn W. White, Supervisor, HFR-SE450, (504) 253-4545

Baton Rouge R.P., 5353 Essen Lane, Suite 220, Baton Rouge, LA 70809
Vacant, Resident in Charge (RIC)
Barbara Wright, BIMO Specialist, HFR-SE4550, (225) 757-7749 FAX (225) 757-7746
John E. Veazey, Regional Shellfish Specialist, (225) 757-7745

Lafayette R.P., 101 Feu Follet Road, Room 148 Lafayette, LA 70508
Francis Guidry, Resident in Charge (RIC), HFR-SE4560, (337) 262-6603 FAX (337) 262-6678

Shreveport R.P., 401 Edwards Street, Suite 223, Shreveport, LA 71101
Randy D. Baxter, Resident in Charge (RIC), HFR-SE4555, (318) 676-3343 FAX (318) 676-3345

Birmingham R.P., 950 22nd Street North, Suite 628, Birmingham, AL 35203
Patricia Smith, HFR-SE3555, (205) 731-0017 FAX (205) 731-0260
Vacant, Resident in Charge (RIC)

Mobile R.P., 3737 Government Blvd., Suite 308, Mobile, AL 36693
Vacant, Resident in Charge (RIC), HFR-SE3565, (251) 441-5161 FAX (251) 441-5162
Samuel L. Collins, CSO

Montgomery-RP, 500 Eastern Blvd., One East Bldg Ste. 201, Montgomery, AL 36117-2044
Brian S. Lynch, Biologics Specialist, HFR-SE3565, (334) 223-7116 FAX (334) 223-7145
Vacant, Resident in Charge (RIC)

Jackson R.P., 100 West Capitol St., Suite 340, Jackson, MS 39269
James W. Blakely, Supervisor, HFR-SE4570, (601) 965-4581 FAX (601) 965-4584

Nashville Branch, 297 Plus Park Blvd., Nashville, TN 37217
Emergency (after hours) Answering Service (615) 781-5385
Howard E. Lewis, Dir., Nashville Branch, HFR-SE340, (615) 781-5388, Ext. 124, FAX (615) 781-5383
M. Anthony Abel I, Supervisor, HFR-SE350, (615) 781-5374, Ext. 111
Michael R. Duran, Supervisor, HFR-SE350, (615) 781-5375, Ext. 116
John M. McInnis, Supervisor, (MEM-RP) HFR-SE3550, (901) 544-0345 Ext. 25 FAX (901) 544-0349
Susan M. Halpenny, Supervisor, (MEM-RP) HFR-SE355Q, (901) 544-0345 Ext. 26 FAX (901) 544-0349
Jane M. Moore, Dir. Travel Management Center (TMC), HFR-SE330, (615) 781-5376 Ext. 134
Sandra S. Baxter, Public Affairs Specialist, HFR-SE345, (615) 781-5372 Ext. 122
R. Thomas Trout, Regional Radiological Health Rep., (615) 781-5380 Ext. 171

Chattanooga R.P., 5715 Uptain Road, 6200 Building, Suite 5503, Chattanooga, TN 37411-5654
Pamela M. Thomas, Resident in Charge (RIC), HFR-SE3540, (423) 855-6630 FAX (423) 855-6632

Knoxville R.P., 412 Cedar Bluff Office Park, Suite 415, North Cedar Bluff Rd., Knoxville, TN 37923
Edward H. Maticka, Resident in Charge (RIC), HFR-SE3545, (865) 545-4601 FAX (865) 545-4602

Memphis R.P., 225 N. Humphreys Blvd., Eaglecrest Bldg., Rm. 2087, Memphis, TN 38120-2149
John M. McInnis, Supervisor, HFR-SE3550, (901) 544-0345 Ext. 25 FAX (901) 544-0349

███████████████████████████ **466 Fernandez Juncos Ave, San Juan, PR 00901-3223**
Main Number (787) 474-9500, Emergency (after hours) Answering Service (787) 729-6844
Donald J. Voeller, District Director, HFR-SE500, (787) 474-9537 FAX (787) 729-6851
Donald Watchko, Dir. Compliance Branch, HFR-SE540, (787) 474-9568 FAX (787) 729-6658
Elizabeth Kage, Dir. Science Branch, HFR-SE560, (787) 474-9525 FAX (787) 729-6884
Vacant, Supervisory Administrative Specialist, HFR-SE530, (787) 474-9503 FAX (787) 729-6809
Nilda Villegas, Public Affairs Specialist, HFR-SE545, (787) 474-9567 FAX (787) 729-6851
Ruth Marcano, Public Affairs Specialist, HFR-SE545, (787) 474-9531 FAX (787) 729-6851
Andres Toro, Dir. Investigations Branch, HFR-SE550, (787) 474-9564 FAX (787) 729-6747

H. Gordon Cox, Supervisor, (787) 474-9508 FAX (787) 729-6747
Jaime E. Pares, Supervisor, (787) 474-9548 FAX (787) 289-7949
Eliezer Ramos, Supervisor, HFR-SE5570, (787) 831-3337/8 FAX (787) 831-3339
Maridalia Torres, Supervisor (787) 474-9565 Fax (787) 729-6747

Mayaguez R.P., #59 Martinex Nadal St., Norte Park Plaza Bldg., Mayaguez, PR 00680
Eliezer Ramos, Supervisor, HFR-SE5570, (787) 831-3337/8 FAX (787) 831-3339

Ponce R.P Social Security Administration, 2190 Ponce By Pass, Ponce, PR 00717-1368
Eliezer Ramos, Supervisor, HFR-SE5570, (787) 812-2243 Ext 3004 FAX (787) 841-3145

St. Thomas R.P. Federal Bldg. #142, St. Thomas, USVI 00802
H. Gordon Cox, Supervisor (340) 715-0971 FAX (340) 715-0980

SOUTHWEST REGION

SW Region, Dallas (DAL-FO), 4040 North Central Expressway, Suite 900, Dallas, TX 75204
Dennis Baker, Regional Food and Drug Dir., HFR-SW1, (214) 253-4902 FAX (214) 253-4965
Elaine Crosby, Special Asst. for Operations HFR-SW2, (214) 253-4940
O.D. Evans, Deputy RFDD, HFR-SW-3, (214) 253-4903
David Arvelo, Small Business Rep. HFR-SW17, (214) 253-4952 FAX (214) 253-4970
Linda Collins, Regional Food Specialist, HFR-SW16, (214) 253-4945
Dennis L. Eastin, Regional Food Specialist,HFR-SW16, (214) 253-4947
W. Lynn Hodges, Regional Food Specialist, HFR-SW16, (214) 253-4948
Rodney Bridge, Regional Milk Specialist, HFR-SW16, (214) 253-4913
A. Mike Davis, Regional Milk Specialist, HFR-SW16, (214) 253-4946
Ronald O. Sims, Regional Milk Specialist, HFR-SW16, (214) 253-4950
David Blevins, Shellfish Specialist, HFR-SW16, (214) 253-4944
Donald L. Walker, Dir. Regional Computer Center (214) 253-4920
Vacant, Regional Radiological Health Representative (214) 253-4930 FAX (214) 253-4960
Scotty Hargrave, Regional Radiation Specialist, HFR-SW19, (214) 253-4932
Michelle Hawkins, Regional Radiation Specialist, HFR-SW19, (214) 253-4933
John Mays, Regional Radiation Specialist, HFR-SW19, (214) 253-4934
Deborah McGee Regional Radiation Specialist, HFR-SW19, (214) 253-4935

Denver Regional Staff, Bldg 20, Denver Federal Center, 6th & Kipling St. Denver, CO 80225-0087
(Mail to: PO Box 25087, Denver, CO 80225-0087)
Robert Antonsen, Radiation Specialist, (303) 236-3025
Mario Seminara, Regional Food Specialist, (303) 236-3026

Kansas City Regional Staff, 11630 West 80th St., Lenexa, KS 66214-3338
Timothy Roddy, Regional Milk Specialist, HFR-SW35, (913) 752-2402 FAX (913) 752-2136
Cynthia Kunkel, Regional Food Specialist, (913) 752-2401 FAX (913) 752-2136
Reggie Cope, Regional Radiation Specialist, (913) 752-2403

St. Louis Regional Staff 12 Sunnen Dr. Ste. 122, St. Louis, MO 63143
Vacant, Regional Public Affairs Specialist, HFR-SW445, (314) 645-1167 Ext. 123 FAX (314) 645-2969
Dennis Butcher, Electro-Optics Specialist, (314) 645-1167 Ext. 160

Arkansas Regional Laboratory, 3900 NCTR Rd., Bldg. 26, Jefferson, AR 72079-9502
Vacant, Laboratory Director, HFR-SW500, (870) 543-4099 FAX (870) 543-4041
John Gridley, Deputy Director., HFR-SW500, (870) 543-4007 FAX (870) 543-4041
Ralph Furth, Supervisory Chemist, HFRSW-560, (870) 543-4045
John Eckert, Supervisory Chemist, HFRSW-560 (870) 543-4025
Himansu Vyas, Supervisory Chemist, HFRSW-560, (870) 543-4026
Russell Fairchild, Supervisory Chemist, HFRSW-560, (870) 543-4045
Frederick Johnson, Ph.D., Supervisory Microbiologist, HFR-SW570, (870) 543-4036

DALLAS DISTRICT, (DAL-DO), 4040 North Central Expressway, Suite 300, Dallas, TX 75204

Main Office Number (214) 253-5200, Emergency (after hours) Answering Service (214) 253-5200
Michael A. Chappell, District Director, HFR-SW100, (214) 253-5201 FAX (214) 253-5318
Maria R. Velasco, Public Affairs Specialist, HFR-SW145, (214) 253-5205
Reynaldo (Ricky) R. Rodriguez, Jr., Dir. Compliance Branch, HFR-SW140, (214) 253-5215 FAX (214) 253-5314
H. Tyler Thornburg, Dir. Investigations Branch, HFR-SW150, (214) 253-5228 FAX (214) 253-5314
Elvia Cervantes, Supervisor, HFR-SW1540, (210) 308-4528 Ext. 11 FAX (210) 308-4548
Dale L. Graham, Supervisor, HFR-SW1580, (713) 802-9095 Ext. 131 FAX (713) 802-0906
Jose Martinez, Jr., Supervisor, HFR-SW1540, (210) 308-4528 Ext. 18 FAX (210) 308-4548
Sharyn K. Miller, Supervisor HFR-SW 1580, (713) 802-9095 Ext. 117 FAX (713) 802-0906
Angela Moak, Supervisor, HFR-SW150, (214) 253-5258 FAX 214) 253-5314
Paul Perdue, Supervisor, HFR-SW150, (214) 253-5248 FAX (214) 253-5314
Lynnette Riggio, Supervisor, HFR-SW150, (214) 253-5260 FAX (214) 253-5314

Austin R.P., 903 San Jacinto, Room 115, Austin, TX 78701
Lance Johnson, Resident in Charge (RIC), HFR-SW1575, (512) 916-5736 FAX (512) 916-5799

El Paso R.P., 700 E. San Antonio Ave. Federal Bldg., Rm. C-407, El Paso, TX 79901
Vivian Garcia, Resident in Charge (RIC), HFR-SW1510, (915) 534-6274 FAX (915) 534-6287

Houston R.P., 1445 Loop West, Suite 420, Houston, TX 77008
Dale L. Graham, Supervisor, HFR-SW1580, (713) 802-9095 Ext. 131 FAX (713) 802-0906
Sharyn K. Miller, Supervisor HFR-SW 1580, (713) 802-9095 Ext. 117 FAX (713) 802-0906
Sheryl Baylor McConnell, Public Affairs Specialist, (713) 802-9095 Ext. 115

Little Rock R.P., Rm. 4122 Federal Bldg.,700 West Capital, Little Rock, AR 72201
Vacant, Resident in Charge (RIC), HFR-SW1590, (501) 324-5257 FAX (501) 324-5080

Oklahoma City R.P., Suite C20, 3800 Classen Blvd, Oklahoma City, OK 73118
Lloyd Payne, Resident in Charge (RIC), HFR-SW1535, (405) 231-4544 FAX (405) 231-4543

San Antonio R.P., 10127 Morocco, Suite 119, San Antonio, TX 78216
Elvia Cervantes, Supervisor, HFR-SW1540, (210) 308-4528 Ext. 11 FAX (210) 308-4548
Jose Martinez, Jr., Supervisor, HFR-SW1540, (210) 308-4528 Ext. 18 FAX (210) 308-4548

Tulsa R.P., 222 S. Houston Street, Suite B, Tulsa, OK 74127
(Mail to: PO Box 3568, Tulsa, OK 74101-3568)
Janice Hickock, Resident in Charge (RIC) HFR-SW1545, (918) 581-7605 FAX (918) 581-7606

DENVER DISTRICT, (DEN-DO), 6th & Kipling St, Building 20, Denver Federal Center, Denver, CO 80225-0087

(Mail to: P.O. Box 25087, Denver, CO 80225-0087) Main Number (303) 236-3017
Emergency (after hours) Answering Service (303) 231-6466 FDA Emergency Contact Cell phone (303) 994-2218
B. Belinda Collins, District Director, HFR-SW200, (303) 236-3016 FAX (303) 236-9670
Aleta Hill, Admin Officer, HFR-SW230, (303) 236-3030, FAX (303) 236-3100
Virlie Walker, Public Affairs Specialist, HFR-SW245, (303) 236-3018 FAX (303) 236-3551
Howard Manresa, Director, Compliance Branch, HFR-SW240, (303) 236-3019, FAX (303) 236-3551
Karen S. Kreuzer, Director, Laboratory Branch, HFR-SW260, (303) 236-3060 FAX (303) 236-9675
Susan J. Miller, Director, Investigations Branch, HFR-SW250, (303) 236-3040 FAX (303) 236-3551
Deborah Hammond, Supervisor, HFR-SW250, (303) 236-3082
Michael J. Quinn, Supervisor, HFR-SW250, (303) 236-3058
Elvin R. Smith, Supervisor, HFR-SW250, (303) 236-3087 FAX (303) 236-3100
Teresa C. Thompson, Supervisor, HFR-SW2520, (801) 524-3190 Ext. 12 FAX (801) 524-3188

Albuquerque R.P., 517 Gold Ave. SW, Rm. 4430, Albuquerque, NM 87103
(Mail to: PO Box 1427, Albuquerque, NM 87103)
Barbara J. White, Resident in Charge (RIC), HFR-SW2500, (505) 248-7395 FAX (505) 248-7394

Salt Lake City R.P., 2090 N. Redwood Road, Suite 80, Salt Lake City, UT 84116
Teresa C. Thompson, Supervisor, HFR-SW2520, (801) 524-3190 FAX (801) 524-3188

KANSAS CITY DISTRICT, (KAN-DO), 11630 West 80th St., Lenexa, KS 66214-3340

Overnight Packages to: 11510 West 80th St., Lenexa, KS 66214-3338
Main Number and Emergency (after hours) Answering Service (913) 752-2100
Charles W. Sedgwick, District Director, HFR-SW300, (913) 752-2144 FAX (913) 752-2111
Barbara J. Blosser, Program Management Officer, HFR-SW330, (913) 752-2466 FAX (913) 752-2495
Amy Meeks, Administrative Officer, HFR-SW330, (913) 752-2472 FAX (913) 752-2487
Ann M. Adams, Dir. Science Branch and Total Diet Research, HFR-SW360, (913) 752-2155 FAX (913) 752-2151
Duane Hughes, Supervisor, Metals Laboratory, (913) 752-2157
Ann Rice, Supervisor, Pesticide Laboratory, (913) 752-2174
LaTonya M. Mitchell, Supervisor, Pesticide Laboratory (913) 752-2731
Joan Nandrea, Supervisor, Mycotoxin Laboratory, (913) 752-2156
Vacant Dir. Compliance Branch, HFR-SW340, (913) 752-2101 FAX (913) 752-2111
Tywanna G. Paul, Public Affairs Specialist, HFR-SW345, (913) 752-2141
John W. Thorsky, Dir. Investigations Branch, HFR-SW350, (913) 752-2423 FAX (913) 752-2413
Gregory D. Dixon, Supervisor, Biologics/Foods Investigations (913) 752-2427 FAX (913) 752-2413
Robert R. Wilson, Supervisor, Device and BSE Investigations (913) 752-2426 FAX (913) 752-2413
Marion Wimberly, Supervisor, Drug Investigations, (913) 752-2786 (913) 752-2413
Eric Nielsen, Supervisor, BIMO and Biologics Investigations, (913) 752-2409)913) 752-2413

Des Moines R.P., Suite 469, 210 S. Walnut St, Des Moines, IA 50309-2109
Dave Miser, Investigator, HFR-SW3510, (515) 323-2760 FAX (515) 323-2762

Davenport R.P., Northwest Bank Building, 101 West Second St. Suite 406, Davenport, IA 52801
John A. Iwen, Resident in Charge (RIC), HFR-SW4505, (563) 326-3323 FAX (563) 326-3608

Omaha R.P., 11061 "I" Street, Bldg. 24, Omaha, NB 68137-1209
Ismael Olvera, Investigator, HFR-SW3515, (402) 331-8536 Ext. 15 FAX (402) 331-9001

Sioux City R.P., Federal Bldg. RM. 112, 320 6th St, Sioux City, IA 51101-1210
Linda K. Cline, Resident in Charge (RIC), HFR-SW3525, (712) 252-0812 FAX (712) 252-0192

Springfield R.P., Suite 707, 901 St. Louis, Springfield, MO 65806-2560
Ted L. Anderson, Resident in Charge (RIC), HFR-SW3530, (417) 865-3944 FAX (417) 831-5058

Wichita R.P., 1861 N. Rock Road, Suite 370, Wichita, KS 67206-1264
Rick Rutherford, Investigator, HFR-SW3535, (316) 684-0953 FAX (316) 686-1042

St. Louis Office, 12 Sunnen Drive, Suite 122, St. Louis, MO 63143-3800
Don Aird, Public Affairs Specialist, HFR-SW445, (314) 645-1167 Ext. 111 FAX (314) 645-2969
David K. Glasgow, Supervisor, HFR-SW450, (314) 645-1167 Ext. 116
James P. McReavey, Supervisor, HFR-SW450, (314) 645-1167 Ext. 133

SOUTHWEST IMPORT DISTRICT (SWI-DO), 4040 North Central Expressway Ste 300, Dallas, TX 75204

Main Number (214) 253-5330
Robert J. Deininger, Director, HFR-SW600 (214) 253-5283
Hector Zuazua, Director, Investigations Branch, Laredo RP HFR-SW-650 (956) 729-9691
Todd Cato, Director, Compliance Branch, HFR-SW640 SWID-DO (214) 253-5284

Brownsville Resident Post 3300 South Expressway 77-83 Room N-126, 78521
Trinidad Barrera, Supervisory, Consumer Safety Officer (SCSO) (956)283-2191
Resident Post: HFR-SW6570 (956) 983-5550 FAX (956) 983-5558

Calexico R.P., 1699 East Carr Road, Calexico, CA 92231
Mail Address: P.O. Box 805 Holtville, CA 92250
Peter Marez, SCSO, HFR-SW6545 (760)768-2590 Ext 27 FAX (760)768-2589

Dallas R.P. 4040 North Central Expressway Ste 300 Dallas, TX 75204
L.B. Booty, SCSO,   HFR-SW 6510   (214) 253-5290   Fax (214) 253-5316

Eagle Pass R. P., Camino Real International Bridge, 500 S. Adams, Eagle Pass, TX 78853
Julio Salazar, SCSO, (956)729-9691 Ext 1103 FAX (956) 729-0997
Luis Soto, Investigator, HFR-SW6560 (830) 758-5550 FAX (830) 758-5551

El Paso R.P., 3600 E. Paisano, Bridge of the Americas, Bldg D, Rm. 101, El Paso, TX 79905
Luis Chavarria, Supervisor, HFR-SW6520 (915) 872-4776 FAX (915) 872-4778
Covers RP – Ysletta, TX; Columbus, NM; Del Rio, TX

Houston R.P., 1445 Loop West, Suite 420, Houston, TX 77008
L.B. Booty, SCSO, (214) 253-5290   Fax (214) 253-5316
Sheila Robinson, Senior Import Specialist, HFR-SW6515 (713) 802-9095 Ext. 120 FAX (713) 802-0906

Laredo R.P., World Trade Bridge, 715 Bob Bullock Loop, Rm. 75, Laredo, TX 78045
Julio Salazar, Supervisor, HFR-SW6530 (956) 729-9691 Ext 1103 FAX (956) 729-0997
Maria E. Perez, Inspector, (956) 729-9691 EXT 1107

Laredo R.P., Columbia Solidarity Bridge, Laredo, TX 78045
Julio Salazar, Supervisor, HFR-SW6530 (956) 729-9691 Ext 1103 FAX (956) 729-0997
Cordelia Carrizalez, CSO (956) 417-5138 Ext 225

Los Indios Resident 100 Los Indios Road   Los Indios, TX 78567
Trinidad Barreras, Supervisory, Consumer Safety Officer (SCSO) (956) 283-2191
Sylvia Ballard, Investigator HFR-SW6535   (956) 361-1403   FAX (956) 361-1403

Nogales R.P., 1777N Frank Reed Road, Suite 2, Nogales, AZ 85621
Adrian H. Garcia, SCSO, HFR-SW6550 (520) 281-1100 FAX (520) 281-1190

Otay Mesa R.P., 9777 Vua de la Amistad, Rm 131   San Diego, CA 92154
Joseph Tracey, SCSO, (619) 661-3198
Resident Post: HFR-SW6564 (619) 661-3273 FAX (619) 661-3216

Otay Mesa R.P., 2320 Paseo de las Americas, Ste 300   San Diego, CA 92154
Robert Rast, SCSO, HFR-SW6540 (619) 661-3196 FAX (619) 661-3195

Pharr R.P., 9901 S. Cage Blvd., Pharr, TX 78577
Trinidad Barreras, SCSO, HFR-SW6565 (956) 283-2191 FAX (956) 283-2192

Rio Grande Resident 317 S. Pete Diaz Ave Rio Grande City, TX 78582
Trinidad Barreras, Supervisory, Consumer Safety Officer (SCSO) (956) 283-2190
Luis Gonzalez, Investigator HFR-SW6585   (956) 487-1144   FAX (956) 487-1148

San Luis R.P., FDA P.O. Box 1450 San Luis, AZ 85349
Peter Marez, SCSO (760)768-2590 Ext 27
Resident Post: HFR-SWR6555 (928)627-9265 FAX (928) 627-2355

Santa Teresa R.P. 170 Pete V. Domenici Hwy   Santa Teresa, NM 88088
Luis Chavarria, Supervisor, HFR-SW6520 (915) 872-4776 FAX (915) 872-4778
David Hayward, CSO HFR-SW6525 (505) 589-4540

Tecate R.P., Hwy 94 & YS/Mexican Border Tecate, CA 91980
Robert Rast, SCSO, HFR-SW6540 (619) 661-3196 FAX (619) 661-3195

PACIFIC REGION

PA Region, San Francisco (SAN-FO), Ste. 1180-N, 1301 Clay St., Oakland, CA 94512-5217
Main Number and Emergency (after hours) Answering Service   (510) 637-3960
Brenda J. Holman, Regional Food and Drug Dir., HFR-PA1, (510) 637-3960 Ext. 118 FAX (510) 637-3976
Mark Roh, DRFDD, HFR-PA1, (510) 637-3960 Ext. 143
Ana M. Osorio, MD, Reg. Medical Officer, HFR-PA18, (510) 637-3960 Ext. 117

Thomas Sidebottom, Special Assistant to RFDD, HFR-PA1, (510) 637-3960 Ext. 130
Marcia Madrigal, Small Business Rep., HFR-PA17, (510) 637-3980 FAX (510) 637-3977
James H. Wyman, Regional Training Officer, HFR-PA14, (510) 637-3960 Ext. 129
Steven Ziser, Program Analyst, HFR-PA14, (510) 637-3960 Ext. 120
Pauline Cummings, Program Support Specialist, HFR-PA1, (510) 637-3960 x146

PA Region Cooperative Programs Staff

Barbara Cassens, Director, Cooperative Programs Staff, HFR-PA13, (510) 637-3960 Ext. 140
Alethea Aranas, Consumer Safety Tech, HFR-PA13, (510) 637-3960 Ext. 112
Steve Himebaugh, Regional Dairy Specialist, HFR-PA16, (510) 637-3960 Ext. 125
Kenneth A. Miles, Rad. Health Rep. HFR-PA16, (510) 637-3960 Ext. 122
Lisa Whitlock, Regional Food Specialist, HFR-PA16, (510) 637-3960 Ext. 127

San Jose, CA Regional Staff 96 North Third Street Rm. 325, San Jose, CA 95112

Frank Eng, Electro-Optics Specialist, HFR-PA19, (408) 291-7548 Ext. 15 FAX (408) 291-7228
Gary Zaharek, Electro-Optics Specialist, HFR-PA19, (408) 291-7548 Ext. 12 FAX (408) 291-7228

Fresno, CA Regional Staff 1752 East Bullard Ave., Suite 102, Fresno, CA 93710

Randy Elsberry, Regional Dairy Specialist, HFR-PA16, (559) 447-3376   FAX (559) 447-3424

Los Angeles, CA Regional Staff 19900 MacArthur Blvd. Suite 300, Irvine, CA 92612-2445

Suzie Kent, Electro-Optics Specialist, HFR-PA19, (949) 798-7657 FAX (949) 798-7750
Richard Ramirez, Regional Food Specialist, HFR-PA16, (949) 979-7775 FAX (949) 979-7771

Puget Sound Regional Staff 1000 2nd Ave. Suite 2400, Seattle, WA 98104

Tim Sample, Shellfish Specialist, HFR-PA36, (206) 553-7001 Ext. 45 FAX (206) 553-7020
Vacant, Shellfish Specialist, HFR-PA36, (206) 553-7001 Ext. 40 FAX (206) 553-7020
Lester Bolan, Regional Dairy Specialist, HFR-PA16, (206) 553-7001 Ext. 31 FAX (206) 553-7020
Belinda Clifton, Regional Dairy Specialist, HFR-PA16, (206) 553-7001 Ext. 18 FAX (206) 553-7020
Sharon Smith, Retail Food Specialist, HFR-PA16, (206) 553-7771 Ext. 15
Carolyn Swanson, Regional Program Management Specialist, HFR-PA16, (206) 553-7001 Ext. 26

Portland, OR Regional Staff 9780 SW Nimbus Ave. Beaverton, OR 97008-7163

Kathryn Kennedy, Regional Food Specialist, HFR-PA16, (503) 671-9711 Ext. 16 FAX (503) 671-9445

Phoenix, AZ Regional Staff 4605 E. Elwood St. Suite 402, Phoenix, AZ 85040

John Marcello, Regional Food Specialist, HFR-PA16, (480) 829-7396 Ext. 35 FAX (480) 829-7677

Spokane, WA Regional Staff 1000 North Argonne, Suite 105, Spokane, WA 99212

Bradley E. Tufto, Retail Food Specialist, (509) 353-2470 Fax (509) 353-2746

REGIONAL INFORMATION TECHNOLOGY STAFF (RITS)

22201 23RD Drive SE, Bothell, WA 98021-4421
Timothy Blair, Dir. Regional Computer Center, HFR-PA35, (425) 483-4952 Fax (425) 483-4996
Timothy Anderson, Computer Specialist, HFR-PA37, (425) 483-4995
Robert Kiesel, Computer Specialist, HFR-PA37, (425) 483-4968
Dang Ngoc-Lan, Computer Specialist, HFR-PA37, (425) 483-4891
Christopher Pratt, Computer Specialist, HFR-PA37, (425) 483-4954
Brad Tenge, Computer Specialist, HFR-PA37, (425) 402-3167

RITS - RO

Gregory Page, Computer Specialist, HFR-PA1, (510) 637-3960 x145

(RITS - San-Do)

Karen Bush, Computer Specialist, HFR-PA37, (510) 337-6778
Elgin Williams, Computer Specialist, HFR-PA37, (510) 337-6889
Ken Chika, Computer Specialist, HFR-PA37, (510) 337-6863

(RITS - Los-Do)

Frank Bonefont, Computer Specialist, HFR-PA37, (949) 798-7621

Gene Calfy, Computer Specialist, HFR-PA37, (949) 798-7619
Ronald Vasquez, Computer Specialist, HFR-PA37, (949) 798-7620

(RITS – PRL-SW)
William Patterson, Computer Specialist, HFR-PA37, (213) 352-7592 Ext. 306

Pacific Regional Laboratory Northwest (PRL-NW), 22201 23rd Dr. SE, Bothell, WA 98021-4421
Emergency (after hours) Answering Service (425) 486-8788
Austin R. Long, Ph.D., Director Pacific Regional Lab-Northwest, PRL-NW, HFR-PA360, (425) 483-4901
Moises O'Neill, Director, Microbiology, HFR-PA360, (425) 483-4879
William Chase, Director, Chemistry, HFR-PA360, (425) 483-4990
Vacant, Director, Seafood Products Research Center, HFR-PA380, (425) 483-4902

Pacific Regional Laboratory Southwest (PRL-SW), 1521 W. Pico Blvd., Los Angeles, CA 90015-2486
Elizabeth A. Keville, Director, Pacific Regional Laboratory Southwest, HFR-PA260, (213) 252-7592, Ext. 214
FAX (213) 252-7511
Ted Dunn, Director, Microbiology, HFR-PA260 (213) 252-7592 Ext. 311
Dennis Farley, Director, Food Chemistry, HFR-PA260 (213) 252-7592, Ext. 301

LOS ANGELES DISTRICT, (LOS-DO), 19900 Mac Arthur Blvd, Ste 300, Irvine, CA 92612-2445
Main Number (949) 798-7600, Emergency (after hours) Answering Service (949) 797-1063
Alonza E. Cruse, District Director, HFR-PA200, (949) 798-7714 FAX (949) 798-7715
Vacant, Dir. Compliance Branch, HFR-PA240, (949) 798-7755 FAX (949) 798-7771
Vacant, Dir. Mgt & Program Support Br., HFR-PA230, (949) 798-7601 FAX (716) 798-7690
Rosario Quintanilla-Vior, Public Affairs Specialist, HFR-PA245, (949) 798-7607 FAX (949) 798-7656
Laurel Eu, Public Affairs Specialist, (949) 798-7609 FAX (949) 798-7656
Vacant, Dir. Domestic Investigations, HFR-PA250, (949) 798-7769 FAX (949) 798-7725
Vacant, Supervisor, HFR-PA252, (949) 798-7790 FAX (949) 798-7794
Vickie Anderson, Supervisor, HFR-PA250, (949) 798-7760 FAX (949) 798-7794
Daniel Cline, Supervisor, HFR-PA250, (949) 798-7675 FAX (949) 798-7750
Jonetta Collins, Supervisor, HFR-PA253, (949) 798-7780 FAX (949) 798-7794
Terri Dodds, Supervisor, HFR-PA250, (949) 798-7794 FAX (949) 798-7794
Vien Le, Supervisor, HFR-PA250 (949) 798-7691 FAX (949) 798-7794
Tanya Malais, Supervisor, HFR-PA250, (949) 798-7719 FAX (949) 798-7750
James Stumpff, Supervisor, HFR-PA2535, (858) 550-3850 Ext. 118 FAX (619) 550-3860
Karen Miller, Complaint Coordinator (949) 798-7701

Canoga Park R.P., 22736 Vanowen St, Rm. 205, Canoga Park, CA 91307-2659 FAX (818) 595-1140

Phoenix R.P., 4605 E. Elwood St, Suite 402, Phoenix, AZ 85040-1948
Terry Conder, Supervisor, HFR-PA2530, (480) 829-7396 Ext. 22 FAX (480) 829-7677
Gilbert Meza, Public Affairs Specialist, Ext. 25 FAX (480) 829-7677

San Diego R.P., 4510 Executive Dr., Suite 225, San Diego, CA 92121-3021
James Stumpff, Supervisor, HFR-PA2535, (858) 550-3850 Ext. 118 FAX (619) 550-3860
Carol Sanchez, Supervisor, HFR-PA2535, (858) 550-3850 Ext. 103, FAX (858) 550-3860
Cell (310) 350-7064

Santa Barbara R.P., 1332 Anacapa St., #120, Santa Barbara, CA 93101-2090
William Bowman, Resident in Charge (RIC), HFR-PA2570, (805) 962-4332 FAX (805) 962-7853

San Pedro Import Operations, 222 W. 6th St., Suite 700, San Pedro, CA 90731-3354
Irene Gomez, Director, Import Operations, HFR-PA256, (310) 831-6123 Ext. 102 FAX (310) 831-5659
George Durgin, Supervisor, HFR-PA256, (310) 831-6123 Ext. 116 FAX (310) 831-5659
Donna Rowland, Supervisor, HFR-PA256, (310) 831-6123 Ext. 109
Richard Guillen, Supervisor, HFR-PA256, (310) 831-6123 Ext. 114
Patty Hankawa, EEPs Implementation Manager (310) 831-6123 Ext. 113

Tucson R.P., 300 W. Congress St., Rm. 4P Box FB55, Tucson, AZ 85701
(520) 670-4765 FAX (520) 670-4769

LAX R.P., 11099 S. LaCienega Blvd., Ste. 215, Los Angeles, CA 90045-6115
(310) 215-2040 FAX (310) 831-5659

SAN FRANCISCO DISTRICT, (SAN-DO), 1431 Harbor Bay Parkway, Alameda, CA 94502-7070
Main Number (510) 337-6700, Emergency (after hours) Answering Service (877) 650-8490
Dennis K. Linsley, District Director, HFR-PA100, (510) 337-6730 FAX (510) 337-6859
Darrell T. Lee, Dir. Compliance Branch, HFR-PA140, (510) 337-6820 FAX (510) 337-6703
Roderick Asmundson, Laboratory Director, HFR-PA160, (510) 337-6898 FAX (510) 337-6704/5
Bernard Wade, Administrative Officer, HFR-PA130, (510) 337-6885 FAX (510) 337-6859
Janet McDonald,Ph.D., Public Affairs Specialist, HFR-PA145, (510) 337-6845 FAX (510) 337-6708
Charles Moss, Dir. Investigations Branch, HFR-PA150, (510) 337-6846 FAX (510) 337-6702
Darlene B. Almogela, Supervisor (510) 337-6769
Darla R. Bracy, Supervisor, HFR-PA150, (510) 337-6773
Janet Codor, Supervisor, Import Operations, HFR-PA152, (510) 337-6786 FAX (510) 337-6707
James F. Foster, Supervisor, HFR-PA150 (510) 337-6797
Kris A. Foster, Supervisor, HFR-PA150, (510) 337-6798
Steve R. Gillenwater, Supervisor, HFR-PA150, (510) 337-6802
James Henry, Supervisor, HFR-PA1500, (559) 447-3376
Lorna F. Jones, Supervisor, HFR-PA150, (510) 337-6818
Ralph J. Kalinowski, Supervisor, HFR-PA150, (510) 337-6819
Kathryn D. Macropol, Supervisor, HFR-PA150, (510) 337-6836
Susan R. Nelson, Supervisor, HFR-PA1525, (916) 930-3674 Ext. 19 FAX (916) 930-3679
Gerald Schwartz, Supervisor, HFR-PA150, (510) 337-6868
Luis A. Solorzano, Supervisor, HFR-PA150, (510) 337-6752
Davina Watson, Supervisor, HFR-PA150, (510) 337-6896
Lynn Wong, Supervisor, HFR-PA1515, (808) 541-2661

Fresno R.P., 1752 E. Bullard, Suite 103, Fresno, CA 93710-5864
James Henry, Supervisor, HFR-PA1500, (559) 447-3376 Ext. 19 FAX (559) 447-3424
Randy Elsberry, Regional Milk Specialist, (559) 447-3376 Ext. 20

Honolulu R.P., Rm. 6-299, P.J.K.K. Bldg, 300 Ala Moana Blvd, Honolulu, HI 96850
(Mail to: PO Box 50061, Honolulu, HI 96850)
After January 2003: 1132 Bishop Street, Suite 500, Honolulu, Hawaii, 96813
Lynn Wong, Supervisor, HFR-PA1515, (808) 541-2661/3 FAX (808) 541-2678

Las Vegas R.P., 600 South Las Vegas Blvd., Rm. 590, Las Vegas, NV 89101
(Mail to: PO Box # 7, 600 South Las Vegas Blvd., Las Vegas, NV 89101)
Anthony E. Keller, Resident in Charge (RIC), HFR-PA1520, (702) 388-6361 FAX (702) 388-6362

Reno R.P., 300 Booth St., Rm. 4111, Reno, NV 89501
Edward D. Harris, Resident in Charge (RIC), HFR-PA1510, (775) 784-5770 FAX (SAME)

Sacramento R.P., 650 Capitol Mall, Room 8-400, Sacramento, CA 95814
Susan R. Nelson, Supervisor, HFR-PA1525, (916) 930-3674 Ext. 19 FAX (916) 930-3679

San Jose R.P., 96 North 3rd St, Suite 325, San Jose, CA 95112
Andrea P. Scott, Supervisor, HFR-PA1530, (408) 291-4350 Ext. 25

Stockton R.P., Rm. 106, 401 N San Joaquin St, Stockton, CA 95202
(Mail to: PO Box 1179, Stockton, CA 95201)
Alice Blair, HFR-PA1535, (209) 946-6306 FAX (209) 946-6021

SEATTLE DISTRICT, (SEA-DO), 22201 23rd Drive SE, Bothell, WA 98021-4421
Main Number and Emergency (after hours) Answering Service (425) 486-8788
Charles M. Breen, District Director, HFR-PA300, (425) 483-4950 FAX (425) 483-4996
Russell Gripp, Dir. Compliance Branch, HFR-PA340, (425) 483-4963
Kristy D. Thies, Director, MPSB, HFR-PA330, (425) 483-4951
Susan Hutchcroft, Public Affairs Specialist, HFR-PA345, (425) 483-4953
Celeste M. Corcoran, Dir. Investigations Branch, HFR-PA350, (425) 483-4971 FAX (425) 483-4996

Richard S. Andros, Supervisor (425) 483-4980
Bryan Baker, Supervisor, Portland R.P. (503) 627-0784
Carol A. Gripp, Supervisor (425) 483-4905
Mark Harris, Supervisor (425) 483-4921
George F. Long, Supervisor, Blaine R.P. (360) 332-4032
Janelle K. Martin, Supervisor (425) 483-4928
David Pettenski, Supervisor (425) 483-4911
Christopher E. Rezendes, Supervisor, Puget Sound R.P. (206) 553-7001 Ext. 21
Robert A. Williams, Supervisor, Helena R.P. (406) 441-1170

Anchorage R.P., Fed. Bldg. US Courthouse, 222 W. 7th Ave. #25, Anchorage, AK 99513-7549
Wayne F. Larson, Resident in Charge (RIC), HFR-PA3500, (907) 271-5018 FAX (907) 271-5014

Blaine R.P., 9935 A Pacific Hwy, Blaine, WA 98230
George F. Long, Supervisor, HFR-PA3530, (360) 332-4032 FAX (360) 332-7771

Boise R.P., 304 N. 8th Street, Rm. 147, Boise, ID 83702
John W. Banks, Resident in Charge (RIC), HFR-PA3505, (208) 334-1051 FAX (208) 334-1053

Eastport R.P. Highway 95 North, Eastport, ID 83826

Helena R.P., Federal Office Building, FDA, 10 West 15th St., Suite 1700, Helena, MT 59626
Robert A. Williams, Supervisor, (406) 441-1170 FAX (406) 441-1171

Sweetgrass R.P., P.O. Box 286, Sweetgrass, MT 59484
(406) 335-3550 FAX 406-335-3551

Portland R.P., 9780 S.W. Nimbus Ave., Beaverton, OR 97008-7163
Bryan Baker, Supervisor, (503) 627-0784 FAX (503) 671-9445
Alan Bennett, Public Affairs Specialist, (503) 671-9332

Portland Airport Office, 7820 NE Holman St., Suite B10, Portland, OR 97218
Gail Kirby, Consumer Safety Inspector, (503) 262-8748 FAX (503) 262-8859

Oroville, R.P. 33637 A. Highway 97, Oroville, WA 98844
509-476-3688 FAX 509-476-3693

Puget Sound R.P., 1000 2nd Ave., Suite 2400, Seattle, WA 98104
Christopher E. Rezendes, Supervisor, (206) 553-7001 Ext. 21

Spokane R.P., 1000 North Argonne, Suite 105, Spokane, WA 99212
Dolores E. Price, Resident in Charge (RIC), (509) 353-2470 FAX (509) 353-2746

Yakima R.P., 905 Goodlander Drive, Selah, WA 98942
Jean Brewer, Resident in Charge (RIC), (509) 697-3855 FAX (509) 697-5283

ORA FIELD PROGRAM MONITORS

ADVERSE DRUG EXPERIENCE (ADE) COORDINATORS:

ATL-DO:	Leah M. Andrews	(404) 253-1285
CHI-DO:	Kathy Haas	(312) 596-4250
CIN-DO:	David C. Radle,	(513) 679-2700 Ext. 124
DAL-DO:	Jose Martinez	(210) 308-4528 Ext. 18
DEN-DO:	Michael J. Kuchta	(303) 236-3059
DET-DO:	George Domingo	(313) 393-8142
FLA-DO:	Susan M. Corrales	(561) 338-7631 Ext. 19
KAN-DO:	Gwyn Dickinson	(913) 752-2446
LOS-DO:	Yumi Hiramine	(818) 595-0016 Ext. 34
MIN-DO:	Sharon Thoma	(612) 334-4100 Ext. 196
NOL-DO:	M. Anthony Abel I, NSV-BR	(615) 781-5374 Ext. 111
NWJ-DO:	Meyer Slobotsky	(732) 940-8946 Ext. 12
NYK-DO:	Upstate: John A. Podsadowski	(716) 551-4461 Ext. 3155
	Downstate: Larry Farina	(516) 921-1601
PHI-DO:	Steven L. Carter	(215) 597-4390 Ext. 4520
SAN-DO:	Marie K. Kinkade	(510) 337-6823
SEA-DO:	Carol A. Gripp	(425) 483-4905
SJN-DO:	Ivonne Ayala	(787) 474-9505

AIDS COORDINATORS:

ATL-DO:	JoAnn Pittman	(404) 253-1272
BLT-DO:	Stephen King	(410) 779-5426
CHI-DO:	Darlene Bailey	(312) 596-4205
CIN-DO:	Ruth E. Weisheit	(330) 273-1038
DAL-DO:	Maria Velasco	(214) 253-5205
DEN-DO:	Virlie Walker	(303) 236-3018
DET-DO:	Evelyn DeNike	(313) 393-8109
FLA-DO:	Lynne Isaacs	(407) 475-4704
KAN-DO:	Tywanna Paul	(913) 752-2141
LOS-DO:	Rosario Vior	(949) 798-7607
MIN-DO:	Stephen Davis,	(414) 771-7114
NOL-DO:	Sandra S. Baxter, NSV-BR	(615) 781-5380 Ext. 122
NWE-DO:	Ellen P. Madigan	(781) 596-7753
NWJ-DO:	Joan Lytle	(973) 526-6035
NYK-DO:	Upstate: Diana D. Monaco	(716) 551-4461 Ext. 3118
	Downstate: Dilcia Granville	(718) 340-7000 Ext. 5445
PHI-DO:	Anitra Brown-Reed	(215) 597-4390 Ext. 4202
SAN-DO:	Mary Ellen Taylor	(510) 337-6888
SEA-DO:	Alan Bennett	(503) 671-9332
SJN-DO:	Nilda Villegas	(787) 474-9567

BIORESEARCH MONITORING PROGRAM (BIMO) MONITORS:

ATL-DO:	Stephanie Hubbard	(404) 253-1290
BLT-DO:	Lynette Salisbury	(410) 779-5446
CHI-DO:	Susan Yuscius	(217) 492-4095
CIN-DO:	Steven P. Eastham	(513) 679-2700 Ext. 123
DAL-DO:	Joel Martinez	(210) 308-4528 Ext. 20
DEN-DO:	Elvin R. Smith	(303) 236-3087
DET-DO:	Nancy Bellamy	(313) 393-8143
FLA-DO:	Brunilda Torres	(407) 475-4718
KAN-DO:	Carl J. Montgomery	(913) 752-2780
LOS-DO:	Ron Koller (Drugs)	(818) 595-0016 Ext. 22
	Allen Hall (Devices)	(858) 550-3850 Ext. 111
	John Gonzales (CVM)	(949-798-7772
MIN-DO:	Sharon Matson	(612) 334-4100 Ext. 189
NOL-DO:	Michael W. Roosevelt	(504) 253-4525

NWE-DO:	Ellen Madigan	(781) 596-7753
NWJ-DO:	Shirley Isbill	(732) 940-8946 Ext. 13
NYK-DO:	(Downstate) Thomas Hansen	(516) 921-1601 Ext. 26
	(Upstate) John Podsadowski	(716) 551-4461 Ext 3155
PHI-DO:	Daniel Tammariello	(412) 644-3394 Ext. 16
SAN-DO:	Darlene Almogela	(510) 337-6769
SEA-DO:	Carol A. Gripp	(425) 483-4905
SJN-DO:	Maridalia Torres	(787) 474-9500 Ext. 9565

BLOOD BANK MONITORS:

ATL-DO:	Vincent M. Williams	(404) 253-2240
BLT-DO:	Linda Mattingly	(410) 779-5443
CHI-DO:	Roger Adams	(217) 492-4095
CIN-DO:	Robert W. Connatser	(513) 679-2700 Ext. 121
DAL-DO:	Al Peacock	(713) 802-9095 Ext. 137
DEN-DO:	Deborah Hammond	(303) 236-3082
DET-DO:	Catherine V. Quinlan	(313) 393-8153
FLA-DO:	Ronnie E. Jackson	(407) 475-4725
KAN-DO:	Lenexa: Gregory D. Dixon	(913) 752-2427
STL:	Robert Nesselhauf	(314) 645-1167 Ext. 132
LOS-DO:	Gene Arcy	(949) 798-7647
MIN-DO:	Mary Ann Ruff	(608) 264-5332
NOL-DO:	Michael W. Roosevelt	(504) 253-4525
NSV-BR:	Michael R. Duran	(615) 781-5375 Ext. 116
NWE-DO:	Ellen P. Madigan	(781) 596-7753
NWJ-DO:	Lisa Harlan	(973) 526-6070 Ext. 6014
NYK-DO:	Elizabeth Jacobson	(914) 682-6166 Ext. 27
PHI-DO:	Luann M. Pallas	(717) 541-9924 Ext. 12
SAN-DO:	Deb Kleinfeld	(510) 337-6825
SEA-DO:	Bryan Baker	(503) 627-0784
SJN-DO:	Gordon Cox	(787) 474-9508

BLOOD REGISTRATION MONITORS:

ATL-DO:	Vincent M. Williams	(404) 253-2240
BLT-DO:	Linda Mattingly	(410) 779-5443
CHI-DO:	Linda E. Whitehead	(312) 596-4246
CIN-DO:	Marianne Allen	(513) 679-2700 Ext. 145
DAL-DO:	Warren L. Landry	(214) 253-5230
DEN-DO:	Deborah Hammond	(303) 236-3082
DET-DO:	Catherine V. Quinlan	(313) 393-8153
FLA-DO:	Ronnie E. Jackson	(407) 475-4725
KAN-DO:	Linda Kuchenthal	(913) 752-2436
LOS-DO:	Kirsten Tharp	(949) 798-7720
MIN-DO:	Kellie L. Westerbuhr	(612) 334-4100 Ext. 245
NOL-DO:	Marion J. Ferrante	(504) 253-4523
NWE-DO:	Ellen P. Madigan	(781) 596-7753
NWJ-DO:	Rosa Brown	(973) 526-6007
NYK-DO:	Upstate: Ann Okon	(716) 551-4461 Ext. 3120
	Downstate: Evelyn Taha	(718) 340-7000 Ext. 5574
PHI-DO:	Steven L. Carter	(215) 597-4390 Ext. 4520
SAN-DO:	Laverne Puckett	(510) 337-6774
SEA-DO:	Bryan Baker	(503) 627-0784
SJN-DO:	Gilbert Andino	(787) 474-9502

CDRH INFORMATION RETRIEVAL SYSTEM (CIRS) LIAISONS:
(contact via e-mail)

ATL-DO:	Christie Traughber
BLT-DO:	Susan Alba
CHI-DO:	Stephanie Bolton
CIN-DO:	Linda Brock
DAL-DO:	Richard Hodgkinson
DET-DO:	Linda Brock
DEN-DO:	William Morris
FLA-DO:	Christie Traughber
KAN-DO:	Patricia Schneider
LOS-DO:	Adriana Garnica and Gene Calfy
MIN-DO:	Stephanie Bolton
NOL-DO:	Pesi Umrigar
NWE-DO:	Scott Lewis
NWJ-DO:	Susan Alba
NYK-DO:	Cliff Klein and Ruben Torres
NYK/BUF:	Susan Denny
PHI-DO:	Susan Alba
SAN-DO:	Elgin Williams
SEA-DO:	Robert Kiesel and Deborah Matthews
SJN-DO:	Damaris Sanchez and Elaine Rivas
SWID:	Richard Hodgkinson
ORA-HQ:	Alan Gion

COMPLAINT COORDINATORS:

ATL-DO:	Mallory W. Lawrence	(404) 253-2243
BLT-DO:	Edette Murfree	(410) 779-5445
CHI-DO:	Kathy Haas	(312) 596-4250
CIN-DO:	David C. Radle	(513) 679-2700 Ext. 124
DAL-DO:	Margarito Uribe	(214) 253-5233
DEN-DO:	Donald L. Bean	(303) 236-3044
DET-DO:	Linda (Smith) Richey	(313) 393-8198
FLA-DO:	Philip DeLisle	(407) 475-4717
KAN-DO:	Eric Nielsen	(913) 752-2409
LOS-DO:	Karen Miller	(949) 798-7701
MIN-DO:	Dirk Mouw	(612) 334-4100 Ext. 184
NOL-DO:	Marie K. Fink	(504) 253-4511
	Betty D. Storey, NSV-BR	(615) 781-5380 Ext. 123
NWE-DO:	Lina Cicchetto	(781) 596-7727
NWJ-DO:	Emma Nesbit	(973) 526-6017
NYK-DO:	Upstate: Joan B. Trankle	(716) 551-4461 Ext. 3171
	Downstate: Marlene Doherty	(718) 340-7000 Ext. 5588
PHI-DO:	Sharon Gordon	(215) 597-9064
SAN-DO:	Charla Stevens	(510) 337-6741
SEA-DO:	Janice D. Laird	(425) 483-4949
SJN-DO:	Gilbert Andino	(787) 474-9502

COMSTAT (COMPLIANCE STATUS INFORMATION SYSTEM) MONITORS: SEE FACTS PROFILE MONITORS

CRIMINAL INVESTIGATIONS MONITORS:

ATL-DO:	Dawn Todd-Murrell	(404) 253-2242
BLT-DO:	Roberta Wagner	(410) 779-5430
CHI-DO:	Gerald Berg	(312) 596-4240
CIN-DO:	Carol A. Heppe	(513) 679-2700 Ext. 120
DAL-DO:	Reynaldo (Ricky) R. Rodriguez, Jr.	(214) 253-5215
DEN-DO:	Susan J. Miller	(303) 236-3040
DET-DO:	John P. Dempster	(313) 393-8141
FLA-DO:	David J. Gallant	(407) 475-4715

KAN-DO:	John Thorsky	(913) 752-2423
LOS-DO:	Terry Conder	(480) 829-7396 Ext. 222
MIN-DO:	Cheryl A. Bigham	(612) 334-4100 Ext. 162
NOL-DO:	F. Dwight Herd, NOL	(504) 253-4522
	Howard E. Lewis, NSV-BR	(615) 781-5388 Ext. 124
NWE-DO:	Michael R. Kravchuk	(781) 596-7799
NWJ-DO:	Diana Amador	(973) 526-6015
NYK-DO:	Wanda Eng	(718) 340-7000 Ext. 5586
PHI-DO:	Peter C. Baker	(215) 597-4390 Ext. 4500
SAN-DO:	Darrell Lee	(510) 337-6820
SEA-DO:	Celeste M. Corcoran	(425) 483-4971
SJN-DO:	Andres Toro	(787) 474-9564

DEVICE MONITORS:

ALT-DO:	Fulton A. Varner	(404) 253-2225
BLT-DO:	Lori Lawless	(410) 779-5442
CHI-DO:	Larry Stringer	(312) 596-4245
CIN-DO:	Guy W. Cartwright	(614) 487-1273 Ext. 11
DAL-DO:	Lynnette Riggio	(214) 253-5260
DEN-DO:	Michael J. Quinn	(303) 236-3058
DET-DO:	James Szelc	(313) 393-8170
FLA-DO:	Ronald T. Weber	(407) 475-4724
KAN-DO:	James P. McReavey	(314) 645-1167 Ext. 133
LOS-DO:	Vickie Anderson	(949) 798-7760
MIN-DO:	Rhonda Mecl	(612) 334-4100 Ext. 190
NOL-DO:	Michael R. Duran, NSV-BR	(615) 781-5375 Ext. 116
NWE-DO:	William Boivin	(781) 596-7783
NWJ-DO:	Toniette Williams	(973) 526-6018
NYK-DO:	Upstate: Ray Kent	(716) 551-4461 Ext. 3126
	Downstate: Otto Vitillo	(516) 921-2869
PHI-DO:	Daniel R. Tammariello	(412) 644-3394 Ext. 16
SAN-DO:	Andrea Scott	(408) 291-4360 Ext. 25
SEA-DO:	David Pettenski	(425) 483-4911
SJN-DO:	Gilbert Andino	(787) 474-9502

DEVICE REGISTRATION MONITORS:

ATL-DO:	Calvin Foulks	(404) 253-2241
BLT-DO:	Lori Lawless	(410) 779-5442
CHI-DO:	Linda E. Whitehead	(312) 596-4246
CIN-DO:	Laureen M. Geniusz	(330) 273-1038
DAL-DO:	Warren L. Landry	(214) 253-5230
DEN-DO:	Nicholas R. Nance	(303) 236-3052
DET-DO:	James E. Szelc	(313) 393-8170
FLA-DO:	Ronald T. Weber	(407) 475-4724
KAN-DO:	Robert Wilson	(913) 752-2426
LOS-DO:	Kirsten Tharp	(949) 798-7720
MIN-DO:	Rhonda Mecl	(612) 334-4100 Ext. 190
NOL-DO:	Marion J. Ferrante	(504) 253-4523
NWE-DO:	William Boivin	(781) 596-7783
NWJ-DO:	Rosa Brown	(973) 526-6007
NYK-DO:	Upstate: Ann Okon	(716) 551-4461 Ext. 3120
	Downstate: Elizabeth Jacobson	(914) 682-6166 Ext 27
PHI-DO:	Steven L. Carter	(215) 597-4390 Ext. 4520
SAN-DO:	Andrea Scott	(408) 291-4350 Ext. 25
SEA-DO:	David A. Pettenski	(425) 483-4911
SJN-DO:	Gilbert Andino	(787) 474-9502

DRUG MONITORS:

ATL-DO:	Leah Andrews	(404) 253-1285
BLT-DO:	Matthew Henciak	(410) 779-5438
CHI-DO:	Nick Lyons	(312) 596-4247
CIN-DO:	Steven P. Eastham	(513) 679-2700 Ext. 123
DAL-DO:	Jose Martinez	(210) 308-4528 Ext. 18
DEN-DO:	Elvin R. Smith	(303) 236-3087
DET-DO:	Patsy Domingo	(313) 393-8145
FLA-DO:	Keith S. Ehrlich	(561) 338-7631 Ext. 11
KAN-DO:	David Glasgow	(314) 645-1167 Ext. 116
LOS-DO:	Virgilio Pacio	(858) 550-3850 Ext. 116
MIN-DO:	Sharon Thoma	(612) 334-4100 Ext. 196
NOL-DO:	M. Anthony Abel I, NSV-BR	(615) 781-5374 Ext. 111
NWE-DO:	Steven Souza	(203) 240-4289
NWJ-DO:	Meyer Slobotsky	(732) 940-8946 Ext. 12
NYK-DO:	Ray Kent	(716) 551-4461 Ext. 3126
PHI-DO:	LuAnn M. Pallas	(717) 541-9924 Ext. 12
SAN-DO:	Darlene Almogela	(510) 337-6769
SEA-DO:	Carol A. Gripp	(425) 483-4905
SJN-DO:	Rebecca Rodriguez	(787) 474-9556

DRUG DEFECT REPORTING MONITORS:

ATL-DO:	Tracy L. Ball	(704) 344-6116
BLT-DO:	Melissa Garcia	(410) 779-5461
CHI-DO:	Kathy Haas	(312) 596-4250
CIN-DO:	David C. Radle	(513) 679-2700 Ext. 124
DAL-DO:	Jose Martinez	(210) 308-4528 Ext. 18
DEN-DO:	Michael J. Kuchta	(303) 236-3059
DET-DO:	Anthony C. Taube	(313) 393-8176
FLA-DO:	Susan M. Corrales	(561) 338-7631 Ext. 19
KAN-DO:	Gwyn Dickinson	(913) 752-2446
LOS-DO:	Richmond Yip	(949) 798-7694
MIN-DO:	Sharon Thoma	(612) 334-4100 Ext. 196
NOL-DO:	M. Anthony Abel I, NSV-BR	(615) 781-5374 Ext. 111
NWE-DO:	Ellen Madigan	(781) 596-7753
NWJ-DO:	Mimi Roa Remache	(973) 526-6019
NYK-DO:	Upstate: John A. Podsadowski	(716) 551-4461 Ext. 3155
	Downstate: Larry Farina	(516) 921-1601
PHI-DO:	Sharon Gordon	(215) 597- 9064
SAN-DO:	Marie K. Kinkade	(510) 337-6823
SEA-DO:	Carol A. Gripp	(425) 483-4905
SJN-DO:	Ivonne Ayala	(787) 474-9505

DRUG EFFICACY STUDY IMPLEMENTATION (DESI) MONITORS:

ATL-DO:	Philip S. Campbell	(404) 253-1280
BLT-DO:	Melissa Garcia	(410) 779-5461
CHI-DO:	Kathy Haas	(312) 596-4250
CIN-DO:	Steven P. Eastham	(513) 679-2700 Ext. 123
DAL-DO:	Jose Martinez	(210) 308-4528 Ext. 18
DEN-DO:	Michael J. Kuchta	(303) 236-3059
DET-DO:	George Domingo	(313) 393-8142
FLA-DO:	Susan M. Corrales	(561) 338-7631 Ext. 19
KAN-DO:	Gwyn Dickinson	(913) 752-2446
LOS-DO:	Virgilio Pacio	(858) 550-3850 Ext. 116
MIN-DO:	Sharon Thoma	(612) 334-4100 Ext. 196
NOL-DO:	M. Anthony Abel I, NSV-BR	(615) 781-5374 Ext. 111
NWE-DO:	Stephen Souza	(860) 240-4289
NWJ-DO:	Meyer Slobotsky	(732) 940-8946 Ext 12
NYK-DO:	Ray Kent	(716) 551-4461 Ext. 3126
PHI-DO:	Steven Carter	(215) 597-4390 Ext. 4520

SAN-DO:	Rochelle Young	(510) 337-6804
SEA-DO:	Carol A. Gripp	(425) 483-4905
SJN-DO:	Ivonne Ayala	(787) 474-9505

DRUG FIELD ALERT MONITORS:

ATL-DO:	Tracy L.Ball	(704) 344-6116
BLT-DO:	Melissa Garcia	(410) 779-5461
CHI-DO:	Kathy Haas	(312) 596-4250
CIN-DO:	Steven P. Eastham	(513) 679-2700 Ext. 123
DAL-DO:	Jose Martinez	(210) 308-4528 Ext. 18
DEN-DO:	Donald L. Bean	(303) 236-3044
DET-DO:	Anthony C. Taube	(313) 393-8176
FLA-DO:	Paul L. Figarole	(813) 228-2671 Ext. 11
KAN-DO:	Gwyn Dickinson	(913) 752-2446
LOS-DO:	Richmond Yip	(949) 798-7694
MIN-DO:	Sharon Thoma	(612) 334-4100 Ext. 196
NOL-DO:	M. Anthony Abel I, NSV-BR	(615) 781-5374 Ext. 111
NWE-DO:	Ellen Madigan	(781) 596-7753
NWJ-DO:	Ray Abrahams	(973) 526-6002
NYK-DO:	Upstate: John Podsadowski	(718) 551-4461 Ext. 3155
	Downstate: Larry Farina	(516) 921-1601
PHI-DO:	Megan M. Lauff	(215) 597-4390 Ext. 4502
SAN-DO:	Marie K. Kinkade	(510) 337-6823
SEA-DO:	Carol A. Gripp	(425) 483-4905
SJN-DO:	Ivonne Ayala	(787) 474-9505

DRUG LISTING MONITORS:

ATL-DO:	Leah M. Andrews	(404) 253-1285
BLT-DO:	Matthew Henciak	(410) 779-5438
CHI-DO:	Linda E. Whitehead	(312) 596-4246
CIN-DO:	Steven P. Eastham	(513) 679-2700 Ext. 123
DAL-DO:	Jose Martinez	(210) 308-4528 Ext. 18
DEN-DO:	Patricia A. Cortez	(303) 236-3086
DET-DO:	George A. Domingo	(313) 393-8142
FLA-DO:	Angela J. Davis	(561) 338-7631 Ext. 10
KAN-DO:	Gwyn Dickinson	(913) 752-2446
LOS-DO:	Kirsten Tharp	(949) 798-7720
MIN-DO:	M. Edith Snyder	(612) 334-4100 Ext. 165
NOL-DO:	M. Anthony Abel I, NSV-BR	(615) 781-5374 Ext. 111
NWE-DO:	Ellen Madigan	(781) 596-7753
NWJ-DO:	Rosa Brown	(973) 526-6007
NYK-DO:	Upstate: Ann Okon	(716) 551-4461 Ext. 3120
	Downstate: Valerie Grecek	(781) 340-7000 Ext. 5572
PHI-DO:	LuAnn M. Pallas	(717) 541-9924 Ext. 12
SAN-DO:	Darlene Almogela	(510) 337-6769
SEA-DO:	Carol A. Gripp	(425) 483-4905
SJN-DO:	Gilbert Andino	(787) 474-9502

DRUG REGISTRATION MONITORS:

ATL-DO:	Leah M. Andrews	(404) 253-1285
BLT-DO:	Matthew Henciak	(410) 779-5438
CHI-DO:	Linda E. Whitehead	(312) 596-4246
CIN-DO:	Steven P. Eastham	(513) 679-2700 Ext. 123
DAL-DO:	Warren L. Landry	(214) 253-5230
DEN-DO:	Patricia A. Cortez	(303) 236-3086
DET-DO:	James E. Szelc	(313) 393-8170
FLA-DO:	Angela J. Davis	(561) 338-7631 Ext. 10
KAN-DO:	Linda Kuchenthal	(913) 752-2436
LOS-DO:	Kirsten Tharp	(949) 798-7720
MIN-DO:	M. Edith Snyder	(612) 334-4100 Ext. 165

NOL-DO:	Marion J. Ferrante	(504) 253-4523
NWE-DO:	Ellen Madigan	(781) 596-7753
NWJ-DO:	Rosa Brown	(973) 526-6007
NYK-DO:	Upstate: Ann Okon	(716) 551-4461 Ext. 3120
	Downstate: Valerie Grecek	(718) 340-7000 Ext. 5572
PHI-DO:	Steven L. Carter	(215) 597-4390 Ext. 4520
SAN-DO:	Darlene Almogela	(510) 337-6769
SEA-DO:	Carol A. Gripp	(425) 483-4905
SJN-DO:	Gilbert Andino	(787) 474-9502

DRUG SAMPLING PROGRAM MONITORS:

ATL-DO:	Penny McCarver	(404) 253-2263
BLT-DO:	Matthew Henciak	(410) 779-5438
CHI-DO:	Bruce McCullough	(312) 596-4260
CIN-DO:	Steve Eastham	(513) 679-2700 Ext. 123
DAL-DO:	Jose Martinez	(210) 308-4528 Ext. 18
DEN-DO:	Elvin R. Smith	(303) 236-3087
DET-DO:	George A. Domingo	(313) 393-8142
FLA-DO:	Paul L. Figarole	(813) 228-2671 Ext. 11
KAN-DO:	David Glasgow	(314) 645-1167 Ext. 116
LOS-DO:	Yumi Hiramine	(949) 798-7672
MIN-DO:	Sharon Thoma	(612) 334-4100 Ext. 196
NOL-DO:	M. Anthony Abel I, NSV-BR	(615) 781-5374 Ext. 111
NWE-DO:	Steven Sousa	(203) 240-4289
NWJ-DO:	Doug Kovacs	(973) 526-6070 Ext. 3006
NYK-DO:	Upstate: John A. Podsadowski	(716) 551-4461 Ext. 3155
	Downstate: Larry Farina	(516) 921-1601
PHI-DO:	LuAnn M. Pallas	(717) 241-9924 Ext. 12
SAN-DO:	Rochelle Young	(510) 337-6804
SEA-DO:	Carol A. Gripp	(425) 483-4905
SJN-DO:	Jorge Guadalupe	(787) 474-9515

FACTS PROFILE MONITORS (formerly Compliance Status Information System (COMSTAT):

ATL-DO:	Calvin Foulks	(404) 253-2241
BLT-DO:	Kevin D. Morrow	(410) 779-5414
CHI-DO:	Linda Whitehead	(312) 596-4246
CIN-DO:	Steven P. Eastham	(513) 679-2700 Ext. 123
DAL-DO:	Pauline Logan	(214) 253-5232
DEN-DO:	Elvin R. Smith	(303) 236-3087
DET-DO:	George Domingo	(313) 393-8142
FLA-DO:	Philip DeLisle	(407) 475-4717
KAN-DO:	Robert Wilson	(913) 752-2426
LOS-DO:	Kirsten Tharp	(949) 798-7720
MIN-DO:	Rhonda Mecl	(612) 334-4100 Ext. 190
NOL-DO:	M. Anthony Abel I, NSV-BR	(615) 781-5374 Ext. 111
NWE-DO:	Ellen Madigan	(781) 596-7753
NWJ-DO:	Shirley Isbill	(732) 940-8946 Ext. 13
NYK-DO:	Downstate: Jim Liubicich	(718) 340-7000 Ext. 5712
	Upstate: Ray Kent	(716) 551-4461 Ext. 3126
PHI-DO:	Steven Carter	(215) 597-4390 Ext. 4520
SAN-DO:	Darlene Almogela (Drugs)	(510) 337-6769
	Andrea Scott (Medical Devices)	(408) 291-4350 Ext. 25
SEA-DO:	David A. Pettenski	(425) 483-4911
SJN-DO:	Ivonne Ayala	(787) 729-6728

FACTS TRAINING CADRE:

ATL-DO:	Sheryl Cruse	(404) 253-1278
BLT-DO:	Gerald Bromley	(804) 379-1627 Ext. 13
CHI-DO:	Larry J. Stringer	(312) 596-4245
CIN-DO:	Robert Connatser	(513) 679-2700 Ext. 121

DAL-DO:	Sandy Ziegler	(214) 253-5237
DEN-DO:	Paul Teitell	(303) 236-3057
DET-DO:	George Domingo	(313) 393-8142
FLA-DO:	Virginia Jackson	(305) 526-2800 Ext. 931
	Shari J. Hromyak	(407) 475-4730
KAN-DO:	Ralph Erickson	(314) 645-1167 Ext. 124
LOS-DO:	Lloyd Lehrer	(714) 798-7777
MIN-DO:	Tony Duran	(612) 334-4100 Ext. 171
NERL:	Phyllis Wilson	(718) 340-7000 Ext. 5378
NOL-DO:	Allen Carman, NOL	(504) 253-4512
	Marie Clendening, NSV-BR	(615) 781-5372 Ext. 129
NWE-DO:	Maureen Donahue	(781) 596-7721
NWJ-DO:	Kimberly Bailey	(973) 526-6023
NYK-DO:	Ray Kent	(716) 551-4461 Ext. 3126
PHI-DO:	Kenneth Gordon	(215) 597-4390 Ext. 4611
SAN-DO:	Randy Plunkett	(510) 337-6858
	Kris Foster	
	FACTS implementation monitor	(510) 337 - 6798
SEA-DO:	Dennis Kawabata	(425) 483-4904
SJN-DO:	Miguel Hernandez	(787) 474-9519
SERL:	Jackie Welch	(404) 253-1200 Ext. 5468
WEAC:	George Varney	(781) 729-5700 Ext. 758

FOOD PROGRAM MONITORS:

ATL-DO:	Mallory W. Lawrence	(404) 253-2243
BLT-DO:	Valerie Wright	(410) 779-5434
CHI-DO:	Bradley Maunder	(312) 596-4244
CIN-DO:	Susan C. Morgan	(330) 273-1038 Ext. 233
DAL-DO:	Paul Perdue	(214) 253-5248
DEN-DO:	Mario Seminara	(303) 236-3026
DET-DO:	Michael V. Owens	(313) 393-8167
FLA-DO:	Kathleen M. Sinninger	(305) 526-2800 Ext. 964
KAN-DO:	Eric Nielsen	(913) 752-2409
LOS-DO:	Carol Sanchez	(858) 550-3850 Ext. 103
MIN-DO:	Anthony Duran	(612) 334-4100 Ext. 171
NOL-DO:	James W. Blakely, JKS-RP	(601) 965-4581
NWE-DO:	Willis I. Cobb	(207) 622-8268
NWJ-DO:	Robert McCullough	(856) 757-5389 Ext.11
NYK-DO:	Upstate: Ray Kent	(716) 551-4461 Ext. 3126
	Downstate: Rick Ferfoglia	(718) 340-7000 Ext. 5587
PHI-DO:	Susan F. Laska	(215) 362-0740 Ext. 21
SAN-DO:	Davina Watson	(510) 337-6896
SEA-DO:	Christopher E. Rezendes	(206) 553-7001 Ext. 21
SJN-DO:	Jaime Pares	(410) 474-9548

FOOD REGISTRATION MONITORS:

ATL-DO:	Mallory W. Lawrence	(404) 253-2243
BLT-DO:	Valerie Wright	(410) 779-5434
CHI-DO:	Linda E. Whitehead	(312) 596-4246
CIN-DO:	Marianne Allen	(513) 679-2700 Ext. 145
DAL-DO:	Warren L. Landry	(214) 253-5230
DEN-DO:	Mary Frances Bodick	(303) 236-3088
DET-DO:	James E. Szelc	(313) 393-8170
FLA-DO:	Kathleen M. Sinninger	(305) 526-2800 Ext. 964
KAN-DO:	Eric Nielsen	(913) 752-2409
LOS-DO:	Carol Sanchez	(858) 550-3850 Ext. 103
MIN-DO:	Tony Duran	(612) 334-4100 Ext. 171
NOL-DO:	Marion J. Ferrante	(504) 253-4523
NWE-DO:	Willis I. Cobb	(207) 622-8268
NWJ-DO:	Vacant	(973) 331-2914

NYK-DO:	Upstate: Ann Okon	(716) 551-4461 Ext. 3120
	Downstate: Richard Ferfoglia	(718) 340-7000 Ext. 5587
PHI-DO:	Steven L. Carter	(215) 597-4390 Ext. 4520
SAN-DO:	Lorna Jones	(510) 337-6818
SEA-DO:	Christopher E. Rezendes	(206) 553-7001 Ext. 21
SJN-DO:	Gilbert Andino	(787) 474-9502

GOVT. VEHICLE MONITORS:

ATL-DO:	Calvin Foulks	(404) 253-2241
BLT-DO:	John Mannara	(410) 779-5408
CHI-DO:	Lillian M. Starr	(312) 596-4183
CIN-DO:	Robert W. Connatser	(513) 679-2700 Ext. 121
DAL-DO:	Stacie McAllister	(214) 253-5259
DEN-DO:	Wendy Hettinger	(303) 236-3041
DET-DO:	Melanie S. Bourcier	(313) 393-8126
FLA-DO:	Stanley Ross	(407) 475-4735
KAN-DO:	Theresa Star	(913) 752-2442
STL:	James McReavey	(314) 645-1167 Ext. 133
LOS-DO:	Edward Whitford	(949) 798-7605
MIN-DO:	Cindy Grindahl	(612) 334-4100 Ext. 138
NOL-DO:	Ella Sue O'Regan, NOL	(504) 253-4544
	Betty Storey, NSV-BR	(615) 781-5380 Ext. 123
NWE-DO:	Alfred N. Levitt	(781) 596-7747
NWJ-DO:	Steve Krause	(973) 526-6022
NYK-DO:	Upstate: Ray Kent	(716) 551-4461 Ext. 3126
	Downstate: Richard Ferfoglia	(718) 340-7000 Ext. 5587
PHI-DO:	Maryann Yates	(215) 597-4390
SAN-DO:	William F. Hutson	(510) 337-6812
SEA-DO:	Donald Martinson	(425) 483-4943
SJN-DO:	Mario Guzman	(787) 474-9516

HAZARD ANALYSIS CRITICAL CONTROL POINT/LOW ACID CANNED FOOD (HACCP/LACF) MONITORS:

ATL-DO:	Mallory W. Lawrence	(404) 253-2243
BLT-DO:	Valerie Wright	(410) 779-5434
CHI-DO:	Darrell E. Luedtke	(847) 249-8632 Ext. 28
CIN-DO:	Susan C. Morgan	(330) 273-1038 Ext. 233
DAL-DO:	Dallas Gilbreath	(214) 253-5231
DEN-DO:	Mary Francis Bodick	(303) 236-3088
DET-DO:	Michael V. Owens	(313) 393-8167
FLA-DO:	Kathleen M. Sinninger	(305) 526-2800 Ext. 964
KAN-DO:	Peter E. Gruman	(913) 752-2771
LOS-DO:	Carol Sanchez	(858) 550-3850 Ext. 103
MIN-DO:	Douglas Nelson	(920) 433-3924
NOL-DO:	Carolyn W. White	(504) 253-4545
NWE-DO:	Willis I. Cobb	(207) 622-8268
NWJ-DO:	Robert McCullough	(856) 757-5389 Ext. 11
NYK-DO:	Upstate: Ray Kent	(716) 551-4461 Ext. 3126
	Downstate: Elizabeth Jacobson	(914) 682-6166 Ext. 27
PHI-DO:	Alfred Puglia	(215) 597-4390 Ext. 4540
	Susan Laska	(215) 362-0740 Ext. 21
SAN-DO:	Lorna Jones	(510) 337-6818
SEA-DO:	Seafood: Christopher Rezendes	(206) 553-7001 Ext. 21
	Juice: Janelle K. Martin	(425) 483-4928
SJN-DO:	Jaime Pares	(787) 474-9548

HEALTH FRAUD MONITORS:

ATL-DO:	Myla D. Chapman	(404) 253-2220
BLT-DO:	Stephen King	(410) 779-5426
CHI-DO:	Kathy Haas	(312) 596-4250
CIN-DO:	David Radle	(513) 679-2700 Ext. 124

DAL-DO:	Reynaldo (Ricky) R. Rodriguez, Jr.	(214) 253-5215
DEN-DO:	Shelly Maifarth	(303) 236-3046
DET-DO:	Evelyn DeNike	(313) 393-8109
FLA-DO:	Martin Katz	(407) 475-4729
KAN-DO:	Marion Wimberly	(913) 752-2786
LOS-DO:	Diane Van Leeuwen	(949) 798-7707
MIN-DO:	M. Edith Snyder	(612) 334-4100 Ext. 165
NOL-DO:	Stacy M. Below	(504) 253-4506
NWE-DO:	Vacant	
NWJ-DO:	Mercedes Mota	(973) 526-6009
NYK-DO:	Upstate: Joan Trankle	(716) 551-4461 Ext. 3171
	Downstate: Marlene Doherty	(718) 340-7000 Ext. 5588
PHI-DO:	Anitra Brown-Reed	(215) 597-4390 Ext. 4202
SAN-DO:	Jeff Watson	(510) 337-6767
SEA-DO:	Carol A. Gripp	(425) 483-4905
SJN-DO:	Nilda Villegas	(787) 474-9567

HUMAN TISSUE REGISTRATION MONITORS:

ATL-DO:	Vincent Williams	(404) 253-2240
BLT-DO:	Gerald Mierle	(804) 379-1627 Ext. 15
CHI-DO:	Linda Whitehead	(312) 596-4246
CIN-DO	Marianne Allen	(513) 679-2700 Ext. 145
DAL-DO:	Warren Landry	(214) 253-5230 Ext. 518
DEN-DO:	Deborah Hammond	(303) 236-3082
DET-DO:	Catherine V. Quinlan	(313) 393-8153
FLA-DO:	Ronnie Jackson	(407) 475-4725
KAN-DO:	Gregory Dixon	(913) 752-2427
LOS-DO:	Kirsten Tharp	(949) 798-7720
MIN-DO:	Kellie Westerbuhr	(612) 758-7161
NOL-DO:	Marion Ferrante	(504) 253-4523
NWE-DO:	Ellen Madigan	(781) 596-7753
NWJ-DO:	Lisa Harlan	(973) 526-6014
NYK-DO:	Elizabeth Jacobson	(914) 682-6166 Ext. 27
	Upstate: Ann B. Okon	(716) 551-4461 Ext. 3120
	Downstate - Evelyn Taha	(718) 340-7000 Ext. 5574
PHI-DO	Kim Crayton-Lee	(215) 597-4390 Ext.4539
SAN-DO:	Deborah Kleinfeld	(510) 337-6825
SEA-DO:	Dolores Price	(509) 353-2470
SJN-DO:	Gilbert Andino	(787) 474-9502

IMPORT PROGRAM MANAGERS:

ATL-DO:	Andrew B. Bevill	(404) 253-2218
BLT-DO:	Dean Cook	(410) 631-0322 Ext 11
CHI-DO:	Stephen D. Eich	(630) 860-1307 Ext. 15
CIN-DO:	Stephen J. Rabe	(513) 679-2700 Ext. 122
DAL-DO	Southwest Import District (SWID)	(214) 253-5283
DEN-DO:	SWID	(214) 253-5283
DET-DO:	Vickie L. Kaiser	(313) 226-5249
FLA-DO:	Kathleen M. Sinninger	(305) 526-2800 Ext. 964
KAN-DO:	SWID	(214) 253-5283
LOS-DO:	Irene Gomez	(310) 831-6123 Ext. 102
MIN-DO:	Catherine Levar	(612) 334-4100 Ext. 247
NOL-DO:	John M. McInnis, MEM-RP	(901) 544-0345 Ext. 25
NSV-BR:	Denise D. Duncan	(901) 544-0345 Ext. 11
NWE-DO:	Frank J. Mazzoni	(781) 596-7754
NYK-DO:	Upstate: Kevin Murray	(716) 551-4461 Ext. 3129
	Downstate: John Moore	(718) 340-7000 Ext. 5460
PHI-DO:	Alfred Puglia	(215) 597-4390 Ext. 4540
SAN-DO:	Janet Codor	(510) 337-6786

| SEA-DO: | Celeste M. Corcoran | (425) 483-4971 |
| SJN-DO: | Carlos I. Medina | (787) 474-9539 |

INTERSTATE TRAVEL SANITATION (ITS) MONITORS:

ATL-DO:	Mallory W. Lawrence	(404) 253-2243
BLT-DO:	Bruce E. Kummer	(410) 779-5439
CHI-DO:	Freed Sharif	(847) 249-8632 Ext. 23
CIN-DO:	Robert Rodriguez	(419) 259-6353
DAL-DO:	Lillie Johnson, HOU-RP	(713) 802-9095 Ext. 128
DEN-DO:	Elvin R. Smith	(303) 236-3087
DET-DO:	Vacant	
FLA-DO:	Diane L. Kelsch	(407) 475-4747
KAN-DO:	Eric Nielsen	(913) 752-2409
LOS-DO:	Michele Douglas	(310) 831-6123 Ext. 150
MIN-DO:	Ken Libertoski	(612) 334-4100 Ext. 244
NOL-DO:	Carolyn W. White	(504) 253-4545
NSV-BR:	David R. Heiar	(615) 781-5380 Ext. 148
NWE-DO:	Frank Mazzoni	(781) 596-7754
NWJ-DO:	Kris Moore	(856) 757-5389 Ext. 19
NYK-DO:	Elizabeth Jacobson	(914) 682-6166 Ext. 27
PHI-DO:	Daniel R. Tammariello	(412) 644-3394 Ext. 16
SAN-DO:	Randall P. Zielinski	(510) 337-6897
SEA-DO:	Janelle K. Martin	(425) 483-4928
SJN-DO:	Jaime Pares	(787) 474-9548

MEDICATED FEED MONITORS:

ATL-DO:	Andrew B. Bevill	(404) 253-2218
BLT-DO:	Karen S. Anthony	(804) 379-1627 Ext. 11
CHI-DO:	Mark Peterson	(217) 492-4095
CIN-DO:	Guy Cartwright	(614) 487-1273 Ext. 11
DAL-DO:	Ed Edmiston	(210) 308-4528 Ext. 16
DEN-DO:	Vacant	(303) 236-3040
DET-DO:	Michigan: Frederic W. French	(616) 233-9311 Ext. 11
	Indiana: William G. Nelson	(574) 288-7222
FLA-DO:	Nicolas Rivera	(813) 228-2671 Ext. 13
KAN-DO:	Robert Wilson	(913) 752-2426
LOS-DO:	John Gonzalez	(949) 798-7772
MIN-DO:	Richard Willey	(414) 771-7167 Ext. 11
NOL-DO:	James W. Blakely, JKS-RP	(601) 965-4581
NWE-DO:	Judy Peterson	(856) 757-5389 Ext. 23
NYK-DO:	Upstate & Downstate: Joe Erdmann	(315) 448-7601
PHI-DO:	Michael O'Meara	(302) 573-6447
SAN-DO:	Karen Robles	(916) 930-3674 Ext. 14
SEA-DO:	Carol A. Gripp	(425) 483-4905
SJN-DO:	Jaime Pares	(787) 474-9548

NADA/ANADA PREAPPROVAL MONITORS:

ATL-DO:	Leah M. Andrews	(404) 253-1284
BLT-DO:	Melissa Garcia	(410) 779-5461
CHI-DO:	Lorelei Jarrell	(312) 596-4216
CIN-DO:	Kathleen Culver	(502) 425-0069
DAL-DO:	Jose Martinez	(210) 308-4528 Ext. 18
DEN-DO:	Michael J. Kuchta	(303) 236-3059
DET-DO:	Vacant	
FLA-DO:	Paul L. Figarole	(813) 228-2671 Ext. 11
KAN-DO:	Shirley Berryman	(913) 752-2108
LOS-DO:	Caryn Everly	(949) 798-7722
MIN-DO:	Sharon Thoma	(612) 334-4100 Ext. 196
NOL-DO:	James W. Blakely, JKS-RP	(601) 965-4581
NWE-DO:	Richard Penta	(781) 596-7765

NWJ-DO:	Nancy Rolli	(732) 940-8946 Ext. 31
NYK-DO:	Upstate: John A. Podsadowski	(716) 551-4461 Ext. 3155
	Downstate: Larry Farina	(516) 921-1601
PHI-DO:	Karen Campbell	(215) 597-4390 Ext. 4204
SAN-DO:	Rochelle Young	(510) 337-6804
SEA-DO:	Carol A. Gripp	(425) 483-4905
SJN-DO:	Myriam Sosa	(787) 474-9563

OASIS LEAD USERS:

ATL-DO:	Frank Roberts	(404) 253-1292
BLT-DO:	Dean Cook	(410) 631-0322 Ext. 11
CHI-DO:	Dorothy Stanback	(312) 596-4218
CIN-DO:	Stephen Rabe	(513) 679-2700 Ext. 122
DAL-DO:	Vacant	
DEN-DO:	Brent Higgs	(801) 524-3190 Ext. 16
DET-DO:	Vickie Kaiser	(313) 226-5249
FLA-DO:	Diashion E. Reid	(407) 475-4755
IO-HQ:	Joseph Tracy	(301) 443-6553
KAN-DO:	Ralph Gray	(913) 752-2105
LOS-DO:	Ruth Rouleau	(310) 831-6123 Ext. 107
MIA-RP:	Lorraine Barnes	(305) 526-2800 Ext. 934
MIN-DO:	Catherine Levar	(612) 334-4100 Ext. 247
NOL-DO:	John M. McInnis, MEM-RP	(901) 544-0345 Ext. 25
NWE-DO:	Patricia Ronan	(781) 596-7775
NYK-DO:	Downstate: Kenneth Klein	(718) 340-7000 Ext. 5478
PHI-DO:	Alfred J. Puglia	(215) 597-4390 Ext. 4540
SAN-DO:	Andrea Cahill	(510) 337-6779
SEA-DO:	Michelle Swanson	(206) 553-7001 Ext. 42
	Shannon Rodriguez	(206) 553-7001 Ext. 16
	Gail Kirby	(503) 262-8771
SJN-DO:	Miguel Hernandez	787) 474-9519

OFFICIAL ESTABLISHMENT INVENTORY (OEI) MONITORS:

ATL-DO:	Sandra Lawrence	(404) 253-2222
BLT-DO:	Vivian D. Gandy	(410) 779-5444
CHI-DO:	Linda E. Whitehead	(312) 596-4246
CIN-DO:	Robert W. Connatser	(513) 679-2700 Ext. 121
DAL-DO:	Warren Landry	(214) 253-5230
DEN-DO:	Michael J. Quinn	(303) 236-3058
DET-DO:	James Szelc	(313) 393-8170
FLA-DO:	Justin Price	(407) 475-4710
KAN-DO:	Robert Wilson	(913) 752-2426
LOS-DO:	Vacant	
MIN-DO:	Calvin Baas	(612) 334-4100 Ext. 116
NOL-DO:	Allen S. Carman, NOL	(504) 253-4512
	Michael R. Duran, NSV-BR	(615) 781-5375 Ext. 116
NWE-DO:	Catherine Hosman	(781) 596-7735
NWJ-DO:	Rosa L. Brown	(973) 526-6007
NYK-DO:	Upstate: Ray Kent	(716) 551-4461 Ext. 3126
	Downstate: Otto Vitillo	(561) 921-1601
PHI-DO:	Steven Carter	(215) 597-4390 Ext. 4520
SAN-DO:	Kathryn Macropol	(510) 337-6836
SEA-DO:	Laura Betts	(425) 483-4965
SJN-DO:	Ivonne Ayala	(787) 474-9505

PRESCRIPTION DRUG MARKETING ACT (PDMA) MONITORS:

ATL-DO:	Leah M. Andrews	(404) 253-1285
BLT-DO:	Karen S. Anthony	(804) 379-1627 Ext. 11
CHI-DO:	Lisa Hayka	(312) 596-4259
CIN-DO:	Steven P. Eastham	(513) 679-2700 Ext. 123

DAL-DO:	Jose Martinez	(210) 308-4528 Ext. 18
DEN-DO:	Michael J. Kuchta	(303) 236-3059
DET-DO:	Patsy J. Domingo	(313) 393-8145
FLA-DO:	Paul L. Figarole	(813) 228-2671 Ext. 11
KAN-DO:	David Glasgow	(314) 645-1167 Ext 116
LOS-DO:	Richmond Yip	(949) 798-7694
MIN-DO:	Charles R. Cote	(608) 264-5332
NOL-DO:	M. Anthony Abel I, NSV-BR	(615) 781-5374 Ext. 111
NWE-DO:	Stephen Souza	(203) 240-1289
NWJ-DO:	Diane Amador	(973) 526-6015
NYK-DO:	Wanda Eng	(718) 390-7000 Ext. 5586
PHI-DO:	Luann M. Pallas	(717) 541-9924 Ext. 12
SAN-DO:	Darlene Almogela	(510) 337-6769
SEA-DO:	Carol A. Gripp	(425) 483-4905
SJN-DO:	Maridalia Torres	(787) 474-9565

PESTICIDE MONITORS:

ATL-DO:	Mallory W. Lawrence	(404) 253-2243
BLT-DO:	Valerie Wright	(410) 779-5434
CHI-DO:	Roger Adams	(217) 492-4095
CIN-DO:	Susan C. Morgan	(330) 273-1038 Ext. 233
DAL-DO:	Dallas Gilbreath	(214) 253-5231
DEN-DO:	Deborah Hammond	(303) 236-3082
DET-DO:	William D. Tingley	(269) 345-3203
FLA-DO:	Kathleen M. Sinninger	(305) 526-2800 Ext. 964
KAN-DO:	C. Richard Pendleton	(913) 752-2103
LOS-DO:	Carol Sanchez	(858) 550-3850 Ext. 103
MIN-DO:	Douglas Nelson	(920) 433-3924
NOL-DO:	Tura L. King	(504) 253-4552
NWE-DO:	Maureen E. Donahue	(781) 596-7721
NWJ-DO:	Robert McCullough	(856) 757-5389 Ext. 11
NYK-DO:	Upstate: Ray Kent	(716) 551-4461 Ext. 3126
	Downstate: Thomas Mooney	(516) 921-2035
PHI-DO:	Michael O'Meara	(302) 573-6447 Ext. 11
SAN-DO:	Luis Solorzano	(510) 337-6752
SEA-DO:	Robert Williams	(406) 441-1170
SJN-DO:	Eliezer Ramos	(787) 831-3337/8 Ext. 13

RECALL COORDINATORS:

ATL-DO:	Arnold Best	(404) 253-1293
BLT-DO:	Kevin D. Morrow	(410) 779-5414
CHI-DO:	Kathy Haas	(312) 596-4250
CIN-DO:	A. Wayne Edwards	(513) 679-2700 Ext. 125
DAL-DO:	Sherrie L. Krolcyzk	(214) 253-5222
DEN-DO:	Donald L. Bean	(303) 236-3044
DET-DO:	Sandra A. Williams	(313) 393-8118
	Miah Schneider	(313) 393-8180
FLA-DO:	Philip DeLisle	(407) 475-4717
KAN-DO:	Michelle Thompson	(913) 752-2425
LOS-DO:	R. Craig Hoover	(949) 798-7730
MIN-DO:	Dirk Mouw	(612) 334-4100 Ext. 184
NOL-DO:	Marie K. Fink	(504) 253-4511
NWE-DO:	Susan E. Liner	(781) 596-7750
NWJ-DO:	Mimi Roa Remache	
NYK-DO:	Upstate: Joan Trankle	(716) 551-4461 Ext. 3171
	Downstate: Maria Caride	(718) 340-7000 Ext. 5577
PHI-DO:	Megan F. Lauff	(215) 597-4390 Ext. 4502
SAN-DO:	Sam Ali	(510) 337-6869
SEA-DO:	Patricia A. Pinkerton	(425) 483-4937
SJN-DO:	Ivonne Ayala	(787) 474-9505

SAMPLE CUSTODIANS:

ATL-DO:	Larry Towers	(404) 253-5315
	Dexter Smith	(404) 253-5316
	Frank Goffigan	(404) 253-5412
DEN-DO:	Gianna Costo	(303) 236-3068
DET-DO:	Charles Teschke	(313) 393-8269
FCC:	Steve Gallagher	(513) 679-2700 Ext. 259
KAN-DO:	Lloyd S. (Butch) Ingram	(913) 752-2483
LOS-DO:	Liberty Kaai	(213) 252-7592 Ext. 201
NRL:	Garnatt Duncan	(718) 340-7000 Ext. 7114
	Daniel Pugh	(718) 340-7000 Ext. 7113
PHI-DO:	William Johns	(215) 597-4390 Ext. 4605
SAN-DO:	Mitchell Bonner	(510) 337-6772
SEA-DO:	PRL-NW: Robert Jones	(425) 483-4991
SERL:	Larry Towers	(404) 253-4007
SJN-DO:	Pedro Kuilan	(787) 474-4777
WEAC:	John Loveter	(781) 729-5700 Ext. 745

SEAFOOD MONITORS:

ATL-DO:	Mallory W. Lawrence	(404) 253-2243
BLT-DO:	Valerie Wright	(410) 779-5434
CHI-DO:	Darrell E. Luedtke	(847) 249-8632 Ext. 28
CIN-DO:	Susan C. Morgan	(330) 273-1038 Ext 233
DAL-DO:	Sharyn K. Miller	(713) 802-9095 Ext. 117
DEN-DO:	Mary Frances Bodick	(303) 236-3088
DET-DO:	Michael V. Owens	(313) 393-8167
FLA-DO:	Kathleen M. Sinninger	(305) 526-2800 Ext. 964
KAN-DO:	Eric Nielsen	(913) 752-2409
LOS-DO:	Debra Fracassa	(949) 798-7653
MIN-DO:	Frank Sedzielarz	(612) 334-4100 Ext. 193
NOL-DO:	Carolyn W. White	(504) 253-4545
NWE-DO:	Willis I. Cobb	(207) 622-8268
NWJ-DO:	Antoinette Ravelli	(856) 757-5389 Ext. 12
NYK-DO:	Elizabeth Jacobson	(914) 682-6166 Ext. 27
PHI-DO:	Peter C. Baker	(215) 597-4390 Ext. 4500
SAN-DO:	Darla Bracy	(510) 337-6773
SEA-DO:	Christopher E. Rezendes	(206) 553-7001 Ext. 21
SJN-DO:	Jaime Pares	(787) 474-9548

STATE CONTRACT MONITORS:

ATL-DO:	Dawn L. Todd-Murrell	(404) 253-2242
BLT-DO:	Nathaniel Esaw	(410) 779-5450
CHI-DO:	Roger J. Adams	(217) 492-4095
CIN-DO:	OH: Guy W. Cartwright	(614) 487-1273 Ext. 11
CIN-DO:	KY: Robert W. Connatser	(513) 679-2700 Ext. 121
DAL-DO:	Sylvia Yetts	(214) 253-5204
DEN-DO:	Paul J. Teitell	(303) 236-3057
DET-DO:	Roger Hartman	(313) 393-8162
FLA-DO:	Justin H. Price	(407) 475-4710
KAN-DO:	Monica Maxwell	(913) 752-2777
LOS-DO:	Vacant	(949) 798-7669
MIN-DO:	David Yost	(612) 334-4100 Ext. 154
NOL-DO:	AL: James W. Blakely, JKS-RP	(601) 965-4581
	TN: M. Anthony Abel I, NSV-BR	(615) 781-5374 Ext. 111
	LA & MS: Allen S. Carman	(504) 253-4512
NWE-DO:	MA: Frank Mazzoni	(781) 596-7754
	RI: Mutahar Shamsi	(781) 596-7778
	CT: Stephen Souza	(203) 240-4289
	VT: Janice Gordon	(802) 951-6240
	NH: Ellen Madigan	(781) 596-7753

	ME: Willie I. Cobb	(207) 622-8268
NWJ-DO:	Robert McCullough	(856) 757-5389
NYK-DO:	Beverly Kent	(716) 551-4461 Ext. 3131
PHI-DO:	Peter C. Baker	(215) 597-4390 Ext. 4500
SAN-DO:	Davina Watson	(510) 337-6896
SEA-DO:	Celeste Corcoran	(425) 483-4971
SJN-DO:	Circe Arana	(787) 474-9504

TISSUE RESIDUE MONITORS:

ATL-DO:	Andrew B. Bevill	(404) 253-2218
BLT-DO:	Dianne Hamilton	(804) 379-1627 Ext. 17
CHI-DO:	Mark Peterson	(217) 492-4095
CIN-DO:	David C. Radle	(513) 679-2700 Ext. 124
DAL-DO:	Ed Edmiston	(210) 308-4528 Ext. 16
DEN-DO:	Michael L. Zimmerman	(505) 248-7393
DET-DO:	Cathie Marshall	(313) 393-8174
FLA-DO:	Christopher T. Smith	(305) 513-4417 Ext. 4835
KAN-DO:	Robert Wilson	(913) 752-2426
LOS-DO:	John Gonzalez	(949) 798-7772
MIN-DO:	Kathy A. Clarke-Girolamo	(715) 344-2868
NOL-DO:	James W. Blakely, JKS-RP	(601) 965-4581
NSV-BR:	Robert E. Hultman	(615) 781-5380 Ext. 153
NWE-DO:	Janice Gordon	(802) 951-6240
NWJ-DO:	Wayne Meyer	(732) 940-8946 Ext. 24
NYK-DO:	Joe Erdmann	(315) 448-7601
PHI-DO:	Michael D. O'Meara	(302) 573-6447 Ext. 11
SAN-DO:	Karen Robles	(916) 930-3674 Ext. 14
SEA-DO:	William C. Hughes	(503) 671-9711 Ext. 13
SJN-DO:	Maria Medina	(787) 474-9540

TRAINING COORDINATORS:

ATL-DO:	Patricia Hudson	(404) 253-2221
BLT-DO:	Nathaniel Esaw	(410) 779-5450
CHI-DO:	Larry J. Stringer	(312) 596-4245
CIN-DO:	Carol A. Heppe	(513) 679-2700 Ext. 120
DAL-DO:	Cynthia Rashid	(214) 253-4949
DEN-DO:	Susan J. Miller	(303) 236-3040
DET-DO:	Roger Hartman	(313) 393-8162
FLA-DO:	Frank R. Goodwin	(407) 475-4707
KAN-DO:	Marion D. Wimberly	(913) 752-2786
	STL: David Glasgow	(314) 645-1167 Ext 116
LOS-DO:	Sandi Velez	(949) 798-7698
MIN-DO:	Rhonda Mecl	(612) 334-4100 Ext. 190
NOL-DO:	Michael W. Roosevelt, NOL	(504) 253-4525
	Marie B. Clendening, NSV-BR	(615) 781-5372 Ext. 129
NWE-DO:	Alfred N. Levitt	(781) 596-7747
NWJ-DO:	Mimi Roa Remache	(973) 526-6019
NYK-DO:	Upstate: Ray Kent	(716) 551-4461 Ext. 3126
	Downstate: Elizabeth Jacobson	(914) 682-6166 Ext. 27
PHI-DO:	Maryann Yates	(215) 597-4390
SAN-DO:	Ralph Kalinowski	(510) 337-6819
SEA-DO:	Laura A. Betts	(425) 483-4965
SJN-DO:	Ivette Roque	(787) 474-9558

VET DRUG LISTING MONITORS:

ATL-DO:	Andrew B. Bevill	(404) 253-2218
BLT-DO:	Karen Anthony	(410) 379-1627 Ext. 11
CHI-DO:	Linda E. Whitehead	(312) 596-4246
CIN-DO:	Steven P. Eastham	(513) 679-2700 Ext 123
DAL-DO:	Ed Edmiston	(210) 308-4528 Ext. 16

DEN-DO:	Vacant	(303) 236-3040
DET-DO:	George A. Domingo	(313) 393-8142
FLA-DO:	Susan M. Corrales	(561) 338-7631 Ext. 19
KAN-DO:	Gwyn Dickinson	(913) 752-2446
LOS-DO:	Kirsten Tharp	(949) 798-7720
MIN-DO:	M. Edith Snyder	(612) 334-4100 Ext. 165
NOL-DO:	James W. Blakely, JKS-RP	(601) 965-4581
NWE-DO:	Janice Gordon	(802) 951-6240
NWJ-DO:	Rosa Brown	(973) 526-6007
NYK-DO:	Upstate: Ann Okon	(716) 551-4461 Ext. 3120
	Downstate: Valerie Grecek	(781) 340-7000 Ext. 5572
PHI-DO:	LuAnn M. Pallas	(717) 541-9924 Ext 12
SAN-DO:	Karen Robles	(916) 930-3674 Ext. 14
SEA-DO:	Carol A. Gripp	(425) 483-4905
SJN-DO:	Jaime Pares	(787) 474-9548

VET DRUG REGISTRATION MONITORS:

ATL-DO:	Andrew B. Bevill	(404) 253-2218
BLT-DO:	Karen Anthony	(804) 379-1627 Ext. 11
CHI-DO:	Linda E. Whitehead	(312) 596-4246
CIN-DO:	Steven P. Eastham	(513) 679-2700 Ext. 123
DAL-DO:	Warren L. Landry	(214) 253-5230
DEN-DO:	Vacant	(303) 236-3040
DET-DO:	James E. Szelc	(313) 393-8170
FLA-DO:	Angela J. Davis	(561) 338-7631 Ext. 10
KAN-DO:	Robert Wilson	(913) 752-2426
LOS-DO:	Kirsten Tharp	(949) 798-7720
MIN-DO:	M. Edith Snyder	(612) 334-4100 Ext. 165
NOL-DO:	Marion J. Ferrante	(504) 253-4523
NWE-DO:	Janice Gordon	(802) 951-6240
NWJ-DO:	Rosa Brown	(973) 526-6007
NYK-DO:	Upstate: Ann Okon	(716) 551-4461 Ext. 3120
	Downstate: Thomas Mooney	(516) 921-1601
PHI-DO:	Steven L. Carter	(215) 597-4390 Ext. 4520
SAN-DO:	Karen Robles	(916) 930-3674 Ext. 14
SEA-DO:	Carol A. Gripp	(425) 483-4905
SJN-DO:	Gilbert Andino	(787) 474-9502

X-RAY MONITORS:

ATL-DO:	Calvin Foulks	(404) 253-2241
BLT-DO:	Gerald Bromley	(804) 379-1627 Ext. 13
CHI-DO:	Matthew J. Sienko	(312) 596-4264
CIN-DO:	R. Terry Bolen	(513) 679-2700 Ext. 138
DAL-DO:	Vacant	
DEN-DO:	Robert Antonson	(303) 236-3025
DET-DO:	Dennis E. Swartz	(313) 393-8156
FLA-DO:	D. Janneth Caycedo	(561) 338-7631 Ext. 23
KAN-DO:	Reggie Cope	(913) 752-2403
LOS-DO:	Ron Alexander	(818) 595-0016 Ext. 35
MIN-DO:	Tony T. Yang	(612) 334-4100 Ext. 199
NOL-DO:	James T. Goertz, Jr.	(504) 253-4508
NSV-BR:	Michael R. Duran	(615) 781-5375 Ext. 116
NWE-DO:	Michael J. Leal	(508) 793-0421
NWJ-DO:	Toniette Williams	(973) 526-6018
NYK-DO:	Otto Vitillo	(516) 921-2869
PHI-DO:	Daniel R. Tammariello	(412) 644-3394 Ext. 16
SAN-DO:	Mike Davila	(510) 337-6788
SEA-DO:	John Hall	(425) 483-4932
SJN-DO:	Jorge Martinez	(787) 474-9533

CHAPTER 3 - FEDERAL AND STATE COOPERATION

CONTENTS

SUBCHAPTER 300 – COOPERATIVE EFFORTS

301　POLICY

The scope of consumer protection is extended by cooperative efforts of federal, state, and local agencies and international cooperation. Procedures to appropriately share responsibilities and cooperate with our consumer protection partners are essential.

Federal, state, and local cooperation shall be fostered whenever possible. The Agency issues the IOM as well as other FDA manuals to international regulators and conformity assessment bodies, and state and local inspectors. FDA fosters cooperation through correspondence, FDA testimony, press releases, reprints from the Federal Register, and distribution of all pertinent policy and regulations issued by FDA which have significance in other regulatory jurisdictions.

Districts, headquarters' offices, and resident post personnel in particular, should maintain liaison with federal, state and local officials.

Follow district policy regarding contacts with appropriate federal, state, county and local officials to exchange information, coordinate operations, and arrange joint inspections. If an assignment calls for joint work with state or local inspectors, make every effort to accomplish this work. See IOM 331. When you travel internationally, follow policy established in the "GUIDE TO INTERNATIONAL INSPECTIONS AND TRAVEL".

302　LAWS, CODES, AGENCIES

Many states have enacted the basic Uniform Food, Drug, and Cosmetic Bill, and others have adopted at least a part of the Uniform Bill. The provisions of these laws are very similar to the 1938 provisions of the Federal Food, Drug, and Cosmetic Act. A few states have enacted the Pesticide Food and Color Additives or Kefauver-Harris type amendments. See IOM 333.

Most states without the Uniform FD&C Act, have laws based on the 1906 Food and Drug Act. Most larger cities have their own ordinances and regulations. A portion of the food supply of the United States is consumed within the state in which it is produced, and is therefore, not directly under the jurisdiction of the Federal Food, Drug and Cosmetic Act as amended. Thus, the various state and local agencies are solely responsible for policing this supply.

The departments of the executive branch of the federal government operate under the laws and regulations which they are specifically responsible for enforcing. Since responsibilities may overlap and be duplicated, operating agreements and liaison between agencies is essential for smooth and efficient governmental operation. Section 702(c) of the FD&C Act recognizes this by providing that the records of any department in the executive branch shall be open to inspection by authorized DHHS personnel.

District management is responsible for maintaining official liaison between FDA and other federal agencies. However, for day by day operations, personal contact between various operating federal investigators, inspectors, and agents is desirable and encouraged.

302.1　Agreements and Memoranda of Understanding (MOU)

To provide for more efficient use of FDA and other agency manpower and resources and to prevent duplication of effort, FDA and various agencies often enter into formal or informal agreements, and/or understandings. These specify areas in which each will assume primary responsibility.

Pertinent parts or paraphrasing of the Agreements and/or MOU which are of particular interest to you as operating inspectors and investigators are listed below. Copies of many of the formal Agreements and Memoranda of Understanding (MOU) are in the FDA Federal Cooperative Agreements Manual (1996 edition) and the FDA International Cooperative Agreements Manual (1996 edition). Your district and most resident posts have copies of these manuals. Refer to them as necessary. Some Agreements and MOU's are listed, for your information and reference, in this Chapter of the IOM under the appropriate agencies. For FDA personnel, the Federal Cooperative Agreements Manual is located on the FDA Gold Disk or for either the Federal or International manuals, a hardcopy can be obtained by contacting the Division of Compliance Information and Quality Assurance (HFC-240) at 301-827-0889. State and local governmental agencies may contact the Division of Federal State Relations (HFC-150) at 301-827-6906. FDA's Office of International Programs (OIP) (HFG-1) will answer your questions about international Agreements and/or Memoranda of Understanding. If you plan to share non-public information with another federal agency, contact HFC-230; with a state agency, contact HFC-150; or with a foreign government, contact HFC-230, who will consult with OIP. The public may obtain a copy of either manual for a fee by contacting the National Technical Information Services (NTIS), U.S. Department of Commerce, 5285 Port Royal Road, Springfield, VA 22161 or by telephoning them at 800-553-6847. Partnership Agreements will be posted on the ORA Internet (See www.fda.gov/ora/partnership agreements/ default.htm.)

303　OTHER GOVERNMENT INSPECTION

General procedures regarding cooperation with other federal, state, and local officials are furnished below.

During establishment inspections determine the specific type of inspection service and inspecting units, such as the name of the federal, state, county, or city health agency or department. Obtain the name and title of the inspectional official, and general method of operation. IOM 538 discusses coverage of grade A Dairy Plants.

303.1 Federal

Compulsory Continuous Inspection - Do not inspect firms, or that portion of a plant, under compulsory, continuous inspection under USDA's Meat Inspection Act, Poultry Products Inspection Act, or Egg Products Inspection Act, except on specific instructions from your supervisor or assignment document.

Ingredients or manufacturing processes common to both USDA and FDA regulated products should be inspected by FDA. See IOM 311.3 for FDA/USDA Agreements in specific areas.

Provide routine FDA coverage of such firms as breweries and wineries, which may be intermittently inspected on a compulsory basis by the U.S. Treasury Department, U.S. Public Health Service, or other agencies.

Voluntary - All products inspected under the voluntary inspection service of the Agriculture Marketing Service (AMS), USDA, and the National Marine Fisheries Service (NMFS), US Department of Commerce, are subject to FDA jurisdiction and are usually given routine coverage; however, formal written Agreements or a Memorandum of Understanding (MOU) between FDA and other agencies are often executed and may govern the agreeing agencies' operations on these type of inspected plants.

303.2 Discussion with Federal Inspector

If you are assigned to cover a federally inspected plant which is under either compulsory or voluntary inspection, check to see if an Agreement or a MOU exists between FDA and the agency involved to determine the obligations of both agencies. When you arrive at the firm:

1. Identify yourself to the inspector(s) and invite him/her to accompany you on the inspection but do not insist on their participation.

2. At the conclusion of the inspection offer to discuss your observations and provide the in-plant inspector with a copy of your Inspectional Observations (FDA 483).

303.3 State and Local

State and local officials usually have extensive regulatory authority over firms in their area regardless of the interstate movement or origin of the food products involved. Joint FDA-State or local inspections are occasionally conducted. These are usually arranged by district administrative or supervisory personnel. See IOM 331.

SUBCHAPTER 310 - FEDERAL AGENCY INTERACTION

This subchapter deals with the interaction of the FDA with other federal agencies. This interaction will be discussed below. Each agency with which FDA has agreements or an MOU is listed separately. Information regarding MOU's and other interactions are discussed as appropriate. Information about the complete MOU or agreement can be found in the appropriate Cooperative Agreements Manual. Listings of all Liaison Officers are included below.

311 U.S. DEPARTMENT OF AGRICULTURE (USDA)

See IOM 303 for procedures to be followed when making inspections of firms under USDA inspection or subject to inspection by USDA.

311.1 Foods Rejected by USDA

All procurement and processing contracts administered by USDA for edible food products require compliance with FDA regulations. The USDA routinely reports to the FDA its findings on lots of flour, cereal, or other products which have been rejected for acceptance into USDA-sponsored programs, based on FDA guidelines. This notification of rejection is routinely furnished to the involved district office. When a district office receives such notification it will determine appropriate follow-up by evaluating the reason for rejection, current priority assignments, and workload.

Samples should not be routinely collected from the USDA rejected material. If a follow-up inspection is made the district will then determine the need for samples or additional action.

311.2 USDA Complaints

Whenever a complaint is received involving any meat-containing product, including such items as soups, combination infant foods, frozen dinners, etc., evaluate the need to contact USDA. Most products containing red meat or poultry are regulated by USDA. The exceptions include: (1) products containing meat from game animals, such as venison, rabbits, etc., (2) meat-flavored instant noodles, and (3) the product "pork and beans" which contain only a small amount of pork fat and for historic reasons is regulated by FDA.

Determine from the consumer whether there is a round "shield" on the label with the USDA establishment number. Alternatively, the establishment number may be identified in the lot number. Red meat products under USDA jurisdiction will often contain the abbreviation "EST" followed by a one to four digit number; poultry products under USDA jurisdiction will contain the letter "P" followed by a number.

FDA reports suspected outbreaks to USDA & CDC. In addition, FDA and CDC have an agreement that FDA will be immediately advised whenever CDC ships botulism antitoxin anywhere in the United States or its possessions. See IOM 314.3 regarding interaction with CDC.

USDA and FDA have an agreement whereby FDA informs a designated USDA Compliance and Evaluation Area Office about any foodborne disease where a meat or poultry product is suspected. Conversely, USDA will alert the FDA district office on suspected products subject to

FDA jurisdiction. In order for your district to alert USDA promptly, check with your supervisor immediately if meat or poultry products are involved in an outbreak you are investigating or which comes to your attention.

311.3 USDA Acts

This is a listing of various USDA Acts under which FDA has been delegated detention authorities for products subject to USDA inspection. See IOM 750 for additional information. See IOM Exhibit 311 for a chart depicting jurisdictional lines for products regulated by FDA and USDA.

Federal Meat Inspection Act (MIA) - Sections 402 and 409(b) of the Federal Meat Inspection Act (MIA) provide FDA representatives may detain meat products subject to the MIA found outside an inspected plant, if they have reason to believe the products are adulterated or misbranded under the FD&C Act. Detention may not exceed twenty (20) days and the items detained shall not be moved by any person from the place of detention until released by the FDA representative.

Poultry Products Inspection Act PPIA - Sections 19 & 24(b) of the Poultry Products Inspection Act (PPIA) provide that FDA representatives may detain poultry products subject to the PPIA found outside an inspected plant, if they have reason to believe the products are adulterated or misbranded under the FD&C Act. Detention may not exceed twenty (20) days and the items detained shall not be moved from the place of detention until released by the FDA representative.

Egg Products Inspection Act (EPIA) - Sections 19 & 23(d) of the Egg Products Inspection Act (EPIA) provide FDA representatives may detain egg products subject to the EPIA found outside an inspected plant, if they have reason to believe the products are in violation of the EPI Act. Detention may not exceed twenty (20) days and the items detained shall not be moved from the place of detention until released by the FDA representative.

311.4 FDA-USDA Agreements & MOUs

MOU's and MOA's with USDA and its various units will be listed and in some cases described below. This first subsection covers MOU's with the USDA, USDA/other agency, and FDA. The following subsections provide information about MOU's with other USDA units.

MOU with:

1. US Department of Commerce and USDA Concerning Inspection of Industrial Fishery Products Intended For Animal 315 Feed Use.

2. USDA, NIH Regarding Importation of Biological Specimens Under US/USSR Scientific Exchange Agreement.

3. USDA Concerning Public Education in the Basics of Food Safety, Nutrition, and Veterinary Medicine.

4. USDA Concerning Sampling & Aflatoxin Testing of Imported Pistachios or Peanuts.

Importers of pistachio nuts voluntarily offer to USDA inspectors before introducing them into U.S. commerce. USDA is responsible for sampling and testing each lot for

aflatoxin, in accordance with procedures prescribed by FDA, and for issuing an analysis certificate for each lot. The Agricultural Marketing Service (AMS) will forward a copy of each certificate to the appropriate FDA District office.

The FDA Liaison Officer is the Director, Office of Compliance, Center for Food Safety and Applied Nutrition, HFS-600 (301-436-2359).

The USDA Liaison Officer is the Chief of Technologies Services Branch, Science Division, AMS (202-690-4025).

5. USDA and DHHS Regarding General War Food Inspection.

Staff units and officials of USDA and FDA shall confer on matters of joint concern. In an immediate post-attack period USDA food inspectors or designated FDA Inspectors may act to inspect and approve foods meeting emergency standards for safety. DHHS/FDA will provide appropriate guidelines for use by USDA personnel in assuring compliance for food inspection in the emergency period. The emergency liaison officers appointed by each agency may be assigned to the other agency's headquarters emergency relocation sites for the purpose of coordinating food inspection services.

The FDA Liaison Officer is the Director, Emergency Operations Center, HFC-160, (301-827-5655).

The USDA Liaison Officer is the Director, Emergency Response Division, Food Safety and Inspection Service (202-501-7515)

6. USDA Regarding the Reduction of Salmonella enteritidis (S.E.) Infection of Humans.

311.5 Agricultural Marketing Service (AMS)/USDA (MOU's)

MOU with:

1. AMS Concerning the Inspection and Grading of Food Products.

This MOU has extensive separation of duties between AMS and FDA.

Both agencies agree to maintain a close working relationship, in the field as well as headquarters. Both agencies will work with industry toward greater efficiency connected with improvement of coding methods. Each agency will designate a central contact point to which communications dealing with this agreement or other issues may be referred to for attention.

The FDA Liaison Officer is the Director, Office of Compliance, Center for Food Safety and Applied Nutrition, HFS-600 (301-436-2359)

The USDA Liaison Officer is the Chief of Technologies Services Branch, Science Division, AMS (202-690-4025).

2. AMS Regarding the Egg Products Inspection Act.

FDA has exclusive jurisdiction over restaurants, institutions, food manufacturing plants, and other similar establishments, that break and serve eggs or use them in their products.

AMS shall notify FDA whenever it has reason to believe that shell eggs or egg products have been shipped in commerce in violation of the act to a receiver for which FDA has exclusive jurisdiction, and notify FDA when applications are made to import shell eggs into the U.S.

FDA will notify AMS so that they can check on the seller of any restricted eggs when it is determined that more restricted eggs than are allowed in U.S. Consumer Grade B. are encountered. FDA will also notify AMS of any unwholesome egg products it encounters, including imported shell eggs which contain restricted eggs not in accordance with USDA regulations and labeling requirements.

The FDA Liaison Officer is the Director, Emergency Operations Center, HFC-160, (301-827-5653).

The FDA Liaison Officer for imported shell eggs is the Branch Chief, Import Branch, Division of Enforcement, Office of Compliance, Center for Food Safety and Applied Nutrition, HFS-606 (301-436-2413).

The USDA Liaison Officer is the Deputy Administrator, Poultry Program, Agricultural Marketing Service (202-720-4476).

3.   AMS Concerning Imported Dates and Date Material.

FDA inspects samples and examines imported dates and date products intended for processing to determine whether they are in compliance with the statute.

AMS, upon request, will provide FDA with a copy of each examination report which will contain information such as that in the FDA Technical Bulletin Number 5, Microanalytical Procedures Manual.

The FDA Liaison Officer is the Director, Division of Natural Products, Microanalytical Branch, Center for Food Safety and Applied Nutrition, HFS-315 (301-436-2401).

The USDA Liaison Officer is the Chief, Processed Products Branch, Fruit & Vegetable Division, Agricultural Marketing Service (202-720-4693).

4.   AMS Concerning Cooperative Efforts for Inspection, Sampling, and Examination of Imported Raisins.

AMS evaluates raisins for grade condition requirements and at the time and place of entry all lots of imported raisins. Upon completion of the examination, AMS promptly notifies the appropriate FDA District Office of any lots found not to meet minimum acceptance criteria because of insect infestation, filth, etc., and any questionable cases regarding the laboratory examination results. At the end of the season, the AMS provides FDA with a copy of each examination report.

FDA accepts, unless it notifies USDA to the contrary, AMS findings on any lot of raisins sampled and inspected by them. FDA will detain any lots of raisins rejected by USDA because they contain insect infestation, etc. See the cooperative agreement manual for details of responsibilities.

The FDA Liaison Officer is the Director, Division of Natural Products, Microanalytical Branch, Center for Food Safety and Applied Nutrition, HFS-315 (301-436-2401).

The USDA Liaison Officer is the Chief, Processed Products Branch, Fruit & Vegetable Division, Agricultural Marketing Service (202-720-4693).

5.   AMS Regarding Aflatoxin Testing Program for In-Shell Brazil Nuts.

Importers of Brazil Nuts voluntarily offer for USDA inspections before introducing them into U.S. commerce. USDA is responsible for sampling and testing each lot for aflatoxin in accordance with procedures prescribed by FDA and for issuing an analysis certificate for each lot. The Agricultural Marketing Service (AMS) will forward a copy of each certificate to the appropriate FDA District office. FDA accepts the certificate and then allows entry of the lots into U.S. commerce provided the aflatoxin level does not exceed the current action level prescribed by FDA.

The FDA Liaison Officer is the Director, Office of Compliance, Center for Food Safety and Applied Nutrition, HFS-600 (301-436-2359).

The USDA Liaison Officer is the Chief of Technologies Services Branch, Science Division, AMS (202-690-4025).

6.   AMS Concerning Aflatoxin in Peanuts.

AMS will use FDA administrative guidelines on objective samples to certify peanuts, recognizing that GMPs remove significant quantities of unfit peanuts and that levels of aflatoxin are reduced by heating. USDA will provide FDA with a copy of the analytical certificate and identification of the applicant on each lot found to exceed 25 ppb of aflatoxin and the analysis certificate on any lot on request. FDA will routinely confirm chemical assays in finished product at 20 ppb by bioassay procedures.

FDA will not formally object to the offering of lots of peanuts to processors where certificates show levels of aflatoxin above 25 ppb but will examine finished products from such lots. Such lots of raw peanuts may be subject to appropriate action in cases where there is lack of assurance that the finished product will comply with current standards.

The FDA Liaison Officer is the Director, Office of Compliance, Center for Food Safety and Applied Nutrition, HFS-600 (301-436-2359)

The USDA Liaison Officer is the Chief of Technologies Services Branch, Science Division, AMS (202-690-4025).

7.   AMS & FSIS and EPA re: Regulatory Activities Concerning Residues of Drugs, Pesticides, and Environmental Contaminants in Foods. Parts of this MOU are discussed below. Information about the complete MOU can be found in the appropriate Cooperative Agreements Manual. The contact offices are as follows:

The FDA Liaison Office is the Director, Division of Natural Products, Microanalytical Branch, Center for Food Safety and Applied Nutrition, HFS-315 (301-436-2401).

The USDA Liaison Office is the Administrator, Food Safety and Inspection Service (202-720-7025).

The EPA Liaison Office is the Office of Pesticide Programs, (703-305-7090), or Health Effects Division, (703-305-7351).

8.   AMS Concerning Salmonella Inspection and Sampling Coverage of Dry Milk Plants.

Parts of this MOU are discussed below. Information about the complete MOU can be found in the appropriate Cooperative Agreements Manual.

USDA has two types of voluntary inspection programs: Plant Inspection Program for USDA Approved for Grading Services, and their Resident Inspection and Grading Program.

Plant Inspection Program (PIP). Under the PIP, dry milk plants are surveyed for approval every three months. This includes a salmonella surveillance testing of the plant's product and environmental material. Product inspection and grading is provided on request and dry milk products produced under this program are eligible to bear the USDA shield.

FDA will accept the AMS Salmonella Surveillance Program results on such plants and the finished dry milk products after shipment from those plants will not be sampled by FDA for Salmonella examinations. This does not preclude FDA sampling dry milk at manufacturing plants using dry milk as an ingredient as a follow-up to consumer complaints, or where the dry milk may have become contaminated or adulterated after leaving the dry milk manufacturer's control. Neither will it preclude FDA inspections of any plant for problems other than Salmonella whether or not such plant produces dry milk products under USDA inspection, or the sampling of their products, including dry milk products, for problems other than Salmonella.

The FDA Liaison Office is the Director, Emergency Operations Center, HFC-160, (301-827-5655).

The USDA Liaison Office is the Chief, Grading Branch, Dairy Division, Agricultural Marketing Service, (202-720-3171) or Chief, Standardization Branch, (202-720-7473).

311.6 Animal Plant Health Inspection Service/USDA (APHIS)

MOU with:
1. APHIS Concerning Mutual Responsibilities for Regulating Biological Products.

Referral and exchange information for purposes of investigation and appropriate legal action. To coordinate investigations and enforcement actions and to avoid duplication of effort, FDA and USDA agree to provide each other with any information which may be germane to either agency's enforcement functions. Information regarding pending investigations and enforcement actions shall be provided to the liaison officers noted below on a regular basis.

The FDA Liaison Office is the Director, Office of Surveillance and Compliance, Center for Veterinary Medicine, HFV-200, (301-827-6647).

The USDA Liaison Office is the Director, Center for Veterinary Biologics, Animal and Plant Health Inspection Service, (301-734-8245).
2. APHIS and NIH Regarding the Care and Welfare of Laboratory Animals.

311.7 Federal Grain Inspection Service/ USDA (FGIS)

MOU with FGIS Concerning Inspection of Grain, Rice, Pulses, and Food Products.

During an FDA inspection of any facility that processes, packs, or holds agricultural products, the investigator and or inspector will request that the FGIS inspector or licensee stationed at a facility accompany him/her during the inspection.

The inspector/investigator will request from FGIS any information concerning quality determinations of specific lots of products against which FDA has taken or may take action.

FDA will notify FGIS of any details concerning serious objectionable conditions found by FDA to exist in processing plants, packing plants, grain elevators, or any other facility where FGIS provides official services.

General matters involving this agreement may be referred to the agencies' liaison officers.

The FDA Liaison Office is the Director, Office of Plant and Dairy Foods and Beverages, Center for Food Safety and Applied Nutrition, HFS-300, (301-436-1700) or Director, Division of Programs and Enforcement Policy, Center for Food Safety and Applied Nutrition, HFS-305, (301-436-1400).

The USDA Liaison Office is the Director, Field Management Division, Federal Grain Inspection Service, Grain Inspection, Packers and Stockyards Administration (202-720-0228).

311.8 Food Safety and Inspection Service/USDA (FSIS)

1. FSIS Pertaining to Class I and Class II Recalls of Food Products that Contain Poultry and/or Meat Products that have been Manufactured in a FSIS Inspected Establishment;

FDA and FSIS agree that they will keep the customary records and make those related to the operation of this agreement available to the other agency. Both agencies will furnish reports of the progress of the work and such other reports as may be mutually agreed upon from time to time between cooperating parties.

The FDA Liaison Officer is the Deputy Director, Emergency Operations Center, HFC-160, (301-827-5660).

The USDA Liaison Officer is the Director, Emergency Planning Office, Food Safety and Inspection Service (301-504-2121)
2. FSIS Concerning Inspection of Food Manufacturing Firms

FDA investigators will attempt to contact any on-site FSIS inspectors when they arrive at a plant, invite them to participate in the inspection and discuss with or report any adverse findings involving meat and poultry products to that inspector prior to leaving the premises.

When report findings are classified "indicated" FDA will provide FSIS with a copy when the plant is also inspected by FSIS.

If the FDA investigator has found unsanitary conditions or otherwise adulterated products, the appropriate FSIS office should be informed by telephone unless the FDA investigator has already reported his findings to the FSIS inspector at the plant.

To any extent possible, consider information provided by FSIS to minimize duplication of effort.

The FDA Liaison Office is the Director, Emergency Operations Center, HFC-160, (301-827-5653)

The USDA Liaison Office is the Deputy Administrator, Field Operations, Food Safety and Inspection Service (202-720-8803).
3. FSIS & AMS and EPA re: Regulatory Activities Concerning Residues of Drugs, Pesticides, and Environmental Contaminants in Foods.

4. FSIS (NE & SE Regional Offices), DE Department of Agriculture, MD Department of Agriculture, PA Department of Agriculture, VA Department of Agriculture and Consumer Services, WV Department of Agriculture Regarding Regulatory Investigations Involving Drug, Pesticide, and Industrial Chemical Residues in Animal Feeds and Meat and Poultry.

5. FSIS and GA Department of Agriculture Regarding Regulatory Investigations Involving Drug, Pesticide, and Toxic Chemical Residues in Animal Feeds and in Meat Tissues.

311.9 Science and Education Administration/USDA (SEA)

MOU with SEA Concerning Educational Programs in the Use of Animal Drugs.

312 U.S. DEPARTMENT OF COMMERCE (DOC)

312.1 Commerce (DOC)

MOU's with DOC and USDA Concerning Inspection of Industrial Fishery Products Intended for Animal Feed Use.

312.2 National Oceanic and Atmospheric Administration (NOAA) - National Marine Fisheries Service (NMFS)

MOU with:
1. NOAA/NMFS Regarding Inspection Programs for Fishery Products - The National Marine Fisheries Service (NMFS) of the National Oceanic & Atmospheric Administration (NOAA), Department of Commerce, operating under the authority of the Agriculture Marketing Act and the Fish & Wildlife Act is responsible for the development and advancement of commercial grade standards for fishery products and better health and sanitation standards in the industry and for furnishing inspection, analytical, and grading services to interested parties. The major purpose is to encourage and assist industry in improving the quality and safety of its products. This MOU outlines joint responsibilities between NOAA and FDA.

See IOM 303 for guidance on joint inspections when inspecting firms under the voluntary NMFS program.

The FDA Liaison Office is the Policy Guidance Branch, Division of Programs and Enforcement Policy, Office of Seafood, Center for Food Safety and Applied Nutrition, HFS-416 (301-436-1415).

The NMFS Liaison Office is the Seafood Inspection Program, Department of Commerce, NOAA (301-713-2355).

2. NOAA/NMFS Concerning Enforcement of Laws - Against Illegal Commerce in Molluscan Shellfish.

FDA will support NMFS Lacey Act investigations to the extent that regulatory authority and resources allow. This may include conducting food sanitation inspections of suspect shellfish shippers, reviewing interstate shipping records and obtaining affidavits to the extent possible, collecting and analyzing shellfish samples to be used as evidence of violations, and removing adulterated shellfish from the marketplace. Refer to the appropriate Cooperative Agreements manual for further discussion of this MOU.

The FDA Liaison Office is the Policy Guidance Branch, Division of Programs and Enforcement Policy, Office of Seafood, Center for Food Safety and Applied Nutrition, HFS-416 (301-436-1415).

The NMFS Liaison Office is the Seafood Inspection Program, Department of Commerce, NOAA (301-713-2355).

312.3 U.S. Patent and Trademark Office (USP&TO)(DOC)

MOU's with:
1. USP&TO/DOC Concerning Orphan Drugs.
2. USP&TO/DOC to Establish a Product's Eligibility for Patent Term Restoration.

313 DEPARTMENT OF DEFENSE (DOD)

FDA has a number of MOU's with DOD and its various elements.

313.1 DOD MOU's

1. DOD Concerning Licensure of Military Blood Banks.
2. DOD Concerning Investigational Use of Drugs, Antibiotics, Biologics, and Medical Devices by DOD.

FDA also has a number of Interagency Agreements (IAG) with DOD to include IAG with:
1. DOD Concerning FDA Responsibility for Quality Assurance of DOD Procured Drugs and Biologics.
2. DOD Regarding Testing of Tea Purchased by DOD.
3. DOD Regarding FDA Quality Assurance Responsibility for DOD Contracts for Medical Devices.

313.2 US Army Corps of Engineers (DOD)

MOU with US Army/Corps of Engineers Concerning Consumer Protection During Natural Disasters.

313.3 US Army Medical Research and Development Command (DOD)

MOU with U.S. Army Medical Research and Development Command Regarding Quality Assurance Support for Medical Material Having Military Application.

313.4 Defense Personnel Support Center (DPSC)

1. MOU with DPSC Concerning Exchange of Information Regarding Food & Cosmetic Recalls and Hazardous Food Situations.
2. The Defense Personnel Support Center purchases vast quantities of foods and drugs for use by the Armed Forces. The products are purchased on contract and must

meet standards and contract specifications to be accepted. Any products failing to meet these specifications are rejected. These are mentioned in IOM 313.1 above.

FDA under the Government-Wide Quality Assurance Program (GWQAP) makes certain inspections and furnishes information as to the capabilities of firms bidding or desiring to bid on government contracts. In areas involving GWQAP activities follow the procedures set forth in that activity. Each district has procedures to be followed in these areas, so when this type operation is involved, you will be given specific sampling or investigational assignments by your district.

Samples shall be collected only from those depots and hospitals selected in advance by the district. DOD Depot and hospital locations must notify their headquarters prior to releasing their stock. Prior to visiting a U.S. Government installation to collect samples of foods, drugs, or medical devices, districts may contact the Division of Medical Products Quality Assurance (DMPQA) (HFC-240) so that the visit can be expedited.

See IOM 407 for information regarding GWQAP samples and IOM 512.3 for information regarding GWQAP FDA 483.

313.5 Department of Navy/Bureau of Medicine and Surgery

MOU with Dept. the Navy/Bureau of Medicine and Surgery Regarding the Microwave Oven Survey.

314 DEPARTMENT OF HEALTH AND HUMAN SERVICES (HHS)

This Agency has a number of MOU's with the Department and other HHS units.

314.1 HHS MOU's

MOU with USDA and HHS Regarding General War Food Inspection.

314.2 Administration for Children, Youth and Families (ACYF)

A MOU with ACYF to Assure the Feeding Programs in Head Start Centers Conform with Federal Food Safety and Sanitation Responsibilities.

314.3 Centers for Disease Control and Prevention (CDC)

MOU with:
1.   CDC Concerning In-Vitro Diagnostics.
2.   CDC Regarding Radiation Emergencies.
3.   CDC Regarding Exchange of Information and Coordination of Actions.
Additional information is being provided here because of the close working agreement to assure the prompt exchange of information on suspected foodborne outbreaks.

Since it is essential that any suspected outbreaks be reported promptly to CDC, communicate any information

you may learn in connection with foodborne outbreaks to your supervisor as soon as possible. See IOM 910 and FMD #64 for procedures on Epidemiological Investigations Alert Reporting Procedures.

1.   Botulism Antitoxin Shipments - CDC is responsible for maintaining and shipping necessary supplies of botulinum antitoxin. When CDC makes a shipment of botulinum antitoxin, CDC will immediately, regardless of the day or time, phone the Emergency Operations (E.O.) Center, ORO, HFC-160, (301-443-1240). The E.O. contact will immediately phone the consignee district to advise them of the shipment.

2.   Outbreaks on Foreign Flag Vessels - If an outbreak involving a foreign flag vessel or a US Flag vessel with an international itinerary comes to your attention, report it to your supervisor immediately who will then report it to EMOPS (301) 443-1240. This situation falls under the jurisdiction of the Foreign Quarantine Section of the Centers for Disease Control and Prevention (CDC) Atlanta, Ga.

3.   Outbreaks Involving Interstate Conveyances - Reports of illness attributed to travel on an interstate conveyance (plane, bus, train, or vessel) are the responsibility of FDA.

When a report of illness is received, you are encouraged to share it with state and local public health officials in case they received additional illness reports. Additionally, the procedures outlined in this Subchapter are to be followed including the following:

Interviews with the ill passenger, family members and/or physician (as applicable), should be in-depth enough to hypothesize whether the carrier may be related to the illness. Factors such as time of onset of symptoms, history of eating suspect foods, and other potential exposures should be considered. The carrier should also be contacted to determine whether other reports of illness have been received. The information developed should be evaluated to determine whether further follow-up is necessary (i.e., the carrier suspect). On those carriers where a reservation system is used, the names and phone numbers of passengers should be obtained to determine if other individuals became ill. It may be necessary to contact other passengers to determine if they consumed any food or water on the trip, and if they became ill in the time period associated with the original complaint.

When a report of additional related or similar illnesses is received, immediately contact the Emergency Operations Center, ORO, HFC-160, (301) 443-1240 and relay the information. Also contact the state epidemiologist of the affected state to report the details of the illness. It may be advantageous to request assistance from them in the epidemiological investigation, particularly if patient specimens are needed to determine the cause.

Recently FDA revised the MOU between FDA and CDC regarding exchange of information and coordination of actions. This MOU provides a framework for coordination and collaborative efforts between the two agencies. It also provides the principles and procedures by which information exchanges between FDA and CDC will take place. The new memorandum supersedes the MOU between CDC and FDA dated 4/1/82. When receiving a request for information from the CDC immediately notify the Director of the Emergency Operations Center, HFC-160, (301) 443-1240 or (301) 827-5660.

"FDA and CDC agree that the following principles and procedures will govern the exchange of nonpublic information between the two agencies. Although there is no legal requirement the FDA and CDC exchange information in all cases, FDA and CDC agree that there should be a presumption in favor of full and free sharing of information between FDA and CDC. Both agencies recognize and acknowledge however that it is essential that any confidential information that is shared between FDA and CDC must be protected from unauthorized public disclosure. See e.g., 21 USC sec. 331(j); 18 USC sec. 1905; 21 CFR Parts 20 and 21; 42 CFR Parts 5 and 5b; and, 42 USC sec. 301(d). Safeguards are important to protect the interests of, among others, owners and submitters of trade secrets and confidential commercial information; patient identities and other personal privacy information; privileged and/or pre-decisional agency records; and information protected for national security reasons. Any unauthorized disclosure of shared confidential information by the agency receiving the information shall be the responsibility of that agency.

a. Routine Requests for Information:

1. The requesting agency must demonstrate, in writing, why it is necessary for it to obtain the requested information.

2. The agency receiving the request for information shall, based upon the sufficiency of the need-to-know demonstration described in section a.1. above, determine whether it is appropriate to share the requested information with the requesting agency.

3. The requesting agency agrees that:

    i. it shall limit the dissemination of shared information it receives to internal agency offices and/or individuals that have been identified in its written request and/or have a need-to-know;

    ii. agree in writing not to publicly disclose any shared information in any manner including publications and public meetings without written permission of the agency that has shared the information;

    iii. if the requesting agency receives a Freedom of Information Act (FOIA) request for the shared information, it will refer the request to the information-sharing agency; and,

    iv. it shall promptly notify the appropriate office of the information-sharing agency when there is any attempt to obtain shared information by compulsory process, including but not limited to a FOIA request, subpoena, discovery request, or litigation complaint or motion.

4. The agency that shares information with the requesting agency shall include a transmittal letter, along with any agency records exchanged, indicating the type of information.

b. Emergency Requests for Confidential Information In cases in which the requesting agency has a need to obtain certain information as soon as possible due to emergency circumstances, such as a foodborne illness outbreak, FDA and CDC may utilize the following procedures:

1. The requesting agency shall indicate orally or in writing to the agency in possession of the relevant information that it has the need to obtain certain identifiable information as soon as possible due to the existence of emergency circumstances and describe what the emergency circumstances are.

2. The requesting agency shall verbally agree to protect from unauthorized public disclosure any and all information that is shared, according to all applicable laws and regulations.

3. The existence of an actual emergency situation shall warrant, as determined by the agency in possession of the requested records, the waiver of the need-to-know demonstration and determination described above in section a1 and a2. However, once the requesting agency has obtained the information it seeks, it shall comply with those procedures set forth in section a3 above.

c. Liaison Officers

1. For FDA:
    Associate Commissioner for Regulatory Affairs
    Contact: Ellen Morrison, Director Emergency Operations Center
    Food and Drug Administration
    5600 Fishers Lane, HFC-160
    Rockville, MD 20857
    (301) 443-1240 or (301) 827-5660

2. For CDC:
    Associate Director for Science
    Dixie E. Snyder, MD
    Centers for Disease Control
    Public Health Service
    Department of Health and Human Services
    Atlanta, GA 30333
    (404) 639-7240

314.4 Health Care Financing Administration (HCFA)

MOU with HCFA Concerning Blood Banking and Transfusion Programs.

314.5 Health Services Administration (HSA)

MOU with HSA Concerning Quality Assurance for Drugs, Biologics, Chemicals and Reagents Procured by HSA.

314.6 National Center for Health Statistics (NCHS)

A MOU with NCHS Regarding Exchange of Information.

314.7 National Institute of Drug Abuse (NIDA)

MOU's with:

1. NIDA Regarding Mutual Responsibilities in Implementing the Jointly Published Narcotic Addict Treatment Regulations.

2. NIDA Concerning Cooperative Interaction in Expediting Domestic Scheduling of Drugs of Abuse.

314.8 National Institutes of Health (NIH)

MOU with:
1. NIH Regarding Anticancer Drugs.
2. NIH and USDA Regarding Importation of Biological Specimens under US/USSR Scientific Exchange Agreement.
3. NIH and APHIS Regarding the Care and Welfare of Laboratory Animals.

315 DEPARTMENT OF JUSTICE

315.1 U.S. Attorney

You may be contacted by the U.S. Attorney's office to discuss possible or pending cases or other matters pertinent to FDA. Notify your supervisor of these contacts. You may be accompanied by your supervisor or a compliance officer.

During any discussion with the U.S. Attorney, inform him that you are qualified to report the facts of whatever case or item being discussed, but inform him that you are a fact witness only and not qualified as an "expert".

315.2 Drug Enforcement Administration (DEA) (Formerly: Bureau of Narcotics)

Memorandum of Agreement, FDA-DEA Field Liaison Policy Guide MOU's with:
1. DEA Regarding Narcotic Treatment Programs.
2. DEA Regarding Liaison Activities.
Informal working relationships which had existed between FDA and DEA have been formalized by mutual agreement between the two agencies.

This agreement provides for files to be made mutually available. If you have any occasion to review DEA files, properly identify yourself to the DEA office wherein the files are located.

If joint inspections are to be made, arrangements will be handled by your supervisor. Do not request joint inspection without prior clearance.

Should you start an Establishment Inspection of a firm and discover a DEA agent is already present, immediately contact him/her. Any conflict of dual presence should be discussed and reconciled. It may be possible to terminate your visit if the DEA agent is obtaining the same information you were obtaining since it will be available from him or her office.

This Memorandum of Agreement provides:
1. Conditions Observed by DEA Agents - DEA agents during their audits of firms may observe conditions of prime interest to FDA. Any of the following conditions observed by an agent will be transmitted to the appropriate FDA District Office by DEA:
    (a) counterfeiting of drugs.
    (b) failure to register as a manufacturer, repacker, or relabeler of drugs.
    (c) presence of improperly labeled, unidentified drugs or other observable deviations of GMPs.
    (d) evidence of contamination of drugs by water or fire damage, foreign materials in bulk containers, or other observable contamination or damage.
2. Conditions Observed by FDA Personnel - During inspections or investigations you may observe conditions of prime interest to DEA. If you observe any of the following conditions report them to your supervisor for transmission to appropriate DEA Field Offices:
    (a) the manufacture or distribution of controlled drugs when there is reason to suspect that the drugs may be intended for diversion to the illicit market.
    (b) producers and wholesalers of controlled drugs who are not registered.
    (c) unusual stock inventories of controlled drugs.
    (d) unusual special order items; e.g., amphetamine "footballs".
    (e) unusual patterns of purchase or distribution of controlled drugs.
    (f) counterfeiting of drugs.

315.3 Federal Bureau of Investigation (FBI)

The FBI, USDA and FDA are authorized to investigate reported tampering of FDA regulated consumer products under the Federal Anti-Tampering Act (FATA), Title 18, USC, Section 1365. In most cases, FDA's authority for such investigations is also found in the FD&C Act.

USDA and the FBI share enforcement of the FATA with FDA as described below:
1. FBI Responsibility - FDA understands that the FBI's primary response in FATA matters will be to investigate particularly those cases that involve a serious threat to human life or if a death has occurred. The FBI will also investigate FATA matters involving threatened tamperings, and actual or threatened tamperings coupled with an extortion demand.

The FBI will rely on FDA to determine if tampering with FDA products has occurred.
2. USDA Responsibility - The USDA will investigate and interact with the FBI on tamperings with products regulated by USDA.

For complete information regarding FBI/FDA actions under FATA, see IOM 970.

316 DEPARTMENT OF LABOR: OCCUPATIONAL SAFETY AND HEALTH ADMINISTRATION (OSHA)

1. The MOU with OSHA Concerns Standards for Electronic Product Radiation.
2. IAG's with OSHA are:
    a. OSHA, CPSC, and EPA Relating to the Regulation of Toxic and Hazardous Substances.
    b. OSHA, CPSC, and EPA Supplemental IAG.

317 DEPARTMENT OF TRANSPORTATION & FEDERAL AVIATION ADMINISTRATION (FAA)

The IAG with FAA Concerns Inspection of Food Service at National Airport.

318   TREASURY DEPARTMENT

Many different agencies operate under the direction of this department. These include the Secret Service, Customs, Service, Internal Revenue Service, and the Bureau of Alcohol, Tobacco, and Firearms. Agreements and MOU's with the Treasury Department will be discussed below.

318.1 Bureau of Alcohol, Tobacco, and Firearms (BATF)

MOU with BATF to Delineate the Enforcement Responsibilities of Each Agency with Respect to Alcoholic Beverages as below.

This MOU confirms that BATF is responsible for testing alcoholic beverages to determine the extent of an adulteration problem and that when FDA learns or is advised that an alcoholic beverage is or may be adulterated, FDA will contact BATF. FDA will provide laboratory assistance and health hazard evaluations, at BATF request. BATF also has responsibility for alcoholic beverage labeling, but does not have authority over wine beverages having less than 7% alcohol by volume (such as most wine coolers).

Based on this MOU, districts should refer all complaints involving alcoholic beverages (distilled spirits, wines, and malt beverage products except the wine beverages mentioned above) to BATF, in a manner similar to that already in effect for referring complaints about meat and poultry to USDA. When a complaint is received from a consumer, it should be entered into FACTS with the disposition "referred to other Federal agency." If the complainant is reporting a suspected tampering, it should be referred to the home district and OCI for follow-up. In all cases, a copy of the FACTS consumer complaint report should be forwarded to the FDA liaison officer with BATF at HFS-301 to facilitate appropriate follow-up between the two agencies at the headquarters level.

The FDA Liaison Officer is the Director, Office of Compliance, Center for Food Safety and Applied Nutrition, HFS-600, (301-436-2359).

The ATF Liaison Office is the Special Programs Branch, (202) 927-8020.

A hard copy of the complaint should also be faxed to the closest BATF Field Office at the address listed below (as of 12/02):

3003 North Central Ave.
Suite 1010
Phoenix, AZ 85012
Tel. (602) 776-5400
Fax (602) 776-5429

350 S. Figueroa St.
Suite 800
Los Angeles, CA 90071
Tel. (213) 894-4812
Fax (213) 894-0105

221 Main Street, 11th Fl.
San Francisco, CA 94105
Tel. (415) 744-7001
Fax (415) 744-9443

607 14th St. NW, Ste. 620
Washington, D.C. 20005
Tel. (202) 927-8810
Fax (202) 927-4024

5225 NW 87th Ave., Ste. 300
Miami, FL 33178
Tel. (305) 597-4800
Fax (305) 597-4797

501 East Polk Street
Suite 700
Tampa, FL 33602
Tel. (813) 228-2021
Fax (813) 228-2111

2600 Century Parkway
Atlanta, GA 30345-3104
Tel. (404) 679-5170
Fax (404) 679-5134

300 South Riverside Plaza
Suite 350 South
Chicago, IL 60608
Tel. (312) 353-6935
Fax (312) 353-7668

600 Martin L. King, Jr. Place
Suite 322
Louisville, KY 40202
Tel. (502) 582-5211
Fax (502) 582-5634

Heritage Place, Ste. 1008
111 Veterans Boulevard
Metairie, LA 70005
Tel. (504) 841-7000
Fax (504) 841-7039

Federal Building
10 Causeway St., Rm. 253
Boston, MA 02222-1047
Tel. (617) 565-7042
Fax (617) 565-7003

G H Fallon Building
31 Hopkins Plaza, 5th Fl.
Baltimore, MD 21201-2825
Tel. (410) 779-1700
Fax (410) 779-1701

1155 Brewery Park Blvd., Suite 300
Detroit, MI 48207-2602
Tel. (313) 393-6000
Fax (313) 393-6054

2600 Grand Ave., Ste. 200
Kansas City, MO 64108
Tel. (816) 421-3440
Fax (816) 421-6511

1870 Minn. World Trade Ctr.
30 East Seventh Street
St. Paul, MN 55101
Tel. (651) 290-3092
Fax (651) 290-3363

6701 Carmel Road, Ste. 200
Charlotte, NC 28226
Tel. (704) 716-1800
Fax (704) 716-1801

241 37th Street
Brooklyn, NY 11232
Tel. (718) 650-4000
Fax (718) 650-4001

37 West Broad St., Ste. 200
Columbus, OH 43215
Tel. (614) 469-5303
Fax (614) 469-5308

US Customhouse, Rm. 607
2nd & Chestnut Sts.
Philadelphia, PA 19106
Tel. (215) 717-4700
Fax (215) 717-4701

5300 Maryland Way
Ste 200
Brentwood, TN 37027
Tel. (615) 565-1400
Fax (615) 565-1401

1114 Commerce Street
Ste 303
Dallas, TX 75242
Tel. (469) 227-4300
Fax (469) 227-4302 (4315)

15355 Vantage Pkwy West
Suite 200
Houston, TX 77032
Tel. (281) 449-2073
Fax (281) 449-2049

915 2nd Ave., Rm. 790
Jackson Federal Building
Seattle, WA 98174
Tel. (206) 220-6440
Fax (206) 220-6446

A copy of the complaint should also be forwarded to the FDA liaison officer with BATF at HFS-301 to facilitate

appropriate follow-up between the two agencies at the headquarters levels.

The FDA Liaison Office is the Director, Office of Field Programs, Center for Food Safety and Applied Nutrition, HFS-600 (202-205-4187).

The ATF Liaison Office is the Special Programs Branch (202-927-8020).

318.2 U.S. Customs Service

MOU with:

1. Customs Service and the FDA Regarding Identifying Roles and Authority Concerning Electronic Products.

2. Customs Service to Establish a Working Relationship for Cooperative Enforcement.

3. Customs Services Regarding the Needs of the Trading Public in Expediting the Collection, Processing and the Use of Import Information.

318.3 Internal Revenue Service (IRS)

MOU with IRS Concerning Legal Actions Taken by FDA Against Alcoholic Beverage Firms for Under filling of Containers.

The FDA Liaison Office is the Division of Enforcement, Office of Field Programs, Center for Food Safety and Applied Nutrition, HFS-605 (202-205-5332).

The ATF Liaison Office is the Chief, Industry Compliance Division (202-927-8100).

318.4 Secret Service

The Secret Service operates under the Treasury Department and is charged with the responsibility of protecting the President of the United States and certain other prominent persons. They also enforce the laws and regulations relating to currency, coins, and obligations and securities of the U.S. and foreign governments.

Authority for Secret Service to request FDA assistance, and for FDA to respond, is derived from the "Presidential Protection Assistance Act of 1976", P.L. 94-524 (90 Stat. 2475-7), Sections 1-10. Section six states in part:

"Executive Departments and Executive Agencies shall assist the Secret Service in the performance of its duties by providing services, equipment, and facilities on a temporary and reimbursable basis when requested by the Director and on a permanent and reimbursable basis upon advance written request of the Director; except that the DOD and the Coast Guard shall provide such assistance on a temporary basis without reimbursement when assisting the Secret Service in its duties directly related to the protection of the President or the Vice President or other officer immediately next in order of succession to the office of the President."

Note: At the present time the Agency is not claiming reimbursement from Secret Service until a study of total costs of our support function is completed.

FDA's authority for entry and inspection is derived from Secret Service authority and its request for FDA assistance. When called upon by the Secret Service to assist with a food service function, FDA's response is that of an advisor. Authority for decisions regarding food and beverages to be consumed by protectees is retained by the Secret Service.

Note: Do Not issue a Notice of Inspection - FDA 482 unless the investigation evolves into the collection of a sample for the enforcement of the FD&C Act. You are in the firm under the Secret Service authority.

FDA may initiate action against products encountered which are suspected of being in violation of the FD&C Act or the FPLA.

a. Liaison - The Secret Service and FDA have an arrangement whereby FDA district officials are alerted by the Secret Service when the President, Vice President or other Protectees are to visit their areas and are to consume prepared meals and Secret Service wants the food service facilities inspected. This is to assure that proper precautions are taken if any meals are to be consumed by these individuals during the stay.

If you are alerted by Secret Service Agents that the President, Vice President or other protectees will visit the area, immediately advise your supervisor in person or by telephone. Since the lead time is often short, the district must be alerted at once so proper arrangements can be made for issuance of inspectional or investigational assignments. Because of security procedures you are not to contact the Secret Service concerning protectee travel prior to notification by them even though you may hear from other sources that a protectee is to visit your area.

As part of this arrangement FDA supplies current rosters, office addresses, and telephone numbers of Regional Food and Drug Directors, District Directors, Station Chiefs, and Residents to the Secret Service Headquarters for dissemination to their field agents.

b. Definitions:

1. Advanced Prepared Food means food that was prepared on location at the food service establishment prior to arrival of the Lead Investigator.

2. Food Service Function means a public event where food will be provided to a protectee.

3. Lead Advance Agent means the Secret Service Agent in charge of all security arrangements. This person is responsible for all sites to be visited by the protectee, and is a representative of the Office of Protective Operations (Secret Service Headquarters).

4. Lead Investigator means the FDA person designated by the FDA district/region to coordinate the investigational activities at the site of a food service function.

5. Person-in-Charge means the available person in the food service establishment authorized to make necessary changes/decisions such as the general manager, executive chef, banquet manager, caterer's representative or other management person.

6. Pre-prepared Food means potentially hazardous food that was received at the food service establishment in a prepared form. Examples would include chicken salad, liver pate, gefilte fish, hors d'oeuvres, etc. which were prepared at another location, and then transported to the food service establishment providing food for the event.

7. Protectee means any person eligible to receive the protection authorized by law.

8. Protective Detail means a team of Secret Service agents responsible for security surrounding public events to be attended by a protectee during a trip. Protective details are assigned and coordinated by Secret Service Headquarters, but may include Secret Service field representatives.

9. District Contact means the Director, Investigations Branch.

10. Site Advance Agent means the Secret Service person responsible for security arrangements at a specific site to be visited by the protectee. This person is part of the protective detail headed by the Lead Advance Agent. Note: the term Site Advance Agent will include any agent designated by the Site Advance Agent to be the contact with the FDA Lead Investigator.

11. Support Personnel means FDA persons deemed necessary by FDA in order to properly inspect a food service function.

c. Purpose - FDA's primary purpose in support of Secret Service is to minimize the possibility of the protectee becoming ill from a food intoxication or foodborne infection resulting from inadequate knowledge of food safety requirements by food service personnel, inadequate facilities, improper operating procedures, or carelessness. FDA is further concerned that food have no visible signs of filth, and that it is prepared in a clean environment.

FDA personnel are not trained to detect deliberate attempts to harm persons by the addition of poisonous or toxic substances to food. The Secret Service retains responsibility for matters involving criminal intent. However, FDA personnel should immediately report to the Site Advance Agent peculiar behavior or suspicious conditions observed during their investigation.

d. Criteria For Requesting FDA Assistance - The decision to request FDA assistance is made by Secret Service Office of Protective Operations (Headquarters). FDA has provided certain criteria to aid Secret Service in determining how they might derive maximum benefit from FDA. Regardless what criteria are used, FDA should always respond to Secret Service requests for assistance. Secret Service considers factors other than the FDA supplied criteria in making its judgment regarding requests for assistance.

e. Scope of Investigation - The focus of the FDA investigation should be on the menu items that the protectee will be served, or from which the protectee will make a selection. Food, facilities, personnel, procedures, etc. are only considered by FDA as they relate to the specific food and beverage items which may be consumed by the protectee. Do not conduct a traditional regulatory type food service inspection. The Food Service EIR (FDA 2420) will not normally be part of the report prepared following this special investigation. State/local regulatory authorities have jurisdiction over food establishments, and have a primary responsibility for public health protection of the general public or participating members or guests of the organization sponsoring the event.

f. Interagency Cooperation - Upon contact by Secret Service and after contacting your supervisor to apprise district management of the Secret Service request, the appropriate state/local regulatory authority should be contacted and encouraged to participate prior to and during the food service function. These officials may offer invaluable assistance because of their familiarity with the establishment and because of their regulation over the establishment on a long-term basis.

g.   District Contact - The district contact should receive Secret Service requests for assistance and initiate the FDA response. If a resident post is contacted directly for assistance, immediately contact your supervisor who will notify the director investigations branch. The director investigations branch will designate the lead investigator and arrange for assignment of support personnel and equipment as required. The lead investigator could be on district or region staff according to district/region policy.

h.   Lead Investigator Qualifications - The best suited investigator (criteria optional) assigned to coordinate investigation of these food service functions should be one who:

1.   possesses OPM "Critical Sensitive" security clearance.

2.   is standardized in the use of the FDA Food Code.

3.   is experienced in Secret Service food service functions, if possible. New personnel should accompany experienced personnel before being assigned as Lead Investigator, if at all possible.

4.   is able and authorized to quickly mobilize an investigational team (FDA/State/Local).

5.   is able and authorized to make quick decisions on important food protection/sanitation questions.

6.   has a background in food microbiology.

i.   Steps for Conducting a Special Secret Service Investigation (District Contact/Lead Investigator).

1.   Verify the call with the Secret Service and obtain from them:

(a) information about the site advance agent with whom FDA is to coordinate its activities. This should include the name(s) of agent(s) assigned, location(s) and telephone number(s).

(b) information about the firm(s) providing food for the food service function, to include:

(1) names of persons-in-charge of food service establishment and caterers.

(2) telephone numbers.

(3) addresses of firm(s).

(4) location where food service function will be held (if different).

(5) date of function.

(6) time of food events during function.

2.   obtain through means prearranged and agreed upon by FDA district/region management:

(a) FDA support personnel needed.

(b) equipment required to conduct special investigation.

3.   contact the person-in-charge at the facility to:

(a) introduce the lead investigator.

(b) advise of purpose and scope of special investigation.

(c) arrange for personal interview to discuss

menu, food preparation schedule and history (times/specific locations in establishment), and any intended use of pre-prepared foods.

(d) obtain telephone number(s) at the site(s) where FDA lead investigator may be reached while on location.

4.   contact state and local regulatory agencies responsible for retail food protection and sanitation. Request participation by inspectional personnel of the local office which provides routine inspectional coverage of the facility where the food service function is being held.

5.   Meet with person-in-charge on location, in order to:

(a) be introduced to other key employees who have responsibility for the target meal or kitchen facilities, i.e. banquet manager, executive chef, maintenance supervisor, etc.

(b) Inform person-in-charge of the names of other FDA, state, or local regulatory personnel to be involved.

(c) obtain the use of an area within the establishment that will become an FDA base of operations. The location should have convenient access to a telephone, but may not be necessary for small functions.

6.   coordinate with Secret Service command post on location, in order to:

(a) inform site advance agent of the names of other FDA, state or local regulatory personnel to be involved.

(b) determine method for final selection of specific meal(s) to be served to protectee(s).

7.   carry out investigation by:

(a) basing judgments on the provisions of the FDA Food Code. In consideration of food sources, food protection, personnel, food equipment/utensils, water, waste disposal, vermin control, storage and use of toxic materials, and other code items as they relate to the food items to be served to the protectee.

(b) taking the history of each item on the menu to be served the protectee. The history for each potentially hazardous food (including advance prepared and pre-prepared Food) must be detailed. Include timetables for preparation and storage, and the names of specific employees involved in its preparation. This will immediately establish parameters needed for FDA to complete a comprehensive, but well focused investigation (See IOM Exhibit 310-A for a chart format to report the history of each item of food served. Copy this Exhibit for use as you see fit.). It is suggested that the lead investigator arrange to have coverage by a regulatory official during the period of meal selection and service.

(c) negotiating with the person-in-charge for any modifications, substitutions, or other changes necessary to achieve the "Purpose" as stated in IOM 318.4 above. Though every effort should be made by the lead investigator to help the person-in-charge and the Secret Service in their efforts to assure that preparation and arrangements for the food service function flow smoothly and efficiently, FDA personnel must be aware that their responsibility is for assuring that all prudent steps have been taken to minimize the risk of foodborne illness to the protectee.

8. Sampling - Samples shall be collected at the discretion of the lead investigator. Two types of samples should be considered.

(a) Typical Meal - In the unlikely event that a protectee (or others) becomes acutely or seriously ill during the hours following a food service function, it could be very helpful to have samples of meals served for analysis. Should this happen, FDA's response should be coordinated with the FDA Emergency Operations Center at 301-827-5653 or 301-443-1240.

FDA under Secret Service authority should request that two complete meals, including beverages, be randomly selected from the meals being served to the head table. This selection should be made by the same person and at the same time head table meals are selected.

If a reception is a planned part of the event, an example of each type of hors d'oeuvres should also be retained.

These meals should be kept intact, covered, and retained under refrigeration by the person-in-charge for 72 hours following the event. Cost of the meals may, at the establishment's option, be invoiced to the organization sponsoring the food service function.

Note: Examples of food items selected in this manner cannot be considered a representative sample of food offered at the function. However, such food examples could be an aid to the FBI and food regulatory personnel, should a suspected food related illness occur.

(b) Food Samples - Occasionally, the lead investigator may elect to collect official samples of a food product because of a selected violation of the FD&C Act or for some other reason. When this is done, issue an FDA 482, Notice of Inspection.

In these cases, samples should be collected in accordance with procedures outline in IOM Chapter 4.

j.   Reporting

1. Verbal Report - The lead investigator shall report to the site advance agent in person or by telephone.

(a) Significant adverse findings should be immediately reported to the site advance agent during the investigation, if resolution of the finding has the potential for disrupting the smooth flow of the food service function.

(b) At the conclusion of the investigation, and prior to leaving the location, notify the site advance agent of FDA conclusions and recommendations. One of the following responses would be normal:

(1) no restrictions recommended. Protectee should be permitted to consume any food or beverage being offered.

(2) a recommendation that the protectee be advised that one or more specifically named items available should not be selected or consumed.

(3) in unusual cases, it may be necessary to recommend that the protectee not eat food prepared for the event, or not drink the water provided.

2. Narrative Report - Following each special investigation conducted for the Secret Service, a narrative report shall be submitted as directed in the Field Reporting Requirements Section of the Retail Food Protection - Federal Compliance Program.

The report is for FDA's internal use and should be a chronological accounting beginning with how and when the Secret Service request was received and concluding with recommendations tendered to the Secret Service, and any F/U actions recommended to or planned by participating State/local food protection agencies.

The narrative report should include time frames, contact persons, a copy of the menu, a description of the investigational process used, adverse findings, corrective steps taken, the selection and retention of typical meals, and how & why official samples (if any) were collected and submitted, and a discussion of other matters of significance in your opinion.

Each narrative report must contain:

(a)   total time on location.

(b)   total time of inspection including, time on location and time necessary for making arrangements in advance, and preparation and submission of required reports. It does not include travel time.

(c)   total travel time and mileage.

319   DEPARTMENT OF VETERANS AFFAIRS VETERANS ADMINISTRATION (VA)

MOU with the VA are:

1.   VA Concerning Exchange of Medical Device Experience Data.

2.   VA Concerning Communications and Cooperation Regarding Clinical Research with Investigational New Drugs and Devices, Including Biologicals.

IAG's with the VA are:

1.   VA Concerning FDA Responsibility for Quality Assurance for Drugs, Biologicals, Chemicals and Reagents Procured by VA.

2.   VA Regarding FDA Quality Assurance Responsibility for VA Contracts for Medical Devices.

320   CONSUMER PRODUCT SAFETY COMMISSION (CPSC)

MOU's with CPSC are:

1.   CPSC Concerning CPSC Use of FDA Documents.

2.   CPSC Regarding Jurisdiction with Respect to Food, Food Containers, and Food Related Articles and Equipment.

IAG's with CPSC are:

1.   CPSC, EPA, and OSHA Relating to the Regulation of Toxic and Hazardous Substances.

2.   Supplement Agreement CPSC, EPA, and OSHA.

321   ENVIRONMENTAL PROTECTION AGENCY (EPA)

The EPA administers many Acts one of them is the National Environmental Protection Act (NEPA). FDA must be guided by this Act when assisting in voluntary destructions, disposal of laboratory wastes, etc.

Do not condone the wanton pollution of waterways, uncontrolled burning, the creation of a public nuisance or other questionable disposal practices. Note that certain products should not be disposed of in a conventional manner (e.g.: sanitary landfill, flushing down the drain, etc.). In particular, certain products that have been banned in the past (chloroform, methapyrilene, hexachlorophene, PCB, etc.), are classified by EPA as hazardous and toxic substances and may require a special method of disposal by a licensed hazardous disposal facility. Any possible hazardous or toxic substance (carcinogen, mutagen, etc.) should not be disposed of without prior consultation by the firm with the U.S. Environmental Protection Agency and/or the regulating state authority. Refer to 21 CFR 25 and the National Environmental Protection Act for guidance regarding the environmental impact of voluntary destructions.

321.1 EPA MOU'S

MOU's with:

1.   EPA Regarding Matters of Mutual Responsibility Under Federal FD&C Act and Federal Insecticide, Fungicide and Rodenticide Act.

2.   EPA Regarding Potable Water on Interstate Conveyances.

The EPA administers a regulatory program in this area but FDA has the responsibility of notifying the ICC headquarters when problems are found. FDA will, if deemed appropriate include conveyances in their inspection/monitoring schedule. Both agencies will coordinate enforcement efforts, thereby avoiding duplication of efforts.

3.   EPA Concerning Control of Drinking Water.

FDA has responsibility for water, and substances in water, used in food and for food processing and bottled drinking water.

FDA will take appropriate regulatory action to control bottled drinking water and water and substances in water, used in food and for food processing.

The FDA Liaison Office is the Division of Programs and Enforcement Policy, Office of Plant and Dairy Foods and Beverages, Center for Food Safety and Applied Nutrition, HFS-305 (301-436-1400).

The EPA Liaison Office is the Drinking Water Technologies Branch, Drinking Water Standards Division (202-260-3022).

4.   EPA Regarding a Cooperative Research Program in Connection with the Development of Neurotoxicity Risk Assessment Procedures.

5.   EPA and USDA (FSIS & AMS) re: Regulatory Activities Concerning Residues of Drugs, Pesticides, and Environmental Contaminants in Foods.

IAG's with EPA are as follows:

1.   EPA, CPSC, and OSHA Relating to the Regulation of Toxic & Hazardous Substances.

2.   Supplement Agreement to IAG Between FDA, EPA, CPSC, and OSHA.

3.   EPA, Office of Pesticides and Toxic Substances regarding auditing of health related toxicity test reports and laboratory records.

If the labeling of articles for control of fleas and ticks for use on pets and other animals contains claims for conditions other than fleas and other external parasites, they may be drugs subject to regulation by FDA. FDA has CPG 7125.28 (641.00) covering products for Control of Fleas and Ticks Containing a Pesticide (3/95). Products containing a pesticide that are generally the responsibility of EPA contain an EPA registration number in the labeling. There is an MOU between FDA and EPA (CPG 7155b.08) to cover this. However, you may want to consult the Center for Veterinary Medicine, Division of Compliance, Gloria J. Dunnavan, Director (301-827-1168) with any questions on shared responsibilities and for assistance with label review.

322   AGENCY FOR TOXIC SUBSTANCES AND DISEASE REGISTRY (ATSDR)

The ATSDR (formerly CDC Superfund) staff has been designated as the lead agency for the DHHS response to chemical emergencies. The CDC ATSDR Public Health Advisors are located at the EPA Regional Offices. These advisors would not only alert your office of chemical emergencies but would be invaluable in answering questions concerning the severity of the problem and discussing protective measures. Under no circumstances, are FDA employees to enter areas designated as hazardous. If it is necessary to contact ATSDR employees, their addresses and phone numbers are listed below:

AGENCY FOR TOXIC SUBSTANCES AND DISEASE REGISTRY (FORMERLY KNOWN AS SUPERFUND)

Louise A. House
EPA Region I
ATSDR
EPA Bldg
60 Westview St.
Lexington, MA 02173
(617) 860-4314

Arthur Black
EPA Region II
Rm 3137C
26 Federal Plaza
New York, NY 10278
(212) 264-7662

Charles J. Walters
EPA Region III
841 Chestnut Bldg
Philadelphia, PA
19106
(215) 597-7291
(303) 294-1063

Robert E. Safay
Air & Waste Mgmt Div.
Region IV
345 Courtland St.
Atlanta, GA 30365
(404) 347-1847

Louise A. Fabinski
Emerg. & Remedial Br.
EPA Region V (M-SHS-6)
77 W. Jackson Blvd
Chicago, IL 60604
(312) 886-0840

George Pettigrew
EPA Region VI (6HE)
1445 Ross Ave.
Dallas, TX 75202
(214) 655-8361

Denise Jordan-Izaguirre
EPA Region VII
Waste Management Branch
726 Minnesota Ave
Kansas City KS 66101
(913) 551-7692

Glenn J. Tucker
ATSDR Region VIII (8HWM-FF)
Waste Management Div.
Suite 500
999 18th St.
Denver, CO 80202

William Q. Nelson
ATSDR Region IX
75 Hawthorne St
Rm 09261
San Francisco, CA 94105
(415) 744-2194

George Thomas
EPA Region X (MSHW113)
1200 6th Ave.
Seattle, WA 98101
(206) 553-2113

Some situations where ATSDR guidance is indicated are mentioned below.

In wrecks the physical impact usually causes most damage. Toxic items in the same load, this is illegal, may rupture and add to the contamination. In train wrecks, other railcars loaded with chemicals, oils or other contaminating materials may rupture and contaminate food and drug products in otherwise undamaged cars. Removal of the wreckage may cause further physical damage or chemical contamination. Exposure to weather may also adversely affect the products.

Do not overlook the possibility that runoff of toxic chemicals from wrecked and ruptured cars may contaminate adjacent or nearby streams supplying water to downstream firms under FDA jurisdiction.

Chemical spills occurring on land or water can pose a serious threat to the environment and contaminate FDA regulated products both directly and indirectly.

Hazardous waste sites also pose a hazard to the immediate environment, as well as offsite, if runoff contaminates nearby surface waters or if leachate contaminates ground water supplies.

323　FEDERAL TRADE COMMISSION (FTC)

The MOU with FTC Concerns Exchange of Information.

324　GENERAL SERVICES ADMINISTRATION

The IAG with GSA regarding food service sanitation in GSA buildings is no longer in force.

325　U.S. NUCLEAR REGULATORY COMMISSION (NRC)

The U.S. Nuclear Regulatory Commission and the U.S. Department of Health and Human Services, Food and Drug Administration signed a MOU on August 26, 1993 (FR Vol. 58, No. 172, 09/08/93, 47300-47303). The purpose of the MOU is to coordinate existing NRC and FDA regulatory programs for medical devices (including utilization facilities used for medical therapy), drugs, and biological products utilizing byproduct, source, or special nuclear material regulated under the Atomic Energy Act of 1954, as amended. These regulatory programs include activities for evaluating and authorizing the manufacture, sale, distribution, licensing, and labeled intended use of such products.

Medical devices affected by this MOU include, but are not limited to: in vitro diagnostic kits (radioimmunoassay); utilization facilities licensed to perform medical therapy; and teletherapy and brachytherapy sources, systems, and accessory devices. Biologicals include, but are not limited to, licensed in vitro diagnostic kits (radioimmunoassay), and certain radiolabeled biologics for in-vivo use. Drugs include all those that contain byproduct, source, or special nuclear material.

The organizations in FDA that are principally responsible for regulating these products are CDRH, CDER, and CBER.

The FDA Liaison Offices are the Center for Devices and Radiological Health, Director, Office of Compliance, HFZ-300 (301-594-4692), Center for Drug Evaluation and Research, Director, Office of Compliance, HFD-300 (301-594-0054), and the Center for Biologic Evaluation and Research, Director, Office of Compliance and Biologics Quality, HFM-600 (301-827-6190).

The NRC Liaison Office is the Director, Office of Nuclear Material Safety and Safeguards (301-504-3352).

326　U.S. POSTAL SERVICE

FDA cooperates with postal authorities in areas of mutual concern. If contacted by postal authorities, extend courtesy and cooperation. In any doubtful situation or incidents involving excessive expenditure of time and/or resources, check with your supervisor.

a.　Change of Address Information - At times during an investigation or inspection it may become necessary to visit local post offices to obtain new or forwarding addresses of individuals involved.

Procedure:

1.　Introduce yourself and display your credentials to the local P.O. clerk or official.

2.　State the information desired.

3.　Present the clerk or official on duty the statement in writing on FDA letterhead using the wording from IOM Exhibit 310-B which may be reproduced or typed on district letterhead.

4.　If you are still refused information or delayed in any manner, contact the nearest U.S. Postal Inspector to handle the matter.

5.　At this time there is no charge for providing this information to a Federal Agency. The regulation promulgating a fee has been stayed.

b.　Postal Box Information - At times during an investigation or inspection it will become necessary to obtain the name and address of the holder of a postal box (PO Box).

Procedure:

1.　Introduce yourself and display credentials to the local P.O. clerk or official.

2.　State the information you desire.

3.　Present the clerk or official the statement in writing on FDA letterhead using the wording from IOM Exhibit 310-B which may be reproduced or typed on district letterhead.

4.　At this time there is no charge for providing this information to a Federal Agency. The regulation promulgating a fee has been stayed.

5.　If you are still refused the information or are delayed in any manner, contact the nearest U.S. Postal Inspector to handle the matter.

The authority for providing forwarding address information to government agencies is defined in 39 CFR 265.6(d)(4)(i) which states as follows:

(4) Exceptions. Except as otherwise provided in these regulations, names or addresses of postal customers will be furnished only as follows:

(i) To a federal, state, or local government agency upon prior written certification that the information is required for the performance of its duties.

Additionally, 39 CFR 265.6(d)(6) may apply: Address verification. The address of a postal customer will be verified at the request of a federal, state, or local government agency.

327   FIRM LOCATIONS

Many firms FDA is required to inspect are difficult to locate, including growers, farms, and other types of operations in rural areas. Directions to these firms can be obtained from many sources, including:

1.   Visits to Post Offices.
2.   If the envelope has a postal meter number and no return address, check with the USPS to determine the name of the firm or holder of that "PB Meter" number.
3.   Visits to local health departments.
4.   Visits to county extension services.
5.   Visits to USDA - Agricultural Stabilization and Conservation Offices of Soil Conservation Service Offices.

Many of these offices have maps of the counties, municipalities, etc. which can be purchased or copied and used with their guidance to find the firms.

After the directions are obtained or the maps copied, copies of the maps with directions can be included in the factory jacket.

328   FEDERAL FOOD SAFETY COALITION

In August, 1999, FDA began an interagency Federal Food Safety Coalition with other federal agencies in an effort to focus on food protection of high-risk populations. The group's objective is to promote the development of effective public health protection systems for food safety within federal programs using the FDA Model Food Code, emphasizing foodborne illness interventions, to reduce the occurrence of the five leading illness risk factors. A formal MOU or partnership has not yet been developed. The initial participating agencies are as follows:

- Dept. of Veterans Affairs, Veterans Health Admin.
- United States Department of Agriculture, Food and Nutrition Service: School Lunch Program, WIC Program, and Infant Formula Program
- Dept. of Justice, Bureau of Prisons
- Dept. of Health and Human Services:
  - Head Start Program
  - Administration on Aging
  - Indian Health Services
  - Health Care Financing Administration
  - Food and Drug Administration, Center for Food Safety and Applied Nutrition

SUBCHAPTER 330 - STATE OPERATIONAL AUTHORITY

331   STATE OPERATIONAL AUTHORITY

Establishment Inspections - All state and local officials have some type of jurisdiction over the food and drug establishments located within their state or local boundaries, regardless of the interstate movement or origin of the products involved. Some states divide the responsibility for food, drugs, etc., among the various agencies within the state. See IOM 333.

Samples - All state laws provide authority to collect samples of food, drug, and other products within the state.

Embargoes - FDA personnel, except in certain situations involving meat, poultry products, egg products and devices do not have embargo or detention powers (See IOM 311.2, 708, and 750).

State laws empower their inspectors to place an immediate embargo on products that are, or are suspected of being, adulterated or misbranded or otherwise in violation of their laws. As a cooperative measure most state agencies will have their inspectors place an embargo at the request of an FDA representative. Do not routinely request such embargo. District assignments may include instructions relative to cooperative embargoes.

In all instances, exercise care in requesting embargoes. The cooperating officials must be notified promptly of the final FDA action on the lot so that records may be updated, required releases issued, and inordinately long holding time prevented.

Embargoes should be considered not as a mere convenience to the Food and Drug Administration but as an important and effective cooperation measure to be applied only when circumstances indicate such action.

Disaster Operations - Following major disasters, FDA regional directors and district directors will arrange for close cooperation with local and state food and drug officials, Health Departments, the Public Health Service and other agencies engaged in comparable work. When requested to do so, FDA district personnel will assist local and state officials during such emergencies. At such times FDA personnel may be temporarily commissioned by local or state authorities and provided the authority to place embargoes (See IOM 945.1).

331.1 FDA Personnel with State Authority

Certain states have designated selected FDA employees as special representatives or agents of the particular state agency. In these cases, they have furnished the FDA individuals with official state credentials. The FDA representatives given this authority will receive instructions and training, by their district, in the proper exercise of the powers conferred on them and must operate within the guidelines established by their district to monitor this authority. This is particularly important whenever state embargo powers may be used.

331.2 Joint Inspections

Joint inspections with state or local inspectors are arranged by the district supervisory personnel. Joint inspections are conducted in the same manner as inspections by FDA alone and findings are discussed with the accompanying inspector. The cooperating inspector may wish to take action against the merchandise or the firm under pertinent local or state laws.

331.3 FDA Commissioned State Personnel

Qualified state regulatory officials may be commissioned to conduct examinations, inspections, investigations, collect samples and to copy and verify records under the Federal Food, Drug, and Cosmetic Act. For additional information, please see Chapter 3 of the Regulatory Procedures Manual (RPM).

332 STATE MEMORANDA OF UNDERSTANDING

The FDA has entered into agreements with various state and local agencies covering a variety of issues and work sharing agreements. At the present time not all the states have entered into agreements with FDA. The following is a alphabetical listing of current MOU's for states, the District of Columbia, and the Commonwealth of Puerto Rico. Complete text of the MOU's is in Federal Cooperative Agreements Manual.

332.1 Alabama (AL)

MOU with AL Department of Public Health Regarding Inspections, Investigations, and Analytical Findings Related to Food Firms. (6/23/92)

332.2 Arizona (AZ)

MOU with AZ Department of Health Services Concerning Food, Device and Drug Firms. (9/28/94)

332.3 Arkansas (AR)

MOU with:
1. AR Department of Health and the AR State Plant Board Regarding Monitoring Pesticide Residues and Mycotoxins in Food and Animal Feed. (5/3/96)
2. AR Attorney General and AR Department of Health Regarding the Inspection of Foods, Drugs, Devices, and Cosmetics. (4/17/92)

332.4 California (CA)

MOU with:
1. CA Department of Food and Agriculture Regarding Monitoring and Enforcement for Pesticide Residues in Raw Agricultural Commodities. (3/31/89)
2. CA Department of Health Services, Food, Drug, and Radiation Safety Division, Food and Drug Branch Concerning the Exchange of Information of Mutual Interest. (1/26/94)
3. CA Department of Health Services concerning the sharing of inventories, planning of work, and exchange of inspection reports and regulatory correspondence relating to blood banks, plasma centers, and the screening, processing, and storage of by-products in the state. (8/17/94)

332.5 Colorado (CO)

MOU with CO Department of Health and CO Department of Law Regarding Inspections of Food, Drug, Cosmetic, and Medical Device Firms. (4/22/92)

332.6 Connecticut (CT)

MOU with CT Department of Consumer Protection Regarding the Coordination of Joint Efforts in Monitoring Pesticide and Industrial Chemical Residues In Foods. (5/16/90)

332.7 Delaware (DE)

MOU with:
1. DE Board of Pharmacy Concerning Regulatory Activities Relating to the Inspection of Drug Manufacturers, Wholesalers, and Distributors. (3/18/88)
2. DE Department of Agriculture, MD Department of Agriculture, PA Department of Agriculture, VA Department of Agriculture and Consumer Services, WV Department of Agriculture, USDA/FSIS - NE & SE Regional Offices Regarding Regulatory Investigations Involving Drug, Pesticide, and Industrial Chemical Residues in Animal Feeds and Meat and Poultry. (9/13/90)
3. DE Division of Public Health Relating to the Food Processing Industry. (8/19/93)

332.8 District of Columbia (DC)

MOU with DC, Department of Consumer and Regulatory Affairs Concerning Public Health Emergencies, Coordination of Consumer Complaint Investigations, Joint Training Efforts, Analytical Assistance, and Mutual Exchange of Inspectional Information. (3/26/96)

332.9 Florida (FL)

MOU with:
1. FL Department of Agriculture and Consumer Services Delineates Activities Relating to the Regulation of Milk, Foods, Medicated Feeds, and Pesticides. (10/16/89)
2. FL Department of Health and Rehabilitative Services Concerning Cooperation in Consumer Protection Activities Such as Foods, Drugs, Medical Devices, Cosmetics, and Radiation Emitting Electronic Products. (6/25/93)
3. FL Department of Agriculture and Consumer Services, USDA FSIS, Involving Drug, Pesticide and Environmental Chemical Residues in Animal Feed, Meats, and Poultry Tissue. (8/23/91)
4. FL Department of Agriculture and Consumer Services Concerning Milk, Foods, Medicated Feeds and Pesticide Residues. (9/28/94)

332.10 Georgia (GA)

MOU with GA Department of Agriculture and USDA/FSIS Regarding Regulatory Investigations Involving Drug, Pesticide, and Toxic Chemical Residues in Animal Feeds and in Meat Tissues. (10/11/90)

332.11 Illinois (IL)

MOU with:

1. IL Attorney General Regarding Development and Implementation of Appropriate Sanctions Concerning Fraud and Deception Involving Foods, Drugs, Devices, and Cosmetic. (12/13/82)

2. IL Department of Public Health Concerning the Monitoring and Investigation of Foodborne Illnesses. (8/18/87)

3. Commercial Feed Regulatory Agencies of the states of Illinois, Indiana, Michigan, Minnesota, North Dakota, South Dakota, and Wisconsin Relating to Animal Feed and the Impact of Animal Feed on Food. (5/24/93)

332.12 Iowa (IA)

MOU with:

1. IA Department of Agriculture & Land Stewardship Relative to Animal Feed Firms. (3/2/93)

2. IA Department of Inspections & Appeals Relative to Wholesale Food Establishments (9/23/93)

332.13 Indiana (IN)

MOU with Commercial Feed Regulatory Agencies of the states of Illinois, Indiana, Michigan, Minnesota, North Dakota, South Dakota, and Wisconsin Relating to Animal Feed and the Impact of Animal Feed on Food (5/24/93)

332.14 Kansas (KS)

MOU with KS Department of Health and Environment Concerning Inspection, Investigation, and Analytical Findings Related to Food and Drug Firms (revised 5/12/95)

332.15 Kentucky (KY)

1. MOU with KY State Board of Pharmacy Regarding Investigations of Drug Distributors Involving Violations of the Prescription Drug Marketing Act of 1987 (PDMA) (7/16/90)

2. CAP with KY Department of Health Services Regarding Milk, Food, Cosmetics, Interstate Travel Sanitation, Radiological Health, Drugs, and Pesticides (revised 6/28/90)

332.16 Louisiana (LA)

MOU with LA Department of Agriculture and Forestry Relating to Food Firms (6/28/94)

332.17 Maine (ME)

MOU with ME Department of Agriculture, Food and Rural Resources Regarding the Coordination of Joint Efforts in Monitoring Pesticide and Industrial Chemical Residues in Foods (3/22/90)

332.18 Maryland (MD)

MOU with:

1. MD Department of Health and Mental Hygiene Concerning the Inspection of Food Processing and Storage

Industries and emergency public health problems of food origin (revised 1/31/89)

2. DE Department of Agriculture, MD Department of Agriculture, PA Department of Agriculture, VA Department of Agriculture and Consumer Services, WV Department of Agriculture, USDA/FSIS - NE & SE Regional Offices Regarding Regulatory Investigations Involving Drug, Pesticide, and Industrial Chemical Residues in Animal Feeds and Meat and Poultry (revised 9/13/90)

332.19 Michigan (MI)

MOU with:

1. MI Department of Agriculture Regarding Inspections, Investigations, and Analytical Findings Related to Food Firms (11/20/91)

2. Commercial Feed Regulatory Agencies of the states of Illinois, Indiana, Michigan, Minnesota, North Dakota, South Dakota, and Wisconsin Relating to Animal Feed and the Impact of Animal Feed on Food (5/24/93)

332.20 Minnesota (MN)

MOU with:

1. MN Department of Agriculture Regarding the Inspection of Food and Medicated Feed Firms (7157.50: 7/29/92)

2. Commercial Feed Regulatory Agencies of the states of Illinois, Indiana, Michigan, Minnesota, North Dakota, South Dakota, and Wisconsin Relating to Animal Feed and the Impact of Animal Feed on Food (5/24/93)

332.21 Missouri (MO)

MOU with:

1. MO Department of Health Regarding Food Inspection, Monitoring of Industry Recalls, Disaster Investigations, HIV Related Issues and Exchange of Inspectional and Analytical Information (revised 5/12/95)

2. MO State Board of Pharmacy to Differentiate Between the Practice of Pharmacy and the Manufacture of Finished Pharmaceuticals (1/16/96)

332.22 Nebraska (NE)

MOU with NE Department of Agriculture Concerning Inspection, Investigations, and Analytical Findings Related to Foods and Animal Feeds Firms (revised 5/23/95)

332.23 New Jersey (NJ)

MOU with NJ Department of Health Regarding Inspection of Drug Firms, Investigations of Drug Related Health Frauds, Analysis of Drug Samples, and Recalls (2/3/86)

332.24 New Mexico (NM)

MOU with NM Department of Health and Environment and NM Department of Agriculture Regarding Coordination of Information and Work-Sharing in Monitoring Pesticide Residues and Mycotoxins in Food and Animal Feed Commodities (revised 4/12/94)

332.25 New York (NY)

Agreement with NY Department of Agriculture and Markets Regarding Coordination of Communications and Work-Sharing to Ensure Prompt and Effective Food-Related Consumer Protection Services (6/20/90)

332.26 North Carolina (NC)

MOU with NC Department of Agriculture of Food and Drug Firms (10/02/92)

332.27 North Dakota (ND)

MOU with Commercial Feed Regulatory Agencies of the states of Illinois, Indiana, Michigan, Minnesota, North Dakota, South Dakota, and Wisconsin Relating to Animal Feed and the Impact of Animal Feed on Food (5/24/93)

332.28 Ohio (OH)

MOU with OH Department of Health Regarding Sharing of Information About Levels of Pesticides in Grade A Milk, Milk Products, Grade A Goat Milk, and Goat Milk Products (1/18/90)

332.29 Oklahoma (OK)

MOU with:
1.   OK Department of Health and the OK Department of Agriculture Concerning Joint Efforts for the Coordination of Information in Monitoring Pesticide Residues and Mycotoxins in Food and Animal Feed Commodities (5/9/88)
2.   OK Attorney General and OK Department of Health Regarding Fraud and Deception Involving Foods, Drugs, Devices, and Cosmetics (8/17/92)
3.   OK Department of Health and the OK Department of Agriculture Concerning Pesticides Residues and Mycotoxins in Food and Animal Feed (1/29/96)

332.30 Oregon (OR)

MOU with OR Dept. of Agriculture Relating to Food Firms (Being Superceded by Partnership Agreement)

332.31 Pennsylvania (PA)

MOU with:
1.   Allegheny County, PA Health Department Concerning Coordination of Inspection of Food Processing, Storage and Service Facilities, and Interstate Carrier Support Facilities (11/18/78)
2.   PA Department of Health Regarding the Inspection of Drug, Device, and Cosmetic Manufacturers, Wholesalers, and Distributors (revised 4/6/88)
3.   PA Department of Agriculture Regarding Regu-

latory Activities Relating to the Inspection of Food Processing and Storage Facilities (revised 11/30/88)
4.   DE Department of Agriculture, MD Department of Agriculture, PA Department of Agriculture, VA Department of Agriculture and Consumer Services, WV Department of Agriculture, USDA/FSIS - NE & SE Regional Offices Regarding Regulatory Investigations Involving Drug, Pesticide, and Industrial Chemical Residues in Animal Feeds and Meat and Poultry (revised 9/13/90)

332.32 Puerto Rico (PR)

MOU with the Commonwealth of Puerto Rico Dept. of Consumer Affairs (DACO) Concerning Cooperative Education Initiatives, Mutual Planning, Sharing Reports of Inspections, Investigations, and Analytical Findings (10/1/93)

332.33 Rhode Island (RI)

MOU with RI Department of Health Regarding the Coordination of Joint Efforts in Monitoring Pesticide and Industrial Chemical Residues in Foods (9/26/90)

332.34 South Carolina (SC)

MOU with:
1.   SC Department of Agriculture Regarding the Inspection of Food and Drug Firms (7/31/92)
2.   SC Department of Agriculture, USDA FSIS, Southeastern Region, Animal & Health Inspection Service, Veterinary Service, and Clemson University Regarding Violative Levels of Drugs, Pesticides and Toxic Chemical Residues in Food Animals (11/08/91)
3.   SC Dept. of Health & Environmental Control Concerning Food Firms (11/12/92)

332.35 South Dakota (SD)

MOU with Commercial Feed Regulatory Agencies of the states of Illinois, Indiana, Michigan, Minnesota, North Dakota, South Dakota, and Wisconsin Relating to Animal Feed and the Impact of Animal Feed on Food (5/24/93)

332.36 Tennessee (TN)

MOU with TN Department of Agriculture Regarding Inspections of Food, Animal Feed, Cosmetic, Medical Device, and Drug Firms (8/25/92)

332.37 Texas (TX)

MOU with:
1.   TX Department of Health Regarding the Regulation of Foods and Drugs Firms (2/11/87)
2.   TX Department of Health; TX Department of Agriculture; and TX Agricultural Experiment Station, Office of the TX State Chemist Regarding the Cooperation, Coordination and Sharing of Pesticide Monitoring Data Concerning Residues in Raw and Processed Agricultural Products (revised 6/3/93)

3.   TX Department of Health Regarding Methadone Programs, Blood Banks, and Plasmapheresis Operations (5/6/94)

332.38 Utah (UT)

MOU with UT Department of Agriculture Regarding the Inspection of Food Firms (4/16/92)

332.39 Virginia (VA)

MOU with:

1.   VA Board of Pharmacy for the Inspection of Drug Manufacturers, Wholesalers, and Distributors (revised 3/29/88)

2.   VA Department of Agriculture and Consumer Services Concerning Inspection of the Food Processing and Storage Industries (revised 2/28/96)

3.   VA Department of Health Concerning the Inspection of the Crabmeat Industry (revised 5/20/88)

4.   DE Department of Agriculture, MD Department of Agriculture, PA Department of Agriculture, VA Department of Agriculture and Consumer Services, WV Department of Agriculture, USDA/FSIS - NE & SE Regional Offices Regarding Regulatory Investigations Involving Drug, Pesticide, and Industrial Chemical Residues in Animal Feeds and Meat and Poultry (revised 9/13/90)

332.40 Washington (WA)

MOU with:

1.   WA State Dept. of Agriculture Regarding Inspection and Grading of Grain, Rice, and Pulses (9/10/81)

2.   WA State Department of Agriculture Regarding Coordination of Information and Work-Sharing in Monitoring Pesticide Residues in Food and Animal Feed Commodities (4/11/91)

3.   WA State Dept. of Agriculture Relating to Food Firms (1/5/93)

332.41 West Virginia (WV)

MOU with:

1.   WV Department of Health Relating to the Inspection of the Food Processing Industry (revised 4/7/88)

2.   WV Department of Agriculture Concerning Regulatory Activities Related to Inspections of Food Storage and Medicated Feed Industries (revised 4/19/88)

3.   DE Department of Agriculture, MD Department of Agriculture, PA Department of Agriculture, VA Department of Agriculture and Consumer Services, WV Department of Agriculture, USDA/FSIS - NE & SE Regional Offices Regarding Regulatory Investigations Involving Drug, Pesticide, and Industrial Chemical Residues in Animal Feeds and Meat and Poultry (revised 9/13/90)

332.42 Wisconsin (WI)

MOU with:

1.   WI Department of Agriculture, Trade and Consumer Protection Relating to Food and Drug Firms (8/24/92)

2.   Commercial Feed Regulatory Agencies of the states of Illinois, Indiana, Michigan, Minnesota, North Dakota, South Dakota, and Wisconsin Relating to Animal Feed and the Impact of Animal Feed on Food (5/24/93)

332.43 Wyoming (WY)

MOU with WY Department of Agriculture Regarding the Inspection of Food, Drug, and Medical Device Firms (3/20/92)

332.44 National Association of State Departments of Agriculture (NSDA)

MOU with NSDA in Order to Provide a Coordinated Structure for the Conduct of Public Education Programs Regarding the Safety and Wholesomeness of the United States Food Supply (3/4/91)

333   STATE AUTHORITIES AND PHONE CONTACT NUMBERS

This section contains information regarding various state enforcement authorities. Some states operate under state laws patterned after the FD&C Act of 1906 or the current FD&C Act. However, most of the states operate under a "Uniform FD&C Act" which was developed by the Association of Food and Drug Officials (AFDO).

States that have adopted the Uniform FD&C Act as their legal guideline have in most cases adopted the entire act. The food authority in most cases includes among other things the adoption of the food and color additive provisions, pesticide residue amendments, enrichment guidance, etc. The Uniform FD&C Act also includes a provision for automatic adoption of changes in the FD&C Act. Some state legislatures have also included this provision in their laws. Some other provisions of the Uniform Act adopted by state include the new drug provisions, medical device laws, and cosmetic requirements.

Some states have also adopted the Association of American Feed Control Officials (AAFCO) model bill as their legal guideline for feed inspections.

In most cases the contact for "Consumer Protection Issues" would be located in the Office of the State Attorney General and would usually cover consumer fraud and other consumer protection issues. The State Attorney General's staff usually has mechanisms to deal with health fraud issues not efficiently dealt with by traditional FDA approaches. Contact your District Health Fraud Monitor for guidance in cooperative efforts with the State Attorney General's staff.

This section of the IOM also contains a current listing of phone numbers for selected program areas within state agencies that regulate products also covered by the FDA. This listing which is alphabetical by state is not all-inclusive. A complete listing of the personnel and programs at the state and local level may be found in the Directory of State

& Local Officials – 2000 which was prepared by the Division of Federal-State Relations (DFSR) (HFC-150) at http://www.fda.gov/ora/fed_state/default.htm. or http://www.fda.gov/ora/fed_state/directorytable.htm.

333.1 Alabama (AL)

Alabama has adopted the FD&C Act of 1906 and the 1970 AAFCO as their legal guideline. The control agencies are Agriculture and Health. They have not adopted the new drug provisions, the medical device law, nor the automatic adoption provisions.

Phone Contact Numbers
```
Epidemiology . . . . . . . . . . . .(334) 206-5325
Food & Drugs . . . . . . . . . . .(334) 240-7202
Pharmacy Practice . . . . . . .(205) 967-0130
Consumer Protection . . . . . .(334) 242-7463
After Hours . . . . . . . . . . . . .(800) 338-8374
```

333.2 Alaska (AK)

Alaska has adopted the Uniform FD&C Act without the automatic adoption provision and have not adopted either AAFCO feed bill. The controlling agencies are Health, Social Services, and Environmental Conservation. Alaska has adopted the various provisions of the Uniform bill.

Phone Contact Numbers
```
Epidemiology . . . . . . . . . . . .(907) 269-8000
Drugs, Devices, Cosmetics  .(907) 465-3090
Foods . . . . . . . . . . . . . . . .(907) 451-2110
Pharmacy Practice . . . . . . .(907) 465-2589
Consumer Protection . . . . . .(907) 269-5206
After Hours . . . . . . . . . . . . .(907) 249-1370
     or . . . . . . . . . . . . . . . . . .(800) 478-2337
```

333.3 Arizona (AZ)

Arizona operates under the Uniform FD&C Act and the 1970 AAFCO Feed Bill. The controlling agencies are Health, Pharmacy and the State Chemist. They have not adopted the medical device law, cosmetics law, nor the automatic adoption provisions of the Uniform FD&C Act.

Phone Contact Numbers
```
Epidemiology . . . . . . . . . . . .(602) 230-5808
Foods . . . . . . . . . . . . . . . .(602) 230-5917
Pharmacy Practice, Drugs  . .(602) 255-5125
Consumer Protection . . . . . .(602) 542-7701
After Hours (HEALTH) . . . . .(602) 494-0493
After Hours (PHARM) . . . . .(602) 995-0128
```

333.4 Arkansas (AR)

Arkansas operates under the Uniform FD&C Act and the 1970 AAFCO Feed Bill. The agencies in control are Health and the Plant Board. They have not adopted the new drug provisions or the automatic adoption provision.

Phone Contact Numbers
```
Epidemiology . . . . . . . . . . . .(501) 661-2227
Drugs, Devices, Cosmetics  .(501) 661-2325
```

```
Foods . . . . . . . . . . . . . . . .(501) 661-2171
Pharmacy Practice . . . . . . .(501) 682-0190
Consumer Protection . . . . . .(501) 682-6150
After Hours (HEALTH) . . . . .(501) 661-2136
```

333.5 California (CA)

California has adopted the Uniform FD&C Act and the 1970 AAFCO Feed Bill along with the automatic adoption provisions of the Uniform FD&C Act. The controlling agencies are Agriculture and Health.

Phone Contact Numbers
```
Epidemiology . . . . . . . . . . . .(510) 622-4500
Foods, Drugs, Devices,
   Cosmetics . . . . . . . . . . . .(916) 445-2263
Pharmacy Practice . . . . . . .(916) 445-5014
Consumer Protection . . . . . .(619) 645-2089
After Hours . . . . . . . . . . . . .(916) 427-4341
```

333.6 Colorado (CO)

Colorado has adopted the Uniform FD&C Act and the automatic adoption provisions of the Uniform FD&C Act. The controlling agencies are Agriculture and Health. They have not adopted either version of the AAFCO Feed Bill.

Phone Contact Numbers
```
Epidemiology . . . . . . . . . . . .(303) 692-2613
Foods, Drugs, Devices
   Cosmetics . . . . . . . . . . . .(303) 692-3620
Pharmacy Practice . . . . . . .(303) 894-7753
Consumer Protection . . . . . .(303) 866-5079
After Hours . . . . . . . . . . . . .(303) 320-9395
```

333.7 Connecticut (CT)

Connecticut has adopted the FD&C Act, the Uniform FD&C Act and the 1958 AAFCO Feed Bill along with the automatic adoption provisions of the Uniform FD&C Act. The controlling agencies are Agriculture and Consumer Protection.

Phone Contact Numbers
```
Epidemiology . . . . . . . . . . . .(860) 509-7995
Food - Health . . . . . . . . . . .(860) 509-7293
Food - Consumer Protection (860) 713-6160
Drugs, Devices, Cosmetics  .(860) 713-6065
Pharmacy Practice . . . . . . .(860) 713-6065
After Hours (HEALTH) . . . . .(860) 509-8000
```

333.8 Delaware (DE)

Delaware has adopted the Uniform FD&C Act and the 1970 AAFCO Feed Bill along with the automatic adoption provisions of the Uniform FD&C Act. The controlling agencies are Agriculture, Health, and Pharmacy. They have not adopted the food and color additive amendments, the pesticide residue amendment, enrichment amendment, new drug provisions, medical device law, and the cosmetics law.

Phone Contact Numbers
```
Epidemiology . . . . . . . . . . . .(302) 739-3033
```

113

Pharmacy Practice, Drugs . .(302) 739-4798
Food . . . .(302) 739-3841
Consumer Protection . . . . . .(302) 577-3250
After Hours . . . .(302) 739-4130

333.9 District of Columbia (DC)

Phone Contact Numbers
Epidemiology . . . .(202) 645-5550
Foods . . . .(202) 727-7250
Drugs, Devices, Cosmetics .(202) 535-2180
Pharmacy Practice . . . .(301) 315-8424
Consumer Protection . . . . . .(202) 727-3500
After Hours . . . .(202) 727-6161

333.10 Florida (FL)

Florida has adopted the Uniform FD&C Act and the 1970 AAFCO Feed Bill along with the automatic adoption provisions of the Uniform FD&C Act. The controlling agencies are Agriculture and Health.
Phone Contact Numbers
Epidemiology . . . .(850) 488-2905
Foods - Agriculture . . . .(850) 488-3951
Foods - Health . . . .(850) 487-0004
Drugs, Devices, Cosmetics .(850) 487-1257
Pharmacy Practice . . . .(850) 414-2969
Consumer Protection . . . . . .(954) 712-4600
After Hours (HEALTH) . . . . .(850) 488-7721

333.11 Georgia (GA)

Georgia has adopted the Uniform FD&C Act and the 1970 AAFCO Feed Bill but not the automatic adoption provisions of the Uniform FD&C Act. The controlling agencies are Agriculture and Pharmacy. They have not adopted the food additive, color additive or pesticide residue amendments.
Phone Contact Numbers
Epidemiology . . . .(404) 657-2588
Foods . . . .(404) 656-3627
Pharmacy Practice, Drugs,
Devices, Cosmetics . . . . . .(404) 656-5100
Pharmacy Licensing . . . . . .(404) 656-3912
Consumer Protection . . . . . .(404) 656-3337
After Hours (Radiation) . . . .(404) 656-4300

333.12 Hawaii (HI)

Hawaii has adopted the Uniform FD&C Act and the 1970 AAFCO Feed Bill along with the automatic adoption provisions of the Uniform FD&C Act. The controlling agencies are Agriculture, Health and the Attorney General.
Phone Contact Numbers
Epidemiology . . . .(808) 586-4586
Foods, OTC Drugs, Devices,
Cosmetics . . . .(808) 586-4725
Pharmacy Practice . . . .(808) 586-2694
Consumer Protection . . . . . .(808) 586-1500
After Hours . . . .(808) 247-2191

333.13 Idaho (ID)

Idaho has adopted the Uniform FD&C Act and the 1958 AAFCO Feed Bill and has not adopted the automatic adoption provisions of the Uniform FD&C Act. The controlling agencies are Agriculture, Health and Pharmacy. They have not adopted the food additive, color additive or pesticide residue amendments of the Act.
Phone Contact Numbers
Epidemiology . . . .(208) 334-5939
Foods . . . .(208) 334-5938
Pharmacy Practice, Drugs . .(208) 334-2356
Devices . . . .(208) 334-5930
Consumer Protection . . . . . .(208) 334-4114
After Hours (Public Health) .(208) 334-4570

333.14 Illinois (IL)

Illinois has adopted the Uniform FD&C Act and the 1958 AAFCO Feed Bill along with the automatic adoption provisions of the Uniform FD&C Act. The controlling agencies are Agriculture and Health. They have not adopted the enrichment provisions of the Act.
Phone Contact Numbers
Epidemiology . . . .(217) 785-7165
Foods, Drugs, Devices,
Cosmetics . . . .(217) 785-2439
Pharmacy Practice . . . .(217) 785-8159
Consumer Protection . . . . . .(217) 782-9020
or . . . .(312) 814-4714
After Hours . . . .(800) 782-7860

333.15 Indiana (IN)

Indiana has adopted the Uniform FD&C Act and the 1970 AAFCO Feed Bill along with the automatic adoption provisions of the Uniform FD&C Act. The controlling agencies are Health and the State Chemist.
Phone Contact Numbers
Epidemiology . . . .(317) 233-7164
Foods . . . .(317) 233-7467
Drugs, Devices, Cosmetics .(317) 233-7467
Pharmacy Practice . . . .(317) 232-1140
Consumer Protection . . . . . .(317) 232-6205
After Hours (HEALTH) . . . . .(317) 233-8115
After Hours (PHARM) . . . . .(317) 232-2960

333.16 Iowa (IA)

Iowa has adopted the 1906 FD&C Act and the 1970 AAFCO Feed Bill along with the automatic adoption provisions of the FD&C Act. The controlling agencies are Agriculture, Health & Appeals, and Pharmacy.
Phone Contact Numbers
Epidemiology . . . .(515) 281-4941
Food . . . .(515) 281-7114
Pharmacy Practice, Drugs
Devices, Cosmetics . . . . . .(515) 281-5944
Consumer Protection . . . . . .(515) 281-5926
After Hours . . . .(515) 281-3231

333.17 Kansas (KS)

Kansas has adopted the Uniform FD&C Act and the 1958 AAFCO Feed Bill and has not adopted the automatic adoption provisions of the Uniform FD&C Act. The controlling agencies are Agriculture and Health.

Phone Contact Numbers
Epidemiology . . . .(785) 296-6536
Foods, Drugs, Devices
  Cosmetics . . . .(785) 296-5599
Pharmacy Practice . . . .(785) 296-4056
Consumer Protection . . . . . .(785) 296-3715
After Hours . . . .(785) 296-0614

333.18 Kentucky (KY)

Kentucky has adopted the Uniform FD&C Act and the 1970 AAFCO Feed Bill along with the automatic adoption provisions of the Uniform FD&C Act. The controlling agencies are Human Resources, Pharmacy, and the University of Kentucky Registration Services.

Phone Contact Numbers
Epidemiology . . . .(502) 564-7243
Foods . . . .(502) 564-7181
Drugs, Devices . . . .(502) 564-7985
Pharmacy Practice . . . .(502) 573-1580
Consumer Protection . . . . . .(502) 696-5389
After Hours . . . .(502) 564-7815

333.19 Louisiana (LA)

Louisiana has adopted the Uniform FD&C Act and the 1970 AAFCO Feed Bill along with the automatic adoption provisions of the Uniform FD&C Act. The controlling agencies are Agriculture and Health. They have not adopted the provisions of the medical device law.

Phone Contact Numbers
Epidemiology . . . .(504) 568-5005
Foods, Drugs, Devices
  Cosmetics . . . .(225) 763-5508
Pharmacy Practice . . . .(225) 925-6496
Consumer Protection . . . . . .(504) 342-9639
After Hours - (AGRIC) . . . . .(504) 925-3763

333.20 Maine (ME)

Maine has adopted the Uniform FD&C Act and the 1970 AAFCO Feed Bill but not the automatic adoption provisions of the Uniform FD&C Act. The controlling agencies are Agriculture and Pharmacy. They have not adopted the food and color additive amendments nor the new drug provisions or the medical device law.

Phone Contact Numbers
Epidemiology . . . .(207) 287-3591
Food . . . .(207) 287-3841
Pharmacy Practice, Drugs
  Cosmetics . . . .(207) 624-8603
Devices . . . .(207) 287-8016
Consumer Protection . . . . . .(207) 626-8800
After Hours - (HUMAN SVCS)(800) 452-1999

333.21 Maryland (MD)

Maryland has adopted the Uniform FD&C Act and the 1970 AAFCO Feed Bill along with the automatic adoption provisions of the Uniform FD&C Act. The controlling agencies are Agriculture and Health. They have not adopted the enrichment provisions of the Act.

Phone Contact Numbers
Epidemiology . . . .(410) 767-6031
Food . . . .(410) 767-8440
Drugs, Devices, Cosmetics . .(410) 764-2890
Pharmacy Practice . . . .(410) 764-4755
Consumer Protection . . . . . .(410) 576-6557
After Hours - Health . . . . . .(410) 243-8700

333.22 Massachusetts (MA)

Massachusetts has adopted the Uniform FD&C Act and the 1970 AAFCO Feed Bill but not the automatic adoption provisions of the Uniform FD&C Act. The controlling agencies are Agriculture and Health. They have not adopted the new drug provisions of the Act.

Phone Contact Numbers
Epidemiology . . . .(617) 983-6800
Foods, Drugs, Devices
  Cosmetics . . . .(617) 983-6759
Pharmacy Practice . . . .(617) 727-0085
Consumer Protection . . . . . .(617) 727-2200
After Hours (HEALTH) . . . . .(617) 522-3700

333.23 Michigan (MI)

Michigan has adopted the Uniform FD&C Act and the 1970 AAFCO Feed Bill but not the automatic adoption provisions of the Uniform FD&C Act. The controlling agencies are Agriculture, Commerce, Licensing and Registration.. They have not adopted the enrichment provisions or the cosmetics law.

Phone Contact Numbers
Epidemiology . . . .(517) 335-8900
Food . . . .(517) 373-1060
Pharmacy Practice, Drugs
  Devices . . . .(517) 373-9102
Consumer Protection . . . . . .(517) 335-0855
After Hours (HEALTH) . . . . .(517) 335-9030
After Hours (AGRIC) . . . . . .(517) 373-1104

333.24 Minnesota (MN)

Minnesota has adopted the Uniform FD&C Act and the 1970 AAFCO Feed Bill but not the automatic adoption provisions of the Uniform FD&C Act. The controlling agencies are Agriculture and Pharmacy. They have not adopted the enrichment provisions, the new drug provisions, the medical device law, nor the cosmetic law.

Phone Contact Numbers
Epidemiology . . . .(612) 676-5414
Food . . . .(651) 296-1590
Pharmacy Practice, Drugs
  Cosmetics . . . .(612) 617-2201

Consumer Protection . . . . . .(651) 296-3353
After Hours . . . .(612) 649-6451
or . . . .(800) 422-0798

333.25 Mississippi (MS)

Mississippi has adopted the 1906 FD&C Act and the 1970 AAFCO Feed Bill but not the automatic adoption provisions of the Uniform FD&C Act. The controlling agencies are Agriculture, Commerce and the State Chemistry Lab. They have not adopted the food additive, color additive, and pesticide residue amendments, nor the new drug provisions or cosmetic law.

Phone Contact Numbers
Epidemiology . . . .(601) 576-7725
Food . . . .(601) 576-7689
Food, Drugs, Devices,
Cosmetics . . . .(601) 325-3324
Pharmacy Practice . . . .(601) 354-6750
Consumer Protection . . . . . .(601) 359-4230
After Hours . . . .(601) 576-7400

333.26 Missouri (MO)

Missouri has adopted the Uniform FD&C Act and the 1970 AAFCO Feed Bill but not the automatic adoption provisions of the Uniform FD&C Act. The controlling agencies are Agriculture and Health. They have not adopted the enrichment provisions of the Act.

Phone Contact Provisions
Epidemiology . . . .(573) 751-6128
Foods, Drugs, Devices
Cosmetics . . . .(573) 751-6102
Pharmacy Practice . . . .(573) 751-0091
Consumer Protection . . . . . .(573) 751-8355
After Hours - Health . . . . . .(573) 751-4674

333.27 Montana (MT)

Montana has adopted the Uniform FD&C Act and the 1970 AAFCO Feed Bill along with the automatic adoption provisions of the Uniform FD&C Act. The controlling agencies are Agriculture and Health.

Phone Contact Numbers
Epidemiology . . . .(406) 444-3986
Foods, Drugs, Devices
Cosmetics . . . .(406) 444-5309
Pharmacy Practice . . . .(406) 444-1698
Consumer Protection . . . . . .(406) 444-3553
After Hours . . . .(406) 444-6911

333.28 Nebraska (NB)

Nebraska has adopted the Uniform FD&C Act and the 1970 AAFCO Feed Bill but not the automatic adoption provisions of the Uniform FD&C Act. The controlling agencies are Agriculture and Health. They have not adopted the new drug provisions nor the medical device and cosmetic laws.

Phone Contact Numbers
Epidemiology . . . .(402) 471-0550

Food . . . .(402) 471-2536
Pharmacy Practice, Drugs
Cosmetics . . . .(402) 471-2115
Consumer Protection . . . . . .(402) 471-2682
After Hours . . . .(402) 471-2927

333.29 Nevada (NV)

Nevada has adopted the Uniform FD&C Act but not the automatic adoption provisions of the Uniform FD&C Act. They have not adopted either version of the AAFCO Feed Bill. The controlling agencies are Agriculture and Health. They have not adopted the enrichment provisions of the Act.

Phone Contact Numbers
Epidemiology . . . . .None
Food, Drugs, Devices
Cosmetics . . . .(775) 687-6353
Pharmacy Practice . . . .(775) 852-1440
Consumer Protection . . . . . .(702) 486-3777
After Hours . . . . .None

333.30 New Hampshire (NH)

New Hampshire has adopted the Uniform FD&C Act and the 1970 AAFCO Feed Bill but not the automatic adoption provisions of the Uniform FD&C Act. The controlling agencies are Agriculture and Health.

Phone Contact Numbers
Epidemiology . . . .(603) 271-4501
Food, Drugs, Cosmetics . . .(603) 271-4589
Pharmacy Practice . . . .(603) 271-2350
Devices . . . .(603) 271-4872
Consumer Protection . . . . . .(603) 271-3643
After Hours - Health . . . . . .(603) 271-5591

333.31 New Jersey (NJ)

New Jersey has adopted the Uniform FD&C Act and the 1970 AAFCO Feed Bill but not automatic adoption provisions of the Uniform FD&C Act. The controlling agencies are Agriculture and Health. They have not adopted the pesticide residue amendment.

Phone Contact Numbers
Epidemiology . . . .(609) 588-7463
Food, Drugs, Devices
Cosmetics . . . .(609) 588-3123
Pharmacy Practice . . . .(973) 504-6450
Consumer Protection . . . . . .(973) 504-6534
After Hours . . . .(609) 392-2020

333.32 New Mexico (NM)

New Mexico has adopted the Uniform FD&C Act and the 1958 AAFCO Feed Bill but not the automatic adoption provisions of the Uniform FD&C Act. The controlling agencies are Agriculture, Environment, Health and Pharmacy. They have not adopted the food additive or color additive amendments.

Phone Contact Numbers
Epidemiology . . . .(505) 827-2389

Food . . . .(505) 841-9450
Pharmacy Practice, Drugs
   Devices, Cosmetics . . . . .(505) 841-9102
Consumer Protection . . . . .(505) 827-6000
After Hours (HEALTH) . . . . .(505) 827-0006
After Hours (ENVIRO) . . . . .(505) 827-9329

333.33 New York (NY)

New York has adopted the Uniform FD&C Act and the 1970 AAFCO Feed Bill along with the automatic adoption provisions of the Uniform FD&C Act. The controlling agencies are Agriculture and Markets, Health, and Pharmacy. They have not adopted the cosmetics law.

    Phone Contact Numbers
      Epidemiology . . . .(518) 473-4436
      Food . . . .(518) 457-4492
      Pharmacy Practice, Drugs
        Devices, Cosmetics . . . . . .(518) 474-3848
      Consumer Protection . . . . . .(212) 416-8300
      After Hours (HEALTH) . . . . .(518) 465-9720

333.34 North Carolina (NC)

North Carolina has adopted the Uniform FD&C Act and both versions of the AAFCO Feed Bills along with the automatic adoption provisions of the Uniform FD&C Act. The controlling agency is Agriculture. They have not adopted the enrichment provisions of the Act.

    Phone Contact Numbers
      Epidemiology . . . .(919) 733-3421
      Foods, Drugs, Devices
        Cosmetics . . . .(919) 733-7366
      Pharmacy Practice . . . .(919) 942-4454
      Consumer Protection . . . . . .(919) 733-7741
      After Hours (Radiation) . . . .(800) 344-0569

333.35 North Dakota (ND)

North Dakota has adopted the Uniform FD&C Act and neither version of the AAFCO Feed Bill but not the automatic adoption provisions of the Uniform FD&C Act. The controlling agencies are Consolidated Laboratories, Health and Pharmacy.

    Phone Contact Numbers
      Epidemiology . . . .(701) 328-2378
      Foods . . . .(701) 328-6150
      Drugs, Devices, Cosmetics . . . . .None
      Pharmacy Practice . . . .(701) 328-9535
      Consumer Protection . . . . . .(701) 328-2811
      After Hours . . . .(701) 328-2121

333.36 Ohio (OH)

Ohio has adopted the Uniform FD&C Act and the 1970 AAFCO Feed Bill but not the automatic adoption provisions of the Uniform FD&C Act. The controlling agencies are Agriculture and Pharmacy.

    Phone Contact Numbers
      Epidemiology . . . .(614) 466-0265

Food . . . .(614) 466-1390
OTC Drugs, Devices
   Cosmetics, Foods . . . .(614) 728-6250
Pharmacy Practice, Rx Drugs(614) 466-4143
Consumer Protection . . . . . .(614) 466-1305
After Hours .NONE

333.37 Oklahoma (OK)

Oklahoma has adopted the Uniform FD&C Act but neither version of the AAFCO Feed Bills nor the automatic adoption provisions of the Uniform FD&C Act. The controlling agencies are Agriculture and Health. They have not adopted the food additive or color additive amendments, the enrichment provisions nor the new drug provisions.

    Phone Contact Numbers
      Epidemiology . . . .(405) 271-3266
      Foods, Drugs, Devices
        Cosmetics . . . .(405) 271-5217
      Pharmacy Practice, Drugs . .(405) 521-3815
      Consumer Protection . . . . . .(405) 521-4274
      After Hours - Health . . . .(405) 271-5221

333.38 Oregon (OR)

Oregon has adopted the Uniform FD&C Act and the 1958 AAFCO Feed Bill along with the automatic adoption provisions of the Uniform FD&C Act. The controlling agencies are Agriculture and Pharmacy. They have not adopted the cosmetics law.

    Phone Contact Numbers
      Epidemiology . . . .(503) 731-4023
      Food . . . .(503) 986-4720
      Pharmacy Practice, Drugs
        Cosmetics . . . .(503) 731-4032
      Consumer Protection . . . . . .(503) 378-6347
      After Hours (HLTH) . . . .(503) 731-4030
      After Hours (PHARM) . . . . .(503) 731-4032

333.39 Pennsylvania (PA)

Pennsylvania has adopted the 1906 FD&C Act and the 1958 AAFCO Feed Bill but not the automatic adoption provisions of the Uniform FD&C Act. The controlling agencies are Agriculture and Health. They have not adopted the food additive, color additive, and pesticide residue amendments nor the enrichment provisions.

    Phone Contact Numbers
      Epidemiology . . . .(717) 787-3350
      Food . . . .(717) 787-4315
      Drugs, Devices, Cosmetics .(717) 787-4779
      Pharmacy Practice . . . .(717) 783-7156
      Consumer Protection . . . . . .(717) 787-9716
      After Hours - Health . . . .(717) 737-5349
      After Hours - (ENVIR PROT).(717) 787-4343

333.40 Puerto Rico (PR)

    Phone Contact Numbers
      Epidemiology . . . .(787) 274-5524

Food, Drugs, Devices
  Cosmetics . . . .(787) 274-7810
Pharmacy Practice . . . .(787) 725-8161
Consumer Protection . . . . . .(809) 723-9583
After Hours . . . .(809) 766-1616

333.41 Rhode Island (RI)

Rhode Island has adopted the Uniform FD&C Act and the 1970 AAFCO Feed Bill along with the automatic adoption provisions of the Uniform FD&C Act. The controlling agencies are Environmental Management and Health.
  Phone Contact Numbers
    Epidemiology . . . .(401) 222-1171
    Foods, Cosmetics . . . .(401) 222-2750
    Pharmacy Practice, Drugs,
     Devices . . . .(401) 222-2837
    Consumer Protection . . . . . .(401) 274-4400
    After Hours - Health . . . . . .(401) 222-5952

333.42 South Carolina (SC)

South Carolina has adopted the Uniform FD&C Act and the 1958 AAFCO Feed Bill but not the automatic adoption provisions of the Uniform FD&C Act. The controlling agencies are Agriculture and Health.

  Phone Contact Numbers
    Epidemiology . . . .(803) 737-4040
    Food . . . .(803) 896-0646
     or . . . .(803) 737-9702
    Drugs, Devices . . . .(803) 935-7817
    Pharmacy Practice . . . .(803) 896-4700
    Consumer Protection . . . . . .(803) 734-9458
    After Hours .NONE

333.43 South Dakota (SD)

South Dakota has adopted the Uniform FD&C Act and the 1970 AAFCO Feed Bill but not the automatic adoption provisions of the Uniform FD&C Act. The controlling agencies are Agriculture, Commerce and Regulations. They have not adopted the new drug provisions, medical device law, nor the cosmetics law.
  Phone Contact Numbers
    Epidemiology . . . .(605) 773-3361
    Food . . . .(605) 773-3364
    Drugs . . . .(605) 773-3697
    Pharmacy Practice . . . .(605) 362-2737
    Consumer Protection . . . . . .(605) 773-3215
    After Hours . . . .(605) 773-3231

333.44 Tennessee (TN)

Tennessee has adopted the Uniform FD&C Act and the 1970 AAFCO Feed Bill but not the automatic adoption provisions of the Uniform FD&C Act. The controlling agency is Agriculture.
  Phone Contact Numbers
    Epidemiology . . . .(615) 741-7247

Foods, Drugs, Devices
  Cosmetics . . . .(615) 837-5155
Pharmacy Practice . . . .(615) 741-2718
Consumer Protection . . . . . .(615) 741-6422
After Hours . . . .(615) 741-0001
  or . . . .(800) 258-3300

333.45 Texas (TX)

Texas has adopted the Uniform FD&C Act and the 1970 AAFCO Feed Bill along with the automatic adoption provisions of the Uniform FD&C Act. The controlling agencies are Health and the State Chemist.
  Phone Contact Numbers
    Epidemiology . . . .(512) 458-7729
    Foods . . . .(512) 719-0232
    Drugs, Devices Cosmetics . .(512) 719-0237
    Pharmacy Practice . . . .(512) 305-8000
    Consumer Protection . . . . . .(512) 463-2185
     or . . . .(214) 969-7639
    After Hours . . . .(512) 458-7111

333.46 Utah (UT)

Utah has adopted the Uniform FD&C Act and the 1970 AAFCO Feed Bill along with the automatic adoption provisions of the Uniform FD&C Act. The controlling agencies are Agriculture and Health. They have not adopted the new drug provisions.
  Phone Contact Numbers
    Epidemiology . . . .(801) 538-6191
    Food . . . .(801) 538-7150
    Pharmacy Practice, Drugs . .(801) 530-6767
    Consumer Protection . . . . . .(801) 538-1331
    After Hours . . . .(801) 782-4412

333.47 Vermont (VT)

Vermont has adopted the Uniform FD&C Act and the 1970 AAFCO Feed Bill along with the automatic adoption provisions of the Uniform FD&C Act. The controlling agencies are Agriculture and Health. They have not adopted the enrichment provisions.
  Phone Contact Numbers
    Epidemiology . . . .(802) 863-7240
    Foods . . . .(802) 863-7220
    Pharmacy Practice, Drugs . .(802) 828-2875
    Consumer Protection . . . . . .(802) 828-3171
    After Hours (HEALTH) . . . . .(802) 863-7200
    After Hours (AGRIC) . . . . . .(802) 828-2500

333.48 Virginia (VA)

Virginia has adopted the Uniform FD&C Act and the 1958 AAFCO Feed Bill but not the automatic adoption provisions of the Uniform FD&C Act. The controlling agencies are Agriculture and Pharmacy.
  Phone Contact Numbers
    Epidemiology . . . .(804) 786-6029
    Foods . . . .(804) 786-8899

Pharmacy Practice, Drugs
Devices, Cosmetics . . . . . .(804) 662-9911
Consumer Protection . . . . . .(804) 786-3344
After Hours . . . .(804) 674-2400
    or . . . .(800) 468-8892

333.49 Virgin Islands (VI)

Phone Contact Numbers
Epidemiology . . . . .NONE
Food . . . .(809) 774-6880
    or . . . .(809) 773-0717
Pharmacy Practice,
Devices . . . .(340) 776-8311
Consumer Protection . . . . . .(809) 774-3130
After Hours . . . . .NONE

333.50 Washington (WA)

Washington has adopted the Uniform FD&C Act and the 1958 AAFCO Feed Bill along with the automatic adoption provisions of the Uniform FD&C Act. The controlling agencies are Agriculture and Pharmacy.

Phone Contact Numbers
Epidemiology . . . .(206) 361-2831
Food . . . .(360) 902-1888
Pharmacy Practice, Drugs
Devices, Cosmetics . . . . . .(360) 236-4825
Consumer Protection . . . . . .(206) 464-7744
After Hours . . . .(360) 361-2914
After Hours (PHARM) . . . . .(425) 747-2939

333.51 West Virginia (WV)

West Virginia has adopted the 1906 FD&C Act and the 1970 AAFCO Feed Bill but not the automatic adoption provisions of the Uniform FD&C Act. The controlling agencies are Agriculture, Health and Pharmacy. They have not adopted the food additives or color additive amendments, the new drug provisions, the medical device law and the cosmetics law.
Phone Contact Numbers
Epidemiology . . . .(304) 558-5358
Food, Drugs . . . .(304) 558-2981
Pharmacy Practice, Drugs . .(304) 558-0558
Consumer Protection . . . . . .(304) 558-8986
After Hours . . . . .NONE

333.52 Wisconsin (WI)

Wisconsin has adopted the Uniform FD&C Act and the 1958 AAFCO Feed Bill along with the automatic adoption provisions of the Uniform FD&C Act. The controlling agencies are Agriculture and Pharmacy. They have not adopted the enrichment provisions, the new drug provisions, the medical device law, and the cosmetics law.
Phone Contact Numbers
Epidemiology . . . .(608) 297-9006
Food . . . .(608) 224-4701

Pharmacy Practice, Drugs
Devices, Cosmetics . . . . . .(608) 266-0483
Consumer Protection . . . . . .(608) 266-3861
After Hours . . . .(800) 943-0003

333.53 Wyoming (WY)

Wyoming has adopted the Uniform FD&C Act and the 1970 AAFCO Feed Bill but not the automatic adoption provisions of the Uniform FD&C Act. The controlling agency is Agriculture.
Phone Contact Numbers
Epidemiology . . . .(307) 777-5596
Food, Drugs, Cosmetics . . .(307) 777-6587
Pharmacy Practice . . . .(307) 234-0294
Consumer Protection . . . . . .(307) 777-5838
After Hours (AGRIC) . . . . . .(307) 777-7701

SUBCHAPTER 340 - INTERNATIONAL AGREEMENTS

340 MEMORANDA OF UNDERSTANDING

The Agency has over the years entered into agreements with foreign governments regarding the quality of foods, drugs, and other products exported to the United States. The following is a listing of these agreements. The complete text of the agreements is in the International Cooperative Agreements Manual. The listing is by country and CPG order. Please also refer to FDA's website at http://www.fda.gov/oia/default.htm for additional information.

340.1 Australia

MOU with:
1. Australia Regarding Dry Milk Products (7156f.01)
2. The Export Inspection Service, Dept. of Primary Industry, Australia Concerning Fresh Frozen Molluscan Shellfish.

340.2   Belgium

MOU with the Ministry of Agriculture of Belgium Represented by the National Dairy Office Concerning the Sanitary Quality of Dry Milk Products.

340.3   Canada

MOU with:
1. Canada Regarding Radiation Emission and Human Exposure from Electronic Products.
2. Canada Covering the U.S. Interstate Travel Sanitation Program and the Canadian Common Carriers Program.
3. Canada Regarding Good Laboratory Practices.
Agreement with:
1. Canada Concerning Exchange of Drug Plant Inspection Information.
2. Canada on Sanitary Control of Shellfish Industry.

119

340.4 Republic of Chile

MOU with:
1.   The Ministry of Economic Development and Reconstruction, Subsecretariate of Fisheries, Republic of Chile Regarding the Safety and Wholesomeness of Fresh and Frozen Oysters, Clams, and Mussels Exported to the United States.
2.   The Agricultural and Livestock Service, Ministry of Agriculture of the Republic of Chile Regarding Cooperation in Establishing and Implementing Emergency Procedures to Ensure the Safety of Fresh Fruit Exported to the United States.

340.5 People's Republic of China (PRC)

MOU with the State Administration of Import and Export Commodity Inspection of the PRC Covering Ceramic ware Intended for Use in Preparation, Serving, or Storage of Food or Drink and Offered for Export to the United States of America.

340.6 Denmark

MOU with the State Quality Control for Dairy Products and Eggs, Etc., Denmark, Concerning Dry Milk Products Exported to The US.

340.7 Finland

MOU with Finland to Establish Certification Requirements for Various Foods to Minimize FDA Audit Sampling of those Foods Exported to the US.

340.8 France

MOU with:
1.   French Ministry of Social Affairs and National Solidarity Office of Pharmaceuticals & Medicines to Exchange Information Regarding Non-clinical Laboratories.
2   The Ministry of Agriculture, Republic of France Regarding Caseins, Caseinates, and Mixtures Thereof Exported to the US.

340.9 Federal Republic of Germany (FRG)

MOU with the Environmental Protection Agency and the Federal Minister of Food, Agriculture, and Forestry, the Federal Minister for Youth, Family Affairs, Women and Health, and the Federal Minister of the Environment, Nature Conservation and Nuclear Safety of the FRG Regarding Good Laboratory Practice.

340.10 Iceland

MOU with The Ministry of Fisheries, Government of Iceland Concerning Fresh and Fresh Frozen Oysters, Clams, and Mussels.

340.11 Ireland

MOU with Ireland Covering Caseins, Caseinates, and Mixtures Thereof Exported to the United States.

340.12 Italy

MOU with the Pharmaceutical Service, Ministry of Health, Republic of Italy Regarding Good Laboratory Practice.

340.13 Japan

Agreement with Japan on Shellfish Sanitation.

340.14 Republic of Korea (ROK)

MOU with:
1.   ROK Regarding Exchange of Toxicological Information Between National Center for Toxicological Research and the Korea Research Institute of Chemical Technology.
2.   ROK Regarding Frozen Molluscan Shellfish for United States Consumption.
Agreement with:
1.   ROK Concerning Cooperation Regarding Fishery Resources.

340.15 United Mexican States (UMS)

MOU with:
1.   The Secretaria De Salud, UMS Regarding Cooperation in the Scientific and Regulatory Areas of Foods, Drugs, Cosmetics, Biologics (Including Blood and Blood Products), and Medical Devices.
2.   The Secretariat of Health of the UMS Regarding Fresh and Frozen Oysters, Clams, and Mussels.
3.   The Secretariat of Agriculture and Water Resources, UMS Regarding Mutual Cooperation in the Regulation of Raw Agricultural products Involved in Commerce Between Mexico and the United States.

340.16 Netherlands

MOU with:
1.   The Directorate General for Agriculture and Food of the Ministry of Agriculture and Fisheries of the Netherlands Concerning Dry Milk Products Exported to the US.
2.   The Ministry of Welfare, Health and Cultural Affairs, The Netherlands, on Good Laboratory Practice.

340.17 New Zealand

MOU with:
1.   Ministry of Agriculture and Fisheries, New Zealand Relative to Exporting Dry Milk Products to the US.
2.   New Zealand Regarding Exportation of Fresh and Fresh Frozen Shellfish to the U.S.

340.18 Northern Ireland

MOU with the Department of Health and Social Security of the UK and Northern Ireland Regarding the Recognition of Inspections of Manufacturers of Medical Devices.

340.19 Norway

MOU with Norway Regarding Rennet Casein Exported to the U.S.

340.20 Philippines

MOU with the Republic of Philippines Concerning Various Food Products Exported from the Philippines to the United States of America.

340.21 Sweden

MOU with:

1.   The Swedish National Board of Health & Welfare Concerning Exchange of Inspectional Information.

2   The Swedish National Board of Health and Welfare and the FDA Concerning Good Laboratory Practices.

3.   The Swedish Government Control Board of Dairy Products & Eggs Concerning Exporting Dry Milk Products to the US.

340.22 Switzerland

1.   MOU with Switzerland Regarding Good Laboratory Practice Inspections and the Reciprocal Recognition of Each Countries GLP Program.

2.   Agreement with Switzerland Regarding United States Acceptance of Swiss Drug Inspections.

340.23 United Kingdom (UK)

MOU with:

1.   The United Kingdom Regarding Fresh and Fresh Frozen Shellfish.

2.   The Department or Health and Social Security of the UK and Northern Ireland Regarding the Recognition of Inspections of Manufacturers of Medical Devices.

3.   The Office of Pesticides and Toxic Substances, U.S.EPA, and the Medical Division of Toxicology and Environmental Protection, United Kingdom Department of Health and Social Security Regarding Good Laboratory Practice.

341   MUTUAL RECOGNITION AGREEMENTS

341.1 European Community

Changes in FDAMA have required that FDA begin the process of acceptance of mutual recognition agreements relating to the regulation of FDA regulated commodities, facilitate commerce in devices between the US and foreign countries and other activities to reduce the burden of regulation and to harmonize regulatory requirements. See Section 803. Additional specific information is available at http://www.fda.gov/oia/homepage.htm.

341.2 Pharmaceuticals and Medical Devices

The first mutual recognition agreement (MRA) to be implemented, The Joint Declaration to the Agreement on Mutual Recognition Between the United States of America and the European Community (MRA) was signed in May 1998. It consists of the following sections:

Framework
Telecommunication Equipment
Electromagnetic Compatibility (EMC)
Electrical Safety
Recreational Craft
Pharmaceutical Good Manufacturing Practices (GMPs)
Medical Devices

It covers both FDA regulated and non-FDA regulated products and is an agreement between the United States and the European Union (EU) representing 15 Member States. It establishes procedures leading to FDA acceptance of inspectional work done by (EU) Regulatory or Competent Authorities (RA/CA) or Notified Bodies termed Conformity Assessment Bodies (CABs) in the MRA. The pharmaceutical annex is based on an assessment of equivalence with the Member States and the medical device annex is based on inspections by non-government firms who are recognized by the Member State regulatory authority. FDA has begun the process of implementing this agreement which has a 3 year transition period before the operational phase.

341.3   Food Products

In July, 1999, the United States and the EC signed the "AGREEMENT BETWEEN THE UNITES STATES OF AMERICA AND THE EUROPEAN COMMUNITY ON SANITARY MEASURES TO PROTECT PUBLIC AND ANIMAL HEALTH IN TRADE IN LIVE ANIMALS AND ANIMAL PRODUCTS". This agreement is very much like a mutual recognition agreement and is based on the equivalence process. It covers a very wide range of human food products, all of animal origin, such as milk and dairy products, seafood, honey, wild game, snails, frog legs and canned pet food. For purposes of this agreement, the EC is considered one "party" and not 15 Member States. Activities to begin assessing equivalence are underway.

SUBCHAPTER 350 - NON GOVERNMENT AGREEMENTS

The Agency has entered agreements with various nongovernmental groups to formulate various programs and guidance. The complete text of these agreements appears in the Federal Cooperative Agreements Manual. These agreements are outlined below.

350.1 Association of Official Analytical Chemists (AOAC)

MOA with AOAC Concerning Analytical Methods.

350.2 National Conference on Interstate Milk Shipments (NCIMS)

MOU with NCIM To Strengthen the Interstate Milk Shippers Program. See IOM 538 regarding inspection at dairy plants covered under the Interstate Milk Shippers Program.

350.3 Interstate Shellfish Sanitation Conference (ISSC)

MOU with ISSC to Improve the Sanitation and Quality of Shellfish by Delineating Responsibilities.

350.4 United States Pharmacopoeia Convention (USP)

Agreement with USP Regarding Review of Revisions to Compendial Requirements for Drugs.

350.5 Conference for Food Protection (CFP)

MOU with the Conference for Food Protection (CFP) to promote input by all stakeholders toward improving food safety.

HISTORY OF MENU ITEMS   DATE: 4/25/84   PLACE: Hyatt Hotel, St. Louis, MO.

MENU ITEM	SUPPLIER	DATE REC'D	PRE-PREPARED	ADVANCE PREPARED	LOCATION	STEPS IN PROCESS	TEMP °F	TIMES	EMPLOYEE(S) INVOLVED
Egg Rolls (Appetizer)	Independent Food St. Louis, MO	4/20	YES		Freezer	Bake	5°-235°F	1400-1730	R. Brown
Ravioli (Appetizer)	Ital-Amer Foods St. Louis Mo	4/21	YES		Freezer	Deep Fry	5°-300°F	1700-1730	B. Black
Cheeses (Appetizer)	Fox Dairy St. Louis MD	4/24	YES		Cooler	Slice	40°F	1350-1450	C. White
Pate (Appetizer)	Joes' Butcher Shop E. St. Louis, IL (Liver)	4/10		Y-4/10 Chef Welsh	Freezer	Thaw / Slice / Plate	5-40°F / 40°F / 40°F	?-1630 / 1600-1630 / 1630-1700	K. Green
Produce (Salad)	Lombardi's St. Louis, MO	4/24			Cooler	Wash / plate / Cool	55°F / 75°F / 75°-40°F	0730 / 0945-1145 / 0945-1130	B. Black & K. Green
Crown Potatos	"	"			"	Slice / Bake / Plate	75°F / 75-235°F / 200°F	0900-1630 / 1030-1200 / 1700-1730	R. Brown & A. Smith
Prime Ribs	Joes Butcher Shop E. St. Louis, IL	4/24			"	Roast / Slice / Plate	36-140°F / 135°F / 130°F	1500-1700 / 1800-1830 / 1830-1900	Chef Welsh / C. White / Chef Welsh
Wine	1983 Chateau St. Juan - Sonoma Valley, CA. / 1980 Marion Cabernet - "								

EXHIBIT 310-A

INVESTIGATIONS OPERATIONS MANUAL

HISTORY OF MENU ITEMS   DATE   PLACE

MENU ITEM	SUPPLIER	DATE REC'D	PRE-PREPARED	ADVANCE PREPARED	LOCATION	STEPS IN PROCESS	TEMP OF	TIMES	EMPLOYEE(S) INVOLVED

Date:

To: Postmaster

ADDRESS INFORMATION REQUEST

Please furnish this agency with the new address, if available, for the following individual or firm, or verify whether or not the address given below is one at which mail for this individual is currently being delivered. If the following address is a post office box, please furnish the street address as recorded on the box holder's application form. In accordance with ASM Section 352.44, please also furnish the name and phone number of the boxholder and if applicable, the name of the person who rented the box.

Name:

Last Known Address:

I certify that the address information for this individual is required for the performance of this agency's official duties.

(Signature of Agency Official)

(Title)

FOR POST OFFICE USE ONLY

( )   Mail is delivered to address given.   New Address:

( )   Not known at given address.

( )   Moved, left no forwarding address

( )   No such address.   Boxholders Street Address

( )   Other (specify)_____

_____

FDA Requesting Office Address

Postmark/Date Stamp

EXHIBIT 310-B   **INVESTIGATIONS OPERATIONS MANUAL**

INSTRUCTIONS FOR COMPLETING IOM EXHIBIT 310-B

If you have already attempted to locate the individual or firm by sending mail marked on the outside of the envelope "DO NOT FORWARD. ADDRESS CORRECTION REQUESTED", without results, then proceed with this form according to the instructions below.

INSTRUCTIONS

1.   Address the request to the Postmaster at the post office of the last known address.

2.   On the lines provided, give the name and last known address, including zip code, of the individual or firm. Do not include any other identifying information such as race, date of birth, social security number, etc.

3.   **The Postal Service provides the service of address verification to Government agencies only. For this reason, the Postal Service requires the signature and title of an agency official to certify that the address information requested is required in the performance of the agency's official duties. The agency official should be if possible, the chief of the office requesting the information. In the interests of efficiency, the signature may be preprinted or rubber-stamped.**

4.   **Type or stamp the agency's return mailing address in the space provided at the bottom of the request. Then, mail or deliver the request to the Postmaster at the post office of the last known address.**

You are not required to submit this request in duplicate or to furnish a return envelope.

THIS TABLE SUMMARIZES INFORMATION CONCERNING JURISDICTION OVERLAP FOR COMMERCIAL PRODUCTS REGULATED BY EITHER OR BOTH FDA AND USDA. IT DOES NOT COVER PRODUCTS MADE FOR ON-SITE CONSUMPTION SUCH AS PIZZA PARLORS, DELICATESSENS, FAST FOOD SITES, ETC. PRODUCTS CARRYING THE USDA SHIELD ARE USDA JURISDICTION.

<----FDA JURISDICTION---->	<------------------------USDA JURISDICTION---------------------->		
21 USC 392(b) Meats and meat food products shall be exempt from the provisions of this Act to the extent of the application or the extension thereto of the Meat Inspection Act. FDA responsible for all non-specified red meats (bison, rabbits, game animals, zoo animals and all members of the deer family including elk (wapiti) and moose)). FDA responsible for all non-specified birds including wild turkeys, wild ducks, wild geese and Emus.	The Meat Inspection Act specifies the species of animal covered and includes carcasses or parts of cattle, sheep, swine, goats, horses, mules or other equines. Mandatory Inspection of Ratites and Squab announced by USDA/FSIS April 2001	The Poultry Products Inspection Act (PPIA) defines the term poultry as any domesticated bird. USDA has interpreted this to include chickens, turkeys, domestic ducks, domestic geese and guineas. The Poultry Products Inspection Act states poultry and poultry products shall be exempt from the provisions of the FD&C Act to the extent they are covered by the PPIA.	The Egg Products Inspection Act defines egg to mean the shell egg of domesticated chicken, turkey, duck, goose or guinea. Grading of shell eggs is done under USDA supervision. (FDA enforces labels/labeling of shell eggs and egg products.)
Products with less than 3% red meat on a wet basis, products with less than 2% poultry on a wet basis and closed-face sandwiches are not subject to mandatory USDA inspection.	Products containing 3% or more meat on a wet basis, open-faced sandwiches.	Products containing 2% or more poultry on a wet basis.	Egg processing plants (egg washing, sorting, egg breaking, and pasteurizing operations) are under USDA jurisdiction.
FDA is responsible for egg containing products and other egg processing not covered by USDA; e.g. restaurants, bakeries, cake mix plants, etc.			Products that are basically known for their egg content are under USDA jurisdiction such as egg rolls for slicing, heat 'n serve omelets, etc.
Cheese pizza, onion and mushroom pizza, meat flavored spaghetti sauce (less than 3% red meat), spaghetti sauce with mushrooms and 2% meat, pork and beans, sliced egg sandwich (closed-face), frozen fish dinner, rabbit stew, shrimp-flavored instant noodles, venison jerky, buffalo burgers, alligator nuggets, noodle soup chicken flavor	Pepperoni pizza, meat-lovers stuffed crust pizza, meat sauces (3% red meat or more), spaghetti sauce with meat balls, open-faced roast beef sandwich, hot dogs, corn dogs, beef/vegetable pot pie	chicken sandwich (open face), chicken noodle soup	

Jurisdiction for products produced under the School Lunch Program, for military use, etc. is determined via the same algorithm although the purchases are made under strict specifications so that the burden of compliance falls on the contractor. Compliance Policy Guide 565.100, 567.200 and 567.300 provide additional examples of jurisdiction. IOM 311 and 750 provide more information on our interactions with USDA and Detention Authority.

CHAPTER 4 - SAMPLING

CONTENTS

SUBCHAPTER 400 - GENERAL

401   AUTHORITY

401.1 Examinations and Investigations

Collecting samples is a critical part of FDA's regulatory activities. Section 702(b) of the Act gives FDA authority to conduct investigations and collect samples. A Notice of Inspection is not always required for sample collections. If during a sample collection, you begin to conduct an inspection (examining storage conditions, reviewing records for compliance with laws and regulations, etc.), issue an FDA 482 and continue your activities. See IOM 501 and 511.

While inspections and investigations may precede sample collection, a sample must ultimately be obtained for a case to proceed, under the law. Proper sample collection is the keystone of effective enforcement action.

FD&C Act - See IOM 701.1 for this information.

PHS Act - See IOM 701.3 for this information.

401.2 Notice of Inspection

Samples are often collected during the course of an establishment inspection or inspection of a vehicle. See IOM 501 & IOM 511.

a.   Carriers - Issue an FDA 482 - Use of Notice of Inspection to the driver or agent when it is necessary to inspect vehicles. See IOM 511.2.

b.   Manufacturers, etc. - An FDA 482. A Notice of Inspection should be issued when samples are collected from lots in possession of a manufacturer, processor, packer or repacker, whether or not regulatory action is intended toward the articles, the dealer, the manufacturer or the shipper.

401.3 Receipt for Sample

Section 704(c) of the FD&C Act requires issuing a receipt describing any samples obtained during the course of an inspection. The receipt is to be issued to the owner, operator, or agent in charge, upon completion of the inspection and prior to leaving the premises. See IOM 513 for special situations. See IOM 412.6 for instructions on completing the form.

401.6 Report of Analysis

Section 704(d) of the FD&C Act requires FDA furnish a report of analysis on any sample of food (including animal food and feed, medicated and non-medicated), collected during an inspection of an establishment where such food is "*** manufactured, processed, or packed ***," if the sample is examined for compliance with Section 402(a)(3) of the Act. Reports of analysis are not required for non-food items examined (rodent pellets, etc.). The servicing laboratory is responsible for furnishing the report of analysis.

402 VALID SAMPLE

A valid sample is the starting point and keystone for most administrative and legal actions. As evidence, the sample must support the government's charge there is a violation of the law. Also, it must conform to the rules on admissibility of evidence. A properly collected and prepared sample provides:

a.   A portion of the lot of goods for laboratory analysis and reserve, a 702(b) reserve portion if appropriate, and/or an exhibit demonstrating the violation represented by the lot.

b.   A report of your observations of the lot.

c.   Labels and labeling, or copies of such, which "accompany" the goods.

d.   Documentary evidence of federal jurisdiction over the lot, information about individuals responsible for the violation, where the violation was committed, and similar data.

e.   Signed statements from persons who may be called upon as witnesses, if there is a subsequent court action.

404   RESPONSIBILITY

Collect every sample as if you will be required to testify in court about everything you did concerning each and every event surrounding the sample collection. Mistakes or deficiencies, however trivial they may seem, can fatally damage the government's case. Be objective, accurate, and thorough.

405   OFFICIAL SAMPLES (21 CFR 2.10)

A sample of a food, drug, or cosmetic is an "Official Sample" if records or other evidence obtained shows the lot from which the sample was collected was:

a.   Introduced or delivered for introduction in interstate commerce, or

b.   Was in or was received in interstate commerce, or

c.   Was manufactured in a territory or the District of Columbia.

A sample of a device, a counterfeit drug, or any object associated with drug counterfeiting, no matter where it is collected, is also an "Official Sample". The statute permits proceeding against these articles, when violative, at any time. See Sections 304(a)(2) Act.

Import Samples are Official Samples and require the same integrity as domestic Official Samples. They must be identified with sample number, collection date and collector's handwritten initials. Interstate documentation is not required, see CPG manual section 110.200 & 110.600. Import Samples need not be sealed, unless District policy dictates, as long as the integrity of the sample is maintained.

Normally, 702(b) portions are not collected for routine Import Samples. However, in situations where a dispute arises or a potential for regulatory action exists, the 702(b) portions should be collected and the sample sealed as described in IOM 453.

405.1 Definition - Official Sample

An Official Sample is one taken from a lot for which Federal jurisdiction can be established. If violative, the Official Sample provides a basis for administrative or legal action. Official Samples generally, but not always, consist of a physical portion of the lot sampled. To be useful, an Official Sample must be:

a.   Accompanied by records establishing Federal jurisdiction, and identifying the persons having knowledge of the lot's movement and custody of the records. (Evidence of Interstate movement is not required for medical device samples, but by policy to be obtained when a seizure, injunction, prosecution or civil penalty is contemplated).

b.   Representative of the lot from which collected.

c.   If a physical sample, large enough to permit proper laboratory examination and provide a 702(b) reserve portion when necessary.

d.   Handled, identified, and sealed in such a manner as to maintain its integrity as evidence, with a clear record of its chain of custody.

405.2 Documentary Samples

In a "Documentary" (or "DOC") sample, no actual physical sample of the product is taken. However, all the other elements of an official sample described in 405 and 405.1 above are present. This official sample consists of the article's labels (or label tracings, photocopies, or photos), accompanying labeling (leaflets, brochures, promotional materials, including Internet websites, etc.) and documentation of interstate movement (freight bills, bills of lading, affidavits, etc. Photos of the product, drawings, sketches or schematics, production records, diagrams, invoices or similar items may also be part of the sample. See IOM Exhibits 430-I and 430-J. As a rule, no FDA 484, receipt for samples is issued during collection of a DOC Sample. See subparagraph 513.1 for physical evidence exception.

A DOC samples is collected when an actual physical sample is not practical (e.g., very large, expensive, complex, permanently installed devices), in instances where the article is no longer available, or there is little need for laboratory examination. A single piece of life support equipment, which must remain in emergency service until a replacement is available, may be sampled in this manner. Another instance where a DOC sample might be collected involves a shipment of product recommended for seizure based on misbranding charges. During availability check, the lot sampled is found to have been distributed; however, a new shipment, identically labeled, is on hand. In this instance, the new shipment may be sampled on a DOC basis since another physical sample and examination is not required. Regulatory action may proceed on the basis of the earlier examination. Thus, only labeling, transportation records, the appropriate dealer affidavits, and an inventory of product on hand need be obtained.

A variation of this procedure involves collecting one or more units and removing (stripping) the original labels/labeling from the product container. It is frequently easier and quicker to collect relatively inexpensive units to field strip than it is to photocopy or photograph all accompanying labels. The sample is handled in exactly the same manner as any other DOC sample, once original labeling has been removed and the remainder of the sample destroyed. A prominent explanation on the C/R alerts reviewers the original units collected were destroyed after the original labeling was removed. This procedure is not appropriate where complete, intact, labeled units are desired for exhibit purposes, even though there is no intention of analyzing the units obtained.

When photos are taken as part of DOC Samples, the rolls of exposed film should - unless developed by yourself - be sent to established commercial film dealers or color processors for developing. Report identity of film processor on the FDA 525. Also see IOM 523.

See IOM 451.5 for guidance on identifying records associated with a DOC sample. Do not officially seal these records, but list them on the C/R. If any photos are taken as part of the DOC sample, the negatives, if any, must be officially sealed per IOM 523.2. See IOM Exhibit 430-I and 430-J for examples of DOC samples. Attach the documents, photo's and negatives along with any other records associated with the sample to the printed FACTS Collection Record. See IOM 439.9.

405.3 In-Transit Samples

In-Transit samples are those collected from lots held on loading/receiving docks of steamships, trucklines, or other common carriers, or being transported in vehicles. The lot is considered to be in-transit if it meets any of the following characteristics:

a.   A Bill of Lading (B/L) or other order to ship a lot interstate has been issued.

b.   The owner/shipper or agent acknowledges, preferably by signed affidavit, he has ordered the lot to be shipped interstate.

c.   The owner or operator of the common carrier acknowledges, preferably by signed affidavit, he has an order from the shipper to move the lot interstate.

405.4 301(k) Samples

Section 301(k) of the FD&C Act is a prohibited act, which can result in any one or more separate legal procedures . A sample collected from a lot of food, drug, device or cosmetic which became adulterated or misbranded while held for sale, whether or not the first sale, after shipment in interstate commerce is often referred to as a "301(k) Sample". The term "301(k) Sample" is misleading, but widely used within FDA to describe certain samples collected from lots which become violative after shipment in interstate commerce.

Since some act took place which resulted in the adulteration or misbranding of a previously nonviolative product, after shipment in interstate commerce, the "301(k)" documentation is incomplete without identifying the act, establishing when and how it occurred, and the person(s) responsible for causing the violation. This feature, more than any other, distinguishes a "301(k) Sample" from the other Official Samples. When you report the sample collection, the responsible party will always be the dealer. See IOM Exhibit 430-I.

For example, to document insect adulteration of a finished product, caused by a live insect population in the processing areas of a food manufacturer such as a bakery, you must document receipt of clean raw material and subsequent adulteration caused by the firm's handling or processing of the raw material. Therefore, you would need to show there was an insect infestation at the firm that either did, or may have contaminated the finished product. You would need to collect a sample of the clean incoming flour, and subsamples at points in the system to demonstrate where insect infestations exist in the system. In situations where sampling may disturb static points in the system which may result in a higher level of adulteration of the finished product than normal, you should sample in reverse.

301(k) samples can also be used to document adulteration (including noncompliance with GMPs) or misbranding of other regulated commodities, including drugs and biologics. If possible, when collecting a 301(k) sample covering a drug product, you should attempt to document 'adulteration' or 'misbranding' of the active ingredient by the firm's actions. In the case of a biologic (for example, whole blood), which has not moved in interstate commerce, document the interstate receipt of the bag, and the firm's subsequent 'adulteration' or 'misbranding' of the anti-coagulant (considered a drug) in the blood bag.

405.5 Induced Sample

An induced sample is an Official Sample ordered or obtained by agency response to some type of advertisement or promotional activity. The sample is procured by mail, telephone, or other means without disclosing any association of the requester or the transaction with FDA. See IOM 425.4 for additional information.

405.6 Undercover Buy

An "undercover buy" is an Official Sample, similar to and obtained in much the same manner as an "induced sample". In an "undercover buy", however, the solicitation is made in person, usually under an alias. Pre-arranged explanations or cover stories are necessary to dispell any suspicions about the requester that may surface in face-to-face discussions. "Undercover buys" are frequently used in investigating complaints of illegal activity where the information cannot be substantiated or refuted through more conventional means.

405.7 Post Seizure (P.S.) Sample

A lot under seizure is in the custody of the U. S. Marshal. If either the claimant or the government desires a sample from the seized lot, for any reason, it may be collected only by court order. In most cases, the order will specify how the sample is to be collected, and may provide for each party to collect samples. If the order was obtained by the claimant, permit the claimant's representative to determine

how his/her sample collection is made. If the method of collection is improper, make constructive suggestions, but do not argue. Report exactly how the sample was drawn. Unless the claimant objects, mark subdivisions he collects with "P.S.", your initials and date. "P.S." Samples are Official Samples.

Do not pay for Post Seizure Samples or any samples collected of a lot reconditioned under a Consent Decree. See IOM 416.1.

405.8 Domestic Import Sample

To record information on FDA's total coverage of imported products, an additional classification of samples, "Domestic Import" or "DI" was devised. These are Official Samples of foreign products, which have passed through customs and are in domestic commerce. The FDA may have previously taken a sample of the product while in import status, or the product may have been permitted entry without being sampled. If sampled while still in import status, the samples collected are import samples, and not "DI" Samples. However, once the product leaves import status, it enters domestic commerce and any sample collected is an Official "Domestic Import" (DI) Sample. Note: When collecting DI Samples, especially if a violation is suspected, attempt to determine the port of entry and importer of record. Report this information on the CR. Include the name of the Country of Origin of the product and the Country Code if known.

A sample is classed as Domestic Import (DI), if any of the following situations apply:

a.   The label declares the product to be from a foreign country.

b.   The label bears the word, "Imported".

c.   Records obtained or reviewed reveal the product originated in a foreign country.

d.   It is known that the product is not grown or produced in the US; it is packed as a single item with few or no other ingredients added, and it is not manipulated in any major manner, which changes the product or its composition. For example, "Olive Oil" imported in bulk and merely repacked with no added ingredients and no manipulation would be a "DI" sample, while pepper which is processed, ground and packed after entry would not. However, retail packages of ground pepper processed and packaged in a foreign country would be "DI" Samples.

e.   Samples of imported raw materials, which are collected before further processing or mixed with other ingredients.

DI samples are significantly different from other official samples in another important respect. Unlike domestic products, where considerable information is readily available on manufacturing and distribution channels, it is frequently difficult to identify the responsible parties for products of foreign origin once they enter domestic commerce. The most practical way is to establish a paper trail of records going back as far as possible in the distribution chain to the actual entry.

Identifying "DI" Samples - When writing the sample number on physical samples of Domestic Import products, documents related to the sample, and the seals, preface the sample number with prefix "DI" in the same manner other sample types are used, such as, "DOC", "FS", "PS", etc.

405.9 Import Sample

Import samples are physical sample collections of products, which originate from another country, collected while the goods are in import status. Import status ends when Customs has cleared an entry for the shipment. See IOM chapter 6.

405.10 Additional Sample

This is a physical sample collected from a previously sampled lot of either a domestic or imported product.

a. Additional Import Samples - The sample collected must have the same sample number as the original sample collected.

b. Additional Domestic Sample - The sample collected may have another sample number, but it must be Flagged as an "ADD" Sample and the original sample number referenced in the "Related Sample" block on the Collection Record.

406 FOOD STANDARDS SAMPLE

Food Standards (FS) samples are collected to provide information on which to base Food Standards. Sample integrity is maintained the same as Official Samples.

Note: Samples of standardized foods are not FS Samples.

407 GWQAP SAMPLES

As part of the Government-Wide Quality Assurance Program (GWQAP), FDA may determine the need for testing samples of medical products procured on Government contracts in order to assure compliance with Federal specifications and the applicable requirements of the FD&C Act.

Whenever FDA determines samples are desired, Office of Enforcement's Division of Compliance Information and Quality Assurance (DCIQA) advises the home district GWQAP coordinator a sample is to be collected, and provides written background and testing instructions. DCIQA normally arranges for DOD/VA/HRSA to ship GWQAP drug samples directly to the home district for processing and analysis. Most device samples are shipped directly to WEAC by DOD/VA/HRSA. District investigators will rarely be requested to collect GWQAP or "GQA" Samples from DOD/VA/HRSA facilities. However, they may occasionally complete a C/R and prepare a "GQA" Sample for the laboratory upon its arrival from DOD/VA/HRSA.

For more information about GWQAP Samples, contact DCIQA at (301) 827-0390.

408 INVESTIGATIONAL SAMPLES

These samples, referred to as "INV Samples", need not be collected from lots in interstate commerce or under federal jurisdiction. They are generally collected to document observations, support regulatory actions or provide other information. They may be used as evidence in court, and they must be sealed and their integrity and chain of custody protected. Examples of INV Samples are:

a. Factory Samples - Raw materials, in-process and finished products to demonstrate manufacturing conditions. Note: Photographs taken in a firm are not samples. They are exhibits except when they are part of a DOC Sample. See IOM 451.4, 522, & 523.

b. Exhibits - Filth exhibits and other articles taken for exhibit purposes during inspections to demonstrate manufacturing or storage conditions, employee practices, and the like.

c. Reconditioning Samples - These are taken from lots reconditioned under a Decree or other agreement to bring the lots into compliance with the law. The sample is taken to determine if reconditioning was satisfactorily performed. These samples should be submitted as Official Samples, rather than INV.

d. Certain Complaint Samples - Injury and illness investigation samples from certain complaints where there is no Federal jurisdiction, or where the alleged violation offers no basis for subsequent regulatory action. Complaint samples from lots for which Federal jurisdiction is clear should be submitted as Official Samples.

When writing the sample number on sub samples, documents related to the sample, and the seals, preface the sample number with "INV" in the same manner as other sample types are used. (e.g. "DOC", "DI").

408.1 Audit/Certification Sample

A sample collected to verify analytical results provided by a certificate of analysis or private laboratory analysis that purports to show a product complies with the FD&C Act and/or regulations. This sample type will usually be used with an import sample.

408.2 Mail Entry Sample

A mail entry sample is a sample of an imported product that enters the U.S. through the U.S. Mail.

408.3 Non-Regulatory Sample

Samples collected and analyzed by FDA for other federal, state, or local agencies of products over which the FDA has no jurisdiction.

SUBCHAPTER 410 - DEALER RELATIONS

410.1 Dealer Definition and Good Will

For sample collection purposes, the dealer is the person, firm (which could include the manufacturer), institution or other party, who has possession of a particular lot of goods. The dealer does not have to be a firm or company, which is in the business of buying or selling goods. The dealer might be a housewife in her home, a physician, or a public agency; these dealers obtain products to use but not to sell. The dealer may be a party who does not own the goods, but has possession of them, such as a public storage warehouse or transportation agency.

Rapport with the dealer is important to the success of your objective. All dealers, including hostile ones, should be approached in a friendly manner and treated with fairness, honesty, courtesy and consideration. A dealer may be called as a Government witness in a court case, and a favorable attitude on his/her part is to be sought. Never use strong-arm tactics or deception, but rather be professional and demonstrate diplomacy, tact, and persuasion. Do not make unreasonable demands.

Introduce yourself to the dealer by name, title and organization; present your credentials for examination, and, if appropriate, issue an FDA 482, Notice of Inspection. See IOM 401.2, 411, 501 and 511. Explain the purpose of your visit. Be prepared to answer the dealer's questions and attempt to relieve any apprehensions, at the same time being careful not to reveal any confidential information. Do not disparage the product, its manufacturer, or shipper. Do not reveal the particular violation suspected unless the dealer is responsible, or unless you ask him/her to voluntarily hold the goods. The very fact we are collecting a sample is often reason enough to arouse the dealer's suspicions about the legality of the product.

410.2 Dealer Objection to Sampling Procedure

If the dealer objects to your proposed sampling technique, attempt to reach a reasonable compromise on a method that will provide a satisfactory, though perhaps not ideal, sample. Assure the dealer you will make every effort to restore the lot to its original state, you are prepared to purchase a whole unit to avoid leaving broken cases, and we will reimburse him/her for additional labor costs incurred as a result of sampling. See IOM 416. If a reasonable compromise cannot be reached, proceed as a refusal to permit sampling.

410.3 Refusal to Permit Sampling

A challenge of FDA authority to collect samples may be raised by a dealer who, for varied reasons, both personal and professional opposes the activities of the agency, or of governmental units in general.

Refusals to permit sample collection commonly emerge unless you can identify a section of the law which specifically authorizes it. The suggested approach for dealing with these individuals is to use patient, tactful persuasion, pointing out that the sample is a part of the investigations authorized in Section 702(b) of the Act. If you have not already done so, issue an FDA 482 - Notice of Inspection as soon as it becomes apparent the dealer will continue to object. Point out and discuss the authorities provided by Sections 702(a), 702(b), 704(a), 704(c), 704(d) and the precedent case mentioned in IOM 701.1. If refusal persists,

point out the criminal prohibitions of Section 301(f) of the Act.

If samples are still refused, leave the premises and contact your supervisor immediately. Refer to IOM 514 and Compliance Policy Guide manual section 130.100 for further discussions on resolving the impasse.

411 NOTICE OF INSPECTION

See IOM 401.2, 501 and 511.

Each time you issue an FDA 482, Notice of Inspection, and subsequently collect a sample, issue the appropriate sample receipt (FDA 472 - Carriers Receipt for Samples or FDA 484 -Receipt for Samples).

411.1 Dealer Responsible For Condition of Lot

An FDA 482 should be issued before collecting samples from firms, carriers, or individuals whom FDA can take regulatory action against for the violative condition of the lot. See IOM 401.1. When in doubt, issue a Notice of Inspection. If there is no EIR, attach a copy of the FDA 482 to the printed FACTS Collection Record. See IOM 439.9.

411.2 Refusals

See IOM 410.2. An FDA 482 must be issued in all sample refusal situations to invoke the applicable provisions of the FD&C Act. The copy of the FDA 482 is to accompany the EIR; a memorandum outlining the facts of the refusal if no EIR is prepared.

411.3 Carrier In-transit Sampling

Caution: See IOM 424 for conditions, which must be met before collecting in-transit samples from common carriers.

When collecting samples from in-transit lots in possession of a commercial carrier, and the only regulatory sanctions possible are against the product itself or parties other than the carrier (e.g., manufacturer, shipper, etc.), furnish the carrier or his agent an FDA 482 modified to read "Notice of Inspection to Collect Samples Only…". See exhibit 510-A2. Attach a copy to the printed copy of the FACTS Collection Record. See IOM 439.9.

411.4 Dealer Requests Notice of Inspection

When inspecting a dealer, and an FDA 482 does not need to be issued, but the dealer requests a Notice of Inspection, issue an FDA 482 modified to read "Notice of Inspection to Collect Samples Only…" See Exhibit 510-B. Attach a copy to the printed FACTS Collection Record. See IOM 439.9.

412 RECEIPT FOR SAMPLES

Any time you collect a physical sample after issuing an FDA 482, Notice of Inspection, always issue the appropriate sample receipt FDA 472 - Carriers Receipt for Samples or FDA 484 , Receipt for Samples.

Always issue an FDA 484 as a receipt for samples of prescription drugs, including narcotics and controlled substances. See IOM 412.4 & 412.5.

412.1 Carriers/In-Transit Lots

Caution: See IOM 424.1 for conditions that must be met before collecting in-transit samples from common carriers.

Complete an FDA 472, Carriers Receipt for Samples, when samples are collected from carriers or while in transit. See IOM Exhibit 410-A. Give the original to the carrier or his agent and route a copy to the appropriate fiscal unit for your district. The fiscal clerk will notify the consignee and consignor that a sample has been collected so the owner can, if desired, bill FDA for the sample.

412.2 Dealer Requests Receipt

When collecting physical samples of regulated products, not in connection with an EI or where no FDA 482 has been issued, do not routinely issue an FDA 484, Receipt for Samples, except for prescription drugs, narcotics, or controlled substances. See IOM 412.4 & 412.5. If any dealer specifically asks for a receipt, prepare and issue an FDA 484 and route a copy with any other records associated with the collection record. See IOM 439.9.

412.4 Narcotic and Controlled Rx Drugs

Regulations of the Drug Enforcement Administration (DEA) impose strict controls and comprehensive record-keeping requirements on persons handling narcotics and controlled substances. As a result, an FDA 484 must be issued for all samples of such drugs collected by FDA.

Each dealer in narcotic and controlled drugs is assigned it's own unique DEA registration number. Any time you collect a sample of a narcotic or controlled drug, be sure the Dealer's DEA Registration Number is entered in the appropriate block of the FDA 484. Double-check the number for accuracy. An error may result in possible investigation for drug shortages.

The complete DEA Registration Number must be entered on the - RECEIPT FOR SAMPLES, given to the person from whom collected, by the collector when samples of narcotic or controlled drugs are collected.

Complete the FDA 484 carefully and completely. Include the trade and chemical name, strength, sample size, container size, lot, batch, or control number, manufacturer's name and address, district address and the sample number on the FDA 484 Receipt for Samples. See IOM Exhibit 410-C.

Always issue the original FDA 484, Receipt for Samples, to the person or firm from whom the narcotic or controlled drugs are obtained. Attach a copy to the printed FACTS Collection Record. See IOM 439.9. Use of the FDA 484 as a receipt for samples of these drugs has the approval of DEA. (See reverse of FDA 484).

412.5 Prescription Drugs (Non-Controlled)

Issue an FDA 484, Receipt for Samples, when samples of prescription legend drugs are collected from dealers,

individuals, or during inspections. Attach a copy of the FDA 484 to the printed FACTS Collection Record. See IOM 439.9.

412.6 Preparation of FDA 484

Complete the blocks on the FDA 484, Receipt for Samples, as follows:

Block 1 - Enter your District address & telephone number including area code.

Block 2 - Enter the complete name and official title of the individual to whom you issue the FDA 484.

Block 3 - Enter date on which you finished collecting the sample. If you spent more than one day on the sample collection, enter the date you completed sampling.

Block 4 - Enter complete Sample Number here. Be sure to include any prefixes such as "DOC", "INV", etc.

Block 5 - Enter firm's legal name.

Block 6 - If the firm is a dealer in narcotics or control drugs, enter their DEA Number here.

Block 7 & 8 - Enter number, street, city, state, and zip code of firm.

Block 9 - Enter a brief description of the article collected, including the number and size of units collected, product name and any identifying brand and code marks.

Block 10 - In certain situations such as for large or expensive device samples, the owner of the article may not want to part with the item. In these instances, FDA may borrow the item and return it later. If the item is borrowed and to be returned, check this box on the FDA 484. Otherwise, check the purchased block even if there is "no charge".

Block 11 - Enter the amount paid for the sample (even if borrowed, the owner may ask rent for it) and check the appropriate box. If there is no charge (always offer payment except for Post Seizure Samples), enter N/C and leave boxes blank. If, as a last resort, it is necessary for you to use your personal check or credit card and this is acceptable to the person, enter amount and check "Cr. Cd." box.

NOTE: Older editions of the FDA 484 do not have a "Cr. Cd." box. If not, write in "Cr. Cd." following the amount.

Block 12 - In instances where payment is made for the Sample, whether actually purchased, borrowed or provided at no charge, and there is no Dealer's Affidavit or any other document executed to show the owner's signature for receipt of payment, obtain the signature of the person receiving payment for the sample.

If Dealer's Affidavit, regular Affidavit or other document is used, the recipient's signature will be on that document so it is not necessary for him to also sign the FDA 484. In this case insert an applicable statement such as "Dealers Affidavit signed" in this block.

Blocks 14, 15, & 17 - Enter your name & title and signature.

412.7 Routing of FDA 484

Original - Give the signed original to the firm, preferably to the individual to whom you gave the FDA 482 & FDA 483. See IOM 412.4 regarding receipts for narcotics and controlled drug samples.

First Carbon - Accompanies the EIR. If no EIR is involved such as when collecting a sample and the dealer specifically requests a receipt, attach it to the original Collection Record. See IOM 412.2, 4, & 5.

Second Carbon - This is an extra copy for use as needed. If not filed in the factory file, or attached to the C/R or not otherwise needed, it may be destroyed.

If exact copies are used instead of carbon copies, then route one exact copy with the EIR and a second as above.

When numerous sub samples are collected, the second carbon or exact copy may be attached to the original C/R to avoid repetition of the sub descriptions. When used for this purpose, be sure the numbers you assign to the physical sub samples matches those on the FDA 484, and that the subs are adequately described. If errors are noted after issuance, handle the same way as instructed under IOM 512.

414 DEALER IDENTIFICATION OF LOT AND RECORDS

Positive identification of sampled lots and the records covering their sales and shipment are essential to legal proceedings. The dealer's identification of a sampled lot and his identification of the records covering I.S. shipment should be factual and specific. If there is a question about accurate identification of the lot or records, determine all facts and establish identification as clearly as possible. Be alert to any identifying marks, which may later be used on the witness stand for positive identification.

414.2 Private Individuals

When collecting Official Samples from private individuals, ask the individual to initial and date the label, wrappings, promotional literature, etc. This will aid in positively identifying the product and related documents in any court proceeding that may develop months, or even years later.
414.3 Seriously Ill Individuals

If you collect samples from a person for contemplated regulatory action, and it is obvious the person is seriously ill, you should attempt to locate and obtain a corroborating statement and identification from someone else. This corroborating witness should have personal knowledge of the facts and be available if the principle witness cannot testify in a legal proceeding.

415 SAMPLING FROM GOVERNMENT AGENCIES

See IOM 313.4 for information.

416 PAYMENT FOR SAMPLES

Payment for all samples, except those collected under authority of a Court Order or Decree shall be offered to the person from whom obtained regardless of the amount. See IOM 416.2.

An exception is import samples. FDA does not pay for Import samples at the time of collection. The importer should bill the District Office. FDA will not pay for violative import samples. See 21 CFR 1.91.

416.1 Post Seizure (P.S.) and Reconditioning Samples Under Court Order

Do not pay for, or offer payment for, any Post Seizure (P.S) or other samples including those from reconditioned lots, if collected under authority of a Court Order or Decree. If the dealer insists on payment before permitting sampling, show him/her the Court Order. If he/she still refuses sampling, contact your supervisor immediately for further instructions. You may be instructed to notify the U.S. Attorney.

416.2 Determining Sample Cost

If you are collecting samples from firms or representatives of firms who have Federal Supply, Veterans Administration or other contracts with the Federal Government, the cost of the sample should be determined by the scheduled price. Inquire of the firm if they are on contract for the item. If so, pay only the scheduled price. Some dealers may wish to charge their regular selling price. However, if the cost of the sample seems excessive, try to persuade the dealer a lower price is more fair. If asked, tell the dealer the government considers a fair price to be the dealer's invoice cost plus a nominal charge (usually 10-15%) for freight, handling and storage.

If unable, through tactful discussion, to convince the dealer to lower the sample cost, do not haggle over the price to be paid. If the cost seems exorbitant, check with your supervisor to determine if the sample size can be reduced, or for further instructions. Whenever there is a disagreement over sample cost, ask the dealer to bill the district and report the circumstances in the Collection Remarks field on your FACTS collection record.

If districts encounter requests for payment for method validation samples (either direct submission by firms to labs or during collection from responsible firms), they should contact the responsible Office of New Drug Chemistry review division, so that communication may take place with the application sponsor. If product is being collected from commercial distribution not in the control of the sponsor/manufacturer, then the district should expect to pay wholesale cost. Expenses for NDA method validation samples should be charge to a PDUFA reimbursable CAN.

416.3 Method of Payment

Costs Billed to District - Billing sample costs to the district is, in many instances, the most practical method of payment. This is particularly true where substantial costs are involved due to large numbers or expensive samples, when samples are collected from third parties such as carriers and public storage warehouses, or when delivery followed by subsequent billing is the dealers normal business practice. If available, obtain the dealer's invoice and submit it to the appropriate fiscal unit for your district.

Sampling from public storage warehouses and common carriers incur s costs, which are normally billed because the owner of the product is unavailable. Determine the identity of the owner or his agent, and estimate the value of the goods sampled. Arrange with the owner or agent to bill the district.

Cash Payment –If you who are authorized to collect samples, you can withdraw an ATM advance using your government credit card whether or not you are in travel status. This authorization is provided on your blanket travel order. The amount of the withdrawal should be limited to the cost of the sample. You should submit your itemized claim for samples along with the ATM fee on an SF 1164, Claim for Reimbursement for Expenditures on Official Business. Include the sample number and submit to your fiscal unit for payment. Any documentation should be provided. Sample costs cannot be charged directly to your government credit card.

416.4 Sampling - Labor Charges

Additional labor, use of forklift, or other assistance may be required to move merchandise, skids, pallets, etc., to properly sample and restore the lot. Usually assistance will be available on the premises, or arrangements can be made with management to employ outside professional help.

There is usually little need to discuss payment when requesting nominal use of labor or equipment. However, if there is an indication management expects payment; attempt to reach a clear understanding of the charges before proceeding. If the charges to be incurred appear reasonable, and the cost is minor (about $25.00 or less), proceed with the work and add the charges to your sample cost. However, if substantial costs are involved, consult with your supervisor before making a commitment to pay.

Where the charges are substantial and have been authorized by your supervisor, arrange for the cost of labor and/or machinery to be billed to the district. Handle these charges separately from the actual cost of the sample. Determine the hourly rate and keep track of time, labor, or machinery actually used. Prepare a short memo outlining the charges and submit it to the appropriate fiscal unit for your district.

418   VOLUNTARY EMBARGO

This section deals solely with a "voluntary" hold on regulated products. See IOM 750 for specific statutory authorities for detaining meat, poultry, egg products, and medical devices.

While there is no specific authority for requesting a voluntary embargo on a lot, voluntary embargoes by a dealer shall be encouraged where the lot sampled is clearly adulterated. By voluntarily holding, the dealer prevents further distribution of suspected violative goods until seizure or other appropriate action can be accomplished.

418.1 Perishable Goods

Except in rare instances, it is generally not practical to hold highly perishable items unless the analysis can be completed within 24 hours. You should confer with your supervisor before requesting a voluntary embargo on perishable items. FDA's policy on sampling perishable imported products can be found at Part 9, Regulatory Procedures manual.

418.2 Obtaining a Voluntary Embargo

When the lot is clearly adulterated, or when instructed to do so by your supervisor, arrange for a voluntary embargo by the dealer. If possible, direct your conversation so that the dealer suggests the embargo. Call the dealer's attention to his/her responsibility under the law, and appeal to his/her sense of public service, integrity, or the health consequences that may be involved.

Always place a time limit on voluntary embargoes using your best estimate of how long it will take to complete the analysis and reach a district decision. Consider such factors as location of the examining lab, difficulty of the analysis required, turnover rate, storage conditions and the perishable nature of the merchandise. Note: Your district's compliance branch can ask for an extension of the voluntary embargo.

Since the action is voluntary, we cannot compel the dealer to do all the things we might ask him/her to do. While requests for voluntary holds are generally granted, a dealer may act or suggest an alternative approach.

If the dealer indicates a reluctance to voluntarily hold the lot, call his/her attention to Section 301(a) of the FD&C Act. If the dealer still refuses, a state embargo may be the next action of choice. See IOM 331 and consult your supervisor.

If the dealer declines to hold the lot, but proposes returning it to the shipper, the dealer should be warned NOT to return the goods to the shipper and advised FDA does not condone shipping violative goods. Direct his/her attention to Section 301(a) of the Act.

If the dealer offers to voluntarily denature or destroy the lot in lieu of voluntary embargo, provide or arrange for supervising the denaturing per IOM 760. If the dealer proposes to recondition the lot, refer him/her to your district compliance branch for approval of his/her method. See IOM 740 and IOM 742.

SUBCHAPTER 420 - COLLECTION TECHNIQUE

Sampling operations must be carried out using techniques that ensure the sample is representative of the lot, the sample of the product is in the same condition as it was before sampling, and that the collection technique does not compromise the compliance status of the lot.

420.1 Responsibility

It is your responsibility to collect your own samples using techniques and methods which will provide the most ideal sample, yet not be objectionable to management. This sub-chapter and the sampling schedules that follow, contain many sampling techniques, but not all. Your training and experience will enable you to become proficient in most sampling operations. However, in new or unusual situations it is your responsibility to use imagination and ingenuity in getting the job done and, if necessary, to consult with your supervisor.

421   LOT RESTORATION & IDENTIFICATION

421.1 Restoring Lot(s) Sampled

Restore lots to their original condition. Do not leave partially filled shipping cases, short weight or short volume containers in the lot after sampling. Do not leave the lot in any condition, which might encourage pilferage, or make it unsalable.

When collecting from either full cases or bulk containers, replace sampled units by back filling from a container selected for that purpose. Avoid contaminating the back-filled units. If necessary, correct the contents declaration on the container(s) from which sampled to reflect the actual contents present. Refer to IOM 410.2 if the dealer objects to back filling because of company policy, different codes involved, or for other reasons. As a last resort, accede to the dealer's wishes and sample intact units, but record the facts in your diary and place a brief explanation on the C/R.

Carefully re-close all containers and shipping cases. (Commercially available glues in spray cans or plastic squeeze-type bottles are an effective means of re-gluing cartons and cases without defacing with tape or other methods.) Re-cooper or reseal barrels and drums, re-sew bags, etc. If necessary, request use of the dealer's employees in helping to restore the lot, or arrange through the dealer to employ outside help. See IOM 416.4.

421.2 Identifying Lot(s) Sampled

Identify each container from which units are taken with the date, your initials and the sample number, or you may complete and affix an FDA 2426, Examination Label, to each shipping case or bulk container sampled. For burlap or woven bags, the FDA 2426 may be glued to tags, and the tags attached to the bags.

Should the dealer object to your identification procedure, attempt to reach a compromise (e.g., placing the ID in an obscure location, etc.). If the dealer still objects, accede to his wishes, but record the facts in your diary.

Positive identification of the containers sampled is important if it becomes necessary to resample the lot(s), or if an embargo, seizure, or other action ensues. It also aids the dealer to differentiate between containers that have been opened by FDA as opposed to those opened by pilferage or torn opened by rough handling. It may be necessary to mark more containers than sampled to assure proper identification of the lot. This can be done by using the Examination Label, a handwritten ID or by using a rubber stamp.

Do not use industrial or permanent type markers on sample containers which allow penetration by ink. Many inks will penetrate to the product and act as a contaminant, interfering with the analysis. Water base markers will run when damp and must be covered with tape. See IOM 451.3 for identification techniques.

Do not permanently identify articles that are borrowed and will be returned to the dealer.

422   SAMPLE SIZE

To determine sample size, first consult your assignment. If the assignment doesn't specify the sample size, follow the guidance in the applicable Compliance Program. The IOM SAMPLE SCHEDULE, should be used if the Compliance Program doesn't state the sample size. If none of these furnish the sample size, consult with your supervisor or the laboratory. Collect sufficient sample to allow for the FDA reserve portion and the 702(b) portion. See IOM 422.2 & 422.3.

422.1 Medical Device Samples

The following table represents the devices for which there are sampling instructions in Compliance Policy Guides:

Device	CPG Reference
Clinical Thermometers	See CPG 7124.20
Condoms	See CPG 7124.21
Surgeons and Patient Exam Gloves	See CPG 7124.31

In addition to providing instructions on sample size, these compliance policy guides provide guidance on criteria to determine adulteration and whether or not regulatory action should be recommended.

422.2 702(b) Requirement

When the sample schedule, assignment or other instruction does not specifically provide for the 702(b) portion, collect a sufficient amount to provide this required portion. You are not required to obtain a 702(b) portion in the following instances exempted by statute or by regulation 21 CFR 2.10(b):

a.   Devices are not included in the statutory requirement of Section 702(b).

b.   The amount available for sampling is less than twice the quantity estimated to be sufficient for analysis, in which case, collect all that is available.

c.   The cost of twice the quantity estimated to be sufficient for analysis exceeds $150.00. (Currently 21 CFR 2.10 uses $50.00 as the amount. However, ORA policy sets a limit of $150.00. If the sample is critical, and the cost exceeds $150.00, check with your supervisor.

d.   Import samples, collected from a shipment being imported or offered for entry into the United States.

e.   The sample is collected from a person named on the label of the article or his agent, and such person is also owner of the article. For example, it is not necessary to obtain a 702(b) portion if the sample is collected from a lot owned by and in the possession of the manufacturer whose name appears on the label.

f.   The sample is collected from the owner of the article or his agent, and the article bears no label, or if it bears a label, no person is named thereon.

Note: Regardless of the exemptions under 21 CFR 2.10(b) listed above, a good rule of thumb to follow for most filth samples, is to collect the 702(b) portion.

422.3 Collecting the 702(b) Portion

Whenever possible, collect separate subdivisions in order to provide the firm a portion as required by Section 702(b). Each duplicate subdivision should be collected from the same bag, box, case, or container. The total sample should be at least twice the quantity estimated to be sufficient for analysis, including a reserve portion for FDA's laboratory. If unable to collect separate subdivisions, assure that the total amount collected for each sample subdivision, or the total amount collected from an undivided sample, is at least twice the amount estimated to be sufficient for analysis. See IOM 427.4.

424   IN-TRANSIT SAMPLES

The exterior of any domestic package thought to contain an article subject to FDA regulation and in the possession, control, or custody of a common carrier may be examined (photographed, information on the outside copied, etc.) and records of the shipment may be obtained. Such package may not be opened either by an FDA employee or by an employee of the common carrier at the request of an FDA employee except as provided below.

The Office of Chief Counsel has advised FDA employees may, without a warrant, open, examine the contents and/or sample a package which is part of a domestic commercial interstate shipment in the possession, control, or custody of a common carrier only if:

1.   The consignor or consignee affirmatively consents to examination and/or sampling of the contents; or

2.   The Agency has reliable information the carrier regularly carries FDA regulated articles, and the facility where the sampling is contemplated is subject to FDA inspection. Reliable information may come from agency files, the carrier itself, other customers of the carrier, etc.

and

the Agency has reliable information a particular package sought to be examined is destined for, or received from another state, and contains an FDA regulated article. [Such information may be found on the exterior of the package and/or shipping documents in specific terms. Information may also come from reliable sources, which establish the consignor is in the business of manufacturing and/or shipping FDA regulated articles using a distinctive type of package (shipping container); and the package in question meets such description and shows the consignor to be such firm.]

Confer with your supervisor on any question concerning the need for a warrant. However, headquarters approval must be obtained because such inspection and sampling

may require a search warrant. Contact the Division of Field Investigations (DFI) (HFC-130) at (301) 827-5653 to discuss the matter. They will coordinate as necessary with Office of Enforcement (HFC-200) and Chief Counsel (GCF-1) and provide further instructions.

If a decision has already been made by the district office to obtain a warrant, follow the procedures outlined in the Regulatory Procedures Manual, Chapter 8.

If a common carrier reports a violative article which it discovers under its own package opening procedures, independent of any request by an FDA employee or any standing FDA cooperative program with the carrier, FDA may still need a warrant to examine the material. Unless all the conditions for independent sampling in 1 or 2 above exist, you must consult with your supervisor, who will arrange for headquarters consultation as outlined above.

Note: Where the identity of an Interstate product is known by virtue of it being visible in bulk, or being in labeled containers or packages which are verified as to contents by shipping records, and where such product is under FDA jurisdiction at a given location, it may be sampled according to established IOM procedures.

Resealing Conveyances - If it is necessary to break the commercial seal to enter a railcar or other conveyance, reseal the door with a numbered self-locking "U.S. Food & Drug" metal seal. Record in your regulatory notes (and on C/R if sample taken) the number of the car or conveyance, the identifying number on any car seals removed, and the number of the FDA metal seals applied.

425   SPECIAL SAMPLING SITUATIONS

Do not collect human or animal biological materials (urine, feces, sputum, blood, blood products, organs, tissue etc.) unless arrangements for special handling and special treatment have been made in advance. Most ORA servicing laboratories are not prepared or certified to handle these materials. In addition to guidance for special sampling situations provided below, sampling guidance may also be found in these areas of the IOM:

IOM 140 - Safety

IOM 143 – Sampling

Sampling Containers for Lemon Oil or Other essential Oils - Plastic or paraffin-coated liners in caps of containers used to hold samples of this type product are not satisfactory in that the plastic or paraffin is soluble in the oils and interferes with the analysis. Use glass, cork, foil covered, or non-plastic, non-paraffin closures.

Sampling medicinal and other gasses - Gasses represent a special sampling situation. Please contact your servicing lab to determine an appropriate sampling container and sample size.

425.1 Complaints, Tampering, Foodborne
Disease, Injury Illness

Detailed instructions for investigating and sampling products in connection with consumer complaints, tampering, foodborne outbreaks, injury and adverse reactions, etc. appear in the following sections of the IOM:

Be cognizant of conserving scarce resources when investigating consumer complaints that do not involve injury, illness, or product tampering. Unnecessary samples waste both operational and administrative resources. Use judgment as to whether or not it is necessary to collect the consumer's portion in situations that do not involve injury, illness, or product tampering. For example, there is little need to collect a physical sample of an insect infested box of cereal from the complainant. Both you and the consumer can readily see it is insect infested. The laboratory would find it insect infested, and the district would merely report the same thing back to the complainant. No practical purpose would be served by either collecting or examining such a sample.

425.2 Recalls

See IOM 800 & IOM 801.2.

425.3 Natural Disasters

See IOM 940.

425.4 Induced Samples

If this type sample is desired your supervisor will provide specific instructions and procedures to be followed. This may involve:

a.   Whether to use your correct name or an alias. Caution: if you use an alias, do not use a similar name or a name with initials the same as yours (e.g., Sidney H. Rogers should not use Samuel H. Right). In addition, do not use a district office or resident post as a return address when ordering products or literature.

b.   Do not telephone your order in from the office or your home phone because the firm may have "Caller ID" and be able to identify your location by the phone number.

c.   Whether to use order blanks contained in the promotional package, advertisement, or promotional activity; or whether false ones will be used.

d.   Whether money orders, your charge plate numbers, bank checks, or your personal checks should be used for payment. It depends on the situation, but money orders are preferred since these do not involve personal accounts.

e.   Where the requested items are to be sent: rented P.O. Box, home address, General Delivery, or other address.

f.   How the address and/or your name is to be recorded on the order blank. A code may be used either in your name or address so any follow-up promotional material sent to that name and address can be keyed to your original order.

When it has been decided to induce a sample and you have discussed the procedures with your supervisor, prepare the order and obtain the money order, or payment document. When all documents for ordering the item(s) are prepared, photocopy all the material, including the addressed envelope, for your record and submit the order.

When the order is received, identify the sample item, all accompanying material such as pamphlets, brochures, etc. (including all wrappings containing any type of printing, identification, numbers, post marks, addresses, etc.), and submit the item and exhibits in the same manner as any other official sample. If payment of the item was by personal check or credit card number, attach a photocopy of the canceled check or credit card receipt if available. You may do this later, after clearance of the check or charge slip.

425.5 Undercover Buy

See IOM 405.6.

426   ASEPTIC SAMPLE

Aseptic sampling is a sampling technique used to assure you are not increasing the microbial load of a product sample by your sampling method. The use of sterile sampling implements and containers and a prescribed sampling method defines aseptic sampling. This method of sampling also assures that you are not contaminating what remains in the container from which you sample. Collecting and delivering samples to the laboratory using aseptic technique, will permit testimony that the bacteriological findings accurately reflect the condition of the lot at the time of sampling and, ideally, at the time of the original shipment. Whenever possible collect intact, unopened containers. Aseptic sampling is often used in the collection of in-line samples, environmental samples, product samples from bulk containers and collection of unpackaged product that is being collected for microbial analysis.

Note: Products in 55 gallon drums, or similar large containers, either aseptically filled or heat processed, should not be sampled while the shipment is en route unless the owner accepts responsibility for the portion remaining after sampling. Try to arrange sampling of these products at the consignee (user) so the opened containers can be immediately used or stored under refrigerated conditions. Use ASEPTIC TECHNIQUE when sampling these products.

For more guidance on aseptic technique, you may consult the course _Food Microbiological Control 10: Aseptic Sampling_, which is available to FDA employees through the ORAU intranet site.

426.1 General Procedures

If it is necessary to open containers, draw the sample and submit it under conditions, which will prevent multiplication or undue reduction of the bacterial population. Follow the basic principles of aseptic sampling technique. Take steps to minimize exposure of product, sampling equipment, and the interior of sampling containers to the environment.

a. Sterilized Equipment - Use only sterilized equipment and containers. These should be obtained from the servicing laboratory or in emergency, at local cooperating health agencies. Pre-sterilized plastic or metal tools should be used. However, if unavailable, the metal tools can be sterilized immediately before use with a propane torch. Permit the tool to cool in the air or inside a sterile container before using. Soaking with 70% alcohol and flaming off is an acceptable method of field sterilization, and may be used as a last resort.

(1) If it is necessary to drill, saw, or cut the item being sampled (such as large frozen fish, cheese wheels, frozen fruit, etc.), if at all possible, use stainless steel bits, blades, knives, etc. Wooden handled sampling instruments are particularly susceptible to bacterial contamination, are difficult to sterilize, and should be avoided.

Caution: Be extremely careful when using a propane torch or other flame when sterilizing tools and equipment. Evaluate the conditions pertaining to explosive vapors, dusty air, flame-restricted areas, firm's policy or management's wishes. The use of supportive devices should be considered when torch is not being hand held. Also be sure all flammable liquids, such as alcohol, in your filth kit are in metal safety cans and not in breakable containers.

(2) If it is necessary to handle the items being sampled, use sterile disposable type gloves (rubber, vinyl, plastic, etc. - surgeon's gloves are good). Use a fresh glove for each sub and submit one unused glove in a sterile container as a control. See IOM 426.5.

(3) Opening Sterile Sampling Containers - Work rapidly. Open sterile sampling containers only to admit the sample and close it immediately. Do not touch the inside of the sterile container, lip, or lid. Submit one empty sterile container similarly opened and closed as a control. See IOM 426.5.

(4) Dusty Areas - Do not collect samples in areas where dust or atmospheric conditions may cause contamination of the sample, unless such contamination may be considered a part of the sample.

426.2 Sampling Dried Powders

Cautions - The proper aseptic sampling of dried milk powder, dried eggs, dried yeast, and similar type products is difficult because they are generally packed in multilayer poly-lined paper bags. These may be stitched across the entire top, may have filler spouts, or the top of the poly-liner may be closed or sealed with some type of "twists".

a. The practice of cutting an "X" or "V" or slitting the bag and folding the cut part back to expose the contents for sampling should not be used because it creates a resealing problem; the opening cannot be properly repaired.

b. Procedure - The following procedure has been approved by the scientific units in Headquarters and should be used when sampling this type product:

(1) Bag and Poly-liner Stitched Together Across Top Seam.

(a) Remove as much dust as possible from the seam end by brushing and then wiping with a cloth dampened with alcohol. Note: This does not sterilize the bag as porous paper cannot be sterilized.

(b) Remove the seam stitching carefully (and dust cover, if any) and spread the walls of the bag and the poly-liner open enough to permit sampling being careful that no extraneous material such as dust, bits of twine, paper, etc., drops into the product.

(c) Carefully scrape off the surface of the product with a sterile device and aseptically draw the sample from the material below.

(d) Carefully reclose the bag and restitch by hand, or by machine if firm or FDA portable sewing machine is available.

(2) Bag Stitched Across Top and Poly-liner Twist-Closed and Sealed with "twist" Device - Wire, Plastic, etc.

(a) Brush, alcohol wipe, and remove stitching as described.

(b) Remove "twist" seal and carefully open poly-liner using caution that no extraneous material drops into the product.

(c) Draw aseptic sample in same manner as in (1)(c) above.

(d) Carefully close the poly-liner with a twisting motion and reseal with "twist" seal arranging it so it will not puncture the poly-liner, and resew bag as in (1)(d) above.

(3) Bags With Filling Spouts. The filling spout will be located at one side of the top stitching and will either pull out to form a top or side spout.

(a) Brush and alcohol wipe the area around the spout and carefully pull it out to reveal the opening. It is better to have the bag on its side while pulling the spout so any dust in the opening falls outside the bag.

(b) Carefully spread the sides of the spout apart and aseptically draw the sample. A trier or long handled device is usually better for this type opening because of the limited opening.

(c) Carefully close the spout with a firm twisting motion and be sure the opening is closed prior to pushing back into the bag.

426.3 Collecting Water Samples

When it is necessary to collect water samples for bacteriological examination, use the following procedures:

a. Use sterile bottles. If dechlorination of sample is necessary, sodium thiosulfate sufficient to provide 100 mg/l should be placed in the clean bottles prior to sterilization. The sodium thiosulfate will prevent the chlorine from acting on the bacteria and assures, when the sample is analyzed, the bacterial load is the same as when collected.

b. Carefully inspect the outside of the faucet from which the sample will be drawn. Do not collect sample from a faucet with leaks around handle.

c. Clean and dry outside of faucet.

d. Let the water run from the fully open faucet for at least 1/2 minute or for 2 or 3 minutes if the faucet is on a long service line.

e. Partially close faucet to permit collecting sample without splashing. Carefully open sample bottle to prevent contamination, as for any other aseptic sampling operation.

f. Fill bottle carefully without splashing and be sure

no water from your hands or other objects enters the bottle. Do not over fill, but leave a small air bubble at top.

g.   Unless otherwise instructed, minimum sample size for bacteriological examination is 100 ml.

h.   Deliver sample to lab promptly. If sample is not examined within 24 hours after collection, the results may be inaccurate.

Note: When documenting specific situations in a plant, you may need to vary this procedure to mimic the actual conditions used by the firm.

426.4 Sample Handling

For frozen samples, pre-chill sterile containers before use and keep frozen with dry ice. Use ordinary ice or ice packs for holding and transporting unfrozen samples that require refrigeration. See IOM 452.5 & 912.3. Under normal circumstances dried products may be shipped unrefrigerated except in cases where they would be exposed to high temperatures, i.e., above 37.8oC (100°F).

Submit samples subject to rapid spoilage (specimens of foods involved in poisoning cases, etc.) by immediate personal delivery to the bacteriologist where feasible.

426.5 Controls

When collecting samples using aseptic technique and the subs are collected using presterilized containers and equipment, submit a number of control subs. If the sampling covers a long period of time you should submit controls which show environmental conditions during the time of sampling. The controls should be collected at the start, during, and at the end of the sampling period. List control subs on your C/R.

Examples of various control subs are:

a.   Sterile Containers - Where sterile containers are used to collect aseptic samples, submit one unopened container, which was sterilized in the same manner as containers used for sampling. Also submit at least one empty sterile container which has been opened and closed in the sampling area.

b.   Sterile Disposable Gloves - If sterile disposable gloves are used to handle the product, submit one unused glove in a sterile container as a control.

c.   Sterile Sampling Equipment - Where presterilized sampling tools are used (e.g., spoons, spatulas, triers, etc.), submit at least one unopened and one opened sampling tool as controls. Place tool, which was opened but not used, in a sterile container for submission.

d.   Bagging or Container Material – Collect control subs of unstained bagging, or portion of container, and product when a sample is collected for rodent contamination. See IOM 427.4.

427   ADULTERATION VIOLATIONS

Since adulteration samples are collected to confirm the presence of filth or other deleterious material, they are generally either larger or more selective than samples collected for economic or misbranding purposes.

When lots appear actionable, it is desirable to list recent sales from the lot in question. Follow up may be necessary as directed by your supervisor.

427.1 Field Examination

Provide a detailed description of observations, physical sub divisions which reflect the violative nature of the lot, and exhibits which corroborate your report of observations.

Record in your regulatory notes, subsequently in C/R Collection Remarks field or Continuation Form, or on Analyst Worksheet FDA 431, the results of your unit by unit examination of the lot. Observations should be specific. Report the general storage conditions, the violative condition of the lot, the physical relationship of the violative lot to other lots in the area, how you conducted the examination and how many units you examined. Wherever possible, record quantitative observations.

Report the number and location of live and dead insects, pellets, or other adulteration discovered inside the containers as well as on their exterior surface. Provide graphic measurements of areas of urine/chemical stains on each container and the extent of penetration. Correlate findings of the unit by unit examination with any photographs and physical subdivisions collected.

Where the field examination is carefully described and documented, the sample collected from obviously violative lots may be reduced to carefully selected exhibits. The field examination and the report of findings will serve as the analysis. In this case prepare an FDA 431, Analyst Worksheet. See IOM Exhibit 420-A.

427.2 Random Sampling

The concept of random "blind" sampling is to yield information about the average composition of the lot. It is employed when you have no information or method of determining which units are violative. Usually the violation is concealed and must be found by laboratory methods.

Sample size is usually described in your assignment, IOM Sample Schedule, Compliance Program, or the applicable schedules. If none of these furnish the sample size, a general rule is to collect samples from the square root of the number of cases or shipping containers but not less than 12 or more than 36 subs in duplicate. If there are less than 12 containers, all should be sampled. Discuss sample size and 702(b) requirements with your supervisor. See IOM 422.2.

427.3 Selective Sampling

In some situations, random sampling is unnecessary or even undesirable. Under these conditions, examine the lot and select the portions which will demonstrate the violative nature of the lot.

In addition to the selective samples collected, exhibits should include diagrams and photographs to demonstrate the violative conditions reported, and which containers were sampled and photographed.

427.4 Sample Criteria

When collecting selective samples of products to show adulteration by filth, be guided by the following minimum requirements for action against the merchandise. Your sample collection should be sufficient to document the extent of the violative conditions and not be limited to this minimum. Even where these minimum prerequisites are not met, you should collect samples as exhibits and evidence, particularly where adulteration under section 402(a)(4) of the FD&C Act may be a factor. Your evidence may be used in a subsequent action against the firm, if corrections are not made.

a. Rodent Contamination

1. There is evidence to show the warehouse is rodent infested and:

(a) Three or more of the bags in the lot are rodent gnawed; or

(b) At least five of the bags in the lot bear either rodent urine stains at least 1/4" in diameter, or two or more rodent pellets; or

(c) The food in at least one container in the lot contains rodent gnawed material, or rodent excreta or urine.

2. Whether or not the warehouse is rodent infested;
IF:

(a) At least three bags bear rodent urine stains of at least 1/4" in diameter which penetrates to the product even though the product cannot be demonstrated to have been contaminated; or:

(b) At least two bags are rodent-gnawed and at least five bags bear either rodent urine stains at least 1/4" in diameter, with or without penetration to the product, or two or more rodent pellets; or:

(c) The food in at least one bag in the lot contains rodent-gnawed material or rodent excreta or rodent urine, and at least five bags bear either rodent stains at least 1/4" in diameter or two or more rodent pellets.

b. Considerations for examining and selectively sampling lots to document rodent urine contamination:

1. Examine suspected urine stains with ultra-violet light in as near total darkness as possible. A minimum of 15 minutes is normally required for the eyes to become properly adjusted to accurately differentiate between rodent stain fluorescence and normal fluorescence of rice and certain other commodities.

2. Wet, fresh or continually wetted runs may fluoresce poorly, but the odor of urine will usually be present and should be described on the C/R. Fresh dry urine stains will fluoresce blue-white, while older stains may be more yellowish/white. Rodent hairs will look like blue/white streaks. Look for the typical droplet pattern because rodents commonly urinate while in motion. Report the presence of droplet patterns on your C/R.

3. Note clearly on C/R if the product or package contains or is directly associated with any of the following:

(a) Dried milk products (contain urea).

(b) Whole grain wheat (contains urea & allantoin).

(c) Animal feeds (urea is usually intentionally added).

4. The following products may be difficult to evaluate because of either natural fluorescence or "quenching" of UV rays, even if contaminated. ("Quenching" refers to a covering up or a decrease in the ability of a product to fluoresce.)

FOODS	NON-FOOD ITEMS
High Gluten Flour (Natural)	Burlap Bags (Quenching)
Nut Meats (Natural)	Bleached Sacks (Natural-White Glow)
Bean Flours (Natural)	Lubricants (Oils & Greases) (Natural-Blue/White to yellow/brown glow)
Brans (Natural)	
Pop & Field Corn (Natural)	Pitches & Tars (Natural-Yellow)
Wheat (Natural)	Detergents & Bleaches (Natural-White)
Starch (Natural)	Sulfide Waste Matter (Natural-Blue/White)
Spices (Natural or Quenching)	

5. Many types of bagging and threading materials will fluoresce under U.V. light, however, the characteristic rodent stain fluorescence can be identified by its yellowish color in contrast to the usual glow of chemical stains.

Note: Corn which fluoresces a "bright greenish-yellow" under blacklight examination is indicative of possible aflatoxin contamination. If normal cracked corn is blacklighted, it fluoresces a bluish white color. See IOM 427.4 "G" below for a blacklight screening procedure.

6. Submit stained portions cut from the bag or container for laboratory confirmation. Note: Small manicure scissors are excellent for removing the stained or gnawed portions of bags and transparent tape is excellent for picking up adhering pellets or small insects.

7. When collecting exhibits of suspected urine stains, a control portions are required. As a general guide, collect the controls from the opposite side of the bag or make the cutting large enough to separate the control area and the stain. Separate the controls from the stains and submit in separate containers. Collect at least 3 container controls for each sample. If the lot consists of different containers or bags of different manufacturers, collect controls to represent each type or manufacturer of the containers.

8. Handle the exhibits carefully and preferably with tweezers or gloves to:

(a) prevent loss of invisible evidence of rodent adulteration, i.e., hairs, adhering food particles and possibly rodent parasites.

(b) prevent chemical contamination of the stain or control areas through handling.

(c) prevent contracting the potential diseases or parasites associated with rodents, i.e., Salmonella (common on fecal material), Leptospirosis and Hanta Virus (urine), mites and fleas (nesting material or heavily traveled runs).

(d) prevent cross-contaminating the control portions with contaminated portions.

9. If possible, take stained cuttings from areas which have not been exposed for extended periods of time to light, in particular, ultraviolet light sources or to intense heat. If you have no alternative or cannot determine the

stained areas' history, note the conditions on the C/R.

10. Certain chemicals in urine are photo-sensitive, therefore; maintain subs in a dark container.

11. Identify the top or external layer of a multi-layer cutting with a pencil. Exception: If there is a possibility that a multi-layer exhibit will separate through pre-analysis handling and shipment, identify all layers with a pencil. (Do not use ink as it often contains urea.) Handle exhibits carefully to prevent loss of microscopic evidence.

12. Submit a minimal amount of product from under the stained area, preferably just the clumped product. This prevents dilution of the contaminated product with uncontaminated product. Collect a product control from an uncontaminated area and submit as a separate sub.

13. Urine stained areas may be photographed under ultra-violet light conditions. Check with your supervisor about the technical aspects of this procedure. Do not mark container surfaces to outline the stained areas when taking either ultra violet or normal photographs. This may contaminate the product by migration through the containers.

14. Controls – When collecting exhibits of suspected urine stains, control portions of the container and the product are required. As a general guide, collect the control from the opposite side of the bag or make the cutting large enough to separate the control area and the stain. Separate the controls from the stains and submit in separate sample containers. Collect controls from at least three containers in the lot where possible.

15. Each sample must consist of the following portions:

a. A piece of unstained bagging, or portion of the container, which does not fluoresce, for controls (minimum three required).

b. A number of pieces of stained bagging, or portion of the container, and any adhering pellets.

c. A small portion of the product directly beneath the stained area. Do not dilute the contaminated product beneath the stain with the non-contaminated product.

d. A portion of uncontaminated product from beneath the unstained bagging, or other container. This serves as a control, and should be collected in duplicate to provide a 702(b) portion. Collect control samples from 3 different containers.

Submit each portion of bagging or container portion, pellets, material from beneath sampled area, control, etc., in separate vial or sub sample container.

c.   Other

1. Where you separate, count, or identify the various elements of an exhibit, (e.g.: sieve & find X number of rodent pellets), maintain the counted portions separate from the other subs. Note on the C/R those subs that were counted, separated, etc.

2. Place cuttings and gnawed holes between 2 pieces of white paper, and then fold, roll, or leave flat and place into a glass container or other suitable container. This will hold the evidence in place and prevent possible loss of hairs or parasites due to static charges. Do not separate a multilayer cutting. Avoid the use of polyethylene containers as insect fragments and rodent hairs may adhere to containers made from this material.

3. Protect the exhibits from being crushed.

d.   Insect Contamination - Note: The criteria below, involving dead insects only, will not be used for action against any food intended to undergo further processing that effectively removes all the dead insects, e.g. processing of cocoa beans.

1. The product contains:

a. One live insect in each of two or more immediate containers; or, one dead insect in each of three or more immediate containers; or, three live or dead insects in one immediate container; plus

b. Similar live or dead insect infestation present on, or in the immediate proximity of, the lot to show a 402(a)(4) violation.

2. The product contains one or more live insects in each of three or more immediate containers.

3. The product contains two or more dead whole insects in at least five of the immediate containers. Note: a situation such as this may follow fumigation of the lot and vacuuming of the exteriors of the bags.

4. The product is in cloth or burlap bags and two or more live or dead insects are present on at least five of the containers. Note: Some live insects must be present. Product need not be shown to have become contaminated.

Note: Fumigate exhibits as necessary being careful the fumigant does not destroy the exhibits or its container. If a fumigant is not available, freeze the sample. If fumigated, report in the Flag Remarks field of the C/R and the FDA-525 that the sample was fumigated and which fumigant was used.

e.   Bird Contamination - If the product is in permeable containers (paper, cloth, burlap, etc.), and

1. The product contains bird excreta in one or more containers, and you feel the insanitary storage conditions will clearly support a 402(a)(4) violation.

2. Bird excreta is present on the exteriors of at least five of the containers, and the product contains bird excreta in one.

3. At least 30% of the number of bags examined, but at least five bags, are contaminated with bird excreta; and at least three of the bags bear excreta stains which penetrate to the product, even though the product may not be contaminated.

Note: In all instances of bird excreta contamination the excreta must be confirmed by positive test for uric acid.

f.   General

1. Collect samples from lots suspected of dry chemical contamination in much the same manner as described above. After collecting a sample of the contents from immediately beneath the suspected area, collect residues from the surface of the bag or container. In the case of infiltration of loosely woven bags, shake or tumble the bag over a large sheet of clean paper to collect the siftings as a sample.

2. When Selective Sampling consists of an actual sample of a product, however small, as distinguished from bag cuttings, rodent pellets, insects, etc., a 702(b) portion must be obtained. In such cases, collect duplicate subs of the product to provide the 702(b) portion. This 702(b) portion is usually not an exact duplicate of the product collected for the Selective Sample, but should be collected from the

same bag, box, or other container of product sampled. Whether collected from a container or bulk, the 702(b) portion should be taken as close as possible to that portion selectively sampled for analysis. Specify for each sub and duplicate collected, the origin, manner in which taken, and the examination to be made.

g. Blacklight Test Screening Procedure for Aflatoxins in Corn

Note: The USDA/FGIS has approved a number of commercial screening tests for detecting aflatoxin contaminated corn. However, these tests usually require a chemical extraction process and are therefore not amenable to FDA field examination procedures.

The blacklight test (also referred to as the bright greenish-yellow Fluorescence (BGYF) test) is a presumptive test used to screen and identify corn lots that should be tested further for aflatoxins. The test is based on BGYF observed under long wave (366 nm) ultraviolet (UV) light produced by the molds Aspergillus parasiticus A. flavus on "living" corn (i.e. corn that has been stored less than 3 months). The growth of these fungi may result in aflatoxin production. Aflatoxins per se do not produce BGYF under long wave UV light. It is thought the BGYF is produced by the reaction of kojic acid formed by the fungi and a peroxidase enzyme from living corn. Corn that has been in storage for a lengthy period of time (3 months or more) may give false positive BGYF. Therefore, determine how long the corn being sampled has been in storage. If it has been in storage over three months, do not use the following field screening procedure.

Essential steps for this blacklight procedure are:

1. A 10 lb. sample representative of the corn lot must be obtained by probing, or by continuously sampling a grain stream.

2. Examine using a 366 nm UV light (portable blacklights meet this criteria).

3. Wear goggles or use a viewer that screens out UV light. Shine the light on the corn sample which has been spread in a single layer on a flat surface in a darkened room.

4. Use a 2 lb. Portion, and carefully observe the entire corn surface one kernel at a time. Examine the entire sample using this procedure.

5. Count all BGYF glowers (kernels or particles that "glow" bright greenish-yellow). Compare the BGYF color with a fluorescent standard, if one is available. Remember normal corn, if it fluoresces, will fluoresce a bluish white.

6. If four (4) or more BGYF particles are detected in the 10 lb screening sample, collect a sample for laboratory analysis.

427.5 Abnormal Containers

See IOM SAMPLE SCHEDULE CHART 2 - LACF for listing can defects.

427.6 In-Line Samples

Mold Samples - During inspections of manufacturers such as canneries, bottling plants, milling operations, etc.,

it may be necessary to collect scrapings or swabs of slime or other material to verify the presence of mold. The sample should represent the conditions observed at the time of collection and consist of sufficient material to confirm and identify mold growth on the equipment. If possible, take photographs and obtain scrapings or bits of suspect material. Describe the area scraped or swabbed, e.g., material was scraped or swabbed from a 2" x 12" area.

Suspected filth, collected from ceilings, walls, and equipment, for mold examination must be kept moist by placing it in a container with a small amount of a 3% formalin solution. Large amounts of slime may be placed in a wide mouth glass jar with either a 1% formaldehyde solution or a 3% formalin. Note: Formalin is normally sold as a standard stock solution of 37%. To obtain the required 3-4% formalin solution, mix 5 ml of the 37% stock solution with 95 ml of distilled water. This will furnish the solution necessary to fix the mold.

Although formaldehyde or formalin are the preservatives of choice you may preserve the subs in either a 50% alcohol solution or in acetic acid (vinegar).

The above instructions apply to the collection of raw material, in-line and finished product samples for mold. However, in-line and finished product subs such as doughs, etc., which may be harmed by the formaldehyde, may be frozen. Check with your laboratory for its recommendation regarding preserving mold samples.

Bacteriological Samples - During inspections of firms producing products susceptible to microbial contamination (e.g., frozen precooked; ready to eat seafood, creme filled goods, breaded items, egg rolls, prepared salads, etc.), proof of adulteration, with fecal organisms, or elevated levels of non-pathogenic microorganisms, must be established. Sampling of raw materials, in-line and finished product is warranted. Follow instructions under IOM 427.7-Products Susceptible to Contamination with Pathogenic Microorganisms, Sampling During Inspection.

427.7 Products Susceptible to Contamination with Pathogenic Microorganisms

A top priority of the agency and CFSAN is to decrease foodborne illness caused by microbial contamination. With the rise of foodborne outbreaks detailed guidance was developed for sample collections and inspections dealing with microbial contamination.

Note: This guidance is intended to augment guidance found in the Compliance Programs listed below. Instructions in current compliance programs and ongoing assignments supersede this guidance. Before conducting inspections under these programs, investigator/analyst teams should be thoroughly familiar with the guidance provided in the appropriate Compliance Program.

For the following Compliance Programs collect samples for microbiological analyses only if:

a. Directed to do so in the current compliance program or ongoing assignments.

b. The firm has a previous history of microbiological contamination (e.g., follow up to illness or injury complaint, recalled/seized product, previous inspectional history, etc.) or

c. Sampling is conducted 'for cause' during an inspection (e.g., inspectional observations warrants collection for microbiological analyses):

1. Domestic and Imported Cheese and Cheese Products (7303.037)

2. Domestic Food Safety (7303.803)

3. Domestic Acidified and Low-Acid Canned Foods (7303.803A)

4. Domestic Fish and Fishery Products (7303.842). Except as directed by the compliance program, you should **not** conduct any in-line, environmental, or finished product sampling, for microbiological concerns, during the inspection. Instead, fully document the lack of HACCP control(s) without physical sampling. If in the investigator's judgment the firm's HACCP plan is extremely inadequate and therefore sampling is warranted, contact CFSAN/OFP/Division of Enforcement and Programs. CFSAN/OFP/Division of Enforcement and Programs will confer with CFSAN/Office of Seafood to determine what in-line sampling will be performed and the type of regulatory action that may be warranted for the situation at hand.

During inspections of these types of firms, or where inspectional observations indicate there may be a microbial contamination problem, whenever possible an investigator/microbiologist team approach should be used.

A bacteriological inspection requires a thorough understanding of critical factors associated with the production of the specific product being inspected. To prove the establishment is being operated in an insanitary manner it is necessary to show the manufacturing operation or conditions at the facility are likely to, or have contributed, to the bacterial load of the product. When feasible, inspections should cover equipment condition before a day's production begins, and the clean-up at the end of the day's production.

For all inspections at firms meeting the criteria previously referenced, environmental swabs, in-line and finished product samples must be collected to document possible or actual routes of contamination of the finished product. Other environmental swabs (e.g., floor drains, walls, etc.) will be collected based upon the investigator's observations of extensive insanitary conditions.

Sampling During Inspection:

1. In-Line Sampling Areas (this is not a comprehensive listing of areas to collect in-line samples, since each firm will be different, depending on processing/packaging techniques and the finished product produced).

Each in-line subsample will consist of approximately 114 g (4 oz), in duplicate (702b portion), if that amount is available (Also see IOM 422.2 - 702(b) Requirement). All in-line samples must be collected aseptically.

"Raw" ingredients used in the manufacturing of finished foods (including those conveyed by bulk tankers) should be considered for sampling to determine the effect of subsequent processing on bacterial content. Of particular concern are raw materials, which can support microbial growth, are not normally cooked or prepared in a manner lethal to pathogenic microorganisms (such as dairy, soy, corn or sugar syrup based products), and adequate controls to ensure the safety of the finished product are not in effect. Since the major portion of some finished food products are not homogeneously contaminated, it may be necessary to collect multiple subsamples of the raw material(s) to establish a reliable microbial base line.

Obtain sequential subsamples with the view of bracketing each step of the processing operation, in particular those steps suspected as routes of product contamination. A series of in-line samples should be collected during the first part of a shift, and a duplicate series during the latter part.

If products or components are heated (e.g., blanched, boiled, etc.) take subsamples immediately before and immediately after heating, before possible insanitary equipment and processing delays contribute to bacterial increases. Particular attention should be given to determine routes of cross-contamination from the raw product to the "heated" product, especially if this heating step is critical to the destruction of pathogenic organisms.

If a product is capable of supporting microbial growth and is not being handled expeditiously, sample before and after this particular processing step.

Take time and temperature measurements of cooking, freezing and cooling procedures. Sample when appropriate to demonstrate possible microbial growth. Large masses of ingredients may cool or warm slowly enough to permit microbial growth.

Improperly cleaned equipment may contaminate the product with bacteria. This may result in either a uniform or a spotty increase in bacterial numbers. If possible, scrapings of questionable material should be in sufficient quantity to be easily weighed and quantitatively diluted, if collected for analysis.

2. Environmental Sampling

"Environmental" swab sampling does not give quantitative results. Because a swab takes a very small sample, microorganisms of significance are often missed. It is important to keep in mind a negative result on a swab will often negate an inspectional observation unless the observation is fully documented. A positive finding will give more support to a fully documented observation.

Environmental swabs from food contact surfaces are to be collected initially (See IOM 427.6). Other environmental swabs (e.g., floor drains, walls, etc.) will be collected based upon the investigator's observations of extensive insanitary conditions.

Document the possible link between the source of an environmental sample and contamination of the food product. For example, if a swab was taken from:

A floor drain - Did cleaning procedures provide "back splash" to the food contact surfaces or product? Were employees observed walking through the area of the floor drain and back to the processing area (how many and when)? Was product dropped on the floor and placed back on the processing line (how many times and when)?

A wall - Did insects (e.g., flies and number) land on the wall and have subsequent contact on the food contact surface or product (how many and when)?

The ceiling area - Is condensate, flaking paint, etc., located over the processing area? Did you observe the condensate dripping on the food surfaces of the processing equipment and/or product?

3.   Finished Product Sampling

Collect finished product from production on the day of the inspection and from the previous day's run. Sampling multiple lots should be considered depending on the type of product and process used. The subsamples should consist of ten (10) retail size containers at least 114g (4 oz) each, in duplicate (702b portion).

If the finished product is also to be analyzed for Salmonella, the number of finished product subs should be 15, 30 or 60, depending upon product classification. See Salmonella Sampling Plan, IOM, Chart 1.

See IOM section 536.2 for inspectional guidance for firms producing products susceptible to contamination with pathogenic/non-pathogenic microorganisms.

427.8 Samples for Viral Analysis

Sample instructions will be issued by the appropriate Center on a case by case basis.

428   ECONOMIC VIOLATIONS

428.1 Net Weight

Field weighing for net weight is primarily to determine the likelihood of short weight units. The laboratory will confirm both tare and net weights.

Equipment - Use either a Gurley, Troemner, or equivalent balance. Check the accuracy of the balance before and after use. If this equipment is not available, or the units exceed their capacities, use commercial scales. If possible, have the commercial scales checked in your presence by the local Sealer of Weights and Measures. If this is not possible, report the name, type of scale, style and capacity, minimum graduations, apparent sensitivity, and date of last sealing and by whom.

Tare Determination - Whenever possible, determine a minimum of six tares selected at random. If empty containers are readily available, or if tares vary widely (e.g.; glass jars), determine at least 12 tares.

Field Examination - Weigh 48 units, if that number is available, selected at random from the square root of the number of cases in the lot with a minimum of 6 and a maximum of 12. Where units are selected from the production line, do so in representative manner. Report the code weighed and if short weight, the quantity in the code. Unless otherwise instructed, do not weigh leaking containers. Identify each unit with the corresponding sub number on the Field Weight Sheet (FDA 485).

Submit the units indicated by the asterisks on the FDA 485 plus twelve additional weighed units for reserve if the average net is below that declared on the label.

Field Weight Sheet - Record weights on Form FDA 485, Field Weight Sheet. See IOM Exhibit 420-B. Submit Field Weight Sheet with the printed FACTS Collection Record.

a.   Individual Captions
(1)   Date - Enter the date weighed.
(2)   Sample No.- Enter the sample number of the C/R.

(3)   Product - Enter the specific name of the product, i.e., macaroni in cellophane, print butter in aluminum wrappers, olive oil in glass, etc. Quote significant portions of the label including the declared net weight.

(4)   Type of Balance - Enter the type of balance used i.e., Gurley, Troemner, etc. If balance used is not FDA equipment, give style, capacity, minimum graduations, etc.

(5)   Responsible Firm and Address - Enter the name and address of the firm most likely responsible for the short weight violation.

(6)   Address Where Weighed - Enter the name and address or location where weighed.

(7)   Warehouse - Enter the type of warehouse where product is stored, i.e., cold storage, truck dock, production line, etc. Enter the temperature and estimate the humidity where possible.

(8)   No. Of - Enter the number of cases, and number and size of units per case in the lot. Enter the number of cases from which subs were weighed and the number of subs weighed from each case. If the units are collected from a production line, estimate the number of units produced of the code weighed.

(9)   Gross Weight - Arbitrarily assign and record the shipping case number from which each sub was weighed. Number each unit submitted to correspond with the sub number on the Field Weight Sheet. Record weights to second decimal place.

(10)   Preliminary Tare - Determine and record tare weights as provided in IOM 428.1. Obtain the preliminary average tare by totaling preliminary tares and dividing by the number of tares weighed.

(11)   Weighing Results
        a.   Determine the average gross weight by totaling gross weights and dividing by the number weighed;
        b.   Enter preliminary average tare from caption 10;
        c.   Determine average net weight by subtracting b from a;
        d.   Enter the declared net weight as stated on the package weighed;
        e.   Determine the shortage by subtracting c from d.

(12)   Preliminary % Short
Enter the preliminary percent short, which is determined by dividing e by d.

(13)   Remarks - Record any observations on the condition of the lot or storage facilities which might affect net weights, (faulty machine sealing of packages, extreme high temperature, extended length of storage, etc.)

(14)   District - Enter the name of the collecting district.
(15)   Employee Signature
(16)   Employee Title

428.2 Volume Determination

Field determination of volume is a screening procedure to determine the likelihood of short volume units in the lot. The laboratory will confirm both tare and net volume.

Free Flowing Liquids - The approximate volume of small containers of free flowing liquids may be obtained by direct measurement. Standardized graduated cylinders calibrated to "contain" a given volume can be obtained from the laboratory. Use the smallest graduate that will hold the volume to be measured. Under no circumstances use a graduate to measure a volume less than 25% of the maximum capacity of the graduate. Proceed as follows:

a.   Select 8 units at random; one from each of 8 cases or otherwise representative of the lot.

b.   Empty contents into calibrated graduate holding the container in a nearly vertical position, but tipping so that the bottom of the container will drain. Allow to drain one minute after stream breaks into drops. Obtain an anti-foaming agent from the laboratory if beer or other product likely to foam is measured.

c.   Hold the graduate vertically with the surface of the liquid level with the eye. Place a shade of some dark material immediately below the meniscus and read volume from the lowest point of the meniscus. A convenient device for this purpose is a collar-shaped section of thick black rubber tubing cut open at one side and of such size as to clasp the graduate firmly.

d.   If no units containing less than declared volume are found, no further determinations are required.

e.   If one or more units containing less than declared volume are found, measure 4 additional units selected as above.

f.   If the total of twelve determinations contains only one short volume unit, be guided by the significance of the average shortage as related to the individual program guideline.

g.   If the total of twelve determinations contains more than one short volume unit, an Official Sample of 48 units should be collected regardless of the average shortage figure.

Viscous Liquids - Direct measurement of viscous liquids or large containers is not practical. Field weigh 48 units as specified in IOM 428.1.

428.3 Labeling

See the document "Guide to Nutritional Labeling and Education Act (NLEA) Requirements" for guidance.

429   ORGANOLEPTIC EXAMINATIONS

Examination of many products may be conducted on the spot without fixed laboratory equipment. These examinations vary from simple visual observations for gross filth, such as rodent pellets in wheat, to the detection of odors of decomposition in seafood. Organoleptic examinations for regulatory purposes shall be made only by those individuals qualified by training or experience to conduct such examinations.

If it is necessary to collect physical sub samples for organoleptic examination and they are collected from bulk, the subs must be packed in glass jars to prevent the product from picking up foreign odors.

Review your Compliance Program Guidance Manual and IOM 427.1 & 620 for field examination techniques which may be applicable to specific products or industry.

429.1 Whole-Bag Screening

When making filth examination by screening shelled peanuts, dried bean, peas and similar products, packed in large containers (i.e., 50-125 lb. bags) use the portable folding whole-bag screens available in your district.

Conduct the examination in a well lighted area. Set up screen and adjust height to permit opening the bags directly onto the high side of the screen. Place another bag or container on the screen's low side to catch the screened product.

Place a sheet of clean butcher or similar paper in screen body to catch screenings and insert screen wire over paper.

Open stitches of bag being examined to permit approximately ten to twenty pound portions to enter onto high side of screen. Gradually work the product across the sieve to the low side and into the receiving container. Do not push large quantities rapidly across screen because insects, eggs, stones, excreta pellets, etc., will be carried along with the product and will not sift through the sieve openings.

Examine the screening from each bag and subjectively report live or dead insects, rodent excreta pellets, or other obvious filth. Submit screenings as separate subs if actionable.

SUBCHAPTER 430 - DOCUMENTATION & C/R

430.1 Authority

Section 703 of the FD&C Act describes FDA's authority to access and copy records of interstate shipment.

430.2 Objective

For FDA to initiate formal legal action, interstate jurisdiction must be established. Most often, this is done by documenting interstate movement of a product by copying records ("getting the records") of a shipment represented by an Official Sample. However, on occasion, jurisdiction can be fixed on a limited list of articles, e.g., counterfeit drugs, medical devices, oleomargarine, through other means.

430.3 Policy

Fully document every Official Sample at the time of collection unless instructed otherwise by the program, the assignment or your supervisor. Current agency policy does not require the collection of records of interstate movement for the issuance of a Warning Letter. Also, the FDA Modernization Act expanded the (rebuttable) presumption of interstate commerce for medical devices to all commodities regulated by FDA. Nevertheless, in any situations where you think a formal legal action may occur, make sure you collect copies of interstate records.

The decision to collect copies of records of interstate commerce in situations involving warning letters may be further covered by District policies or situations. As an example, in cases where the records are readily available and the site is located a long distance from an FDA office, it may be better to collect copies of the records at the time the sample is collected. This will ensure FDA has the records in the event a different action is chosen and you will have saved resources in their collection.

Collection Records - Sample Collections are recorded in the Field Accomplishments and Compliance Tracking System (FACTS). Individuals who may be assigned to collect samples should routinely obtain in advance, a supply of FACTS sample numbers, to be used by the collector to identify samples in the field, prior to accessing FACTS to prepare a sample collection record.

430.4 Responsibility

Document samples in accordance with procedures in this Sub-Chapter being certain the copies of records obtained cover the product sampled.

Do not remove the dealer's only copy of records. Whenever possible, photocopy or mechanically copy records, if duplicates are not available. Reproductions should be reviewed to ensure all relevant information is readable.

It is possible to enhance the clarity of photocopies from poor originals (e.g., second or third carbon copies, copies in blue ink, etc.) by overlaying the "original" document with one or two clear yellow plastic sheets. These clear yellow plastic sheets are available at most stationary stores.

If the above procedure does not enhance the copied document, pen and ink additions should be made. Records copied on FDA forms must be accurate and legible.

If you are documenting a shipper violation at a dealer, it is your responsibility to show the storage conditions did not contribute to the violation. Obtain an affidavit describing handling of the goods after receipt, and any other information which supports the violation.

In cases where the product does not move Interstate but is formulated from I.S. raw materials, government jurisdiction may be established by documenting the I.S. nature of the major raw materials. This is done by linking copies of records for the I.S. raw material with the production of the final product, by affidavit from a knowledgeable and responsible firm official. See IOM Exhibit 430-M.

Note: In the case of imported products which have been released to commerce, documentation of the sample should also include the port of entry and the importer of record to facilitate investigation by the home district if necessary.

430.5 Sample Records Identification

Copies of all records obtained and attached to the collection record (including those pertaining to the interstate movement of the lot(s)) must be identified with the sample number, collection date, and collector's handwritten name or initials. See IOM 451.5.

If the firm maintains their records on film or electronically, see IOM 527.1.

431 EVIDENCE REQUIRED

When documenting violative situations, consider whether you have established FDA's jurisdiction, documented interstate commerce, shown a violation, and determined responsibility for the violation. The contemplated legal action determines the extent of documentation. A preponderance of evidence is required to prevail in a civil action, such as a contested seizure, as opposed to a criminal prosecution, which requires evidence establishing guilt beyond a reasonable doubt.

431.1 Seizure

For a seizure action, FDA must establish jurisdiction over the product, show its interstate movement and document a violation.

Obtain copies of any document proving the article was introduced into or in interstate commerce, or held for sale after shipment in interstate commerce. Collect copies of the best records available, without extensive search or travel. See section 304(a)(1) of the FD&C Act.

431.2 Injunction or Criminal Prosecution

The proof required depends on the violation of Section 301 of the FD&C Act.

Introduction Into I.S. - Proof is required showing introduction into interstate commerce on or about a certain day by a specific person of a specific consignment of the article. In addition, delivery for introduction into I.S. requires proof the seller had knowledge the purchaser intended to introduce the article into interstate commerce. See Section 301(a) or (d) of the FD&C Act.

Adulteration or Misbranding in Interstate Commerce - Proof is required showing that a specific consignment was in interstate commerce and was rendered violative by a specific person on or about a certain date while therein. See Section 301(b) of the FD&C Act.

Receipt in I.S. - Proof is required showing receipt of a violative consignment in interstate commerce on or about a certain date, along with evidence to show specific delivery thereafter by a specific person. It is essential to show the violative condition of the shipment was known to the consignee before the delivery or proffered delivery. Whether it was sold or given away is immaterial. See Section 301(c) of the FD&C Act.

Manufacture Within a Territory - Proof is required of manufacture within any territory by a specific person on or about a certain date. See Section 301(g) of the FD&C Act.

False Guaranty - Proof of the giving on or about a certain date of a specific guaranty and proof of its falsity; usually a specific sale (and delivery) on or about a definite date to the holder of the guaranty. Interstate commerce is not required, except evidence the consignee normally engages in some interstate business. See Section 301(h) of the FD&C Act and 21 CFR 7.13, 201.150 & 701.9.

Dealer Violation - Proof of interstate origin of the article, and proof of a specific manipulation which adulterates or misbrands the article, on or about a certain date by a specific person. See FD&C Act Section 301(k).

431.3 Complaint or Injury Samples

Generally samples collected from complainants during investigation of injuries or foodborne out-breaks are investigational in nature and not documented. However, if the nature of the contamination or adulteration is such that regulatory action may be warranted, the interstate nature of the sample should be documented. Affidavits from the consumer, retailer, and wholesaler should be obtained.

At times even though you may not be able to obtain physical portions of the involved item, a Documentary Sample can be collected by photographing the container, contents, labels, codes, etc., and obtaining necessary affidavits and interstate records. See IOM 408 for sample criteria on complaint samples.

During investigations of alleged tampering incidents, complainants must be advised of the provisions of the Federal Anti-Tampering Act (FATA). A general discussion of the FATA, its provisions for investigation, filing of false reports, and tampering can be useful and informative to those individuals.

Prior to concluding your interview of the complainant, obtain a signed affidavit attesting to the circumstances of the complaint. See IOM 975.4.

432 DOCUMENTING INTERSTATE SHIPMENTS

The minimum set of records ordinarily submitted with a sample will consist of a copy of the invoice covering the sale of the lot to the dealer, the transportation record showing interstate commerce, and an affidavit signed by the dealer, which identifies both the lot sampled and the applicable records. See IOM 430.3 and 430.5.

432.1 Sales Records

An invoice does not establish interstate commerce and thus federal jurisdiction. It does not prove actual movement. However, it may provide information as to the value of the goods, carrier, date of shipment, etc. and bear a Food and Drug type guarantee. Collect copies of the invoice to show the owner's intent to sell the product and tie other records to the sample. If the invoice covers numerous items, copy entries covering items sampled and indicate omissions by asterisks. Copy the invoice on the FDA 1662. See IOM Exhibit 430-A. If the invoice bears a Food & Drug guarantee, copy the guarantee on the back of the FDA 1662. Other records which may be substituted in the absence of an invoice are copies of purchase orders, receiving records, canceled checks, correspondence, etc.

Invoices covering in-transit shipments usually are not available. Document any available transportation record that establishes the lot to be in interstate commerce. Be sure to name the shipper and consignee if known. Where positive identification of a shipment cannot be made by personal observation, obtain a statement from the carrier's agent identifying the shipment sampled as having been delivered by the consignor on a certain day for delivery to the consignee. Include in this statement reference to the particular transportation record covering the shipment. The transportation record will generally be available after the shipment is delivered.

Where the sample is taken from a vehicle or dock as the vehicle is loaded, and there are no unusual circumstances which must be explained in a regular affidavit, use the FDA 1664b, Affidavit (In-Transit Sampling). See IOM Exhibit 430-L.

432.2 Transportation Records for Common Carrier Shipments

Mandatory Access to Interstate Records - Section 703 of the FD&C Act [21 USC 373] provides for mandatory access to and copying of all records showing interstate movement of commodities subject to the Act. This is provided the request is in writing, and the records are in the possession of common carriers, or persons receiving or holding such commodities.

Section 704(a) of the FD&C Act [21 USC 374a] provides mandatory access, upon presenting your credentials and issuing a written notice of inspection, to documents covering the interstate movement of, non-prescription drugs for human use, prescription drugs and restricted devices. The authority applies to inspection of any factory, warehouse, establishment, or consulting laboratory in which prescription drugs, nonprescription drugs for human use, or restricted devices are manufactured, processed, packed or held.

Note: At times, you may have only the name of the carrier (trucking company), with no address or phone number. If you are unable to locate the trucking company, contact the local office of the Office of Motor Carrier Safety, Federal Highway Administration, Department of Transportation. If you furnish this office the name of the trucking company, they will be able to provide the address and phone number. The DIB has the phone number of the local offices of the OMCS as part of a MOU between DOT and FDA.

Refusal to Permit Access to Records in Possession of Common Carriers - Refusal to permit access to and copying of all records showing interstate movement of articles subject to FDA jurisdiction is unlawful provided the request for such permission is issued in writing. You cannot state that the law requires the records be furnished to FDA unless you also explain it is required only after a written request is issued. If refused, after providing a written request, politely explain the law requires the records to be furnished. You are more likely to get the records through courteous persuasion and tact than through stressing the force of law.

Written Request for Records - If a carrier, consignee, or any other person refuses to supply I.S. records, and it is apparent he will not do so without a written request, report the facts to your supervisor. Do not routinely issue a written request for I.S. records since evidence so obtained may not be used in the criminal prosecution of the person from whom obtained.

If the request is being made of a carrier who has no responsibility for the violation, issue a written request only after approval by District Management. When authorized by your supervisor to issue a written request, prepare a statement, using the following guidance, or as otherwise directed by your supervisor:

"Pursuant to Section 703 of the Federal Food, Drug, and Cosmetic Act (21 U.S.C. 373) permission is hereby requested for access to and copying of all records showing quantity, shipper, and consignee, showing movement in interstate commerce and/ or the holding after interstate movement of_____."

Clearly identify the specific lots which are the subject of the request, the firm and the individual to whom the request is given.

Bill of Lading - The shipper, who delivers the goods to the carrier for shipment, prepares The Bill of Lading. It is an order for the carrier to move the goods. When the carrier's agent signs the Bill of Lading he acknowledges receipt for the shipment. The carrier's office in city of origin of shipment maintains a copy of the Bill of Lading. Information normally included is the name and address of shipper, name and address of consignee, date of shipment, name of carrier, vehicle number, and a description of the goods. Copy Bill of Lading on Section II of the FDA 1662. See IOM Exhibit 430 A.

Freight Bill - This record is prepared by the transportation company for the purpose of collecting freight charges. It includes the same information found on the Bill of Lading, plus additional data about the carrier's handling of the shipment and cost involved. Railroads prepare Freight Bills at their destination offices, where copies can be made. Steamship and airlines combine the Bill of Lading and Freight Bill into one form. Copies are filed at both origin and destination offices of these carriers. Truck lines prepare Freight Bills at the origin office and both origin and destination offices should have copies. The dealer should have a Freight Bill if he received the goods directly in interstate commerce.

Copy Freight Bills on Section II of the FDA 1662. Enter the type of shipping record in block 21. Section I and II may be executed together on one sheet. If only one section is used, leave the other section blank, and submit the entire page.

Waybill - The transportation company uses the Waybill in its own operations, and it accompanies the shipment during transit. Copies are not given to the shipper or consignee, but can be obtained from the carrier. Other transportation records are generally more readily available than Waybills. Air Freight Waybill numbers are designed so that the originating line and point of origin are encoded in the Waybill number itself. Each airline has a numerical code description, indicated by the first two digits of the number. The three letters, which next follow indicate the point of origin. For example, Waybill No. 01LGA, designates American Airlines (01) as the carrier, and La Guardia Field (LGA) as the point of origin. Most airline offices have a copy of "Official Air Freight Transmittal Manual", which lists the codes. Other express shipping companies, such as Federal Express, and United Parcel Service have their own codes.

Copy Waybills on the FDA 1662.

432.3 Mail or Parcel Service Shipments

Always attempt to collect the original wrappings showing cancellation of origin office and address sticker. Record the facts obtained from the dealer on the FDA 463, Affidavit (Parcel Post/Service). Before the individual signs the statement he should be asked to affirm he affidavit is true and accurate. A statement to that effect can also be added at the conclusion of the affidavit. See IOM Exhibit 430-C.

Note: Shipments made by "Express Mail" do have a shipping record maintained. These are:

a. Express Mail - Form A - used for Post Office to Post Office service.

b. Express Mail - Form B - used for Post Office to Addressee service.

c. Express Mail - Form C - used for Airport to Airport service.

Obtain copies of the Postal Service record from the consignee, if possible, or from the Post Office to document shipments using Express Mail Service.

432.4 Shipment by Privately-Owned Conveyance

Obtain on the FDA 463a, Affidavit, a dealer's statement setting forth the facts, including the date and manner of receipt. The affidavit by the dealer may not be evidence, since the dealer lacks personal knowledge of the point of origin. Ascertain the name and home address of the driver of the conveyance, vehicle license number, the name and address of the driver's employer or the owner of the conveyance and the driver's license number. Obtain an Affidavit, from the driver setting forth the facts of the shipment. See IOM Exhibit 430-D.

432.5 In-Transit Sampling Affidavit

See IOM 405.3 and 424 for definition and sampling procedures. When obtaining samples from in-transit lots, if it is a straightforward uncomplicated sample requiring no unusual explanations, use the FDA 1664b, Affidavit (In-Transit Sampling). See IOM Exhibit 430-L. Otherwise, use the regular Affidavit, FDA 463a.

433   AFFIDAVITS

Statements on various affidavit forms may be obtained from persons who have dealt somehow with the goods sampled, know material facts relating to the movement of the goods, and/or to events affecting their condition. Such facts, recorded in writing and signed by the person who can testify in court to those facts, can be used either to establish federal jurisdiction or fix the responsibility for a violation. The statement may identify documents proving I.S. movement of goods sampled; they may name the person who could testify to the identity of the goods sampled: and they may certify the sample collected is from the lot of goods covered by the records.

433.1 Affidavit (Dealer/Warehouseman)

The FDA 1664, Affidavit (Dealer/Warehouseman), is used to document the dealer or warehouseman identification of the lot and related records. See IOM Exhibit 430-E. Fill in all blanks on the form as applicable. There are sufficient blanks for listing up to three invoices and up to three shipping records covering the lot in question. Any unused blanks should be lined out, and strike out the words or letters in parentheses which are not applicable.

Be certain the dealer knows what he is signing. Before the individual signs the statement, he/she should be asked to affirm the affidavit is true and accurate. A statement to that effect can also be added at the conclusion of the affidavit. See IOM Exhibit 430-C.

You should only sign the affidavit AFTER the affiant has signed it. The wording above your signature is, "Subscribed and sworn to before me at ***" Subscribed, in this context means to attest by signing. Thus, your signature is attesting to the fact the affiant has read and understood the statement and has confirmed that the statement is the truth. You MUST NOT sign an affidavit until after the affiant swears (affirms) to you the written statement he/she has signed is true. If more than one FDA employee is present, they may also sign the affidavit. The dealer may be provided a copy of an affidavit if he/she requests it and it has been signed.

Also see IOM 433.2 for conditions not amenable to use of the FDA 1664.

433.2 Affidavit (FDA 463a)

Unusual sampling situations may present circumstances that do not lend themselves to presentation on the FDA 1664 or 1664b. In these situations, record the facts on an FDA 463a, Affidavit.

Preparation - There is no prescribed format for composing the statement. However, you should positively identify the affiant by name, title, and address at the beginning of the statement and show why he/she is qualified to make the statement. The facts should be arranged in an order roughly paralleling that of the FDA 1664. The most manageable narrative describes the events and circumstances chronologically. Whatever format is used, the recorded facts must be intelligible to the reader unfamiliar with the transaction. See IOM Exhibit 430-C, 430-G, and 430-M.

Ascertain all the facts and record those which are material, relevant, and to which the affiant can affirm.

Narrate the facts in the words of the affiant, using the first person singular. Do not use stilted terms such as, "that" as in the expression " that I am the president of.." If the statement is long and complex, break it down into logical paragraphs.

Have the affiant read the statement and make necessary corrections before signing the affidavit. Mistakes that have been corrected and initialed and numbered by the affiant are an indication he/she has read and understood the statement. A concluding paragraph in the affiant's own handwriting declaring he/she read and understood the statement are valuable safeguards to counter the possibility he/she might later claim he/she did not know what he/she was signing.

Before the individual signs the statement, he/she should be asked to affirm the affidavit is true and accurate. A statement to that effect can also be added at the conclusion of the affidavit. See IOM Exhibit 430-C.

You should only sign the affidavit AFTER the affiant has signed it. The wording above your signature is, "Subscribed and sworn to before me at ***" Subscribed , in this context means to attest by signing. Thus, your signature is attesting to the fact that the affiant has read and understood the statement and has confirmed that the statement is the truth. You MUST NOT sign an affidavit until after the affiant swears (affirms) to you the written statement he/she has signed is true. If more than one FDA employee is present, they may also sign the affidavit. The dealer may be provided a copy of an affidavit if he/she requests it and it has been signed.

You and the affiant should sign all pages of a multi-page affidavit.

Refusal to Sign - Even if it is apparent the dealer will refuse to sign a statement setting forth the facts he/she has revealed, the statement should be prepared as described above. Either read the statement to the dealer or have him/her read it. Request the dealer to correct and initial by his/her own hand any errors. Elicit from him/her an acknowledgement the statement is true and correct. Ask him/her to write in his/her own hand at bottom of the statement "I have read this statement and it is true, but I am not signing it because...". Failing that, declare at the bottom of the affidavit that you recorded the facts above as the dealer revealed them, that the dealer read the statement, and avowed the statement to be true.

Be aware, in situations involving confidential informants, the affiant may be reluctant to sign a statement, which reveals his or her identity. See IOM 518 for guidance on interviewing confidential informants.

433.3 Affidavit (Jobber)

Form FDA 664a is used to document movement of goods from a jobber to a dealer. See IOM Exhibit 430-F. Complete all blanks as applicable. There are sufficient blanks to list up to three invoices and three shipping records. Line out any unused blanks and strike out all words and letters in parentheses, which are not applicable.

Be sure the jobber knows what he/she is signing. Before the individual signs, he/she should be asked to affirm the affidavit is true and accurate. A statement to that effect can also be added at the conclusion of the affidavit. See IOM Exhibit 430-C.

You should only sign the affidavit AFTER the affiant has signed it. The wording above your signature is, "Subscribed and sworn to before me at ***" Subscribed, in this context means to attest by signing. Thus, your signature is attesting to the fact that the affiant has read and understood the statement and has confirmed that the statement is the truth. You MUST NOT sign an affidavit until after the affiant swears (affirms) to you the written statement he/she has signed is true. If more than one FDA employee is present, they may also sign the affidavit. The dealer may be provided a copy of an affidavit if he/she requests it and it has been signed.

See IOM Exhibit 430-F.

435 LABELS AND LABELING

No sample documentation is complete without copies of the label and labeling. No special effort is needed to obtain copies of the label when it is on the individual units collected. However, the goods may be accompanied by labeling which is not affixed to the product. In this case, you must obtain copies of all labeling. Although your sample assignment may not specifically request the collection of accompanying labeling, determine if such labeling exists, and if it is present, collect it.

Collect at least four copies of all labeling, if there is a sufficient stock on hand. Mount individual copies or sets of labeling so they can be reviewed by various individuals located in separate offices. Do not collect the actual labeling if only one copy is available. To do so may remove the offending literature and thus correct the misbranding or you may misbrand the product yourself, by removing legally mandated information. Photographs or other copies must be made in this case.

435.1 Labels & Labeling

These are defined as:

a.   Label - A display of written, printed, or graphic matter upon the immediate container of an article.

b.   Labeling - All labels and other written, printed, or graphic matter upon any article or any of its containers or wrappers, or accompanying such article. Labeling includes such material as circulars, booklets, placards, displays, window streamers, books, article reprints, etc., that supplement or explain a product and /or are part of an integrated distribution system for the product. If the labeling and the product are in functional proximity at a point of sale, provide diagrams or photographs of this relationship. If the labeling and the product are found at a manufacturer or distributor, document the role that the labeling will play in the distribution of the product (e.g. to whom will it be sent and when).

Dealer Identification - Request the dealer (Note: a manufacturer may be considered a dealer if the product being sampled is located at the manufacturer) identify collected copies of accompanying labeling with his initials and the date. This will identify these copies of labeling if they are introduced in court later. Prepare a dealer's affidavit on the FDA 463a, covering the relationship of the labeling to the goods. This affidavit should include the following information.

a.   Description of Labeling - Describe briefly each piece of literature by name of identifiable quote, i.e., Leaflet, "Do You Have Tired Blood" or Window Streamer, "Amazing New Tranquilizer". State the quantity of such labeling on hand.

b.   Location of Labeling - Report the location of each different piece of literature and how much of each is at that location.

c.   Method of Distribution - Determine how the labeling is made available to the public. Describe how it is displayed such as: for voluntary pick-up; mailed to prospective customers; distributed without being displayed, etc.

d.   Source of Labeling - Describe whether the labeling was sent to the dealer by the shipper of the goods or if the dealer prepared the labeling himself or if it originated from another source. It is important to document this point to fix responsibility in the event the agency wishes to pursue action against that individual. It is not necessary to determine or fix responsibility in order to seize the goods. Document the shipment of the labeling if a source other than the dealer supplied the labeling.

e.   Instructions to Dealer - The manufacturer or shipper often provide sales promotion instructions to the dealer. Obtain copies of such instructions if available.

435.2 Bulk Shipments

Do not remove the label from bulk containers such as drums, barrels, and large bags, if this results in misbranding the article. Remove and submit an identical label from an empty container if available. Photograph or trace the label if none other is available.

Note: Besides using tracing paper, it is possible to trace a label on a piece of plastic, similar to a document protector, using either a ball point pen or stylus. If it is difficult to read, filling in the tracing with a marker, may highlight the tracing.

435.3 Unlabeled or Partially Labeled Lot

The regulations provide for controlled shipment in IS commerce of unlabeled goods. It is a violation to ship unlabeled goods unless:

a.   The shipper operates the establishment where the article is to be processed, labeled or repacked, or

b.   If the shipper is not the operator of the establishment, he must first obtain from the owner a written agreement signed by the operator. The agreement must contain the post office addresses of both parties and describe the specifications and the processing, labeling, or repacking procedures, in sufficient detail to insure that the article will not be adulterated or misbranded within the meaning of the Act, upon completion of the processing, labeling or repacking.

Determine if there is a labeling agreement and obtain copies of pertinent correspondence. See 21 CFR 101.100, 201.150, and 701.9.

Documentation - Collect both unlabeled and relabeled units or specimens of the label to be affixed. Collect specimens of any shipping case labels and any labeling which accompanied the original shipment.

Obtain evidence showing how the lot was labeled at the time of receipt; how the misbranding occurred, and who was responsible. Use photographs and diagrams if necessary to portray the present condition of the lot. If any of the lot has been resold, collect documentary evidence of the resale.

439 REPORTING SAMPLE COLLECTIONS

For each sample collected prepare a FACTS Sample Collection Record. See IOM Exhibits 430-H through 430-L for examples. Sample collection data may be entered either from an FDA office or from a remote location in the field using a laptop computer and modem. If change is needed to the data in the FACTS Firms table that relates to the sample collection, e.g., the firm's name or address has changed; you (the collector) should update the FACTS firm table before completing the sample collection record.

After collection data is entered into the FACTS system, you (the collector) must check the record for accuracy and completeness, send it to a supervisor for review, if appropriate, and then sign it electronically. The original data will be stored and permanently associated with this record. Any future changes to the FACTS database reference tables, such as the firm files, employee name, data codes, etc., will not alter the original data in the electronically-signed sample collection record.

Only you (the collector) have editing privileges for the signed original sample collection record. You may modify the original record but must electronically sign each revision. All modifications of the original record are permanently retained as part of the original record. A permanent electronic record trail is created, capturing and retaining every change to original and subsequent records. If retrieval of the sample collection data is needed, the original record and all changes to the original record can be retrieved.

439.1 Flag

The following situations require an entry in the Sample Flags screen in FACTS See IOM Exhibit 430-H. **Note: If a sample is collected for compliance purposes, it must be flagged "Compliance," in addition to the flags listed below.**

See the Other Codes Section of the Data Codes Manual for an explanation of the flags.

➢ **"301(k) Sample"** - See IOM 405.4.

➢ **"Complaint Sample"** - Use this flag for any sample collected from a complainant during follow-up investigation.

➢ **"Dealer Voluntarily Holding"** - This flag alerts the reviewer the lot is being voluntarily held. Enter how long or if under state embargo in the Flag Remarks field.

➢ **"Exhibit Sample"** - When sample is to be used exclusively for court exhibit without analysis.

➢ **"Factory Food Sample"** - Flag as "Factory Food Sample" when sample(s) of any item, used in the production of any food product, are taken during the EI. See IOM 408.

➢ **"Fumigated"** - Enter name of fumigant in Flag Remarks field.

➢ **"Inv. Samples of Filth Exhibits"** - Enter the product code of the filth exhibits (obtained from the Data Codes Manual) in the Product Code field of the FACTS Sample Collection Screen. **Note the product code for exhibits consists of the Industry Code followed by "YY-99" or "Y--99" as below.**

Example: Filth Exhibits of gnawings, pellets, wood splinters, etc.

In a food plant = 52YY-99
52 = Misc. food related items
Y = Exhibits
Y = Sub class - None

- = Dash
99 = Evidence exhibits n.e.c.

In a drug plant = 66Y--99
66 = Misc. drug related
Y = Exhibits
- = Dash
- = Dash
99 = Evidence exhibits n.e.c.

Other industries: Handled in same manner using applicable industry code from the Data Codes Manual.

➢ **"Pesticide Sample"** - After flagging a pesticide sample, the basis for sampling must be entered in the Flag Remarks field as either "Pesticide Compliance" or "Pesticide Surveillance". Additionally, the name of the county and state, or country where grown must be entered in the appropriate fields in the Collection Record.

Pesticide Episode - An "episode" is defined as a violative pesticide (or other chemical contaminant) finding and all samples collected in follow-up to that finding. All samples must be associated with one responsible firm (grower, pesticide applicator, etc.) and one specific time period (e.g. growing season). The following examples are provided for clarification of this definition:

(a)   Samples of cantaloupes from Mexico reveal violative residues. Any destination point samples or subsequent compliance samples from the same shipper or grower would along with the original sample be considered an episode.

(b)   Grower Jones has violative residues of chlorothalonil on collards for which there is no tolerance. Field samples, I.S. samples, and packing shed or warehouse samples of these collards would all be part of the same episode.

(c)   Grower Jones also has violative residues of omethoate on kohlrabi about two months later. This is a separate episode.

(d)   Along with the omethoate on kohlrabi, Grower Jones has violative residues of omethoate on beets. Normally this would be considered a separate episode from the previous episode. However, if information were available showing that both residues resulted from the same application of the pesticide or the residues were closely related in some other way, the beets might be considered as part of the kohlrabi episode.

(e)   Grower Smith has violative residues of disulfon and permethrin on kale. This would be considered as one episode because only one commodity is involved.

Note: The detention without physical examination procedures provide for recommending detention based on a single violative pesticide finding. See RPM 601.2(b) Under these procedures we may anticipate that the number of compliance samples collected in follow-up to a violative finding may diminish appreciably and, in most cases, will be limited to occasional audit samples. These samples should also be linked to the sample number (episode number) of the original violative sample that prompted the automatic detention. This episode number will be indicated in the applicable Import Alert.

The Episode Number will be the sample number of the first violative sample collected in a series of samples and is used to identify the other related samples within an episode. The district must assure that the Episode Number is used within the district and any other districts which follow-up to the original violative sample. This number must appear in the **Episode Number** field of the FACTS CR.

➢ **"Reconditioned"** - When collected in connection with a reconditioning operation in accordance with a court order.

➢ **"Sampled in Transit"** - Use when the sample is collected from a carrier or while in transit. Indicate this flag in the Collection Remarks field. See IOM 405.3 and 424.

➢ **"Split Sample"**- When sample is divided between two or more laboratories.

➢ **"Survey No. ___ "** - use this flag for any sample collected under the Drug Surveillance Program (CPGM 7356.008)

➢ **"Survey Sample"** - Use this flag for any sample collected under a Compliance Program, which directs samples be collected as part of a survey, or if an assignment to collect the sample(s) indicates the sample(s) are "Survey" sample(s).

439.2 Type Identification

When applicable, using the list of values, choose one of the following to complete the Sample Type field in FACTS. Identify any documents associated with the sample, and the sample itself, with the corresponding abbreviation followed by the FACTS sample number.

➢ **"Additional Analysis"** - ADD - To identify a physical sample collected from a previously sampled lot. Do not report or document as an "ADD Sample" those instances when only additional records or documentation are obtained for the sample.

➢ **"Documentary Sample"** - DOC – To identify an official sample comprised of documents and photographs, collected without a physical portion. Do not use this designation to identify a physical sample for which you wish to delay analysis. See IOM 405.2 and Exhibits 430-I and 430-J.

➢ **"Domestic Import"** - DI To identify samples collected of foreign products, which have passed through Customs and entered domestic commerce. See IOM 405.8.

➢ **Food Standards Sample** - F.S.- To identify samples collected to provide information on which to base Food Standards. See IOM 406.

➢ **"Investigational Sample"** – INV – To identify samples collected to document observations and/or where interstate commerce does not exist or is not necessary. See IOM 408.

➢ **"Post Award Sample"** – GQA – To identify samples collected as part of GWQP. See IOM 407.

➢ **"Post Seizure Sample"** - P.S. – To identify samples collected from a lot under seizure. See IOM 405.7.

439.8 Preparation

The collection record (C/R) is the starting point and the basic reference for all actions and considerations based on the sample. It contains or bears direct reference to every important point about the sample and the lot from which it was collected. See IOM 430-H, I, J, K & L for examples.

Individual Fields - Complete the individual fields on the FACTS Sample Collection Screen as indicated. The following fields must be completed to save the sample information; Sample Class; Sampling District; Collector; Collection Date; Sample Basis; Sample Type; FIS Sample Number; Sample Description; Product Code; Product Description; Resp. Firm Type; Resp. Firm FEI Number; PAC; Sample Origin; and CR& Records Sent To. The fields described below are listed in alphabetical order to facilitate locating the instructions.

➢ **Accomplishment Hours:** Enter the accomplishment data for every sample collected, by clicking on the "clock" icon at the FACTS task bar. In the Accomplishment hours screen, enter the PAC by selecting from the list of values and type in the number of hours spent collecting the sample. Also enter all PACs that were entered in the Collections PACs field on page 2 of the collection record. If another person is involved in the collection, add their time by clicking on the "Add" button. See IOM exhibit 430-K.

➢ **Analytical Assignment:** After saving a collection record, the system will prompt you for analytical assignment data. Enter lab analysis data (PAC and PAF) for your sample. The analytical PAC and PAF may be different from the collection PAC and PAF. Enter split sample data on separate lines. For DOC samples leave this field blank. Do not enter any data in this form if the sample is being delivered to a non-FACTS lab.

➢ **Brand Name:** Enter the Brand Name of the product. Carrier name: Enter name if known.

➢ **Collection Date:** Enter the date using the format - mm/dd/yyyy. **Note: the default date is today's date. Be careful not to use the default date if the sample was not collected on the date the CR is created. Only one date can be entered; if the sample collection was accomplished over several days, use one date. Be consistent. This date should be used to identify the physical sample and any records attached to the CR.**

➢ **Collection Method:** Describe how you collected the sample. Relate the number and size of the sampled units to show how each was taken, e.g., "Two cans from each of 12 previously unopened cases selected at random." Note any special sampling techniques used. E.g.: "Subs collected using aseptic technique and placed in sterile glass jars or whirl-packs" or "Sub samples collected from bulk containers and each sub placed in paper bag, plastic bag, glass jar, etc." See IOM 451.1 regarding sub identification.

➢ **Collection PACs:** Enter the Program Assignment Code (PAC), which is most correct, from the list of values. If the PAC on your assignment is not listed, discuss with your supervisor or FACTS Lead User.

➢ **Collection Reason:** Enter the complete reason for collection giving the suspected violation, or analysis desired. Identify any interdistrict, regional, headquarters initiated, assignment document(s) in sufficient detail so the document can be located, if necessary. If the sample was collected during an inspection to document violations found, state that and indicate the date of inspection. See IOM exhibits 430-I and 430-K.

➤ **Collection Remarks:** Enter any remarks you feel are necessary. Describe any special circumstances. If a 704(d) letter is indicated, include the name and title of the most responsible person at the firm to which the letter should be addressed. If the sample is an in-transit sample, state the sample was collected in-transit, from whom sampled (e.g. driver & carrier firm), and where sampled. If the dealer firm is a consumer, the name and address of the consumer should be entered in the Collection Remarks field, and the consumer's state in the State field. You may use a "CR Continuation Sheet", FDA 464a if you need more space.

➤ **Collector:** Your name should appear here by default.

➤ **Collector's ID on Package/Document:** As the Sample Collector, quote your identification placed on the packages, labels, etc., e.g., "2235 10-7-98 SHR". See IOM 451.3. When multiple units are collected, all or at least a portion should be labeled as subsamples. Subsample numbers need to be included on the C/R and in the EIR.

➤ **Collector's ID on Seal:** Quote your identification used on the Official Seal applied to the sample, e.g., "2235 10-7-98 Sidney H. Rogers". See IOM 453.1. If you use the FDA metal seal, enter the words "Metal Seal" followed by the seal identification and number, e.g., "U.S. Food & Drug 233", entering the actual number of the seal used. Samples need to be kept under lock or in your possession, until sealed. The Collection Remarks field needs to describe any discrepancy between the date sealed and the date collected. Normally, the sample should be sealed on the same day as collected.

➤ **Consumer Complaint Number:** If the sample relates to a consumer complaint, enter the complaint number.

➤ **Country of Origin:** Select the Country of Origin, if known.

➤ **County:** Select the County where the sample was collected.

➤ **CR & Records Sent to:** Enter the division or district office to which you will send the CR and records. This should be the office, which is most likely to initiate any regulatory action.

➤ **CRx/DEA Schedule:** Choose the appropriate schedule from the list of values, if applicable.

➤ **Dairy Permit Number:** Enter if applicable.

➤ **Date Shipped:** Enter date in the format, mm/dd/yyyy.

➤ **Documents Obtained:** Click on this button to enter Document Type, Document Number, Document Date and Remarks for any records collected to support a violation or show interstate movement of the product sampled. Enter an identifying number and date for invoices, freight bills, bills of lading, etc. Include the name and title of person signing any affidavits in the Remarks field. See IOM 430-I. Episode Number: Enter an episode number if applicable. See IOM 439.1.

➤ **Estimated Value:** Enter the estimated wholesale value of the lot remaining after sampling. Obtain this information from invoice or other records. (This is not the value to be used for seizure bond purposes.) Estimate value if you have no documentary reference. For DOC samples (see Exhibits 430-I & 430-J), indicate the estimated value of the lot. If the DOC sample is collected to document a lot that has already been shipped, estimate the value, or obtain a figure from your documentation, which represents what was shipped. Many times a DOC sample is collected merely to establish interstate commerce, in those situations, the value of the goods that traveled, or will travel, in interstate commerce is what is needed.

➤ **FEI Number:** The FEI number is a 10-digit unique identifier, which is used to identify firms associated with FDA regulated products. Use the Build button to query the database and find an FEI for firms associated with your sample. If one does not exist, FACTS will assign one to the firm. Take care in entering search criteria to avoid creating unnecessary FEI numbers. **You must enter an FEI for a dealer on every CR, unless you check the box indicating the dealer is a consumer.**

➤ **Firm Name:** This will be filled in by FACTS when you select an FEI.

➤ **Firm Type:** Using the list of values, select one of the following with for each FEI entered, with respect to the product sampled:

"Dealer" – This is always the firm from which the sample was collected. **There must be a dealer entered on every CR**, unless you check the box indicating the dealer is a consumer. **Note: this is not the same as the *establishment type* of the firm identified by the FEI. There are circumstances where you may identify the same firm as the dealer and another establishment type, such as when collecting a plant in-line sample.**
 Note: If the dealer firm is a consumer, the name and address of the consumer should be entered in the Collection Remarks field, and the consumer's state in the State field. When the sample is an in-transit sample (see IOM 405.3), enter the consignee of the lot as the dealer and state in **collection remarks** the sample was collected in-transit, from whom sampled (e.g. driver & carrier firm), and where sampled.
 "Grower" – Select if the FEI identifies a producer of a raw agricultural commodity.

"Harvester" – Use for an FEI identifying the harvester of the product sampled.

"Ingredient Supplier" – This should be used to identify a firm which supplied a raw material or component. For example, when documenting a 301(k) situation.

"Manufacturer" – Use this with an FEI, which identifies the manufacturer of the product sampled. **Note: this may be the same as the dealer when a product is sampled at a manufacturer. In that case, you can enter the FEI twice and identify it as both the manufacturer and the dealer.**

"Shipper" – The shipper is the firm responsible for causing the interstate movement of the product.

➤ **FIS Sample Number:** Enter the last two digits of the fiscal year. The remainder of the number will be assigned by FACTS. Note: FIS sample numbers will no longer be required when the FIS is turned off.

➤ **Food Canning Establishment:** Enter if applicable.

➤ **How Prepared:** Explain how the sample was prepared prior to submission to the laboratory; how you identified some or all the units; and how you wrapped and sealed the sample. Note any special preparation methods such as fumigation, frozen, kept under refrigeration, etc, and the form in which the sample was delivered to the laboratory, e.g. in paper bags, original carton, etc. If coolants or dry ice were used, indicate so here.

➤ **Lot Size:** Enter the amount of goods on hand before sampling as determined by your inventory of the lot. Include the number of shipping cases and the size of the components, e.g., 75 (48/12 oz.) cases, 250/100 lb. burlap bags, 4/100,000 tab drums, 24 cases containing 48/12/3 oz. tins. If accompanying literature is involved, describe and state the amount on hand. For DOC samples (see Exhibit 430-I and 430-J), also indicate the lot size, e.g. "one x-ray machine" or "50000 syringes and 1000 promotional brochures."

➤ **Manufacturing Codes:** Click on this button to enter and identify all codes, lot numbers, batch control codes, etc., shown on labels, cartons and shipping containers. Enclose the code in quotes, e.g. "code". Enter any expiration dates in the Exp Date field. For DOC samples (see IOM Exhibit 430-J), indicate serial number, lot numbers, etc., e.g. "serial number "ABC" stamped on metal ID plate".

➤ **National Drug Code:** Enter if applicable

➤ **Payment Method:** Select one of the following from the from the list of values: "Billed"; "Borrowed"; "Cash"; "Credit Card"; "No Charge"; "Voucher".

➤ **Product Code:** Enter the 7-digit product code. Use the product code build feature or your data codes manual. When 301(k) samples are collected, the full product code of the finished product must be entered. See IOM exhibit 430-I. See IOM 439.1for product codes for filth or evidence exhibits.

➤ **Product Description:** Enter the common or usual name of the product, i.e., aspirin tablets, chocolate candy bars, or alfalfa sprouts, etc. For identification, enter the type of container, i.e., Glass Ampoule, Bulk, Multilayer or paper bag, etc.

➤ **Product Label:** Quote pertinent portions of the label such as brand name, generic name, quantity of contents, name and address of manufacturer or distributor, code, etc. In the case of drugs, quote the potency, active ingredients and indicate whether Rx or non-Rx. Quote sufficiently from accompanying literature to identify. In the case of a Documentary Sample, sufficiently describe the article to identify what is sampled.

When the product sampled is packaged in a carton, shipping case or similar container, quote the pertinent labeling from the container.

When quoting from a label, or labeling, use exact spelling, capitalization, punctuation, arrangement, etc., as found on the original label(ing). Use asterisks to indicate any omissions.

➤ **Product Name:** This field is completed by FACTS when you select the product code.

Recall Number: If the sample relates to a recall, enter the recall number.

➤ **Receipt Issued:** Select "FDA472", "FDA484", or "None" from the list of values.

➤ **Related Samples:** This field is used to identify a sample number to which other sample information can be linked. When you collect more than one sample from a single shipment or there is more than one sample relating to a possible regulatory action, designate one sample as the "lead" sample. Enter that sample number in this field of the collection record for each related sample. Other related sample numbers should be listed in the Collection Remarks field.

➤ **Resp. Firm Type:** Choose the appropriate type from the list of values for the firm most likely to be responsible for a violation. For a 301(k) sample the responsible firm should be "Dealer". You should only enter one firm with the firm type you designate as the responsible firm type.

Sample Basis: Choose "Compliance" or "Surveillance" from the list of values.

➤ **Sample Class:** Make a selection from the following list of values: "Collaborative Study"; "Criminal Investigation"; "District Use Sample"; "Normal Everyday Sample"; "Petition Validation"; "Quality Assurance"; "State Partnership"; "Total Diet".

➤ **Sample Cost:** Enter the cost of the sample. If no charge, enter 0. If, as a last resort, you use your personal credit card to pay for the sample, enter the amount paid in this field and select "Credit. Card" in the Payment Method field. If you are unable to determine the cost of the sample and the firm states they will bill you later, enter the estimated cost in this field and state that it is an estimate in the Collection Remarks field.

➢ **Sample Delivered Date:** Enter the date on which the sample was delivered to the laboratory or for shipment. For DOC samples, you must leave this field blank. If you make an entry, you must enter a laboratory.

➢ **Sample Delivered To:** Enter to whom you delivered the physical sample. If delivered to your own sample custodian under seal, show delivery to servicing laboratory or sample custodian. If delivered to an analyst, report e.g., "In person to Analyst Richard R. Doe." If you shipped the sample, enter the name of the carrier to whom the sampled was delivered. Enter the Government Bill of Lading Number, if used. If shipment is by parcel post, give the location of the post office, e.g., "P.P., Austin, TX." For a DOC sample, leave this field blank. . If the sample is being sent to a non-FACTS laboratory, enter the laboratory here.

➢ **Sample Description:** Briefly describe the sample, i.e., three unopened, 200 tablet bottles, or documentary sample consisting of records, literature and photographs, etc.
Sample Flags: Click on this button to choose an appropriate flag using the list of values. See IOM 439.1 and exhibit 430-H.

➢ **Sample Number:** Select a pre-assigned sample number, using the list of values button, or the system will enter a sample number when the record is saved.

➢ **Sample Origin:** Choose "Domestic" or "Domestic/Import" from the list of values.

➢ **Sample Sent To:** Choose appropriate lab from the list of values. Select the laboratory to which you are sending the sample. If you are splitting the sample among multiple laboratories for various analyses, enter each laboratory separately. Generally, in that case you will have more than one PAC code. If, because of your assignment, you are aware the sample should be forwarded to a second laboratory after the first analysis is complete, include that information in the Collection Remarks field. However, you should only enter a laboratory in this field if you are sending the sample there, not if the laboratory will be expected to forward it. For a DOC sample, leave this blank. If the sample is to be sent to a non-FACTS lab, leave this field blank, enter the lab in the Sample Delivered To field, print a copy of the collection record and enclose it in the FDA 525 attached to the sample.

➢ **Sample Type:** Make a selection from the list of values. You can enter only one value. If more than one type applies, choose one and indicate the other in remarks. If the sample is a domestic import, be sure to enter "DI", so that you can enter the foreign manufacturer. See IOM 439.2.

➢ **Sampling District:** Make a selection from the list of values. This is the district that actually collects the sample. State: Select the State where the sample was collected.

➢ **Status:** This field is pre-filled by the system as "In-Progress". Select "Ready for Review", from the list of values, when you are ready to send the record to your supervisor for review, if you are required to do so. After supervisory review, if appropriate, change the status to "Complete". This will cause the electronic signature form to be activated.

➢ **Storage Requirements:** Select from the following list of values: Ambient; Frozen; Refrigerated.

Any information that needs to be included regarding the sample and cannot be documented via FACTS, should be documented on the FDA 464a, C/R Continuation Sheet. For example, pictorial descriptions of a field exam for a filth sample; or a description of relative documents and what they demonstrate regarding the subject lot of a documentary sample; etc.

439.9 Routing

Anyone who has user access to the FACTS system has access to the electronic records contained therein, including sample collection records. Individuals requiring sample collection data can query the system and retrieve data, based on the query parameters. In those cases where an individual needs to receive immediate notification of a sample collection, you may communicate the sample number via E-mail, telephone, or another means to a user, and the user may then query the system and obtain the desired data. It is not always necessary to print paper copies of FACTS sample collection records for those who have access to FACTS.

Routing Records Accompanying Sample Collection Record – Print a copy of the Collection Record in FACTS. Attach original records to the printed FACTS Collection Record and route, through your supervisor, to the district office compliance unit most likely to take regulatory action. When requested, additional copies should be routed, attached to a routing slip, marked "records to accompany CR _____(number), as requested." Include a copy of the printed FACTS Collection Record in the FDA 525 if it is available at the time of sample shipment.

When a sample is to be billed, route a copy of the FDA 484,if issued, annotated with the FACTS sample number to the appropriate fiscal unit for your district. If possible at the time of collection, provide the FACTS sample number to the firm and request that this number be placed on the billing invoice. If no sample number is available, ask the firm to identify the bill with your name as the collector to help the fiscal unit match the bill to the sample record in FACTS. The fiscal unit will have access to the sample collection record in FACTS to obtain detailed sample information.

SUBCHAPTER 450 - SAMPLING: PREPARATION, HANDLING, SHIPPING

450.1 Objective

The preparation, handling, and shipping of samples is your responsibility, and must be carried out in a manner which assures the sample's integrity and supports testimony that the sample examined was the same sample you collected from the shipment you documented.

As few persons as possible should handle the sample to reduce the likelihood of compromising sample integrity. See the Laboratory Procedures Manual (LPM), Chapter 4,4.1 for information about relinquishing samples.

451   IDENTIFYING MARKS

451.1 Sub Samples

Identify a representative number of sub samples (subs) with the sample number, collection date and your handwritten initials. If individual sub identity must be maintained, assign and mark each sub with a separate Arabic numeral. In some comprehensive inspections or investigations it may be important to correlate the manufacturing control code with the sub number.

When a variety of articles are included under one sample number, fully identify each sub and describe them on the C/R. Factory exhibits should be fully identified and, where appropriate, correlated with inspectional observations, manufacturing procedures, and/or routes of contamination. See IOM 412.7 for using the FDA 484 - Receipt for Samples as a memo to accompany C/R to describe subs collected.

When multiple subs are taken from cases, bales, boxes, etc. in the lot, Arabic numerals and letters in combination may be used for identification. For example: if two cans are taken from each case in the lot, the cans may be marked as subs 1a, 1b, 2a, 2b, etc. to identify the subs as coming from case #1, case #2, etc. If the second can or container taken from each case is the 702(b) portion, it is desirable that all duplicate portions be sealed separately from the FDA portion. This fact should be so noted on the cases and C/R.

If multiple sub samples are to be collected, it may be advantageous to place identifying information such as sub number, sample number, and collection date on peel-off labels, tape, etc. in advance of sampling to save valuable time. Your initials must be in your own handwriting.

451.2 Borrowed Samples

Although most samples are purchased, some may be borrowed, non-destructively examined, and returned to the owner. These samples must be handled carefully to avoid defacing or damaging the product.

Identify borrowed samples so the identification can be removed with no damage to the product, i.e. a sticker label that can be peeled off.

451.3 Identification Techniques

Mark a representative number of sub samples with the sample number, collection date and your written initials. Similarly identify any outer packaging, labels or circulars. If more than one person is involved in collecting the sample, the person preparing and signing the C/R initials the subs. Reinsert circulars removed from packages. See IOM 421.2 for procedures on identifying lots from which sampled.

Transparent tape such as Scotch Magic Transparent tape accepts ball point ink and may be used on glossy items such as glass, plastic, tin, etc. Glass, such as bottles, vials and ampoules, may be identified by using a very fine pointed felt or nylon marking pen and covering the identification with transparent tape for protection.

Do not use tape on very small containers such as ampoules, which must be snapped or broken to remove the contents for analysis. Tape wrapped around the container may interfere with assay.

Do not use permanent type markers when identifying subs in absorbent containers if the ink may penetrate into the product thus contaminating the sample.

Diamond or carbide tipped stylus pencils may be used to mark tin, glass, etc. Do not use diamond or carbide tipped stylus to mark products in glass under pressure (i.e., carbonated beverages).

451.4 Photographs

Unless they are part of a DOC Sample, photographs are exhibits to an EIR, report of investigation, or complaint. They are not samples. Photos taken during inspections and investigations are not described on a C/R, but are submitted as exhibits with the EIR. Photographs related to DOC Samples, i.e., labeling, records, product, etc. are identified with the sample number, collection date, and handwritten initials on the border or backside. See IOM 523.2. Attach the photos to the printed FACTS Collection Record. See IOM 439.9.

In describing photographs, do not mark the face of the print. Narrative descriptions may be placed on the mounting paper next to the print or, if explanatory graphics are required, use a plastic overlay. See IOM 523.2 for negative identification and submission procedures.

451.5 Records - Accompanying Literature and Exhibits

Identify all copies of sample records, accompanying literature, and exhibits with the sample number, collection date and your handwritten initials as described in IOM 451.1.

452   SAMPLE HANDLING

All samples must be handled, packaged, and shipped to prevent compromising the identity or integrity of the sample. Samples must be packed with shock absorbing materials to protect against breakage of containers or damage to Official Seals. Frozen samples must remain frozen; perishable products may be frozen, if freezing doesn't interfere with the planned analysis, products requiring refrigeration (e.g., fresh crabmeat for bacteriological analysis) should be shipped in ice. Use your experience and knowledge (and that of your supervisor, if necessary) to determine the most appropriate packing and shipping method.

452.1 Fumigation

See IOM 143.1 for safety precautions.

a.   General - As soon as possible, freeze any sample containing, or suspected to contain live insects, as long as freezing will not change or damage the product or break the container. If freezing is inappropriate to maintaining the integrity of the sample, fumigation may be carried out using air tight containers (such as a mason-type jar with inner ring, or a polypropylene container with air tight lid), with sufficient fumigant to kill the insect infestation. Contact your servicing laboratory for alternative fumigants.

Moth crystals, containing paradichlorobenzene (PDB), is an alternative fumigant. Do not use mothballs or moth flakes containing naphtha or naphthalene. Do not use moth crystals in or near plastics, particularly Styrofoam/ polystyrenes as crazing or melting may occur. Other alternative fumigants include: liquid household ammonia or ethyl acetate, either of which can be used to dampen a cotton ball and placed in an appropriate container; or cut small portions of commercial pesticide strips.

Follow safety precautions when fumigating samples. **Contact your local servicing laboratory or MSDS for the appropriate protective gear and handling of fumigants.**

Guidance is as follows:

1.   Carry all alcohols, fumigants, and other hazardous liquids in approved safety containers.

2.   When fumigants or preservatives are used, limit your exposure to these chemicals. Minimize transfer and exposure time. Avoid getting chemicals on hands or clothing. DO NOT MIX CHEMICALS.

3.   Insure DOT guidelines are followed when mailing or shipping samples containing fumigant or preservative. Exceptions for small quantities are listed in 49 CFR 173.4. If the samples are sent via Federal Express, the International Air Transport Association (IATA) dangerous goods regulations must be met. (Call 1-800-238-5355, extension 922-1666 for specific instructions for shipment.)

4.   The sample identification data on your packaging, the FDA-525 and C/R, must always identify the fumigant and method of fumigation, and/or preservative used.

5.   Material Safety Data Sheets (MSDS) for each chemical fumigant or preservative used must be available at each duty site and enclosed with the shipped sample. Read and follow all instructions and precautions listed on the MSDS.

b.   Procedures for fumigation - Place a small amount of fumigant, in an airtight container. Separate the fumigant from the sample with a piece of paper, paper napkin, or unscented facial tissue. Put specimen or product into container and seal tightly. Do not re-open container unless absolutely necessary. If possible, use a glass container with

a lined screw lid. A mason-type jar with inner ring is also acceptable.

c.   `Exceptions to Fumigation - When submitting samples or exhibits to show live infestation, do not fumigate. Consult with your supervisor or your servicing laboratory PRIOR to sending or bringing a live infestation into the laboratory to permit preparation for proper handling and storage. Do not fumigate sample when submitting samples for pesticide residue analysis.

d.   Preservation Liquids - Insects may be killed and preserved in 70% ethyl alcohol or a 1:1 mixture of 70% ethyl alcohol and glycerine (may be labeled glycerol). These chemicals can be obtained from your servicing laboratory. Do not collect rodents or animal tissues unless specifically instructed. Insure all vials or bottles of preservation liquids are tightly sealed to avoid leakage. Identification labels may be placed in containers, but must be written in India ink or 2H pencil only. Keep all preservation liquids away from excessive heat or open flame.

Identify preservative used on FDA 525, C/R, and on sample container. Enclose a copy of the MSDS with the shipped sample. Follow DOT and IATA guidelines when shipping or mailing samples with preservatives as stated under fumigants.

452.2 Labeling

Samples collected for label review only should be officially sealed in clear plastic bags. This will permit cursory review and, if necessary, photocopying of the container label and reduce the need to break the seal each time the label is examined.

452.3 Samples for Pathological Examination

Tissue samples are not routinely collected for microscopic or pathological examination. Authorization must be obtained from the appropriate Center before collecting samples of this material.

When assigned to collect tissue samples, unless directed otherwise by the program, the assignment, or your supervisor, cut the tissue into 1/4 inch pieces and preserve in 10% buffered formalin, or in other suitable preservatives as directed. Do not freeze the sample since frozen tissue is not suitable for pathological studies.

452.4 Small Sample Items

Samples in small vials, bottles, boxes and similar type containers may be placed inside the FDA 525 envelope after identification. When the envelope is used as the sample package, place the official seal across the glued flap and the blank face of the form.

If the sample container (vial, bottle, etc.) is officially sealed, it may be placed in the same FDA 525 together with copies of the assignment.

452.5 Frozen Samples

Containers - Pre-chill sterile containers before collecting frozen samples. Transfer liquids in glass to expandable containers before freezing. If the liquid must be frozen in glass, leave sufficient headspace to allow expansion. If freezer facilities are not available or if the sample is to be shipped, pack with dry ice in insulated cartons.

Dry ice and insulated cartons may be obtained from ice cream or dry ice dealers, and economical polystyrene (Styrofoam) containers are available at most variety stores. However, while Styrofoam containers have excellent insulating qualities, they will not withstand shipping abuse unless protected by sturdy outer cartons.

Note: If your district desires the return of Styrofoam freezer chests or ice packs used in shipping samples, note this fact on the C/R and FDA 525.

Dry Ice - Caution: Dry ice is potentially dangerous and requires caution in handling and shipping. Do not handle with unprotected hands; transport in your car without adequate ventilation; or place inside tightly closed metal, glass, plastic, or similar type containers that do not breathe. If it is necessary to use this type container, adequately vent to prevent pressure build up.

Note: If a sample is to be analyzed for ammonia contamination, it must not be shipped frozen in dry ice. Use other methods of freezing, if frozen shipment is necessary.

Shipping Frozen Samples - If using a U.S. Government Bill of Lading, it is important to give a full and accurate description of the sample for rate purposes. If more than one commodity is in the shipment, describe and enter each separately.

In all packages where dry ice is used, distribute the dry ice equally on all sides of the sample package using pieces as large as possible. Be sure the container is insulated on all six sides and tape all edges securely to assist in insulating the carton. Do not place dry ice inside officially sealed packages.

Freezing by dry ice is not effective for more than forty-eight hours. For overnight shipments, use at least one pound of dry ice per pound of sample. Increase the amount for longer hauls or unusually warm weather. (Note: When samples are in plastic type containers, the dry ice must be wrapped in paper to prevent direct contact with the plastic. The extreme cold generated by the dry ice may cause plastic to become brittle and rupture.)

Shipments made via Federal Express Corporation (FEC), Priority I, Purolator, Airborne or by other fast air express carriers, will be delivered to consignees early the next business day. Tests have shown the following amounts of dry ice will be adequate when this method is used:

For samples already in frozen state: five to ten pounds of dry ice depending on sample size is normally sufficient. For samples requiring only to be refrigerated: A minimum of ten pounds of dry ice is sufficient.

Note: The dry ice may freeze the edges of the product, so if it is imperative no part of the sample becomes frozen, use coolants other than dry ice. Mark the FDA 525 that dry ice was used.

See IOM 454.8f when shipping sample packages containing hazardous or toxic items, including dry ice, by air.

Control - To prove the shipment did not thaw in transit, place a jar or leak proof plastic bag of chipped ice in the shipment adjacent to the sample package, but not within the officially sealed package.

452.6 Refrigerated (Not Frozen) Samples

Maintain refrigerated (not frozen) samples in a refrigerator at 4.4°C (40°F) or below. Use either wet ice or some type of "Ice Pak", "Liquid Ice", "Sno-Gel", "Kool-It", or similar products to maintain the required temperature range.

Place Ice Packs, etc., in sealed plastic bags to protect samples from possible contamination should the container break, the ice melt, or the refrigerant penetrate the sample. Use Styrofoam insulated shipping cartons for shipping samples to the laboratory.

Control – If it is necessary to show the sample temperature did not go above the desired or specified temperature, you can use one of several methods, such as including a pre-chilled, shaken down, maximum reading thermometer or commercially available indicators. Take care to place the thermometer outside of the sealed sample package and attempt to place in an area anticipated to be likely to reach the highest temperature. Describe the method used on your C/R.

453 OFFICIAL SEALS

Domestic samples, regardless of type, shall be sealed with form FDA 415a, Official Seal, or, in some situations with the FDA "metal Sea". See IOM 453.6 for use of metal seals. See also IOM 405.2.

Note: With the approval of your supervisor and laboratory, it is not necessary to affix an official seal to a sample that will be in the sample collector's continuous personal custody until it is submitted personally to an analyst. This procedure should be reserved for emergencies and high priority situations. The sample should be submitted the same day it is collected with the subs properly identified. The C/R must state you personally delivered the sample to "Analyst _____"or other appropriate staff member.

Make every effort to prepare and submit your samples on the date collected so the C/R, sub identification, and the final official seal bear the same date, and thus enhance sample integrity. However, if you cannot finish the sample preparation on the same day collected, you must explain in the C/R Collection Remarks field what steps you took to protect the integrity of the sample, e.g., officially sealed and locked in supply cabinet, locked in safe, etc.

Never place more than one sample in the same officially sealed package.

453.1 Preparation

Inscribe FDA 415a, official seal, with the district office name, sample number, the date applied, your signature, printed name and title. See IOM Exhibit 450-A. The seal must bear only one signature. If more than one person is involved in collecting the sample, the person preparing and signing the collection record must sign the seal.

453.2 Application

Seal the sample package so that it cannot be opened at any point without evidence of tampering. If the surface of the sample container is of such construction or condition that the FDA-415a, official seal, will not adhere (e.g., waxed carton, frosted over, sweating, etc.), wrap or place sample in a container to which the official seal will hold. See IOM 453.6.

When using the self-adhering seals, the surface on which the seal is to be placed must be clean and dry. The seal must be rubbed when affixed to generate heat and help it bond.

453.3 Sealing Method

There are many acceptable methods of officially sealing samples. Because of the wide variety of shapes and sizes of samples, and the ingenuity you may have to apply to package and packaging situations, explicit methodology will not be detailed here. Your supervisor, your on-the-job training, and your developing experience will familiarize you with the most effective methods.

453.4 Protecting the Official Seal

Protect the sealed surface by wrapping the package securely with heavy wrapping paper for mailing or shipment.

If your officially sealed package is not further wrapped for shipping and the tape(s) and official seal are thus exposed, you must protect the Official Seal from damage during shipment by:

a.   Covering the official seal with a sheet of heavy wrapping paper or heavy clear plastic (e.g. from a document protector) of sufficient size to cover the surface of the official seal.

b.   Tape the protective paper or heavy clear plastic securely around the edges so it cannot come loose and expose the official seal. Do not paste or glue the paper or plastic to the face of the official seal since this will obliterate the official seal when removed.

c.   When you protect the official seal by heavy paper, write "FDA Seal Underneath", or similar wording across the protective paper. This alerts the receiving custodian the official seal is underneath, and to take care when removing the protective paper. If you cover and protect the seal with heavy clear plastic, the sample custodian will be able to copy the necessary information off the seal without removing the protective cover.

453.5 Broken Official Seals and "Temporary Seals"

Reseal the sample whenever you break the official seal. Each seal used on the sample will be submitted with the records associated with the collection record, properly initialed and dated, to provide a continuous history.

There is only one class of seal: an "official seal". Anytime a sample is sealed with the FDA 415a, or with the FDA Metal Seal, the item is "officially sealed". An officially sealed sample must sometimes be reopened to prepare it for submission to the laboratory, or for some other legitimate reason. In that situation, the original seal must show the date

it was broken. When the sample is ready to be resealed the new seal must show the date it is applied. This procedure must be followed each time the official seal on a sample is broken. Each seal will show the history of the date it was applied and broken. See instructions in Exhibit 450-A. Indicate in the collection remarks field of the FACTS C/R the fact that the seal was broken and reapplied and attach the broken seal to the printed FACTS C/R. This provides an unbroken, documented chain of custody.

453.6 Metal Seals

Where it is impossible to use the paper official seal, the numbered self-locking "U.S. Food and Drug" metal seal may be used. This seal is effective for use on wooden crates, drums, baskets, etc., where the FDA 415a cannot be used. Record the number of the metal seal used on the CR. See IOM 424 for instructions on the use of the metal seal to reseal railroad cars or conveyances. When a supply of these seals is needed by your district, contact the Division of Field Investigations (DFI) (HFC-130) at (301) 827-5653.

453.7 Sealing Non-Sample Items

Although the primary purpose of the official seal is for sealing samples, there are times when the official seal may be used to officially seal items other than samples. The FDA metal seal is often used to seal rail cars or vehicles as indicated in IOM 424.

When directed by your supervisor, you may use an official seal to seal questionable or suspicious bioresearch records encountered during an inspection or investigation to prevent tampering or to preserve their integrity. As explained in the applicable compliance program, the procedure must have the approval of the bioresearch monitoring staff (HFC-230) prior to implementation.

454   SAMPLE SHIPMENT

When you cannot personally deliver a sample to the examining laboratory, ship it by the most economical means commensurate with the need for rapid handling. See IOM 454.2 & 454.6 for special information on shipments to FDA Headquarters' laboratories.

FDA collects a wide variety of samples, many of which are unstable, toxic or hazardous material, e.g., etiological agents, radiation products, chemical, hard swells, etc. Use safety precautions in handling and shipping commensurate with the hazard. See IOM 454.8.

454.1 Sample Package Identification

a.   Form FDA 525 - Place the FDA 525, sample package identification, near the official seal. For small containers or surfaces that will not accommodate the FDA 525, you can tie it to the sample package by using twine through the eyelet. Do not affix the FDA 525 on the outside of the shipping carton or under the official seal. Enclose a copy of the assignment document in the FDA 525 envelope and provide the following information on the FDA 525:

1.   District or Headquarters' laboratory to which the sample is directed, City, State, and unit symbol (e.g., SRL, HFD-400, HFS-300, etc.).

2.   Date.

3.   Your district and symbol.

4.   Sample Number.

5.   Name and address of the firm most likely responsible for any suspected violation.

6.   Product Identification.

7.   Address of dealer firm.

8.   Enter the reason for collection. (Copy from C/R.) Provide reference to any sampling assignment.

9.   Provide information as to the analysis to be made.

10.   Enter any pertinent remarks. Note if your district desires the return of any freezer chests, ice packs, or maximum/minimum thermometers used.

11.   Provide any special storage instructions. Mark appropriate block and enter suggested refrigeration temperature if necessary. Elaborate in Remarks if necessary.

12.   Print your name.

See IOM 452.4 and the reverse side of the FDA 525 when using the FDA 525 as a sample package. See IOM 454.3f for information to include with the FDA 525 for medical device samples.

b.   Outer Wrapper - Always place the words, "SAMPLE NO. _____" followed by the actual FACTS or OASIS sample number(s) on the outside of the package near the address label. This alerts the receiving mail room that the package contains a sample and must go to the sample custodian.

454.2 Routing of Samples

In general, samples will be submitted to your district's designated servicing laboratory, except as directed by the Compliance Program, assignment or your supervisor. The following provides general guidance for sample submission.

a.   Vitamin & Nutritional Labeling - Submit to FDA, Science Branch (HFR-SE680), 60 Eighth St. N.E., Atlanta, GA 30309.

b.   Radiopharmaceuticals for Sterility - Submit samples to WEAC.

c.   Tissue Residues - Submit to the Denver District Tissue Residue Lab.

A complete, current listing of designated servicing laboratories can be found in the current ORA Field Workplan as Appendix III. This appendix is comprised of a table designating the servicing laboratories for each collecting district and for each compliance program or subpart.

454.3 Samples to Administration Laboratories

When shipping samples to headquarters or other special laboratories use the following procedures:

a.   **Samples for National Center for Drug Analysis, Center for Microbiological Investigations, or Headquarters' Division analysis alone.**

1.   Do not forward original C/R and records.

2.   Enclose a copy of the assignment memorandum in the FDA 525 envelope.

3.   Affix the FDA 525 to the officially sealed sample package.

4.   Submit the Original C/R and records to the home district, or forward to the home district if other than the collecting district.

b.   **Split Samples - Where the sample examination is split between a Headquarter's Division, the National Center for Drug Analysis, the Center for Microbiological Investigations and a district lab:**

1.   Follow the above procedures on the portion sent to a Headquarter's laboratory or NCDA, or CMI.

2.   Submit Original C/R and records to the servicing laboratory, whether or not the home district.

c.   **Center for Food Safety and Applied Nutrition (CFSAN).**

Note: Unless specifically directed by a Compliance Program or an assignment, do not submit samples to the CFSAN without approval of the Office of Compliance, Division of Field Programs, Compliance Programs Branch, HFS-636 at (301) 436-2061. Send samples to CFSAN at the following address:

Food and Drug Administration
5100 Paint Branch Parkway
College Park, Maryland 20740

CFSAN Laboratories are as follows:

1.   Office of Cosmetics and Colors

   a.   Division of Science and Applied Technology (HFS-125)
   3650 Concorde Parkway, Suite 200
   Chantilly, VA 20151

   Note: Temporary location until College Park, MD laboratories are completed. This laboratory conducts chemical and/or toxicological analyses of all cosmetic complaint samples needed for medical evaluation.

   b.   Division of Programs and Enforcement Policy (HFS-105) - Conducts color analysis of foods/drugs/cosmetics.

2.   Office of Nutritional Products, Labeling, and Dietary Supplements

   Division of Research and Applied Technology (HFS-840) - Conducts examinations related to food standards and food technology. Analyzes conventional foods for requirements of nutritional properties where special skills and expertise are not available in the field.

3.   Office of Applied Research and Safety Assessment

   Division of Molecular Biology (HFS-025) - Analyses foods when the chemical methodology is under development or unusual equipment or skills are required, such as radioactivity analysis/migration of food additives from blood packaging materials. Microbiologically examines samples for potential food pathogens by rapid molecular biological testing using DNA probes, PCR and DNA fingerprint analysis.

4.   Office of Plant and Dairy Foods and Beverages

   a.   Division of Natural Products, Microanalytical Branch (HFS-315) - Examines foods for bacterial contamination if field laboratory facilities are not available.

b.   Division of Natural Products (HFS-345) - Analyzes foods for non-nutritive components, including toxins.

c.   Division of Pesticides and Industrial Chemicals - (HFS-335) - Conducts examinations related to industrial chemicals contamination, including pesticides, toxic elements and radionuclides.

d.   Division of Microbiological Studies (HFS-515) - Conducts examinations related to Food Standards and food technology investigations, including the intended effect of food additives and the integrity of packaging.

5.   Office of Seafood

Division of Science and Applied Technology (HFS-425) - Conducts decomposition, toxicity and parasite analysis of seafood where special skills or equipment required for analysis are not available in the field.

6.   Office of Food Additive Safety

Division of Chemistry Research and Environmental Review (HFS-245) – Analyses foods and food packaging materials for direct and indirect food additives where special skills and expertise are not available in the field.

d.   **Center for Drug Evaluation and Research**

1.   Division of Pharmaceutical Analysis (DPA)

a.   Testing and Research, Division of Pharmaceutical Analysis (DPA) (HFD-920)
Food & Drug Administration
Sample Room 3329
8301 Muirkirk Road
Laurel, MD 20708

Conducts drug bioassay potency testing. Send samples only on request, or with prior approval. HFD-920 analyzes all heparin and insulin samples and all drugs and devices requiring toxicological analysis and evaluations of related injuries. Note: When shipping refrigerated, frozen, or perishable items, requiring prompt attention, notify the sample room, at (301) 594-5870 (or 5866) per IOM 454.5.

b.   Antimicrobial Drugs Branch (HFD-473)
Division of Pharmaceutical Analysis (DPA)
Food & Drug Administration
Sample Room 3329
8301 Muirkirk Road
Laurel, MD 20708

Conducts testing of all antibiotic products for composition, toxicity, etc. Note: When shipping refrigerated, frozen, or perishable items, requiring prompt attention, notify the FDA Washington, DC, sample room, at (202) 205-4034 per IOM 454.5.

c.   Center for Drug Analysis (HFH-300)
Division of Pharmaceutical Analysis (DPA)
US Courthouse & Customhouse Bldg.
1114 Market Street, Room 1002
St. Louis, Missouri 63101

Examines surveillance drug samples collected and shipped under current program directives.

e.   **Center for Biologics Evaluation and Research**
Sample Custodian (ATTN: HFM-235)
Room 175
5516 Nicholson Lane
Kensington, MD 20895

Examines and reviews biological products not covered by a Compliance Program. Prior to shipping a sample, the district should notify either the Sample Custodian, (301) 594-6517, or the Surveillance and Policy Branch, (301) 594-1070, who in turn will notify the Sample Custodian.

f.   **Center for Devices and Radiological Health (CDRH)**

WEAC (see 1. below) is the primary laboratory for devices and radiation-emitting products. The CDRH OST laboratory accepts medical devices and radiation-emitting products for testing, but only after assignment or approval from CDRH, Office of Compliance. Note: Include in the FDA 525 envelope a copy of the manufacturers finished device specifications test methods and acceptance/rejection criteria.

1.   Send samples for sterility analysis to:
Winchester Engineer and Analytical Center (WEAC)
109 Holton Street (HFR-NE400)
Winchester, MA 01890-1197
Director, Martin J. Finkelson
Telephone: (781) 729-5700 ext. 749 or 721
FAX: (781) 729-3593

2.   Send bioburden analysis samples to WEAC. Send bioindicator analysis samples to WEAC.

3.   Send device and GWQAP device samples for physical and engineering analysis to WEAC.

4.   Send in-vitro diagnostic device samples to WEAC.

5.   Send devices used for antibiotic susceptibility testing (including discs) requiring performance testing to WEAC.

6.   Send Southwest and Pacific Region condom and glove samples to the Pacific Regional Laboratory (PRS)

7.   Send all other condom and glove samples to WEAC.

8.   Send radiological health samples to :
CDRH/OST Sample Custodian HFZ-105
12725 Twinbrook Parkway, Room 210
Rockville, MD 20852
Telephone: (301) 827-4723
FAX: (301) 827-4731

Note: Contact Electronic Products Branch, HFZ-342, (301) 594-4654 prior to collection and shipment of any radiological product sample.

g.   **Center for Veterinary Medicine**
Division of Compliance (HFV-230)
7500 Standish Place (MPN II)
Rockville, MD 20855
(301) 827-1168

Samples of veterinary products, not specifically covered by one or more of the CVM Compliance Programs, can be sent to the above address for review, evaluation, and comment. This includes documentary samples, and labels/labeling and advertising materials. There are no laboratory facilities at MPN II. If you have questions about sampling or sample destinations, contact HFV-230 and/or the applicable program contact.

h.   **Central Region, Philadelphia**
Center for Microbiological Investigations
(HFR-MW400)
240 Hennepin Ave.
Minneapolis, MN 55401

Conducts sterility testing of drugs (including injectable vitamins), surgical gut, etc., when district tests indicate contamination.

454.4 Sample Shipment to Outside Agencies

Do not ship any samples outside FDA unless your assignment, applicable program, or your supervisor specifically instructs you to do so.

454.5 Notifying Receiving Laboratories

When frozen, perishable, or high priority items are shipped, notify the receiving district or lab by telephone, or e-mail, that you have shipped the sample. Provide the following information:

a. Sample Number
b. Name of Product
c. Number of Parcels in Shipment
d. Carrier's Name
e. Carrier's Waybill Number
f. Carrier's Train, Truck, Bus, or Flight Number
g. Estimated Time and Date of Arrival
h. Relevant Remarks, i.e., "Sufficient Dry Ice to maintain frozen until 8:00 AM, (date)"
i. Place the name and telephone number of the person that is to receive the sample on the outer shipping carton near the address with instructions to the carrier to contact the above named individual upon arrival of the package.

Note: When shipping refrigerated, frozen, or perishable items requiring prompt attention to the Division of Drug Biology, Antimicrobial Drugs Branch (HFD-473), notify the FDA Sample Room, at (202) 205-5284.

454.6 Method of Shipment

Note: If samples are shipped to headquarters laboratories by bus lines, delivery of the sample must be specified on the bus bill.

Use the most economical method of shipment consistent with the need for special handling. Shipping costs may be reduced by packing samples addressed to the same consignee into a larger carton or by "piggy-backing" (taping a number of larger boxes together and shipping them as one package). Make sure the total package is within the carrier's weight and size limits.

454.7 Parcel Post

When samples are shipped by parcel post, do not exceed the parcel post limits as to size and weight.

a. Package Limits
(1) From a first class post office to a first class post office: Weight - 40 lbs.
Size - 84 in. length and girth combined.
(2) Mailed at or addressed to a second or lower class post office: Weight - 70 lbs.
Size - 100 in. length and girth combined.
b. Address Labels - The use of franked labels and envelopes is no longer allowed. Affix proper postage to envelope or address label after using district or resident post postal scale and meter. If no postal meter is available, use the resident post postage scale to weigh the envelope

or package and add the proper postage using postage stamps. If no stamps are available purchase them from the post office and claim reimbursement on your voucher. Obtain a receipt for the stamps or postage, if required by your District Office.

If the package is addressed to an FDA unit, show the FDA routing symbol following the name of the FDA unit.

Note: Wrap parcels shipped "Registered Mail" in kraft paper because the postal service must affix an ink stamp seal to each closure point. Do not wrap the outer package with tape that has a shiny or glossy surface (e.g., masking tape, filament tape, scotch type tape, etc.).

454.8 Common Carrier

Certain Department of Transportation (DOT) regulations exist pertaining to carrier inspection of packages. Instruct the carrier to contact the shipper (FDA) prior to any package inspection requires breaking the official seal. Carriers have broken FDA official seals for package inspection during transit, thereby compromising the sample integrity.

If an FDA 3082 - Shippers Declaration for Dangerous Goods is executed for shipments of restricted items, place a statement in the special handling section that breaking an FDA official seal is not authorized, and to contact the shipper (FDA) if there are any questions regarding the shipment. See IOM Exhibit 450-C.

a. Shipment - You must decide how your samples are shipped. The judgment must be based on your knowledge of the practices and performance of the transportation based on your knowledge of the practices and performance of the transportation firms in your area. As a general rule, Parcel Post, United Parcel Service, or current GSA contract carrier should be used for small packages and other express or comparable carriers for packages too large for PP, UPS, or current GSA contract carrier. Before using motor express lines and passenger bus lines determine that their schedules and delivery practices are satisfactory and reliable. Bus lines must not be used for shipments to Washington, DC offices unless delivery at the destination address is specified.

Air express or air freight shall be used only for samples requiring extremely rapid handling or where more economical means of shipment are not available or feasible. Air freight service is offered by the individual air lines and, although usually not as convenient as express, is more economical and should be used especially for shipments of 50 lbs. or more.

b. Designated Carriers - You may ship by any carrier you wish with the objective of obtaining the best possible service at the most economical rate.

Always indicate on the carrier's shipping document that the shipment is a U.S. Government shipment.

c. Government Bill of Lading - Prepare Form SF-1103, Government Bill of Lading (GBL), for shipments made by common carrier except as described below. Distribute GBL as follows:
Give the Carrier:
Original (White) Form SF-1103
Shipping Order (Pink) Form SF-1104

Freight Waybill Original (White) Form SF-1105
Freight Waybill Carriers Copy (White) Form SF-1106

Submit the remaining 4 copies "Memoranda Copy" (Yellow), Form SF-1103a, and the "Memorandum Copy" (Blue), Form SF-1103b, to your district.

If available, obtain the transportation costs or the rate from the carrier and enter it in pencil on the copies submitted to the district.

d. Commercial Bill of Lading - The use of commercial forms (in lieu of GBL's) and procedures for small shipments is subject to the limitations and instructions set forth in the following paragraphs. The use of commercial forms shall be limited to those carriers that have a letter of agreement with FDA or GSA.

The use of commercial forms is to be applied only to the following types of shipments:

1. Shipments for which the transportation charges ordinarily do not exceed $100.00 per shipment and the occasional exception does not exceed that monetary limitation by an unreasonable amount.

2. Single-parcel shipments via express, courier, small package, or similar carriers, without regard to shipping cost, if the parcel shipped weighs 70 lbs. or less and does not exceed 108 inches in length and girth combined.

3. Multi-parcel shipments via express, courier, small package or similar carriers for which transportation charges do not exceed $250.00 per shipment.

e. Address Labels - Affix a completed address label, form HHS-409, U.S. Government shipment to each shipping carton. Use the street address of the consignee, do not use the post office box numbers, since carriers usually will not deliver to PO box numbers. If the package is going to an FDA unit, include the FDA routing symbol in the consignee address. If shipment is made under the GSA-Carrier Agreement, strike out the information on GBLS in the lower left corner of the form since a GBL is not used.

f. Shipment of Hazardous or Toxic Items - The Department of Transportation (DOT) regulations require certain packaging, forms, certifications, declarations, and/or statements covering shipment of hazardous or toxic items. Except for dry ice, most of the samples of hazardous or toxic materials we ship are classified as "ORM-D, Consumer commodity". Both dry ice classified as "9", and ORM-D classifications require a certification/declaration for shipment by air but not for shipment by surface transportation.

Shipments containing dry ice - use the dedicated Dry Ice Sticker (available from the carrier - for an example see IOM Exhibit 450-D). Complete the bottom portion of the sticker and note the amount of dry ice in kilograms. In addition to the label, the package itself must be clearly marked in 1" block letters: "DRY ICE; 9; UN1845".

g. Contact the carrier involved to execute the necessary forms, certification/declarations, packaging, marking, etc. required for the particular shipment or hazardous or toxic items.

Always pack liquid products in sufficient cushioning and absorbent material to absorb any breakage which might occur. Check with the Post Office or other carriers regarding shipment of liquids.

h. Hard swells may explode. Wrap them heavily in paper and cushioning material for shipment and submit promptly.

i. Observe special precautions when shipping products in pressurized containers to avoid exposure to excessive heat. Air shippers who ship in non-pressurized planes may also have special requirements for this type container. Check Post Office and carrier for regulations, precautions, or restrictions before shipping products in this type container.

j. Special precautions for both packaging and shipping radioactive substances must be observed. If necessary, consult your supervisor, the regional radiological health representative, WEAC or the applicable program.

Note: The compliance program for radioactive drugs directs the manufacturer to ship samples via their normal mode of transportation to WEAC. The Nuclear Regulatory Commission (NRC) requires that firms manufacturing radioactive drugs ship only to NRC licensed consignees. WEAC's NRC license number is 20-08361-01 Exp. Date 2-28-2006. This license number should be used for any shipments of radioactive products to WEAC.

454.9 Certified and First Class Mail

Where speed is essential and a record of receipt of the sample is desired, small samples may be sent by express mail or certified air mail, or, in situations where speed is a factor but the receipt is not necessary, by first class air mail. Where other methods of shipment do not suffice, larger samples may be shipped certified or first class as a last resort. Normally do not use certified or first class for routine samples.

455 PAYMENT OF SHIPPING CHARGES

a. Cash Payment - Agencies have authority to use imprest funds (pay cash) for Cash On Delivery (COD) payment of transportation charges. See IOM 454.8a and IOM 454.8d.

1. Shipments between districts may be shipped COD when the conditions cited above are met.

2. Shipments to headquarters may be shipped COD but you must enter on the firm's commercial bill of lading that the FDA billing unit is as follows:
Food and Drug Administration
Accounting Branch (HFA-120)
5600 Fishers Lane
Rockville, MD 20857

b. Other Means of Payment - If you do not pay cash or the shipping cost exceeds those circumstances in IOM 454.8d, you must use one of the following payment methods:

1. Postal meter or postage stamps - You can use these for shipments under 70 lbs/ when it is cost effective.

2. Billed shipments - Those shipments meeting the criteria in IOM 454.8a and IOM 454.8d and are billed by an invoice from the carrier.

3. Government Bill of Lading (GBL) - If the other methods discussed above are not appropriate, a GBL must be issued at the time of the shipment.

In an emergency, if you are without a GBL or the carrier refuses to accept a GBL at the time of shipment, you can convert the carrier's invoice to a GBL after the completion of the shipment. Avoid this procedure if at all possible.

DEPARTMENT OF HEALTH AND HUMAN SERVICES PUBLIC HEALTH SERVICE FOOD AND DRUG ADMINISTRATION		DISTRICT ADDRESS AND PHONE NO. 300 S. Riverside Plaza, Suite 550 South Chicago, Il 60606	

TO:	NAME AND TITLE OF INDIVIDUAL John B. Carr, Driver	DATE 11/6/98
	NAME AND ADDRESS OF CARRIER Transcontinental Trucking, 10 Front St. Dallas TX, 75204	SAMPLE NUMBER 2358

CONSIGNEE AND ADDRESS (Street, City, State and ZIP Code) XYZ Wholesale 111 S. Water Market Chicago, IL 60601	CONSIGNOR AND ADDRESS (Street, City, State, and ZIP Code) Best Yet Packing Co. 3 first St. Young Town, TX 75002

SAMPLES (S) REMOVED FOR EXAMINATION		WAYBILL OR FREIGHT BILL NUMBER
AMOUNT OF SAMPLE	PRODUCT	
2 Cases (48 ct)	Lettuce - Best Yet Brand	A-23764

SAMPLE COLLECTOR'S NAME Sylvia H. Rogers	TITLE Investigator	SIGNATURE *Sylvia H. Rogers*

FORM FDA 472 (6/82)   PREVIOUS EDITION MAY BE USED UNTIL
SUPPLY IS EXHUASTED.   CARRIER'S RECEIPT FOR SAMPLE

DEPARTMENT OF HEALTH AND HUMAN SERVICES PUBLIC HEALTH SERVICE FOOD AND DRUG ADMINISTRATION	**1. DISTRICT ADDRESS & PHONE NUMBER** 850 Third Avenue Brooklyn, NY 11232 718-340-7000

2. NAME AND TITLE OF INDIVIDUAL	3. DATE	4. SAMPLE NUMBER
Richard R. Frost, General Manager	12-4-98	2558

5. FIRM NAME	6. FIRM'S DEA NUMBER
Quality Wholesale Drug Co.	AB3632918

7. NUMBER AND STREET	8. CITY AND STATE (Include Zip Code)
3146 Front St.	Brooklyn, NY 11232

9. SAMPLES COLLECTED (*Describe fully. List lot, serial, model numbers and other positive identification.*)

The following samples were collected by the Food and Drug Administration and receipt is hereby acknowledged pursuant to Section 704(c) of the Federal Food, Drug, and Cosmetic Act [21 U.S.C. 374(c)] and/or Section 532(b) of the Federal Food, Drug, and Cosmetic Act [21 USC 360ii(b)] and/or 21 Code of Federal Regulations (CFR) 1307.02 . Excerpts of these are Quoted on the reverse of this form.
(**NOTE**: *If you bill FDA for the cost of the Sample(s) listed below, please attach a copy of this form to your bill.*)

One box of 25 - 1 cc ampules, Diloudid HCl (hydromorphone) 2mg/cc, lot # 0103213 manufactured by Knoll Pharmaceutical Co., Orange NJ.

10. SAMPLES WERE	11. AMOUNT RECEIVED FOR SAMPLE	12. SIGNATURE (*Persons receiving payment for sample or person providing sample to FDA at no charge.*)
☐ PROVIDED AT NO CHARGE X☐ PURCHASED ☐ BORROWED (*To be returned*)	X☐ CASH ☐ BILLED ☐ VOUCHER ☐ CREDIT CARD $15.00	*Richard R. Frost*

14. COLLECTOR'S NAME (*Print or Type*)	15. COLLECTOR'S TITLE (*Print or Type*)	17. COLLECTOR'S SIGNATURE
Sylvia A. Rogers	Investigator	*Sylvia A. Rogers*

FORM FDA 484 (5/98)   PREVIOUS EDITION IS OBSOLETE   **RECEIPT FOR SAMPLES**   PAGE 1 OF 1 PAGES

See IOM Exhibit 510C for the Reverse of FDA 484.

EXHIBIT 420-A

INVESTIGATIONS OPERATIONS MANUAL

FLAG

ANALYST WORKSHEET	1. PRODUCT		2.. SAMPLE NUMBER

3. SEALS ☐ INTACT ☐ NONE ☐ BROKEN	4. DATE REC'D	5. RECEIVED FROM	6. DISTRICT OF LABORATORY

7. DESCRIPTION OF SAMPLE

8. NET CON-TENTS	☐ NOT APPLICABLE DECLARE/UNIT _____ ☐ NOT DETERMINED AMOUNT FOUND _____ _____ UNITS EXAMINED % OF DECLARED _____	9. LABEL-ING	_____ ORIGINAL(S) SUBMITTED _____ COPIES SUBMITTED ☐ NONE

10. SUMMARY OF ANALYSIS

(See page 2 of IOM Exhibit 420-A for instructions on preparation of this form).

11. RESERVE SAMPLE

12.a. ANALYST SIGNATURE *(Broke Seal ☐)*	13. WORK-SHEET CHECK	a. BY
b.		b. DATE
c.		14. DATE REPORTED

FORM FDA 431 (5/84)   PREVIOUS EDITION IS OBSOLETE   PAGE   OF   PAGES

ANALYST WORKSHEET – PREPARATION

Block #

1. Name of product examined.

2. Enter complete sample number.

3. Check "None" since it is a Field Examination and no seals are involved.

4. Enter date sample received. For Field Examination of the sample, this will be the date you made the examination.

5. Insert "Field Examination."

6. Enter your District name. District symbol, e.g. ATL, SAN, SJN, etc. is acceptable. Do not use District mailing codes.

7. Describe the product examined.

8. Check applicable box or enter information in blanks.

9. Check applicable box.

10. Describe the examination performed, how made and results.

11. If applicable, describe and enter amounts.

12. Sign. Do not check "Broke Seal" box since no seal is involved.

13. This is for check analysis, so leave blank.

14. Enter date the form was prepared.

DEPARTMENT OF HEALTH, EDUCATION, AND WELFARE PUBLIC HEALTH SERVICE FOOD AND DRUG ADMINISTRATION	1. DATE 4-15-99
	2. SAMPLE NUMBER 55532

3. PRODUCT Spaghetti in plastic bags: "Genoa Semolina Vermicelli***Delmonico Foods, Inc. San Francisco, Calif.***Net Weight 12 ozs."	4. TYPE OF BALANCE Gurley

5. RESPONSIBLE FIRM AND ADDRESS Delmonico Foods, Inc. 4701 Canal Street San Francisco, California	6. ADDRESS WHERE WEIGHED Medicine Bow Wholesalers 23 Railroad Ave. Cheyenne, Wyoming

7. WAREHOUSE	a. TYPE Wholesale Grocery Warehouse	b. TEMPERATURE 80 F	c. HUMIDITY est. 20%

8. NO. OF	a. CASES IN LOT 325 48/12 oz.	b. CASES SAMPLED 12	c. SUBS WEIGHED FROM EACH CASE 4 from each of 12 cases

9. GROSS WEIGHT *(Submit a minimum of 12 subs with at least one from each case examined. Submit the subs indicated by asterisks adding others where necessary to identify additional subs submitted. Determine six tares. Where tares may vary wildly, determine up to 12 where practical.)*

CASE NO.	SUB NO.	GROSS WEIGHT	CASE NO.	SUB NO.	GROSS WEIGHT	CASE NO.	SUB NO.	GROSS WEIGHT	CASE NO.	SUB NO.	GROSS WEIGHT
1	1	11.40	4	13	12.08	7	25	11.32	10	37	12.00
1	2	11.72	4	14	11.68	7	26	12.00	10	38	12.04
1	3	11.60	4	15	11.42	7	27	11.34	10	39	11.64
1	4	11.30	4	16	12.40	7	28	11.34	10	40	11.72
2	5	11.32	5	17	11.32	8	29	11.34	11	41	12.10
2	6	11.40	5	18	11.34	8	30	11.40	11	42	11.70
2	7	12.00	5	19	11.40	8	31	11.40	11	43	11.40
2	8	11.38	5	20	11.42	8	32	11.36	11	44	11.50
3	9	11.34	6	21	12.02	9	33	12.04	12	45	11.32
3	10	11.40	6	22	11.70	9	34	12.00	12	46	11.30
3	11	11.42	6	23	12.08	9	35	11.38	12	47	11.24
3	12	12.02	6	24	12.10	9	36	11.36	12	48	11.36
TOTAL		138.30			140.96			138.28			139.32
								GRAND TOTAL			556.86

10. PRELIMINARY TARE				11. WEIGHING RESULTS	
TARE NO.	WEIGHT	TARE NO.	WEIGHT	a. AVERAGE GROSS	11.60
1	0.22	4	0.23	b. PRELIMINARY AVERAGE TARE	.22
2	0.22	5	0.21	c. AVERAGE NET	11.38
3	0.21	6	0.22	d. DECLARED NET	12.00
	0.65	TOTAL	0.66	e. SHORTAGE	.62
		GRAND TOTAL	1.31	12. PRELIMINARY % SHORT	5.2%
NUMBER OF TARE WEIGHED			6	13. REMARKS *(List observations of lot or storage conditions affecting net weights.)* Lot has been in storage since 4-1-99.	
PRELIMINARY AVERAGE TARE			0.22		

14. DISTRICT DENVER	15. EMPLOYEE SIGNATURE *Sidney H. Rogers*	16. EMPLOYEE TITLE Investigator

FD FORM 485 (11/72)   PREVIOUS EDITION MAY BE USED UNTIL SUPPLY IS EXHAUSTED   FIELD WEIGHT SHEET

1. LOCATION Pine Bluff, Arkansas	2. NAME OF SAMPLE COLLECTOR Sylvia A. Rogers	3. DATE COLLECTED 10-8-99	4. SAMPLE NUMBER 55566

SECTION I – COPY OF INVOICE

5. CONSIGNOR (Name, Street, City, and State) Captain Sam Seafood, Inc. 719 Butler Ave. New Orleans, LA	6. CONSIGNEE (Name, Street, City, and State) Razor Back Super Market 1207 Little Rock Dr. Pine Bluff, AR	

7. GUARANTEE -----see reverse-----	8. INVOICE NUMBER 477	9. INVOICE DATE 9-20-99

10 QTY	11 UNIT SIZE	12 DESCRIPTION OF ARTICLE(S)	13 UNIT PRICE		14 TOTAL	
10 cs	24/ 4 1/2 oz.	Horseshoe Brand Canned Medium Shrimp	2	84	56	80
5 cs.	10/ 5 lb.	Frozen Green Hills 21-25 Shrimp	1	10	275	00
		****************************				
5cs.	24/ 8 oz	Horseshoe Brand Canned Cove Oysters	5	25	52	50
		****************************				
2 cs.	6/ 4 lb.	Frozen C&P Small Shrimp	1	50	72	00
			15. TOTAL		642	80

SECTION II - COPY OF SHIPPING RECORD

16. SHIPPER (Name, Street,, City, and State) Captain Sam Seafood, Inc. NOLA	17. CONSIGNEE (Name, Street, City, and State) Razor Back Super Market 1207 Little Rock Dr. Pine bluff, AR

18. CARRIER (Name, City, and State) Sea Breeze Trucking, Inc. NOLA

19. CAR OR EQUIP NO Van 109	20. WAYBILL DATE AND NO. N/A	21. TYPE OF RECORD (Specify) F/B	22. RECORD NO. 06641	23. RECORD DATE 9-20-99
24. SHIPPED FROM (City and State) NOLA	25. ROUTE N/A			26. DATE SHIPPED 9-20-99

27 DESCRIPTION OF ARTICLE(S)	28 NO. PKGS.	29 WEIGHT	30 RATE	31 CHANGES
Canned Food	20	300	172	5.16
Frozen Seafood	8	350	224	7.84

32. RECEIVED BY P. Monteux s/s	33. DATE REC'D 9-26-99	34. TOTAL	28	650		13.00

FORM FD-1662 (12/74)   PREVIOUS EDITION MAY BE USED   COPY OF INVOICE AND SHIPPING RECORD

EXHIBIT 430-B   INVESTIGATIONS OPERATIONS MANUAL

AFFIDAVIT *(Parcel Post/Parcel Service)*	SAMPLE NO. 2358

STATE OF Colorado	COUNTY OF Pueblo

Before me, <u>Sidney H. Rogers</u> an employee of the Department of Health and Human Services, Food and Drug Administration, designated by the Secretary, under authority of the Act of January 31, 1925, 43 Statutes at Large 803; Reorganization Plan No. IV, Secs. 12-15, effective June 30, 1940; Reorganization Plan No. 1 of 1953, Secs. 1-9, effective April 11, 1953; and P.L. 96-88, Sec. 509, 93 Statutes at Large 965 (20U.S.C.3508), effective May 4, 1980; to administer or take oaths, affirmations, and affidavits, personally appeared <u>Joseph D. Bullard</u> in the county and state aforesaid, who, being duly sworn, deposes and says: (I) (My firm) received on or about the <u>10th</u> day of <u>July</u>, 19<u>99</u>, in response to an order previously given by <u>me Two (packages, cartons, etc.)</u> consisting in whole or in part of a product designated <u>"4 ounces NET***Johnson's Eye Ease***Reservation Special"</u> via: (parcel post, United States mail) (United Parcel Service) from <u>Old Indian Herb Co. 294 N. Blackfoot St., Boise, Idaho 30854</u> and covered by attached copy of invoice number <u>C-20</u> dated <u>7-2-99</u>; after unpacking the goods the (parcel post) (parcel service) wrapper was destroyed; and on the <u>12th</u> day of <u>July</u>, 19<u>99</u>, Inspector/Investigator <u>Rogers</u> obtained from me a sample consisting of <u>10-4 oz. bottles of Johnson's Eye Ease coded "J-638" on the bottle label</u>, shipped and described as aforesaid and for which he paid me the sum of <u>$25.00</u> in (cash) (voucher) (billed).

Remarks: <u>I first learned of this product while reading the January 1999 issue of "The Retired Engineer." I use it to relieve the burning and itching in my eyes after working in the heat and dryness.</u>

AFFIANT'S SIGNATURE AND TITLE
Joseph D. Bullard

FIRM'S NAME AND ADDRESS *(Include ZIP Code)*

Subscribed and sworn to before me at <u>Crow, Colorado</u> this <u>13th</u> day of <u>July</u>, 19<u>99</u>.
(City & State)

<u>Sidney H. Rogers</u>
(Employee's Signature)

Employee of the Department of Health and Human Services designated
under Act of January 31, 1925, Reorganization Plan IV effective June
30, 1940; Reorganization Plan No. 1 of 1953, effective April 11, 1953;
and P.L. 96-88, effective May 4, 1980.

FORM FDA 463 (4/83)   PREVIOUS EDITIONS ARE OBSOLETE

AFFIDAVIT	SAMPLE NO. 2558

STATE OF Oregon	COUNTY OF Klamath

Before me, Sidney H. Rogers, an employee of the Department of Health and Human Services, Food and Drug Administration, designated by the Secretary, under authority of the Act of January 31, 1925, 43 Statutes at Large 803; Reorganization Plan No. IV, Secs. 12-15, effective June 30, 1940; Reorganization Plan No. 1 of 1953, Secs. 1-9, effective April 11, 1953; and P.L. 96-98, Sec. 509, 93 Statutes at Large 965 (20 U.S.C. 3508), effective May 4, 1980; to administer or take oaths, affirmations, and affidavits, personally appeared George F. Thompson in the county and State aforesaid, who, being duly sworn, deposes and says:

I am George F. Thompson, D.O. and as such I am knowledgeable about the purchase and use of medical products in use by me at my medical practice. I live at 2207 Timberlane Ave., Klamath Falls, Oregon. In response to an Ad in the August 1992 "Cascade Sun," I ordered from Los Gatos Associates, 920 Apricot St., San Jose, CA, four (4) Energizer Devices for use in my practice.

On 8-20-99, Mr. George Hughes, Abrico Ave., Klamath Falls, Oregon, delivered to my office the four devices all labeled in part: "Isotope Energizer***Model MARK I***Distributed By: Los Gatos Associates, San Jose, Calif." The device serial numbers are 2904, 2906, 2907 and 2908. Mr. Hughes picked up these devices in San Jose for me as he makes regular trips there in his pickup truck to buy fruit.

On 9-2-99, U.S. Food and Drug employee, Sydney H. Rogers, took photographs and copied the labeling of these four Energizer devices located in my office located at 2209 Timberline Ave., Klamath Falls, Oregon.

George F. Thompson, D.O. read this affidavit and avowed it to be true but declined to sign it.
Sidney H. Rogers

AFFIANT'S SIGNATURE AND TITLE
George F. Thompson, D.O.

FIRM'S NAME AND ADDRESS *(Include ZIP Code)*

Subscribed and sworn to before me at _____ this _____ day of _____, 19 __.
(City & State)

_____
(Employee's Signature)

Employee of the Department of Health and Human services designated under Act of January 31, 1925, Reorganization Plan IV effective June 30, 1940; Reorganization Plan No. 1 of 1953, effective April 11, 1953; and P.L. 96-88 effective May 4, 1980.

FORM FDA 463a (4/83)   PREVIOUS EDITONS ARE OBSOLETE   PAGE __1__ OF __1__ PAGES

EXHIBIT 430-D   INVESTIGATIONS OPERATIONS MANUAL

AFFIDAVIT	SAMPLE NO. 55555

STATE OF **OREGON**	COUNTY OF **KLAMATH**

Before me, <u>Sidney H. Rogers </u> an employee of the Department of Health and Human Services, Food and Drug Administration, designated by the Secretary, under authority of the Act of January 31, 1925, 43 Statutes at Large 803; Reorganization Plan No. IV, Secs. 12-15, effective June 30, 1940; Reorganization Plan No. 1 of 1953, Secs. 1-9, effective April 11, 1953; and P.L. 96-88, Sec. 509, 93 Statutes at Large 965 (20U.S.C.3508), effective May 4, 1980; to administer or take oaths, affirmations, and affidavits, personally appeared <u> George W. Hughes </u> in the county and state aforesaid, who, being duly sworn, deposes and says:

I live at 482 Abricia Ave., Klamath Falls, Oregon. On October 18, 1999, my neighbor, Dr. Samuel Thompson, asked me to pick up some medical instruments from a firm in Santa Rosa, California for him. Later that same day I drove to Santa Rosa in my 1997 Dodge Ram pick-up truck which has Oregon license plates, number FAS 682.

The next morning, October 19, 1999, I drove to Charles Brown & Associates at 920 Grape St., Santa Rosa, California and picked up 4 cartons bearing the label: "Fancy Medical Device, quantity 1." Each carton contained a medical device.

I drove back to Klamath Falls, Oregon after picking up a load of wine for my wine cellar, and arrived home on or about 11:00 PM.

The next morning, October 20, 1999, I delivered the 4 cartons to Dr. Samuel Thompson at his office, 2209 Timberline Ave., Klamath Falls, Oregon.

I did not charge Dr. Thompson for the pick-up and delivery because I make regular trips to pick up wine in Santa Rosa for my wine cellar.

AFFIANT'S SIGNATURE AND TITLE
George W. Hughes. Owner

FIRM'S NAME AND ADDRESS *(Include ZIP Code)*
Hughes Wine Cellar, 482 Abrecia, Ave., Klamath Falls OR, 97210

Subscribed and sworn to before me at <u>Klamath Falls, Oregon</u> this <u>4th</u> day of <u>November, 19 99</u>.
(City and State)

Sidney H. Rogers

_____
(Employee's Signature)

Employee of the Department of Health and Human Services designated under Act of January 31, 1925, Reorganization Plan IV effective June 30, 1940; Reorganization Plan No. 1 of 1953, effective April 11, 1953; and P.L. 96-88, effective May 4, 1980.

FORM FDA 463a (4/83)   PREVIOUS EDITIONS MAY BE USED   PAGE 1 OF 1 PAGES

AFFIDAVIT *(Dealer/Warehouseman)*	SAMPLE NO. 55563
STATE OF ARKANSAS	**COUNTY OF** JEFFERSON

Before me, ___Sidney H. Rogers___ , an employee of the Department of Health and Human Services, Food and Drug Administration, designated by the Secretary under authority of the Act of January 31, 1925, 43 Statutes at Large 803; Reorganization Plan No. IV, Secs. 12-15, effective June 30, 1940; Reorganization Plan No. 1 of 1953, Secs. 1-9, effective April 11, 1953; and P.L. 96-88, Sec. 509, 93 Statutes at Large 965 (20 U.S.C. 3508), effective May 4, 1980, to administer or take oaths, affirmations and affidavits, personnally

appeared ___Henry O'Rourke___ , in the county and State aforesaid, who, being duly sworn, deposes and says: The sample

consisting of _Two Cases (24/8 oz. Each) Horseshoe Brand Canned Cove Oysters_ collected by the

above FDA employee on _3-10-99_ was from shipment(s) received by us from _Captain Sam Seafood, Inc. New_

Orleans, LA on _3-7-99_ and so identified to the collector:

That the copy of invoice(s):

NUMBER	DATE	NUMBER	DATE	NUMBER	DATE
1) 06641	3/6/99	2) 06643	3/7/99	3)	

and (copy of) shipping record(s):

TYPE: (B/L, F/B)	NUMBER	DATE	ISSUING FIRM OR CARRIER
1) F/B	4778	3/6/99	Acme Freight Lines, Inc. NOLA
2) F/B	A-9321	3/7/99	Thru-Fast Lines, Little Rock, AR
3)			

which were identified and furnished the collector, cover this (these) shipment(s):

That said shipment(s) was (were) entered for the account of ___N/A_____ .
_____ under Lot no._____ .

The collector paid me the sum of $ _21.32_____ (in cash) ~~(by voucher) (to be billed)~~ for the sample.

REMARKS

AFFIANT'S SIGNATURE & TITLE
          Henry O. O'Rourk, Warehouse Manager Plant #12

FIRM *(Name and address, include ZIP Code)*
          Southeastern Seafood Distributors, Inc. #4 Canal Street Dock Red River Basin Area, Little Rock, AR 72901

Subscribed and sworn to before me at _Little Rock, AR_____ this _10th_ day of _March_, 19 _99_.
                             (City and State)

Sidney H. Rogers
   (Employee's Signature)
Employee of the Department of Health and Human Services designated
under Act of January 31, 1925, Reorganization Plan IV effective
June 30, 1940; Reorganization Plan No. 1 of 1953, effective April 11, 1953;
and P.L. 96-88, effective May 4, 1980.

FORM FDA 1664 (4/83)   **PREVIOUS EDITIONS ARE OBSOLETE**

177

EXHIBIT 430-F   **INVESTIGATIONS OPERATIONS MANUAL**

AFFIDAVIT *(Jobber)*	SAMPLE NO. 55576
STATE OF PENNSYLVANIA	COUNTY OF PHILADELPHIA

Before me, ___Sylvia A. Rogers___ , an employee of the Department of Health and Human Services, Food and Drug Administration, designated by the Secretary under authority of the Act of January 31, 1925, 43 Statutes at Large 803; Reorganization Plan No. IV, Secs. 12-15, effective June 30, 1940; Reorganization Plan No. 1 of 1953, Secs. 1-9, effective April 11, 1953; and P.L. 96-88, Sec. 509, 93 Statutes at Large 965 (20 U.S.C. 3508), effective May 4, 1980, to administer or take oaths, affirmations and affidavits, personnally

appeared ___Patrick T. Palmer___ , in the county and State aforesaid, who, being duly sworn, deposes and says: The lot of ___325 cases,___ (24/ 4 ½ oz. cans of Jolly Miller Canned Mushrooms

:

which we invoiced and sold to Patriot Markets, Inc. Frankford Pennsylvania   ,

on 4-12-99 was a portion/all of a parcel shipped to us by Northern Light Foods, Inc. Duluth, Minnesota   .
and is covered by submitted (copy of) invoice(s):

NUMBER	DATE	NUMBER	DATE	NUMBER	DATE
1) 3914	4/4/99	2)		3)	

And (copy of) shipping record(s):

TYPE: (B/L, F/B)	NUMBER	DATE	ISSUING FIRM OR CARRIER
1) B/L	20018	4/5/99	Northern Freight Carriers
2)			
3)			

REMARKS

AFFIANT'S SIGNATURE & TITLE
Patrick T. Palmer Warehouse Manager

FIRM *(Name and address, include ZIP Code)*
Liberty Wholesale Grocers, 3210 11ᵗʰ Ave. Frankford, PA 19105

Subscribed and sworn to before me at Frankford, PA   this 28ᵗʰ day of April , 19 99.
               (City and State)

Sylvia A. Rogers
   (Employee's Signature)
Employee of the Department of Health and Human Services designated
under Act of January 31, 1925, Reorganization Plan IV effective
June 30, 1940; Reorganization Plan No. 1 of 1953, effective April 11, 1953;
and P.L. 96-88, effective May 4, 1980.

FORM FDA 1664a (4/83)   PREVIOUS EDITIONS ARE OBSOLETE

AFFIDAVIT	SAMPLE NO. 55545

STATE OF TENNESSEE	COUNTY OF SHELBY

Before me, _____Sidney H. Rogers_____ , an employee of the Department of Health and Human Services, Food and Drug Administration, designated by the Secretary under authority of the Act of January 31, 1925, 43 Statutes at Large 803; Reorganization Plan No. IV, Secs. 12-15, effective June 30, 1940; Reorganization Plan No. 1 of 1953, Secs. 1-9, effective April 11, 1953; and P.L. 96-88, Sec. 509, 93 Statutes at Large 965 (20 U.S.C. 3508), effective May 4, 1980, to administer or take oaths, affirmations and affidavits, personally appeared ___George R. Applegate___ , in the county and State aforesaid, who, being duly sworn, deposes and says:

I am manager of John's Curb Market, 342 East Johnson St., Memphis, Tennessee. As such, I have knowledge of purchasing and receipt of products at the market.

On September 2, 1999, FDA Investigator Sydney H. Rogers collected from my firm a sample consisting of six – 4 pound cans of Red River Brand Pure Sorghum. This sorghum was collected from a lot of six cases, each containing 4 – 4 pound buckets (cans) purchased by me from Ted Buymore who regularly sells sorghum in this area. Ted delivered this lot of six cases to my market on August 28, 1999 in a red panel GM truck with Alabama license plates. I do not know the license number.

AFFIANT'S SIGNATURE AND TITLE

George R. Applegate, Manager

FIRM'S NAME AND ADDRESS *(Include ZIP Code)*

John's Curb Market, 342 East Johnson St., Memphis, Tenn. 38110

Subscribed and sworn to before me at __Memphis, Tennessee__ this _2nd_ day of __September__ , 19 _99._
             (City and State)

            Sidney H. Rogers .
                     (Employee's Signature)

Employee of the Department of Health and Human Services designated under Act of January 31, 1925, Reorganization Plan IV effective June 30, 1940; Reorganization Plan No. 1 of 1953, effective April 11, 1953; and P.L. 96-88, effective May 4, 1980.

FORM FDA 463a (4/83)   **PREVIOUS EDITIONS MAY BE USED**   **PAGE 1 OF 1 PAGES.**

EXHIBIT 430-H

INVESTIGATIONS OPERATIONS MANUAL

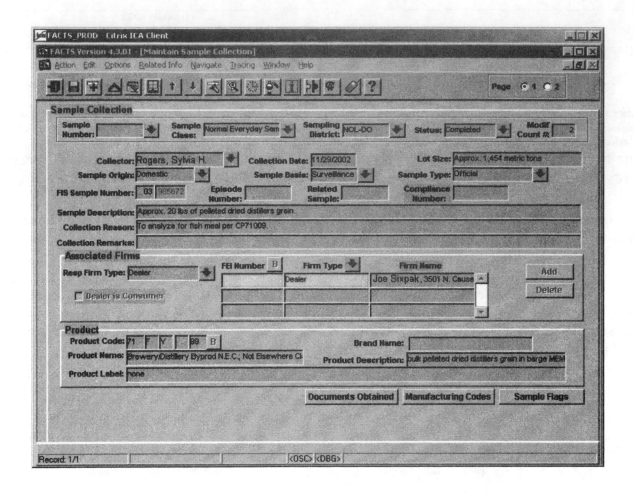

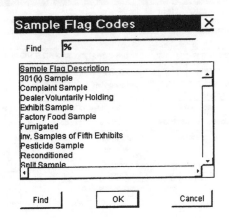

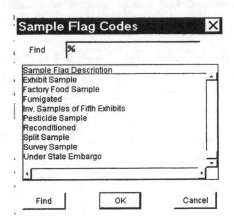

EXHIBIT 430-I   **INVESTIGATIONS OPERATIONS MANUAL**

FACTS V.2   ▼ ⬍

Action   Edit   Options   Related Info   Navigate   Window   Help

| Sample Number: | 2340 ⬇ | Sample Class: | Normal Everyday Sam ⬇ | Sampling District: | CHI-DO ⬇ | Status: | In Progress ⬇ | Modif Count # |

Collector: Sylvia H. Rogers ⬇   Collection Date: 09/25/2000   Lot Size: 125 CS/12 BTLS/100 TAB

Sample Origin: Domestic ⬇   Sample Basis: Compliance ⬇   Sample Type: Documentary ⬇

FIS Sample Number: 00 308358   Episode Number: Related Sample: Compliance Number:

Sample Description: Sample consists of photographs and copies of records documenting interstate commerce and cGMP deficiencies for Wilaprin Art

Collection Reason: Collected during EI of dealer, dated 9/20-25/2000 to document interstate commerce and cGMP deviations. No analysis needed.

Collection Remarks: See EIR of dealer and FDA-483 , dated 9/20-25/2000 for more information. FDA-483 points 1-12 discuss deviations specific to th

Associated Firms

Resp Firm Type: Dealer ⬇

☐ Dealer is Consumer

FEI Number B	Firm Type ⬇	Firm Name
3000901032	Dealer	Wilson Pharmaceutical, 300 S
3000901033	Ingredient Supplier	Woleske Chemical, 100 W. Ma

Add
Delete

Product

Product Code: 60 L B A 05 B   Brand Name: Wilaprin Arthritis Formula

Product Name: Aspirin (Analgesic); Human N/Rx Comb Ingr; Pr   Product Description: Aspirin Non-Rx Combination Tablet

Product Label: Finished product is labeled in part: "***WILAPRIN ARTHRITIS FORMULA 500 Tablets***Active Ingredients: Acetylsalicylic Acid ... 5

[Documents Obtained] [Manufacturing Codes] [Sample Flags]

FACTS V.2   ▼ ⬍

Action   Edit   Options   Related Info   Navigate   Window   Help

| Sample Number: | 2340 ⬇ | Sample Class: | Normal Everyday Sam ⬇ | Sampling District: | CHI-DO ⬇ | Status: | In Progress ⬇ | Modif Count # |

Collection Method: Copies of records collected during EI, dated 09/20-25/2000. Photographs taken 09/23/2000.

State: IL ⬇   County: COOK ⬇   Country of Origin: United States ⬇

Estimated Value: $4500.00   Sample Cost: $.00   Payment Method: No Charge ⬇   Receipt Issued: None ⬇

Carrier Name: Roadway   Date Shipped: 06/06/1999   Consumer Complaint Number: Recall Number:

How Prepared: All records and photographs identified as below and submitted to Supervisory Investigator. Negatives and extra photos placed in 525

Collector's ID On Package/Document: "DOC 2340 9/25/00 SHR"   Collector's ID On Seal: "DOC 2340 9/25/00 Sylvia H. Rogers"

Sample Delivered To: Sample Delivered Date:

CR & Records Sent To: CHI-DO ⬇   Storage Requirement: ⬇

Dairy Permit Number: Food Canning Establishment: ☐ 704 (d) Sample

National Drug Code: CRx/DEA Schedule: ⬇   ☐ 702 (b) Portion Collected

Collection PACs

PAC Code ⬇	Description
56002	DRUG PROCESS INSPECTIONS(DPI)

Add

Physical Sample Sent To ⬇

Add
Delete

Count "0   <List>

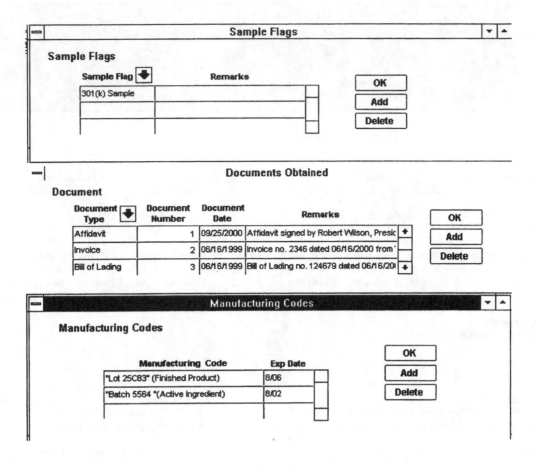

EXHIBIT 430-I3   INVESTIGATIONS OPERATIONS MANUAL

Food and Drug Administration Office of Regulatory Affairs
Collection Report

For Sample 2340

This is an accurate reproduction of the original electronic record as of 10/14/2000

Flag
301 (k) Sample

Flag Remarks

Episode Number	**Orgin**	**Basis**	**Sample Type**	**FIS Smpl Num**	**Status**
	Domestic	Compliance	Documentary	00908358	In Progress

FEI	**Date Collected**	**Product Code**	**Responsible Firm**	**PAC**	**Hours**
3000901032	09/25/2000	60LBA05 Dealer		56002	8

Related Smpl Num Position Class 2 **Sampling District** CHI-DO **NDC Number** **Permit Number** **Storage Rqrmnt.**

Dealer is Consumer No **Crx/DEA Schedule** **Recall Num** **Consumer Compl. Num** **Brand Name** Wilaprin Arthritis Formula

Product Description
Aspirin Non-Rx Combination Tablet

Product Label
See continuation

Reason for Collection
Collected during EI of dealer,dated 9/20-25/2000 to document
Interstate commerce and cGMP deviations. No analysis needed

MFG Codes
"Lot 25C83" (Finished Product)
"Batch 5564"(Active Ingredient)

Expiration Date
8/06
8/02

Firm Legal Name	**Address**	**Type of Firm**	**Firm FEI**	**FCE**
Wilson Pharmaceutical	300 Riverside Chicago, IL 60606 US	Dealer	3000901032	
Woleske Chemical	100 W. Main Kansas City,MO 64111 US	Ingredient Supplier	3000901033	

Size of Lot	**Est. Value**	**Rcpt Type**	**Date Shipped & Doc. Ref.**
125 CS/12 BTLS/100 TAB	$4,500	None	06/06/1999

Description of Sample
Sample consists of photographs and copies of records documenting interstate commerce and cGMP deficiencies for Wilaprin Arthritis Formula

Method of Collection
Copies of records collected during EI, dated 09/20-25/2000. Photographs taken 09/23/2000.

How Prepared
See continuation.

Collector's Identification on Package and/or Label
"DOC 2340 9/25/00 SHR"

Collector's Identification on Seal
"DOC 2340 9/25/00 Sylvia H. Rogers"

Sample Delivered To

Date Delivered

Orig C/R & Records To CH-DO

Lab w/Split Sample

Lab

Document Number	**Document Date**	**Document Type**	**Document Remarks**
1	09/25/2000	Affidavit	Affidavit signed by Robert Wilson, President
2	06/16/199	Invoice	Invoice no. 2346 dated 06/16/2000 from Woleske Chemical, Kansas, MO for 1 -250 lb drum of Acetylsalicylic Acid, batch 5564
3	06/16/2000	Bill of Lading	Bill of Lading no. 124679 dated 06/16/2000 from Roadway, Inc. Smith Center Kansas for shipment of

Date: 10/14/2000   **Page:** 1 of 3

		250 lbs of Acetylsalicylic Acid from Woleske Chemical, Kansas City, MO to Wilson Pharmaceutical, Inc. Chicago, IL.
4	Other	Raw Material Inventory Card for Acetylsalicylic Acid Batch no 5564
5	Other	Photographs of labeling for bulk 250 lb. Drum of Acetylsalicylic Acid, Batch 5564
6	Other	Wilson Pharmaceuticals Batch Record for Wilaprin Arthritis Formula, lot 25C83-25 pages. (contains Copies of all labeling distributed with lot 25C83)

Remarks
See EIR of dealer and FDA-483, dated 9/20/25/2000 for more information. FDA-483 points 1-12 discuss deviations specific to this product.

Payment Amount	Payment Method	704(d) Sample	702/(b) Portion	Collector's Name
$0.00	No Charge	No	No	Silvia H. Rogers

Name of Signer	Date & Time of Signature	Meaning
	ET	

EXHIBIT 430-I4   INVESTIGATIONS OPERATIONS MANUAL

Food and Drug Administration Office of Regulatory Affairs
Collection Report

For Sample 2340

This is an accurate reproduction of the original electronic record as of 10/14/2000

Continuation:

Product Label
Finished product is labeled in part: "***WILLAPRIN ARTHRITIS FORMULA 500 Tablets***Active Ingredients: Acetylsalicylic Acid…500 mg, Caffeine…32 mg.*** 100 Tablets*** Lot 25C83*** EXP 8/06***Wilson Pharmaceuticals, Chicago, IL 60606***". 12 bottles are placed in a case, labeled in part: "***WILLAPRIN ARTHRITIS FORMULA***Wilson Pharmaceuticals***Lot 25C83***EXP 8/06***"
Active ingredient documented is Acetylsalicylic Acid packaged in 250 lb drum, labeled in part:"***Acetylsalicylic Acid, USP***Batch No 5564***Use by 8/02**Woleske Chemical, Kansas City, MO 64111***"

How Prepared
All records and photographs identified as below and submitted to Supervisory Investigator. Negatives and extra photos placed In 525, sealed as below and submitted to Supervisor.

Date: 10/14/2000   **Page:** 3 of 3

FACTS V.1 - [Maintain Sample Collection]   _ 🗗 ✕

Action   Edit   Options   Related Info   Navigate   Tracing   Window   Help   _ 🗗 ✕

Page ⊙ 1 ○ 2

Sample Collection

Sample Number: 2357 ⬇	**Sample Class:** Normal Everyday Sam ⬇	**Sampling District:** MIN-DO ⬇	**Status:** In Progress ⬇

Collector: Silvia H. Rogers ⬇   **Collection Date:** 10/08/1998   **Lot Size:** One X-ray unit.

Sample Origin: Domestic ⬇   **Sample Basis:** Compliance ⬇   **Sample Type:** Documentary ⬇

FIS Sample Number: 99 | 901862   **Episode Number:**   **Related Sample:**

Sample Description: No physical sample obtained. Sample consists of photographs and records.

Collection Reason: FU to Assembler's Report. Possible violation X-Ray Performance Standard.

Collection Remarks: No shipping record issued. Unit was picked up at manufacturer by Dealer.

Associated Firms

Resp Firm Type: Manufacturer ⬇

☐ **Dealer is Consumer**

FEI Number **B**	Firm Type ⬇	Firm Name
3000900973	Manufacturer	Acme X-ray Corp., 20 Spruce
3000900974	Dealer	Dr. Gunther Krankheit, 555 5th

Add

Delete

Product

Product Code: 80 | L | | | DQ | B   **Brand Name:** Acme X-ray Corp.

Product Name: General Medical Devices   **Product Description:** General purpose diagnostic x-ray unit.

Product Label: Serial # "1234" stamped on metal plate.

Documents Obtained | Manufacturing Codes | Sample Flags |

Count: *1

FACTS V.1 - [Maintain Sample Collection]   _ 🗗 ✕

Action   Edit   Options   Related Info   Navigate   Tracing   Window   Help   _ 🗗 ✕

Page ○ 1 ⊙ 2

Sample Collection

Sample Number: 2357 ⬇	**Sample Class:** Normal Everyday Sam ⬇	**Sampling District:** MIN-DO ⬇	**Status:** In Progress ⬇

Collection Method: Sample consists of dealer affidavit, invoice, and 8 photographs of the X-ray unit.

State: MN ⬇   **County:** CAMDEN ⬇   **Country of Origin:** ⬇

Estimated Value: $5000.00   **Sample Cost:** $.00   **Payment Method:** No Charge ⬇   **Receipt Issued:** None ⬇

Carrier Name: **Date Shipped:**   **Consumer Complaint Number:**   **Recall Number:**

How Prepared: Photographs developed by Speed Foto 21, 4th Street, Brooklyn, NY. Photographs & records identified as below. Negatives officially :

Collector's ID On Package/Document: "DOC 2357 10/8/98 SHR"   **Collector's ID On Seal:** "DOC 2357 10/8/98 Silvia H. Rogers"

Sample Delivered To: United States Mail, Minnea: **Sample Delivered Date:** 10/08/1998

CR & Records Sent To: NYK-DO ⬇   **Storage Requirement:** Ambient ⬇

Dairy Permit Number: **Food Canning Establishment:**   ☐ **704 (d) Sample**

National Drug Code: **CRx/DEA Schedule:** ⬇   ☐ **702 (b) Portion Collected**

Collection PACs

PAC Code ⬇	Description		Sample Sent To ⬇	
82Z800	SHORT TERM ASSIGNMENTS/CDRH INITIATE	**Add** / **Delete**	CDRH-LABS	**Add** / **Delete**

Count: *1

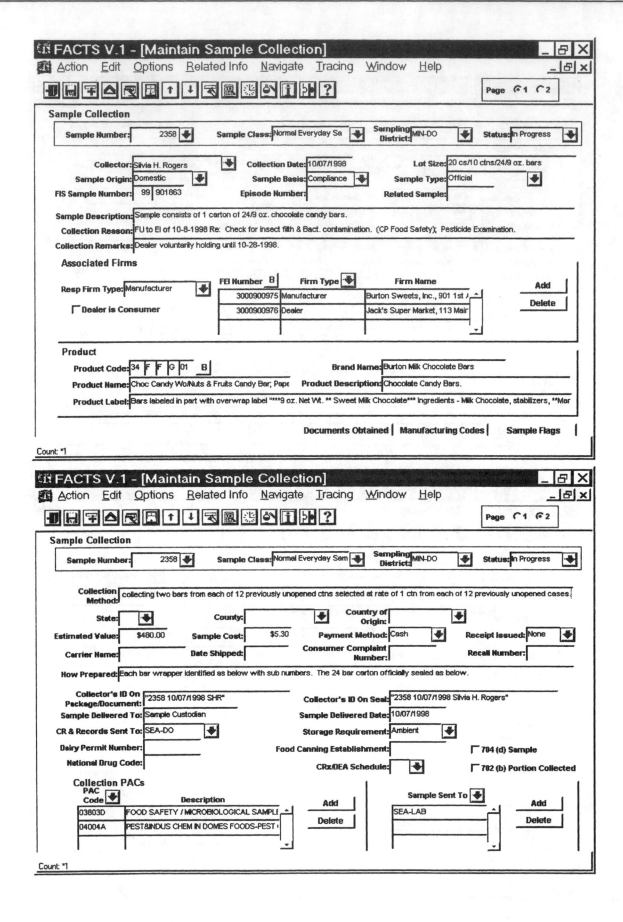

Accomplishment Hours ✕

| Accomplishment Hours |

Operation

Operation Code: 31 — Sample Collection   **Work Subject / Title:** Ad Hoc Collection

Sample Number: 2358

Assignment Status: In Progress   **Status Date:** 10/08/1998   **Reimbursable:** ☐

Assignees Accomplishment Hours

Collector	Employee Name	Position Class	Home District	PAC	Hours
☑	~~Silvia H. Rogers~~		MIN-DO	03803D	2.0
☑	Silvia H. Rogers		MIN-DO	04004A	2.0
☐	Harold I. Richards		MIN-DO	03803D	2.0
☐	Harold I. Richards		MIN-DO	04004A	2.0
☐					
☐					

Total Hours : 8.0

Add
Delete
Duplicate

EXHIBIT 430-L   INVESTIGATIONS OPERATIONS MANUAL

AFFIDAVIT *(In-transit Sampling)*	SAMPLE NO. 55522

STATE OF UTAH	COUNTY OF UINTAH

Before me, ___Sylvia A. Rogers___ , an employee of the Department of Health and Human Services, Food and Drug Administration, designated by the Secretary under authority of the Act of January 31, 1925, 43 Statutes at Large 803; Reorganization Plan No. IV, Secs. 12-15, effective June 30, 1940; Reorganization Plan No. 1 of 1953, Secs. 1-9, effective April 11, 1953; and P.L. 96-88, Sec. 509, 93 Statutes at Large 965 (20 U.S.C. 3508), effective May 4, 1980, to administer or take oaths, affirmations and affidavits, personnally

appeared ___Wayne J. Ellmore___ , in the county and State aforesaid, who, being duly sworn, deposes and says: I am employed by ___Trans-National Truck Lines, Tulsa, OK___ ,
(Carrier or firm name, city & state)

_____ as Driver _____ .
(Title of position)

On ___October 14, 1999___ , at ___Vernal, Utah___ the above named FDA employee collected a sample consisting of
(Date)   *(City & state where sampled)*

Two crates (48 heads per crate) of Polar brand Iceberg lettuce packed by Delbert Brothers Lettuce
(Description and number of units sampled)

Suppliers, Fresno, CA _____ .

from ___Tractor Trailer #321, Oklahoma Lic. #3672TR, 1999___ ,
(Enter type and number & License number of truck, bus, RR car, airplane, etc. or Firm name and shipping dock

_____ from shipment(s) of goods consigned to or being shipped to ___Mid Central___ ,

address if from dock

Distributors, 33 Front St., Minneapolis, Minnesota _____ .
(Consignee name and address)

The aforesaid sampled shipment(s) was (were) identified to the FDA collector by ___Wayne J. Ellmore___ ,
(Name of individual making identification)

Truck Driver _____ .
(Title of person making identification)

(Copy of) Shipping Record(s) F/B _____ , number ___A-32196___ ,
(Type record – B/L, Waybill, etc.)

dated ___10/14/99___ , issued by ___Trans-National Truck Lines___ ,

which were identified by ___Wayne J. Ellmore, Driver___ ,
(Name & title of individual identifying records)

and furnished to the FDA collector cover this (these) shipment(s).

AFFIANT'S SIGNATURE
Wayne J. Ellmore

Subscribed and sworn to before me at ___Vernal, Utah___ this 14th day of ___October___ , 19 99.
(City and State)

Employee of the Department of Health and Human Services designated

under Act of January 31, 1925, Reorganization Plan IV effective
June 30, 1940; Reorganization Plan No. 1 of 1953, effective April 11, 1953;
and P.L. 96-88, effective May 4, 1980

Sylvia A. Rogers .
(Employee's Signature)

FORM FDA 1664b (4/83)   PREVIOUS EDITIONS ARE OBSOLETE

AFFIDAVIT		SAMPLE NO. 55533
STATE OF KANSAS	COUNTY OF SEDGWICK	

Before me,_____Sidney H. Rogers_____, an employee of the Department of Health and Human Services, Food and Drug Administration, designated by the Secretary under authority of the Act of January 31, 1925, 43 Statutes at Large 803; Reorganization Plan No. IV, Secs. 12-15, effective June 30, 1940; Reorganization Plan No. 1 of 1953, Secs. 1-9, effective April 11, 1953; and P.L. 96-88, Sec. 509, 93 Statutes at Large 965 (20 U.S.C. 3508), effective May 4, 1980, to administer or take oaths, affirmations and affidavits, personnally appeared __Joseph H. Roe__, in the county and State aforesaid, who, being duly sworn, deposes and says:

I am the Vice President in charge of production of the Doe Bottling Co., Inc., 123 Main, Thistown, Kansas 67201; and as such I have knowledge of the raw material receiving and use, and carbonated beverage production at this firm.

The sample consisting of two cases, 48- 10 ounce bottles, of Kola Cola, coded ABCD, collected by Investigator Rogers on November 15, 1999 was from a lot of 2668 cases produced by this firm on October 7, 1999. The copies of our production records for October 7, 1999 consist of a Syrup Room Report dated 10-6-99, a two-page Production Report dated 10-7-99, an undated in-line Control record, and a Finished Drink Control Record dated 10-7-99. Copies of these records were provided to the investigator and cover our production of this lot.

The above described lot was made in part from a portion of a lot of bulk liquid sugar received October 3, 1999 from the Sweet Sugar Co., Boise, Idaho, in railroad tank car ATSF 98765, unloaded October 6, 1999. The copies of the Sweet Sugar Co. invoice number 468 dated Sept. 26, 1999; freight waybill number UP-3579 dated Sept. 27, 1999 issued by the Union Pacific Railroad Co.; and our receiving report number 01-23 dated October 3, 1999 were provided to the investigator and cover this shipment.

The above described lot was also made in part from a portion of a lot of Kola Cola syrup base received September 23, 1999 from the Kola Cola Co., Thattown, Texas. The copies of Kola Cola Co. invoice number KCO1928 dated Sept. 20, 1999; freight bill number X-98125 dated Sept. 21, 1999 issued by Speedy Truck Line Co.; and our receiving report number 01-01 dated Sept. 23, 1999 were provide to the investigator and cover this shipment.

The above described lot of Kola Cola was identified to the investigator by William S. Doe, Production Supervisor. I identified and provided copies of the records to the investigator.

AFFIANT'S SIGNATURE AND TITLE

Joseph H. Roe, Production Vice President

FIRM'S NAME AND ADDRESS *(Include ZIP Code)*

Doe Bottling Co., Inc. 123 main, Thistown, Kansas, 67201

Subscribed and sworn to before me at _Thistown, Kansas_ this _15th_ day of _November_ , 19 _99_.
(City and State)

Sidney H. Rogers .
(Employee's Signature)

Employee of the Department of Health and Human Services designated under Act of January 31, 1925, Reorganization Plan IV effective June 30, 1940; Reorganization Plan No. 1 of 1953, effective April 11, 1953; and P.L. 96-88, effective May 4, 1980.

FORM FDA 463a (4/83)   PREVIOUS EDITIONS MAY BE USED   PAGE 1 OF 1 PAGES.

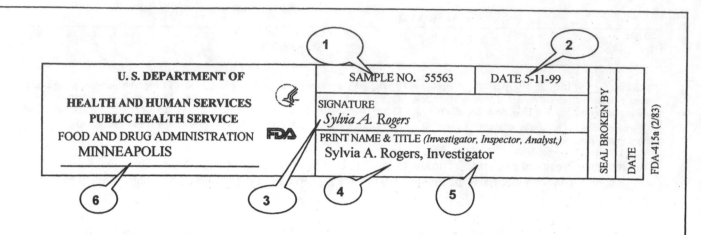

1   Insert Sample Number. When applicable, use prefix, e.g. "Inv", "FS", "DOC", "PS", etc. (See IOM 439.2)

2   Insert date sealed. Use figures, month, day, year. (See #7 below when seal is broken for any purpose).

3   Sign your usual signature.

4   Print your name same as signature. (A rubber name stamp may be used if desired but use it carefully and do not smear.)

5   Print your title

6   Print your district – spell out – do not use district abbreviations or symbols. (A rubber stamp may be used.)

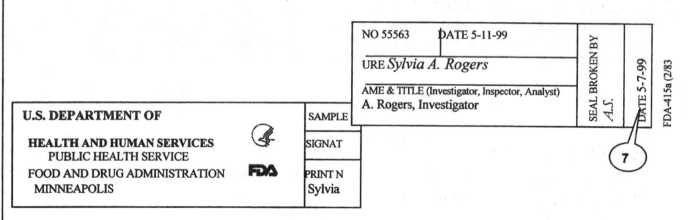

7   When seal is broken for any purpose, initial here and enter the date broken. Submit broken seal with sample records.

SHIPPER'S DECLARATION FOR DANGEROUS GOODS

Shipper US Food and Drug Administration 6601 N.W. 25th St. Room 236 Miami, FL 33122	**Air Waybill No.** Delta 7012-6140 Page _1___ of _1__ Pages Collection Report Number 2555

Consignee Food and Drug Administration 60 Eighth Street Atlanta, GA 30309	**U.S. GOVERNMENT** **SHIPMENT**

Two completed and signed copies of this Declaration must be handed to the operator.	**WARNING** Failure to comply in all respects with the applicable Dangerous Goods Regulations may be in breach of the applicable law, subject to legal penalties. This Declaration must not, in any circumstances, be completed and/or signed by a consolidator, a forwarder or an IATA cargo agent.

TRANSPORT DETAILS

This shipment is within the limitations prescribed for *(delete non-applicable)*	Airport of Departure MIAMI, FL
~~PASSENGER AMD CARGO AIRCRAFT~~ ~~CARGO AIRCRAFT ONLY~~	

Airport of Destination Atlanta, GA	Shipment Type *(Delete non-applicable)* **NON-RADIOACTIVE** ~~RADIOACTIVE~~

<u>NATURE AND QUANTITY OF DANGEROUS GOODS</u>

Dangerous Goods Identification

PROPER SHIPPING NAME OF ARTICLE as listed in the Restricted Articles Tariff Federal Aviation Regulations or IATA Restricted Articles Regulation. Specify each article separately.	Class or Division	UN or ID No.	Subsidiary Risk	Quantity and Type of Packing	Packing Inst.	Authorization
DRY ICE 9CARBON DIOXIDE SOLID)	ORM A OR 9	UN 1845	N/A	5 Fiberboard Cartons Net weight 20 lbs. Dry Ice each Carton	173. 615 or 615	
		Note: Include these notations on all Dry Ice shipments.				

Additional Handling Information

DO NOT OPEN THIS PACKAGE, IF PROBLEMS ARISE, CONTACT SHIPPER AT (305) 555-3344

I hereby declare that the contents of this consignment are fully and accurately described above by proper shipping name and are classified, packed, marked and labeled, and are in all respects in the proper condition for transport by air according to the applicable International and National Government Regulations.	**Name/Title of Person Signing** Sidney H. Rogers Investigator
	Place and Date Miami, FL (9-8-99)
	Signature *(See warning above)* *Sydney H. Rogers*

FORM FDA 3062 (3/83)   PREVIOUS EDITION IS OBSOLETE.

EXHIBIT 450-C   **INVESTIGATIONS OPERATIONS MANUAL**

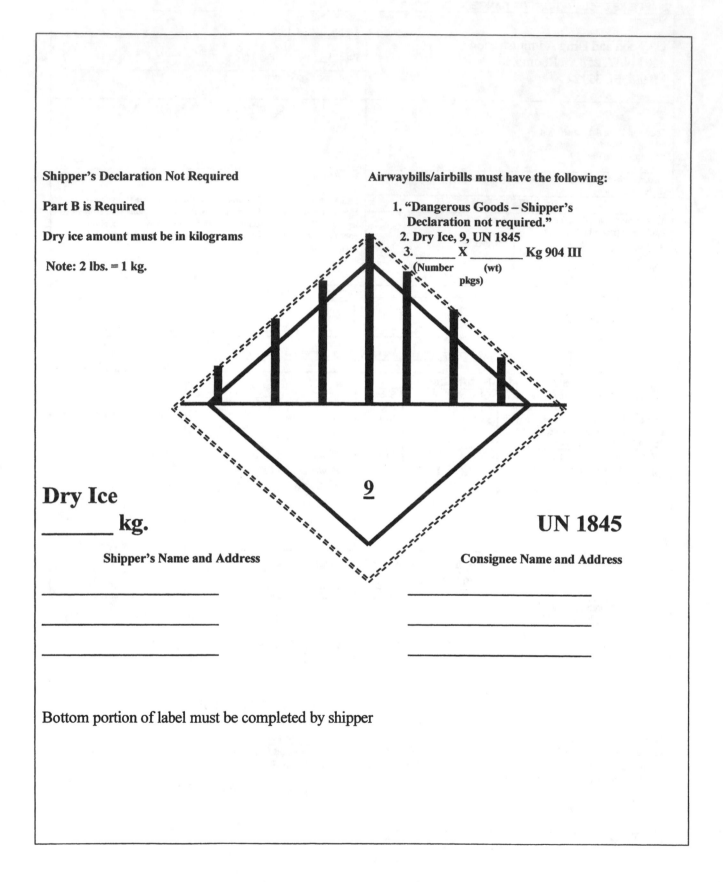

Shipper's Declaration Not Required

Part B is Required

Dry ice amount must be in kilograms

 Note: 2 lbs. = 1 kg.

Airwaybills/airbills must have the following:

1. **"Dangerous Goods – Shipper's Declaration not required."**
2. **Dry Ice, 9, UN 1845**
3. _____ X _____ Kg 904 III
   (Number   (wt)
    pkgs)

Dry Ice
_____ kg.

UN 1845

Shipper's Name and Address

_____

_____

_____

Consignee Name and Address

_____

_____

_____

Bottom portion of label must be completed by shipper

SALMONELLA SAMPLING PLAN

PURPOSE:

To determine the presence of Salmonella in processed foods intended for human consumption.

APPLICABILITY

This sampling plan is applicable to the inspection of either a continuing series of production lots or to isolated lots consisting of an identifiable collection of process units (cans, bags, packages, or similar units). This plan is for use by FDA for regulatory purposes.

FOOD CATEGORIES:

Foods are listed in three categories based on the number of Salmonella hazards and whether a food is to be consumed by infants, the aged, or infirm.

The three defined Salmonella Hazards of foods are:

    1.   The food or an ingredient of the food is a significant potential source of Salmonella;.

    2.   The manufacturing process does not include a controlled step that destroys Salmonella; and

    3.   The food has significant potential for microbiological growth if "abused" in distribution or by consumers.

Classification of Foods:

Foods have been classified into three food Categories for regulatory sampling purposes. The foods are listed in the Categories by Product Code sequence.

NOTE: For products not listed, check with your supervisor. The District will request categorization from the Office of Field Programs/Center for Food Safety and Applied Nutrition (HFS-600), or, when time is of essence, the District will make the categorization and obtain later concurrence from CFSAN.

Category I

This includes all foods that would normally be in Category II except that they are intended for consumption by the aged, the infirm, and infants.

Category II

This includes the foods that would not normally be subjected to a process lethal to Salmonella between the time of sampling and consumption. Examples are as follows:

PRODUCT CODE	FOOD ITEM
03	Bread, rolls, buns, sugared breads, crackers, custard and cream filled sweet goods
05	Breakfast cereals, ready to eat
07	Pretzels, chips and specialty items
09	Butter and butter products; pasteurized milk and raw fluid milk and fluid milk products for consumption; pasteurized and unpasteurized concentrated liquid milk products for consumption; dried milk and dried milk products for consumption
12	Cheese and Cheese products
13	Ice cream from pasteurized milk and related products that have been pasteurized; raw ice cream mix and related unpasteurized products for consumption.
14	Pasteurized and unpasteurized imitation dairy products for consumption
15	Pasteurized eggs, egg products from pasteurized eggs; unpasteurized eggs and egg products from unpasteurized eggs for consumption without further cooking
16	Canned and cured fish, vertebrates; other fish products; fresh and frozen raw oysters and raw clams, shellfish and crustacean products; smoked fish, shellfish and crustaceans for consumption
17	Unflavored gelatin
20-22	Fresh, frozen and canned fruits and juices, concentrates and nectars; dried fruit for consumption; jams, jellies, preserves and butters
23	Nuts and nut products for consumption
26	Oils consumed directly without further processing and oleomargarine
27	Dressings and condiments (including mayonnaise) salad dressing and vinegar
28	Spices including salt; flavors and extracts
29	Soft drinks and water
30	Beverage bases
31	Coffee and tea
33	Chewing gum and candy
34	Chocolate and cocoa products
35	Pudding mixes not cooked prior to consumption, gelatin products
36	Syrups, sugars and honey
38	Soups
39	Prepared salads

Category III

This includes the following foods that would normally be subjected to a process lethal to Salmonella between the time of sampling and consumption. Examples are as follows:

02	Whole grain, processed grain and starch products for human use
04	Macaroni and noodle products
16	Fresh and frozen fish; vertebrates (except that eaten raw); fresh and frozen shellfish and crustaceans (except raw oysters and raw clams for consumption); other aquatic animals (including frog legs)
24	Fresh vegetables, frozen vegetables, dried vegetables, cured and processed vegetable products normally cooked before consumption
26	Vegetable oils, oil stock and vegetable shortening
35	Dry dessert and pudding mixes that are cooked prior to consumption
37	Frozen dinners, multiple food dinners
45-46	Food chemicals (direct additives)

SAMPLE COLLECTION

Each sub will consist of a minimum of 100 gm (approx 3.53 oz). The usual subsample is a consumer size container of a product. Subsamples should be obtained at random to insure that the total sample is representative of the lot. When a lot consists of identifiable subdivisions (e.g., different codes), sub samples should be obtained from subdivisions in the proportion that the subdivisions are to the whole lot.

More than one subsample may be collected from large institutional or bulk containers when the number of sub samples required exceeds the number of containers in the lot. A subsample will consist of more that one container when the lot consists of containers smaller than 100 gms (e.g., 4 - 25 gm containers is a subsample).

When a sample is collected by transferring it to sample containers, a sample control must be submitted which consists of an empty sample container that is exposed to the same conditions under which the sample is collected. See IOM 426.2 and 426.4 on controls. Use aseptic technique when sampling from bulk containers.

SAMPLE SIZE

The following sample sizes also apply to the finished product portion of in-line samples when analyzed for Salmonella. Each subsample will consist of at least 100 gms (approx 3.5 oz).

The number of subsamples includes the 702(b) portion.

FOOD CATEGORY	NUMBER OF SAMPLE UNITS (SUBS)
I	60
II	30
III	15

SAMPLE SUBMISSION

Submit all samples collected to your district's microbiological servicing laboratory unless directed otherwise by your supervisor or assignment. See IOM 454.2

SAMPLING SCHEDULE FOR CANNED AND ACIDIFIED FOODS

I. Canned Foods

A. Field Examination

1. Routinely examine warehouse stock for evidence of leaking cans, wet cases, swollen cans, swarms of fruit flies around isolated pallets, etc.

2. When the inspectional evidence indicates the probability of under processed lots, or lots with excessive defective units, conduct a visual examination of warehouse stock. Give preference to the examination of the lot that was processed incorrectly. However, any lot produced using the process, and preferably warehoused at least 14 days, should be examined.

3. A lot to be examined will be one production code.

4. Each field examination will consist of a maximum of 576 containers. However, a minimum of 192 containers may be examined if 3 or more abnormal containers are found.

a. Flippers. Only one end is slack or slightly bulged and the end remains flat if pressed in. Cans which bulge when sharply and squarely struck end-down on a flat surface are flippers, provided that the bulged end remains flat when pressed. Flippers result from a lack of vacuum.

b. Springers. One end of a can bulges. Manual pressure on the bulged end forces the opposite and out or the same end will spring out with release of pressure. If both ends bulge, but only one will remain flat when pressed, the can is a springer. Springers result from moderate positive pressure in the can. Buckling or extensive denting of the side wall may produce a springer.

c. Swells. Both ends of the can are bulged. Neither end will remain flat without pressure. Soft swells yield to manual pressure, but no impression can
be made manually on hard swells. Swells result from positive pressure in the can usually because of spoilage
of the contents. Some swells, especially in acid products, may result from chemical reaction between the contents and the container.

NOTE: Other abnormalities or defects, should be reported on C/R, but not counted as "abnormal containers" for the purposes of the sequential field examination. These other defects include visibly leaking cans, severe dents around seams, gross seam defects, severely rusted containers, etc.

5. Follow the chart on the next page for the field examination.

6. Unless the inspectional evidence of improper processing or non-compliance with the GMP's can be related to specific production lots, conduct no field examinations during the inspection. However, if inspectional evidence or other examination results indicate problems, conduct *field examinations* using the large chart on the next page for guidance.

B. Sample Size
1. Investigational
a. Samples for laboratory examination will consist of all abnormal and 12 normal containers. The sample will include as many abnormal containers as were found during your field

exam(e.g., if 21 abnormal containers are observed during the examination, the sample will consist of 21 abnormal and 12 normal containers). Do not collect leakers, but report the number noted.

It may be necessary to collect samples of any other defects noted such as seam defects to support observations and document the severity of the defects. In some cases, photographs may be a suitable substitute for collection of physical subsamples.

b. Report the results of the field examination in the EIR and as a Field Exam in FACTS. If a sample is collected, on the C/R. Identify, by sub-sample number, the condition of each container in the sample (e.g., sub-sample 1 - flipper; sub-sample 2 - hard swell; --------sub-sample x – normal).

UNCASED CONTAINERS		PACKED 48/CASE		PACKED 24/CASE		PACKED 12/CASE		PACKED 6/CASE		
LOT SZ CONTAIN.	NO. TO EXAMINE	LOT SIZE (CASES)	CASES TO EXAMINE	LOT SIZE (CASES)	CASES TO EXAMINE	LOT SIZE (CASES)	CASES TO EXAMINE	LOT SIZE (CASES)	CASES TO EXAMINE	NUMBER ABNORMAL CONTAINERS TO DISCONTINUE
192 or less	all	1 - 4	all	1 - 8	all	1 - 16	all	1 - 32	all	3
193 - 288	192	4 - 6	4	8 - 12	8	16 - 24	16	32 - 48	32	5
289 - 384	all - 298	6 - 8	6	12 - 16	12	24 - 32	25	48 - 64	all - 50	6
385 - 576	363	8 - 12	8	16 - 24	15	32 - 48	30	64 - 96	61	7
577 - 912	433	12 - 19	9	24 - 38	18	48 - 76	36	96 - 152	72	8
913 - 1488	480	19 - 31	10	38 - 62	20	76 - 124	40	152 - 248	80	9
1489 - 3408	529	31 - 71	11	62 - 142	22	124 - 284	44	248 - 568	88	10
3409 or more	576	71 or more	12	142 or more	24	284 or more	48	568 or more	96	11

*For a given lot size, when the specified number of abnormal containers is found, discontinue the examination and collect the abnormals ONE NORMAL CONTAINER TAKEN FROM EACH OF 12 CASES. Open additional cases, if necessary, to meet this requirement. When the maximum number of containers/cases have been examined, always collect a sample as directed above, if one or more abnormal containers have been found. IT IS ABSOLUTELY NECESSARY TO INCLUDE ON THE COLLECTION REPORT THE LOT SIZE, THE NUMBER CONTAINERS EXAMINED, AND THE NUMBER OF ABNORMAL CONTAINERS FOUND BY TYPE (E.G., HARD SWELLS)

2. Official

NOTE: Products in 55 gallon drums, or similar large containers, either aseptically filled or heat processed should not be sampled while the shipment is enroute unless the owner accepts responsibility for the portion remaining in the opened containers. Arrange sampling of these products at the consignee (user) so the remaining portion can be immediately used or stored under refrigeration. Always use ASEPTIC TECHNIQUE when sampling these types of products.
A lot is defined as one production code.

Collect each subdivision in duplicate from a separate case, if possible. Mark subs 1a, 1b, 2a, 2b, etc. Collect as follows:

	Size of Lot	Min total cans	Cans/case
906 gm (2 lbs.) Net weight and smaller	Up to 50 cases	48	2 from 24
	More than 50 cases	96	2 from 48
Over 906 gm (2 lbs)	Up to 600 cases	48	2 from 24
	More than 600 cases	72	2 from 36

a. Filth, Micro, etc. (Includes 702(b) portion)

b. Standards Assay (Includes 702(b) portion)
NOTE: Sample sizes listed below are based upon the requirements of the Standards (21 CFR 145.3)

When sampling products, which are likely to be non-uniform throughout the lot because of variations from standards of quality, identity, fill-of-container, grade, etc., collect each subdivision in the triplicate from a separate case. Mark subs 1a, 1b, 1c, 2a, 2b, 2c, etc. Collect as follows:

	Number of cans or packages	Min total cans	Cans/case
1 kg (2.2 lbs) Net weight or less	4800 or less	48	3 from 16
	4801 to 24,000	72	3 from 24
	24,001 to 48,000	96	3 from 32
	48,001 to 84,000	144	3 from 48
	84,001 to 144,000	264	3 from 88
	144,001 to 240,000	384	3 from 128
	Over 240,000	600	3 from 200
Greater than 1 kg (2.2lbs), but less than 4.5 kg (10 lbs.)	2400 or less	48	3 from 16
	2401 to 15000	72	3 from 24
	15001 to 24000	96	3 from 32
	24001 to 42000	144	3 from 48
	42001 to 72000	252	3 from 88
	72001 to 120,000	384	3 from 128
	Over 120,000	600	3 from 200
Greater than 4.5 kg (10 lbs)	600 or less	48	3 from 16
	601 to 2000	72	3 from 24
	2001 to 7200	96	3 from 32
	7201 to 15000	144	3 from 48
	15001 to 24000	252	3 from 88
	24001 to 42000	384	3 from 128
	Over 42000	600	3 from 200

3. Acidified Foods(Metal or Glass)
A lot is defined as one production code.

Samples must be collected randomly from the entire lot. **Sample size does not include 702(b) portion.**

 # 10 size containers – Randomly select 1 normal container from each of 12 randomly selected cases (if available) in the lot.
 # 2 ½ and smaller –Randomly select 2 normal containers from each of 12 randomly selected cases (if available) in the lot. Sample size is 24 containers.

For acidified products, the equilibrium pH determines whether the product will support organisms of public health significance. Spoilage in such products is usually due to inadequate heat treatment to kill spoilage organisms. When abnormal containers of acidified products are found during domestic plant inspections, the Investigator should determine the cause of spoilage through inspectional observations and/or record review. It will not ordinarily be necessary to collect samples of abnormal containers of domestic acidified products, unless the reason for the abnormality has potential health hazard significance; the reason cannot be determined; or , the lot contains 1% or more abnormal containers and is intended for shipment or has already been partially shipped. However, since inspectional follow-up is not practical for imported acidified products, always collect abnormal containers to serve as a basis for determining progressive decomposition or product adulteration.

When collection of abnormal containers is indicated, conduct an examination following the sequential plan provided for canned foods. Collect all abnormal containers (up to a maximum of 24) in addition to the normal containers collected for pH determination. Indicate on the C/R the total number of containers examined and the number of each type of abnormality and defect observed. Also indicate the estimated percentage of abnormal containers in the lot.

PESTICIDE SAMPLES
(Includes 702(b) portion)
DO NOT FUMIGATE PESTICIDE SAMPLES

INTRODUCTION

The objectives of FDA's pesticide monitoring program are to gather information on levels and incidence of pesticide residues in the nation's food supply and to initiate enforcement action against shipments of food and feed found to contain illegal pesticide residues. To meet both objectives, it is necessary to collect samples of food and feed for pesticide residue analysis. These instructions describe procedures for collecting samples of raw agricultural commodities and processed commodities. The procedures apply to domestic and import shipments. The instructions include a separate set of procedures for collecting samples for special investigations such as determining levels of pesticide residues in soil, water, and growing crops.

Pesticide sample sizes no longer differentiate between Surveillance and Compliance Samples. All pesticide samples will be collected as directed below. Remember to include the state and county or country of origin in the Flag. See IOM 439.1.

For appraisal purposes, you must Flag each Domestic and Import Sample as to the basis for sampling in accordance with the definitions below.

Pesticide Compliance Sample. Collected on a selective basis as a result of inspectional or other evidence of suspected misuse of a pesticide on a food or feed commodity or as a follow-up to a "Pesticide Surveillance Sample" that was found to contain actionable levels of pesticide residues. Flag "Pesticide Compliance".

Pesticide Surveillance Sample. Collected on an objective basis where there is no evidence or suspicion of pesticide misuse on a food or feed commodity. Flag "Pesticide Surveillance".

1. GENERAL SAMPLING INSTRUCTIONS

SAMPLE SIZES FURNISHED IN THIS SCHEDULE APPLY TO BOTH DOMESTIC AND IMPORTED FOOD AND FEED COMMODITIES.

GENERAL SAMPLING SCHEDULE

Lot Size (Cases Crates, boxes, etc)	No. 900 gm (2 lb) subs	Total Sample Size kg (lbs)
12 or less	5	4.5 kg (10)
13 to 18	6	5.4 kg (12)
19 to 30	7	6.3 kg (14)
31 to 56	8	7.3 kg (16)
57 to 190	9	8.2 kg (18)
over 190	10	9.0 kg (20)

Unless instructed otherwise minimum sub size will be 900 gms (2 lbs).

2. FRESH PRODUCE

Districts have the option to collect 1 intact shipping case [minimum of 9 kg (20 lbs)] or a total of 9 kg (20 lbs) from one or more large containers of fresh produce from packing sheds or large produce warehouses. This "one case" option may be used on domestic Pesticide Surveillance Samples, if the collector can be assured that the "one case" collected is representative of the lot or field. If the collector is not assured of this, collect the samples as indicated in the General Sampling Schedule above. This "one case" sampling does not apply to large items such as melons.

NOTE:

If "one case" option is used for surveillance samples of domestic produce, describe in the Remarks Section of the CR, the basis for determining that the sample is representative of the lot or field.

ALL SURVEILLANCE SAMPLES OF FRESH IMPORTED PRODUCE, EXCEPT GRAPES FOR SULFITES, WILL CONSIST OF ONE CASE, BAG, BALE, BOX, ETC.

3. GRAPES FOR SULFITES

Collect approximately 900 - 1800 gms (2 - 4 lbs) of grapes [10/100 - 200 gm (1/4 to 1/2 lb) subs]. Each subsample will consist of individual grapes, not bunches, and will be collected from different lugs (cases) on as many different pallets in the lot as possible. No grapes that are damaged during the sampling procedure should be included in the sample. However, grapes with damage prior to sampling may be included in the sample.

If sulfiting pads are present, grapes sampled should be selected from areas closest to and directly under the pad.

Monitoring activities should be focused upon lots of grapes with the highest potential for violative sulfite residues.

Direct efforts to lots of grapes sulfited through fumigation or to lots with multiple fumigations especially towards the end of the harvesting season and also to lots with significant numbers of damaged grapes (split, crushed, or unusually wet, if such damage is apparent).

Sample lots of grapes sulfited through use of sulfiting pads, with or without additional fumigation. If at all possible, sample lots subjected to the following conditions, which could cause high sulfite residues:

Lots subjected to unrefrigerated storage of 2 or more hours during warm weather.

Unusual shipping conditions (ships at seas during heavy storms.

Lots with significant numbers of damaged grapes.
Lots containing evidence of sulfite pad damage sufficient to cause spilling of sulfiting agent onto grapes.

Special Sample Handling

Place sample in tightly closed airtight glass mason jar(s) or sealed plastic bag(s). Although no effort should be made to commingle subsamples, more than one subsample may be placed in the same container for shipping convenience.

Appropriate cooling procedures are:

Place samples in shipping container or cooler with sufficient ice or other refrigerant to keep sample refrigerated until arrival at the laboratory. Sample should be placed immediately in a refrigerator at or below 7°C. If sample is not to be analyzed within a few hours, the sample should be placed in a freezer, which is maintained at or below -20°C.

or

Place sample in container with sufficient dry ice to keep sample frozen until arrival at the lab, sample should be placed in freezer upon arrival at laboratory.

4.   FLUID MILK PRODUCTS

Retail Containers

Use General Sample Schedule. Sub size will be 1 retail unit (1 pt, 1 qt, 1/2 gal, etc.). When the retail container is less than 16 ozs, collect 2 units per sub.

Bulk Tank Trucks

Collect two (2) qts from each bulk tank after agitation.

5.   MANUFACTURED DAIRY PRODUCTS

Concentrated Liquid Milk Products

Use General Sample Schedule. Subsample size will be 1 retail unit. If retail unit container size is less than 16 ozs, collect 2 retail units per sub.

Dried Milk Products, Cheese, Ice Cream, and Related Dairy Products

Use General Sample Schedule, using the following subsample sizes:

Container Size	Minimum Units Per Sub
Less than 16 oz (pt)	2
Over 1 pint	1
Less than 453 gms (1 lb)	2
453 gms (1 lb) thru 10.9 kg (24 lbs)	1
11.4 kg (25 lbs) or more in bags or drums. Use Aseptic Technique	453 gm (1 lb) From each unit sampled

6.   EGGS AND EGG PRODUCTS

Liquid or Frozen Eggs

Use General Sample Schedule. Subsample size will be 1 pt liquid or 1 qt packed shavings from drillings. Subs will be collected using aseptic technique.

Dried Egg Products

Use General Sample Schedule. Use same sub sizes as in 4.b. Dried Milk Products. Use Aseptic Technique.

Shell Eggs

Retail Packages (1 doz.) - Use General Sample Schedule - Sub size 1 dozen

Commercial Cases

15 cases or less - 1 dozen from each case, minimum 2 dozen - maximum 10 dozen

16 cases or more - 1 dozen from each of 10 random cases

Grower Samples or lots that can be identified to a specific grower - 6 dozen

7.   FISH AND SHELLFISH PRODUCTS

NOTE: THIS SAMPLE SIZE FURNISHES SUFFICIENT FISH FOR HEAVY METAL ANALYSIS.

Packaged Fish, fresh, frozen, smoked, cured, or shellfish (except oysters)

Collect 12 subs - minimum sub size is 453 gms (1 lb)

Bulk Fish - .453 - 1.35 kg (1 - 3 lb)/fish

Collect 12 subs, each sub to consist of 453 gm (1 lb) of edible fish

Bulk Shellfish (except oysters)

Collect 12 - 453 gm (1 lb) subs

Canned Fish and Shellfish Products (except oysters)

Collect 12 subs - 5 cans per sub

Other Fish and Shellfish Products

Oysters - Collect 12 1 pint subs

Fish Flour and Meal

Use Compliance Sample Schedule. For containers 11.4 kg (25 lbs) or larger, collect 900 gms (2 lbs) per sub

SWORDFISH FOR HEAVY METALS

These sample sizes **must** be used whenever sampling swordfish, either for audit, surveillance, or compliance purposes.

Whole Fish (dressed, head removed)

Characterize lot in terms of fish sizes, i.e., small, medium, and large. The following dressed weight ranges are used for classification:

Small Fish - Weighs less than 36.4 kg (80 lbs)

Medium Fish - Weighs 36.4 - 54.5 kg (80 - 120 lbs)

Large Fish - Weighs more than 54.5 kg (120 lbs)

For lots consisting of 12 or more fish, the representative sample to be collected will be determined by the following formula:

$$ns = (n)(Ns)/N$$

ns = the number of fish in a given weight range from which subsamples must be taken

n = total number of subsamples to be collected from the lot. (In using this formula n will always equal 12)

Ns = the number of fish in a given weight range in the lot

N = the total number of fish in the lot

Example: If a lot consists of 25 fish and is characterized as: 5 small fish [less than 36.4 kg(80 lbs)], 15 medium fish [36.4 - 54.5 kg (80 - 120 lbs)], and 5 large fish [greater than 54.5 kg (129 lbs)], the sample should be collected as follows:

small fish $\dfrac{(12)(5)}{25} = 2.4 = 2$

medium fish $\dfrac{(12)(15)}{25} = 7.2 = 7$

Large fish $\dfrac{(12)(5)}{25} = 2.4 = 2$

TOTAL SAMPLE: 11 sub samples

Usually, the total sample will consist of 12 subsamples. However, due to rounding numbers of subsamples determined by the formula may be 11 or 13 in some instances. The total sample should consist of the specific number of sub samples determined by the formula in all cases.

Each sub sample should consist of approximately a .453 kg (1 lb) steak cut from just below the nape of the fish. Care should be taken to avoid mutilation of fish. The individual fish from which the private laboratory takes the sub sample should be identified with a tag or other suitable method. This will permit FDA to take audit samples from the same fish sampled by the private laboratories.

For lots consisting of 12 or less fish, collect 1 sub from each fish.

Swordfish Loins (slabs or sides cut from dressed whole fish which has been boned or trimmed).
Use the same formula stipulated for whole fish, with the exception that the following weight ranges should be used to characterize the lot:

Small fish loins = weighs 9.1 - 18.2 kg (20 - 40 lbs)

Medium fish loins) = weighs 18.2 - 36.4 kg (40 - 80 lbs)

Large fish loins = weighs over 36.4 kg (80 lbs)

Swordfish Steaks
Collect 12 sub samples, i.e., 12 steaks, at random from different containers in the lot (as many as possible)

Canned Swordfish
Collect 12/453 gm (1 lb) sub samples at random

8. RETAIL CONTAINERS CANNED, FROZEN AND DRIED FOODS

Use General Sample Schedule - Sub size is 900 gms   (2 lbs)

9. GRAINS AND FLOUR FOR HUMAN USE

Use General Sample Schedule. For containers 11.4 (25 lbs) or larger take 900 kg (2 lbs) per sub

10. HAY, FEEDS, SILAGE, AND BY-PRODUCTS FOR ANIMAL FEED

Use General Sample Schedule. Collect 900 gm (2 lbs) per sub. When sampling from bulk, collect 10 - 900 gm (2 lb) subs to yield a 9.1 kg (20 lb) sample.

11. SPECIAL INVESTIGATIONS

Growing Crops
Superimpose an imaginary grid on the field dividing it into approximately 100 areas. Randomly select 10 areas to form a representative sample of the field. Collect one pound subs from each area. Combine to form a composite. If a sample is being collected to document drift, etc. DO NOT composite subs. In addition, diagram the field in the Remarks Section of the C/R and indicate sub number where each sub was collected.

For leafy vegetables, such as lettuce, cabbage, etc. INV Samples collected in the growing field should be representative of local commercial harvesting practices If the local practice is to strip outer leaves at the time of harvest, this practice should be followed when collecting field samples. In head lettuce, for example, the lettuce may be packed directly into shipping cartons in the field, in which case 6 or 8 outer leaves are left on the head to be removed at the retail outlet. In other instances, each head is stripped of 2 or 3 outer leaves and individually wrapped in plastic, placed in shipping cartons, and the consumer receives the produce in this condition. Describe sampling method on C/R and describe how packing shed handles produce prior to shipping (e.g., washing, waxing, stripping, etc.).

Soil Samples

Collect soil samples from fields according to the following 3x3 grid diagram:

	a	b	c
1	o	o	o
2	o	o	o
3	o	o	o

Sample at the 9 locations indicated by the "o". If the field being sampled is very large, you may have to sample it using a 4x4, 5x5, or even larger grid pattern.

Subs are to be placed in clean quart glass jars, which have beenwashed in water, rinsed in methanol, and air dried. If methanol is not available, use washed, air dried jars and submit an empty jar as a control. Note on CR that jars were or were not rinsed with methanol.

Obtain two "6 in" deep plugs (1-2 in. in diameter from each sampling location. Place two plugs from each location in cleaned glass jars, place clean aluminum foil over top of jar and seal with screw cap.

Soil samples should be submitted to the lab a 4°C (39°F) or below.

Water Samples - Collect 3 quarts of water from the same sampling source (e.g., faucet, stream, lake, etc.) and place in cleaned, washed and methanol rinsed jars as described under "Soil Samples".

Submit water samples to lab at 4°C (39°F) or below.

GENERAL

Official Samples **shall** be collected whenever feasible unless they are not required to accomplish the objective of the assignment. Investigational Samples **shall** be collected only when Official Samples are not readily available.

See IOM Sample Schedule Chart 4, Wheat Carload Sampling for guidance in the collection of samples by trier from railcars and trucks.

Consult with your supervisor in cases of doubt as to sample cost, size, or collection technique.

When collecting samples in glass jars, line the lids with aluminum foil which has been certified by the laboratory as contaminant free or use teflon lined lids.

If shipment of shell eggs is required and breakage may result during transit, subs may be broken, shells discarded, and liquid magma collected in clean glass jars. Each sub jar should be properly identified.

Samples collected at Packing Sheds should be representative of the produce as shipped in commerce. DO NOT strip outer leaves from subs collected at packing sheds from bulk lots, shipping cartons ready for shipment, intransit lots or at final destination. If the packing shed practice is to strip outer leaves prior to shipment, follow this practice when collecting the samples. Describe the sampling method on the C/R.

DO NOT USE magic markers, etc. to identify sub bags, because the ink may affect assay results. Use stick on labels to identify sub bags.

Collect samples in the container in which the dealer is packaging the product. If the dealer is packaging the product in plastic bags, collect sample in these bags. If the firm is not packing the product, collect the samples in paper bags, cardboard cartons, etc. Do not use plastic bags as this may interfere with the analysis, unless the bags are certified as contaminant free by your district laboratory.

Samples must be delivered as promptly as possible to the laboratory if regulatory action is to be taken against actionable lots.

Hold samples in cold storage until ready to be shipped or delivered to the laboratory only if normally held or shipped under refrigeration in commercial practice.

Use aseptic technique, where applicable, when collecting samples of finished products from bulk containers.

If the "one case" option is used to sample domestic fresh produce from a lot or field, report in the Remarks Section of the C/R, the facts used to determine that the one case is representative of that lot or field.

REMEMBER SURVEILLANCE SAMPLES OF IMPORTED FRESH PRODUCE, EXCEPT FOR SAMPLES OF GRAPES FOR SULFITES, SHOULD BE ONE CASE.

WHEAT CARLOAD SAMPLING

I.   SAMPLING NORMAL CARS

CAUTION: WHEN USING A GRAIN PROBE, BE CAREFUL NOT TO CLOSE THE TRIER COMPARTMENT DOORS ON YOUR FINGERS.

Collect samples only of specific assignment.

A.   Equipment

1.   Double tube compartmented trier, 60 in. long
2.   Sampling cloth at least 60 in. long
3.   1000 ml plastic graduate
4.   Paper bags or other suitable containers capable of holding more than one quart of sample and **do not** use canvas bags.
5.   Fumigant, chloroform or paradichlorobenzene (mothballs)
6.   Absorbent cotton or equivalent
7.   FDA Metal Car Seals for resealing railroad cars
8.   Aluminum ladder
9.   Block and tackle to open railcar door

B.   Drawing Sample

Principal sources of grain samples are railcars, barges, and trucks. Draw 5 probes (in duplicate) for each sample taken as described below. However, if the sample is to be Field Examined, an initial sample of 5 probes drawn as indicated below will be sufficient.

Probe samples from railcars and trucks as follows:

1.   Probe #1 - From Center of car
2.   Probe #2 - From 3-5 feet back from door post toward end of the car and approximately 2 feet from the side of the car.
3.   Probe #3 - From 3-5 feet from the same end of the car, but approximately 2 feet from the opposite side of car as Probe #2.
4.   Probe #4 - Same as Probe #2, but opposite end of car.
5.   Probe #5 - Same as Probe #3, but opposite end of car.

Sketches I and II below are alternatives showing the approximate sampling locations.

```
        I                    II

           5          5
           o          o
     4                      4
     o                      o
           1          1
           o          o
           2          2
           o          o
     3                      3
     o                      o
```

Insert trier in the grain at an angle of about 10° from the vertical, with the slot up and closed. Open slots, give trier 2 or 3 short up and down motions, so that the openings will fill. Close slots (SEE CAUTION AT BEGINNING OF SCHEDULE), withdraw trier and carefully empty over sampling cloth. The cloth should be long enough to catch product from each compartment separately when you open the trier compartment doors; e.g. about 6 feet long.

C.   Field Examination

Examine each pocket of the probe separately, looking for evidence of pink wheat, rodent pellets, insect damage and uneven loading or plugging. Note any insect infestation and record types of insects and whether live or dead. Count and report for each probe the number of rodent pellets, or rodent pellet fragments. Follow procedure in I.C.2 below. Count as pellets any that are sufficiently large to be readily identified by size, shape, surface coating, and/or presence of rodent hairs. Report the number of rodent pellets per sub. Measure the volume of each sub (probe) in quarts and calculate the average number of pellets per quart per I.C.2.a below. Place pellets from each sub in separate vials and submit with each wheat sub. Place each of the wheat subs in clean, suitable containers such as ice cream cartons or temporarily in clean paper bags.

Do not use canvas bags or take glass jars into railcars.

Substantially larger loads will require additional probing or larger samples taken from falling grain during loading or unloading operations.

Submit all suspect samples to laboratory for confirmatory analysis.

1.   Non-Violative Samples. When field examination shows sample as non-violative, return grain to the car, unless collected for pesticide analysis. Report results in the Remarks Section of the C/R.

2.   Violative Samples

a.   Rodent Pellet Contamination. The guideline for determining whether wheat is violative due to rodent contamination is:

"9 mg or more rodent excreta pellets and/or fragments of rodent excreta pellets per kg of wheat."

NOTE: Since it is impractical to weigh rodent pellets and wheat in the field, the following estimations can be used. Mouse pellets average approximately 8.7 mg each and a kilogram of wheat about 2.35 pints. This translates roughly as 1 pellet per quart of wheat or 1/2 pellet per pint.

Where your field examination reveals one or more rodent pellets (or you can estimate that sufficient fragments of rodent pellets exist to equal one pellet) in a quart of wheat, take duplicate probes to furnish the claimants portion. Take the duplicate probes from the same locations as the original probes. Place the duplicates in separate containers and identify these to correspond with the original probes.

b.   Pink Wheat. Where evidence of pink wheat or other fungicide treated wheat is found, collect 15 probe samples. Take 5 probes from each end of the car and 5 probes from the center of the car. Submit the three 5-probe portions separately, using new clean containers.

c.   **Insect Damaged Kernels.** The violative status of these samples should be established by laboratory analysis. When any evidence of insect damage is revealed by cursory examination, collect duplicate samples and submit for laboratory analysis.

3.   **Resealing Cars**   See IOM 424.2.

4.   **Procedures for Actionable Cars.**   If field examination reveals an average of one or more rodent pellets per quart or gross evidence of insect-damaged kernels, evidence of plugging, or "pink wheat" contamination, determine any movement of the car or other disposition of the grain and notify your supervisor immediately.

5.   **Preparation of Sample for Laboratory Analysis.** If a sample can be delivered to the laboratory promptly and confirmatory analysis handled expeditiously, fumigation of the FDA probes is not necessary. The claimant's portion of the sample, however, must be fumigated. Otherwise fumigate all probes with chloroform or other suitable fumigant. Use about 5 ml per pint of wheat if transferred to glass jars. If in ice cream-type containers, use at least 10 ml. **DO NOT** pour fumigant directly on the grain, saturate a piece of absorbent cotton or blotting paper with the fumigant and add to each container. Label to show sample as fumigated and include name of fumigant on label. Officially seal all probes. Keep upright so that fumigant vapors will migrate down through the grain.

D.   **Special Reporting**

Submit an Analyst Worksheet (FDA-431) for each sample analyzed and found in compliance. See IOM 427.1

If field examination shows the sample is possibly actionable, report analytical results in Remarks Section of the C/R.

II.   **SAMPLING PLUGGED CAR**

If uneven loading, layering or "plugging" is suspected, contact your supervisor as to whether to sample or not. A 'plugged' car is a railcar, truck, or barge load of grain where the contamination is suspected of being in only one portion or layer of grain. Plugging is usually the deliberate mixing of violative grain below the surface or in isolated pockets of grain.

A.   **Equipment**
     Equipment needed is the same as in 1.A. above except:
1.   Double tube grain probe must have individual compartments permanently separated.
2.   Small containers of sufficient size to hold the contents of each compartment of each grain probe.

B.   **Procedure**

1.   In the Remarks Section of the C/R, draw a diagram showing actual "plugging" pattern suspected.
2.   Each <u>sample</u> consists of thirty probes of grain with each probe compartment maintained as a separate sub. Each

sample thus consists of 300-330 subs depending on whether a 10 or 11 compartment probe is used and if grain depth is sufficient to insert the probe to fully cover all compartments of the probe.

3.   Probe each load and number the probes as follows:

     1 4 7 10 13 16 19 22 25 28
     2 5 8 11 14 17 20 23 26 29
     3 6 9 12 15 18 21 24 27 30

4.   Identify the subs by probe number plus compartment letter starting with small "a" as the compartment nearest the tip of the probe.
     Example:

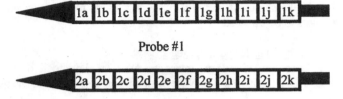

Probe #1

Probe #2

4.   Submit sample to your district's servicing laboratory. See IOM 454.2.

IMPORTED WHITEFISH SAMPLING SCHEDULE

GENERAL

This Sample Schedule objective is to maintain import lot integrity from time of importation thru FDA inspection or examination and final action.

Shipments will be special manifested from non-lab ports to DO cities and other cities designated by the DD as FDA inspection points. These shipments will arrive in Customs bonded trucks under seal applied by Customs at the port of entry. Customs Entry documents and commercial invoice will accompany each shipment. The commercial invoice contains a description of the lots in the shipment and will serve as a guide in the selection of the lots to be sampled.

1. Special Manifested Shipments:

a. Determine if seals are intact and record seal number.

b. FDA metal seals may be broken and lots checked against invoice.

c. Customs seals may be broken only if authorized by Customs.

d. Lots which are not to be examined will be released by completing the "MAY PROCEED" block of the FDA-701.

e. Sample lots to be examined by using either the Single or Sequential Sampling Plan depending on whether examination is made at the DO Lab or at the dock. The Sequential Plan can only be used where additional fish are immediately available for cutting.

2. Definition of a Lot & Selection for Examination.

a. A lot is defined as "Each group of fish of a distinct size, listed in the invoice as from a distinct lake, will be considered as a separate lot. Where an invoice does not list lakes of origin of boxes of fish in a shipment, fish of the same size and kind will be considered to comprise a single lot. When the size of the fish or lakes of origin in a shipment are not specified, the shipment will be treated as a single lot."

b. Limit sampling to lots containing 5 or more boxes unless deliberate splitting up of lots is suspected.

c. Basis for Sampling. Select lots for sampling on either a "selective" or "objective" (random) basis. The criteria in selective sampling may be prior knowledge or suspicion that fish listed as from a given lake are likely to have excess cysts; that the shipper has been known to manipulate shipments; etc. Regardless of the reason for selective
sampling, record the basis for sampling each lot in your examination report. Simply list the basis as "selective" or "objective" next to the results of each lot sampled.

d. Normally, select boxes in a lot for sampling at random. However, where there's evidence of layering, selectively sample the suspect boxes.

a. Imported samples of whitefish & related fish for parasites. The sampling schedules estimate lot quality more precisely, thereby reducing the likelihood of passing a lot which should be detained, or vice versa, due to an inadequate sample.

SCHEDULE A below is a single sample plan for use in collecting samples for examination in the district lab or other location where it is impossible or undesirable to return and obtain additional fish.

SCHEDULE B below contains sequential sampling plans for use when the exam is made at a customs office or a carrier's dock where you have immediate access to the lot and can obtain additional fish, if necessary.

The sequential plan for lots of 20 to 100 boxes is presented in tabular form. the sequential sample plan for lots of 100 or more boxes is presented in a sampling chart. For small lots of 5-20 boxes, a sequential sample plan is not feasible. All import sampling plans are based on lot size and the sizes of the fish in the lot.

When lots are very good or very poor quality, in terms of cyst infestation, double sample plans require a smaller sample size on the average than single sampling plans, to reach a decision.

b. Domestic Samples for Parasites.

1. For Laboratory Examination.

Lots of 11 or more boxes; Collect at least 25 fish from a representative number of boxes.

For small lots, under 11 boxes; Collect 12 fish from a representative number of boxes.

2. For Examination in Other Than Laboratory.

Cut a preliminary sample in accordance with the appropriate double sampling plan, Schedule B. Cut the additional sample where indicated or bring the additional sample to the laboratory for examination.

3. Sampling Schedule.

SCHEDULE A - SINGLE SAMPLE PLAN

Number of Boxes in Lots	NUMBER OF KG'S (POUNDS) IN A SAMPLE 1/		
	Jumbo or Large 2/	Medium 2/	Small 2/
5 - 19 boxes	12.7 Kg (28lbs)	10.5 Kg (23lbs)	7.3 Kg (16lbs)
20 - 100 boxes	24 Kg (73lbs)	20.5 Kg (45lbs)	15 Kg (33lbs)
100 or over	32 Kg (70lbs)	25.5 Kg (56lbs)	17.8 Kg (39lbs)

1/ When an invoice does not designate the size of the fish in the shipment and inspection reveals more than one size in the lot, use sampling plan for medium fish.

2/ RANGE OF WEIGHT OF FISH IN EACH SIZE CLASS:
      SMALL   Under 675 gms (1 1/2lbs)
      MEDIUM 675 gms (1 1/2lbs) & under 1.4 Kg (3lbs)
      LARGE   1.4 Kg (3lbs) & under 1.8 Kg (4lbs)
      JUMBO   Over 1.8 Kg (4lbs)

SCHEDULE B - SEQUENTIAL SAMPLE PLAN

1. Limited to lots of 20 - 100 boxes. 454 Kg (1000lbs) to 2272 Kg (5000lbs)

Size of Fish 1/	Size of preliminary Sample	Cysts/45.5 Kg (100lbs) in Preliminary Sample			Size of ADD'L SMPL	Cysts/45.5 Kg (100lbs) in sample	
		PASS	DETAIN	TAKE ADD'L SMPL		PASS	DETAIN
Large & Jumbo	16 Kg (35lbs)	30 or less	70 or more	31-69	28.6Kg (63lbs)	49 or less	50 or more
Medium					19.5 Kg (43lbs)		50 or more
	12.3 Kg (27lbs)	26 or less	67 or more	27-66		49 or less	
					11.8Kg (26lbs)		50 or more
Small							
	8.2 Kg (18lbs)	38 or less	61 or more	39-61		49 or less	

1/ When an invoice does not designate the size of the fish in the shipment and inspection reveals more than one size in the lot, use sampling plan for medium fish.

2/ For lots of 100 boxes or over, use the Sequential Sampling Chart for the particular size fish in the lot.

WHITEFISH SEQUENTIAL SAMPLING PLAN (WHEN LOT SIZE EXCEEDS 100 BOXES)

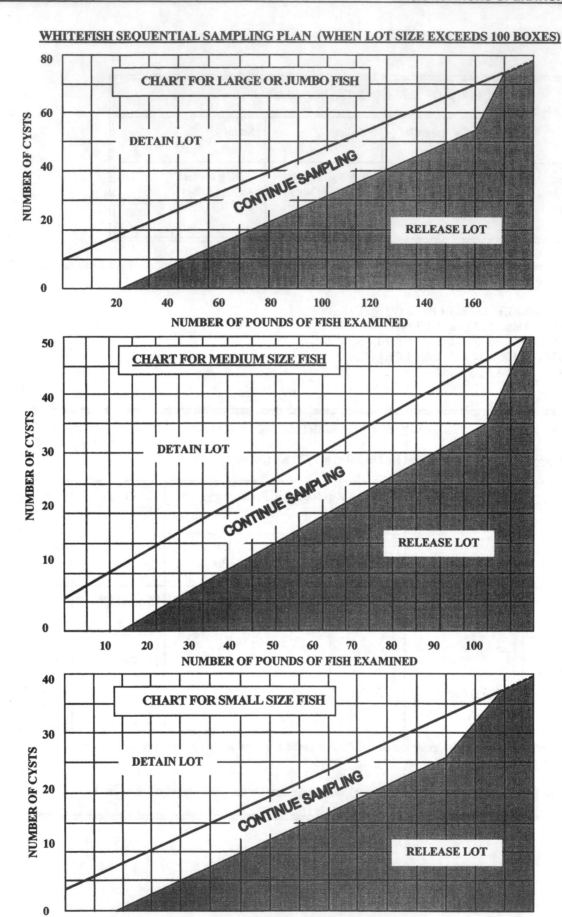

MYCOTOXIN SAMPLE SIZES

PRODUCT SAMPLE SIZES FOR MYCOTOXIN ANALYSIS
(Includes 702(b) portion - each sample unit, contains product for the reserve portion, no duplicate subs are necessary)
NOTE: COMPLIANCE SAMPLE SIZES MAY DIFFER FROM SURVEILLANCE SAMPLE SIZES.

PRODUCT	PACKAGE TYPE	LOT SIZE	NUMBER OF SAMPLE UNITS*	UNIT SIZE (minimum)	TOTAL SAMPLE SIZE (minimum)
Peanut Butter (smooth)	Consumer or bulk	NA	24	225 gm (8 oz)	5.4 Kg (12 lbs)
			12	454 gm (1 lb)	5.4 kg (12 lbs)
Peanut Butter (Crunchy) Peanuts shelled roasted, or unroasted, Peanuts ground for topping	Consumer or bulk	NA	INITIAL SAMPLE		
			10	454 gm (1 lb)	4.5 kg (10 lb)
			AS FOLLOW-UP TO POSITIVE ANALYSIS		
			48	454 gm (1 lb)	21.8 kg (48 lbs)
Peanuts, roasted in shell (only for domestic runner variety)	Consumer or bulk	NA	INITIAL SAMPLE		
			15	454 gm (1 lb)	6.8 kg (15 lbs)
			AS FOLLOW-UP TO POSITIVE ANALYSIS		
			75	454 gm (1 lb)	34 kg (75 lbs)
Tree nuts (except in-shell Brazil Nuts and all pistachio nuts in import status) shelled, in-shell slices, pieces, or flour	Consumer or bulk	NA	INITIAL SAMPLE		
			10	454 gm (1 lb)	4.5 kg (10 lb)
			AS FOLLOW-UP TO POSITIVE ANALYSIS		
			50	454 gm (1 lb)	22.7 kg (50 lbs)
Tree nuts - paste			12	454 gm (1 lb)	5.4 kg (12 lbs)
Brazil Nuts in-shell (in import status)	Bulk	<200 bags 201-800" 801-2000"	20 40 60	454 gm (1 lb) " "	9 kg(20 lbs) 18 kg (40 lbs) 27 kg (60 lbs)
Pistachio nuts in-shell (in import status)	Bulk	multiples of 34,100 kg (75,000 lbs)	20 % of units	---	50 lbs for each multiple of 34,100 kg (75,000 lbs) or less
Pistachio nuts shelled (in import status)		SAME	SAME	---	25 lbs for each multiple of 34,100 kg (75,000 lbs) or less
Corn - shelled, meal flour or grits	Consumer or bulk	NA	10	454 gm (1 lb)	4.5 kg (10 lbs)

209

PRODUCT	PACKAGE TYPE	LOT SIZE	NUMBER OF SAMPLE UNITS*	UNIT SIZE (minimum)	TOTAL SAMPLE SIZE (minimum)
Oil seed meals - Peanut meal, cottonseed meal	Bulk	NA	20	454 gm (1 lb)	9 kg (20 lbs)
Edible seeds** melon pumpkin, sesame, etc	Bulk	NA	**INITIAL SAMPLE** 10	454 gm (1 lb)	4.5 kg (10 lb)
			AS FOLLOW-UP TO POSITIVE ANALYSIS 50	454 gm (1 lb)	22.7 kg (50 lb)
Ginger Root dried whole	Bulk	"n" units	Sq root "n"	---	6.8 kg (15 lbs)
ground	Consumer	NA	16	16-28 gm (1 oz)	4.5 kg (10 lbs)
Milk - whole, skim low fat	Consumer	NA	10	454 gm (1 lb)	4.5 kg (10 lbs)
	Bulk	NA	---	---	4.5 kg (10 lbs)
Small grains - wheat sorghum, barley, etc	Bulk	NA	10	454 gm (1 lb)	4.5 kg (10 lbs)
Dried fruit** - e.g.: Figs	Consumer or bulk	NA	**INITIAL SAMPLE** 10	454 gm (1 lb)	4.5 kg (10 lb)
			AS FOLLOW-UP TO POSITIVE ANALYSIS 50	454 gm (1 lb)	22.7 kg (50 lb)
Mixtures containing commodities susceptible to mycotoxin contamination	Consumer	NA			
Commodity particles relatively large			50	454 gm (1 lb)	22.7 kg (50 lbs)
Commodity particles relatively small			10	454 gm (1 lb)	4.5 kg (10 lbs)

NOTE: Containers for samples of unprocessed, intact nuts, seeds, or grains must be sufficiently porous to provide for dissipation of moisture produced by respiration of the nut, seed, or grain.

*   To be collected from as many random sites in the lot as possible. For surveillance samples, you may combine subs prior to shipping to the laboratory. For compliance samples, you must maintain sub integrity.

**   Optional sampling program for seeds or dried fruit with a low incidence of contamination. Take initial 10 x 454 gm (1 lb) sample. If any aflatoxin is detected, resample 50 x 454 gm (1 lb) sample for determination of contamination level on which to base regulatory judgement.

CANNED FRUIT - FILL OF CONTAINER - AUTHENTIC PACK

Collect samples only on a specific assignment or during inspections when it appears that the firm is not filling the containers to capacity.

A.   <u>INVESTIGATIONAL SAMPLES</u>: Authentic Pack Preparation.

       Procedure for preparing authentic factory packs.

       1.   Remove 72 cans, 3 at a time, from packing line <u>after</u> fruit has been added and <u>before</u> syruping.

       2.   Mark 24 cans with the sub numbers A-1, A-2, A-3, etc.; 24 cans with sub numbers B-1, B-2, B-3; and 24 cans with sub numbers C-1, C-2, C-3, etc. See IOM 451.3.

       3.   Drain water from the "B" subs by inverting each can for 10 seconds, holding the fruit so it doesn't fall out.

       4.   Obtain gross weight of each can and record data for each series of sub on 3 separate FDA-485 - Field Weight Sheets.

       5.   Add additional fruit of the same kind and style to the "C" subs until the cans are filled to capacity. **Do not** tamp the contents or crush the fruit.

       6.   Record the number of fruit pieces added where the size of the fruit makes the procedure reasonable. **Do not** make time consuming counts of small pieces of fruit or berries.

       7.   Obtain the gross weight of the "C" subs after additional fruit is added and record on "C" series Field Weight Sheet.

       8.   Return all 72 cans to the filling line for syruping, exhausting, sealing, etc. in normal cannery operation.

       9.   Remove cans after cooking and cooling.

     10.   Identify cans with a single INV Sample number.

     11.   Attach FDA-485 - Field Weight Sheets to C/R.

B.   <u>OFFICIAL SAMPLES</u>

       See Sample Schedule Chart 2 for sample size.

C.   <u>SPECIAL REPORTING AND PRECAUTIONS</u>

       1.   Report coding of cans and shipping cases.

       2.   Obtain label specimen(s) for the slack filled products.

       3.   Report shipments made before the inspection or since previous inspection in the same canning season.

       4.   **Do not** prepare Authentic Factory Samples when the cannery is packing for USDA fill-of-container certification unless:

         a.   USDA inspection is not continuous.
         b.   USDA Certification is for quality only.
         c.   USDA recommendations for weights are not being followed.

D.   <u>SAMPLE SUBMISSION</u>

       Submit samples to your district's designated workplan servicing laboratory.

IMPORTS - COFFEE, DATES AND DATE MATERIAL

1. Coffee - Wharf Examination - Note: Wharf Examine a minimum of six bags of coffee beans regardless of lot size. If a significant number of defective beans or significant contamination is found during the examination of these six bags, continue the examination using the following schedule, which applies for both Wharf Examination and samples for laboratory analysis:

LOT SIZE	NO. BAGS TO BE SAMPLED
100 or less	6 bags
101-200	10 bags
201-1000	15 bags
over 1000	20 bags

Sample each bag with a trier, collecting 1/2 pt. of beans from the top and 1/2 pt. from the bottom of the bag. The total quantity of beans taken from each bag must be the same, since both wharf and laboratory examinations are to be performed on a composite sample of all beans collected.

Shake each sub on a #8 sieve nested in a pan. Dump the sifted beans from each sub into a bag of sufficient size to hold and permit mixing all of the subs collected from the lot. Composite the subs. Do not maintain individually.

(a) Macroscopic Filth
Examine the siftings for macroscopic filth (live and dead whole insects, excreta pellets, extraneous material and sweepings), reporting findings for each sub separately. See IOM 427.4.

Transfer macroscopic filth, including all sifted material to a second bag and submit to the laboratory for confirmation. If live insect infestation is encountered, fumigate the filth portion containing the insects and the composite coffee bean sample. Report fumigant on CR and FDA-525. The lot will be detained if a live insect infestation is encountered, however, proceed with the defect bean examination since the reconditioning process will depend on the results.

(b) Defect Bean Examination
Thoroughly mix the composite sample of coffee beans and remove three-hundred beans at random. Examine each individual bean visually (or at a 5X magnification) for insect tunneling and mold damage. Count as moldy only those beans with 1/4 or more of the surface being moldy. Note: Each district office has examples of the various types of reject beans.

(c) Accept the lot if twenty or less rejects are found and discard the sample. Report your wharf examination into FACTS; no Sample Collection Report is necessary.

(d) If twenty-one or more rejects are detected, return beans examined to the composite and submit to the laboratory. You may discontinue the examination when twenty-one rejects are detected.

When a sample is submitted to the laboratory, all wharf examination time is reported as a field exam in FACTS and the sample collection time is reported as an import sample collection. All necessary documents for an import sample collection must be completed.

2. Dates & Date Material - Filth

Sample according to the following schedule:

NUMBER OF SUBSAMPLES REQUIRED**

NO. CONTAINERS IN LOT*	WHOLE DATES	DATE MATERIAL
100 or less	3	4
101 - 600	8	6
601 - 1,200	14	8
1,201 - 2,000	26	10
2,001 - 2,800	36	12
2,801 - 6,000	44	14
6,001 - 9,600	56	16
9,601 - 15,000	68	18
Over 15,000	82	22

* Schedule is based upon unit containers weighing between twenty and one-hundred pounds. For containers exceeding one-hundred pounds each, consider as two or more containers. For example, a one-hundred and fifty pound container is considered as two containers; a three-hundred pound container as three containers, etc.

** Each subsample should consist of two-hundred to three-hundred dates or two pounds of date material.

(a) Identify each subsample separately. Each lot will be a separate sample.

(b) Do not sample jujubes as dates. These are usually labeled as Chinese Red Dates, Dried Red Dates, or Honey Dates. Jujubes are not considered to be misbranded when called Chinese Red Dates, etc., because of the long standing use of these names. Sample jujubes following the above schedule, except duplicate subs are not necessary.

(c) If live insects are noted, include these as part of the sample collected and report on the C.R. which subs contained the insects and how many insects, adult or larvae, were noted. If live infestation is noted, place all subs from the lot sampled in clear glass jars and fumigate. Report what the fumigant used on the FDA-525 and the C.R.

SAMPLING SCHEDULE FOR COLOR
CONTAINING PRODUCTS
COLOR ADDITIVES

The following schedule provides general guidance for collecting samples of foods and cosmetics to determine whether non-permitted colors are present, rather than to determine the actual level of a particular color. This schedule was developed with the assumption that color distribution in the lot will be homogeneous. In the case of heterogeneous products, your supervisor should contact Center for Food Safety and Applied Nutrition, Office of Field Programs, Division of Enforcement (HFS-605) to determine sample size.

Sample size given includes the 702(b) portion.

INDUSTRY CODE		SAMPLE SIZE
		(DO NOT COMMINGLE CODES) (Min. 225 gm (8 oz)/pkg Unless otherwise specified)

GRAIN AND BAKING

02	Whole grains, Milled Grain Products and Starch	2 retail packages
03	Bakery Products, Doughs, Bakery Mixes, and Icings	2 retail packages
04	Macaroni and Noodle Products	2 retail packages
05	Cereal Preparations Breakfast Foods	2 retail packages
07	Snack Food Items (Flour, Meal, or Vegetable Base)	2 retail packages

DAIRY

09	Milk, Butter, and Dried Milk Pdts	Liquid Pdts: 2 pts where possible Solid: 2 packages
12	Cheese and Cheese Products	2 retail packages
13	Ice Cream and Related Products	6 items per sample (If item is single serving; ie., cup, popsicle, bar, etc.) 2 pt containers where possible, or 1 quart or 1/2 gal
14	Filled Milk and Imitation Milk Products	2 pints

EGGS

| 15 | Egg and Egg Pdts | 2 dozen whole eggs (e.g. colored hard boiled Easter eggs) 2 retail pkg of egg pdts |

FISH

| 16 | Fishery/Seafood Pdts | 2 retail packages. Any collection of smoked salmon should be selective, based on inspectional evidence |

MEAT & SIMULATED MEAT PRODUCTS

| 17 | Meat, Meat Products and Poultry | 2 retail packages |
| 18 | Vegetable Protein Pdts | 2 retail packages |

FRUIT, NUT AND VEGETABLE PRODUCTS

20-22	Fruit & Fruit Pdts	2 retail packages canned or glazed. 12 fresh fruit (e.g., oranges, etc.).
23	Nuts & Edible Seeds	2 retail packages
24-25	Vegetable & Vegetable Products	2 retail packages
26	Vegetable Oils & Olive Oil	Liquids - 2 pints Solids - 2 retail packages

DRESSINGS AND SPICES

| 27 | Dressings & Condiments | 2 retail packages |
| 28 | Spices, Flavors, & Salts | Extracts - 2 pints Solids - 2 retail packages |

BEVERAGES

29	Soft Drinks & Waters	6 Retail Units (Cans, Bottles, Packets)
30	Beverage Bases, Concentrates, and Nectars	Liquids - 1 pint Solids (Powder mix, packets) – 6 Consumer Pkg Solids - 2/225 gm (8 oz) or larger containers
31	Coffee and Tea	2 retail packages
32	Alcoholic Beverages	2 pints or 1 quart

CONFECTIONS AND DESSERTS

33	Candy w/o chocolate, Candy Specialties, and Chewing Gum	2 retail packages
34	Chocolate & Cocoa Pdts	2 retail packages
35	Gelatin, Rennet,	6 pkgs - smallest

	Pudding Mixes, & Pie Fillings	consumer size
36	Food Sweeteners (Nutritive)	2 pints

MULTIPLE FOODS, SOUPS, SALADS, BABY FOOD AND DIETARY

37	Multiple Food Dinners Gravies, Sauces and Specialties (Total	Single Serving Dinners, etc - 4 pkgs Two Consumer Pkgs when 1 pkg serves more than 2
38	Soups	Same as 37 Above
39	Prepared Salad Products	Same as 37 Above
40	Baby (Infant and Junior) Food Pdts	Sufficient retail pkgs to total at least 454 gm (1 lb) of food
41	Dietary Conventional Foods and Meal Replacements	Same as 37 Above

COLORS AND COSMETICS

50	Color Additives for Foods Drugs, and Cosmetics	1. Straight Color 28 gm (1 oz) powder. 2. Color Mixtures 110 gms (4 oz) Liq, paste or powder. If mixture contains over 50% pure dye, 55 gm (2 oz) is sufficient
53	Cosmetics	Four retail packages of the same lot code for each shade (color) in the product line, if the product is strongly colored. (e.g., Lipsticks, hair coloring products, eye mascara, eye liners, make up pencils of all types) Sufficient number of retail packages to equal 1 lb or 1 pt of sample if the product is lightly colored. (e.g., creams, lotions, shampoos, bath products, shaving preparations, and perfumes.) Note: Always collect a minimum of two retail units of each product.

MISCELLANEOUS

	Bulk Items (Any bulk food or cosmetic)	Dry - 454 gm (1 lb) Liquid - Min 36 fl oz

DRUG SAMPLING SCHEDULES
(Does not include Antibiotic Preparations)

STERILITY TESTING VITAMINS, DEVICES, & DRUGS

Type of Product	Sample Size[1]	
	INV Sample[2]	Official [702(b) & Check][3]
DRUGS	36	86
DEVICES	46	106

LEGEND:
1. Double sample size requirements when individual containers are 2 ml (2 gm) or smaller.
2. INV sample includes units (30 for Drugs & 40 for devices) for examination and 6 units for bacteriostasis.
3. Official Sample includes units (30 for drugs & 40 for devices) for examination, units (30-40) for check, 20 units for 702(b) and 6 for bacteriostasis.

Note: If a lot is aseptically filled into 200 finished units or less, sample no less than 10% of lot.

DISSOLUTION TEST - USP & NF

Unless directed otherwise by your assignment or supervisor, submit samples to your normal servicing laboratory.

SAMPLE SIZE

Collect a 200 tablet portion for drug potency analysis by the collecting district lab, plus a separate 100 tab portion to be split for dissolution testing

MICROBIOLOGICAL EXAMINATION OF DRUGS (Other than for Sterility)

PRODUCT	MINIMUM SAMPLE SIZE (Includes 702(b) portion)	
	Sub Size	Nos. of Subdivisions
Dosage Form Drugs (See #1 below), Bulk Drugs, or Raw Materials for Manufacturing	90 gm or 90 ml	10

SAMPLING INSTRUCTIONS

1 Contact the laboratory (which has microbiological testing capabilities) serving your district for sample size requirements before sampling dosage form drugs containing less than 3 grains, 200 mg, or 25% of the suspect ingredient.

2. Use aseptic technique when collecting samples from raw materials or bulk containers. Implements and sample containers used must be sterile. Submit controls. See IOM 446 thru 446.4.

3. Submit samples to the laboratory with microbiological testing capabilities which serves your district unless directed otherwise.

215

VITAMIN SAMPLING

VETERINARY PRODUCTS, FEEDS, & BY-PRODUCTS FOR ANIMAL FEEDS

A.   GENERAL

This sampling schedule may be used as a guide in the collection of surveillance or compliance samples resulting from district assignments or as a follow-up to violative inspections and/or investigations.   Before collecting follow-up samples to violative inspections or investigations, contact your supervisor since it may be necessary for your district to consult with the Atlanta Center for Nutrient Analysis (HFR-SE680) when unscheduled compliance sampling is contemplated.

B.   SAMPLE PRODUCT, SIZE, & SPECIAL INSTRUCTIONS

Vitamin-mineral testing, sampling instructions and information. Sample size includes 702(b) portion.

Unless excessive cost is a factor, collect at least 3 intact containers from each lot or control number. When sampling from bulk lots, collect appropriate subs from a minimum of 3 different bulk containers in the lot.

DOSAGE FORM VITAMIN-MINERAL PREPARATIONS (Single/Multiple Ingredients)

PRODUCT	NO. SUBSAMPLES	MINIMUM TOTAL SAMPLE SIZE	REMARKS
Injectables	3 vials/amps	30 ml	Split samples for sterility testing (60 vials/amps)
Tabs/Caps	3 retail units	300 Tabs/Caps	Split sample for micro tests (10/50 tab/cap subs)
Liquids	3 retail units	4 fl. oz.	Split sample for micro tests (10/2 fl. oz. subs)
3 retail units	112	gm (4 oz)	Same as above

FEEDS & BY-PRODUCTS FOR ANIMAL FEEDS (Vitamin-Mineral Claims)

Vitamin A & D Concentrates, Supplements & (A&D feeding	3 retail units(1/2 gal or less)	3 lbs (1.4 kg) 3 pints	Limit samples to those products containing at least 800 units/g Vit A and/or 80 Feeds units/g Vit D
Vitamin B_2 (Riboflavin) Concentrates, Supplements, & feeds	Same	Same	Limit samples to those products containing at least 20 mg/lb
Vitamin B_{12} (Cyanocobalamin) Concentrates, Supplements & feeds	Same	Same	Limit samples to those products containing at least 1 mg/lb
Multiple Vitamins Concentrates, Supplements, & feeds.	Same	Same	Limit samples to those products meeting vitamin levels listed above.

C. SAMPLE SUBMISSION
Submit all samples for Vitamin Potency analysis to the Atlanta Center for Nutrient Analysis (HFR-SE680).
Submit samples for filth analysis, microbiological examination, sterility, etc. to your district servicing laboratory.

MEDICATED ANIMAL FEEDS SAMPLING

1. Medicated Premixes
   A. Investigational Samples (INV Samples)

   To demonstrate suspected drug carryover or other chemical contamination during manufacturing, collect 1-900 gm (2 lbs) of static residual material in the equipment, and the finished product premixes.

   B. Official Physical Samples 702(b) Portion Included

   For expensive premixes or components, collect a total of 3/170 gm (6 oz) subs; One sub from each of 3 containers. In the case of premixes packaged in plastic, e.g., mini-packs, follow instructions under bagged premixes.

   1. Bagged Premixes

   Collect 10 - 454 gm (1 lb) subs from each lot. Sample all bags in lots under 10 bags, for a total of 10 subs from the lot.

   Collect 454 gm (1 lb) subs from at least 10 different bags selected at random in lots of more than 10 bags.

   2. Bulk Premixes

   Collect at least 10 - 454 gm (1 lb) subs, from different locations in the lot providing a minimum total sample of 4.5 Kg (10 lbs).

   C. Documentary Samples (DOC Sample) - Refer to IOM 405.12 for guidance on the collection of DOC Samples.

II. Medicated Feeds
   A. Investigational Samples (INV Sample)

   Collect 1 - 900 gm (2 lb) of static residual material in the equipment and correlate with finished feed samples to show that residues are being carried over into the finished product.

   B. Official Samples (Includes 702(b) portion)

   1. Bagged Complete Feed

   Collect a total sample of not less than 2.3 Kg (5 lbs) from each lot. Collect 454 gm (1 lb) subs sampling all available bags from lots of 10 bags or less. If lot size is greater than 10 bags, collect 454 gm (1 lb) from each of 10 bags selected at random.

   2. Bulk Complete Feed

   Collect at least 10 - 454 (1lb) subs from different points in the bulk lot to obtain a minimum total sample of 4.5 kg (10 lbs).

   3. Concentrates/Supplements

   If the concentrate or supplement is relatively inexpensive, follow the sampling procedures for complete feeds. Limit sampling of more expensive drug materials, concentrates, or supplements to no more than 3 containers taking a 170 gm (6 oz) or 6 fl. oz. sub from each of the 3 containers.

   C. Documentary Samples (DOC Sample)

   1. Feed Subject to MFA Approval - Collect DOC Samples of products processed without required MFA approval. Where the plant does not ship in IS commerce, but ingredients are received from IS sources, document the IS nature of drug ingredients and the "Held For Sale" status of the finished feed. Labeling of drug ingredients must be submitted.

   2. Misbranded Products - Collect a DOC Sample for misbranding or labeling deficiencies. The failure to provide warning and/or withdrawal statements which could present danger to animals or man, or gross evidence of false and misleading therapeutic claims, are factors for consideration.

III. Sampling Precautions (See IOM CHART 4)
   A. Insert the trier the full length of the bag when sampling bagged premixes, or complete feeds.

   B. Clean trier between sampling the different lots of premixes or complete feeds.

   C. Place subs in clean airtight container, preferably clean glass jars.

   D. DO not fumigate samples intended for potency analysis, drug carryover or cross-contamination.

IV. Sample Submission
   Submit samples to your district's servicing laboratory or as directed by your assignment or supervisor. See IOM 454.2.

CHAPTER 5 - ESTABLISHMENT INSPECTION

CONTENTS

SUBCHAPTER 500 - INSPECTION INFORMATION

501   AUTHORITY TO ENTER AND INSPECT

See IOM 701 for discussion of statutory authority.

FDA Investigator's Responsibility - Your authority to enter and inspect establishments is predicated upon specific obligations to the firm as described below. It is your responsibility to conduct all inspections at reasonable times and within reasonable limits and in a reasonable manner. Proceed with diplomacy, tact and persuasiveness.

Credentials - Display your credentials to the top management official be it the owner, operator, or agent in charge. See IOM 511.

NOTE: Although management may examine your credentials and record the number and your name, do not permit your credentials to be photocopied. Federal Law (Title 18, U.S.C. 701) prohibits photographing, counterfeiting, or misuse of official credentials.

Written Notice - After showing the firm's representative your credentials, issue the original, properly executed, and signed FDA 482, Notice of Inspection, to the top management official. Keep the carbon copy for submission with your report.

Written Observations - Upon completing the inspection and before leaving the premises, provide the highest management official available your inspectional findings on an FDA 483 - Inspectional Observations. See Section 704(b) of the FD&C Act and IOM 512 & 516.

Receipts - Furnish the top management official the original of the FDA-484 - Receipt for Samples describing any samples obtained during the inspection. See IOM 513.

Written Demand for Records - In low-acid canned food and acidified food EI's, an FDA 482a - Demand for Records is required under 21 CFR 108.35(h) and 21 CFR 108.25(g) to obtain records required by 21 CFR 113 and 114.

Written Request for Information - In low-acid canned foods and acidified foods EI's, an FDA 482b, Request for Information, is required under 21 CFR 108.35(c)(3)(ii) and 21 CFR 108.25(c)(3)(ii) to obtain information concerning processes and procedures required under 21 CFR 113 and 114.

It is your obligation to fulfill these requirements because failure to do so may prevent use of evidence and information obtained during the inspection.

501.1 Business Premises

Authority to inspect firms operating at a business location is described in IOM 501 and requires issuing management an FDA 482, Notice of Inspection, and presenting your credentials. A warrant for inspection is not necessary unless a refusal or partial refusal is encountered or anticipated.

501.2 Premises Used for Living Quarters

All inspections where the premises are also used for living quarters must be conducted with a warrant for inspec-

tion unless:

Owner Agreeable - The owner or operator is fully agreeable and offers no resistance or objection whatsoever or;

Physically Separated - The actual business operations to be inspected are physically separated from the living quarters by doors or other building construction. These would provide a distinct division of the premises into two physical areas, one for living quarters and the other for business operations, and you do not enter the living area.

501.3 Facilities where Electronic Products are Used or Held

Section 537(a) of the Radiation Control for Health and Safety Act of 1968 (P.L. 90-602) provides the FDA with the authority to inspect the facilities of manufacturers in certain circumstances.

It is lawful for FDA personnel to enter the facilities of an electronic product distributor, dealer, assembler or user for the purpose of testing an electronic product for radiation safety when the entry is voluntarily permitted. Congress has not specifically prohibited FDA from conducting such voluntary examinations and such examinations would clearly agree with the congressional declaration of purpose expressed in section 532(a) of the RCH&S Act.

Under the Medical Device Authority, electronic products utilized in human and/or veterinary medicine, e.g., x-ray, laser, ultra-sound, diathermy, etc. can be considered prescription devices. In these cases the authority of Section 704 of the FD&C Act can be used to obtain entry to inspect the user facility. If the Medical Device Authority is utilized, credentials must be displayed and a FDA 482, Notice of Inspection, must be issued.

501.4 Multiple Occupancy Inspections

You are required to issue a Notice of Inspection, FDA 482, to each firm inspected. When firms have operations located in different sites or buildings, you should use judgment to determine when multiple FDA 482 forms need to be issued. For sites located a distance apart, it is preferable to issue an FDA 482 to the most responsible person at each site. One rule of thumb that can be used is if the sites or buildings are within walking distance, your original Notice of Inspection can be considered sufficient to cover both. During your initial interview with management, when you issue the FDA 482, make sure you clearly indicate the facility and sites you intend to inspect. If management requests separate notices, cooperate and issue them. There is no harm in issuing more than one to cover a single inspection operation at multiple sites as long as you clearly explain the situation in your narrative report.

The following instructions are to be followed when more than one firm operates in the same facility and apply to situations covered by 21 CFR 201.1(c) et al.

1.   Issue one FDA 482, Notice of Inspection, for the location inspected, but list all known firms using that location. Issue the FDA 482 to the person in charge. If multiple firms are represented on site by separate people, give

them each a copy of the FDA 482. If necessary issue additional FDA 482(s).

If you later determine other firms besides those listed on the original FDA 482 are using the facility, issue a revised FDA 482 to cover those firms.

2.   Inspect the firm premises according to your assignment including each firm listed on the FDA 482.

(a)   Ask to examine records of each firm. If there are no records for a firm on site, report that fact.

(b)   If the lessee firm's records are on site but they have no representative available and the lessor firm states permission to examine records must come from elsewhere, request them to quickly obtain permission for record examination and offer to provide a copy of the FDA 482.

(c)   Determine individual responsibility for each firm operating on the premises at the time of the inspection. Give detailed information of the responsibilities between the lessee/lessor firms.

3.   Closeout discussion with management should be conducted with all firm representatives present at the same time. However, if requested by the firm(s), the discussion may be done separately.

4.   Report the inspection into FACTS as one inspection using the FEI/Registration number of the lessor firm.

5.   One EIR will be written incorporating all of the facts into one narrative. Each firm's separate operations should be reported under a separate EIR heading for that firm's operations.

501.5 Authority for Examinations and Investigations

Section 702(a) of the FD&C Act authorizes examinations and investigations for the purpose of enforcing the Act.

501.6 Authority to Implement Section 702(e)(5) of the FD&C Act

Background - Section 702(e) contains certain authorities relating to counterfeit drugs including the authority to seize ("confiscate") counterfeit drugs and containers, counterfeiting equipment, and all other items used or designed for use in making counterfeit drugs prior to the initiation of libel proceedings. This authority has been delegated, with certain restrictions, to holders of official credentials consistent with their authority to conduct enforcement activities. Additional authority in 702(e) to make arrests, to execute and serve arrest warrants, to carry firearms, or to execute seizure by process under Section 304 of the FD&C Act have not been delegated.

The agency does intend to utilize the authority contained in Section 702(e) to execute and serve search warrants, but such use does not require delegation from the ACRA.

Section 702(e)(5) contains authority for such delegated persons to confiscate all items which are, or which the investigator has reasonable grounds to believe are, subject to seizure under Section 304(a)(2). Items subject to seizure, and thus to confiscation under Section 702(e)(5), includes most things associated with counterfeit drugs. Confiscation authority does not, however, extend to vehicles, records, or items (i.e. the profits) obtained as a result of counterfeiting.

Scope - Under this delegation, with supervisory concurrence and prior to the initiation of libel proceedings, investigators and inspectors are authorized to confiscate: (1) any counterfeit drug, (2) any container used to hold a counterfeit drug, (3) any raw material used in making a counterfeit drug, (4) any labeling used for counterfeit drug, (5) any equipment used to make a counterfeit drug including punches, dies, plates, stones, tableting machines, etc., (6) any other thing which you have reasonable grounds to believe is designed or used in making a counterfeit drug.

NOTE: You and your supervisor must be constantly aware of the potential dangers involved in confiscating property from individuals. Special care should be taken to ensure your safety. Arranging for teams of investigators to conduct the investigation, or arranging for assistance by local police, or other agencies with police powers, should be considered in planning the confiscation of counterfeit materials.

Inspectional Guidance - Guidance provided for implementing the authority to confiscate drug counterfeits is as follows:

1.   The authority is not to be utilized unless there has been an agency determination the drug to be confiscated is a counterfeit and it is a drug which "without authorization, bears a trademark, *** or any likeness" of a legitimate product. The determination usually is based upon evidence supplied by the firm whose product is being counterfeited. A written agency determination will issue to the District Director from the Office of Enforcement, in conjunction with the Office of Regional Operations, and the Center for Drug Evaluation and Research.

2.   When engaged in counterfeit investigations, you should proceed as follows upon encountering items to be confiscated.

(a)   Evaluate safety needs and check the location to ensure it is safe to proceed. Do not attempt to remove an item by force. If it appears there will be resistance, contact the local police, or other agencies with police powers for backup, if not already done in advance.

(b)   Inventory the items to be confiscated.

(c)   Prepare a written receipt and offer it to the person in charge.

(d)   Remove the items, if possible, from the premises (if they cannot be removed, secure them under seal).

(e)   Place all items removed under lock at a secure location. In most cases, confiscated items will be stored at the district or resident post office until they are seized.

Follow up Guidance - After items are confiscated, certain actions must be taken to bring confiscated items under the control of the court. Proceed as follows:

1.   After an item is confiscated, immediately notify your supervisor.

2.   Supervisors must then notify the appropriate compliance units of the items confiscated.

3.   Compliance units should initiate seizure proceedings against any items confiscated.

4.   ORO/DFI should be advised of any action utilizing this authority.

Search Warrants - Section 702(e)(2) contains authority to execute and serve search warrants. Proceed as instructed by your district after a search warrant has been obtained.

501.7 Products Imported Under the Provisions of Section 801(D)(3) of the FFD&CA

The FDA Export Reform and Enhancement Act of 1996 (PL 104-134 and 104-180) amended the FFD&CA by adding Section 801(d)(3) ("Import for Export") which permits the importation of unapproved drug and medical device components, food additives, color additives, and dietary supplements intended for further incorporation or processing into products destined for export from the United States. At time of entry the importer must declare the initial owner or consignee intends to incorporate the imported articles into products destined for export. In addition, the initial owner or consignee must keep records showing the use of the imported articles, and must be able to provide upon request a report showing the disposition or export of the imported articles. An article imported under this section and not incorporated or further processed must be destroyed or exported by the owner or consignee. Failure to keep records or to make them available to FDA, making false statements in such records, failure to export or destroy imported articles not further incorporated into finished products, and introduction of the imported article or final product into domestic commerce are Prohibited Acts under Section 301(w).

(NOTE: FDA is in the process of drafting regulations specifying the reporting and record keeping requirements for Section 801(d)(3). Draft Guidance for Industry was published for comment in the Federal Register on June 12, 1998. Until regulations take effect, districts should refer to the following:)

Filers making entry under the Import for Export provisions must either identify entry submissions with Affirmation of Compliance "IFE" (Import for Export), or supply FDA with written documentation stating the product is entered under the Import for Export provisions. Districts receiving such written documentation will forward it to the home district of the initial owner or consignee for incorporation into the appropriate Establishment File.

Before conducting an Establishment Inspection, contact your district's designated individual with access to OASIS/EEPS Reports to obtain a printout of any import entries made by the establishment under the Import for Export provisions through OASIS. In addition, check the Establishment file for copies of any Import for Export documents forwarded from the district where entry was filed. During the inspection examine the firm's records to determine the disposition of any items identified at time of entry as intended for incorporation into products for export. Document any instances in which such products were introduced into domestic commerce or cannot be accounted for.

502   INSPECTIONAL APPROACH

An establishment inspection is a careful, critical, official examination of a facility to determine its compliance with laws administered by FDA. Inspections may be used to obtain evidence to support legal action when violations are found, or they may be directed to obtaining specific information on new technologies, good commercial practices, or data for establishing food standards or other regulations.

The kind and type of inspection you conduct will normally be defined by the program, assignment, or your supervisor; according to the following definitions:

Comprehensive Inspection - directs coverage to everything in the firm subject to FDA jurisdiction to determine the firms compliance status; or

Directed Inspection - directs coverage to specific areas to the depth described in the program, assignment, or as instructed by your supervisor.

See IOM Subchapter 140 for information on safety, use of protective gear, dealing with potential hazards and other safety issues.

502.1 Depth of Inspection

The degree and depth of attention given various operations in a firm depends upon information desired, or upon the violations suspected or likely to be encountered. In determining the amount of attention to be given in specific cases, consider:

1.   The current Compliance Program,
2.   Nature of the assignment,
3.   General knowledge of the industry and its problems,
4.   Firm history, and
5.   Conditions found as the inspection progresses.

502.2 Signing Non-FDA Documents

Occasionally a firm will request you sign various documents including:

1.   A waiver which will exempt the firm from any responsibility or liability should an accident occur and you are injured on the firm's premises,

2.   Form letters concerning access to confidential information the firm does not want released,

3.   Information/data you request during the inspection be put into writing, etc.

If you receive such a request, inform the firm you are not authorized to sign such documents, letters, requests, waivers, etc., but will report the firm's request in your EIR. The use of common sense is expected with this procedure. All FDA employees are authorized to sign-in and sign-out at a firm and to comply with security measures employed by the firm, including documenting the removal/replacement of seals to inspect vehicles and containers. See IOM 424 & 453.6. Obviously, the key issue is you are not authorized to waive, without supervisory approval, any of FDA's rights to inspect, sample, photograph, copy, etc. or to sign any interstate shipping record document which could infer the firm could not be prosecuted under the Act.

502.3 Technical Assistance

If you determine specialized technical assistance is necessary in conducting inspections of new technologies, products or manufacturing procedures, it may be available through Regional or National experts, other ORA components or Center scientists and engineers. If specialized skills are necessary and are not available locally or through your Region, contact the Division of Field Investigations, (HFC-130) at (301) 827-5653. See FMD 142 and IOM 271.2 for additional information.

502.4 Team Inspections

The use of teams to conduct inspections may be beneficial. Very often individuals well versed in an analytical or inspectional technique or technology can provide assistance and advice.

When inspection teams are involved in an inspection, one investigator will be designated as the team leader by the inspecting district or by the Division of Field Investigations (DFI/HFC-130) if a headquarters directed special inspection is involved. The team leader is in charge of the inspection and bears the overall responsibility for the inspection and the EIR. A team may consist of multiple investigators, laboratory personnel and other FDA employees, and your supervisor/coach, who may participate as part of the ORA Quality Assurance program.

Each team member is responsible for preparing those portions of the report pertaining to his/her activities. Team members shall identify their portion of the report so they can later identify that portion as the part he/she performed and reported. Since reports should be written in the first person, one system might be to head each portion with a statement "The following operation(s) was/were observed and reported by Investigator _____", who can then report in the first person.

All team members must sign the original EIR. Ideally, all team members should sign the FDA 483, if one is issued. However, issuance of the FDA 483 should not be delayed, in the absence of a team member's signature. See IOM 512 for instructions for signing a multi-page FDA 483.

The Team Leader shall be responsible for:

1. Issuing unused diary notebooks for taking notes during the EI or investigation to headquarters personnel on the team. He/she is also responsible for instructions on their use, if necessary, and when the report is finished, for obtaining the headquarters individual's signature on the original EIR and completed and properly identified diaries and submitting them to the supervisor for filing. See IOM 193.

2. Directing the overall inspection to accomplish the objectives of the assignment including;

(a) planning the inspection,

(b) scheduling and coordinating team members' pre-inspection preparations,

(c) determining, to the extent possible, the firm will be open and operating,

(d) planning for needs of visiting scientists if applicable. When the team leader is not familiar with all the processes or technology involved in the inspection, provide for primary coverage of selected areas by other team members,

(e) determining an orderly, efficient, and effective approach and sequence to be used and discussing the inspection plan with the team,

(f) modifying the inspection plan as necessary during the EI, to permit following leads, documenting evidence, etc.,

(g) setting team policy on how communications with the firm are to be handled,

(h) discussing personal conduct in dealing with headquarters personnel as necessary,

(i) assuring an early understanding by team members of their roles in note taking and reporting,

(j) assuring communications are open among team members, especially if the team is allowed to separate and work independently,

(k) reviewing inspection progress at least daily, discussing remaining objectives with the team members, and setting objectives for the following day,

(l) continually assessing the progress of the inspection to evaluate how the inspectional approach is working and to keep the district supervisor advised of the inspection's progress,

(m) providing guidance and direction to team members as necessary,

(n) advising each team member of reporting responsibilities and dates when drafts are to be provided,

(o) following up promptly on any delays or failures to report as required, and

(p) assisting the supervisor with further follow up, as indicated.

3. Making sure any person who joins the team after the inspection has started presents credentials and issues a Notice of Inspection, FDA 482, to the firm prior to actually taking part in the EI;

4. Completing and/or correcting the computer generated coversheet;

5. Preparing the Summary of Findings;

6. Completing all headings of an administrative nature in the narrative report;

7. Compiling and submitting the complete final report; and

8. Resolving any disputes or differences of opinion among the team members, including items, which may be listed on the FDA 483.

503 INSPECTION OF FOREIGN FIRMS

Inspectional requirements apply to all inspections, including foreign inspections. However, there are some exceptions. For instance the FDA 482 is not required, unless the firm is a US Military facility.. Be guided by relevant Compliance Programs and the Guide to International Inspections and Travel Manual for other differences. See IOM 111.2.

504 INSPECTIONAL PRECAUTIONS

Our concern over microbiological contamination emphasizes the need for you to be alert to criticism or allegations that you may have contributed to or caused contamination at a firm. This is especially important in drug firms and high-risk food firms, among others. You must adhere to good sanitation practices to refute any such criticisms. You could also unknowingly introduce or spread disease during inspections of or visits to animal production or sale facilities, conducting environmental investigations at poultry layer facilities, conducting dairy farm inspections or audits of state activities, investigating tissue residue reports or working in the veterinary bioresearch area. See IOM section 519 for information outlining precautions for you to follow.

Exercise caution in all activities in the firm. Follow the firm's sanitation program for employees and wash and sanitize hands, shoes, vehicles and equipment as indicated. Restrict unnecessary movement between various areas in plants and when possible, complete your activities in one area before moving to the next.

When inspecting areas where sterility is maintained or sterile rooms are located (especially in pharmaceutical or device firms), follow the sterile program required of the firm's employees. In general it is unnecessary to enter sterile rooms except in the most extraordinary circumstances. These areas are usually constructed to provide visual monitoring. Take no unsterile items with you (notebook, pencils, etc.). In this type of situation you can enter your observations in your diary immediately after leaving the sterile area.

Always use aseptic techniques, including hand sanitizing, when collecting in-line and raw material samples, as well as finished product samples for microbiological examination. See IOM 426.

Do not use or consume a firm's products at any of a firm's facilities. This could be interpreted as accepting a product as being satisfactory and could possibly embarrass you and the Agency, both during the inspection and in the future. In general, consuming food products in a manufacturing area is considered an objectionable practice.

When conducting inspections of firm's using chemicals, pesticides, etc., ask to review the Material Safety Data Sheets (MSDS) for the products involved to determine what, if any, safety precautions you must take. This could include the use of respirators or other safety equipment.

504.1 Clothing

Wear clean coveralls or other protective clothing for each inspection and if circumstances dictate, use a clean pair when returning from lunch, or upon entering certain machinery or critical areas.

Remove and secure all jewelry, pens, pencils, notebook, etc., so they cannot fall into the product or machinery. Do not depend on clips on pens, etc., to hold these items in your outer pockets.

Clean protective clothing should be either individually wrapped or placed in clean plastic bags and taped to pro-

tect from contamination. If the package has been sterilized, protect the package from possible contamination or puncture. The package should not be opened until you are ready to use the clothing. After use, clothing should be turned inside out as it is removed, and immediately placed in clean paper or plastic bags to prevent spread of contamination until washed and/or sterilized.

Use disposable hair and head coverings throughout the inspection and disposable hand and foot coverings in areas where floor tracking or cross contamination may be a factor. Use hard hats and other protective devices where the situation dictates.

If reusable protective boots are used, wash and sanitize before each use. Always use sterile disposable boot covers when entering machinery such as dryers or where unavoidable contact with product is a factor.

When discarding contaminated disposable head and boot coverings, it is suggested they be placed with used clothing for proper disposal after leaving the plant area.

See IOM 519.1 for protective clothing and equipment necessary when visiting livestock or poultry producing areas.

504.2 PHS Recommendations - Basic Sanitary Practices

FDA personnel are not required by law to have health certificates, take physical exams or submit to requirements, which ensures their compliance with sanitary procedures in the performance of their official duties. However, it is critical you adhere to basic sanitation practices. See IOM 169.6.

The U.S. Public Health Service has designed a model sanitation code for use by state and local governments at their option. This code, "United States Public Health Service Food Service Sanitation Ordinance and Code", is contained in DHEW Publication No. (FDA) 78-2081 - "Food Service Sanitation Manual; - 1976". Your district has copies of the manual for use if necessary.

504.3 Representatives Invited by the Firm to View the Inspection

While conducting an inspection, you may find the firm's management has invited individuals who are not directly employed by the firm to view the inspectional process (e.g., representatives from the press, trade associations, consumer groups, congressional staff, other company officials).

Regardless of whom the firm invites to observe the progress of an inspection, the presence of outside representatives should not disrupt the inspectional process. You should continue to conduct the inspection in a reasonable fashion. The presence of these individuals should have no impact on the manner in which the inspection progresses except you should take precautions to preserve the confidentially of any information you may have obtained as a result of the Agency's statutory authority. This is especially true when the inspection is recorded via videotaping, other photography, and/or audio recordings.

It is the Agency's position that while the investigator must protect privileged information provided to him/her during the inspection, it is the firm's responsibility to protect privileged/confidential information observed or recorded by those individuals invited by the firm.

SUBCHAPTER 505 - GENERAL PROCEDURES & TECHNIQUES

The procedures and techniques applicable to specific inspections and investigations for foods, drugs, devices, cosmetics, radiological health, or other FDA operations are found in part in the IOM (inspectional and investigational policy/procedure), various Guides to Inspections of... (a "how to" guidance series), and the Compliance Program Guidance Manual (program specific instructions). Some procedures and techniques which may be applicable to overlapping areas or operations are as follows:

505.1 Candling

Candling is defined as: "to examine by holding between the eye and a light, especially to test eggs in this way for staleness, blood clots, fertility and growth." Like most techniques learned through the food inspection programs, there are uses for this technique in other program areas such as looking for mold in bottled liquids which could be drugs, devices or biologics. Candling can also be useful in the examination of original documents to see below white-out or to look for over-writing.

Many types of products lend themselves to inspection by some type of candling. For these products, firms generally have candling equipment which may be built into the production lines or may be a separate operation.

Where checking products by candling, it may be possible to utilize the firm's candling equipment. Various other light sources for candling are also available including overhead projectors. Exercise care when using overhead projectors and protect the glass surface and the lens from scratches and damage. All candling is best accomplished when light outside the item being candled is masked so the light passes through the object rather than being diffused around it. A heavy paper or cardboard template can be quickly prepared at the time candling is done.

505.2 Label Review

Do not undertake a critical review of labels unless instructed by the assignment, program, or your supervisor. Limit your comments to the mandatory label requirements required by the Acts. However, if after review of the formula, it is obvious an active ingredient or an otherwise mandatory ingredient statement does not appear on the label, such discrepancy may be called to management's intention. See also IOM 512.1 regarding labeling for blood and blood products.

If asked for other label comments, refer the firm to the appropriate Center to obtain a label review.

When the labeling is suspect or when you are requested to collect labels/labeling, collect three copies of all labels and accompanying literature for further review. For medical devices, if there is a question regarding the need for a new 510(k) or PMA supplement, it is essential the label and labeling be collected.

505.3 Field Exams

A field examination is an on-site examination of a domestic product (or a foreign product in domestic channels of trade) sufficient in itself to determine if the product is in compliance with the Acts enforced by FDA.. A field exam can be conducted of any commodity in any location. If the examination does not reveal a violation or the appearance of a violation, a sample of the lot is usually not collected. If your exam reveals a violation or potential violation, you should collect an official sample. With the implementation of FACTS, your time spent conducting the field exam is reported even if you do collect a sample. Only the actual time spent in the collection of the sample would be reported as sample time.

Instructions on how to conduct a field exam are contained in "Guides To The Inspection of ***" and Compliance Programs. The Sample Schedules in Chapter 4 also provide guidance on lot examinations for special situations.

SUBCHAPTER 510 - INSPECTION PROCEDURES

510   PRE-INSPECTIONAL ACTIVITIES

Prior to the start of any inspection or investigation there are a number of activities, which should be conducted. These will differ based on whether this is an inspection or an investigation. All planned inspections should include a review of the establishment's factory jacket (if one exists), and registration and listing (if applicable) information. The purpose of this review is to determine the location of the establishment and obtain an overview of the establishment's operations and products as well as an understanding of their compliance history.

If the inspection or investigation is a directed assignment from a Center, ORA headquarters or another district, read it and attached materials to assure you understand the assignment. If the inspection or investigation is being conducted in part or solely as a recall follow-up or complaint, refer to Chapter 8 (Recalls) or Chapter 9 (Investigations) of the IOM for additional guidance.

You should also review the applicable Compliance Program(s) prior to the start of your inspection or investigation. ORA's Division of Field Investigations (DFI) has written numerous Inspection Guides to assist you in conducting inspections of various types of establishments, products or processes. You should become familiar with the appropriate guides prior to the start of the inspection and utilize them as needed throughout the inspection. The Centers have issued numerous guidance documents for industry. These documents are normally posted to the appropriate Center's Internet and Intranet web sites. Detailed references are listed by program area in Chapter 10 of the IOM.

Sub-chapters 530-570 of the IOM contain additional, program specific pre-inspectional activities, which you should follow.

Pre-Announcements - Pre-announcements are mandatory for all medical device inspections in accordance with the criteria and instructions below and BIMO sponsor/monitor inspections per DFI Field Alert #6. In all other program areas, pre-announcements may be made at the discretion of the district. If you are going to visit facilities where live-stock (including poultry) or wild animals are housed or processed, review IOM 519. In general, it may be inappropriate to pre-announce inspections of food establishments, blood banks, source plasma establishments and some BIMO inspections, but this too is subject to district discretion. If a district believes pre-announcing an inspection of an establishment will facilitate the inspection process then the procedures below for doing pre-announcements for medical device inspections should be followed. ORA's primary purpose for pre-announcing is to assure the appropriate records and personnel will be available during the inspection. It is not to make an appointment for the inspection. It should not be referred to as an appointment to inspect. When doing a pre-announcement, it is important you communicate to the establishment the purpose of the inspection and a general idea of the records you may wish to review. If you find neither the appropriate personnel nor records available, note this in your Establishment Inspection Report (EIR). The District may use this data in the future when considering whether this establishment should be eligible for pre-announced inspections.

The following is the general outline for pre-announcement of medical device inspections. You are advising the establishment's management of the date and time you will be arriving at the establishment to conduct the inspection. The establishment has no authority to negotiate this. If you, as the investigator, feel the need to accommodate the establishment's request, be sure there are sound reasons for doing so and report them in your inspection report.

A. Basic Premises

1.   Pre-announcement of inspections is to be applied only to establishments that meet specific criteria.   Pre-announcement may be considered for establishments that manufacture both drugs and devices or biologics and devices. The eligibility of an individual establishment for pre-announced inspection is at the discretion of the inspecting office using clearly described criteria. (See section B.). The district does not have the discretion to decide the types of medical device establishments eligible for pre-announcement, but may decide the specific establishments' eligibility because they meet the criteria.

2.   The pre-announcement should generally be no less than 5 calendar days in advance of the inspection. Should a postponement be necessary, the decision as to rescheduling rests with the investigator/team, but the new inspection date should not be later than 5 calendar days from the original date. Inspections may be conducted sooner than 5 calendar days if requested by or acceptable to the establishment and if this date is acceptable to the investigator/team.

3.   To participate in the pre-announcement portion of the program, establishments are expected to meet the commitment to have appropriate records and personnel available during the inspection.

4.   Pre-announced inspections will not limit an investigator's authority to conduct the inspection. Inspections will be as thorough as necessary.

B. Criteria for Consideration

When deciding whether an establishment qualifies for a pre-announced inspection, you must consider whether both the type of inspection and the establishment's status meet the following specific criteria.

1.   Type of Inspection: Only the following types of inspections are appropriate:

a.   Pre-market inspections (PMA, 510(k)),

b.   Foreign inspections,

c.   Quality System/Good Manufacturing Practice (QS/GMP) inspections:

*   Biennial routine inspections,

*   Initial inspections of new facilities or newly registered establishments, and

*   Initial inspections under new management and/or ownership.

d.   Recall follow-up inspections at manufacturer, initial importer, or U.S. designated agent.

Other types of inspections do not normally qualify. Inspection types where pre-announcement is not generally appropriate include: Government-Wide Quality Assurance (GWQAP) inspections with short deadlines; immediate and urgent responses to complaints, immediate and urgent follow-up to information from any source, and immediate hazard-to-health, recall follow-up inspections.

2.   Eligibility Criteria: Establishment's eligible for pre-notification should meet the following requirements:

a.   Non-violative QS/GMP inspection histories (inspections classified as no action indicated (NAI) or voluntary action indicated (VAI)). For VAI, adequate corrections of conditions observed and listed on FDA 483 during the previous inspection were verified and did not lead to any further agency action.

b.   To remain eligible for pre-announced inspections, establishments must have a history of having individuals and/or documents identified in previous pre-announced inspections reasonably available at the time of the inspection.

C. Procedures

1.   The investigator designated to conduct the inspection will contact the most responsible individual at the facility. You should leave a message requesting a return call if the most responsible person at the facility is unavailable at the time the call is made. The district should use good judgment as to what is a reasonable time frame to await the return call.

2.   Changes in dates should be kept to a minimum. If a change is made, a new date should be provided as soon as possible, which will facilitate the inspection and accommodate the investigator's schedule.   The establishment should provide a valid reason for requesting a change in the start date. A valid reason should be the same as you would accept if presented with the information during an unannounced inspection.

3. Inform the establishment as to the purpose, estimated duration, and the number of agency personnel expected to take part in the inspection. The products or processes to be covered should be described if this will facilitate and be consistent with the objectives of the inspection.

4. When known, specific records/personnel will be requested at the time the inspection is pre-announced.

5. The notification should be as specific as reasonably possible and specify the date for the start of the inspection.

Include in your EIR whether or not the inspection was pre-announced and include information on any difficulties experienced in notification or accessing records or personnel, which should have been available as a result of pre-announcing the inspection. For medical device establishment inspections, if not pre-announced, describe briefly in the EIR why not. If an establishment should become ineligible for pre-announcement, the endorsement of the EIR should include this statement. This information will be necessary for making a determination regarding future pre-announced inspections of the establishment. In addition, it is advisable to inform the establishment during the current and subsequent inspections of the action(s), which may have caused them to be ineligible for pre-announcement.

Sub-chapters 530-570 of the IOM contain additional, program specific pre-inspectional activities, which you should follow.

511 NOTICE OF INSPECTION

Upon arrival at the firm locate the owner, operator or agent in charge of the establishment. This should be the top Management Official on site. Be certain of this individual's status. Introduce yourself by name, title and organization. Show your credentials to this person and present a properly signed, completed, original of the FDA 482, Notice of Inspection, including the attachment page "Resources for FDA Regulated Businesses". This attachment provides information for the firm in the event it has disagreements or complaints. See IOM Exhibit 510-A.

If additional Agency personnel accompany you during the inspection, they must show their credentials to the top Management Official upon arrival at the site. A new FDA 482, Notice of Inspection must be issued. Submit the carbon copy of the FDA 482(s) with your EIR. Explain the purpose of your visit. Readily accept any management offer to have a representative accompany you on the inspection.

For multiple occupancy inspections in drug establishments, refer to IOM 501.4. Inspections of multiple firms, which are separate legal entities, should be reported under separate EIRs.

If faced with a refusal, or partial refusal of inspection proceed as outlined in IOM 514.

Any time a FDA 482 is issued, also issue FDA 484, Receipt for Samples, if you collect any samples at the firm. See IOM 513. See IOM 401.1 & 401.2 for instructions for issuance of the FDA 482 in certain sampling situations.

See IOM 401.1 for issuance of a FDA 482 for sample collections only. The FDA 482 may be amended "To Collect Samples Only" as shown in IOM Exhibit 510-A2.

If you have concerns of when to or when not to issue the FDA 482, discuss with your supervisor.

511.1 Multiple Date Inspections

If your inspection covers more than one day, advise management at the close of each day you have not finished the inspection and when you will return. Do this each day until you finish the inspection. A FDA 482 is not required for each day of an inspection or when different individuals are interviewed. If there will be an extended period of time (i.e., a week or longer) before you can return to the firm to complete the inspection, be sure management is aware of the delay and discuss with your supervisor whether or not you need to issue another FDA 482.

511.2 Inspection of Vehicles

If vehicles are present which are owned or leased by the firm being inspected and it is necessary to inspect the vehicles, the inspection of these is covered by the FDA 482, Notice of Inspection, you issued to the firm.

If vehicles (trucks, trailers, RR cars, etc.) which are not owned or leased by the firm are present and inspection is necessary, a separate FDA 482, Notice of Inspection, is required:

1. Issue the FDA 482 to the driver of the vehicle.

2. If the driver is not present and if, after a diligent search, he cannot be located, issue a separate FDA 482 jointly to the firm being inspected and to the firm whose name appears on the cab. Enter the license number of the vehicle on the FDA 482. Give the original FDA 482 to the firm and leave a copy in the cab of the vehicle.

3. If there is no cab present, prepare a separate FDA 482 modified to read "*** to inspect unattended vehicle ***" and issue it to the firm being inspected as the "agent in charge" of the vehicle. Enter the license number of the vehicle, trailer or RR car number, etc., on the FDA 482. Should the firm being inspected refuse to accept the Notice, leave it in a conspicuous place in the vehicle. Describe the circumstances in your EIR.

511.3 Follow-Up Inspections by Court Order

At times you may be instructed to conduct inspections of firms by authority of an injunction or other court order. This situation provides separate and distinct inspectional authority involving both the authority of the court order and the authority of Section 704 of the FD&C Act, each providing independent courses of action.

When assigned to conduct inspections under these situations, obtain a copy of the injunction or other court order bearing the filing stamp and all relevant signatures. Prior to starting the inspection study the order thoroughly for any special instructions of the court. Your supervisor will assist you in determining the depth of the inspection necessary to cover all of the court requirements.

Take a clearly legible copy of the court decree (not necessarily a certified copy) with you to the firm to be inspected.

Present your credentials in the same manner as for any other EI. Issue the FDA 482, Notice of Inspection, modified to read, "Notice of Inspection is hereby given under authority of injunction (provide here the injunction number and/or other identification) against the firm and pursuant to Section 704 ***". Show the person to whom the FDA 482 was issued a copy of the Order, and, read the following statement to that person.

"This inspection is being conducted under the authority of injunction (add the injunction number and/or other identification) (or other court order) granted by the United States District Court against this firm on (date). The inspection will cover all items specified in the decree. In addition to the inspection authority granted in the court decree, I am issuing you a Notice of Inspection under the authority of Section 704 of the Federal Food, Drug and Cosmetic Act which authorizes inspections of firms subject to that Act."

If, the firm refuses access to records, facilities, or information for which the decree provides inspectional authority, read the pertinent section(s) or portion of the order to the person refusing so there will be no misunderstanding as to the requirements of the decree. If the person still refuses, report the facts to your supervisor as soon as possible so the court can be promptly advised of the situation. See IOM 514 for information on handling refusals.

At the conclusion of the inspection and a FDA 483 is to be issued and you are using Turbo EIR, follow the Turbo instructions to get injunction specific cites on the FDA 483.

When you prepare your EIR, describe the sequence of events in detail including exactly what happened and how you handled the situation. This documentation will help support any charge of violating the court order and/or Section 704 of the FD&C Act.

The court order may require a report to the court. Discuss this with your supervisor since the district will normally handle this part of the requirement.

511.4 Conducting Regulatory Inspections When the Agency is Contemplating Taking, or is Taking, Criminal Action

You should not issue a Notice of Inspection if the agency is contemplating taking, or is taking, criminal action against a firm without first discussing the matter with your Supervisory Investigator. Federal Rules of Evidence may not permit using evidence in a criminal matter if it is knowingly obtained under administrative authorities such as Section 704 of the FD&C Act. It is the responsibility of the office generating the inspection assignment to inform the District if a criminal action is ongoing or contemplated. Once alerted, the Supervisory Investigator will then obtain advice from the Office of Chief Counsel and, once obtained, will assign the inspection to the Investigator(s).

Decisions to inspect under such circumstances should be based on considerations of whether or not the request is consistent with FDA's responsibility to assure articles are not produced or distributed in violation of the Federal Food, Drug, and Cosmetic Act or other Federal law within FDA's jurisdiction. It would be lawful to conduct an inspection to identify such violative products and to determine if corrective action was necessary to bring such products into compliance. However, it would be an abuse of the regulatory inspection authority for FDA to conduct a regulatory inspection under that authority for the sole purpose of gathering evidence of criminal violations. Such an abuse is unlawful, and could have significant consequences.

This is because, in general, the Fourth Amendment to the United States Constitution prohibits searches without a warrant. One exception to the warrant requirement includes the inspection of industries long subject to close supervision and inspection, which are conducted under a statute that dispenses with the need for a warrant. Because such inspections are not subject to advance scrutiny for probable cause, as would be an inspection conducted pursuant to a criminal warrant, the Supreme Court has warned government entities not to use administrative inspections to search for criminal violations in an effort to sidestep the Fourth Amendment. So long as the Agency conducts the administrative inspection in good faith for a valid, non-criminal purpose, evidence gathered in such inspections generally may be used in a criminal prosecution. However, the facts of each case are unique, and employees involved must carefully document the Agency's purpose in conducting the inspection.

Because the Agency's underlying purpose in conducting an inspection ultimately will determine whether the inspection was conducted in good faith to pursue a valid, non-criminal purpose it is important to document the non-criminal purpose for an inspection undertaken under these circumstances. The need for and extent of such documentation is at a minimum when the non-criminal purpose of the inspection is evident and compelling, for example, when the purpose is to determine articles are being produced in conformity with the Food, Drug, and Cosmetic Act. The need to document the non-criminal purpose of the regulatory inspection increases as the likelihood of criminal prosecution increases. For example, there would be an increased need to document the regulatory purpose of an inspection if the matter has been referred to the Department of Justice for grand jury investigation.

There may be occasions when neither the office generating the inspection assignment nor the District conducting the inspection is aware the Office of Criminal Investigations is conducting a criminal investigation of a firm that is the subject of a regulatory inspection. The Office of Criminal Investigations may determine it is not in the interest of the agency to disclose to other components of FDA the existence of its investigation, as long as the Office of Criminal Investigations is not involved in the agency decision to conduct a regulatory inspection. However, the Office of Criminal Investigations and other components of FDA may also share information as set out below.

511.5 When Evidence of a Criminal Violation is Discovered in the Course of a Regulatory Inspection

There may also be occasions where you are conducting a regulatory inspection at a facility, and, in the course of that inspection, you discover evidence of a criminal violation. If this occurs, you should continue the regulatory inspection as you would under normal circumstances. Document the observation and notify your supervisor. Evidence of the observation could be used in a criminal investigation, and the evidence could legally be disclosed to criminal investigators.

If you know criminal investigators are conducting a criminal investigation, your supervisor should notify the criminal investigators of any such observations. If you do not know of any ongoing criminal investigation, your supervisor should refer the information for review by the Office of Criminal Investigations. See the current Regulatory Procedures Manual (RPM). If the regulatory inspection is Center-directed (such as a bio-research monitoring inspection, a pre-approval inspection, or an inspection related to data integrity issues) your supervisor should immediately notify the Center involved of the referral to the Office of Criminal Investigations.

The discovery of evidence of a criminal violation may also be relevant to FDA's responsibility to assure articles are being produced in conformity with the Food, Drug, and Cosmetic Act. Additional inspections may be warranted. Such inspections should be planned and documented in accordance with the preceding section, "Conducting Regulatory Inspections When the Agency is Contemplating Taking, or is Taking, Criminal Action."

511.6 Use of Evidence Gathered in the Course of a Criminal Investigation

The extent to which information gathered in the course of a criminal investigation may be shared with other components of FDA will vary with each case. Investigators should determine the extent of information sharing in accordance with the following guidelines.

Information and evidence gathered in the course of a criminal investigation may be shared with regulatory personnel, subject to two reservations:

1. Information obtained pursuant to grand jury subpoena or testimony may not be shared. Disclosure of such information to anyone other than individuals identified by the Department of Justice attorney involved could subject the individual making the improper disclosure to sanctions for contempt by the court. Only the court can authorize disclosure beyond these parameters. Information obtained by other means (search warrant, cooperative witnesses, surveillance, etc.) may be shared, subject to the following paragraph.

2. There may be a need to protect the confidentiality of the criminal investigation. For example, disclosure to regulatory investigators might prematurely disclose the existence of the criminal investigation or the identity of confidential informants. However, whenever you are calculating the need to protect the confidentiality of information gathered in the course of a criminal investigation through means other than the grand jury, you must consider whether it will be in the interest of public health to protect the confidentiality of that information.

Criminal investigators should consult their supervisors to determine whether disclosure should be made to regulatory investigators.

511.7 Use of Evidence Voluntarily Provided to the Agency

Criminal and regulatory investigators may share information and evidence voluntarily provided to FDA, without use of the regulatory inspection authority, search warrant, or subpoena. If criminal investigators decide not to share such information because of a need to protect the confidentiality of the criminal investigation, they should consider the potential impact on the public health of protecting the confidentiality of that information.

511.8 Concurrent Administrative, Civil, and Criminal Actions

It may be appropriate to seek administrative and/or civil remedies against a firm or individual under investigation for criminal violations. There are many issues involved in determining whether such actions may proceed concurrently, or whether certain actions should proceed first. Each situation must be evaluated on an individual basis. If administrative and/or civil remedies are under consideration against a firm or individual also under investigation for criminal violations, representatives from the Center responsible for evaluating the administrative and/or regulatory action should meet with the Office of Criminal Investigations Headquarters staff to issues related to the timing of administrative, civil, and criminal actions. The Office of Criminal Investigations and other components of FDA may share information subject to the reservations set out earlier.

511.9 Working with a Grand Jury

Finally, if you are assigned to work with a grand jury, you should not participate in a regulatory inspection or other regulatory matter involving the same firm or individual(s). Such participation is contrary to long standing agency policy, might be unlawful, and could result in sanctions against the investigator and the agency. You should not participate in any regulatory matters that could result in improper disclosure of grand jury information, even after the grand jury investigation is closed. Grand jury proceedings remain secret even after they are concluded. Under no circumstances should you undertake such participation without first obtaining clearance from the Department of Justice attorney or the Office of Chief Counsel attorney assigned to the grand jury case. See IOM 705 for additional information on Grand Jury proceedings.

512 REPORTS OF OBSERVATIONS

The FORM FDA 483 INSPECTIONAL OBSERVATIONS is intended for use in notifying the inspected establishment's top management in writing of significant objectionable conditions, relating to products and/or processes, which were observed during the inspection. The issuance of written inspectional observations is mandated by law and ORA policy. Only report significant observations on the FDA 483.

Observations of lessor significance should be discussed with firm management and properly reported in the narrative report. As of 1997, ORA established a policy of adding "annotations" to the FDA 483. See IOM 512.3.

With the roll-out of Turbo EIR, an automated FDA 483 and EIR reporting system, the traditional FDA 483 is created electronically. Turbo EIR must be used to generate the FDA 483 and write the EIR for any inspection where applicable cite modules exist. Turbo EIR must not be used to create a FDA 483 during an inspection of a firm involving multiple commodity areas and FDA 483 cites do not exist for ALL of the commodity areas for which observations need to be included on the FDA 483. You must be able to write the entire FDA 483 using Turbo EIR. You cannot use Turbo to write the EIR if a FDA 483 was issued to the firm and it was NOT generated using Turbo EIR. NOTE: Turbo EIR can be used to write the EIR for any inspection not involving issuance of a FDA 483.

It is not necessary to complete all headings of the FDA 483, when multiple page 483's are issued. Complete all headings on the first page and, on subsequent pages, only those necessary to identify the firm and dates inspected. You must sign the FDA 483 and sign the first and last pages of a multi-page FDA 483. Pages between the first and last may be signed or initialed. For Turbo FDA 483s the last page must be signed and all other pages initialed. If conducting a team inspection, each member of the team present at the issuance of the FDA 483 must sign the first and last pages of a multi-page FDA 483 and sign or initial all remaining pages in the appropriate area.

Report all significant objectionable conditions noted during the inspection by issuing a FDA 483, Inspectional Observations. See IOM Exhibit 510-B. Be alert for specific guidance in assignments or Compliance Programs which may supplement the following general instructions. FDA 483's should be issued at the conclusion of the inspection and prior to leaving the premises. However, in preparing some complex FDA 483's, it may be necessary to leave the premises and return at a later date to issue and discuss your inspectional observations. In this case, you should advise the firm's management your inspection has not been completed and you will return to issue the FDA 483 and discuss inspectional findings. There must not be unreasonable and unwarranted delays in issuing and discussing the FDA 483. During the inspection, you must not show the firm's management a draft, unsigned copy of the FDA 483 or an electronic copy of the FDA 483 on your computer screen. You must issue only a signed FDA 483 at the closeout discussion with management. It is appropriate for you to discuss potential objectionable conditions with the firm's management on a daily basis or as you observe them. Prepare the FDA 483 as follows:

District Office address and phone number - Legibly print the district address on copies in advance if desired. Include District Office commercial telephone number and area code.

Name and Title of individual to whom report is issued - Enter legal first name, middle initial and last name and full title of the person to whom the form is issued.

Firm name - Enter full, legal name of the firm, including any abbreviations, quotation marks, dashes, commas, etc.

Street address, city, state and Zip Code - Enter street address, city, state and Zip Code. (Not P.O. Box unless P.O. Box is part of the address such as on a Rural Route).

Date(s) of inspection - Enter actual or inclusive date(s) of inspection.

FEI Number - If the Firm Establishment Number is on the assignment, enter it here. If not readily available, leave blank.

Type of establishment inspected - Enter the types of the establishment, such as bakery, cannery, wholesale warehouse, drug repackager, salvage warehouse, etc.

Employee(s) signature and Employee(s) name & title - Each member of an inspection team should sign the FDA 483. However, absence of a team member at the conclusion of an inspection need not prevent issuance of the FDA 483. See IOM 502.4. If you use an electronically generated FDA 483, assure you have an exact copy of the original for the District files. An unsigned photocopy or printed copy is unacceptable.

Signature Policy - Until electronic signatures have been fully implemented, you will initial all pages of a multi-page FDA 483 next to the Date of Issue and you will sign the front and final pages. Ideally, the FDA 483 is signed by all members of an inspection team. If some members of the inspection team are not available when the FDA 483 is issued, you, as the lead investigator, must sign the FDA 483 as above, initial the remaining pages of a multi-page FDA 483, and fully explain in the EIR why the FDA 483 was not signed by all members of the inspection team. You should follow your district policy in determining the need for all members to initial each page of the FDA 483. The official FDA 483 is the printed, pen/ink signed, exact duplicate of the issued original. This is the copy maintained with the EIR (see IOM 512.5). There are only three possible exact duplicates of any issued FDA 483, which are to be maintained in the official file:

1). The original, signed FDA 483 issued to the firm,

2) The modified, signed FDA 483 if the original FDA 483 issued contains an error and/or is annotated, and

3). The signed FDA 483 addendum issued after departing the firm.

RETAIN FOR THE OFFICIAL FILE A SIGNED, ISSUED EXACT DUPLICATE OF ALL FDA 483s ISSUED DURING YOUR INSPECTION.

Date issued - Enter date the form is actually issued to the firm's management.

"During an inspection of your firm (I) (We) observed" - Enter your reportable observations succinctly and clearly. Conditions listed should be significant and must relate to an observed or potential problem with the facility, equipment, processes, controls, products, employee practices, or records. "Potential problems" must have a reasonable likelihood of occurring based upon observed conditions or events. Do not cite deviations from draft Agency policy statements or directly refer to Agency guidance documents in your written observations. You should contact your supervisor to discuss and resolve questionable observations prior to the issuance of the FDA 483. Good judgment is necessary when deciding whether conditions are objectionable in view of their relation to other conditions or controls at the given time and place. When there is continued uncertainty about the significance of one or more observations, these should not be listed. They should however be discussed with the firm's management and reported in the EIR.

If the firm maintains satisfactory controls as intended by the regulations, but does so by alternate means, it may be possible no adverse condition will result. See 21 CFR 820.1(e) regarding petitions for exemption or variance from device GMP's.

To make the FDA 483 observations more concise, avoid unnecessary redundancy. Items of the same nature should be grouped together. Examples should be given if a condition with broad or general scope is described. Write the observations in clear and descriptive terms, including locations, dates of occurrence, frequency of occurrence, lot numbers, etc., as appropriate. When reviewing records, the FDA 483 observations should include the number of records of a given type examined, for example, "Two out of 50 records examined were * * *."

If you discover an error on the FDA 483 at the time of issuance, correct and initial all copies of the FDA 483. Note: if the FDA 483 was created in Turbo, all corrections/additions/deletions MUST be made in Turbo. This procedure does not pertain to adverse conditions noted and then corrected during the inspection. Observations of this type should remain on the FDA 483. If a discrepancy is discovered after you leave the firm, discuss it with your supervisor. If necessary, an additional FDA 483 will be prepared as an addendum to the original, limiting it to correction of those discrepancies. This FDA 483 addendum should be personally delivered to the firm for discussion. If personal delivery is impossible it should be transmitted by mail including a full explanation. A copy of the letter and FDA 483 addendum should be included with the EIR. In addition, you must call the person to whom the original FDA 483 was issued, to discuss the change. Document your discussion on the FDA copies of the FDA 483 and in the EIR. The Inspectional Observations (FDA 483) is of critical importance to both the Agency and regulated industry. Individual FDA 483s may become public through publishing in industry trade press, FOI inquiries, Headquarters postings and other means.

If an error(s) is found on a signed, issued Turbo FDA 483, you must follow these instructions. Changes made to correct information in the text of the observation will show on the face of the final printed FDA 483. Deletions will remain visible but will be crossed out and additions added, preferably in a different font. If an entire observation is removed, incidental text will be used to add the statement "An observation concerning * * * was removed based on discussion with management."

512.1 Reportable Observations

Review Sections 402, 501, 601, & 704 of the FD&C Act. Include specific factual observations of:

1. Foods, drugs, devices, or cosmetics consisting in whole or in part of filthy, putrid, or decomposed substances.

2. Undesirable conditions or practices, bearing on filth or decomposition, which may reasonably result in the food, drug, device, or cosmetic becoming contaminated with filth.

3. Insanitary conditions or practices which may reasonably render the food, drug, device, or cosmetic injurious to health.

4. Careless handling of rodenticides or pesticides.

5. Results of field tests (organoleptic examination of fish, crackout of nuts, etc.) if the results revealed adulteration.

6. Observations of faulty manufacturing, processing, packaging, or holding, of food, drug, or device products as related to current good manufacturing practice regulations including inadequate or faulty record keeping.

7. Observations of faulty can closures and/or deviations from recommended processing times and temperatures.

8. Observations indicating non-conformity with commitments made in a New-Drug Application (or NADA) or in an antibiotic certification or certification exemption form.

9. Observations, forming the basis for product non-acceptance under the Government Wide Quality Assurance Program (GWQAP). See IOM 512.3.

10. Deviations from blood and blood products labeling requirements as specified in 21 CFR 606.121 and 21 CFR 640.

11. Deviations from the animal proteins prohibited in ruminant feeds requirements (21 CFR 589.2000), including labeling deviations.

12. Deviations from IRB regulations (21 CFR 56) and Good Laboratory Practices regulations (21 CFR 58).

13. Observations indicating drug misuse, failure to maintain proper drug use records, and/or poor animal husbandry practices during tissue residue investigations. See the applicable Compliance Program(s) for guidance.

14. Observations indicating non-conformity with the Medical Device Reporting requirements as specified in 21 CFR 803; the Medical Devices Reports of Corrections and Removals requirements as specified in 21 CFR 806; and the Medical Device Tracking requirements as specified in 21 CFR 821.

15. Observations indicating noncompliance with medical device pre-market notification requirements and pre-market approval requirement under FD&C Act sections 510(k) and 515 respectively, should only be made with the prior confirmation of CDRH and/or CBER.

16. 21 CFR PART 200.10 does allow reporting observations noted at a contract facility to the contracting facility. Before doing this, check with your supervisor to determine if this is appropriate.

17. Observations indicating non-compliance with LACF/Acidified food registration and failure to file scheduled processes. Before doing this, verify lack of such, as covered in CPGM 7303.803A

512.2 Non-Reportable Observations

Do not report opinions, conclusions, or characterize conditions as "violative." The determination of whether any condition is violative is an agency decision made after considering all circumstances, facts and evidence. See IOM

516 involving discussions with management at which time opinions may be discussed.

Do not quote Regulations (e.g., specific CFR sections) when listing items.

Do not report observations pertaining to:

1. Label and labeling content, except per IOM 512.1, items 9, 10 & 11 above.

2. Promotional materials.

3. The classification of a cosmetic or device as a drug.

4. The classification of a drug as a new drug.

5. Non-conformance with the New Drug Regulations, 21 CFR 312.1 (New Drugs for Investigational Use in Human Beings: Exemptions from Section 505(a)) unless instructed by the particular program or assignment.

6. The lack of registration required by Section 510 of the FD&C Act.

7. Patient names, donor names, etc. If such identification is necessary, use initials, code numbers, record numbers, etc.

8. Corrective actions. Specific actions taken by the firm in response to observations noted on the FDA 483 or during the inspection are not listed on the FDA 483, but are reported in the EIR. Except as described in IOM section 512.3.

512.3 Annotation of the FDA 483

Annotation of the FDA 483 is required for all medical device inspections. It is left to the district's discretion whether they wish to annotate the FDA 483s in other program areas. Annotations of FDA 483s for inspections in other program areas may be done if both the establishment and the investigator/team believe annotation will facilitate the inspection process. When a FDA 483 is annotated it must be done in accordance with the guidance that follows.

When annotating the FDA 483, it is to be done at the time of issuance to acknowledge an establishment's promised or completed corrective action. The annotations are succinct comments about the status of the FDA 483 item. They are added by the Investigator at the time the FDA 483 is issued and are limited to 4 phrases: reported corrected, not verified; corrected and verified; promised to correct; and, under consideration. The establishment should review the annotations on this issued FDA 483 to ensure there are no misunderstandings about promised corrective actions. (BIMO inspections are generally excluded from annotations.)

When annotating the FDA 483, inform the establishment of the annotation program at some point prior to the final discussion with management. Determine from management whether they wish to have their FDA 483 observations annotated. It is voluntary on the part of the establishment. If the establishment does not want one or more observations annotated, you must honor the request.

The actual annotation of the FDA 483 must occur during the final discussion with management. It is not permissible to pre-print or pre-format the annotations onto the FDA 483 form. The annotations can be made after each observation, at the end of each page of the FDA 483 or at the bottom of the last page of the FDA 483 prior to the investigator's signature.

Regardless of whether an establishment's FDA 483 is annotated, investigators and analysts will discuss all observations with the management of the establishment as they are observed, or on a daily basis, to minimize surprises, errors, and misunderstandings when the FDA 483 is issued. This discussion will include those observations, which may be written on the FDA 483 and those that will only be discussed with management during the closeout meeting. Industry may use this opportunity to ask questions about the observations, request clarification, and inform the inspection team what corrections have been or will be made during the inspection process. Investigators are encouraged to verify the establishment's completed corrective actions as long as the verification does not unreasonably extend the duration of the inspection.

The following details the requirements and procedures for the annotations of the FDA 483:

1. During your discussion of the FDA 483 item, ask the establishment if they want the entire FDA 483 or portions annotated using the specific comments as listed in #2 below. If so, place the annotation on the FDA 483 based on the comment of the establishment and your knowledge. The establishment does not initial or sign the FDA 483 or annotations.

A reportable item will not be deleted from the FDA 483 because the establishment has promised or completed a corrective action. The investigator will continue to have the latitude to delete the observation if the establishment's response to the observation clearly shows the observation is in error or to clarify the observation based on additional information provided.

2. If the establishment has promised and/or completed a corrective action to an FDA 483 observation prior to the completion of the inspection, all copies of the FDA 483 should be annotated (either following each observation or at the end of the FDA 483) with one or more of the following comments, as appropriate:

- Reported corrected, not verified.
- Corrected and verified.
- Promised to correct.
- Under consideration.

The term "verified" means "to confirm; to establish the truth or accuracy". In this case, you must do the verification. In some situations, you will not be able to verify the corrective action unless there is further district or Center review or until there is another inspection of the establishment.

The actual wording of these annotations may be slightly modified as long as the original meaning is not lost. The establishment's stated objections to any given observation or to the FDA 483, as a whole should not be annotated on the FDA 483.

3. If an observation made during a prior inspection has not been corrected or is a reoccurring observation, it is appropriate to note this on the FDA 483. Note: This is not an annotation, it would normally appear as a header to the observation or as part of the current observation itself.

4. All corrective actions taken by the establishment and verified by FDA should be discussed in detail in the Establishment Inspection Report (EIR) and reported using the Compliance Achievement Reporting Systems (CARS).

Where the investigator and the establishment have "agreed to disagree" about the validity of an observation, you may annotate this observation with "Under consideration" or with no annotation based on the establishment's desire. If they would prefer no annotation, do not annotate it. The EIR should include the establishment's objections to the observation and the fact the establishment declined to have the observation annotated.

When an establishment has promised corrections and furnishes a date or timeframe (without a specific date) for completion, then you may add "by xxx date" or "within xxxx days or months" in the annotation. The establishment can, and should, follow-up their annotation to the FDA 483 with a written response. If they cannot meet a commitment made in the annotation, they can explain it in the written response. The establishment also has the option to not comment at the time the FDA 483 is presented and leave their commitments to their written response.

512.4 Government Wide Quality Assurance Program (GWQAP)

When performing product acceptance examinations under the GWQAP, you must discuss all deficiencies with management and report these deficiencies in writing on the FDA 483. This includes all deficiencies related to the FD&C Act as well as deficiencies in complying with contract requirements, which result in non-acceptance. There must be a clear differentiation on the FDA 483 between these two types of deficiencies.

Enter the FD&C type deficiencies (GMP deviations, etc.) first on the FDA 483. If there are deficiencies in contract provisions, draw a line across the sheet and add a heading "The Following Additional Contract Non-Conformances Were Observed." Enter each deficiency, which forms a basis for non-acceptance, followed by the reference to the applicable contract requirement or specification.

512.5 Distribution of the FDA 483

Be sure all copies of the FDA 483 are legible and distribute as follows:

Original - Before leaving the premises at the end of the EI present the original to the individual who received the FDA 482 "Notice of Inspection" if that person is present and qualifies as "most responsible." If that person is not available or is outranked by someone else, present it to the individual who meets the definition of owner, operator, or agent in charge.

Copies - Submit the two remaining exact copies with your EIR. One of these copies may be sent to the top management of the firm including foreign management, unless the individual to whom you gave the original is the top official of the firm. With Turbo, only the signed, and any modified/amended copy(ies) should be attached to the EIR package.

If the inspection covered vehicles as described in IOM 511.2, leave an exact copy of the list of observations with the firm being inspected. The original will be sent by your district to the firm owning or leasing the vehicle. You must make every effort to obtain the name and address of the vehicle owner. Usually the firm name is on the vehicle; however, it may require a trace of the vehicle license number. Discuss with your supervisor before taking this step. See IOM 432.2.

513 RECEIPT - FACTORY SAMPLES

You must issue an FDA 484, Receipt for Samples, if you collect any physical sample during an inspection. At the end of the EI and prior to leaving the premises, issue the original FDA 484 to the same individual who received the FDA 482. (See IOM 412) If this person is not available, give it to someone else who meets the definition of owner, operator, or agent in charge. Submit an exact copy with the EIR. Do not comment on type of examination expected or promise a report of analysis.

513.1 Items Requiring Receipt

Issue FDA 484 for any item of food, drug, device, or cosmetic actually removed from the establishment.

NOTE: A receipt must always be issued to anyone from whom you obtain Rx drugs. This includes individuals as well as firms. See IOM 412.5 and IOM 439.8(23).

The following are examples of exhibit materials also requiring a Receipt for Samples:
1. Air filter pads,
2. Rodent pellets, and
3. Any other physical evidence actually removed from the plant.

513.2 Items Not Requiring Receipt

Do not issue a FDA 484 for:
1. Items or materials examined during the inspection but not removed from the establishment (report adverse results of analysis of materials on FDA 483 as indicated in IOM 512.1),
2. Labels or promotional material, or
3. Photographs taken during the inspection.
4. Record(s): including production, quality control, shipping and interstate records.

Firm's management may request copies of documents or records you obtain from their firm. There is no objection to supplying them.

See IOM 527.5 for procedures when a firm requests a receipt for records copied during an inspection or investigation.

514 INSPECTION REFUSAL

Refusal as used in your IOM means refusing to permit an inspection or prohibiting you from obtaining information to which FDA is entitled under the law. See IOM 410.3 for information regarding refusal to permit sampling.

In the case of a refusal you must show your conduct was reasonable, fair, and you exercised reasonable precaution to avoid refusal. You must have shown your credentials and given the responsible individual a properly prepared and signed Notice of Inspection, FDA 482.

Inspection refusals may take several forms:

1.   Refusal of Entry - when you are faced with a refusal of entry, call the person's attention to the pertinent sections of the Acts (Sections 301(f) & 704 of the FD&C Act and Section 351(c), 360A(a), (b) & (f); 360B(a); and 361(a) of the Public Health Service Act. Portions of these are listed on the front and back of the FDA 482. If entry is still refused, leave the completed FDA 482, leave the premises and telephone your supervisor immediately for instructions.

2.   Refusal of Information - if management objects to the manner of the inspection or coverage of specific areas or processes, do not argue the matter but proceed with the inspection. However, if management refuses information to which FDA is entitled under law, call attention to Section 301(f) of the FD&C Act or applicable sections of the PHS Act. If management still refuses, proceed with the inspection until finished. It is not an inspection "refusal" when management refuses to provide formula information, lists of shipments, codes, etc., except where specifically required by the law. If the refusal is such you cannot conduct a satisfactory inspection, discuss with your supervisor if a Warrant for Inspection should be requested.

3.   Refusal after Serving Warrant - If you have been refused entry, obtained a warrant, tried to serve or execute it and are refused entry under the warrant, inform the person, the warrant is a court order and such refusal may constitute contempt of court. If the warrant is not then immediately honored (entry and inspection permitted), leave the premises and promptly telephone the facts to your supervisor.

If you have served the warrant and during the inspection you encounter partial refusal or resistance in obtaining access to anything FDA is authorized to inspect by the warrant, inform the firm that aspect of the inspection is part of a court order and refusal may constitute contempt of court. If the warrant is not then immediately honored, leave the premises and promptly telephone the facts to your supervisor.

All refusals to permit inspection must be reported in your EIR under the "Refusals" heading.

514.1 Hostile and Uncooperative Interviewees

More often than not, investigations or inspections are conducted in a reasonable atmosphere. Nonetheless, there will be times you are confronted by unfriendly or hostile persons.

Your activities must always be conducted with tact, honesty, diplomacy, and persuasiveness. Even though you must at times adopt a firm posture, do not resort to threats, intimidation, or strong-arm tactics.

Many times a hostile or uncooperative attitude on the part of individuals being interviewed results from fear, timidity, or previously distasteful encounters with law enforcement personnel. In most cases a calm, patient, understanding and persuasive attitude on your part will overcome the person's reluctance or hostility. Often the mere fact you patiently listen while individuals share their views will make them receptive to your quest.

Normally you have no way to determine the nature of the individuals you meet. However, there are often indicators, which can alert you, such as:

1.   Establishment inspection reports may show situations where investigators encountered belligerent or hostile individuals.

2.   Discussions and conversations with FDA, federal, state and local inspectors and investigators may reveal instances where uncooperative individuals and problem situations were encountered.

3.   The nature of the assignment, program or information requested may indicate some degree of caution is needed.

4.   A firm located in an area with a reputation for unfriendliness to law enforcement personnel should alert you some employees of the firm may be less than cooperative during the investigation.

If you find yourself in a situation which, in your judgment, indicates violence is imminent, stop the operation and make an exit as soon as possible. Immediately report the facts to your supervisor.

The FDA recognizes there are situations where it is advisable to take precautions for your personal safety. In those, consult your supervisor. Some procedures, which may be utilized to minimize the danger, include:

1.   Inspections or investigations carried out by a team of two or more persons.

2.   Request assistance from local law enforcement agencies prior to or during investigations.

3.   In potentially hazardous investigations such as methadone, two investigators may be used and personnel from the U.S. Drug Enforcement Administration, State, or local law enforcement agencies may be requested to accompany you.

In instances when you are actually assaulted or threatened, you should immediately notify your supervisor. The district should immediately notify the local office of the Federal Bureau of Investigations and the U.S. Attorney's office in the jurisdiction where the incident occurred. Also, the District should notify the Office of Security, HFA-204, at 301-443-8995 (FAX 301-443-9399).

If you are physically attacked, you have the same recourse as any other citizen as well as the benefit of federal laws protecting government officials while in the performance of their official duties.

It is a federal crime for anyone to kill, assault, resist, oppose, impede, intimidate, or interfere with, a federal official in the performance of their official duties.

In case of assault or threat against you, notify your supervisor immediately, so the facts can be submitted to the Federal Bureau of Investigations and the U.S. Attorney's office for immediate action.

The referenced sections in Title 18 of the U.S. Code are:

1.   Title 18 U.S.C.A. Section 111, which provides:

"111. Assaulting, resisting, or impeding certain officers or employees.

Whoever forcibly assaults, resists, opposes, impedes, intimidates, or interferes with any person designated in Section 1114 of this title while engaged in or on account of the performance of his official duties, shall be fined not more than $5,000 or imprisoned not more than three years, or both.

Whoever, in the commission of any such acts uses a deadly or dangerous weapon, shall be fined not more than $10,000 or imprisoned not more than ten years, or both. **** ".

2.   Title 18 U.S.C.A. Section 1114, which provides: "1114. Protection of officers and employees of the United States.

Whoever kills ***** or any officer or employee of the Department of Health and Human Services or of the Department of Labor assigned to perform investigative, inspection, or law enforcement functions while engaged in the performance of his official duties, shall be punished as provided under sections 1111 and 1112 of this title. ****".

See Title 18 of the US Code Sections 111 and 1114 for the complete text.   See also IOM 140.

515   INSPECTION WARRANT

A refusal to permit inspection invokes a criminal provision of the FD&C Act [Sec. 301(f)]. Depending on the individual situation, instances of refusal may be met by judicious use of inspection warrants.

Instructions for obtaining warrants are contained in the Regulatory Procedures Manual, Chapter 6-00. See your supervisor for information and instructions.

You are operating as an agent of the court when you serve an inspection warrant and it must be executed expeditiously once served. See IOM 514 for guidance on how to handle any refusal after obtaining a warrant.

In situations where a potential problem is anticipated with the service of a warrant, the District should consider sending a Supervisory Consumer Safety Officer or Compliance Officer and a U.S. Marshal with the Investigator to assist and supervise the serving of the warrant.

After obtaining an Inspection Warrant, return to the firm and:

1. Show your credentials to the owner, operator, or agent in charge,

2.   Issue the person a written Notice of Inspection (FDA 482),

3.   Show that individual the original signed Inspection Warrant,

4.   Give him/her a copy (not the original) of the warrant.

The copy you provide need not be signed by the issuing judge, but the judge's name should be typed on the copy.

Follow the procedures of the court or U.S. Attorney involved, if their methods differ from the above.

When an inspection is made pursuant to a warrant, a Return showing the inspection was completed must be made to the Judge (or U.S. Commissioner or Magistrate) who issued the warrant. The Return, executed on the original warrant, should be made promptly and usually no later than 10 days following its execution.

516   DISCUSSIONS WITH MANAGEMENT

After completion of the inspection, meet with the highest ranking management official possible to discuss your findings and observations. The FDA 483 is not a substitute for such discussion since there may be additional questionable practices or areas not appropriate for listing on this form.

During the discussion be frank, courteous and responsive with management. Point out the observations listed on the FDA 483 are your observations of objectionable conditions found during the inspection, and explain the significance of each. Try to relate each listed condition to the applicable sections of the laws and regulations administered by the FDA. You should inform management during the closeout discussion the conditions listed may, after further review by the Agency, be considered to be violations of the Food, Drug and Cosmetic Act. Legal sanctions, including seizure, injunction, civil money penalties and prosecution, are available to FDA if establishments do not voluntarily correct serious conditions.

Do not be overbearing or arbitrary in your attitude or actions. Do not argue if management voices a different view of the FDA 483 observations, or of your opinions. Explain, in your judgment the conditions you observed MAY be determined by the FDA, after review of all the facts, to be violations. Make clear the prime purpose of the discussion is to call attention to objectionable practices or conditions, which should be corrected.

Obtain management's intentions regarding correcting objectionable conditions. They may propose corrections or procedural changes and ask you if this is satisfactory. If this involves areas where your knowledge, skill, and experience are such that you know it will be satisfactory, you can so advise management. Do not assume the role of an authoritative consultant. In areas where there is any doubt, you must explain to management you cannot endorse the proposed corrections. Advise the individuals FDA will supply comments if the establishment will submit its request and its proposed corrections or procedures in writing to the district office.

Concentrate on what needs to be done rather than how to do it. Do not recommend the product or services of a particular establishment. If asked to suggest a product or consulting laboratory, refer the inquirer to a classified directory or trade publications and or organizations.

Report in your EIR all significant conversations with management or management representatives. In most instances it is not necessary to quote management's response verbatim. Paraphrasing the replies is sufficient. However, if the situation is such that quoting the reply or replies is necessary, enclose them in quotation marks.

516.1 Protection of Privileged Information

You have certain responsibilities under the FD&C Act, Section 301(j); Sections 359(d) & 306(e) of the Public Health Service Act; and Section 1905 of the Federal Confidential Statute (18 U.S.C. 1905) regarding protection of confidential material obtained during your official duties.

Do not volunteer information about other firms or their practices. Ignore casual exploratory questions or remarks from management about competitors or their processes. Your casual and seemingly innocuous remarks may reveal privileged information. Therefore, be alert and avoid voluntarily or unknowingly divulging information, which may be privileged or confidential and possibly compromise FDA's and your own integrity.

Management often request copies of any documents or records you obtain from their firm. There is no objection to your supplying these. When management requests copies of photos taken by you in a plant, follow IOM 523.3.

You may encounter situations when management invites outside individuals to observe the inspectional process (e.g., representatives from the press, trade associations, congressional staff, other company officials). As discussed in Section 504.3 of the IOM, the presence of representatives invited by the firm should not disrupt the inspectional process. You are to continue the inspection in a reasonable manner.

If the firm allows invited individuals to photograph, videotape, or prepare audio recordings during the inspection, you should make every effort to protect privileged information in your possession. However, it is the Agency's position that it is the firm's responsibility to protect confidential and/or proprietary information observed or recorded by those individuals invited by the firm.

516.2 Refusals of Requested Information

Should management refuse to provide any reasonable request for information, which is not specifically required by the law, determine the reasons for the denial and report the details in the EIR. Types of refusals of interest to FDA and refusal codes to be entered in FACTS are listed in the FDA Data Codes Manual. Refusal codes' data are used when reporting to Congress. See IOM 514.1 for instructions in dealing with hostile and/or uncooperative interviewees.

517 CONSUMER COMPLAINTS

Prior to conducting any inspection, you should review the FACTS system and the factory jacket becoming familiar with all FDA Complaint/Injury forms. Be especially alert for ones marked "Follow-Up Next Inspection" and make sure you investigate these during your inspection.

During the inspection, discuss these complaints with management without revealing the complainant's name(s). Determine if the firm has had similar complaints on the same product. Determine what action the firm has taken to identify the root cause of the problem and to prevent a recurrence in the future. See IOM 593.3 (#14) for reporting instructions.

518 INTERVIEWING CONFIDENTIAL INFORMANTS

When you are faced with a situation involving sources of information who want to remain anonymous, please contact your supervisor and follow the procedures here. If your management concurs with the decision to utilize a confidential source, it is particularly important you take the necessary steps to keep the identity of the source, and any information which could lead to the identity, confidential. For purposes of this subchapter, a confidential source is a person who provides information that may be of assistance to FDA without necessarily becoming a party to the actual FDA investigation. If you believe the information provided by the source could lead to a criminal investigation, please contact the Office of Criminal Investigations (OCI).

I. How to handle the first contact. When you interview a person who may become a confidential source use the following procedures.

A. Type of meeting. Try to schedule a personal interview with the person rather than a telephone interview. At a face-to-face interview you can assess the person's demeanor, body language, overall presentation, and truthfulness.

B. Meeting location. The place and time of the interview should be the choice of the person, unless there is a concern with personal safety. If the person's suggested location is unsuitable, the investigator should suggest the location. When you conduct the interview off FDA premises, notify your supervisor of your destination, purpose, and estimated time of return. When an off-site interview has been completed, check-in with your supervisor.

C. Interviewing methods/techniques. It is strongly recommended you have two investigators conduct interviews of a confidential source. The lead investigator conducts the interview, while the second investigator takes notes and acts as a witness to the interview. You should:

1. prepare carefully for the interview. The investigators should develop the questions they intend to ask the person during the interview, e.g., "establish motivation," and record and number the questions to be asked in their diaries prior to the interview. This preparation assists in documenting the interview process and reduces the amount of note taking needed during the interview. The investigators also should discuss their interviewing strategy, and determine the method by which they will consult with each other during the interview and (during extensive interviews) share the interviewing and note-taking responsibilities;

2. have the person tell the story chronologically, placing complex situations into logical order; and

3. if the person makes allegations, ask him or her how he or she knows the allegations are true.

--How were they in a position to know?

--Did they personally see, hear, or write about the information/incident?

--Can they provide proof of the allegations?

D. Establish motivation. At the end of the interview ask the person why he or she is divulging this information. This may reveal their motive(s):

1. Is the person a disgruntled current or former employee who harbors a grudge?

2. Is the person looking for some type of whistle-blower reward or notoriety?

3. Does the person just want to do the right thing?

4. Is the person involved in actual or prospective litigation about or related to the information?

E. Anonymity. If the person is requesting anonymity, inform him or her FDA:

1. will not divulge his or her identity, the occurrence of the interview, or the sensitive information provided to FDA if the information could lead to the identity of the person, unless FDA is required to disclose the information by law, e.g., the investigation leads to a hearing or trial and he or she is required to testify, and

2. will try to corroborate all information provided by the person, minimizing the chances he or she must later testify. However, testifying remains a possibility.

F. Ask the person for names of other persons who might be willing to speak with you about the allegations and corroborate their story.

II. Protect the identity of the source.

A. Collection of information. Obtain sufficient personal information necessary to enable you to contact the person for follow up if needed. However, to maintain the confidentiality of the person, do not include the person's identifier information such as gender, name, address, and phone number in the memorandum of interview. You should assign the confidential source a code name or number and use the identifier in memoranda and other communications relating to the confidential source (see item 2.C. below).

B. Access. Know who is authorized by District procedure to access the information, and restrict access by others accordingly. Share the minimum amount of information necessary to meet the purpose of the disclosure.

C. Storage. Each District should establish procedures, in addition to those listed below, to properly store confidential information. The following list contains information related to storage procedures.

1. Use security measures necessary to protect the confidentiality of personal information, whether it is in hard copy or electronic form, on FDA premises, in an FDA home-based computer, or in any other form. Use whatever means necessary and appropriate to physically safeguard the information, such as storing in a safe, or locked file cabinets, or password-coded computers, etc.

2. When referring to the source in any manner (orally, in writing, electronically, etc.), consider using code to identify the source. For example, use a number rather than the individual's name, to identify the source. Personal privacy information should be safeguarded. Use discreet subject headers in the file labels as appropriate.

3. Remove personal information from a file only after you have noted in the file your name, date, etc. Promptly return that information to the file.

D. Disclosure. Do not disclose information from or about the source, unless the disclosure complies with the law and FDA's procedures. Do not share non-public information outside of the Freedom of Information (FOI) process, unless the sharing is done according to our regulations and procedures. Refer FOI requests to your FOI officer (see item (3) below). See also IOM Subchapter 130. The following information relates to disclosures of information from or about a confidential source.

1. Make duplicates of the personal information only to the extent necessary for authorized disclosure (inside or outside of FDA). Do not leave the copy machine unattended.

2. Make only authorized disclosures of the information, regardless of the manner of disclosing (oral, written, etc.). Do not use mobile telephones or leave voice mails with the information. Avoid transmitting the non-public information by facsimile or e-mail.

3. If you receive a FOI request for information from or about a source consult with your supervisor immediately. Disclosure to a non-FDA government official of information from or about a source may be disclosed only if permitted by law and FDA procedures, and after consulting your supervisor and, if needed, OCI.

4. Immediately retrieve information from or about a source is inadvertently disclosed.

E. Destruction. Destroy personal information by shredding or similar means which physically destroys the record and/or, if the information is in electronic form, makes it unreadable.

Office of Chief Counsel. After a matter has been referred to the Office of Chief Counsel (OCC) for litigation or enforcement action, consult with OCC if you are interested in contacting the source.

519 ANIMAL HUSBANDRY-GROWERS - PRODUCERS

This section is FDA's guidance when you visit any type of facility where any domestic or wild animals are housed or transported. If a firm has more restrictive controls, follow those in addition to the controls cited below as long as they do not interfere with your assignment needs. The controls and procedures are intended to prevent you from becoming a vector or carrier of animal diseases, to prevent the spread of animal disease, and to set a good example for stockmen, growers and industry servicemen. A number of chronic diseases, such as Johne's Disease, bovine virus diarrhea (BVD) and others exist in domestic animals which you can unknowingly spread. Any inspectional contact with herds of livestock (including poultry) or non-domesticated animals exposes you to potential claims of introducing or spreading disease. This could occur between sections of a single site, such as poultry houses, or between different sites or farms. The potential also exists for the introduction of disease from an animal processing plant, such as a slaughterhouse or renderer to a live animal facility. You can prevent this by following appropriate cleaning and disinfection steps between facilities. Generally, a break of 5 days or more between sites is sufficient to eliminate concern about transmission of infectious agents.

These precautions, biosecurity measures, are necessary in two types of situations. The first is when there is no known disease present and your actions are precautionary. This section primarily addresses those kinds of activities. The other situation involves known or suspected disease outbreaks or more notorious disease conditions such as salmonella in eggs, infectious Laryngotrachetis, foot and mouth disease, vesicular stomatitis, and blackhead which can be highly contagious and spread from one group of animals to another by movement of people and objects between infected and non-infected groups. In these cases, special precautions must be taken to make sure you are not an unknowing vector for the spread of disease. See IOM 519.3

If you will only be inspecting an office or house away from areas where animals are housed or kept, clean and suitable street attire may be sufficient. Be aware if you visit any area of a facility where animals have been, you should always sanitize, clean or change footwear and it may be necessary to change outerwear before visiting another animal site to prevent any possibility of transmission of disease.

Your vehicle may also transport infection if you drive through contaminated areas.

519.1 Pre-Inspection Activities

When you know you are going to visit or inspect any animal production or holding facility, consider contacting the State Veterinarian and/or the Regional APHIS office to determine if there are any areas in the state under quarantine or special measures to control animal diseases. APHIS office locations can be found on their website: http://www.aphis.usda.gov/vs/area_offices.htm. The State Veterinarian will be listed under Government Listings in your phone book and is listed at http://www.fda.gov/ora/fed_state/directorytable.htm. Regional Milk Specialists frequently working with State counterparts in the Interstate Milk Shippers program should contact these sources at least quarterly for updates. Ask for any special controls or procedures they recommend. Follow any guidance they offer in addition to the precautions in this section. You should also consider pre-notification of the facility following guidance in IOM 510, Pre-Announcement, unless your assignment does not allow pre-notification. If you elect to pre-announce the inspection, in addition to the normal contact, ask to speak with the person at the facility responsible for their biosecurity measures and find out what they require of employees and visitors. If their requests do not interfere with your ability to do your job, follow their requests as we do when inspecting sterile manufacturing facilities.

Make sure your vehicle is clean and has been recently washed. Commercial car washes are adequate as long as you check to make sure any dirt, manure or other debris, which may be present from a previous site, has been removed. Some facilities may require additional disinfection of tires upon entry to the premises. Ensure tires and floor mats are clean. Consider designating places in your vehicle for storage of clean, unused supplies and dirty or used supplies.

In addition to your normal inspectional tools, obtain the following equipment and supplies from your district:

1.   Laundered or disposable coveralls or smocks (coveralls are suggested because they give better coverage). If you are going to visit multiple facilities in one day or trip, obtain sufficient quantities so you can change into clean or unused clothing between each site.

2.   Disposable plastic gloves, rubber boots, which can be sanitized, and disposable shoe/boot covers. Rubber boots over which you place disposable shoe/boot covers are preferred.

3.   Reusable cloth or plastic laundry bag(s) for clothing to be laundered. (Disposable bags can be used.)

4.   Soap, water and disposable or freshly laundered individual hand (or paper) towels.

5.   Sanitizing solution(s) and equipment (brushes, bucket, tray, measuring devices, etc.) to permit you to properly sanitizing hands, boots, equipment and your vehicle. Most disinfectants will require removing organic matter before use and good brushes are essential to remove dirt from boots and other objects.

Make sure any equipment you take with you has been thoroughly cleaned and sanitized as necessary. Clip boards, briefcases, flashlights, inspectional sampling tools, coolers, brushes, buckets and other objects should be cleaned between uses as necessary and between visits to any suspected infected facilities. Disposable equipment should be used to the fullest extent possible.

Maintain copies of any applicable Material Safety Data Sheets (MSDS) for disinfectants with you in your vehicle. If the firm's management requests information on the disinfectants you are using, they may read or copy these MSDS. Be familiar with the instructions and precautions concerning use of disinfectants. Any disinfectant should be effective against known or suspected microbiological agents.

In the event of a foreign animal disease, contact the USDA, APHIS Veterinary Services area Veterinarian in Charge for additional precautions and procedures to follow. (See 519.3)

519.2 General Inspection Procedures

Always begin each day with a clean vehicle free from any visible dirt or debris. During the day, take precautions to minimize contamination of your vehicle. If your vehicle becomes obviously dirty with adhering mud or manure, clean it before visiting another animal facility. When you arrive at a facility where animals are located, check to see if there are designated parking spots or pads for visitors. If so, park your vehicle there unless directed otherwise by the firm. If there is no guidance, park well away from all areas housing animals. When you arrive, inquire about or reconfirm any biosecurity measures the firm employs. Confirm your actions are suitable and follow expectations of the facility when this does not interfere with your inspection ability. Follow steps requested by the firm to remove contamination from vehicles, which may include troughs or pools of disinfectants for tires or other control measures. Avoid driving through manure, mud or wastewater at these sites.

In general, entry to animal housing or feeding areas, corrals, calf pens, hospital pens or special treatment facilities should be avoided unless the assignment requires their inspection or there are specific reasons requiring entry. If you must visit the feeding area occupied by livestock or birds, first determine if any groups are infected with disease. Arrange to visit the known non-disease areas first. Do not handle any animals unless official duty requires such contact. Before leaving the area where you parked your car, put on protective clothing as described and proceed with the purpose of your visit; sanitizing hands (and gloves if worn) and boots as necessary during the visit or inspection.

• General procedures:

1. **Wear rubber boots or other suitable footwear, which you disinfect upon arriving at the site and prior to departure. It is preferable to also place disposable foot coverings over your footwear, regardless of the type, after you have disinfected them. If the firm has foot-baths, use them. Boots and footwear should be disinfected with any of the agents identified at the end of this subsection using a good brush. Clean and disinfect the brush(es) and bucket you use for these activities.**

2. Wash your hands with soap and water. If you are visiting a facility where a known animal disease is present or the firm's biosecurity protocol requires, wear disposable gloves.

3. Wear disposable or freshly laundered coveralls, when appropriate. Some facilities may provide disposable coveralls and require visitors to shower in and shower out at their facilities. If requested by the firm and facilities are provided, you should follow those requests.

4. Wear appropriate head coverings, as necessary. If you wear a head covering, clean and disinfect between facilities or use disposable head coverings.

5. Minimize any materials you carry with you such as notebooks, flashlights, etc. to what is required. Consider keeping these things in clean plastic bags or containers between uses. Disinfect any of these types of items as best you can between visits to facilities or between different animal-housing areas.

6. If you are visiting production units with animals of multiple ages, always try to work from the youngest to the oldest.

7. Avoid direct contact with livestock or wild animals, bodily fluids or animal byproducts when visiting facilities.

8. Regional Milk Specialists, Milk Safety Branch and State Training Team staff frequently working with State counterparts in the Interstate Milk Shippers program shall follow any biosecurity measures the firm employs, any biosecurity measures the State employs, and as a minimum shall follow the coded memoranda issued by CFSAN Milk Safety Branch on this subject.

Upon completing your assignment in a given animal area, return to the same area where you donned protective clothing. Remove disposable shoe/boot covers and gloves, if applicable, and place them in a disposable paper or plastic laundry bag. Clean and sanitize boots/footwear. Remove the protective clothing, if applicable, by peeling it off inside out. (This keeps the surfaces exposed to contamination on the inside.) Place all disposable items in a disposable laundry bag for disposal back at your office. If the firm has special containers for disposing of such articles, it is preferable to leave them there rather than transport them back to the office. Place reusable coveralls or other reusable protective clothing in a separate laundry bag for disposition at the office.

Follow guidance on biosecurity provided in the applicable Compliance Program or "Guide to the Inspection of "****" in addition to precautions in this Section.

Repeat these procedures for each separate location visited or inspected.

Purchase commercially available solutions for disinfecting objects or consult with your servicing laboratory. Commercial products such as Nolvosan, Efersan, One Stroke Environ or Virkon-S may be used as long as they are registered by EPA for the intended purpose. Lye or chlorine based cleaners and disinfectants may also be used.

The following formula for household bleach may be used. Mix 3/4 cup (6 oz) of liquid bleach (5.25%) in one gallon of water (128 oz). This solution will be approximately 1:20 dilution. Formulations of household bleach, which are more concentrated than 5.25% are commercially available. Dilute accordingly to these directions. A more concentrated 1:10 solution (1-oz bleach to 9-oz water) may be used with decreased contact time required. Dilutions should be prepared fresh daily and protected from light.

You should read the label and be familiar with directions and precautions, such as removing any organic matter from objects to be disinfected, for any disinfectant you use. In the absence of directions or for chlorine solutions you prepare: 1. Remove visible dirt from the object (boots, tools, tires, etc.). 2. Wipe, brush or scrub surfaces with the solution and keep wet for 2 minutes. 3. Allow to air dry or dry with previously sterilized toweling.

519.3 Special Situation Precautions

If you are required to inspect or visit a facility known or suspected to be involved in a contagious animal disease an outbreak or otherwise identified as having diseased animals, contact the Center for Veterinary Medicine and/or Center for Food Safety and Applied Nutrition for additional precautions which may be necessary before you visits these sites. Your activities may be limited to visiting a single site in a day, taking extra-ordinary decontamination steps, ensuring you do not visit or inspect another facility for 5 or more days following the visit to the contaminated site or other steps. APHIS may have special restrictions or precautions for you to follow. The State Veterinarian may also request you follow additional requirements. During inspections of poultry operations where salmonella contamination is known or suspected, you should make sure you contact CFSAN directly for specific procedures to follow. Additional decontamination steps will be required.

SUBCHAPTER 520 - EVIDENCE DEVELOPMENT

520   TECHNIQUES

The recognition, collection, and effective presentation of admissible evidence is essential to successful litigation. Tangible evidence is required to support your observations and reports of violative conditions.

Although the inspectional procedures to detect adulteration and contamination, etc., are described under specific headings in the IOM, the same procedures and/or techniques may also apply to other areas. For instance, the procedures to detect contamination from filth, insects, rodents, birds, etc., described in IOM 530 may also apply to drugs or other products. Your experience and training assists you in making this transition and enables you to detect possible violative conditions.

Keep in mind the policy annunciated in the 4/23/1991 memorandum from the Director, Office of Compliance: The lack of a violative physical sample is not a bar to pursuing regulatory and/or administrative action providing the CGMP deficiencies have been well documented. Likewise, physical samples found to be in compliance are not a bar to pursuing action under CGMP charges.

521 FACTORY SAMPLES

Samples of raw materials or finished products collected during inspections provide the necessary key to establish routes of contamination. They also document the character of products packed prior to the inspection. Collect Factory Samples for laboratory examination only when they contribute to confirming the suspected violation. Be selective since negative reports of analysis of food samples are required under Section 704(d) of the Act and might give management a false picture of the firm's operation.

When possible collect duplicate sub samples to provide for the 702(b) portion of the sample. See IOM 422.1 & 427.4f for additional guidance and 21 CFR 2.10 for exemptions regarding the collection of duplicate portions.

522 EXHIBITS

Impressive exhibits are extremely effective and important forms of evidence to establish existence of violative conditions or products. They should relate to insanitary conditions contributing or likely to contribute, filth to the finished product, or to practices likely to render the product injurious or otherwise violative. Diagrams of the establishment, floor plans, flow charts, and schematics are useful in preparing a clear concise report and in later presentation of testimony. A small compass is useful in describing exact locations of objectionable conditions in the plant, in your diagrams, and locations from which samples were taken, etc. See IOM Exhibit 510-C.

Describe and submit under one INV Sample Number all exhibits (except photographs) collected during the inspection or investigation. Identify and number individual subs and officially seal all samples collected.

Examples of exhibits include:
1. Live and dead insects.
2. Insect frass, webbing, and insect chewed materials; nesting material of rodents and/or other animals; and other behavioral evidence of the presence of insects, rodents and other animals.
3. Samples of components or ingredients, in-process materials and finished products or dosage forms.
4. Manufacturing and control devices or aids.
5. Physical samples if possible and practical or, photographs with descriptions of scoops, stop-gap expediencies, other unorthodox manufacturing equipment or makeshift procedures. If photos are taken, follow the procedures described in IOM 523.
6. Evidence showing the presence of prohibited pes-

ticide residues. A method of swabbing for prohibited pesticide residues was published in Laboratory Information Bulletin # 1622. Excerpts are quoted as follows:

Apparatus - Four dram size glass vials, 95% ethanol, and cotton swabs preformed on 6" long wooden handles. Keep uncontaminated in a clean plastic bag.

Procedure - Blow away loose dirt or debris from approximately a 3" x 3" selected area. Measure approximately 2 cm of 95% ethanol in vial, dip swab into ethanol, press out excess on inside of vial and roll moist swab back and forth firmly across the selected area. Return swab to vial, swirl in alcohol, press out excess on inside of vial and again roll moist swab across the same area 90∞ to the previous swabbing. Re-insert swab into vial, break off swab handle and cap the vial with the swab inside.

When swab sub-samples are submitted, also submit a blank control sub consisting of an unused swab placed in a capped vial containing 2 cm of the same alcohol that was used for the other swabs.

Describe the type of material swabbed (cardboard carton, metal table top, rubber inspection belt, etc.) and the area covered. A reasonable area is approximately 10 sq. inches. Always try to establish a definite link in the chain of subsamples leading towards the highest level of contamination. If possible, identify the pesticide suspected. Be sure to include a floor plan with the areas sampled identified.

523 PHOTOGRAPHS - PHOTOCOPIES

Photos taken during EI's are not classified as INV Samples. They are exhibits. No C/R is used for photos taken unless the photos are part of an Official Sample. See IOM 405 for information on Official Samples.

Since photographs are one of the most effective and useful forms of evidence, every one should be taken with a purpose. Photographs should be related to insanitary conditions contributing or likely to contribute filth to the finished product, or to practices likely to render it injurious or otherwise violative.

CAUTION: Evaluate the area where flash photography is contemplated. Do not use flash where there is a potentially explosive condition; e.g. very dusty areas or possible presence of explosive or flammable vapors. In these situations use extremely fast film and/or long exposure time instead of flash.

Examples of conditions or practices effectively documented by photographs include:
1. Evidence of rodents or insect infestation and faulty construction or maintenance, which contributes to these conditions.
2. Routes of, as well as, actual contamination of raw materials or finished products.
3. Condition of raw materials or finished products.
4. Employee practices contributing to contamination or to violative conditions.
5. Manufacturing processes.
6. Manufacturing and various control records showing errors, substitutions, penciled changes in procedure, faulty practices, deviations from GMP's, NDA's, or other protocols, altered or inadequate assays or other control proce-

dures and any variation from stated procedure. See IOM 527.1 for identification of records.

7.   Effluent contamination of water systems. See IOM 532 for techniques in photographing this type of contamination.

When photographing labels, make sure your picture will result in a legible label with printing large enough to be read by an unaided eye. Photograph whited out documents by holding a flashlight against the whited out side and taking a close up photo of the reverse using high-speed film. This will produce a photo with a mirror image of the whited out side.

If you use a Polaroid camera or color slide film, explain the facts in your EIR or on the C/R to alert reviewers that there are no negatives.

523.1 In-Plant Photographs

Do not request permission from management to take photographs during an inspection. Take your camera into the firm and use it as necessary just as you use other inspectional equipment.

If management objects to taking photographs, explain that photos are an integral part of an inspection and present an accurate picture of plant conditions. Advise management the U. S. Courts have held that photographs may lawfully be taken as part of an inspection.

If management continues to refuse, provide them with the following references:

1.   "Dow Chemical v. United States, 476 U.S. 227 (1986) This Supreme Court Decision dealt with aerial photographs by EPA, but the Court's language seems to address the right to take photographs by any regulatory agency. The decision reads in part, "** When Congress invests an agency with enforcement and investigatory authority, it is not necessary to identify explicitly each and every technique that may be used in the course of executing the statutory mission. ***"

2.   "United States of America v. Acri Wholesale Grocery Company, A Corporation, and JOSEPH D. ACRI and ANTHONY ACRI, Individuals", U.S. District Court for Southern District of Iowa. 409 F. Supp. 529. Decided February 24, 1976.

If management refuses, advise your supervisor so legal remedies may be sought to allow you to take photographs, if appropriate. If you have already taken some photos do not surrender film to management. Advise the firm it can obtain copies of the photos under the Freedom of Information Act. See IOM 523.3.

523.2 Photo Identification and Submission

One of the most critical aspects about photographs or videotapes is the ability for the agency to provide testimony clearly verifying the authenticity of the conditions depicted in the photograph or video. It makes no difference if the photo is a 35 mm print from acetate negatives, a Polaroid photo, a digital photo or video taken with a video recorder. You must create a trail, starting with the taking of the photo, confirming its original accuracy and establishing a record describing the chain of custody. To do this, you must make sure each photograph is described in your diary or regulatory notes in sufficient detail to assure positive correlation of the photo or video with your inspection findings. One way you can do this is to photograph a card with your name, district address and phone number as the first frame or picture on a roll of film or in the digital record. This will help identify the film or file and assist in tracking if it is lost or becomes separated from its identification envelope during processing or storage. Proper procedures will also allow the agency to provide evidence confirming the authenticity of the photographs or video recording in the event you are not able to testify personally.

1.   Prints - Identify each print on the margin with exhibit number, firm name (or DOC Sample Nos., if DOC Sample), date taken, and your initials. Do not place any identifying marks on the picture area of the print. (Some photo developing firms are supplying borderless prints. For this type print, place identification along the back bottom edge of the print and mount the print so that the identification can be read without removing the print from the mounting paper. Place a narrative description on the mounting paper next to the print and attach as exhibits to the EIR and/or route with other records associated with a DOC Sample.)

2.   Color Slide Identification - If color slides are used, identify each slide, in the same manner as for prints. Districts may have special mounting frames for color slides, so the narrative description of each slide must be in the body of the report with proper reference to exhibits, or, each description may be placed on sheets of paper following the mounting frames and properly referenced.

3.   Negative Identification - Identify the edge of at least two negative strips, with the same information as for prints using a 3/16" strip of pressure sensitive tape. Place all negatives in a FDA-525 envelope. Complete blocks 2, 3, (4 if DOC Sample), 5, 7, and 12 and seal with an Official Seal, FDA-415a. If negatives are not part of a DOC Sample, enter firm name in the Sample Number block.

4.   Digital Photographs or Video Recordings - The initial file or video record must be handled and protected just as if it is a photograph negative. Unused disks or videotapes should generally be used to capture the photograph or video and, for subsequent copies of the original file/recording. The initial file containing the digital picture or video must be write-protected, identified with a label with the firm name (or Sample number if it is being submitted as part of an official sample), date taken, and your initials. The original must be officially sealed in a FDA-525 envelope or similar envelope. If you use a larger, unfranked envelope, identify the envelope with your name, title, home district, date, firm name, firm address (include zip code), description of the contents of the envelope, and marked in large, bolded letters **"STORE AWAY AND PROTECT FROM MAGNETIC FIELDS"**. You may place more than one disk in a single FDA-525 as long as you state on the envelope how many disks are in the envelope. The same procedure can be used if there is more than one videotape. If this original envelope is opened, a chain of custody must be recorded and a new seal(s) used after each entry to the envelope.

If the digital camera you use has a built-in or special disk for storing optical images, you can download the picture to a clean, unused disk and treat this first copy as the original disk. Your diary or regulatory notes must contain an entry you performed this first copy and verified the copy by viewing the photo(s) was an accurate copy of the original picture you took. This "original copy" should be treated just as if it is the original. When you need to place the photo file into a document or otherwise copy it, or perform any manipulation of the file or recording, do this only using a copy of the original and not the original. When you sign the report, memorandum or other agency document, your signature certifies you are saying the content of the document, including any photographic images, is true and accurate to the best of your ability.

Submit the sealed FDA-525 as an exhibit to the EIR, with the Investigative Report as an attachment, or with the other associated records with a DOC Sample.

523.21　Preparing and Maintaining Digital Photographs as Regulatory Evidence

A digital photo's chain of custody (and authenticity) must be assured and protected with the following procedure:

1. Prior to using the digital camera, verify the date and time stamp is correct and there are no images stored on the memory media.

2. The camera and the storage media used must be handled in a manner to protect your evidence and maintain the trail of the "chain of custody" for the evidence you have collect. For example: The camera and storage media shall be in the investigator's personal possession at all times or held under lock/key in a secure storage area. Any additional storage media with images shall also remain in the investigator's personal possession until transferred to permanent storage media. Where necessary, document these facts in your diary or written report (EIR, CR etc).

3. As soon as practical, the investigator will create a master of the digital photos. Some cameras will capture images directly to a (Write-once Compact Disk Recordable (CD-R)), the CD-R from these cameras becomes the original CD-R. Identify, date and initial the CD-R as an original image record. If a CD-R/W was used, the images must be copied to a CD-R to create a master with files that can not be altered. Follow additional instructions for creating and finishing a CD-R in step 4 below.

4. If the camera requires downloading of images to a CD-R, download all the images from the digital camera to an unused CD-R or other electronic storage media to create a master. The images should be transferred to a file format maintaining the image resolution at the time the image was captured. If possible, avoid the use of any file compression in transferring the images to the CD-R. Prior to preparing the CD-R or transferring image files you must verify that the computer you are using is set to the correct date and time. The CD-R shall be made permanent in a format readable by any CD-R reader.

5. Where applicable, document in your diary the verification and identification of each photographic image comparing them to your diary notes, which were recorded at the time the photographs were taken.

6. You should make only one copy from each original or master and make any additional copies using the first copy from the original or master. No more than one copy should be made from the original or master in order to preserve the original or master as a pristine set.

7. Prior to making the initial working copy from the original or master, the original or master should be identified as you would with photo negatives with the firm name, (or Sample Number), date and your initials. It is important to identify the original or master as soon as possible to prevent possible mix up of original or master with any copies. The CD-R should be identified on the non-recording side using a permanent felt marker. After making the initial working copy, the original or master should be placed in a suitable package, officially sealed and store the officially sealed CD-R or other electronic storage media until submitted with the written report (EIR, CR etc). If the images are captured or transferred to diskettes, refer to Section 527.3 for the handling of diskettes. If possible, the investigator (who took the photos and will authenticate them at trial) should store the sealed CD-R or other electronic storage media until it is submitted with the written report. If you break the seal for any reason this must be documented on the broken seal and in your diary or written report and with the package subsequently resealed.

8. Working copies should be used to print photos, insertion into EIR, cropped, otherwise manipulated or to be included in a referral.

9. Steps taken for any unusual manipulation of photo images must be documented in a diary or written report (EIR, CR, etc). For example: Superimposing over a important area of the image, image enhancement, composite images, etc.

523.3　Photograph Requests

Do not routinely advise firms they may have copies of photos. However, if management of the firm initiates the request, advise them it is possible to obtain copies of photographs taken in their plant under the Freedom of Information Act. Any request should be sent to The Food and Drug Administration, at the address listed on the FDA 482 or FDA 483. The firm must bear the cost of duplicating the photographs.

Since photographs are records in an investigative file, they are not available under the Freedom of Information Act until the file is closed.

Do not discourage firms from taking their own photographs at the same time and of the same scenes as you.

524　RECORDINGS

Under normal circumstances recording devices will not be used while conducting inspections and investigations. However, some firms are now recording and/or video taping, the inspection and/or the discussion with management portion of the inspection. These firms should be advised we do not object to this procedure, but we will also record the discussion to assure the accuracy of our records. Occasionally a firm's management may record the serving of an inspection warrant or, in a hostile situation, may want to record everything. In such cases, depending on the circumstances, you may prepare your own recording in parallel with the firm's recording. Do not depend on the firm to provide a duplicate of their recordings.

Use a clear tape cassette and identify the tape verbally as follows:

"This is Investigator _____ of the U.S. Food and Drug Administration speaking in the (state location) of (firm name), (address), (city), (state), and (zip code). It is now a.m./p.m. on (date). Present are (list individuals present with title). This discussion is being recorded by both the representative of (firm name) and by me. We are going to discuss the inspectional findings of an inspection conducted at this firm on (inclusive dates)."

At the close of the discussion and prior to leaving the firm, the recording will be verbally identified as follows:

"This is Investigator _____ speaking. It is now _____ a.m./p.m. on (date). This was a recording of the discussion with management at the conclusion of an inspection of (firm name & address) conducted on (dates).

If the recording covers a different situation, the identification should be modified accordingly. If the representative of the firm refuses permission to record the discussion, continue with your discussion and report the facts in your EIR.

The tape cassette must be identified with the firm name, date of the inspection, and investigator's name. Districts have the option of transcribing the tape and making the transcription an exhibit for the EIR. However, the tape itself must be made a permanent part of the EIR as an exhibit.

525   RESPONSIBLE INDIVIDUALS

The identification of those responsible for violations is a critical part of the inspection, and as important as determining and documenting the violations themselves. Responsibility must be determined to identify those persons to hold accountable for violations, and with whom the agency must deal to seek lasting corrections.

Document and fully report individual responsibility whenever;

1.   It is required by the assignment,
2.   Inspectional findings suggest the possibility of regulatory action, or
3.   Background information suggests the possibility of regulatory action.

Under the Medical Device Quality System regulation (21 CFR 820.20), if the management at the firm is not exercising the controls required by the regulation, the deviations may be cited on your FDA 483.

525.1 Discussion on Duty, Power, Responsibility

Duty - An obligation required by one's position; a moral or legal obligation.

Power - Possession of the right or ability to wield force or influence to produce an effect.

Responsibility - An individual who has the duty and power to act is a responsible person.

Three key points to consider are:
1. Who had the duty and power to detect the violation?
2. Who had the duty and power to prevent the violation?
3. Who had the duty and power to correct the violation?

525.2 Inspection Techniques – How to Document Responsibility

Always determine and report the full legal name and title of persons interviewed, who supplied relevant facts and the name/title/address of top management officials to whom FDA correspondence should be directed.

Obtain the correct name and correct title of all corporate officers or company officials. Obtain pertinent educational and experience backgrounds, and the duties and powers of the officers and employees in key managerial, production, control, and sanitation positions. Ascertain the experience and training of supervisory personnel, in terms that will describe their qualifications to carry out their responsibilities.

There are numerous ways to establish and document responsibility. Evidence may be obtained during interviews and record review specifically intended to determine responsibility. Cover and report items such as:

1.   Organizational charts,
2.   Statements by individuals admitting their responsibility or attributing responsibility to others,
3.   Company publications, letters, memos and instructions to employees, and
4.   The presence or absence of individuals in specific areas at specific, significant times, and their observed activities directing, approving, etc.

In order to establish relationships between violative conditions and responsible individuals, the following types of information, would be useful:

1.   Who knew of conditions?
2.   Who should have known of the conditions because of their specific or overall duties and positions?
3.   Who had the duty and power to prevent or detect the conditions, or to see they were prevented or detected?
4.   Who had the duty and power to correct the conditions, or to see they were corrected? What was done after person(s) learned of the conditions? Upon whose authority and instructions (be specific)?
5.   What orders were issued (When, by whom, to whom, on whose authority and instructions)?
6.   What follow up was done to see if orders were carried out (when; by whom; on whose authority and instructions)?
7.   Who decided corrections were or were not complete and satisfactory?
8.   What funding, new equipment, new procedures were requested, authorized or denied in relation to the conditions; who made the requests, authorizations, or denials.

Duties and power related to general operations should be established to supplement the specific relationships to violations. Examples of operational decisions that indicate responsibility are:

1. What processing equipment to buy.
2. What raw materials to purchase.
3. What products to produce and what procedures to follow in production?
4. Production schedules - how much to produce, what to make, when to stop or alter production?
5. What production controls to be used?
6. What standards are set for products, raw materials, processes?
7. How to correct or prevent adverse conditions; how much to spend and whom to hire to correct or prevent adverse conditions; when to clean up?
8. How products will be labeled; what products to ship; label approval?
9. When to reject raw materials or products; when to initiate a recall; acceptable quality levels for products?
10. When to hire or fire personnel?
11. Who will accept FDA 482, Notice of Inspection; refuses inspection; accept Inspectional Observations, FDA 483?
12. Who designed and implemented the quality assurance plan; who receives reports of Q.A.; who acts or should act upon the reports?
13. Who is responsible for auditing other facilities, contractors, vendors, GLP sites, etc.?
14. In the firm's business relationships, who signs major contracts, purchase orders, etc?

In some circumstances, documenting of individual responsibility requires investigative techniques that lead to sources outside the firm. These sources may include contractors, consultants, pest control or sanitation services, local health officials and others. Copies of documents between the firm and outside parties may help establish responsibilities. Do not overlook state officials as another possible source of information in selected cases.

During the course of the inspection you may observe persons who hold responsible positions and/or influence in the firm whose abilities or judgment may be affected by an obvious infirmity, handicap, or disability. If it is obvious the infirmity adversely affects the person's responsibilities or duties that are under FDA oversight, describe in your EIR the extent of the infirmity and how it relates to the purported problem or adverse condition.

526   GUARANTEES AND LABELING AGREEMENTS

Review the Code of Federal Regulations, 21 CFR 7.12, 7.13, 101.100(d), 201.150, and 701.9, for information concerning guarantees and labeling agreements.

Guaranty - Certain exemptions from the criminal provisions of the FD&C Act are provided where a valid guarantee exists as specified in Section 303(c) of the FD&C Act. Obtain a copy of any Food and Drug guarantee, which the firm claims to use relating to a violation noted during your inspection. No person may rely upon any guaranty unless he has acted merely as a conduit through which the merchandise reached the consumer.

Labeling Agreement - Products regulated by FDA are normally expected to be completely labeled when intro-

duced into or while in interstate commerce. Under certain conditions exemptions are allowed when such articles are, in accordance with trade practices, to be processed, labeled, or repacked in substantial quantity at an establishment other than where originally processed or packed. Sections 405, 503(a) and 603 of the FD&C Act also provide exemptions from complete labeling for products.

To enjoy this exemption, the shipment must meet one of the following:
1. The shipper must operate the establishment where the article is to be processed, labeled or repacked; or
2. If the shipper is not the operator of the establishment, he must first obtain from the owner a written agreement signed by and containing the post office addresses of such persons and such operator and containing such specifications for the processing, labeling or repacking of such articles as will insure that such article will not be adulterated or misbranded within the meaning of the Act, upon completion of the processing, labeling or repacking.

Submit copies and dates of labeling agreements where unlabeled articles are shipped in interstate commerce.

527   RECORDS OBTAINED

Many types of inspections and investigations require collection of copies of records to document evidence of deviations. In some cases, this may involve voluminous copies of Good Manufacturing Practice (GMP) records, commitments made in the Pre-Approval process, adherence to the requirements of the Low Acid Canned Food regulations or other areas. Copies of records are also obtained to document interstate commerce, product labeling and promotion, and to identify the party or parties responsible for a variety of actions. All documents become part of the government's case should it go to litigation.

Normally, during litigation proceedings, the best evidence rule prevails in court, whereby the copy of the record in the custody of the government can be authenticated, if the original record is not produced by the custodian of the record.

It is imperative the government witness [usually the collector of the record(s)] be able to testify where, when and from whom the copies were obtained, and that the copy is a true copy of the source document, based on their review of the source document.

527.1 Identification of Records

Articles used as evidence in court cases must be marked to assure positive identification. This includes all records as noted in IOM 527, and any others for evidence in administrative or judiciary proceedings. When identifying and filing records, you must assure the record is complete and no identification method or filing mechanism covers, defaces or obliterates any data on the record/document.

It is imperative you identify the records used as evidence so you can later testify the documents entered as evidence are the very ones you obtained. See IOM 527.2. You should always review source documents to assure the records you obtained are an accurate representation (copy) of the source document. Record in your Regulatory Notes the when, where, and from who copies are obtained so you can properly prepare for testimony as needed.

527.2 Identifying Original Paper Records

NOTE: Policy Changes - In keeping with other regulatory and enforcement agencies' policies, the mandatory identification of the original or source document copied during an inspection or investigation is no longer routinely required. IOM 451.5 covers identification of records collected and submitted as part of a sample collection.

When you collect an Official or Documentary (or "DOC") Sample, each page of the copied records will become part of the collection report and should be identified as noted in this section and as in IOM 430.5. This includes records of interstate commerce, manufacturing deviations, label and labeling violations, or any other record copied which may become "evidence.

While it is no longer routinely required for you to identify the original or source record(s), you must verify the copy of the record(s) you received is an accurate reproduction of the original or source record(s). You must be able to testify your copy is an exact duplicate of the original or source record. You should record in your diary you authenticated copies of records you obtain so you can provide this testimony during any trial proceedings.

To ensure you are able to positively identify the specific copies you received during your inspection or investigation and to avoid any filing mix-up, you must identify the copies you obtained. This identification will cover records submitted in support of the inspection or investigation, and include all those submitted whether it is an Establishment Inspection Report (EIR) or a narrative memorandum.

You should identify records/exhibits submitted with an EIR using at least the Exhibit number, firm name, date(s) of the inspection, and your initials. This should be done in such a way that you will be able to clearly identify the copy of specific record(s) you obtained. If some type of label is used, it must be permanently applied so any removal will be obvious. Records submitted with a Collection Report will be similarly identified with the sample number, date of collection, but with your handwritten initials. Records submitted with a memorandum will include a phrase or firm or subject name to tie them to the investigation, the date(s) of the investigation and your initials.

There are occasions when a single record may include hundreds of sheets of bound paper. Abbreviated methods of identification may be used for bound documents by fully identifying the first and last few pages. In some cases, firm's clearly mark each page with the sequential and total pages number (e.g., page 6 of 10, 7 of 10, etc.) and this allows you to fully mark only a few pages in the beginning and end of the exhibit.

All pages must be identifiable if not in bound documents. One example of a shortened method of identifying individual exhibits containing a large number of pages (usually more than 25) is to fully identify the first few and last few pages with at least the exhibit number, date and your initials. Then identify the remaining pages with the page num-

ber of the total page numbers, and your initials, e.g., "5 of 95 SHR". This may not be acceptable if you have more than one exhibit consisting of exactly 95 pages.

Whatever method is used, you must assure the document is complete and is always identifiable. This is so you can testify as to the "where", "when" and "from whom" the copies were obtained, and that the copy is a true copy of the source document based on your review of the source document. The identification method should allow any reviewer to determine if the document is complete or pages or parts are missing.

527.3 Filmed or Electronic Records

When attempting to obtain records, you may find they are stored on microfilm, microfiche, or some form of a computerized management information system as electronic records.

Microfilm/Microfiche and electronic information - You may encounter records stored on microfilm/microfiche or as electronic records on a computer system. Hard copy records obtained during the course of the inspection from these sources are handled the same as any hard copied records following procedures outline in IOM 527, 527.1 and 527.2.

NOTE: See CPG Section 130.400 for Agency Policy concerning microfilm and/or microfiche records. 21 CFR Part 11 contains information concerning Electronic Records and Electronic Signatures and may be of value to you.

Electronic information received on CD-R, or other electronic storage media - You may obtain electronic information, databases, or summary data from a firm's databases during an establishment inspection. The methods used must maintain the integrity of the electronic data and prevent unauthorized changes.

Electronic data, such as blood bank databases, drug production records, medical device complaints, service records, returned products and other records are often dynamic data files with real time updating. Information from these files is generally provided at the time of the inspection. Your request may require the firm to develop one or more custom queries to provide the requested information. You must assume the query logic is not validated and take appropriate action to ensure the data is accurate and no data has been accidentally omitted due to a programming logic error occurring at the firm.

When appropriate, a copy of electronic data can be obtained on one or more CD-R, or other electronic storage media. If you provide the diskettes to the firm, use only new, previously unused and preformatted diskettes. An additional safeguard is to request the firm reformat the disk on their own computer to assure it is usable and "clean".

Any request for electronic information on a CD-R, or other electronic storage media must be made with a computer application in mind and the data obtained must be useful. Request for electronic information should be in a format compatible with software applications knowledgeable to you and available from the Agency. Converting files into different file formats is difficult and should not be attempted without the necessary knowledge and availability of conversion type programs where applicable. If help is needed for file conversion, assistance may be available within the district, region or from DFI HFC-130.

Any CD-R or other electronic storage media containing electronic information received during the course of an inspection should be considered and handled as master copies. The firm may or may not retain a copy of the information provided during the course of an inspection. Ask the individual providing the copy(s) to provide actual CD-R or other electronic storage media labeling information, such as filename(s), date and other information to facilitate their later identification of the CD-R or other electronic storage media and the data provided on the CD-R or other electronic storage media. The name of the appropriate software and version used to ensure readability of the information should also be maintained with the copy of the electronic information.

You should perform a virus scan of the master CD-R or other electronic storage media according to Agency requirements. Each master diskette should be write-protected, labeled and identified as you would any hard copy document.

There are no guarantees the files provided on CD-R or other electronic storage media will be useable data. It is your responsibility to make a working copy of each master CD-R or other electronic storage media. Before making any working copies from the master CD-R or other electronic storage media, confirmation should be made that the write-protection has been activated on each master diskette. You will need to use a computer to view the copied files and verify each file contains the information requested and the information is useable to you. Some electronic data files may be too large to open from a CD-R or other electronic storage media and must be loaded on a hard disk before opening. If this is the case, the file should be put on a subdirectory before opening and viewing.

As a general practice, any findings developed from electronic information provided by the firm should be requested in a hard copy format. The hard copy provided by the firm should then be used as an exhibit to support the investigator's observation. This will preclude or limit any errors that may have occurred from the investigator querying of the electronic information.

The master CD-R, diskettes or other electronic storage media, should be secured to assure the integrity of the data when used in a subsequent enforcement action. Identify the master copy as an exhibit, write-protect diskettes, and place in a suitable container, e.g., FDA-525, and officially seal. Mark the FDA-525 or other container as containing diskettes and to "Protect from magnetic fields." The diskette(s) should be stored as part of the exhibits with the original EIR. See IOM 594.1.

527.4 Requesting and Working with Computerized Complaint and Failure Data

The auditing of FDA regulated firms has found that an increasing number of firms are developing and maintaining computerized complaint and failure data to meet GMP

record requirements. Records, hardcopy and electronic, are becoming increasingly voluminous. The auditing of information contained in computerized databases is generally most effectively accomplished with the use of a computer.

Computer auditing of computerized complaints and failure data may require the transfer of electronic data to CD-R or other electronic storage media for you to use in your computer. You should use a computer and application software familiar to you to query information obtained in electronic format. You should not use the audited firm's equipment or personnel to perform extensive queries or manipulation of the audited firm's own computerized data.

527.41 Computerized Complaint and Failure Data

Requesting and obtaining electronic data on CD-R or other electronic storage media is becoming more common during the course of routine inspections. Providing computerized data on electronic media is advantageous to both you and the firm and can result in shorter inspection time. These types of databases contain large numbers of records, which can be easily and quickly queried if they are in electronic format. Inspection time would be lengthened if all such information was only provided in hardcopy format. It may result in you reentering all of the hardcopy data into a new database or reviewing volumes of documents. Be aware if the firm should generate custom software to provide requested electronic records, it would be difficult for you to validate or verify the firm's algorithm used to extract the requested data and ensure that records were not accidentally or deliberately omitted due to programming logic errors, data entry errors, etc.

527.42 Requesting Computerized Data

Before requesting a copy of computerized data, you should determine several things including information about the size and contents of the database, the program used by the firm, and the program you will use, among others. The following steps are useful in preparing for an electronic record request.

1. Determine the firm's application program used to maintain the data of interest. This may be in a DOS compatible application program such as Access, Excel, Dbase, Paradox, Lotus 123 or others. It is best to obtain data files in a format compatible with application programs you will be using. Large data files with record counts in excess of 10,000 records are best converted to file formats that can be used by programs designed to handle such large databases. There are spreadsheet record limits in some commercial programs that would not allow these application programs to handle much over 5,000 records. Check the program you plan to use to ensure it can handle the file size you will be using.

2. Most large and real-time data files reside in mainframe or network systems requiring programming and downloading to a PC using an [Structured Query Language (SQL)] SQL format. Although data may be captured and

downloaded in an SQL format, not all spreadsheet or database application software can load an SQL file. In addition, it may be difficult or impossible to manipulate data in that format. Problems can also be encountered downloading data from Apple computers to an IBM format. Successful conversions are possible if the firm selects the proper conversion format or you have conversion software designed to convert from an Apple to an IBM platform.

3. You may need to request an ASCII (American Standard Code for Information Interchange) text/flat file format. ASCII format is an industry standard, which assigns a unique code to every printable, keyboard, and screen character. An ASCII file should be stripped of all non [-] standard codes that are used by specific application programs for fonts, underlining, tabs, etc. The ASCII text file can be imported by all application programs, and once imported, can be restructured for the specific application program. ASCII delimited is the format of choice, with ASCII fixed length as an alternative. Care must be exercised in specifying a hard carriage return at the end of each line to be DOS compatible, or additional conversion may be necessary before the file is useable.

4. You should determine what fields of information are routinely captured by the firm. This can be accomplished by requesting a printout of the data structure of the data file or observing the inputting of data at a computer terminal or workstation. It is common for databases to contain numbers or other coded information requiring translations from look up tables to give meaningful text. You should determine if information fields contain coded data, and if so, a code breakdown should be obtained. Information about code breakdowns should be located in the SOPs for that computerized system. Also be aware in relational databases, there may be linking data fields that exist in other tables that should also be considered in the overall data request.

5. If the files are too large to fit on a disk, file compression must be used. If possible, ask that the firm prepare the data in a compression format that is self-extracting. Self-extracting files are executable files and should be virus scanned before and after executing. All CD-R, diskettes or other electronic storage media should be scanned prior to being used on any FDA computer. Whatever compression utility is used, make sure you have the software to manipulate the files as needed.

6. You should always get the total record count of the data file provided by the firm. This count should be verified any time the file is loaded, converted, manipulated, or queried.

527.43 Identification and Security of CD-R, Diskettes or Other Electronic Storage Media

You should follow these steps to ensure proper identification and security of CD-R or other electronic storage media:

1. Label each CD-R or other electronic storage media
   a. Firm name
   b. Date and your initials
   c. Initials by a representative of the firm (optional)

If you provide the diskettes to be used, use only new and preformatted diskettes from an unopened box.
   d. The name of the appropriate software and version to ensure readability of the information
2. Make a working copy of CD-R or other electronic storage media
   a. Write protect the original diskette
   b. Virus scan the original diskette
   c. Copy the original CD-R or other electronic storage media

The original CD-R or other electronic storage media should not be used for manipulating data so as to maintain the integrity of the CD-R or other electronic storage media and data. **NOTE:** If a virus is detected, do not remove the virus from the source diskette provided by the firm. This may become evidence if it is suspected that the firm intentionally transferred the virus. Attempt to obtain another, uninfected copy of the data file from the firm.

Create a subdirectory on the computer hard drive
   a. Transfer data from the virus-free, working copy of the CD-R or other electronic storage media to your hard drive.
   b. Virus scan any decompressed files before and after decompression. (Some virus scan software will scan compressed files but it is safer to scan all foreign files
   c. You have now transferred confidential information to the hard drive and that information must be protected.
   d. Upon completion of the use of the data, the file must be deleted and totally overwritten with a utility to wipe the data from the hard drive. A delete file operation is not adequate to totally remove the data from the hard drive.
   e. Do not leave confidential files in any shared directories or e-mail.

527.44 Data Integrity of Records Provided by Firm

Many manufacturers are using computers to store records concerning complaints, failure data, returned goods, servicing, testing results and others. Record traceability and data integrity are always concerns when you copy or use computerized data.

1. It is difficult to determine what records are to be designated as originals or copies of original records. It is important, when obtaining hardcopy or copy of computerized data, for you to capture some method of dating. The date of an electronic file can be captured by recording the date and time from a file listing in DOS or with File Manager in Windows. This may not always be possible, but some attempt should be made to date and time stamp electronic data.

2. Requests for most information from manufacturers will require the use of some custom software routine to generate the Investigator's requested information. Any data generated at the request of an Investigator should always be considered custom data. The firm will seldom validate or verify software routines used to generate data in response to your request. You should request a copy of any software program or scripts used to generate the computerized data provided. The request for the software program is not a

request for a copy of the application program but a request for the special commands or programs created within the application program for the querying and extraction of data into a new data file. You should review the command structure to ensure it includes all data related to your request.

527.45 Electronic Information for Official Documentation

During your use of queried data, if you find a violative situation, you should request the firm prepare a hardcopy report of the specific data that depicts the situation. (Do not request an entire copy of the data base and do not rely on the digital database or your extractions from the data to serve as official documentation.) Any records of interest, such as complaints, failure information, etc., noted from querying the computerized data should be copied from original hardcopy documents to support the findings in the database. You should also maintain the procedures or commands you used to find the violative situations in the data base. Follow procedures in IOM 527.3 for maintaining and identifying original disks.

527.5 Listing of Records

If management requests a list of the copies of records you obtain, prepare it in duplicate and leave the original with the firm. Many firms prepare duplicate copies of documents requested during our inspections. In the interests of conserving inspectional time, you may ask the firm to prepare the list of copies concurrently with the photocopying and you then verify the accuracy. Do not use form FDA-484, Receipt for Samples. Describe the circumstances in your report including the name and title of the individual to whom you gave the list. Submit the duplicate list with your report as an Exhibit.

527.6 Patient and/or Consumer Identification on Records

During the course of many types of inspections and investigations you will review and collect records which specifically identify (by name) patients or consumers. Under most state Privacy Laws this information is confidential. Some firms we inspect may mistakenly believe this information is not releasable to the federal government. However, Federal laws preempt State laws; with few exceptions we are entitled to review and copy the complete record, including the identifying patient/consumer names. The Agency is then required to maintain the confidentiality of the records/files, as with any confidential record you collect. Any disclosure of the information contained in the record(s) can only be by Law, i.e., judge's order, disclosure, Congressional order, etc.

General, routine guidance is as follows:

a. For records copied as a result of injury or complaint investigation, where you obtain patient identification, the identification should remain intact and stored in the official FDA files. Frequently, medical releases must be obtained from a complainant, consumer or "next-of-kin". At least one

or two extra should be obtained and stored in the files.

b. For methadone inspections, continue the Agency policy of deleting patient identification specific to the patient (name, SSN, Driver License #, etc.).

c. For any inspection/investigation involving a regulation required Informed Consent, such as clinical investigations, IRBs, bioequivalence testing, etc., patient identification should remain intact and stored in the official FDA files.

d. For most others, such as MQSA, plasmapheresis, blood donations, etc., only the patient initials and unique identifier supplied by the firm (such as donor number, donation number, etc.) need be routinely retained in the FDA files.

It is not uncommon for a firm to voluntarily purge the documents of the pertinent identifiers as they are copied. You must verify (by direct comparison to the original document) you received an accurate reproduction of the original, minus the agreed to purging, prior to accepting the copy.

As with any inspection there are times when the specific identifiers must be obtained, copied and retained, such as if/when further interview of the patient/consumer could be necessary. If in doubt, obtain the data. It is always easier to delete later than to return to obtain the information, especially in the few cases where questionable practices may result in the loss of the information.

All documents obtained containing confidential identifiers will be maintained as all documents obtained by FDA containing confidential information, i.e., in the official FDA files. Confidential identifiers may be flagged in the official FDA files for reference by reviewers to assure no confidential data are released under FOIA.

528   REQUEST FOR SAMPLE COLLECTION

There are times one district will request another district to collect surveillance or compliance samples for it. The requesting district should provide as much of the following information as is available on specific shipments, using the FACTS Create Assignment Screen. See IOM Exhibit 550 A.

The following fields must be completed in order to save the assignment: Requesting Organization, Priority, Subject, POC Name, Op Code, Accomp Org, Num of Ops, and PAC. When you create a sample collection assignment, which will require laboratory analysis, you should also create an assignment for the laboratory, using operation 41.

The screen is organized in sections. The Assignment section has the following fields:

Compliance Number: Enter the Compliance Number if known. This will make it easier to tie all associated activities together if the District is considering a compliance action. You can generate a compliance number after completing the mandatory fields on the Maintain Inspection Results screen.

ORA reqd: This field only applies to assignments generated by Centers or other organizations outside of ORA. It will indicate whether or not ORA concurrence is required for the assignment.

ORA Cncrnc Num: This field is for the requesting organization (other than an ORA component) to indicate ORA concurrence for the assignment.

POC Name: This field Indicates the point of contact in the requesting organization for the assignment.

Priority: Choose High or Routine

Remarks: This is a free form field, which should briefly describe the assignment.

Reporting Method: Indicate how the other district should notify the contact of problems with or status of the assignment. For example: e-mail, phone, etc.

Requesting Organization: Enter your District Office, if you are requesting a sample from another district or other appropriate FACTS organization.

Requestor Completion Date: Enter the completion date desired, using the format, MM/DD/YYYY.

Subject: Enter a subject for the assignment. It may be helpful to create a subject others will recognize as related to a specific action, for example a firm or product name. The Operations section has the following fields:

Estmtd Hours: Enter the number of hours you believe the assignment should take. This is done to assist the collecting district in planning their work.

Estmtd Smpl Cost: Enter the estimated sample cost, if known.

Op Code: Enter the operation code for the assignment. If you are requesting a sample collection, it is 31.

Requester Remarks: Enter as many details about the sample collection as you can. Include: date of shipment, number and size of units or amount, codes, carrier (routing and freight bill number), invoice number, and name of responsible firm with date of inspection (if one occurred).

Rqstr Prty: Enter High or Routine. This will default to the same data entered in the Assignment section if it was prepared first.

Subject: This will default to the same data entered in the Subject field in the Assignment section if it was prepared first.

The Organizations section contains the following fields.

➤ **Accomp Org:** Enter the District or other FACTS organization you are requesting collect the assignment. If you are completing the sample analysis assignment, be sure to enter a laboratory.

➤ **Num of Ops:** Enter the number of sample collections or analyses you are requesting from the organization identified in the previous field.

➤ **Perf Orf (Adhoc Work):** If the performing organization is part of the accomplishing organization you are in, you may enter the performing organization here. If you are requesting the sample of another District, you will probably leave this blank.

The PACS & Products section of the form contains fields for entering the assignment PAC and Product code.

Enter the FEI number(s)/CFN(s) of the firm or firms from which the sample is to be collected in the Firms & Cross References section. See IOM 439.8.

529   POST-INSPECTION NOTIFICATION LETTERS

Issuance of Post-inspection notification letters have been discontinued in all program areas. See FMD 145.

SUBCHAPTER 530 - FOOD

530   FOOD INSPECTIONS

Food plant inspections are conducted to evaluate the methods, facilities, and controls used in manufacturing, storage and distribution of foods.

530.1 Preparation and References

Before undertaking an inspection:

1.   Review the district files of the firm to be inspected and acquaint yourself with the firm's history, related firms, trade marks, practices and products. The review will identify products difficult to manufacture, require special handling, special processes or techniques, and hours of operation, which is especially important in bacteriological inspections. Remove, for subsequent investigations and discussion with management, Complaint/Injury Reports - FDA-2516 & 2516a, which are marked for follow-up during the next inspection. See IOM 517.

2.   Become familiar with current programs relating to the particular food or industry involved and relevant DFI inspection guides. These are referenced in Chapter 10 of the IOM. If the commodity you are covering is not contained in an inspection guide, then use the Guide entitled "INSPECTIONAL METHODS (INTERIM GUIDANCE) OCTOBER 1996".

3.   Understand the nature of the assignment and whether it entails certain problems, e.g., Salmonella or other bacteriological aspects.

4.   Review the FD&C Act Chapter IV - Food.

5.   Review and become familiar with the various parts of 21 CFR pertaining to foods. 21 CFR 110 GMP's on foods, 21 CFR 108 & 113 on Thermally Processed Low-Acid Foods Packaged in Hermetically Sealed Containers, and 21 CFR 114 Acidified Foods are of particular importance.

6.   Review reference materials on food technology and other subjects available in the District Inspectional Reference Library.

7.   If you are assigned to inspect food-service establishments under the FDA - Secret Service Agreement, you should use the most current copy of the "Food Code" and be standardized in its use. All Regional Food Service Specialists and most Interstate Travel Sanitation Specialists are standardized in use of the code.

8.   Be familiar with the "Food Chemicals Codex". See IOM 533.

530.2 Seafood HACCP

In December 1995, the Food and Drug Administration (FDA) issued seafood regulations based on the principles of Hazard Analysis and Critical Control Point (HACCP). The FDA issued these regulations to ensure safe processing and importing of fish and fishery products. Seafood HACCP inspections should follow the guidance in this subchapter supplemented with these additional Seafood

HACCP inspection specific guidance documents:
1.   Current Compliance Programs.
2.   Fish and Fishery Products Hazards & Control Guide (Second Edition)
3.   HACCP Training Materials
4.   HACCP Regulation for Fish and Fishery Products - Question and Answers (Issue Three, Revised January 1999)

530.3 Inspectional Authority

See IOM 701 for broader information on this topic.
Authority to Obtain Records & Information in LACF & Acidified Foods Plants:
1.   Written Demand for Records - FDA's regulation in 21 CFR 113 requires commercial processors of low-acid foods packaged in hermetically sealed containers to maintain complete records of processing, production and initial distribution. 21 CFR 114 requires the same of commercial processors of acidified foods. 21 CFR 108.25(g) and 21 CFR 108.35(h) provide that a commercial processor shall permit the inspection and copying of the records required by 21 CFR 113 and 21 CFR 114 by duly authorized employees of FDA. The demand for these records must be in writing on an FDA 482a, Demand for Records, signed by you and must identify the records demanded.
To obtain the records:
1.   Prepare a FDA 482a, "Demand for Records", listing the records demanded. Describe the processing records to be reviewed and/or copied as accurately as you can, e.g., "All thermal process and production records mandated by 21 CFR 113 (or 114 if applicable) for the foods (state name of food) processed at this plant on (specific date or period of time)". If only a specific record is desired list it specifically as follows: e.g., "Fill Weight Records for #2 Filling Machine for the period 4-15-87 through 6-7-87." (b) Sign the form. (c) Issue the original to the same person to whom the FDA 482, "Notice of Inspection", was issued. (d) Submit the carbon copy with your EIR.
2.   Written Request for Information - 21 CFR 108.35(c)(3)(ii) states commercial processors engaged in thermal processing of low-acid foods packaged in hermetically sealed containers shall provide FDA with any information concerning processes and procedures necessary by FDA to determine the adequacy of the process. 21 CFR 108.25(c)(3)(ii) requires the same of commercial processors of acidified foods. The information in this regulation is the data on which the processes are based. Many processors will not have this information and in fact 21 CFR 113.83 requires only that the person or organization establishing the process permanently retain all records covering all aspects of establishing the process. The processor should, however, have in his files a letter or other written documentation from a processing authority delineating the recommended scheduled process and associated critical factors.
You may encounter situations where you believe control of certain factors is critical to the process and there is no evidence to document these factors were considered when the process was established (e.g., a change in formulation which could effect consistency). It is appropriate to issue a written request for a letter or other written documentation from a processing authority, which delineates the recommended scheduled process and associated critical factors. This represents the processing authority's conclusions and should correlate with the filed process.
If you believe control of certain factors are critical to the process and are not delineated in the process authority's recommendation or the filed process, obtain all available information about the situation. Include the name of the person or organization who established the process and the specific practices of the firm. This information should be included in your report and forwarded by your District to the Center for Food Safety and Applied Nutrition, Division of Enforcement (HFS-605) for review, as soon as possible. If the process establishment data and information is deemed necessary by the center, they will either request it directly from the processor or will direct the district to request it. I f requested to obtain the information:
1.   Prepare a FDA 482b - Request for Information listing the specific information requested. Specify each product involved by food product name and form, container size and processing method.
2.   Sign the form.
3.   Issue the original to the same person to whom the FDA 482, "Notice of Inspection", was issued.
4.   Submit the carbon copy with your EIR.

531   PERSONNEL

Management - Follow the guidance described in IOM 525 when documenting individual responsibility including obtaining the full name and titles of the following individuals:
1.   Owners, partners, or officers.
2.   Other management officials or individuals supplying information.
3.   Individuals to whom credentials were shown and FDA 482, Notice of Inspection, and other inspectional forms issued.
4.   Individuals refusing to supply information or permit inspection.
5.   Individuals with whom inspectional findings were discussed or recommendations made.
Regulations require plant management take all reasonable measures and precautions to assure control of communicable disease, employee cleanliness, appropriate training of key personnel, and compliance by all personnel with all requirements of 21 CFR 110.10, 113.10, and 114.10.
Determine if adequate supervision is provided for critical operations where violations are likely to occur if tasks are improperly performed.
Employees - Improper employee habits may contribute to violative practices in an otherwise satisfactory plant. Observe the attitude and actions of employees during all phases of the inspection. Observe employees at their work stations and determine their duties or work functions. Note whether employees are neatly and cleanly dressed and whether they wear head coverings which properly cover their hair.

Determine if employees working with the product have obvious colds, or infected sores, cuts, etc. Under no circumstance should you swab a sore, touch or remove a bandage from an employee in an attempt to obtain bacteriological data. To do so is a violation of personal privacy, possibly hazardous to you and/or the employee, and usually provides little useful data.

Note whether employees eat while on duty.

Observe and record insanitary employee practices or actions showing employees handling or touching unsanitized or dirty surfaces and then contacting food products or direct food contact surfaces. Such practices might include employees spitting, handling garbage, placing their hands in or near their mouths, cleaning drains, handling dirty containers, etc. and then handling food product without washing and sanitizing their hands. Observe whether employees comply with plant rules such as, "No smoking", "Keep doors closed", "Wash hands before returning to work", etc. See IOM 536.2.

Be alert to employees handling insanitary objects, then quickly dipping their hands in sanitizing solutions without first washing them. Depending upon the amount and type of filth deposited on the hands during the handling of insanitary objects, such attempts at sanitizing are questionable at best. Sanitizers work most effectively on hands, which have been first cleaned by washing with soap and water.

Conversations with employees doing the work may provide information on both current and past objectionable practices, conditions and circumstances. These should be recorded in your notes.

Where appropriate, determine employee education and training. Also determine type, duration, and adequacy of firm's training programs, if any, to prepare employees for their positions and to maintain their skills. See IOM 593.3.

532   PLANTS AND GROUNDS

Environment - Observe the general nature of the neighborhood in which the firm is located. Environmental factors such as proximity to swamps, rivers, wharves, city dumps, etc., may contribute to rodent, bird, insect or other sanitation problems.

Plant Construction, Design and Maintenance - Determine the approximate size and type of building housing the firm and if suitable in size, construction, and design to facilitate maintenance and sanitary operations. Check placement of equipment, storage of materials, lighting, ventilation, and placement of partitions and screening to eliminate product contamination by bacteria, birds, vermin, etc. Determine any construction defects or other conditions such as broken windows, cracked floor boards, sagging doors, etc. which may permit animal entry or harborage.

Inspect toilet facilities for cleanliness, adequate supplies of toilet paper, soap, towels, hot and cold water, and hand washing signs. Check if hand washing facilities are hidden, or if located where supervisory personnel can police hand washing.

Determine who is responsible for buildings and grounds maintenance. Many facilities such as docks, wharves, or other premises are owned and maintained by other firms, municipalities, or individuals for lease for manufacturing operations. Determine who is legally responsible for repairs, maintenance, rodent proofing, screening, etc. Evaluate the firm's attitude toward maintenance and cleaning operations.

Waste Disposal - Waste and garbage disposal poses a problem in all food plants depending upon plant location and municipal facilities available.

Check the effectiveness of waste disposal on the premises and ensure it does not cause violative conditions or contribute toward contamination of the finished products. Check for in-plant contamination of equipment and/or product, if its water is supplied from nearby streams, springs, lakes or wells.

Suspected dumping of sewage effluent into nearby streams, lakes, or bay waters near water intakes can be documented by color photographs and water soluble fluorescein sodium dye. Place approximately two ounces dye, which yields a yellowish red color, into the firm's waste system and/or toilets, as applicable, and flush the system. The discharge area of the effluent becomes readily visible by a yellowish-red color on the surface of the water as the dye reaches it. Color photographs should be taken.

Determine collecting or flushing methods used to remove waste from operating areas. If water is used, determine if it is recirculated and thus may contaminate equipment or materials.

Determine the disposition of waste materials that should not be used as human food such as rancid nuts, juice from decomposed tomatoes, etc.

Determine the disposition of waste, garbage, etc., which contain pesticide residues. Determine how this is segregated from waste material which contains no residues and which may be used for animal feed.

Plant Services - If applicable, check steam generators for capacity and demand. Demand may reach or exceed the rated capacity, which could effect adequacy of the process. Check boiler water additives if steam comes in direct contact with foods.

Check central compressed air supply for effective removal of moisture (condensate) and oil. Determine if any undrained loops in the supply line exist where condensate can accumulate and become contaminated with foreign material or microorganisms.

533   RAW MATERIALS

Source - List in a general way the nature of raw materials on hand. Itemize and describe those, which are unusual to you, or involved in a suspected violation (copy quantity of contents and ingredient statements, codes, name of manufacturer or distributor, etc.). Be alert for additives and preservatives. Evaluate the storage of materials. Determine the general storage pattern, stock rotation and general housekeeping. Materials should be stored so they are accessible for inspection. Thoroughly check ceilings, walls, ledges, and floors in raw material storage areas for evidence or rodent or insect infestation, water dripping or other adverse conditions.

Handling Procedure - Determine if growing conditions relative to disease, insects, and weather are affecting the raw material. Check measures taken for protection against insect or rodent damage. Raw materials may be susceptible to decomposition, bruising or damage, e.g., soft vegetables and fruits delivered in truckload lots. Determine the holding times of materials subject to progressive decomposition.

Condition - Evaluate the firm's acceptance examination and inspection practices including washing and disposition of rejected lots. Where indicated, examine rejected lots and collect appropriate samples and report consignees.

Determine the general acceptability of raw materials for their intended use and their effect on the finished product. Raw stocks of fruits or vegetables may contribute decomposed or filthy material to the finished product. Be alert for use of low quality or salvage raw materials. Check bags, bales, cases and other types of raw material containers to determine signs of abnormal conditions, indicating presence of filthy, putrid or decomposed items. Check any indication of gnawed or otherwise damaged containers, to ascertain if material is violative. Be alert to contamination of raw materials by infested or contaminated railroad cars or other carriers.

Document by photographs, exhibits or sketches any instances where insanitary storage or handling conditions exist.

Food Chemicals Codex - Any substance used in foods must be food-grade quality. FDA regards the applicable specifications in the current edition of the publication "Food Chemicals Codex" as establishing food-grade unless FDA publishes other specifications in the Federal Register.

Determine whether firm is aware of this publication and whether or not they comply.

534   EQUIPMENT AND UTENSILS

By arriving before processing begins, you are able to evaluate conditions and practices not otherwise observable before plant start-up. This includes adequacy of clean-up, where and how equipment is stored while not in use, how hand sanitizing solutions and food batches are prepared and if personnel sanitize their hands and equipment before beginning work.

Dirty or improperly cleaned equipment and utensils may be the focal point for filth or bacterial contamination of the finished product. Examine all equipment for suitability and accessibility for cleaning. Determine if equipment is constructed or covered to protect contents from dust and environmental contamination. Open inspection ports to check inside only when this can be done safely. Notice whether inspection ports have been painted over or permanently sealed.

Observe the firm's filtering systems and evaluate the cleaning methods (or replacement intervals of disposable filters) and schedules. Check types of filters used. There have been instances where firms have relied on household furnace type filters.

Check the sanitary condition of all machinery. Determine if equipment is cleaned prior to each use and the method of cleaning. If the firm rents or leases equipment on a short-term basis, report prior cleaning procedures. Equipment may have been used for pesticides, chemicals, drugs, etc.,

prior to being installed and could therefore be a source of cross-contamination.

Inspect conveyor belts for build-up of residual materials and pockets of residue in corners and under belts. Look in inspection ports and hard-to-reach places inside, around, underneath, and behind equipment and machinery for evidence of filth, insects, and/or rodent contamination. Chutes and conveyor ducts may appear satisfactory, but a rap on them with the heel of your hand or a rubber mallet may dislodge static material, which can be examined. See IOM 427.6 for procedure on taking In-line Sample Subs.

Determine how brushes, scrapers, brooms, and other items used during processing or on product contact surfaces are cleaned, sanitized and stored. Evaluate the effectiveness of the practices observed.

Be alert for improper placement or inadequately protected mercury switches, mercury thermometers, or electric bulbs. Breakage of these could spray mercury and glass particles onto materials or into processing machinery.

If firm is using U.V. lamps for bacteria control, check if it has and uses any method or meters to check the strength of U.V. emissions. If so, obtain methods, procedures, type equipment used, and schedule for replacement of weak U.V. bulbs.

In plants where chlorine solution is piped, check on type of pipe used. Fiberglass reinforced epoxy pipe has been observed to erode inside through the action of the chlorine solution. This poses a threat of contamination from exposed glass fibers. Pipes made with polyester resin do not deteriorate from this solution.

Observe sanitizing practices throughout the plant and evaluate their effectiveness, degree of supervision exercised, strength, time, and methods of use of sanitizing agents. Determine the use, or absence of, sanitizing solutions both for sanitizing equipment and utensils as well as for hand dipping. If chlorine is used, 50 ppm - 200 ppm should be used for equipment and utensils, while a 100 ppm will suffice for hand dipping solutions. Sanitizing solutions rapidly lose strength with the addition of organic material. The strength of the solution should be checked several times during the inspection.

535   MANUFACTURING PROCESS

Where helpful to describe equipment and processes, draw flow plans or diagrams to show movement of materials through the plant. Generally a brief description of each step in the process is sufficient. List all quality control activities for each step in the process and identify Critical Control Points. Provide a full description when necessary to describe and document objectionable conditions, or where the assignment specifically requests it.

Observe whether hands and equipment are washed or sanitized after contact with unsanitized surfaces. For example:

1.   Workers do general work, then handle the product;

2.   Containers contact the floor, then are nested or otherwise contact product or table surfaces;

3.   Workers use common or dirty cloths or clothing for wiping hands;

4. Product falls on a dirty floor or a floor subject to outside foot traffic and is returned to the production line.

Be alert for optimum moisture, time and temperature conditions conducive to bacterial growth.

In industries where scrap portions of the product are re-used or re-worked into the process (e.g., candy and macaroni products), observe the methods used in the re-working and evaluate from a bacteriological standpoint. Re-working procedures such as soaking of macaroni or noodle scrap to soften or hand kneading of scrap material offers an excellent seeding medium for bacteria.

When a product is processed in a manner which destroys micro-organisms, note whether there are any routes of recontamination from the "raw" to the processed product (e.g. dusts, common equipment, hands, flies, etc.).

535.1 Ingredient Handling

Observe the method of adding ingredients to the process. Filth may be added into the process stream from dust, rodent excreta pellets, debris, etc. adhering to the surface of ingredient containers. Evaluate the effectiveness of cleaning and inspectional operations performed on the materials prior to or while adding to the process. Determine specific trimming or sorting operations on low quality or questionable material. Observe and report any significant lags during the process or between completion of final process and final shipping. For example, excessive delay between packing and freezing may be a factor in production of a violative product.

535.2 Formulas

The Act does not specifically require management to furnish formula information except for human drugs, restricted devices and infant formulas. Nonetheless, they should be requested especially when necessary to document violations of standards, labeling, or color and food additives. Management may provide the qualitative formula but refuse the quantitative formula.

If formula information is refused, attempt to reconstruct formula by observing:
1. Product in production,
2. Batch cards or formula sheets,
3. Raw materials and their location.

Any refusal to furnish requested information is reported in your EIR under the refusal heading.

535.3 Food Additives

Refer to the food additives program in the CPGM (Chapter 9) for instructions on conducting establishment inspections of firms manufacturing food additive chemicals. Information is also available in DFI's "Guide to the Inspection of Manufacturers of Miscellaneous Food Products - Volume 2.

When making food plant inspections direct your evaluation of food additives only to those instances of significant violation or gross misuse.

Routine inspectional coverage will be directed primarily to the following two types of additives:
1. Unauthorized and illegal as listed in the Food Additive Status List (safrole, thiourea, et al), and
2. Restricted as to amount in finished food.

Because of special problems, exclude the following additives from coverage during routine inspections:
1. Packaging materials,
2. Waxes and chemicals applied to fresh fruit and vegetables,
3. Synthetic flavors and flavoring components except those banned by regulations or policy statements (these products will be covered under other programs), and
4. Food additives in feeds (these products will be covered under other programs).

The Food Additives Status List (FASL) contains an alphabetical listing of substances, which may be added directly to foods or feeds and their status under the Food Additives Amendment and Food Standards. In addition, a few unauthorized or illegal substances are included. See IOM Appendix A.

You may encounter substances not included in the Food Additives Status List (FASL). Such substances will include:
1. Obviously safe substances not on the list of items generally recognized as safe (GRAS), which are not published in the regulations, i.e., salt, cane sugar, corn syrup, vinegar, etc.;
2. Synthetic flavoring substances because of their indefinite status;
3. Substances pending administrative determination,
4. Substances granted prior sanction for specific use prior to enactment of the Food Additives Amendment.

Give primary attention to unauthorized substances. Document and calculate levels of restricted-use additives in finished food only where gross misuse or program violations are suspected as follows:
1. List ingredients, which may be restricted substances or food additives, and determine their status by referring to the current FASL. Report complete labeling on containers of these substances.
2. Obtain the quantitative formula for the finished product in question.
3. Determine the total batch weight by converting all ingredients to common units.
4. Calculate the theoretical levels in the final product of all restricted or unauthorized ingredients from the formula by using the Food Additives Nomographs. See IOM Exhibit 530-B.
5. Determine probable level of restricted ingredients by observing the weight of each ingredient actually put into the batch.

535.4 Color Additives

Evaluate the status of all colors observed during each food establishment inspection by using the Color Additives Status List. The list provides the current status and use limitations of most colors likely to be found in food, drug, device, or cosmetic establishments. See IOM Appendix A.

Stocks of delisted and uncertified colors may be found in the possession of manufacturers where there is no evidence of misuse. Advise the firm of the status of these colors. If management wishes to voluntarily destroy such colors, witness the destruction and include the facts in your EIR. If the firm declines to destroy the colors, determine what disposition is planned, e.g., use in non-food products.

Where decertified or restricted-use colors are used in manufacturing food, drug, device, or cosmetics products, proceed as follows:

1. Collect an Official Sample consisting of the color and the article in which it is being used. Make every effort to collect interstate shipments of the adulterated product before attempting to develop a 301(k) or 301(a) case. When regulatory action is an alternative, obtain sufficient interstate records to cover both the color and the basic ingredients of the manufactured product. Refer to IOM Sample Schedule, Chart 9 - Sampling Schedule for Color Containing Products for guidance.

2. Document the use of decertified colors after the decertifying date. Documentation should include batch formula cards, employee statements, code marks indicating date of manufacture, color certification number, etc. The presence of color in the finished product will be confirmed by your servicing laboratory.

535.5 Quality Control

The objective of quality control is to ensure the maintenance of proper standards in manufactured goods, especially by periodic random inspection of the product. Your inspection should determine if the firm's quality control system accomplishes its intended purpose. Establish responsibility for specific operations in the control system. Determine which controls are critical for the safety of the finished product.

Inspection System - Determine what inspectional control is exercised over both raw materials and the processing steps. Such inspection may vary from simple visual or other organoleptic examination to elaborate mechanical manipulation. Determine what inspection equipment is used, i.e., inspection belts, sorting belts, grading tables, ultraviolet lights, etc. Ascertain its effectiveness, maintenance or adjustment schedules. Where indicated, determine the name of the manufacturer of any mechanical inspection device and the principles of its operation.

Evaluate the effectiveness of the personnel assigned to inspection operations. Determine if the inspection belts or pick-out stations are adequately staffed and supervised.

Determine the disposition of waste materials, which are unfit for food or feed purposes.

Laboratory Tests - Describe routine tests or examinations performed by the firm's laboratory and the records maintained by the firm. Determine what equipment is available in the laboratory and if it is adequate for the purpose intended. If the firm uses a consulting laboratory, determine what tests are performed and how often. Review laboratory records for the period immediately preceding the inspection.

Manufacturing Code System - Obtain a complete description of the coding system with any necessary keys for interpretation. Provide an example by illustrating the code being used at the time of the inspection. (See 21 CFR

113.60(c) and 114.80(b)). Report coding systems, which require the use of ultra-violet light for visibility. Hermetically sealed containers of low acid processed food must be coded in a manner clearly visible. (See 21 CFR 113.60). Check 21 CFR 113 and 114 for regulations on coding for the type plant you are inspecting.

535.6 Packaging and Labeling

Evaluate storage of packaging materials including protection from contamination by rodents, insects, toxic chemicals or other materials. Appraise the manner in which containers are handled and delivered to the filling areas. Determine if there is likelihood of chipping of glass or denting, puncturing, tearing, etc., of packaging materials. Observe the preparation of containers prior to filling. Consider any washing, steaming, or other cleaning process for effectiveness. Determine, in detail, the use of air pressure or other cleaning devices.

Quantity of Contents - If slack fill is suspected, weigh a representative number of finished packages. See IOM 428 for net weight procedure. Sets of official weights are available in the district servicing laboratory. These may be used to check the accuracy of firm's weighing equipment.

Labeling - Check the sanitary condition of labelers and equipment feeding cans to, and away from, the labeler. Determine if old product is present on any equipment which touches the can end seams, in the presence of moisture carry-over from the can cooling operation. Check availability of floor drains in the labeling area. Absence of floor drains could indicate infrequent cleaning of the equipment unless it is physically moved to another area for cleaning.

Determine what labels are used and what labeling is prepared or used to accompany or promote the product. Obtain specimens of representative labels and labeling including pamphlets, booklets, and other promotional material. Obtain 3 copies of labels and labeling believed to be violative.

Nutritional Labeling - See document "Guide to Nutritional Labeling and Education Act (NLEA) Requirements" for guidance.

536   SANITATION

Documented observation of the conditions under which food products are processed, packed, or stored is essential to the proper evaluation of the firm's compliance with the law. This involves the determination of whether or not insanitary conditions contribute to the product being adulterated with filth, rendered injurious to health, or whether it consists in whole or in part of a filthy, putrid or decomposed substance.

Observations that dirt, decomposed materials, feces or other filthy materials are present in the facility and there is a reasonable possibility these filthy materials will be incorporated in the food are also ways of determining products may have become contaminated.

536.1 Routes of Contamination

It is not sufficient to document only the existence of insanitary or filthy conditions. You must also demonstrate how these conditions contribute or may contribute to contaminating the finished product. Investigate and trace potential routes of contamination and observe all means by which filth or hazardous substance may be incorporated into the finished product. For example, defiled molding starch in a candy plant may contribute filth to candy passing through it, or filth in insect or rodent contaminated raw materials may carry over into the finished product. (See 21 CFR 110.37(f)). Subchapter 420 contains instructions on sample collection techniques for adulteration violations. Sample sizes for adulteration violations can be found in the applicable DFI "Guide to Inspections of ***" or in DFI's Inspectional Methods (Interim Guidance) (10/96).

Insects - Insect contamination of the finished product may result from insect infested raw material, infested processing equipment or insanitary practices, and by insanitary handling of the finished product. When routes of contamination with insect filth are encountered, identify the insects generally, e.g., weevils, beetles, moths, etc. If quantified, identify as to species. You must be correct in your identification. See IOM Appendix C.

Rodents - Rodent contamination of the finished product may result from using rodent defiled raw materials, exposure to rodents during processing, and by rodent depredation of the finished product. When evidence of rodents are discovered, you should thoroughly describe its composition, quantity, estimated age and location. Explain its significance and potential for product contamination.

Pesticides - Pesticide contamination of the finished product may be the result of mishandling of food products at any stage in manufacturing or storage. The use of toxic rodenticides or insecticides in a manner, which may result in contamination, constitutes an insanitary condition. Where careless use of these toxic chemicals is observed, take photographs and provide other documentation showing its significance in relation the food products.

Additional guidance can be found in 21 CFR as follows:
1. Part 110.20(b) - Plant Construction and Design,
2. Part 110.40(a) - Equipment and Utensils,
3. Part 110.35(c) - Pest Control,
4. Part 110.10(b) - Personnel Cleanliness.

Additional guidance can be found in 40 CFR Part 185 - Tolerances For Pesticides in Food Administered by The Environmental Protection Agency as follows:
1. Part 185.3475 - Fumigants for grain-mill machinery, and
2. Part 185.3480 - Fumigants for processed grains used in production of fermented malt beverages.

Be alert for:
1. Possible PCB contamination. Articles containing PCB's (e.g., transformers, PCB containers stored for disposal, electrical capacitors) must be marked with prescribed labeling to show they contain PCB. No PCB-containing heat exchange fluids, hydraulic fluids or lubricants are allowed used in food plants. All PCB storage areas must be marked to show the presence of PCB's. Observe food plant transformers for possible leakage. If observed, determine if food items are stored in the area, and sample for PCB contamination. If PCB's are encountered in a food establishment, immediately advise management this is an objectionable condition and advise your supervisor .
2. Possible mix-up of pesticides or industrial chemicals with food raw materials.
3. Improperly stored pesticides or industrial chemicals (lids open, torn bags in close proximity to foods, signs of spillage on floors, pallets, shelves, etc.).
4. Incorrect application methods including excessive use. Many pesticide labels give instructions for use and precautions on the container.
5. Improper disposal or reuse of pesticide or industrial chemical containers.
6. Evidence of tracking powder or improper use of bait stations or baited traps.
7. Improper handling of equipment. Movable or motorized equipment used for handling possible chemical contaminants should not be used for handling food products unless they are thoroughly decontaminated. For example, fork-lifts moving pallets of pesticides should not also be used to move pallets of flour, etc.
8. Use of unauthorized pesticides.
9. Use of foods treated with pesticides and marked "Not For Human Consumption" (e.g., Treated seed wheat, etc.).
10. Noticeable odor of pesticides.
11. Careless use of machinery lubricants and cleaning compounds.
12. Chemical contaminants in incoming water supply.

When inspecting products with a known potential for metals contamination, determine whether the firm tests for such contamination in raw materials.

Determine who administers the firm's rodent and insect control program. Determine responsibility for the careless use of toxic materials.

If pesticide misuse is suspected, obtain the following information;
1. Name of exterminator and contract status,
2. Name of pesticide,
3. Name of pesticide manufacturer,
4. EPA registration number,
5. Active ingredients, and
6. Any significant markings on pesticide containers.

Fully document the exact nature of any pesticide or industrial chemical contamination noted or suspected. If samples are collected to document misuse, exercise caution to prevent contamination of the immediate area of use, product or yourself.

Other - Contamination of food products by bats, birds and/or other animals is possible in facilities where food and roosting facilities are available. Examine storage tanks, bins, and warehousing areas to determine condition and history of use. There have been instances where empty non-food use containers were used for food products.

536.2 Microbiological Concerns

During the inspection, you must fully identify likely sources and possible routes of contamination of the product. See IOM section 427.7 for instructions on sampling for pathogens. Before and during processing, become completely familiar with the flow of the process and determine the potential trouble spots, which may be built into the operation. To document the establishment is operating in an insanitary manner, it is necessary to show the manufacturer has contributed to the bacterial load of the product. If there are several products being prepared at once, do not try to cover the entire operation during one inspection. Select the product which has the greatest potential for bacterial abuse or which poses the greatest risk for the consumer.

It is extremely important each EIR contain complete, precise, and detailed descriptions of the entire operation. The EIR must be able to stand alone without the analytical results, which serve to support the observations.

Observations made during the inspection must be written in clear and concise language. The EIR will be reviewed in conjunction with analytical results of in-line, environmental and finished product samples. Based on this review and other information, which may be available, the district must then decide if the total package will support a recommendation for regulatory action.

Each inspection/process will be different, but the techniques for gathering the evidence will be the same. However, the critical points in the operation should always be defined and special attention given to these areas.

Depending on the type of product being produced and the process being used, it may be useful to record the time each critical step takes from beginning to end of the entire processing period with correlating temperature measurements. This should be done especially for products, which would support the growth of microbial pathogens. During the entire inspection, be aware of and document delays in the processing of the product (e.g., **temperature** of product prior to, during and after the particular processing step, **and the length of time** the product has been delayed prior to the next step).

Some products receive a thermal process at the end of production, which may reduce bacterial counts to or near zero. Include detailed observations of heating step, temperature, length of time, controls and documentation used/not used by the firm. Even in the presence of end-product thermal processing, there is a regulatory significance to insanitary conditions prior to cooking, coupled with increases in bacterial levels demonstrated through in-line sampling.

Processing Equipment: Document the addition, or possible addition of pathogenic microorganisms from accumulated material due to poorly cleaned and/or sanitized processing equipment

Observe and report the firm's clean up procedures and the condition and cleanliness of food contact surfaces before production starts, between production runs and at the end of the day. Document any residue on food contact surfaces of equipment, especially inside complex equipment not easily cleaned and sanitized. Report firms clean-up procedures in depth, since it may lend significance to insanitary conditions of residues on the plant machinery which are left to decompose overnight or between shifts.

Where possible, observe equipment both before and after cleaning to assess it adequacy. Observations of residues on plant machinery can dramatically document the addition of pathogenic microorganisms, if present, into the product.

Identify any vectors of contamination (e.g. birds, rodents, insects, foot traffic, etc.), and describe sources and the routes of contamination from them to the product. Support this with your actual observations.

Employee practices: document any poor employee practice and how they have or would provide a route for contaminating the product. For example, did employees (number/time of day) fail to wash and sanitize their hands at the beginning of processing, after breaks, meals, or after handling materials likely contaminated with a microbial pathogen, etc.; and then handle the finished product. Did employees handle product in an insanitary manner (cross contaminating raw product with cooked product, etc., how many, how often,).

536.3 Storage

Evaluate the storage of finished products in the same manner as for raw materials. Determine if products are stored to minimize container abuse, facilitate proper rotation, and adherence to the storage requirements. This includes refrigeration temperatures, critical temperature tolerance, aging of products, and proper disposition of distressed stock.

Food Transport Vehicles - During food sanitation inspections, (See IOM 511.2 regarding issuance of FDA 482, Notice of Inspection while inspecting vehicles.), conduct inspections of food transport vehicles to include:
1. Evidence of insanitary conditions,
2. Conditions which might lead to food adulteration,
3. Physical defects in the vehicle,
4. Poor industry handling practices.
The following types of transport vehicles should be covered:
1. Railroad boxcars, both refrigerated and non-refrigerated, and hopper cars.
2. Any type of truck used to transport foods; both refrigerated and non-refrigerated.
3. Use extreme caution, if it is necessary to inspect tank railcars or tank trucks. Usually this coverage will be limited to determining what was transported in the tank previously and was the tank cleaned and/or sanitized as necessary between loads.
4. Vessels used to transport food in I/S commerce. Direct coverage primarily to intercoastal type vessels, including barges.
Coverage should be limited to food transport vehicles used for long haul (I/S) operations. Long haul vehicles are defined as those which travel at least 150 miles between loading and unloading or which do not return to the point of loading at the end of the day.

Regulatory actions are possible if unfit cars are loaded and, as a result of loading, adulteration occurs. Fully document any violations noted with appropriate samples and photographs. When vehicle insanitation is observed, it is imperative the carrier's and shipper's responsibility for the food adulteration be documented by appropriate evidence development, such as;

1.   The nature and extent of the conditions or practices, and

2.   The mechanical or construction defects associated with the food transport vehicle.

3.   Individual responsibility for vehicle or trailer cleaning, vehicle assignments, load assignments, etc.

If gathering evidence about a single carrier, seek a series of occurrences at numerous locations involving as many different shippers as possible.

Basically two types of vehicles will be covered:

Vehicles at Receivers - When inspecting receivers of food products, examine the food transport vehicle prior to or during unloading. Make a preliminary assessment of food product condition, then inspect the vehicle after unloading to determine its condition and whether the unloaded food may have been contaminated during shipment. If the food appears to have been adulterated, collect a sample(s) for regulatory consideration. Samples collected from vehicles, which have moved the product in interstate commerce are official samples. You may also collect Documentary (DOC) Samples from the vehicle to substantiate the route of contamination.

Vehicles at Shippers - When inspecting shippers of food products, examine the food transport vehicle just prior to loading to determine its sanitary/structural conditions. If the vehicle has significant sanitation or structural deficiencies, notify the shipper of these conditions and of the possibility of product adulteration. If the shipper loads food aboard the vehicle, alert your supervisor so he/she can contact the FDA District where the consignee is located for possible follow-up. You may also collect samples from the load. These samples will become official when the bill of Lading is issued.

537   DISTRIBUTION

Interstate Shipping - Report the general distribution pattern of the firm. Review shipping records or invoices to report shipment of specific lots. If access to invoices or shipping records is not possible, observe shipping cartons, loading areas, order rooms, address stencils, railroad cars on sidings, etc., to determine customer names, addresses and destination of shipments. If no products are suspect, obtain a listing of the firm's larger consignees.

Promotion and Advertising - Determine the methods used to promote products and how the products reach the ultimate consumer. Determine what printed promotional materials are used and whether they accompany the products or are distributed under a separate promotional scheme. Check on the possibility of oral representations, i.e., door-to-door salesmen, spieler, etc. and obtain copies of brochures, pamphlets, tearsheets, instructions to salespersons, etc. Where indicated, obtain the lecture schedule of any promotional lecture program. If applicable, determine the general pattern of the media used for promotion and advertising.

Recall Procedure - Determine the firm's recall procedure. Audit enough records to determine the effectiveness of established procedures. Report if there is no recall procedure.

Complaint Files - Review the firm's complaint files. Where possible, copy the names and addresses of representative complainants; include a brief summary of each significant complaint in the EIR.

Identify who reviews complaints and their qualifications. Describe the criteria used by the firm in evaluating the significance of complaints and how they are investigated. Determine if records are kept of oral and telephone complaints. See IOM 517 for discussion of complaints with management and IOM 593.3 for reporting of complaints in the EIR.

Complaints may not be filed in one specific file, but may be scattered throughout various files under other subject titles including Product name; Customer name; Injured party name; Adjustment File; Customer Relations; Repair orders, etc.

During the inspection investigate all complaints contained on FDA-2516 & FDA-2516a forms in the firm's district factory jacket. See IOM 517, 530.1 & 593.3.

538   OTHER GOVERNMENT INSPECTION

Federal – See IOM 300 for general procedures on cooperating with other Federal, State, and local officials.

During Establishment Inspections determine the specific type of inspection service and inspecting units, which cover the firm, such as the name of the federal, state, county, or city health agency or department. Obtain the name and title of the inspectional official, and general method of operation.

Do not inspect firms, or those portions of the plant, subject to compulsory, continuous inspection under USDA's Meat Inspection Act, Poultry Products Inspection Act, or Egg Products Inspection Act, except on specific instructions from your supervisor or assignment document.

Ingredients or manufacturing processes common to both USDA and FDA regulated products should be inspected by FDA. See IOM 311.3 for FDA-USDA Agreements in specific areas.

Provide routine FDA coverage of such firms as breweries and wineries, which may be intermittently inspected on a compulsory basis by the U.S. Treasury Department, U.S. Public Health Service, or other agencies.

All products inspected under the voluntary inspection service of the Agriculture Marketing Service (AMS), USDA, and the National Marine Fisheries Service (NMFS), US Department of Commerce, are subject to FDA jurisdiction and are usually given routine coverage. However, formal written Agreements or Memoranda of Understanding between FDA and other agencies are often executed and may govern the agreeing agencies' operations on this type inspected plants. When assigned this type of plant for inspection, always check to see if an Agreement or a Memorandum of Understanding exists between FDA and the agency involved to determine the obligations of both agencies. See IOM 301.2 & 310.

If you are assigned to cover a Federally Inspected plant which is under either compulsory or voluntary inspection, present your credentials and an FDA 482 "Notice of Inspection" to management and:

1. Identify yourself to the inspector(s) and invite him/her to accompany you on the inspection but do not insist on their participation.

2. At the conclusion of the inspection offer to discuss your observations and provide the in-plant inspector with a copy of your Inspectional Observations (FDA 483).

State and Local - State and local officials usually have extensive regulatory authority over firms in their area regardless of the interstate movement or origin of the food products involved. Joint FDA-State or local inspections are frequently conducted. These are usually arranged by district administrative or supervisory personnel. See IOM 302 and 330.

Grade A Dairy Plant Inspections – If you are assigned to do an inspection or sample collection at a dairy firm in the Grade A program or a firm which has products labeled and sold as Grade A, you should verify the need to complete the assignment with your supervisor and the Regional Milk Specialist. Grade A plants and most products labeled as Grade A are inspected by state inspectors or FDA's Regional Milk Specialists and you should not inspect these products. Firms in the Grade A program and covered by the Interstate Milk Shippers (IMS) program are identified in the Interstate Milk Shippers List of Sanitation Compliance and Enforcement Ratings book published every year by the Milk Safety Branch, HFS-626. The reference lists the specific plant and each product covered under the IMS program. These products are covered by a MOU between the FDA and the states, which places primary inspectional responsibility with the state.

There are situations where you will need to conduct an inspection in a Grade A plant and cover products they manufacture which do not carry the "Grade A" designation (such as juices). If the plant is an IMS shipper and has fluid or other products rated as acceptable they may also manufacture optional products and label them as Grade A, without having those product lines covered in the IMS program. Fluid products, sour cream, cultured milk products and yogurt are not optional products. Optional products include cottage cheese, condensed milk/whey and dry milk/whey and may be labeled as Grade A. As an example, some firms are listed in the IMS Sanitation Compliance and Enforcement Ratings book who manufacture cottage cheese and label it as Grade A, but is not specifically covered under the Grade A inspection program. As long as the plant is listed and has one or more products rated as acceptable in the Grade A program, they can manufacture a product and label it as Grade A without having the particular product line covered in the IMS program. In those situations, the product will not be shown in the Enforcement Ratings book and you should cover its production, labeling, etc.

539   FOOD STANDARDS

The Federal Food, Drug, and Cosmetic Act requires the Secretary of Health & Human Services to promulgate reasonable definitions and Standards for food to promote hon-

esty and fair dealing in the interest of consumers. When a Standard becomes effective, it establishes the common or usual name for the article, defines the article and fixes its standard of identity. It is then the official specification for the food. The food industry actively participates in the development of a Standard, and supplies much of the data upon which the regulation is based.

The Food Standards (FS) Inspection is made to obtain data for use, together with information from other sources in developing a Food Standard. Food Standard inspections are also made to determine a firm's compliance with food standards regulations, when manufacturing a standardized food.

539.1 Food Establishment Inspection

Food Standard (FS) inspection assignments usually originate from CFSAN. When an inspection is planned for the purpose of collecting data to support a proposed food standard regulation, the district may elect to advise the firm, if the CFSAN has not already done so. If the firm selected does not choose to cooperate, it may be necessary to visit additional plants in order to obtain the desired information. Selection of additional firms should be done in consultation with the CFSAN.

Some firms often contend their entire process and formulas are "trade secrets". Attempt to persuade management the term "trade secret" should only be used to cover the process and/or quantitative-qualitative formulation which is truly unique to the firm. In instances where the firm is reluctant to release any of the information requested, point out FDA will, within the limits of the Freedom of Information Act, make every effort to preserve the confidentiality of the composition, make-up, and production levels of the product through the use of codes, which cannot be traced back to the firm. Include as much of the compositional and processing information as you can in the body of the report, without violating the firm's confidence.

539.2 Food Inspection Report

FS EIR's may be used as exhibits at public hearings and are subject to review by any interested party.

Three copies of the report are prepared. The original and one copy will be submitted to the CFSAN and one copy kept for the district file. Sign the original and duplicates of the first and last pages of each report sent to the Center.

Divide the report into three sections:

1.   Establishment Inspection Record (EI Record) - In order to relate the sections of the report to each other and to any assignments, and to assure any parts of the reports made public will not be identified as to the name of the firm or individuals therein, each district will set up a master list of numbers. One number will be assigned to each establishment covered, e.g., "BLT FS-3". For each FS Inspection place the assigned number next to the firm name on the EI Record. All other pages of the report shall be identified only by this number, the name of the commodity, and date. Example: "EIR Frozen Fish Sticks 10-3-87 BLT FS-3". This indicates a FS EI of frozen fish sticks conducted by Baltimore District on 10-3-87 in a plant designated as #3.

Where a producer may be reluctant to release any of the information requested, point out the FDA will, within the limits of the FOIA, make every effort to preserve the confidentiality of the composition, make-up, and production levels of his product through the use of codes, which cannot be traced back to the firm.

2. <u>Body of Report</u> - Prepare the body of the report following the narrative outline as for any other food EIR except for the restrictions below.

The body of the FS report should also contain information in regard to the approximate annual value and volume as well as the percent of interstate business for each product covered. This is necessary because the coversheet, which contains this information, identifies the firm and will not be made public. Processes and the listing of raw materials used by the firm, which are not restricted by the term "trade secret" should be included. Any opinions, recommendations, or other information obtained or offered by individuals interviewed should be reported. Any suggestions made by individuals interviewed regarding what should be placed in the Standards for the products covered should be included. All individuals interviewed, firm name, etc. should have an identifying code assigned.

The body of the report should not include names and titles of individuals, (including USDA, USDI, or other inspectors), trade secret information, labeling, trade names, formulas, sample numbers, firm name or location of plant (other than by state or region), shipments, or other distribution information, legal status, or regulatory history. This information will be placed in the "Special Information" section of the report.

3. <u>Special Information Section</u> - this is a separate attachment to the EIR which lists the names and titles of individuals (including other government inspectors) and firms with a reference code for each. The EIR should refer only to "Mr. A.," "Mr. B.," "Firm X," "Firm Y", etc. Do not use the firm or individual's actual initials in the body of the report. Include all information excluded from the body of the report and mount all labels obtained during the EI Labels may be quoted in the body of the report, but do not identify the firm. List the "Special Information Sheet" in the FACTS endorsement section as an enclosure.

Supplemental Reports - If, because of an additional visit or visits to the same firm on the same project, it is necessary to prepare another EIR, flag the report with the same number as assigned to the original report. For example, mark the EI Record "BLT FS-3 Supplemental Report", and the remaining pages, "EIR Frozen Fish Sticks 10-25-87 BLT FS-3 Supplemental Report."

539.3 Violative Inspections

When an inspection made in connection with the Food Standards project shows insanitary or other conditions which are not germane to the assignment or in the District's opinion suggests regulatory action, an appropriate narrative of the violative conditions should be prepared as a Regulatory Addendum.

SUBCHAPTER 540 - DRUGS

540   DRUG INSPECTIONS

Authority for inspection is discussed in IOM 701. FFD&CA Section 501(a)-(d) describe the ways in which a drug may be or may become adulterated. Section 502 does much the same, with respect to drug labeling. Therefore, the purpose of a drug inspection is:

1. to determine and evaluate a firm's adherence to the concepts of sanitation and good manufacturing practice;

2. to assure production and control procedures include all reasonable precautions to ensure the identity, strength, quality, and purity of the finished products;

3. to identify deficiencies which could lead to the manufacturing and distribution of products in violation of the Act, e.g., non-conformance with Official Compendiums, super/sub potency, substitution;

4. to obtain correction of those deficiencies;

5. to determine if new drugs are manufactured by essentially the same procedures and formulations as specified in the New Drug Approval documents; and

6. to determine the drug labeling and promotional practices of the firm.

7. to assure the firm is reporting NDA field alerts as required by 21CFR314.81.

8. to determine if the firm is complying with the requirements of the Prescription Drug Marketing act (PDMA) and regulations.

540.1 Preparation and References

Become familiar with current programs related to drugs. Determine the nature of the assignment, i.e., a specific drug problem or a routine inspection, and if necessary, consult other district personnel, such as chemists, microbiologists, etc. Review the district files of the firm to be inspected including:

1. Establishment Inspection Reports,
2. District Profiles,
3. New and Investigational Drug Applications,
4. Sample results,
5. Complaints,
6. Regulatory files,
7. Antibiotic Applications.
8. Drug Quality Reports (DQRS) & NDA Field Alert Reports (FARS)

During this review identify products which:

1. Are difficult to manufacture,
2. Require special tests or assays, or can not be assayed,
3. Require special processes or equipment, and
4. Are new drugs and/or potent low dosage drugs.

Review the factory jacket and all complaint forms (FDA-2516 and FDA-2516a) which are marked follow-up next inspection. These complaints are to be investigated during the inspection and discussed with management. See IOM 516.

Become familiar with current regulations and programs relating to drugs. When making GMP inspections, discuss with your supervisor the advisability of using a microbiologist, analyst, engineer, or other technical personnel to aid in evaluating those areas of the firm germane to their expertise. Review the FD&C Act, Chapter V, Drugs and Devices. Review parts of 21 CFR 210/211 applicable to the inspection involved and Bioavailability (21 CFR 320).

Review the current editions of the United States Pharmacopeia (USP), and Remington's Pharmaceutical Sciences for information on specific products or dosage forms. Also IOM Chapter 10 provides a consolidated list of pertinent guides and guidelines which may be applicable during drug inspections.

Review 21 CFR 201 "Prescription Drug Marketing", 21 CFR "Guidelines for State Licensing of Rx Drug Distributors", and Compliance Programm 7356.022, Enforcement of the Prescription Drug Marketing Act (PDMA).

540.2 Inspectional Approach

In-depth inspection of all manufacturing and control operations is usually not feasible or practical. An audit approach is recommended in which therapeutically significant drugs and those drugs, which are difficult to manufacture, are covered in greater detail.

The bioavailability regulations, 21 CFR 320, cover those drugs, which are therapeutically significant and for which manufacturing changes can affect efficacy. Some manufacturers have difficulty in complying with the dissolution specifications established for many products. Also, significant problems are not uncommon with timed release or delayed release drugs requiring multiple dissolution (release) tests.

If reworked products are encountered, validation of their manufacturing procedures and justification for reworking should be reviewed. Written investigation reports, which are required for any product failing to meet an established specification, should also be reviewed and evaluated.

For those drug manufacturers marketing a number of drugs posing potential bioavailability problems, identify suspect products by:

1. Reviewing the firm's complaint files early in the inspection to determine relative numbers of complaints per product.

2. Inspecting the quarantine and/or rejected product storage area to identify rejected product.

3. Examining annual reviews performed under 21 CFR 211.180(e) to determine those products which have a high reject rate.

4. Reviewing summaries of laboratory data or laboratory workbooks.

Attempts should also be made to determine the attitude or philosophy of top management and how they react to problems, such as, batch rejections, and how they investigate product failures.

541   DRUG REGISTRATION & LISTING

Registration and listing is required whether or not interstate commerce is involved. See Exhibit 540-A and IOM 771.1 for additional information.

Two or more companies occupying the same premises and having interlocking management are considered one establishment and usually will be assigned a single registration number. See IOM 501.4 - Multiple Occupancy Inspections for additional information.

Vitamin manufacturers are required to register unless their products are used solely in food supplements and do not become drugs or components of drugs. In most cases, bulk vitamin manufacturers should register unless they can demonstrate the ultimate use and labeling of their products in foods or food supplements. Independent laboratories providing analytical or other laboratory control services on commercially marketed drugs must register.

The FACTS will indicate if the establishment is registered for the current year. If you determine registration and listing is required, advise your supervisor. After checking for past registration, cancellation, etc., the district will provide the firm with the proper forms and instructions.

542   PROMOTION AND ADVERTISING

21 CFR 202.1 which pertains only to prescription drugs, covers advertisements in published journals, magazines, other periodicals, and newspapers, and advertisements broadcast through media such as radio, television, and telephone communication systems. Determine what department or individual is responsible for promotion and advertising and how this responsibility is demonstrated. Ascertain what media (radio, television, newspapers, trade journals, etc.) are utilized to promote products.

Do not routinely collect examples of current advertising. Advertising should be collected only on assignment, or if, in your opinion, it is clearly in violation of Section 502(n) of the FD&C Act or 21 CFR 202.1.

543   GUARANTEES AND LABELING AGREEMENTS

Determine the firm's policies relative to receiving guarantees for raw materials, and issuing guarantees on their products. Also determine firm's practices regarding shipment of unlabeled drugs under labeling agreements. See IOM 526.

544   NEW DRUGS, ANTIBIOTICS, INVESTIGATIONAL DRUGS

544.1 Drug/Dietary Supplement Status

In instances where the drug/dietary supplement status of a product is unclear, the investigator should collect all related labeling and promotional materials including pertinent Internet web sites. This labeling and promotional material is often useful in determining the intended use of a product (See 21 CFR 201.128). Labeling, promotional materials and Internet web sites often contain information, for example, disease claims, that can be used to determine the intended use of a product and thereby if it is a dietary supplement or a drug and an unapproved new drug.

Further, the presence of synthetic ephedrine HCl, or the manipulation of red yeast rice to increase the presence of lovastatin, can exclude a product from being considered a dietary supplement within the meaning of the FD&C Act, 201(ff).

Check the current programs in your CPGM, Section 505 of the FD&C Act and 21 CFR 314.1 for required information. You may take the District's copy of the NDA into the plant as a reference during the inspection.

Document and report all deviations from representations in the NDA even though they may appear to be minor.

Antibiotics - Provide the same inspectional coverage as for other drugs. Refer to the approved antibiotic application to facilitate your evaluation of the firm's operation.

Investigational Drugs - Follow the instructions in pertinent programs in your CPGM or as indicated in the specific assignment received.

Clinical Investigators and/or Clinical Pharmacologists - Inspections in this area will be on specific assignment previously cleared by the Administration. Follow guidance in the CPGM or assignment.

545   BIORESEARCH MONITORING

Inspectional activities in the bio-research monitoring programs include In Vivo Bio-equivalence, Good Laboratory Practice (GLP), Sponsor/Monitor (S/P), Clinical Investigators (CI), Institutional Review Boards (IRB), and Radioactive Drug Research Committees (RDRC). In most instances, inspections conducted under these programs will be done on assignment from the respective Center and occasionally with the assistance of a Center's Bio-research Monitoring review staff. Refer to the Compliance Program for each of the areas. Become familiar with all associated regulations. Bio-research Monitoring inspections routinely issue from CDER, CDRH, and CBER. Some issue from CFSAN and CVM.

During team inspections with center personnel, the investigator is the team leader. See IOM 502.3. Districts should make the initial classification of inspections and the Center issuing the assignment will make the final decision after review.

546   Adverse Event Reporting

21 CFR Parts 310.305, 314.80, and 314.98 require reporting of adverse events occurring in connection with the use of marketed FDA regulated human drug products. Responsible firms include holders of NDAs and ANDAs, and applicants, and manufacturers, packers and distributors of marketed prescription drug products that are not the subject of approved NDAs or ANDAs. Firms must maintain current Standard Operating Procedures (SOPs) and must maintain records of documents related to adverse events. Responsible firms must submit the event information to FDA in reports. The events must be evaluated to determine if they have had a serious outcome such as death, disability, hospitalization, life threatening, or were included in the current labeling for the product.

For headquarters-initiated investigations, field investigators should contact the assigning Office of Compliance staff prior to beginning the investigation to obtain specific instructions and current documents to be used during the investigation.

549   DRUG INSPECTION REPORT

In 2000, FDA assembled a workgroup to review the content of pharmaceutical reports for human, veterinary and biological pharmaceuticals. The workgroup developed a number of recommendations intended to improve the content of such reports. Information from the workgroup and any applicable Compliance Programs can be used to help you prepare an acceptable report. This guidance outlines the inspection report content for an inspection conducted to meet the statutory obligation, i.e., a full inspection. It does not cover the reporting requirements for a limited inspection with a narrow focus, such as a complaint follow-up or investigation into a recall. In those cases, use your judgment and guidance in the Investigations Operations Manual (IOM) about the amount of reporting required.

The information is not arranged by report section headings. You can use the existing section headings in Section 590 or other headings as appropriate. The facts should be presented in a logical manner with similar data grouped together. Some information such as the firm name & central file number may be placed in the report header. You can combine section headings. When you do, cover the items requested under each heading description in the combined heading.

You will see a few items listed which are duplicative of information contained in FACTS. Your reports may be distributed to other, non-FDA parties, such as the European Union, who do not have access to FACTS, but will still need this information. It is included in the description of the narrative deliberately to serve the needs our non-FDA partners.

The workgroup developed two lists of information. The first was termed "Core Elements" and consisted of recommendations for information to be included in every inspection report. The second was called "General Elements", identifying topics and areas the group believed should be covered for every complete inspection. In any report, full reporting of objectionable conditions is a requirement.

In some cases, you may wish to indicate the information requested is already in an FDA inspection report. When you do this, refer only to one report and specify the report by date. Do not simply say "see previous report". Do not refer to multiple "previous reports" to avoid the need for positively reporting information. You also need to determine if the end users of your report, such as a Center Compliance Officer, will have access to that report. If not and the information is needed, include it in your report whether or not it is already in the District file.

For each of the Element Areas, guidance about the expected content of the section is provided. This additional guidance covers areas such as depth of reporting, diagrams and exhibits to assist in explaining the inspection, etc. This format does not require full and detailed narratives for every area for every inspection. The firm's state of compliance, the previous inspectional report and information, complexity of operations and other aspects all are determinants in how much reporting will be necessary. In many cases, brief summaries addressing the format areas will be sufficient.

CORE ELEMENTS

The narrative report may be supplemented with coversheets, appendices, annexes, files, report of observations, or exhibits, which provide all the information necessary to make administrative and regulatory decisions. Long reports should include a Table of Contents.

Name of Firm & Site Address - Report the firm's complete legal name, street address of inspected facility, fax and phone numbers, and e-mail address. Note if there are other facilities and the location of a headquarters if different.

FDA Registration Number - A unique number assigned to each company or firm manufacturing or processing drugs intended for the United States and its territories. Include, if different, the Firm Establishment Identifier (FEI) and Central File Number (CFN).

Reason for the Inspection & Scope - State the reason and scope of the inspection referring to any assignment or request for special coverage. You may reference applicable Compliance Programs, pre-approval request, elaborate on a "for cause" inspection request or other reason. Include the time period of the firm's operations covered by your inspection.

Date, Classification and Findings of Previous Inspection - Provide the requested information, summarizing the previous inspection findings. If this information is from a foreign inspection and you have access to the prior report or information, report the same information and note, which Regulatory Authority was responsible for the report.

Actual Dates of Inspection - Specify which specific days you were present in the firm. (This may be in the report header.) Bracketed listing is not acceptable, e.g. 9/1-25/XX. Name of all Investigators - Names of Investigators, analysts, etc., present for any part of the inspection. If investigators are from multiple districts or offices, specify their home offices.

Persons Interviewed and Individual Responsibility - List the relevant individuals who answered questions regarding the inspection or who have the appropriate responsibility, authority, and knowledge to prevent, detect, and/or correct objectionable conditions. Report the following:

Full name, title and authority of person shown credentials and receiving FDA 482 and all other FDA forms.

Full name, title and areas of responsibility of key officers, plant personnel and individuals interviewed.

Where to send correspondence: The names, titles, mailing addresses, and responsibility, where appropriate, for the key operating personnel and top management to whom all FDA correspondence should be sent.

For foreign inspections, include name, street and mailing address, e-mail address, voice and fax phone numbers of US Agent/Broker.

Changes Since Last Inspection - Report significant changes of personnel, management, equipment, manufacturing, documentation, and/or procedures of areas being inspected. Include address changes in premises and any changes to procedures in an application or DMF/VMF filing.

If you become aware of significant changes in areas not covered during the inspection, report those also.

Summary of Inspection and Findings - This portion of the report will include information on corrections made following the last inspection, what products and processes were covered, significant findings and any objectionable conditions.

Status of Previously Objectionable Conditions - You should determine if all corrective actions promised from a previous inspection were completed. If the firm did not make promised corrections, identify those and include the firm's reason for the failure to do so. Identify and document any continuing objectionable conditions. Corrective actions should also be compared with any inspectional findings to assure the issue has truly been corrected.

Products Produced and Covered - Describe the products and dose forms manufactured by the firm (e.g. Tablets, non-sterile API synthesis, injectables). A list of all products manufactured should be collected and attached. For foreign firms, identify which products are shipped to the US and the primary US consignees. Identify which products and types were covered during the inspection.

Processes/Systems covered - Describe the firm's manufacturing processes, systems and operations relevant to your inspection. Summarize the processes covered during the inspection. The use of layouts, flow plans, schematics, etc. is encouraged. A detailed description of operations may be necessary when related to deviations from GMPs or application commitments, or when significant changes in the manufacturing operations have occurred.

PDMA Coverage - Describe what sample loss, theft, or diversion reports were covered during the inspection. Describe the firm's sample audit and security systems, including a review of the firm's SOP's. Significant problems that may contribute to the firm's inability to adequately monitor sample distribution via sales representative, mail or common carrier should be addressed under objectionable conditions.

Manufacturing codes - Report the firm's manufacturing code and the interpretation of the code. If same as the previous report, you may refer to that report by date.

Complaints/Product Defects - Describe any significant product complaints and/or defects, which may result in the product failing its release or stability specifications or may jeopardize the end product user. This includes NDA Field Alerts.

Returned / Salvaged Goods - Summarize the scope of products returned to the manufacturer because of quality defects. Include information about how the firm salvages returned goods. Any returns related to objectionable conditions or GMP deviations should be explained in your discussion of objectionable conditions.

Recall/Withdrawal Operations - Describe any company removal or correction of a marketed product not reported to FDA or covered in a prior report.

Refusals - Describe any refusal by the firm.

Objectionable Conditions - Report on each objectionable condition (verbal and/or listed on the FDA 483) including a clear description of each, its impact on the product and batches or lots involved, and any relationship to other products or processes. Reference any exhibits to the conditions as they are discussed in the narrative. When you have a large number of objectionable conditions and a long FDA 483, include an FDA 483 cross-referenced to exhibits to aid review. Note if the condition was found during a previous inspection. Identify the person(s) with knowledge, duty and power to prevent, detect and/or correct each condition. Relate any compliance samples to conditions as you discuss them in your report.

Samples Collected - Report and describe any samples collected during your inspection. If the inspection was performed because of information from prior sample results include this in the description of the scope of inspection.

Discussion of Observed Conditions with Management (exit interview) - Report the discussion of all objectionable conditions from your daily inspection review and the discussion with management at the conclusion of the inspection. During your discussions, you should summarize the inspectional findings and explain the nature of observed deviations. The firm's management should be asked to respond to the conditions but a response is not mandatory.

List of Objectionable Conditions (FDA 483) including firm's annotation - At the end of the inspection, a List of Inspectional Observations (e.g., FDA 483) is issued to the most responsible individual at the firm. The observations should be factual, concise and free of any opinions.

Report the Full Name, title and responsibility of all persons present during the discussion of the FDA 483 and/or other observed conditions. State the date the FDA 483 was issued and the location if different than the inspected site.

Discussions with Management including firm's responses - Report promises of corrections and time frames. Clearly identify those conditions which were corrected during your inspection. If the firm intends to provide a written response later, report when they expect to send this.

List of Attachments and Exhibits - Attachments to your report include FDA forms (when issued) and should include the assignment documents. Supporting records, reports, procedures, batch records, Organizational Charts, Label Specimens, Batch Records, etc, collected to support possible deviations are generally considered evidence and must be properly identified and submitted according to Section 527. All exhibits should be referenced in the narrative.

GENERAL ELEMENTS

It may be necessary to include this additional information for initial inspections, when there has not been a complete narrative for a number of years or for other reasons. You need not repeat information in these sections contained in one of the Core Element areas and you may combine Core and General Elements where appropriate.

Table of Contents - For long reports, list report sections with page numbers.

Firm History - Report on the company structure, legal status, affiliations with other companies and any recent mergers or acquisitions. Report any trade names used, products handled by the company, and types of products manufactured. List the names and titles of owners, partners, corporate officers, and other key corporate officials and describe the firm's organizational structure.

Planned Future Changes - Describe details of any proposed site changes or significant changes to the company's operation.

U.S. Agent/Broker - Report the name, title, physical and mailing address, phone and fax number and e-mail address of any US Agent or broker who represents the company when dealing with FDA.

Consultants - For individuals hired by the firm to provide guidance and advice, obtain their names, addresses, and qualifications. Identify those associated with key or critical processes such as sterilization validation.

Customers - For foreign inspections, list US consignees to whom the firm's product is shipped. For API and component manufacturers, this includes consignees who use the product in their manufacturing of products intended for the US market, if known. For domestic firms, identify the general types of customers and provide the names and addresses for several regular customers of a few of the firm's products.

Areas and Functions not Inspected - Generally describe any areas or processes of the firm that were not covered during your inspection.

Description of Facility - Describe the overall layout of the facility. Include critical facility features or equipment such as the HVAC system, room classifications, sterilization equipment, systems design for cross contamination prevention and other specialty designs. A diagram may be included.

Equipment - Generally describe the firm's manufacturing equipment. Equipment is not expected to be described in detail unless it is new, significantly changed, related to a deviation from GMPs, or requested in the inspection assignment. This section would include information about qualification, calibration, maintenance, cleaning and validation. Your descriptions can be presented in subheadings if the information is extensive.

Training Program - Obtain a description of the firm's training program for production and testing personnel. This should document if personnel are adequately trained to perform the specific operations within the firm, and reflect if personnel performing the manufacturing operations are trained in GMPs.

Component & Materials Control - Report procedures for the receipt, storage, and analysis of materials, including containers and closures, used to produce product. Describe procedures for the control of released, quarantined, and rejected materials for raw materials, containers, closures, in-process material and finished products.

Reprocessing/Reworking - Describe the procedures used to reprocess or rework non-conforming material to bring it into compliance with specifications. This could include the repeating of a step or steps in the normal processing sequence. It may involve a method, which is not part of the validated process, or may not be part of the firm's NDA or NADA. If you encounter reprocessing/reworking, report if the procedure is approved and the process validated.

Adverse Event Reports - Describe the firm's reporting procedures (including designated office with final authority) for receipt, tracking, surveillance and control activities. Include a brief summary of what you reviewed.

Water Systems - Describe the major components of any water system used in manufacturing or processing, especially Purified Water and Water for Injection (WFI) Systems. Include qualification and validation studies, plus maintenance and monitoring programs. System schematics may be attached as necessary.

Computer Systems - Describe the functions and validation program for all computer systems used to control manufacturing, control electronic record keeping and signatures, or any other GMP function. Include data integrity, data security, and prevention of improper data manipulation.

Packaging & Labeling - The label, labeling and promotional materials are a critical part of determining a product's intended use. In instances where a regulatory action is being considered based on product labels, labeling, and/or other promotional materials, including any Internet websites, it is imperative all such documentation be collected. This would include all written, printed or graphic matter upon the immediate container of an article or accompanying such article [the product's label and labeling, see FD&C Act, 201(k) and (m) and Section 435.1 of this manual]. Accompanying labeling could include for example, brochures, pamphlets, circulars, and flyers, as well as audio and video tapes. The investigator should also review and copy all related Internet web sites for information concerning, for example, promotional statements made for the firm's products. In cases where there may be a dispute about whether a product is a drug or a dietary supplement, all materials which claim a product can be used for the treatment of any disease should be collected.

Scale-Up Procedures - Describe the firm's procedures for scaling up from pilot to commercial size production. Determine if equipment is available, parameters & specifications for full-scale production have been established, and if not, how the firm plans to establish them.

QA / QC Systems - Describe the firm's organization, responsibilities, and procedures for quality control and quality assurance. Describe any deviations from regulatory or application requirements, or the firm's own quality control requirements.

Contracting Services/Vendors - Describe the location, site name and any manufacturing, laboratory or other testing operations performed at other sites. Include the firm's procedures to audit contractors and vendors.

Product Reviews/Discrepancy/Failure Evaluation and Reporting Systems - Describe how the firm conducts its "annual product review" and summarize your coverage of one or more of these activities. Summarize the firm's procedures for documenting and investigating systems, production, testing deviations, failures from validated processes and Out of Specification (OOS) results.

Testing/Laboratory Operations - Describe testing operations performed to assure product quality. Include all procedures and record keeping, sampling, testing or examination of components, in-process materials, finished product, containers and closures, stability tests, OOS laboratory investigation procedures, validation of methods, reference standards, and calibration of analytical equipment. (See 19, Contracting)

Specific areas of laboratory focus include:

Analytical Laboratories - Information about the structure of the firm's laboratories (QC, QA, R&D, and Microbiology),

their locations, and the identification of different operations performed in these laboratories. The description may also include listing of instruments and equipment in these laboratories, as well as the names of supervisors or the organizational charts of these laboratories.

Lab Equipment Calibration & Qualification - A summary of the instruments used to test and monitor regulated products (number, types, and brands). Includes qualification, calibration and maintenance records reviewed, including in-house and vendor logbooks. Microbiology sections may include laboratory autoclave and depyrogenation oven equipment certification or qualification. Laminar flow hoods, biosafety cabinets, pH meters, autoclaves, isolators, incubators, refrigerators or freezers including daily temperature records as well as maintenance or repairs, etc.

Microbiology Quality Control & SOPs - Suitability of specialty laboratory, procedures, equipment or facilities such as sterility testing and bacterial endotoxin testing; qualification of production equipment; depyrogenation tunnel/oven endotoxin challenges, biological indicators. Review of the qualification of production disinfectants using microbial challenges.

Stability Testing, Protocol & Storage Conditions - An evaluation of the firm's stability program which includes the review of applicable SOPs, assuring that the firm is adhering to application commitments, proper sampling and storage conditions.

Sample Accountability & Tracking - A description of the firm's sampling procedures including sample receipt, tracking, and storage in the laboratory.

Sampling and Testing for Acceptance and Rejection of Raw Materials - A description of the firm's sampling and testing protocols for the acceptance or rejection of raw materials (components, containers and closures) to be used in manufacturing of the pharmaceutical products.

Analyst's Notebooks - Review SOP's relating to analysts' notebooks, data recording, etc. .A review of the accuracy and completeness of the data recorded in analysts' notebooks or worksheets should be done and include review of raw data from associated chromatography, spectra, etc. and other sources generated by laboratory instruments. This review encompasses all analytical testing performed in the laboratory including raw material testing of active ingredients and excipients, in-process, release, stability testing, etc.

Standards/Reagents/Chemicals/Media - A description of the firm's testing, standardization, handling, and storage of laboratory reference standards, standard solutions, media, reagents, and chemicals. For a microbiology laboratory, the following may be included: media preparation and formulation, sterilization, storage, growth promotion, bacteriostasis/fungistasis testing, culture handling, storage or identification, etc. Media uses such as analytical testing, environmental and personnel monitoring, production media fills, and growth support for biological indicators must also be documented. Included are outside media, reagent, or equipment suppliers, etc.

Analytical Method Validation - A description of the firm's method validation program. Review should include: accuracy, precision, specificity, detection limit, limit of quantification, linearity, range, ruggedness, and robustness.

Computer System Validation - Information, which identifies any computer systems used to perform critical functions in the laboratory. A definition of each system should include both hardware and software descriptions along with a description of the functionality of each system. The validation status of each system will be reviewed which will include evaluation of: Developmental validation documentation (if appropriate); change control of software, hardware and associated end user SOP's; Backup systems for controlling software and data files; Security systems to protect program and data integrity; and System design controls which ensure traceability for any altered records. It is important to ensure the Quality Unit at the firm is involved with establishing and maintaining control over all critical computer system related activities.

Method Transfer - Information regarding the proper analytical method transfer from R&D laboratories to the QC or contract laboratories where actual analytical testing is conducted. Includes information about the written method transfer protocol, any method-specific training provided to the analysts involved in performing the methods transfer work at the receiving laboratory, any difficulties experienced by the receiving lab, any correspondence between the coordinating and receiving labs regarding any deviation issues during the official transfer process. Also, report any observations or comments regarding the analytical work, raw analytical data or summary report.

OOS Results - Information about the adequacy of the laboratory's protocol for the handling and investigation of out of specification (OOS) test results. The assessment should include discussion about the relevant areas, such as: procedures for reporting laboratory errors, responsibilities of laboratory personnel, retesting/resampling, timeframes, requirements for additional testing, guidance regarding when to expand the investigation to an outside laboratory, final evaluation of all test results, conclusions, investigation records, and follow up procedures. In addition, if raw analytical data for any OOS investigation(s) is reviewed, any deficiencies or deviations found should be discussed.

Training Protocol for Lab Personnel - Description of the firm's training program for laboratory personnel. Records should be complete to ensure that personnel are adequately trained to perform specific laboratory functions within the firm.

Contract Testing Lab - The written agreement or contract between a contract servicing laboratory and a pharmaceutical company must be reviewed to ensure the agreement states the responsibilities of the contract lab as far as tests performed, the number of tests to be performed, procedures related to OOS results, and the methodology to be used to perform the test(s). Review and generally report in what form and how results are reported to the receiving laboratory. Review the firm's control of all pertinent operations as discussed above in this section.

Stability Program - Evaluate the company's stability program. Include discussions of deficiencies in SOPs, sampling, chamber maintenance, chamber temperature and humidity specifications, and any stability sample failures.

Records/Reports/Documentation Control - Describe the firms procedure for creation, approval and maintenance of required procedures, records, etc. for production, control, or distribution of pharmaceutical products. This includes raw data and other items such as annual product reviews, complaints, recalls and returned or salvaged drug product records. Includes electronic record / signature compliance. Includes QC control, approval, and review.

SUBCHAPTER 550 - DEVICES

550 DEVICE INSPECTIONS

See IOM 701 for discussion of statutory authority. The term "device" is defined in Sec. 201(h) of the FD&C Act. In-vitro diagnostics (21 CFR 809) are devices, as defined in 201(h) of the Act, and may also be biological products subject to Section 351 of the PHS Act.

Inspections involving devices should be made only by those individuals qualified by training and experience in the device area. Electronic product radiation is defined in 21 CFR 1000. Because of the specific nature of inspections and investigations involving radiation, only personnel who have special training in this field should be assigned such work. However, others may participate for training purposes. Specific Compliance Programs designate the type of individual and special training required for work in these areas.

CAUTION: Radiation-emitting devices and substances present a unique hazard and risk potential. Every effort should be taken to prevent any undue exposure or contamination. Monitoring devices must be used whenever radiation exposure is possible. Investigators should also be on the alert for, and avoid contact with, manufacturing materials and hazards associated with the manufacturing of many types of devices, which may present a threat to health, e.g., ethylene oxide, high voltage, pathogenic biomaterials, etc. See IOM 140 for additional safety information.

550.1 Technical Assistance

Each region and some districts have engineers and radiological health personnel available for technical assistance and consultation. Do not hesitate to make use of their services.

Engineers, quality assurance specialists, and expert investigators in ORA/ORO/Division of Field Investigations (DFI), Medical Device Group, HFC-130, (301) 827-5653, are available for on-site consultation and assistance in problem areas. The division's medical device group is also available by telephone for consultation and to answer questions regarding regulation and program interpretation and QS/GMP application. Additionally, the CDRH Office of Compliance enforcement divisions (organized by device product) can be contacted as necessary.

WEAC has various personnel (biomedical, sterility, electronic, materials, mechanical, nuclear and plastics engineers) available for telephone consultation and on-site assistance. They can be reached at (617) 729-5700.

550.2 Sample Collection During Inspection

Because of the limited funds available for samples and the relatively high cost of device samples, it is essential you consider, in consultation with your supervisor, the following factors before collecting a physical sample of a device:

1.   If follow-up to a QS/GMP deviation, will sampling demonstrate the deviation and/or a defective product? Documentary Samples may be more suitable for QS/GMP purposes.

2.   Likelihood of the analysis showing the device is unfit for its intended use.

3.   Samples costing over $250.00.

4.   Laboratory capability to analyze the sample. See IOM 454.3f for sample routing information.

If you are still uncertain, discuss with your supervisor and contact the CDRH Laboratory or WEAC (781)729-5700 for assistance.

Contact CDRH for assistance as follows:

1.   In-vitro Diagnostic Devices - Office of Science & Technology (HFZ-113).

NOTE: Device samples do not require 702(b) portions. Include in the FDA 525 and with the C/R, if destined for different locations, a copy of the firm's finished device specifications, test methods and acceptance and/or rejection criteria.

550.3 Types of Inspections

General device inspections will be conducted under various Compliance Programs found in the Compliance Program Guidance Manual. The majority of these will be QS/GMP inspections, but often the reason for the inspection will vary. For example, inspections may be conducted to assist the pre-market clearance process (PMA or Class III 510(k)), to specifically address MDR concerns, or to assure in-depth coverage of an aspect of manufacturing (sterility). The following describes some of these inspections.

551   MEDICAL DEVICE QUALITY SYSTEM/GOOD MANUFACTURING PRACTICES

Section 520(f) of the Act provides the Agency with authority to prescribe regulations requiring that the methods used in, and the facilities and controls used for, the manufacture, packing, storage, and installation of medical devices conform to good manufacturing practices. The medical device Quality System/Good Manufacturing Practices Regulation (QS/GMP)(21 CFR 820) became effective on June 1, 1997.

21 CFR 820 is established and promulgated under the authority of Sections 501, 502, 510, 513, 514, 515, 518, 519, 520, 522, 701, 704, 801 and 803 of the FD&C Act (21 U.S.C. 351, 352, 360, 360c, 360d, 360e, 360h, 360i, 360j, 360l, 371, 374, 381 and 383). Failure to comply with the provisions of 21 CFR 820 renders a device adulterated under Section 501(h) of the Act.

The regulations promulgated under 21 CFR 820 establish minimum requirements applicable to finished devices,

as defined in 820.1(a). This regulation is not intended to apply to manufacturers of components or parts of finished devices, but instead recommended to them as a guide. In some special cases, components have been classified as finished devices (dental resins, alloys, etc.) and are subject to the QS/GMP. Manufacturers of human blood and blood components are not subject to this part, but are subject to 21 CFR 606.

The QS/GMP includes regulations regarding Purchasing Controls, 21 CFR 820.50, Receiving, In-process and Finished Device Acceptance, 21 CFR 820.80, and Traceability, 21 CFR 820.65, that require finished device manufacturers exercise more control over the components they use in their devices. The preamble of the QS/GMP states: "Since FDA is not regulating component suppliers, FDA believes that the explicit addition to the CGMP requirements of the purchasing controls...is necessary to provide the additional assurance that only acceptable components are used." And "...inspections and tests, and other verification tools, are also an important part of ensuring that components and finished devices conform to approved specifications." It further states, "...traceability of components must be maintained so potential and actual problem components can be traced back to the supplier."

The medical device QS/GMP is an umbrella GMP that specifies general objectives rather than methods. It is left to the manufacturer to develop the best methods to meet these objectives. You must use good judgment in determining compliance with the QS/GMP, keeping in mind that it is an umbrella GMP and all requirements may not apply or be necessary. The purpose of the QS/GMP is to assure conformance to specifications and to ensure that all requirements that will contribute to assuring the finished device meets specifications are implemented. You should not insist that a manufacturer meet non-applicable requirements. Refer to IOM Exhibit 550-A for types of establishments that are required to comply with the QS/GMP.

551.1 Pre-Inspectional Activities

Prior to the start of any medical device inspection, the factory jacket or establishment history of the establishment should be reviewed.   You should review the previous inspectional findings and subsequent correspondence between the establishment and FDA; any MDR or consumer complaints where it was determined follow-up would occur at the next inspection; and any notifications of recalls since the last inspection.

The following on-line databases should be queried through the CDRH Information Retrieval System (CIRS):

-For Medical Device Reporting (MDR) data (MAUDE),

-Registration and Listing data, and

-510(k) and PMA summary data (OSCAR);

These databases are accessible to users with individual accounts. Accounts can be requested through the district or regional CIRS liaisons to DFI/Alan Gion (301) 827-5649.

MDR data most useful in preparing for an inspection includes specific MDRs for the manufacturer (i.e., query by establishment's short name) for the time frame since the last inspection, or MDRs for the generic devices manufactured by that establishment (i.e., query by product code) for some reasonable time frame. This data assists you in determining potential problem areas in the manufacture or design of the device, or lot or batch specific issues.

The establishment's reported registration and listing data should be verified during any GMP inspection to assure there have been no changes and the registration and listing data was accurately reported. Changes or inaccuracies should be immediately reported to the district medical device registration and listing monitor. See also Field Management Directive (FMD) 92.

510(k) and PMA data assists you in determining what devices the establishment is manufacturing and whether any new devices have been designed or changed since the last inspection. This data is useful in focusing the inspection on new or changed devices as well as devices that are higher risk devices, i.e., Class II or III versus Class I.

IOM 510 should be followed in regards to pre-announcement of medical device inspections.

551.2 High-Risk Devices

There is a designation for devices that are surgically implanted or intended to support or sustain human life and whose failure, when used in accordance with instructions provided in the labeling, could reasonably be expected to result in significant injury or illness. This group of devices is designated as high risk (previously listed as significant risk and critical devices).

When identifying high-risk devices, FDA uses recommendations received from the Device GMP Advisory Committee and the device classification panels. The selection of high-risk devices is independent of the classification of devices into Class I, II, III. High-risk devices are those identified by CDRH as such and appear as an attachment to the Compliance Program, 7382.845, Inspection of Medical Device Manufacturers, (combines the list of significant risk and critical devices.)

551.3 Quality Audit

The inspectional approach for identifying inadequate auditing of a quality assurance program is limited by the agency's policy, which prohibits access to audit results. The policy is stated in CPG 7151.02. Under the QS/GMP regulation (21 CFR 820.180 (c)) this prohibition extends to evaluations or audits of suppliers, 21 CFR 820.50(a), and Management Reviews conducted per 21 CFR 820.20. Evidence of inadequate auditing may be discovered without gaining access to the written audit reports. See the Guide to Inspections of Medical Device Manufacturers or Guide to Inspections of Quality Systems for inspectional guidance.

The preamble to the QS/GMP specifically states, "FDA will review the corrective and preventive action procedures and activities performed in conformance with those procedures without reviewing the internal audit reports. FDA wants to make it clear that corrective and preventive actions, to include the documentation of these activities, which result from internal audits and management reviews

are not covered under the exemption at 820.180(c)." Therefore, these corrective and preventive actions and documentation are not excepted from inspectional scrutiny.

The QS/GMP regulation (21 CFR 820.180(c)) requires a manufacturer to certify in writing that audits and reaudits have been conducted whenever requested to do so by an investigator. Investigators through their supervisors should consult with CDRH (HFZ-306) prior to requesting such certification.

551.4 Records

FDA has distinct authority under section 704(e) of the Act to inspect and copy records required under section 519 or 520(g). Investigators should only collect copies of documents as necessary to support observations or to satisfy assignments. Manufacturers who have petitioned for and obtained exemption from the QS/GMP are not exempted from FDA authority to review and copy complaints and records associated with investigation of device failures and complaints.

You may advise manufacturers they may mark as confidential those records they deem proprietary to aid FDA in determining which information may be disclosed under Freedom of Information.

Records must be maintained for as long as necessary to facilitate evaluation of any report of adverse performance, but not less than two years from the date the device is released for distribution. Records required by the Radiation Control for Health and Safety Act must be maintained for five years. It is permissible to retain records in photocopy form, providing the copies are true and accurate reproductions.

551.5 Complaint Files

Complaints are written or oral expressions of dissatisfaction with finished device identity, quality, durability, reliability, safety, effectiveness or performance. Routine requests for service would not normally be considered complaints. However, service requests should be reviewed to detect complaints, and as part of any trend analysis system, and to comply with 820.20(a)(3).

FDA has the authority to require a device firm to open its complaint files, and review and copy documents from the file.

Provisions in the FD&C Act pertaining to FDA review of records are:

1. For restricted devices the FD&C Act in Section 704(a)(2) extends inspection authority to records, files, papers, processes, controls and facilities bearing on restricted medical devices. See FD&C Act Sec. 704 for a full explanation and for a list of the items, e.g., financial data, which are exempt from disclosure to FDA.

2. For all devices, including restricted devices, refer to Section 704(e) of the FD&C Act, which provides for access to, copying and verification of certain records.

3. Section 519 of the FD&C Act requires manufacturers, importers, or distributors of devices intended for human use to maintain such records, and provide information as the Secretary may by Regulation reasonably require.

4. Section 520(g) of the FD&C Act covers the establishment of exemptions for devices for investigational use and the records which must be maintained and open for inspection.

QS/GMP requirements for complaint files are found in 21 CFR 820.198. GMP requirements for complaint files first became effective on December 18, 1978. The Quality System Regulation, which went into effect on June 1, 1997, added to and modified the requirements for complaint handling. The regulation contains a provision that records maintained in compliance with the QS/GMP must be available for review and copying by FDA (21 CFR 820.180). Complaint files are QS/GMP required records, therefore, the manufacturer must make all complaints received on or after December 18, 1978 and the records of their investigation available for FDA review and copying. EIRs should contain enough information to allow cross-referencing between complaints and MDRs.

21 CFR Part 803/804 require medical device manufacturers to report deaths, serious illnesses, and serious injuries to FDA for which a device has or may have caused or contributed, and manufacturers must also report certain device malfunctions. The MDR reportable events must be maintained in a separate portion of the complaint files or otherwise clearly identified. These complaints must be investigated to determine whether the device failed to meet specifications; whether the device was being used for treatment or diagnosis; and the relationship, if any, of the device to the reported incident or adverse event.

When a firm determines complaint handling will be conducted at a place other than the manufacturing site, copies of the record of investigation of complaints must be reasonably accessible at the actual manufacturing site.

551.6 In Vitro Diagnostics

By memorandum, dated April, 9, 1999, CBER's Office of Compliance requested that the next inspection of all IVD manufacturers conducted after April 9, 1999 include the completion of an IVD Manufacturer Questionnaire (see Exhibit 550 B).

FDA has identified a potential problem in performing a comprehensive evaluation of occurrences with the human blood and/or blood products that are imported into the U.S., which are regulated by CBER, for further processing into IVDs, which are regulated by CDRH. Currently, neither CBER nor CDRH has a tracking database to establish where and from whom the IVD manufacturers are receiving their imported blood and/or blood products. It cannot be determined at this time if these blood and/or blood products entering the U.S. have had suitable FDA examination or meet blood GMP requirements (21 CFR 606).

CBER has developed a questionnaire to be used during inspections of IVD manufacturers. It is to be used 1) if the IVD manufacturers are using human blood and/or blood products in their IVDs, and if so, 2) what is the source of the product. Information from the IVD manufacturer questionnaire will be evaluated, and tracked in a database, by CBER, Division of Case Management, Import/Export Team.

CBER requests the following:

1. Begin immediately to incorporate the IVD Manufacturer Questionnaire, Exhibit 550 B, into the scheduled QS/GMP inspections for all medical device IVD manufacturers. (Unless the information requested is to be sent electronically, please print the information requested on the form for easier review.)

2. Describe the specifications of the IVD manufacturer for acceptance of the human blood and/or blood products, i.e., standard operating procedure (SOP) or contractual agreements (21 CFR 820.50).

You should incorporate the IVD Manufacturer Questionnaire into all QS/GMP inspections until each establishment has been evaluated using the questionnaire. Either fax the completed form to (301) 594-0940 or mail to FDA/CBER/Office of Compliance and Biologics Quality/Division of Case Management/HFM-610; 1401 Rockville Pike: Rockville, MD 20852-1448; Attention: Import/Export Team. If there are any questions regarding this request contact HFM-610 at (301) 827-6201, or FAX (301) 594-0940.

552 STERILE DEVICES

Inspections of sterile device manufacturers are conducted per Compliance Program 7382.845, as a production process under the Production & Process Control Subsystem. See the Guide to Inspections of Quality Systems for further guidance.

553 LABELING

Specific labeling requirements for in vitro diagnostics (IVDs) are contained in 21 CFR 809.10.

1. Part 809.10(a) contains explicit labeling requirements for the individual IVD containers, and for the outer package labeling and/or kit labeling. Part 809.10(b) contains special labeling requirements for the product insert, which must be included with all IVD products. These two sections also contain the requirements for: lot numbers, allowing traceability to components (for reagents) or subassemblies (for IVD instruments); stability studies for all forms of the product; an expiration date, or other indication to assure the product meets appropriate standards; and, the requirements for establishing accuracy, precision, specificity and sensitivity (as applicable).

2. Part 809.10(c) lists the labeling statements required for IVDs which are being sold for investigational and research use. Determine whether the firm is limiting the sale of IVDs, labeled as such, to investigators or researchers. Document any questionable products, and submit to CDRH for review.

Warning and caution statements recommended for certain devices, along with certain restrictions for use, are described in 21 CFR 801. This same section also contains the general labeling regulations, which apply to all medical devices.

554 GOVERNMENT-WIDE QUALITY ASSURANCE PROGRAM (GWQAP)

Inspections under the GWQAP are conducted upon request by OE, Division of Compliance Information Quality Assurance (HFC-240). Each assignment is specific and may involve more than a single compliance program. These inspections should be completed within 6 days from the date of the receipt from HFC-240. Specific questions arising during or as a result of these inspections should be directed to HFC-240.

555 CONTRACT FACILITIES

Device manufacturers may employ the services of outside laboratories, sterilization facilities, or other manufacturers (i.e., injection molders, packagers, etc). In such cases, the finished device manufacturer is responsible for assuring these contractors comply with the QS/GMP and the product or service provided is adequate. These contractors are subject to FDA inspection and the QS/GMP regulation.

Determine how a manufacturer evaluates and selects potential contractors for their ability to meet the manufacturer's requirements, as required by 820.50, Purchasing Controls. Conducting audits can be an effective method for assessment. However, not all contractors allow audits. Audits may not be feasible in some instances. In other instances the activity the contractor is conducting may not have a significant impact on the device safety or function; therefore, expending the resources necessary to audit the contractor may not be warranted.

Evaluations may be accomplished by other means such as requesting that the potential contractor fill out a questionnaire about their quality system, asking other customers of the contractor about their experiences with the firm, or basing assessments on past performance. Evaluations must be documented. The extent to which a manufacturer has evaluated a contractor, as well as the results of the evaluation, should govern the degree of oversight exercised over products and services supplied by the contractor.

556 SMALL MANUFACTURERS

When inspecting one-person or very small manufacturers for compliance with the QS/GMP master record and written procedure requirements, the investigator should realize that detailed written assembly, process, and other instructional procedures required for larger firms may not be needed. In a small firm, division of work is at a minimum, with one person often assembling and testing the finished device. In many cases, blueprints or engineering drawings could be an adequate procedures. The QS regulation requires that certain activities be defined, documented and implemented. The regulation does not require separate procedures for each requirement and often several requirements can be met with a single procedure. The complexity of the procedures should be proportional to the complexity of the manufacturer's quality system, the complexity of the organizational structure and the complexity/risk of the finished device being produced. In assessing the need for detailed or lengthy written procedures, the investigator should make judgments based on training and experience of the individuals doing the work and the complexity of the manufacturing process. However, this does not mean small manufacturers have any less responsibility for complying with the QS regulation or assuring safe and effective devices are produced.

557 BANNED DEVICES

Section 516 of the FD&C Act provides a device for human use may be banned by regulation (21 CFR 895) if it presents substantial deception or an unreasonable and substantial risk of illness or injury. Investigators should become familiar with this regulation. When you determine, during an inspection or investigation, that banned devices are being distributed, the distribution, manufacture, etc. should be documented as for any other violative product.

559 DEVICE INSPECTION REPORTS

This section describes two EIR formats, detailed and abbreviated, for use during surveillance and follow-up inspections not related to pre-market submissions. The detailed EIR was developed to assure all evidence is there to support a regulatory or administrative action. The abbreviated EIR is intended for non-violative inspections. Both formats will allow FDA to meet its regulatory partners needs in a global arena. For all GMP medical device inspection reports, headings in the report may be added, but not omitted. Additions can be made to address needs of other CPs such as 7383.001 and 7383.003 for pre-market and post-market PMA inspections and Class III 510(k) pre-clearance inspections.

In an abbreviated report, much less detail is expected. In addition, if it is not an initial inspection and no changes have been made since the previous fully reported inspection, many of the section prompts will not apply, do not include the section. The section entitled Additional Information will accommodate remarks that do not fit elsewhere.

ABBREVIATED INSPECTION REPORT

Information in this section should be included in every inspection report as applicable. The Header of each device EIR should include the FEI #, firm name, full address, initials of investigator(s) and date(s) of inspection.

Summary - Report the reason for the inspection (e.g., compliance program, by assignment, etc.). Report the scope of the inspection (comprehensive, limited, sample collection only, etc.). The date(s) and summary of the findings (include classification) of the previous inspection and the firm's response/corrective actions. The products, systems and processes covered during the current inspection (in brief). The types of records and documents reviewed (in brief). Include a summary of the current findings and a summary of management's response or corrections.

Administrative Data - The firm name, address, phone, FAX and e-mail address. Report the names and titles of the Investigator(s), Analyst(s), etc. The inclusive date(s) of the current inspection, i.e., list the actual dates in the plant. If a team inspection and some individuals came and went during the inspection, indicate dates in plant for each team member. The names and titles of persons to whom Federal credentials were shown. The names and titles of the persons to whom any FDA forms were issued during the inspection. (FDA 482, 483, 484, etc.) If this was a team inspection, report who wrote which section of the EIR. Report changes to hours of operation (include seasonal variations); changes to registration status.

History - If not the initial inspection of the firm: Include only changes to legal status of the firm (e.g. sole owner, partnership, or corporation.) If a corporation, in which state and when was it incorporated. List parent corporation, corporate address, subsidiaries. Include a summary of any regulatory actions taken as a result of the last inspection.

Interstate Commerce - Report changes in the previous estimate of the percentage of products shipped outside of the state, (or exported to the U.S.) and the basis of the estimate. Report changes in the firm's Promotion and Distribution Patterns.

Products and Labeling - Include changes in the firm's catalog of products, or list of representative number of currently marketed products subject to FD&C Act or other statute enforced by FDA or counterpart state agency. Report changes of Brand Names used. Collect full labeling (product and case labels, inserts, brochures, manuals, promotional materials of any type) for any changes. Documentation of any changes to applicable statutory guaranty given or received.

Responsibility - Report with whom you dealt, and in what regard (both during and prior to the start of the inspection), describe roles and authorities of responsible individuals and names and titles of individuals who supplied you with information. Report any changes in responsibilities from the last inspection: Who is the most responsible individual at the firm under inspection? Report the responsible head or designated correspondent, and names and titles of owners, partners, and corporate officers.

Copy of public annual report, if any and names and titles of key operating personnel.

Copy of relevant labeling agreement, if any. See IOM 526. Names, titles and address(es) of top management official(s) to whom correspondence should be addressed (FMD 145, PIN letter, W/L, etc.). Who has the duty, responsibility, and power to prevent, detect, and correct the violation(s), and how is this demonstrated and/or documented? See IOM 525.2.

The full chain of command including organizational chart (create if necessary).

Manufacturing/Design Operations - If not an initial inspection, report only changes to the firm's general overall operations, including significant changes in equipment, processes, or products since previous inspection. Include schematics, flow plans, photographs, formulations and diagrams, if useful.

For ALL inspections: for CAPA - indicate which data sources were available for review and which were actually covered/reviewed. Include a brief statement regarding coverage or non-coverage of applicable Tracking require-

ments, MDRs, sterilization and Reports of Corrections and Removals. For ALL Level 2, 3 and For Cause inspections: for P&PC – indicate which production processes were covered/reviewed. Under design controls – indicate which design project(s) was covered.

Manufacturing codes - If changed (or this is an initial inspection), a full description of the manufacturing coding system, and a key to interpretation of codes. If unchanged, a statement that the system is the same as described in reports on file at the District. Indicate the date of the EIR in which the codes are fully explained.

Complaints (If Applicable) - Note: The complaints included in this portion of the EIR are those that were reported to the FDA by consumers, health care professionals, industry, etc. – Not the complaints received by the firm, unless they are of such significance they should have been. Obtain details of deaths, injuries or other significant consumer/trade complaints, DPPR's, MDR's, MedWatch reports, or recalls if appropriate. Report your follow-up of consumer/trade complaints, DPPR's, MDR's, MedWatch reports or recalls identified in the district factory jacket for coverage. Describe the relationship of consumer/trade complaints, DPPR's, MDR's, MedWatch reports to specific objectionable conditions observed. If Returned Goods were examined, describe findings. If not examined, so indicate.

Objectionable Conditions - [those written (i.e., appear on the FDA 483) and those verbally discussed with management at the conclusion of the inspection].

Before listing and discussing observations, include a statement identifying which team member (if applicable) was responsible for the observation. List and discuss each observation and its relevance. Cross-reference each to exhibit(s) and sample(s). All violations or deficiencies should be supported by evidence. Include management's response or any corrective action taken for each observation and include time frames given for corrections to be taken, if any.

For each observation based on sampling of records, indicate which Sample Table and level of confidence was used and the actual number of records sampled. If the number sampled is different than the actual number reviewed, so indicate. List and describe any additional items not provided in writing, such as: questionable labeling practices, e.g., commercialization of products covered by IDE or IND; fraudulent health claims; lack of approved or cleared PMA, 510(k), NDA, ANDA, etc. This includes all verbal observations deemed of the same significance as the observations on the FDA 483.

NOTE: Indicate any exhibits, samples, etc. pertaining to these "verbal" observations.

Refusals - Furnish full details of all refusals of reasonable requested information encountered during the inspection.

General discussion with management - Furnish names and titles of all those present, including those who participated via electronic media and so describe. Include name and title to whom FDA 483 was issued. A description of each warning, recommendation, or suggestion given to the firm, and to whom given.

Additional information - If this is not an initial inspection, report changes only: Describe contractors used and for what purpose. Describe suppliers (major raw material, active ingredient, etc.) used and their products.

Include here those pertinent facts, which do not fit well into any other section of the EIR. (For firms located in foreign countries, include information relative to lodging and travel; for domestic firms, include information relative to location of firm if difficult to find; etc.)

Voluntary corrections - A brief description of improvements initiated by the firm in response to a previous report of observations or a warning letter. Voluntary destructions, recalls, and similar actions since prior inspection or during this inspection. (Include recalls to specific objectionable conditions observed.) Your follow-up to recalls identified during the inspection (may reference Attachment B recall report). Identify the person(s) responsible for the corrections.

Exhibits and Samples Collected - List by an assigned exhibit and sample #. Briefly describe or title each exhibit and sample collected.

Attachments - List and attach all FDA forms issued to the firm or created as part of the inspection. (Notice of Inspection, Inspectional Observations, Receipt for Samples, Affidavits, etc.). List and attach all associated assignment documentation by title, date, issuer. List and attach copies of any associated reports (Recall Attachment B Report; Complaint Follow-up Report, related informant or other investigation report or memo, etc.)

DETAILED INSPECTION REPORT

Report the following in addition to the items listed in Abbreviated Report section. The same section headings should be used.

Administrative - Report the full name and title of in-plant inspectors from other government agencies. Hours of operation (include seasonal variations). Registration status and applicable registration number.

History - Legal status of the firm (e.g. sole owner, partnership, or corporation.) If a corporation, in which state and when was it incorporated. List parent corporation, corporate address, subsidiaries. A summary of prior regulatory actions and prior warnings (do not cite any action that was only recommended but not approved.)

Interstate Commerce - An estimate of the percentage of products shipped outside of the state, (or exported to the U.S.) and the basis of the estimate. Examples of I.S. shipments of violative product(s); or if no such shipments, I.S. shipments of major components of violative products -- with complete I.S. documentation in either case. Promotion and Distribution Patterns.

Products and Labeling - A current catalog of products or a list of a representative number of currently marketed, products subject to FD&C Act or other statute enforced by FDA or counterpart state agency. List Brand Names used. Full labeling (product and case labels, inserts, brochures, manuals, promotional materials of any type) for those products.

Manufacturing/Design Operations - Include a general overall description of the firm's operations, including significant changes in equipment, processes, or products since previous inspection. List the name and address where design activities occur if different from manufacturing site.

Include their responsibilities. Include name and address of specification developer if different from either of the above. Include their responsibilities. Describe manufacturing operations by sub-system covered in your inspection (Management Controls, Design Controls, Production and Process Controls, Corrective and Preventive Action Controls, Material Controls, Facility and Equipment Controls, and Records/Documents/Change Controls.) If a sub-system is not specifically covered during the EI, you do not need to separately describe the general operations of that sub-system.

Manufacturing codes - Include description of the system used for identification to maintain control during the manufacturing process, as well as the codes used for traceability (for applicable finished devices).

Complaints - If Returned Goods were examined, describe findings. If not examined, so indicate.

Additional information - Be sure to include names and addresses of all applicable third-party installers or servicing organizations used by the manufacturer. Include their responsibilities

SUBCHAPTER 560 - BIOLOGICS

560   DEFINITION

A "biological product" means any virus, therapeutic serum, toxin, antitoxin, vaccine, blood, blood component or derivative, allergenic product, or analogous product, or arsphenamine or its derivatives (or any trivalent organic arsenic compound), applicable to the prevention, treatment, or cure of diseases or injuries of man. Additional interpretation of the statutory language is found in 21 CFR 600.3. Biological products are either drugs or devices, depending on their use and mode of action.

Veterinary biologicals are subject to the animal Virus, Serum, and Toxin Act which is enforced by USDA (21 U.S.C. 151-158).

561   BIOLOGICS INSPECTIONS

FDA has developed a strategy known as "Team Biologics", a reinvention of the agency's approach to inspectional coverage of biological products. Team Biologics consists of the "Blood Bank Cadre" and the "Core Team." The periodic cGMP inspections and compliance operations of plasma fractionated products, biotechnology derived therapeutics, allergenic products, vaccines, and biological in vitro diagnostic devices are now led by investigators and compliance officers in the Core Team. The investigators in the Cadre perform inspections of blood banks, plasmapheresis centers, tissue banks, and other blood establishments. The Cadre members report to their ORA District. The Core Team investigators report to ORO headquarters; Core Team compliance officers report to OE. See IOM 701 for a discussion of statutory authority. CBER maintains the lead for pre-licensing inspections of biological products.

Biological products are regulated under the authority of Section 351 of the Public Health Service Act and under the

Food, Drug and Cosmetic Act, as drugs or devices. Blood and blood products for transfusion are prescription drugs under the FD&C Act. Recovered plasma and source plasma intended for manufacturing non-injectable products and in-vitro diagnostics, e.g., HIV home collection kits, are devices.

Section 351(d) of the PHS Act provides for licensure of biologic establishments and products and inspection of the licensees. Most biological drugs are licensed. Radioactive biological products require NDAs (21 CFR 505) unless they have an unrevoked and unsuspended license issued prior to August 25, 1975.

The investigational new drug application regulations (21 CFR 312) also apply to biological products subject to the licensing provisions of the PHS Act. However, investigations of blood grouping serum, reagent red blood cells, and anti-human globulin in-vitro diagnostic products may be exempted (21 CFR 312.2(b)).

For blood bank and plasmapheresis center inspections use the CGMPs for Blood and Blood Components (21 CFR 606) as well as the general requirements for biological products (part 600), the general biological standards (part 610), and the additional standards for human blood and blood products (Part 640.) The drug GMPs (21 CFR 210/211) also apply to biologic drugs. In the event it is impossible to comply with both sets of regulations, the regulation specifically applicable to the product applies. This would generally be Section 606 and 640 regulations in the case of blood banks or plasma centers.

FDA is in the process of revising the regulation of human tissues, cells, and cellular and tissue-based products. CBER currently regulates human tissue intended for transplantation under 21 CFR Part 1270. This is tissue recovered, processed, stored, or distributed by methods which does not change tissue function or characteristics and is not currently regulated as a human drug, biological product, or medical device. Examples of such tissues are bone, skin, corneas, ligament and tendon. Part 1270 requires tissue establishments to screen and test donors, to prepare and follow written procedures for the prevention of the spread of communicable disease, and to maintain records. Human cells, tissues, and cellular and tissue based products (HCT/Ps) are covered under 21 CFR 1271.

Blood and human tissue establishments are sensitive to maintaining confidentiality of donor names. The mere reluctance to provide records is not a refusal. However, FDA has the authority under both the PHS and the FD&C Act to make inspections and 21 CFR 600.22 (g) provides for copying records during a blood establishment inspection. For prescription drugs, section 704 of the FD&C Act specifically identifies records, files, papers, processes, controls, and facilities as being subject to inspection.

If you encounter problems accessing records, explain FDA's authority to copy these records. IOM 514 should be followed if a refusal is encountered. When donor names or other identifiers are necessary, they may be copied, but the information must be protected from inappropriate release. See IOM 527.6.

The inspectional objective is to ensure biological products are safe, effective, and contain the quality and purity

they purport to possess and are properly labeled. Facilities will be inspected for conformance with:

1.   Provisions of the PHS Act and FD&C Act,
2.   GMPs in 21 CFR 210-211, 600-680, and 820,
3.   FDA Policies, which include guidance to the blood and blood products industry, and the Compliance Policy Guides Chapter 2.

561.1 Preparation

Review the district files of the facility to be inspected and familiarize yourself with its operation and compliance history. Review:

1.   Appropriate Compliance Programs and related Compliance Policy Guides (CPG), Chapter 2.
·   NOTE: Federal Cooperative Agreements Manual; MOU with the Department of Defense, and MOU with Health Care Financing Administration (HCFA) on transfusion services;
2.   Correspondence from the firm depicting any changes since the last inspection;
3.   Firm's registration and product listing information;
4.   DFI's Guide to Inspections of Source Plasma Establishments, Guide to Inspections of Blood Banks, and Guide to Inspections of Infectious Disease Marker Testing Facilities.
5.   Error and Accident Reports, Adverse Reaction Reports, complaints, and recalls;
6.   Guideline for Quality Assurance in Blood Establishments, (July 14, 1995).
7.   Draft Guideline for the Validation of Blood Establishment Computer Systems (September 28, 1993).

Through guidance documents, CBER sets forth its inspection policy and regulatory approach. A list of these documents is attached to the current Compliance Programs (CP).

The OSHA regulation 29 CFR 1910.1030 December 6, 1991, was intended to protect health care workers from bloodborne pathogens, including those involved in the collection and processing of blood products. The regulation defines expectations for the use of gloves, hand washing facilities, decontamination of work areas, waste containers, labeling and training of employees and exemptions for volunteer blood donor centers. FDA Investigators should adhere to these safety guidelines during inspections or related activities in establishments that process biologically hazardous materials.

Become familiar with the OSHA regulations and their applicability to 21 CFR 606.40(d)(1) & (2), which require the safe and sanitary disposal for trash, items used in the collection and processing of blood and for blood products not suitable for use. Consult your district biologics monitor for copies of the above references. Additional copies may be obtained from ORO, Division of Field Investigations (DFI), Biologics Group, HFC-130, (301) 827-5653 or see CBER's web site at http://www.fda.gov/cber.

561.2 Inspectional Approach

Use the compliance programs and Guides to Inspection of Blood Banks, Source Plasma Centers and Infectious Disease Marker Testing Facilities for inspectional guidance.

The EIR must clearly identify the areas covered. The report should include a summary of the inspection, the FDA 482, the FDA 483, if issued, and required FACTS EI Record.

Particular attention should be given to error and accident reports indicative of problematic areas or processes, adverse reactions, transfusion associated AIDS (TAA), and hepatitis and HIV lookback procedures. For additional information regarding TAA, see Compliance Program 7342.001. The follow-up investigations to such reports should also be covered.

Complaints, in particular those involving criminal activity, must be promptly investigated and coordinated with other agency components as needed.

A multi-layered system of safeguards has been built into the blood collection, manufacturing and distribution system to assure a safe blood supply. Refer to CP 7342.001 and 7342.002 for a discussion of the systems approach to inspection.

An example of such an approach is the coverage of infectious disease testing and control, including test procedures and interpretations of test results, decisions leading to the release of products, and donor deferrals. Investigators should also check on product returns, which may indicate possible GMP deficiencies.

If Investigators encounter products not specifically referenced in the regulations, they should contact CBER/OCBQ/ Division of Inspections and Surveillance for guidance.

561.3 Regulations, Guidelines, Recommendations

Guidance documents for industry are sent directly from CBER or made available on the CBER web site or via CBER's FAX Information System. The contents of most of these documents are incorporated into the establishment's SOPs and/or license applications or supplements. Also, DFI has issued Blood Bank, Source Plasma Establishment and Infectious Disease Marker Testing Facility Inspectional Guides to be used by investigators during inspections.

Deviations from the guides must not be referenced on a FDA 483. However, since these documents are often related to specific GMP requirements, in most cases deviations can be referenced back to the GMP. If a deviation is observed during an inspection and the investigator relates it to the regulations or law, then the item may be reported on the FDA 483. During the discussion with management, the relationship of the deviation to the regulation or law, or accepted standard of industry, should be clearly explained.

If an establishment indicates that it has not received any of these documents, provide the CBER web site and CBER FAX Information System telephone number.

If a firm claims approval for an alternative procedure, it should be able to produce the written approval letter. Approved alternative procedures may be verified by contacting CBER/Division of Blood Applications.

561.4 Technical Assistance

Several regions and some districts have specialists in biologics who are available for technical assistance and consultation. Do not hesitate to avail yourself of their services.

The services of expert investigators in ORA/ORO/ Division of Field Investigations (DFI), Biologics Group, HFC-130, (301) 827-5653, are available for telephone or on-site consultation and assistance in problem areas.

CBER/OCBQ, Division of Inspections and Surveillance (HFM-650), (301)827-6220, can provide technical assistance on blood banking principles, testing issues, and can coordinate assistance with other CBER offices.

562 REGISTRATION, LISTING AND LICENSING

See IOM 773.1.

Registration and Listing - Most transfusion services are exempt from registration under 21 CFR 607. This includes facilities approved for Medicare reimbursement and engaged in the compatibility testing and transfusion of blood and blood components, but which neither routinely collect nor process blood and blood components. Such facilities include establishments:

1.   Collecting, processing and shipping blood and blood components under documented emergency situations,

2.   Performing therapeutic phlebotomy and therapeutic plasma exchange after which the product is discarded,

3.   Preparing recovered human plasma and red blood cells,

4.   Pooling products/platelets for in-house transfusion,

5.   Thawing frozen plasma or cryoprecipitate for transfusion.

Although FDA transferred the routing inspection responsibility for these establishments to the Health Care Financing Administration (HCFA), the FDA retains legal authority to inspect them if warranted. Districts should conduct inspections jointly with the HFCA regional liaison. If a routine inspection determines an establishment is a HCFA obligation, FDA's inspection should be terminated and reported as such. See Federal Cooperative Agreements Manual - FDA/HCFA Memorandum of Understanding.

Tissue establishments manufacturing HCT/Ps currently regulated under 21 CFR Part 1270 must register and list. Manufacturers of HCT/Ps not currently regulated under 21 CFR Part 1270 as well as establishments manufacturing HCT/Ps currently regulated as medical devices, drugs or biological drugs registered with FDA may register in advance of the January 21, 2003 effective date, but will not be subject to the regulations inspections until then. Establishments not required to register are listed in 21 CFR 1271.15.

Laboratories that perform infectious disease testing on blood or blood components establishments are an FDA obligation and should be in the active OEI. Clinical laboratories are specifically exempted from registration by 21 CFR 607.65(g), but this does not exempt them from FDA inspections. Such laboratories should be encouraged to register voluntarily if performing any testing used by blood establishments to determine the suitability of donors or blood product quality. Inspections should focus on activities relevant to these testing or irradiation operations.

Inspection of military blood banks is a responsibility of the field. These facilities are required to meet the same standards as other blood banks although military emergencies may require deviations from the standards. A separate license is held by each branch of the service; although each individual establishment may be licensed or unlicensed, all are required to register. Districts should notify the appropriate military liaisons 30 days before inspection of a military facility. For additional information on inspection of government establishments, see Compliance Program 7342.001, the Federal Cooperative Agreements Manual, and the MOU with Department of Defense Regarding Licensure of Military Blood Banks.

Field Management Directive 92, Agency Establishment Registration and Control Procedures, details the registration process within the agency. Refer to FDA Compliance Policy Guides, Chapter 2, Sub-chapter 230 (230.110), for additional information on registration.

Ensure the firm's current registration forms reflect actual operations.

Biologic License - See IOM 773.2. Prior to granting a license, field personnel and CBER jointly conduct a pre-license inspection of the firm for compliance with the firm's license application and regulations. Copies of CBER's pre-license inspection reports are forwarded to the districts and should be part of the firm's file.

Approval of Biological Devices - There must be a pre-approval inspection (PAI) of the establishment for compliance with the QS/GMP regulation and the firm's PMA. For licensed devices, CBER conducts the PAI. Devices used in the collection and testing of blood for transfusion are approved/cleared through the PMA/510(k) authorities. ORA Investigators customarily inspect the CBER regulated devices, which are subject to PMA/510(k) applications.

563 RESPONSIBLE INDIVIDUALS

In licensed establishments, the applicant or license holder may designate an authorized official(s) to represent the applicant to the FDA in matters of compliance. The FDA 482 and any 483 should be issued to the most responsible person on the premises at the time of inspection. An exact copy of the FDA 483 should also be forwarded to the top official of the firm if that person did not receive the FDA 483. The designation as authorized official does not necessarily mean that individual is the most responsible for any non-compliance of the firm. In licensed or unlicensed facilities, establish and document all individuals responsible for violations and their reporting structure in the organization.

564 TESTING LABORATORIES

Blood establishments may use outside testing laboratories to perform required testing. Laboratories conducting testing for licensed blood banks are usually licensed. CBER may approve the use of a non-licensed laboratory to do required testing, provided the lab is capable of performing the tests and the lab registers with CBER prior to CBER approving the licensing arrangement. Laboratories performing required testing for Source Plasma manufacturers must either be (1) licensed or (2) meet the standards of the Clinical Lab Improvement Act (CLIA) and be qualified to perform the required testing. Clinical laboratories are specifically exempted from registration, but are encouraged to voluntarily register. Laboratories performing testing for manufacturers of blood and blood components are FDA inspectional obligations whether or not they are exempt from registration.

Guidance for inspecting testing laboratories is included in the appropriate Compliance Programs. Coordinate the inspection of non-registered laboratories with HCFA regional office contacts. If a testing laboratory is located outside of the district, request an inspection by the appropriate district office.

565 BROKERS

Blood establishments may use brokers to locate buyers for products such as recovered plasma or expired red blood cells. These articles are used for further manufacture into products such as clinical chemistry controls and in-vitro diagnostic products not subject to licensure. Fractionators also use brokers to locate suppliers of plasma under the short supply provisions (21 CFR 601.22). During inspections, determine if the facility is selling products to any brokers. If brokers are used, determine if the brokered products are shipped to a facility operated by the broker or directly to the consignee.

Brokers who take physical possession of blood products and engage in activities considered manufacturing or labeling are required to register and are included in the OEI for routine inspection under the blood bank compliance program. Brokers who only arrange sales of or store blood and blood components, but do not engage in manufacturing activities are not required to register.

SUBCHAPTER 570 - PESTICIDES

570 PESTICIDE INSPECTIONS

The objective of a Pesticide Inspection is to determine the likelihood of excessive residues of significant pesticides in or on products in consumer channels, and to develop sources of information for uncovering improper use of pesticide chemicals.

This requires directing coverage to two major areas:
1. Pesticide practices in the production and processing of field crops.
2. Application of pesticide chemicals in establishments storing and processing raw agricultural products.

Pesticide coverage must be provided during all food establishment inspections. Coverage of raw agricultural products will generally be on a growing-area basis.

Problem areas include:
1. Improper use of pesticides around animals - gross misuse of sprays and dips in animal husbandry may result in pesticide residues in foods.
2. Use of contaminated animal feeds - waste and spent materials from processing operations may contain heavy concentrations of pesticide residues, which were

present in the original commodity. See Compliance Policy Guide 575.100

3. Past pesticide usage - past pesticide practices on growing fields. Past use of persistent pesticides may result in excessive residues in the current food crop. You may need to check on pesticide usage for several years prior to an incident to ensure you gather enough information. Some pesticides last for many years in the environment.

571 CURRENT PRACTICES

Cooperative Activities - important sources of information relative to evaluating the "Pesticide Environment" include:

1. At the start of the growing season, spray schedules recommended for each crop by county agents, state experiment stations, large pesticide dealers, farmers cooperatives, et al should be obtained.

2. Visits to agricultural advisors may provide information relative to heavy infestation of insect pests and fungal infections on specific crops in specific areas.

3. Daily radio broadcasts in most agricultural areas may provide information on spray schedules, insect pests, harvesting and shipping locations, etc.

4. Field employees of fruit and vegetable canning and freezing plants usually recommend spray schedules, pesticides, and harvesting schedules for products produced by contract growers.

5. United States Weather Bureau Offices and their reports will provide data on weather conditions, which may effect insect growth and their development, size of fruit or leaf growth, and dissipation of pesticide chemicals.

6. USDA Market News Service daily price quotations, and weekly quotations in trade magazines provide information regarding harvesting schedules since market prices are indicators of how quickly a crop will be harvested in a given area. Growers who have the opportunity to obtain high prices may harvest their crops without regard to recommended pre-harvest intervals.

7. State Colleges of Agriculture seminars or short courses on food and vegetable production may alert you to significant departures from usual agricultural practices. Prior approval to attend such meetings should be secured from your supervisor.

8. Pesticide suppliers and distributors may provide information on spray practices, schedules, and the name and address of growers, etc.

NOTE: The U.S. Department of Agriculture has a Pesticide Data Program (PDP), which provides data on pesticide use and residue detection. This program helps form the basis for conducting realistic dietary risk assessments and evaluating pesticide tolerances. Coordination of this program is multi-departmental, involving USDA, EPA and FDA, covered by a MOU (Federal Cooperative Agreements Manual). As a part of this program USDA collects data on agricultural chemical usage, and factors influencing chemical use, and collects pesticide residue data through cooperation with nine participating states. USDA provides this data to EPA, FDA and the public. Several USDA publications are listed below as reference material.

The contact point at USDA for pesticide residue matters is:

Martha Lamont, Chief
Residue Branch, Science Division
Agricultural Marketing Service, USDA
8700 Centreville Road, Suite 200
Manassas, VA 221110
(703)-330-2300

Reference materials - the following reference materials provide background and data necessary or helpful in evaluating current practices. This material should be available at the District office.

1. Pesticide Chemicals - Regulations under the Federal Food, Drug and Cosmetic Act on tolerances for pesticides in food administered by the Environmental Protection Agency (EPA). (See 40 CFR 185)

2. EPA's Pesticide Regulations - Tolerances for Raw Agriculture Products. (See 40 CFR 180)

3. EPA's Rebuttable Presumption Against Registration (RPAR) List.

4. Pesticide Index. - By William J. Wiswesser. A publication containing information on trade names, composition and uses of commercial pesticide formulations.

5. The Daily Summary or Weekly Summary. News releases and reports from USDA.

6. USDA's Weekly Summary Shipments-Unloads.

7. Agricultural Economic Report No. 717 Pesticide and Fertilizer Use and Trends in U.S Agriculture (May 1995)

8. Annual Pesticide Data Summary (http://vm.cfsan.fda.gov/~dms/pesrpts.html).

9. Reports from USDA's Crop Reporting Board.

10. USDA's Pesticide Assessment Reports.

572 GROWERS

Preliminary investigation of growing areas at the start of the season will provide data necessary for district work planning including production schedules, types and acreage of crops, pesticides used and the names and addresses of growers and shippers.

Growing Dates - The significant growing dates relative to pesticide usage are as follows:

1. Planting date,

2. Date of full bloom, and

3. Date of edible parts formation.

Harvest Dates - The dates of the anticipated harvest season will provide planning information relative to pre-harvest application and shipping.

Acreage - This will provide volume information for work planning.

Pesticide Application - ascertain the actual pesticide application pattern for each crop. Look for objective evidence to document actual grower practice. Check the grower's supply of pesticide chemicals, look for used pesticide containers, visit his source of supply, etc. Check spraying and dusting practices. Establish if pesticide chemicals are used in such a manner that excessive residues might result.

The following information provides a basis for evaluating pesticide usage:

1.   Pesticide Chemical Applied - List the common name if there is no doubt as to the chemical identity of the pesticide. Include labeling indications and instructions.

2.   Method of Application - Describe the method of application i.e., ground rig, airplane, greenhouse aerosol, hand, etc.

3.   Formulation - Describe the formulation i.e., wettable powder, emulsifiable concentrate, dust, granules, aerosol, etc. Express as pounds of active ingredient per gallon or percent wettable powder.

4.   Number of Applications and Dates.

5.   Rate of Last Application - Calculate the amount of active ingredient per acre.

6.   Pre-Harvest Interval (PHI) - Calculate the number of days between the day of the last application of pesticide and the harvest date or anticipated harvest date. Compare to the PHI.

7.   Visible residue on growers crop.

8.   Summary of Usage - Determine the USDA Summary Limitations and evaluate the responsible usage.

Pesticide Misuse/Drift/Soil Contamination - Pesticide residues, which exceed established tolerances, action levels, or "regulatory analytical limits" may be caused by pesticide misuse which can include:

1.   Excessive application of a chemical on a permitted crop.

2.   Failure to follow labeled time intervals between the last pesticide application and harvest.

3.   Use of a non-approved pesticide on a crop.

4.   Failure to wash a crop when pesticide labeling requires it (e.g., for certain EBDC's).

Other conditions, which may cause illegal residues, include spray drift and soil contamination.

Drift may be documented by determining which crops and pesticides have been grown/used in fields adjacent to those sampled. Determine direction of prevailing winds and wind condition on the day of spraying. Selective sampling will aid in determining if drift occurred. Compliance Samples collected to document pesticide drift should be Flagged and noted in block 16 of the CR as "Drift Sample - Maintain as Individual Subs".

Soil contamination by compounds, which are relatively stable in the environment, may cause systemic uptake of the compounds by growing crops. Follow-up investigations to violative samples may, in some limited cases, include soil samples as an attempt to determine the source of the contaminant. Do not routinely collect soil samples.

573   PACKERS AND SHIPPERS

Follow the same general procedure as in IOM 572. Observe and report the following:

1.   Treatment Before Shipping - This may include stripping of leaves, washing, vacuum cooling, application of post-harvest preservative chemicals, use of cartons with mold-inhibiting chemicals, waxes, colors, fumigation, etc.

2.   Identification of Growers' Lots - Determine procedure or methods used to maintain the identity of each grower's lot. Provide the code and key if any.

3.   Labeling - Quote labeling or brand names.

4.   Responsibility - Determine whether the packer or shipper knows what sprays have been used on the products shipped.

574   PESTICIDE SUPPLIERS

Pesticide suppliers should be visited routinely during growing-area coverage. They may provide valuable information about pesticides being used on various crops in the growing area. Some suppliers may suggest spray schedules or advise growers about pesticide usage.

Determine what representations were made by the manufacturer of pesticide chemicals for which there is only a temporary tolerance or experimental permit. Get copies of any correspondence relating to sale and use of these products. Obtain names of growers to whom sales are made if such sale was not for use on acreage assigned under the experimental permit. Collect Official Samples of any crops treated with the pesticide.

575   PESTICIDE APPLICATORS

Pesticide applicators may provide valuable information about pesticides being used on various crops in the growing area. Interview several pesticide applicators, particularly those using airborne equipment. Determine the pesticide chemicals, their formulation, and on what crops they are currently being applied. Determine who supplies the pesticides and how they are prepared to assure proper concentration. If state law requires the applicator to keep a record of each spray application, request permission to review such records. Determine what steps are taken to assure drift on adjoining crops does not result in violative residues. Where there is likelihood of drift, collect Selective Samples from adjoining fields.

576   SAMPLE COLLECTIONS

See IOM Sample Schedule Chart 3 - Pesticides.

SUBCHAPTER 580 – VETERINARY MEDICINE

580   CVM WEBSITE

The Center for Veterinary Medicine has its own website at: www.fda.gov/cvm. The website contains an alphabetical listing of topics under "Index"; a listing of current and planned Guidance Documents; and on line access to the "GreenBook" database listing animal drug approvals. There is a "search" feature allowing you to search for documents containing various words or phrases. The website also contains organizational information for the Center and an explanation of the various laws and regulations which the Center enforces. Information on the website can provide guidance for inspectional efforts related to CVM obligations.

581   VETERINARY DRUG ACTIVITIES

CVM is responsible for inspections of therapeutic and production drugs, and Active Pharmaceutical Ingredients (APIs). Therapeutic drugs are used in the diagnosis, cure, mitigation, treatment or prevention of disease. Production drugs are used for economic enhancement of animal productivity. Examples include: growth promotion, feed efficiency and increased milk production.

Preapproval inspections are conducted pursuant to pending NADA or ANADA applications.

Post approval inspections of veterinary drugs are conducted to determine compliance with the Current Good Manufacturing Practices (CGMPs) for Finished Pharmaceuticals under 21 CFR Part 211. These cGMPs apply to both human and veterinary drugs. Information on veterinary drugs approved can be found in the "Greenbook" database accessed through CVM's website at: www.fda.gov/cvm.

API's are active pharmaceutical ingredients. Many of the APIs used to manufacture dosage form drugs are imported from foreign countries. The intended source for an API must be indicated in NADA/ANADA submissions for new animal drug approvals. Any change in a source for an API would require a supplement to the application.

Extra label drug use refers to the regulations in 21 CFR Part 530 codified as a result of the Animal Medicinal Drug Use Clarification Act (AMDUCA) of 1994. These regulations set forth the requirements for veterinarians to prescribe extra label uses of certain approved animal and human drugs and the requirements for the existence of a valid veterinarian/client/patient relationship (VCPR). The regulations under 21 CFR Part 530 address issues regarding extra label use in non-food as well as food producing animals. 21 CFR 530.41 contains a list of drugs that cannot be used in an extra label fashion in food-producing animals. During an inspection or investigation if you encounter any situations on extra label use of the listed drugs, you should contact CVM's Division of Compliance (HFV-230) (301-827-1168).

The regulations under 21 CF Part 530 also address compounding of products from approved animal or human drugs by a pharmacist or veterinarian. The regulations clearly state compounding is not permitted from bulk drugs. This would include APIs. CVM has an existing CPG on Compounding of Drugs for Use in Animals (CPG 7125.40; Chapter 608.400). A copy can be found on CVM's website. The Division of Compliance (HFV-230) has issued assignments to conduct inspections of firms, including internet pharmacies, who may be engaged in the practice of manufacturing under the guise of pharmacy compounding. You should contact the Division of Compliance (HFV-230) at 301-827-1168 to report instances of compounding or to seek guidance on inspectional issues, or regulatory and enforcement policies.

582   MEDICATED FEEDS AND TYPE A ARTICLES

Animal feed is defined under section 201(w) of the FD&C Act. CVM is responsible for control of medicated and non-medicated animal feeds, Type A medicated articles and pet foods.

The regulations for animal food labeling are in 21CFR Part 501. The regulations for medicated feed mill licensure are in 21CFR Part 515. The cGMPs for Medicated Feeds are in 21CFR Part 225. The cGMPs for Type A Articles are in 21 CFR Part 226.

Inspections are routinely conducted of medicated feed mills and manufacturers of Type A Medicated Articles.

If you have questions related to cGMPs and enforcement policies and strategies concerning Medicated Feeds and Type A Articles you should contact the CVM/Division of Compliance (301-827-1168).

Guidance on pet food labeling requirements can be found on CVM's website.

583   BSE ACTIVITIES

CVM is responsible for FDA's educational and regulatory activities involving BSE. BSE is "Bovine Spongiform Encephalopathy" and is often referred to as "mad cow disease." BSE information can be found on the CVM website at: www.fda.gov/cvm. CVM has four Guidance Documents in place dealing with BSE (67-70, dated February 1998). The Guidance Documents address renderers, protein blenders, feed manufacturers, distributors and on farm feeders.

Questions on inspectional assignments and regulatory activities in the BSE area should be addressed to the CVM/Division of Compliance (HFV-230) at 301-827-1168.

584   TISSUE RESIDUES

The presence of violative drug residues in food from slaughtered animals is a human health concern. Tissue residue investigations/inspections are performed in response to reports of violative drug residue levels found in tissue sampled at slaughter by the USDA.

Tissue residues are commonly caused by the medication of animals prior to marketing and failure to follow the withdrawal times. When a new animal drug is approved the manufacturer must conduct studies to accurately determine withdrawal times. Allowable tolerances for residues of new animal drugs in food can be found in 21CFR Part 556.

For information on tissue residue violations and activities you should contact the CVM/Division of Compliance (HFV-230, 301-827-1168).

585   VETERINARY DEVICES

Medical devices for animal/veterinary use are not subject to the premarket approval requirements like human medical devices. Once an animal use device is marketed the Center is concerned with safety and efficacy of the veterinary device. CVM often recommends firms use the human device GMPs in controlling the manufacturing of animal use devices. CVM also suggests labeling be sent in for review by the Division of Compliance (HFV-230) to avoid misbranding. Regulatory questions for veterinary/animal use devices should be directed to the CVM/Division of Compliance (HFV-230).

586   ANIMAL GROOMING AIDES

Cosmetic articles intended to cleanse and beautify animals are referred to as "animal grooming aides." The definition of "cosmetic" under section 201(I) of the FD & C Act refers only to use of such articles in humans and does not include products for animal use.

If animal grooming aides are labeled with either direct or implied therapeutic claims, however, they may be considered as drugs under section 201(g) of the Act or even as new animal drugs under section 201(v) of the Act. Grooming aides formulated only to cleanse or beautify animals are not subject to the provisions of the Act. However, the Center is still concerned over the safety of such products and tracks complaints and adverse reactions.

Questions on labeling and regulatory concerns should be directed to the Division of Compliance (HFV-230). To report complaints or adverse reactions involving animal grooming aides or to determine the complaint history of a particular product you should contact the Division of Surveillance (HFV-210).

587   BIORESEARCH MONITORING

CVM issues assignments to the field to conduct inspections of animal drug studies, including both therapeutic and production drugs. This would include inspections of clinical investigators, sponsor monitors and to determine compliance with the Good Laboratory Practices Regulations. Currently there is no requirement for animal drug studies to be controlled by any sort of institutional review board (IRB).

CVM BIMO inspectional assignments are issued by the CVM/Division of Compliance (HFV-230). The regulations for new animal drugs for investigational use can be found in 21CFR Part 511. Guidance Documents in the BIMO area may be found on the CVM website at: www.fda.gov/cvm.

For information or guidance on bioresearch monitoring program activities and assignments you should contact Dottie Pocurull at 301-827-6664.

SUBCHAPTER 590 - REPORTING

590   ESTABLISHMENT INSPECTION REPORT (EIR)

The EIR consists of the following in this order: a printed copy of the FACTS Establishment Inspection Record (EI Record) including, at least, the endorsement with the EIR distribution printed at the bottom of the "endorsement" section of the EI Record; carbon or other copies of FDA forms issued during the inspection such as the FDA 482, FDA 483, and FDA 484; investigator's narrative report; copy of assignment if available; exhibits; and/or any additional material attached and referred to in the narrative report. Regarding the use of checklists (such as the BSE Checklist), the original raw data completed checklist should be submitted with the EIR. If you maintain the data in your diary, rather than entering directly on the form, then enter on the electronic copy. A printed copy from FACTS becomes the data to include with the EIR.

No copies of inspection reports will be maintained other than in headquarters, district, and resident post files. The signed original report is maintained in the district office or in the case of foreign inspections in the appropriate Center HQ office.

591   ENDORSEMENT

The endorsement of the establishment inspection is prepared by the supervisor. Some supervisors may have the investigator prepare proposed endorsements. Endorsements should fit in the available space provided in FACTS. If the endorsement exceeds the 2000 character space provided in FACTS, a separate endorsement should be prepared, fully identifying the firm with a Summary of the Endorsement included in FACTS. The FACTS EI Record will be printed and used as the endorsement and routing document to accompany the EIR. See also IOM 593.1.

Normally the endorsement consists of:

1.   The reason for the EI, i.e., workplan, or assignments from headquarters. State the subject of the assignment and reference. If the assignment was issued hard copy (i.e. not through FACTS), it should be attached to the EIR following the narrative. Include the FACTS assignment number and compliance tracking number if applicable.

2.   A brief history of previous findings including classification of previous EI, any action taken by the district and/or corrective action taken by the firm in response to inspectional observations from the previous inspection.

3.   A concise summary and evaluation of current findings and samples collected.

4.   Refusals, voluntary corrections or promises made by the firm's management.

5.   Classification and follow-up consistent with inspectional findings and Agency policy including notification of other districts and headquarters as warranted.

The Compliance Status Information System (COMSTAT) was a separate Agency database summarizing Quality Systems regulation (QS/GMP) and current Good Manufacturing Practices (cGMP) regulations for facilities, which manipulate drug, device, and biological products. QS or GMP status of firms inspected is now entered into the FACTS database. The Profile Data is submitted electronically to the Division of Compliance Information and Quality Assurance (DCIQA), HFC-240, following an inspection. DCIQA should be notified via hardcopy, e-mail or FAX as soon as an inspection reveals a violative QS or GMP situation, which may result in regulatory action. Often this may occur before the inspection has concluded.

See Exhibit 590-D. The COMSTAT Guidance to Field and Centers document replaced Chapter 15 of the GWQAP Manual and can be accessed from the DCIQA web site at http://web.ora.fda.gov.

591.1 Compliance Achievement Reporting System (CARS)

FACTS is used to report achieved and verified compliance actions, which are not the result of a legal action. A compliance achievement is the observed repair, modification, or adjustment of a violative condition, or the repair, modification, adjustment, relabeling, or destruction of a violative product when either the product or condition does not comply with the Acts enforced by the FDA. There are three criteria for reporting into the CARS system:

1. The detection or identification of the problem. A problem may be observed by FDA, other federal officials, or by state or local authorities and referred to FDA; and as a result of an inspection, investigation, sample analysis, or detention accomplished by ORA or states under contract to ORA.

2. The correction of the problem. The correction is directly attributable to the efforts of ORA or state officials under contract to ORA (involving contract products only); and is unrelated to the filing of a legal action, i.e., seizure, prosecution, injunction.

3. The verification of the correction of the problem. The correction is verified by the FDA, other federal officials or state or local authorities and reported in writing to the FDA; and is based on an inspection, investigation, sample analysis, or letter from a firm to FDA certifying the problem has been corrected.

Only when the corrective action(s) has been verified should a CARS be reported. The data elements are those entered/coded in FACTS (See IOM Exh. 590 B):

PAC. See the Data Codes Manual. Should there be insufficient space to code all corrections verified on an occasion, record the most significant corrections.

PROBLEM TYPE. The problem type is the problem(s) identified during the operation(s). Use the List of Values (LOV) found in this field on the Compliance Achievement Reporting Screen. If 'Other' is chosen, you must include an explanation in the 'Remarks" field.

3. CORRECTIVE ACTION. The action the establishment took to correct the identified problem. Use the LOVs found in this field on the CARS screen. If "Other" is selected, you must include an explanation in the "Remarks" field.

4. VERIFICATION DATE. Use the date the corrective action(s) is verified, either through an establishment inspection, an investigation, or a letter from the establishment certifying the corrections have been made. Include documentation to verify the action such as repair receipts/plans.

5. CORRECTING ORGANIZATION. The FDA, other federal agency, or state or local authority, which observed the verified correction. Use the LOVs found in this field on the CARS screen.

6. REPORTING DISTRICT. The FDA, other federal agency, or state or local authority, which is actually inputting the verified correction. Use the LOVs found in this field on the CARS screen.

7. REASON FOR CORRECTION. The action the FDA took to make the correction happen. Use the LOVs found in this field on the CARS screen. If 'Other' is chosen, you must include an explanation in the 'Remarks' field.

592 FACTS ESTABLISHMENT INSPECTION RECORD (EI Record)

Instructions for completion of the FACTS (Field Activities and Compliance Tracking System) EI Record will be included in future revisions. Until such time consult with your supervisor and District Lead FACTS user(s). See IOM Exhibits 590 A & B. The FACTS Profile Data instructions and FACTS generated assignment are attached as IOM Exhibits 590 C & D.

Inspectional accountable time in FACTS consists of the hours devoted to file reviews (operational preparation), actual inspectional, investigational, audit, etc. time (onsite), document (exhibit) preparation and EIR (report) write-up. Accountable time does not include travel time. One occasional exception could be when more than one participant in an inspection/investigation travel together and discuss/prepare while in route. Other accountable time operations are listed in the FDA Data Codes Manual.

593 NARRATIVE REPORT

The narrative report is the written portion of the EIR, which accurately describes the investigator's inspectional findings. All reports must be prepared as stand-alone documents outside of FACTS. Your Establishment Inspection Report (EIR) must:

1. Be factual, objective, and free of unsupportable conclusions.
2. Be concise while covering the necessary aspects of the inspection.
3. Not include opinions about administrative or regulatory follow-up.
4. Be written in the first person.
5. Be signed by all FDA and commissioned personnel participating in the inspection. See IOM section 502.4 when more than one FDA or commissioned person participated in the inspection.

593.1 Non-Violative Establishments

Investigators should use abbreviated, stand-alone, narrative reports for non-violative establishments, unless directed otherwise by their supervisor, the assignment or the Compliance Program involved.

Abbreviated reports, with the exception of drug and medical device GMP inspection reports, may consist only of a "Summary of Findings Report" as a separate narrative. The Summary of Findings Report may not be written solely in the FACTS provided "Summary" heading. The summary must include:

1. The reason for the inspection;
2. The date, classification and findings of the previous inspection;
3. The actual inclusive dates of the inspection (these may be included as part of a header or in the body of the EIR.)
4. The name of the person to whom credentials were shown and the Notice of Inspection was issued and the person's authority to receive the Notice. Explain if you were

unable to show credentials or issue forms to top management;

5.   The scope of the inspection; i.e., comprehensive or limited; and a brief description of the products, processes or systems covered during the inspection; the manufacturing codes and if necessary their interpretation.

6.   The significant findings if any;

7.   Management's response or corrections;

8.   Warnings given to management; and

9.   The investigator's handwritten signature.

593.2 Violative Establishments

All violative EIR's must in addition to the information required for non-violative reports contain the following:

1.   the objectionable conditions or practices described in sufficient detail so someone reading the report will clearly understand the observation(s) and significance.

2.   the objectionable conditions or practices cross-referenced to FDA 483 citations, samples collected, photographs, or other documentation including exhibits attached to the EIR.

3.   information as to when the objectionable conditions or practices occurred, why they occurred, and who is or was responsible, developed to the highest level in the firm.

593.3 Individual Narrative Headings

There are many acceptable ways of organizing a narrative report. The key is to cover the required information cited in IOM 593.1 and 593.2 or as required by the assignment or Compliance Program. Because of FDA's agreements with international governments in the areas of drugs and medical devices, standardized abbreviated and detailed reports with specified headings will be used. See IOM 549 and 559.

The appropriate use of headings should not result in repetition of the same information in different sections. Investigators are encouraged to create headings as necessary to present their inspectional findings in the most concise manner.

For short reports, some may find a single heading such as Summary of Findings is all that is needed (exception, see IOM 593.1). For some situations, investigators may use a sequential approach in which their findings are discussed in the same order as and correlated with each of the FDA 483 citations. Include all required information as each citation is discussed.

There are EIR headings commonly used and many investigators choose to rely on a "standard" set of such headings. However, with the roll-out of Turbo EIR, an automated FDA 483 and EIR reporting system, the traditional headings have been modified in a generic abbreviated and detailed report format. Even with Turbo, be guided by your District requirements or procedures to prepare EIRs. Each inspection is different and all headings may not be necessary.

Turbo EIR should be used to generate the FDA 483 and write the EIR for any inspection where applicable cite modules exist. Turbo EIR must not be used to create a FDA 483

during an inspection of a firm involving multiple commodity areas and FDA 483 cites do not exist for ALL of the commodity areas for which observations need to be included on the FDA 483. You must be able to write the entire FDA 483 using Turbo EIR. You cannot write the Turbo EIR if a FDA 483 was issued to the firm and it was **NOT** generated using Turbo EIR. NOTE: Turbo EIR can be used to write the EIR for any inspection not involving issuance of a FDA 483.

In Turbo there are two generic EIR formats detailed and abbreviated. The generic EIR can be expanded and certain sections can be made optional from program to program. The detailed generic EIR was developed to provide a best case scenario based on FDA's need for information to assure all evidence is there to support a domestic, violative inspection case. Because this generic EIR format needs to be harmonized for use by non-US countries who may share reports with FDA or with each other, the detailed format is best used for VAI and OAI inspections. These inspections require more detailed reporting to assure the compliance officer has sufficient information from which to make their compliance decision.

The generic abbreviated EIR is intended for inspections FDA classifies as NAI. Because of the harmonization of the report format, the abbreviated report may be slightly more than FDA would currently use. Domestic VAI inspections for which no further regulatory action is anticipated (i.e., no Warning Letter will issue) may be written using the abbreviated format based on supervisory and compliance officer input.

To fully appreciate the differences in the EIRs, attention needs to be given to the depth of the reporting. In an abbreviated report, much less detail is expected to describe the specifics.

EIRs for OOB or non-OEI may be much more abbreviated than described here.

ABBREVIATED INSPECTION REPORT

The following headings appear in the Turbo generic report format for an Abbreviated Inspection Report:

Summary - provide the reason for the inspection (e.g. compliance program, by assignment, etc.); the scope of the inspection (comprehensive, limited, sample collection only, etc.). Include: the firm's name, address, phone, FAX and e-mail address; the names and titles of the Investigator(s), Analyst(s), etc.; the inclusive date(s) of the current inspection, i.e., list the actual dates in the plant; the date(s) and summary of the findings of the previous inspection and the firm's response/corrective actions; and the names and titles of persons to whom Federal credentials were shown; the names and titles of the persons to whom any FDA forms were issued during the inspection (FDA 482, 483, 484, etc.).

List the products, systems and processes covered during the current inspection, and the types of records and documents reviewed. Provide a summary of the current findings and a summary of management's response or corrections.

Administrative Data - The firm name, address, phone, FAX and e-mail address. Report the names and titles of the Investigator(s), Analyst(s), etc. The inclusive date(s) of the current inspection, i.e., list the actual dates in the plant. If a team inspection and some individuals came and went during the inspection, indicate dates in plant for each team member. The names and titles of persons to whom Federal credentials were shown. The names and titles of the persons to whom any FDA forms were issued during the inspection. (FDA 482, 483, 484, etc.) If this was a team inspection, report who wrote which section of the EIR. Report changes to hours of operation (include seasonal variations); changes to registration status.

History - If not the initial inspection of the firm, include only changes to legal status of the firm. If a corporation, list in which state and when the firm was incorporated. List the parent corporation, corporate address and any subsidiaries. Provide a summary of any regulatory actions taken as a result of the last inspection. Include any relevant recalls, etc. since the last inspection.

Business Operations - Report changes to hours of operation (include seasonal variations). Report changes to registration status.

Interstate Commerce - Report changes in the previous estimate of the percentage of products shipped outside of the state (or exported to the U.S.) and the basis of the estimate. Report changes in the firm's promotion and distribution patterns.

Jurisdiction - Include changes in the firm's catalog of products, or list of representative number of currently marketed products subject to FD&C Act or other statute enforced by FDA or counterpart state agency. Report changes of Brand Names used. Collect full labeling (product and case labels, inserts, brochures, manuals, promotional materials of any type) for any changes. Provide documentation of any applicable statutory guaranty given or received.

Responsibility - Report with whom you dealt, and in what regard (both during and prior to the start of the inspection). Describe roles and authorities of responsible individuals, including the names and titles of individuals providing you with information.

If this is not an initial inspection, report only changes to the following:
Who is the most responsible individual at the inspected firm? Who is the responsible head or designated correspondent? Report names and titles of owners, partners, and corporate officers. Obtain a copy of public annual report, if any. List the names and titles of key operating personnel. Obtain a copy of relevant labeling agreement, if any. See IOM 526. Provide the names, titles and addresses of top management official(s) to whom correspondence should be addressed (FMD 145, PIN letter, W/L, etc.). Who has the duty, responsibility, and power to prevent, detect, and correct violation(s), and how is this demonstrated and/or documented? See IOM 525.3. Report the chain of command; include an organizational chart (create if necessary).

Manufacturing/Design Operations - If not an initial inspection, report only changes to the firm's general overall operations, including significant changes in equipment, processes, or products since previous inspection. Include schematics, flow plans, photographs, formulations and diagrams, if useful.

Manufacturing Codes - If changed (or this is an initial inspection), describe the manufacturing coding system, and a key to interpretation of codes. If unchanged, include a statement the system is the same as described in reports on file at the District. Indicate the date of the EIR in which the codes are explained.

Complaints (if applicable) - Note: The complaints included in this portion of the EIR are those reported to the FDA by consumers, health care professionals, industry, etc. – Not necessarily the complaints received by the firm. Describe injuries or other significant consumer/trade complaints, DPPR's, MDR's, MedWatch reports, or recalls, if appropriate. Report your follow-up of consumer/trade complaints, DPPR's, MDR's, MedWatch reports or recalls identified in the district factory jacket for coverage. Correlate consumer/trade complaints, DPPR's, MDR's, MedWatch reports to specific objectionable conditions observed. The reporting of your review of the firm's complaint file(s) should be reported under a separate section, such as "Complaint File(s)."

Objectionable Conditions (those written and provided to management at the conclusion of the inspection) - If any observations were provided to management in writing at the conclusion of the inspection list each observation. Provide a detailed discussion of each observation and its relevance. Cross-reference each observation to your exhibit(s) and sample(s) collected. Identify the responsible party for each violation. Identify which team member (if applicable) was responsible for the observation. Report management's response to each item and time frames given for corrections and/or any corrective action taken for each observation.

NOTE: Observations of a verbal nature should be reported in sufficient detail under the General Discussion with Management (correlate any Exhibits, samples, etc. to any "verbal" observations).

Refusals - Provide full details of all refusals of requested information received during the inspection, including who made the refusal and, if available, why the refusal was given.

General Discussion with Management - Report the names and titles of all present, including those present via electronic media (describe). Include the name and title to which the FDA 483 was issued. Provide additional discussion items not provided in writing at the conclusion of the inspection such as: questionable labeling practices, commercialization of products covered by IDE or IND, fraudulent health claims, registration deviations, lack of approved PMA, 510(k), NDA, ANDA, etc. These include all verbal observations deemed not to merit inclusion on the FDA 483 (IOM 512). A description of each warning, recommendation, or suggestion given to the firm, and to whom given. Management's general responses to the inspection and/or to groups of items listed on the report of observations or discussed at the conclusion of the inspection.

Additional Information - If this is not an initial inspection, report changes only. Describe contractors used and for what purpose. Describe suppliers (major raw material, active ingredient, etc.) used and for what. Report pertinent facts, which do not fit another section of the EIR. (For firms located in foreign countries, include information relative to lodging and travel; for domestic firms, include information relative to location of firm if difficult to find; etc.).

Voluntary Corrections - Provide a brief description of improvements initiated by the firm in response to a previous inspection, report of observations and/or a warning letter. Report voluntary destructions, recalls, and similar actions since the prior inspection or during this inspection. Report any follow-up to recalls identified during the inspection (may be by referencing Attachment B recall report). Include recalls to specific objectionable conditions observed. Provide the identity of person(s) responsible for the corrections. Report any appropriate voluntary corrections in FACT CARS.

Exhibits and Samples Collected - List all exhibits attached. See IOM 594, Exhibits. Include a listing of any samples collected. Briefly, describe or title each exhibit and sample number attached.

Attachments - Attachments as referred to here are any material attached to and referred to in the EIR, which are not evidentiary in nature; such as assignments, Center provided protocols, etc. See IOM 527.2 for identification of non-evidentiary material attached to the EIR. Documents attached to the EIR will be referred to in the EIR and listed here, such as the FDA 482, FDA 483, copy of the FDA 463a, etc.; but such documents/forms must not be numbered, altered from their issued state, bear adhesive identification labels, etc. See the opening sentence of IOM 594. List and attach copies of associated reports (Recall Attachment B Report, etc.).

Signature - All participants must sign the final narrative portion of the EIR. The prescribed format is to type each persons name, title, and district (or other affiliation) below the signature. In some cases immediate signature by all participants is not possible. An example as to how this can be accomplished is to forward an electronic "draft" copy of the EIR for all to read and approve, then followed or accompanied by the original signature sheet. When signed, return to the lead investigator for proper filing and routing. When using this method, a photocopy of the original signature page is made with the lead investigator's signature and temporarily attached to the EIR.

DETAILED INSPECTION REPORT

The following headings appear in the Turbo generic report format for a Detailed Inspection Report in addition to the format for an Abbreviated Inspection Report. NOTE: There is no provision to report only if there are changes, all data should be reported.

Summary - See the heading for the Abbreviated Inspection report, and if more than one person wrote the EIR, identify who wrote each portion.

History - Report the legal status of the firm (e.g., sole owner, partnership, corporation). If a corporation, in which state and when it was incorporated. List the parent corporation, corporate address and subsidiaries. Include a summary of the firm in terms of regulatory actions, recalls, and prior warnings. Do not report any action only recommended but not approved.

Business Operations - Report the hours of operation (include seasonal variations). Report the firm's registration status and the registration number.

Interstate Commerce - An estimate of the percentage of products shipped outside of the state, (or exported to the U.S.) and the basis of the estimate. Examples of I.S. shipments of violative product(s); or if no such shipments, I.S. shipments of major components of violative products — with complete I.S. documentation in either case. Include promotion and distribution patterns.

Jurisdiction - Obtain a current catalog of products, or a list of a representative number of currently marketed, violative products subject to FD&C Act or other statute enforced by FDA or counterpart state agency. List the Brand Names used. Collect full labeling (product and case labels, inserts, brochures, manuals, promotional materials of any type) for those products. Document any applicable statutory guaranty given or received.

Responsibility - Report with whom you dealt, and in what regard (both during and prior to the start of the inspection), describe roles and authorities of responsible individuals and the names and titles of individuals who supplied you with information. Who is the most responsible individual at the firm under inspection? Report the responsible head or designated correspondent, and the names and titles of owners, partners, and corporate officers. Obtain a copy of public annual report, if any. Names and titles of key operating personnel. Copy of relevant labeling agreement, if any. See IOM 526. Name(s), title(s) and address(es) of top management official(s) to whom correspondence should be addressed (FMD 145, PIN letter, W/L, etc.). Who has the duty, responsibility, and power to prevent, detect, and correct the violation(s), and how is this demonstrated and/or documented? See IOM 525.3. Report the full chain of command including organizational chart (create if necessary).

Manufacturing/Design Operations - Provide a general overall description of the firm's operations, including significant changes in equipment, processes, or products since previous inspection. Attach schematics, flow plans, photographs, formulations and diagrams, if useful.

Manufacturing Codes - See the same heading under the Abbreviated Inspection Report.

Complaints (if applicable) - See the same heading under the Abbreviated Inspection Report. In addition, if Returned Goods are examined, describe findings. If not examined, so indicate.

Objectionable Conditions (those written and provided to management at the conclusion of the inspection) - See the same heading under the Abbreviated Inspection Report.

Refusals - See the same heading under the Abbreviated Inspection Report.

General Discussion with Management - See the same heading under the Abbreviated Inspection Report.

Additional Information - Describe contractors used and for what purpose. Describe suppliers (major raw material, active ingredient, etc.) used and for what. Report pertinent facts, which do not fit in any other section of the EIR. (For firms located in foreign countries, include information relative to lodging and travel; for domestic firms, include information relative to location of firm if difficult to find; etc.).

Voluntary Corrections - See the same heading under the Abbreviated Inspection Report.

Exhibits and Samples Collected - See the same heading under the Abbreviated Inspection Report. NOTE: For complex inspections include a cross-reference form the FDA 483 and verbal observations to applicable exhibits and samples.

Attachments - See the same heading under Abbreviated Inspection Report.

Signature - See the same heading under Abbreviated Inspection Report.

For EIRs not written in Turbo, the general headings should be used as guidance format. There are other pertinent headings, which may be used for reports of inspections for which no Turbo EIR format is available, such as foods and medicated feed inspections. These may include:

Guarantees & Labeling Agreements - Submit copies of, or list and give dates of, specific documents. See IOM 526.

Firm's Training Program - The firm's training programs are of particular significance where inspectional findings find people may not be adequately trained.

Raw Materials and Components - List names and sources of new or unusual components or raw materials.

Recall Procedures - Describe plans and procedures for removing products from marketing channels if necessary.

Promotion and Distribution - Describe the firm's general promotion and distribution patterns. Document shipments of any suspect product(s).

594   EXHIBITS

Exhibits are materials collected from the firm and do not include FDA forms or copies of assignments. Exhibits should contribute to the objective of the assignment and the clarity of the report. They may include flow-plans, schematics, layouts, etc. If the materials collected from the firm are not needed as exhibits, they should be destroyed in accordance with district policy. Submit four copies of new or suspect labeling or other material collected as exhibits for labeling purposes. These should be mounted in a manner so complete sets are submitted, i.e. labels 1-10 in each of three sets. Identify records, labeling and documents with at least the Exhibits' number, date of EI and your initials. See IOM 527.2.

594.1 Electronic information

Electronic information, databases or summary data from databases may be obtained from firms and evaluated during the course of an EI. This data may form the basis for observations or information included in the EIR. It is preferable to include a printed version and/or a summary of the data as an exhibit. When it is included as an exhibit to the EIR, it should be stored so as to protect the integrity of the data. See Section 527.3 for procedures for collecting and identifying electronic data. Electronic media should be protected from extreme temperatures and most magnetic fields. Additional precautions may be necessary and you should be guided by your district procedures for storage of electronic data.

595   ADDENDUM TO EIR

If your EIR requires correcting or clarification after it has been finalized, signed and distributed, you should prepare an addendum, with your supervisor's approval. The addendum should clearly identify itself with the EIR being added to, explain the necessity for the addendum, and clearly define what section(s) and page(s) are being revised. The addendum must be signed by the preparer.

EXHIBIT 510 A   INVESTIGATIONS OPERATIONS MANUAL

| DEPARTMENT OF HEALTH AND HUMAN SERVICES
PUBLIC HEALTH SERVICE
FOOD AND DRUG ADMINISTRATION | 1. DISTRICT ADDRESS & PHONE NO.
Rm 508 Federal Office Building
30 U.N. Plaza
San Francisco, CA 94102 | | |

	2. NAME AND TITLE OF INDIVIDUAL Robert K. Thompson, Plant Manager	3. DATE 5-15-85	
TO	4. FIRM NAME Garden City Nut Shellers	5. HOUR	8:30 a.m. p.m.
	6. NUMBER AND STREET 2704 Sellers Ave		
	7. CITY AND STATE & ZIP CODE San Jose, CA 95131	8. PHONE # & AREA CODE (408)123-4567	

Notice of Inspection is hereby given pursuant to Section 704(a)(1) of the Federal Food, Drug, and Cosmetic Act [21 U.S.C. 374(1)][1] and/or Part F or G, Title III of the Public Health Service Act [42 U.S.C. 262-264][2]

9. SIGNATURE (Food and Drug Administration Employee(s))	10. TYPE OR PRINT NAME AND TITLE (FDA Employee(s)) Sidney H. Rogers, Investigator

[1]Applicable to portions of Section 704 and other Sections of the Federal Food, Drug, and Cosmetic Act [21 U.S.C. 374] are quoted below:

Sec. 704. (a)(1) For purposes of enforcement of this Act, officers or employees duly designated by the Secretary, upon presenting appropriate credentials and a written notice to the owner, operator, or agent in charge, are authorized (A) to enter, at reasonable times, any factory, warehouse, or establishment in which food, drugs, devices, or cosmetics are manufactured, processed, packed, or held, for introduction into interstate commerce or after such introduction, or to enter any vehicle being used to transport or hold such food, drugs, devices, or cosmetics in interstate commerce; and (B) to inspect , at reasonable times and within reasonable limits and in a reasonable manner, such factory, warehouse, establishment, or vehicle and all pertinent equipment, finished and unfinished materials, containers and labeling therein. In the case of any factory, warehouse, establishment, or consulting laboratory in which prescription drugs, nonprescription drugs intended for human use, or restricted devices are manufactured, processed, packed, or held, the inspection shall extend to all things therein *(including records, files, papers, processes, controls, and facilities)* bearing on whether prescription drugs, nonprescription drugs intended for human use, or restricted devices which are adulterated or misbranded within the meaning of this Act, or which may not be manufactured, introduced into interstate commerce, or sold, or offered for sale by reason of any provision of this Act, have been or are being manufactured, processed, packed, transported, or held in any such place, or otherwise bearing on violation of this Act. No inspection authorized by the preceding sentence or by paragraph (3) shall extend to financial data, sales data other then shipment data, pricing data, personnel data *(other than data as to qualifications of technical and professional personnel performing functions subject to this Act)*, and research data *(other than data, relating to new drugs, antibiotic drugs and devices and, subject to reporting and inspection under regulations lawfully issued pursuant to section 505(i) or (k), section 507(d) or (g), section 519, or 520(g), and data relating to other drugs or devices which in the case of a new drug would be subject to reporting or inspection under lawful regulations issued pursuant to section 505(j) of the title).* A separate notice shall be given for each such inspection, but a notice shall not be required for each entry made during the period covered by the inspection. Each such inspection shall be commenced and completed with reasonable promptness.

Sec. 704(e) Every person required under section 519 or 520(g) to maintain records and every person who is in charge or custody of such records shall, upon request of an officer or employee designated by the Secretary, permit such officer or employee at all reasonable times to have access to and to copy and verify, such records.

Sec. 704(f)(1) A person accredited under section 523 to review reports under section 510(k) and make recommendations of initial clssifications of devices to the Secretary shall maintain records documenting the training qualifications of the person and the employees of the person for handling confidential information, the compensation arrangements made by the person, and the procedures used by the person to identify and avoid conflicts of interest. Upon the request of an officer or employee designated by the Secretary, the person shall permit the officer or employee, at all reasonable times, to have access to, to copy, and to verify, the records.

Section 512 (l)(1) In the case of any new animal drug for which an approval of an application filed pursuant to subsection (b) is in effect, the applicant shall establish and maintain such records, and make such reports to the Secretary, of data relating to experience and other data or information, received or otherwise obtained by such applicant with respect to such drug, or with respect to animal feeds bearing or

[2]Applicable sections of Parts F and G of Title III Public Health Service Act [42 U.S.C. 262-264] are quoted below:

Part F – Licensing – Biological Products and Clinical Laboratories and ******

Sec. 351(c) "Any officer, agent, or employee of the Department of Health & Human Services, authorized by the Secretary for the purpose, may during all reasonable hours enter and inspect any establishment for the propagation or manufacture and preparation of any virus, serum, toxin, antitoxin, vaccine, blood, blood component or derivative, allergenic product or other product aforesaid for sale, barter, or exchange in the District of Columbia, or to be sent, carried, or brought from any State or possession into any other State or possession or into any foreign country, or from any foreign country into any State or possession."

Part F - ****** Control of Radiation.
Sec. 360 A (a) "If the Secretary finds for good cause that the methods, tests, or programs related to electronic product radiation safety in a particular factory, warehouse, or establishment in which electronic products are manufactured or held, may not be adequate or reliable, officers or employees duly designated by the Secretary, upon presenting appropriate credentials and a written notice to the owner, operator, or agent in charge, are thereafter authorized (1) to enter, at reasonable times any area in such factory, warehouse, or establishment in which the manufacturer's tests (or testing programs) required by section 358(h) are carried out, and (2) to inspect, at reasonable times and within reasonable limits and in a reasonable manner, the facilities and procedures within such area which are related to electronic product radiation safety. Each such inspection shall be commenced and completed with reasonable promptness. In addition to other grounds upon which good cause may be found for purposes of this subsection, good cause will be considered to exist in any case where the manufacturer has introduced into commerce any electronic product which does not comply with an applicable standard prescribed under this subpart and with respect to which no exemption from the notification requirements has been granted by the Secretary under section 359(a)(2) or 359(e)."

(b) "Every manufacturer of electronic products shall establish and maintain such records (including testing records), make such reports, and provide such information, as the Secretary may reasonably require to enable him to determine whether such manufacturer has acted or is acting in compliance with this subpart and standards prescribed pursuant to this subpart and shall, upon request of an officer or employee duly designated by the Secretary, permit such officer or employee to inspect appropriate books, papers, records, and documents relevant to deter-mining whether such manufacturer has acted or is acting in compliance with standards prescribed pursuant to section 359(a)."

****

FORM FDA 482 (9/00)   PREVIOUS EDITION IS OBSOLETE   NOTICE OF INSPECTION

"The Secretary may by regulation (1) require dealers and distributors of electronic products, to which there are applicable standards prescribed under this subpart and the retail prices of which is not less than $50, to furnish manufacturers of such products such information as may be necessary to identify and locate, for purposes of section 359, the first purchasers of such products for purposes other than resale, and (2) require manufacturers to preserve such information. Any regulation establishing a requirement pursuant to clause (1) of the preceding sentence shall (A) authorize such dealers and distributors to elect, in lieu of immediately furnishing such information to the manufacturer to hold and preserve such information until advised by the manufacturer or Secretary that such information is needed by the manufacturer for purposes of section 359, and (B) provide that the dealer or distributor shall, upon making such election, give prompt notice of such election (together with information identifying the notifier and the product) to the manufacturer and shall, when advised by the manufacturer or Secretary, of the need therefor for the purposes of Section 359, immediately furnish the manufacturer with the required information. If a dealer or distributor discontinues the dealing in or distribution of electronic products, he shall turn the information over to the manufacturer. Any manufacturer receiving information pursuant to this subsection concerning first purchasers of products for purposes other than resale shall treat it as confidential and may use it only if necessary for the purpose of notifying persons pursuant to section 359(a)."

Sec. 360 B.(a) It shall be unlawful-
   (1) ***
   (2) ***
   (3) "for any person to fail or to refuse to establish or maintain records required by this subpart or to permit access by the Secretary or any of his duly authorized representatives to, or the copying of, such records, or to permit entry or inspection, as required or pursuant to section 360A."
***

Part G – Quarantine and Inspection

Sec. 361(a) "The Surgeon General, with the approval of the Secretary is authorized to make and enforce such regulations as in his judgement are necessary to prevent the introduction, transmission, or spread of communicable diseases from foreign countries into the States or possessions, or from one State or possession into any other State or possession. For purposes of carrying out and enforcing such regulations, the Surgeon General may provide for such inspection, fumigation, disinfection, sanitation, pest extermination, destruction of animals or articles found to be so infected or contaminated as to be sources of dangerous infection to human beings, and other measures, as in his judgement may be necessary."

(Reverse of Form FDA 482)

FORM FDA 482 (9/00)

EXHIBIT 510 A1   **INVESTIGATIONS OPERATIONS MANUAL**

ATTACHMENT TO FDA 482

Resources for FDA Regulated Businesses

The U.S. Food and Drug Administration strives to protect, promote and enhance the health of the American people, while minimizing the regulatory burden on the industries it regulates. You have a right to disagree with any agency decision, action, or operation without fear of retaliation. You also have a right to be treated with appropriate courtesy and respect. If you are dissatisfied with any agency decision or action, you may appeal to the supervisor of the employee who made the decision or took the action. If the issue is not resolved at the first supervisor's level, you may request that the matter be reviewed at the next higher supervisory level. This process may continue through the agency's chain of command.

To resolve a problem with your company's interaction with FDA, or if you have questions or concerns about FDA rules or procedures, we suggest that you first write or call your district office to explain your concerns. If you are not satisfied with the help provided by the district office, you may take your complaint or concern to the regional office. If that effort is not satisfactory, contact FDA's Office of the Chief Mediator and Ombudsman for further assistance and guidance.

Contact the **District Office** if you have a concern or question about an inspection, an import or export issue, or any other action taken by an FDA field representative. The District Office will provide you with the name and phone number of someone who will review the matter and provide assistance.

District	Telephone	District	Telephone
Atlanta	(404) 253-1164	Minneapolis	(612) 334-4100
Baltimore	(410) 779-5454	New England	(781) 596-7700
Chicago	(312) 353-5863	New Jersey	(973) 526-6000
Cincinnati	(513) 679-2700	New Orleans	(504) 253-4500
Dallas	(214) 253-5200	New York	(718) 340-7000
Denver	(303) 236-3017	Philadelphia	(215) 597-4390
Detroit	(313) 393-8100	San Francisco	(510) 337-6700
Florida	(407) 475-4700	San Juan	(787) 474-9500
Kansas City	(913) 752-2100	Seattle	(425) 486-8788
Los Angeles	(949) 798-7600	Southwest Import	(214) 253-5330

Contact the **Regional Office** for further help if you were not able to effectively resolve the issue with the assistance of the district office. Telephone numbers for the regional offices and a list of the states covered by each region are on the Internet at http://www.fda.gov/ora/hier/ora_field_names.txt.

Contact the **Office of the Chief Mediator and Ombudsman** at 301-827-3390 if you have been unsuccessful in resolving a problem at the district and regional levels. The office's home page is on the Internet at http://www.fda.gov/oc/ombudsman/homepage.htm.

The Small Business Administration also has an ombudsman. The **Small Business and Agriculture Regulatory Enforcement Ombudsman** and 10 Regional Fairness Boards receive comments from all kinds of small businesses about federal agency enforcement actions and annually evaluate the enforcement activities, rating each agency's responsiveness to small business. If you wish to comment on the enforcement actions of FDA, call 1-888-734-3247. The ombudsman's home page is on the Internet at http://www.sba.gov/ombudsman.

Small Business Guide to FDA
Internet at http://www.fda.gov/ora/fed_state/small_business/sb_guide/intro.html

Office of Regulatory Affairs (ORA)
Internet at http://www.fda.gov/ora/ora_home_page.html

Food and Drug Administration (FDA)
Internet at http://www.fda.gov

| DEPARTMENT OF HEALTH AND HUMAN SERVICES
PUBLIC HEALTH SERVICE
FOOD AND DRUG ADMINISTRATION | 1. DISTRICT ADDRESS & PHONE NO.
Rm 5003 Federal Office Building
909 1st Ave.
Seattle, WA 98174 (206)442-5304 | | |

TO

2. NAME AND TITLE OF INDIVIDUAL Howard M. Allgreen, Pharmacist-Owner	3. DATE 5-16-85		
4. FIRM NAME Darlings Drug Store	5. HOUR	2:00	a.m. p.m.
6. NUMBER AND STREET 312 Main Street			
7. CITY AND STATE & ZIP CODE Medford, OR 97501	8. PHONE # & AREA CODE (503)765-4321		

∨ TO COLLECT SAMPLES ONLY

Notice of Inspection is hereby given pursuant to Section 704(a)(1) of the Federal Food, Drug, and Cosmetic Act [21 U.S.C. 374(1)][1] and/or Part F or G, Title III of the Public Health Service Act [42 U.S.C. 262-264][2]

9. SIGNATURE *(Food and Drug Administration Employee(s))*	10. TYPE OR PRINT NAME AND TITLE *(FDA Employee(s))* **Sidney H. Rogers, Investigator**

FORM FDA 482 (9/00)   PREVIOUS EDITION IS OBSOLETE   NOTICE OF INSPECTION

EXHIBIT 510 B   INVESTIGATIONS OPERATIONS MANUAL

DEPARTMENT OF HEALTH AND HUMAN SERVICES
FOOD AND DRUG ADMINISTRATION

DISTRICT OFFICE ADDRESS AND PHONE NUMBER	DATE(S) OF INSPECTION
Minneapolis District 240 Hennipin Ave. Minneapolis, MN 55401 (612) 787-3904	Jan. 5-7, 2000
	FEI NUMBER 0000112233

NAME AND TITLE OF INDIVIDUAL TO WHOM REPORT IS ISSUED

TO: William S. Gundstrom, Vice President Production

FIRM NAME	STREET ADDRESS
Topline Pharmaceuticals, "T.L.P."	2136 Elbe Place

CITY, STATE AND ZIP CODE	TYPE OF ESTABLISHMENT INSPECTED
Jackston, MN 55326	Tablet Repacker

DURING AN INSPECTION OF YOUR FIRM (I) (WE) OBSERVED:

List your observations in a logical and concise manner.

(See IOM 512, 512.1, & 512.2)

SEE REVERSE OF THIS PAGE	EMPLOYEE(S) SIGNATURE *Sidney H. Rogers*	EMPLOYEE(S) NAME AND TITLE *(Print or Type)* Sidney H. Rogers, Investigator	DATE ISSUED 1-07-00

FORM FDA 483 (8/00)   PREVIOUS EDITION MAY BE USED.   INSPECTIONAL OBSERVATIONS   PAGE *1* OF *1* PAGES

The observations of objectionable conditions and practices listed on the front of this form are reported:

1. Pursuant to Section 704(b) of the Federal Food, Drug and Cosmetic Act, or

2.   To assist firms inspected in complying with the Acts and regulations enforced by the Food and Drug Administration.

Section 704(b) of the Federal Food, Drug, and Cosmetic Act (21 USC 374(b)) provides:

"Upon completion of any such inspection of a factory, warehouse, consulting laboratory, or other establishment, and prior to leaving the premises, the officer or employee making the inspection shall give to the owner, operator, or agent in charge a report in writing setting forth any conditions or practices observed by him which, in his judgement, indicate that any food, drug, device, cosmetic in such establishment (1) consists in whole or in part of any filthy, putrid, or decomposed substance or (2) has been prepared, packed, or held under insanitary conditions whereby it may have become contaminated with filth, or whereby it may have been rendered injurious to health. A copy of such report shall be sent promptly to the Secretary."

(Reverse of Form FDA 483)

FORM FDA 483 (8/00)

EXHIBIT 510 C   INVESTIGATIONS OPERATIONS MANUAL

DEPARTMENT OF HEALTH AND HUMAN SERVICES PUBLIC HEALTH SERVICE FOOD AND DRUG ADMINISTRATION	1. DISTRICT ADDRESS & PHONE NUMBER 850 Third Ave. Brooklyn, NY 11232 718-340-7000		

2. NAME AND TITLE OF INDIVIDUAL Richard R. Frost, Gen. Mgr.		3. DATE 12/4/98	4. SAMPLE NUMBER 32528

5. FIRM NAME Quality Wholesale Drug Co.	6. FIRM'S DEA NUMBER AB3632918	

7. NUMBER AND STREET 3146 Front St.	8. CITY AND STATE (Include Zip Code) Brooklyn, NY 11232

9. SAMPLES COLLECTED (Describe fully. List lot, serial, model numbers and other positive identification)

___The following samples were collected by the Food and Drug Administration and receipt is hereby acknowledged pursuant to Section 704(c) of the Federal Food, Drug, and Cosmetic Act [21 U.S.C. 374(c)] and/or Section 532(b) of the Federal Food, Drug and Cosmetic Act [21 USC 360ii(b)] and/or 21 Code of Federal Regulations (CFR) 1307.02. Excerpts of these are quoted on the reverse of this form.

(NOTE: *If you bill FDA for the cost of the Sample(s) listed below, please attach a copy of this form to your bill.*)

One box of 25-1cc ampoules, Diloudid HCL (hydromorphone) 2 mg/cc, lot # 0103213 manufactured by Noll Drug Co., Orange, NJ.

10. SAMPLES WERE ☐ PROVIDED AT NO CHARGE ☐ PURCHASED ☐ BORROWED (To be returned)	11. AMOUNT RECEIVED FOR SAMPLE ☐ CASH ☐ BILLED ☐ VOUCHER ☐ CREDIT CARD	12. SIGNATURE (Person receiving payment for sample or person providing sample to FDA at no charge.) Dealer Affadavit signed
13. COLLECTOR'S NAME (Print or Type) Sylvia A. Rogers	14. COLLECTOR'S TITLE (Print or Type) Investigator	15. COLLECTOR'S SIGNATURE *Sylvia A. Rogers*

FORM FDA 484 (5/98)   PREVIOUS EDITION is obsolete.   **RECEIPT FOR SAMPLES**   PAGE **1** OF **1** PAGES

Section 704(c) of the Federal Food, Drug, and Cosmetic Act [21 U.S.C. 374(c)] is quoted below:

"If the officer or employee making any such inspection of a factory, warehouse, or other establishment has obtained any sample in the course of the inspection, upon completion of the inspection and prior to leaving the premises he shall give to the owner, operator, or agent in charge a receipt describing the samples obtained."

Section 332(b) of The Federal Food, Drug and Cosmetic Act [21 USC 360 ii (b)]is quoted in part below:

"Section 532(b) in carrying out the purposes of subsection (a), the Secretary is authorized to –

        (1) ***

        (2) ****

        (3) ****

        (4) procure (by negotiation or otherwise) electronic products for research and testing purposes, and sell or otherwise dispose of such products."

21 Code of Federal Regulations 1307.02 is quoted below:

"1307.02 Application of State law and other Federal law.

Nothing in this chapter shall be construed as authorizing or permitting any person to do any act which such person is not authorized or permitted to do under other Federal laws or obligations under international treaties, conventions or protocols, or under the law of the State in which he/she desires to do such act nor shall compliance with such be construed as compliance with other Federal or State laws unless expressly provided in such other laws."

Therefore, in the event any samples of controlled drugs are collected by FDA representatives in the enforcement of the Federal Food, Drug, and Cosmetic Act, the FDA representative shall issue a receipt for such samples on FDA form FDA 484, RECEIPT FOR SAMPLES, to the owner, operator, or agent in charge of the premises.

Report of analysis will be furnished only where samples meet the requirements of Section 704(d) of the Federal Food, Drug, and Cosmetic Act [21 U.S.C. 374(d)] which is quoted below:

"Whenever in the course of any such inspection of a factory or other establishment where food is manufactured, processed, or packed, the officer or employee making the inspection obtains a sample of such food, and an analysis is made of such sample for the purpose of ascertaining whether such food consists in whole or in part of any filthy, putrid, or decomposed substance, or is otherwise unfit for food, a copy of the results of such analysis shall be furnished promptly to the owner, operator, or agent in charge."

(Reverse of Form FDA-484)

EXHIBIT 530 B

INVESTIGATIONS OPERATIONS MANUAL

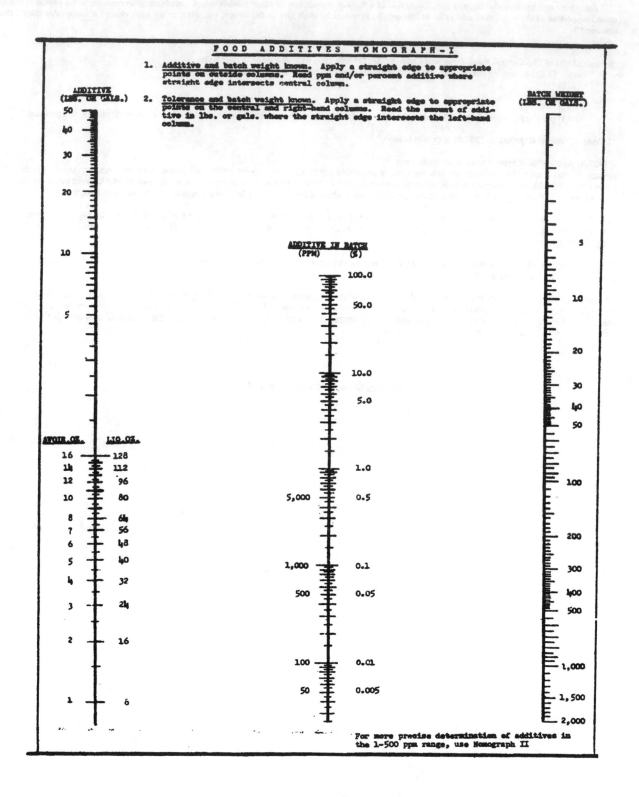

FOOD ADDITIVES NOMOGRAPH-I

1. Additive and batch weight known. Apply a straight edge to appropriate points on outside columns. Read ppm and/or percent additive where straight edge intersects central column.

2. Tolerance and batch weight known. Apply a straight edge to appropriate points on the central and right-hand columns. Read the amount of additive in lbs. or gals. where the straight edge intersects the left-hand column.

For more precise determination of additives in the 1-500 ppm range, use Nomograph II

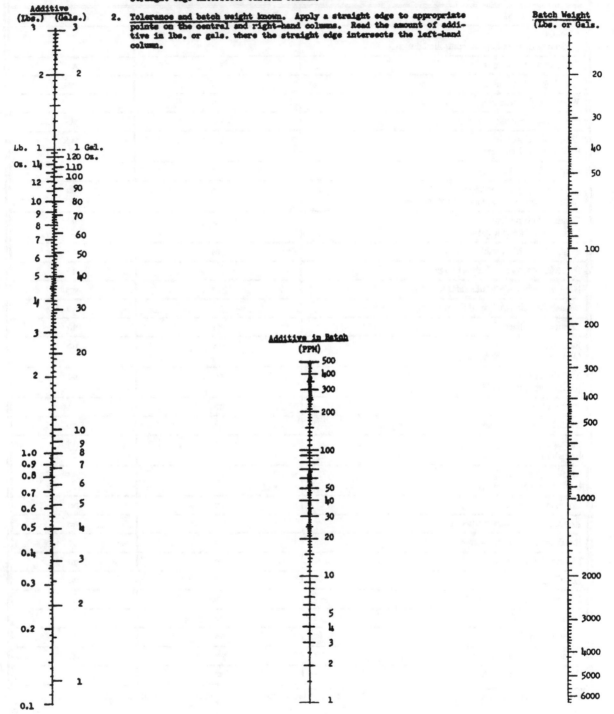

FOOD ADDITIVES NOMOGRAPH-II

1. <u>Additive and batch weight known.</u> Apply a straight edge to appropriate points on outside columns. Read ppm and/or percent additive where straight edge intersects central column.

2. <u>Tolerance and batch weight known.</u> Apply a straight edge to appropriate points on the central and right-hand columns. Read the amount of additive in lbs. or gals. where the straight edge intersects the left-hand column.

EXHIBIT 540

INVESTIGATIONS OPERATIONS MANUAL

SUMMARY OF REGISTRATION AND LISTING REQUIREMENTS FOR THE MANUFACTURE OR DISTRIBUTION OF HUMAN PHARMACEUTICALS

TYPE OF FIRM	REGISTRATION STATUS	LISTING STATUS
Manufacturer [including homeopathic & controlled drugs]	yes	yes
Contract Manufacturer	yes	yes*
Own Label Distributor	no	yes
Wholesale Distributor	no	no
Own Label Repacker	yes	yes
Own Label Relabeler [including recirculizer]	yes	yes
Contract Relabeler	yes	no
Contract Testing Laboratory [dosage forms & active ingredient release]	yes	no
Contract Testing Lab [doing non-release tests]	no	no
Contract Sub-Manufacturer	yes	no
IND Manufacturer [Clinical Drugs]	no	no
NDA and ANDA Manufacturer	yes	yes
Sponsor/Monitors/Clinical Investigator	no	no
Contract Sterilizer	yes	no
Fulfillment Packager [adding substantive labeling]	yes	no
Mail Order House [adding insubstantial labeling]	no	no
Printing House	no	no
Medical Gas Transfiller	yes	yes
First Aid/Rescue Squad [transfilling for own use]	no	no
Medical Gas Transfiller [operating out of a van]	yes	yes
Contract Assembler	yes	no
Active Drug Substance Manufacturer	yes	yes
Excipient Drug Manufacturer	no	no
Manufacturer of Research Drugs	no	no
Drug Importer	no	no
Foreign Drug Manufacturer	voluntary	yes
Methadone Clinic	no	no
Retail Pharmacy	no	no
Manufacturing Pharmacy	yes	yes
Regional Admixture Pharmacy	yes	no

*Products packaged/marketed under the contract manufacturer's own label must be listed by the Contract Manufacturer.

SUMMARY OF REQUIREMENTS FOR THE MANUFACTURE OR DISTRIBUTION OF SUBSTANTIALLY EQUIVALENT MEDICAL DEVICES

OPERATION	SUBMIT 510(k)	REGISTER	LIST	COMPLY W/ GMP
1. MANUFACTURE AND DISTRIBUTE DEVICE	YES: 807.81(a)	YES: 807.20	YES: 807.20(a)	YES
2. CONTRACT MANUFACTURER OF *FINISHED* DEVICES	NO: 807.81(a)	YES: 807.20(a)(2)	NO: 807.20(a)(2)	YES
3. MANUFACTURER MODIFIES DEVICE OR NEW INTENDED USE AND DISTRIBUTE	NO: PREAMBLE NO. 17 & 18, FR 8-23-77 YES: 807.81(a) (3) WITH SIGNIF. CHANGE IN DEVICE OR USE	YES: 807.20(a)(2)	YES: 807.20(a)	YES
4. DIST. U.S. MADE DEVICE: NO SPECIFICATION INITIATION	NO: 807.81(a)	NO: 213 of FDAMA	NO	NO
5. SPECIFICATION INITIATOR AND DISTRIBUTE ONLY	YES: 807.81(a)	YES: 807.20(a)(1) PREAMBLE NO. 5, FR 8-23-77	YES: 807.20(a)(1)	YES: 820.181, etc.
6. SPECIFICATION CONSULTANT ONLY; NO DISTRIBUTION	NO	NO: PREAMBLE NO. 5, FR 8-23-77	NO	NO
7. RELABELER OR REPACKER: DISTRIBUTE UNDER OWN NAME	NO: 807.85(b): NO CHANGE TO DEVICE OR EXISTING LABELING	YES: 807.20(a)(3)	YES: 807.20(a)(3) PREAMBLE NO. 7, FR 8-25-78	YES
8. KIT ASSEMBLER USING *PRE*LABELED & *PRE*PACKAGED DEVICES ONLY	NO: NO CHANGE IN DEVICE OR EXISTING LABELING OTHER THAN ADDING DIST. NAME & ADDRESS	NO	NO	NO
9. KIT ASSEMBLER CHANGES INTENDED USE (801.4) OR *PRE*PACKAGED/*PRE*LABELED DEVICES	YES: 807.81(a)	YES: 807.20	YES: 807.20	YES: 820.120, 820.130, etc.
10. KIT ASSEMBLER CHANGES OF *PRE*PACKAGED/*PRE*LABELED DEVICES	NO: IF NO SIGNIFICANT CHANGE TO LABELING OR DEVICE; OTHERWISE YES: 807.81(a)(3)(I)	YES: 807.20(a)(3)	YES: 807.20(a)(3)	YES
11. MANUF. ACCESSORY, COMPONENT AND PACKAGE & LABEL FOR HEALTH PURPOSE TO END USER	YES: 807.81(a)	YES: 807.20(a)(5) PREAMBLE NO. 7, FR8-25-78	YES: 807.20(a)(5)	YES
12. MANUF. COMPONENTS & DIST. ONLY TO FINISHED DEVICE MFR.	NO: 807.81(a)	NO: 807.65(a)	NO	USE AS GUIDE: 820.1
13. *CONTRACT* MFR. OF SUBASSEMBLY OR COMPONENT (SEE NO. 11, ACCESSORY)	NO	NO	NO	PRIMARY MFR. MUST SEE THAT GMP IS MET PREAMBLE NO. 33, FR 7-21-78
14. *CONTRACT* PACKAGER OR LABELER	NO	NO	NO	PRIMARY MFR. MUST SEE THAT GMP IS MET PREAMBLE NO. 33, FR 7-21-78
15. *CONTRACT* STERILIZER	NO	YES	NO	YES
16. MANUFACTURE CUSTOM DEVICE (DOMESTIC OR FOREIGN)	NO: 807.85(a)(1) & (2)	YES	YES	YES: ALSO SEE 520(b); 520(f)
17. FOREIGN MFR. SELLING DIRECT TO U.S. USER	YES: 807.81(a)	NO: ENCOURAGED TO: 807.40(a)	YES: 807.40(b)	YES
18. FOREIGN MFR. SELLING THROUGH INITIAL DISTRIBUTOR	YES: 807.81 FOREIGN MFR. HAS PRIMARY RESPONSIBILITY, BUT MAY DELEGATE TO AN INIT. DIST.	NO: ENCOURAGED TO: 807.40(a)	YES: UNLESS SOLE INIT. DIST. LISTS, 807.40(a)	YES
19. INITIAL DISTRIBUTOR OF DEVICE	YES: 807.81(a) or 807.85(b) UNLESS 510(k) HAS BEEN FILED BY FOREIGN MANUFACTURER OR ANOTHER INIT. DIST.	YES: 807.20(a)(4) PROVIDE NAME & ADDRESS OF FOREIGN MFRS. 807.22(c)(3)	NO: UNLESS INIT. DIST. DEVELOPS SPECS OR REPACK/RELABELS 807.22(c) OR IF AUTHORIZED 807.40(b)	YES: 807.3(d), 820.198, 820.20(a)(3) etc.
20. INSTALLER-MFR.'S AGENT	NO	NO	NO	YES: 820.152
21. INSTALLER-USER	NO	NO	NO	NO: FOR X-RAY SEE 1020.30(d) REPORT
22. DEVICE BEING INVESTIGATED UNDER IDE	EXEMPT: 812.1(a)	EXEMPT: 812.1(a)	EXEMPT 812.1(a)	EXEMPT: BUT MUST HAVE A QA SYSTEM: 812.5, 812.20(b), 812.27; 812.140(b): SEE 501C
23. MFR. BUYS MANUFACTURING RIGHTS FOR DEVICE (SEE NO. 3)	NO: PREAMBLE 18 FR 8-23-77 ONLY IF SAME TYPE OF MANUF. EQUIP. IS USED AND NO SIGNIF. CHANGE TO DEVICE	YES: 807.20(a)(2) IF NOT ALREADY REGISTERED	SEND LETTER TO FDA PER 807.30(b)(5) & 807.26	YES

IVD MANUFACTURER QUESTIONNAIRE
PLEASE PRINT

FIRM NAME:_____

ADDRESS:_____

_____

CENTRAL FILE NUMBER:_____

FDA DISTRICT OFFICE:_____

1. Does the firm use human blood and/or blood products in the manufacturer of the IVD(s)?

    _____NO   _____YES (If "NO", questionnaire is complete)

2. Are human blood and/or blood products **imported** for incorporation into the IVD(s)?

    _____NO   _____YES

If yes, list the foreign countries where the products were collected and provide the name(s) and address(es) of the foreign establishment(s).

_____

_____

_____

3. Are human blood and/or blood products obtained from a broker for incorporation into the IVD(s)?

    _____NO   _____YES

If yes, list the name(s) and address(es) of the broker(s).

_____

_____

_____

4. If question 2 and/or 3 above is answered "yes", please complete page 2 of this form.

IMPORTED BLOOD/BLOOD PRODUCTS
REPORTING FORM

PRODUCT: (CHECK ALL APPLICABLE)

Container type - please circle

_____ HUMAN WHOLE BLOOD   (TUBES   BOTTLES   BAGS)

_____ HUMAN RED BLOOD CELLS   (TUBES   BOTTLES   BAGS)

_____ HUMAN PLASMA   (TUBES   BOTTLES   BAGS)

_____ HUMAN SERUM   (TUBES   BOTTLES   BAGS)

_____ HUMAN RECOVERED PLASMA (FOR MANUFACTURING USE
            ONLY - INJECTABLES)

_____ HUMAN RECOVERED PLASMA (FOR MANUFACTURING USE
            ONLY - NONINJECTABLES)

_____ HUMAN SOURCE PLASMA (FOR MANUFACTURING USE ONLY -
            INJECTABLES)

_____ HUMAN SOURCE PLASMA (FOR MANUFACTURING USE ONLY -
            NONINJECTABLE)

CRITERIA: (PLEASE CIRCLE)

1. SPECIFICATIONS OF THE IVD MANUFACTURER FOR ACCEPTANCE
    OF THE HUMAN BLOOD/BLOOD PRODUCTS (21 CFR 820.50):

            SOP   CONTRACTUAL AGREEMENT

2. DO THE PRODUCTS AND TESTING SPECIFICATIONS LISTED IN #1
    ABOVE MATCH THE SHIPPING DOCUMENTATION? YES   NO
                                (Check a representative sample)

3. DEPENDING ON THE TYPE OF PRODUCT IMPORTED, DOES IT MEET
    THE CRITERIA FOR IMPORTATION STATED IN THE REGULATORY
    PROCEDURES MANUAL, CHAPTER 9, (IMPORT OPERATIONS/
    ACTIONS)? YES   NO   (Check a representative sample)

COMMENTS: (attach additional pages as needed)

_____

_____

Fax the completed questionnaire to CBER, Office of Compliance and Biologics Quality, Division of Case Management
(HFM-610), Import/Export Team at (301)594-0940.

EXHIBIT 590 A

INVESTIGATIONS OPERATIONS MANUAL

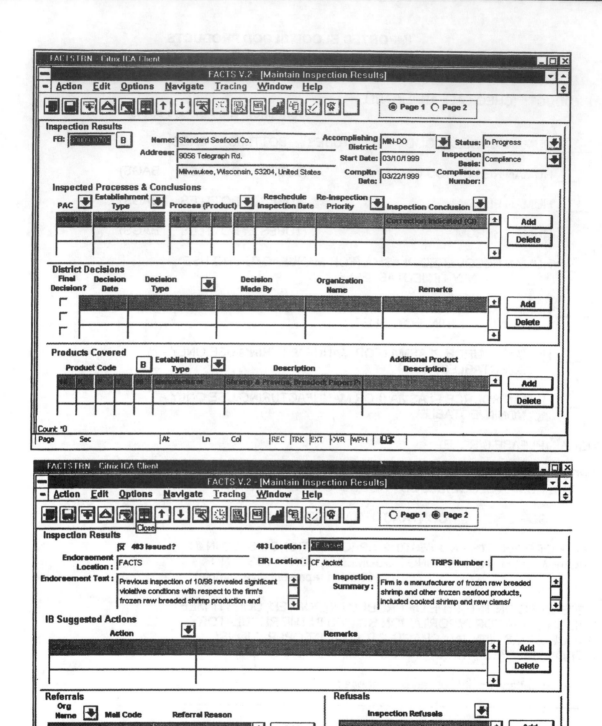

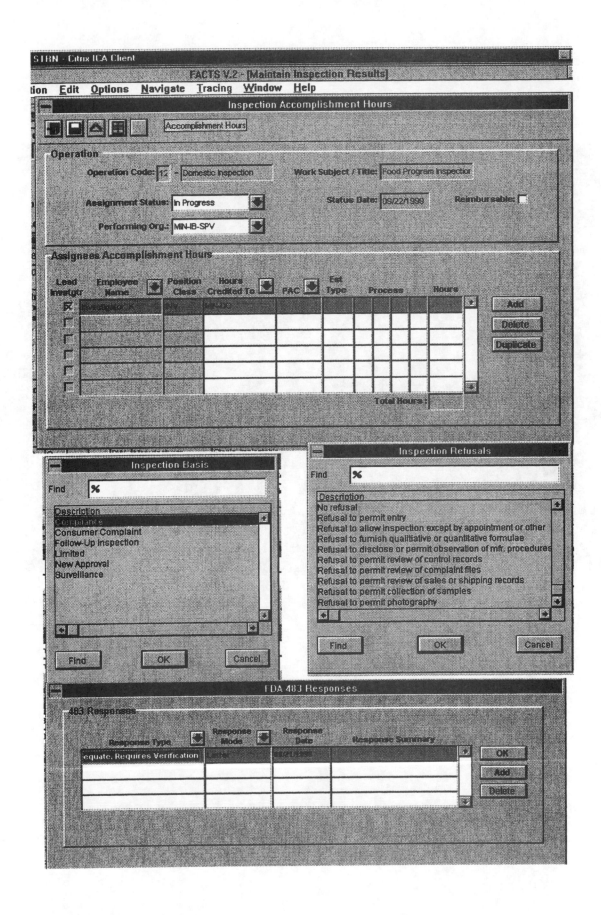

EXHIBIT 590 A   INVESTIGATIONS OPERATIONS MANUAL

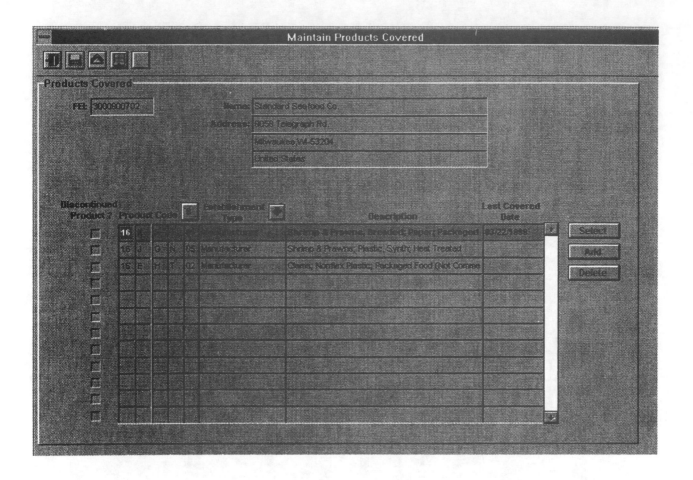

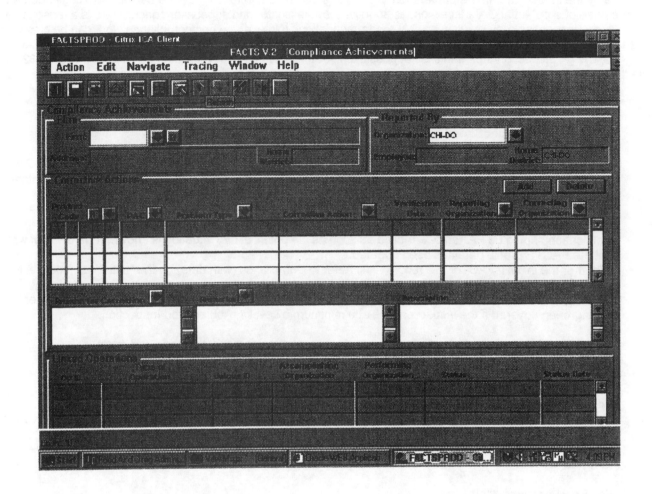

EXHIBIT 590 C   INVESTIGATIONS OPERATIONS MANUAL

Updating Profile Data in FACTS

(This information is provided by DCIQA, formerly MPQAS)

Profile data must be updated in FACTS to establish or update a firm's profile information (see profiling criteria below). This should be by the investigator in the preparation of the inspection record in FACTS before setting "awaiting endorsement." Or in the case of a potential OAI inspection, as soon as the investigator and supervisor concur there is a reasonable probability the inspection may result in an OAI recommendation. (Note: an ad hoc compliance work can be created at the same time a profile is set to "FI.") For foreign inspections, a CI/Potential OAI situation should be entered into FACTS during the foreign inspection trip. If this is not possible, FAX the Potential OAI Notification to HFC-240 at (301)827-0343 while the inspection is in progress.

The FACTS investigator role:

For Domestic Inspections:
Record in "initial" an "AC" for inspections classified as NAI or VAI.
Record in "initial" an "FI" immediately upon determining the inspection may be classified as OAI. HFC-240 requires a hard copy or e-mail documentation of all Potential OAI Notifications as soon as the "FI" is entered into FACTS.

For Foreign Inspections:
Notification should be FAXed or e-mailed as soon as the potential OAI situation is known, regardless of whether or not the FACTS profile data has been updated.
Whether the initial is "AC" or "FI" record "Will Refer to Compliance (with date)" in the "Initial" remarks section.

NOTE: For all Device inspections (foreign or domestic) record all applicable profiles for the establishment as having been covered if the inspection was at a minimum a Level 1, Abbreviated Inspection.

For all Drug inspections done utilizing the top-down, systems approach, the same will apply.

The FACTS IB supervisor role:

For Domestic Inspections:
In the case of a NAI or VAI inspection set the "Record Final" status to "AC" when endorsing the inspection in FACTS.
In the case of a potential OAI inspection the supervisor adds, "referred to Compliance (with date)" in the "Initial" remarks section.

For Foreign Inspections:
The supervisor verifies the investigator has properly completed his/her role. (Compliance, in the appropriate Center, will set the "Record in Review" status when they receive the EIR and "Record Final" when they finish their review.)

DO NOT record "Final" for any profile class at the District level for any foreign inspection record.

For Biologics Core Team OAI Inspections (Foreign and Domestic):
The Team's compliance officers in OE will set the "Record in Review" status when they receive the EIR and "Record Final" status when they finish their review and consultations with CBER.

The FACTS District compliance role:
For potential OAI inspections, set FACTS to Record in Review as soon as the inspection is submitted to compliance branch for evaluation.
Use the Remarks box to keep track of the progress of the review. Include in "remarks" if the action is submitted to a Center or Counsel (date) for further review or opinion.
After the final evaluation, close the inspection in Final with the District's decision. Include type of action taken and date of action.

Profile Process

1. Prior to the inspection, the investigator should review the firm's profile information and, if possible during the inspection, evaluate the firm's capability to produce products in the listed profile class(es). Cover as many profile classes as possible.

2. Update information for all the profile classes covered during the inspection. (When performing a top-down, systems-type inspection for medical devices and drugs (pilot GMP program) all profile classes applicable to the establishment and its products can be considered to have been covered by the inspection.)

3. Add any new profile classes.

4. Include the last date of the inspection and the compliance status. Use the remarks column to clarify information, to note product specific problems, and/or to note any regulatory action recommended or taken and the date of such action.

5. When a firm no longer manufactures products in a listed profile class, "Discontinue" those class(es) in the profiles screen of FACTS. Contact DCIQA (HFC-240) if the wrong profile class code was used, e.g., PRF instead of OPT for contact lenses/glasses. In order to remove the wrong PC from the history in FACTS, it must be deleted (not to be confused with a discontinued PC).

6. When profile classes BMI, NEC SOL, or MIS are used to identify product(s) not elsewhere classified, be sure to use the remarks section to identify the product(s).

7. Make name and/or address changes using FACTS Firm Maintenance.

8. When a firm is doing business under a different name, use FACTS Firm Maintenance to list DBAs.

9. If a firm is found to be unacceptable by a district (or in the case of foreign inspections, by the Center), any regulatory action recommended and the date must be noted in the remarks section of "In Review" in FACTS. The same is true for "Record Final." The remarks section must include any regulatory action taken and the date. This block is updated accordingly as the work travels through the compliance subsystem of FACTS.

10. If the deficiencies are product(s) specific within a profile class, and the overall profile class status is considered acceptable, the initial profile status should be made "AC" and the initial remarks status should be made "FI" for the product specific item. Note in the remarks section the reason for the product specific status (include the product(s) when possible) and referred to compliance for review. Compliance should then either concur with the initial product specific "FI," reach a conclusion as to the warranted regulatory action to be taken, or make the product acceptable and enter as "AC" as the final profile status. If compliance concurs with the initial "FI" and concludes the product specific item is unacceptable, the final remarks status should be made "UN" and the remarks section updated with the regulatory action and the date action taken. Remarks section should state the other products in the profile class are acceptable.

11. When a profiled firm goes out of business, changes operations, or discontinues production of FDA regulated products, record the appropriate information in the FACTS OEI and remember to remove the profile required flag.

12. Update Operation type from drop down menu:

    a. For devices: If a firm makes sterile products , include the appropriate profile class(es) for the product(s) manufactured and, whether the sterilization is performed on-site or by a contract sterilizer, include the appropriate sterilization profile class code. Use the Remarks box to indicate "on-site sterilization" or "off-site sterilization" as appropriate. For off-site sterilization include the name of the sterilizer, city and state/country in Remarks.

    b. If a firm is a contract sterilizer only, use the appropriate sterilization profile class code, and note in the remarks column "contract sterilizer only."

    c. If a firm is a control-testing laboratory for its own products do not use CTL. If the firm does validation, stability, etc., work for other firms, use the CTL profile class code and from the "Operation Type" drop down menu choose "Control Testing Lab Also" and indicate in the remarks section "Drug," "Device," or "Biologic.

    d. If a firm is a control testing laboratory only, use the CTL profile class code and from "Operation Type" drop down menu choose "Control Testing Lab Only" and indicate in the remarks section "Drug," "Device," "Biologics" (or a profile status combination of the three, e.g., "Drugs and Devices") as appropriate.

13. The use of "Others" as found on the Profile Status (Final) pull down menu.

    a. When a firm is operating under a **Consent Decree** the Final profile status should be "Others" rather than acceptable or unacceptable. The Remarks Status field should reflect the status of the current inspection (acceptable or unacceptable) and the Remarks field should elaborate on the current inspection and state that the firm is operating under consent decree (date). The consent decree information should be carried forward to each new inspection until the consent decree is lifted. If and when it is lifted use the remarks section to record consent decree lifted and the date it was lifted.

    b. When a firm is operating under an **Application Integrity Policy** (AIP) the final profile status should be "Others" rather than acceptable or unacceptable. The Remarks Status field should reflect the current inspection (acceptable or unacceptable) and the Remarks field should state that the firm is under AIP on a product by product basis. If feasible list the product(s) under AIP. This should be carried forward to each new inspection under the AIP until it is removed. Use the "Remarks" section to record removal of the AIP and the date.

EXHIBIT 590 C   **INVESTIGATIONS OPERATIONS MANUAL**

14. The Inspection Date never changes. For profiling purposes it is the last date of the inspection entered in the EI record. The Status Date is the date the status was initially entered. The Status date provides an audit trail and should not be backdated or changed.

15. There are times the district's course of action for an OAI inspection is not to immediately issue a Warning Letter or take regulatory action, but instead seek compliance via an alternative means. For these cases, the profile status for the OAI inspection should not be finalized. Instead, the compliance officer should enter the "record in review" as "pending" and track the action in the "remarks" field. If a reinspection is required, the investigator must **"uncheck" the profile required box on the "Maintain Inspection Results Screen" before entering the information of the inspection. Unchecking the profile required box avoids the "normal requirement" to update the profile for the inspection.** If this inspection is found to continue to be OAI, the investigator should note in the Remarks field and indicate the reinspection is referred to compliance. The compliance officer has the responsibility to update the Remarks in "record for review" and track any corresponding action on the Profile screen via the Original Inspections Result Screen. When a compliance action is taken, e.g., Warning Letter issued, Compliance should access the original Maintain Profile Screen through the original Inspections Result Screen and enter the firm's "Final" profile status. This prevents two screens open concurrently and dissuades entering a final status of "unacceptable" when alternative corrective action is taken. The "record in review" "pending" status can remain open for as long as required and can be edited repeatedly, until a final decision is made.

NOTE: The GMP "Last Final Status" field [top portion of profile screen-Profile Classes] should always be OT for firms under a Consent Decree or Application Integrity Policy. Setting the Profile Status (in Final) to "Others" will accomplish this.

16. When to use profile status codes HO (hold) and PN (pending):

    a. PN – Compliance work is being done on the item. Use for all work sent to Compliance. Remarks should be updated to reflect overall status, action and action status.

    b. HO – Used for any compliance work referred to ORA/HQ, OCC or Centers for review. Could be used for a number of reasons that cause any compliance component to stop work on the item, e.g., awaiting policy decisions, temporary abeyance, etc.

Establishment Profile Criteria

Profile the following device, biologic, human and veterinary drug establishments:

Manufacturer	Makes a new or a changed product from one or more ingredients.
Remanufacturer	A person who processes, conditions, renovates, repackages, restores, or performs any other act to a finished device that significantly changes the device's performance or safety specifications or intended use.
Reprocessor	A person who performs remanufacturing operations on a single-use device.
Packer/ Repacker	The establishment packs a product or products into different containers without making any changes in the form of the product.
Labeler/ Relabeler	An establishment which affixes the original labeling to a product or changes in any way the labeling on a product without affecting the product or its container.
Contract Sterilizers	Performs sterilization or irradiation of products or components of products regulated by FDA on a contract basis.
Control Testing Laboratories	Performs production quality control work related to products regulated by FDA on a contract basis.
Assemblers of Medical Device Kits	Person or establishment responsible for assembling finished devices into medical device kits.
Tissue Establishments	Manufacturers of tissues, cellular or tissue-based products regulated as devices subject to QS/GMPs, and those regulated as biological products (under section 351 of the PHS Act) subject to drug GMPs should be profiled. See CBER website: http://www.fda.gov/cber/tissue/tislist2.htm
Specification Developer	A person who initiates or develops specifications for a device that is distributed under the establishment's own name but is manufactured by a second person.

EXHIBIT 590 C

INVESTIGATIONS OPERATIONS MANUAL

The following establishment and operation types are not profiled.

Blood Banks
Methadone Clinics
Manufacturers of "Research Use Only" Products
Pharmacies and Retail firms
Distributors
Plasmapheresis Centers
Custom Device Manufacturers
Veterinary Medical Device Firms
X-ray Assemblers
Mammography Clinics
Manufacturers of General Purpose Articles (Devices)
Physicians Offices, Hospitals and Clinics
Laser Light Shows/Television and Microwave Oven Manufacturers
Suntanning Establishments
Device Component Manufacturers
Clinical Investigators/Bioresearch Monitoring
Tissue firms inspected under 21 CFR 1270, (see CBER website: http://www.fda.gov/cber/tissue/tislist2.htm)
Any Non-GMP Inspection

For more information contact your District Profile Coordinator, DCIQA [(301)827-0390] or the DCIQA web page on the ORA Intranet.

Profile Class Codes with Definitions:

BIOLOGICS

AEV	ANTITOXINS, ANTIVENINS, ENZYMES, AND VENOMS
AFP	ANIMAL DERIVED FRACTIONATION PRODUCTS
ALP	ALLERGENIC PRODUCTS
BGR	BLOOD GROUPING REAGENTS
BMI	BIOLOGICAL PRODUCTS NOT OTHERWISE CLASSIFIED (LAL, BLOOD COLLECTION BAGS WITH ANTI-COAGULANT, ETC., WHEN USING THIS PROFILE CLASS NOTE SPECIFIC PRODUCT(S))
BTP	BIOLOGICAL THERAPEUTIC PRODUCTS
CBS	COMPUTER BIOLOGICAL SOFTWARE
HFP	HUMAN DERIVED FRACTIONATION PRODUCTS
SMC	SOMATIC CELLULAR PRODUCTS
TIS	HUMAN TISSUE REGULATED BY FDA
TOX	TOXOIDS/TOXINS
TRP	THERAPEUTIC RECOMBINANT PRODUCTS
VBP	VACCINE BULK PRODUCT
VFP	VACCINE FINISHED PRODUCT
VIV	IN VIVO DIAGNOSTICS
VTK	VIRAL MARKER TEST KIT

DRUGS

ADM	AEROSOL DISPENSED MEDICATION
CBI	BIOTECHNOLOGY CRUDE DRUGS
CEX	PLANT/ANIMAL EXTRACTION CRUDE DRUG
CFN	NON-STERILE BULK BY FERMENTATION CRUDE DRUGS
CFS	STERILE BULK BY FERMENTATION CRUDE DRUGS
CHG	CAPSULES, PROMPT RELEASE
CRU	CRUDE BULK DRUGS (NON-SYNTHESIZED)
CSG	CAPSULES, SOFT GELATIN
CSN	NON-STERILE BULK BY CHEMICAL SYNTHESIS
CSS	STERILE BULK BY CHEMICAL SYNTHESIS
CTL	CONTROL TESTING LABORATORIES (WHEN USING THIS PROFILE CLASS NOTE IN REMARKS "DRUGS")
CTR	CAPSULES, MODIFIED RELEASE
GAS	MEDICAL GAS (INCLUDES LIQUID OXYGEN)
LIQ	LIQUIDS (INCLUDES SOLUTIONS, SUSPENSIONS, ELIXIRS, TINCTURES, ETC.)
LVP	LARGE VOLUME PARENTERALS
NEC	NOT ELSEWHERE CLASSIFIED (WHEN USING THIS CLASS, NOTE THE SPECIFIC PRODUCT(S))
OIN	OINTMENTS, NON-STERILE (INCLUDES CREAMS, JELLY, PASTE, ETC.)
POW	POWDERS (INCLUDES ORAL AND TOPICAL)
SNI	STERILE NON-INJECTABLE
SUP	SUPPOSITORIES

SVL	SMALL VOLUME PARENTERALS (LYOPHILIZED)
SVS	STERILE-FILLED SMALL VOLUME PARENTERAL DRUGS
SVT	TERMINALLY STERILIZED SMALL VOLUME PARENTERALS
TCM	TABLETS, PROMPT RELEASE
TCT	TABLETS, DELAYED RELEASE
TDP	TRANSDERMAL PATCHES
TTR	TABLETS, EXTENDED RELEASE

NOTE: CCS and SVP are no longer used.

DEVICES

BBP	BLOOD AND BLOOD PRODUCTS FOR FURTHER MANUFACTURING(reinstated 1/01)
CCR	CLINICAL CHEMISTRY REAGENTS (INCLUDES DIAGNOSTIC TAPES, STICKS, ETC.)
COH	COMPUTER HARDWARE
COS	COMPUTER SOFTWARE (OTHER THAN BIOLOGICS)
CSP	CHEMICAL STERILIZATION
CTL	CONTROL TESTING LABORATORIES (WHEN USING THIS PROFILE CLASS, NOTE IN REMARKS "DEVICE")
DKA	DEVICE KIT ASSEMBLER
ELE	ELECTRICAL ASSEMBLY
FSP	FILTRATION STERILIZATION
GLA	GLASS OR CERAMIC FABRICATION AND ASSEMBLY
GSP	GAS STERILIZATION (ETO, PROPYLENE OXIDE)
HCP	HEMOTOLOGY AND COAGULATION PRODUCTS (reinstated 1/01
HSP	DRY HEAT STERILIZATION
MED	MEDIA (INCLUDES MICROBIOLOGICAL AND TISSUE CULTURE, GROWTH MEDIA AND ACCESSORIES, INCLUDING INGREDIENTS)
MIS	NOT ELSEWHERE CLASSIFIED (NOTE SPECIFIC PRODUCT(S) IN REMARKS)
MTL	METAL FABRICATION AND ASSEMBLY
OPT	OPTIC FABRICATION AND ASSEMBLY (CONTACT AND OTHER LENSES, EYEGLASS, ETC.)
PBM	PROCESSED BIOLOGIC MATERIAL (reinstated 1/01)
PRF	PLASTIC OR RUBBER FABRICATION AND ASSEMBLY
RIP	RADIOIMMUNOASSAY PRODUCTS
RSP	RADIATION STERILIZATION
SIP	SEROLOGICAL AND IMMUNOLOGICAL PRODUCTS (INCLUDES BACTERIAL TYPING, RHEUMATOID FACTORS, PREGNANCY KITS, IVD other than VIRAL MARKER TEST KITS, ETC.)
SOL	DEVICE SOLUTIONS AND GELS (INCLUDES CONTACT GELS, DIALYSIS SOLUTIONS, DENTAL PASTES, ADHESIVES, ETC.)
SSP	STEAM STERILIZATION
SPD	SPECIFICATION DEVELOPERS
TSP	FRACTIONAL TYDALLIZATION STERILIZATION
TXT	TEXTILE FABRICATION AND ASSEMBLY
WOD	WOOD FABRICATION AND ASSEMBLY
WSP	WATER STERILIZATION

EXHIBIT 590 D

INVESTIGATIONS OPERATIONS MANUAL

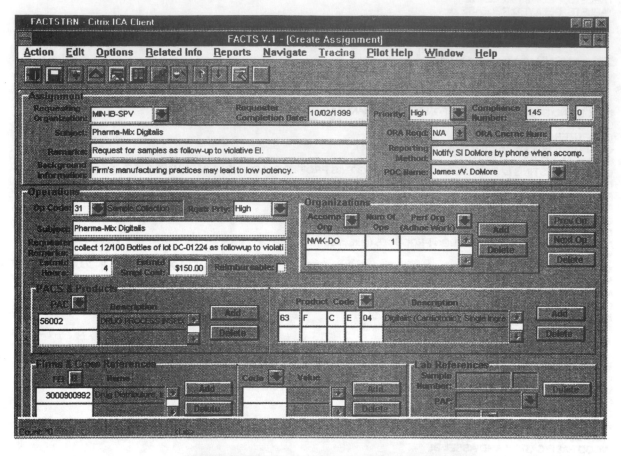

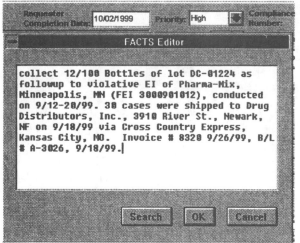

CHAPTER 6 - IMPORTS

CONTENTS

NOTE: All FDA notices are now computer generated and can be located in OASIS. Specific form notices, e.g., FD-172, Notice of Sampling, FD-718, Detention, Release, FD-717 etc., are no longer being issued. Also, the Import Procedures can be located on FDA's WWW Internet site: HTTP://WWW.FDA.GOV.

SUBCHAPTER 600 - IMPORTS

601 AUTHORITY

Section 801 of the FD&C Act authorizes FDA examination of foods, drugs, cosmetics and devices offered for entry into the United States. Section 536 of the FD&C Act authorizes refusal of radiation emitting products which fail to comply with the requirements of Section 534 (h) of the Act. 19 CFR 151.4 of the U.S. Customs regulations authorizes employees of FDA to examine or take samples of entry merchandise released under immediate delivery. The procedures outlined cover imported merchandise subject to, but not limited to, the following Acts/Regulations:

• Federal Food, Drug, and Cosmetic Act
• Fair Packaging and Labeling Act
• Nutrition Labeling and Education Act (NLEA)
• Import Milk Act/Filled Milk Act
• Federal Caustic Poison Act
• Radiation Control for Health and Safety Act
• Public Health Service Act, Part F, Subpart 1, Biologic Products
• Title 21 CFR Subpart E - Imports and Exports (1.83), etc.
• Title 19 CFR Customs Duties (authority to sample delegated by Custom Regulations, etc.)

602 PRODUCTS IMPORTED UNDER THE PROVISIONS OF SECTION 801(D)(3) OF THE FFD&CA

The FDA Export Reform and Enhancement Act of 1996 (PL 104-134 and 104-180) amended the FFD&CA by adding Section 801(d)(3) ("Import for Export") which permits the importation of unapproved drug and medical device components, food additives, color additives, and dietary supplements intended for further incorporation or processing into products destined for export from the United States. Section 801(d)(3) was subsequently amended by Section 322 of the Public Health Security and Bioterrorism Preparedness and Response Act of 2002 (Bioterrorism Act), (PL 107-188), which specified certain requirements that an importer had to satisfy in order to import a product under this Section.

These requirements include:

1. a statement that confirms the intent to further process such article or incorporate such article into a product to be exported

2. the identification of all entities in the chain of possession of the imported article

3. a certificate of analysis "as necessary to identify the article" (unless the article is a device)

4. a bond providing for liquidated damages in the event of default, in accordance with U.S Customs. This bond remains in effect until the final product is exported or destroyed and thus the usual Customs entry bond is not sufficient. A Temporary Import Bond (TIB) or such other bond as designated by U.S. Customs must be executed.

In addition, the initial owner or consignee must keep records showing the use of the imported articles, and must be able to provide, upon request, a report showing the disposition or export of the imported articles. An article imported under this section, and not incorporated or further processed, must be destroyed or exported by the owner or consignee. Failure to keep records or to make them available to FDA, making false statements in such records, failure to export or destroy imported articles not further processed into finished products, and introduction of the imported article or final product into domestic commerce are Prohibited Acts under Section 301(w).

Filers making entry under the Import for Export provisions must either identify entry submissions with Affirmation of Compliance "IFE" (Import for Export), or supply FDA with written documentation stating the product is entered under the Import for Export provisions. In all cases, a Certificate of Analysis (as necessary) and identification of all involved entries must be submitted in writing to the import district. The import district should forward all written documentation to the home district of the initial owner or consignee for incorporation into the appropriated Establishment File.

(See IOM Section 501.7 for Domestic follow-up to importations under Section 801(d)(3).) (see Regulatory Procedures Manual, Chapter 9 Subchaper - Import for Export-www.fda.gov/ora/compliance_ref/rpm_new2/ch9impex.html).

603 INSPECTOR/INVESTIGATOR ROLE

When performing import operations, you may be assigned field examinations or sample collections in response to potentially violative conditions found during field examinations. Import Alerts, FIARS, Monthly Detention Reports, and local intelligence should also be used to support sampling and field examination.

604 GLOSSARY OF IMPORT TERMS

Refer to the Regulatory Procedures Manual (RPM) glossary for a more complete listing of import terms. Below is some common import language:

American Goods Returned - Goods produced in the U.S. which are exported, and then returned to the U.S. They are considered imports. (See Sec. 801(d)(1).)

Bonded Warehouse - A warehouse in the U.S. where imported merchandise is stored under bond prior to being offered for entry.

Break-Bulk Cargo - Cargo transported in individual units, such as bags or cartons, which are not containerized.

Consumption Entry (CE) - The entry document submitted to customs by the importer when imported merchandise is offered for use.

Container - A unit used for storage and transportation of cargo.

Date Collected - The date an import sample is collected.

Date of Arrival - The date a carrier transporting imported cargo arrives in the U.S.

Date of Availability - The date imported cargo is available/accessible for sampling by FDA. Goods may not be available for sampling as soon as they arrive in the U.S., due to the way the items were shipped/stored.

Detention - A temporary administrative action taken by

FDA against articles offered for entry which are not or appears not to be in-compliance with the laws FDA administers. Detained articles can be released if brought into compliance, refused entry, or seized if not brought into compliance.

Detention Without Physical Examination – An action directed against specific products manufactured or shipped by specific foreign firms. "Import Alerts" list products which may be detained without physical examination due to their violative history or potential.

Domestic Import (DI) Sample - A sample of an imported article collected after it has been released from import status. See IOM 405.8.

Entry - A formal offering of specific merchandise into the U.S.

Entry Documents (Entry Package) - A group of documents describing the articles offered for importation, which includes consumption entry form, commercial invoice, manifest, etc. Entry documents include all electronic entries filed through customs automatic commercial system covering FDA regulated products.

Filer - A Customs term used to identify the individual or firm responsible for filing an entry.

Formal Entry - As defined by Customs regulations, an entry whose value is $2,000.00 or greater. It must be covered by an entry bond.

Foreign Trade Zones - Areas set aside in the U.S. by U.S. Customs Service, to hold or otherwise manipulate goods for an unlimited period of time awaiting a favorable market in the U.S. or nearby countries, without being subject to U.S. Customs entry, payment of duty, tax, or bond.

Immediate Delivery (ID) - An entry document filed with Customs by the importer. An ID allows the importer to take immediate possession of the goods and allows him 10 days to file the Consumption Entry (CE).

Import Alerts - Guidance documents concerning unusual or new problems affecting import coverage which direct application of sanctions. They are available on the internet at www.fda.gov/ora/fiars/ora_import_alerts.html.

Importer of Record - Importer or his/her representative responsible for assuring an entry of goods is in compliance with all laws affecting the importation. The redelivery bond issued for the entry will be in the name of the importer of record.

Import Sections (536, 801 and 802) - Those sections of the Federal Food, Drug, and Cosmetic Act containing the Import/Export Provisions.

Import Status - The standing of an article in the import system which is not yet released.

Informal Entry - As defined by Customs Regulations, an entry whose value is less than $2,000.00 and, usually not imported under bond.

Intransit Entry (IT) - An entry document filed with Customs by the importer. It allows the merchandise to move from the port of unloading to its destination, under Customs bond, and allows the importer thirty days to file a CE. The merchandise is usually inspected by FDA at the destination point (port of entry).

Line (Line Item) - Each portion of an entry which is listed as a separate item on an entry document. An importer may identify merchandise in an entry in as many portions as he chooses, except each item in the entry having a different tariff description and rate must be listed separately.

Lot - An entry, group of entries, or a portion of an entry of merchandise which can clearly be defined as appropriate for FDA sampling and examination purposes.

Marks - Words or symbols, usually including the country of origin, marked on cartons, bags, and other containers of imported merchandise for identification purposes. A Customs requirement.

Port (Point) of Entry - The Customs location where the Consumption Entry is made. This may or may not be at the Port of Unloading (the point of physical entry into the U.S.)

Redelivery Bond (AKA Entry Bond) - A bond posted by the importer of record with Customs, currently in the amount of three times the value of the imported product, to insure redelivery of the product for examination, reconditioning, export, or destruction.

Stripping (Of Containers) - The removal of articles from a "Container" for examination or sampling.

Supervisory Charges - The charges for FDA supervision of the reconditioning and examination of articles after detention. (See 21 CFR 1.99).

Warehouse Entry (WE) - An entry document filed with Customs by the importer which allows the goods to go immediately into a bonded warehouse.

SUBCHAPTER 610 - IMPORT PROCEDURES

611 SCOPE

These procedures cover imported merchandise.

612 DIVISION OF AUTHORITY

FDA determines if an article is in compliance with the Acts enforced by FDA. It also determines whether or not the article can be brought into compliance with the appropriate statute and authorizes reconditioning for that purpose.

Supervision over the reconditioning is exercised by either FDA or Customs as mutually arranged. At ports in reasonably close proximity to an FDA office, supervision is ordinarily exercised by FDA. At remote ports supervision may be exercised by Customs.

The refusal of admission, exportation, or destruction of merchandise is carried out under the direction of Customs. However, at some ports the actual supervision of the destruction of violative merchandise may be conducted by FDA pursuant to a local FDA/Customs agreement.

613 ENTRIES

613.1 Formal Entries

All articles offered for entry into the U.S. and subject to the Acts enforced by FDA, with a value greater than $2000 (current), are considered formal entries. They are subject to bond requirements, which include a condition for the redelivery of the merchandise, or any part of it, upon demand by Customs at any time, as prescribed for in the Custom's regulations in force on the date of entry. (See 21 USC 381(b), 19 CFR Part 113). The bond is filed with Customs which, in case of default, takes appropriate action to effect the collection of liquidated damages provided for in the bond after consultation with FDA. (See 19 CFR Section 113.62(k) and 21 CFR Section 1.97).

Notification of the Customs entry is generally accomplished by electronic submission through the Customs Automated Commercial System (ACS). Non-electronic entries are submitted directly to FDA. Electronic entries received by FDA may be reviewed on screen (OSR) to determine if further action is needed, or if full documentation must be submitted. For entries requiring further review, FDA will be provided the appropriate Customs Entry documents (CF 3461/3461ALT, or other Customs entry forms) along with a copy of the invoice, etc. If an entry is not filed electronically, these documents will be submitted to FDA at the time Customs entry is made, in accordance with local port operations.

613.2 Informal Entries

Normally, informal entries (value less than $2000 currently) do not require posting a redelivery bond. All informal entries of articles subject to FDA jurisdiction, entered electronically, are forwarded to FDA through the Customs/FDA ACS interface. Informal entries not filed electronically are processed as paper entries. When an informal entry is sampled, Customs may be requested to convert it into a formal consumption entry.

613.3 Mail/Personal Baggage

In the case of imports by mail or personal baggage, FDA districts should arrange for coverage with their local Customs International Mail Office or border crossing office. This should include agreements designating who is responsible for coverage, when (how often), etc. Customs is responsible for examination of personal baggage. If an article subject to FDA review is encountered, the Customs officer will determine if it should be brought to the attention of the local FDA office. Personal importations meeting the criteria of a formal entry will be processed in accordance with normal non-electronic entries. Generally, since most personal importations are small in size and value, guidance has been developed for evaluating these importations. (See RPM Chapter "Coverage of Personal Importations".)

"Section 321 entries" for Customs are those entries with a value of $200 or less. Generally, this form of entry applies to articles which pass free of duty and tax, as defined in 19 C.F.R. 101.1(o), and imported by one person. Customs and FDA may conduct periodic "blitzes" to determine the volume and type of FDA-regulated merchandise admitted under "Section 321 entries." The use of the 321 entry process should not apply to multiple shipments covered by a single order or contract, sent separately for the express purpose of securing free entry and avoiding compliance pertinent law or regulation.

613.4 Entry Processing

FDA district offices generally receive notification of all formal and informal entries subject to FDA's jurisdiction at ports of entry located in its territory. However, through the use of Custom's Automated Commercial System and FDA's Operational and Administrative System for Import Support (ACS/OASIS) some electronic entries may be forwarded to off-site districts for processing during certain periods of time, i.e., late night coverage of air carrier hubs. The means of receiving notification for non-ABI/OASIS entries can be arranged through local Customs/FDA District agreements.

The most satisfactory and efficient means of getting notification is through FDA's OASIS system. Electronic entries processed through this system are electronically screened against criteria established by FDA for coverage. Automated Broker Interface (ABI) filers using the Customs ACS for cargo release are required to provide FDA information on entries subject to its jurisdiction submitted through ACS.

Customs' ACS uses guides established by each Federal agency to identify which commodities are subject to their jurisdiction. These guides are known as Other Government Agency (OGA) flags. FDA flags are identified as FD0, FD1 and FD2. FD0 indicates the article, even though subject to FDA regulation, may be released without further presentation of entry information to FDA. For entries flagged FD1, the commodity may or may not be subject to FDA regulation. The filer may, based on information received from the importer regarding the intended use of the commodity, specify the entry is not subject to FDA regulation and "Disclaim" the entry. Otherwise, FDA required information must be submitted. FDA review of "Disclaimed" entries is performed periodically to confirm the accuracy of the declaration. Entries covered by an FD2 flag must include FDA required information.

Electronic entries for Customs review includes all mandatory Customs entry required information, i.e., entry number, entry date, importer identification, port of entry, vessel/voyage information, filer identification, Harmonized Tariff System (HTS) code for product description, information on foreign shipper, country of origin, quantity, value, etc. Through the screening process in ACS, Customs determines if the article is subject to FDA examination (see OGA flag identifications above).

FDA's electronic screening of the Customs ABI/ACS entry requires the filer to provide the following information.
1.   FDA product code. (FDA's product code is not the same as the HTS codes used for Customs screening purposes.)
2.   The "Manufacturer's Identification" (MID) code (a Customs designation) of the foreign manufacturer. The MID consists, at a minimum, of the 2 letter identification of the foreign country, the name of the foreign firm, generally made up of the first three letters of the first and second names of the firm, where applicable. Up to 4 numbers, if present in the address, and the first three letters of the city where the firm is located. This code is subsequently transmitted to FDA's screen as the un-coded identified firm.

3. The MID information of the foreign shipper, including city and country. (Which may or may not be the same as the foreign manufacturer.) and

4. The country of origin. (Which may be different from the country of origin identified for Customs purposes.)

FDA has also established Affirmation of Compliance (AofC) codes which are designed to provide FDA reviewers with information concerning the imported article (example: medical device listing number). Use of the AofC is voluntary, and may or may not provide for a more expeditious screening of the entry.

In OASIS, the FDA forms identified as: "Notice of Sampling," "Release Notice," "Notice of Detention and Hearing," and "Notice of Refusal of Admission," are no longer issued as specific forms. OASIS generates a "Notice of FDA Action" providing information on the actions taken regarding a particular entry line. The notice identifies the specific line(s) of the entry, where appropriate, with the description of the sample collected or intended for sampling, specific line(s) identified as detained, and/or the specific line(s) identified as released, refused, etc. As the status changes for a particular line, a new "Notice of FDA Action" is issued to advise the appropriate individuals of the changes. The use of the designation "Product Collected by FDA," "Detained," "Released," "Refused," etc., or similar wording on the "Notice of FDA Action," meet the requirements of the wording of the law and regulation when applied to "giving notice thereof to the owner or consignee." See Exhibit 610-C.

OASIS notices are designed to be mailed to the addressees. A copy of each notice is produced with the filer, importer of record, and consignee on the addressee line. (If the same firm fills one or more of those functions, only one copy is produced for the firm.) Notices are official documents which provide FDA decisions on entries. The distribution of the notices is made by FDA, not the filer, to ensure proper notification to the parties involved (i.e., FAX, express pick-up services, postal service, etc.). The intention is for FDA to distribute to the responsible firm without an intermediary.

614   SAMPLING

614.1 Ports Covered by FDA

For electronic entry submissions, if the filer receives a message indicating FDA review, the filer will provide appropriate entry information to the FDA office having jurisdiction over the port of entry. For those entries submitted by paper, all appropriate entry documents should be included with the package sent to the local FDA office.

After evaluating the entry, if FDA decides to collect a sample, the appropriate individuals/firms will be provided with a Notice for Sampling and advised:

1. if the entry is to be held intact for FDA examination or sampling;
2. only those designated items need be held; etc.

614.2 Ports not Covered by FDA

For those ports where Customs does not maintain its ACS electronic entry process, and FDA does not generally cover the port under its normal operating schedule, the responsible FDA district office will coordinate coverage with the responsible Customs Port manager to assure FDA notification. If FDA decides to examine or sample articles being entered through such a port, Customs, the importer, and broker will notified.

Generally, for these entries, examination and/or sampling can take place at the point of destination. Under certain conditions, however, FDA may ask Customs to collect a sample at the point of entry for forwarding to the FDA servicing laboratory. Appropriate information on the entry, sample requirement, and requirements for holding the entry will be provided to the Customs officials and importer by the responsible district.

614.3 Entry Sampling

If no examination or sample is requested, FDA will notify Customs and the filer (who is responsible for notifying the importer, or other designated parties). This electronic notification is called a "May Proceed Notice," and indicates the shipment may proceed without further FDA examination. In the ACS/OASIS process, this may occur as a result of the initial FDA/OASIS screening, or after the district performs an "On-Screen-Review". (NOTE: Since the article is allowed entry without FDA examination, should the article, at a later time, be found in violation of the law, the Agency is not prevented from taking legal action because the article was allowed admission by FDA without examination at the time of importation. [See 21 USC 334(d).])

If an examination or sample is requested, FDA notifies Customs, broker or filer, importer, or other designated parties, either through the electronic entry system or other form of notification, (Notice of FDA Action) to hold the entry, and will identify the specific product(s) to be sampled, etc.

614.4 Notice Of Sampling

When a sample is collected by FDA, a Notice of FDA Action is issued to the importer of record, consignee, and filer. If Customs collects the sample for FDA, the district will enter the entry information into OASIS and issue the Notice of FDA Action

For those entries where specific lines (items) of an entry are not sampled or examined, the Notice of FDA Action will be amended to indicate which lines (items) "May Proceed." (See RPM chapter "Notice of Sampling" for detailed guidance.)

614.5 Payment For Samples

The FDA will pay for all physical samples found in compliance or collected as an audit of private laboratory reports of analysis submitted to FDA in response to detention (See 21 CFR 1.91). (NOTE: This does not apply in the case of an audit sample collected to document reconditioning). See IOM 416.2 for guidance on sample costs.

Billing for reimbursement should be made to the FDA district office in whose territory the shipment was offered for import. FDA will not pay for a sample if the article is initially found to be in violation, even though it is subsequently released. For this reason, do not pay for samples at the time of collection.

Samples taken in connection with the supervision of a reconditioning are not paid for by FDA.

615   PROCEDURE WHEN PRODUCTS CANNOT BE SAMPLED OR EXAMINED

If the entry is still under control of the district inspection operations, and the sample collection can not be completed, the district may annotate the notice to the filer and importer no product was collected, and return the entry to the flier designating the entry "May Proceed." If the designated product was part of a multi-line entry where other products were collected, the notice issued for the other items sampled will be appropriately updated with the release of the product not sampled.

In the OASIS system, when a notice is issued for the collection or examination of a product, and neither operation is accomplished, the filer will be advised through a revised Notice indicating the article is given a "May Proceed" status. The system will print a status of "May Proceeded" in the Line Summary and also print a detail section "Lines Which May Proceed."

In OASIS, the following are definitions used to describe "May Proceed" or "Release" actions:

May Proceed: "Product may proceed without FDA examination. FDA has made no determination the product complies with all provisions of the Food, Drug, and Cosmetic Act, or other related acts. This message does not preclude action should the products later be found violative." (No compliance decision has been made.)

Release: "The product is released after FDA examination. This message does not constitute assurance the product complies with all provisions of the Food, Drug and Cosmetic Act, or other related Acts, and does not preclude action should the product later be found violative." (A compliance decision has been made.)

Districts will follow the appropriate guidance under each of the above procedures, according to their import operations.

616   PROCEDURE WHEN NO VIOLATION IS FOUND

If the shipment is found in compliance after examination, the importer of record, consignee (where applicable), filer, and Customs are notified with a Notice of Release. The shipment may be admitted. (See RPM chapter "Notice of Release" for detailed guidance) .

617   PROCEDURE WHEN VIOLATION IS FOUND

617.1 "Notice of Detention & Hearing"

If examination of the sample or other evidence indicates the article appears to be in violation, and detention is the course of action chosen by the district, the filer, owner and consignee, where applicable, are advised of such action by "Notice of Detention and Hearing." The Notice will specify the nature of the violation charged and designate a site for the owner or consignee (or authorized representative) to appear at a hearing. These hearings are informal meetings with the district, designed to provide the respondents an opportunity to present evidence supporting admissibility of the article. Ordinarily the respondents are allowed 10 working days to appear. However, if for some compelling reason the district determines ten (10) working days are insufficient, this time period may be extended. On the OASIS generated "Notice of FDA Action", this date is identified under the caption "Respond By". A copy of this Notice is also sent to Customs. (See RPM chapter "Notice of Detention and Hearing".)

617.2 Response To "Notice of Detention & Hearing"

Response to the Notice of Detention and Hearing may be made personally, by representative or by mail. The importer may present evidence supporting the admissibility of the article, request refusal of admission, propose an effective manner of reconditioning, or a method to remove the product from the authority of the Act.

617.3 Request for Authorization to Relabel or Perform Other Acts

FDA may authorize relabeling or other remedial action upon the timely submission of an "Application for Authorization to Relabel or To Perform Other Action," (FD Form 766 – See Exhibit 610-A). Application may also be made by letter and the execution of a good and sufficient bond by the owner or consignee (See 21 USC 381(b)). The redelivery bond on file with the District Director of Customs for the particular importation applies to any re-labeling or other action authorized, and a new bond will not have to be filed.

After review of the application, FDA will notify the importer of its approval or disapproval. If approved the original application will be returned outlining the conditions to be fulfilled and the time limit within which to fulfill them will be noted. Notification to other parties will be made where appropriate. A copy will be retained in the district files. (See RPM chapter "Response to Notice of Detention and Hearing", and RPM chapter "Reconditioning" for detailed guidance).

617.4 Inspection After Completion of Authorization to Bring Article Into Compliance

After the re-labeling or reconditioning operation has been completed, the applicant will submit the "Importer's Certificate" (the reverse side of Form FDA 766, Exhibit 610-A) or advise the district reconditioning is complete. At this point, FDA may conduct a follow-up inspection and/or sampling to determine compliance with the terms of the authorization, or it may accept the statement from the importer with no further follow-up. The follow-up inspection and/or sampling may be made by FDA or Customs, depending on agreements between the district and the local Customs. The "Report of Inspector" (reverse side of FDA 766, Exhibit 610-A), or other appropriately completed summary of reconditioning, should be forwarded to the appropriate FDA office.

617.5 Procedure When Conditions of Authorization Have Been Fulfilled

If the conditions of the authorization have been fulfilled, the district will notify the owner or consignee by Notice of Release. This notice is usually identified as "Originally Detained and Now Released." A copy is also sent to Customs and filer. Where there is a non-admissible portion (rejects), they must be destroyed or re-exported under FDA or Customs supervision. A Notice of Refusal of Admission should be issued for the rejected portion. FDA may include in its approval of the reconditioning a provision for the non-admissible portions (rejects) of the reconditioning to be destroyed and not exported

617.6 Procedure When Conditions of Reconditioning Have Not Been Fulfilled

If the initial attempt at reconditioning is unsuccessful, a second attempt should not be considered unless a revised method of restoration shows reasonable assurance of success.

If the conditions of the authorization have not been fulfilled, a "Notice of Refusal of Admission" is issued to the importer, consignee, where applicable, to the filer, and to Customs.

617.7 Procedure after hearing - "Notice of Release"

If, after presentation of testimony, the district determines the article should be released, the importer of record and consignee are issued a "Notice of Release". The Notice will declare the detained goods may be admitted. The Notice will also be identified "Originally Detained and Now Released" and, where appropriate, explain the reason for the change of action. A copy of the Notice is sent to Customs, and all parties receiving the Notice of Sampling/Notice of Detention. (See RPM chapter "Notice of Release" for detailed guidance.)

617.8 Procedure after hearing - "Refusal of Admission"

When the importer requests the district issue a notice of refusal of admission, or the district decides the shipment still appears to be in violation, the importer, owner, and consignee where applicable, are issued a "Notice of Refusal of Admission." On this Notice, the charge(s) is stated exactly as shown on the original (or amended) Notice of Detention and Hearing. A copy of the Notice is also sent to Customs. (See RPM chapter "Notice of Refusal of Admission" for detailed guidance.)

The Notice of Refusal provides for the exportation or destruction of the shipment, under Customs supervision, within 90 days of the date of the notice, or within such additional time as specified by Customs Regulation. Under OASIS, the Notice will also contain language which includes reference to the requirement for redelivery, and contain all the above required information concerning the product and charge(s). The FDA file remains open until the district receives notification indicating the merchandise.

Was either destroyed or exported. FDA is responsible for the protection of the U.S. public regarding foods, drugs, cosmetics, etc. until the violative article is either destroyed or exported.

617.9 Payment of Costs of Supervision of Relabeling and/or Other Action

After completion of the authorized relabeling or other action, FDA will submit a detailed statement of expenses incurred, including travel, per diem or subsistence, and supervisory charges, on Form FDA 790 (See Exhibit 610-B, Charges for Supervision) of officers of employees of the FDA regarding the supervision of the authorized relabeling or other action to Customs National Finance Center. The expenses shall be computed on the following basis:

- Inspector's time
- Analyst's time
- Per diem allowance
- Travel other than by auto - actual cost of such travel
- Travel by auto (mileage, toll fees, etc.)
- Administrative support

When OASIS is fully operational, the supervisory charges submitted to Customs will be processed by OASIS, and the form FDA 790 will no longer be used. (See RPM chapter "Supervisory Charges" for detailed guidance.)

Customs, upon receipt of the charges for supervision, will send a notice for payment to the identified importer of record. The expenses shall include charges of supervision of destruction of the article or rejects. The remittance by the owner or consignee shall be to Customs. Payment of supervisory charges should not be accepted by FDA district offices.

617.10 Exportation of Merchandise Refused Admission

Exportation of refused merchandise is done under Customs supervision. However, if after a reasonable time,

FDA has not received notification of exportation or destruction, the district should investigate the status of disposition. Districts should also consider, under certain conditions, verifying the refused goods have been held intact pending exportation or destruction, or that re-export actually occurred. Guidance on refusals to be verified may change, based on the reason for detention.

617.11 Bond Action

Under the provisions of the Act (section 801(b)) and Customs regulations (19 CFR 113.62) a bond is required for all conditionally released articles offered for importation. This bond provides relief to the government on the default of the conditions of the bond and the payment of liquidated damages in the amount specified in Customs notice of assessment of liquidated damages for failure to redeliver such merchandise.

Bond actions are taken when an entry is distributed prior to FDA release and can not be redelivered, or when an article has been detained and refused and the article is not destroyed or exported in accordance with the requirements of the law.

If district has evidence the entry, or any portion of an entry subject to FDA jurisdiction, was disposed of in violation of the terms of the appropriate Act, or its regulations, or of the terms of the bond, (see 19 CFR Section 113.62(k)) they should immediately contact the appropriate Customs office.

The district, upon receiving evidence the refused article was not exported or destroyed should immediately investigate the matter. Send a detailed statement showing the importer's liability under the redelivery bond or other applicable customs bond to the responsible Customs office. If the facts warrant, and the article was under detention, and the Notice of Refusal of Admission has not been issued, immediately issue a Notice of Refusal to the owner or consignee, with a copy to Customs.

Upon the receipt of an application for relief (appeal for Mitigation or Cancellation of Assessed Liquidated Damages) Customs may agree to mitigate the amount of damages. However, in cases involving FDA merchandise, Customs does not usually mitigate unless FDA is in full agreement with the action. It is FDA's policy to always seek 100% penalty [see 21 CFR section 1.97(b)]. (See RPM chapter "Bond Actions" for detailed guidance.)

SUBCHAPTER 620 - REVIEW OF RECORDS

620 GENERAL

"Records review" is the initial examination provided the importer's documentation (including any electronic entry filing information.) This operation is performed on every entry of regulated product to determine if additional action, such as sampling, is necessary. (Review of electronic filings follows the same decision-making criteria applied to hard-copy entry filings.) At this point, one of four decisions is made:

1.   Release the lot, or
2.   Detain the lot, or
3.   Examine the lot by Field Examination, or Sampling, or
4.   Verify registration, listing, declarations, certifications, etc. where applicable.

The decision will be supported by:
1.   Electronic screening on entry information,
2.   Computerized information (FIARS, local/regional data systems),
3.   Import Alerts,
4.   Monthly Detention List,
5.   Past history,
6.   Compliance Program Guidance Manual,
7.   Assignments, and
8.   Local assignments and programs (e.g., Regional Pesticide Sampling Plan).

See Regulatory Procedure Manual (RPM) Chapter 9 for additional guidance concerning the review/processing of entries of specific types of commodities, including products under detention without physical examination.

Record reviews are reported into PODS as Entry Reviews.

SUBCHAPTER 630 - FIELD EXAMINATION

630 GENERAL

A field examination is simply an on-the-spot examination or field test performed on a product to support a specific decision. It may be conducted on products discharged from vessels on to the wharves (piers), pier sheds, and other locations; products in trucks, trains, freezers, and containers, etc., at border entry points; or on products set aside for FDA examination. Some compliance programs don't address field examinations. Nevertheless, field examinations are appropriate for certain problems and/or commodities and should be conducted.

A field examination involves actual physical examination of the product for such things as storage or intransit damage, inadequate refrigeration, rodent or insect activity, lead in dinnerware (Quick Color Test – QCT), odor and label compliance

A field examination does not have the same level of confidence as a laboratory examination. Consequently, more rigorous standards of acceptance are applied than those used for formal regulatory levels. For example, if the formal action guideline for whole insects is 10 per 100 gms in product X, you may sample product X when your field examination shows only one or two insects per 100 gms. The decision to sample is, to some degree, left to your discretion. In most instances, it should be based on findings significantly lower than specified by the formal guideline.

A field examination begins when the physical examination is started. Do not include, as reported Field Examination time, the time to locate the lot or travel time.

Time spent in locating the lot is reported as import investigation.

See Section 504.3 for suggestions on what to do when conducting a field examination and the firm responsible for the products invites individuals who are not directly employed by the firm to observe the examination.

631 FIELD EXAMINATION SCHEDULE

A Field Examination should include a physical examination of a minimum of five containers (cases, cans, bags, etc.) of a product, or as directed by Compliance Programs, specific product examination schedules (e.g., LACF), or other guidance.

When you conduct any field examination of a product's label or labeling, in addition to the specific items discussed in the following sections, be alert for any overlabeling where a product name or identify may have been changed; products without mandatory English labeling; changes in expiration date or lot numbers or similar questionable practices. If you encounter any of these items, collect an example and discuss the appropriate action with your supervisor.

632 FIELD EXAMINATIONS - FOODS

632.1 Food Sanitation

<u>Microbiological</u> - field examinations can not be used for suspected microbiological contamination.

<u>Filth & Foreign Objects</u> - field examine only those product/container combinations in which you can physically view and examine the product, e.g., products which can be probed, products in see-through containers, etc. See IOM Chapter 429 and 505, et al for some specific guidance on performing field examinations.

<u>Low acid and other Canned Foods</u> - See IOM SAMPLE SCHEDULE CHART 2.

<u>Decomposition in Non-sealed Foods</u> - This can include organoleptic examination for fish, seafood, frozen eggs, etc.

632.2 Pesticides, Industrial Chemicals, Aflatoxins, & Toxic Elements

Field examinations can not be performed for these materials, except for metals in dinnerware.

NOTE: Districts should use the Quick Color Test (QCT) field examination of dinnerware to determine if follow-up sampling is required.

632.3 Food and Color Additives

The only valid field examination which can be performed for these materials is a visual examination through the container and a label review for the mandatory labeling requirements, i.e., is a color additive declared for a product without natural coloring; determining if an additive declaration includes its function, for example, "Sodium Benzoate as a preservative".

NOTE: Label examination of products to determine whether there is a declaration of certain food and/or color

additives must be reported as an import investigation.

632.4 Nutrition and Nutrition Labeling

The only valid field examination which can be performed for this type of problem is a label examination for the mandatory labeling requirements. See the "Guide to Nutritional Labeling and Education Act (NLEA) Requirements" document.

632.5 Food Economics (On consumer size containers only.)

Label Examination – Review labels for all aspects of the labeling requirements.

Net contents - See IOM 428.1

Food Standards - The only valid field examination which can be performed for Food Standards is a label examination for the mandatory labeling requirements of a particular Food Standard.

NOTE: Label examinations of products to determine if the labeling meets the mandatory labeling requirements for a particular Food Standard must be reported as an Import Investigation.

632.6 Cosmetics

The only valid field examination which can be performed for these products is a label examination for the mandatory labeling requirements. The most important are:
1.   Ingredient Labeling (21 CFR 701.3),
2.   Prohibited ingredients (21 CFR 700.11 through 700.23 and 250.250),
3.   Non-permitted color additives,
4.   Warning Statements (21 CFR 740.11 and 740.12) (Prohibited fully halogenated chloroflurocarbon propellants).

NOTE: Label examinations of products to determine whether their labeling declares certain ingredients must be reported as an Import Investigation.

633 FIELD EXAMINATION - DRUGS

When you conduct field examinations of drugs (bulk drugs and finished dosage forms) ensure you check:
1.   Labeling compliance (e.g., Reye Syndrome warning)
2.   Probable contamination
3.   Tamper Resistant Packaging Requirements

633.1 Labeling

Bulk drugs and finished dosage forms should be evaluated for compliance with the Drug Listing Act, 21 CFR 207.40. Refer to the Drug Listing Compliance Program.

633.2 Contamination

Drugs should be examined for container integrity, e.g.: cracked vials, ampoules, bottles, etc.

633.3 Samples

A decision to collect samples for Drug Listing Act compliance evaluation should be made in accordance with the drug listing C.P. The nature of samples to be taken from lots where the drug substance or finished product has been subjected to actual or suspected contamination, should be decided on a case-by-case basis.

633.4 Special Instructions

Field examinations may be made of drug lots to obtain information in determining the new drug status of a given shipment. Districts should contact the Division of Labeling and Non-Rx Drug Compliance, Import/Export International Drug Team, (HFD-316) for guidance.

634 FIELD EXAMINATIONS - DEVICES

Medical device field exams include electrode lead wires, patient cables, labeling, and physical damage. Lead wires and patient cable exams should conform to applicable standards set forth in 21CFR Part 898.

635 FIELD EXAMINATIONS - BIOLOGICS

Review the biologics section of Chapter 9 of the RPM and the Import Alert regarding biologics prior to conducting any field examinations of biological products.

In general, products controlled by Center for Biologics Evaluation and Research (CBER) do not require field examination, because they are licensed under Section 351 of the PHS Act. In addition, lot release procedures pursuant to 21 CFR 610.2 apply to many products, such as vaccines.

Products imported under IND Applications are also monitored, but due to the small volumes involved, no specific guidance is necessary.

Shipments of biologics which are not licensed, or are not directly related to an active IND (or, in the future, licensure), should be examined for:
1. Labeling
2. Consignee
3. Manufacturer
4. Intended use

Contact CBER/OC/Division of Case Management (HFM-610) for guidance.

636 FIELD EXAMINATIONS - VETERINARY PRODUCTS

Field examinations of veterinary drugs are visual examinations to determine potential misbranding or adulteration. This may include examination for: (1) Container Integrity, (2) Labeling Compliance, and (3) Product adulteration. Dosage form drugs must be examined to determine if they are new animal drugs. If the products are new animal drugs, you need to determine if an approved NADA/ANADA exists or if there is a valid INAD exemption in place. You should consult with CVM's Division of Compliance (HFV-230) regarding the status of imported veterinary products

(301-827-1168).

Bulk New Animal Drug substances and Active Pharmaceutical Ingredients (APIs) may be legally imported only if destined to the holder of an approved NADA or INAD exemption. You will need to consult with the Center for the status of particular drugs.

Entries of prescription animal drugs for use by the consumers (laymen) must be examined for labeling content, consignee (name and address) and to determine if a valid prescription/order exists from an appropriately licensed veterinarian. The Center (301-827-1168) should have records of any exemptions or permission granted for personal imports.

Devices intended for animal do not require premarket approval. However, they are still subject to examinations for misbranding violations. Animal devices must bear adequate directions for use and label claims must not be false or misleading. You should consult with CVM for guidance (301-827-1168).

Animal feeds and feed components, including pet foods should be examined for conformance with all applicable and appropriate food labeling requirements, drug claims, food additive violations and use of banned or objectionable ingredients as well as filth and foreign objects. You should consult with CVM on individual issues and to determine specific requirements (301-827-1168).

Cosmetics for animals are referred to as "animal grooming aids". While the Center does not actively pursue enforcement actions with animal grooming aids, the products are expected to be safe, effective and properly labeled. The labels and labeling of any incoming animal grooming aids are subject to examination and review for potential instances of misbranding. Consult with the Center for appropriate guidance. The Division of Compliance (301-827-1168) can answer regulatory and enforcement questions. The Division of Surveillance (301-827-0158) tracks reporting of complaints and adverse reactions, including those for animal grooming aides.

CVM does regulate animal biologic products. They are considered as drugs. However, the Center does not regulate animal vaccines. The vaccines are regulated by USDA/APHIS.

Contact the CVM Division of Compliance (HFV-230), the Enforcement and Regulatory Policy Team, with general questions on the importation of veterinary products. You should be aware of various Import Alerts, Compliance Policy Guides or Guidance Documents as they affect individual import situations. See CVM website at: www.fda.gov/cvm for additional information or notifications on current import situations

637 FIELD EXAMINATIONS – RADIOLOGICAL HEALTH

Field Examinations for imported electronic products consist of reviewing the Entry Documents and FDA-2877, Declaration for Products Subject to Radiation Control Standards, to determine if they are properly completed and accurate. This applies to each shipment of electronic products for which performance standards exist. Performance standards, covering ionizing, optical, microwave and acoustic radiation-emitting products, are specified in 21 CFR 1020 through 1050.

For electronic products, physical samples may only be collected on specific assignment. DTR/DER recommendations are to be submitted when the Field Examination indicates the product may not be in compliance and detention is recommended.

Import coverage for radiation emitting products is provided for in a CDRH Compliance Program. Do not collect physical samples except on specific assignment, or with concurrence of CDRH.

SUBCHAPTER 640 - IMPORT SAMPLE COLLECTION

641   GENERAL

In general, the difference between Official Domestic and Import Samples is that import samples do not require official seals or collection of a 702(b) reserve portion. However, these are district options. There will be instances when the collection of a reserve portion and an official seal is warranted, i.e., when enforcement action (e.g., seizure, injunction, prosecution) is contemplated. Many sample sizes are provided in the Sample Schedule Section (Chapter 4). When using the sample sizes furnished elsewhere in this manual, do not collect the duplicate portion of the sample unless directed by your district.

FDA does not pay for import samples at the time of collection. The Importer should be told to bill the responsible district. FDA will not pay for violative import samples, per 21 CFR Part 1.91   See IOM 614.5.

When collecting IMPORT "ADDITIONAL Samples", the original Import C.R. Number should be used. Under OASIS, this will be the entry number with appropriate line information, etc.

Import Samples are compliance samples, except for those collected for pesticide analysis. These MUST BE FLAGGED either "Pesticide Surveillance" or "Pesticide Compliance" depending on the basis for sampling. See IOM Sample Schedule Chart 3 (Chapter 4) for guidance.

642   PROCEDURES

Review the submitted entry (electronic or hard copy documentation) to assure the location of the product(s) is known and the lots are available for FDA examination/ sampling before initiating action. The general description of the shipment in the entry documentation submitted to FDA should match the description of the product(s) in the invoice from the broker.

643   TECHNIQUES

Follow guidance furnished in IOM SubChapter 420 - Collection Technique.

644   IMPORT FORMS PROCEDURES

Because forms are now generated electronically by OASIS, individuals performing field examination or sample collections should follow guidance provided in the OASIS Training Manual, or consult their lead OASIS personnel.

645   SAMPLE COLLECTION REPORTS

For every sample collected, a corresponding electronic collection report must be completed in OASIS. You are responsible for making sure the date collected, quantity collected, unit of weight, and description of text fields are completed accurately. The description text should reflect your District's current policy. Prior to saving the report, you should ensure the calculated cost accurately reflects the quantity collected. If it does not, you should make the necessary corrections to the quantity by accessing the line detail of the entry summary of the line being sampled. (See IOM Exhibit 640-A.)

SUBCHAPTER 650 - FILER EVALUATIONS

651   GENERAL

Since we now handle the majority of entries utilizing the OASIS system, evaluation of the data submitted by the electronic filers is done on a periodic basis. These audits of submitted data are done on a periodic basis depending on the number of entries, quality of the data and other factors. You should follow DIOP policy in the conduct of these evaluations.

EXHIBIT 610 A PAGE 1 of 2   INVESTIGATIONS OPERATIONS MANUAL

SUBMIT IN TRIPLICATE *(Submit in QUADRUPLICATE if you desire copy returned to you.*

APPLICATION FOR AUTHORIZATION TO RELABEL OR TO PERFORM OTHER ACTION OF THE FEDERAL FOOD, DRUG, AND COSMETIC ACT AND OTHER RELATED ACTS

FORM APPROVED: OMB No. 0910-0025
EXPIRATION DATE: Date: October 31, 2000

Paper work Reduction Act Statement An agency may not conduct or sp9onsor, and a person is not required to respond to, a collection of information unless it displays a currently valid OMB control number. Public reporting burden for this collection of information is estimated to average 24 hours (minutes) per respons, including time for reviewing instructions, searching existing data sources, gathering and maintaining the necessary data, and completing and reviewing the collection of information. Send comments regarding the burden estimate or any other aspect of this collection of information to:

OS Reports Clearance Officer
ASMB/Budget/DIOE (0910-0025)
HHH Building, Room 531-H
200 Independence Avenue, SW
Washington, DC 20201

Please DO NOT RETURN this form to this address.

TO: DIRECTOR _____ District	DATE	SAMPLE NO.
Application is hereby made for authorization to bring the merchandise below into compliance with the Act.	PRODUCT	
	ENTRY NO.	ENTRY DATE

CARRIER	AMOUNT AND MARKS

Redelivery bond has been posted by the applicant. The merchandise will be kept apart from all other merchandise and will be available for inspection at all reasonable times. The operations, if authorized, will be carried out at:

_____ and will require about _____ days to complete. A detailed description of the method by which the merchandise will be brought into compliance is given in the space below:

We will pay all supervisory costs in accordance with current regulations.

FIRM NAME	ADDRESS OF FIRM
APPLICANT'S SIGNATURE	

ACTION ON APPLICATION

TO: *(Name and Address)*	DATE

Your application has been   ▢ Denied because: ▢ Approved with the following conditions

Time limit within which to complete authorized operations: _____
When the authorized operations are completed, fill in the importer's certificate on the reverse side and return this notice to this office.

SIGNATURE OF DISTRICT DIRECTOR	DISTRICT	DATE

FORM FDA 766 (12/97)   (SEE BACK)

IMPORTER'S CERTIFICATE

PLACE	DATE

I certify that the work to be performed under the authorization has been completed and the goods are now ready for inspection at:

_____

_____.

The rejected portion is ready for destruction under Customs' supervision and is held at: _____

_____.

TYPED NAME OF APPLICANT	SIGNATURE

REPORT OF INVESTIGATOR / INSPECTOR

TO PORT DIRECTOR OR DISTRICT DIRECTOR	DATE

I have examined the within-described goods and find them to be the identical goods described herein, and that they have been:
_____ on: _____ , 19 _____ , as
authorized, except:

DATA ON CLEANED GOODS

Good Portion: _____

Rejections: _____

Loss (if any) _____

Did importer clean
entire shipment? _____

Time and cost of
Supervision

INSPECTING OFFICER	DATE

DIRECTOR OF DISTRICT

Disposed of as noted above.

DIRECTOR OF CUSTOMS	DATE

FORM FDA 766 (12/97)   (BACK)

EXHIBIT 610 B

INVESTIGATIONS OPERATIONS MANUAL

CHARGES FOR SUPERVISION ☐ Federal Food, Drug, And Cosmetic Act, Section 801 (b) and (c) ☐ 21 CFR 1005.24				DATE		

TO: *(Insert Address)*
DISTRICT DIRECTOR OF CUSTOMS

FROM: *(Insert Address)* DHHS, PHS,
FOOD AND DRUG ADMINISTRATION

PRODUCT	FDA SAMPLE NO.
CARRIER	ENTRY NO.
IMPORTER OF RECORD	ENTRY DATE
CONSIGNEE	

The following is a list of charges incurred by this Agency for supervision of operations performed in accordance with the above-designed Act or regulation. You are requested to collect payment, including any expenses incurred by your Department, for deposit into Treasury Miscellaneous Receipts.

Under Section 801(c), default of payment shall constitute a lien against future importation made by the owner or consignee.

TYPE OF CHARGES	UNIT			CHARGE PER UNIT	TOTAL CHARGE
	HOURS	DAYS	MILES		
INVESTIGATORS TIME					
ANALYSTS TIME					
PER DIEM, PAID PER GOVERNMENT TRAVEL REGULATIONS					
AUTOMOBILE USE					
OTHER TRANSPORTATION EXPENSES *(itemize)*					
MISCELLANEOUS EXPENSES *(itemize)*					
GRAND TOTAL					

REMARKS

FORM FDA 790 (7/82)   PREVIOUS EDITION MAY BE USED UNTIL SUPPLY IS EXHAUSTED.

EXAMPLE

United States Food and Drug Administration
Los Angeles District Office

Notice of FDA Action[1]

Entry Number: 112-9861457-6

Notice Number: 2
November 6, 1996

Filer:
FBN Freight Services   Attention: George
500 Canal St.
New Orleans LA 70130

>

Port of Entry: 2704, Los Angeles,
Carrier: NOL RUBY
Entry Date: November 2, 1996
Arrival Date: November 4, 1996

Importer of Record: Shipley'S Donut Shop Inc., Lafayette, LA
Consignee: a: Shipley'S Donut Shop Inc., Lafayette, LA
            b: Specialty Commodities Inc., Fargo, ND

___

HOLD DESIGNATED

Notify FDA of Availability

Summary of Current Status of Individual Lines

Document: 1   Invoice: PRAC004

@ LINE ACS/FDA	Product Description	Quantity	Current Status
* a 001/001	PINEAPPLE, DEHYDRATED	500 CT	RELEASED 11-6-96
* a 002/001	DEHYDRATED GINGER SLICES	10 KG	Product Collected by FDA 11-06-96
* b 003/001	PAPAYA, DEHYDRATED	10 KG	Detained 11-06-96

* = Status change since the previous notice. Read carefully the sections which follow for important information regarding these lines.
@ = Consignee id

___

[1]This example of a Notice of FDA Action is a model and should not be considered all inclusive. The format and wording in the actual Notice of FDA Action issued by districts from the Operational and Administrative System for Import Support (OASIS) may appear different.

323

EXHIBIT 640-A

INVESTIGATIONS OPERATIONS MANUAL

Notice of FDA Action
Entry Number: 112-9861457-6

Notice Number: 2
Page: 2

FDA will not request redelivery for examination or sampling, if the products not released by FDA are moved, following USCS conditional release to a location within the local metropolitan area or to a location approved by the FDA office at the number below.

All products in this entry not listed above may proceed without FDA examination. This notice does not constitute assurance the products involved comply with provisions of the Food, Drug, and Cosmetic Act or other related acts, and does not preclude action should the products later be found violative.

Please provide documentation concerning all products in this entry to the FDA office below. Include the USCS document (e.g., CF-3461 or CF-7501) and commercial invoice for these products, annotated to show the ACS/FDA line numbers sent electronically.

Also, advise FDA upon actual availability, and include date, location, and warehouse control number, where applicable, for all lines in this entry.

Jennifer A Thomas, Inspector
U.S. Food & Drug Administration   (213) 555-1212
2nd and Chestnut Streets (HFR-MA100)
Philadelphia, PA 19106

DETENTION WITHOUT EXAMINATION

The following products are subject to refusal pursuant to the Federal Food Drug and Cosmetic Act (FD&CA), Public Health Service Act (PHSA),or other related acts in that they appear to be adulterated, misbranded or otherwise in violation as indicated below:

LINE ACS/FDA	Product Description	Respond By
003/001	Product: PAPAYA, DEHYDRATED	November 26, 1996

FD&CA Section 402(a)(1), 801(a)(3); ADULTERATION
The article appears to be held in a container containing a poisonous or deleterious substance which may render it injurious to health.

FD&CA Section 402(a)(2)(B), 801(a)(3); ADULTERATION
The article appears to be a raw agricultural commodity that bears or contains a pesticide chemical which is unsafe within the meaning of Section 408(a). The article appears to contain quinalphos.

Jennifer A Thomas, Inspector
U.S. Food & Drug Administration   (213) 555-1212
2nd and Chestnut Streets (HFR-MA100)
Philadelphia, PA 19106

You have the right to provide oral or written testimony, to the Food & Drug Administration, regarding the admissibility of the article(s) or the manner in which the article(s) can be brought into compliance. This testimony must be provided to FDA on or before the dates shown above.

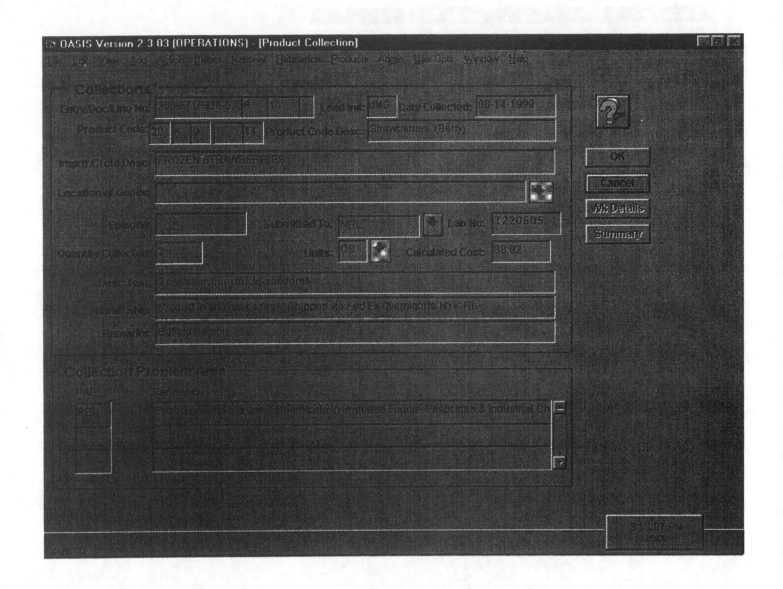

EXHIBIT 640-A   INVESTIGATIONS OPERATIONS MANUAL

OASIS Version 4.1.01 (OPERATIONS) - [Entry Query]

File   Edit   View   Add   Action   District   National   Reference   Products   Admin   User Opts   Help

Entry Query   KDS

555   -   [   ]   -   [   ]   Current Entry Status: Hold Desg/Others Go/Notify

                          Filer: Fiddledee Dee Co., Inc., Los Angeles, California

                                                                                          Execute Query

Importer of Rec: AcmeFish Company   Clear

Port of Entry: Los Angeles, Los Angeles, CA   Cancel

Port of Unlading:

Carrier:

Carrier Type: Arrival Date: 06-25-2002

Lead Customs Commodity Team #   Date Received: 06-25-2002

Filer Contact: Est. Liq. Date: 09-23-2002   Commercial :

Remarks:

Doc/Line Suffix	Product Description	Activity	Date of Activity	Resp Per.
1 - 1 -	FROZEN IQF SLIPPER LOBSTER TAIL	Cert of Export Recd	12-04-2002	KFM
2 - 1 -	FROZEN WAHOO FILLETS 100 CTNS / 50 LB	MPro Issued	07-01-2002	FR
3 - 1 -	FROZNE MAHI MAHI FILLETS 400 CTNS / 50 LB	MPro Issued	07-01-2002	FR
- -				
- -				

Mail / Baggage

Rescind:

Disclaimed Lines

Line #		Hts Code
- -		
- -		

Record: 1/1   <OSC> <DBG>

Start   OASIS Version 4.1.01 (...

Line Details

Line Information

Entry No: 555-0352712-3

Importer of Record: Union Fish Company, Alameda, CA, US

Doc/Line#: 1 - 1   Suffix: [ ]   HTS: 0306110000

Date Available Information

Expected: 06-25-2002   Actual: 07-02-2002   Storage status: [ ]

Product Information

Product Code: 16 - J - G - T - 08   Country of Origin: Taiwan, Republic Of China

Product Code Desc: Slipper Lobster,Plastic, Synth,Packaged Food (Not Commercially Sterile)

Importer Desc: FROZEN SLIPPER LOBSTER TAIL   441 CTNS / 6 BAGS / 5 LB

Corrected Desc: FROZEN IQF SLIPPER LOBSTER TAIL

Brand Name: TAIMEN   Package/Can Codes: Lot#93398, Size 4/6oz

Quantity: Total: 13230 Pounds (avdp); 441 Carton; 6 Bag; 5 Pounds (avdp)   **Q**

Value of Goods: 86704.00   A of C [ ]   **A**

Firm Information

Manufacturer: 3003070527   Ching Yi Cheng Ind. Co Ltd, Kaohsiung, -, TW

Shipper: 1000254526   Taimen Foods Corp, Kaohsiung, -, TW

Consignee: 1000522867   Union Fish Company, Alameda, CA, US

NextRec

Entry Details

Trans\Cont Id's: [ ]

Location of Goods: US Growers #1 3141 E 44th St, Vernon

Cancel

Record: 1/?

<OSC> <DBG>

Start OASIS Version4.1.01 (...

EXHIBIT 640-A   INVESTIGATIONS OPERATIONS MANUAL

SAMPLES COLLECTED

LINE ACS/FDA	Product Description	Est. Cost
001/001	PINEAPPLE, DEHYDRATED	$ 15.00

Sample: 10 KG Collected 1 KG from each of 10 cartons

LINE ACS/FDA	Product Description	Est. Cost
002/001	DEHYDRATED GINGER SLICES	$ .23

Sample: .1 KG Collected approximately 4 ounces from one carton.

LINES RELEASED

LINE ACS/FDA	Product Description
001/001	PINEAPPLE, DEHYDRATED

These products are released. This notice does not constitute assurance that the product released complies with all provisions of the Food, Drug, and Cosmetic Act, or other related Acts, and does not preclude action should the product later be found violative.

Notice Prepared by: Thomas J. DiNunzio (QA5)
                      U. S. Food and Drug Administration

CHAPTER 7 - REGULATORY

CONTENTS

SUBCHAPTER 700 - STATUTORY AUTHORITY

701   STATUTORY AUTHORITY

Various acts specify the authority conferred on the Secretary of DHHS. This authority is delegated by regulations to the Commissioner of Food and Drugs, and certain authorities are delegated further by him.

701.1 Federal Food, Drug, and Cosmetic Act

This Act, as amended, and its regulations provide the basic authority for most operations.

Examinations, Investigations, and Samples - Collecting samples is an important and critical part of FDA's regulatory activities. While inspections and investigations may precede sample collection, a case under the law does not normally begin until a sample has been obtained. Proper sample collection is the keystone of effective enforcement action.

The basic authority for FDA to take samples falls under the statutory provisions of section 702(a) of the FD&C Act [21 USC 372(a)], which authorizes examinations and investigations for the purposes of this Act.

Section 702(b) of the FD&C Act [21 USC 372(b)] requires FDA to furnish, upon request, a portion of an official sample for examination or analysis to any person named on the label of an article, the owner thereof, or his attorney or agent. In a precedent case, "United States v. 75 Cases, More or Less, Each Containing 24 Jars of Peanut Butter, the U.S. Circuit Court of Appeals for the Fourth Circuit held the taking of samples is authorized under section 702(b) of the Act, since this section "clearly contemplates the taking of samples." See Kleinfeld and Dunn 1938-1949 at 126. The FD&C Act also refers to samples in sections 704(c) and 704(d) [21 USC 374(c) and 374(d)].

Authority to Enter and Inspect - Section 704 of the Food, Drug & Cosmetic Act provides the basic authority for establishment inspections. This authorizes you to enter, and to inspect at reasonable times, within reasonable limits, and in a reasonable manner, establishments or vehicles being used to process, hold or transport food, drugs, devices or cosmetics. The statute does not define, in specific terms, the meaning of "reasonable". FDA's establishment inspection procedures maintain this authority extends to what is reasonably necessary to achieve the objective of the inspection.

Food Inspections - Authority to inspect food plants resides in the general inspectional authority of section 704 of the FD&C Act.

The Infant Formula Act of 1980 added new authority to the FD&C Act. Section 412 extends the definition of adulteration to include specific nutritional, quality and good manufacturing control requirements. It also mandates a firm make available batch records, quality control records, nutrient test data and methodology, and similar documents for examination and copying. Section 704(a)(3) gives investigators the right to examine and copy these records.

Device Inspections - Section 704(a) of the FD&C Act provides the general inspectional authority to inspect medical device manufacturers. The Medical Device Amendments of 1976 provided additional authority to inspect records, files, papers, processes, controls, and facilities to determine whether restricted devices are adulterated or misbranded. The Amendments also provide FDA authority, under section 704(e), to inspect and copy records required under section 519 or 520(g).

Limitations - Section 704 of the FD&C Act provides authority for FDA to conduct inspections of factories, warehouses, establishments, and vehicles, and all pertinent equipment, finished and unfinished materials, containers, and labeling therein where food, drugs, devices, or cosmetics are manufactured or held. This section does not include a provision to inspect records within those facilities, except for inspections of prescription drugs, nonprescription drugs intended for human use, and restricted devices, as stipulated in 704(a)(1)(B), or inspections of infant formula described in 704(a)(3).

Keep in mind that several other sections of the Act or of regulations also include provision for inspection and copying of required records. For example, 505(k) provides authority to access and copy records required for new drug applications and abbreviated new drug applications, 512(k)(2) and 512(m)(5) provide access and copying of records regarding new animal drug and medicated feed permits, HACCP regulations in 21 CFR 123 for fish and fishery products provide for access and copying of required records.

Some firms will allow access to files and other materials for which the FD&C Act does not give mandatory access, but retain the right to later refuse. Management may propose the following alternatives:

1. That inspections to obtain data from these files be made without issuing an FDA-482, Notice of Inspection. You cannot agree to this because the act requires the notice be issued before the inspection.

2. That when data is provided, you are advised in writing it is being given voluntarily. In this instance accept the written or oral statement, and include it as part of the EIR.

Management may insist answers to specific questions be provided by the firm's legal department or other administrative officers. In some instances, management may request questions be submitted in writing. In these cases, try to obtain answers necessary to complete the inspection. Do not submit lists of questions unless specifically instructed to do so by your supervisor.

Examinations - The authority for obtaining samples of radiation-emitting electronic products for testing is provided in Section 532(b)(4) of the Act.

Electronic Radiation Inspections - The authority to inspect factories, warehouses, and establishments where electronic products are manufactured or held is provided in Section 537(a) of the Act. This authority is limited; FDA must find "good cause" that methods, tests, or programs related to radiation safety (such as noncompliance with a standard) may be inadequate or unreliable. If there is no finding of "good cause," inspections must be voluntary unless another authority, such as Section 704(a) for medical devices, exists. The authority to inspect books, papers, records, and documents relevant to determining compliance with radiation standards is provided in Section 573(b) of the Act. The Electronic Product Radiation Control prohibited acts and enforcement authorities are specified in Sections 538 and 539 of the Act.

701.2 Selected Amendments to the FD&C Act

The FDA Modernization Act of 1997 (FDAMA) - A major amendment of the FD&C Act focused on reforming the regulation of food, drugs, medical devices, and cosmetics. A few important provisions of this amendment are to streamline and speed up approval processes, to harmonize regulation of biological and drug products where feasible, to support risk-based regulation of medical devices, and to implement good guidance practices to ensure meaningful public participation in development of agency guidance documents.

Prescription Drug Amendments of 1962 - Amends the FD&C Act to require prescription drug manufacturers to prove to FDA the effectiveness of their products before marketing.

Mammography Quality Standards Act of 1992 - Amends the Public Health Service Act to establish the authority for the regulation of mammography services and radiological equipment.

Medical Device Amendments of 1992 - Amends the FD&C Act with respect to Medical Devices.

Nutritional Labeling and Educational Act of 1990 - Amends the FD&C Act to prescribe nutrition labeling for foods.

Prescription Drug Amendments of 1992 - Amends the FD&C Act to coordinate Federal and State regulation of wholesale drug distribution.

Prescription Drug Marketing Act of 1987 - Amends the FD&C Act to ban the re-importation of drugs produced in the United States, to place restrictions on the distribution of drug samples, and to ban certain resale of drugs by hospitals and other health care entities.

Prescription Drug User Fee Act of 1992 - Amends the FD&C Act to authorize human drug application, prescription drug establishment, and prescription drug product fees.

Animal Drug Availability Act (ADAA) of 1996 - Deals with evidence of effectiveness and pre-submission conferences, limitations on residues, import tolerances, feed mill licenses and veterinary feed directives (VFDs).

Animal Medicinal Use Clarification Act (AMDUCA) of 1994 - Allows veterinarians to prescribe extra label uses of certain approved animal drugs and approved human drugs for animal use under certain conditions including existence of a valid veterinary/client/patient relationship (VCPR). The implementing regulations for AMDUCA can be found in 21 CFR Part 530.

Generic Animal Drug and Patent Term Restoration Act (GADPTRA) of 1988 - Addresses submission of abbreviated new animal drug applications (ANADAs) before generic animal drugs can be legally marketed. See section 774.3 for additional information.

Safe Medical Device Act of 1990 - Amends and provides additional authority to FDA for regulating devices. The Act provides for such things as: user reporting of deaths and serious injuries; reclassification of certain devices; provisions for mandatory reporting of recalls initiated by manufacturers and additional authority to order the recall of devices; civil penalties; incorporation of the RCHSA into the FD&C Act; and, device design validation requirements. It also contains specific time frames for writing regulations to implement provisions of the Act. The provisions to order the recall of devices, to notify users, to temporarily suspend premarket approval of a device and to impose civil penalties became effective immediately.

701.3 Other Acts

See IOM 708 and IOM 311.2 for special authorities involving detentions under the Federal Meat Inspection, Poultry Products Inspection, and Egg Products Inspection, Acts.

Anabolic Steroids Control Act of 1990 - Amends the Controlled Substances Act by adding Anabolic Steroids to Schedule III of section 202(c).

Fair Packaging and Labeling Act (FPLA) - An Act to prevent the use of unfair or deceptive methods of packaging or labeling of certain consumer commodities.

Federal Anti-Tampering Act - Prohibits certain tampering with consumer products (18 USC 1365). See IOM 970 for guidance on tampering investigations.

Federal Import Milk Act - Regulates the importation of raw and pasteurized bovine milk and cream from foreign producers.

Federal Caustic Poison Act - Primarily a labeling Act specifying warnings and precautionary statements on labeling of certain household caustic preparations.

Poison Prevention Packaging Act - Provides for special packaging to protect children from serious personal injury or serious illness resulting from handling, using, or ingesting household substances.

Public Health Service Act (PHS) - Sampling; Specific authority for taking samples appears in the PHS Act and/or its implementing regulations for radiation emitting electronic products. For electronic products and biological products, which are also medical devices or drugs under the FD&C Act, the sampling authority of both Acts exists.

Section 351(c) of Part F, Title III of the Public Health Service (PHS) Act [42 USC 262(c)] authorizes inspections of biological establishments (vaccines, serum, and blood). Authority to collect samples and records is found in 21 CFR 600.22.

Section 361(a) of Part G of the PHS Act [42 USC 264] authorizes inspection and other activities for the enforcement of 21 CFR 1270, Human Tissue Intended for Transplantation, and 21 CFR 1240, Interstate Quarantine Regulations. Part 1240 covers the mandatory pasteurization for all milk in final package form intended for direct human consumption; the safety of molluscan shellfish; the sanitation of food service; and food, water, and sanitary facilities for interstate travelers on common carriers.

701.4 Code of Federal Regulations (CFR)

Regulations (published daily in the Federal Register) are codified annually into volumes by Title, Part, and section number. The Food and Drug Regulations are contained in Title 21, Parts 1-1299 For example, the specific regulation covering drug GMPs appears as "21 CFR 211". That is, Title 21, Part 211.

702 DEFINITIONS

The following terms are used in assignments, correspondence, and various procedures described in this manual and used throughout FDA.

Civil Number - A docket number used by US district courts to identify civil cases (seizure and injunction).

Citation (Cite) - The section 305 Notice is a statutory requirement of the FD&C Act. It provides a respondent with an opportunity to show cause why he should not be prosecuted for an alleged violation. Response to the notice may be by letter, personal appearance, or an attorney(s).

Criminal Number - A docket number used by the US district courts to identify criminal cases (prosecutions).

FDC and INJ Numbers - The number used by the Chief Counsel's office to identify FDA cases.

Complaint For Forfeiture - A document furnished to the U.S. attorney for filing with the clerk of the court to initiate a seizure.

Home District - The district in whose territory the alleged violation of the Act occurs, or in whose territory the firm or individual responsible for the alleged violation is physically located. The original point from which the article was shipped, or offered for shipment, as shown by the interstate records, is usually considered the point where the violation occurred; and the shipper of such article, as shown by such records, may be considered to be the alleged violator.

Where actions against a firm are based on goods which became violative after interstate shipment was made, or after reaching its destination (such as 301(k) violations), the dealer in whose possession the goods are sampled may be considered the violator, and the location of this dealer determines the "Home District".

Nolle Prosequi (Nol-Pros) - The prosecutor or plaintiff in a legal matter will proceed no further in prosecuting the whole suit or specified counts.

Nolo Contendere (Nolo) - A plea by a defendant in a criminal prosecution meaning "I will not contest it".

Seizing District - The district where seizure is actually accomplished. The seizing district is not necessarily the collecting district, as in the case of intransit samples.

Subpoena Duces Tecum - A writ commanding a person to appear in court bringing with him certain designated documents or things pertinent to the issues of a pending controversy.

Supervising District - The district which exercises supervision over reconditioning lots in connection with seizure actions.

704 SEIZURE

Seizure is a civil action directed against specific offending goods. Originally designed to remove violative goods from consumer channels, it was intended primarily as a remedial step; however, the sanction often has a punitive and deterrent effect.

District Recommendation - The district considers all evidence, including any establishment inspection, sample collection, and analytical results. If indicated, seizure is recommended to headquarters.

Headquarters - Except for certain direct seizure authority, district seizure recommendations are referred to the appropriate center for approval. If approved, the case is referred to the Office of Enforcement (HFC-200) which then requests the Chief Counsel to initiate seizure action.

Department of Justice - The Food and Drug Division of the Department's Office of Chief Counsel reviews and forwards the seizure action to the U.S. attorney in whose judicial district the violative goods are located, through the seizing district. The U.S. attorney files a Complaint For Forfeiture addressed to the U.S. district court, setting forth the facts of the case and calling for the "arrest" of the goods. This Complaint is filed with the appropriate district court.

U.S. District Court - The court orders the arrest of the goods by issuing a monition and warrant to the U.S. marshal, directing seizure of the goods.

The marshal seizes the goods, which then become the property of the court. You may be asked to assist the marshal in the seizure. If so, submit a memorandum to your district office covering this activity.

Claimant & Options - Any person who has an interest in the goods may appear as claimant or to intervene, and claim the goods.

Abandonment - If no claimant appears within a specified time, (return date), then the U.S. attorney requests a Default Decree of Condemnation and Forfeiture, in which the court condemns the goods and directs the U.S. marshal to destroy or otherwise dispose of the goods. Usually, the District assists the marshal in determining the method of disposal, and you may be asked to help in the actual disposition. Any disposition must be in accordance with the National Environmental Protection Act (NEPA).

Reconditioning for Compliance - A claimant may appear and propose the goods be reconditioned to bring them into compliance. After the FDA agrees to the method of reconditioning, the court issues a Decree of Condemnation permitting reconditioning under the supervision of the FDA, after a bond is posted. Salvage operations may include:

1. cleaning, reworking, or other processing,
2. relabeling, or
3. denaturing.

Contested Seizure - A claimant may file an answer to the complaint and deny the allegations. The issues then go to trial.

District Follow-up - The district monitors the progress of the seizure and forwards appropriate reports to the headquarters.

705   PROSECUTION

Prosecution is a criminal sanction directed against a firm and/or responsible individuals. They can be pursued at two levels: misdemeanor or felony. A prosecution is punitive, with the view of punishing past behavior and obtaining future compliance.

Section 305 Notice - The section 305 Notice is a statutory requirement of the Act. It provides a respondent with an opportunity to explain why he should not be prosecuted for the alleged violation. Response to the notice may be by letter, personal appearance or attorney.

Under certain circumstances, the Agency will refer prosecution (or for further investigation) without first providing the opportunity for presentation of views in accordance with section 305 [See 21 CFR 7.84(a)(2) and (3)].

The facts developed at the hearing are reviewed, along with other evidence, and the district prepares a recommendation the case be:

1.   placed in permanent abeyance, with no further action, or

2.   placed in temporary abeyance, in which case the decision is delayed pending additional evidence, or for other reasons, or

3.   requests, with RFDD concurrence, ad hoc meeting when there is an indication of potential felony charges or the case is especially unusual, or

4.   forwarded to the Justice Department for prosecution.

The district recommendation is reviewed by Headquarters units in the light of current policy and procedure. If prosecution is indicated, the case is forwarded to the Office of Chief Counsel (OCC) for review. If the Chief Counsel agrees, the matter is forwarded to the Department of Justice (DOJ) where it is reviewed again. If DOJ concurs, the case is forwarded to the appropriate U. S. Attorney. Non-concurrence results in return of the case to FDA.

Information - An Information is a legal document filed in misdemeanor actions identifying the defendants and setting forth the charges. The Information is forwarded to the appropriate U.S. Attorney, who then files the legal instruments. A trial date is set by the court. Ideally, trial preparation is a collaboration between representatives of the U. S. Attorney's office, OCC, the District and the involved Center.

Grand Jury Proceedings - The Justice Department must proceed by indictment in all felony cases. Evidence in possession of the government is presented to the grand jury which decides if it is sufficient to warrant prosecution. If the grand jury returns a "True Bill", and the defendant pleads not guilty at the arraignment, preparation for trial begins.

The deliberations of a federal grand jury are secret, and only those whom the court has placed under Rule 6(e) of the Federal Rules of Criminal Procedure may be privy to the grand juries activities. Consequently, if you have been designated under the Rule, you may not divulge your knowledge of grand jury affairs to anyone, including colleagues or supervisors, unless they, too, have been placed under the Rule. Strict adherence to the rule of grand jury secrecy protects not only the integrity of the government's investigation, and the validity of any indictment the grand jury might return, but the rights of the person accused. See IOM 511.9 Working with a Grand Jury.

When you are assigned to work with, or for, a grand jury and are instructed as part of that assignment to conduct an inspection or an investigation, do not issue a Notice of Inspection (FDA-482) (See IOM 511.4 Conducting Regulatory Inspections When the Agency is Contemplating Taking, or is Taking, Criminal Action). Check with district management and the Assistant U.S. Attorney or Chief Counsel attorney involved, prior to initiating this type of assignment. Also, refer to IOM 511.4, 511.5, 511.6, 511.7, 511.8 and 511.9.

District Follow-up - Appropriate reports are made to the Administration when the case terminates. Follow-up may involve inspections either of a routine nature or as directed by the court.

706   INJUNCTION

An injunction is a civil restraint issued by the court to prohibit violations of the Act. Injunction is designed to stem the flow of violative products in I.S., and to correct the conditions in the establishment.

Injunction actions must be processed in strict time frames. Therefore, you may be requested to conduct an inspection to determine the current condition of a firm and to obtain specific information required for the injunction.

Temporary Restraining Order (TRO) - Upon presentation of evidence, the U.S. district court may issue an order restraining defendant from certain acts, for a specific length of time. This period may be extended by order of the court.

Hearing for Injunction - Prior to the expiration of the TRO, if one is involved, the U.S. Attorney, assisted by the district, presents evidence to support an injunction.

Consent Decree of Injunction - The defendants may, following conferences with the U.S. Attorney, consent to a decree of preliminary or permanent injunction. If not, the issue goes to trial.

Trial for Injunction - A preponderance of evidence is required to support an injunction. This differs from a prosecution, which requires evidence establishing guilt "beyond a reasonable doubt". Trial is before the district court. There is no trial by jury, unless demanded by the defendant. In violations of injunction (contempt), the action is brought under the Rules of Criminal Procedure.

Preliminary or Permanent Injunction - A preliminary or permanent injunction enjoins a firm or individuals from continuing a specific violation(s). The terms of the injunction specify the steps to be taken to correct the violations at issue.

District Follow-up - Generally, the district will police an injunction to assure the terms of the decree are met. This may include routine inspections or actual supervision of compliance activities dictated by the terms of the injunction.

707   EMERGENCY PERMIT CONTROL

Section 404 of the FD&C Act provides for the issuance of temporary permits prescribing the conditions governing the manufacture, processing or packing of certain classes of foods. It applies to foods subject to contamination by injurious microorganisms, where such contamination cannot be adequately determined after such articles have entered interstate commerce.

708   DETENTION POWERS

Sections 402 and 409(b) of the Federal Meat Inspection Act, sections 19 and 24(b) of the Poultry Products Inspection Act, sections 5(d), 19, and 23(d) of the Egg Products Inspection Act, and section 304(g) of the Federal Food, Drug and Cosmetic Act provides certain detention powers.

In essence, articles subject to the Federal Meat Inspection Act or the Poultry Products Inspection Act that are believed to be adulterated or misbranded under the FD&C Act may be detained.   FDA representatives may detain articles subject to the Egg Products Inspection Act, which are suspected to be in violation of that statute.

Devices may be detained under the FD&C Act for a maximum of thirty days when there is reason to believe they are adulterated or misbranded under the FD&C Act.
See IOM 750 for inspectional procedures, which must be followed, in exercising the detention authority.

709   COURTROOM TESTIMONY

Effective testimony, whether it be in court before a judge or jury, grand jury or opposing counsel at a deposition, is a result of quality investigative skills; the ability to prepare factual and informative investigative reports; and thorough preparation for being a fact witness.

As a witness, you are required to testify from memory, but you are allowed to refer to diary notes, reports and memoranda, when necessary to refresh your recollection. For this reason, and the fact they are available to opposing counsel, the Agency insists your notes, reports and the like always be accurate, organized and complete.

There is little difference in giving testimony in court, in a deposition or before a grand jury. In a deposition, testimony is given upon interrogation by opposing counsel, under oath, before a court reporter. Be guided by your (the Government's) attorney in preparing for a deposition. Once completed, the deposition is available to all persons interested in the case, and is available for use at trial.

In a grand jury, testimony is given under oath to a group of jurors who determine whether sufficient evidence exists to charge someone with a felony (See IOM 705).

709.1 Testimony Preparation

The following suggestions may be helpful in preparing to provide testimony in court, before a grand jury or at a deposition:
1.   Carefully and thoroughly reviewing your diary notes, inspection reports and all samples collected.
2.   Be neat in your personal appearance; dress conservatively in business attire, and be well groomed.
3.   When you take the witness stand, get comfortable, sit erectly and carefully look around to familiarize yourself with the court surroundings.

4.   Tell the truth. If asked, do not hesitate to admit you have discussed your testimony in advance with the U.S. Attorney's office.
5.   Be sure you understand the question before you answer. If you don't understand the question, request clarification. Take your time. Give each question such thought as required to understand and formulate your answer. Do not answer questions too quickly. Give your attorney time to raise an objection in case it is a question you should not answer. Answer questions clearly and loudly enough so everyone can hear you. Look at the jury and address your remarks to it so all jury members will be able to hear and understand you. Speak directly and authoritatively, and do not use ambiguous phrases such as, "I guess so", "I believe," etc. Do not be afraid to say, "I don't know".
6.   Be polite and serious at all times. Give an audible answer to all questions. Do not nod your head yes or no.
7.   Do not lose your temper, even if baited by an attorney. Do not spar with examining attorneys; answer questions frankly, factually and confidently, then stop. Do not answer questions, which have been objected to until the court rules on the objection. Do not volunteer information.
8.   If you make a mistake answering a question, correct it immediately. If a question can't be truthfully answered with a yes or no, you have the right to explain your answer. If you are asked questions about distances, time or speed, and your answer is only an estimate, be sure you make that clear.
9.   If a recess is declared while you are on the stand, keep to yourself. Do not discuss your testimony with anyone except on special instructions from the U.S. Attorney or his/her assistant.
10.   Be natural, be yourself. Do not be intimidated by personalities.

709.2 Interviewing Persons Under Arrest

Miranda Warning - In the Agency's normal course of operation, it is not necessary to read a person their rights, (i.e.: Miranda warnings) because the Agency does not routinely interview individuals who are in custody (under arrest). Miranda warnings are not necessary, during discussions with management when conducting inspections, during investigational interviews, or during a section 305 meeting because the individuals being interviewed are not in custody, and are free to leave at any time.

In certain situations, however, FDA personnel may interview someone who is already in custody. In this case, the individual must be given their Miranda rights.

When this situation is encountered, copy page 1 of IOM Exhibit 700-A. If the subject cannot speak/read English, you must arrange for a form in the appropriate language. Read this material to the individual, preferably in the presence of another person, and then have them sign and date the waiver statement. Submit the signed statement with your report. If the individual refuses to sign the statement, indicate this on the unsigned statement, and identify the witness on the document. Submit the unsigned statement with your report.

SUBCHAPTER 710 - RECONDITIONING AND DESTRUCTION

710   POLICY

Sections 304 and 801 of the FD&C Act provide the legal basis for reconditioning or destruction of goods under domestic seizure or import detention.

Reconditioning and destruction are the means whereby goods are brought into compliance with the law, or permanently disassociated from their intended use. Manpower may not be expended on supervision of reconditioning and destruction of goods except under administrative controls, detention, or emergency and disaster operations. See IOM 940 for operations in disasters.

FDA does not seek or condone the destruction of books or other publications. FDA policy and practice tries to be sensitive to the potential First Amendment issues associated with the regulation of books and other printed materials that function as labeling of a product. See Compliance Policy Guide 140.100. In the context of judicial enforcement, disposition of any labeling subject to the court's jurisdiction is determined by the court. In a voluntary compliance situation, the disposition is the prerogative of the manufacturer, distributor, wholesaler, or retailer. Agency policy does not authorize field employees to direct or limit the options for disposition of violative labeling or other printed materials in such circumstances. Good judgement should always be exercised in such matters.

Section 536(b) of the Act provides authority for electronic products to be reworked if FDA determines they can be brought into compliance with radiation performance standards. Therefore, reconditioning of radiation-emitting products must be approved by CDRH, Office of Compliance, prior to implementation to assure compliance with performance standards. If a foreign manufacturer conducts the reconditioning, the district should notify both the importer/consignee and the foreign manufacturer's agent of all FDA actions.

711   DEFINITIONS

Reconditioning - The reworking, relabeling, segregation, or other manipulation which brings a product into compliance with the law, whether or not for its original intended use.

Destruction - The procedures involved in rendering a product unsalvageable. Destruction may be accomplished by burning, burial, etc.

Denaturing - Decharacterization of a product, whereby it is made unusable for its originally intended purpose.

712   DISASTERS

Reconditioning and destruction of contaminated merchandise in times of disasters can assume national proportions and is handled differently than normal operations.

Instructions for operations pertaining to reconditioning and destruction during non-attack type disasters is covered in IOM 940.

SUBCHAPTER 720 - CONSENT DECREE

720   POLICY

Seized goods may be released under bond, by court order to be destroyed or brought into compliance. The order normally provides for supervision of the operation by FDA. Release of the bond depends upon your certification the court order has been satisfactorily executed.

Do not undertake reconditioning until you are certain a court order has been entered, bond posted, and goods released by the marshal. Be certain the identity and amount of goods corresponds with that seized. Be sure you are familiar with the terms of the court order.

Reconditioning or destruction may, at times, be permitted without continuous supervision. However, the lot must be checked before operations start, rechecked intermittently and upon completion. Supervision must be sufficient to assure none of the lot was diverted. All of the goods involved in the action, including reconditioned goods as well as discarded material such as screenings, old labels, etc., must be accounted for. If organoleptic examination will not permit a judgement regarding the degree of compliance, collect suitable samples for laboratory examination. If the reconditioning process does not appear to comply with the order, immediately advise the claimant and your supervisor.

721   RELABELING

Before permitting any relabeling operation, be sure FDA has approved the proposed new label. Provide an accounting of disposition of the old labels. Submit three (3) copies of the new label and three (3) copies of the old label with your report of the operation.

722   REWORKING

Before permitting any manipulation, determine the proposed process has been approved by your district. This includes ensuring the facilities and equipment to be used are sanitary and effective for the proposed process. Report the yield of the reworked product.

723   SEGREGATION

Thoroughly examine goods set aside as legal, and submit samples for laboratory examination, if indicated. Follow up on disposition of reject material to prevent illegal diversion. Describe the method of destruction of unfit material resulting from the segregation process.

724   DESTRUCTION

Supervise and describe the method of destruction of goods, labels, labeling, etc. and report the amount destroyed.

725 DISPOSITION OF REJECTS

Arrange for reject materials to be destroyed in an approved manner, under your supervision. The method of disposition will have already been approved by the District, and in some cases set out in the Consent Decree.

726 RELEASE OF GOODS

Do not authorize release of reconditioned goods, unless specifically directed by your supervisor. Formal release is normally handled by district headquarters.

729 REPORTING

Promptly submit a detailed report upon conclusion of the operation. Where the operation is prolonged, submit interim progress reports. Include the following information in your report of the operation:

1.   identification of the case (sample number, court number, FDA number, product and claimant).

2.   description of the method of reconditioning or destruction.

3.   disposition of rejects; explanation for unaccounted goods.

4.   findings of field examinations.

5.   exhibits and samples collected. Do not pay for samples collected during reconditioning operations conducted under a Consent Decree.

6.   expenses, including time spent in supervision and travel, mileage, per diem, and incidental expenses.

SUBCHAPTER 730 - DEFAULT DECREE

730 POLICY

When no claimant appears in a seizure case, the court issues a Default Decree of Condemnation condemning the goods. It may or may not specify the manner of disposal. Disposition, whether by destruction, distribution to charitable institutions or sale by salvage must be approved and monitored by the Government.

Primary responsibility for disposition of seized lots following a default decree lies with the U.S. Marshal's Office.

FDA inspectional personnel frequently accompany the marshal to witness the operation. Although you are there in an advisory capacity, assist the marshal in every way to assure compliance with the court order.

739 REPORTING

Promptly submit a written report of your observations upon completion of the operation. See IOM 729.

SUBCHAPTER 740 - COMPLIANCE ACHIEVEMENT

740 POLICY

FDA uses a blend of industry voluntary correction and regulatory actions to help achieve industry compliance.

A voluntary corrective action is defined as the observed voluntary repair, modification, or adjustment of a violative condition, or product. For purposes of this definition, violative means the product or condition does not comply with the Acts or associated regulations enforced by the Agency.

Voluntary destruction in lieu of seizure of small lots of violative goods shall be encouraged, where the proposed method is adequate. Supervision of voluntary segregation and denaturing of violative goods shall not be provided, except where it can be accomplished with dispatch, minimal inspectional resources, and in a manner consistent with procedures outlined in this Sub Chapter.

The most extensive actions in this area usually occur in disaster situations. Follow instructions in IOM Subchapter 940 - Disaster Procedures.

Do not engage in actual destruction, reconditioning, repair, modification, etc. of goods. This is the responsibility of the owner or dealer. You are in the capacity of witness only. Samples should be collected of violative goods prior to voluntary destruction to support subsequent action against the responsible individuals. Take photographs where applicable. See IOM 591.1 and IOM 749.

741 DESTRUCTION

Before you supervise destruction, be sure management is aware the action is voluntary and that you are acting only as a witness. See IOM 749.

Witness all destructions personally, making certain that destroyed goods are rendered totally unsalvageable for food, drug, device, etc. use. Keep in mind personal and public safety. Exercise proper precautions in dealing with potentially dangerous substances and situations. Comply with local ordinances regarding the disposition of garbage and trash.

Note certain products should not be disposed of in a conventional manner (e.g.: sanitary landfill, flushing down the drain, etc.). In particular, certain products which have been banned in the past (chloroform, methapyrilene, hexachlorophene, PCB, etc.), are classified by EPA as hazardous and toxic substances and may require a special method of disposal by a licensed hazardous disposal facility. Any possible hazardous or toxic substance (carcinogen, mutagen, etc.) should not be disposed of without prior consultation by the firm with the U.S. Environmental Protection Agency and/or the regulating state authority. Refer to 21 CFR 25 and the National Environmental Protection Act for guidance regarding the environmental impact of voluntary destructions.

741.1 DEA Controlled Drugs

FDA and DEA have a written policy to permit FDA representatives, in certain situations, to witness the destruction of DEA controlled drugs. The procedures and instructions to follow when these drugs are destroyed are:

DEA Approval - FDA and the Drug Enforcement Administration (DEA) have a mutual, written policy concerning witnessing the destruction of drugs under the distribution control of DEA. This provides for FDA, upon receiving a request to witness such destruction, to advise the DEA regional office and obtain approval for the action. If approval is requested by telephone and verbally approved, the approval should be reduced to writing for the record.

Procedure - The necessity for FDA personnel to witness destruction of DEA controlled drugs will normally happen only when FDA is already present in the firm, encounters DEA controlled drugs, and is requested to witness destruction, or when DEA controlled drugs are to be destroyed at the same time FDA is witnessing destruction of drugs not under DEA control.

If you are in a firm either making an inspection or to witness destruction of drugs under FDA's distribution control, and the firm requests you also witness destruction of DEA controlled drugs, do not commit yourself. Telephone your supervisor for instructions. You will be advised whether or not to proceed after your district communicates with DEA. In all other situations refer the requester to DEA.

If the request to witness the destruction is approved, observe the destruction, and prepare DEA Form DEA 41, as follows:

1. List each dosage form of each drug on a separate line. Calculate amounts for columns 6 and 7.
2. Line out the inappropriate sentences in the paragraph following line 32.
3. Date and sign the form.
4. Type or print your name, title, and district under your signature.

Prepare the original only and submit it to your district for transmittal to DEA.

742 RECONDITIONING

The supervision of voluntary segregation of violative goods without the regulatory safeguards of seizure should be avoided. Voluntary segregation and destruction of violative lots should be encouraged; but under no circumstances should you supervise the voluntary segregation and salvage of unfit goods, regardless of the nature of the violation or the size of the lot. Be sure management is aware the segregation is its responsibility. Collect samples where indicated, and/or advise the dealer or owner of his responsibilities under the law. If the dealer decides to voluntarily destroy any lot, refer him to the National Environmental Protection Act (NEPA). See IOM 741.

749 REPORTING

Report any voluntary correction of a problem unrelated to a district recommendation for regulatory action.

749.1 Documenting Voluntary Destruction

Prior to supervising voluntary destruction, prepare a statement on the firm's letterhead or on an FDA 463a, Affidavit, providing the following information.

1. voluntary nature of the action, with you as a witness.
2. name of the product, including applicable code marks.
3. condition of the lot.
4. amount.
5. method of destruction.
6. signature of responsible individual.

749.2 Compliance Achievement Reporting

The following are examples of compliance actions to be described in the report, EI Record, and reported into the Compliance Achievement Reporting System in FACTS (Exhibit 590-B) per Data Codes Manual or district office SOP's:

Violative Products - Voluntary destruction by the person in possession of any violative product.

Destruction by Cooperating Officials - Destruction of violative products by a cooperating food or health official, where such product was discovered by and reported to such official by FDA when those officials were doing work for FDA under contract. Do not report formal condemnation by cooperating officials in the usual course of their independent work.

Manufacturer's Raw Materials - Voluntary destruction of manufacturer's raw materials during the course of an inspection. For example, decomposed cream or filthy milk.

Capital Improvements - Significant improvements correcting a violative condition such as new equipment, rodent-proofing, etc. These should be reported at follow-up inspections where actual improvement has been accomplished or committed, and the improvement is the result of a previous FDA observation or suggestion and not as a result of a seizure, injunction or prosecution.

Correction of GMP Deviations - During an inspection the investigator observes GMP deficiencies have been corrected since the previous EI. These corrections are based on the previous FDA 483.

Formula/Label Correction - Based on a sample analysis, consumer complaint, etc., a product formula or label is corrected.

Additional Personnel - Employment of personnel for quality improvement or improved quality control.

Educational and/or Training - Initiation of an educational and/or training program among employees or producers, or other general industry movement to improve conditions.

Do not report:

1. Recalls, although voluntary, because they are already recorded elsewhere (FACTS).
2. Corrections which are not directly attributable to the efforts of FDA, or states under contract to FDA.
3. Corrections as a result of a seizure, injunction or prosecution.

For products involving the field compliance testing of diagnostic X-Ray equipment, use form FDA 2473a to report these actions, as directed by the Compliance Program. Submit the completed form to your district. Your district will submit a copy to the CDRH, Office of Compliance and maintain a copy for the district files.

SUBCHAPTER 750 - DETENTION ACTIVITIES

750 OBJECTIVES

The objective of the detention is to protect the consumer by preventing the presence of or to provide for removal from commerce of meat, poultry, egg products, or devices, which are adulterated or misbranded. The various Acts described in this sub section provide certain detention powers for FDA. Pertinent sections of the Meat Inspection Act (MIA), Poultry Products Inspection Act (PPIA), Egg Products Inspection Acts (EPIA), and the Food, Drug, and Cosmetic Act (FD&C Act), and its Regulations pertaining to detentions, are printed on the reverse of page 1 of the FDA 2289, Detention Notice (IOM Exhibit 750-A).

750.1 Federal Meat Inspection Act

See IOM 311.3 for information.

750.2 Poultry Products Inspection Act

See IOM 311.3 for information.

750.3 Egg Products Inspection Act

See IOM 311.3 for information.

750.4 Food Drug and Cosmetic Act

See FD&C Act section 304(g).

Section 304(g) of the Federal Food, Drug, and Cosmetic Act provides FDA with authority to detain a device believed to be adulterated or misbranded. You should become familiar with this section and the regulations implementing it. See 21 CFR 800.55. At the present time, these regulations apply only to devices intended for human use.

750.5 Definitions

Meat Products and Poultry Products - For FDA purposes, Meat Products & Poultry Products are defined as the carcasses of cattle, sheep, swine, goats, horses, mules, other equines, or domesticated birds, parts of such carcasses, and products made wholly or in part from such carcasses, except products exempted by U.S.D.A. because they contain a relatively small amount of meat or poultry products (e.g.; meat flavored sauces, pork & beans, etc.). Examine labels for USDA Shield or coding information to help determine if it is a USDA product.

Egg and Egg Products - The term "egg" means the shell egg of the domesticated chicken, turkey, duck, goose, or guinea.

The term "Egg Products" means any dried, frozen, or liquid eggs, with or without added ingredients, excepting products which contain eggs only in relatively small proportion or historically have not been, in the judgement of the Secretary, considered by consumers as products of the egg food industry, and which may be exempted by the Secretary under such conditions as he may prescribe to assure the egg ingredients are not adulterated and such products are not represented as egg products. This would be done on a case by case basis by USDA.

Device - Section 201(h) of the FD&C Act defines a device as follows: "The term "device" *** means an instrument, apparatus, implement, machine, contrivance, implant, in-vitro reagent, or other similar or related article, including any component, part, or accessory, which is:

1. recognized in the official National Formulary, or the United States Pharmacopoeia, or any supplement to them,

2. intended for use in the diagnosis of disease or other conditions, or in the cure, mitigation, treatment, or prevention of disease, in man or other animals, or

3. intended to affect the structure or any function of the body of man or other animals, and which does not achieve any of its principal intended purposes through chemical action within or on the body of man or other animals and which is not dependent upon being metabolized for the achievement of any of its principal intended purposes."

751 INSPECTIONAL PROCEDURE

Direct attention to meat, poultry, or egg products only when found during your regular operations; when so instructed in a C/P; following up on complaints; or, on other assignments as directed by your supervisor.

Placing Detention - Consider detention when so instructed by your supervisor, and only when in your judgement it appears the product will not be held voluntarily and arrangements cannot be made for local, state, or USDA authorities to take control.

751.1 Criteria for Detention

The criteria listed are for your guidance in judging whether or not the product or products should be detained. Detention may be made when all of the requirements listed for the particular items are met.

For products subject to the Meat Inspection Act or the Poultry Products Inspection Act the requirements are:

1. The article meets the jurisdictional requirements of section 304 of the FD&C Act and is in commercial channels.

2. The article is located in an establishment which does not have USDA meat or poultry inspection service.

3. The article is intended for human food channels or could be readily diverted into such channels.

4. The article appears to be adulterated or misbranded under the FD&C Act.

NOTE: For any contemplated detentions based on misbranding or adulteration under section 402(b) of the FD&C Act, check with your supervisor. These must be cleared with the Center for Food Safety and Applied Nutrition.

For products subject to the Egg Products Inspection Act the requirements are:

1.   The article, whether or not in interstate commerce, is located in an establishment which does not have USDA Egg Products Inspection Service.

2.   The article is intended for human food channels or could be readily diverted into such channels.

3.   There is reason to believe the article is in violation of the Egg Products Inspection Act.

For Devices the requirements are;

1.   You have reason to believe the device is adulterated or misbranded.

2.   There is no reasonable assurance the device will not be used, moved, altered, or tampered with in any manner before the FDA can take appropriate legal action.

3.   The device is intended for human use.

751.2 Detention Procedure

Immediate Action - After assuring yourself the criteria for detention are met, immediately advise your supervisor of the situation. The information you must furnish should consist of that requested in blocks numbered 2, 4, 5, 7, 8, 10, 11, 13, 15, 17, 18, 19, 20, 22 and 24 on the Detention Notice, FDA 2289. See IOM 751.3. For devices mark #22 and #24 N/A.

If your supervisor instructs you to detain the article, proceed as in IOM 751.3, and 751.4.

Executing The Detention - When you have been authorized by your supervisor to place a detention proceed as follows:

1.   If the product is not currently stored under proper conditions to maintain its integrity, or if devices are stored in such a way as to interfere with the firm's operation, arrange for proper storage as follows:

(a)   Maintain surveillance on in-transit products and detain after products are placed in storage if possible.

(b)   Arrange for the custodian (dealer) to place the product in proper storage if custodian will agree.

(c)   If neither (a) nor (b) is possible, place product under detention and, except for devices, remove it to proper storage facility. Notify the custodian of the place of storage (block 16 on the FDA 2289) and advise your supervisor of the necessity for including this information in the letter to the owner.

After a device is detained, it may not be moved unless specific procedures are followed. Consult your supervisor for guidance.

2.   Personally inform the immediate custodian, at the highest management level, that the article is under U.S. detention, and if a device, that record keeping requirements of 21 CFR 800.55(k) are in force.

3.   Prepare the "Notice of Detention, FDA-2289", as instructed in IOM 751.3 and issue page 1, the original, to the custodian named. If the product is a device, point out the appeal rights of the owner, which are listed on the back of Page 1 of the FDA-2289.

4.   Affix a sufficient number of "Detention Tag, FDA-2290", to the article in a manner to assure visibility.

751.3 Detention Notice FDA 2289

The Detention Notice, FDA 2289, is a pre-numbered five-part snap-out form, constructed and arranged to serve as a Notice of Detention and as a report of the action.

Preparation of Detention Notice - Print or type the information in the appropriate blocks. The first page blocks to be filled in are those numbered 1 through 12, 15 and 16. Once page 1 is completed, signed and issued to the custodian, it becomes an official document and the detention period begins.

You must immediately complete the additional pages of the Notice of Detention (2 through 5) and submit them to your supervisor, for processing the action. Blocks to be typed on these pages are items 13, 14 and 17 through 26. See IOM Exhibit 750-A.

Preparation of Page 1.

1.   DISTRICT ADDRESS, PHONE NUMBER, NAME OF DISTRICT DIRECTOR - This may be typed in advance.

2.   NAME OF CUSTODIAN - Obtain the name of the highest-ranking official of the firm at the place of detention, and issue to him. Page 1 of the FDA 2289 is to be issued to the person named in this block.

3.   DETENTION NOTICE NUMBER - This is pre-stamped on each form. Any correspondence or subsequent actions should reference this number.

4.   TITLE OF CUSTODIAN - Insert proper official title such as president, warehouse manager, etc. Do not use courtesy titles.

5.   TELEPHONE NO. - Insert the office telephone number including area code.

6.   DATE AND HOUR DETAINED - Insert actual date and time you hand the original to the custodian. The period of detention begins when you issue the original to that person.

7.   FIRM NAME - Enter the legal name of the custodial firm.

8.   ADDRESS - Use complete street name, city, state and Zip Code of custodial firm.

9.   MAXIMUM DETENTION _____ DAYS - Enter "20" unless devices are involved. For devices enter either "20" or "30", as instructed by your supervisor.

10.   NAME OF DETAINED ARTICLE - Use the actual name of the actual product e.g., "Beef Pot Pies with mushrooms" not just "Pies". "Dr. Z's Tongue Depressors", not just "device".

11.   SIZE OF DETAINED LOT" - Indicate number of cases or other type container or article and subordinate containers, e.g., 2000 cases/24/#2 cans, 250 half sides pork carcasses, 500/fore quarters veal, 95 crates/50 lbs. whole fryers, 25/30 lb. cans frozen eggs, etc.

12.   DETAINED ARTICLE LABELED - Quote enough labeling so the article can be positively identified. Include product numbers, lot numbers, serial numbers, control codes, grade marks, etc.

13.   APPROXIMATE VALUE OF LOT - This is the wholesale or invoice value of the merchandise. Estimate if there is no documentary reference you can quote.

14.   SAMPLE NUMBER(S) - List numbers of any samples taken in connection with the detention.

15. REASON FOR DETENTION - Describe the apparent violation and briefly list evidence available to substantiate it. If the product is a device, always state not only the section of the FD&C Act the device is believed to violate, but the particulars of the violation as well. Discuss the reasons for detention with your supervisor when you obtain the permission to detain a device. See Page 4 of IOM Exhibit 750-A.

16. DETAINED ARTICLE STORED AT - In most instances this will be the same as the custodial firm indicated in blocks 7 and 8. However, if the product has been moved to another location, enter the name and address of the firm and location where it finally comes to rest and will stay until the detention is terminated. Once the product is detained, it is unlawful to move it without direct authority from FDA except that devices may be moved and processed under 21 CFR 800.55 (h)(2) pursuant to section 304(g)(2)(B) of the FD&C Act.

NAME OF FDA EMPLOYEE - Print or type.

SIGNATURE - Sign the form.

TITLE - Enter your title.

Preparation of Page 2 through 5 - The blocks on pages 2 through 5 are identical and completion of these constitutes your report on the detention, unless directed otherwise by your supervisor.

17. NAME AND ADDRESS OF ARTICLE OWNER - This will probably be the same as the custodian's. However, they may differ in the case of public warehouses or consigned goods. Enter the name and address, including zip code, of the actual owner.

18. NAME AND ADDRESS OF INITIAL SHIPPER OR SELLER - Enter name and address of person or firm who first shipped or sold the product.

19. NAME AND ADDRESS OF SUBSEQUENT SHIPPERS OR SELLERS - If products have passed through more than one firm prior to coming to your attention, list these firms.

20. NAME OF CARRIERS - List carrier or carriers involved, starting with the one who first picked up the article.

21. DATE LOT SHIPPED - Use date on a shipping document, not the invoice date.

22. NAME AND ADDRESS OF PACKING PLANT - Enter firm name and address of the plant where products were actually packed, processed, manufactured or assembled. For devices enter "N/A"

23. DATE LOT RECEIVED - Self-explanatory.

24. PACKING PLANT U.S.D.A. NO. - All plants under U.S. Department of Agriculture inspections are numbered. This number is placed on products packed or processed in that particular plant. Enter the complete number. For devices enter "N/A".

25. DESCRIPTION OF SAMPLE - Describe sample collected in connection with the detention operations. This will be the same as on the C/R.

26. REMARKS - Elaborate on items wherever necessary. List any recommendations you made to the custodian for special storage such as refrigerated, frozen, etc.

Distribution of FDA-2289 - The five-part snap-out is distributed as follows:

Page 1, original - Give to custodian.

Page 2,3,4 - Turn in to your district immediately using the fastest means possible.

Page 5 - Retain in your possession.

751.4 Detention Tag FDA 2290

This tag is a warning and identification device intended to be affixed to the detained products.

Preparation - As soon as you have issued the Detention Notice, fill out Detention Tags, FDA 2290, following the instructions below. See IOM Exhibit 750-B.

Front of Tag.

"DETENTION DATE AND HOUR" - Copy the date and hour of detention from block #6 of the Detention Notice.

"DETENTION NOTICE NO. DN" - Copy the exact number from block #3 of the Detention Notice.

"MAXIMUM DETENTION _____ DAYS" - Copy the number of days from block #9 of the Detention Notice.

"NAME FDA EMPLOYEE" - Print or type.

"SIGNATURE" - Sign.

"TITLE" - Enter your title.

Reverse of Tag.

"NAME OF DETAINED ARTICLE" - Enter the name exactly as in Block #10 of Detention Notice.

"DETAINED ARTICLE LABELED" - Copy enough from Block #12 of Detention Notice to identify the product.

"SIZE OF DETAINED LOT" - Copy from Block #11 of Detention Notice.

Use of Tag - Complete and affix tags so they are visible on several sides of the lot detained. Use sufficient tags to give adequate warning the lot is under U.S. Detention and must not be used, moved or tampered with, in any manner.

Each tag has a self-locking pin, the point of which should be firmly inserted in an appropriate seam, border, flap, or other area of the container or product, and pulled sharply downward to engage the top curve of the pin. Do not just lay tags on the articles. Secure them to the containers or products. If locking pin cannot be used, tape or tie the tag firmly onto the container or item.

Advise the custodian that Detention Tags have been affixed, the reason for the detention and, in the case of devices, advise the custodian the lot may not be moved without written permission of the Agency. In-process devices may be completed without permission. See 21 CFR 800(h)(2) for instructions.

751.5 Termination of Detention

When final action has been taken on the detention, you will be authorized to terminate the detention. This will occur when one of the following conditions has been met.

1. The article has been brought into compliance, denatured or destroyed under appropriate supervision.

2. For USDA products the USDA, state, county, or local authorities have accepted jurisdiction and control of the article.

3. For USDA products, it has been determined there is no significant violation of the FD&C Act, or of the Egg Products Inspection Act, whichever is applicable, and the

USDA has been notified that FDA intends to terminate the detention.

4.   Twenty consecutive days have expired (or 20 or 30 days, for devices), counting from the day and hour of detention of the product.

5.   Seizure or other legal action has been accomplished.

6.   The District Director or the Regional Food and Drug Director orders the termination.

Removal of Detention Tags - As soon as you are authorized to terminate the detention, proceed to where the detained material is stored, personally remove and completely destroy all detention tags. Do not merely throw them in the trash.

Issuance of Detention Termination Notice FDA 2291 - As soon as you have removed all detention tags, tell the custodian the article is no longer under detention. Immediately prepare a Detention Termination Notice by filling out blocks 1 through 10, 12, 13, and the bottom of the form to include name, title and signature. Give the original, (page 1), to the custodian. This terminates the detention.

Complete the remaining blocks on page 2. Use the "Remarks" section to elaborate on pertinent information such as supervision, reconditioning, destruction accomplished, etc. The Detention Termination Notice, FDA 2291 together with Detention Notice, FDA 2289 will, unless instructed otherwise, constitute the complete report on the detention. See IOM Exhibit 750-C.

752   SAMPLING

Official samples of articles involved in this type operation are collected, prepared, and submitted, in the same manner as any other regulatory samples.

753   SUPERVISION OF RECONDITIONING, DENATURING, OR DESTRUCTION

Methods and procedures for reconditioning, denaturing, or destruction, will be proposed to the district by the owner of the merchandise. Do not take any action on this unless you are authorized by your supervisor. The district officials will determine the adequacy of the proposed method. If satisfactory, you will be advised of the procedure and authorized to monitor the action.

When the operation is satisfactorily completed, and when authorized, terminate the detention as indicated in IOM 751.5.

The results of the reconditioning, denaturing or destruction may be described in the "Remarks" section on the Detention Termination Notice, FDA 2291, if desired. See IOM Exhibit 750-C.

759   REPORTING

Except in unusual situations. or unless instructed otherwise by your supervisor, the Detention Notice, FDA 2289, the Detention Notice Termination, FDA 2291, and the FACTS Collection Record, are designed to provide all information required to report the action from detention to termination.

SUBCHAPTER 760 - DENATURING

760   OBJECTIVE

The basic purpose of denaturing is to prevent salvage or diversion of violative materials for human consumption.

761   DIVERSION TO ANIMAL FEED

Carefully consider any situation before agreeing to diversion of contaminated foods to animal feed. The indiscriminate use of contaminated food for livestock may constitute a hazard to such livestock, as well as humans.

When denaturing human foods for animal feed purposes, contact the Center for Veterinary Medicine, Division of Compliance (HFV-236) to determine if the product may be converted safely to animal feed.

Rodent or Bird Contaminated Foods - Diversion of rodent or bird contaminated foods for animal feed is authorized only when the contaminated product is treated by heat to destroy Salmonella organisms. In the case of wheat and other grains containing rodent excreta, a suitable heat process may be used or the product is examined bacteriologically and shown not to contain Salmonella.

Moldy Food - If processors insist on salvage of moldy grain or foods for animal feed use, it must be done under proper supervision, and provide for:

1.   treatment by dry heating to destroy viable spoilage microorganisms (generally, this will result in grain having a toasted color and odor), and

2.   evidence it does not contain mycotoxins, and

3.   evidence, by animal feeding studies, the product is safe for animal use.

Pesticide Contamination - Foods contaminated by pesticides residues should not be diverted to animal food use unless a determination is made which assures illegal residues will not result in the food animal or their food products, e.g., meat, milk, eggs.

762   DECHARACTERIZATION FOR NON-FOOD OR FEED PURPOSES

The choice of methods, should be made by considering the type of the denaturant, the physical properties of the diverted material, and the ultimate use of the article.

SUBCHAPTER 770 - REGULATORY SUBMISSIONS

Subchapter 770 provides information on the procedures for obtaining information and filing applications with the agency. These will be covered by Center. The filing and registration requirements are directed by the FD&C Act and its implementing regulations. They are filed, in most cases, by industry (e.g.: drug registration, LACF registration & process filing, ANDA's, etc.).

771   CENTER FOR DRUG EVALUATION AND RESEARCH (CDER)

The FD&C Act and its regulations require the filing of certain forms by firms which produce human drugs and drug related products. The requirements and procedures for these are described below.

771.1 Registration and Listing

Owners or operators of all drug establishments not exempt under Section 510(g) of the FD&C Act or 21 CFR 207.10, that engage in the manufacture, preparation, propagation, compounding, or processing of a drug or drugs, including blood products, and biologicals, are required to register each such establishment and to submit a list of every drug in commercial distribution, whether or not the output of such establishment or any particular drug so listed enters interstate commerce. Briefly, registration is accomplished by submitting an FDA 2656 (Registration of Drug Establishment). The drug listing and subsequent June and December updating shall be on form FDA 2657 (Drug Product Listing). In lieu of an FDA 2657, tapes for computer inputs may be submitted, if equivalent in all elements of information specified on the FDA 2657 after initial FDA review and approval of the formats.

Registration and Listing is required whether or not interstate commerce is involved. Detailed registration instructions appear in 21 CFR 207.

An establishment shall register the first time on the form FDA 2656 - Registration of Drug Establishment. The forms may be obtained from: Food and Drug Administration, Center for Drug Evaluation and Research, Office of Management/Division of Management and Budget, Product Information Management Branch (HFD-058), 5600 Fishers Lane, Rockville, MD 20857.

The completed FDA 2656 should be mailed to: Food and Drug Administration, Center for Drug Evaluation and Research, Office of Management/Division of Management and Budget, Product Information Management Branch (HFD-058), 5600 Fishers Lane, Rockville, MD 20857.

General information and questions can be addressed by: Phone: (301) 594-1086 or Mail: Food and Drug Administration, Center for Drug Evaluation and Research, Office of Management/Division of Management and Budget, Product Information Management Branch (HFD-058), 5600 Fishers Lane, Rockville, MD 20857. See IOM Exhibit 540-A for types of drug operations that require registration and listing.

771.2 Investigational New Drug Application (IND)

An application which a drug sponsor must submit to FDA before beginning tests of a new drug on humans. The IND contains the plan for the study and is supposed to give a complete picture of the drug, including its structural formula, animal test results, and manufacturing information. Detailed instructions for the submission of IND's can be found in 21 CFR 312.

771.3 New Drug Application (NDA)

A New Drug Application is an application requesting FDA approval to market in interstate commerce a new drug for human use. The application must contain among other things, data from clinical studies needed for FDA review from specific technical viewpoints, including chemistry, pharmacology, biopharmaceutics, statistics, and microbiology (for anti-infective drugs only). Detailed instructions for the submission of NDA's can be found in 21 CFR 314.

771.4 Abbreviated New Drug Application (ANDA)

A simplified submission permitted for a duplicate of an already approved drug. ANDAs are for products with the same or very closely related active ingredients, dose form, strength, administration route, use, and labeling as a product already shown to be safe and effective. An ANDA includes all the information on chemistry and manufacturing controls found in a new drug application (NDA), but does not have to include data from studies in animals and humans. It must, however, contain evidence the duplicate drug is bioequivalent to the previously approved drug. Information concerning the submission of ANDA's can be found in 21 CFR 320.

772   CENTER FOR DEVICES AND RADIOLOGICAL HEALTH (CDRH)

The FD&C Act, its amendments, and the regulations promulgated under the Act, require the filing of certain forms and submission of certain data by those involved in the production (and in some cases the use) of medical devices and radiological products. Within the CDRH, the Division of Small Manufacturers Assistance (HFZ-220) has been charged with responsibility for providing information and assistance to industry in complying with these requirements. The general requirements are discussed below, as are several issues unique to CDRH submissions.

772.1 Device Registration and Listing

Section 510 of the FD&C Act and 21 CFR 807 describe the establishment registration, device listing, and premarket notification requirements and specify conditions under which establishments are exempt from these requirements.

Manufacturers of finished devices (including device specification developers, reprocessors of single use devices), repackers and relabelers, foreign exporters and initial distributors of imported devices, are required to register their establishments by submitting a form FDA 2891. After initial submission, annual registration is accomplished by use of the Center for Devices & Radiological Health (CDRH) computer generated FDA 2891(a). Component manufacturers are not required to register if the components are sold to registered device establishments for assembly into finished devices. Registration and listing is required, however, if the component is labeled for a health care purpose and sold to medical or clinical users. Optical laboratories, clinical laboratories, dental laboratories, orthotic and prosthetic appliance assemblers, hearing aid dispensers and others who, using previously manufactured devices, perform a service function for physicians, dentists, other licensed practitioners or their patients, are exempt from establishment registration if they are located in the United States. X-ray assemblers are exempt from establishment registration. An exemption from registration does not excempt an establishment from inspection under Section 704 of the FD&C Act.

Each establishment (except contract manufacturers & contract sterilizers located in the United States, and initial distributors of imported devices) required to register must list their devices. Device listing is accomplished using a form FDA-2892; the same form is used to update listing information.

All foreign establishments (including manufacturers and foreign exporters) are required to notify FDA of the name, address, phone and fax numbers, and e-mail address of their United States agent. The United States agent must reside or have a physical place of business in the United States. Post office boxes, answering services and machines are not allowed.

Establishments are required to register and list, even if interstate commerce is not involved. Foreign establishments must register, list and submit a United States agent notification prior to exporting to the United States.

An establishment must initially register on the form FDA 2891, and list on form FDA 2892 which may be obtained from:

1. FDA Internet site: http://www.fda.gov/cdrh/reglistpage.html.

2. CDRH, Division of Small Manufacturers, International and Consumers Assistance (HFZ-220), 1350 Piccard Drive, Rockville, MD 20850, (800) 638-2041 ext. 102 or (301) 443-6597 ext. 102. Please note this is an automated publications' request line. Caller must leave name, address, phone number and publications needed.

A sample United States agent notification letter may be obtained from:

1. FDA Internet site: http://www.fda.gov/cdrh/reglistpage.html.

2. CDRH, Division of Small Manufacturers, International and Consumers Assistance (HFZ-220), 1350 Piccard Drive, Rockville, MD 20850, (800) 638-2041 ext. 102 or (301) 443-6597 ext. 102. Please note this is an automated publications' request line. Caller must leave name, address, phone number and publications needed.

General information and policy questions can be addressed by:

1. Sending an e-mail message to RLPROGRAM@cdrh.fda.gov.

2. Writing to or calling Food and Drug Administration, Center for Devices and Radiological Health, Office of Compliance/Division of Program Operations, Registration and Listing Program (HFZ-308), 9200 Corporate Blvd., Rockville, MD 20850, (301) 827-4555, press 3, then 1.

772.2 Investigational Device Exemption (IDE) Regulation

The IDE regulation in 21 CFR 812 contains requirements for sponsors, Institutional Review Boards (IRBs) and Clinical Investigators. Additional requirements are found in 21 CFR 50, Informed Consent, and 21 CFR 56, IRB's. All Sponsors of device clinical investigations must have an approved IDE, unless specifically exempted by the regulation. Sponsors who have an approved IDE are exempt from requirements on labeling, registration and listing, premarket notification, performance standards, premarket approval, GMPs except the design control provisions, banning of devices, restricted devices, and color additives.

Provisions for obtaining an IDE, and the sections of the regulations, with which sponsors, investigators, and IRBs must comply, differ according to the risks posed by the device. Sponsors of nonsignificant risk devices must obtain IRB approval, and are subject to a limited number of provisions; sponsors of significant risk (See 21 CFR 812.3(m).) investigations are subject to the entire regulation.

There are investigations, described in 21 CFR 812.2(c) that are exempt from the IDE regulation. Exempted investigations apply to devices and diagnostics, which meet the criteria in the regulation. These devices are, however, still subject to other regulatory requirements of the Act, such as labeling, premarket approval of Class III devices, and GMPs (as stated in the preamble to the IDE regulation).

A Sponsor who knows a new device is not "substantially equivalent" to a preamendment device, or who is not sure if a device is "substantially equivalent" without conducting a clinical investigation, must obtain an approved IDE to conduct the clinical investigation. After collecting clinical data, a sponsor who desires to market a device must either submit a premarket notification (510k) or premarket approval application to FDA. A premarket notification may be submitted if the sponsor believes the data supports a finding of substantial equivalence.

Certain radiation-emitting electronic devices that are investigational are also subject to radiological health regulations, 21 CFR 1000 through 1050.

Transitional devices, must have an approved IDE in order to be investigated.

Sponsors, Monitors, IRBs, Investigators, and Non-Clinical Toxicological Laboratories will be covered under the Bioresearch Monitoring Program. FDA has the authority to inspect and copy records relating to investigations. Records identifying patients by name will be copied only if there is reason to believe adequate Informed consent was not obtained, or investigator records are incomplete, false, or misleading.

772.3 Premarket Notification - Section 510(k)

The Medical Device Amendments of 1976 require device manufacturers to notify the CDRH at least 90 days before commercially distributing a device. This is known as a "Premarket Notification" or a "510(k)" submission. "Commercial distribution", for practical purposes, means the device is held for sale. These 501(k) requirements do not apply to Class I devices unless the device is intended for a use which is of substantial importance in preventing impairment of human health, or to any Class I device that presents a potential unreasonable risk of illness or injury. See section 510(l) of the FD&C Act.

A manufacturer must submit a Premarket Notification to FDA in any of the following situations:

1.   Introducing a device into commercial distribution for the first time.

2.   Introducing a new device or product line for the first time, which may already be marketed by another firm.

3.   Introducing or reintroducing a device with significant changes or modifications affecting the safety or effectiveness of the device. Such changes or modifications could relate to design, material, chemical composition, energy source, manufacturing method, or intended use.

These requirements do not apply to "custom devices." A "custom device" is a device made exclusively for, and to meet the special needs of, an individual physician or health professional, or for use by an individual patient named in the order of a physician or dentist (such as specially designed orthopedic footwear). A "custom device" is not generally available in finished form for purchase; and is not offered through labeling or advertising for commercial distribution.

Refer to IOM EXHIBIT 550 for types of medical devices, which require 510(k) submissions. The investigator should document for CDRH review failures to submit required 510(k)s.

772.4 Premarket Approval

Class III devices are required to undergo premarket approval in accordance with the provisions of Section 515 of the Act. Premarket approval for a device is initiated with the submission of an application to FDA. Prior to approval of a premarket approval application (PMA), or a supplemental PMA, FDA has the authority to inspect the applicant's facilities and those records pertinent to the PMA.

C/P 7383.001 contains specific guidance on performing PMA pre-approval and post-approval inspections.

Inspections of manufacturing facilities are usually required prior to approval of a Premarket Approval Application. A full GMP inspection may not be necessary if there has been a recent satisfactory inspection covering a device similar to the PMA device.

Requests for PMA inspections issue from HFZ-306. The assignments will request the firm be inspected for compliance with the GMP regulations, and with their commitments in the PMA.

772.5 Classification of Devices

All medical devices subject to the FD&C Act will be classified into one of the following:

Class I - General - Devices for which general controls (i.e., the controls in Section 501, 502, 510, 516, 518, 519 and 520 of the FD&C Act) provide reasonable assurance of safety and effectiveness.

Class II - Special Controls - Devices for which the general controls, by themselves, are insufficient to provide reasonable assurance of safety and effectiveness of the device, and for which there is sufficient information to promulgate special controls, necessary to provide such assurance.

Class III - Premarket Approval - Devices which:

1.   cannot be placed into Class I or II because insufficient information exists to provide assurance of safety and effectiveness, and cannot be placed into Class II because too little data exists to support the promulgation of Special Controls, and

2.   are purported or represented to be for use in supporting or sustaining human life, or for a use which is of substantial importance in preventing impairment of human health, or

3.   presents a potentially unreasonable risk of illness or injury.

Unless they are determined substantially equivalent to devices distributed prior to the 1976 Medical Device Amendments, devices proposed for marketing after May 28, 1976, fall automatically into Class III. Class III medical devices marketed before May 28, 1976, and the substantially equivalent devices marketed after that date, remain subject to the premarket notification requirements until required to have an approved PMA. Petitioners can request to have such devices reclassified into Class I or II. Transitional devices, those regulated as new drugs before May 28, 1976, are automatically assigned to Class III.

Manufacturers who have questions regarding the classification of a device can write CDRH under Section 513(g) of the FD&C Act and request an opinion as to the status of the device.

772.6 Requests for GMP Exemption and Variances

Section 520f(2)(A) of the FD&C Act allows manufacturers, trade organizations, or other interested persons to petition for exemption or variance from all or part of the GMP. Filing a petition does not defer compliance with the GMP requirements, and petitions will not be processed while an investigation is ongoing, or while regulatory action is pending.

Some Class I devices have been exempted from the GMP through the classification process. Each classification panel was required to consider the Class I devices reviewed by that panel and recommend if they should be exempt from the GMP. Devices exempted from the GMP by the classification process are published in classification regulations in the Federal Register.

Devices labeled or otherwise represented as sterile are not eligible for exemption from the GMP regulation. A sterile device is subject to all GMP requirements pertinent to sterility and sterilization processes.

No exemptions will be granted from 21 CFR 820.198 - Complaint Files, which requires the device manufacturer to have an adequate system for complaint investigation and follow-up. This Policy extends to 820.180 - General Requirements, which gives authorized FDA employees access to complaint files, device related injury reports, and failure analysis records for review and copying.

When FDA has granted a manufacturer an exemption from one or more GMP requirements, the manufacturer still has the responsibility to implement appropriate quality control measures to assure the finished device has the quality it purports to possess, as stated in Section 501(c) of the FD&C Act. A manufacturer who has been granted a GMP exemption is still subject to inspection under Section 704(a) of the FD&C Act, and may be subject to regulatory action if devices are adulterated or misbranded.

772.7 Medical Device Reporting

The Medical Device Reporting (MDR) regulation and the changes mandated by the Safe Medical Devices Act of 1990 (SMDA) is a mandatory information reporting system. It requires manufacturers, importers, and users of medical devices to report to FDA certain adverse experiences caused or contributed to by their devices. This program is administered by the Center's Office of Surveillance and Biometrics. The regulation requires a report be submitted to FDA whenever a manufacturer or an importer becomes aware of information that its device:

1. may have caused or contributed to a death or serious injury, or

2. has malfunctioned and, if the malfunction recurs, is likely to cause or contribute to a death or serious injury.

Under the SMDA of 1990, user facilities must report device-related deaths to FDA and to the manufacturer, if known. User facilities must also report device-related serious illnesses and injuries to the manufacturer, or to FDA if the manufacturer is unknown. In addition, SMDA also requires user facilities to submit to FDA, on an annual basis, a summary of all reports submitted.

The CDRH Division of Small Manufacturers Assistance and the Office of Surveillance and Biometrics should be contacted for further guidance about the MDR regulation. Inspections for compliance with the MDR regulation are conducted following the guidance contained in the MDR Compliance Programs. When reviewing the manufacturers complaint files, look for complaints, which are reportable, and have not been reported by the manufacturer.

772.8 Radiation Reporting

Prior to introduction of products into commerce, manufacturers of radiation-emitting electronic products must submit radiation safety Product Reports if the product is listed and marked in Table 1 of 21 CFR 1002.1. (Non-medical radiation products have NO registration and listing requirements, but the same type of information is included in these reports.) These are premarket documents but there is no timeframe for review and manufacturers do not have to wait for clearance. However, these documents must be processed by CDRH, Office of Compliance to provide rapid import entry of electronic products. Radiation Product Reports provide technical specifications, how products comply with standards, and radiation testing and quality control programs to support the firm's (self)-certification of compliance of each product.

In addition, manufacturers must file annual reports (if specified in Table 1), defect or noncompliance reports when appropriate (similar to recall notices), and accidental radiation occurrence reports when appropriate (similar to, and sometimes replaced by, Medical Device Reports (MDRs)).

773 CENTER FOR BIOLOGICS EVALUATION AND RESEARCH (CBER)

The requirements for the registration and licensing of biological products fall under both the Public Health Service Act (PHS) and the FD&C Act.

773.1 Registration and Listing

See also IOM 562.

Registration and listing forms, FDA 2830, Blood Establishment Registration & Product Listing, and FDA 3356, Establishment Registration & Listing for Human Cells, Tissues, and Cellular and Tissue-Based Products (HCT/Ps), are provided by CBER to industry. Instructions for completing these documents are on the reverse side of these forms along with establishment and product definitions. FDA 2830 forms are available through the district office and the CBER, Division of Blood Applications (HFM-375). Form 3356 is also available though CBER and the district office. Updated forms are also available at: http://forms.psc.gov/forms/FDA/fda.html and on the CBER Tissue Action Plan website at: http://www.fda.gov/cber/tissue/docs.htm. Registration and listing is required whether or not interstate commerce is involved. (See IOM 562)

Human Blood & Blood Products:

1) Who must register - Section 510 of the FD&C Act and 21 CFR 607 delineate the requirements and exemptions relating to the registration of establishments engaged in the collection, manufacturing, preparation, or processing of human blood or blood products. Registration and listing are required whether or not interstate commerce is involved. Fixed blood collection sites which have supplies or equipment requiring quality control or have an expiration date, e.g., copper sulfate, centrifuges, etc., or are used to store donor records, must register. Temporary collection sites, to which all blood collection supplies are brought on the day of collection and are completely removed from the site at the end of the collecting period (except beds, tables, and chairs) and blood mobiles, are not required to register. Licensed firms however, must supplement their establishment license applications for use of bloodmobiles (motorized vehicles for blood and blood component collection and storage). All Military blood bank establishments are required to register. (MOU with Department of Defense [Federal Cooperative Agreements Manual] Regarding Licensure of Military Blood Banks.) Brokers, who take physical possession of blood products, such as in storage, pooling, labeling, or distribution, are required to register.

2) When to register - Such establishments must register within five days after beginning operations and must submit a list of blood products they distribute commercially.

3)   How to register - To register a Form FDA 2830 must be completed. Refer to Compliance Policy Guide (CPG) 230.110 for additional information on registration.

4)   Where to mail completed forms - Mail completed legible forms to: Food and Drug Administration, Center for Biologics Evaluation and Research, Division of Blood Applications (HFM-375), 1401 Rockville Pike, 200N, Rockville, MD 20852-1448.

5)   General Information and Questions -
Phone: (301) 827-3546

Mail: Food and Drug Administration, Center for Biologics Evaluation and Research, Division of Blood Applications, (HFM-375), 1401 Rockville Pike, 200N, Rockville, MD 20852-1448.

Human Cells, Tissues, Cellular/Tissue-Based Products (HCT/P):

1)   Who must register - Establishment registration and exemptions are covered under 21 CFR 1271. Establishments that manufacture HCT/Ps currently regulated under 21 CFR Part 1270 (e.g., bone, skin, corneas, and fascia) must register and list by May 4, 2001. Manufacturers of HCT/Ps not currently regulated under 21 CFR Part 1270 (e.g., reproductive cells and tissue and hematopoietic stem cells) may register in advance of the January 21, 2003 effective date, but will not be subject to the regulations inspections until then. Establishments manufacturing HCT/Ps currently regulated as medical devices, drugs or biological drugs registered with FDA using forms FDA 2891, or 2656 respectively will begin to register and list with FDA using Form 3356 on January 21, 2003. Establishments not required to register are listed in 21 CFR 1271.15.

2)   When to register - Such establishments must register within five days after beginning operations and must submit a list of each HCT/P manufactured.

3)   How to register - To register a Form FDA 3356 must be completed.

4)   Where to mail completed forms - Mail completed legible forms to: Food and Drug Administration, Center for Biologics Evaluation and Research, (HFM-305), 1401 Rockville Pike, 200N, Rockville, MD 20852-1448, Attention: Tissue Establishment Registration Coordinator. Or it may be submitted electronically according to form instructions.

5)   General Information and Questions -
Phone: (301) 827-3546

Mail: Food and Drug Administration, Center for Biologics Evaluation and Research, 1401 Rockville Pike, 200N, Rockville, MD 20852-1448.

773.2 Biologic License

Licensure is a requirement for manufacturers under section 351 of the Public Health Service Act only if products are shipped interstate. Establishments apply for licensure directly to the CBER. An establishment license may cover multiple sites. For each and every product they ship in interstate commerce, firms must obtain a product license. For example, a firm may have an establishment license with product licenses for Red Blood Cells and cryoprecipitate, and also manufacture additional products not shipped interstate for which they do not obtain a license.

What is Reportable - Significant proposed changes in location, equipment, management and responsible personnel. Alterations in manufacturing methods and labeling of any product, for which a license is in effect, or for which an application for license is pending, must be reported.

When to Report - In the case of an emergency, not less than 30 days in advance of the time such changes are intended to be made (21 CFR 601.12(a)).

Where to send Reports - Food and Drug Administration, Center for Biologics Evaluation and Research, Division of Blood Applications, (HFM-375), 1401 Rockville Pike, 200N, Rockville, MD 20852-1448.

774   CENTER FOR VETERINARY MEDICINE (CVM)

Requirements for registration and filing of various applications by firms which manufacture animal drugs, feeds, and other veterinary products are required by the FD&C Act.

774.1 Registration and Listing

Owners or operators of all drug establishments, not exempt under section 510(g) of the Act or subpart D of 21 CFR 207, who engage in the manufacture, preparation, propagation, compounding, or processing of a drug or drugs are required to register. Also, they must submit a list of every drug in commercial distribution, except that listing information may be submitted by the parent, subsidiary, and/or affiliate company for all establishments when operations are conducted at more than one establishment, and there exists joint ownership and control among all the establishments. Registration of animal drug firms is handled by the Center for Drug Evaluation and Research (CDER). CVM maintains its own animal drug listing database.

Who must register - Owners and operators of establishments engaged in manufacture or processing of drug products must register and list their products.

When to register - The owner or operator of an establishment must register within 5 days after beginning of the operation and submit a list of every drug in commercial distribution at that time. Owners or operators of all establishments engaged in drug activities described in 21 CFR 207.3(a)(8) shall register annually, within 30 days after receiving registration forms from the FDA.

How to register - An establishment registers the first time on the form FDA 2656 - Registration of Drug Establishment. The forms may be obtained from: Food and Drug Administration, Center for Drug Evaluation and Research, Office of Management/Division of Management and Budget, Product Information Management Branch (HFD-058), 5600 Fishers Lane, Rockville, MD 20857.

Where to mail completed forms - The completed FDA-2656 should be mailed to: Food and Drug Administration, Center for Drug Evaluation and Research, Office of Management/Division of Management and Budget, Product Information Management Branch (HFD-058), 5600 Fishers Lane, Rockville, MD 20857.

For information on registered firms - CVM's Registration Monitor is Lowell Fried (HFV-214), 7500 Standish Place,

Rockville, MD 20855, (301) 827-0165. You may make inquiries on registration status of individual firms through Mr. Fried.

For information on animal drug listing - CVM maintains its own database for animal drug listing. You may make inquiries for information through Lowell Fried (HFV-214), (301) 827-0165.

774.2 Medicated Feed Mill License (FML)

Who must register - The manufacture of a Type B or Type C medicated feed containing a Category II drug, from a Type A medicated article, must hold an approved license (FDA 3448). The mill must be registered with the Food and Drug Administration, Information Management Team, HFD-095, to obtain a Central File Number (CFN or CF number) and be operating in compliance with Good Manufacturing Practices as described in 21 CFR 225 by passing an inspection conducted by FDA or a designated party.

How to obtain a license application - Form FDA 3448 is available on the Center for Veterinary Medicine's web page. See http://www.fda.gov/cvm/forms/forms.html or from the Food and Drug Administration, Center for Veterinary Medicine, Division of Animal Feeds (HFV-220), 7500 Standish Place, Rockville, MD 20855.
Where to mail completed forms - Mail completed legible form to the Division of Animal Feeds at the address above. Supplemental applications also go to the above address.

General Information & Questions -
Phone: (301) 827-0170.
Mail: Food & Drug Administration, Center for Veterinary Medicine (HFV-220), 7500 Standish Place, Rockville, MD 20855.

774.3 Abbreviated New Animal Drug Application (ANADA)

The Generic Animal Drug and Patent Term Restoration Act amended the FD&C Act to provide for the approval of generic copies of previously approved animal drug products. The generic product may be approved by providing evidence it contains the same active ingredients, in the same concentration, as the approved article, and is bioequivalent. The information is submitted to the FDA in the form of an Abbreviated New Animal Drug Application or ANADA.

How to file - An ANADA must be submitted to FDA on the form FDA 356V. The format and content of the application must be in accordance with the policies and procedures established by FDA's Center for Veterinary Medicine. The application must be filled out completely in triplicate and submitted to the address below.

Where to obtain forms - ANADA's also use the form FDA 356 which can be obtained from: Food and Drug Administration, Center for Veterinary Medicine (HFV-12), 7500 Standish Place, Rockville, MD 20855.

Where to mail completed forms - Completed legible applications should be mailed to: Food and Drug Administration, Center for Veterinary Medicine (HFV-199), 7500 Standish Place, Rockville, MD 20855.

General Information & Questions - Assistance and additional information can be obtained by writing or calling Dr. Lonnie Luther.
Phone: (301) 295-8623.
Mail: Food and Drug Administration, Center for Veterinary Medicine (HFV-102), 7500 Standish Place, Rockville, MD 20855

774.4 New Animal Drug Application (NADA)

A new animal drug is any drug intended for use in animals other than man. Manufacturers of new animal drugs must complete a New Animal Drug Application (NADA), and receive approval prior to distribution.

How to file - Applications must be submitted on a form FDA 356. The applications must be signed by the applicant or by an authorized attorney, agent, or official. The application must be filled out completely, in triplicate, and submitted to the address below.

Where to obtain forms - NADA's use form FDA 356 which can be obtained from: Food and Drug Administration, Center for Veterinary Medicine (HFV-12), 7500 Standish Place, Rockville, MD 20855.

Where to mail completed forms - Completed NADA's should be mailed to: Food and Drug Administration, Center for Veterinary Medicine (HFV-199), 7500 Standish Place, Rockville, MD 20855.

General Information & Questions - General information or questions can be answered by mail or phone by contacting Dr. Lonnie Luther.
Phone: (301) 295-8623.
Mail: Food and Drug Administration, Center for Veterinary Medicine (HFV-102), 7500 Standish Place, Rockville, MD 20855

775 CENTER FOR FOOD SAFETY AND APPLIED NUTRITION (CFSAN)

The FD&C Act and its regulations require certain firms to register and to file scheduled processes, while other firms are requested to do this voluntarily. CFSAN provides guidance and assistance as described below.

775.1 Low Acid Canned Food (LACF) / Acidified Foods (AF) Food Canning Establishment (FCE) Registration

Food Canning Establishments (FCE) (foreign and domestic) engaged in the manufacture of Low Acid Canned Food/Acidified Foods (LACF/AF) offering their products for interstate commerce within the United States are required by 21 CFR Parts 108, 113, and 114 to register their facility with the FDA using form FDA 2541 and file scheduled process information for their products using forms FDA 2541a, "Food Process Filing for All Methods Except Low-Acid Acid Aseptic Systems".

Who must register - All commercial processors of LACF and AF products located in the US, and all processors in other countries who export their LACF or AF into the US must register their processing plants with the FDA.

Wholesalers, importers, distributors, brokers, shippers, etc. are not required to register and file scheduled process information. However, they must ensure the processing firms they represent comply with all registration and process filing requirements.

When to register - Commercial LACF and AF processors in the US must register with FDA not later than 10 days after first engaging in the manufacture, processing, or packing of AF or LACF. Processors in other countries must register before offering any such products for import into the US.

How to register - To register with FDA, processors must complete and submit the FCE Registration Form (FDA 2541) for each processing establishment location.

The pink copy of the FCE Registration form will be returned to the firm or its authorized representative upon assigning of the five-digit FCE number to the plant. For domestic plants, a yellow and blue copy of the FCE Registration Form will be forwarded to the Investigations Branch of the FDA District Office in which the plant is located. The yellow copy is to be used for notifying the LACF Registration Coordinator of the firm's assigned CFN and the blue copy is for the District's Investigations Branch records.

FCE registration information changes - Manufacturers must notify the FDA of any changes to their FCE registration information. These notifications should be for changes in firm name, ownership, street name and number when the plant does not actually change location, preferred mailing address, or authorized representative. This can be accomplished through a letter or submission of a FCE Registration Form listing "Change of Registration Information" and the type of change requested.

Where to mail completed forms - Mail completed legible forms to: LACF Registration Coordinator (HFS-618), Center for Food Safety and Applied Nutrition, 5100 Paint Branch Parkway, College Park, MD 20740-3835.

General Information and Questions -
Contacts: Nathaniel L. Murrell and Renee Duckett Green
Phone: 301 436-2411; FAX: (301) 436-2669
e-mail: LACF@CFSAN.FDA.GOV
Mail: Center for Food Safety & Applied Nutrition, (HFS-618), 5100 Paint Branch Parkway College Park, MD 20740-3835.

Registration changes (street number, authorized representatives, etc.) can also be sent to the above address.

775.2 FCE Process Filing of LACF/AF Processors

In addition to processors registering their establishments with the FDA, processors must also submit and file scheduled process information for their LACF/AF products with the FDA. That information must be submitted on forms FDA 2541a or FDA 2541c. Processes must be filed no later than 60 days after registration and prior to packing a new product or, in the case of firms in other countries, before importing their products into the United States.

It is the responsibility of the manufacturer and/or its authorized representative to ensure the design process used is safe from a standpoint of public health significance

and will destroy or inhibit the growth of microorganisms. This is accomplished through the consultation of and recommendations by a process authority. Documentation that scheduled processes are delivered should be maintained through appropriate and accurate record keeping. Forms and documentation must be presented in English.

Process filing information consists of the following:
1.   FCE number to the plant,
2.   Submission Identifier (SID) number to identify a specific form submitted by the manufacturer,
3.   Governing regulation (LACF – 21 CFR 108.35/113 or AF – 21 CFR 108.35/114),
4.   Food name or description, which includes form or style of the product (whole, sliced, diced, etc.) and packing medium (in water, in brine, in tomato sauce, etc.),
5.   Container type,
6.   Process Establishment Source, and
7.   Container dimensions in inches and/or capacity.

775.3 Cosmetics

VOLUNTARY REGISTRATION OF COSMETIC PRODUCT ESTABLISHMENTS (21 CFR 710)

Who should register - The owner or operator of a cosmetic product establishment, which is not exempt under 21 CFR 710.9, and engages in the manufacture or packaging of a cosmetic product, is asked to register each such establishment, whether or not the product enters interstate commerce. This request extends to any foreign cosmetic product establishment whose products are exported for sale in any State as defined in section 201(a)(1) of the FD&C Act. No registration fee is required.

Time for registration - The owner or operator of an establishment entering into the manufacture or packaging of a cosmetic product should register the establishment within 30 days after the operation begins.

How and where to register - The FDA 2511 - Registration of Cosmetic Product Establishment is available from the FDA, Office of Cosmetics and Colors, Division of Programs and Enforcement Policy (HFS-106), 5100 Paint Branch Parkway, College Park, MD 20740-3835, or at any FDA district office. The completed form should be mailed to the FDA Division of Programs and Enforcement Policy (HFS-106).

Information requested - The FDA 2511 requests information on the name and address of the cosmetic product establishment, including post office ZIP code; all business trading names used by the establishment; and the type of business (manufacturer and/or packer). The information requested should be given separately for each establishment.

General information and questions - Call (202) 418-3414. An instruction is sent with the forms.

VOLUNTARY FILING OF COSMETIC PRODUCT INGREDIENT COMPOSITION STATEMENT (21 CFR 720)

Who should file - Either the manufacturer, packer, or distributor of a cosmetic product is requested to file a FDA-512 Cosmetic Product Ingredient Statement, whether or not the product enters interstate commerce. The request extends to any foreign manufacturer, packer, or distributor of a cosmetic product exported for sale in any State as defined in section 201(a)(1) of the FD&C Act. No filing fee is required.

Times for filing - Within 180 days after forms are made available to the industry, the FDA 2512 should be filed for each cosmetic product being commercially distributed as of the effective date of this part. The FDA-2512 should be filed within 60 days after the beginning of commercial distribution of any product not covered within the 180-day period.

How and where to file - The FDA 2512 and FDA 2514 - Discontinuance of Commercial Distribution of Cosmetic Product Formulation are obtainable on request from the FDA, Office of Cosmetics and Colors, Division of Programs and Enforcement Policy (HFS-106), 5100 Paint Branch Parkway, College Park, MD 20740-3835 or at any FDA district office. The completed form should be mailed or delivered according to instructions provided with the form to: Cosmetic Product Statement, Food and Drug Administration, Division of Programs and Enforcement Policy, (HFS-106), 5100 Paint Branch Parkway, College Park, MD 20740-3835.

General information and questions -
Phone: (202) 418-3414.

775.4 Color Certification Program

Request for Certification - A request for certification of a batch of color additive (straight, repack, lake) should be submitted in duplicate. Formats for these requests are found in 21 CFR 80.21. The fee prescribed in 21 CFR 80.10 should accompany the request, unless the firm has established with the FDA an advanced deposit to be used for prepayment of such fees.

A sample accompanying a request for certification must be submitted under separate cover, and should be addressed to the Food and Drug Administration, Color Certification Branch (HFS-107), 5100 Paint Branch Parkway, College Park, MD 20740-3835.

Where to mail request - Mail or deliver the request to the Food and Drug Administration, Division of Programs and Enforcement Policy (HFS-106), 5100 Paint Branch Parkway, College Park, MD 20740-3835.

General information and questions –
Phone: (703) 266-4601

Contact the Food and Drug Administration, Division of Programs and Enforcement Policy (HFS-106), 5100 Paint Branch Parkway, College Park, MD 20740-3835.

Costs - There is a fee for services provided (analytical work) which will vary based on type (straight, repack, lake), weight, number of batches, etc. See 21 CFR 80.10.

775.5 Infant Formula

Who should register - There are three types of notifications:

1. First Notification - All manufacturers of infant formula sold in the US, and any manufacturer of a "new infant formula", must register with FDA no less than 90 days before it is introduced into interstate commerce.

The first notification shall include:

(a)   the quantitative formulation of the infant formula,

(b)   a description of any reformulation of the formula or change in processing of the infant formula,

(c) assurances the infant formula meets regulations and, as demonstrated by the testing required under quality factors, and

(d)   assurances the processing of the infant formula complies with regulations.

2.   Second notification - This notification is given to FDA after the first production of an infant formula, and before its introduction into interstate commerce. The manufacturer shall submit a written verification which summarizes test results and records demonstrating such formula complies with regulations.

3.   Third notification - This notification must be sent to FDA if a change in the formulation or processing of the formula may adversely affect the article.

Where to mail notifications - Notifications should be sent to: Food and Drug Administration, Office of Nutritional Products, Labeling and Dietary Supplements, Division of Nutrition Science and Policy, HFS-831, 5100 Paint Branch Parkway, College Park, MD 20740-3835.

General information and questions -
Phone: 301-436-1450.

775.6 Interstate Certified Shellfish (Fresh and Frozen Oysters, Clams, and Mussels) Shippers

Persons interested in receiving general information about the National Shellfish Sanitation Program - Contact: Food and Drug Administration, Office of Seafood, HFS-400, 5100 Paint Branch Parkway, College Park, MD 20740 Phone: (301) 436-2300; FAX: (301) 436-2599

Persons interested in technical assistance about the National Shellfish Sanitation Program - Contact: Food and Drug Administration, Division of Cooperative Programs (HFS-628), 5100 Paint Branch Parkway, College Park, MD 20740
Phone: (301) 436-2144; FAX: (301) 436-2672

Persons interested in receiving the Interstate Certified Shellfish Shippers List (ICSSL) - Contact: Charlotte V. Epps. Mail: Food and Drug Administration, Division of Cooperative Programs (HFS-625), 5100 Paint Branch Parkway, College Park, MD 20740
Phone: (301) 436-2154; FAX: (301) 436-2672

775.7 Interstate Milk Shippers (IMS)

Rules for inclusion in the IMS List - All Grade A milk shippers certified by State Milk Sanitation Rating authorities as having attained an acceptable sanitation compliance and enforcement rating are include in the IMS list. These ratings are based on compliance with the requirements of the "USPHS/FDA Grade A Pasteurized Milk Ordinance (PMO) and/or the Grade A Condensed and Dry Milk Products and Condensed and Dry Whey Ordinance (DMO)" and are made in accordance with the procedures set forth in "Methods of Making Sanitation Rating of Milk Shippers" and the "Procedures Governing the Cooperative State-Public

Health Service/ Food and Drug Administration Program of the National Conference on Interstate Milk Shippers". The IMS List is published semi-annually and updated monthly on the FDA website. To obtain a free copy of the IMS List contact:

> Food and Drug Administration
> Milk Safety Branch (HFS-626)
> Division of Cooperative Programs
> 5100 Paint Branch Parkway
> College Park, MD 20740

General Information and Questions.

Contact: Milk Safety Branch (HFS-626), Division of Cooperative Programs, Food and Drug Administration, 5100 Paint Branch Parkway, College Park, MD 20740 Phone: (301) 436-2175; FAX: (301) 436-271

YOUR RIGHTS

Place _____

Date _____

Time _____

Before we ask you any questions, you must understand your rights.

You have the right to remain silent.

Anything you say can be used against you in court.

You have the right to talk to a lawyer for advice before we ask you any questions and to have him with you during questioning.

If you cannot afford a lawyer, one will be appointed for you before any questioning if you wish.

If you decide to answer questions now without a lawyer present, you will still have the right to stop answering at any time. You also have the right to stop answering at any time until you talk to a lawyer.

WAIVER OF RIGHTS

I have had read to me this statement of my rights and I understand what my rights are. I am willing to make a statement and answer questions. I do not want a lawyer at this time. I understand and know what I am doing. No promises or threats have been made to me and no pressure or coercion of any kind has been used against me.

Signed _____

Witness: _____

Witness: _____

Time: _____

EXHIBIT 700-A   INVESTIGATIONS OPERATIONS MANUAL

SUS DERECHOS

Lugar _____
Fecha _____
Hora _____

Antes de hacerle pregunta alguna, Ud. debe entender lo que son sus derechos.

Ud. tiene el derecho de mantener silencio.

Culquier cosa que diga Ud. puede ser usada en su contra en un tribunal.

Ud. tiene el derecho de consultar con un abogado para que éste le aconseje antes de que le hagamos las preguntas y también tiene derecho a la presencia del abogado durante el interragatorio.

Si Ud. no puede pagar los gastos de un abogado, se le asignara uno antes de iniciarse el interragotorio, si así lo desea Ud.

Si Ud. se decide a contestar las preguntas ahora sin la presencia del abogado, Ud. tiene todavía el derecho de negarse a contestar en cualquier momento. Ud. tiene también el derecho de interrumpir las contestaciones en cualquier momento hasta que haya consultado con un abogado.

RENUNCIA A LOS DERECHOS

Me han leído esta declaración de mis derechos y entiendo lo que son. Estoy despuesto a hacer una declaración y a contestar las preguntas. No quiero que esté presente un abogado en este momento. Tengo conciencia de lo que hago. No se me han hecho ni promesas ni amenazas y no se has ejercido presión alguna en mi contra.

Firmado _____

Testigo: _____

Testigo: _____

Hora: _____

DEPARTMENT OF HEALTH AND HUMAN SERVICES PUBLIC HEALTH SERVICE FOOD AND DRUG ADMINISTRATION DETENTION NOTICE	1. DISTRICT ADDRESS, PHONE NUMBER, NAME OF DISTRICT DIRECTOR 850 Third Ave. Brooklyn, NY 11232 Thomas Gardine (718) 340-7000

2. NAME OF CUSTODIAN TO: Mr. William Jantz		3. DETENTION NOTICE NUMBER
4. TITLE OF CUSTODIAN Warehouse Manager, Division II	5. TELEPHONE NO. 716- 843-7066	DN **60006**

7. FIRM NAME Amoure Cold Storage Co., Inc.	6. DATE AND HOUR DETAINED 1-30-99	10:45 a.m. p.m.

8. ADDRESS *(Street, City, State, ZIP code)* 245 Dockage St. Buffalo, NY 14206	9. MAXIMUM DETENTION Twenty (20) _____ DAYS

Pursuant to Sections 402 and 409(b) of the Federal Meat Inspection Act; Sections 19 and 24(b) of the Poultry Products Inspection Act; Sections 19 and 23(d) of the Egg Products Inspection Act; or Section 304(g) of the Federal Food, Drug, and Cosmetic Act, the merchandise listed below is hereby detained for the period indicated and must not be used, moved, altered or tampered with in any manner during that period (except that device may be moved and processed under 21 CFR 800.55(h)(2) pursuant to Section 304(g)(2)(B) of the latter Act) without the written permission of an authorized representative of the Secretary of the U.S. Department of Health and Human Services.

10. NAME OF DETAINED ARTICLE Beefy Brand Beef Pot Pie with Mushrooms	11. SIZE OF DETAINED LOT 1600cs/24 – 1 lb. 2 oz tins

12. DETAINED ARTICLE LABELED *(Include Master Carton Label)*
Tins lbld in part "Beefy Brand Pot Pie***ingredients: Selected beef, choice green peas, carrots, selected Idaho potatoes, Mushrooms***Gravy***1 lb. 2 oz.***Packed by Burly Products Co.***Kansas City, MO EST 223" Tins in cs lbld similarly.

15. REASON FOR DETENTION Estimated 10% of tins swelled and/or leaking.	16. DETAINED ARTICLE STORED AT *(Name, Address, ZIP code)* Amoure Cold Storage Co., Inc. Warehouse 3B, 321 Dockage St. Buffalo, NY 14206

Sections 402 and 409(b) of the federal Meat Inspection Act is quoted below:

   "Sec. 402. Whenever any carcass, part of a carcass, meat or meat food product of cattle, sheep, swine, goats, horses, mules, or other equines or any product exempted from the definition of a meat food product, or any dead, dying, disabled, or diseased cattle, sheep, swine, goat, or equine is found by any authorized representative of the Secretary upon any premises where it is held for purposes of, or during or after distribution in, commerce or otherwise subject to Title I or II of this Act, and there is reason to believe that any such article is adulterated or misbranded and is capable of use as human food, or that it has not been inspected, in violation of the provisions of Title I of this Act or of any other Federal law or the laws of any State or Territory or the District of Columbia, or that such article or animal has been or is intended to be, distributed in violation of any such provisions, it may be detained by such representative for a period not to exceed twenty days, pending action under Section 403 of this Act or notification of any Federal, State, or other governmental authorities having jurisdiction over such article or animal, and shall not be moved by any person, firm, or corporation from the place at which it is located when so detained, until release by such representative. All official marks may be required by such representative to be removed from such article or animal before it is released unless it appears to the satisfaction of the Secretary that the article or animal is eligible to retain such marks. (21 U.S.C. 672.)

Sec. 409.

   (b) The detainer authority conferred by Section 402 of this Act shall apply to any authorized representative of the Secretary of Health and Human Services for purposes of the enforcement of the Federal, Food, Drug, and Cosmetic Act with respect to any carcass, part thereof, meat, or meat food product of cattle, sheep, swine, goats, or equines that is outside any premises at which inspection is being maintained under this Act, and for such purposes the first reference to the Secretary in Section 402 shall be deemed to refer to the Secretary of Health and Human Services. (21 U.S.C. 679)"

Sections 19 and 24(b) of the Poultry Products Inspection Act is quoted below:

   "Sec. 19. Whenever any poultry product, or any product exempted from the definition of a poultry product, or any dead, dying, disabled, or diseased poultry is found by an authorized representative of the Secretary upon any premises where it is held for purposes of, or during or after distribution in, commerce or otherwise subject to this Act, and there is reason to believe that any such article is adulterated or misbranded and

(Continued on the reverse of this form)

NAME OF FDA EMPLOYEE *(Type or Print)* Sylvia A. Rogers	TITLE *(FDA Employee)* Investigator	SIGNATURE *(FDA Employee)* *Sylvia A. Rogers*

FORM FDA 2289 (11/89)	PREVIOUS EDITION MAY BE USED	**DETENTION NOTICE 1**

EXHIBIT 750-A   INVESTIGATIONS OPERATIONS MANUAL

is capable of use as human food, or that it has not been inspected, in violation of the provisions of this Act or of any other Federal law or the Laws of any State or Territory, or the District of Columbia, or that it has been or is intended to be, distributed in violation of any such provisions, It may be detained by such representative for a period not to exceed twenty days, pending action under Section 20 of this Act or notification of Any Federal, State, or other governmental authorities having jurisdiction over such article or poultry, and shall not be moved by any person, from The place at which it is located when so detained, until released by such representative. All official marks may be required by such representative To be removed from such article or poultry before it is released unless it appears to the satisfaction of the Secretary that the article or poultry is Eligible to retain such marks."

Sec. 24.

"(b) The detainer authority conferred by Section 19 of this Act shall apply to any authorized representative of the Secretary of Health and Human Services for purposes of the enforcement of the Federal Food, Drug and Cosmetic Act with respect to any poultry carcass, or part or product thereof, That is outside any official establishment, and for such purposes for first reference to the Secretary in Section 19 shall be deemed to refer to the Secretary of Health and Human Services."

Sections 19 and 23(d) of the Egg Products Inspection Act is quoted below:

"Sec. 19. Whenever any eggs or egg products subject to the Act, are found by any authorized representative of the Secretary upon any premises and there is reason to believe that they are or have been processed, brought, sold, possessed, used, transported, or offered or received for sale or transportation in violation of this Act or that they are in any other way in violation of this Act, or whenever any restricted eggs capable of use as human food are found by such a representative in the possession of any person not authorized to acquire such eggs under the regulations of the Secretary, such articles may be detained by such representative for a reasonable period but not to exceed twenty days, pending action under Section 20 of this Act or notification of any Federal, State, or other governmental authorities having jurisdiction over such articles and shall not Be moved by any person from the place at which they are located when so detained until released by such representative. All official marks may be required by such representative to be removed from such articles before they are released unless it appears to the satisfaction of the Secretary That the articles are eligible to retain such marks."

"Sec. 23(d). The detainer authority conferred on representatives of the Secretary of Agriculture by Section 19 of this Act shall apply to any authorized representative of the Secretary of Health and Human Services for the purposes of paragraph (d) of Section 5 of this Act, with respect to any eggs or egg products that are outside any plant processing egg products."

Section 304(g) of the Food, Drug and Cosmetic Act is quoted below:

"(g)(1) If during an inspection conducted under Section 704 of a facility or a vehicle, a device which the officer or employee making the inspection has reason to believe is adulterated or misbranded is found in such facility or vehicle, such officer or employee may order the device detained (in accordance with regulations prescribed by the Secretary) for a reasonable period which may not exceed twenty days unless the Secretary determines that a period of detention greater than twenty days is required to institute an action under Subsection (a) or Section 302, in which case he may authorize a detention period of not to exceed thirty days. Regulations of the Secretary prescribed under this paragraph shall require that before a device may be ordered detained under this paragraph the Secretary or an officer or employee designated by the Secretary approve such order. A detention order under this paragraph may require the labeling or marking of a device during the period of its detention for the purpose of identifying the device as detained. Any person who would be entitled to claim a device if it were seized under Subsection (a) may appeal to the Secretary A detention of such device under this paragraph. Within five days of an appeal of a detention is filed with the Secretary, the Secretary Shall after affording opportunity for an informal hearing by order confirm the detention or revoke it.
"(2)(A) Except as authorized by subparagraph (B), a device subject to a detention order issued under paragraph (1) shall not be moved by any person from the place at which it is ordered detained until -
"(i) released by the Secretary, or
"(ii) the expiration of the detention period applicable to such order, whichever occurs first.
"(B) A device subject to a detention order under paragraph (1) may be moved -
"(i) in accordance with regulations prescribed by the Secretary, and
"(ii) if not in final form for shipment, at the discretion of the manufacturer of the device for the purpose of completing the work required to put it in such form."

Section 800.55(g)(1)-(2) of Title 21, Code of Federal Regulations, is quoted below as notice of opportunity for appeal and a regulatory hearing:

"(g) **Appeal of a detention order.** (1) A person who would be entitled to claim the devices, if seized, may appeal a detention order. Any appeal shall be submitted in writing to FDA District Director in whose district the devices are located within 5 working days of receipt of a detention order. If the appeal includes a request for an informal hearing, as defined in Section 201(y) of the Act, the appellant shall request either that a hearing be held within 5 working days after the appeal is filed or that the hearing be held at a later date, which shall not be later than 20 calendar days after receipt of the detention order.

(2) The appellant of a detention order shall state the ownership or proprietary interest the appellant has in the detained devices. If the detained devices are located at a place other than an establishment owned or operated by the appellant, the appellant shall include documents showing that the appellant would have legitimate authority to claim the devices if seized."

Any informal hearing on an appeal of a detention order shall be conducted as a regulatory hearing under 21 CFR Part 16, with certain exceptions Described in 21 CFR § 800.55(g)(3).

FORM FDA 2289 (11/89)   (BACK)

DEPARTMENT OF HEALTH AND HUMAN SERVICES PUBLIC HEALTH SERVICE FOOD AND DRUG ADMINISTRATION **DETENTION NOTICE**	1. DISTRICT ADDRESS, PHONE NUMBER, NAME OF DISTRICT DIRECTOR 850 Third Ave. Brooklyn, NY 11232 Thomas Gardine (718) 340-7000

2. NAME OF CUSTODIAN TO: Mr. William Jantz		3. DETENTION NOTICE NUMBER DN **60006**	
4. TITLE OF CUSTODIAN Warehouse Manager, Division II	5. TELEPHONE NO. 716- 843-7066	6. DATE AND HOUR DETAINED 1-30-99	10:45 a.m. p.m.
7. FIRM NAME Amoure Cold Storage Co., Inc.			
8. ADDRESS *(Street, City, State, ZIP code)* 245 Dockage St. Buffalo, NY 14206		9. MAXIMUM DETENTION Twenty (20) _____ DAYS	

Pursuant to Sections 402 and 409(b) of the Federal Meat Inspection Act; Sections 19 and 24(b) of the Poultry Products Inspection Act; Sections 19 and 23(d) of the Egg Products Inspection Act; or Section 304(g) of the Federal Food, Drug, and Cosmetic Act, the merchandise listed below is hereby detained for the period indicated and must not be used, moved, altered or tampered with in any manner during that period (except that device may be moved and processed under 21 CFR 800.55(h)(2) pursuant to Section 304(g)(2)(B) of the latter Act) without the written permission of an authorized representative of the Secretary of the U.S. Department of Health and Human Services.

10. NAME OF DETAINED ARTICLE Beefy Brand Beef Pot Pie with Mushrooms	11. SIZE OF DETAINED LOT 1600cs/24 – 1 lb. 2 oz tins
12. DETAINED ARTICLE LABELED *(Include Master Carton Label)* Tins lbld in part "Beefy Brand Pot Pie***ingredients: Selected beef, choice green peas, carrots, selected Idaho potatoes, Mushrooms***Gravy***1 lb. 2 oz.***Packed by Burly Products Co.***Kansas City, MO EST 223" Tins in cs lbld similarly.	13. APPROXIMATE VALUE OF LOT $19,000.00
	14. SAMPLE NUMBER 55566

15. REASON FOR DETENTION Estimated 10% of tins swelled and/or leaking.	16. DETAINED ARTICLE STORED AT *(Name, Address, ZIP code)* Amoure Cold Storage Co., Inc. Warehouse 3B, 321 Dockage St. Buffalo, NY 14206

17. NAME AND ADDRESS OF ARTICLE OWNER Big Midget Food Chains General Offices – Chicago, Illinois Local Agent – Big Midget, Division 132 2234 Lake drive, Buffalo, NY 14238	18. NAME AND ADDRESS OF INITIAL SHIPPER OR SELLER Burly Products Co. 1921 Packer Avenue Kansas City, MO 64309
19. NAME AND ADDRESS OF SUBSEQUENT SHIPPERS OR SELLERS *(Continue in Remarks, if necessary)* Big Midget Food Chains, Chicago, IL, lot shipped by Burly from KC to Chicago to Big Midget Warehouse 1st & 2nd Ave. Then shipped by Big Midget to Amoure, Buffalo.	20. NAME OF CARRIERS KC to Chicago via Overland Transport, KC, MO Chicago to Buffalo via IS Cartage, Chicago
	21. DATE LOT SHIPPED 1-13-99 to Chicago; 1-20-99 to Buffalo
22. NAME AND ADDRESS OF PACKING PLANT Burly Products Co., Inc. 1921 Packer Avenue Kansas City, MO 64309	23. DATE LOT RECEIVED 1-23-99 in Buffalo
	24. PACKING PLANT USDA NO. EST 223

25. DESCRIPTION OF SAMPLE
Sample consists of 2 cs/24/1 lb. 2 oz. tins taken at rate of 2 tins from each of 24 previously unopened cases selected at random from the lot. Of the 48 tins taken, 24 were swollen to some degree and 12 of these were leaking. The other 24 were normal.

24. REMARKS *(List any recommendations made to custodian for special storage requirements, i.e., refrigeration, frozen, etc.)*
Entire lot was removed from initial location at Amoure Cold Storage Warehouse #2A, 245 Dockage St. to same firm's warehouse #3B at 321 Dockage St., Buffalo, NY, where detention was placed in effect.

NAME OF FDA EMPLOYEE *(Type or Print)* Sylvia A. Rogers	TITLE *(FDA Employee)* Investigator	SIGNATURE *(FDA Employee)* *Sylvia A. Rogers*

FORM FDA 2289 (11/89)   PREVIOUS EDITION MAY BE USED   DETENTION NOTICE 3

EXHIBIT 750-B   INVESTIGATIONS OPERATIONS MANUAL

DEPARTMENT OF HEALTH AND HUMAN SERVICES
PUBLIC HEALTH SERVICE
FOOD AND DRUG ADMINISTRATION

U.S. DETAINED

The lot of goods to which this tag is affixed is

DETAINED BY THE
UNITED STATES GOVERNMENT

In accordance with the provisions of Section 402 and 409(b) of the
Federal Meat Inspection Act; Sections 19 and 24(b) of the Poultry Products
Inspection Act; Sections 19 and 23(d) of the Egg
Products Inspection Act; or Section 304(g) of the Federal Food,
Drug and Cosmetic Act, must not be used, moved, altered
Or tampered with in any manner for the period indicated
(except that devices may be moved and processed under
21 CFR 800.55(h)(2) pursuant to section 304(g)(2)(B) of the latter
act) without the written permission of an authorized
representative of the Secretary of the U.S. Department of
Health and Human Services.

WARNING: Removal, alteration or mutilation of this Tag or
Violattion of any of the above conditions is punishable by fine or imprisonment
or both.

SEE REVERSE OF THIS TAG
FOR DESCRIPTION OF
DETAINED MERCHANDISE

DETENTION DATE	& HOUR 10:45a.m.	DETENTION NOTICE NO.
1-30-2000	p.m.	DN 70007

MAXIMUM DETENTION

_____31____DAYS

NAME FDA EMPLOYEE *(Print or type)*

Sidney H. Rogers

SIGNATURE *(FDA Employee)*
Sidney H. Rogers

TITLE *(FDA Employee)*
Investigator

FORM FDA 2290 (4/86) Prev. Ed. May Be Used
DETENTION TAG

U.S. DETAINED.

NAME OF DETAINED ARTICLE.
Beefy brand pot pie with mushrooms

DETAINED ARTICLE LABELED

"Beefy Brand Pot Pie net wt. 1 lb. 2 oz.
packed by Burly Products Co.
Inc.***Kansas City, MO. EST 223"

SIZE OF DETAINED LOT

1600 cs/28/1 lb. 2oz. tins

SEE REVERSE

DEPARTMENT OF HEALTH AND HUMAN SERVICES PUBLIC HEALTH SERVICE FOOD AND DRUG ADMINISTRATION	1. DISTRICT ADDRESS, PHONE NUMBER, NAME OF DISTRICT DIRECTOR 850 Third Ave. Brooklyn, NY 11232 Thomas Gardine (718) 340-7000	

TO:	2. NAME OF CUSTODIAN Mr. William Jantz	3, DETENTION NOTICE NUMBER **DN 60006**	

4. TITLE OF CUSTODIAN Warehouse Manager, Division II	5. DATE AND HOUR DETAINED 1-30-99	10:45 a.m. p.m.

6. FIRM NAME Amoure Cold Storage Co., Inc.	7. DATE AND HOUR DETENTION TERMINATED 2-6-99	8:35 a.m. p.m.

8. ADDRESS (Street, city, and state) 245 Dockage St. Buffalo, NY	9. ZIP CODE 14206

The merchandise listed below which, pursuant to Sections 402 and 409(b) of the Federal Meat Inspection Act; Sections 19 and 24(b) of the Poultry Products Inspection Act; Sections 19 and 23(d) of the Egg Products Inspection Act; or Section 304(g) of the Federal Food, Drug, and Cosmetic Act, was detained on the above date and bears the above detention number, is hereby released and the detention is terminated.

10. NAME OF DETAINED ARTICLE Beefy Brand Beef Pot Pie with Mushrooms	11. SIZE OF DETAINED LOT 1600cs/24 – 1 lb. 2 oz tins

12. DETAINED ARTICLE LABELED (Include Master Carton Label)
Tins labeled in part with paper labels: "Beefy Brand Pot Pie***ingredients: Selected beef, choice green peas, carrots, selected Idaho potatoes, Mushrooms***Gravy composed of: Water, beef stock, and flour***Net Wt. 1 lb. 2 oz.***Packed by Burly Products Co.***General Offices Kansas City, MO EST 223" Tins in cases labeled in part: "***24/ 1 lb 2 oz tins Beefy Pot Pies***EST 223***"

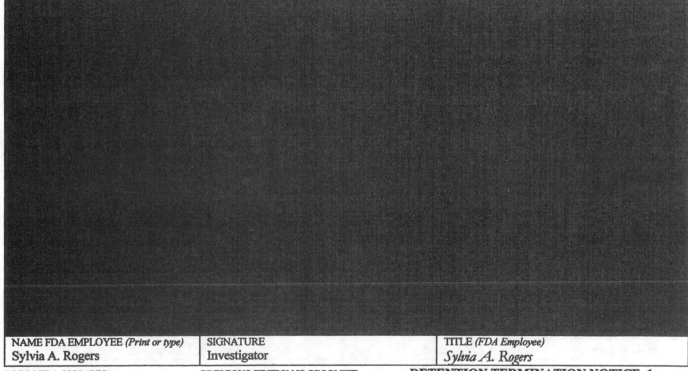

NAME FDA EMPLOYEE (Print or type) Sylvia A. Rogers	SIGNATURE Investigator	TITLE (FDA Employee) Sylvia A. Rogers

FORM FDA 2291 (6/82)   PREVIOUS EDITION IS OBSOLETE   **DETENTION TERMINATION NOTICE 1**

EXHIBIT 750-C   INVESTIGATIONS OPERATIONS MANUAL

DEPARTMENT OF HEALTH AND HUMAN SERVICES PUBLIC HEALTH SERVICE FOOD AND DRUG ADMINISTRATION	1. DISTRICT ADDRESS, PHONE NUMBER, NAME OF DISTRICT DIRECTOR 850 Third Ave. Brooklyn, NY 11232 Thomas Gardine (718) 340-7000	

TO:	2. NAME OF CUSTODIAN Mr. William Jantz	3, DETENTION NOTICE NUMBER DN 60006	

4. TITLE OF CUSTODIAN Warehouse Manager, Division II	5. DATE AND HOUR DETAINED 1-30-99	10:45 a.m. p.m.

6. FIRM NAME Amoure Cold Storage Co., Inc.	7. DATE AND HOUR DETENTION TERMINATED 2-6-99	8:35 a.m. p.m.

8. ADDRESS (Street, city, and state) 245 Dockage St. Buffalo, NY	9. ZIP CODE 14206

The merchandise listed below which, pursuant to Sections 402 and 409(b) of the Federal Meat Inspection Act; Sections 19 and 24(b) of the Poultry Products Inspection Act; Sections 19 and 23(d) of the Egg Products Inspection Act; or Section 304(g) of the Federal Food, Drug, and Cosmetic Act, was detained on the above date and bears the above detention number, is hereby released and the detention is terminated.

10. NAME OF DETAINED ARTICLE Beefy Brand Beef Pot Pie with Mushrooms	11. SIZE OF DETAINED LOT 1600cs/24 – 1 lb. 2 oz tins

12. DETAINED ARTICLE LABELED (Include Master Carton Label)
Tins labeled in part with paper labels: "Beefy Brand Pot Pie***ingredients: Selected beef, choice green peas, carrots, selected Idaho potatoes, Mushrooms***Gravy composed of: Water, beef stock, and flour***Net Wt. 1 lb. 2 oz.***Packed by Burly Products Co.***General Offices Kansas City, MO EST 223" Tins in cases labeled in part: "***24/ 1 lb 2 oz tins Beefy Pot Pies***EST 223***"

REMARKS

The Culmore County Health department assumed jurisdiction of the product at 8:35 AM on 2-6-99 when it was released form US detention. The entire 1600 case lot was hauled on 2-6-99 by the ACE Trucking Co., 2993 Longway Place, Buffalo, NY, from Amoure Cold Storage Co., Warehouse #3B, 321 Dockage St., Buffalo, NY, to the county landfill at Port Road and Culmore County Road #8 where the lot was dumped, crushed by bulldozers, buried in a ditch, and covered with approximately five feet of earth.

The entire operation was supervised by Culmore County Health Department Inspectors Robert J. Sandi and Henry D. Larky and FDA Investigator Sylvia A. Rogers.

FDA supervision time and expenses:
    Inspectional time – 6 hours
    Mileage – 22 miles in US Gov't car G11-396

Sylvia A. Rogers
Sylvia A. Rogers
Investigator

NAME FDA EMPLOYEE (Print or type) Sylvia A. Rogers	SIGNATURE Investigator	TITLE (FDA Employee) *Sylvia A. Rogers*

FORM FDA 2291 (6/82)   PREVIOUS EDITION IS OBSOLETE   DETENTION TERMINATION NOTICE 2

CHAPTER 8 - RECALL ACTIVITIES

CONTENTS

SUBCHAPTER 800 - RECALLS

801   DEFINITIONS

801.1 Recall

A Recall is a firm's removal or correction of a marketed product that FDA considers to be in violation of the laws it administers, and against which the Agency would initiate legal action (e.g., seizure). Recall does not include a market withdrawal or a stock recovery. See the Agency recall policy outlined in 21 CFR 7.1/7.59 - Enforcement Policy - General Provisions, Recalls (Including Product Corrections) - Guidance on Policy, Procedures, and Industry Responsibilities.

Recall Classification - Means the numerical designation, i.e., I, II, or III, assigned by the FDA to a particular product recall to indicate the relative degree of health hazard presented by the product being recalled.
There are three possible classifications.

Class I - A situation in which there is a reasonable probability that the use of, or exposure to, a violative product will cause serious adverse health consequences or death.

Class II - A situation in which use of, or exposure to, a violative product may cause temporary or medically reversible adverse health consequences or where the probability of serious adverse health consequences is remote.

Class III - A situation in which use of, or exposure to, a violative product is not likely to cause adverse health consequences.

Recall Type - A designation based on whether the recall is Voluntary, FDA Requested (at the request of the Commissioner or his designee), or ordered under section 518(e) or the Act.

Recall Strategy - A planned specific course of action to be taken in conducting a specific recall, which addresses the depth of recall, need for public warnings, and extent of effectiveness checks for the recall.

Depth of Recall - Depending on the product's degree of hazard and extent of distribution, the recall strategy will specify the level in the distribution chain to which the recall is to extend, i.e., wholesaler, retailer, user/consumer.

Recall Number - Number assigned by a responsible Center for each recalled product they initiate. This number consists first of a letter designating the responsible Center (see letter Codes below), a 3-digit sequential number indicating the number of recalls initiated by that Center during the fiscal year, and a 1-digit number (the Center for Devices and Radiological Health (CDRH) uses 2-digit numbers) indicating the fiscal year the recall was initiated. For example: F-100-2 identifies the 100th recall initiated by the Center for Food Safety and Applied Nutrition (CFSAN) in FY-2002. The following letters are used to identify the Centers.

Letter	Center/Office
F	Foods – CFSAN
D	Drugs – Center for Drug Evaluation and Research (CDER)
Z	Medical Devices & Radiological Health – CDRH
V	Veterinary Medicine – Center for Veterinary Medicine (CVM)
B	Biologics – Center for Biologics Evaluation and Research (CBER)
N	Medical Devices (Voluntary Safety Alerts & Notifications)
A	Audit Numbers issued by the District performing the recall, the Centers, Office of Enforcement (Division of Compliance Management and Operations [DCMO], or the Division of Field Investigations (DFI) to monitor recalls requiring audit checks.

801.2 Medical Device Notification

__Notification Order__ - An order issued by FDA requiring notification under section 518(a) of the Act. The directive issues when FDA determines a device in commercial distribution, and intended for human use, presents an unreasonable risk of substantial harm to the public health. The notification is necessary to eliminate the unreasonable risk of such harm, and no more practicable means is available under the provisions of the Act to eliminate such risk.

__Notification__ - A communication issued by the manufacturer, distributor, or other responsible person in compliance with a Notification Order. It notifies health professionals and other appropriate persons of an unreasonable risk of substantial harm to the public health presented by a device in commercial distribution.

801.3 Medical Device Safety Alert

This is a communication voluntarily issued by a manufacturer, distributor, or other responsible person (including FDA). It informs health professionals and other appropriate persons of a situation which may present an unreasonable risk to the public health by a device in commercial distribution.

NOTE: Medical Device Notifications and Safety Alerts as described in IOM 801.2 & 801.3 are to be handled by the Districts as recalls. They will go through the stages of alert, recommendation, classification, field notification, firm notification letter, firm effectiveness checks and status reports, FDA audit checks, and termination recommendations.

801.4 Human Tissue for Transplantation

FDA may issue an order for recall, retention, and destruction of human tissue intended for transplantation upon a finding the tissue may be in violation of the regulations in 21 CFR 1270. However, firms are usually afforded an opportunity to take corrective actions voluntarily. The procedures for recall, retention, and destruction in 21 CFR 1270.43 will be used when the FDA finds it necessary to ensure the suitability of human tissue for transplantation. FDA intends to invoke this section when there is evidence a tissue establishment failed to voluntarily address a violation related to tissue suitability, such as the source of the human tissue, the adequacy of the testing or screening of the human tissue, or the adequacy of donor selection. (See 21 CFR Part 1270.43).

SUBCHAPTER 810 - RECALL NOTIFICATION / INSPECTION

If FDA learns of a questionable product which may lead to a recall, an inspection is made to determine the firm's course of action. This inspection should include a determination of the root cause(s) of the problem(s).

NOTE: In all discussions of violative or potentially violative products with the responsible firm, make it clear FDA is not requesting recall action. FDA requested recalls are authorized only by ORA, or by delegation of authority such

as Drug Efficacy Study Implementation (DESI) recall requests.

When an investigation determines there is no evidence of manufacturing or distribution problems, but a firm has removed products from the market as a result of actual or alleged tampering with individual units, the action will be considered a Market Withdrawal. A market withdrawal means a firm's removal or correction of a distributed product which involves a minor violation that would not be subject to legal action by the FDA or which involves no violation, e.g., normal stock rotation practices, routine equipment adjustments and repairs, etc.

810 INSPECTION PROCEDURES

An important part of your job is to identify the "root cause" for the recall and assure the firm has implemented procedures to prevent it from reoccurring. In some cases, management will have conducted its own analysis and reached conclusions about the problem and its cause. The initial judgments about the problem are not always correct nor discriminating enough to identify the underlying causes. You need to verify the steps taken were sufficient in depth and scope and reflect the correct conclusions about both the problem and correction.

Determine if the firm conducted a failure analysis using techniques such as fault tree analysis or failure mode analyses. Did it consider things such as the length of time the product has been manufactured and sold, complaints or returns for the same or similar problems, any reworking of product prior to release or distribution which may have been due to the same or similar problems and, process or personnel changes which occurred about the time the problem appeared.

For all recall inspections, in addition to verifying the identification of the "root cause":

1. Issue a Notice of Inspection (FDA 482)
2. Discuss the suspected problem with management and review the firm's complaint file.
3. Investigate all areas, control points and/or circumstances which may have a bearing on the product's deficiency.
4. Fully develop individual responsibility for the problem.
5. Review batch records, processing logs and/or other types of records for violative lots and associated lots.
6. Review and obtain copies of the firm's quality control/analytical data.
7. Determine any actions the firm has taken, is taking, or has planned to take to prevent similar occurrences. If corrective action is not underway, determine the firm's timetable for achieving correction.
8. Determine what action the firm has taken or plans to take, and the time frames involved, regarding questionable product(s) remaining in commerce.

810.1 Recall Decision Follow-up

If the firm has decided to recall, do the following:
1. Request that management obtain their FDA District's review of recall correspondence and any press releases

before they are issued to prevent misunderstandings between the firm, its customers, and the FDA. This suggestion is voluntary on the part of the firm and is not required.

2. If the firm requests guidance in preparing recall communications, provide it in accordance with your District policy. See Chapter 7 of the RPM and IOM Exhibit 810-A for an example of recall communications.

3. See Attachment B of the Regulatory Procedures Manual Chapter 7 and 21 CFR 7.46a(1)-(9) for information to be obtained.

4. Obtain an Official Sample of the recalled product. (See IOM section 814 for the collection of samples for electronic products or medical devices.)

5. Obtain a complete distribution list of all shipments of the suspect lot(s), including foreign distribution.

6. Obtain specimens or copies of all labels and labeling associated with the recalled product.

7. Obtain complete copies of all recall communications issued or planned including the text of phone conversations, and submit them to your District's recall coordinator.

8. Advise the firm on how the returned products should be handled. FDA must witness or otherwise verify the reconditioning or destruction of the products returned under the recall.

9. Take any other steps necessary in your judgment, or that your District requires.

NOTE: At this early stage there usually has not been a recall evaluation by the appropriate Center. In the absence of such an evaluation, avoid suggesting the firm extend its recall efforts.

811   FOOD RECALLS

Experience with food recalls dictates specific information be obtained from firms which have used recalled material in the production of another product. This is necessary to decide if the recall must be extended to a new product(s). In those instances, the following are some areas to be covered:

1. Incoming ingredient quality control procedures.

2. Quality control over ingredients at the time of use, and the products in which the ingredients are used.

3. A detailed description of the methods used in preparation and packaging of the processed product.

4. How the finished product is stored and shipped.

5. Labeling of product, and any cooking instructions for consumer or purchaser.

6. Quality control testing of the finished product. Detail any test(s) performed by firm.

7. For products produced in USDA plants, determine if the USDA was notified of the suspect incoming ingredient? Did USDA determine what testing was done by the firm?

This information must be evaluated by CFSAN (HFS-607) prior to the initiation of any sub-recall.

811.1 Interstate Milk Shippers

The FDA will not ordinarily be involved in the classification and auditing of Interstate Milk Shippers (IMS) product recalls where such actions have been, or are being, handled expeditiously and appropriately by the State(s). However, the FDA district office in which the recalling firm is located must be assured that all States involved in an IMS plant's recall are participating in ensuring removal of the product from commerce and that, when appropriate, States issue warnings to protect the public health.

In the event that FDA determines that the States are unable to effect the recall actions necessary, the Agency will classify, publish, and audit the recall, including issuance of a public warning when indicated.

812   MEDICAL DEVICE RECALLS

Medical device may result from manufacturing defects, labeling deficiencies, failure to meet premarketing requirements [PMA, 510(k)], packaging defects or other nonconformance problems. How firms identify the causes of medical device recalls and corrective action activities is essential to the analysis of medical device failures and the determination of the effectiveness of the medical device GMP program. It is also useful in evaluating the medical device program, and for directing attention to problem areas during inspections. 21CFR Part 806.1 requires device manufacturers and importers to report certain actions concerning device corrections and removals. They must also maintain records of all corrections and removals regardless of whether such corrections and removals are required to be reported to FDA. (See 21 CFR Part 806.1). Failure to report as required by 21 CFR 806.1 is a violation and should be listed on the FDA-483, "Inspectional Observations." This may be included in a direct reference Warning Letter.

Each device manufacturer or importer must submit a written report to FDA of any correction or removal of a device initiated by such manufacturer or importer, if one was initiated:

1.   To reduce a risk to health posed by the device; or

2.   To remedy a violation of the Act caused by the device which may present a risk to health, unless the information has been provided according to 21 CFR 806.10 (f), or the correction or removal action is exempt from the reporting requirements under 21 CFR 806.1(b).

Collection of complaint, PMA and 510(k) related information is necessary to determine compliance with the GMP requirements. During recall follow-up inspections, answers should be obtained to the questions below, in addition to routine recall information. For firms where it has been established a manufacturing defect led to the recall, conduct a complete GMP evaluation of the manufacturing operations. Report such inspections into FACTS as "qualifying" GMP inspections.

Problem Identification

1.   How did the firm identify the nonconformance which led to the recall, e.g., complaint, in-house data, etc.

2.   If the recall was due to a device defect, did the firm conduct a documented failure analysis of the device, using such techniques as fault tree or failure mode analyses? If so, report whether these results were provided for review.

(a)   Did the firm determine the failure mechanism, e.g., shorted component, incomplete weld, etc.?

(b) If not, how did firm determine the cause of the nonconformance?

(c) If not, what rationale does the firm have for not conducting a failure analysis?

3. Did the firm determine at what phase of the device life cycle the nonconformance occurred, i.e., design, manufacturing, storage, use, etc., and the actual cause of the nonconformance, for example, software design error, process out of specifications, employee error, user misuse, etc.? What evidence does the firm have to support the determination?

4. Did the firm determine if the nonconformance resulted in an injury or death?

5. If a component was responsible for the defect, determine if the same component was used in other devices manufactured by the firm. If so, has the firm conducted an analysis to assure the defect in the component will not have a deleterious effect on the operation of the other device(s)?

6. If a component was responsible for the device defect, what other device manufacturers use the same component (and especially the same lot number of the component)? Has the manufacturer of the recalled device notified the component manufacturer? Has the component manufacturer contacted its other customers about the problem?

7. Why was the component defective? Did the manufacturer of the component change the specifications without notifying the finished device manufacturer? Did the component fail to meet its release specifications?

NOTE: A visit to the component manufacturer may be needed to adequately answer questions 5, 6 and 7. Before doing so, confirm with CDRH and your supervisor that the matter is egregious enough to warrant this "next step."

8. Did the finished device manufacturer have an incoming component/raw material sampling and testing procedure? If not, why not?

9. If the manufacturer recalled the device because the labeling was inaccurate, or the wrong labeling was applied to the device (label mix-up) determine the following:

(a) What quality system procedures should have been established to prevent the problem?

(b) If the label or instructions for use were inaccurate, was the inaccuracy introduced in the design stage, or was it due to a printing problem?

10. If the device has been on the market for a year or more, and the manufacturer claims the problem is the result of design:

(a) Why is the problem just now showing up? How many reports concerning the problem did the firm receive before deciding a recall was necessary? Does the firm have a procedure established for determining if a recall is necessary, and if so, did it follow the procedure? Obtain a copy of the procedure.

(b) If the firm doesn't provide rational answers to the above questions, determine if they explored other possible causes for the problem?

(c) Was the design feature which caused the problem included in the design of the device that was the subject of a premarket submission?

(d) If the design feature which caused the problem is part of the original design, did the manufacturer recall all products manufactured since the device was introduced to the market? If not, why not?

(e) If the problem was introduced via a design change, did the manufacturer follow established design change or change control procedures? If yes, are the procedures adequate? Was the nature of the problem such that it should have been anticipated, and the design verification/ validation study fashioned to detect the problem?

(f) Has the manufacturer recalled all products distributed since the design change was introduced? If not, why not?

Corrective Action

1. Describe the corrective action taken to correct the immediate problem, e.g., redesign, modify SOP, process validation, etc.

2. Did the firm qualify/validate the corrective action?

3. Did the firm establish responsibility to assure that the corrective action would be implemented and satisfactorily completed?

4. What action did the firm take to prevent recurrence of the nonconformance, e.g., training, increased process monitoring, etc.

5. Was the nonconformance information provided to those responsible for the areas in which the nonconformance occurred?

6. Did the firm determine if the nonconformance extended to other devices?

7. Did the firm determine if changes were needed in procedures and, if so, did it validate and implement the changes?

8. Has the manufacturer taken appropriate corrective action?

Complaint and Medical Device Reporting (MDR) Reporting

1. Determine if adequate complaint investigations were performed as required by 21 CFR 820.198(b). Also, determine if the investigation verified the complaint was a failure of the device to meet any or all of its specifications.

2. For complaints related to the recall, the firm should have made a determination whether the events are MDR reportable. Any event associated with a death or serious injury must be reported under MDR. Malfunctions likely to cause or contribute to a death or a serious injury are also reportable under MDR. Document the firm's explanations for the events they believe are nonreportable. Failure to submit required MDR reports are violations, and should be listed on the FDA-483 at the completion of the inspection.

Provide adequate documentation with the EIR to cross-reference complaints with associated MDRs.

Device Information - Obtain the 510(k) or PMA number for each device under recall. If there is no 510(k) or PMA, determine if the device is a pre-enactment device (i.e., in commercial distribution prior to May 26, 1976). If multiple devices are being recalled, obtain this information for each device model or catalog number under recall.

813   DRUG RECALLS

813.1 Recalls of Human Drug Products

If the recalled product is covered by an New Drug Application (NDA) or Abbreviated New Drug Application (ANDA), determine if the defective product involves the type of problems shown under CFR 314.81 (b)(1) (i) and (ii). Also note whether or not the firm reported the problem to the FDA district office that is responsible for the firm within 3 working days of its receipt of the information, as required by that section.

813.2 Recalls of Veterinary Drug Products

Veterinary Drug Products Recalls are classified by and health hazard evaluations are obtained through CVM's Division of Compliance (HFV-230), Gloria J. Dunnavan, Director. To inquire about specific veterinary drug product recalls or to obtain information on how to proceed, contact the Division at (301) 827-1168 or contact Barbara Rodgers at (301) 827-0356.

814   SAMPLE COLLECTION

Collection of samples for regulatory consideration is at the discretion of District management. Consult your supervisor and/or compliance branch for guidance. If a sample is indicated, only collect documentary samples for electronic products or medical devices, unless otherwise instructed.

If, after consulting with the Centers, it is determined that a product must be examined physically for health hazard evaluation, ship an appropriate sample to the designated Center office by the most expeditious and practical means available. Notify the Center of the time and method you sent the product and its estimated time of arrival.

815   RECALL ALERT

When a District learns of or confirms a recall situation exists or is planned, they will give the appropriate Center Recall Office and OE/DCMO (HFC-210) a twenty-four hour alert. See Chapter 7 of the RPM.

816   RECOMMENDATION FOR RECALL NUMBER

A memorandum should be prepared as soon as the recall number is available, and transmitted to your District's R&E Coordinator through your Supervisor. Do not wait for writing, typing and submission of the EIR. A copy of the memo may be attached to your EIR as an exhibit, so the information need not be repeated in the body of the report. From the time the recall alert is sent to the appropriate Center, the district has five days to submit the Recall Recommendation (ten days if the recall is completed). See Attachment B to Chapter 7 of the RPM.

1.   **Product**

For each recalled product, provide: its name; type (e.g. tablet, sugar coated); strength; sizes; form; route of administration; shipping or unit package; and a brief description of the product and its use. If it is a drug product, indicate whether it is a prescription (Rx) or Over-the-Counter (OTC) product. If product labeling does not indicate how the product is to be used, and the health hazard is dependent on use, consult the firm's catalog, the Red Book, or similar sources for that information.

For each recalled product also provide: the brand name; name, address, and type of responsible firm on label; number and description of private labels. Complete copy of all labeling (including product inserts or information sheets). These must be sent to the appropriate Center by an expeditious method.

2.   **Code**

List all lot and/or serial numbers, catalog numbers, product numbers, packer or manufacturer numbers, etc., which appears on the product or its labeling.

3.   **Recalling Firm/Manufacturer**

Provide complete name and address of the recalling firm, and identify the type of firm, i.e., manufacturer, importer, broker, repacker, own label distributor. Provide complete name and address of the manufacturer, if different from the recalling firm. Also identify firms which processed or handled the product, or supplied components which might have been responsible for the problem. Indicate which firm(s) appear(s) responsible for the violation.

4.   **Reason for Recall Recommendation**

Provide detailed information as to how the product is defective and violates the FD&C Act or related statutes.

(a)   Include any analytical findings in qualitative and/or quantitative terms, whether from the firm or FDA analysis, and which laboratory was involved.

(b)   Provide inspectional (e.g., GMP) or other evidence, where appropriate.

(c)   List in chronological order any complaints, injuries, or associated problems with the product. Include any MDR's that have been submitted.

If firm management was advised of FDA findings, and the problem was discussed with them, report their reactions and plans. If the firm advised FDA of the problem, report and explain firm's own analytical results and how it learned of the need for a recall.

Explain all State involvement in the recall, including sample collection or analysis, recall agreement or initiation, recall monitoring, and product disposition.

For DESI related recalls, use the following terminology: "Federal Register Publication (date), Drug Efficacy Study Implementation."

In cases where a veterinary drug product is recalled due to subpotency prior to labeled expiration date provide the following information:

(a)   The firm's stability testing plan (including the analytical methodology) which established the labeled expiration date.

(b)   Specific batch numbers in the stability studies, and assay values that are the basis of the firm's recall.

(c)   Potency specifications which the firm uses for recall purposes.

(d)   Final assay values for the active ingredients which were the basis of the initial release of the batch.

Note if information regarding stability data on file with the firm, and the Quality Control (QC) procedures used by the firm to determine the potency of the active ingredients, is available in the EIR.

5.   Volume of Product In Commerce

Provide total volume of product(s) distributed. Provide estimate of amount and availability of stocks remaining on market, at all levels. (Indicate whether this is the firm's or FDA's estimates.) Include product expiration dates or shelf life expectancy.

NOTE: If recommendation is for an FDA Requested Recall, assure there is, in fact, product remaining in commerce.

6.   Distribution Pattern

Report the areas of distribution, the number of direct accounts, the approximate percentage of each type consignee, and the percentage of product sent to each type of consignee. List foreign countries and U.S. Government military and/or civil units/agencies to which product(s) were distributed. If various labels are involved, describe any differences in distribution pattern.

Where there were any Defense Personnel Support Center (DPSC), Department of Veterans Affairs (DVA), or other government agency sales/distribution, the consignee list should be submitted separately through your District's R&E Coordinator to OE/DCMO. Show if these were direct or contract sales. If contact sales, report the contract number, contract date, and implementation date.

7.   Firm's Recall Strategy

Describe the firm's planned recall strategy. Comment on the adequacy of this strategy from your District's viewpoint, and evaluate the firm's ability to accomplish an effective recall. See Sections 7.42 and 7.46 of 21 CFR, Part 7, which set forth information to be obtained from the firm which will be evaluated by the Center. The firm's strategy should include the intended course of action when an account which distributed the recalled product is found out of business. Include the date the recall was initiated, if already underway

8.   Firm Official

Report the name, title, location, and telephone number of the firm official who should be contacted concerning the recall.   In case of potential Class I or FDA requested recalls, also provide this information for the firm's chief executive officer (CEO).

9.   District Audit Program

Report what actions have already been taken (FDA inspections, sample collections, etc.). Provide specific recommendations for the appropriate Center's action, where appropriate.

Provide details of any publicity issued or planned by FDA, the firm, the State, or local government.

Provide your District's proposed program for monitoring the recall. Include time table for reviewing the recall status and the level and type of audit checks which will verify the recall's effectiveness.

10.   Recommending Official

Name and title of your District's recommending official.

SUBCHAPTER 820 - MONITORING RECALLS

821   INSPECTIONS TO MONITOR RECALL PROGRESS

It may be necessary to re-inspect the firm between the initiation and closeout of a recall to monitor its progress and verify the recalled product's disposition. These visits are limited inspections; issue an FDA-482, Notice of Inspection, at each one. Request recalling firms to submit periodic status reports to FDA . See 21 CFR 7.53.

822   FDA RECALL AUDIT CHECKS

822.1 Definition

A recall audit check is a personal visit, telephone call, letter, or a combination thereof, to a consignee of a recalling firm, or a user or consumer in the chain of distribution. It is made to verify all consignees at the recall depth specified by the strategy have received notification about the recall and have taken appropriate action.

822.2 Level of Audit Checks

Level A - 100% of the total number of consignees to be contacted.

Level B - Greater than 10% but less than 100% of the total number of consignees to be contacted.

Level C - 10% of the total number of consignees to be contacted.

Level D - 2% of the total number of consignees to be contacted.

Level E - No effectiveness checks.

NOTE: A statistical audit plan may be directed by the Center involved.

822.3 Sub-Account Checks

If a recall strategy includes sub-recall by a firm's direct accounts, sub-recall checks will be made following the above levels, as instructed by the Center and your supervisor.

822.4 Conducting the Check

Your assignment contains the necessary details of the recall, recall strategy, and a list of accounts to be checked. The Center will indicate how checks will be made, i.e., visit, phone calls, record checks, etc. Obtain at least the following information, plus any additional information requested by the monitoring district or your home District:

1.   Name and title of person interviewed.

2.   Was notification received, understood, and followed?

3.   Date and method of notification.

4. Amount of recalled product on hand at time of notification.

5. Amount returned and the method of return.

6. Amount destroyed and method of destruction.

7. Amount presently on hand and its status (held for sale, awaiting return, etc.).

8. Date of anticipated return or destruction, and planned method (if applicable).

9. Was sub-recall conducted? (If so, obtain a list of consignees from which to select your sub-recall check locations).

10. Have injury reports or complaints been received? If so, report details.

When you conduct an audit check by visit, you should visit the storage sites for the recalled product and check the shelf stock to ensure all recalled product has been identified, removed from areas of use and properly quarantined. In firms where products are stored in multiple locations, a sufficient number should be checked to verify the consignee properly found and removed all product subject to the recall. This is especially important in Class I recalls and you should check each storage site.

822.5 Audit Check Reporting

The narrative results of your audit check should be reported on an FDA 3177, "Recall Audit Check Report" form. See IOM Exhibit 820-A. Districts have the option of using computer generated audit check forms or hard copies. The FDA 3177 is a three-part form, which is basically self-explanatory. If necessary, instructions for completing it may be found in RPM, Part 5, Exhibit X5-00-8. It is distributed as follows:

Original - Monitoring district.

Yellow Copy - Accomplishing district files.

Pink Copy - District Use

Version 2 of FACTS allows you to enter the amount of time and other data information. When you complete Recall Audits, you should report your time using the "Miscellaneous Operations Accomplishment Hours" screen. You do not need to report the information on the 3177 unless your District SOP requires this. Until some other reporting procedure is developed, continue to report audit checks using the FD-3177 form or memorandum.

822.6 Ineffective Recalls

If your audit check discloses recalled product being held for sale, or a requested sub-recall has not been initiated, document the responsibility for failure to follow recall instructions. This is particularly important if the account received the recall notice and ignored it. An Official Sample should be collected from these remaining products. If in doubt, contact your supervisor or R&E Coordinator. Encourage the consignee to follow the recalling firm's instructions. If a sub-recall is justified, obtain a commitment and details of the firm's sub-recall effort. Get distribution information for follow-up sub-account audit checks.

823   RECALL TERMINATED / RECALL COMPLETED

823.1 Definitions

Recall Terminated - A recall will be terminated when the FDA determines that all reasonable efforts have been made to remove or correct the violative product in accordance with the recall strategy, and when it is reasonable to assume that the product subject to the recall has been removed and proper disposition or correction has been made commensurate with the degree of hazard of the recalled product. Written notification that a recall is terminated will be issued by the appropriate District office to the recalling firm.

Recall Completed - For monitoring purposes, the FDA classifies a recall action "Completed" when all outstanding product, which could reasonably be expected is recovered, impounded, or corrected.

823.2 Closeout Inspection

The final monitoring step is a limited inspection made to verify recall closeout by the recalling firm. A memorandum or limited EIR should be prepared. See Attachment D of Chapter 7 of the RPM for the format. Portions of this format (i.e., Section II and certain items in Section III) will be completed by your supervisor, R&E Coordinator, or compliance officer, depending upon your District's policy.

During the closeout inspection, you should witness destruction or reconditioning of the recalled product when possible. If you are unable to witness the destruction or reconditioning, obtain written documentation from the firm and/or any state or local government agencies which may have witnessed or otherwise verified product disposition. The disposal of large amounts of contaminated or hazardous items may require the firm to file an Environmental Impact Statement (EIS), or pre-disposal processing to render the goods harmless. Do not agree to witness destruction without resolution of these issues. Obtain a "Letter of Voluntary Destruction" from the firm whenever you witness this operation. See IOM 749.1.

SUBCHAPTER 830 - SPECIAL RECALL SITUATIONS

830 General

There are several special recall situations which may require you to deviate from the normal recall procedures. Seek your supervisor's or R&E Coordinator's guidance on these. Examples include:

1. Products in the possession of U.S. Defense Installations.

2. NDA and NADA withdrawals.

3. National Academy of Science (NAS)/Nuclear Regulatory Commission (NRC) (DESI) recalls of drugs judged ineffective.

4. Recalls involving jurisdiction of more than one Federal Agency (e.g., FDA/EPA, FDA/Consumer Product Safety Commission (CPSC), etc.).

EXHIBIT 810-A Page 1 of 3   INVESTIGATIONS OPERATIONS MANUAL

MODEL DRUG RECALL LETTER

John Doe Laboratories
Somewhere, U.S.A. 12345

> Control Division
> Date _____

(red print) -- URGENT: DRUG RECALL -- Nonsterile injectable

Re: List 1234, Cyanocobalamin Injection Lot No. 4321

Recent tests show that the above lot number of this product is not sterile and, therefore, represents a potential public health hazard. Consequently, we are recalling this lot from the market. Other lot numbers are not involved.

Please examine your stocks immediately to determine if you have any of Lot 4321 on hand. If so, discontinue dispensing the lot and promptly return via parcel post, to our New York City Plant; ATTENTION: RETURNED GOODS.

(NOTE: If a sub-recall is indicated in a particular recall situation, the following paragraph should be added:)

> "If you have distributed any of lot 4321, please immediately contact your accounts, advise them of the recall situation, and have them return their outstanding recalled stocks to you. Return these stocks as indicated above."

You will be reimbursed by check or credit memo for the returned goods and postage.

Please return the enclosed card immediately providing the requested information.

This recall is being made with the knowledge of the Food and Drug Administration. The FDA has classified this recall as class _____ (if classified).

We appreciate your assistance.

> John Doe
> President

PLEASE FILL OUT AND RETURN

We do not have any stock of List 1234, Cyanocobalamin
Injection Lot No. 4321 on hand. ☐

We have requested our accounts to return their stocks of this
Merchandise to us. ☐

We are returning _____ bottles of List 1234, Lot No. 4321

Name _____

Address _____

City _____ State _____ Zip Code _____

First Class
Permit No. 2

BUSINESS REPLY MAIL

No Postage Stamp Necessary if mailed in U.S.A.

Postage will be paid by:

JOHN DOE LABORATORIES
Somewhere, U.S.A. 12345-0909

Henry Doe
Director, Quality Control

EXHIBIT 810-A Page 3 of 3

INVESTIGATIONS OPERATIONS MANUAL

FIRST CLASS MAIL

JOHN DOE LABORATORIES

A. B. C. Pharmacy
Anywhere, U.S.A.

(red print) URGENT DRUG RECALL

1. RECALL INFORMATION

a. RECALL NUMBER

b. RECALLING ESTABLISHMENT

c. RECALLED CODE(S)

d. PRODUCT

2. PROGRAM DATA (CHECK BOX IF PREVIOUSLY SUBMITTED)
(DO NOT COMPLETE IF REPORTED UNDER FDA 2123)

a. ACCOMP DISTRICT CODE	b. HOME DISTRICT CODE	c. OPERATION CODE	d. OPERATION DATE (MM/DD/YY)
		17	

e. CENTRAL FILE NUMBER OF RECALLING ESTABLISHMENT

f. PAC CODE

g. EMPLOYEE			h. TYPE	# OF CHECKS	HOURS
HOME DIST.	POS. CLASS	NUMBER	VISITS		
			PHONE		

3. AUDIT ACCOUNTS

a. DIRECT

b. SUB-ACCOUNT (SECONDARY)

c. SUB-ACCOUNT (TERTIARY)

PHONE NO. _____

PHONE NO. ___ _____

PHONE NO. _____

4. CONSIGNEE DATA   Contacted by:
☐ Phone   ☐ Visit   ☐ Other

a. NAME OF PERSON CONTACTED, TITLE & DATE

b. TYPE CONSIGNEE

☐ Wholesaler   ☐ Physician
☐ Retailer   ☐ Hospital   ☐ Other
☐ Processor   ☐ Pharmacy
☐ Consumer   ☐ Restaurant

c. DOES (DID) THE CONSIGNEE HANDLE RECALLED PRODUCT?

☐ YES   ☐ NO

5. NOTIFICATION DATA

a. FORMAL RECALL NOTICE RECEIVED?
(If "No" skip to item 6c.)

☐ YES   ☐ NO   ☐ CANNOT BE DETERMINED

b. RECALL NOTIFICATION RECEIVED FROM:

☐ Recalling Firm
☐ Direct Account
☐ Sub-Account
☐ Other (Specify)

c. DATE NOTIFIED

d. TYPE OF NOTICE RECEIVED (e.g. letter, phone)

6. ACTION AND STATUS DATA

a. DID CONSIGNEE FOLLOW THE RECALL INSTRUCTIONS? (If "No", discuss in item 10 action taken upon FDA contact)

☐ YES   ☐ NO

b. AMOUNT OF RECALLED PRODUCT ON HAND AT TIME OF NOTIFICATION

c. CURRENT STATUS OF RECALLED ITEMS
☐ Returned   ☐ Destroyed
☐ Corrected   ☐ None on Hand
☐ Was Still Held for Sale/Use *
☐ Held For Return/Correction *
* = Ensure Proper Quarantine/Action

d. DATE AND METHOD OF DISPOSITION

7. SUB-RECALL NEEDED?
Did Consignee Distribute to any other Accounts?
(If "Yes" give Details in "Remarks" or Memo)

☐ YES   ☐ NO

8. AMOUNT OF RECALLED PRODUCT NOW ON HAND

9. INJURIES/COMPLAINTS

IS CONSIGNEE AWARE OF ANY INJURIES, ILLNESS, OR COMPLAINTS?

☐ INJURY   ☐ COMPLAINT
☐ ILLNESS   ☐ NONE

If answer is other than "None", report details in a separate memo to monitoring district and copy to E.O.B. (HFC-162)

10. REMARKS (Include action taken if product was still available for sale or use)

SIGNATURE OF CSO/CSI

DISTRICT

DATE OF CHECK

TO:

DATE

SIGNATURE OF SCSO OR R&E COORDINATOR

ENDORSEMENT

FORM FDA 3177

CHAPTER 9 - INVESTIGATIONS

CONTENTS

SUBCHAPTER 900 - INVESTIGATIONS

901 INVESTIGATIONS GENERAL

This Chapter contains specific information on many types of investigations and each section provides additional guidance for you on how to investigate particular issues, special reporting requirements and where additional assistance can be obtained. Recall work, a special type of investigation, is covered in Chapter 8. There is an on-line training course in Investigations which covers many types of investigations and provides additional information.

An investigation is an information gathering activity you conduct for many different reasons. The purpose of any investigation is to determine and document facts concerning a particular issue so the Agency can make informed and sound decisions. Investigation is a general term and can apply to a very general activity or a specific type of infor-

mation gathering process. Some specific types of investigations include a complaint investigation, a disaster investigation, a health fraud investigation and a product tampering investigation. Investigations can be distinguished from inspections because usually you will not need to issue an FDA 482, you will be working somewhere other than a manufacturing plant, you may be visiting retail establishments, consumers, other government agencies. On rare occasions, you may be conducting an investigation without advising individuals you are a FDA employee. Keep in mind that investigations can not all be categorized and there will be times when you do issue an FDA 482, such as when you are at a manufacturing site or doing work similar to an inspection. Experience gained on the job will help you determine the proper course of action for these special situations.

Reporting an investigation is almost always done using a memorandum. The format is not as defined in sections as an inspection report. A good rule of thumb to follow is to first summarize what you did, why or give the reason for the investigation and briefly state the findings. After this, you can go into detail about how you conducted the investigation and what you found. Reporting the course of your investigation and your findings chronologically works in many situations. For long narratives, using headings will make it easier for the reader to follow your reporting. Some types of investigations have forms that need to be completed in addition to the narrative.

SUBCHAPTER 902 - COMPLAINTS

902 COMPLAINTS - GENERAL

A complaint is notification that a product in commercial distribution may be in violation of the laws and regulations administered by FDA.

Complaints are received from various sources, including consumers, other government agencies, Congress on behalf of their constituents, trade associations, etc. Complaints should be promptly acknowledged in written format, by telephone or visit. See Field Management Directive FMD-119.

Consumers contacting field offices with complaints of injury or illness should receive a prompt, courteous response and assurance their complaints will receive appropriate consideration. An immediate follow-up may be warranted when there is an indication of a serious illness or injury.

Obtain sufficient information to enable evaluation of the complaint, determination of appropriate follow-up, and, if possible, enough facts to permit further FDA evaluation and response without subsequent contact with the complainant. If a complaint cannot be resolved immediately, determine if the complainant expects further contact. If so, report the best time to reach the complainant. For complaints involving special nutritional products, i.e., infant formula, medical foods and dietary supplements, complete the FACTS Adverse Event Questionnaire, See Exhibit 900-D. See IOM 902.3 for additional instructions regarding special nutritional complaints.

The Emergency Operations Center (EOC) HFC-160, (301) 443-1240 must be notified immediately of all significant injury, illness and tampering complaints. The EOC must also be notified of all complaints regarding infant formula/baby food.

Significant injury/illness includes, but is not limited to any life threatening event; seizures; severe respiratory distress syndrome including broncho-constriction or bronchospasm; acute asthmatic attacks, anaphylactic or hypotensive episodes; unconsciousness or coma, or any event requiring medical treatment. Also to be included are behavioral or mood disorders of sufficient intensity to alter the daily activities of the consumer. These complaints require immediate and thorough follow-up, unless specifically directed otherwise by the EOC. The Emergency Operations Center is also to be kept advised of the status of all such follow-up investigations. Information about complaints nationwide is available in FACTS and from the EOC and may be helpful in determining appropriate follow- up.

Complaints concerning products which do not present a hazard to health must be investigated by the home district during the next planned inspection of the responsible firm.

If the complaint concerns a matter not under FDA jurisdiction, or one which would more properly be handled by another agency, refer the complainant to the appropriate organization whenever possible.

902.1 Complaint Categories

Complaints can be divided into two categories:

Injury/Illness Complaints - A complaint indicating a serious injury, illness, hospitalization, or death requires immediate reaction. It will, in all likelihood, require immediate investigation, including the accumulation of epidemiological data and prompt liaison with other appropriate federal, state and local agencies.

A complaint that clearly indicates an illness resulting from consuming a FDA regulated product, and manifested by symptoms such as nausea, fever or diarrhea, should receive prompt follow-up by FDA or cooperating officials. Conversely, some illnesses are considered psychological in nature, e.g., a consumer finds a foreign object in a product and becomes ill because it is revolting. For purposes of conducting follow-up and reporting to headquarters, these should be handled as non-injury/illness complaints and do not need to be reported to the Emergency Operations Center.

Non-Injury/Illness Complaints - These do not require immediate follow-up at the consumer level. Follow-up may include examining the parent lot, referral to another FDA district, state, or local agency, or, deferral until the next regularly scheduled inspection. Examples include mold in beverages, obvious filth or insects in canned goods, etc. It may be possible that adequate investigation would be contacting the dealer, advising them of the nature of the complaint and requesting notification of action taken. Non-injury/illness complaints do not need to be reported to the Emergency Operations Center unless product tampering is suspected or the product is a baby food or infant formula.

902.2 Infant Formula and Baby Food

There is a continued sensitivity to all reported incidents involving infant formula or baby food. All complaints involving either infant formula or baby food are to be thoroughly investigated on a high-priority basis. This will include follow-up at the doctor or hospital (if an injury/illness is involved), with the collection and analysis of appropriate samples. Complaints involving baby food that is regulated by USDA should be referred to USDA for appropriate follow-up. See IOM 910.3 and 311.2.

There are two exceptions for collecting samples as part of the follow-up to infant formula/baby food complaints:

1. Complaints involving outdated product in the marketplace, with no associated injury or illness. These do require investigation to assure all outdated product has been removed from the identified retail and/or wholesale source.

2. Complaints involving an illness associated with normal appearing product, but follow-up investigation discloses a physician's diagnosis that the event does not appear to be product related, or that the event was an allergic response to a properly labeled product.

Also see the following:

1. IOM 902.3 Special Nutritional Product Injury/Adverse Reaction

2. IOM 910 - Foodborne Outbreaks

902.3 Special Nutritional Product Injury/ Adverse Reaction

Definition - Special nutritional products include dietary supplements, infant formulas and medical foods.

The Dietary Supplement Health and Education Act of 1994 (See DSHEA) defined the term "dietary supplement" to mean a product, intended to supplement the diet, that contains one or more dietary ingredients, i.e., vitamins, minerals, herbs or other botanicals, amino acids, and dietary substances for use by man to increase the total dietary intake, as well as a concentrate, metabolite, constituent, extract, or combination of any of the dietary ingredients. Under DSHEA, a dietary supplement is a food which must be labeled as a "dietary supplement", and cannot be represented for use as a conventional food or the sole item of a meal or diet.

DSHEA also removes dietary ingredients from coverage under the food additive provisions of the FD&C Act. Rather, DSHEA places the burden on the Agency to prove a dietary supplement or dietary ingredient is adulterated before the product can be removed from the marketplace.

A crucial source of information on potentially unsafe products is the Agency's consumer complaint system. It is extremely important that FDA conduct appropriate investigations and follow-up on complaints of illness or injury attributed to dietary supplement products. The instruction and guidance provided below must be followed when conducting follow-up on complaints involving adverse reactions to special nutritional products.

Causes - Injuries or other adverse reactions may be associated with the use of products which:

1. Vary markedly from the declared potency or concentration.

2. Contain deleterious substances accidentally included in their manufacture.

3. Have changed composition or become contaminated after shipment.

4. Are mislabeled as to identity, warnings or instructions for use.

5. Have not been used according to label instructions or the directions of the manufacturer or prescriber.

6. Are dangerous when used according to directions.

Procedures - When investigating adverse events attributed to CFSAN monitored products:

1. Complete the adverse event questionnaire during the initial consumer contact, e.g., telephone report of complaint, or soon thereafter. Information already contained in the FACTS Consumer Complaint Report need not be duplicated on the questionnaire. (See IOM Exhibit 900-D)

2. Obtain a release of information for medical records for all serious adverse events during the initial consumer contact or shortly thereafter. (Please refer to section 902.7 Medical Records.)

3. Document a complete description of the incident including the sequence of events.

4. Describe in detail the nature of the injury.

5. Obtain detailed information including names, addresses, and dates for any hospitalizations, emergency room visits or physician visits.

6. Obtain photographs of the victim's injuries, if significant.

7. Document names of other persons involved, such as lawyers, insurance agents, etc.

8. Obtain complete details on the product involved.

9. Obtain detailed information of how the product was used, including frequency, in what amounts, concomitant treatments, and whether administered by the user or someone else.

10. Document the source of the product.

11. Obtain copies of all labeling/inserts.

NOTE: Contact the Office of Scientific Analysis and Support, CFSAN Adverse Events Reporting System (CAERS) Staff, CAERS-HFS-702, 301-436-2405, for all questions pertaining to field follow-up requests or medical guidance on investigations of adverse reactions associated with CFSAN monitored products. CAERS will coordinate with the office experts.

Current policy requires all decisions to collect samples of CFSAN monitored products be made by CFSAN's Office experts, following review and evaluation of the complaint. The field offices are NOT to collect any samples of CFSAN monitored products associated with complaints (either consumer portions or intact retail units) unless specifically directed by CFSAN. Should questions arise, contact CAERS.

Sample Collection - Investigators should refer to the appropriate compliance program (Medical Foods CP 7321.002, Infant Formula CP 7321.006, Dietary Supplements CP 7321.008) for sampling guidance when samples are necessary.

When following up on adverse events relating to infant formula or baby food, please refer to Section 902.2 for guidance.

902.4 Complaints Involving Alcoholic Beverages

All tampering complaints involving alcoholic beverages should be entered as a consumer complaint in FACTS. The Emergency Operations Center and OCI should be notified immediately. For all other complaints involving alcoholic beverages, please see IOM 318.1 for guidance.

902.5 Emergency Operations Center Guidance

As unique situations arise, the Emergency Operations Center (HFC-160), (301) 443-1240, provides guidance concerning the type of follow-up to be made; except as noted above for special nutritional products. This guidance should be kept on file by the district consumer complaint coordinator.

902.6 Interviews

The key to thorough consumer complaint investigations is complete interviews with the complainant and/or others knowledgeable about the incident (other family members, health professionals, law enforcement officials, etc.).

The basic information to be obtained is in the FACTS Consumer Complaint Report which replaces the 2516 and the Consumer Complaint Follow-Up Report which replaces the 2516a. See IOM Exhibit 900-A and 900-B. It is important to accurately determine the sequence of events leading up to the complaint. This includes a 72-hour food history (for food related illness); whether the complainant used the product before (cosmetic or drug products); condition of the product when purchased or consumed (tampering complaints, mold in foods, possible mishandling, product abuse in the home, etc.); and storage of the products (if filth is the subject of the complaint).

There are additional considerations with injury/illness complaints. The prior medical history of the complainant may provide indications regarding allergies, drug side effects or drug-food/drug-drug interactions which may be responsible for the illness or injury. Medical verification should be sought in these situations. Food illnesses are frequently associated with the most recent food consumed, food that didn't appear or smell right, or a food consumed only by the ill person. Additional interviews may be required to identify other suspect foods, especially if the food implicated is not a likely vehicle for illness. Familiarity with items previously associated with illness or injuries is helpful in pursuing the investigation; such as pet turtles or occupational sources for Salmonella; incompatibility of soft contact lenses with lens solution or other eye products not specifically approved for use with them; production of acetic acid by aspirin as it decomposes; and the bitter or burning taste of calcium chloride-contaminated frozen ice cream novelties. Consider that individuals differ in sensitivity to bacterial levels or toxins, and not everyone using or consuming a contaminated product will show symptoms.

The complainant may request a copy of your investigative report or sample results. Inform the complainant that they can receive the results of any sample collected from them, in accordance with the Freedom of Information Act (FOIA), after the Agency has determined that there is no consideration of criminal prosecution or such consideration has occurred and the matter is closed. Also inform them there may be a slight charge for the investigatory report as required by the FOI Regulations. See IOM 134.

902.7 Medical Records

In investigating complaints where a health professional was seen by the complainant, contact the health professional concerning the nature of the alleged illness/injury, and the relationship to the product. You may occasionally find the complainant has not mentioned the product as a potential cause of the illness or injury to the health professional. Use judgment as to the usefulness of collecting medical records.

If collection of medical records is necessary, use the FDA 461, Authorization for Medical Records Disclosure, signed by the patient or someone authorized to act for the patient. See IOM Exhibit 900-C. The FDA 461 is not required to obtain records from the Department of Defense (DOD) medical facilities. Identify yourself to the Commanding Officer of the facility or representative and request authorization to examine and copy records. DOD Directive 6040.2, Release of Information from Medical Records, authorizes release of medical information to government agencies.

NOTE: Many states require statements concerning other subjects besides those covered on the FDA 461. If the hospital does not accept the FDA version of the Authorization for Medical Records Disclosure, obtain and complete one of their forms for use at their facility.

Collect all medical records pertinent to the investigation.

902.8 Sample Collection

A thorough investigation will provide information to form a hypothesis as to the cause of the illness or injury and will assist in determining what sample(s) to collect. Adequate samples should be collected immediately, while they are available. Do not overlook sampling any product which may be remotely implicated in the incident. See Section 902.3 for guidance on sampling dietary supplements.

In addition to the consumer portion, intact containers of products of the same lot should be collected from the retail and wholesale levels. These samples provide more useful information regarding the product in consumer channels, and may prove useful in any future legal action. Refer to IOM 425.1 for information concerning collection of consumer portions.

902.9 Recording Complaints/Follow-ups

The FACTS Consumer Complaint Report and Follow-Up Report are used for recording and investigating all complaints (except drug reactions – see IOM 922), unless pre-

viously reported through one of FDA's other post-marketing surveillance systems. See IOM Exhibits 900-A & 900-B.

SUBCHAPTER 910 - INVESTIGATION OF FOODBORNE OUTBREAKS

910   FOODBORNE OUTBREAKS

If you become aware of a foodborne outbreak, contact the Emergency Operations Center (EOC) 301-443-1240 immediately. Generally, epidemiological investigations are conducted by state and local public health authorities. Epidemiological investigative techniques have been established to assist in determining the cause of a foodborne outbreak or illness. The information presented describes the standard methods for gathering and evaluating data. In fact, these techniques are useful in investigating all types of complaints.

910.1 Outbreaks on Foreign Flag Vessels

If a suspect outbreak involving a foreign flag vessel or a US flag vessel with an international itinerary comes to your attention, report it to your supervisor and the Emergency Operations Center 301-443-1240 immediately. The Centers for Disease Control and Prevention (CDC) assumes primary jurisdiction for foreign flag (non-US registry) and US flag vessels with international itineraries entering the US and traveling in US waters. See IOM 314.3.

910.2 Outbreaks Involving Interstate Conveyances

Reports of illness attributed to travel on an interstate conveyance (plane, bus, train, or vessel) are a shared responsibility of FDA and CDC. When a report of illness is received, notify the Emergency Operations Center at 301-443-1240 and you are encouraged to share the report with state and local public health officials. The following procedures are to be coordinated with local/state public health officials:

Interviews with the ill passenger, family members (well and ill), caregivers, and/or health professional (as appropriate) should be sufficiently probative to hypothesize if the food, water or an environmental transmission is related to the illness. Transmission of illnesses, particularly viral diseases, by ill employees and contaminated environmental surfaces can result in illness carryover between successive trips and should be considered. Factors such as time of onset of symptoms, symptoms, food history for the 72 hours prior to onset of the first symptom, any clinical laboratory results, and other potential exposures should be documented. The carrier should also be contacted to determine if other reports of illness have been received (passengers and employees). Obtain any illness logs from the carrier. The information developed should be evaluated to determine if further follow-up is necessary. On those carriers where a reservation system is used, obtain the names and phone numbers of passengers. It may be necessary for the state/local health authorities, CDC or FDA to contact other passengers to determine if they became ill.

If additional cases are uncovered during these contacts, immediately notify the EOC and the state and local public health authorities in all of the affected states. FDA will work cooperatively with these authorities and request their assistance in conducting an epidemiological investigation and collecting patient specimens. Note: If at any time the local/state public health officials are unable to assist with an investigation, notify the EOC, who will contact CDC and request assistance in the epidemiological investigation.

910.3 Cooperation with Other Agencies

One of FDA's functions is to assist local, State, and other Federal agencies in conducting investigations, collecting samples, and conducting plant inspections if warranted.
In addition to state and local health departments, the following federal agencies may also become involved in investigating foodborne disease outbreaks:

1. U.S. Department of Agriculture (USDA),
Centers for Disease Control and Prevention (CDC), and Environmental Protection Agency (EPA)

Whenever a complaint is received involving any meat-containing product, including such items as soups, combination infant foods, frozen dinners, etc., evaluate the need to contact USDA. Most products containing red meat or poultry are regulated by USDA. The exceptions include:

1. Products containing meat from game animals, such as venison, rabbits, etc.;
2. Meat-flavored instant noodles;
3. The product "pork and beans" (which contain only a small amount of pork fat and is regulated by FDA); and
4. Closed face sandwiches.

Determine from the consumer if there is a round "shield" on the label with the USDA Establishment Number. Alternatively, the establishment number may be identified in the lot number. Red meat products under USDA jurisdiction will often contain the abbreviation "EST" followed by a one to four digit number; poultry products under USDA jurisdiction will contain the letter "P" followed by a number.

IOM 311 and 314.3 provide information for reporting suspected outbreaks to USDA & CDC. In addition, FDA and CDC have an agreement that FDA will be immediately advised whenever CDC ships botulism antitoxin anywhere in the United States or its possessions.

Whenever the source water is suspected as a likely origin of the agent of an illness outbreak, Environmental Protection Agency (EPA) should be notified. For example, when investigating a foodborne outbreak on a vessel passenger conveyance, you may find the water used in food preparation to be from a land-based source or from an onboard water treatment plant. Both of these sources would fall under EPA jurisdiction. See IOM 321.

910.4 Outbreaks Associated with Salmonella Enteritidis (SE) in Eggs

All reports regarding SE outbreaks, including any epidemiological and environmental data associated with whole shell eggs are to be referred to the Emergency Operations Center, 301-443-1240, (emergency.operations@fda.gov@ ora.fda.gov). The EOC will notify CFSAN Outbreak Coordination Staff immediately, who will serve as the lead CFSAN contact.

911   FOLLOW-UP GUIDANCE

Preparation - Investigator kits with proper equipment should be maintained in the district to facilitate immediate investigation of foodborne outbreaks. The kits should be restocked on a schedule recommended by FDA laboratory personnel to ensure continued sterility of sampling equipment. A supply of Carey-Blair tubes should be readily available as part of the investigation kit. These tubes provide a transport medium that will help preserve the environmental and food swabs.

If an alert or complaint indicates a large outbreak, inform your servicing laboratory immediately that samples will probably be collected and give the approximate time they are expected to arrive at the laboratory. This will assist laboratory managers planning work schedules, equipment and supplies.

Each district may have individuals specifically trained in epidemiological investigations who can provide advice on investigations. If not, consult with the Emergency Operations Center at (301) 443-1240 and the state and local public health authorities.

Interviews - health professionals, hospital personnel, or consumers may report suspected cases of foodborne illness. Regardless of the source of the report, the diagnosis must be verified by a thorough case history and, if possible, by examination of appropriate food samples and clinical specimens. This verification is done by public health professionals.

Upon contacting the affected person, identify yourself and explain the purpose of the visit or call. Neat attire, pleasant manner of speech, professional attitude and confidence in discussing epidemiology and control of foodborne illnesses are important in developing rapport with an affected person or family. Exhibit a genuine concern for persons affected, and be sincere when requesting personal and confidential information. Communicate a sense of urgency, and emphasize the positive contribution already made by the complainant toward the control and prevention of foodborne illness.

Set your level of communication based on the person being interviewed. Tact is essential. Phrase your questions so the person(s) interviewed will describe their illness, and the foods and events which they feel were associated with it, in their own way. Never suggest answers by the way you phrase your questions.

Ask specific questions to clarify the affected person's comments. Realize people are sometimes sensitive to questions about age, gender, special dietary habits, ethnic group, excreta disposal and housing conditions. Phrase questions thoughtfully. Some information may usually be deduced from observations, but if doubt remains, confirm your hypothesis by asking questions. Information on recent travel, gatherings, or visitors may indicate common sources or events.

Gather information about all meals and snacks eaten seventy-two hours before onset of illness. The food, even the meal, which precipitated the illness, might not be obvious. The type of illness will sometimes give a clue.

If the first and predominant symptoms are nausea and vomiting, concentrate questions on foods eaten recently. If the first and predominant symptoms are diarrhea and abdominal cramps, foods eaten six to twenty hours before onset of illness are suspect.

If diarrhea, chills and fever predominate, foods eaten twelve to seventy-two hours before onset of illness are suspect.

Remember that these suggestions relate to common foodborne illnesses. The more unusual illnesses often present different clinical patterns. For instance, some illnesses such as Typhoid Fever and Hepatitis A, have incubation periods greater than 72 hours. Refer to IOM Exhibit 910-C.

Use this detailed interview approach with every person identified in the initial complaint or alert, even though some may not have been ill, until you have sufficient information to determine if there is a foodborne disease outbreak.

Medical Records - Physicians' and hospitals' records can be useful in verifying reported signs, symptoms and other clinical data and can sometimes rule out the possibility of foodborne illness. See IOM 902.7 and IOM Exhibit 900-C.

912   SAMPLING PROCEDURES

CAUTION: Never taste any of the food products, and handle all samples with caution to prevent accidental ingestion of even minute amounts of the contaminated or suspect product.

912.1   Sample Collection

During investigations of foodborne diseases, cooperate with other health officials in collecting samples of items that may be associated with the outbreak.

Use a menu or data from an attack-rate table to determine which of the foods from the implicated meal are most suspect, and collect samples of them. Check storage areas for items that may have been overlooked. Check garbage for discarded foods or containers. Suspect foods often are discarded by an operator if he thinks someone may have become ill as a result of eating in his establishment. Because one of the primary tasks of the investigator is to prevent further illness, take appropriate action to prevent distribution or serving of any suspect food until it has been proven safe. If no foods remain from the suspect meal or lot, try to collect samples of items prepared subsequently to the suspect lot, but in a similar manner. Collect ingredients or raw items used in the suspect food. Determine supplier,

distribution, and code information on ingredients and packaged foods to aid any investigation of the same lot in distribution channels.

Collect samples aseptically. If foods are to be examined for organophosphate pesticides or heavy metals, do not use plastic containers. Use glass jars with foil lined lids because substances from the plastic can leach into the food and interfere with analysis.

The following are examples of articles normally collected:

1.   Remaining portions of all suspect foods;
2.   Parent stocks of suspect foods;
3.   Insecticides, rodenticides, or other poisons which may be involved.
4.   Suspect food containers such as cans, bottles, etc.;
5.   Utensils or materials used in the preparation and storage of the suspect food;
6.   Table scrapings and food residues from equipment such as slicing machines, cutting boards, etc.

NOTE: Clinical specimens such as vomitus, stools, swabs of nasal and throat passages or open sores or lesions of food workers are collected by local, state, or CDC health officials or private physicians.

912.2 Sample Size

In general, follow the IOM SAMPLE SCHEDULE in Charts 1, 2, & 3 (IOM, Chapter 4). Where only small amounts of items remain, such as bits of left-overs, empty containers with adhering particles, etc., collect all or as much as possible by scraping from utensils, equipment or containers. It may also be necessary to collect the empty container(s). See IOM 913.6.

912.3 Sample Handling

Record the temperature of the room, refrigerator, or warmer in which the food was stored, and record the temperature of the food that remains after a sample is collected.

Inform the laboratory of the type and number of samples, and discuss methods to preserve and transport samples, time of arrival, and the person who will receive the shipment.

Samples of products frozen at the time of collection should be maintained frozen until analyzed. Samples of perishable foods, which are not frozen at the time of collection, should be cooled rapidly to a temperature of 4.4°C (40°F) and maintained at this temperature if they can be analyzed within eight hours. If analysis cannot be started within eight hours, and you suspect microbial contamination, contact your servicing microbiology laboratory for proper handling procedures.

Transport refrigerated or frozen samples to the laboratory in insulated containers, packed with an appropriate refrigerant to maintain the desired temperature during transit. Send samples to the laboratory by the most expeditious means. Clearly mark: "PERISHABLE FOOD SAMPLE FOR MICROBIAL EXAMINATION - RUSH," "PRIORITY." Label specimens according to applicable regulations governing transport of hazardous material. See IOM 454.8f.

If the suspect food is a commercial product, examine the original package or container for coding information to identify the place and time of processing. Your district may notify all agencies responsible for regulating the products alleged or suspected to have caused the illness. Collect additional packages bearing the same code number for analyses for microorganisms, toxins, seam defects, vacuum, leaks, or other conditions. Be specific as possible in requesting the type of analysis.

913 EPIDEMIOLOGICAL ASSOCIATIONS

Conduct a preliminary evaluation of your epidemiological data as soon as possible. If your data suggests an outbreak has occurred, develop a hypothesis about the causal factors. Test your hypothesis by obtaining additional information to prove or disprove its validity.

913.1 Outbreak Determination

An outbreak is an incident in which two or more individuals have the same disease, have similar symptoms, or excrete the same pathogens; and there is a time, place, and/or person association between these individuals. A foodborne disease outbreak results from ingestion of a common food by such individuals. However, a single case of suspected botulism, mushroom poisoning, paralytic shellfish poisoning, rare disease, or a disease which can be definitely related to ingestion of a food, may be considered as an incident of foodborne illness which warrants investigation.

Sometimes it will be obvious from an initial report that a foodborne disease outbreak has occurred, simply because of the number of individuals displaying certain symptoms at or near the same time. Many complaints, however, involve illness in only one or two individuals, and determining a particular food was responsible, or its consumption and the onset of illness was only coincidental, is often difficult. Certain diseases that are highly communicable from person to person, such as epidemic viral gastroenteritis, or those associated with a common place, such as carbon monoxide poisoning, may simulate a foodborne illness.

If additional complaints connected with the same food or eating establishment are received, food is almost certainly involved. A food-related or enteric disease alert/complaint log assists in determining if similar complaints have been received.

Time associations primarily refer to onset of similar illnesses within a few hours or days of each other. Place associations deal with buying foods from the same place, eating at the same establishment, residing at the same place, or attending the same event. Person associations have to do with common experiences, such as eating the same foods or being of the same age, gender, ethnic group, occupation, social club, or religion. Once some of these associations become obvious, verify the outbreak by identifying and interviewing other individuals who were at risk by virtue of their association with the ill persons.

913.2 Assistance

If the outbreak affects a large number of individuals or food establishments, consult with your supervisor regarding the need to seek assistance from other health professionals. A team consisting of an epidemiologist, microbiologist or chemist, sanitarian, and others may be required to make a sufficiently detailed foodborne illness investigation. Such personnel may be provided by local, state or provincial, or national agencies concerned with health, food and drug, environment, fish or agriculture.

913.3 Additional Case History Interviews

Seek and interview additional individuals both ill and well, who had time, place, or person associations with the identified cases. If the suspect meal was served during a particular occasion, determine the name of the person in charge. That person may have a list of names, addresses, and telephone numbers of persons who attended. Obtain menus of suspect meals as soon as possible. Additional cases may be identified by checking reservation books and credit card receipts. Review the districts food-related, enteric disease alert/complaint log for recently received complaints which may be related to the outbreak. Consult with your supervisor as to further contact with other health agencies, hospital emergency rooms, poison control centers, and local physicians to find additional cases. At this stage of the investigation, interviews can be accelerated by reviewing the event itself to stimulate each individual's memory. Inquire about specific symptoms known to be common to the suspected syndrome, and mention each food served at the event or meal.

The number of individuals to be interviewed depends on the proportion of attendees who are probably affected. As a rule of thumb, if no more than 100 people attended the meal, an effort should be made to interview everyone. If several hundred were present, a random, representative number should be interviewed.

Prepare a separate FDA 3042, Food Illness Investigation Report, for each person interviewed. See IOM Exhibit 910-B. The FDA 3042 is intended as a guide to supplement a complete narrative report. Do not be restricted to this form in obtaining details during investigations. Information can be extracted from this form to compile an Attack Rate Table to pinpoint the suspect food. See IOM Exhibit 910-A.

913.4 Establishment Investigation

When a botulism or other foodborne outbreak is reported, and an establishment is inspected, the initial impact of the incident can create confusion at the plant, and conflicting instructions if too many individuals become involved. To reduce the confusion, one investigator should be designated as the team leader. A supervisor should be the coordinator for overall district activities, and the district contact for headquarters personnel. All communications from FDA field or other offices to the firm's management should be channeled through the supervisor. The lead investigator should be responsible for all phases of the physical inspection of the facilities, and briefing the supervisor as to his progress. See IOM 502.4.

Upon arrival at the establishment where the suspect food was processed or prepared, the implicated meal was served, identify yourself to the person in charge and state your purpose. Emphasize the purpose of the investigation is to determine what contributed to the outbreak, so preventive measures can be taken. Attempt to create a spirit of cooperation. Consider the position, feelings, and concerns of the manager and his staff; defensive reactions are common.

Many factors could have contributed to contamination before foods came under the control of the manager. Assure him these possibilities will also be investigated. Inform the manager of the activities proposed and benefits which may be gained for educating his workers.

Review of distribution records and examination of warehouse stock are two important aspects of a botulism follow-up inspection. Each of these operations should be monitored by an investigator reporting directly to the team leader. These two monitoring investigators are responsible for all reports from their assigned areas, regardless of the number of investigators assisting them. Field examination should also include an inventory by code of all stock on hand. When conducting field examinations follow instructions in IOM Sample Schedule Chart 2 (IOM, Chapter 4).

When preparing the report, follow instructions in IOM 502.4.

913.5 Food Employee Interviews

If a food is already suspect, interview separately all persons who were directly involved in processing, preparing, or storing of the food and others who could have observed preparation and storage. Ask questions in a sequence that discloses the flow of food from the time it was received until it was served or distributed. Especially inquire about foods that were prepared several hours or days before being served with the suspect meal. Ask similar questions, suitably modified, of the managers or workers who were involved in producing, transporting, processing, preparing, or storing food at other levels of the food chain, as well as individuals who prepared the food at home.

Food workers who fear criticism or punitive action because of their possible role in the outbreak do not always accurately describe the food handling as it actually happened. Their descriptions should be plausible, account for possible sources of contamination, and indicate possibilities of survival and potentials for growth of pathogens. If the description does not contain all the information desired, rephrase the questions and continue the inquiry. Seek confirmation of one person's story by talking to others who have knowledge of the food operation, or by watching the food preparation or processing practices. Be alert for inconsistencies among the accounts, as told by different individuals.

913.6 Possible Contamination Source

It is important to have an understanding of the pathogen and the factors that contribute to the contamination that resulted in the foodborne illness. Some pathogens, such as Shigella, are associated with human fecal contamination, while other pathogens, may be more commonly associated with a particular food source (e.g. raw meat and E. coli O157:H7). Exhibit 910-C and microbiologists can help provide useful information on sources and contributing factors.

Pests are a possible contamination source and can be an indication of poor hygiene, sanitation, food storage, handling and preparation practices. These pests include certain rodents, flies, cockroaches or other pests that:

1.   Occur around human settlements.
2.   Occur indoors as well as outdoors.
3.   Are attracted to potential sources of pathogens (garbage, drains, excrement, etc.) and to human food.
4.   Travel back and forth between possible sources of pathogens and food or food contact surfaces.

Evaluate whether a pest is a potential contributing factor to the outbreak by comparing your direct observations of pest activity combined with other evidence of pest activity (excreta, urine, gnawing, etc.) to the above criteria. A pest species that appears to meet all four of the above criteria is a possible source of pathogen contamination. It is helpful to collect specimens of any insect pest that meets these criteria for identification to determine if the pest species is one that is known to carry foodborne pathogens. See Appendix C.

Raw poultry, pork, and other meats are often contaminated when they come into kitchens. If any of these agents are suspected in an outbreak, samples of meat and poultry, meat scraps, drippings on refrigerator floors, and deposits on saws or other equipment can sometimes be helpful in tracing the primary source. Swabbing food contact surfaces of equipment (as tables, cutting boards, slicing machines) which had contact with the suspect food may establish links in the transmission of contamination. This is especially true if a common utensil or piece of equipment is used for raw and cooked foods. Swab these surfaces with sterile swabs, moistened with a sterile solution (such as sterilized 0.1% peptone water or buffered distilled water). Break off the tip of the swab into a tube containing 5 to 10 ml of this solution or into a tube of enrichment broth for specific pathogens. Samples or swabs from air filters, drains, vacuum sweepings, food scrap piles, dried deposits on equipment, and dead ends of pipe lines may reflect the presence of organisms previously in the establishment.

Evaluate the cleanliness, manner, and frequency of cleaning equipment. Seek possible routes of cross-contamination between raw and cooked foods. As ingredients may be the initial source of pathogens, determine which were added before, and which were added after any cooking or heat processing.

Workers can be a source of foodborne pathogens. Enterotoxigenic Staphylococcus aureus strains are carried in the nostrils of a large percentage of healthy persons. They are also found on the skin and occasionally in feces. Clostridium perfringens can be recovered from the feces of most healthy persons. Workers are sometimes infected with other enteric pathogens. Employee food safety training and knowledge should be investigated. Poor hygiene practices among food workers (e.g. not washing their hands) continues to be a major contributing factor to foodborne illnesses. See IOM Exhibit 910-C. If the same type of pathogenic organism is recovered from a fecal specimen of a worker and the suspect food, do not immediately conclude the worker was the source. A worker who ate some of the implicated food could be one of the victims. A history that includes a skin infection (boil or carbuncle) or a gastrointestinal or respiratory disturbance preceding the preparation of the suspect food would be more incriminating. Employee attendance and sick leave records may provide additional information.

Look for pimples, minor skin inflammation, boils and infected cuts and burns on unclothed areas of the body; ask if there are any infections in other areas.

913.7 Pathogen Growth Factors

In addition to tracing sources of contamination, the circumstances which permitted survival and growth of foodborne pathogens in the implicated foods must be identified. This information is vital to develop preventive measures. Factors usually contributing to outbreaks of specific foodborne illnesses are cited in IOM Exhibit 910-C. Identify these factors by careful and diligent interviews of food workers; close observation of employees' food handling practices; checking temperatures of foods during processing and equipment in which the foods were held; and by conducting studies to determine time-temperatures relationships during processing and storage. Consider times and temperatures which were involved in freezing, thawing, cooking or thermal processing, hot and cold holding, chilling, reheating, and any other steps in the processing operations. It is important to know the survival and growth characteristics of the pathogen that caused the illness outbreak. For example, viruses do not replicate outside of the body and therefore will not "grow" regardless of the temperature. However, their survival characteristics should be considered. You should consult with a microbiologist or the Emergency Operations Center prior to your investigation in order to understand the characteristics of the pathogen and focus on the relevant contributing factors.

914   ANALYZING DATA/HYPOTHESIS FORMULATION

Organize and group the data obtained from the interviews of both ill or well individuals. From appropriate calculations and analyses, the illness can be classified, the hypothesis tested as to whether the outbreak was associated with a common source, a vehicle can be determined, and the necessity for further field or laboratory investigation can be decided.

914.1 Epidemic Curve

An epidemic curve is a graph which depicts the distribution of onset times for the initial symptoms of all cases that occurred in a disease outbreak. The unit of time used in the construction of the graph depends on the disease, or the period covered by the outbreak. For example, use a scale in days or weeks for Hepatitis A; and a scale in hours for staphylococcal food poisoning.

The epidemic curve assists in determining whether the outbreak originated from a common-source, such as food, or person-to-person propagation. A common-source epidemic curve is characterized by a sharp rise to a peak; with the fall usually being less abrupt. The curve continues for a period approximately equal to the duration of one incubation period of the disease. A person-to-person curve is characterized by a relatively slow, progressive rise. The curve will continue over a period equivalent to the duration of several incubation periods of the disease. (Exhibit 910-E)

914.2 Symptoms Determination

Determine predominant symptoms by constructing a table as illustrated below:

Frequency of symptoms

Symptoms	Number of Cases	Percent with Symptoms (N = 20)
Vomiting	17	85
Nausea	12	60
Diarrhea	12	60
Abdominal cramps	6	30
Headache	3	15
Fever	2	10

The percent of ill persons who manifest each symptom is obtained by dividing the number of individuals reporting a given symptom by the number of individuals reporting any symptom (twenty in this example), and multiplying by one-hundred.

This information helps determine whether the outbreak was caused by an agent that produces a neurological, enteric, or generalized illness. Either infections or intoxications will be suggested. Such information can identify suspect foods and indicate appropriate laboratory tests.

914.3 Incubation Periods

The incubation period is the interval between ingestion of a food contaminated with enough pathogens to cause illness and the appearance of the initial symptom of the illness. Calculate this interval for each case. Individual incubation periods will vary because of individual resistance to disease, differing amounts of food eaten, uneven distribution of the infectious agent or toxin throughout the food, and other factors.

The shortest and longest incubation periods give a range. Calculate the median incubation period, the mid-value of a list of individual incubation periods when ordered in a series from the shortest to the longest or the average of the two middle values if such series contains an even number of values. The median, rather than the mean, is used because the former is not influenced by exceptionally short or long incubation periods which are sometimes reported in outbreaks of foodborne illness.

The median and range of the incubation period, coupled with information regarding predominant symptoms, form bases upon which to judge whether the disease in question is an infection or an intoxication and thereby determine what laboratory tests should be done. See Exhibit 910-C.

914.4 Attack Rate Table

Complete the Food-Specific Attack Rate Table. It provides an easy way to compare the percentage of ill persons who ate each food with the percentage of ill persons who did not eat each food. The attack rate table is useful in identifying the food responsible for an outbreak or illness. This food will usually have the highest attack rate, percent ill, in the column for persons who ate the food and the lowest attack rate in the column for persons who did not eat the food; it will also have the greatest difference between the two rates. See IOM Exhibit 910-A.

914.5 Tracebacks of Foods Implicated in Foodborne Outbreaks

Traceback investigations are important epidemiological tools that are used to determine the source of food implicated in foodborne outbreaks. Traceback investigations may prevent further sale and distribution of contaminated food. Commonly, states or local government agencies conduct the initial epidemiological investigation of foodborne outbreaks and identify suspect (interstate) product(s) requiring tracebacks. In some cases FDA may be asked to assist another agency with a traceback investigation.

If a request for an inter-state traceback investigation is received by a District Office, it should be referred to the Emergency Operations Center (301) 443-1240. The Emergency Operations Center and CFSAN will review the epidemiological data and hazard analysis or environmental assessment before initiating a traceback investigation. The EOC will issue traceback assignments to the appropriate district(s). The EOC will coordinate and issue inter-district assignments for traceback investigations. The field should use the FDA Guide to Tracebacks of Fresh Fruits and Vegetables Implicated in Epidemiological Investigations, dated April 2001, unless otherwise directed by DFI or the EOC.

915 REPORTING

Your district will follow Field Management Directive FMD-119 for proper reporting of epidemiological investigations. Promptly submit a complete narrative of the investigation in memorandum, including references to exhibits, samples, medical records, and laboratory reports. There is no prescribed reporting format, but it should be in a logical order.

Submit copies of any written reports and documents for all INJURY or ILLNESS complaints involving all CFSAN

products (see section 902) except cosmetics to:
Food and Drug Administration
CFSAN/OSAS
CAERS Staff (HFS-700)
5100 Paint Branch Pkwy
College Park, MD 20740
Attn: Consumer Complaint Coordinator
(Note: CFSAN Offices will move to College Park, MD between October 2001 and March 2002. See on-line directories for change in address.)

Refer to IOM Section 928 for submission of cosmetic complaints.

Illness/injury complaints involving special nutritional products (refer to IOM 902.3) must be accompanied by a completed FACTS Adverse Event Questionnaire (Exhibit 900-D) when forwarded to CFSAN.

If additional follow-up on any complaint involving a CFSAN product is necessary, the Division of Field Program Planning and Evaluation (HFS-635) will issue an assignment.

916 REFERENCES

1. "Procedures to Investigate Foodborne Illness" Int'l Assoc. of Milk, Food and Environmental Sanitarians, Inc., Ames, Iowa 50010.
2. "Diseases Transmitted by Foods" CDC, Atlanta, GA. 30333.
3. "Procedures to Investigate Waterborne Illness" Int'l Assoc. of Milk, Food and Environmental Sanitarians, Inc., Ames, Iowa 50010.
4. "Epidemiology Man and Disease" J.P. Fox, M.D., and L.R. Elveback, PhD, MacMillan Publishing Co., N.Y., N.Y. - 1970.
5. FMD 119 - Consumer Product Complaints System.
6. Regulatory Procedures Manual Chapters 5 - 10.
7. "Control of Communicable Diseases Manual," American Public Health Association, Washington, D.C. 20001-3710.

SUBCHAPTER 920 - INVESTIGATION - INJURY & ADVERSE REACTION - BIOLOGICS,DRUGS, DEVICES, COSMETICS, VETERINARY PRODUCTS

921 INVESTIGATIONS

The purpose for investigating injury and adverse reactions to drugs, devices, biologics and cosmetics is to determine the cause of, and to prevent additional injury or adverse reaction to the consuming public.

Injury and adverse reaction complainants should receive a prompt, courteous response, and assurance their complaints will receive appropriate consideration. An immediate follow-up should be made when there is an indication of a serious injury or adverse reaction.

When investigating injuries or adverse reactions, do not make comments or enter into discussions with firms as to the involvement of particular products, unless specifically instructed to do so. Many adverse reactions come to FDA through the MedWatch system, which is operated on a voluntary basis with the reports held confidential. Divulging information before the reports are confirmed or denied is inappropriate, and not to be done.

While investigating complaints, there may be occasions when either the consumer, or the firm responsible for the marketing of a product, contact the press. In those instances, when the complainant (other than the manufacturer or the firm responsible for the marketing of the suspected product) contacts the local press, follow instructions found in Section 161. When the responsible firm invites the news media to observe the inspectional process, follow instructions found in Section 504.3.

Personnel routinely receiving complaints should be particularly sensitive to those involving recently approved drugs, devices and biologics. Clinical trials may not have identified all possible adverse reactions, and FDA's approving Center may want to reconsider current labeling, modify directions for use, establish registries for monitoring, or withdraw approval based on the most recent information.

Procedures - When investigating all injuries and adverse reactions:

1. Complete a FACTS Consumer Complaint Report and FACTS Follow-up Report (replaces the FDA 2516 and 2516a) to record and investigate all complaints, unless previously reported through one of FDA's other post marketing surveillance systems such as MedWatch. For special nutritionals, complete the FACTS Adverse Event Questionnaire. For cosmetics, complete the Cosmetics Adverse Event Report. See IOM Exhibits 900-A, 900-B, 900 –D, 900-E.

2. Provide complete details on the product involved, including brand name and identity statement with all qualifiers appearing on the label and code marks. In device cases, obtain a wiring diagram or furnish a complete description. Take photographs, if appropriate.

3. Identify the source of the offending article.

4. Provide details of how the product was used, including frequency, in what amounts, other on-going treatments, any known previous adverse reactions or pre-existing allergies and whether applied by the user or someone else. Determine if label directions were followed. Obtain copies of all labeling/inserts. Also, be alert for medical research or literary reviews the reporting party may have conducted or relied upon, and collect copies of such research or reviews. The device community has various publications of frequency of types of adverse events investigated and findings.

5. Obtain a complete description of the incident (sequence of events) and the nature of the injury or adverse reaction, including date, time, location and symptoms or description of injury.

(a) Include any hospital or physician's records available, and identify pre-existing conditions which may have a bearing on the injury or adverse reaction.

(b) Obtain photographs of the victim's injuries, if significant. See IOM 902.7 for the procedures used to obtain medical records.

6. List names of other persons involved, such as beauty salon operators, medical personnel, lawyers, insurance agents. Obtain their views on the injury or adverse reaction. The views of an attending physician are important because they may vary markedly from those of the patient.

7. Ask the consumer if an attempt to report the adverse reaction to the product manufacturer has been made, and the nature of the manufacturer's response, if known.

8. Any other consumer complaints, injuries or alleged adverse reactions reported to the manufacturer concerning the product.

9. If necessary, obtain distribution information of the implicated lot(s) from the manufacturer.

922 DRUGS - INJURY OR REACTIONS

Drug injuries or reactions, either human or veterinary; result from the use of products which may:

1. Vary markedly from declared potency.

2. Contain deleterious substances.

3. Are mislabeled as to identity, warnings, or instructions.

4. Have been mistaken for other drugs despite proper labeling.

5. Have changed composition, or become contaminated after shipment.

6. Are dangerous when used according to directions.

7. Have not been used in accordance with label directions or directions from the prescriber.

8. Have been improperly administered, or administered without the necessary precautions.

9. Have been contaminated with objectionable microorganisms, soaps or cleaning solutions.

10. Have been misidentified.

11. Be labeled as sterile drugs, but are found to be non-sterile.

Investigative Procedures - The following procedures should be followed for investigating suspected drug-induced birth defects or other adverse drug reactions:

1. If the complaint concerns a suspect, drug-induced birth defect, obtain only the information requested on the FDA 3500 MedWatch form, and submit this information to MedWatch (HFD-410). See Exhibit 920-A.

2. If the complaint concerns a suspected adverse drug reaction, determine if it is one already listed in the product labeling or if the reaction might be due to a drug defect.

(a) If it is an adverse drug reaction, and there is no evidence of a defective drug product, obtain only the information requested on the FDA 3500 form and submit it to MedWatch (HFD-410).

(b) If the adverse reaction is suspected of being associated with a defective drug product, a complete investigation should be conducted. The FDA 3500 form should be completed and submitted to MedWatch (HFD-410). Copies of all reports should be forwarded to appropriate ORO and Center offices for review and evaluation.

(c) If it cannot be determined that the adverse reaction is specific to the drug, and/or related to a drug defect, a limited investigation should be conducted to determine if the reaction falls under 2a or 2b above.

In all cases of suspect drug-induced adverse reactions, the Center will review the information on the FDA 3500 form, and will issue assignments to the field if additional information is needed.

923   DEVICES - INJURY

The cause of medical device injuries may originate with the manufacturer, operator, user, or from other factors including, but not limited to the transportation or installation of the device.

923.1 Mechanical, Electrical or Electromechanical Devices

Injuries caused by mechanical, electrical or electro-mechanical devices may result from devices that:
1.   Do not conform to specifications due to:
(a) mistreatment (e.g., damage in transit), or
(b) failure to comply with good manufacturing practices.
2.   Malfunction because:
(a) of incorrect installation,
(b) have not been used in accordance with labeled instructions,
(c) have been used/installed with accessories or parts which are not compatible,
(d) have been used under conditions which interfere with their ability to function (e.g., electromagnetic interference (EMI), fluid seepage into electrical circuits, etc.),
(e) have been damaged during use, or
(f) random failures.
3.   Have not been adequately designed for intended use (e.g., unstable, poor structural integrity, sharp or pointed surfaces, electrical leakage, etc.).
4.   Do not contain adequate directions or warnings.
5.   Are intended to be sterile but are nonsterile.
6.   Fail or deteriorate for any reason.

923.2 Devices for Implant

Causes of injuries which may result from implanted devices include those listed in IOM 923.1. The term installation, as used above, does not include implantation. Injuries also may result because the materials used in the implant are not biocompatible, thereby causing an adverse tissue reaction and/or deterioration of the implant.

923.3 In Vitro Diagnostic Devices

Certain In Vitro Diagnostics (IVD) are instruments, such as gas chromatographs and automated blood analyzers, and much of the information under IOM 923.1 is applicable. Injuries to patients from IVD products may, in many cases, be considered indirect, because they are due to complications resulting from misdiagnosis or delays in patient treatment due to incorrect test results. Examples of IVD failures include false positives, false negatives and erratic results. Poor performance or failure may be due to poor manufac-

turing practices or user error.
Manufacturing problems include:
1.   Process errors and mix-ups (e.g., varying fill in kit components, improper ingredient addition, etc.).
2.   Labeling does not contain adequate directions or warnings, or contains incorrect information.
3.   Labeling mix-ups
4.   Contamination, making the product unusable or causing misdiagnosis.
User errors include:
1.   Failure to follow label directions
2.   Use of unclean or poorly calibrated laboratory equipment.
3.   Improper storage of reagents

923.4 Investigative Procedures

When investigating incidents implicating a medical device, you must first confirm whether or not the device was a contributing factor. An appropriate follow-up, such as inspection at the manufacturer, may be necessary.

Current agency policy defers regulation to the Department of Transportation (DOT) of automotive adaptive equipment which are medical devices. Consumer complaints or other reports concerning these devices should be referred to DOT.

Copies of EIR's, FACTS Consumer Complaint Report and Follow-Up Report, including documentation and related materials, for all device consumer complaints should be sent to HFZ-343.

Reports received through the Medical Device Reporting system are not considered to be consumer complaints and are tracked through a system maintained by CDRH. A FACTS Consumer Complaint Report should not be completed for any incident that CDRH has requested follow-up on via MDR, unless you originally were advised of the incident by a consumer and initiated a FACTS Consumer Complaint Report at that time. For additional information concerning MDR reports, see the applicable Compliance Program in the CPGM.

Interview the victim, physician(s), and any other individual(s) who witnessed or has knowledge of the incident. When conducting an investigation at a hospital, be sure to contact and inform the administrator of the purpose of the investigation.

Obtain the following information for devices:
1.   A complete description of the incident (sequence of events) and the injury, including:
(a) Type, model, serial number and manufacturer of the device.
(b) Details of the alleged incident, including: number of people involved; symptoms, onset time & duration and outcome; date & time of occurrence; reports of other investigating agencies and their conclusions, e.g., fire marshal or OSHA reports; similar incidents which may have resulted in injury; all operational SOP's, written or unwritten.
2.   Copies of medical records and/or laboratory records. Use an FDA 461, Authorization for Medical Records Disclosure, IOM Exhibit 900-C, signed by the patient or other authorized person, when obtaining these records.

Official cause of death, death certificate and/or autopsy report, if indicated.

4. Determine if the device malfunctioned, and the cause.

5. The condition of the device at the time of use. Review its maintenance history, including responsibility for maintenance (past and present), special service calls, repairs, whether component warning or safety systems were functional, maintenance records, changes or corrections accomplished just prior to or immediately after the incident, and who performed the activity. An interview with bio-engineering department personnel may be indicated.

6. Who has access to the device, and if individuals using the device are familiar with its operation?

7. The results of any examination or inspection of the device by the hospital or other party to determine the cause of the incident.

8. Whether there are other devices of the same model number or lot number on the premises.

For In Vitro Diagnostics, determine:

1. What are the results of the test used for? (Screening, therapeutic drug monitoring, epidemiological information, monitoring the course of disease, susceptibility testing, etc.)

2. The clinical value or worth of the test (is it diagnostic, does it only aid in diagnosis).

The report of the investigation and related documentation is extremely important and must be promptly submitted. The report will be used by CDRH Medical and Scientific Review Staff in their health hazard evaluation.

For Dialysis Injury or Deaths, in addition to the general device investigative procedures,

1. Obtain the following information:

(a) Determine time of incident, i.e., at beginning of procedure, or after several hours of operation.

(b) Actions taken by staff, the number of patients normally treated, medications given, etc.

(c) Whether reuse of the dialyzer is practiced (manual or automated).

(d) Contact and interview maintenance personnel, where appropriate. Verify there is a maintenance schedule.

(e) Verify whether checks on alarm systems were performed prior to each start up and at any other critical stages in the operation, and how often. Determine the last time temperature and/or other alarm systems were calibrated.

2. Verify when the dialysis facility filed a User Facility Report (UFR) in compliance with SMDA90.

3. Describe the type of water treatment devices used to make the dialysate. Verify who services and maintains the water treatment system, including off-site regeneration systems. Determine when these services were performed and recorded (name & times), in relationship to the incident. Report, for off-site regeneration systems, whether the resin bed regeneration was "medical use only" or mixed with other uses.

4. Where a dialysis center practices reuse of dialyzers, determine the type of disinfectant method used (manual or automated), type of disinfectant used (formaldehyde, renalin, glutaraldehyde, etc.) and review the service and maintenance records for proper procedure including names, dates and time.

924 BIOLOGICS - INJURY, REACTION OR FATALITY

Reactions or symptoms of illness may occur in association with the administration of vaccines and other biological products. The Center for Biologics Evaluation & Research (CBER) is interested in all unexpected clinical responses to a biological product, as well as any expected responses of unusual frequency or severity. In some cases, a reaction or illness could occur because the product may:

1. Vary from declared potency.

2. Have been contaminated during manufacturing, shipment, or after shipment.

3. Be mislabeled.

4. Not have been given according to directions.

5. Not have been stored under proper conditions.

6. Have been provided to the wrong person.

7. Contain substances innocuous to most people, but which the recipient is unable to tolerate (anti-Kidd, anti-Duffy), or contains substances not usually present in such a product which stimulate an adverse response in the recipient (HLA antibodies).

924.1 Professional Reporting System for Vaccine Adverse Reactions

The National Childhood Vaccine Injury Act of 1986, 42 USC 201, was passed to achieve optimal prevention of childhood infectious diseases through immunization. At the same time, it was intended to minimize the number and severity of adverse reactions to vaccines routinely administered to children. This law requires health care providers and vaccine manufacturers to report certain adverse events which occur following the administration of specific vaccines. The vaccines and reportable events are listed in the table "Reportable Events Following Vaccination". See IOM Exhibit 920-C. The Department of Health and Human Services (DHHS) has established a Vaccine Adverse Events Reporting System (VAERS) to accept all reports of suspected adverse events after the administration of any vaccine, in all age groups, including but not limited to those in the table.

The Vaccine Adverse Event Reporting System (VAERS) is administered under a joint FDA/CDC contract with ERC Bio-Services Corporation, Rockville, MD. The system utilizes a preaddressed and postage paid form (Form VAERS-1) for reporting adverse events which occur subsequent to vaccine administration. See IOM Exhibit 920-D.

924.2 Investigation/Reporting

When a biologics reaction/injury complaint is received by the district office (DO), a preliminary investigation should be conducted. CBER should be consulted before initiating any follow-up which extends beyond the complainant, and in some cases even before the complainant interview.

All complaints initially received by the District Office must be recorded on the FACTS Consumer Complaint Report. When interviewing the complainant about a biologics complaint /injury, obtain:

1. Complete description of the complaint/injury.
2. Onset and duration of the reaction/injury.
3. Name of product administered, include date & time of administration.
4. Manufacturer and lot number of product, if available.

At this point, it is generally unnecessary to conduct interviews beyond the complainant, or obtain records, until a preliminary review has been conducted. It is important to rapidly communicate the basic information about the incident, implicated product, lot, license number, manufacturer, and presence of intact units to the Center and the EOCcontact. Immediately, CBER offices will advise whether reactions are expected or unexpected, and the level of investigation, including sample collection and analysis, necessary. Further follow-up is unnecessary until it has been determined the reaction/injury is not unexpected, or has not already been reported through other channels.

Vaccine Products - If the complaint involves an adverse reaction of any kind, then a Form VAERS-1 (IOM Exhibit 920-D) should be sent to the complainant. The form should be completed by the complainant's physician, if at all possible, or by the complainant, if the physician will not cooperate. The completed VAERS Reporting Form should be mailed directly to the address on the form. When you send a VAERS form to a complainant, note this fact in the Remarks Section of the FACTS Consumer Complaint Report.

If the complaint does not involve an adverse reaction, obtain the necessary information to allow the Center to make an informed decision on follow-up at the manufacturer. A VAERS Form will not be sent to the complainant in the case of a non-adverse reaction injury.

Biological Products - If the complaint is an adverse reaction to a product, an FDA 3500, MedWatch Form (See IOM Exhibit 920-A) must also be completed and forwarded to the complainant for completion by their physician. If the physician will not cooperate by completing the FDA-3500, request the complainant to do it. Assist the complainant in completing the FDA 3500, if necessary. Note in the "Remarks" section of the FACTS Consumer Complaints Report that the FDA 3500 was forwarded to the complainant.

If the complaint does not involve an adverse reaction, obtain information necessary to permit the Center or home district to make an informed decision on follow-up at the manufacturer. If a complainant desires further information, refer them to CBER, Office of Biostatistics and Epidemiology at (301) 827-3974.

If the complaint is a fatality where blood or a blood component is implicated, notify CBER, Office of Compliance and Biologics Quality, as soon as possible (21 CFR 606.170). This is required of the collecting facility, in the event of a donor reaction, and by the facility which performed the compatibility tests, in the event of a transfusion reaction. An investigation of the incident shall be conducted by either HCFA or FDA, based on the type of facility involved, for example, transfusion service, blood bank, plasma center or hospital.

925   COSMETICS - INJURY OR REACTION

Injuries or adverse reactions may arise from cosmetics which:

1. Are inherently dangerous or which may prove harmful or injurious to a consumer;
2. Are due to ingestion, primary irritation of skin, eye, or mucous membranes (including the lungs and urinary tract) applied topically, or which may be due to an individual sensitization reaction or allergic response;
3. Have undergone formulation changes, or other chemical or microbiological contamination while in the possession of the manufacturer, dealer, distributor, or end user;
4. Are mislabeled because they contain unlisted ingredients, lack instructions for safe use, or lack any necessary warning statements;
5. Have been misused.

Investigative Procedure - Limit complaint follow-ups to those involving:

1. Severe or unusual skin irritation or allergic reaction, eye irritation, urogenital tract or respiratory tract irritation, or apparent toxicity;
2. Reports of unusually large numbers of adverse events, even when the event is less severe;
3. Labeling violations which may constitute health hazards; or,
4. Suspected microbiological contamination.

Prior to conducting follow-up on any cosmetic complaint, including sampling, the district should contact the Cosmetic Adverse Event Monitoring (CARM) Program Coordinator, Division of Programs and Enforcement Policy (HFS-105), Office of Cosmetics and Colors at (202) 418-3414. That office will provide guidance concerning any investigation and reporting. If unable to contact that office, the district should proceed to investigate reports initiated on those complaints involving serious adverse reactions, and pursue contact with the CARM Program Coordinator later. The FACTS Consumer Complaint Cosmetic Report should be used for Adverse Events relating to cosmetics (Exhibit 900-E). See the applicable Compliance Program in the CPGM.

926   VETERINARY PRODUCTS - COMPLANTS/ADVERSE REACTIONS

Complaints and adverse reactions associated with veterinary products including animal drugs, medicated feeds, medical devices for animals, grooming aids (cosmetic items for animals) are handled through the Division of Surveillance (HFV-210) 301-827-6642. Veterinarians, animal owner and firms may report problems to their local FDA offices, the EOC, or directly to the Center for Veterinary Medicine. The District and the EOC will complete a FACTS Consumer Complaint Report and advise the complainant to complete a FDA 1932s "Veterinary Drug Adverse Experience, Lack of Effectiveness or Product Defect Report". The form and instructions are available at www.fda.gov/cvm.

For information on the history of reported problems for particular products, contact the Adverse Drug events Coordinator at the Division of Surveillance 301-827-0158.

927   SAMPLE COLLECTION

Collect a sample of the product which caused the injury and an official sample from the same lot. Collect the same and other lot codes, if available. Check with your supervisor if you have any doubt as to the appropriateness of collecting a particular sample.

See IOM 454.3 for routing of injury and complaint samples to the laboratory.

Device Samples - Obtain Center concurrence prior to collecting any device samples.

Biological Samples - Do not collect samples of the suspect product until an evaluation of the preliminary information on the injury/reaction has been made by CBER (Licensed products) or the Home District (Unlicensed Products, Plasma and Blood Products).

Cosmetic Samples - Products such as depilatories, permanent hair dyes, home permanents, deodorants, hair straighteners, etc. are known to cause adverse reactions. Samples of these products should not be collected except in cases of alleged severe or unusual injury, e.g., multiple complaints. In case of obvious allergic type reactions, samples should not be collected. Most cosmetic products which get into the eye will cause temporary eye irritation and in such cases, a sample generally should not be collected.

Collect samples associated with consumer complaints in which microbiological contamination is suspected.

928   REPORTING

Prompt reporting is essential. You may save the lives of others.

Reporting Forms - Field personnel must report all consumer complaints in FACTS. In addition, for adverse reactions or injury associated with drugs, medical devices, cosmetics, biologics (except vaccines), provide complainants with an FDA 3500 MedWatch form (IOM Exhibit 920-A) and provide the consumer with the MedWatch web address: www.fda.gov/medwatch. Prior to sending a MedWatch form to the complainant, enter the FDA FACTS consumer complaint number in the box below the Triage Unit Sequence # in the upper right corner of form FDA 3500.

For veterinary product complaints, provide complainants with an FDA 1932a "Veterinary Drug Adverse Experience, Lack of Effectiveness or Product Defect Report" available at www.fda.gov/cvm.

For adverse reactions to vaccine products, provide complainants with form VAERS-1 (IOM 924.2, IOM Exhibit 920-D).

Routing Reports - A copy of the FACTS consumer complaint report and your narrative report(s), including any copies of medical or injury reports obtained must be submitted by your district as follows:

Drug complaints and injuries to:
MedWatch
The FDA Medical Products Reporting Program (HFD-410)
Food and Drug Administration
5600 Fishers Lane
Rockville, MD 20857

Medical Device & Radiological Product complaints and injuries to:
Food & Drug Administration
Center for Devices and Radiological Health
Division of Surveillance Systems (HFZ-530)
1350 Piccard Drive
Rockville, MD 20850

Cosmetics (including products that are both drugs and cosmetics) complaints and injuries to:
Food and Drug Administration
Center for Food Safety and Applied Nutrition
Office of Cosmetics & Colors
CARM Program Coordinator
Cosmetic Programs & Regulations Branch (HFS-106)
200 "C" Street, S.W.
Washington, D.C. 20204
(Note: CFSAN Offices will move to College Park, MD between October 2001 and March 2002. See on-line directories for change in address.)

Foods and Dietary Supplements Complaints, Injury Reports and Adverse Events to:
Food and Drug Administration
CFSAN/OSAS
CAERS Staff (HFS-700)
5100 Paint Branch Pkwy
College Park, MD 20740
Attn: Consumer Complaint Coordinator
(Note: CFSAN Offices will move to College Park, MD between October 2001 and March 2002. See on-line directories for change in address.)

Veterinary injuries or adverse reaction reports to:
Food and Drug Administration
Center for Veterinary Medicine
Division of Surveillance (HFV-210)
7500 Standish Place
Rockville, MD 20857

Biologics - Licensed Products (includes vaccines), except for source plasma and blood products:
The receiving district will complete the FACTS consumer complaint report and fax a copy to HFM-650 at 301-443-3874, select HFM-650 in the referrals box and then electronically forward to the home district. The home district will select "Surveillance for Next EI" as the final disposition and close the complaint. CBER will issue an assignment if follow-up is needed.

Biologics - Unlicensed Product, Plasma and Blood & Blood Products: The receiving district will complete and electronically forward the FACTS consumer complaint to the home district and send a hard copy to HFM-650. The home district will determine if any follow-up is needed and issue an appropriate assignment. Advice is available from HFM-650 at (301) 594-1911.

Biologics injury/adverse reaction narrative reports are forwarded to:
Food and Drug Administration
Center for Biologic Evaluation and Research
Office of Compliance
1401 Rockville Pike, Suite 400S
Rockville, MD 20852

NOTE: In addition, check the "Notify DEIO" box in FACTS for al injury and adverse reaction complaints. For serious injury/illness reports, please notify the Emergency Operations Center immediately at 301-443-1240.

SUBCHAPTER 940 - DISASTER PROCEDURES

The objective of FDA investigations in the aftermath of non-attack disasters is to determine whether or not foods, drugs including biologics, cosmetics and devices affected by the catastrophe are safe for human use; and if not, to effectively remove them from commerce.

In disaster operations, FDA will assist state, local and other federal agencies in removing contaminated or unfit merchandise from the market.

941   DISASTER TYPES

The types of natural and man-made disasters which affect FDA operations are:

Floods   Earthquakes
Hurricanes   Volcanoes
Tornadoes   Chemical Spills
Wrecks   Riots & Disorders
Fires Explosions   Bioterrorism

942   RESPONSIBILITY & COORDINATION

State and local officials usually assume direct responsibility, as their laws and regulations can be immediately invoked, however FDA assistance is often requested. Except in unusual circumstances, FDA responsibilities are to assist the state and local health agencies in removing, destroying or reconditioning affected merchandise.

In situations involving interstate movement of merchandise; large interstate firms; areas in which state or local political ramifications are anticipated; or when state or local health officials so request; FDA may assume the primary role in the operation.

943   PREPARATION

Personal Safety - In a disaster or pending disaster the personal protection of yourself and your family is your primary concern. Provide for your own safety as you perform your FDA duties in a disaster area. Inoculations and protective clothing should be considered. See IOM 141 and 169.6.

Disasters produce dangerous situations. e.g.; high water, escaping gases, fallen electrical lines, damaged buildings, falling rubble, etc., so care and extra safety precautions must be observed. If you become sick or injured, you become another problem to already overworked health officials.

CAUTION: In situations where electrical power has been out for an extended period of time, and firms attempt to salvage frozen or refrigerated products using dry ice, do not enter these areas without first providing for proper ventilation and/or obtaining oxygen breathing apparatus.

Inspectional & Investigational Preparation - After taking care of yourself and family, and being properly equipped and supplied, you are ready to begin disaster operation. Stock your car in the same manner as for any inspectional activities; however, consider the extra amounts of materials needed in the particular situation.

Extra gasoline and oil, drinking water, communication equipment (cellular and satellite phones, email, etc.), battery powered radios, lighting equipment (battery flashlights, propane or gasoline lanterns, etc), extra film, medical supplies and materials of an emergency nature must be provided if power facilities and normal distribution channels are disrupted. Consideration must also be given to your own sleeping and eating needs.

Review the Model Food Salvage Code, 1984 Recommendation of the Association of Food and Drug Officials and the U.S. Department of Health & Human Services for guidance.

944   PRELIMINARY INVESTIGATION

Initial Information - FDA usually learns of disasters, or impending disasters from weather agencies, news media, public health agencies, civil defense units, or law enforcement organizations. Initially, there is little anyone can do, other than monitor the course and severity of a disaster, until the situation becomes sufficiently stabilized for personnel to move into the area to survey damage.

Initial Procedures - FDA's initial course of action is to contact state and local officials, offer assistance, and begin to coordinate the mobilization of personnel and resources necessary to handle the emergency.

If you are in an area when a disaster strikes or is imminent, advise your supervisor on the situation by the fastest means possible. In the initial stage of the operation you may be the only FDA representative on the scene. If this is the case, contact the state or local officials and offer your services, advising them you have alerted or will alert your district as soon as possible. Keep your supervisor informed.

Each district has a disaster plan which will be implemented in applicable situations. As the situation develops, you will receive instructions from your supervisor.

945   FIELD OPERATIONS

Inspectional and investigational activities will normally be conducted with other FDA personnel and state or local counterparts.

Once personnel are mobilized and assignments issued, your operational procedures will be similar, regardless of the type of disaster. You will be searching out, identifying and investigating foods, drugs, devices, and cosmetics for actual or possible contamination and taking the necessary steps to preclude their use until they are released, reconditioned, or destroyed.

A rapid physical survey must first be made of the disaster area to determine the extent of damage, and the amounts and kinds of merchandise involved.

CAUTION: Although procedures in this subchapter do not cover disasters resulting from nuclear attack, it is possible you may discover products suspected of contamination by radioactive materials in the disaster area. If you suspect the presence of radioactive materials, take no action on the materials yourself, but have the area cordoned off at once. Notify the command official and immediately contact your supervisor to alert the regional radiological health representative and the state radiation control agency. Follow their instructions.

When in doubt as to the condition of any materials affected, request holds or embargoes pending final outcome of further examinations. See IOM 945.2.

945.1 Embargoes

See IOM 331 and 750.
FDA has no embargo powers except as specified in:
1. The Federal Meat Inspection Act;
2. The Poultry Products Inspection Act;
3. The Egg Products Inspection Act; and
4. Certain parts of the FD&C Act, namely Section 304(g).

In emergency situations, state and local embargoes are an effective tool. Embargoes can be employed immediately and, the merchandise held, destroyed, or reconditioned without time consuming delays. Some state and local embargo powers are limited as to time and/or amounts. In these cases, the use of federal injunction and seizure action must not be overlooked. State or local agencies may also confer their embargo authority to FDA personnel for the duration of the emergency.

945.2 Field Examination & Samples

During all your investigational activities examine the lots affected for obvious adulteration, decomposition, contamination, or physical damage. Use your camera extensively, and collect samples whenever indicated. Judge the extent of field examination and sample collections necessary, based on the nature and magnitude of the disaster.

In major catastrophes, large numbers of samples may not be necessary because of obvious visible contamination and the emergency disposition powers invoked by state and local officials. In minor local disasters, such as fires, riots, train, truck, or shipwrecks, lots may be held pending outcome of examinations, so extensive sampling may be required.

Examine cans or jars for physical damage (rusty, burst seams, holes, ripped, etc.), and for visible adulteration from filth, oil or chemicals, and defaced labels. In addition, examine jars and bottles for sediment or other visible filth under cap crimps and cap lugs. When a lid is removed, sediment or micro-contamination may be drawn into the container by internal vacuum. Discard any jars you open for examination. Visible contamination under lids may be photographed or lids may be used as exhibits as conditions permit.

Plastic, paper, cloth bags, and cardboard containers must be examined for physical damage and contamination.

Stocks of devices must be examined for contamination, water, heat, mechanical, physical, electrical, or chemical damage. If any doubt exists as to whether or not devices have been affected, experts should be consulted or utilized.

Examine bulk containers and their contents, including underground storage tanks. Examine material in rail cars, truck trailers, and storage silos. Be especially alert for rail car and trailer movement. These quickly disappear, as clean-up crews arrive.

945.3 Flooding

All flood water, regardless of its source, must be considered a polluting medium because of overflowing sewers, outhouses, decomposing livestock, street run-off water, etc.

Depending on the extent of the flood, first determine the locations of the major stocks of regulated products. Food and drugs will normally receive first priority. As stocks of goods are located, rapidly survey the extent of damage, then concentrate on affected materials. Use your camera extensively. Examine the walls of buildings and storage areas and the top and sides of stacked or tiered goods for flood water residue, debris, and the usually well defined high-water mark. Merchandise stacked above this line is still of concern because other problems probably exist, e.g. vermin defilement, failure of refrigeration, thawing of frozen items, etc.

Make arrangements to have any suspect material embargoed by local officials, or held pending final disposition. Management is usually cooperative and willing to do things it may not normally do to get back to normal operations as quickly as possible. Cooperate with management, but avoid hasty decisions.

Much merchandise is quickly rendered unsuitable for human consumption by water action. Items such as bread, cakes, cookies, candies, bulk flour, sugar, bulk liquids, and similar items not in jars or hermetically sealed containers can often be immediately hauled to disposable areas and destroyed.

Determine areas which have lost power. In facilities such as frozen food firms, frozen or refrigerated warehouses, etc., check the sites for length of down-power and condition of the merchandise. If power is restored in time to avoid thawing, or prevent spoilage of refrigerated items, and products were not inundated, or otherwise affected, there is no need for further examination.

Even though flood waters may not have inundated the firm, the situation may have caused sewer and waste lines to back-flush into basements and immediately drain out again. Debris or sewage particles along walls and on low floor surfaces or presence of sewage odors are evidence of backflushing.

Grain, cottonseed, soybeans, dried bean products, peanuts, and similar products may become flood damaged in terminal elevators, on farms, and in flat storage facilities. In addition to flood water contamination, molding products may develop mycotoxin contamination. Examine susceptible products and facilities for damage, inundation and mold.

Rodent activity may increase in flooded areas as the vermin seek food and shelter. Be alert to rodent defilement on products.

As lots of goods are checked, embargoed or released and the immediate situation returns to normal, firms will want to start operating. Prior to their beginning operations, examine equipment and processing facilities for pollution, and its aftermath. Plant operation must not be permitted unless proper cleanup and sanitizing is performed.

945.4 Hurricanes & Tornadoes

Investigate following the guidance in IOM 945.3 In addition, examine merchandise for evidence of physical damage caused by flying particles and crushing by debris. Physical damage to product containers may be extensive. Broken or leaking containers of materials such as chemicals, oils, fertilizers, etc., may have contaminated materials subject to FDA coverage. Also see IOM 945.6 on chemical contamination from various sources.

945.5 Fires, Explosions, Riots

FDA operations following these disasters are usually localized and do not normally involve a large number of personnel or extended resources.

Examine stocks for exposure to excessive heat, physical damage from flying particles and falling debris, and lack of refrigeration in down-power areas. Examine for water damage from fire fighting activities and handle these as a flooding situation. Also, be alert for possible pollution from using non-potable water in fire fighting.

Fire fighting often involves use of chemicals, so examine merchandize for residues from possible toxic fire extinguishing materials, and question fire authorities regarding this issue.

In addition, chemical contamination in fire disasters can also be present from other sources, including:

1.   Stored chemicals rupturing from heat or from impact of falling debris.

2.   Spraying or leaking chemicals (liquid, powder, dust, granules) as damaged containers are being removed or salvaged from the fire area.

3.   Tracking of chemical material from contaminated areas to other areas by fire crews or others.

4.   Burning or melting plastic containers and/or insulation and other building materials.

5.   Leaking fuels, storage batteries, anti-freeze, etc., from burning, damaged or overheated equipment.

6.   Chemicals from melting or vaporizing electrical insulation and, in particular, cooling chemicals from leaking or exploding electrical transformers. Large commercial transformers are often directly involved in the fire area and may leak or explode from the heat, spreading toxic liquid chemicals (some transformer oils contain concentrations of PCB) over a large area, even contaminating products in non-fire areas.

945.6 Chemical Spills, Hazardous Waste Sites, Wrecks

See IOM 321 for information.

Chemical spills occurring on land or water can pose a serious threat to the environment and contaminate FDA regulated products both directly and indirectly.

In wrecks, the physical impact usually causes most damage. Toxic items in the same load may rupture and add to the contamination. In train wrecks, other railcars loaded with chemicals, oils or other contaminating materials may rupture and contaminate food and drug products in otherwise undamaged cars. Removal of the wreckage may cause further physical damage or chemical contamination. Exposure to weather may also adversely affect the products.

Do not overlook the possibility that runoff of toxic chemicals from wrecked and ruptured cars may contaminate adjacent or nearby streams supplying water to downstream firms under FDA jurisdiction.

Hazardous waste sites also pose a hazard to the immediate environment, as well as off-site, if runoff contaminates nearby surface waters or if leachate contaminates ground water supplies.

945.7 Earthquakes

Extreme care must be exercised when working in earthquake areas. Do not enter severely damaged buildings.

Most damage from an earthquake comes from the after shocks, falling debris, and resulting fires and flooding. Items under FDA jurisdiction are most likely to suffer physical damage, spoilage from lack of refrigeration, and/or fire and flood damage.

946 BIOTERRORISM

Guidance to the Field on Bioterrorism (10/17/2001)

When a District is notified of a suspected bioterrorism event (including anthrax events) involving an FDA regulated product, they will notify Emergency Operations (EO) (301-443-1240) and the local OCI office immediately. EO will then notify the appropriate FDA Center, the HHS Office of Emergency Preparedness (OEP) and OCI headquarters. OCI will then notify FBI and/or local law enforcement. If EO or any other FDA office gets a report, EO will notify the offices above as well as the District Office involved. Notification of the state officials will occur at the direction of EO or OCI.

It is vital that the person taking the initial report obtain complainant contact information as well as detailed information about the event. This is the same information that is regularly collected for consumer complaints and used to record the complaint in FACTS. Complainants should be instructed to call local police (911) and follow police instructions.

If a bioterrorism act is suspected, FDA staff should not collect or accept samples from any local, state, or law enforcement agency as such actions will be coordinated by OCI and the FBI, as appropriate. If an FDA product is suspected in a tampering, please call EO immediately. In the event that FBI/OCI determine the product is not suspect, EO will issue further guidance to the District Office.

947   PRODUCT DISPOSITION

In every disaster situation orderly disposition of affected merchandise poses problems. Lots under embargo, or voluntarily held pending examination or analysis, must be secured until the examination or analysis is completed, and a decision to release is made. If the material can be released, it is returned to the owner. If contamination is obvious and state or local officials condemn the lots, arrangements must be made for disposition. Mixed adulterated and non-adulterated materials must be held for segregation and disposition.

Depending on the circumstances and the magnitude of the disaster, segregation, destruction or reconditioning of affected goods may be accomplished in the immediate area. However, the materials may be moved to distant locations for further manipulation.

FDA normally opposes movement of affected goods since control of the lots is difficult. However, in cases of wide spread disasters, reconditioning centers established in non-disaster areas may be the most efficient way to handle the problem. Decisions of this nature will be made by command or headquarters officials. Should the materials be moved, arrangements must be made for their control. Short moves might necessitate guards on the vehicles to prevent diversion, while longer ones may be by regular carriers with control by shipping records, sealed railroad cars, bonded truckers, etc.

A situation not usually encountered during our normal operations is the problem of scavengers. Handling scavengers and preventing their activity is a police matter. Nevertheless, it ties in closely with your operations in disasters, and plans must be formulated for the protection of merchandise detained, released, or awaiting disposition at the disposition site.

In disasters, local police forces are usually augmented by State and County Police, National Guard, State Militia or private security forces. Arrangements should be made by the disaster command officials for guarding of affected merchandise. If this has not been done, you should make the recommendation.

Segregation - The condition of certain goods may be difficult to ascertain since one often has no way of determining how excessive heat, humidity or disaster conditions affected package contents. Smoke damaged containers of one material may not be of concern, while for other materials, it may be cause for condemnation. Rules for each product in each situation are impossible. Your decisions in disaster areas should be based on experience, review of the laboratory results if possible, and input from your state/local counterparts and superiors.

The segregation process often creates a multitude of problems, especially when insurance claims-agents and salvage firms become involved. You are not to segregate materials yourself. This is the responsibility of the owner or his agent. You should advise them what constitutes releasable conditions. After segregation, you may be instructed to advise them what can and cannot be released based on your examination and/or laboratory results.

Destruction - It is not your responsibility to say how condemned goods are to be destroyed. This is a concern of the owner and the state or local health agencies who condemned the lots. Many times, however, FDA will be asked to aid in or recommend destruction methods. The most common destruction method is crushing and dumping in a land fill in approved areas. See IOM 710 and 740. Destruction methods usually are worked out with state or local officials. The final decision in major operations may be required of the command officials or higher headquarters, especially if the environmental impact is significant.

Control materials to be destroyed, and protect them from pilfering at destruction sites.

947.1 Reconditioning

Often, merchandise affected may be reconditioned depending on the condition of the product, its container, type product, intended use, and extent and kind of contamination.

Any reconditioning must be closely supervised, with proper safeguards for merchandise accountability. Procedures must be such that control over the operation is complete, with proper disposition of the rejected portion and the material reconditioned to the satisfaction of all health officials.

Certain articles which cannot be salvaged for human or animal use might be of use in non-food or non-feed industries. Examples of such products are:

Butter for soap stock
Meat & Poultry products for technical oil production
Oils & nuts for technical oil production
Flour for glue or wall board construction
Grains and fruits (especially dried) for industrial alcohol
Fish for fertilizer
Eggs for tannery use

However, these must be denatured to render them unfit for food or feed use. Firms must be required to account for the amounts denatured and keep records as to whom sold and for what final use. Examination of the product at its final destination and/or a spot check may be required to assure it is utilized in non-food or non-feed products.

947.2 Relabeling

Relabeling will be permitted, if all the following conditions are met.

1.   The new label contains all mandatory information, is not misleading in any way, and conforms with the Act in all other aspects;
2.   Label codes are carried over to the new label;
3   The product is not contaminated; and
4.   The container has its original integrity.

947.3 Ammonia Leaks

Refer to IOM 144.2 for guidance prior to entering any area where an ammonia leak has occurred.

If products involved in an ammonia leak are to be salvaged/reconditioned, cover the following points:

1.   Cases of food should be removed from ammonia spill rooms as soon as possible.

2.   Food packages should be removed from master corrugated cases as soon as possible. Ammonia appears to be absorbed by the corrugated cases.

3.   Food products should be recased and moved to storage areas free of ammonia and other products.

4.   When sampling ammonia contaminated products use IOM Sample Schedule Chart 3 for guidance.

The following barrier characteristics of packaging materials exposed to ammonia will help in deciding if food products may be salvaged or reconditioned.

1.   Kraft and other types of paper are very permeable.

2.   Plastic films (polyethylene, saran, cryovac, etc.) are fairly good barriers.

3.   Water glaze (ice) on food will absorb ammonia and the washing action by melting ice may eliminate ammonia.

4.   Waxed paper overwrap and waxed cardboard boxes are very permeable.

5.   Loose packed Individually Quick Frozen (I.Q.F.) Foods are more susceptible than block frozen foods.

6.   Glass, metal and heavy aluminum foil packages are excellent barriers.

947.4   Perishable Products

Milk is extremely perishable, and is highly susceptible to bacterial contamination. Any attempts at salvage are risky. Retail cartons of milk are not to be salvaged. Storage vats or sealed tanks of milk in processing plants must be closely examined and tested before release. If milk has been affected by flood waters, it should be condemned.

Fresh fruits and vegetables which have been inundated by flood waters cannot be adequately cleaned. Most are subject to rapid spoilage.

Merchandise requiring refrigeration or freezing which has been immersed in flood waters cannot be reconditioned. The same applies to meats or poultry which have been without refrigeration and may be in a decomposing state.

The following is general guidance in determining when frozen or refrigerated products cannot be reconditioned.

1.   Product is contaminated.

2.   Products which have been thawed, and there is evidence of decomposition.

3.   Products which have thawed and represent a potential public health hazard.

4.   Products which have not been maintained at temperatures appropriate to individual product requirements.

5.   Products meeting criteria in the following sections regarding types of containers.

947.5 Reconditioning Plastic, Paper, Cardboard, Cloth and Similar Containers

Goods packed in these containers which have been water damaged usually cannot be reconditioned. (In some instances, sugar has been permitted to be returned to a refinery for reprocessing, but each case must be decided individ-

ually). Fire and/or smoke damaged material may be permitted to be relabeled if contents have not been affected.

General rules for reconditioning of products in these types of containers are:

1.   The product is not contaminated and the product is not highly susceptible to bacteriological contamination.

2.   If the external container is torn, the interior liner must be intact, and the external container must be repaired or replaced to eliminate possible contamination of the product.

3.   Soiled containers may be cleaned, if the product is not damaged and the container can be cleaned.

4.   Foods from torn packages, where the product has been exposed but not obviously subjected to contamination, may be repackaged.

5.   Water, chemical or other liquid damage, where the exterior package may be replaced, providing the internal containers were not affected and the external containers can be replaced without contaminating the product.

6.   Fire damaged goods (wet, burned, heavy smoke contamination, or toxic fumes) are generally not reconditionable.

NOTE: Foods for infants, the aged or infirm, and drug products must be strictly controlled to assure the product is acceptable.

947.6   Reconditioning Screw-top, Crimped-cap, and Similar Containers

Products in containers with screw-caps, snap-lids, crimped-caps (soda pop bottles), twist-caps, flip-top, snap-open, and similar type closures must not be reconditioned. Sediment and debris from flood water becomes lodged under the cap lips, threads, lugs, crimps, snap-rings, etc. and is impossible to remove, especially after it has dried. If these container/closure systems are affected only by fire or smoke, but the contents are not affected by the heat, they may be relabeled.

General rules for reconditioning are:

1.   Product is not contaminated, or rendered unfit for food.

2.   Soiled containers may be reconditioned if soil can be removed, and it does not involve the closure or contents.

3.   Rust on closure: No rust allowed; surface rust may be removed by buffing or other suitable means.

4.   Cap or crown dents: slight indentations obviously not affecting the rim seal would be reconditionable.

5.   If there is evidence of exposure to extreme temperatures or pressures (hurricanes-tornadoes), products are not reconditionable.

6.   If there is soil around the closure, products are not reconditionable.

7.   If submerged in water, chemicals, or other liquids, products are not reconditionable.

8.   If container/closure are defective or not properly sealed, products are not reconditionable.

947.7 Reconditioning Hermetically Sealed (Top & Bottom Double Seam) Cans

Products in this type container which have been exposed to fire and smoke, and which are not damaged by the heat or exposed to water contamination, may be relabeled.

This type container, having been immersed in water, may be reconditioned and relabeled under controlled conditions and supervision as follows:

1.   Inspect cans;
2.   Remove labels;
3.   Wash containers in soap or detergent solution, brushing as necessary;
4.   Rinse in potable water;
5.   Buff to remove rust. Heavily rusted cans are to be discarded.
6a.   Disinfect by immersion in a solution of sodium hypochlorite containing not less than 100 ppm available chlorine or other equivalent disinfectant,

or

6b.   If product will stand it, immerse in 212oF water, bring the temperature of the water back to 212oF and maintain the temperature at 212oF for at least five minutes, then remove and cool to 95oF,
7.   Dry thoroughly, and
8.   Relabel.

General Rules for reconditioning canned foods are:

1.   The product is not contaminated. ·
2.   No rust is allowed. Surface rust may be removed, by buffing, electrolysis, or other suitable means.
3.   Cans soiled by dirt, smoke, etc., may be reconditioned if the product is not contaminated and the container can be cleaned by an acceptable method.
4.   Water contaminated cans may be reconditioned if subjected to an approved bactericidal treatment and dried promptly.
5.   If can dents consist of insignificant paneling or slight dents not affecting the double seam, or cracking the can corrugation, and not causing the can end to bulge, reconditioning is possible.
6.   Leaking cans, cans with open seams, severely damaged seams, cans which are abnormal (i.e., swollen or flipper) and cans with defective closures are not reconditionable.
7.   Cans exposed to extreme temperature are not reconditionable.
8.   Cans crushed to the point that the can body is extensively creased, paneled or dented on the seams can not be reconditioned.

947.8 Reconditioning Devices

Radiation Type Devices - Radiation producing products such as x-ray equipment, TV sets, and microwave ovens are relatively complex, expensive, sensitive devices. Any of these type devices which have been inundated by flood waters, exposed to fire, heat, mechanical or physical damage such as falling debris, chemically corroded, or electrically damaged must be checked by expert personnel. They will decide whether the device can be repaired or reconditioned by the manufacturer and/or re-tested for compliance.

Do not release any of these type devices, but report the situation to your supervisor so arrangements can be made for appraisal. The regional radiological health representative will normally be the individual contacted by your district in this type situation.

Medical Devices & Diagnostic Products - Do not attempt any reconditioning of these type products.

Any medical devices or diagnostic products which have been affected by disaster forces should not be released. Advise your supervisor of the facts so the district officials can obtain any necessary advice and guidance from the Center for Medical Devices and Radiological Health.

948   REPORTING

There is no prescribed format for narrative reporting of disaster operations. Consult with your supervisor as to your district's preference. The report should briefly describe the onset of the disaster, its magnitude, and your activities. Include cooperation with officials, planning operations, and the logical sequence of your activities.

Your report must contain exhibits consisting of photographs, diagrams, records, references to samples, and any other items necessary for proper presentation of the operation. Refer to RPM Chapter 5-10 - Emergency Procedures, for guidance on reporting natural disasters and civil disorders. Attach copies of any FDA forms issued, especially the use of FDA-2809, Natural Disaster Report, listing amounts of materials destroyed and the method of destruction. See IOM 749. Prepare charts and lists as necessary to provide documentation of all affected lots destroyed, reconditioned, or released. Include kinds and amounts of materials segregated, released, reconditioned, and destroyed and method of reconditioning and/or destruction.

Record time and FACTS data following instructions in the Data Codes Manual.

SUBCHAPTER 950 SURVEILLANCE

950   SURVEILLANCE PROCEDURES

Instructions for planned surveillance activities are found in your Compliance Program Guidance Manual. During your inspectional, investigational, and other activities, be alert to anything which may be new or unusual or interesting from FDA's viewpoint such as:

1.   New firms;
2.   New products;
3.   New production and distribution practices;
4.   New equipment and industrial processes;
5.   Seasonal practices;
6.   Industry trends;
7.   Recent or on-going construction and plans for future expansion;
8.   Proposed products;
9.   New ideas the firm is contemplating;
10.   New products in the development stage;
11.   Activities about a firm's competitor;
12.   Plans for consolidation, mergers, diversification, etc.;

13. Equipment failures or malfunction possibly affecting other firms, faulty design of equipment, incompatibility of ingredients, faulty process design, equipment manufacturers' recommendations which violate proper manufacturing precautions, health fraud (quackery), etc.

14. Health Fraud (Quackery) is defined as "the deceptive promotion, advertisement, distribution or sale of articles, intended for human or animal use, which are represented as effective to diagnose, prevent, cure, treat or mitigate disease, or provide a beneficial effect on health, but which have not been scientifically proven safe and effective for such purposes." See CPG: Chapter 1.

Use the FDA-457, Product/Establishment Surveillance Report, to report any of the items listed above. Include any other ideas/observations you may consider worthy of reporting. FDA must keep abreast of new ideas, trends, or contemplated changes in the industries we regulate as well as problems with possible broad impact.

951   FDA 457 PREPARATION

Report product or establishment surveillance on the FDA 457, Product/Establishment Surveillance Report, and submit it to your supervisor. See IOM Exhibit 960-A. Prospective new establishments must be verified for appropriateness before inclusion in the active FEI. See Field Management Directive (FMD) 130.

Complete blocks 1 through 18 and 22 through 26 of the FDA 457 for product surveillance or blocks 1,6, 8 through 10, and 18 through 26 of the FDA 457 for establishment surveillance. Your supervisor or reviewing official will complete blocks 27 through 30. For a human drug firm or product which has not actually entered the market, enter the information in the REMARKS Section.

The following number designations correspond to identically numbered blocks on the FDA 457.

"1.   HOME DISTRICT" - Enter the name of the home district of the new firm or firm producing the product reported. See IOM 702 for definition of home district.

"2.   REPORTING UNIT SYMBOL" - Enter your district symbol here, e.g., " ATL-DO", "BOS-DO", "LOS-DO", etc. If units other than field units report on the form, their mailing symbol goes here.

"3.   CENTRAL FILE NO." - Enter the central file number if readily available. Otherwise, leave blank.

"4.   J.D./T.A." - Leave blank.

"5.   COUNTY" - Leave blank.

"6.   DATE" - Enter date you prepare the FDA 457.

"7.   PRODUCT CODE" - Enter the 7-character Product Code from the Data Codes Manual.

"8.   OPERATION" - Enter operation code from the Data Codes Manual. For surveillance it is 13.

"9.   PROGRAM ASSIGNMENT CODE" - Enter the Program/Assignment Code (PAC) from the Data Codes Manual.

"10.   HOURS" - Enter the time spent on this operation, including time for preparing the report, through FACTS. Report time to the nearest 1/4 hour in fractions, not decimals. Do not report travel time.

"11.   IDENTIFICATION" - Enter the generic name of the product and quote enough of the label to properly identify

the item, including the firm name and address.

"12.   MANUFACTURER CONTROL CODES" - Enter all codes, lot numbers, batch codes, etc., found on the containers, labels, wrappers, packages, cases, etc. and indicate whether the number is located on the label, containers, case, etc.

"13.   AMOUNT ON HAND" - List lot size (amount of the products) on hand or available. If count cannot be made, make an estimate and so indicate.

"14.   DATE LOT RECEIVED" - Determine & enter the date the dealer received the lot(s).

"15.   ESTIMATED VALUE" - This is the invoice value of the amount on hand at the time you observed it. Estimate, if not readily available.

"16.   SAMPLE NO(s)" - Enter sample number(s) of any relevant samples collected. If no samples are collected, enter "None".

"17.   DEALER" - List name and complete address including the ZIP code of dealer who owns or has custody of the product.

"18.   DISTRIBUTOR   MANUFACTURER   SHIPPER OTHER" - Check applicable box or boxes and list name, complete address, ZIP code and telephone number, including area code.

"19.   ESTABLISHMENT TYPES/INDUSTRY CODES" - Enter up to three establishment types with up to six industry codes each for the establishment.

"20.   ESTABLISHMENT SIZE" - Enter gross dollar value of the annual production of all FDA regulated products made or manipulated in the establishment.

"21.   INFORMATION OBTAINED BY" - Check the applicable box to indicate how the FEI information was obtained.

"22.   REMARKS" - Enter explanatory information here.

"23.   REPORT PREPARED BY" - Type or print your name and title.

"24.   EMPL NO." - Enter your employee number.

"25.   PC" - Enter your Position Classification code.

"26.   SIGNATURE" - Enter usual signature.

"27.   REPORTING UNIT ACTION" - Your supervisor or reviewing official completes this section by checking the applicable box.

"28.   NAME OF REVIEWING OFFICIAL" - Typed or printed name of person reviewing the report.

"29.   TITLE" - Title of reviewing official.

"30.   DATE REVIEWED" - The reviewing official enters date report was reviewed.

Complete reverse side of the FDA 457 by checking the appropriate box(es).

952   FDA 457 ROUTING

Submit all FDA 457's to your supervisor for review, assignment, or routing as indicated:

1.   Human Drug Surveillance - Submit a copy of the FDA 457 to the Center For Drug Evaluation & Research (HFD-323).

2.   Veterinary Drug Surveillance - Submit a copy of the FDA 457 to the Center for Veterinary Medicine, (HFV-236).

3.   Device Surveillance - Submit a copy of the FDA 457 to the Office of Medical Devices (HFZ-331).

4.   Foods Surveillance - Submit a copy of the FDA 457 to the home district.

5.   Other Products - Submit a copy of the FDA 457 to the home district.

SUBCHAPTER 960 - INVESTIGATIONAL RESEARCH

961   RESEARCH ASSIGNMENTS

"Investigational Research" is investigation to discover and interpret facts, or to revise accepted theories and practices in the light of new facts, to improve investigational operations.

Investigational Research may be proposed by you, or assigned by your supervisor, and must be submitted for approval on the FDA l609, Research Project Record. To formally propose research, complete this form and submit the original and two copies to your supervisor. After branch approval, original is retained by the branch research coordinator; one copy to the researcher; and one copy to HFC-132. Approval authority, except for research under the Science Advisor Research Associate Program (SARAP), is at the branch director level. SARAP projects are considered on a competitive basis and approved at headquarters. Investigational personnel are eligible to compete for SARAP approvals. Instructions and conditions for SARAP proposals are provided in the "ORO Research Programs" booklet.

Numerical and alpha listings of active laboratory and investigational research projects will be computer generated at headquarters and supplied to the districts on a semi-annual basis. To prevent duplications, check these listings (in possession of the science branch research coordinator) prior to proposing projects.

962   JOINT RESEARCH PROJECTS

Project proposals involving significant analytical requirements must be approved in advance by the appropriate laboratory. Whenever investigational research requires analysis of samples, consider submitting a joint investigational/laboratory project proposal and final report. In these instances, request your supervisor to assist in arranging such joint projects.

When proposed research projects involve engineering assistance beyond that which is available within the district, request this through your supervisor from the Domestic Operations Branch/Division of Field Investigations (HFC-130). DFI Engineers may be available to assist on a specific short term basis, and to work with field investigators on joint projects, or may initiate investigational research independently.

963   RESEARCH PROJECT IDENTIFICATION CODE

Project Codes are assigned by the district investigations branch research coordinator after project approval. You should assure a correct code has been assigned before beginning work under the approved project. The project code will reveal the district, the research category, and sequential project number (1 through 99) within the category for the district.

964   RESEARCH PROJECT PROGRESS REPORTS

You must submit semi-annual progress reports for each ongoing research project. Each researcher shall initiate this form for each active project in April and October to reach DFI (HFC-130) by April 15th and October 15th respectively.

965   TERMINATION OF RESEARCH PROJECTS

Report project termination on FDA 1609 and FDA 1609a. Enter a summary of the completed project on the FDA 1609, including actions taken and publication, if any. If a paper has been prepared for publication, include the abstract.

The complete project report, with supporting data, may be on plain-paper continuation sheets to the FDA 1609, or may be a separate memorandum attached to the FDA 1609. Submit FDA 1609a to accompany a termination FDA 1609, to summarize the concluding semi-annual period of work on the project and to report final time expenditures. The minimum number of termination forms and project report copies is original plus two. After branch action, original is retained by the branch research coordinator; one copy by researcher; and one copy by HFC-132.

966   PRIORITY

Investigational research, after project approval, will be considered in relative priority to other assignments. Always keep your supervisor apprised when you are working on research projects. Whenever possible, such work should be done with other assignments for efficient operations. When research projects are urgently needed, or of substantial scope and duration, you may request supervisory approval of appropriate continuous periods for uninterrupted work. The "Research Priority" entered in block # 9 of the FDA-1609a indicates relative priority to other research, not the priority relative to regulatory and compliance assignments. You should complete regulatory and compliance work while avoiding, as best you can, delays in completing approved research projects. See your supervisor to help determine priorities.

967   DATA REPORTING

Investigational research time is reported into PODS, using a distinctive Program/Assignment Code (PAC). See the Data Codes Manual. Use FDA 2123, Program Data Sheet, reporting as Operation 01, Research.

On the FDA 2123, under item 10, a total of 20 spaces can be read by the computer program. Enter the Investigational Research Project Identification Code for a total of seven spaces. Column 8 may contain either a dash (-) or intra-laboratory code to identify a special laboratory group. An abbreviated research project name will be entered in remaining columns.

If laboratory personnel are working on investigational research projects, follow laboratory procedures for reporting time, while using the Investigational Research Project Identification Code.

SUBCHAPTER 970 - TAMPERING

971   AUTHORITY & RESPONSIBILITY

FDA is authorized to investigate reported tampering of FDA regulated consumer products under the Federal Anti-Tampering Act (FATA), Title 18, USC, Section 1365. See IOM Exhibit 970-A. In most cases, the authority for such investigations is also found in the FD&C Act.

The Office of Criminal Investigations (OCI) has the primary responsibility for all criminal investigation of tampering/threat incidents of products. The District Offices and the OCI Field Office must coordinate responses to tamperings to ensure initial investigative steps are taken in a timely and efficient manner.

In those incidents where OCI does not, or cannot, initiate a criminal investigation because of resource limitations, the District Offices will determine, in consultation with OCI, the proper follow-up.

The purpose of these investigations is to determine if tampering has occurred; the seriousness of the problem; the quantity of affected products on the market; the source of the tampering; and quick removal from consumers or commerce of any contaminated product. The Office of Criminal Investigations will seek to identify and initiate criminal prosecution of those persons responsible for criminal activity associated with tampering/threat incidents.

FDA will investigate reports of tampering associated with FDA regulated products. Priority will be given to reports of death, illness, injury, or a potential health hazard. Adhere to existing procedures and instructions as outlined in the IOM and RPM when conducting tampering investigations, inspections, sample collections, special investigations, and related activities including interviews, record examination, direct observation, affidavits, etc. Additional guidance on investigational authority under FATA can be found in IOM 976.

972   COORDINATION WITH OTHER GOVERNMENT AGENCIES

Federal - USDA and the FBI share enforcement of the FATA with FDA as described below:

1.   FBI Responsibility - The FBI has concurrent jurisdiction under the Federal Anti-Tampering Act over products regulated by FDA. The FDA understands the FBI's primary interest in the Federal Anti-Tampering Act (FATA) matters will be to investigate, particularly, those cases which involve a serious threat to human life or a death. The FBI will also investigate FATA matters involving threatened tamperings, and actual or threatened tamperings coupled with

an extortion demand. The OCI Field Office will coordinate referrals to the FBI in accordance with agency policy.

2.   USDA Responsibility - The USDA will investigate and interact with the FBI on tamperings with products regulated by USDA. The OCI Field Office will coordinate referrals to the FBI in accordance with IOM 973.

State and Local - Isolated incidents of tampering not investigated by OCI and not meeting the criteria for FBI or USDA follow-up, may be referred to the appropriate state or local investigative agencies, after consultation with the OCI Field Office as outlined in IOM 973. Assistance should be provided to cooperating officials as necessary or where requested.

973   REFERRALS

All reports of tampering or tampering threats must be immediately reported to the appropriate OCI Field Office and the Emergency Operations Center.

974   HEADQUARTERS CONTACT

The Emergency Operations Center HFC-160, (301) 443-1240, is the focal point for communications, especially in those tampering cases where regional/national coverage is necessary. Alert the EOC immediately to all suspected or confirmed tampering incidents, whether or not there is an injury/illness involved, especially if media attention will be initiated by any source.

975   INVESTIGATION

Information on matters under investigation by OCI should not be released without prior discussion and concurrence of the OCI Field Office. See IOM 161 for additional information concerning dealing with the media in investigative matters.

975.1 General Procedures

Tampering incidents historically have occurred in unpredictable forms and products. Standard operating procedures, in most cases, will suffice for these investigations. As events take place, specific instructions for some investigations may be provided by headquarters and/or your district. Expeditious resolution is important, especially when a health hazard may be involved.

Attempt to answer the following questions as rapidly as possible:

1.   Has tampering occurred, or can the condition of the product be explained by other means?

2.   Is death, injury, or illness associated with the report and, if so, does it appear to be caused by the product tampering?

3.   Does the incident appear to be isolated, or widespread?

4.   Is it likely other, similarly affected FDA regulated products remain in distribution, and if so, what is the extent and magnitude of distribution?

5.   If not isolated, could the product tampering have

occurred at the production facility or in the distribution chain?

6.   Can specific persons or points in the distribution chain be identified as possibly causing the problem?

When tampering, threat or false report is evident, or highly suspect, use the concepts listed below which are appropriate for the situation. Be sure to coordinate your efforts with the OCI Field Office.

975.2 Interviews

It is often advantageous to work in pairs during interviews with complainants. Conduct interviews in a location which reduces unnecessary interruptions or distractions. Establish rapport with the person or persons being interviewed to put them at ease. Listen to the person. Let them first tell the story in their own way. Listen carefully to each facet. Be genuine and at ease. After hearing the entire story, ask them for more information to fill in details. Ask for clarification of key points.

Obtaining details and requesting clarification of key points allows you to obtain an idea of the validity of the person's story through comparison of the accuracy of the details with previous information supplied.

Note-taking may put the person being interviewed on edge. If this appears to be the case, do not take notes until you request clarification of key points. Ask who was with the person, what happened in the store, any problems noted with the product at the store, and other questions which will provide you with more information on when, where, or why events took place, who was present, etc. If two investigators are involved in the interview, one should take notes while the other asks the questions.

During interviews watch for changes in attitudes, body language, hesitation in speech, etc., as you observe and listen to the person being interviewed. Describe your observations of body language and personal characteristics in your report.

975.3 Sampling

NOTE: Whenever a sample is collected for suspected tampering, you must collect an authentic sample of the same product. It should be from the same lot and code, if at all possible. The sample size for the authentic portion is at least 6 intact units.

Collect any containers a suspect may have handled as they placed the tampered product on the shelf. Preparation of the sample and the shipping method should be carefully selected to insure the integrity and security of the samples. Coordinate with the Office Of Criminal Investigations (OCI) and the Forensic Chemistry Center (FCC) on correct sample packaging.

When handling product containers or other evidence associated with tampering, take care to avoid adding or smearing fingerprints by wearing cotton gloves, using tongs, forceps, or by picking the container up by opposing corners. Identify product containers carefully and in as small an area as possible. Do not open outer containers to identify inner containers or inserts.

When sampling or handling product, be alert for traces of evidence such as hair, dust, paint chips, glass fragments, etc. Secure such evidence in a separate container such as a glass vial, small manila envelope or plastic bag.

Samples should be packed to avoid movement of the product container within the bag. Individual dosage units from previously opened containers can be protected by removing them from their container utilizing a spoon or forceps. Secure them in separate containers so they do not rub or smear possible evidence. Further guidance can be found in the FBI "HANDBOOK OF FORENSIC SCIENCE" which has been supplied to each district. As a precaution, rubber gloves may be worn inside of cotton gloves as protection against toxic or caustic substances.

Ship samples with extreme care to insure their integrity. Thoroughly describe your sample and its characteristics on the C/R to facilitate the analysis. Include any descriptive terms used by individuals associated with the complaint. If special instructions to preserve fingerprints or for further handling are indicated, they should be noted on the C/R and FDA-525. If speed is imperative consider hand delivery to the lab.

975.4 Complainant

When visiting the complainant, use the standard consumer complaint procedures set forth in the IOM. Plan and think through the reasons for and goals for your visit before approaching the complainant. Listen carefully to the complainant. Review background of the complainant for history of complaints or law suits filed. Background checks are appropriate when district management has strong suspicions concerning the validity of the complaint or the potential for the complaint being used to defraud. It is often advantageous to work in pairs while interviewing complainants.

When collecting samples from the complainant, document them as official samples, including an affidavit describing the circumstances involved in the purchase and use of the product.

When investigating at a complainants residence, obtain permission from the occupant to examine trash containers for discarded product labeling and/or containers which can be utilized to further investigations. Be alert to sources of contamination in the residence which are similar to the contaminants found in the product. Be sure to examine other containers of the same product in the residence with the owners permission and sample them if suspect. Obtain permission to examine medicine cabinets if a drug dosage form is involved.

It is possible individuals you contact may not be aware of the provisions of the FATA. A general discussion of the FATA, its provisions for investigation, filing of false reports, and tampering can be useful and informative to those individuals. Prior to concluding your interview of the complainant, obtain a signed affidavit attesting to the circumstances of the complaint, as directed by IOM 431.3 and 975.1. Include a statement in the affidavit similar to the following, "I have been informed of the provisions of the Federal Anti-Tampering Act and also that the providing of false information to the federal government is illegal." It is permissible to pre-type this statement at the bottom of an Affidavit, FDA 463a, and photocopy it before use if you have a large number of tampering complaints to investigate.

975.5 Retail Stores

When investigating a tampering report at a retail store or other source of product, the local police department can be of assistance and provide advice. Before instituting any activities at the scene, protect the area to preserve any evidence on the store shelves, floor or adjacent areas and products. Discuss with the firm's management, and/or the personnel doing the stocking of the shelves, how material is received and handled prior to being placed on shelves.

Document the area using photographs of the product shelves, surrounding area, and any shots which would provide information on the product, its location and store layout. Samples of materials in the area that may be applicable to the investigation are to be collected. Because suspects are thought to handle multiple product containers when placing a tampered product on a store shelf, a diagram of the container relationships to each other should be prepared and individual containers given subsample numbers.

Be observant of persons present in the store, as guilty parties are thought often to return to such location, especially when the agency or news media are present. Be alert to statements of store personnel about activities they have observed. Obtain descriptions of the actions, dress and physical characteristics of persons the employees have noted exhibiting unusual/notable behavior in the store. Ascertain if the firm has a closed circuit TV monitoring system and if they maintain tapes, if so, these may be a source of leads. Obtain information about employees terminated in past year, employee problems, or shoplifters who may wish to cause problems in the store.

975.6 Manufacturer and Distribution System Follow-up

The key to a successful investigation or inspection is to clearly define the objectives of the operation and to examine each facet of the establishment in light of the objective(s). Aspects of the production/distribution system to inspect for leads may include, but not be limited to the following:

Manufacturing Sites

1.   Age of facility, and date when production of the first batch of the product under investigation was initiated.

2.   List of other facilities which produce the product under investigation.

3.   For drugs, list by strength, size of container, name, dosage form, and number of packages per shipping case, all products manufactured or processed at the facility. If products handled are repackaged at this facility, give the name and address and method of receipt from the product source.

4.   Obtain the names, titles, addresses, office and residence telephone numbers of representatives of the company, including that of the Chief Executive Officer (CEO), who are specified as contacts for various aspects of the event under investigation. State whether these representatives are members of an established management team to deal with such events, or have they been identified for the particular instance at hand.

5.   Contract packagers, if any, should be described by name, location and products handled.

6.   For the suspect lot, give its lot number, the size of the lot, size and type of containers in which it was packaged, its history of production and distribution beginning with the date of weighing of the raw material, and the dates and description of steps in processing.

7.   Describe any locations within the facility where an employee could have access to the contaminant being investigated.

8.   Describe the characteristics of the suspected contaminant within the facility, its container type, its brand and generic name, its lot number, size of container, whether the container is full, or partially full and the approximate amount remaining.

9.   Describe security for the suspected contaminant including limitations of access, where it is stored, and responsibility for controlling access to the material.

10.   Describe what legitimate use, if any, the facility has for the suspected contaminant in each of the locations found.

11.   Determine how often the material is used and whether or not a log of its use is maintained.

12.   If a log is maintained, obtain a copy showing its use and discuss with plant management the legitimacy of each such use.

13.   Determine whether the firm verifies use and use rates and has a method of determining explanations for any discrepancies noted.

14.   Have samples of the suspect contaminant been obtained by the FDA or other agencies, and if so, what are the results of analysis?

15.   Does the firm test for the contaminant under investigation?

16.   What method is utilized for such testing, and at what frequency?

17.   List the facility's sources of raw materials for the suspect lot/product.

18.   Evaluate the raw material storage conditions to determine the potential for manipulation of materials.

19.   Describe the lot numbering system, any plant identification numbers, and expiration dates placed on retail products and cases.

20.   If any product for export is processed at this plant, describe any differences from domestic products.

21.   If the product under investigation has tamper resistant packaging (TRP), determine the type of system utilized, and if the system utilized has been evaluated to determine if breaching is possible. If breaching is possible, describe. Describe lot numbers or code numbers placed on TRP and security measures taken for TRP materials on hand and those sent to contract packagers. Determine whether TRP materials are accountable.

22.   If the plant process includes collection of samples for examination on the production line or by laboratory facil-

ities, discuss where the samples are maintained, who has access to them, and their disposition.

23.   Report dates and description of each step in processing, including identification of storage locations between steps. Obtain estimates of flow rates and volume of materials in hoppers and drums at key stages. Determine distances between production areas or between processing equipment at critical points. This information can be useful for statistical evaluation of the likelihood of contamination at various points in the process.

24.   Include a description of the in-process lot numbering systems for each phase of manufacturing, security for each process and/or product while in storage and during processing.

25.   In some types of processes, there are provisions for an individual to ensure sufficient product is placed in each container being filled. If this is the case in the plant under inspection, describe the circumstances and security for this process.

26.   Determine whether the facility hires part-time employees, or transfers employees from one location to another on a temporary basis. Were any were present during production of the suspect lot?

27.   Describe provisions for determining reliability of employees.

28.   Determine if employees can move from area to area within the facility. Describe any restrictions on their movements and if enforced.

29.   Describe laboratory control tests and in-process tests performed on the finished packaged product and in-process materials. Determine if reserve samples are retained of all lots.

30.   Determine how rejects and reworked materials are handled.

31.   Describe any unusual events which may have taken place during the period when the suspect material was in the facility.

32.   Determine if the firm has a plan to safeguard against tampering as part of its Q.A. program. If so, determine the implementation date of this plan and review any periodic assessment reports for potential problem areas.

Distribution Facilities - It may be necessary to obtain the following information at each level in the distribution chain:

1.   Amount of suspect lot on hand at time of inspection.

2.   Obtain the turnover rate for the product under investigation.

3.   Amount of suspect lot received, and any variations from amount consigned to the facility.

4.   Date received.

5.   How received.

6.   Name and type of carrier which delivered the product. Determine security of the vehicle or container while in-transit.

7.   Obtain distribution history of the suspect lots.

8.   Describe the distribution area covered by the facility being inspected and the number of accounts served, whether they are retail or wholesale.

9.   Determine if the facility handles any cash and carry orders.

10.   Determine if the facility will accept returns and how are they handled.

11.   Describe stock rotation practices and how they can be assured.

12.   Determine if lot numbers of products distributed can be traced.

13.   Describe the method of packing of shipments; for example, plastic tote bins sealed with nylon tape, intact cartons only, cases are split, etc.

14.   Describe the methods of shipment utilized by the warehouse.

15.   Describe personnel practices, problems and other information on visitors, contractors, etc.

It is often advantageous to chart a pictograph or a time line chart of the distribution system which shows basic information on each level in the distribution chain and distances between each link in the chain. It is also often worthwhile to prepare a time-line chart showing the progression of the suspect lot through the manufacturing process to the source of the complaint, including the significant steps in the manufacture and distribution of the suspect product.

Security - Obtain the following information. However, when preparing the EIR, do not report the details of the security system, since an inadvertent release could compromise a facilities security system. Discuss with your supervisor how to report this information.

1.   General security arrangements, including the number of guards, their shifts, locations, and whether or not they patrol the facility.

2.   Describe any closed circuit TV systems, their locations, and any physical barriers to prevent access to the plant grounds and its facility.

3.   Describe who is logged in and out of the facility and whether or not employees must display identification badges upon entry. If plant employees are issued uniforms by color or design, which designate their work station locations, also describe.

4.   Determine whether visitors, contractor representatives, cleaning crews, etc., are subject to movement tracking or control, and if any were present during production of the suspect product.

5.   If the suspect product was particularly vulnerable to in-plant tampering during certain stages of handling, identify particular employees who had access to product during these stages and interview them individually. There may be occasions when line employees may be able to remember suspicious activities on the part of co-workers or others working in the area when suspect lots were being produced.

6.   Describe the security measures taken for the processing area after hours, during work breaks, and at meal times. Be alert to those periods when in-process containers are left unattended on a packing/production line.

7.   Describe any employee relations problems such as layoffs, firings, probations, adverse actions, etc.

976   RECORD REQUESTS

Occasionally, your investigation may require you to obtain information not specifically authorized under the FD&C Act, e.g., distribution records of food products, production records for OTC drugs or foods, etc. Seek to obtain such records if the following criteria have been met, or if, in the opinion of your supervisor, district, or headquarters, it is necessary to do so:

1.   The apparent tampering incident may be serious and is assigned a high priority by your supervisor, district and/or agency, and;

2.   The data sought is normally of the type FDA is trained to evaluate and have access to in other areas of routine FD&C Act activities, e.g., production records, formulas, distribution records, etc., and;

3.   The requested data is likely to be necessary to the successful resolution of the investigation, and;

4.   Other alternatives to obtain the information are not as readily available.

If a request for data is made, you should direct it to the most responsible individual at the location. Explain clearly and concisely your need for the data. Do not issue a written request unless you have specific supervisory/district concurrence to do so.

977   REFUSALS

All refusals encountered during tampering investigations should be documented using existing procedures. Refusals of requests should include documentation the criteria in IOM 976 were met and the firm was aware of the non-routine nature of the request. The lack of precedent in this area suggests thorough documentation to allow appropriate compliance review and follow-up. A search warrant, subpoena or other court order may be appropriate in some circumstances. The feasibility and necessity of these actions should be discussed with the OCI Field Office before such action is initiated.

978   REPORTING

Complete the FACTS Consumer Complaint Report and the FACTS Complaint Follow-up Report for all tampering complaints received. See IOM Exhibits 900-A & 900-B. Note: Time reporting should occur through FACTS.

All completed and/or resolved reports of tampering incidents should be provided to the EOC (HFC-160) to develop background information for agency use. If the investigation is of a continuing nature, the agency may require interim reports on a case by case basis.

Critique each interviewing session to determine how it could have been improved. Was your purpose achieved, was your own performance satisfactory, and what were the actions and activities of the person interviewed?

SUBCHAPTER 980 - OFFICE OF CRIMINAL INVESTIGATIONS (OCI)

981   OCI PROCEDURES

The Office of Criminal Investigations (OCI) has the primary responsibility for all criminal investigations conducted by the FDA.

OCI has been designated the authority to administer the consensual electronic surveillance program for the Office of Regulatory Affairs. To comply with FDA policy and Department of Justice requirements, District Directors must contact the appropriate OCI Field Office Special Agent in Charge (SAC) prior to initiating any electronic surveillance.

981.1 Reports of Criminal Activity

All reports of confirmed or suspected criminal activity must be reported to the appropriate OCI field office or resident office as soon as possible. The OCI field office will conduct investigations when criminal activity is suspected and resources are available. In those instances where OCI does not, or cannot, initiate a criminal investigation, the District Offices will determine, in consultation with OCI, the proper follow-up.

981.2 Liaison with Law Enforcement Community

OCI is the FDA's liaison component with the law enforcement community for criminal investigations and related matters. All contacts concerning requests or questions related to criminal matters by federal, state, or local law enforcement agencies or others at the District or Regional level should be made through or referred to the local OCI Field Office Special Agent in Charge (SAIC). Similarly, contacts to FDA Headquarters or Centers should be referred to the Assistant Director (AD) Investigative Operations Division (IOD) at OCI Headquarters. When FDA personnel receive information or requests from law enforcement or other agencies concerning criminal activity, they should obtain the caller's name, organization, request and refer the caller to the appropriate OCI component. After referring the caller to OCI, contact the affected OCI unit to provide them with the caller's information. This will ensure OCI is not caught by surprise. FDA personnel should not respond to inquiries concerning criminal investigations, including questions seeking confirmation FDA is or is not conducting a criminal investigation.

981.3 Consensual Electronic Surveillance

OCI has been designated the authority to administer the consensual electronic surveillance program for the FDA. To comply with FDA Policy and Department of Justice requirements, all FDA personnel must contact the appropriate OCI Field Office SAIC to request approval before any electronic surveillance; this includes recording consensual telephone conversations. FDA Headquarters and Center personnel should contact OCI Headquarters, AD IOD for approval requests.

981.4 Postal Mail Cover

OCI is also the point of contact for any request for a mail cover through the U.S. Postal Inspection Service. A mail cover provides a written record of all data appearing on the outside of any class of mail to obtain information for:

1. Protecting national security.
2. Locating a fugitive.
3. Obtaining evidence of the commission or attempted commission of a crime punishable by more than one year in prison. A mail cover may not be used in non-criminal investigations, except in those cases involving a civil forfeiture of assets related to violations of criminal laws.

982   OCI REPORTING

ORA has developed special forms to facilitate reporting to OCI. This system provides a standard method for both reporting case information and referring a criminal case to OCI.

The Case Initiation/Information (CII) Form (IOM Exhibit 980-A), with instructions, is to be used by the districts to forward information concerning new, ongoing or past criminal case information for data entry.

The Supplemental Investigation Report Form (IOM Exhibit 980-B) is to be used to provide additional information as criminal cases develop. After the initial report is submitted, updating information will be provided to OCI via this form. These supplemental reports should be submitted whenever something of significance develops, or at least every 45 days after a case number is assigned.

The Subject Identifier Form (IOM Exhibit 980-C), with instructions, will be utilized to provide specific information concerning ongoing criminal investigation suspects.

If you have any doubts about whether or not information or a case needs to be referred to OCI, contact your District management for guidance.

NOTE: You may reproduce the IOM Exhibit for use if you do not have a supply of forms.

982.1 Case Referrals

Cases and potential cases are referred to OCI using the applicable form(s), which are forwarded to the Special Agent In Charge (SAIC) at the appropriate OCI field office. The forms will then be forwarded to OCI Headquarters, Investigations Operations unit, for review and assignment of a case number. This case number will be a unique identifier, and the number will be subsequently provided to the reporting district.

If a case is referred to OCI, a cover memo is to be prepared covering the referral and salient case facts. This will lessen duplication, and keep districts and OCI field offices aware of allied investigations across the field.

982.1 Case Closing

When a case is closed, a closing synopsis will be provided to OCI. If the case is closed by judicial action, provide the specifics of the action, listing charges, judicial district, arrest/indictment dates, trial dates, prosecutors, trial results, sentence/fines, etc.

SUBCHAPTER 990 - GENERAL INVESTIGATION REPORTING

The current Field Accomplishment and Compliance Tracking System (FACTS) Investigation fields of "Summary" and Endorsement" cannot be printed and may not have enough space to include all necessary data. Therefore, in each case where a hard copy is required, use the reporting method described below. The FACTS Summary and Endorsement should be annotated to indicate the location of the actual report and endorsement, i.e., "see KAN-DO files," "see FACTS Consumer Complaint #," etc.

Following the completion of an investigation, you will prepare a written report of the investigation as directed by your supervisor, which records all pertinent data, including referencing of firms and attachments/exhibits, samples collected, etc. Use memorandum format, with appropriate supervisory endorsement and routing. For consumer complaints complete the FACTS Complaint Follow-Up Report. See IOM 902, 902.9 and 922. For surveillance activities, use Surveillance Report form (FDA 457). See IOM 951. In other situations use methods directed by your District.

In those instances where FACTS is used for simple data/time entry under the Investigation Operation, and when you may not need a written report (examples: OEI improvement or pesticide surveillance), then enter sufficient information in the appropriate FACTS fields. The fields are those necessary for your supervisor to endorse the entry.

FACTS Operation 13, Investigation, will be used for inspections where the firm is Out of Business (OOB), not Official Establishment Inventory (NOEI), or where no inspection was made. Currently, this requires a written, hard copy memorandum [or a printed endorsement-type document] and supervisory endorsement for inclusion in your District's files. In the case of OOB and NOEI, this is required for the appropriate filing personnel to know to remove the active files and send to the record center or storage per District procedure. For "no inspection made" the information in the file, especially the reason, may be helpful to future investigators.

FACTSPROD - Citrix ICA Client

FACTS Version 3.1.01 - [Maintain Consumer Complaints]

Action   Edit   Options   Navigate   Tracing   Window   Help

Page ● 1 ○ 2

Maintain Consumer Complaints

Complaint Number:

Complaint Date: 09/24/2001

Receiving Org: ORO

Accomp. District:

Status:

Complainant Name (Last, First):

Street Address:

City:

State:

Zip Code:

Province:

Mail Code:

Country:

Phone (Home):

Phone (Work):

How Received:

Complaint Source:

Source POC:

Source Phone:

Complaint Description:

Adverse Event Result:

Attended Health Professional?

Health Care Prov.

Adverse Event Date:

Emergency Room/Outpatient visit?

ER Info.

Injury / Illness:

Required Hospitalization?

Hospital Info.

Complaint Reported To?

Notify DEIO/EMOPS?   Notification Date:

Need addnl. FDA Contact?

Remarks:

Received by: Rogers, Sydney

Complaint Symptoms

Symptoms	System Affected	Onset Time	Onset Time Unit	Duration	Duration Time Unit	Remarks	
							Add
							Delete

Count: 0   <List>

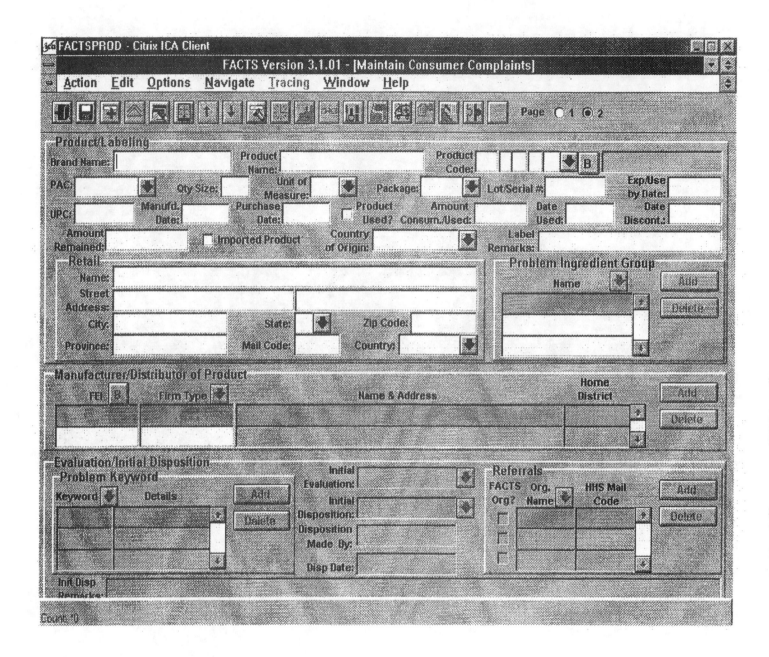

FACTS PROD - EthalICs Client

FACTS Version 4.3.01 – [Maintain Consumer Complaint Follow-Up/ Related Complaints]

Action   Edit   Options   Navigate   Tracing   Window   Help

Maintain Consumer Complaint Follow-Up/ Related Complaints

Complaint Number: 15435   Receiving Org: NOL-DO   Accomplishing District: NOL-DO   Status: Follow Up Requ

Complainant Name: TOGERSON, BARBAR   Complaint Date: 11/13/2002   Initial Disposition:

Product Code: 65 A C Y 99   Product Name: TABLETS   PAC Code: 66R601

Requested Operations/ Related Complaints

Op Id	Operation	Assignment Number	Accomplishing Organization	Performing Organization	Sample Number	PAF	Status	Status Date	Related Complaint #
226321	Domestic Invest	368037	NOL-DO	NOLIBSUPV 3			Assigned	11/14/2002	

Group
Ungroup

Evaluation & Final Disposition

Responsible Firm

FEI: B   Firm Type: Consumer   Follow-Up Disposition:

Name: Disposition Made By: Date:

Address:

Home District: **Follow Up Sent To**

FACTS Org?   Org. Name   HHS Mail Code   Add

DEPARTMENT OF HEALTH AND HUMAN SERVICES
PUBLIC HEALTH SERVICE
FOOD AND DRUG ADMINISTRATION

FOOD & DRUG ADMINSTRATION
850 THIRD AVE.
BROOKLYN, NY 11232
AUTHORIZATION FOR MEDICAL RECORDS DISCLOSURE

Authorizacion Para Revelar Expiendte Medico

TO WHOM IT MAY CONCERN:

You are hereby authorized to furnish the United
States Food and Drug Administration all information
And copies of any and all records you may have
Pertaining to (my case) the (case of

A Quien Pueda Interesar:

Por la presente se le authoriza proveer a la
Administracion de Drogas y Alimentos de Estados
Unidos toda informacion y copias de cualquira y
todos los documentos que usted pueda tener con
relaccion a (mi caso) (el caso de

MISS MARY ELLEN PERTILLO
(Name)

DAUGHTER
(Relationship to you)

including, but not limited to, medical history,
physical reports, laboratory reports and
pathological slides, and X-ray reports and films.

_____
(Nombre)

_____
(Parentesco)

incluyendo, pero no limitado a, historial medico,
examenes fisicos, informes de laboratorio, laminillas
de patologia, placas e informes de radiologia.

Anthony Oliver Pertillo   **7-8-99**
(Signature) (Firma)   *(Date) (Fecha)*

Sidney H. Rogers   **7-8-99**
(Witness) (Testiso)   *(Date) (Fecha)*

FORM FDA 461 (7/82)

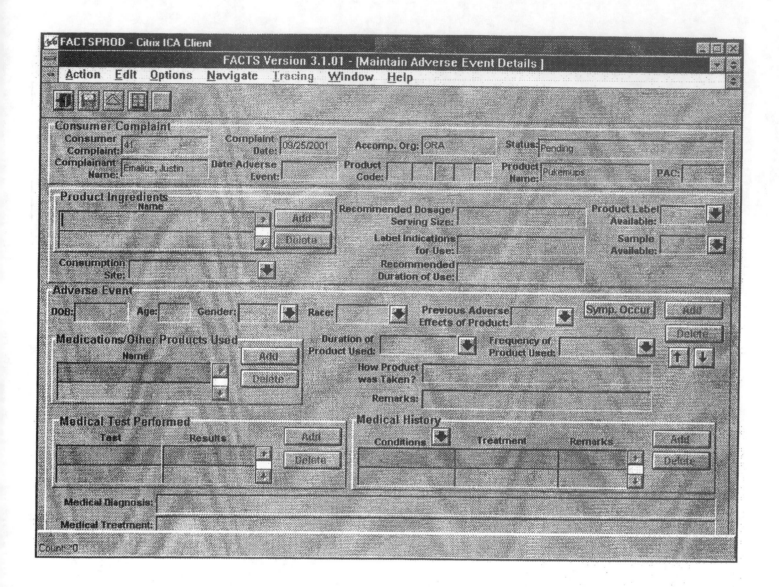

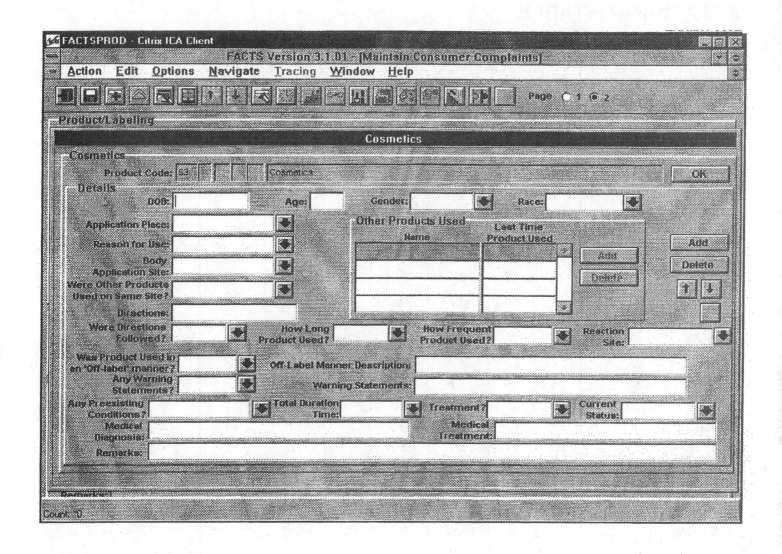

ATTACK RATE TABLE

Food or Beverage	Group A Persons Who Ate Specified Foods				Group B Persons Who Did Not Eat Specified Foods			
	Ill	Not Ill	Total	Attack Rate %	Ill	Not Ill	Total	Attack Rate %
Baked ham…….	29	17	46	63	17	12	29	59
Spinach………..	26	17	43	60	20	12	32	62
Mashed potato...	23	14	37	62	23	14	37	62
Cabbage salad...	18	10	28	64	28	19	47	60
Jell-O…………..	16	7	23	70	30	22	52	58
Rolls…………..	21	16	37	57	25	13	38	66
Brown bread…..	18	9	27	67	28	20	48	58
Milk……………...	2	2	4	50	44	27	71	62
Coffee…………..	19	12	31	61	27	17	44	61
Water…………..	13	11	24	54	33	18	51	65
Cakes…………..	27	13	40	67	19	16	35	54
Ice cream (van.).	43	11	54	(80)	3	18	21	(14)
Ice cream choc.)	25	22	47	53	20	7	27	74
Fruit salad………	4	2	6	67	42	27	69	61

To compute the attack rate in per cent, divide the number who became ill by the number who ate the food item and multiply by 100. (In the above example, baked ham 29 ÷ 46 x 100 = 63%). The offending food will show the greatest difference between the two attack rate percentages. The offending food should have a higher attack rate in "Group A" and a lower attack rate in "Group B". For example, in the table above, the attack rate for persons who ate vanilla ice cream (the offending food in the outbreak cited) was 80% while the attack rate for persons who did not eat vanilla ice cream was 14%. The disparity between the persons in "Group A" and "Group B" is the important point.

DEPARTMENT OF HEALTH AND HUMAN SERVICES
PUBLIC HEALTH SERVICE
FOOD AND DRUG ADMINISTRATION

FOOD ILLNESS INVESTIGATION

1. NAME OF PERSON	3. OCCUPATION
Jon R. Done	Teacher – High School

2 ADDRESS	a. STREET	4. AREA CODE & TELEPHONE NO.	5. AGE	6. SEX
	321 Main St. N.W.	(515) 557-2145	35	M
	c. CITY, STATE & ZIP CODE	7. DID THE PERSON EAT ANY OF SUSPECT MEAL?	X YES	☐ NO
	Centerville, IA 52411	8. DID THE PERSON BECOME ILL	X YES	☐ NO

9. FOOD INGESTED (Names and types, Trade names, frozen, canned, dried, etc.)	10. METHOD OF FOOD PREPARATION	11. QUANTITY INGESTED	12. INGESTED a. DATE	12. INGESTED b. TIME	13. CODES OF SUSPECT CONTAINER
"Yummy Brand"	Consumed as Purchased	2 oz	9-22-99	6:30 am	XYZ-74
Cream-Filled Donut					
"Better Brand" Canned	" " "	4 oz	9-22-99	6:30 am	3-2-3-A
Orange Juice					
"ABC" Corn Flakes	" " "	2 oz	9-22-99	6:30 am	None
"Best" Dairy Grade A Milk	" " "	10 oz	9-22-99	6:30 am	None

(Continue on additional forms if necessary.)

14	a. SYMPTOMS (check)	b. DATE BEGAN	c. TIME BEGAN	d. HOURS DURATION	15 PHYSICIAN	a. NAME
	NAUSEA					Thomas Meedic, M.D.
						b. STREET ADDRESS 323 Broad St. N.W.
SYMPTONS	VOMITING					c. CITY Centerville / d. STATE IA
	X DIARRHEA	9-22-99	2:30 p.m.	6		e. ZIP CODE 52412 / f. AREA CODE & TELEPHONE NO. (515) 532-3334
	X FEVER	9-22-99	2:30 p.m.	6	16 HOSPITAL	a. NAME N/A
	X PROSTRATION	9-22-99	2:30 p.m.	6		b. STREET ADDRESS _____
	PARALYSIS					c. CITY _____ / d. STATE _____
	X OTHER (See Remarks)	9-22-99	2:30 p.m.	8		e. ZIP CODE _____ / f. AREA CODE & TELEPHONE NO. _____

17. REMARKS *(Use reverse side if necessary)*
Only product available for sampling was the cream filled donuts which were sampled as
INV 99-123-456. 14. cramps

18. DATE OF INVESTIGATION	19. OFFICE	20. INVESTIGATOR'S NAME	21. INVESTIGATOR'S TITLE
9-23-99	KAN-DO	Sidney H. Rogers	Investigator

FORM FDA 3042 (12/87)   PREVIOUS EDITION MAY BE USED

CLASSIFICATION OF ILLNESSES ATTRIBUTABLE TO FOODS
(A CLASSIFICATION BY SYMPTOMS, INCUBATION PERIODS, AND TYPES OF AGENTS[1,2])

DISEASE	ETIOLOGIC AGENT AND	INCUBATION OR LATENCY	SIGNS & SYMPTOMS	FOODS INVOLVED[3]	SPECIMENS TO COLLECT	FACTORS THAT CONTRIBUTE OUTBREAKS

UPPER GASTROINTESTINAL TRACT SIGNS AND SYMPTOMS (NAUSEA, VOMITING) OCCUR FIRST OR PREDOMINATE

INCUBATION (LATENCY) PERIOD USUALLY LESS THAN ONE HOUR
FUNGAL AGENTS

DISEASE	ETIOLOGIC AGENT AND	INCUBATION OR LATENCY	SIGNS & SYMPTOMS	FOODS INVOLVED	SPECIMENS TO COLLECT	FACTORS THAT CONTRIBUTE OUTBREAKS
Gastrointestinal irritating group mushroom poisoning	Possibly resin-like substances in some mushrooms (mushroom species are different than those cited on pp. -- & --.)	30 minutes to 2 hours	Nausea, vomiting, retching, diarrhea, abdominal cramps	Many varieties of wild mushrooms	Vomitus	Eating unknown varieties of mushrooms, mistaking toxic mushrooms for edible varieties

CHEMICAL AGENTS

DISEASE	ETIOLOGIC AGENT AND	INCUBATION OR LATENCY	SIGNS & SYMPTOMS	FOODS INVOLVED	SPECIMENS TO COLLECT	FACTORS THAT CONTRIBUTE OUTBREAKS
Antimony Poisoning	Antimony in gray enamelware	Few minutes to 1 hour	Vomiting, abdominal pain, diarrhea	High-acid foods and beverages	Vomitus, stools, urine	Using/buying antimony-containing utensils, storing high-acid foods in gray enamelware
Cadmium Poisoning	Cadmium in plated utensils	15 to 30 minutes	Nausea, vomiting, abdominal cramps, diarrhea, shock	High-acid foods & beverages, candy love beads or cake decorations	Vomitus, stools, urine, blood	Using/buying cadmium-containing utensils, storing high-acid foods in cadmium-containers, ingesting cadmium-containing foods
Copper Poisoning	Copper in pipes and utensils, old dairy white metal	Few minutes to few hours	Metallic taste, nausea, vomiting (green vomitus), abdominal pain, diarrhea	High-acid foods and beverages, ice cream (ices) and beverages.	Vomitus, gastric washings, urine, blood	Storing high-acid foods in copper utensils or using copper pipes for dispensing high-acid beverages, faulty back-flow prevention valves in vending machines
Fluoride poisoning	Sodium fluoride in insecticides	Few minutes to two hours	Salty or soapy taste, numbness of mouth, vomiting, diarrhea, abdominal pain, pallor, cyanosis dilated pupils, spasms, collapse, shock	Any accidentally contaminated food, particularly dry foods, such as dry milk, flour, baking powder & cake mixes	Vomitus, gastric washings	Storing insecticides in same area as foods, mistaking pesticides for powdered foods
Lead poisoning	Lead in earthenware pesticides, putty, plaster, cans with lead solder seams	30 minutes or longer	Mouth and abdominal pain, milky vomitus, black or bloody stools, foul breath, shock blue gum line	Beverages stored in lead containing vessels, any accidentally contaminated food	Washings, stools, blood, urine	Storing high-acid foods in lead-containing vessels, storing pesticides in same area as food, imported canned high-acid foods with faulty seams
Tin poisoning	Tin in tinned cans	30 minutes to two hours	Bloating, nausea, vomiting, abdominal cramps, diarrhea, headache	High-acid foods and beverages	Vomitus, stools, urine, blood	Using uncoated tin containers for storing acidic foods. Very high tin concentrations are required to cause illness.
Zinc poisoning	Zinc in galvanized containers	Few minutes to few hours	Mouth and abdominal pain, nausea, vomiting, dizziness	High-acid foods and beverages	Vomitus, gastric washings, urine, blood, stools	storing high-acid foods in galvanized cans

INCUBATION (LATENCY) PERIOD 1 TO 6 HOURS
BACTERIAL AGENTS

DISEASE	ETIOLOGIC AGENT AND	INCUBATION OR LATENCY	SIGNS & SYMPTOMS	FOODS INVOLVED	SPECIMENS TO COLLECT	FACTORS THAT CONTRIBUTE OUTBREAKS
Bacillus cereus Gastroenteritis (emetic form, mimics staphylococcal intoxication)	Exotoxin of *B. cereus* organism in soil (strains differ from diarrheal form)	0.5 to 5 hours	Nausea, vomiting, occasionally diarrhea	Boiled or fried rice, pasta, cooked cornmeal dishes, porridge	Vomitus, stool	Storing cooked foods at room temperature, storing cooked foods in large containers in refrigerators, preparing foods several hours before serving
Staphylococcal intoxication	Exo-enterotoxins A, B, C, D & E of *Staphylococcus aureus*, staphylococci from skin, nose & lesions of infected humans and animals and from udders of cows	1 to 8 hours, mean 2 to 4 hours	Nausea, vomiting, retching, abdominal pain, diarrhea, prostration	Lower water activity foods (a_w), e.g. cheese, whipped butter, ham, meat & poultry products, cream filled pastry, food mixtures, leftovers, dry milk	Vomitus, stools, rectal swabs, carriers nasal swabs, swabs of lesions, anal swab	Inadequate refrigeration, workers touching cooked food, preparing food several hours before serving, workers with infections containing pus, holding foods at warm (bacterial incubating) temperatures, fermentation of abnormally low-acid foods

CHEMICAL AGENTS

Nitrite poisoning[4]	Nitrites or nitrates used as meat curing compounds or ground water from shallow wells	1 to 2 hours	Nausea, vomiting, cyanosis, headache, dizziness, weakness, loss of consciousness, chocolate brown colored blood[4]	Cured meats, any accidentally contaminated food exposed to excessive nitrification	Blood	Using excessive amounts of nitrites or nitrates in foods for curing or for covering up spoilage, mistaking nitrites for common salt and other condiments, improper refrigeration of fresh foods.

TOXIC ANIMALS

Diarrhetic shellfish poisoning (DSP)	Okadaic acid and other toxins produced by dino-flagellates, Dinophysis acuminata and other species	0.5 to 12 hours commonly < 3 hrs	Diarrhea, nausea, vomiting, abdominal cramps, chills, fever, headache	Mussels, clams, scallops	Gastric washings	Harvesting shellfish from waters with high concentration of Dinophysis

INCUBATION (LATENCY) PERIOD USUALLY 7 TO 12 HOURS
FUNGAL AGENTS

Cyclopeptide and Gyromitrin groups of mushroom poisoning	Cyclopeptides and Gyromitrin in some mushrooms	6 to 24 hours average 6 - 15 h	Abdominal pain, feeling of fullness, vomiting, protracted diarrhea, loss of strength, thirst, muscle cramps, feeble rapid pulse, collapse, jaundice, drowsiness, dilated pupils, coma, death	Amanita phalloides A. verna, Galerina antumnalis, Gyromitra esculenta (false morels) and similar species of mushrooms	Urine, blood, vomitus	Eating certain species of Amanita, Galerina, and Gyromitra mushrooms, eating unknown varieties of mushrooms, mistaking toxic mushrooms for edible varieties

BURNING MOUTH, SORE THROAT AND RESPIRATORY SIGNS AND SYMPTOMS OCCUR

INCUBATION (LATENCY) PERIOD LESS THAN 1 HOUR
CHEMICAL AGENTS

Calcium chloride Poisoning	Calcium chloride freezing mixture for Frozen dessert bars	Few minutes	Burning lips, mouth, throat, vomiting	Frozen dessert bar	Vomitus	Splashing of freezing mixture onto popsicles while freezing; cracks in molds allowing CaCl$_2$ to penetrate popsicle syrup
Sodium hydroxide poisoning	Sodium hydroxide in bottle washing compounds, detergents, drain cleaners or hair straighteners	Few minutes	Burning of lips, mouth, and throat; vomiting, diarrhea, abdominal pain	Bottled beverages	Vomitus	Inadequate rinsing of bottles cleaned with caustic

INCUBATION (LATENCY) PERIOD 12 TO 72 HOURS
BACTERIAL AGENTS

Beta-hemolytic streptococcal infections	Streptococcus pyrogenes from throat and lesions of infected humans	1 to 3 days	Sore throat, fever, nausea, vomiting, rhinorrhea, sometimes a rash	Raw milk, foods containing eggs	Throat swabs, vomitus	Workers touching cooked foods, workers with infections containing pus, inadequate refrigeration, inadequate cooking or reheating, preparing foods several hours before serving

LOWER GASTROINTESTINAL TRACT SIGNS AND SYMPTOMS (ABDOMINAL CRAMPS, DIARRHEA) OCCUR FIRST OR PREDOMINATE

INCUBATION (LATENCY) PERIOD USUALLY 7 TO 12 HOURS
BACTERIAL AGENTS

Bacillus cereus enteritis (diarrheal form, mimics C. perfringens)	Enterotoxin of B. cereus. soil organism (strain differs from emetic form)	6 to 16 hours	Nausea, abdominal pain, diarrhea, some reports of vomiting	Cereal products, custards, sauces, starchy foods, e.g. pasta, potatoes, and meatloaf	Stools, vomitus	Inadequate refrigeration, holding of foods at warm (bacterial incubation) temperatures, preparing foods several hours before serving, inadequate reheating of leftovers
Clostridium perfringens gastroenteritis	Endo-enterotoxin formed during sporulation of C. perfringens in intestines, organism in feces of infected humans, other animals, and in soil	8 to 22 hours, mean 10 hours	Abdominal pain, diarrhea	Cooked meat, poultry, gravy, sauces and soups	Stools	Inadequate refrigeration, holding foods at warm (bacterial incubation) temperatures, preparing foods several hours before serving, inadequate reheating of leftovers

INCUBATION (LATENCY) PERIOD USUALLY 12 TO 72 HOURS
BACTERIAL AGENTS

Aeromonas diarrhea	Aeromonas hydro-*phila*	1 to 2 days	Water diarrhea, abdominal pain, nausea, chills, headache	Fish, shellfish, snails, water	Stools	Contamination of foods by sea or surface water
Campylobacteriosis	*Campylobacter jejuni*	2 to 7 days, mean 3 to 5 days	Diarrhea, (often bloody), severe abdominal pain, fever anorexia, malaise, headache, vomiting	Raw milk, raw clams and shellfish, water poultry and meat	Stools, rectal swab, blood	Drinking raw milk, eating raw or undercooked shellfish, inadequate cooking or pasteurization
Cholera	Endemic in temperate U.S. coastal sea water. *V.cholerae* serogroup 01 classical and El Tor biotypes; serogroup O139	1 to 5 days, usually 2 - 3 days	Profuse, watery diarrhea (rice-water stools), vomiting abdominal pain, dehydration, thirst, collapse, reduced skin turgor, wrinkled fingers, sunken eyes, acidosis	Raw fish & shellfish foods washed or prepared with contaminated water	Stools, rectal swabs	Obtaining fish & shellfish from sewage contaminated waters in endemic areas, poor personal hygiene, infected workers touching foods, inadequate cooking, using contaminated water to wash or freshen foods, inadequate sewage disposal, using night soil as fertilizer
Cholera-like vibrio gastroenteritis	Non 01/O139 *V. cholerae* ,& related species, eg, *V. mimicus, V. fluviallis, V. hollisae*	2 to 3 days	Watery diarrhea (varies from loose stools to cholera-like diarrhea)	Raw shellfish, raw fish	Stools, rectal swabs	Eating raw shellfish or raw fish, inadequate cooking, cross contamination
Pathogenic Escherichia coli Diarrhea (THREE FORMS):						
Enterotoxigenic *E. coli* (ETEC) Gastroenteritis	Enterotoxigenic strains E. coli	10 to 72 hours, usually 24 to 72 hrs	Watery diarrhea, abdominal cramps, nausea, malaise, low grade fever	Water, semi-soft cheeses, foods requiring no further heating	Stools, rectal swab	Infected workers touching foods, inadequate refrigeration, inadequate cleaning and disinfection of equipment
Enterohemorrhagic *E. coli* (EHEC) Gastroenteritis	O157:H7 E. coli Verotoxins	3 to 9 days, mean 4 days	Bloody diarrhea, severe abdominal cramping, complications- Hemolytic Uremic Syndrome (HUS), kidney failure	Raw ground beef, raw milk, cheese	Stools, rectal swabs	Infected workers touching foods, inadequate refrigeration, inadequate cooking, inadequate cleaning and disinfection of equipment
Enteroinvasive *E. coli* (EIEC) Gastroenteritis	Enteroinvasive strains of E. coli	10 to 72 hours	Severe abdominal cramps, watery diarrhea, vomiting malaise, complications – HUS, kidney failure	Raw milk, raw ground beef, cheese	Stools, rectal swabs	Infected workers touching foods, inadequate refrigeration, inadequate cooking, inadequate cleaning and disinfection of equipment
Salmonellosis	Various serotypes of *Salmonella* from feces of infected humans and other animals	6 to 72 hours, mean 18 to 36 hours	Abdominal pain, diarrhea, chills, fever, nausea, vomiting, malaise	Poultry, meat and their products, egg products, other foods contaminated by salmonellae	Stools, rectal swabs	Inadequate refrigeration, holding foods at warm (bacterial incubation) temperatures, inadequate cooking and reheating, preparing foods several hours before serving, cross contamination, inadequate cleaning of equipment, infected workers touching cooked foods, obtaining foods from contaminated sources
Shigellosis	*Shigella flexneri, S. dysenteriae, S. sonnei, & S. boydii* from feces of infected humans	24 to 72 hours	Abdominal pain, diarrhea, bloody & mucoid stools, fever	Any contaminated foods, frequently salads, water	Stools & rectal swab	Infected workers touching foods, inadequate refrigeration, inadequate cooking and reheating
Vibrio parahaemolyticus Gastroenteritis	*V. parahaemolyticus* from sea water or seafoods	2 to 48 hours, mean 12 hours	Abdominal pain, diarrhea, nausea, vomiting, fever, chills, headache	Raw seafoods, shellfish	Stools, rectal swabs	Inadequate cooking, inadequate refrigeration, cross contamination, inadequate cleaning of equipment, using seawater in food preparation
Yersiniosis	*Yersinia enterocolitica, Y. psuedotuberculosis*	24 to 36 hours	Severe abdominal pain, fever, headache malaise, sore throat may mimic appendicitis	Milk, tofu, water, pork	Stools, blood	Inadequate cooking, contamination after pasteurization, contamination of foods by water, rodents, other animals

VIRAL AGENTS

Astrovirus gastro-enteritis	Astroviruses from human feces	1 to 2 days	Diarrhea, sometimes accompanied by one or more enteric signs or symptoms	Ready-to-eat foods	Stools, acute and convalescent blood	Failure to wash hands after defecation, infected person touching ready-to-eat foods, inadequate cooking or reheating
Acute viral Gastroenteritis (Small round structured virus)	Norwalk-like viruses, Calici-viruses	1 to 3 days (Norwalk-like virus mean 36 hours)	Nausea, vomiting, abdominal pain, diarrhea, low grade fever, chills, malaise, anorexia, headache	Clams, oysters cockles, green salad pastry, frostings, ice, cut fruit salads	Stools, acute and convalescent blood sera	Polluted shellfish growing waters, poor personal hygiene, infected persons touching prepared foods, foods not requiring further cooking, contaminated waters

PARASITIC AGENTS

Amebic Dysentery (Amebiasis)	*Entamoeba histolytica* from feces of infected humans	5 days to several months; mean 3 to 4 weeks	Abdominal pain, constipation or diarrhea	Raw vegetables and fruit	Stools	Poor personal hygiene, infected workers touching food, inadequate cooking
Anisakiasis	*Anisakis simplex Pseudoterranova decipiens*	4 to 6 hours	Stomach pain, nausea, vomiting, abdominal pain, diarrhea, fever	Rock fish, herring, cod, squid	Stools	Ingestion of raw fish, inadequate cooking
Beef tapeworm infection (Taeniasis)	*Taenia saginata* from flesh of infected cattle	3 to 6 months	Vague discomfort, hunger pain, loss of weight, abdominal pain	Raw or insufficiently cooked beef	Stools	Lack of meat inspection, inadequate cooking, inadequate sewage disposal, sewage contaminated pastures
Cryptosporidiosis	*Cryptosporidium parvum*	1 – 12 days, usually 7 days	Profuse watery diarrhea, abdominal pain, anorexia, low grade fever, vomiting	Apple cider, water	Stools, intestinal biopsy	Inadequate sewage or animal waste disposal, contamination by animal manure, contaminated water, inadequate filtration of water
Cyclosporiasis	*Cyclopsora cayetanensis*	1 – 11 days, typically 7 days	Prolonged watery diarrhea, weight loss, fatigue, nausea, anorexia, abdominal cramps	Raspberries, lettuce, basil, water	Stools	Sewage contaminated irrigation or spraying water suspected; washing fruits with contaminated water; possibly handling foods that are not subsequently heated
Fish tapeworm infection (Diphyllobothriasis)	*Diphyllobothrium latum* from flesh of infected fish	5 to 6 weeks	Vague gastrointestinal discomfort anemia may occur	Raw or insufficiently cooked fresh water fish	Stools	Inadequate cooking, inadequate sewage disposal, sewage contaminated lakes
Giardiasis	*Giardia lamblia* from feces of humans	1 to 6 weeks	Abdominal pain, mucoid diarrhea, fatty stools	Raw vegetables and fruits, water	Stools	Poor personal hygiene, infected workers touching foods, inadequate sewage disposal
Pork tapeworm infection (Taeniasis)	*Taenia solium* from flesh of infected swine	3 to 6 months	Vague discomfort, hunger pains, loss of weight	Raw or insufficiently cooked pork	Stools	Lack of meat inspection, inadequate cooking, inadequate sewage disposal, sewage contaminated pastures

NEUROLOGICAL SIGNS & SYMPTOMS (VISUAL DISTURBANCES, TINGLING, PARALYSIS) OCCUR

INCUBATION (LATENCY) PERIOD USUALLY LESS THAN 1 HOUR
FUNGAL AGENTS

Ibotenic acid group of mushroom poisoning	Ibotenic acid and and muscinol in some mushrooms	0.5 to 2 hours	Drowsiness and dizziness, state of intoxication, confusion, muscular spasms, delirium, visual disturbances	*Amanita muscaria, A. pantherina* and related species of mushrooms	Vomitus	Eating *Amantia muscaria* and related species of mushrooms, eating unknown varieties of mushrooms, mistaking toxic mushrooms for edible varieties
Muscarine group of mushroom poisoning	Muscarine in some mushrooms	15 minutes to 2	Excessive salivation, perspiration, tearing, reduced blood pressure, irregular pulse, pupils constricted, blurred vision, asthmatic breathing	*Clitocybe dealbata, C. rivulosa,* and many other species of *Inocybe* and *Boletus* mushrooms	Vomitus	Eating muscarine group of mushrooms, eating unknown varieties of mushrooms, mistaking toxic mushrooms for edible varieties
Organophosphorous poisoning	Organic phosphorous insecticides such Parathion, TEPP, Diazinon, Malathion	Few minutes to few hours	Nausea, vomiting, abdominal cramps, diarrhea, headache, nervousness, blurred vision, chest pain, cyanosis, confusion, twitching, convulsions	Any accidentally contaminated food	Blood, urine, fat biopsy	Spraying foods just before harvesting, storing insecticides in same area as foods, mistaking pesticides for powdered foods

411

TOXIC ANIMALS

Paralytic shellfish Poisoning (PSP)	Saxitoxin and similar toxins from plankton *Alexandrium* species which are consumed by shellfish	Few minutes to 30 minutes on average, may take up to 2 hrs	Tingling, burning, numbness around lips and finger tips, giddiness, incoherent speech, respiratory paralysis, sometimes fatal	Bivalve molluscan shellfish, e.g., clams mussels, viscera of crabs and lobsters	N/A	Harvesting shellfish from waters with a high concentration of *Alexandrium*
Tetradon poisoning Aka Fugu (puffer Fish) poisoning	Tetrodotoxin from intestines and gonads of puffer type fish	10 minutes to 3 hrs	Tingling sensation of fingers & toes, dizziness, pallor, numbness of mouth and extremities, gastrointestinal symptoms hemorrage and desquamation of skin, eyes fixed, twitching, paralysis, cyanosis sometimes fatal	Puffer-type fish	N/A	Eating puffer-type fish, failure to effectively remove intestines and gonads from puffer-type fish if they are to be eaten
Neurotoxic shellfish Poisoning (NSP)	Brevetoxins from from *Gymnodinium* species	few minutes to few hours	Paresthesia, reversal of hot and cold temperature sensations, nausea, vomiting, diarrhea	Shellfish (mussels, clams) from S.E.. coastal waters	Gastric washings	Harvesting shellfish from waters with high concentration of *Gymnodinium* species of dinoflagellates
Amnesic Shellfish Poisoning (ASP) or Domoic Acid	Domoic acid from diatoms (Toxin is heat stable)	30 min. to 24 hrs for gastrointestinal symptoms, neurological symptoms within 48 hrs	Initially nausea, vomiting, abdominal pain, diarrhea, neurological signs include: confusion, memory loss, disorientation, seizure, coma, death may occur	Shellfish (mussels, clams), finfish (anchovies), viscera of crabs and lobsters	N.A.	Harvesting shellfish, crabs and finfish from waters which experience plankton blooms releasing domoic acid in the harvesting area
Diarrhetic shellfish Poisoning (DSP)	LISTED PREVIOUSLY					THIS IS NOT A NEUROLOGICAL ILLNESS, BUT IS INCLUDED HERE FOR EASE OF REFERENCE WITH ALL SHELLFISH POISONINGS.

PLANT TOXICANTS

Jimson weed	Tropane alkaloids in Jimson weed	Less than 1 hour	Abnormal thirst, photophobia, distorted sight, difficulty in speaking, flushing, delirium, coma, rapid heart beat	Any part of a plant, tomatoes grafted to Jimson weed stock	Urine	Eating any part of Jimson weed or eating tomatoes from tomato plant grafted to Jimson weed stock
Water hemlock Poisoning	Resin and cicutoxin in hemlock root	15 to 60 minutes	Excessive salivation, nausea, vomiting, Stomach pain, frothing at mouth, irregular breathing, convulsions, respiratory paralysis	Root of water hemlock *Cicuta virosa* and *C. masculate*	Urine	Eating water hemlock, mistaking water hemlock root for wild parsnip, sweet potato or carrot

INCUBATION (LATENCY) PERIOD 1-6 HOURS
CHEMICAL AGENTS

Chlorinated hydrocarbon poisoning	Chlorinated hydrocarbon insecticides such as aldrin, chlordane, ddt, endrin, lindane, & toxaphene	30 minutes to 6 hrs	Nausea, vomiting, paresthesis, dizziness muscular weakness, anorexia, weight loss, confusion	Any accidentally contaminated food	Blood, urine, stools gastric washings	Storing insecticides in same area as food, mistaking insecticides for powdered food

TOXIC ANIMALS

Ciguatera Poisoning	Ciguatoxin in intestines, roe, gonads & flesh of tropical marine fish	3 to 5 hours, sometimes longer	Tingling & numbness about mouth, metallic taste, dry mouth, gastrointestinal symptoms, watery stools, muscular pain, dizziness, dilated eyes, blurred vision, prostration, paralysis, reversal of hot and cold temperature sensations sometimes fatal	Numerous species of tropical fish		Eating liver, intestines, roe, gonads, or flesh of barracuda, large jacks & amberjacks, grouper and other species of tropical reef fish; usually large reef fish are more commonly toxic

INCUBATION (LATENCY) PERIOD USUALLY 12 TO 72 HOURS
BACTERIAL AGENTS

Botulism	Neurotoxins A, B, E & F of *Clostridium botulinum* spores found in soil & animal intestines	2 hours to 8 days, mean 18 to 36 hrs	Vertigo, double or blurred vision, dryness of mouth, difficulty in swallowing, speaking and breathing, descending muscular weakness, constipation, pupils dilated or fixed, respiratory paralysis, gastrointestinal symptoms may precede neurological symptoms. frequently fatal	Home canned low acid foods, vacuum packed fish; fermented fish eggs, fish and marine mammals	Blood, stool	Inadequate heat processing of canned foods and smoked fish, uncontrolled fermentation

INCUBATION (LATENCY) PERIOD GREATER THAN 72 HOURS
CHEMICAL AGENTS

Mercury poisoning	Methyl & ethyl mercury compounds from industrial waste and organic mercury in fungicides	1 week or longer	Numbness, weakness of legs, spastic paralysis, impairment of vision, blindness, coma	Grains treated with mercury containing fungicide; pork, fish, & shellfish exposed to mercury compounds	Urine, blood, hair	Streams polluted with mercury compounds, feeding animals grains treated with mercury fungicides, eating mercury treated grains or animals fed such grains
Triorthocresyl Phosphate Poisoning	Triorthocresyl phosphate used as extracts or as substitute cooking oil	5 to 21 days, mean 10 days	Gastrointestinal symptoms, leg pain, ungainly high stepping gait, foot and wrist drop	Cooking oils, extracts and other foods contaminated with triorthocresyl phosphate	N/A	Using compound as food extractant or as cooking or salad oil

GENERALIZED INFECTION SIGNS AND SYMPTOMS (FEVER, CHILL, MALAISE, ACHES) OCCUR

INCUBATION (LATENCY) PERIOD GREATER THAN 72 HOURS
BACTERIAL AGENTS

Brucellosis	*Brucella abortus, B. melitensis, and B. suis* from tissues & milk of infected animals	7 to 21 days	Fever, chills, sweats, weakness, malaise, headache, muscle and joint pain, loss of weight	Raw milk, goat cheese	Blood	Failure to pasteurize milk, livestock infected with brucellae
Typhoid fever	*Salmonella* Typhi from feces of infected humans	7 to 28 days, mean 14 days	Malaise, headache, fever, cough, nausea, vomiting, constipation, abdominal pain, chills, rose spots, bloody stools	Shellfish, foods contaminated by workers, raw milk, cheese, watercress, water	Stools, rectal swabs blood	Infected workers touching foods, poor personal hygiene, inadequate cooking, inadequate refrigeration, inadequate sewage disposal, obtaining foods from unsafe sources, harvesting shellfish from sewage contaminated areas
Listeriosis	*Listeria monocytogenes* from soil, manure, silage and environment	3 to 21 days, maybe longer	Low grade fever, flu-like illness, stillbirths, meningitis, encephalitis, sepsis, fatalities occur	Cole slaw, milk, cheese, animal products	Blood, urine, cerebrospinal fluid	Inadequate cooking, failure to properly pasteurize milk, prolonged refrigeration, immunosuppressed, pregnant, aged persons, and neonates are at high risk
Vibrio vulnificus Septicemia	*Vibrio vulnificus* from sea water	16 hr mean < 24 hr	Malaise, chills, fever, prostration, cutaneous lesions, fatalities occur	Raw shellfish and crabs	Blood	Eating raw shellfish, inadequate cooking, persons with liver damage are at high risk

VIRAL AGENTS

Hepatitis A (Infectious hepatitis)	Hepatitis A virus from feces, urine, blood of infected humans and other primates	10 to 50 days, mean 25 days	Fever, malaise, lassitude, anorexia, nausea, abdominal pain, jaundice	Shellfish, any food contaminated by hepatitis viruses, water	Urine, blood	Infected workers touching foods, poor personal hygiene, inadequate cooking, harvesting shellfish from sewage contaminated waters, inadequate sewage disposal

(Note: Hepatits E is an emerging viral pathogen. It has similar incubation periods and symptoms as Hepatitis A and can be transmitted in foods.)

PARASITIC AGENTS

Angiostrongylaisis (eosinophilic meningoencehplalitis)	*Angiostrongylus cantonensis* (rat lung worm) from rodent feces and soil	14 to 16 days	Gastroenteritis, headache, stiff neck and back, low-grade fever	Raw crabs, prawns, slugs, shrimp & snails	Blood	Inadequate cooking, ingesting raw food
Toxoplasmosis	*Toxoplasma gondii* from tissue and flesh of infected animals	10 to 13 days	Fever, headache, myalgia, rash	Raw or insufficiently cooked meat (rare)	Biopsy of lymph nodes, blood	Inadequate cooking of meat of sheep, swine and cattle

413

Trichinosis	*Trichinella spiralis* (roundworm) from flesh of infected swine or bear	4 to 28 days, mean 9 days	Gastroenteritis, fever, edema about eyes, muscular pain, chills, prostration, labored breathing	Pork, bear meat, walrus flesh	Muscle biopsy	Eating raw or inadequately cooked pork or bear meat, inadequate cooking or heat processing, feeding uncooked or inadequately heat processed garbage to swine

ALLERGIC TYPE SYMPTOMS (FACIAL FLUSHING, ITCHING) OCCUR

INCUBATION (LATENCY) PERIOD LESS THAN 1 HOUR
BACTERIAL (AND ANIMAL) AGENTS

Scombroid Poisoning or Histaminosis	Histamine-like substance produced by proteus sp. or other bacteria from histidine in fish flesh	Few minutes to 1 hr	Headache, dizziness, nausea, vomiting, peppery taste, burning throat, facial swelling and flushing, stomach pain, itching of skin	Tuna, mackerel, Pacific dolphin (known as the mahi on the Pacific coast of the U.S.), jack, anchovy, marlin, swordfish, bluefish, sometimes from ripened cheese	Vomitus	Inadequate refrigeration of scombroid fish and improper curing of cheese

CHEMICALS

Monosodium glutamate (MSG) poisoning	Excessive amounts of monosodium glutamate (MSG)	Few minutes to 1 hr	Burning sensation in back of neck, forearms chest, feeling of tightness, tingling, flushing, dizziness, headache, nausea	Foods seasoned with MSG	N/A	Using excessive amounts of MSG as flavor intensifier.
Nicotinic acid (niacin) poisoning	Sodium nicotinate used as a color preservative	Few minutes to 1 hr	Flushing, sensation of warmth, itching abdominal pain, puffiness of face and knees	Meat or other food in which sodium nicotinate has been added	N/A	Using sodium nicotinate as color preservative
	Dietary supplements of niacin used chronically	A few days to a few a few months	Impairment of liver function (elevated transaminases), can result in fulminant liver failure	High potency dietary supplements, especially when used in multiples (500mg or more per day)	N/A	Dietary supplements of niacin can cause similar acute symptoms as niacin, but seldom does because of infrequent use at high doses

INCUBATION (LATENCY) PERIOD 1 TO 6 HOURS
TOXIC ANIMALS

Hypervitaminosis A	Vitamin A containing foods or dietary supplements	Acute: 1 to 6 hours	Headache, gastrointestinal symptoms, dizziness, collapse, convulsions, desquamation of skin	Liver & kidney of arctic mammals	Blood	Eating liver & kidney from cold region animals
		Chronic: days to months or years	Chronic use can cause liver disease, including cirrhosis	High potency dietary supplements, especially with chronic use	N/A or Blood?	Chronic usage of dietary supplements containing 25,000 IU vitamin A or more per day

1. Symptoms and incubation periods will vary with the individual and group exposed because of resistance, age, and nutritional status of individuals, number of organism or concentration of poison in ingested foods, amount of food ingested, pathogenicity and virulence of strains of microorganisms or toxicity of chemical involved. Several of the illnesses are manifested by symptoms in more than one category and have an incubation range that overlaps the generalized categories.

2. A more detailed review can be found in:
    A. Bryan, F.L. 1982, Diseases Transmitted by Foods (A classification and summary), second edition, Centers for Disease Control, Atlanta, GA.
    B. Rhodehamel, E.J., Editor, 1992, "Foodborne Pathogenic Microorganisms and Natural Toxins", Third Edition, Food and Drug Administration, Washington, D.C.
    C. Bryan, F.L., Chairman, Committee on Communicable Diseases Affecting Man, 1999, "Procedures to Investigate Foodborne Illness" Fifth edition, International Association of Milk, Food, and Environmental Sanitarians, Inc., Ames, IA

3. Samples of any of the listed foods that have been ingested during the incubation period of the disease should be collected.

4. Carbon monoxide poisoning may simulate some of the diseases listed in this category. Patients who have been in closed care with motors running or have been in rooms with improperly vented heaters are subject to exposure to carbon monoxide.

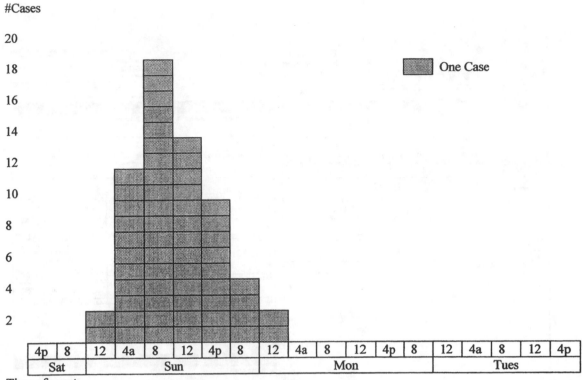

Epidemic curve of a common-source outbreak

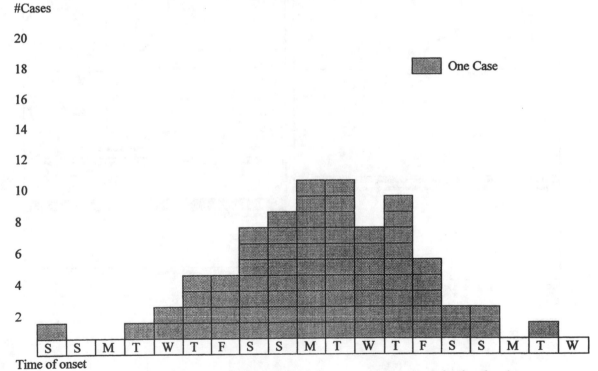

Epidemic curve of a person-to-person transmitted outbreak

MED**W**ATCH

THE FDA MEDICAL PRODUCTS REPORTING PROGRAM

For VOLUNTARY reporting
by health professionals of adverse
events and product problems

Form Approved: OMB No. 0910-0291 Expires:12/31/94
See OMB statement on reverse

FDA Use Only

Triage unit
sequence #

Page ____ of ____

A. Patient information

1. Patient Identifier	2. Age at time of event: or _____ Date of birth:	3. Sex ☐ female ☐ male	4. Weight ____ lbs or ____ kgs
In confidence			

B. Adverse event or product problem

1. ☐ Adverse event   and/or   ☐ Product problem (e.g., defects/malfunctions)

2. Outcomes attributed to adverse event
(check all that apply)

☐ death _____ (mo/day/yr)
☐ life-threatening
☐ hospitalization – initial or prolonged

☐ disability
☐ congenital anomaly
☐ required intervention to prevent permanent impairment/damage
☐ other: _____

3. Date of event (mo/day/yr)	4. Date of this report (mo/day/yr)

5. Describe event or problem

6. Relevant tests/laboratory data, including dates

7. Other relevant history, including preexisting medical conditions (e.g., allergies, race, pregnancy, smoking and alcohol use, hepatic/renal dysfunction, etc.)

C. Suspect medication(s)

1. Name (give labeled strength & mfr/labeler, if known)
#1 _____
#2 _____

2. Dose, frequency & route used #1 #2	3. Therapy dates (if unknown, give duration) from/to (or best estimate) #1 #2

4. Diagnosis for use (indication) #1 #2	5. Event abated after use stopped or dose reduced #1 ☐yes ☐no ☐doesn't apply #2 ☐yes ☐no ☐doesn't apply

6. Lot # (if known) #1 #2	7. Exp. date (if known) #1 #2	8. Event reappeared after reintroduction #1 ☐yes ☐no ☐doesn't apply #2 ☐yes ☐no ☐doesn't apply

9. NDC # (for product problems only)
_____

10. Concomitant medical products and therapy dates (exclude treatment of event)

D. Suspect medical device

1. Brand name

2. Type of device

3. Manufacturer name & address	4. Operator of device ☐ health professional ☐ lay user/patient ☐ other: _____

6. model # _____ catalog # _____ serial # _____ lot # _____ other #	5. Expiration date (mo/day/yr) 7. If implanted, give date (mo/day/yr) 8. If explanted, give date (mo/day/yr)

9. Device available for evaluation?   (Do not send to FDA)
☐ yes   ☐ no   ☐ returned to manufacturer on _____ (mo/day/yr)

10. Concomitant medical products and therapy dates (exclude treatment of event)

E. Reporter (see confidentiality section on back)

1. Name, address & phone #

2. Health professional? ☐ yes ☐ no	3. Occupation	4. Also reported to ☐ manufacturer ☐ user facility ☐ distributor
5. If you do NOT want your identity disclosed to the manufacturer, place an " X " in this box. ☐		

FDA

Mail to: MEDWATCH
5600 Fishers Lane
Rockville, MD 20852-9787

or FAX to:
1-800-FDA-0178

FDA Form 3500 (6/93)   Submission of a report does not constitute an admission that medical personnel or the product caused or contributed to the event.

ADVICE ABOUT VOLUNTARY REPORTING

Report experiences with:
- medications (drugs or biologics)
- medical devices (including in-vitro diagnostics)
- special nutritional products (dietary supplements, medical foods, infant formulas)
- other products regulated by FDA

Report SERIOUS adverse events. An event is serious when the patient outcome is:
- death
- life-threatening (real risk of dying)
- hospitalization (initial or prolonged)
- disability (significant, persistent or permanent)
- congenital anomaly
- required intervention to prevent permanent impairment or damage

Report even if:
- you're not certain the product caused the event
- you don't have all the details

Report product problems – quality, performance or safety concerns such as:
- suspected contamination
- questionable stability
- defective components
- poor packaging or labeling

How to report:
- just fill in the sections that apply to your report
- use section C for all products except medical devices
- attach additional blank pages if needed
- use a separate form for each patient
- report either to FDA or the manufacturer (or both)

Important numbers:
- 1-800-FDA-0178   to FAX report
- 1-800-FDA-7737   to report by modem
- 1-800-FDA-1088   for more information or to report quality problems
- 1-800-822-7967   for a VAERS form for vaccines

If your report involves a serious adverse event with a device and it occurred in a facility outside a doctor's office, that facility may be legally required to report to FDA and/or the manufacturer. Please notify the person in that facility who would handle such reporting.

Confidentiality: The patient's identity is held in strict confidence by FDA and protected to the fullest extent of the law. The reporter's identity may be shared with the manufacturer unless requested otherwise. However, FDA will not disclose the reporter's identity in response to a request from the public, pursuant to the Freedom of Information Act.

FDA Form 3500-back   **Please Use Address Provided Below – Just Fold In Thirds, Tape and Mail**

**Department of
Health and Human Services**
Public Health Service
Food and Drug Administration
Rockville, MD 20857

Official Business
Penalty for Private Use $300

BUSINESS REPLY MAIL
FIRST CLASS MAIL   PERMIT NO. 946   ROCKVILLE, MD

POSTAGE WILL BE PAID BY FOOD AND DRUG ADMINISTRATION

MEDWATCH
**The FDA Medical Products Reporting Program
Food and Drug Administration
5600 Fishers Lane
Rockville, MD 20852-9787**

NO POSTAGE
NECESSARY
IF MAILED
IN THE
UNITED STATES
OR APO/FPO

REPORTABLE EVENTS CHART

VACCINE		EVENT	INTERVAL FROM VACCINATION
DPT,DPT/POLIO, Combined, P	A.	Anaphylaxis or anaphylactic shock	24 hours
	B.	Encephalopathy (or encephalitis)*	7 days
	C.	Shock-collapse, or hypotonic-Hyporesponsive collapse*	7 days
	D.	Residual seizure disorder	(See Aids to Interpretation)*
	E.	Any acute complication or sequela (including death) of above events	No limit
	F.	Events in vaccines described in mfr's package insert as contraindications to additional doses of vaccine** (such as convulsions)	(See package insert)
Measles, Mumps & Rubella; DT, Td. Tetanus Toxoid	A.	Anaphylaxis or anaphylactic shock	24 hours
	B.	Encephalopathy (or encephalitis)* vaccines; 7 days for DT, Td, & Toxoids	15 days for measles, mumps, & rubella
	C.	Residual seizure disorder	(See Aids to Interpretation)*
	D.	Any acute complication or sequela (including death) of above events	No limit
	E.	Events in vaccines described in mfr's package insert as contraindications to additional doses of vaccine** (such as convulsions)	(See package insert)
Oral Polio	A.	Paralytic poliomyelitis	
		-In non-immunodeficient recipient	30 days
		-In an immunodeficient recipient	6 months
		-In a vaccine-associated community case	No limit
	B.	Any acute complication or sequela (including death) of above events	No limit
	C.	Events in vaccines described in mfr's package insert as contraindications to additional doses of vaccine** (such as convulsions)	(See package insert)
Inactivated Polio Vaccine	A.	Anaphylaxis or anaphylactic shock	24 hours
	B.	Any acute complication or sequela (including death) of above events	No limit
	C.	Events in vaccines described in mfr's package insert as contraindications to additional doses of vaccine** (such as convulsions)	(See package insert)

418

*AIDS TO INTERPRETATION

*

Shock-collapse or hypotonic-hyporesponsive collapse may be evidenced by signs or symptoms such as decrease in or loss of muscle tone, paralysis (partial or complete), hemiplegia, hemiparesis, loss of color or turning pale white or blue, unresponsiveness to environmental stimuli, depression of or loss of consciousness, prolonged sleeping with difficulty arousing, or cardiovascular or respiratory arrest.

Residual seizure disorder may be considered to have occurred if no other seizure or convulsion unaccompanied by fever or accompanied by a fever less than 102°F occurred before the first seizure or convulsion after the administration of the vaccine involved.

And, if in the case of measles-, mumps-, or rubella-containing vaccines, the first seizure or convulsion occurred within 15 days after vaccination OR in the case of other vaccine, the first seizure or convulsion occurred within 3 days of vaccination.

AND, if two or more seizures or convulsions unaccompanied by fever or accompanied by fever of less than 102°F occurred within 1 year after vaccination.

The terms seizure and convulsion include grand mal, petite mal, absence, myoclonic, tonic-clonic, and focal motor seizures and signs. Encephalopathy means any significant acquired abnormality of, injury to, or impairment of function of the brain. Among the frequent manifestations of encephalopathy are focal and diffuse neurologic signs, increased intracranial pressure, or changes lasting at least 6 hours in level of consciousness, with or without convulsions. The neurologic signs and symptoms of encephalopathy may be temporary with complete recovery, or they may result in various degrees of permanent impairment. Signs and symptoms such as high-pitched and unusual screaming, persistent inconsolable crying, and bulging fontanel are compatible with an encephalopathy, but in and of themselves are not conclusive evidence of encephalopathy. Encephalopathy usually can be documented by slow wave activity on an electroencephalogram.

**

The health-care provider must refer to the CONTRAINDICATION section of manufacturer's package insert for each vaccine.

VACCINE ADVERSE EVENT REPORTING SYSTEM

24 Hour Toll-free information line 1-800-822-7967

Patient identity kept confidential

		For CDC/FDA Use Only
		VAERS Number _____
		Date Received _____

Patient Name:	Vaccine administered by (Name):	Form completed by (Name):
Last First M.I.	Responsible Physician	Relation to ☐ Vaccine Provider ☐ Patient/Parent Patient ☐ Manufacturer ☐ Other
Address	Facility Name/Address	Address (if different from patient or provider)
City State Zip	City State Zip	City State Zip
Telephone no. (_____)	Telephone no. (_____)	Telephone no. (_____)

1. State	2. County where administered	3. Date of birth mm / dd / yy	4. Patient age	5. Sex ☐ M ☐ F	6. Date form completed mm / dd / yy

7. Describe adverse event(s) (symptoms, signs, time course) and treatment, if any	8. Check all appropriate:
	☐ Patient died (date ___/___/___ mm dd yy)
	☐ Life threatening illness
	☐ Required emergency room/doctor visit
	☐ Required hospitalization (_____ days)
	☐ Resulted in prolongation of hospitalization
	☐ Resulted in permanent disability
	☐ None of the above

9. Patient recovered ☐ YES ☐ NO ☐ UNKNOWN	10. Date of vaccination	11. Adverse event onset
12. Relevant diagnostic tests/laboratory data	mm / dd / yy Time _____ AM PM	mm / dd / yy Time _____ AM PM

13. Enter all vaccines given on date listed in no. 10

Vaccine (type)	Manufacturer	Lot number	Route/Site	No. Previous doses
a.				
b.				
c.				
d.				

14. Any other vaccinations within 4 weeks of date listed in no. 10

Vaccine (type)	Manufacturer	Lot number	Route/Site	No. Previous doses	Date given
a.					
b.					

15. Vaccinated at: ☐ Private doctor's office/hospital ☐ Military clinic/hospital ☐ Public health clinic/hospital ☐ Other/unknown	16. Vaccine purchased with: ☐ Private funds ☐ Military funds ☐ Public funds ☐ Other /unknown	17. Other medications

18. Illness at time of vaccination (specify)	19. Pre-existing physician-diagnosed allergies, birth defects, medical conditions (specify)

20. Have you reported this adverse event previously? ☐ No ☐ To health department ☐ To doctor ☐ To manufacturer	22. Birth weight _____ lb. _____ oz.	23. No. of brothers and sisters

21. Adverse event following prior vaccination (check all appropriate, specify)				24. Mfr. / imm. proj. report no.	25. Date received by mfr. / imm. proj.
	Adverse Event	Onset Age	Type Vaccine	Dose no. in series		
☐ In patient						
☐ In brother or sister					26. 15 day report? ☐ Yes ☐ No	27. Report type ☐ Initial ☐ Follow-Up

Health care providers and manufacturers are required by law (42 USC 300aa-25) to report reactions to vaccines listed in the Vaccine Injury Table. Reports for reactions to other vaccines are voluntary except when required as a condition of immunization grant awards.

Form VAERS-1

Fold in thirds, tape & mail. (DO NOT STAPLE FORM.)

NO POSTAGE
NECESSARY
IF MAILED
IN THE
UNITED STATES
OR APO FPO

BUSINESS REPLY MAIL
FIRST CLASS MAIL   PERMIT NO. 1895   ROCKVILLE MD

POSTAGE WILL BE PAID BY ADDRESSEE

VAERS
the ERC BioServices Corporation
A Division of Ogden Biomedical Services Group
1155 First Street, Suite 130
Rockville, MD 20850-V788

DIRECTIONS FOR COMPLETING FORM

(Additional pages may be attached if more space is needed.)

GENERAL

- Use a separate form for each patient. Complete the form to the best of your abilities. Items 3, 4, 7, 8, 10, 11, and 13 are considered essential and should be completed whenever possible. Parents/Guardians may need to consult the facility where the vaccine was administered for some of the information (such as manufacturer, lot number or laboratory data.)
- Refer to the Vaccine Injury Table (VIT) for events mandated for reporting by law. Reporting for other serious events felt to be related but not on the VIT is encouraged.
- Health care providers other than the vaccine administrator (VA) treating a patient for a suspected adverse event should notify the VA and provide the information about the adverse event to allow the VA to complete the form to meet the VA's legal responsibility.
- These data will be used to increase understanding of adverse events following vaccination and will become part of CDC Privacy Act System 09-20-0136, "Epidemiologic Studies and Surveillance of Disease Problems". Information identifying the person who received the vaccine or that person's legal representative will not be made available to the public, but may be available to the vaccinee or legal representative.

SPECIFIC INSTRUCTIONS

Form Completed By: To be used by parents/guardians, vaccine manufacturers/distributors, vaccine administrators, and/or the person completing the form on behalf of the patient or the health professional who administered the vaccine.

Item 7: Describe the suspected adverse event. Such things as temperature, local and general signs and symptoms, time course, duration of symptoms diagnosis, treatment and recovery should be noted.

Item 9: Check "YES" if the patient's health condition is the same as it was prior to the vaccine, "NO" if the patient has not returned to the pre-vaccination state of health, or "UNKNOWN" if the patient's condition is not known.

Item 10 and 11: Give dates and times as specifically as you can remember. If you do not know the exact time, please indicate "AM" or "PM" when possible if this information is known. If more than one adverse event, give the onset date and time for the most serious event.

Item 12: Include "negative" or "normal" results of any relevant tests performed as well as abnormal findings.

Item 13: List ONLY those vaccines given on the day listed in Item 10.

Item 14: List ANY OTHER vaccines the patient received within four weeks of the date listed in Item 10.

Item 16: This section refers to how the person who gave the vaccine purchased it, not to the patient's insurance.

Item 17: List any prescription or non-prescription medications the patient was taking when the vaccine(s) was given.

Item 18: List any short term illnesses the patient had on the date the vaccine(s) was given (i.e., cold, flu, ear infection).

Item 19: List any pre-existing physician-diagnosed allergies, birth defects, medical conditions (including developmental and/or neurologic disorders) the patient has.

Item 21: List any suspected adverse events the patient, or the patient's brothers or sisters, may have had to previous vaccinations. If more than one brother or sister, or if the patient has reacted to more than one prior vaccine, use additional pages to explain completely. For the onset age of a patient, provide the age in months if less than two years old.

Item 26: This space is for manufacturers' use only.

1. HOME DISTRICT BOS	2. REPORTING UNIT SYMBOL NOL	3. CENTRAL FILE NO. 1234567	4. J.D./T.A. ----	5. COUNTY ----	6. DATE 8-2-99
7. PRODUCT CODE 45AF-19	8. OPERATION 13	9. PROGRAM ASSIGNMENT CODE 09001			10. HOURS 1/2

11. IDENTIFICATION *(Quote pertinent labeling including Establishment name and address)*
"NO CLUMP" BRAND ANTI-CAKING AGENT
CLUMPLESS CORP. 3214 WHARF AVE.
WALTHAM, MA 02154

12. MANUFACTURER CONTROL CODES *(Labels, packaging and shipping containers)* BAGS CODED: "AC 123171"	13. AMOUNT ON HAND 1200/100# BAGS	14. DATE LOT RECEIVED 7-15-99
	15. ESTIMATED VALUE $ 24,000.00	16. SAMPLE NO(s). NONE

17. DEALER *(Name, street address, city, state, and ZIP code)* CREOLE INDUSTRIES 239 CANAL ST. NEW ORLEANS, LA 70130	18. ☐ DISTRIBUTOR ☐ SHIPPER ☒XX MANUFACTURER ☐ OTHER *(Name, street address, city, state, ZIP code, and telephone)* CLUMPLESS CORP. 3214 WHARF AVE. WALTHAM, MA 02154 (617) 765-4321

19. ESTABLISHMENT TYPE(s)	INDUSTRY CODE						20. ESTABLISHMENT SIZE *($ VOLUME)*	21. INFORMATION OBTAINED BY *(Check one)*	
	1	2	3	4	5	6			
a. Manufacuturer	45								MAIL
b.									TELEPHONE
c.								XXX	VISIT

22. REMARKS

23. REPORT PREPARED BY *(Type or print name and title)* Sidney H. Rogers, Investigator	24. EMPLOYEE NO. 075	25. PC 2	26. SIGNATURE *Sidney H. Rogers*

27. REPORTING UNIT ACTION XX☐ REFERRED TO HOME DISTRICT X☐ ADD TO ACTIVE OEI ☐ COLLECT OFFICIAL SAMPLE ☐ ROUTINE FOLLOW-UP ☐ REFERRED TO STATE OR ☐ INSPECT OTHER FEDERAL AUTHORITIES ☐ REINSPECT ☐ MAKE INVESTIGATION ☐ NO ACTION ☐ REFERRED TO HDQTRS _____ *(Routing Symbol)*	28. NAME OF REVIEWING OFFICIAL *(Type or print)* Harry Abelman
	29. TITLE Supervisory Investigator 30. DATE REVIEWED 9-2-99

FORM FDA 457 (5/90)   PREVIOUS EDITION MAY BE USED   **PRODUCT/ESTABLISHMENT SURVEILLANCE REPORT**

	SUSPECTED VIOLATIONS *(Check appropriate box)*		
	HEALTH		
DRUGS – DEVICES	Dangerous under any condition of use: 502(j).		Inadequate directions for use: 502(f)(1).
	Dangerous when sold indiscriminately: 502(f).		Failure to bear list of active ingredients: 502(e).
	Dangerous on account of excessive dosage: 502(j).		Possible variation from professed standard: 501(b), (c), (d).
	Dangerous because of inadequate warnings: 502(f)(2).		Vitamin preparations – possible variation from professed standard: 501(b), (c), (d).
	Drugs dangerous on account of impurities: 501(a)(2), (3), 502(j).		Extravagant therapeutic claims: 502(a)[1]

[1] *If descriptive or promotional material employed in sale of product bears or contains extravagant therapeutic claims, indicate (in REMARKS on front or in separate memo) source, how received, and how employed in sale of product. See Section 201(m), Labeling: 301(b), 301(k), Prohibited Acts.*

☐ HYGIENIC

ECONOMIC

| Deceptive packaged: 502(I). | | Suspect short weight or volume: 502(b) |

☐ NEW DRUG

	HEALTH		
FOODS	Presence of poisons: 402(a)(1), (2).		Therapeutic claims for food: Subject to 502.
	Dangerous and non-nutritive substances *(confectionery)*: 402(d)		Vitamin claims: 403(a), (j). May also be subject to 502.
	Poisonous containers: 402(a)(6).		Special dietary foods: 403(j)
	HYGIENIC		
	Stored under insanitary conditions: 402(a)(4).		Suspected filth or decomposition: 402(a)(3).
	ECONOMIC		
	Deceptive packaging: 403(d).		Failure to declare mandatory statements: nonstandardized foods: 403(e), (f), (I), (k).
	Short weight or volume: 403(e)(2).		Standardized foods, misbranding or nonconformity: 403(g), (h).
	Misrepresentation in labeling: 403(a). See 201(m).	X	**New Product, New Manufacturer**

COSMETICS	Dangerous cosmetics: 601(a).		Adulteration: 601.
	Misbranding: 602		

OTHER	EXPLAIN		

FORM FDA 457 (5/90) (BACK)

423

<u>FEDERAL ANTI-TAMPERING ACT</u>
Public Law 98-127 – OCT. 13, 1983
98th Congress

An Act
To amend title 18 of the United States Code to prohibit certain tampering with consumer products, and for other purposes. (Oct. 13, 1983, [S. 216])

Be it enacted by the Senate and House of Representatives of the United States of America in Congress assembled, That this Act may be cited as the "Federal Anti-Tampering Act". (Federal Anti-Tampering Act. 18 USC 1365 note.)

SEC. 2 Chapter 65 of title 18 of the United States Code is amended by adding at the end thereof the following new section:

"**§ 1365. Tampering with consumer products**

"(a) Whoever, with reckless disregard for the risk that another person will be placed in danger of death or bodily injury and under circumstances manifesting extreme indifference to such risk, tampers with any consumer product that affects interstate or foreign commerce, or the labeling of, or container for, any such product, or attempts to do so, shall-

"(1) in the case of an attempt, be fined not more than$25,000 or imprisoned not more than ten years, or both;

"(2) if death of an individual results, be fined not more than $100,000 or imprisoned for any term of years or for life, or both;

"(3) if serious bodily injury to any individual results, be fined not more than $100,000 or imprisoned not more than twenty years, or both; and

"(4) in any other case, be fined not more than $50,000 or imprisoned not more than ten years, or both.

"(b) Whoever, with intent to cause serious injury to the business of any person, taints any consumer product or renders materially false or misleading the labeling of, or container for, a consumer product, if such consumer product affects interstate of foreign commerce, shall be fined not more than $10,000 or imprisoned not more than three years, or both.

"(c)(1) Whoever knowingly communicates false information that a consumer product has been tainted, if such product or the results of such communication affect interstate or foreign commerce, and if such tainting, had it occurred, would create a risk of death or bodily injury to another person, shall be fined not more than $25,000 or imprisoned not more than five years, or both.

"(2) As used in paragraph (1) of this subsection, the term 'communicates false information' means communicates information that is false and that the communicator knows is false, under circumstances in which the information may reasonably be expected to be believed.

"(d) Whoever knowingly threatens, under circumstances in which the threat may reasonably be expected to be believed, that conduct that, if it occurred, would violate subsection (a) of this section will occur, shall be fined not more than $25,000 or imprisoned not more than five years, or both.

"(e) Whoever is a party to a conspiracy of two or more persons to commit an offense under subsection (a) of this section, if any of the parties intentionally engages in any conduct in furtherance of such offense, shall be fined not more than $25,000 or imprisoned not more than ten years, or both.

"(f) In addition to any other agency which has authority to investigate violations of this section, the Food and Drug Administration and the Department of Agriculture, respectively, have authority to investigate violations of this section involving a consumer product that is regulated by a provision of law such Administration or Department, as the case may be, administers.

"(g) As used in this section-

"(1) the term 'consumer product' means-

"(A) any 'food', 'drug', 'device', or 'cosmetic', as those terms are respectively defined in section 201 of the Federal Food, Drug, and Cosmetic Act (21 U.S.C. 321); or

"(B) any article, product, or commodity which is customarily produced or distributed for consumption by individuals, or use by individuals for purposes of personal care or in the performance of services ordinarily rendered within the household, and which is designed to be consumed or expended in the course of such consumption or use;

"(2) the term 'labeling' has the meaning given such term in section 201(m) of the Federal Food, Drug, and Cosmetic Act (21 U.S.C. 321(m));

"(3) the term 'serious bodily injury' means bodily injury which involves-

"(A) a substantial risk of death;

"(B) extreme physical pain;

"(C) protracted and obvious disfigurement; or

"(D) protracted loss or impairment of the function of a bodily member, organ, or mental faculty; and

"(4) the term 'bodily injury' means-

"(A) a cut, abrasion, bruise, burn, or disfigurement;

"(B) physical pain;

"(C) illness;

"(D) impairment of the function of a bodily member, organ, or mental faculty; or

"(E) any other injury to the body, no matter how temporary.".

SEC. 3. The table of sections at the beginning of chapter 65 of title 18 of the United States Code is amended by adding at the end thereof the following new item:

"1365. Tampering with consumer products.".

INSTRUCTIONS

DISTRICT OFFICE - CASE INITIATION/INFORMATION
REQUEST

GENERAL INSTRUCTIONS: This form may be legibly handwritten, typed, or recreated on your word processor. Please address all the questions. If the information is not applicable or unknown, enter "N/A" or "unknown" in the appropriate block. Additional pages may be attached if necessary, but please insert the appropriate topic number on the attachments (i.e. #7 Product Name). You may elect to attach other documents to this form, such as memoranda regarding the investigative status, Center or GC letters, information from victims, etc. Whenever possible, please provide copies of promotion literature, advertising, and labels for the products involved.

Supplemental information may be submitted in a memo format and must include items 1,m 2, 3 (if known), 4, 5, and 15 of the District Office Case Initiation/Information Report. (Exhibit 980-B is an example of a Supplemental Investigation Report which may be used in lieu of the memo format.)

1. OCI Field Office/SAIC: Identify the OCI field office to which this report is being submitted.
2. District Office: Identify the DO submitting the report.
3. Case Number: This requires an OCI case number which will be assigned by HQ OCI.
4. Date: Provide the date submitted (month/day/year).
5. Title of Case: Provide the common name used to refer to this case. (i.e. Doc's Clinic or John Doe, M.D.)
6. Type of Case: Provide a concise statement such as "Counterfeit Vet Drugs" or " Manufacture and Sale of GHB".
7. Product Name(s): List all products that are subject of the case. Provide generic, common, and trade names of all products, if known.
8. Probable Violations: Cite the titles and sections of the US Code.
9. Origin/Date of Case: Explain how and when FDA became aware of the criminal activity being investigated.
10. Primary Geographic Location: Comment on the locations where you believe the bulk of the investigative activity may be needed.
11. Other Agency Involvement/Interest: Provide the names and location of the agencies and agents (if known) who may be working on this case.
12. OCL or U.S. Attorney Involved: If any DOJ attorney has been assigned any aspect of this case, provide his/her name and telephone number.
13. Center and GC Points of Contact RE this Case: Provide the name and telephone numbers of appropriate Center or OGC personnel if any, who have been involved in this case.
14. Commitment of Other Agencies/DOJ: Explain other agencies role in the case. Identify lead agency, contact names, and telephone numbers. Estimate the number of agents or other resources which have been agreed to or assigned by other agencies.
15. District Office Contact/Telephone Number: Provide the name and telephone number of the FDA employee who is most knowledgeable about the case.
17. Date: Date signed by District Director or designee.
18. SAIC Comments: Reserved for field office SAIC
19. SAIC Signature/Date Received: Reserved for field office SAIC.
20. Date to OCI HQ: Reserved for field office SAIC
21. Synopsis: Write a brief synopsis of the criminal activity and the investigation to date. Include comments on any judicial action taken to date (search warrants, seizures, injunctions, indictments, arrests, etc.). It is not necessary to repeat information provided elsewhere in the report. If you wish, a separate memorandum may be attached. You may also elect to provide copies of other reports which contain the requested information. If appropriate, comment on samples collected, lab results, and known injuries or hazards related to the product(s) involved.
22. Investigative Plan/Strategy: Comment on the basic plan for the conduct of the investigation. Provide an estimate of FDA resources such as the number and location of FDA investigators assigned to this case, and how long the investigation is expected to take.

DISTRICT OFFICE
CASE INITIATION/INFORMATION REPORT

1. OCI FIELD OFFICE/SAIC:	2. DISTRICT OFFICE	3. CASE #:	4. DATE:

5. TITLE OF CASE:

6. TYPE OF CASE:

7. PRODUCT NAME(S):

8. PROBABLE VIOLATIONS:

9. ORIGIN/DATE OF CASE:

10. PRIMARY GEOGRAPHIC LOCATION OF INV. ACTIVITY:

11. OTHER AGENCY INVOLVEMENT/INTEREST:

12. OCL OR U.S. ATTORNEY INVOLVED:

13. CENTER AND GC POINTS OF CONTACT RE THIS CASE:

14. COMMITMENT OF OTHER AGENCIES/DOJ:

15. DISTRICT OFFICE CONTACT/PHONE NUMBER:	16. DISTRICT DIRECTOR:	17. DATE:

18. SAIC COMMENTS:

19. SAIC SIGNATURE/DATE RECEIVED:	20. DATE TO OCI HQ:

427

DISTRICT OFFICE

CASE INITIATION/INFORMATION REPORT

DISTRICT OFFICE:	CASE #:	DATE:

21. SYNOPSIS OF CRIMINAL ACTIVITY BEING INVESTIGATED:

DISTRICT OFFICE

CASE INITIATION/INFORMATION REPORT

DISTRICT OFFICE:	CASE #:	DATE:

21. INVESTIGATIVE PLAN/STRATEGY:

DISTRICT OFFICE

SUPPLEMENTAL INVESTIGATION REPORT

1. CASE TITLE:	2. CASE #:	3. OCI FIELD OFFICE/SAIC:
4. DISTRICT OFFICE:	5. INVESTIGATOR:	6. DATE:

7. **DETAILS**

INSTRUCTIONS - SUBJECT IDENTIFIER FORM

GENERAL INSTRUCTIONS: This form may be legibly handwritten, typed, or recreated on your word processor. Please address all the questions. If the information is not applicable or unknown, enter "N/A" or "unknown" in the appropriate block. Use separate form for each individual or business activity. Relationships between business entities and/or individuals should be explained in the comments section (block #32). **PROVIDE ALL AVAILABLE INFORMATION**

1.   Case Number: Provide the case number if one has been previously assigned. If this form is being submitted with the Case Initiation/Information Report form, OCI will assign the case number.
2.   D.O. Contact Name/Phone #: Provide the name and telephone number of the FDA employee who is most knowledgeable about this case.
3.   Date: Provide the date the form is completed and submitted to OCI.
4.   Last Name : Self Explanatory
5.   First Name: Self Explanatory
6.   Middle Name: Self Explanatory
7.   AKA: Self Explanatory
8.   Occupation: Provide the occupation of the subject if known, i.e. pharmacist, doctor, importer, etc.
9.   DOB: Must be numerical (month/date/year)
10.   POB: If the subject's POB was in the U.S., identify the State. If the subject's POB was in a foreign country, identify the country.
11.   Race/Sex: (A)sian, (B)lack, (C)aucasian, (H)ispanic, (O)ther; (F)emale (M)ale
12.   Height: Feet/inches
13.   Weight: pounds
14.   Eyes/Color: Blu = Blue, Brn = Brown, Blk = Black, Grn = Green, Gry = Grey
15.   Hair/Color: Brn = Brown, Blk = Black, Bln = Blonde, Gry = Grey
16.   Address: If a subject's exact address is unknown, provide city, state or metro area he/she is believed to be located. If the address provided is a former address, add a comment explaining the dates the subject was at the address provided. Give all known addresses including P.O. Boxes, mail drops, etc.
17.   Zip: Provide correct zip code.
18.   Telephone numbers: Enter known telephone number(s) for the subject precede by the appropriate code (i.e. H = home, W = work, C = Cellular, P = pager, F = fax) [e.g. H 703-321-7890, W 301-345-1234, C 301-132-5670]
19.   Social Security Number: Self Explanatory
20.   FBI #: Self Explanatory
21.   State/Local: Self Explanatory
22.   Passport #: Self Explanatory
23.   Other: Enter other identifying law enforcement numbers such as police numbers, TECS, NADDIS, prison number, etc. and department or agency.
24.   Vehicle: Self Explanatory
         Make
         Model
         Color
         Tag #
         State
         Drivers license #:
         State
25.   VIN Number: Vehicle Identification Number

26.   Known to Investigator: Insert the name and contact telephone number of the FDA investigator who best knows the subject through either personal contact and/or investigation.
27.   Firm or Corporate Name: Self Explanatory
28.   EIN: Employer Identification Number (tax ID number)
29.   Address: Provide location or primary address used by the corporation. List any other known addresses used, including P.O. Box, mail drops, etc. in the comments section (#32).
30.   Zip: Correct zip code is required for computer searches.
31.   Telephone Numbers: Enter known telephone number(s) for the firm preceded by the appropriate code (i.e. W = work, C = Cellular, P = pager, F = fax).
32.   Inv./SA Comments: Comment on the individual's or firm's involvement in the activity being investigated. Include relationships to other individuals or business entities. Also, use this section to provide any raw intelligence regarding this subject.

DISTRICT OFFICE
SUBJECT IDENTIFIER FORM
(ATTACH ADDITIONAL PAGES IF NECESSARY)

1. CASE NUMBER:	2. D.O. CONTACT NAME/PHONE #:	3. DATE:

4. LAST NAME:	5. FIRST NAME:	6. MIDDLE:

7. AKA:	8. OCCUPATION:

9. DOB:	10. POB:	11. RACE/SEX:	12. HT:	13. WT:	14. EYES:	15. HAIR:

16. ADDRESS:	17. ZIP:

18. PHONE NUMBERS: (H)OME (W)ORK (C)ELLULAR (P)AGER (F)AX

19. SSN:	20. FBI #:	21. STATE/LOCAL:	22. PASSPORT:	23. OTHER:

24. VEHICLE:	MAKE:	MDL:	COLOR:	TAG #:	STATE:	DRIVERS LIC:	STATE:

25. VIN NUMBER:	26. KNOWN TO INVESTIGATOR:

27. FIRM CORPORATE NAME:	28. EIN:

29. ADDRESS	30. ZIP:

31. PHONE NUMBERS: (H)OME (W)ORK (C)ELLULAR (P)AGER (F)AX

32. INV./SA COMMENTS:

FOR OCI USE ONLY

33. DATE/SIGNATURE REC'D SAIC OCI:	34. DATE/SIGNATURE SENT TO OCI INV. DIV:

35. DATE RECEIVED OCI INV. DIV.:	36. REVIEWED BY:

37. ACTION TAKEN:

38. SAIC –INV. DIV.:	39. DATE:	40. ASSIGNED CASE NUMBER:

41. DATA ENTRY MADE BY:	42. DATE:

CHAPTER 10 - REFERENCE MATERIALS

SUBCHAPTER 1000 - LAW, REGULATION, AND GUIDANCE

This chapter will help you to locate regulatory references and FDA staff.

The Bioterrorism Act of 2002, the Medical Device User Fee and Modernization Act of 2002 (MDUFMA), the FDA Modernization Act of 1997, the International Conference on Harmonization (ICH), the Mutual Recognition Agreement (MRA), national emergencies and initiatives, and other forces continue to impact FDA inspectional operations as changes in law, regulation, guidance and internal procedures issue. For example, as ICH members (Japan, U.S. and European Union) reach consensus agreements, ICH guidelines are adopted by all three governments. In the United States, they may replace outstanding FDA guidance in the medical device, human and animal drug areas. The new Bioterrorism Act of 2002 requires, among other things, that food firms register. The 2002 MDUFMA authorizes FDA to charge user fees for medical device premarket review; it allows third party medical device inspections, sets out new regulatory requirements for single-use devices, and directs FDA to establish the Office of Combination Products.

To be effective, FDA regulators must understand the difference between regulatory requirements and guidance. Laws, or statutes, enacted by Congress and regulations, or rules, promulgated by Federal agencies contain regulatory requirements.

FDA's guidance documents for industry serve purposes different from laws and regulations. The purposes of guidance documents are to:

1)   Provide assistance to the regulated industry by clarifying requirements that have been imposed by Congress or issued in regulations by FDA and by explaining how industry may comply with those statutory and regulatory requirements, and

2)   Provide specific review and enforcement approaches to help ensure that FDA's employees implement the agency's mandate in an effective, fair, and consistent manner.

The term "guidance documents" includes documents prepared for FDA staff, applicants/sponsors, and the public that: (1) relate to the processing, content, and evaluation/approval of submissions; (2) relate to the design, production, manufacturing, and testing of regulated products; (3) describe the agency's policy and regulatory approach to an issue; or (4) establish inspection and enforcement policies and procedures.

Guidance documents do not include documents relating to internal FDA procedures, agency reports, general information documents provided to consumers, speeches, journal articles and editorials, media interviews, press materials, warning letters, or other communications directed to individual persons or firms. FDA procedures issued for staff to follow, such as the IOM, are internal procedures intended to direct your activities and you are to follow them.

Guidance documents for industry do not establish legally enforceable rights or responsibilities and are not legally binding on the public or the agency. Rather, they explain how the agency believes the statutes and regulations apply to certain regulated activities. For a more detailed explanation of the background to the development, issuance and use of guidance documents in the February 27, 1997 Federal Register Volume 62 Number 39, see http://www.fda.gov/cder/guidance/fr27fe97-85.htm. To access 21CFR115 Good Guidance Practices, see http://www.access.gpo.gov/nara/cfr/waisidx_01/21cfrv1_01.html. Also see http://www.fda.gov/cdrh/ohip/guidance/1323.pdf to access the CDRH Manual for the Good Guidance Practices (GGP) Regulation – Final Guidance for FDA Staff (2/01). For a comprehensive list of FDA current guidance documents, see http://www.fda.gov/opacom/morechoices/industry/guidedc.htm.

The Federal Register is the official daily publication for rules, proposed rules, and Notices of federal agencies and organizations as well as Executive Orders and other Presidential documents. The Code of Federal Regulations (CFR) is a codification of the general and permanent rules published in the Federal Register by the Executive Departments and agencies of the Federal Government. Most regulations enforced by FDA are located in Title 21 of the CFR. For a listing of all titles in the U.S Code, see http://www4.law.cornell.edu/uscode/#TITLES.

SUBCHAPTER 1010 - SOURCES OF INFORMATION

1011 INVESTIGATOR TRAINING AND CERTIFICATION

ORA's Investigator certification program provides a focused training plan for the ongoing professional development of agency investigators. The program is designed to address the specific needs of agency District Offices by providing a structured mechanism for investigators to maintain the required levels of competency.

Performance certification promotes uniformity in investigator training and experience. The program is designed to promote the efficient use of (ORA) training resources. Investigators who complete the requirements of the program will be formally recognized as meeting the competencies required at the specific certification level achieved. Additional information on ORA's Investigator Certification program, including procedure documents and forms for certification in specific commodity areas, is available on the ORA U website. See http://web.ora.fda.gov/dhrd/Certification/certification.htm.

In addition to managing the investigator certification program through ORAU, the Division of Human Resource Development (DHRD) (HFC-60) manages and coordinates with Regions and Districts, the ORA staff's overall ongoing professional development training through in person and web-based courses, broadcasts, and video conferences. For more information on available training on the ORAU see http://web.ora.fda.gov/dhrd/.

1012 CONTACTING FDA EMPLOYEES

Easily finding colleagues you need to contact can make your work life more productive. See IOM Chapter 2 the organization of FDA offices, including a directory of ORA field offices and program managers. The Office of Regulatory Affairs organizational directory (blue pages) is available in electronic format. See http://www.fda.gov/ora/inspect_ref/iom/IOMORADIR.html. At the end of the blue pages, find a listing of District program monitors. For FDA Center staff directories:

CFSAN – See http://www.cfsan.fda.gov/~dms/srchbfd.html.
CBER – See http://www.fda.gov/cber/inside/org.htm
CDRH – See http://www.fda.gov/cdrh/organiz-info.html. For a list of resource staff by topic of specialization in the Division of Small Manufacturers, Consumer and International Affairs, see
http://www.fda.gov/cdrh/dsma/dsmastaf.html#
DSMICA_Staff
CVM – See http://www.fda.gov/cvm/aboutcvm/aboutcvm.html
CDER – See http://www.fda.gov/cder/directories/reference_guide.htm. For a list of resource staff by topic of specialization, in the CDER Division of Manufacturing and Product Quality, (HFD-320) see
http://www.fda.gov/cder/dmpq/csotable.htm

To obtain contact information for an FDA employee in your e-mail directory, find the name, then click on "properties" for telephone number and office designation. If the telephone number listed is inaccurate for an FDA employee you wish to contact, call the FDA Personnel Locator at telephone number (301) 443-1544 for an update.

You may also search the Department of Health and Human Services electronic employee directory, which includes FDA and all other HHS staff. See http://directory.psc.gov/employee.htm. See IOM Chapter 3 for other Federal agency and State contact information, or to check the Directory of State and Local Officials on the FDA web site, see http://www.fda.gov/ora/fed_state/directorytable.htm.

1013 INTERNET AND INTRANET

The FDA Internet Web site, (see http://www.fda.gov) provides access to FDA references in electronic format: laws, regulations, policy, guidance, correspondence, reports and other publications. From the FDA home page link to "Laws FDA Enforces", the "Code of Federal Regulations", the "Federal Register", and "FDA Manuals and Publications". See http://www.fda.gov/opacom/laws/lawtoc.htm. Under the heading "FDA Manuals and Publications" is a link to a comprehensive list of current FDA guidance documents. See http://www.fda.gov/opacom/morechoices/industry/guidedc.htm.

Two features will facilitate your navigation of the FDA website, For the FDA "Website Index", see www.fda.gov/opacom/hpchoice.html. To access the FDA "Website Map", see www.fda.gov/sitemap.html.

Subscribe to various FDA e-mail lists for updates on web postings. See www.fda.gov/emaillist.htm.

To access FDA libraries see http://intranet.fda.gov/library/. To access the FDA intranet homepage see http://intranet.fda.gov/index.cfm?index=2.

1014 FDA ON DISK

Another electronic source of regulatory references is the FDA Gold Disk. The Gold Disk is a CD-ROM produced and maintained by the Office of Enforcement, Division of Compliance Information and Quality Assurance (HFC-240) Steven Kendall (510) 337-6840. To order a Gold Disk, contact San Francisco District, Gwen Wong, (510) 337-6890. FDA personnel who do not have access to an FDA network server can use the Gold Disk in an off-line mode. It may also be available on your local district server. Check with your computer support personnel. The FDA gold disk is a convenient source of FDA regulatory references in electronic format when Internet access is not available. It contains, for example, the Federal Food Drug and Cosmetic Act, Title 21 CFR, Compliance Policy Guides, Enforcement Reports, Talk Papers, Import Alerts, Investigations Operations Manual, Regulatory Procedures Manual, selected Compliance Programs, the Food Code, and listings of approved drug products. The Gold Disk is not releasable under FOI and is not available to the public. It is for FDA use only. The subset of the Gold Disk available to state and local agencies (but not releasable under FOI) is the Eureka Disk. To order this, contact Paul Raynes in the ORA Division of Federal-State Relations (DFSR) at (301) 827-2910.

1015 ELECTRONIC-FAX INFORMATION SYSTEMS

FDA fax information systems issue documents twenty-four hours a day, seven days a week on request from the following sources:

Medical Devices: (800) 899-0381
Biologics: (888) 223-7329 or (301) 827-3844
Human/Animal Drugs and Foods: none

Follow the directions by the automated attendant to receive a faxed list of references and their order numbers. Next, request specific documents by number as indicated on the index.

1016 FDA/ORA MANUALS AND REPORTS

ORA headquarters and the OC Office of Information Resources Management support a change to electronic, not paper editions of manuals, because they are easier to issue, revise and distribute. As part of the ORA Quality Management System, ORA HQ supports electronic manual dissemination through developing Intranet master lists or indices for directives used by ORA. See http://web.ora.fda.gov/qms/ or contact Patricia Maroni-Benassi at (301)827-0389 or pmaroney@ora.fda.gov for more information. During the transition from paper to electronic manuals, a limited selection and number of paper manuals will be available as follows:

1. Compliance Policy Guides: Limited number of 2001 paper manuals available by contacting Don Vasbinder at (301) 827-0414 or at dvasbind@ora.fda.gov; for on line CPGs, see http://www.fda.gov/ora/compliance_ref/cpg/default.htm
2. Compliance Program Guidance Manual (CPGM): No paper manuals; for on-line CPGM, see http://web.ora.fda.gov/oe/cprogr/default.htm
3. Data Codes Manual: No paper manuals; for electronic lists of program assignment codes and establishment type codes contact ORM/DPEM.
4. Enforcement Notes: No paper reports; for on-line reports, see http://www.fda.gov/opacom/Enforce.html
5. Field Management Directives - No paper manual; for on-line FMD, see http://www.fda.gov/ora/inspect_ref/fmd/default.htm
6. Guide to International Inspections and Travel - No paper manual; for on-line access see http://www.fda.gov/ora/inspect_ref/giit/default.htm
7. Inspector's Technical Guides - No paper manual; for on-line guides, see http://www.fda.gov/ora/inspect_ref/itg/itgtc.html
8. International Cooperative Agreements Manual - No paper manual: for on-line manual see http://www.fda.gov/oia/default.htm
9. Investigations Operations Manual - Paper manuals available by contacting Alan Gion, ORA/ORO/Division of Field Investigations at (301) 827-5649. For on-line IOM see http://www.fda.gov/ora/inspect_ref/IOM/default.htm
10. Laboratory Procedures Manual (LPM) - No paper manuals; for on-line LPM see http://www.fda.gov/ora/science_ref/lpm/lpmtc_dec02.html
11. Regulatory Procedures Manual (RPM) - Limited 2002 paper manuals by contacting Office of Enforcement; for on-line RPM see http://www.fda.gov/ora/compliance_ref/rpm_new2/
12. Recalls and Safety Alerts – No paper copies; for on-line alerts, see http://www.fda.gov/opacom/7alerts.html
13. Staff Manual Guide: No paper manual; for on-line manual see http://intranet.fda.gov/oirm/manuals/
14. State and Federal Cooperative Agreements: No paper copies: to access on line, see http://www.fda.gov/ora/partnership_agreements/default.htm

1017 FORMS AND OTHER PUBLICATIONS

The FDA Forms Catalog contains a list of FDA forms and the information necessary to order them. The FDA Public Use Forms Catalog is available on the FDA web site. See http://www.fda.gov/opacom/morechoices/fdaforms/fdaforms.html. Order paper copies of FDA forms from the USDA Consolidated Forms and Publications Distribution Center, Beltsville Service Center 6351 Ammendale Road in Beltsville, MD 20705. Phone or fax orders will not be accepted. Forms may be ordered electronically. To obtain a customer number necessary to order forms electronically, or for other questions concerning FDA forms, contact:

FDA/Office of the Commissioner/Office of Information Resources Management/Division of Information Services and Policy
Elizabeth Sands, Forms Management Officer, (HFA-250)
5600 Fishers Lane, Room 16B-26
Rockville, MD 20857
(301) 827-1480
FAX (301) 594-0060
Or e-mail to esands@oc.fda.gov.

The Department of Health and Human Services (DHHS) Program Support Center, 16071 Industrial Drive, Gaithersburg, MD 20877 maintains a limited selection of FDA forms and publications. To access the PSC forms download site, see http://forms.psc.gov/. To search their catalog, see https://propshop.psc.gov/shopping/formspubs.asp#_/. For questions, contact Danny Saum at PSC at (301) 443-7634.

1018 REGULATORY REFERENCES AND THE GENERAL PUBLIC

The general public must make a request under the Freedom of Information Act (FOIA) in order to obtain certain FDA documents requiring redaction. See IOM 134 and IOM 135 for additional information on FOIA. For instructions to the public on how to file an FOIA request, see www.fda.gov/foi/foia2.htm. Many FDA documents are available to the public without an FOIA request. The public can purchase paper editions of various agency manuals, such as the Food Code and Compliance Program Manuals if ordered by product number from the National Technical Information Service (NTIS). Instruct industry representatives to locate publication numbers by conducting a search by topic on the National Technical Information Service (NTIS) web site; see www.ntis.gov. For additional information on NTIS publications, contact:

National Technical Information Service
Technology Administration
U.S. Department of Commerce
Springfield, VA 22161
Order Desk: (703) 605-6000
Fax: (703) 605-6900

To access the U.S. Government Bookstore on-line, see http://bookstore.gpo.gov/, or see http://bookstore.gpo.gov/locations/index.html for locations of on-site U.S. government bookstores. The public may also obtain FDA documents from the FDA automated FAX information services listed in section 1015 of Subchapter 1010. FDA references are also available to the public in electronic format from the FDA web site. See www.fda.gov. From the FDA homepage, link to special information for consumers, industry, health professionals, patients, state and local officials. For example, direct industry to the FDA industry web page; see http://www.fda.gov/oc/industry.

Those regulated by FDA may contact their ORA Regional Small Business Representative for an explanation of how FDA requirements apply to specific circumstances. SBRs also locate relevant references, make referrals, conduct or participate in workshops and conferences, or make non-regulatory audits on request. See

http://www.fda.gov/ora/fed_state/Small_Business/regional.htm. for a list of SBRs and the regions they serve.

Direct industry inquiries in accordance with District policy either to appropriate District personnel; to the ORA Small Business Representative for your region; or to an FDA industry assistance office in the appropriate Center. See http://www.fda.gov/ora/fed_state/Small_Business/sb_guide/centerco.htm for contact information on CDER, CBER, CDRH, CFSAN and CVM business assistance offices and Center Ombudsmen.

In CDRH, the Division of Manufacturers, International and Consumer Affairs (DSMICA) staff specializes in industry assistance. For a list of DSMICA resource staff showing area of special knowledge, see http://www.fda.gov/cdrh/dsma/dsmastaf.html#DSMICA_Staff. For FDA drug manufacturing queries, a list of resource staff in the CDER Division of Manufacturing and Product Quality, (HFD-320) identifies each staff member by area of knowledge. See http://www.fda.gov/cder/dmpq/csotable.htm.

SUBCHAPTER 1020 - SPECIAL REGULATORY REFERENCES BY PRODUCT CATEGORY

1021 FOOD AND COLOR ADDITIVES

1021.1 Food Additives Status List

The Food Additives Status List is intended to include food and drug additives and their use limitations as specified in regulations promulgated under the FD&C Act, under Sections 401 (Food Standards) 409 (Food Additives) and 512 (Animal Drugs) with some exceptions. See IOM Appendix A. You may encounter substances not included in the Food Additives Status List as follows:
1. Obviously safe substances not on the list of items generally recognized as safe (GRAS) which are not published in the regulations.
2. Synthetic flavoring substances because of their indefinite status.
3. Those pending administrative determination.
4. Substances granted prior sanction for specific use prior to enactment of the Food Additives Amendment.
5. Food contact substances (including secondary direct additives) that are the subject of an effective notification. For the inventory of effective notifications for food contact substances, see
http://www.cfsan.fda.gov/~dms/opa-fcn.html
For a list of FDA publications on food additives, see http://vm.cfsan.fda.gov/~dms/industry.html#add.

1021.2 Color Additives Status List

The Color Additives Status List provides the current status and use limitations of most colors likely to be found in food, drug, device, or cosmetic establishments. See IOM Appendix A. To access Color Additives for Medical Devices (11/95), see http://www.fda.gov/cdrh/ode/575.pdf. To access the FDA Color Additives web page see http://www.cfsan.fda.gov/%7Edms/col-toc.html.

1022 FOOD

For up to date references on food, food additive and cosmetic requirements and guidance, periodically check the Center for Food Safety and Applied Nutrition's web site. See http://vm.cfsan.fda.gov/list.html.

For food and cosmetic guidance documents, see http://www.cfsan.fda.gov/~dms/guidance.html.

1022.1 Food - General

1. Action Levels for Poisonous or Deleterious Substances in Human Food and Animal Feed (Revised 8/00): Lists action levels for unavoidable poisonous or deleterious substances, which are established by the FDA to control levels of contaminants in human food and animal feed. See http://vm.cfsan.fda.gov/~lrd/fdaact.html.
2. Allergens: CPG 555.250 FDA Statement of Policy on Labeling and Preventing Cross-Contact of Food Allergens (4/01) see http://www.fda.gov/ora/compliance_ref/cpg/cpgfod/cpg555-250.htm.
3. BSE: Guidance for Industry: The Sourcing and Processing of Gelatin to Reduce the Potential Risk Posed by Bovine Spongiform Encephalopathy (BSE) in FDA Regulated Products for Human Use (9/97) see http://www.fda.gov/opacom/morechoices/industry/guidance/gelguide.htm.
4. Botanicals: Letter to Manufacturers Regarding Botanicals and Other Novel Ingredients in Conventional Foods (1/01) see http://www.cfsan.fda.gov/~dms/ds-ltr15.html2.
5. Defect Action Levels (Revised 5/98) - Lists levels of natural or unavoidable defects in foods that present no health hazards for humans - see http://vm.cfsan.fda.gov/~dms/dalbook.html.
6. Filth in Food - Sec. 555.600 - Filth from Insects, Rodents, and Other Pests in Foods (CPG 7120.18) (12/02). See http://www.fda.gov/ora/compliance_ref/cpg/cpgfod/cpg555-600.html.
7. Food Code (Revised 2001): a compendium of model food safety guidelines for retail operations and institutions that is based on the latest science. The Food Code is used as a reference by the more than 3,000 state and local regulatory agencies that oversee food safety in restaurants, grocery stores, nursing homes, and other institutional and retail settings. See http://vm.cfsan.fda.gov/~dms/foodcode.html.
8. Fruits and Vegetables: Guide to Minimize Microbial Food Safety Hazards for Fresh Fruits and Vegetables; (3/00) see http://www.foodsafety.gov/~dms/prodguid.html.
9. Frozen Dessert Processing Guidelines (10/89) - Available from CFSAN/Office of Field Programs/Division of Cooperative Programs/Milk Safety Branch (HFS-626), Bob Hennes at 301-436-2175.
10. Health Claims: Guidance for Industry: Qualified Health Claims in Labeling of Conventional Foods and Dietary Supplements (12/02) See

http://www.cfsan.fda.gov/~dms/hclmgui2.html.
11. Labeling: Food Labeling Guide (6/99update) See http://vm.cfsan.fda.gov/~dms/flg-toc.html
12. Labeling: Food Labeling Questions and Answers Volume 1 - See http://www.cfsan.fda.gov/~lrd/qa2.html
13. Labeling: Food Labeling Questions and Answers Volume 2 - See http://www.cfsan.fda.gov/~frf/qaintro.html
14. Pesticides: Glossary of Pesticide Chemicals (10/01) lists Title 40 CFR tolerances of pesticide chemicals in food and animal feed - See http://vm.cfsan.fda.gov/~frf/pestglos.html
15. Pesticides: Pesticide Residues in Food and Feed – Enforcement Criteria Sec. 575.100 (CPG7141.01) (Rev. 3/95) See http://www.fda.gov/ora/compliance_ref/cpg/cpgfod/cpg575-100.html
16. Security: Field Instructions for "Food Producers, Processors, Transporters and Retailers; Food Security Preventive Measures Guidance"and "Importers and Filers: Food Security Preventive Measures Guidance" See http://www.cfsan.fda.gov/~dms/secguid3.html
17. Security: Guidance for Industry: Food Producers, Processors, Transporters and Retailers; Food Security Preventive Measures Guidance (1/02) See http://www.cfsan.fda.gov/~dms/secguid.html
18. Security: Guidance for Industry: Food Security Preventive Measures Guidance (1/02) See http://www.cfsan.fda.gov/~dms/secguid2.html

1022.2 Hazard Analysis Critical Control Points (HACCP)

1. Hazard Analysis and Critical Control Point (HACCP) Principles and Application Guidelines (8/97) See http://vm.cfsan.fda.gov/~comm/nacmcfp.html#execsum
2. Juice HACCP regulation – Questions and Answers, See http://www.cfsan.fda.gov/~comm/juiceqa.html
3. Juice HACCP Regulator Training (9/02) See http://www.cfsan.fda.gov/~comm/juiceman.html
4. Juice – Draft Guidance for Industry: Standardized Training Curriculum for Application of HACCP Principles to Juice Processing 10/02 See http://www.cfsan.fda.gov/~dms/juicgui5.html
5. Juice - Draft Guidance for Industry: Bulk Transport of Juice Concentrate and Certain Shelf Stable Juices (10/02) See http://www.cfsan.fda.gov/~dms/juicgui4.html
6. Draft Guidance for Industry: Juice HACCP Hazards and Controls Guidances, First Edition (9/02) See http://www.cfsan.fda.gov/~dms/juicgui3.html
7. Guidance for Industry: Exemptions from the Warning Label Requirements for Juice – Recommendations for Effectively Achieving a 5-Log pathogen Reduction (updated 10/02) See http://www.cfsan.fda.gov/~dms/juicgui6.html
8. For additional information on juice HACCP, see http://www.cfsan.fda.gov/~comm/haccpjui.html#regulation

9. Seafood HACCP Guidance Fish and Fisheries Products Hazards and Controls Guidance, Third Edition, see http://www.cfsan.fda.gov/~comm/haccp4.html

10. Questions and Answers: HACCP Regulations for Fish and Fishery Products, See http://www.cfsan.fda.gov/~dms/qa2haccp.html

11. Seafood HACCP Transition Guidance (12/99) See http://www.cfsan.fda.gov/~comm/seaguide.html

12. Seafood HACCP Refusal of Inspection or Access to HACCP Records Pertaining to Safe and Sanitary Processing of Fish and Fishery Products Guidance (7/01) See http://www.cfsan.fda.gov/~comm/seaguid3.html

13. Domestic Seafood HACCP report, See http://www.cfsan.fda.gov/~dms/sea3501a.html

14. For more information on seafood HACCP, See http://www.cfsan.fda.gov/~comm/haccpsea.html

1022.3 Bioengineered Foods

1. Center for Food Safety and Applied Nutrition, Biotechnology Home Page, See http://vm.cfsan.fda.gov/~lrd/biotechm.html

2. Voluntary Labeling Indicating Whether Foods Have or Have Not Been Developed Using Bioengineering – Draft Guidance (1/01) See http://vm.cfsan.fda.gov/~dms/biolabgu.html

3. Federal Register of 1/18/01, Premarket Notice Concerning Bioengineered Foods (1/01) See http://www.cfsan.fda.gov/~lrd/fr010118.html

4. Federal Register of 5/29/92, Statement of Policy: Foods Derived From New Plant Varieties, pp. 22984-23005 (10/00) See http://vm.cfsan.fda.gov/~lrd/bio1992.html

5. FDA's Policy for Foods Developed by Biotechnology; CFSAN Handout 1995 see http://www.cfsan.fda.gov/~lrd/biopolcy.html

6. Biotech Foods Questions & Answers 6/92 see http://vm.cfsan.fda.gov/~lrd/bioqa.html

1022.4 Seafood

1. Seafood HACCP Guidance Fish and Fisheries Products Hazards and Controls Guidance, Third Edition (6/01) See http://www.cfsan.fda.gov/~comm/haccp4.html

2. Questions and Answers: HACCP Regulations for Fish and Fishery Products (1/99) See http://www.cfsan.fda.gov/~dms/qa2haccp.html

3. Seafood HACCP Transition Guidance (12/99) see http://www.cfsan.fda.gov/~comm/seaguide.html

4. Seafood HACCP Refusal of Inspection or Access to HACCP Records Pertaining to Safe and Sanitary Processing of Fish and Fishery Products Guidance (7/01) See http://www.cfsan.fda.gov/~comm/seaguid3.html

5. Domestic Seafood HACCP Report, Revised Instructions FDA Form 3501 (2/01) see http://www.cfsan.fda.gov/~dms/sea3501a.html

6. For more information on seafood HACCP see http://www.cfsan.fda.gov/~comm/haccpsea.html

7. Guidance Document for Trace Elements in Seafood - Arsenic, Cadmium, Chromium, Lead, Nickel (1993) see http://www.cfsan.fda.gov/~frf/guid-sf.html

8. National Shellfish Sanitation Program Model Ordinance (11/00): represents the Agency's current thinking on the safe and sanitary control of the growing, processing, and shipping of molluscan shellfish for human consumption, see http://vm.cfsan.fda.gov/~ear/nsspotoc.html

9. Interstate Certified Shellfish Shippers List, see http://vm.cfsan.fda.gov/~ear/shellfis.html

1022.5 Food Inspection Guides

Food inspection guides are available from DFI. Also, see http://www.fda.gov/ora/inspect_ref/igs/iglist.html. They include:

1. Guidance on Inspections of Firms Producing Food Products Susceptible to Contamination with Allergenic Ingredients (8/01) See http://www.fda.gov/ora/inspect_ref/igs/allergy_inspection_guide.htm

2. Food Allergen Inspection Training for Regulators (10/01) see http://www.cfsan.fda.gov/~dms/alrgtrn.html

3. Guide to Nutritional Labeling and Education Act (NLEA) Requirements (2/95) See http://www.fda.gov/ora/inspect_ref/igs/nleatxt.html

4. Guide to Inspections of Computerized Systems in the in the Food Processing Industry (3/98) See http://www.fda.gov/ora/inspect_ref/igs/foodcomp.html

5. Guide to Inspections of Grain Product Manufacturers (12/98) See http://www.fda.gov/ora/inspect_ref/igs/grain.html

6. Guide to Inspections of Interstate Carriers and Support Facilities (4/95) See http://www.fda.gov/ora/inspect_ref/igs/icsf.html

7. Guide to Inspections of Miscellaneous Food Products Volume I (5/95) See http://www.fda.gov/ora/inspect_ref/igs/foodsp.html

8. Guide to Inspections of Manufacturers of Miscellaneous Food Products, Volume II (9/96) See http://www.fda.gov/ora/inspect_ref/igs/foodsp2.html

9. Guide to Inspections of Dairy Product Manufacturers (4/95) See http://www.fda.gov/ora/inspect_ref/igs/dairy.html

10. Guide to Inspections of Acidified Food Manufacturers (5/98) See http://www.fda.gov/ora/inspect_ref/igs/acidfgde.htm

11. Guide to Inspections of Low Acid Canned Food Manufacturers, Part 1 (11/96) Administrative Procedures and Scheduled Processes See http://www.fda.gov/ora/inspect_ref/igs/lacfpt1/lacfpt101.html

12. Guide to Inspections of Low Acid Canned Food Manufacturers, Part 2 Processes and Procedures (4/97) See http://www.fda.gov/ora/inspect_ref/igs/lacfpt2/lacfpt201.html

13. Guide to Trace Back of Fresh Fruits and Vegetables Implicated in Epidemiological Investigations (7/98) See http://www.fda.gov/ora/inspect_ref/igs/epigde/epigde.html

1022.6 CFSAN Databases

1. Everything Added to Food in the United States (EAFUS) see http://www.cfsan.fda.gov/~dms/eafus.html
2. List of "Indirect"Additives Used in Food Contact Substances, see http://www.cfsan.fda.gov/~dms/opa-indt.html
3. Inventory of Effective Premarket Notifications for Food Contact Substances see http://www.cfsan.fda.gov/~dms/opa-fcn.html
4. Food Contact Substance Cumulative Daily Intake/Acceptable Daily Intake database, see http://www.cfsan.fda.gov/~dms/opa-edi.html. This database cites the regulation where a food contact substance appears.
5. Summary of all GRAS notices - see http://www.cfsan.fda.gov/~rdb/opa-gras.html
6. Partial List of Enzyme Preparations Used in Food (7/01) see http://www.cfsan.fda.gov/~dms/opa-enzy.html
7. Partial List of Microbial Derived Ingredients Used in Food (7/01) see http://www.cfsan.fda.gov/~dms/opa-micr.html

CFSAN Office of Management Systems (HFS-676) maintains an internal database of Low Acid Canned Food/Acidified Food registered establishments and scheduled processes. To gain access and further information about this database, ORA personnel should contact Michele Baucum ORA/ORM at 301-827-1573.

1023 DIETARY SUPPLEMENTS

To access the FDA's dietary supplement web site, see http://www.cfsan.fda.gov/~dms/supplmnt.html. References there include:

1. Dietary Supplement Health and Education Act of 1994 (12/95) synopsis, see http://vm.cfsan.fda.gov/~dms/dietsupp.html
2. Overview of Dietary Supplements (4/99) see http://vm.cfsan.fda.gov/~dms/ds-oview.html
3. Labeling of Dietary Supplements CFSAN web page, see http://www.cfsan.fda.gov/~dms/ds-labl.html
4. Guidance for Industry: Statement of Identity, Nutrition Labeling, and Ingredient Labeling of Dietary Supplements Small Entity Compliance guide. (1/99) See http://vm.cfsan.fda.gov/~dms/ds-label.html
5. List of warnings and safety information, see http://vm.cfsan.fda.gov/~dms/supplmnt.html
6. Guidance for Industry: Qualified Health Claims in Labeling of Conventional Foods and Dietary Supplements (12/02) see http://www.cfsan.fda.gov/~dms/hclmgui2.html
7. Structure/Function Claims, Small Entity Compliance

Guide (1/02) see http://www.cfsan.fda.gov/~dms/sclmguid.html
8. Guidance for Industry - Statement of Identity, Nutrition Labeling and Ingredient Labeling of dietary Supplements – Small entity Compliance Guide (1/99) see http://www.cfsan.fda.gov/~dms/ds-label.html
9. Guidance for Industry: Iron-Containing Dietary Supplements and Drugs: Label Warning and Unit Dose Packaging (11/97) see http://www.cfsan.fda.gov/~dms/secgiron.html

1024 COSMETICS

1024.1 Cosmetic References

For FDA's Cosmetic web site see http://www.cfsan.fda.gov/~dms/cos-toc.html. Specific cosmetic references include:
1. Cosmetics Handbook (1992): FDA requirements and policies for safe production and accurate labeling of cosmetics. See http://vm.cfsan.fda.gov/~dms/cos-hdbk.html
2. Cosmetic Good Manufacturing Practice Guidelines: See http://vm.cfsan.fda.gov/~dms/cos-gmp.html
3. FDA's Cosmetic Labeling Manual (10/91): Contains information on FDA's requirements and policies for safe production and accurate labeling of cosmetics. See http://www.cfsan.fda.gov/~dms/cos-lab1.html
4. Information Materials for the Food and Cosmetics Industries: A catalogue of cosmetic publications. See http://vm.cfsan.fda.gov/~dms/industry.html#cos

1024.2 Cosmetic Inspection Guides

1. Cosmetic Guide to Inspections of Cosmetic Product Manufacturers (2/95) See http://www.fda.gov/ora/inspect_ref/igs/cosmet.html

1025 DEVICES

1025.1 CDRH Regulatory References

The Center for Devices and Radiological Health (CDRH), Division of Small Manufacturers Assistance (DSMA) (HFZ-220) maintains Fax Back, a fax on demand system to provide medial device related FDA references. The telephone numbers to access this system are (800) 899-0381 or (301) 827-0111. For up-to-date medical device references, see http://www.fda.gov/cdrh/index.html. See www.fda.gov/ora , the ORA home page for up-to-date medical device publications and guidance materials. For an alphabetized index of CDRH references, including product specific references, see http://www.accessdata.fda.gov/scripts/cdrh/cfdocs/cfTopic/topicindex/topindx.cfm. One selection in the index is a list of Good Guidance Practices Documents, organized by issuing CDRH Office/Division/Branch.

References available from the CDRH fax information system or the CDRH web site include:
1. 510(k): 510(k) Manual Premarket Notification

Regulatory Requirements for Medical Devices (8/95)
See http://www.fda.gov/cdrh/manual/510kprt1.html

2. 510(k): Deciding When to Submit a 510(k) for a Change to an Existing Device (1/97) See http://www.fda.gov/cdrh/ode/510kmod.html

3. 510(k) Sterility Review Guidance K90-1 Final Guidance for Industry and FDA (8/02) See http://www.fda.gov/cdrh/ode/guidance/361.html

4. 510(k): Medical Device Exemptions 510(k) and GMP Requirements (11/00) See http://www.accessdata.fda.gov/scripts/cdrh/cfdocs/cfpcd/315.cfm

5. 510(k): Guidance or the Content of Premarket Submissions for Software Contained in Medical Devices (5/29/98) See http://www.fda.gov/cdrh/ode/57.html

6. Classification of Medical Devices: FDA Classification of Medical Devices See http://www.fda.gov/cdrh/devadvice/313.html

7. Classification of Medical Devices: Medical Device Product Code Classification Database See http://www.fda.gov/cdrh/prodcode.html

8. Consensus Standards: Guidance on the Recognition and Use of Consensus Standards (6/01) See http://www.fda.gov/cdrh/ost/guidance/321.html

9. Design: Design Control Guidance for Medical Device Manufacturers (3/97) See http://www.fda.gov/cdrh/comp/designgd.html

10. Design: Do it By Design an Introduction to Human Factors in Medical Devices See http://www.fda.gov/cdrh/humfac/doit.html (9/93)

11. Design: Device Use Safety: Incorporating Human Factors in Risk Management (7/00) See http://www.fda.gov/cdrh/humfac/1497.html

12. Design: New Model Medical Device Development Process (7/98) See http://www.fda.gov/cdrh/pmat/newmod.html

13. Import Alerts on Medical Devices, see http://www.fda.gov/ora/fiars/ora_import_med.html

14. IVD: Guideline for the Manufacture of In Vitro Diagnostic Products (1/94) See http://www.fda.gov/cdrh/comp/918.pdf

15. Labeling: Medical Device Labeling guidance: Suggested Format and Content draft 8/97 See http://www.fda.gov/cdrh/ode/labeling.html

16. Labeling: Regulatory Requirements for Medical Device Manufacturers (8/89) See http://www.fda.gov/cdrh/dsma/470.pdf

17. Labeling: Guidance for Industry: Alternative to Certain Prescription Device Labeling Requirements (1/00) See http://www.fda.gov/cdrh/comp/rxlabeling.html

18. Labeling: Human Factors Principles for Medical Device Labeling (9/93) see http://www.fda.gov/cdrh/dsma/227.html

19. MDR: Medical Device Reporting for Manufacturers (amended 3/00) See http://www.fda.gov/cdrh/manual/mdrman.html

20. MDR: Medical Device Reporting for User Facilities (4/96) See http://www.fda.gov/cdrh/mdruf.pdf

21. MDR: Medical Device Reporting Forms and Instructions See http://www.fda.gov/cdrh/mdr/mdr-forms.html

21. MDR: Medical Device Reporting Alternative Summary Reporting (ASR) Program (10/00) See http://www.fda.gov/cdrh/osb/guidance/315.html

22. MDR: User Facility Reporting Bulletins See http://www.fda.gov/cdrh/fusenews.html

23. PMA: Premarket Approval Manual (1/98) See http://www.fda.gov/cdrh/dsma/pmaman/front.html

24. Quality Systems: Medical Device Medical Device Quality Systems Manual: A Small Entity Compliance Guide First Edition HHS Publication FDA 97-4179 – See http://www.fda.gov/cdrh/dsma/gmp_man.html

25. Quality Systems: The FDA and Worldwide Quality System Requirements Guidebook for Medical Devices". compiled by FDA/CDRH' Kimberly Trautman. The book offers guidance on the medical device QS/GMPs and shows their relationship to ISO 9001.

26. Registration: Guidance for Industry: Instructions for Completion of Medical Device Registration and Listing Forms 2891, 2891a and 2892 See http://www.fda.gov/cdrh/dsma/rlman.html

27. Registration and Listing: FOIA Releasable Registration and Listing Files; See http://www.fda.gov/cdrh/comp/estregls.html

28. Re-use of Single Use: Enforcement Priorities for Single-Use Devices Reprocessed by Third Parties and Hospitals (8/00) See http://www.fda.gov/cdrh/reuse/1168.html

29. Re-use of Single Use: Reprocessing Single Use Devices: Final Guidance for Industry and FDA Staff - Frequently Asked Questions about the Reprocessing and Reuse of Single-Use Devices by Third-Party and Hospital Reprocessors; (7/01) see http://www.fda.gov/cdrh/ohip/guidance/1333.html; Three Additional Questions (9/02) see http://www.fda.gov/cdrh/ohip/guidance/1408.html; Two Additional Questions,(12/02) see http://www.fda.gov/cdrh/ohip/guidance/1427.html

30. Re-use of Single Use: Changes in Enforcement of FDA's Requirements for Single Use Devices (9/01) See http://www.fda.gov/cdrh/reuse/reuse-letter-092501.html and for Reuse Home Page see http://www.fda.gov/cdrh/Reuse/index.html

31. Software: Final Guidance for Industry and FDA: General Principles of Software Validation (1/02) See http://www.fda.gov/cdrh/comp/guidance/938.html

32. Software: Guidance for Industry, FDA Reviewers and Compliance on Off-the-Shelf Software Use in Medical Devices (9/99) See http://www.fda.gov/cdrh/ode/guidance/585.html

33. Tracking: Guidance for Industry and FDA Staff on Medical Device Tracking (1/00) See http://www.fda.gov/cdrh/modact/tracking.html

1025.2 Device Inspection Guides

Inspection guides covering medical devices are available from DFI (HFC-130) at 301-827-5653. Also see http://www.fda.gov/ora/inspect_ref/igs/iglist.html "Guides to Inspections of:"for Medical Devices references such as:

1. Guide to Inspections of Medical Device

Manufacturers(12/97). See http://www.fda.gov/ora/inspect_ref/igs/med_dev_mnfct/toc.html

2. Guide to Inspections of Quality Systems (8/99) See http://www.fda.gov/ora/inspect_ref/igs/qsit/qsitguide.htm

3. Guide to Inspections of Foreign Medical Device Manufacturers (9/95) See http://www.fda.gov/ora/inspect_ref/igs/fordev.html

4. Guide to Inspections of Electromagnetic Compatibility Aspects of Medical Device Quality Systems (12/97) See http://www.fda.gov/ora/inspect_ref/igs/elec_med_dev/emc1.html

5. Mammography Quality Standards Act (MQSA) Auditor's Guide (1/98) See http://www.fda.gov/ora/inspect_ref/igs/mqsa.html

6. Guide to Bioresearch Monitoring Inspections of In Vitro Diagnostic Devices (3/98) See http://www.fda.gov/ora/inspect_ref/igs/bimoivd.html

7. Glossary of Computerized System and Software Development Terminology (8/95) See http://www.fda.gov/ora/inspect_ref/igs/gloss.html

1025.3 CDRH Databases

For a list of and links to CDRH public access databases, see http://www.fda.gov/cdrh/databases.html. They include a searchable database of CDRH guidance documents, a listing of medical devices in commercial distribution, a database of registered firms, a listing of FDA – recognized consensus standards, and a product classification database. To access the CDRH public database of medical devices which may have malfunctioned or caused a death or serious injury during the years 1992 through 1997, see http://www.fda.gov/cdrh/mdrfile.html. The web site also contains a public database of the Device Experience Database (MAUDE) for a reports of adverse events involving medical devices since June 1993. To access the FDA internal registration and listing 510(k), PMA, MDR and Maude databases through the CDRH Information Retrieval System (CIRS) you must acquire an individual account by contacting your District CIRS liaison. See the ORA Field Program Monitors listing in the Chapter 2 of the IOM to locate your District CIRS liaison. To access the CDRH internal M204 data system on radiation-emitting electronic products, request the District computer liaison to contact the CDRH Office of Compliance for an account and instructions.

1026 BIOLOGICS

1026.1 CBER Regulatory References

A current listing of the Center for Biologics Evaluation and Research (CBER) regulatory references is available through CBER's Fax Information System at (301) 827-3844 or (888) 223-7329 (U.S. only). The automated attendant guides the caller through a menu of directions to receive an index of the available materials. With this index, callers can order specific documents by number from the following categories:

1. Federal Register publications
2. General
3. Guidance

4. Guidance (FR Notice)
5. Guideline
6. ICH Guidelines
7. Information Sheets
8. Letter
9. Lists
10. Points to Consider
11. Recall/Withdrawal/Safety

For the topic index of CBER references, see http://www.fda.gov/cber/cberac.htm. For an index sorted by type of CBER publication, see http://www.fda.gov/cber/publications.htm. These references include:

1. Bioengineered Plants: Guidance for Industry: Drugs, Biologics, and Medical Devices Derived from Bioengineered Plants for Use in Humans and Animals (9/02) see http://www.fda.gov/cber/gdlns/bioplant.htm

2. Container Closure Systems: Guidance for Industry: Container Closure Systems for Packaging Human Drugs and Biologics-Chemistry Manufacturing Controls Documentation (7/99) see http://www.fda.gov/cber/gdlns/cntanr.htm

3. Human Tissue: Preventive Measures to Reduce the Possible Risk of Transmission of Creutzfeldt Jakob Disease (CJD) and Variant Creutzfeld-Jakob Disease (vCJD) by Human Cells, Tissues, and Cellular and Tissue-Based Products (HCT/Ps)(6/02) see http://www.fda.gov/cber/gdlns/cjdvcjd0602.htm

4. Human Tissue: Guidance for Industry: Validation of Procedures for Processing of Human Tissues Intended for Transplantation (3/02) see http://www.fda.gov/cber/gdlns/tissval.htm

5. Postmarket Adverse Experiences: Draft Guidance for Industry: Postmarketing Safety Reporting for Human Drug and Biological Products including Vaccines March 2001 See http://www.fda.gov/cder/guidance/4177dft.pdf

1026.2 Blood and Blood Products Inspection Guides and Industry Guidance

For a complete list of inspectional guides available from DFI, see http://www.fda.gov/ora/inspect_ref/igs/iglist.html. Blood and blood products inspection guides are:

1. Blood Bank Inspections (9/94) - See http://www.fda.gov/ora/inspect_ref/igs/blood.html

2. Source Plasma Establishments (4/01) - See http://www.fda.gov/ora/inspect_ref/igs/Source_Plasma/default.htm

3. Infectious Disease Marker Testing Facilities (10/96) See http://www.fda.gov/ora/inspect_ref/igs/infdis.html

CBER has mailed many guidance documents relative to Blood Banks directly to Blood Establishments. These guidance documents are listed in the Compliance Program Guidance Manual, Inspection of Licensed and Unlicensed Blood Banks. Also, to access these on the CBER Blood web page, see http://www.fda.gov/cber/blood.htm. They include:

1. Blood Components: Guidance for Industry: An Acceptable Circular of Information for the Use of Human Blood and Blood Components (10/02) See http://www.fda.gov/cber/gdlns/circbld.htm
2. Donors: Guidance for Industry: Recommendations for Deferral of Donors and Quarantine and Retrieval of Blood and Blood Products in Recent Recipients of Smallpox Vaccine (Vaccinia Virus) and Certain Contacts of Smallpox Vaccine Recipients (12/02) See http://www.fda.gov/cber/gdlns/smpoxdefquar.htm
3. Donors: Guidance for Industry: Recommendations for the Assessment of Donor Suitability and Blood and Blood Product Safety in Cases of Known or Suspected West Nile Virus Infection (10/02) see http://www.fda.gov/cber/gdlns/wnvguid.htm
4. Donors: Draft Guidance for Industry: Streamlining the Donor Interview Process: Recommendations for Self-Administered Questionnaires (4/02) see http://www.fda.gov/cber/gdlns/donorsaq.pdf
5. Blood Components: Draft Guidance for Industry: A Modified Lot-Release Specification for Hepatitis B Surface Antigen (HBSAg) Assays Used to Test Blood, Blood Components, and Source Plasma Donations (4/02) see http://www.fda.gov/cber/gdlns/hbslotrel.htm
6. Donors: Draft Guidance for Industry: Use of Nucleic Acid Tests on Pooled and Individual Samples of Donors of Whole Blood and Blood Components for Transfusion to Adequately and Appropriately Reduce the Risk of Transmission of HIV-1 and HCV (3/02) see http://www.fda.gov/cber/gdlns/hivhcvnatbld.htm
7. Donors: Draft Guidance for Industry: Precautionary Measures to Reduce the Possible Risk of Transmission of Zoonoses by Blood and Blood Products from Xenotransplantation Produce Recipients and Their Contacts (12/99) see http://www.fda.gov/cber/gdlns/zooxeno.htm

1026.3 Other Biologics Inspection Guides

1. Guide to Inspections of Viral Clearance Processes for Plasma Derivatives (3/98) See http://www.fda.gov/ora/inspect_ref/igs/viralcl.html
2. Biotechnology Inspection Guide (11/91) See http://www.fda.gov/ora/inspect_ref/igs/biotech.html

1026.4 CBER Databases

1. Vaccine Adverse Event Report System (VAERS): a public access database of adverse events that occur after the administration of US licensed vaccines. Reports are received from: patients, parents, health care providers, pharmacists, and vaccine manufacturers. See http://www.fda.gov/cber/vaers/database.htm
2. The Adverse Event Reporting System (AERS) is a public access database designed to support the FDA's post-marketing safety surveillance program for all approved drug and therapeutic biologic products. The FDA receives adverse drug reaction reports from manufacturers as required by regulation. Health care professionals and consumers send reports voluntarily through the MedWatch program. See http://www.fda.gov/cder/aers

1027 DRUGS

1027.1 CDER Regulatory References

CDER regulatory references including a complete list of CDER Guidance Documents are available on the CDER Regulatory Guidance web site, see http://www.fda.gov/cder/regulatory/default.htm and from the Drug Information Branch at 301-827-4573. To access the web site of the International Conference on Harmonization (ICH) to learn more about quality references under development by the U.S., European Union (EU) and Japan, see http://www.ich.org/ich1bis.html.

1. ANDA's Blend Uniformity Analysis (8/99) Draft Guidance for Industry: see www.fda.gov/cder/guidance/2882dft.htm
2. Aseptic Processing: Guideline on Sterile Drug Products Produced by Aseptic Processing (6/87, reprinted 6/91) See http://www.fda.gov/cder/guidance/old027fn.pdf
3. Aseptic Processing: Draft Preliminary Concept Paper on Sterile Drugs Produced by Aseptic Processing (9/02) see http://www.fda.gov/cder/dmpq/aseptic-cp.pdf
4. BACPAC I Intermediates in Drug Substance Synthesis: Bulk Actives Post Approval Changes: Chemistry, Manufacturing, Controls and Documentation (2/01) Guidance for industry See http://www.fda.gov/cder/guidance/3629fnl.htm
5. Botanical Drug Products: Guidance for Industry: Botanical Drug Products (Draft 8/00) See http://www.fda.gov/cder/guidance/1221dft.htm
6. Compressed Medical Gases Guideline (2/89) See http://www.fda.gov/cder/guidance/cmgg89.htm
7. Compressed Medical Gas: Fresh Air 2000, A Look at FDA's Medical Gas Requirements, see http://www.fda.gov/cder/dmpq/freshair.htm
8. Computerized Systems Used in Clinical Trials (4/99) See http://www.fda.gov/ora/compliance_ref/bimo/ffinalcct.PDF
9. Container Closure Systems for Packaging Human Drugs and Biologics (5/99) See http://www.fda.gov/cder/guidance/1714fnl.htm
10. Dioxin: Possible Contamination of Drugs and Biological Products - Guidance for Industry (8/99) See http://www.fda.gov/cder/guidance/3310fnl.pdf
11. Drug Master Files Guideline (9/89) See http://www.fda.gov/cder/guidance/dmf.htm
12. Drug Master Files for Bulk Antibiotic Drug Substances Guidance (11/99) See http://www.fda.gov/cder/guidance/3276fnl.pdf
13. Expiration Dating of Solid Oral Dosage Forms Containing Iron (6/97) See http://www.fda.gov/cder/guidance/1807fn1.pdf
14. ICH Q1A Stability Testing of New Drug Substances and Products Rev. 1 (8/01) See http://www.fda.gov/OHRMS/DOCKETS/98fr/930139gd.pdf
15. ICH Q1D Guidance for Industry: Bracketing and Matrixing Designs for Stability Testing of New Drug

Substances and Products (1/03) See
http://www.fda.gov/cder/guidance/4985fnl.pdf

16. ICH Q1E Draft Consensus Guideline - Evaluation of Stability Data, see http://www.fda.gov/OHRMS/DOCKETS/98fr/02d-0237-gdl0001-vol1.pdf

17. ICH Q1F Draft Consensus Guideline – Stability Data for Registration in Climactic Zones 3 and 4, see http://www.ich.org/pdfICH/Q1Fstep2.pdf

18. ICH Q3AR Draft Revised Guidance on Impurities in New Drug Substances (Draft 7/00) in FR Vol. 65 No. 140, see http://www.fda.gov/OHRMS/DOCKETS/98fr/072000b.txt

19. ICH Q3BR Draft Revised Guidance on Impurities in New Drug Products (Draft 7/00) in FR Vol. 65 No. 139, see http://www.fda.gov/OHRMS/DOCKETS/98fr/071900a.txt

20. ICH Q3C Guidance for Industry on Impurities: Residual Solvents (12/97) in FR Vol. 62, NO. 247, December 24, 1997, page 67377, see http://www.fda.gov/cder/guidance/Q3Cfinal.htm

21. ICH Q5A Quality of Biotechnological Products: Viral Safety Evaluation of Biotechnology Products Derived from Cell Lines of Human or Animal Origin in FR Vol. 63, No. 185, 9/24/98 see http://www.fda.gov/ohrms/dockets/98fr/092498c.txt

22. ICH Q6A Specifications: Test Procedures and Acceptance Criteria for New Drug Substances and New Drug Products: Chemical Substances, in FR Vol. 65, No. 251 on 12/29/00, see http://www.fda.gov/OHRMS/DOCKETS/98fr/122900d.htm

23. ICH Q6B Guidance on Specifications: Test Procedures and Acceptance Criteria for Biotechnological/Biological Products in FR Vol. 64 No. 159 on 8/18/99, see http://www.fda.gov/OHRMS/DOCKETS/98fr/081899a.txt

24. ICH Q7A Guidance for Industry: Good Manufacturing Practice Guidance for Active Pharmaceutical Ingredients (8/01) See http://www.fda.gov/cder/guidance/4286fnl.htm

25. Inhalation Drug Products: Guidance for Industry: Nasal Spray and Inhalation, Solution, Suspension and Spray Drug Products (Draft 5/99) See http://www.fda.gov/cder/guidance/4234fnl.htm

26. Orange Book: Approved Drug Products with Therapeutic Equivalents See http://www.fda.gov/cder/ob/default.htm

27. Out of Specification Test Results: Guidance for Industry: Investigation of Out of Specification Test Results for Pharmaceutical Production (Draft 9/98) See http://www.fda.gov/cder/guidance/1212dft.pdf

28. Post-approval Changes: Guidance for Industry: Changes to an Approved NDA or ANDA (11/99) See http://www.fda.gov/cder/guidance/2766fnl.pdf

29. Post-approval Changes: Guidance for Industry: SUPAC-IR: Immediate-Release Solid Oral Dosage Forms: Scale-Up and Post Approval Changes: Chemistry, Manufacturing Controls, In Vitro Dissolution Testing, and In Vivo Bioequivalence Documentation (11/95) See http://www.fda.gov/cder/guidance/cmc5.pdf

30. Post-approval Changes: Guidance for Industry: SUPAC-MR: Modified Release Solid Oral Dosage Forms Scale-Up and Postapproval Changes: Chemistry, Manufacturing and Controls; In Vitro Dissolution Testing and In Vivo Bioequivalency Documentation (9/97) See http://www.fda.gov/cder/guidance/1214fnl.pdf

31. Post-approval Changes: Guidance for Industry: SUPAC-IR/MR Immediate Release and Modified Release Solid Oral Dosage Forms Manufacturing Equipment Addendum (1/99) See http://www.fda.gov/cder/guidance/1721fnl.pdf

32. Post-approval Changes: Guidance for Industry: SUPAC-IR: Questions and Answers about SUPAC-IR Guidance (2/97) See http://www.fda.gov/cder/guidance/qaletter.htm

33. Post-approval Changes: Guidance for Industry: SUPAC-SS: Nonsterile Semisolid Dosage Forms: Scale-UP and Post-Approval Changes: Chemistry, Manufacturing and Controls; In Vitro Release Testing and In Vivo Bioequivalence Documentation (5/97) see http://www.fda.gov/cder/guidance/1447fnl.pdf

34. Post-approval Changes: Guidance for Industry: SUPAC-SS Manufacturing Equipment Addendum (Draft 12/98) See http://www.fda.gov/cder/guidance/1722dft.pdf

35. Postmarket Adverse Experiences: Guideline for Postmarketing Reporting of Adverse Drug Experiences [Docket No. 85D-0249] March 1992 See http://www.fda.gov/medwatch/safety/ade/t_cder.htm

36. Postmarket Adverse Experiences: Guidance for Industry: Postmarketing Adverse Experience Reporting for Human Drug and Licensed Biological Products - Clarification of What to Report August 1997 See http://www.fda.gov/medwatch/report/guide2.htm

37. Postmarket Adverse Experiences: Draft Guidance for Industry: Postmarketing Safety Reporting for Human Drug and Biological Products including Vaccines March 2001 See http://www.fda.gov/cder/guidance/4177dft.pdf

38. Validation: Guideline on the Preparation of Investigational New Drug Products (Human and Animal) (3/91) see www.fda.gov/cder/guidance/old042fn.pdf

39. Validation: Guideline on General Principles of Process Validation (5/87) See http://www.fda.gov/cder/guidance/pv.htm

40. Validation: Compliance Policy Guide 7132c.08 (8/93) Process Validation Requirements for Drugs Subject to Premarket Approval See http://www.fda.gov/ora/compliance_ref/cpg/cpgdrg/cpg490-100.html

41. Validation: Guidance for Industry: Submission Documentation for Sterilization Process Validation in Applications for Human and Veterinary Drug Products (11/94) see http://www.fda.gov/cder/guidance/cmc2.pdf

42. Validation: Guideline on Validation of the Limulus Amebocyte Lysate Test as an End Product Endotoxin Test for Human and Animal Parenteral Drugs, Biological Products, and Medical Devices (12/87) See http://www.fda.gov/cder/guidance/old005fn.pdf

43. Validation: Guidance for Industry: Analytical Procedures and Methods Validation Chemistry, Manufacturing, and

Controls Documentation (Draft 8/00) See
http://www.fda.gov/cder/guidance/2396dft.htm
44. Validation: Final Guidance for Industry and FDA:
General Principles of Software Validation (1/02) See
http://www.fda.gov/cdrh/comp/guidance/938.html

1027.2 Human Drug Inspection Guides

Inspectional guides covering human and animal drug
manufacturing and testing that are available from DFI. See
www.fda.gov/ora, Inspectional References, include:

1. Guide to Inspection of Computerized Systems in Drug
    Processing (2/83) See
    http://www.fda.gov/ora/inspect_ref/igs/csd.html
2. Glossary of Computerized System and Software
    Development Terminology See
    http://www.fda.gov/ora/inspect_ref/igs/gloss.html
3. Guide to Inspections of High Purity Water Systems
    (7/93) See
    http://www.fda.gov/ora/inspect_ref/igs/high.html
4. Guide to Inspections of Lyophilization of Parenterals
    (7/93) See
    http://www.fda.gov/ora/inspect_ref/igs/lyophi.html
5. Guide to Inspections of Microbiological Pharmaceutical
    Quality Control Laboratories (7/93) See
    http://www.fda.gov/ora/inspect_ref/igs/micro.html
6. Guide to Inspections of Pharmaceutical Quality Control
    Laboratories (7/93) See
    http://www.fda.gov/ora/inspect_ref/igs/pharm.html
7. Guide to Inspections of Validation of Cleaning
    Processes (7/93) See
    http://www.fda.gov/ora/inspect_ref/igs/valid.html
8. Guide to Inspections of Dosage Form Drug
    Manufacturers - CGMP's (10/93) See
    http://www.fda.gov/ora/inspect_ref/igs/dose.html
9. Guide to Inspections of Oral Solid Dosage Forms
    Pre/Post Approval Issues for Development and
    Validation (1/94) See
    http://www.fda.gov/ora/inspect_ref/igs/solid.html
10. Guide to Inspections of Sterile Drug Substance
    Manufacturers (7/94) See
    http://www.fda.gov/ora/inspect_ref/igs/subst.html
11. Guide to Inspections of Topical Drug Products (7/94)
    See http://www.fda.gov/ora/inspect_ref/igs/topic.html
12. Guide to Inspections of Oral Solutions and
    Suspensions (8/94) See
    http://www.fda.gov/ora/inspect_ref/igs/oral.html
13. Guide to Inspections of Foreign Pharmaceutical
    Manufacturers (5/96) See
    http://www.fda.gov/ora/inspect_ref/igs/fordrug.html
14. Guide to Inspections of Bulk Pharmaceutical
    Chemicals (9/91) See
    http://www.fda.gov/ora/inspect_ref/igs/bulk.html
15. Biotechnology Inspection Guide (11/91) See
    http://www.fda.gov/ora/inspect_ref/igs/biotech.html
16. Enforcement of the Postmarketing Adverse Drug
    Experience Reporting Regulations See
    http://www.fda.gov/cder/aers/chapter53.htm

1027.3 Veterinary Regulatory References

The Center for Veterinary Medicine (CVM) regulatory
and informational references are available on the CVM
website. See http://www.fda.gov/cvm/default.htm CVM web
site references include guidance documents - See
http://www.fda.gov/cvm/guidance/published.htm#docu-
ments, and Compliance Policy Guides (CPGs) as well as
an index of topics. Copies of regulatory references may
also be obtained from the CVM's Communications Staff
(HFV-12), MPN IV, 7519 Standish Place, Rockville, MD
20855, or by calling (301) 827-4410. CVM also maintains
a fax back system at (301) 827-6635 to deliver requested
documents by fax. CVM references include:

1. Guidance for Industry No. 85: Good Clinical Practices
    (VICH GL9) (5/01) See
    http://www.fda.gov/cvm/guidance/guide85.doc
2. Guidance for Industry No. 105: Computerized Systems
    Used in Clinical Trials (4/99) See
    http://www.fda.gov/ora/compliance_ref/bimo/ffinalcct.htm
3. Animal Drug Manufacturing Guidelines No. 42 A series
    of 4 guidelines revised 1994) See
    http://www.fda.gov/cvm/guidance/admguidelinetoc.html
4. CPG Sec. 608.400 (7125.40) Compounding of Drugs
    for use in Animals, See http://www.fda.gov/ora/
    compliance_ref/cpg/cpgvet/cpg608-400.html
5. Drug Stability Guideline No.5: (4th Revision 12/90) See
    http://www.fda.gov/cvm/guidance/guide5part1.html
6. Guidance for Industry No. 73: Stability Testing of New
    Veterinary Drug Substances and Medicinal Products"
    VICH GL3 (9/99) See
    http://www.fda.gov/cvm/guidance/guide73.doc
7. Guidance for Industry No. 74: Stability Testing of New
    Veterinary Dosage Forms VICH GL4 (9/99) See
    http://www.fda.gov/cvm/guidance/guide74.doc
8. Guidance for Industry No. 75: Stability Testing:
    Photostability Testing of New Veterinary Drug
    Substances and Medicinal Products VICH GL5 (9/99)
    See http://www.fda.gov/cvm/guidance/guide75.doc
9. Guidance for Industry No. 83: Chemistry,
    Manufacturing and Controls Changes to an Approved
    NADA or ANADA: Draft Guidance (6/99) See
    http://www.fda.gov/cvm/guidance/dguide83.pdf
10. Guidance for Industry No. 57: Preparation and
    Submission of Veterinary Master Files (1/95) see
    http://www.fda.gov/cvm/guidance/guide57.html
11. Guidance for Industry No. 92: Impurities In New
    Veterinary Drug Substances (7/99) See
    http://www.fda.gov/cvm/guidance/fguide92.doc
12. Guidance for Industry No. 48: Submission Docu-
    mentation for Sterilization Process Validation in
    Applications for Human and Veterinary Drug Products
    (11/94) See http://www.fda.gov/cder/guidance/cmc2.pdf
13. Guidance for Industry No. 93: Impurities In New
    Veterinary Medical Products (7/99) See
    http://www.fda.gov/cvm/guidance/fguide93.doc
14. Guidance for Industry No. 64: Validation of Analytical
    Procedures: Methodology (7/99) See
    http://www.fda.gov/cvm/guidance/guida64.doc
15. Guidance for Industry No. 99: Stability Testing Of

Biotechnological/Biological Veterinary Medicinal Products VICH GL17: (3/01) See http://www.fda.gov/cvm/guidance/fguide99.doc

16. Guidance for Industry No. 100: Impurities: Residual Solvents in New Veterinary Medicinal Products VICH GL18: (5/01) See http://www.fda.gov/cvm/guidance/guide100.doc

17. Guidance for Industry No. 126: BACPAC I: Intermediates in Drug Substance Synthesis Bulk Actives Post approval Changes: Chemistry, Manufacturing, and Controls Documentation (2/01) See http://www.fda.gov/cder/guidance/3629fnl.htm

18. Guidance for Industry No. 67: Small Entities Compliance Guide for Renderers (2/98) See http://www.fda.gov/cvm/guidance/guidance67.pdf

19. Guidance for Industry No. 68: Small Entity Compliance Guide for Protein Blenders, Feed Manufacturers and Distributors (2/98) See http://www.fda.gov/cvm/guidance/guidance68.pdf

20. Guidance for Industry No. 69: Small Entities Compliance Guide No. for Feeders of Ruminant Animals With On-Farm Feed Mixing Operations (2/98) See http://www.fda.gov/cvm/guidance/guidance69.pdf

21. Guidance for Industry No. 70: Small Entity Compliance Guide for Feeders of Ruminant Animals Without On-Farm Feed Mixing Operations (2/98) See http://www.fda.gov/cvm/guidance/guidance70.pdf

22. Guidance for Industry No. 72: GMPs for Medicated Feed Manufacturers Not Required to Register and be Licensed with FDA (5/98) See http://www.fda.gov/cvm/guidance/guideline72.html

23. Draft Guidance for Industry No. 77: Interpretation of On-Farm Feed Manufacturing and Mixing Operations (9/98) See http://www.fda.gov/cvm/guidance/onfadefi.html

24. Guidance for Industry No. 76: Questions and Answers BSE Feed Regulations (7/98) See http://www.fda.gov/cvm/guidance/guida76.htm

25. CPG Sec. 689.100 (7126.41) Direct Fed Microbial Products See http://www.fda.gov/ora/compliance_ref/cpg/cpgvet/cpg689-100.html

26. Guidance for Industry No. 120: Veterinary Feed Directive Regulation (3/01) See http://www.fda.gov/cvm/guidance/guide120.doc

27. Guidance for Industry No. 91: Stability Testing for Medicated Premixes (VICH GL8) (3/00) See http://www.fda.gov/cvm/guidance/fguide91.doc

28. Guideline No. 23: Medicated Free Choice Feeds: Manufacturing Controls (7/85) See http://www.fda.gov/cvm/guidance/guide23.html

Refer to these documents for additional guidance applicable to veterinary drug manufacture:

1. Guideline on General Principles of Process Validation (5/87) See http://www.fda.gov/cder/guidance/pv.htm

2. Guideline on Sterile Drug Products Produced by Aseptic Processing (reprinted 6/91) See http://www.fda.gov/cder/guidance/old027fn.pdf

3. Compliance Policy Guide 7132c.08 (8/93) Process Validation Requirements for Drugs Subject to

Premarket Approval See http://www.fda.gov/ora/compliance_ref/cpg/cpgdrg/cpg490-100.html

10127.4 Veterinary Drug Inspection Guides

Drug Inspection Guides listed in IOM subchapter 1027.2 apply to inspections of both human and veterinary drugs with regard to application of 21CFR 211 Current Good Manufacturing Practice for Finished Pharmaceuticals.

1027.5 CDER and CVM Databases

1. CDER public access drug firm annual registration status: see www.fda.gov/cder/dfars/default.htm

2. CDER public access National Drug Code Query (NDCQ) System: The NDCQ contains human drug products that have completed the listing process in accordance with the applicable federal law. The information is as reported by the listing firm. See http://www.fda.gov/cder/ndc/database/Default.htm

3. The Adverse Event Reporting System (AERS) is a public access database designed to support the FDA's post-marketing safety surveillance program for all approved drug and therapeutic biologic products. The FDA receives adverse drug reaction reports from manufacturers as required by regulation. Health care professionals and consumers send reports voluntarily through the MedWatch program. See http://www.fda.gov/cder/aers and see http://www.fda.gov/medwatch/index.html

4. Orange Book – public access database provides searches for approved human drug products by proprietary name, active ingredient, applicant holder, or application number. See www.fda.gov/cder/ob/default.htm

5. Green Book – public access database provides search for approved animal drug products by application number, sponsor. See http://www.fda.gov/cvm/greenbook/greenbook.html

6. Inactive Ingredient Database – searchable database of inactive drug ingredient sin FDA-approved drug products, see http://www.accessdata.fda.gov/scripts/cder/iig/index.cfm

1028 BIORESEARCH

1028.1 Bioresearch Regulatory References

The FDA Office for Good Clinical Practice web page, see http://www.fda.gov/oc/gcp/default.htm and/or the FDA Office of Regulatory Affairs Bioresearch Monitoring web page, see http://www.fda.gov/ora/compliance_ref/bimo contain a series of FDA bioresearch monitoring regulatory references, including:

1. Application Integrity Policy Information See http://www.fda.gov/ora/compliance_ref/aip_page.html

2. Bioresearch related Compliance Policy Guides: see http://www.fda.gov/ora/compliance_ref/bimo/default.htm

3. Clinical Investigators and IRBs: FDA Information

Sheets: Guidance for Institutional Review Boards and Clinical Investigators (1998) See http://www.fda.gov/oc/ohrt/irbs/default.htm

4. Clinical Investigators and IRBs: Dear Colleague Letter on 1998 update of FDA Information Sheets (2/99) See http://www.fda.gov/oc/ohrt/irbs/tocltr.html

5. Human Cloning: FDA Letter to Institutional Review Boards on Human Cloning (10/26/98) See http://www.fda.gov/oc/ohrt/irbs/irbletr.html

6. Clinical Investigators: Disqualified/Restricted/Assurances List for Clinical Investigators See http://www.fda.gov/ora/compliance_ref/bimo/dis_res_assur.htm

7. Computerized Systems: Guidance for Industry: Computerized Systems Used in Clinical Trials (4/99) See http://www.fda.gov/ora/compliance_ref/bimo/ffinalcct.htm

8 Debarment: List of Debarred Individuals See http://www.fda.gov/ora/compliance_ref/debar/default.htm

9. Good Laboratory Practice: Guidance for Industry Good Laboratory Practice Regulations Management Briefings Post Conference Report (8/79 - updated 11/98) See http://www.fda.gov/ora/compliance_ref/bimo/q_as.htm

10. Good Laboratory Practice: Guidance for Industry: Good Laboratory Practices Questions and Answers (6/81) See http://www.fda.gov/cder/guidance/old004fn.pdf

11. ICH E6: Good Clinical Practice (4/96) Guidance for Industry See http://www.fda.gov/cder/guidance/959fnl.pdf

12. ICH E8: Guidance on General Considerations for Clinical Trials published in FR Vol. 62 No. 42 12/17/97 See http://www.fda.gov/cder/guidance/1857fnl.pdf

13. Informed Consent: Draft Guidance for Institutional Review Boards, Clinical Investigators, and Sponsors: Exception from Informed Consent Requirements for Emergency Research, (3/00) See http://www.fda.gov/ora/compliance_ref/bimo/err_guide.htm

14. Monitoring Clinical Investigations: Guidance for Industry: Guideline for the Monitoring of Clinical Investigations (1/88 - updated 11/98) See http://www.fda.gov/ora/compliance_ref/bimo/clinguid.html

15. Veterinary Clinical Trials: Guidance for Industry No. 58: Good Target Animal Study Practices: Clinical Investigators and Monitors (5/97). See www.fda.gov/cvm/guidance/clgfinal.pdf

16. Veterinary Clinical Trials: Guidance for Industry No. 85: VICH GL9 (5/01) Good Clinical Practice: See http://www.fda.gov/cvm/guidance/guide85.doc

1028.2 Bioresearch Inspection Guides

1. Techniques for Detecting False Data During Bioresearch Monitoring Inspections (1/03) is available from DFI (HFC-130) at 301-827-5653.

1029 MISCELLANEOUS

1029.1 Computer References

1. Clinical Trials: Guidance for Industry: Computerized Systems Used in Clinical Trials (4/99) See http://www.fda.gov/ora/compliance_ref/bimo/ffinalcct.htm

2. Consensus Standard: Recognized Consensus Standard – Software Lifecycle Processes, see http://www.accessdata.fda.gov/scripts/cdrh/cfdocs/cfStandards/Detail.CFM?STANDARD_IDENTIFICATION_NO=233

3. Drug Manufacturing: Compliance Policy Guide Section 425. 100 (7132a.17) Computerized Drug Processing: CGMP Applicability to Hardware and Software (9/87) See http://www.fda.gov/ora/compliance_ref/cpg/cpgdrg/cpg425-100.html

4. Drug Manufacturing: Compliance Policy Guide Section 425. 200 (7132a.12) Computerized Drug Processing: Vendor Responsibility (9/87) See http://www.fda.gov/ora/compliance_ref/cpg/cpgdrg/cpg425-200.html

5. Drug Manufacturing: Compliance Policy Guide Section 425. 300 (7132a.15) Computerized Drug Processing: Source Code for Process Control Application Programs (4/87) See http://www.fda.gov/ora/compliance_ref/cpg/cpgdrg/cpg425-300.html

6. Drug Manufacturing: Compliance Policy Guide Section 425. 400 (7132a.07) Computerized Drug Processing: Input/Output Checking (9/87) See http://www.fda.gov/ora/compliance_ref/cpg/cpgdrg/cpg425-400.html

7. Drug Manufacturing: Compliance Policy Guide Section 425.500 (7132.08) Computerized Drug Processing: Identification of Persons on Batch Production and Control Records (9/87) See http://www.fda.gov/ora/compliance_ref/cpg/cpgdrg/cpg425-500.html

8. Electronic Records: Compliance Policy Guide Section 160. 850 (7153.17) Enforcement Policy: Electronic Records; Electronic Signatures (5/99) See http://www.fda.gov/ora/compliance_ref/cpg/cpggenl/cpg160-850.htm

9. Electronic Records: Draft Guidance for Industry: 21 CFR Part 11 Electronic Records: Maintenance of Electronic Records (7/02) See http://www.fda.gov/cber/gdlns/esigmaint.htm

10. Electronic Records: Draft Guidance for Industry: 21 CFR Part 11 Electronic Records – Time Stamps (2/02) See http://www.fda.gov/cber/gdlns/esigtime.htm

11. FDA Draft Policy for the Regulation of Computer Products (11/89) See http://www.fda.gov/cdrh/ode/351.pdf

12. Glossary of Computerized System and Software Development Terminology (8/95) See http://www.fda.gov/ora/inspect_ref/igs/gloss.html

13. Medical Device: 510(k)s, PMAs: Guidance for the Content of Premarket Submissions for Software Contained in Medical Devices (5/98) See http://www.fda.gov/cdrh/ode/57.html

14. Medical Device: Computer-Controlled Potentially High-

Risk Medical Devices - List of Device Types (8/99) See http://www.fda.gov/cdrh/yr2000/cdrh/phrds/phrds.html

15. Medical Device: Guidance for Industry, FDA Reviewers and Compliance: Off-the-Shelf Software Use in Medical Devices (9/99) See http://www.fda.gov/cdrh/ode/guidance/585.html

16. Validation: Final Guidance for Industry and FDA: General Principles of Software Validation (1/02) See http://www.fda.gov/cdrh/comp/guidance/938.html

For a compilation of FDA regulatory and informational references on 21CFR Part 11 Electronic Records; Electronic Signatures, see http://www.fda.gov/ora/compliance_ref/part11.

1029.2 Computer Inspection Guides

1. Guide to Inspections of Computerized Systems in Drug Processing (2/83) See http://www.fda.gov/ora/inspect_ref/igs/csd.html

2. Guide to Inspections of Computerized Systems in the Food Processing Industry (3/98) See http://www.fda.gov/ora/inspect_ref/igs/foodcomp.html

3. Guidance for FDA Investigators: Application of Medical Device GMPs to Computerized Devices and Manufacturing Processes (5/92) See http://www.fda.gov/cdrh/comp/guidance/247.pdf

1029.3 Combination Products

The Medical Device User Fee and Modernization Act of 2002 directed FDA to establish the Office of Combination Products to better regulate those products which do not fall neatly into the drug, device, biologic or food categories. For information on how FDA determines product jurisdiction and regulates combination products through intercenter agreements see http://www.fda.gov/oc/ombudsman/pj.htm. To read the intercenter agreements see http://www.fda.gov/oc/ombudsman/bio-dev.htm, (CBER-CDRH); see http://www.fda.gov/oc/ombudsman/drug-dev.htm, (CDRH-CDER), see http://www.fda.gov/oc/ombudsman/drug-bio.htm, (CBER-CDER) and see http://www.cfsan.fda.gov/%7Edms/ds-inter.html (CFSAN-CDER). To read about jurisdictional updates, see http://www.fda.gov/oc/ombudsman/updates.html.

1029.4 Health Fraud References

To access the FDA CFSAN website on health fraud, see http://www.cfsan.fda.gov/~dms/wh-fraud.html.

To obtain Health Fraud Bulletins in the following list, contact the CDER Office of Compliance/Division of Labeling and Non-Prescription Drug Compliance/Non-Traditional Drug Compliance Team (HFD-314) Joel Aronson (301) 594-0070:

1. Request for Limited Inspection Re: Homeopathic Products (Drug Study Bulletin #I - 10/26/84)

2. Removal of Caffeine and Phenylpropanolamine Combination Products from the OTC Market (Drug Study Bulletin #2 - 11/9/84)

3. Homeopathic Drugs (Drugs & Biologics Fraud Bulletin #3 - 12/11/84)

4. Class Action Cholecystokinin (CCK) (Drugs & Biologics Fraud Bulletin #4 - 2/22/85)

5. Implementation of class action to issue Regulatory Letters to all firms marketing DHEA (Drugs & Biologics Fraud Bulletin #5 - 3/28/85)

6. OTC products on the market offered for Oral Chelation Therapy (Drugs & Biologics Fraud Bulletin #6 - 7/1/85)

7. Marine Lipids (Health Fraud Bulletin #7 - 3/25/88 revision)

8. Products containing Nonoxynol-9 which claim to prevent AIDS - request for investigation and recommendations (Drugs & Biologics Fraud Bulletin #8 - 8/30/85)

9. "Colostrum" Products (Health Fraud Bulletin #9 - 1/15/87)

10. Fraudulent AIDS Products (Health Fraud Bulletin #10 - 7/15/87)

11. Immune System Products (Health Fraud Bulletin #11 - 8/17/87)

12. Beta-Carotene for Cancer (Health Fraud Bulletin #12 - Undated)

13. Transdermal Patches (Health Fraud Bulletin #13 - 2/3/89)

14. Products for the Treatment of Systemic Candida infections (Health Fraud Bulletin #14 - 5/l9/89)

15. Vitamin & Mineral Products for the Prevention or Treatment of Diseases of the Eye (Health Fraud Bulletin #15 - 7/13/90)

16. Products containing nonoxynol-9 as a single entity; nonoxynol-9 and para-chlorametaxylenol (PCMX) as a combination (Health Fraud Bulletin #16 - 5/14/91)

17. Prescription Homeopathic Products Marketed Over-the-Counter (Health Fraud Bulletin #17 - 6/9/92)

18. Cholesterol Related to Cardiovascular Disease (Health Fraud Bulletin #18 - 3/22/93)

19. Colloidal Silver (Health Fraud Bulletin #19 - 10/7/94)

20. OTC Treatments for Benign Prostatic Hypertrophy (Non-Traditional Drug Bulletin #20 - 3/18/97)

21. Attention Deficit Hyperactivity Disorder (Non-Traditional Drug Bulletin #21 6/27/97)

22. Herbal Alternatives to Fen-Phen (Non-Traditional Drug Bulletin #22 - 10/8/97)

23. OTC Drug Products for Impotence and Sexual Dysfunction (Non-Traditional Drug Bulletin #23 - 6/11/98)

SUBCHAPTER 1030 - CFR'S

1031 LIST OF PARTS OF TITLE 21 CFR

This subchapter lists the parts of Title 21 Code of Federal Regulations: Food and Drugs, Chapter I, Food and Drug Administration. Title 21 contains nine volumes as follows:

Volume 1 Parts 1-99
Volume 2 Parts 100-169
Volume 3 Parts 170-199
Volume 4 Parts 200-299
Volume 5 Parts 300-499
Volume 6 Parts 500-599

Page citations in the following lists refer to Title 21 CFR revised as of April 1, 2002.

21 CFR SUBCHAPTER A - GENERAL

Bolded list entrees indicate those regulations reprinted in their entirety in IOM Appendix B.
Volume 1

21 CFR SUBCHAPTER B - FOOD FOR HUMAN CONSUMPTION
Volume 2

21 CFR SUBCHAPTER B - FOOD FOR HUMAN CONSUMPTION (CON'T.)
Volume 3

1032   CFR SECTIONS AFFECTING OTC DRUGS

1032.1 Alphabetical Listing of Sections

1032.2 OTC Final Monographs Listed Alphabetically

FOOD ADDITIVE STATUS LIST

FOREWORD

This Food Additives Status List organizes additives found in many parts of 21 CFR into one alphabetized list. Additives included are those specified in the regulations promulgated under the FD&C Act, under Sections 401 (Food Standards), and 409 (Food Additives). The list also includes selected pesticide chemicals from 40 CFR 180 for which EPA has set tolerances in food. FDA enforces those tolerances. Within the space available, the Food Additives Status List includes use limitations and permitted tolerances for each additive. For complete information on its use limitations, refer to the specific regulation for each substance. To access 21 CFR, see http://www.access.gpo.gov/nara/cfr/index.html. To access 40 CFR 180, "Tolerances and Exemptions from Tolerances for Pesticide Chemicals in Food", see http://www.access.gpo.gov/nara/cfr/waisidx_01/40cfr180_01.html. New regulations and revisions are published in current issues of the Federal Register as promulgated. To access the Federal Register, see http://www.access.gpo.gov/su_docs/aces/aces140.html. Also refer to the CFSAN website on Food Additives and Premarket Approval to review several FDA databases of additive categories. See http://www.cfsan.fda.gov/~lrd/foodadd.html. For example, EAFUS (Everything Added to Food in the United States) is a helpful reference within the limitations described at the beginning of the database.

The Food Additive Status List omits certain categories of additives. Here are the omissions:

1. Obviously safe substances not cited in a regulation as Generally Recognized as Safe (GRAS). You may find such substances on an FDA web site, see http://www.cfsan.fda.gov/~rdb/opa-gras.html. It contains GRAS notifications received from companies since 1998, and FDA' s response.

2. Synthetic flavoring substances in 21CFR 172.515. The CFR does not contain a complete list of permissible flavorings. Certain trade groups such as the Flavor Extract Manufacturers Association have established expert panels to evaluate and make determinations on the GRAS status of their products. If you need help in determining the acceptability of a flavoring after consulting 21 CFR 172.515, contact CFSAN Office of Food Additive Safety (HFS-200) at (202) 418-3100.

3. Those pending administrative determination.

4. Substances granted prior sanction for specific use prior to enactment of the Food Additives Amendment. For additional information on these substances, contact the CFSAN Office of Food Additive Safety (HFS-200) at (202) 418-3100.

5. Indirect food additives, 21 CFR Parts 175, 176, 177, & Part 178 (except that sanitizing agents for food processing equipment as listed in 178.1010 are included in the Food Additives list.) Be aware that as a result of the Food Quality Protection Act of 1996 and Antimicrobial Regulation Technical Corrections Act of 1998, EPA now has jurisdiction over sanitizing solutions applied to permanent or semi-permanent food contact surfaces, other than food packaging.

To look up indirect food additives in Parts 175, 176, 177 and 178 go to FDA's "List of Indirect Additives Used in Food Contact Substances" See http://www.cfsan.fda.gov/~dms/opa-indt.html. Use it to locate the regulation in which its use is fully described.

FDA has recently implemented a new way to market, called "Premarket Notification", for certain food contact substances. These notifications are effective only for the manufacturer or supplier identified in the notification. A list of effective notifications is available on the FDA website. See http://www.cfsan.fda.gov/~dms/opa-fcn.html.

6. Color additives, 21 CFR Parts 70, 71, 73, 74, 80 & 82. Go to the Color Additives Status List following the Food Additives Status list in Appendix A.

NOTE: The Food Additives Status List is provided only as a quick look-up on the use limitations for a food additive or pesticide chemical. It is possible that mistakes or omissions could have occurred. Additionally, there may be cases where the agency has offered interpretations concerning specific provisions of the regulations. For example, in the case of boiler water additives or other minor ingredients, processing aids, or indirect additives, FDA has not objected, in certain cases, to the substitution of ammonium, calcium, magnesium, potassium, or sodium salts for each other when only one is listed in a regulation. The Food Additive Status list is updated annually, so it may not reflect the latest information. For all these reasons, take care before advising a firm that a use of a particular food additive is prohibited or otherwise limited. Read the actual regulation. If there are any doubts or if a particular situation is unclear, you or your supervisor should consult with the CFSAN, Office of Food Additive Safety (HFS-200) at (202) 418-3100, or the Division of Petition Review (HFS-265) at (202) 418-3042, or the Division of Food Contact Substance Notification Review HFS-275 at (202) 418-3080, or the Division of Biotechnology and GRAS Notice Review HFS-255 at (202) 418-3090.

Please send corrections or additions to the list, to Alan Gion FDA/Division of Field Investigations (DFI) (HFC-130), 5600 Fishers Lane, Room 13-64,Rockville, Maryland 20857 or e-mail them to IOM@ORA.FDA.GOV.

ABBREVIATIONS USED

<u>Type</u>   (kind, effect or use of additive)

AC	Anticaking agent
AF	Antifoaming (or defoaming) agent
AOX	Antioxidant
BC	Boiler compound
BL	Bleaching agent or flour-maturing agent
B&N	Buffer and neutralizing agent
CTG	Component or coating for fruits & vegetables
DS	Dietary supplement
EMUL	Emulsifier
ENZ	Enzyme
ESO	Essential oil and/or oleoresin (solvent free)
FEED	substances under the Food Additives Amendment added directly to feed
FLAV	Natural flavoring agent
FL/ADJ	Substance used in conjunction with flavors
FUM	Fumigant
FUNG	Fungicide
HERB	Herbicide
HOR	Hormone
INH	Inhibitor
MISC	Miscellaneous
NAT	Natural substances and extractives
NNS	Non-nutritive sweetener
NUTR	Nutrient
NUTRS	Nutritive Sweetener
PEST	Pesticide other than fumigant
PRES	Chemical preservative
SANI	Sanitizing agent for food processing equipment
SDA	Solubilizing and dispersing agent
SEQ	Sequestrant
SOLV	Solvent
SP	Spices, other natural seasonings & flavorings
SP/ADJ	Spray adjuvant
STAB	Stabilizer
SY/FL	Synthetic flavor
VET	Veterinary drug, which may leave residue in edible tissues of animals or in edible animal products

<u>Status</u>

BAN	Substances banned prior to the Food Additives Amendment (FAA) because of toxicity. These substances are underlined

FS	Substance permitted as optional ingredient in a standardized food
GRAS	Generally recognized as safe. Substances in this category are by definition, under SEC. 201(s) of the FD&C Act, not food additives. Most GRAS substances have no quantitative restrictions as to use, although their use must conform to good manufacturing practices. Some GRAS substances, such as sodium benzoate, do have a quantitative limit for use in foods.
GRAS/FS	Substances generally recognized as safe in foods but limited in standardized foods where the standard provides for its use.
<u>ILL</u>	Substances used or proposed for use as direct additives in foods without required clearance under the FAA. Their use is illegal. These substances are underlined.
PD	Substance for which a petition has been filed but denied because of lack of proof of safety. Substances in this category are illegal and may not be used in foods.
PS	Substance for which prior sanction has been granted by FDA for specific uses. There are a number of substances in this category not listed herein because they have not been published in the FEDERAL REGISTER.
REG	Food additive for which a petition has been filed and a regulation issued.
REG/FS	Food additive regulated under the FAA and included in a specific food standard.

<u>Other</u>

&	and
amt	amount
art	artificially
avg	average
ca	about, approximately
calc	calculated
CFR	Code of Federal Regulations
cnd	canned
cond	conditions
comb.	w/ in combination with; combined with
comp	component
ctg	coating for fruits, vegetables, tablets
do	Same CFR reference as appears earlier in paragraph
dr	dried

455

F.R.	Federal Register
g	gram(s)
GMP	In accordance with good manufacturing practices; or sufficient for purpose; or quantity not greater than required.
incl	including
mfr	manufacture
mg	milligram(s)
min	mineral
ml	milliliter
nonstdzd	nonstandardized
Part	Refers to Part number under Title 21 CFR
pdt	product
pdtn	production
pest	pesticide
pkg	packaging
ppm	parts per million
prepns	preparations
res	residue
sp	diet special dietary
suppl	supplement
sw	sweetened
tabs	tablets
temp	temporary
veg	vegetable(s)
w/	with
w/o	without
wt	weight
X-ref	cross reference
<	less than
<	less than or equal to
>	greater than
>	greater than or equal to
+	plus

A

Acacia (gum arabic) - STAB, GRAS/FS, See Reg Part 135, Frozen Desserts; Part 169, Food Dressings and Flavorings; Part 169.179, Vanilla Pwd - 184.1330

Acephate - PEST, REG, 40CFR 180.108

Acesulfam potassium - NNS, REG, See Regulation - 172.800

Acetic acid - B&N/FEED, GRAS/FS, Part 133, Cheese; Part 582.1005, In animal feed practices; 184.1005, 172.814

Acetic anhydride - MISC, REG, In modifying food starch - 172.892

Acetone - SOLV, REG, 30 ppm - As residual solvent in spice oleoresins 173.210

Acetone peroxides - BL, REG/FS, GMP, Part 137, Cereal Flours -172.802

Acetyl-(p-nitrophenyl)-sulfanilamide - FEED, REG, See: Sulfanitran

N-Acetyl-L-Methionine (free, hydrated, or anhydrous, or sodium or potassium salts) - NUTR, REG, In foods, except infant foods and foods containing added nitrites/nitrates - 172.372

Acetylated monoglycerides - EMUL, REG, GMP, Used in food, food processing, food pkg or food stg equipment - 172.828

Acidified sodium chlorite solutions - REG, Used as an antimicrobial agent in a spray or dip solution for processing poultry and raw agricultural commodities (RAC's) at levels that result in sodium chlorite concentrations between 500 and 1,200 ppm, in combination with any GRAS acid at levels sufficient to achieve a solution pH of 2.3 to 2.9. Treatment of the RACS shall be followed by a potable water rinse, or by blanching, cooking or canning. Used in a prechiller or chiller tank in poultry processing at levels that result in sodium chlorite concentrations between 50 and 150 ppm, in combination with any GRAS acid at levels sufficient to achieve a solution pH of 2.8 to 3.2. Used as an antimicrobial agent in a spray or dip solution for processing of red meat, red meat parts, organs, and processed, comminuted or formed meat food products at levels that result in sodium chlorite concentrations between 500 and 1,200 ppm, in combination with any GRAS acid at levels sufficient to achieve a solution pH of 2.5 to 2.9. Used as an antimicrobial agent in water and ice to rinse, wash, thaw, transport, or store seafood at sodium chlorite concentrations between 40 and 50 ppm, in combination with any GRAS acid levels sufficient to achieve a solution pH 2.5 to 2.9, provided that any seafood that is intended to be consumed raw is subjected to a potable water rinse prior to consumption. - 173.325

Acifluorfen, Sodium - Sodium salt of acifluorfen; tolerances for residues-40 CFR 180.383

Aconitic acid (equisetic acid, citridic acid, achilleic acid) - SY/FL, GRAS/FS - 184.1007

Acrolein - MISC, REG, In modifying food starch - 172.892

Acrylamide - acrylic acid resin - MISC, REG, < 5 ppm by wt of juice - Used in clarifying beet sugar or cane sugar juice and liquor or corn starch hydrolyzate - 173.5; < 10 ppm by wt of liquor or hydrolyzate; FEED, REG, GMP, As a thickener & suspending agent in non-medicated aqueous suspensions intended for addition to animal feeds - 573.120

Acrylamide-Sodium Acrylate Resin - MISC, REG, 173.5, Boiler Water Additive - 173.310, 172.710 - Adjuvants for pesticide use dilutions

Acrylic Acid 12-acrylamido-2,2-propionic sulfonic acid copolymer - BC, REG, GMP, Boiler water - 173.310

Acrilonitrile copolymers - 180.22

Adjuvants for pesticides use dilutions - ADG/PEST, REG, Surfactants and adjuvants added to pesticide use dilutions to growing crops - 172.710

Adipic acid - B&N/FEED, GRAS, GMP, In animal feed practices - 582.1005 - FLV, GRAS - 184.1009

Adipic anhydride - MISC, REG, In modifying food starch - 172.892

Agar-agar - MISC, GRAS/FS, GRAS - 184.1115 - 0.8% - In baked goods and baking mixes; 2.0% - In confections & frostings; 1.2% - In soft candy; 0.25% - In all other candy; Part 135, Frozen Desserts; Part 150 Art Swt Jelly & Preserves

Aklomide (2-chloro-4-nitro-benzamide) - FEED, REG, 4.5 ppm - In liver & muscles of uncooked edible tissue - 556.30; 3 ppm - In skin w/fat of chickens - 556.30 - Use 558.35

Alachlor - REG, Residues in or on agricultural commodities – 40CFR 180.249

DL-Alanine - FL/ADJ, REG, 1% of pickling spice - As a flavor enhancer for sweeteners in pickling mix - 172.540

L-Alanine - NUTR, REG - 172.320

Albendazole - VET, REG, Use in cattle as suspension - 520.45a; Use in cattle as paste - 520.45b; 0.2 ppm - As residue in uncooked edible cattle tissue - 556.34 (aminosulfone metabolite); 0.6 ppm - As residue in uncooked edible cattle muscles - 556.34; 1.2 ppm - As residue in uncooked edible cattle liver - do; 1.8 ppm - As residue in uncooked edible cattle kidney - do; 2.4 ppm - As residue in uncooked edible cattle fat - do

Alcohol, Denatured Formula 23A - MISC, REG - 73.1 - Diluent in color additive mixtures for coloring shell eggs

Alcohol, SDA-3A - MISC, REG - 73.1 - Diluent in color additive for marking food

Alcohols/Phosphate Esters of Same Mixture - MISC, REG - 173.315, May be used at a level not to exceed 0.2 percent in lye-peeling solution to assist in the lye peeling of fruit and vegetables.

Aldicarb - PEST, REG - Tolerances for Residues 40 CFR 180.269

Alfafa, Extract - GRAS - 182.20

Alfalfa herb and seed - SP/ESO, GRAS - 182.10

Algae, brown (kelp), or red - NAT, GRAS, REG – 184.1120, 184.1121 and 172.365

Alginic Acid and Salts -
    Ammonium alginate - MISC, REG, Boiler Water Additive -173.310
    Calcium alginate - GRAS - 184.1187
    Potassium alginate - GRAS - 184.1610
    Sodium alginate - GRAS, REG - 184.1724, Boiler Water Additive - 173.310
    Alginic acid - GRAS, 184.1011

Algin - STAB, GRAS/FS, Part 133, Cheeses; Part 135, Frozen Desserts; Part 150 Jellies and Preserves;

Alkanomide produced by condensation of coconut oil fatty acids and diethanolamine - MISC, REG, < 0.2% by wt application rate - In delinting of cottonseeds - 173.322

n-Alkyl (C12-C18) benzyldimethyl-ammonium chloride -cpds, av mol wt 351-380 - SANI, REG, < 200ppm or 150-400 ppm - Of active quaternary compound in the sanitizing solution - 178.1010

n-Alkyl (C12-C14) dimethylethylbenzyl ammonium chloride - SANI, REG, 200 ppm - Of active quaternary compound in the sanitizing solution - 178.1010

-alkyl--hydroxy-poly(oxyethylene) - MISC, REG, < 3 ppm in the flume water - In flume water for washing sugar beets prior to slicing operations - 173.315; < 0.3% by wt application rate - In delinting of cottonseeds - 173.322

Alkylene Oxide Adducts of Alkyl Alcohols - MISC, REG, <0.2% in lye peeling - Assist in lye peeling of fruits and vegetables - 173.315

Allspice - SP/ESO, GRAS - 182.10 and 182.20

Allspice oil and oleoresin - ESO, GRAS - 182.20

Almond, bitter - ESO, GRAS, Free from prussic acid - 182.20

Aloe - FL/ADJ, REG, GMP, Used only in conjunction w/flavors - 172.510

Alpha-acetolactate decarboxylase - ENZ, REG.GMP enzyme preparation (derived from Bacillus subtillis modified by recombinant methods to contain gene coding for enzyme from B. brevis), Used as a processing aid in the production of alcoholic malt beverages and distilled liquors – 173.115.

Alpha-amylase -ENZ, REG, used to modify food starch - 172.892

Alpha-galactosidase from Morteirella vinaceae var raffinoseutilizer - ENZ, REG, No residue in finished product - Used in the production of sugar (sucrose) from sugar beets and increase sucrose yield in molasses - 173.145

Althea flowers or root (marshmallow root) - FL/ADJ, REG, GMP - Used only in conjunction w/flavors - 172.510

Aluminum ammonium sulfate - B&N, GRAS - 182.1127

Aluminum calcium silicate - AC, GRAS/FS - 182.2122 - < 2% by wt - Table salt; Part 169.179, Vanilla Powder

Aluminum nicotinate - DS, REG, As a source of niacin in foods for special dietary use - 172.310

Aluminum phosphide (phosphine) - FUM, REG, Tolerances for Residues - 40 CFR 180.225

Aluminum potassium sulfate - B&N, GRAS

Aluminum salts of fatty acids - MISC, REG, GMP - Binder, emul, and AC agent - 172.863

Aluminum sodium sulfate - B&N, GRAS

Aluminum stearate - AF, REG, X-ref - Defoaming agent comp - 173.340 (Used in processing beet sugar & yeast)

Aluminum sulfate - MISC, GRAS, Part 582 - Animal feed; REG, <2.0% in combo. w/<2.0% of 1-octenyl succinic anhydride - In modifying food starch - 172.892; FEED,GMP/GRAS - 582.1125

Ambergris - MISC, GRAS

Ambrette (seed) - SP/ESO, GRAS - 182.10 and 182.20

Amino Acids –172.320

p-Aminobenzoic acid - MISC, GRAS, <30 mg per day

Aminoglycoside 3'phosphotransferase II – 173.170

Aminopeptidase from Lactococcus lactis - MISC, GRAS - To make cheddar cheese and protein hydrolysates - 184, 1985

Amitraz - PEST, REG, see 40CFR 180.287

Ammonia - PEST,REG, Exemptions from the requirement of a tolerance - 40 CFR 180.1003

Ammoniated cottonseed meal - FEED, REG, <20% of total ration - In feed of ruminants as source of protein and non-protein nitrogen - 573.140; <10% of total ration for laying chickens - In feed of chickens as source of protein and non-protein nitrogen (573.140)

Ammoniated glycyrrhizin, licorice, or glycyrrhiza - MISC, FS, GMP, See Licorice

Ammoniated rice hulls - FEED, REG, <20 % of total ration - In feed of beef cattle as source of crude fiber and sole source of non-protein nitrogen - 573.160

Ammonium alginate - STAB, GRAS; BC, REG, GMP - In boiler water - 173.310

Ammonium bicarbonate - B&N, GRAS/FS, Part 163, Cacao Pdts; Part 582 - Animal feeds - 184.1135

Ammonium carbonate - B&N, GRAS/FS, Part 163, Cacao Pdts; Part 582 - Animal feeds - 184.1137

Ammonium caseinate - MISC, FS, Part 136, Bakery Products

Ammonium chloride - MISC, FS/GRAS, Part 136, Bakery Pdts - 184.1138

Ammonium hydroxide - B&N, GRAS/FS, Part 163, Cacao Pdts; Part 582 - Animal feeds - 184.1137, 184.1139

Ammonium persulfate - MISC, REG, <0.075% - Modifier for food starch - 172.892; <0.05% sulfur dioxide

Ammonium phosphate (mono- and dibasic) - B&N, GRAS/FS, Part 136, Bakery Pdts; Part 582 - Animal feeds - 184.1139, 184.1141, 184.1141a, 184.1141b

Ammonium saccharin - NNS, See Saccharin

Ammonium sulfate - MISC, GRAS, GMP - 184.1143

Amoxicillin - VET, REG, 0.01 ppm - In uncooked edible tissues of cattle - 556.38; In milk - 556.38; Use: As Powder & Bolus

Ampicillin - VET, REG, 0.01 ppm neg residues - In uncooked edible tissues of cattle & swine; In milk - 556.40;

Amprolium   (1-(4-amino-2-n-propyl-5-pyrimIdinyl-methyl)-2- picolinium chloride hydrochloride) alone or comb/w other drugs and antibiotics - FEED/VET, REG, 1 ppm - In uncooked liver and kidneys of chickens, turkeys, and pheasants as a residue - 556.50; 0.5 ppm - In uncooked muscle meat of chickens, turkeys, calves, pheasants as a residue - 556.50; 8 ppm - In egg yolks as a residue - 556.50; 4 ppm - In whole eggs as a residue - 556.50; 2 ppm - In uncooked fat of edible tissues of calves - 556.60; Use in drinking water - 520.100; REG - Coccidiostats for feed uses, See 558.55, 558.58, 558.60, 558.62, 558.76, 558.78, 558.128, 558.248, 558.274, 558.460, 558.530

Amylase from Aspercillgus Oryzae - ENZ, REG - 137.105, 137.155, 137.160, 137.165, 137.170, 137.175, 137.180, 137.185, 137.200, 137.205

Amyloglucosidase Enzyme Product - ENZ, REG, <0.1% by Wt. of gelatinized starch - 173.110 - Degrading gelatinized starch into constituent sugars, in the production of distilled spirits & vinegar

Amyris - FL/ADJ, REG, GMP, Used in conjunction w/flavors - 172.510

Angelica (root, stem, seed) - SP/ESO, GRAS - 182.10 and 182.20

Angola weed - FL/ADJ, REG, GMP, In alcoholic bev only - 172.510

Angostura (cusparia bark) - ESO/SP, GRAS - 182.10 and 182.20

Anhydrous ammonia - FEED, REG, > 16% but < 17% ammonia in feed premix - Source of crude fiber & non-protein nitrogen - 573.180

Animal protein hydrolysate, cond - FEED, REG, Source of animal protein - 573.200

Anise, Star Anise - SP/ESO, GRAS

Anoxomer - AOX, REG, 5000 ppm - 172.105

Antibiotics for growth promotion and feed efficiency - FEED, REG, See Bacitracin Methylene Disalicylate; See Bacitracin Zinc, Bambermycins, Chlortetracycline, Erythromycin thiocyanate, Lincomycin, Monensin, Oleandomycin, Oxytetracycline, Tylosin, Virginiamycin;

Anthracite Coal, Sulfonated - MISC, REG - 173.25 - Ion Exchange Resins, Meeting requirements of ASTM method D388-38, Class 1, Group 2

Apramycin - REG, 0.1 ppm - In uncooked muscle of swine - 556.52; 0.3 ppm - In swine liver - do; 0.4 ppm - In kidney & fat of swine - do; Use: Drinking water - 520.110

Apricot kernel (persic oil) - NAT, GRAS

Arabinogalactan - EMUL, REG, GMP, In essential oils, non-nutritive sweeteners, flavor bases, non-standardized dressings, and pudding mixes - 172.610; MISC, REG, GMP, Comp of microcapsules for flavoring oils - 172.230

Arginine (l form only) - NUTR/DS, REG - 172.320

Arnica flower extract - FL/ADJ, REG, GMP, In alcoholic beverages only - 172.510

Arsanilic acid - FEED, REG, (See Arsenic) In poultry feed - 558.55; 558.58; 558.62; 558.248; 558.680; PEST, REG,

Tolerances for Residues - 40 CFR 180.550

Arsenic - FEED, REG, 2 ppm - As residue in liver & kidney of swine - 556.60; 2 ppm - As residue in edible bypdts of chickens & turkeys - do; 0.5 ppm - As residue in muscle meat of chickens & turkeys, in eggs, & in muscle meat and by-products (other than kidney & liver) of swine - do

Artemisia - FL/ADJ, REG, GMP, Finished food thujone free - 172.510

Artichoke leaves - FL/ADJ, REG, GMP, In alcoholic beverages only - 172.510

Asafoetida - ESO, GRAS - 182.20

Ascorbic acid - PRES, GRAS, GMP - 182.3013; DS, GRAS, GMP - 182.5013; NUTR, GRAS, GMP - 182.8013; MISC, GRAS/FS, Part 137, Cereal Flours; 150.141, 150.161, Art Sw Jellies & Preserves; 155.200 - Canned Mushrooms & Artichokes

Ascorbyl palmitate - PRES, Status under review, contact CFSAN.

Asparagine (l-form) - NUTR/DS, REG - 172.320

Aspartame - NUTRS, REG, GMP, Sweetening agent, sugar substitute uses stated in - 172.804. Sugar substitute tablets, breakfast cereals, chewing gum, dry bases for beverages, instant coffee and tea beverages, gelatins, puddings, fillings, and dairy product analog toppings, ready-to-serve nonalcoholic flavored beverages, tea beverages, fruit juice based drinks where food standards permit such use, fruit flavored drinks and ades, imitation fruit flavored drinks and ades, frozen stick-type confections and novelties, breath mints, hard and soft candy, refrigerated ready-to-serve gelatins, puddings, and fillings, fruit wine beverages with EtOH <7%, yogurt-type products where aspratame is added after pasteurization and culturing, refrigerated flavored milk beverages, frozen desserts, frostings, toppings, fillings, glazes and icings for precooled baked goods, frozen, ready-to-thaw-and-eat cheesecakes, fruit and fruit toppings, frozen dairy and nondairy frostings, toppings, and fillings, fruit spreads, fruit toppings, and fruit syrups, malt beverages with <7% EtOH and containing fruit juice, baked goods and baking mixes 0.5 wt.-% of ready-to bake products or of finished formulation and prior to baking.

Aspartic acid (l-form) - NUTR/DS, REG - 172.320

Aspergillus Niger - MISC, REG, For Fermentation Production of Citric Acid - 173.280

Avermectin B1 and its delta-8.9-isomer 40CFR 449

Azaperone - VET, REG, Use: Swine (Injection) - 522.150

Azodicarbonamide - BL, REG/FS, 45 ppm in flour - Part 137, Cereal Flours & 172.806

B

Bacitracin, manganese bacitracin, zinc bacitracin, Bacitracin methylene disalicylate - FEED/VET, REG, 0.5 ppm (neg res) - As residue in meat and meat by-products of cattle, poultry, pheasants, quail, and swine and in milk & eggs - 556.70; For feed use see 558.55, 558.58, 558.62, 558.76, 558.78, 558.274, 558.430, 558.460, 558.530, 558.680;

Bacteria (harmless, lactic acid producing; propionic acid producing) - MISC, FS, Part 133, Cheeses; Part 166, Margarine

Bacterial Catalase - See Catalase, Bacterial

Bakers Yeast Glycan - EMUL/STAB, REG, <10,000 organisms/gm by APC - 169.150, Salad Dressings; 172.898 as emulsifier; <10 yeast & molds/gm - Thickener, stabilizer or texturizer; < 5% - In salad dressings, 172.898; GMP, In frozen dessert analogs, sour cream analogs, cheese spread analogs, and in cheese- flavored and sour cream-flavored snack dips - 172.898

Bakers Yeast Protein (Saccharomyces Cerevisiae) - NUTR, REG, <10,000 organisms/gm by APC - In foods as Nutrient supplement, 172.325; <10 yeast and mold/gm in final product

Balm (lemon balm) - SP/ESO, GRAS - 182.10 and 182.20

Balsam of Peru - ESO, GRAS - 182.20

Bambermycins - FEED, REG, For feed uses in chickens, turkeys, & swine - 558.95

Basil - ESO, GRAS - 182.20

Basil (bush and sweet) - SP, GRAS - 182.10

Bay, Bay leaves - SP/ESO, GRAS - 182.10 and 182.20

Bay, (Myrcia Oil) - ESO, GRAS - 182.20

Beeswax (bleached, white wax) - MISC, GRAS

Beeswax (yellow wax) - MISC, GRAS - 184.1973

Beeswax, white (cire d'abeille) - FL/ADJ, REG, GMP, In conjunction with flavors - 172.510

Benomyl - FUNG, REG, Pesticid, Tolerances for residues - 40 CFR 180.294

Bensulfuron methyl HERB, REG, Tolerances for residues 40 CFR 180.445

Bentazon - REG, 40 CFR 180.355

Bentonite - FEED, GRAS, GMP 21CFR 582.1155

Benzathine cloxacillin - VET, REG, 0.02 ppm - As residues in milk - 556.115; Use: Infusion - 526.363

Benzene - MISC, REG, 1.0 ppm - In modified hop extract for beer - 172.560

Benzoic Acid - PRES, GRAS, 0.1%

Benzoin Resin - FL/ADJ, REG, GMP, In conjunction with flavors - 172.510, 73.1

Benzophenone

Benzoyl Peroxide - BL, FS, Part 137, Cereal Flours; Part 133 for milk to be used in certain cheeses

Bergamot (bergamot orange) - ESO, GRAS - 182.20

Beta-carotene - NUTR, GRAS, GMP, Use: Direct human food ingredient - 184.1245

BHA (butylated hydroxyanisole) - AOX/FS, GRAS, 0.02% - Of fat or oil content, incl essential (volatile) oil, of food, incl oleomargarine - Part 166, Margarine; AOX, REG, 10 ppm, alone or w/BHT - In potato granules - 172.110; 32 ppm - In mixed diced, glaceed fruits - 172.110; 50 ppm, alone or w/BHT - In dry breakfast cereals, sweet potato flakes, dehydr potato flakes or shreds - 172.110; 90 ppm in mix or <2 ppm in prep food - In dry mixes for beverages and desserts - 172.110; 200 ppm alone or w/BHT - In emulsion stabilizers for shortenings; 0.1% - In active dry yeast - 172.110; AOX, REG,0.1% alone or w/BHT and/or propyl gallate - In chewing gum base - 172.615; AOX, REG, 0.1% of defoamer - For proc. beet sugar & yeast - 173.340; AOX, REG, 0.5% of essential volatile oil - For use in flavoring substances - 172.515; AOX, REG, In mastitis form, for dairy cattle - 526.820

BHT (butylated hydroxytoluene) - AOX, GRAS, 0.02% - Of fat or oil content, incl essential oil, of food, incl oleomargarine Part 166 - Margarine; FS, 33 ppm in rice - In enriched parboiled rice - Part 137.350; FS, <0.02% in oleomargarine - In any animal fat ingredient permitted in oleomargarine not to exceed 0.02% by wt of such animal fat content, Part 166 - Margarine; AOX, REG, 10 ppm alone or w/BHA - In potato granules - 172.115; 50 ppm alone or w/BHA - In dry breakfast cereals, sweet potato flakes, dehydr potato flakes or shreds - 172.115; 200 ppm alone or w/BHA - In emul stab for shortenings - 172.115; REG, 0.1% alone or w/BHA and/or propyl gallate - In chewing gum base - 172.615; REG, 0.1% of defoamer - For proc. beet sugar & yeast - 173.340; REG, In mastitis form, for dairy cattle - 526.820

Bicarbonate of soda - B&N, GRAS/FS - 137.270, Self-rising Cornmeal

Bifenthrin - PEST, REG, Tolerances for Residues 40 CFR 180.442

Bile salts & Ox Bile Extract - SDA, GRAS - 184.4560

Bioflavonoids, citrus - DS, ILL, Any claim for special dietary use renders the food misbranded (VitaSafe case)

Biotin - NUTR/DS, GRAS, GMP - 182.5159; 182.8159

1,1-Bis(p-chlorophenyl)-2,2,2,-trichloroethanol - PEST, REG, Tolerances for Residues - 40 CFR 180.163

Bitter almond - ESO, GRAS, Free of prussic acid - 182.20

Biuret, feed grade - NUTR, REG, GMP, In feed for ruminants except those producing milk for human consumption - 573.220

Blackberry bark extract - FL/ADJ, REG, In conjunction w/flavors only - 172.510

Boiler water additives - Ammonium alginate, cobalt sulfate, lignosulfonic acid, monobutyl ether of polyoxyethylene glycol or potassium tripolyphosphate, sodium carboxymethylcellulose, sodium glucoheptonate, sodium humate, sodium metasilicate, sodium metabisulfite, polyoxypropylene glycol, polyoxyethylene glycol, potassium carbonate, sodium acetate, sodium alginate, sodium aluminate, sodium carbonate, sodium hexametaphosphate, sodium hydroxide, sodium lignosulfonate, sodium nitrate, sodium phosphate (mono-, di-, tri-), sodium polyacrylate, sodium polymethacrylate, sodium silicate, sodium sulfate, sodium sulfite (neutral or alkaline), sodium tripolyphosphate, tannin (incl quebracho extract), tetrasodium EDTA, tetrasodium pyrophosphate, 1-hydroxyethylidene-1, 1-diphosphonic acid and its sodium & potassium salt - BC, REG, GMP, In steam contacting food - 173.310
Hydrazine - BC, REG, In steam contacting food
Acrylamide-sodium acrylate resin - BC, REG, 0.05% of acrylamide monomer - In steam contacting food
Cyclohexylamine or Morpholine - BC, REG, <10 ppm - In steam contacting food except milk and milk products
Octadecylamine - BC, REG, <3 ppm - In steam contacting food except milk and milk productsDiethylaminoethenol - BC, REG, 15 ppm - In steam contacting food except milk and milk products
Trisodium nitrilotriacetate - BC, REG, <5 ppm in feed water - In steam contacting food except milk and milk products
Polymaleic acid and/or its sodium salt - BC, REG, Total < 1 ppm in feed water - In steam contacting food
Sorbitol anhydride esters (a mixture of sorbitan monostearate, polyoxyethylene (20) sorbitan mono stearate (polysorbate 60) and polyoxyethylene (20) sorbitan monolaurate (polysorbate 20) - BC, REG, Each component < 15 ppm in steam contacting food

Bois de rose - ESO, GRAS - 182.20

Boldus leaves - FL/ADJ, REG, In alcoholic beverages only - 172.510

Borax - MISC, ILL, No petition filed, Illegal for use in foods incl. wax ctg for fruits and vegetables. MID permits use in export meats.

Boron - MISC, REG, <310 ppm - In modified hop extract from sodium borohydride - 172.560

Boronia flowers - FL/ADJ, REG, GMP, In conjunction w/flavors only - 172.510

Bromelin or Bromelain (spelling optional) - MISC, MIA, To soften tissue of meats; ENZ, REG, As an enzyme preparation (optional ingredient) in bakery products - 136

Bromides, inorganic - FUM, REG, X-ref - Inorganic bromides

Brominated vegetable oil - STAB, INTERM/REG, <15 ppm - In fruit flavored beverages where not precluded by a standard - 180.30

Bryonia root - FLA/ADJ, REG, GMP, In alcoholic beverages only - 172.510

Bucha leaves oil - FL/ADJ, REG, GMP, In conjunction w/flavors only - 172.510

Buckbeen leaves - FL/ADJ, REG, GMP, In alcoholic beverages only - 172.510

Buquinolate - FEED, REG, 0.4 ppm - In liver, kidney & skin of chickens - 556.90; 0.1 ppm - Residue in muscle of chickens - do; 0.5 ppm - Residues in uncooked yolk of eggs - do; 0.2 ppm - Residues in uncooked whole eggs - do; Feed use in chickens, see 558.62, 558.530 & 558.105

Butadiene styrene rubber - MISC, REG, In chewing gum base - 172.615

Butane, n-butane, iso-butane - MISC, GRAS - 184.1165

Butoxy monoether of mixed (ethylene-propylene) polyalkylene glycol - SANI, REG, GMP, Adequate drainage - 178.1010

n-Butoxypolyoxyethylene polyoxypropylene glycol - AF, REG, GMP, X-ref - Defoaming agent component (used in processing beet sugar) - 173.340

Butter Starter distillate - FLAV, FL/ADJ, GRAS, GMP - 184.1848

Butyl acetate

Butyl Alcohol - MISC, REG - 73.1, 172.560 - Modified hop extract

1,3-Butylene glycol - SOLV, REG, GMP, In nat & syn flavoring substances except where standards preclude use - 173.220, 573.225. Used in the manufacture of sausage casings as a formulation aid and processing aid - 172.712.

Tert-Butylhydroquinone (TBHQ) - AOX, REG - 172.185, 0.02% of fat or oil content, incl essential (volatile) oil, of food

2(p-tert-Butylphenoxy) cyclohexyl 2-propynyl sulfite - PEST, REG, See Propargite

Butyl rubber - MISC, REG, Component of chewing gum base - 172.615

Butyl stearate - AF, REG, X-ref - Defoaming agent component (used in proc. beet sugar & yeast) - 173.340

C

Cacao - ESO, GRAS - 182.20

Cadmium sulfide - COLOR, ILL, Prior sanction for use as colorant in polystyrenes withdrawn - FD 1-8-69

Caffeine - MISC, GRAS, 0.02% - Cola-type beverages

Cajeput - FL/ADJ, REG, GMP, In conjunction with flavors - 172.510

Calamus, root, oil or extract - FLAV, ILL, Illegal in foods

Calcium acetate - SEQ, GRAS - 184.1185

Calcium alginate - STAB, GRAS - 184.1187

Calcium ascorbate - PRES, GRAS - 182.3189

Calcium bromate - BL, FS, <0.0075 part for each 100 parts by wt of flour used - Part 136 - Bakery Products

Calcium bromide - SANI, REG, <200 ppm avail halogen - Adequate drainage - 178.1010

Calcium carbonate - MISC, GRAS/FS, Part 137, admixed w/benzoyl peroxide for bleaching flour; Part 136, Bakery Pdts; Part 135, Frozen Desserts; Part 582, Animal feeds; 184.1191; EMUL, REG, Comb w/any other optional emulsifying ingredients listed in 169.115 including sodium hexametaphosphate; DS/NUTR, GRAS, GMP - 182.5191, 182.8191

Calcium caseinate - MISC, FS, Part 135, Frozen Desserts except water ices; Part 133, Creamed Cottage Cheese

Calcium chloride - MISC, GRAS/FS, 184.1193, Parts 131, 133, 150, 155 & 156 in Evaporated Milk; Cheese & Cheese Products; Part 133; VET, REG, For use in mastitis formulations for treating dairy animals - 526.820

Calcium citrate - MISC, GRAS/FS, Part 133, Process Cheese, Cheese Food & Spread, Part 150, Art Sw Fruit Jelly Preserves & Jam, Parts 155 & 156, certain canned vegetables; Part 31; Part 582 - Animal feeds; DS/NUTR, GRAS,GMP - 182.5195, 182.8195

Calcium cyclamate - NNS, ILL, Removed from GRAS List 10-21-69. Legal only in products complying with drug provisions of the law.

Calcium diacetate - SEQ, GRAS, See calcium acetate

Calcium dioxide (Ca peroxide) - MISC, FS, Part 136

Calcium disodium ethylenediamine-tetraacetate [(calcium ethylenedinitrilo) tetraacetate]; calcium disodium EDTA - AF, REG, 25 ppm - Fermented malt beverages - 172.120; Antigushing agent; MISC, 60 ppm - Spice extractives in soluble carriers; Color & flavor; 100 ppm - Pecan pie filling, promote color retention; 340 ppm - Clams (cooked-canned), promote color retention; 800 ppm - Dry Pinto beans, promote color retention; 310 ppm - Promote color retention in dried lima beans (cooked, canned); 275 ppm - Crabmeat (cooked- canned), retard struvite formation, promote color retention; 250 ppm - Shrimp (cooked-canned), retard struvite formation, promote color retention; 33 ppm - Promote flavor in carbonated soft drinks; 110 ppm - Promote color retention in canned white potatoes; 200 ppm - Mushrooms (cooked, canned); 220 ppm - In pickled cucumbers or pickled cabbage; To promote color, flavor & texture retention; 100 ppm - Promote color retention in artificially colored lemon-flavored and orange-flavored spreads; 100 ppm - Potato salad, preservative; 75 ppm alone or comb with disodium EDTA - French dressing, mayonnaise, and salad dressing; non-standardized dressings and sauces, preservative; 100 ppm alone or comb /w disodium EDTA - Sandwich spread, preservative; 200 ppm by wt of egg yolk portion - Egg product that is hard-cooked & consists, in a cylindrical shape, of egg white w/an inner core of egg yolk, preservative; 25 ppm - In distilled alcoholic beverages - 172.120, promote stability of color, flavor and or product clarity; PRES, REG/MIA, 75 ppm - Oleomargarine - Part 166; 365 ppm - Promote color retention in legumes (all cooked canned, other than dried lima beans, pink beans and red beans) – 172.120

Calcium gluconate - MISC, GRAS/FS, GMP - 184.1199; Part 150, Art Sw Jelly & Preserves; Part 582, Animal feeds

Calcium glycerophosphate - NUTR/DS, GRAS, GMP - 182.8201, 182.5201

Calcium hexametaphosphate - SEQ, GRAS status under review

Calcium hydroxide - MISC/B&N, GRAS/FS, Part 155, Canned Peas; Part 135, Frozen Desserts; Part 582, Animal feeds - 184.1205

Calcium hypochlorite - SANI, REG, <200 ppm avail Cl - Adequate drainage - 178.1010; MISC, REG, < 0.036% Cl of dry starch - In modifying food starch for use in batter for commercially processed foods - 172.892

Calcium iodate - MISC, FS, <0.0075 parts for each 100 parts by wt. of flour used - Part 136, Bakery Pdts; NUTR.

GRAS - 184.1206

Calcium iodobehenate - DS, GRAS, Animal Feed - 582.80

Calcium lactate - MISC, GRAS/FS, Parts 136, Bakery Pdts; Part 150, Art Sw Jelly & Preserves; Part 155, Canned Veg; Part 582, Animal Feeds - 184.1207; MISC, GRAS/FS, < amount which yields 0.051% calcium by wt in finished food - Improve crispness in canned bean sprouts, See Part 155.200

Calcium lactobionate - MISC, REG, GMP, Firming agent in dry pudding mixes - 172.720

Calcium lignin sulfonate (and/or sodium salt) - FEED, REG, <4 % of finished pellets - As sole pelleting aid in animal feeds - 573.600; < 11% - Surfactant in molasses used in feeds as a source of metabolizable energy - 573.600

Calcium lignosulfonate - SP/ADJ, REG, GMP, Dispersing agent and stabilizer in pesticides for pre- or post-harvest use on bananas - 172.715

Calcium orthophosphate - B&N, FS, GMP GRAS - See calcium phosphate (tribasic)

Calcium oxide - MISC, GRAS/FS, Part 135 Frozen Desserts; Part 582, Animal feeds; DS/NUTR, GRAS, GMP - 182.5210, 182.8210, 184.1210

Calcium pantothenate - NUTR/DS, GRAS, GMP, 182.5212, 184.1212

Calcium pantothenate (calcium chloride double salt of) d- or dl-form - DS, REG, GMP, Label of additive container or any intermediate premix prepared there-from shall contain name of the additive and the concentration of additive expressed as pantothenic acid - 172.330

Calcium periodate - FEED, REG, Nutr source of iodine in salt for livestock - 573.240

Calcium peroxide (Same as calcium dioxide) - MISC, FS, <0.0075 parts for each 100 parts wt. of flour used - Parts 136, Bakery Pdts

Calcium phosphate (mono-) - MISC, GRAS/FS, Part 150, Art Sw Jelly & Preserves; Part 155.200, Cnd Potatoes, Cnd Green or Red Sw Peppers, Canned Carrots; Part 155.190(a), Canned Tomatoes; Part 136, Bread; Part 582, Animal feeds

Calcium phosphate (mono-, di-) - NUTR/MISC, GRAS/FS, Part 137, Cereal Flours and other standardized foods

Calcium phosphate (mono-, di, or tribasic) - MISC, GRAS/FS, Part 150, Art Sw Jelly and Preserves; Part 136, Bread; DS/NUTR, GRAS, GMP - 182.5217, 182.8217

Calcium propionate - PRES, GRAS/FS, Part 136 Bakery Pdts; Part 133, Cheeses; Part 150, Art Sw Fruit Jelly & Preserves -184.1221, 184.1784

Calcium pyrophosphate - NUTR/DS, GRAS, GMP - 182.5223, 182.8223

Calcium saccharin - NNS, INTERIM, See Saccharin

Calcium salt of partially dimerized rosin - CTG, REG, GMP, X-ref - Coating on fresh citrus fruit - 172.210

Calcium salts - MISC, FS, 0.026% - Part 155.190(k), Cnd Tomatoes; Part 155.200, Canned Potatoes, Green or Red Sweet Peppers, Lima Beans, Carrots; Part 136, Enriched Bread, Rolls & Buns

Calcium salts of fatty acids - MISC, REG, GMP - Binder, emul, and AC agent - 172.863

Calcium silicate (including synthetic) - AC, FS, <2% - Part 169.179 Vanilla Powder; AC, REG, GMP, Max 2% in foods except 5% in baking powder - 172.410; <2% - In animal feeds - 573.260

Calcium sorbate - PRES, GRAS - 182.3225

Calcium stearate - AC, REG/FS, <2% by wt. - Part 169.179, Vanilla Powder; AF, REG, GMP, In beet sugar and yeast - 173.340; MISC, GRAS, GMP - 184.1229

Calcium stearate, feed grade - FEED, REG, GMP, As anticaking agent in feeds - 573.280

Calcium stearoyl-2-lactylate - MISC, REG/FS, <0.5 part/100 parts flour - Part 136, Bakery Pdts - 172.844; MISC, REG, <0.05% - As a whipping agent in liquid & frozen egg whites; MISC, REG, <0.5% - As a whipping agent in dried egg whites; MISC, REG, <0.3% by wt of finished pdt - As whipping agent in whipped vegetable oil topping; REG, <0.5% - As conditioning agent in dehyd potatoes - do

Calcium sulfate - MISC, GRAS/FS; Part 133, Cheese and Related Cheese Pdts; Part 137, Cereal Flours; Part 136, Bakery Pdts; Part 135, Frozen Desserts; Part 150, Art Sw. Jelly & Preserves; Part 155, Cnd Vegetables; Part 156, Cnd Tomatoes - 184.1230

Calendula - SP, GRAS - 182.10

Calumba root - FL/ADJ, REG, GMP - In alcoholic beverages only - 172.510

Camomile, camomile flowers English, Roman, German, Hungarian - SP/ESO, GRAS - 182.10 and 182.20

Camphor tree - FL/ADJ, REG, GMP, Comp of flavors - safrole free - 172.510

Cananga - ESO, GRAS - 182.20

Candida lipolytica - ENZ, REG, Fermentation organism for production of citric acid - 173.165

Candida guilliermondii - ENZ, REG, Complete absence - Fermentation production of citric acid - 173.160

Candelilla Wax - CTG, GRAS, GMP - 184.1976

Canola oil - MISC, GRAS, X-Ref - Rapeseed oil, Raw Erusic Acid

Capers - SP, GRAS - 182.10

Caproic acid - MISC, REG, <1% aliphatic acids - In peeling soln for fruits & veg - 173.315

Caprylic acid - PRES, GRAS, In cheese wraps; MISC, REG, <1% aliphatic acids - In peeling soln for fruits & vegs - 173.315

Capsicum - SP/ESO, GRAS - 182.10 and 182.20

Captan - PEST, REG, Tolerances for Residues - 40 CFR 180.103

Caramel - MISC, GRAS - 182.1235

Caraway - SP/ESO, GRAS - 182.10 and 182.20

Caraway, black (black cumin) - SP, GRAS - 182.10

Carbadox - FEED, REG, ZERO - Residues in uncooked edible tissue of swine using procedures in 556.100; FEED, REG, Feed Use: 558.115

Carbarsone (not USP) - FEED, REG, 0.025% to 0.0375% in the feed - In feed for turkeys - 558.680, 558.120; FEED, REG, 2 ppm - As residue in edible byproducts of chicken & turkeys - 556.60; 0.5 ppm - As residue in muscle meat of chickens & turkeys & eggs - do

Carbaryl - INSECT, REG, Tolerances for Residues 40 CFR 180.169

Carbofuran - PEST, REG, Tolerances for Residues I40 CFR 180.254

Carbohydrase enzyme derived from Aspergillus niger - ENZ, REG. GMP, For removal of visceral mass in clam processing or shell from shrimp - 173.120

Carbohydrase enzyme derived from Rhizopus Oryzae - ENZ, REG. Used in the production of dextrose - 173.130

Carbomycin - FEED, REG, ZERO - Residues in edible tissues of chickens - 556.110; Use in comb/w oxytetracycline HCl - 520.1660a (Drinking Water)

Carbon dioxide - MISC, GRAS - 184.1240

Carbon monoxide - MISC, REG, 4.5% by volume - In gas combustion product - 173.350

Carbon disulfide - FUM, REG, Tolerances for Residues - 40 CFR 180.467

Carboxymethylcellulose - STAB, FS, Part 133, Cheeses; Part 135, Frozen Desserts; Part 169, Dressings for Foods & Flavorings; GRAS

Cardamom (cardamon) - SP, GRAS - 182.10

Cardamom Oleoresin - ESO, GRAS, 182.20

Cardamom seed (cardamon) - ESO, GRAS - 182.20

Carnauba wax - MISC, GRAS - 184.1978

Carob bean - ESO, GRAS - 182.20

Carob bean extract - ESO, GRAS -182.20

Carob bean gum (locust bean gum) - STAB/EMUL, FA/FS, Part 133, Cheeses; Part 135, Frozen Desserts; Part 169 Dressings for Foods; Part 150, Art Sw Jelly & Preserves; GRAS -184.1343

Carotene - NUTR/DS, GRAS, GMP, 182.5245 - 182.8245

Carrageenan and its ammonium, calcium, potassium, or sodium salts - STAB, REG, GMP, In foods, except for those standardized food that do not provide for such use - 172.620, 172.626; STAB, REG/FS, <0.8% by wt of finished cheese - Part 133, various sections, Cheese Prdts

Carrageenan or carrageenan salts with Polysorbate 80 - MISC, REG, 500 ppm polysorbate 80 in final food containing the additives - For producing foods in gel form - 172.623 (See 172.620, 172.626, & 172.840 for specifications)

Carrot - ESO, GRAS - 182.20

Cascara sagrada - FL/ADJ, REG, GMP, In conjunction with flavors - 172.510

Cascarilla bark - ESO, GRAS - 182.20

Cassia, cassia bark (Chinese, Padang or Batavia, Saigon) - SP/ESO, GRAS - 182.10 and 182.20

Cassie flowers - FL/ADJ, REG, GMP, In conjunction w/flavors - 172.510

Castoreum - MISC, GRAS - 182.50

Castor Oil - MISC, REG, < 500 ppm in hard candy - A release and anti-sticking agent - 172.876; GMP, Comp. protect ctg vit & min tabs. Meet Specs in USP XIX; FL/ADJ, REG, GMP, In conjunction w/flavors - 172.510

Catalase, Bacterial (derived from Micrococcus lysodeikticus) - ENZ, REG/FS, < 20 ppm of the wt of the milk treated - To destroy hydrogen peroxide in mfr of cheese - 173.135; 133.113;

Catechu, black - FL/ADJ, REG, GMP, In conjunction with flavors - 172.510

Cayenne pepper - SP, GRAS - 182.10

Cedar, White (arborvitae) leaves and twigs - FL/ADJ, REG, GMP, Finished food thujone free, Used in conjunction with flavors - 172.510

Ceftiofur - VET, REG, 3.0 ppm - Use as sterile powder - 522.313; Residue in muscle - 556.113; 9.0 ppm - Residue in kidney - do; 6.0 ppm - Residue in liver - do; 12.0 ppm - Residue in fat - do

Celery seed - SP/ESO, GRAS - 182.10 and 182.20

Cellulase enzyme derived from Aspergillus niger - ENZ, REG, GMP, For removal of visceral mass in clam processing and shell from shrimp - 173.120

Cellulose gum - STAB, GRAS/FS, X-ref - Sodium Carboxymethylcellulose

Cellulose triacetate – MISC, GMP, Fixing agent for the immobilization of lactase for use in reducing the lactose content of milk – 173.357

Centaury (centrurium) herb - FL/ADJ, REG, GMP, In alcoholic beverages only - 172.510

Cephapirin, sodium - VET, REG, 0.02 ppm - Residues in milk, 556.115; Use - 529.365; 0.1 ppm - Residues in uncooked edible tissues of cattle - 556.115; Use: Infusion - 529.365

Cephapirin benzathine - VET, REG, 0.02 ppm - As residue in milk - 556.115; Use: Infusion - 526.363

Cetyl Alcohol, synthetic - MISC, REG, GMP, See Fatty alcohols, synthetic - 172.864

Chamomile Flower - SP, REG - 182.10

Chamomile Flower, English, Oil - ESO, REG - 182.20

Chemicals for controlling micro-organisms in cane sugar and beet sugar mills - REG 173.320

Chemicals used in delinting cottonseed - 173.322

Chemicals used in washing fruits & vegs. or to assist in peeling fruits and vegs. Polyacrylamide, Potassium bromide, Sodium dodecylbenzenesulfonate, Sodium hypochlorite, sodium 2-ethyl-l- hexylsulfate, sodium n-alkylbenzene sulfonate, sodium mono- and dimethyl-naphthalene sulfonates- mol wt 245-260, Alkylene oxide adducts of alkyl alcohols and phosphate esters of alkylene oxides. Adducts of alkyl alcohols mixtures - MISC, REG, Use of chemicals followed by rinsing to remove residues. X-ref - Individual chemicals, 173.315 limits amounts of some in wash water

Cherry-laurel leaves - FL/ADJ, REG, GMP, In conjunction w/flavors only; <25 ppm prussic acid - 172.510

Cherry-laurel water - FL/ADJ - 172.510

Cherry, pits, extract - FL/ADJ, REG, GMP, In conjunction w/flavors only; <25 ppm prussic acid - 172.510

Cherry, wild, bark - ESO, GRAS - 182.20

Chervil - ESO/SP/FLAV, GRAS - 182.10

Chervil extract -ESO, GRAS - 182.20

Chestnut leaves/extract - FL/ADJ, REG, In conjunction w/flavors - 172.510

Chewing gum base, MISC, REG, GMP, Chicle, chiquibul, crown gum, gutta hang kang, jelutong, massaranduba balata, massaranduba chocolate, nispero, lechi caspi, pendare, perillo, rosidinha, Venezuelan chicle, Leche de vaca, Niger gutta, tunu, chilte, natural rubber, glycerol ester of tall oil resin, etc. - 172.615

Chicle - MISC, REG, Comp of chewing gum base - 172.615

Chicory - ESO, GRAS - 182.20

Chilte - MISC, REG, Chewing gum base - 172.615

Chilquibul - MISC, REG, Comp of chewing gum base - 172.615

Chirata (Chiretta, East Indian Bolonong) & herb extract - FL/ADJ, REG, GMP, In alcoholic beverages only - 172.510

Chives - SP, GRAS - 182.10

Chloramphenicol - VET, REG, ZERO - Drug in any form may not be used in food (meat, milk, and egg) producing animals

Chlorhexidine dihydrochloride - VET, REG, ZERO - Residue in edible tissues of calves - 556.120

Chlorimuron ethyl - PEST, REG, Tolerance for Residues 40 CFR 180.429

Chlorine & chlorine dioxide - BL, FS, GMP, Part 137, Cereal Flours

Chlorine dioxide - MISC, REG, Used as an antimicrobial agent in poultry process water at a concentration not to exceed 3 ppm residual chlorine dioxide. Used as an antimicrobial agent in water used to wash fruits and vegetables thatt are not raw agricultural commodities at a level not to exceed 3 ppm residual chlorine dioxide - 173.300

Chlorine dioxide, stabilized - SANI, REG, For use as rinse for food processing equipment - 178.1010

Chlorobutanol - VET, REG, ZERO - In milk from dairy animals from use of mastitis formulations - 526.820; As residues - 556.140

Chlorofluorocarbon-113 - MISC, REG, GMP, To cool or freeze chickens - 173.342

Chloromethylated aminated styrene di-vinylbenzene resin - MISC, REG, 500 ppm in sugar liquor - To clarify sugar liquor - 173.70

2-Chloro-4-nitrobenzamide - FEED, REG, See Aklomide Chloropentafluoroethane alone or comb/w carbon dioxide nitrous oxide, propane, or octafluorocyclobutane - MISC, REG, Used as a propellant and aerating agent in food except where food standards preclude use - 173.345

2-(m-Chlorophenoxy) propionic acid - PEST, REG, Tolerances for Residues - 40 CFR 180.325

Chlorpyrifos-methyl - INSECT, REG, 90 ppm - As residue in/or on barley milling fraction - Tolerances for Residues 40 CFR 180.419

Clorsulon - VET, REG, Use: As a drench for cattle - 520.462; 1.0 ppm - As residue in uncooked edible muscle tissue of cattle - 556.163; 2.0 ppm - As residue in uncooked liver - do; 3.0 ppm - As residue in kidney - do; 4.0 ppm - As residue in uncooked cattle fat - do; As injection for cattle; combination with Ivermectin - 522.1193

Chlortetracycline - FEED/VET, REG, 4 ppm - Residues in uncooked kidneys of chickens & turkeys; 1 ppm - In uncooked muscle, liver, fat & skin of chickens and turkeys as residue - 556.150; ZERO - Residues in eggs - 556.150; 4 ppm - Residues in uncooked kidney of swine - 556.150; 2 ppm -Residues in uncooked liver of swine - 556.150; 1 ppm - Residues in uncooked muscle of swine - 556.150; 0.2 ppm - Residues in uncooked fat of calves - 556.150; 4 ppm - Residues in uncooked liver & kidneys of calves - 556.150; 1 ppm - Residues in uncooked muscle & fat of calves - 556.150; 0.1 ppm - In uncooked kidney, liver, and muscle of beef cattle & non-lactating dairy cows as residue; ZERO - Residue in uncooked fat - 556.150; ZERO - Residue in milk - 556.150; 1 ppm - Residues in uncooked kidney of sheep - 556.150; 0.5 ppm - Residues in uncooked liver of sheep - 556.150; 0.1 ppm - Residues in

uncooked muscle of sheep - 556.150; For feed use: 558.55, 558.58, 558.105, 558.128, 558.175, 558.274, 558.368, 558.430, 558.530, 558.680

Chlortetracycline - FEED, REG, Sulfa: 0.1 ppm (neg residue) - Residue in uncooked edible tissues of swine, 556.690;
+Procaine Penicillin - Penicillin: 0 - Residue in uncooked edible tissues of swine, 556.510;
+Sulfathiazole - Chlortetracycline: 4 ppm - Residue in uncooked edible tissue of swine kidney - 556.150; 2 ppm - Residue in uncooked edible tissue of swine liver - 556.150; 1 ppm - Residue in uncooked edible tissue of swine muscle - do; 0.2 ppm - Residue in uncooked edible tissue of swine fat - do; Uses & other information - 558.155

Chlortetracycline - FEED, REG, Sulfa: 0.1 ppm (neg residue) - Residues in uncooked edible tissues of cattle & swine - 556.670
+Procaine Penicillin - Penicillin: 0 - Residue in uncooked edible tissues of swine - 556.510
+Sulfamethazine - Chlortetracycline: - 4 ppm - Residue in uncooked kidney of swine, 556.150; 2 ppm - Residue in uncooked liver of swine, 556.150; 1 ppm - Residue in uncooked muscle of swine, 556.150; 0.2 ppm - Residue in uncooked fat of swine - 556.150; Uses & other information, 558.145

Chlorpyrifos - PEST, REG, - Tolerances for Residues 40 CFR 180.342

Choline bitartrate - NUTR/DS, GRAS, GMP - 182.5250, 182.8250

Choline chloride - NUTR/DS, GRAS, GMP - 182.5252. 182.8252

Choline xanthate - FEED, REG, GMP, For poultry, swine & ruminants - 573.300

Chymosin enzyme preparation derived from E. Coli K-12 - ENZ, GRAS, GMP, As a stabilizer & thickener - 184.1685; derived from Aspergillus niger - ditto.

Cinchona bark, red or yellow - FL/ADJ, REG, < 83 ppm total - Cinchona alkaloids in finished beverage - 172.510

Cinnamon & bark & leaf, Ceylon, Chinese, and Saigon - O/SP, GRAS, 182.10 and 182.20

Cinnamyl anthranilate - SYL/FL, BAN, ZERO - 189.113

Cinnamyl formate

Cire d'abielle - FL/ADJ, REG, GMP, X-ref Beeswax, white - 172.510

Citric acid - SEQ/B&N, GRAS/FS- 182.1033, 182.6033 - GMP, Part 169, Dressings; Part 133, Part 146 Canned Fruite Juices; Cheese; Part 166, Oleomargarine; FEED,

GRAS, GMP, Part 582.1033 - Animal feeds; REG - 172.755, 173.165

Citronella - ESO, GRAS - 182.20

Citrus bioflavonoids - DS, ILL, Any claim for special dietary use renders the food misbranded (Vitasafe Case)

Citrus peels - ESO, GRAS - 182.20

Civet (zibeth, zibet, zibetum) - ESO, GRAS - 182.20

Clary (clary sage) - SP/ESO, GRAS - 182.10 and 182.20

Clopidol (3,5-Dichloro-2,6-dimethyl-4-pyridinol) - FEED, REG, 0.02 ppm - Residues in milk - 556.160; 0.2 ppm - Residues in cereal grains, vegs, fruits, meat of cattle, sheep and goats, and in edible tissues of swine - 556.160; 1.5 ppm - Residues in liver of cattle, sheep & goats - 556.160; 5 ppm - Residues in muscle of chicken & turkeys - 556.160; 5 ppm - Residues in liver & kidneys of chickens & turkeys - 556.160; Uses in chicken & turkey feeds - 558.175

Clopyralid - HERB, REG, Tolerances for residues - 40 CFR 180.431

Cloxacillin - VET, REG, 0.01 ppm - Residues in milk; uncooked edible tissue of cattle - 556.165

Clove, bud, leaf, and stem - ESO, GRAS - 184.1257

Clover - SP/ESO, GRAS - 182.10 and 182.20

Cloves - SP, GRAS - 184.1257

Coatings on fresh citrus fruits - CTG, REG, GMP - 172.210

Cobalt (acetate, carbonate, chloride, oxide, sulfate) - NUTR, GRAS, As nutritional dietary supplement in animal feed - 582.80

Cobaltous salts (acetate) - MISC, ILL, Illegal for use, 172.260 revoked chloride, sulfate) 8/12/66

Coca (decocainized) - ESO, GRAS - 182.20

Cocoa butter substitute from palm oil - GRAS, GMP - In the following food categories: confections and frostings; coatings of soft candy; sweet sauces and toppings - 184.1259

Cocoa butter substitute from coconut oil, palm kernel oil or both - ESO, REG, Coating material for vitamins, citric acid, succinin acid and spices. In lieu of cocoa butter in sweets - 172.861

Cocoa with dioctyl sodium sulfosuccinate for manufacturing -FLV,REG, 75 ppm of finished beverage -0 172.520

Coffee - ESO, GRAS - 182.20

Cognac oil, white and green - MISC, GRAS - 182.50
Cola nut - ESO, GRAS - 182.20

Colloidal Silicon dioxide - AC, REG, X-ref - Silicon dioxide

Combustion product gas - MISC, REG, GMP, To displace or remove oxygen in processing, stg, or pkging of beverage pdts and other foods, except fresh meats - 173.350

Condensed animal protein hydrolysate - FEED, REG, < 5% poultry feed - For use - 573.200; < 10% cattle feed

Copaiba - FL/ADJ, REG, GMP, In conjunction w/flavors - 172.510

Copals, Manila - MISC, REG, 73.1 - Diluents in color additive mixtures

Copolymer condensates of ethylene oxide and propylene oxide - STAB, REG, GMP, Stabilizing agent in flavor concentrates; processing aid and wetting agent w/DSS for fumaric acid - 172.808; MISC, REG, 0.5% by weight of flour - In yeast leavened bakery products as a dough conditioner, if Standards permit its use - 172.808; Part 136 - Bakery Products; < 0.05% - Surfactant and defoaming agent in scald baths for poultry defeathering - 172.808

Copper - PEST, REG, Tolerances for residues - 40 CFR 180.538; exemption from the requirement of a tolerance - 40 CFR 180.1021

Copper (carbonate, chloride, gluconate, hydroxide, ortho -phosphate, oxide, pyrophosphate, sulfate) - NUTR, GRAS, As nutritional dietary supplement in animal feed; PEST, REG, Tolerances for Residues - 40 CFR 180.136.

Copper gluconate - NUTR/DS, GRAS, GMP, In any food - 182.5260, 182.1260

Copper (cuprous) iodide - NUTR/DS, GRAS, <0.01% - In table salt as a source of dietary iodine - 184.1265

Copper sulfate - NUTR/SUPPL, GRAS, GMP, Processing aid - 184.1261

Coriander - SP/ESO, GRAS - 182.10 and 182.20

Cork, oak - FL/ADJ, REG, GMP, In alcoholic beverages only - 172.510

Corn dextrin - NUTRS, GRAS, GMP - 184.1277

Corn gluten - GRAS, GMP - 184.1321

Corn silk - ESO, GRAS - 182.20

Corn sugar - NUTRS, GRAS, GMP - 184.1857

Corn syrup - NUTRS, GRAS, GMP - 184.1865
Corn Syrup, High Fructose - NUTRS, GRAS, GMP - 182.1866

Costmary - FL/ADJ, REG, GMP, In alcoholic beverages only - 172.510

Costus root - FL/ADJ, REG, GMP, In conjunction w/flavors - 172.510

Cottonseed & soybean fatty acids - MISC, REG, GMP - In foods as a lubricant, binder, defoaming agent & component in manufacture of other food grade additives - 172.860

Cottonseed flour (cooked and partially defatted) - MISC, REG, See 172.894 for specifications

Cottonseed Products (modified) - MISC, REG, 60 ppm N-hexane < 1% fat by wt of finished product - Decorticated ground cottonseed kernels - I72.894

Coumaphos (0,0-Diethyl o-3-chloro-4-methyl-2-oxo-2H -1-benzo pyran-7-yl phosphorothioate) - Tolerances for Residues 40 CFR 180.189; Uses in cattle & chicken feeds - 558.185

Coumarin - SY/FS, BAN, Any food containing coumarin added as such or as a constituent of tonka beans or tonka extract is adulterated.

Coumarone-idene resin - CTG, REG, < 200 ppm fresh wt basis on fruit - As protective coating for fruit - 172.215

Crambe meal, heat toasted - 573.310

Cryolite (Sodium aluminum fluoride) - fluorine compounds - Tolerances for Residues 40 CFR 180.145

Cubeb - FL/ADJ, REG, MP, In conjunction w/flavors - 172.510

Cumin (cummin) - SP/ESO, GRAS - 182.10 and 182.20

Cumin, black (black caraway) - SP, GRAS - 182.10

Cuprous iodide - NUTR/DS, GRAS, 0.01% - In table salt as a source of dietary iodine -184.1265

Curacao orange peel (orange, bitter, peel) - ESO, GRAS - 182.20

Curdlan - MISC, EMUL, STAB, REG/FS, GMP - 172.809

Currant black, buds & leaves - FL/ADJ, REG, GMP, In conjunction w/flavors - 172.510

Cusparia bark - ESO, GRAS - 182.20

Cyano(3-phenoxy phenyl)-methyl-4-chloro-alpha-(1-methylethyl) benzeneacetate - PEST, REG, 20 ppm - As

residue in apple pomace to be used in animal feeds - 561.97; PEST, REG, Tolerances for Residues - 40 CFR 180.379

Cyclamates - NNS, ILL, NOT LEGAL IN FOOD

Cyclohexane - MISC, REG, 73.1 - Diluents in color additive mixtures

Cyclohexylamine - BC, REG, 10 ppm in steam - Except in steam in contact with milk and milk products - 173.310

Cyfluthrin - INSECT, REG, Tolerances for Residues 180.436

Cyhexatin - INSECT, REG, Use: In animal feed - Tolerances for Residues 40 CFR 180.144

Cyromazine - PEST, REG, Tolerances for Residues 40 CFR 180.414

Cysteine (l-form) - MISC, FS, 0.009 parts per 100 parts flour by wt. - Part 136 - Bakery Products; 184.1271; 184.1272; NUTR/DS, REG - 172.320

Cysteine (l-form) monohydrochloride - MISC, GRAS - 184.1272 - Used to supply up to 0.009 part of total L-cysteine per 100 parts of flour in dough as a dough strengthener

Cystine (l form) - NUTR/DS, REG - 172.320

D

Damar Gum (Shorea dipterocarpaceae) - Diluents in color additives - 73.1

2,4-D (2,4-dichlorophenoxyacetic acid) - PEST, REG, 2 ppm - Tolerances for Residues - 40 CFR 180.142

Damiana leaves - FL/ADJ, REG, GMP, In conjunction w/flavors - 172.510

Dandelion, dandelion root - ESO, GRAS,

Dandelion, fluid extract (Taraxacum spp.) - GRAS - 182.20

DDVP - FEED, REG, See Dichlorvos

Decalactone alone or comb/w dodecalactone - FLAV, REG, <10 ppm alone or <20 ppm comb - As artificial flavoring in oleomargarine. Part 166 - 172.515

Decanoic Acid - SANI, REG, 109 - 218 ppm total fatty acids - Component of sanitizing solution - 178.1010, Coating for fruits and vegetables - 172.210, Fatty acids - 172.860, Defoaming agents - 173.340

1-Decanol - SYN fatty alcohol - 172.864

Decoquinate - FEED, REG, 2 ppm - In uncooked edible tissue, other than skeletal muscle, of chicken and goats as a residue - 556.170; 1 ppm - In skeletal muscle of chickens as a residue - 556.170; Use: In dry and liquid medicated feed - 558.195

Decyl alcohol, synthetic - MISC, REG, GMP, See Fatty alcohols, synthetic - 172.864

Defoaming agents and components Dimethylpolysiloxane, polyoxyethylene 40 monostearate, Polysorbate 60, Polysorbate 65, propylene glycol alginate, silicon dioxide, sorbitan monostearate, aluminum stearate (For use in processing beet sugar and yeast only - 173.340);, butyl stearate, BHA, BHT, calcium stearate, fatty acids, hydroxylated lecithin, isopropyl alcohol, magnesium stearate, mineral oil, petrolatum, odorless light petroleum hydrocarbons, Petroleum waxes, Synthetic isoparaffinic petroleum hydrocarbons, Oxystearin, Polyethylene glycol, Polyoxyethylene (600) dioleate, Polyoxyethylene (600) monoricinoleate, polypropylene glycol, polysorbate 80, potassium stearate, propylene glycol mono & diesters of fats and fatty acids, soybean oil fatty acids - hydroxylated; tallow - hydrogenated, oxidized, or sulfated; hydrogenated tallow alcohol. n-Butoxypolyoxyethylene (AF, REG, For use in processing beet sugar only - 173.340); polyoxypropylene glycol formaldehyde, sodium polyacrylate, synthetic petroleum wax, oleic acid from tall oil fatty acids - AF, REG, In foods. See individual chemicals for uses and limitations - 173.340

Defoaming agents, butter, oleomargarine, lard, corn oil, coconut oil, cottonseed oil, mono- and diglycerides of fat-forming fatty acids - AF, REG/FS, GMP, In fruit butters, jellies, preserves and related products - Part 150

Dehydroacetic acid or its Na salt - PRES, REG, 65 ppm as the acid - In cut or peeled squash - 172.130

Demeton, alone or comb/w 0,0 diethyl S-2-(ethylthio) ethyl phosphorodithioate - PEST, REG, Tolerances for Residues - 40 CFR 180.183

Dextrans (avg mol wt <100,000) - MISC, GRAS

Diacetyl - SY/FL, GRAS, GMP - 184.1278

Dextrin - GRAS - 184.1277

Dexztrose - GRAS -84.1857

Diacetyl tartaric acid esters of mono- and diglycerides of edible fats or oils, or edible fat-forming fatty acids - EMUL, GRAS/FS, Part 136, Bakery Products - 184.1101

2,4-Diamino-5(6-methylveratryl)pyrimidine - FEED, REG, See Ormetoprim

Di-N-alkyl(C8-C18-from coconut oil) dimethyl ammoniumchloride - PEST, REG, 5% by weight - 172.710

Dialkanolamide (1 mole of methyl laurate w/ 1.05 mole of diethanolamine) - MISC, REG, < 2 ppm in flume - Used in flume water for washing sugar beets prior to slicing operation - 173.315

Diammonium phosphate - FEED, REG, < 2.0% of crude protein in total daily ration - Source of non-protein nitrogen & phos in ruminant feeds. See 573.320

Diatomaceous earth - FEED, REG, 2% - As an inert carrier or anti-caking agent in animal feed - 573.340

2,2-Dibromo-3-nitrilopropionamide - PRES, REG, 2.0 - 10.0 ppm in raw cane or beets - Used alone for control of microorganisms in cane and beet sugar mills, byproducts not for use in animal feeds - 173.320

Dicalcium phosphate - NUTR/FS, GRAS/FS, Part 137; XREF calcium phosphate

Dicamba - HERB, REG, Tolerances for Residues - 40 CFR 180.227

Dichlorodifluoromethane - MISC, REG, GMP, Direct contact freezing agent for foods - 173.355; With ethylene oxide as fumigant for ground spices

3,5-Dichloro-2,6-dimethyl-4-pyridinol - See Clopidol

Dichloroisocyanuric acid - SANI, REG, <100 ppm avail halogen - Adequate drainage - 178.1010

2,4-dichlorophenoxyacetic acid - PEST, REG, See 2,4-D

Dichlorvos (2,2-dichlorovinyl dimethyl phosphate or DDVP) - FEED, REG, 0.1 ppm - In edible tissues of swine - 556.180; Use & other information - 558.205: 520.600; PEST, REG, Tolerances for Residues - 40 CFR 180.235

Diethanolamide condensate from soybean oil fatty acids (C16-C18) - Adjuvants for pesticide use dilution - 172.710

Diethanolamine condensate from stripped coconut oil fatty acids (C10-C18) - Adjuvants for pesticide use dilution -172.710

Diethylaminoethanol - BC, REG, 15 ppm - X-ref; Boiler water additives - 173.310

Diethylene glycol monoethyl ether - SANI, REG, GMP, Adequate drainage - 178.1010

Diethylenetriamine - Ion-exchange membranes - 173.20

Diethylenetriamine crosslinked with epichlorohydrin - Ion-exchange resins - 173.25

Diazinon (O,O-Diethyl O-(2-isopropyl-6-methyl-4-prim-idinyl) phosphorothioate - FEED, REG, GMP, In feed handling establishments for crack/crevice and spot treatment - PEST, REG, Tolerances for Residues - 40 CFR 180.153

Diethylamino-cellulose - MISC, GMP, Fixing agent for the immobilization of glucose isomerase for use in the manufacture of high fructose corn syrup, in accordance with Sec. 184.1372 – 173.357

Diethylstilbestrol (DES) - FEED, BAN, Not legal for animal use (drug or feed)

Diethyl pyrocarbonate (DEPC) - INH, ILL, Not legal in food

Diethyl tartrate

Difenzoquat - PEST, REG, Tolerances for Residues 40 CFR 180.369

Dihydrosafrole - SY/FL, PD/ILL, Not legal in food

3,5-Diiodosalycylic acid - DS, GRAS, Animal feed

Dilauryl thiodipropionate - AOX, GRAS, 0.02% of fat or oil incl essential oil content of food - 182.3280

Dill - SP/ESO, GRAS - 184.1282

Dill, Indian - FL/ADJ, REG, GMP, In conjunction w/flavors only - 172.510

Dimethipin - GROWTH REG, REG, Tolerances for Residues - 40 CFR 180.406

Dimethoate including its oxygen analog - PEST, REG, Residues for Tolerances - 40 CFR 180.204

Dimethylamine-Epichlorhydrin Copolymer - REG, 150 ppm - Decolorizing agent in clarification of sugar liquors and juices - 173.60

2,2-Dimethyl-1,3-benzodioxol-4-ol methylcarbamate - PEST, REG, GMP, Treating crack /crevices or spot treatment in feed manufacturing or other related facilities; Tolerances for Residues - 40 CFR 180.530

Dimethyl dialkyl (C14-C18) ammonium chloride - MISC, REG, <700 ppm by wt of sugar solids - Decoloring agent in the manufacture of sugar, alkyl groups (C14-C18) derived from tallow - 173.400

Dimethyl dicarbonate - MISC, REG, Microbial control agent in the following beverages under normal circumstances of bottling, canning, or other forms of final packaging, where the viable microbial load has been reduced to 500 microorganisms per milliliter or less by current good manufacturing practices such as heat treatment, filtration,

or other technologies prior to the use of dimethyl dicarbonate: 1) In wine, dealcoholized wine, and low alcohol wine in an amount not to exceed 200 parts per million. (2) In ready-to-drink teas in an amount not to exceed 250 parts per million. (3) In carbonated or noncarbonated, nonjuice-containing (less than or equal to 1 percent juice), flavored or unflavored beverages containing added electrolytes (5-20 milliequivalents/liter sodium ion (Na+) and 3-7 milliequivalents/liter potassium ion (K+)) in an amount not to exceed 250 parts per million. (4) In carbonated, dilute beverages containing juice, fruit flavor, or both, with juice content not to exceed 50 percent, in an amount not to exceed 250 parts per million - 172.133

Dimethylethanolamine - Component of Ion-exchange membranes - 173.20

0,0,-Dimethyl S[4-oxo-1,2,3-benzo-triazin-3(4H)-yl)methyl] phosphorodithioate (Guthion) - PEST, REG, Tolerances for Residues - 40 CFR 180.154

Dimethyl phosphate of 3-hydroxy-N,N-dimethyl-cis-crotonamide - PEST, REG, Tolerances for Residues - 40 CFR 180.299

Dimethylpolysiloxane - AF, REG, ZERO - In milk - 173.340; 110 ppm - In dry gelatin dessert mixes; 250 ppm - In salt for cooking purposes; 10 ppm - In other food in its ready-for-consumption state, 145.180(a), Cnd Pineapple; 146.185(a), Cnd Pineapple Juice

Dimetridazole - FEED/VET, REG, ZERO - NOT LEGAL FOR ANIMAL USE

Di-N-alkyl(C8 - C10)dimethyl-ammonium chloride - SANI, REG, 150 ppm - Of active quaternary compound in the sanitizing solution - 178.1010

Di-n-alkyl(C8 - C10)dimethyl-ammonium chloride, n-alkyl(C12 - C18) benzyldimethyl-ammonium chloride, ethyl alcohol and alpha-(p-nonyl-phenyl) -omega-hydroxypoly (oxyethylene) - SANI, REG, 150 - 400 ppm - For use as components of sanitizing solution to be used on food contact surfaces - 178.1010

3,5-Dinitrobenzamide - FEED, REG, ZERO - In edible tissues and by-products of chickens; As residue 556.220; Feed use - 558.376

2,4-Dinitro-6-octylphenyl crotonate+2,6-dinitro-4- octylphenyl crotonate - FUNG/PEST, REG, Tolerances for Residues - 40 CFR 180.342

Dioctyl sodium sulfosuccinate - SDA, REG/FS, <0.5% of wt of gums or hydrophilic colloids - As solubilizing agent for gums & hydrophilic colloids used in food as stabilizing or thickening agents - 172.810; <0.4% by wt - In cocoa for manufacturing - 163.117, 172.810; 75 ppm - In finished beverage made with cocoa with DSS - 172.520; 15 ppm in finished gelatin - Wetting agent in fumaric acid acidulated gelatin desserts, including: Dry Gelatin Desserts; 10 ppm in finished beverage or fruit juice drink - dry beverage base, and fruit juice drinks when standards of identity do not preclude such use - 172.810; 25 ppm of finished beverage - As emulsifying agent for cocoa fat in non-carbonated bev containing cocoa - do; REG, <0.5 ppm per percent of sucrose - Processing aid in mfr of sugar - 172.810 <25 ppm in final molasses - Diluents in color additives, 73.1 - Copolymer condensates of ethylene oxide and propylene oxide, 172.808

Dipotassium phosphate - SEQ, GRAS/FS, Part 133.169, Past Process Cheese - 182.6285

Diquat - HERB, REG, Tolerances for Residues - 40 CFR 180.226

Disodium cyanodithioimidocarbonate - MISC, REG, 2.5 ppm in raw cane - For control of micro-organisms in cane sugar mills - 173.320; <2.9 ppm in raw cane or sugar beets - With potassium N-methyldithiocarbamate for control of micro- org in cane sugar and beet sugar mills - 173.320

Disodium EDTA (Disodium ethylenediaminetetraacetate) - MISC, REG/FS, 100 ppm - Promote color retention in frozen white potatoes, incl cut potatoes - 172.135; 110 ppm - Canned potatoes 155.200; 165 ppm - For color retention in cnd cooked legumes (all cooked, canned other than black-eyed peas) or kidney beans; 315 ppm - Promote color retention in dried banana comp of ready-to-eat cereal pdts; 145 ppm - Promote color retention in canned black-eyed peas, 155.200; 500 ppm - Promote color retention in canned strawberry pie filling, Part 145; 150 ppm - w/iron salts as a stabilizer for Vitamin B12 in liquid multivitamin preparations; 50 ppm - In gefilte fish balls; 36 ppm - As cure accelerator in cooked sausage; MISC, REG, 75 ppm alone or w/Ca disodium EDTA - In non-standardized dressings, sauces; French dressings, mayonnaise, salad dressing - 172.135; 100 ppm alone or w/Ca disodium EDTA - In sandwich spread; 0.1% by wt of the dry sweeteners - As a sequestrant in non-nutritive sweeteners; FEED, REG, <240 ppm in feed - Used to solubilize trace minerals which are added to animal feeds - 573.360

Disodium cyanodithioimidocarbonate - For control of micro-organisms in cane sugar and beet sugar mills - 173.320

Disodium ethylenebisdithiocarbamate - PRES, REG, 3.0 ppm in raw cane - w/Na dimethyldithiocarbamate for control of microorganisms in mills - 173.320; 3.0 ppm in raw cane or sugar beets - w/ethylenediamine and Na dimethyldithiocarbamate for control of micro-org. in cane sugar and beet sugar mills - ibid

Disodium guanylate - MISC, REG/FS, GMP, Part 155, Cnd Vegs - 172.530

Disodium inosinate - FL/ADJ, REG, GMP, Part 155, Cnd Vegs - 172.535

Disodium phosphate (X-ref - Sodium phosphate, mono, di-, & tri-) - SEQ, GRAS/FS, Part 137.305, Enriched Farina; 136.3, Bakery Pdts; EMUL, GRAS/FS, 139, Alimentary Pastes; 131.130 NFDM; 133, Cheeses, Various; 135.30, Ice Cream; 150, Art Sw Jelly

Diuron (3-(3,4 dichlorophenyl)-1,1-dimethylurea) - PEST, REG, 4 ppm - In dried citrus pulp for livestock feed applic of the pesticide to growing citrus fruits - 561.220

Dodecylbenzenesulfonic acid - SANI, REG, <400 ppm in soln - Adequate drainage; May be used on glass containers for holding milk - 178.1010

a-(p-Dodecylphenyl)-omega-hydroxypoly(oxyethylene) - PEST, REG, GMP, Adj for pesticide use - 172.710

Dog grass (quackgrass, triticum) - ESO, GRAS - 182.20

Dulcin - NNS, ILL - Not legal in food

Dulse - NAT, GRAS

E

EDTA - See Calcium disodium EDTA and Disodium EDTA

EDTA, Tetrasodium - Components of boiler water additives - 173.310 - washes for peeling fruits and vegetables, 173.315

Efrotomycin - VET, FEED, - Swine to improve feed efficiency - 558.235

Elder Flowers - SP/ESO, GRAS - 182.20, 182.10

Enanthic acid - MISC, REG, <1% aliphatic acids - In peeling soln for fruits & vegs - 173.315

Endosulfan - PEST, REG, Tolerances for Residues - 40 CFR 180.182

Enzyme-modified soy protein - MISC, FD, GMP, Foaming agent in soda water

Enzymes, carbohydrase & cellulase, from Aspergillus niger - ENZ, REG, GMP, For removal of visceral mass in clam processing - 173.120

Enzymes from Aspergillus oryzae - ENZ, FS, Part 136, Bakery Pdts

Enzymes from plant and animal sources - ENZ, GRAS, GMP - GRAS affirmation of the following: bromolein - 184.1024, catalase - 184.1034, ficin - 184.1316, animal lipase - 184.1415, malt - 184.1443a, pancreatin 184.1583, pepsin - 184.1595, trypsin - 184.1914

Enzymes (for milk clotting) from Endothis parasitica, Bacillus cereus, Mucor pusillus, Mucor miehei Cooney

et Emerson, or **Aspergillus oryzae** modified by recombinant aspartic proteinase enzyme from **Rhizomucor miehei** - ENZ, REG, GMP, For use in preparation of standardized cheese or cheese products, except enzyme from **B cereus** is not suitable for cheese in Sec. 133.195, 133.196 - 173.150

Enzyme-Modified Fats - FLAV/ADJ, GRAS, GMP - 184.1287

Epichlorohydrin - MISC, REG, < 0.1% with propylene <10% added in combination or in any sequence - Residual propylene chlorohydrin < 5 ppm in food starch modified - 172.892; < 0.1% followed by propylene oxide < 25% - 172.892

Epoxidized soybean oil - STAB, REG, Not to exceed 1 percent - Use as a halogen stabilizer in brominated soybean oil - 172.723

Erythorbic acid - PRES, GRAS/FS, X-ref - Isoascorbic acid

Erythromycin, Erythromycin thiocyanate or phosphate - FEED, REG, ZERO - In uncooked edible tissues of chickens, turkeys - 556.230; 0.125 ppm - In uncooked edible tissue of beef cattle, and in milk - 556.230; Use: In drinking water as phosphate - 522.842; 0.1 ppm (neg res) - In uncooked edible tissues of swine; 0.025 ppm - In uncooked eggs as residue - 556.230; Use: 558.55, 558.58,558.62, 558.248, 558.680

Esterase-lipase from Mucor miehei - ENZ, REG, GMP, Flavor enhancer in cheese, fat, oils, milk products - 173.140

Estradiol - VET, REG, Use: Implant in cattle (steers/heifers) - 522.840

Estradiol benzoate - VET, REG, ZERO*** - In uncooked edible tissues and by-products of heifers, lambs & steers as residue - 556.240; Use as implants - 522.842; In combination w/testosterone propionate - 522.842; In combination w/progesterone - 522.19406; ***Tolerances in the Part Per Trillion (ppt) range have been established for these residues - See 556.240

Estradiol valerate - VET, REG, ZERO - Use: As implant in combination with progesterone - 522.1940; **NOT TO BE USED WITH VEAL CALVES**

Estragole (or esdragol, estragon, esdragon, tarragon) - SP/ESO, GRAS - 182.20

Ethalfluralin - HERB, REG, Tolerances for Residues -40 CFR 180.416

Ethephon - PEST, REG, Tolerances for Residues - 40 CFR 180.300

Ethion (0,0,0',0-tetraethyl S,S' methylene bisphosphorodithionate) - PEST, REG, Tolerances for Residues - 40 CFR 180.173

Ethopabate - FEED, REG, 1.5 ppm - In uncooked liver & kidneys of chickens as residue - 556.260; 0.5 ppm - In uncooked muscle of chickens as residue - 556.260; Feed uses - 558.55, 558.58, 558.62, 558.76, 558.78, 558.248, 558.460, 558.530

Ethoxylated mono- and di- glycerides - MISC, REG, Total not to exceed 0.5% of flour used - In yeast leavened bakery products as a dough conditioner and as an emulsifier in pan-release agents for yeast-leavened bakery products - 172.834; EMUL, REG, Not to exceed 0.45% by wt. of finished topping - In whipped vegetable oil toppings and topping mixes - 172.834; Not to exceed 0.5% by wt. of finished icing - In icing & icing mixes - 172.834; Not to exceed 0.2% by wt of finished dessert - Emulsifier in frozen desserts, 172.834; Part 135, Frozen Desserts; Not to exceed 0.4% by wt of finished vegetable fat-water emulsions - In solid state, edible fat water emulsions as Coffee Creamer Substitute - 172.834; Not to exceed 5% of dry ingredients - In cakes & cake mixes - 172.834

Ethoxyquin - FEED/AOX, REG, 5 ppm from use in forage crops - In uncooked fat of meat from animals except poultry - 172.140l; 3.0 ppm (0.0003%) - In or on uncooked liver & fat of poultry; 0.5 ppm (0.00005%) - In or on uncooked muscle meat of animals; 0.5 ppm (0.00005%) - In poultry eggs; Zero - In milk - 172.140; 150 ppm - In animal feed, fish food, and canned pet food - 573.380, 573.400; AOX, REG, 100 ppm - For preserving of color in prod of chili powder, ground chili, and paprika - 172.140; PEST,REG, Tolerances for Residues - 40 CFR 180.178

Ethyl acetate - SY/FS, MISC, REG, GMP, GRAS - 182.60, In decaffeination of coffee & tea - 173.228

Ethyl Alcohol (Ethanol) - INH, GRAS - 184.1293, 2.0% by wt - On pizza crusts prior to baking - 170.3; SANI, REG, GMP, Adequate drainage - 178.1010

Ethyl cellulose - MISC, REG, GMP, As binder or filler in dry vitamin prepns or component of protective ctg for vit & min tabs, or as fixative in flavor compounds - 172.868; 573.420; In anima diamine dihydroiodide - DS, GRAS, Animal feed

Ethylene dibromide - FUM, REG, < 50 ppm inorganic bromide - X-ref fumigant for grain-mill machinery

Ethylene dichloride - SOLV, REG, 30 ppm - In pdtn of spice oleoresins - 173.230; MISC, REG, < 0.2 ppm in flume water - Used in flume water for washing sugar beets prior to slicing operation - 173.315; FUM, REG, X-ref fumigant for grain-mill machinery; SOLV, REG, 300 ppm in extracted by-products - In extraction processing of animal by-products for use in animal feeds - see section 573.440; PEST, REG, GMP, Adjuvant for pesticide use - 172.710

Ethylene glycol monobutyl ether - SANI, REG, GMP, Adequate drainage - 178.1010; MISC, REG, < 1 ppm in flumewater - Used in flume water for washing sugar beets prior to slicing operation - 173.315

Ethylene oxide - FUM, REG, Tolerances for Residues 40 CFR 180.151

Ethylene oxide copolymer condensates - REG, 172.808; STAB, REG- 300 ppm by wt - Foam stabilize in fermented malt beverages - 172.770

Ethylene oxide polymer, alkyl adduct - MISC, REG, NTE 0.2 percent in lye-peeling solution to assist in the lye peeling of fruits and vegetables - 173.315

Ethylene oxide polymer, alkyl adduct, phosphate ester - MISC, REG, NTE 0.2 percent in lye-peeling solution to assist in the lye peeling of fruits and vegetables - 173.315

Ethylene oxide/propylene oxide copolymer REG, SDA - See specs section 172.808; MISC, Defoaming agent - 173.340 for use as prescribed in 172.808

Ethylene oxide/propylene oxide copolymer, alkyl adduct - MISC, REG, NTE 0.2 percent in lye-peeling solution to assist in the lye peeling of fruits and vegetables - 173.315

Ethylene oxide/propylene oxide copolymer, alkyl adduct, phosphate ester - MISC, REG, NTE 0.2 percent in lye-peeling solution to assist in the lye peeling of fruits and vegetables - 173.315

Ethyl 4,4'-dichlorobenzilate - INSECT, REG, 5.0 ppm - As residue in/on citrus fruits - 180.109; 0.5 ppm - As residue in fat, meat, meat by-products of sheep & cattle - do
Ethyl ester of fatty acids - MISC, REG, Comp of coatings for raisins - 172.225

Ethyl formate - SY/FL, GRAS, GMP, (See specs 184.1295); FL/ADJ

Ethyl methylphenylglycidate - GRAS, SY/FL, GMP - 182.60

Ethyl-4-hydroxy-6,7-diisobutoxy-3-quinoline carboxylate - FEED, REG, X-ref - Buquinolate

S-{2-(Ethylsulfinyl)ethyl}O-O-dimethyl phosphorothioate - PEST, REG, Tolerances for Residues - 40 CFR 180.330

Ethyl vanillin - SY/FL, GRAS/FS, Part 163, Chocolate and Cacao Pdts; Part 169, Vanilla Extract and Related Pdts - 182.60, 182.90

Eucalyptus globulus leaves - FL/ADJ, REG, GMP, In conjunction w/flavors - 172.510

Eucheuma cottonii extract - MISC, EMUL, STAB, REG, GMP, FS, See carrageenan - 172.620

Eucheuma spinosum extract - MISC, EMUL, STAB, REG, GMP, FS - 172-620

Eugenol - SY/FL, GRAS - 184.1257

Exfoliated hydrobiotite (Verxite) - FEED, REG, <5% wt. finished feed - In poultry, swine or ruminant feed as anticaking, blending agent, pelleting aid or nonnutritive carrier for incorporation of nutrients - 573.1000; <1.5% - Anticaking, blending agent, etc. in dog feed - 573.1000

F

Famphur (0,0-dimethyl 0-p(dimethyl-sulfamoyl) phenyl phos phorothioate) - PEST/VET, REG, Use: In animal feed - 558.254; As pour on liquid - 524.900; As paste in combination with Levamisole - 520.1242g

Fatty acids - one or any mixture of straight chain monobasic carboxylic acids & assoc. fatty acids from edible fats and oils (capric, caprylic, lauric, myristic, oleic, palmitic, and stearic acids) - MISC, REG, GMP, In foods as a lubricant or binder;comp in mfr of other food-grade additives - 172.860; REG, GMP, Defoaming agent comp used in processing beet sugar and yeast - 173.340

Fatty acids, salts of (aluminum, calcium, magnesium, potassium, and sodium) - MISC, REG, In foods as binder, emulsifier, and anticaking agent - 172.863; FEED, REG, GMP, 573.640; CTG, REG, X-ref - coatings on fresh citrus fruit - 172.210

Fatty alcohols, synthetic hexyl, octyl, decyl, lauryl, myistyl, cetyl, and stearyl alcohols - MISC, REG, As substitutes for the corresponding naturally derived fatty alcohols permitted in foods by existing regulations - 172.864

Fenarimol - FUNG, REG, 2 ppm - As residue in/on wet or dry apple pomace - Tolerance for Residues 40 CFR 180.421

Fenbendazole - VET, REG, 0.8 ppm - Residues in Cattle liver - 556.275; Use: Cattle (Suspension) - 520.905a; (Powder) - 520.905d; (Block) - 520.905e; (Feed) - 558.258

Fendrazen - potassium salt; Tolerances for Residues - 40 CFR 180.423

Fennel, common - SP, GRAS - 182.10

Fennel, sweet (Finochio, Florence) - SP/ESO, GRAS - 182.10, 182.20

Fenoxaprop-ethyl - PEST,HERB, REG, Tolerances for residues- 40 CFR 180.430

Fenprostalene - VET, REG, 10 ppb - Residues in uncooked edible muscle - 556.277; 20 ppb - Residues in uncooked edible liver - do; 30 ppb - Residues in uncooked edible kidney - do; 40 ppb - Residues in uncooked edible fat - do; 100 ppb - Residues at the injection site - do; Use as injection: Induce abortion: Feedlot heifers - 522.914; Estrus control: Beef/non-lactating dairy cattle - 522.914

Fenridazon - PEST, REG, Tolerances for Residues - 40 CFR 180.423

Fenthion - PEST/VET, REG, Tolerances for Residues - 40 CFR 180.214; As pour on liquid - 524.920

Fenugreek - SP/ESO, GRAS - 182.10, 182.20

Fermentation derived milk-clotting enzyme - ENZ, REG, In production of cheese for which permitted by standards of identity - Part 133; Limited to certain organisms, (See specs in 173.150)

Fermented ammoniated condensed whey - See Whey, fermented ammoniated condensed

Ferric ammonium chloride - NUTR, GRAS, GMP - 184.1296

Ferric chloride - NUTR, GRAS, GMP - 184.1297

Ferric citrate - NUTR, GRAS, GMP - 184.1298

Ferric phosphate - NUTR/DS, GRAS, GMP - 182.5301, 184.1301

Ferric pyrophosphate - NUTR/DS, GRAS, GMP - 182.5304, 184.1304

Ferric sodium pyrophosphate - NUTR/DS, GRAS, GMP - 182.5306

Ferric sulfate - NUTR, GRAS, GMP - 184.1307

Ferrous ascorbate - NUTR, GRAS, GMP - 184.1307a

Ferrous carbonate - NUTR, GRAS, GMP - 184.1307b

Ferrous citrate - NUTR, GRAS, GMP - 184.1307c

Ferrous fumarate - DS, REG, Consistent w/good nutrition practices - Used as source of dietary iron in special dietary foods - See section 172.350

Ferrous gluconate - NUTR/DS, GRAS, GMP - 182.5308, 184.1308

Ferrous lactate - NUTR/Color fixative for ripe olives, GRAS, GMP -184.1311, DS, GRAS, GMP - 182.5311.

Ferrous sulfate - NUTR/DS, GRAS, GMP - 182.5315, 184.1315

Fir ("pine" & "balsam") needles and twigs - FL/ADJ, REG, GMP, In conjunction w/flavors - 172.510

Fish protein concentrate, whole - DS, REG, (See specs in 172.385)

Fish protein isolate - DS, REG, (See specs in 172.340)

Flavoring substances, natural - FLAV, REG, GMP - 172.510

Fluazifop-butyl - PEST, REG,- Tolerances for Residues - 40 CFR 180.411

Fluometuron - HERB, REG, Tolerances for Residues - 40 CFR 180.229

Fluorine - containing compounds (Sodium, potassium, or calcium fluoride) - MISC, PD, ILL - Petition for extension in dietary supplements terminated in of 7-1-73. Addition of fluorine compounds to foods limited to that from fluoridation of public water supplies and to that resulting from the fluoridation of bottled water within limits set in 103.35. Refer to section 170.45 for statement of policy.

Fluoridone - HERB, REG, Tolerances for Residues - 40 CFR 180.420

Folic acid (folacin) - NUTR, REG, May be added to foods subject to a standard of identity when standard of identity provides for addition of folic acid. May be added 400 µg per serving to breakfast cereals, to infant formla 4 µg per 100 kcal of infant formula, 1 mg/1 lb. of corn grits, to foods represented as meal-replacement products 400 µg/serving if the food is a meal-replacement that is represented for use once/day or 200 µg/serving if the food is a meal-replacement that is represented for use more than once/day. May be added to medical food at levels not to exceed the amount necessary to meet the distinctive nutritional requirements of the disease or condition for which the food is formulated, and for food for special dietary use not to exceed the amount necessary to meet the special dietary needs for which the food is formulated - 172.345.

Food additives for use in milk producing animals for treatment of bovine mastitis - VET, REG, 528.820 - See BHA & BHT

Food starch, modified - MISC, REG, GMP, See 172.892. Add "amylolytic enzymes" to various chemicals permitted in modifying food starch that are listed in the regulation.

Food starch esterified with n-octenyl succinic anhydride treated with beta-amylase; For useas a stabilizer or emulsifier in non-alcoholic beverages and beverage bases

Formaldehyde (paraformaldehyde) - PRES, REG, Comp of defoaming agent - 173.340; MISC, REG, GMP, In animal feeds composed of oilseed meals and animal fat - 573.460; See also formalin

Formalin - FUNG, REG, Use: In water of salmon, trout, largemouth bass, catfish and bluegills - 529.1030; See also formaldehyde

Formesafen Sodium - PEST, REG, Tolerances for Residues - 40 CFR 180.433

Formetanate hydrochloride - PEST, REG, Tolerances for Residues - 40 CFR 180.276

Formic acid (x-ref - Ethyl formate) - PEST, REG, 2.25% of Silage on a dry basis -or- 0.45% when direct cut, 573.480; Preservative for silage. Silage not to be fed to livestock within 4 weeks of treatment. GRAS, GMP - 186.1316

Fumaric acid and its calcium, magnesium, potassium, and sodium salts - MISC, REG/FS, GMP, (See specs in 172.350); Part 150.140, Fruit jellies; Part 150.160, Fruit preserves

Fumaric acid-Ferrous salt - DS, REG, Consistent w/good nutrition practices - X-ref Ferrous fumarate

Fumigants (Carbon tetrachloride with either carbon disulfide or ethylene chloride, with or without pentane; or methyl bromide) - FUM, REG, Tolerances for Residues (bromide) - 40 CFR 180.123 and 40 CFR 180.123a,

Fumigants for Grain Mill Machinery, Tolerances for Residues - 40 CFR 180.519;

Fumigants for Processed Grains used in production of fermented malt beverages, Tolerances for Residues - 40 CFR 180.522

Furazolidone - VET, REG, ZERO NOT PERMITTED FOR USE IN ANIMAL FEEDS - USE WITHDRAWN 8/23/91

Furcelleran - MISC, EMUL, STAB, REG/FS, GMP, 133.128; 172.655 Part 135.30, Ice Cream

Furcelleran, salts of ammonium, calcium, potassium, or sodium - MISC, EMUL, STAB, REG/FS, GMP - 172.660 Part 135.30, Ice Cream

G

alpha-Galactosidase from morteirella vinaceae raffinoseutilizer ENZ, REG, For use in the production of sucrose from sugar beets - 173.145

Galanga (galangal root) - SP/ESO, GMP, GRAS - 182.10, 182.20

Galanga, greater - FL/ADJ, REG, GMP, In alcoholic beverages only - 172.510

Galbanum - FL/ADJ, REG, GMP, In conjunction w/flavors only - 172.510

Gambir (catechu, pale) - FL/ADJ, REG, GMP, In conjunction w/flavors only - 172.510

Garlic - SP/ESO, GRAS, GMP, 182.10, 182.20, 182.1317

Gas, combustion product - MISC, REG, X-ref - Combustion product gas - 173.350

Gellan Gum - MISC, REG, As a stabilizer & thickener; (See specs in 172.665)

Genet Flowers - FL/ADJ, REG, GMP, In conjunction w/flavors only - 172.510

Gentian rhizome & roots - FL/ADJ, REG, GMP, In conjunction w/flavors only - 172.510

Gentian, stemless - FL/ADJ, REG, GMP, In alcoholic beverages only - 172.510

GENTIAN VIOLET - FUNG, REG, VET, PROHIBITED FROM USE IN ANIMAL FEEDS - 589.1000

Gentamicin Sulfate - VET, REG, 0.1 ppm - Residues in uncooked edible tissue of turkey - 556.300; Residues in swine muscle - do; 0.3 ppm - Residues in swine liver - do; 0.4 ppm - Residues in swine fat & kidney - do; Use: Oral Solution, 520.1044a, 520.1044b; Soluble Powder 520.1044c; Injection, 524.1044;

Geraniol (3,7-dimethyl-2,6 and 3,6-octadien-1-ol) - SY/FL, GRAS - 182.60

Geranium - SP/FLAV/ESO, GRAS - 182.20

Geranium, East Indian or rose - ESO, GRAS - 182.20

Geranyl acetate (geraniol acetate) - SY/FL, GRAS - 182.60

Geranyl isobutyrate

Germander, chamaedrys or golden - FL/ADJ, REG, GMP, In alcoholic beverages only - 172.510

Ghatti gum - EMUL, GRAS, Limited to 0.2 percent of foods defined in § 170.3(n)(3) and 0.1 percent in all other foods; (See specs in 184.1333)

Gibberellic acid and its potassium salt - MISC, REG, <2 ppm - In malt; <0.5 ppm - In finished malt beverage; ZERO - In distilled spirits - 172.725

Gigartina extracts - MISC, EMUL, STAB, REG, FS, See Carrageenan - 172.620

Ginger - SP/ESO, GRAS - 182.10, 182.20

Gluconate salts of Ca and Na - MISC, FS, See limitations on use levels for Ca salt in 184.1199; GMP, Na salt 182.6757

Glucono delta-lactone - MISC, GRAS, GMP, FS, As curing or pickling agent, leavening agent, sequestrant, or pH control agent (See specs in 184.1318)

Glutamic acid (or hydrochloride) - NUTR/DS, REG, (See specs in 172.320); GRAS as a salt substitute in 182.1045 and 182.1047

Glutamic acid, condensed extracted fermentation product - FEED, REG, <5% of total ration - Protein supplement in poultry feed - 573.500; <10% of feed - Protein supplement in cattle feed

Glutamine - NUTR, REG, (See specs in 172.320)

Glutaraldehyde - MISC, GMP, Fixing agent for the immobilization of gloucose isomerase for use in the manufacture of high fructose corn syrup, in accordance with Sec. 184.1372 – 173.357

Glycerin - MISC, GRAS/FS, GMP, Part 169, Food Flavorings, 182.1320; Part 582 - Animal feeds

Glycerin, synthetic - MISC, REG, GMP, In food. (See 172.866 for specs)

Glycerol - See glycerin

Glycerol ester of gum rosin - MISC, REG, GMP, Softener for chewing gum base (See specs in 172.615)

Glycerol ester of partially dimerized rosin - MISC, REG, GMP, Comp of chewing gum base (See specs in 172.615)

Glycerol ester of partially hydrogenated gum or wood rosin - MISC, REG, GMP, Comp of chewing gum base (See specs in 172.615)

Glycerol ester of polymerized rosin - MISC, REG, GMP, Softener for chewing gum base (See specs in 172.615)

Glycerol ester of tall oil rosin - MISC, REG, GMP, Softener for chewing gum base (See specs in 172.615)

Glycerol ester of wood rosin - MISC, REG, GMP, Softener for chewing gum base (See specs in 172.615)

Glycerol ester of partially dimerized rosin - MISC, REG, GMP, Softener for chewing gum base - 172.615

Glycerol ester of partially hydrogenated gum or wood rosin - MISC, REG, GMP, Softener for chewing gum base - 172.615

Glycerol ester of polymerized rosin - MISC, REG, GMP, Softener for chewing gum base - 172.615

Glycerol ester of tall oil resin - MISC, REG, GMP, Softener for chewing gum base - 172.615

Glycerol ester of wood rosin - MISC, REG, <100 ppm - Beverages - 172.735; GMP, Softener for chewing gum base - 172.615

Glycerol (glyceryl) tributyrate (tributyrin, butyrin) - SY/FL, GRAS, GMP - as flavoring agent and adjuvant - 184.1903

Glyceryl behenate - MISC, GRAS, GMP, As formulation aid in tablets - 184.1328

Glyceryl-lacto esters of fatty acids - EMUL, MISC, REG, GMP - 172.852

Glyceryl monooleate - MISC, GRAS, SY/FL, GMP, As flavoring agent and adjuvant - 184.1323

Glyceryl (glycerol) monostearate (monostearin) - MISC, GRAS/FS, GMP, 184.1324; <2% of product - Macaroni products - 139.110; <3% of product - Noodle products - 139.150

Glyceryl palmitostearate - GRAS, GMP, Use as a formulation aid in excipients for tabs - 184.1329

Glyceryl triacetate (triacetin) - MISC, SY/FL, GRAS, GMP. As flavoging agent and adjuvant - 184.1901

Glyceryl tristearate - MISC, REG, See Reg - 172.811

Glycine - MISC, REG, 0.2% of fin bev or bev base - Masking agent for saccharin in beverages & bases - 172.812; STAB, 0.02% - In mono- and diglycerides - 172.812; NUTR - 172.320

Glycoryrrhiza - SP/ESO, GRAS, See Reg - 184.1408

Glycyrrhizin, ammoniated - ESO, GRAS/FS, See Reg - 184.1408

Gonadorelin - VET, REG, Use: As injection for cattle - 522.1077

Gonadotropin (Serum) and Gonadotropin (Chorionic) - VET, REG, Use: As injection for cattle - 522.1079

Grains of paradise - SP, GRAS, GMP - 182.10

Grapefruit - ESO, GRAS, GMP - 182.20

Ground Limestone - GRAS, GMP - 184.1409

Guaiac - FLAV, REG, GMP, In alcoholic bevs only - 172.510

Guarana - FL/ADJ, REG, GMP, In conjunction w/flavors - 172.510

Guar gum - STAB, GRAS/FS, See Reg - 184.1339; Parts 133, Cheese (to include cold pack cheese food); Part 135, Ice Cream; Part 169, Dressing for Foods; Part 150, Art Sw Jelly & Preserves

Guava - ESO, GRAS, GMP - 182.20

Gum arabic (Acacia) - STAB, GRAS/FS, GMP, See Reg - 184.1330; Part 169, Dressings for Foods; Part 135, Ice Cream; Part 169, Vanilla Powder

Gum ghatti - STAB, GRAS/FS, < 0.2% As emulsifier in non-alcoholic bevs - 184.1333; < 0.1% in all other foods - 184.1333

Gum gluten - STAB, FS, GMP, Part 139, Macaroni Products

Gum karaya - STAB, GRAS/FS, See Reg - 184.1349; Part 133, Cheese; Part 169, Dressings for Foods; Part 135, Ice Cream; Part 150, Art Sw Fruit Jelly & Jam

Gum tragacanth - STAB, GRAS/FS, See Reg - 184.1351; Part 133, Cheese; Part 135, Ice Cream; Part 169, Dressings for Foods; Part 150, Art Sw Fruit Jelly & Jam

Gums (natural) of vegetable origin - MISC, REG, GMP, Chewing gum base - 172.615

Guta Hang Kang - MISC, REG, GMP, Chewing gum base - 172.615

Guthion - PEST, REG, See (O,O.-dimethyl-S[4-oxo-1,2,3-benzotriazin-3-(4H)-yi methyl]phosphorodithioate)

H

Halofuginone hydrobromide - FEED, REG, Use: In broiler chicken feed - 558.625; 0.1 ppm - As residue in uncooked edible tissues of chickens - 556.308; 0.3 ppm - As residue in uncooked liver of chicken - do; 0.2 ppm - As residue in uncooked skin (w/fat) of chicken - do

Haloxon - VET, REG, 0.1 ppm - Residues in edible tissues of cattle, sheep, & goats: 556.310; Use - 520.1120

Haw, black bark - FL/ADJ, REG, GMP, In conjunction w/flavors only - 172.510

Helium - MISC, GRAS - 184.1355

Hemicellulose extract - FEED, REG, GMP, As a source of metabolizable energy in animal feed - 573.520

Hemlock needles & twigs - FL/ADJ, REG, GMP, In conjunction w/flavors only - 172.510

Heptylparaben (n-heptyl p-hydroxybenzoate) - INH, REG, 12 ppm - In -fermented malt beverages to inhibit microbiological spoilage, 172.145; 20 ppm - In non-carbonated soft drinks and fruit based beverages when allowed by

established standards of identity - 172.145; PRES, REG, <12 ppm - In fermented malt beverages - 193.285

Hexachlorophene - VET, REG, Permission in animal products restricted - 500.46

Hexane - SOLV, REG, 25 ppm as residue - In spice oleoresins (173.270); 2.2% by weight - As residue in hops extract, extract added before or during cooking of beer - 173.270; MISC, REG, 25 ppm - In modified hop extract for beer - 172.560; MISC, REG, 5 ppm as residue in fish protein isolate - 172.340

Hexakis (2-methyl-2-phenylpropyl) distannoxane - PEST, REG, Tolerances for Residues - 40 CFR 362

Hexitol oleate - EMUL,ILL - No petition filed. Was used as an ice cream emulsifier.

Hexyl alcohol, synthetic - MISC, REG, GMP, See Fatty alcohols, synthetic - 172.864

Hexythiazox - ACRACIDE, REG, Tolerances for Residues - 40 CFR 180.448

Hickory bark - ESO, GRAS, GMP - 182.20

Histidine (l form only) - NUTR/DS, REG, Food Additive Reg - 172.320

Hop extract, modified - FLAV, REG, GMP, In beer - 172.560

Hops - ESO, GRAS, GMP - 182.20

Horehound (hoarhound) - SP/ESO, GRAS, GMP - 182.10, 182.20

Horsemint - ESO, GRAS, GMP - 182.20

Horseradish - SP, GRAS, GMP - 182.10

Hyacinth Flowers - FL/ADJ, REG, GMP, In alcoholic bevs only - 172.510

Hydrazine - BC, REG, ZERO - For steam contacting food - 173.310

Hydriodic acid - SANI, REG, <25 ppm I2 in soln – Adequate drainage - 178.1010

Hydrobiotite, exfoliated - FEED, REG, See Verxite - 573.1000

Hydrochloric acid - MISC, REG, GMP, Modifier for food starch - 172.892; B&N, GRAS/FS - 182.1057; Acidifier in skim milk - 131.1444 and cottage cheese making - 133.129 and Cnd Tom Prods Processing - 155 and dried eggs - 160.105 and dried egg yolks - 160.185 and modified hop extract - 172.560; In animal feed practices - 582.1057

Hydrocortisone (as acetate or sodium succinate) - VET, REG, 10 ppb neg res - In milk as residue - 556.320; VET, REG, In mastitis formulation - 556.820

Hydrogen Cyanide - FUM, REG, Tolerances for Residues - 40 CFR 180.130

Hydrogen peroxide - MISC, REG, Used in combination with acetic acid to form peroxyacetic acid 59 ppm in wash water for fruits and vegetables that are not raw agricultural commodities- 173.315.

Hydrogenated corn syrup - REG, GMP, In dog/cat foods as humectant - 573.530

Hydrogenated menhaden oil - GRAS, GMP - 184.1472

Hydrolyzed leather meal - FEED, REG, 1% by wt of feed - In swine feed - 573.540

Hydrolyzed vegetable protein - FLAV, FS, GMP, 161.190, Cnd Tuna; Part 155, Vegetables

1-Hydroxyethylidene-1,1-di-phosphonic acid - MISC, REG, GMP, Used with peroxyacetic acid for washing fruits and vegetables that are not raw agricultural commodities at levels < 4.8 ppm in wash water - 173.315

a-Hydro-omega-hydroxy-poly (oxyethylene) poly (oxypropylene) (minimum 15 moles) poly (oxyethylene) block co-polymers - AF, REG, <0.05% by wt - As surfactant & defoaming agent in scald baths > 125o F for poultry defeathering, then potable water rinse - 172.808; < 5 gm per hog - As foam control and rinse adjuvant in hog dehairing machines - 172.808

a-Hydro-omega-hydroxy-poly(oxyethylene)poly(oxy-propylene)(53-59 moles) poly(oxyethylene)(14-16 moles) block copolymer, (mol wt 3500-4125) - SDA, REG, 10 ppm total in finished beverage or fruit juice drink - In combination with dioctyl sodium sulfosuccinate - 172.810, 172.808

a-Hydro-omega-hydroxy-poly (oxyethylene) Poly (oxy propylene) (55-61 moles) Poly (oxyethylene) block copolymers, (mol. wt. 9,760-13,200) - SDA/STAB, REG, GMP, Solubilizer and stabilizer in flavor concentrates - 172.808

a-Hydro-omega-hydroxy-poly(oxyethylene) poly(oxy-propylene) (51-57 moles) Poly(oxyethylene) block copolymer (Mol. wt. 14,000) - MISC, REG, <0.5% wt. of flour used - Dough conditioner 172.808

1-Hydroxyethylidene-1,1-diphosphonic acid - REG, May only be used with peroxyacetic acid, < 4.8 ppm in wash water for fruits & vegs that are not raw agricultural commodities- 173.315.

Hydroxylated lecithin - EMUL, FS, Part 136, Bakery Products; REG, GMP, In foods except standardized foods not providing for such use - 172.814; AF, REG, GMP, Defoaming agent for processing beet sugar and yeast - 173.340

4-Hyddroxymethyl-2,6-di-tertbutylphenol - REG antioxidant alone or in combination with other antioxidants so total antioxidants do not exceed .02 per cent of oil or fat content of the food – 172.150

Hydroxypropyl cellulose - MISC, REG, GMP, EMUL, STAB - 172.870

Hydroxypropyl methylcellulose - EMUL, REG/FS, GMP - 172.874; Part 169, Dressings; Part 135, Fr Desserts

8-hydroxyquinoline sulfate - MISC, BAN, Was used as comp. of a cottage cheese coagula

Hygromycin B - FEED, REG, ZERO - In eggs of poultry and in uncooked edible tissues & by-products of swine and poultry as residue - 556.330, 558.55, 558.58, 558.76, 558.78, 558.128, 558.274, 558.460, 558.625, 558.630, 558.680

Hyssop - SP/ESO, GRAS - 182.10, 182.20; Use in chicken & swine feeds

I

Iceland moss - FL/ADJ, REG, GMP, In alcoholic beverages only - 172.510

Imazalil - FUNG, REG, Tolerances for Residues - 40 CFR 180.413

Imazethapyr - HERB, REG, Tolerances for Residues - 40 CFR 180.447

Immortelle - ESO, GRAS, GMP - 182.20

Imperatoria - FL/ADJ, REG, GMP, In alcoholic bevs only - 172.510

Inorganic bromides present as a result of fumigation of processed foods with organic bromides, and/or from use on raw product - FUM, REG, Tolerances for Residues - 40 CFR 180.123 and 40 cFR 180. 123a; 40 CFR 180.199

Inositol - NUTR/DS, GRAS, GMP, 182.5370, 184.1370

Insoluble Glucose Isamase enzyme preparations - ENZ, GRAS, GMP, 184.1372

Interim Tolerances PEST, REG, Tolerances in Residues - 40 CFR 180.319

Intrinsic Factor complex (Liver-stomach concentration) - DS, ILL., See section 250.201 - X-ref; Liver-stomach concentrate

Invert sugar - NUTR, GRAS/FS, GMP - 184.1859; Part 145 Canned fruit; Part 146 Canned fruit juices; Part 169 Food dressings and flavorings

Iodine - SANI, REG, <25 ppm I2 in soln - Adequate drainage - 178.1010

Iodine (from potassium iodide) - DS, REG - 172.375, <0.225 mg I2 per day - w/o reference to age or physical state; <0.045 mg I2 per day - infants; <0.105 mg I2 per day - children <4 years old; <0.225 mg I2 per day - adults and children > 4 years; <0.3 mg I2 per day - Pregnant or lactating women

Iodine (calcium iodate, calcium iodobehenate, cuprous iodide, 3,5-diiodo- salicylic acid, ethylenediamine dihydroiodide, potassium iodate, potassium iodide, sodium iodate, sodium iodide, thymol iodide) - NUTR, GRAS, As nutritional dietary supplement in animal feed - 582.80

Iodinated casein - FEED, REG, 100 - 200 gms/ton - In duck feed - 558.295; 1/2 to 1 1/2 lb/100 lb body weight - In dairy cow feed - 558.295

Ion exchange membranes - MISC, REG, In production of grapefruit juice - 173.20

Ion exchange resins - MISC, REG, For purification of food and water - 173.25

Iprodione - FUNG, REG, Tolerances for Residues - 40 CFR 180.399

Ipronidazole - FEED, REG,ZERO - NOT LEGAL FOR ANIMAL USE; VET, REG, ZERO, do - NADA WITHDRAWN 1-17-89

Irish Moss and extract of - X-ref - Carrageenan

Iron (ascorbate, carbonate, chloride, citrate, fumarate, gluconate, lactate, oxide, phosphate, pyrophosphate, sodium pyrophosphate, sulfate, reduced iron) - NUTR, DS, GRAS, As nutritional dietary supplement in animal feed - 582.80; X-Ref Ferric and Ferrous listings

Iron ammonium citrate - AC, REG, <25 ppm - In salt for human or animal consumption - 172.430, 573.560

Iron-choline citrate complex - FEED, REG, GMP, As source of iron - 573.580; NUTR/DS, REG, In foods for sp diet use - 172.370

Iron (harmless salts of) - NUTR, FS, Part 137, Flour; Part 139, Macaroni & Noodles; Part 136, Bakery Pdts

Iron, elemental - NUTR/DS, GRAS, GMP - 184.1375

Iron, reduced DS, GRAS, GMP - 182.5375

Iron salts - X-ref; Ferric and Ferrous listings

Irradiated enzymes - MISC, REG, Dose not to exceed 10 kilograys - Control of microorganisms - 179.26

Irradiated food - MISC, REG, Dose not to exceed 1 kilogray - To control arthropod pests in any food or to inhibit maturation of fresh foods - 179.26

Irradiated meats - MISC, REG, Minimum dose 44 kilogram - For sterilization of frozen, packaged meats, NASA - 179.26

Irradiated pork - MISC, REG, Min. dose 0.3 kilograys. Max dose 1 kilogray - Control of Trichinella spiralis - 179.26

Irradiated poultry - MISC, REG, Dose not to exceed 30 kilograys - To control pathogens in fresh or frozen uncooked poultry - 179.26

Irradiated poultry feed - FEED, REG, Dose range 2 to 25 kilogray gamma radiation from cobalt-60 - to render poultry feed salmonella negative - 579.40

Irradiated yeast - NUTR, FS, Part 137.305 - Enr Farina, source of Vit D.

Irradiated spices, herbs & seasonings - SP, REG, Dose not to exceed 30 kilograys - Control of microorganisms - 179.26

Irradiation - 579.22 and 179; also see "Radiation"

Isoascorbic acid - PRES, GRAS, X-ref - Erythorbic acid - 182.3041

Isobutane - GRAS, MISC, propellant, aerating agent - 184.1165

Isobutylene-isoprene copolymer - MISC, REG, GMP, Comp of chewing gum base - 172.615

Isobutylene resin, polyisobutylene - MISC, REG, GMP, Comp of chewing gum base - 172.615

Isoleucine (I form only) - NUTR/DS, REG, Food Additive Reg - 172.320

Isoparaffinic petroleum hydrocarbons, synthetic - MISC, REG, GMP, 172.882

Isopropanol, isopropyl alcohol - SOLV, REG, <250 ppm as residue in modified hop extract - 172.560; <50 ppm as residue - In mfr of spice oleoresins - 173.240; 6 ppm - In mfr of lemon oil - 173.240; 2% by wt - In hop extract as residue from extraction of hops in mfr of beer - 173.240; AF, REG, GMP, Comp of defoaming agent for processing beet sugar and yeast - 173.340; SANI, REG, GMP, Adequate drainage - May be used on food processing equip and on food-contact surfaces - 178.1010(b)(17); SANI, REG, < 40 ppm - Adequate drainage; May be used on food processing equip and on glass containers for holding milk - 178.1010(b)(7)

Isopropyl citrate - GRAS/FS, <0.02% - 182.6386; <0.02% in oleomargarine - 166.110

Iva - FL/ADJ, REG, GMP, In alcoholic beverages only - 172.510

Ivermectin - VET, REG, 15 ppb - As a residue in liver of cattle and reindeer - 556.344; 20 ppb - As a residue in liver of swine - 556.344; Use: As injection for cattle; Combination with clorsulon - 522.1193; Use: Cattle (Paste) - 520.1192; Use: Cattle, swine, reindeer (Injection) - 522.1192

J

Jasmine - ESO, GRAS - 182.20

Jelutong - MISC, REG, GMP, as chewing gum base - 172.615

Juniper (berries) - ESO, GRAS - 182.20

K

Karaya gum - STAB, GRAS/FS, See Reg - 184.1349; X-ref - Gum Karaya

Kelp - DS, REG, <0.225 mg I2 per day - w/o reference to age or physical state; <0.045 mg I2 per day - Infants; <0.105 mg I2 per day - <4 years old; <0.225 mg I2 per day - Adults and children > 4 years old; <0.30 mg I2 per day - Pregnant or lactating women; Source of iodine in foods for special dietary use prepared from Macrocystis pyrifera, Laminaria digitata, Laminaria saccharina, and Laminaria cloustoni - 172.365

Kelp (see algae, brown) - NAT, GRAS, GMP - 184.1120, 172.365

Kola nut - ESO, GRAS, GMP - 182.20

L

Labdanum - FL/ADJ, REG, GMP, In conjunction w/flavors - 172.510

Lactase Enzyme Preparation from Kluyveromyces lactis - ENZ, GRAS, GMP - 184.1388

Lactic acid - B&N, GRAS/FS - 184.1061, Part 136, Bakery Pdts; Part 133, Cheese; Part 135, Frozen Desserts; Part 150, Fruit Butters, Jellies & Preserves; In animal feed practices - 582.1061

Lactofen - PEST, REG, Tolerances for Residues - 40 CFR 180.432

Lactose - NUTRS, FS, Nutritive Sweetener - 168.122; Part 133 (133.124, 133.178, 133.179) - Cheeses; 169.179 - Vanilla powder; 169.182 - Vanilla-vanillin powder

Lactose, Hydrolyzed - NUTRS, FS, Nutritive Sweetner; Part 133 (133.124, 133.178, 133.179) - Cheeses

Lactylated fatty acid esters of glycerol and propylene glycol - EMUL, REG, GMP, In food as an emulsifier, plasticizer, or surface active agent - 172.850

Lactylic esters of fatty acids - EMUL, REG, GMP, For use in foods where standards do not preclude use - 172.848

Lactylic stearate - MISC, REG/FS, < 0.5 part/100 parts flour - Part 136, Bakery Pdts - alone or comb/w calcium stearoyl -2-lactylate, sodium stearyl fumarate or succinylated monoglycerides - I72.844

Lanolin - MISC, REG, GMP, Comp of chewing gum base - 172.615

Lasolocid sodium - FEED, REG, 0.05 ppm - Res in edible tissues of chicken - 556.347; Use - 558.311; 4.8 ppm - Res in cattle liver - 556.347; Use: Feed Suppl, Finished Feed, Premix, Liquid Feed Suppl - 558.311

Lasalocid sodium - FEED, REG, 10.3 ppm - Res in skin of chicken - 556.347(a); 7.2 ppm - Res in chicken liver - 556.347(a); 0.7 ppm - Res in cattle liver - 556.347(a); Use in chicken, cattle & sheep feed products (finished feeds, suppls, premixes, & liquid feed suppls) - 558.311

Latex (butadiene styrene rubber) - MISC, REG, GMP, Comp of chewing gum base - 172.615

Laurel berries, leaves - ESO, GRAS - 182.20

Laureth 23 - See Polyoxyethylene (23) Lauryl Ether

Lauric acid - MISC, REG - CTG fresh fruit - 172.210, 172.860; AF - 173.340

Lauryl alcohol, synthetic - MISC, REG, GMP - See Fatty Alcohols, synthetic - 172.864

alpha-Lauryl-omega-hydroxypoly (oxyethylene) (avg. mol wt 400) - SANI, REG, GMP, Adequate drainage; May be used on beverage containers including milk containers & equipment - 178.1010

Lavandin - ESO, GRAS - 182.20

Lavender - SP/ESO, GRAS - 182.10; 182.20

Lavender, spike - ESO, GRAS - 182.20

Leather meal, hydrolyzed - FEED, REG, 1% by wt of feed - In swine feed - 573.540

Lecithin, hydroxylated lecithin - MISC, GRAS/FS - 184.1400, Part 163, Cacao Pdts; Part 136, Bakery Pdts; Part I66, Oleomargarine; Part 133, Cheese Pdts; Part 582 - Animal feeds; REG, GMP, Comp of defoamer - 173.340;

EMUL, REG, GMP, In foods where standards do not preclude use - 172.814

Lemon, lemon peel - ESO, GRAS - 182.20

Lemon balm (See Balm) - ESO, GRAS - 182.20

Lemon grass - ESO, GRAS - 182.20

Lemon-verbena - FL/ADJ, REG, GMP, In alcoholic beverages only - 172.510

L-Leucine - NUTR/DS, REG, Food Additive Reg - 172.320; MISC, REG, 3.5% of tab wt - In aspartame tabs as lubricant -558.240

Levamisole hydrochloride - VET/FEED, REG, 0.1 ppm neg res - In edible tissues of cattle, sheep & swine as res - 556.350; Use & other information: Feeds (cattle & swine)- 558.315; Dosage forms - 520.1242, 524.900, 558.254; Injection as phosphate - 522.1244

Licorice and derivatives (ammoniated glycyrrhizin, glycyrrhiza) - FLAV, GRAS, < 0.05% Baked goods - Flavor, Flavor enhancer, a surface active agent; < 0.1% - Alcoholic Beverages; < 0.15% - Nonalcoholic Beverages; < 1.1% - Chewing Gum; < 16.0% - Hard Candy; < 0.15% - Herbs & Seasoning; < 0.15% - Plant Proteins; < 3.1% - Soft Candies; < 0.5% - Vitamins & Minerals; < 0.1% - All other food - 184.1408

Lignin sulfonate, ammonium, calcium, magnesium, sodium includes lignin from Abaca - FEED, REG, < 4% of finished pellets - Sole pelleting aid in animal feeds - 573.600; As binding agent in flaked grains; < 11% of molasses - As a surfactant in molasses used in feeds

Lime (citrus) - ESO, GRAS - 182.20

Limestone, Ground - GRAS, GMP - 184.1409
Linaloe wood - FL/ADJ, REG, GMP, In conjunction w/flavors - 172.510

Linear undecylbenzenesulfonic acid - MISC, REG, < 3.0 ppm in flume water - Used in flume water for washing sugar beets before slicing operation - 173.315

Lincomycin hydrochloride - VET/FEED, REG, 0.15 ppm neg res - Res in milk - 556.360; 0.1 ppm neg res - In edible tissues of chickens & swine - 556.360: Uses & Info - 558.58; 558.145; 558.105; 558.195; 558.355; 558.680; 558.511; 558.515; 558.530; 558.530; As soluble powder in drinking water - 520.1263b/c; In swine & chicken feeds - 558.325; As injection - 522.1260;

Linden flowers - SP/ESO, GRAS - 182.20

Linden leaves - FL/ADJ, REG, GMP, In alcoholic beverages only - 172.510

Linoleic acid - NUTR/DS, GRAS, GMP, Prepared from edible fats & oils & free from chick-edema factor - 182.5065, 184.1065

Liver-stomach concentrate w/ intrinsic factor complex - DS, ILL, Any food containing the intrinsic factor is adulterated - PART 250.201(f)

Locust bean - ESO, GRAS - 182.20

Locust (carob) bean gum - STAB, GRAS/FS, X-ref - Carob bean gum - 184.1343, Part 133 (133.178, 133.179), Cheeses; Part 135, Frozen Desserts; Art Sw Jellies & Preserves, Part 150; Dressings for Food, Part 169

Lovage - FL/ADJ, REG, GMP, In conjunction w/flavor - 172.510

Lungmoss - FL/ADJ, REG, GMP, In conjunction w/flavors - 172.510

Lupulin - ESO, GRAS - 182.20

L-Lysine - NUTR/DS, REG - 172.320

M

Mace - SP/ESO, GRAS - 182.10

Madurimicin ammonium aka "CYGRO" - FEED, REG, Use: In feed - 558.340; 0.24 ppm - Safe concentrate in muscle - 556.735; 0.72 ppm - Safe concentrate in liver - do; 0.48 ppm - Safe concentrate in skin/fat - do; 0.38 ppm - Res in fat of chicken - do; VET, REG, Use in chicken feeds - 558.340; 0.24 ppm - As res in uncooked chicken muscle tissue - 556.375; 0.72 ppm - As res in uncooked chicken liver - do; 0.48 ppm - As res in uncooked chicken skin - do; 0.48 ppm - As res in uncooked chicken fat - do

Magnesium carbonate - B&N, GRAS/FS - 184.1425; Part 163, Cacao Pdts; Part 137, Cereal Flours; Part 133, Cheeses; Part 155, Cnd Peas; Part 135, Frozen Desserts: Part 582 - Animal Feeds
Magnesium chloride - B&N, GRAS/FS; 172.560, Modified Hop Extract - 184.1426

Magnesium cyclamate - NNS, ILL, Removed from the GRAS list 10-21-69, Legal only in pdts complying with drug provision of the law - 189.135

Magnesium hydroxide - MISC, GRAS/FS - 184.1428; Part 155, Cnd Peas; Part 582 - Animal Feeds

Magnesium oxide - MISC, GRAS/FS, GMP - 184.1431; Part 163, Cacao Pdts; Part 155, Cnd Peas; Part 135 Frozen Dessert; DS/NUTR, GRAS, GMP - 182.5431; Part 582 - Animal feeds

Magnesium phosphate (di-, tri- basic) - NUTR/DS, GRAS, GMP - 182.5434, 184.1434

Magnesium silicate - AC, GRAS/FS, GMP - 182.2437; < 2.0% - In table salt; Part 169.179, Vanilla Powder

Magnesium stearate - MISC, GRAS, GMP - 184.1440; As migratory substance from pkg materials when used as a stabilizer; AF, REG, Defoaming agent comp - 173.340; anti-caking agent -172.863

Magnesium sulfate - NUTR/DS, GRAS, GMP - 182.5443, 184.1443

Maidenhair fern - FL/ADJ, REG, GMP, In Alcoholic Beverages only - 172.510

Malathion - PEST, REG, Tolerances for Residues - 40 CFR 180.111

Maleic hydrazide - PEST, REG, Tolerances for Residues - 40 CFR 180.175

Malic acid, L-malic acid - MISC, GRAS/FS, GMP - 184.1069; < 3.4% - Nonalcoholic Beverages; < 3.0% - Chewing Gum; < 0.8% - Gelatins, Puddings & Fillings; < 6.9% - Hard Candy; < 2.6% - Jams & Jellies; < 3.5% - Processed Fruits & Juices; < 3.0% - Soft Candy; < 0.7% - All other food; 131.144, Acidified Skim Milk; 146.113, Cnd Fruit Nectars; Part 150 (150.141, 150.161), Fruit Pdts; Part 169 (169.115, 169.140, 169.150), Dressings & Flavorings; Part 582 - Animal feeds

Malt (extract) - ESO, GRAS

Malt syrup (malt extract) - FLAV, GRAS, GMP - 184.1445; nutrs in Part 133 (133.178, 133.179, 133.180); comp of color additive caramel - 73.85

Maltodextrin - GRAS, GMP - From corn and potato starch -184.1444

Maltose - NUTRS, Part 133 (133.124, 133.178, 133.179, 133.180) - Cheeses
Mandarin oil - ESO, GRAS - 182.20

Maneb, coordination product of zinc ion - PEST, REG, Tolerances for Residues - 40 CFR 180.110

Manganese bacitracin - FEED, REG, See Bacitracin, manganese

Manganese chloride - DS/NUTR, GRAS, GMP - 182.5446, 184.1446

Manganese citrate - DS/NUTR, GRAS, GMP - 182.5449, 184.1449

Manganese gluconate - DS/NUTR, GRAS, GMP - 182.5452, 184.1452

Manganese glycerophosphate - DS/NUTR, GRAS, GMP - 182.5455, 182.8455

Manganese hypophosphite - DS/NUTR, GRAS, GMP - 182.8458

Manganese sulfate - DS/NUTR, GRAS, GMP - 182.5461, 184.1461

Manganese salts (acetate, carbonate, chloride, soluble citrate, gluconate, ortho-phosphate, dibasic phosphate, sulfate, oxide) - NUTR/DS, GRAS, In animal feed - 582.80

Manganous oxide - DS/NUTR, GRAS, GMP - 182.5464

Mannitol - NUTR, GRAS/INTERIM, < 98.0% - Pressed Mints; < 5.0% - Hard Candy; < 31.0% - Chewing Gum; < 40.0% - Soft Candy; < 8.0% - Frostings; < 15.0% - Jams & Jellies; < 2.5% - all other food; Label "Excess consumption may have laxative effect" if daily ingestion < 20 g mannitol, In foods - 180.25

Maple, mountain - FL/ADJ, REG, GMP, In conjunction w/flavors - 172.510

Marigold, pot - SP, GRAS - 182.10

Marjoram, pot - SP, GRAS - 182.10

Marjoram, sweet - SP/ESO, GRAS - 182.10, 182.20

Massaaranduba balata - REG, GMP, Comp of chewing gum base - 172.615

Massaaranduba chocolate - REG, GMP, Comp of chewing gum base - 172.615

Materials used as fixing agents in the immobilization of enzyme preparations – 173.357

Mate - ESO, GRAS - 182.20

Melengestrol acetate - FEED, REG, ZERO - In edible tissues & by-products of cattle as a res - 556.380; Use in cattle feeds - 558.342, 558.542

Melissa (see Balm) - ESO, GRAS - 182.20

Menadione - DS, PD, Extension for use as a dietary suppl w/limit of 1 mg/day revoked 3/22/63. No food additive regulation authorizing use of menadione in prenatal suppls or any other food pdt issued

Menadione dimethylphyrimdinol bisulfite (2-hydroxy-4, 6- dimethyl pyrimidinol salt of menadione) - FEED, REG, 2.0 g/ton - As nutritional suppl in chicken & turkey feed for prevention of vitamin K deficiency 573.620; 10.0 g/ton - In swine feed - 573.620

Menhaden oil (hydrogenated and partially hydrogenated) - NUTR, GRAS - 184.1472

Menthol - ESO, GRAS - 182.20

Menthyl acetate - ESO, GRAS - 182.20

N-(Mercaptomethyl) phthalimide S-(O,O-dimethylphos-phorodithioate) and its oxygen analog - VET/PEST, REG,Tolerances for Residues - 40 CFR 180.261; Use: Liquid - 524.1742

Metalaxyl - FUNG, REG, 5.0 ppm - Tolerances for Residues - 40 CFR 180.408

Metaldehyde - PEST, REG, Tolerances for Residues 40 CFR 180..523

Methacrylic acid-divinyl benzene copolymer - MISC, REG, GMP - Carrier for Vitamin B12 in nutritional suppls - 172.775

Methanearsonic acid - FEED, REG, See arsenic - In/on cottonseed hulls, 561.280; PEST, REG - Tolerances for Residues - 40 CFR 180.289

Methidathion - INSECT, REG, Tolerances for Residues - 40 CFR 180.298

Methionine (L- & -DL forms) - NUTR, REG - 172.320, DL form not for infant foods; Animal Feeds - 582.5475

Methionine hydroxy analog and its calcium salts - NUTR/DS, GRAS, Animal feeds - 582.5477

Methoprene - FEED/ADD, REG,Tolerances for Residues - 40 CFR 180.359

Methyl alcohol residues - SOLV, REG, < 50 ppm - As residual solvent in mfr of spice oleoresins; < 2.2% by wt - In hop extract for beer - 173.250; < 100 ppm - In modified hop extract for beer - 172.560

Methyl bromide - FUM, REG, Tolerances for Residues - 40 CFR 180.123, 40 CFR 180. 123a

Methylcellulose (USP methylcellulose) - MISC, GRAS/FS, Except methoxy content - 27.5 & 31.5% dr wt basis - 182.1480; Part 150 (150.141, 150.161), Fruit Butters, Jellies; VET, REG, For use in mastitis formulation for treating dairy animals - 526.820

Methylene chloride - SOLV, REG, < 30 ppm - As residual solvent in mfr of spice oleoresins - 173.255; < 10 ppm - In decaffeinated roasted coffee & decaffeinated soluble (instant) coffee; < 2.2% - As res in hop extract. Extract added before or during cooking of beer; MISC, REG, < 5 ppm - In modified hop extract for beer - 172.560

Methyl ester of rosin - partially hydrogenated - MISC, REG, GMP, As a constituent of chewing gum base - 172.615

Methyl esters of fatty acids produced from edible fats & oils - MISC, REG, < 3% wt of aqueous & < 200 ppm raisins - In dehydrating grapes to produce raisins, > 90% methyl esters of fatty acids; < 1.5% unsaponifiable material - 172.225

Methyl esters of higher fatty acids - FEED, REG, In animal feed - 573.640

Methyl ethyl cellulose - MISC, REG, GMP, In food as aerating, emulsifying & foaming agent - 172.872

Methyl glucoside - coconut oil ester - MISC, REG, GMP, In mfr of sucrose & dextrose - 172.816; FEED, REG, < 320 ppm - Used as surfactant in molasses intended for use as comp of animal feeds - 573.660

Methylparaben (methyl-p-hydroxybenzoate) - PRES, GRAS/ FS - 184.1490; < 0.1% by wt - Part 150, Art Sw Jelly (150.141) & Preserves (150.161); REG, ZERO - Res in milk from dairy cows treated with mastitis formulations - 556.390; Use & Info - 526.820

Methyl prednisolone - VET, REG, 10 ppb - Res in milk - 556.400

Metolachlor - HERB, REG, Tolerances for Residues - 40 CFR 180.368

Metoserpate hydrochloride - VET, REG, 0.02 ppm neg res - In edible tissues of chickens - 556.410: Use - 520.1422

Metsulfuron methyl - HERB, REG, Tolerances for Residues - 40 CFR 180.428

Microcapsules - MISC, REG, GMP, For flavoring oils & spices, Capsules contain succinylated gelatin, arabinogalactan, silicon dioxide, glutaraldehyde, n-octyl alcohol & petroleum wax - 172.230

Microcrystalline cellulose - MISC, FS, Unlisted GRAS

Microparticulated protein product - MISC, GRAS, GMP, Thickener & texturizer in frozen dessert-type pdts. May not be used to replace milk fat in standardized frozen desserts. - 184.1498

Milk Clotting Enzymes – 173.150 see Enzymes

Mimosa (black wattle) flowers - FL/ADJ, REG, GMP, In conjunction w/flavors only - 172.510

Mineral oil, white (Use limitations include all petroleum hydrocarbons that may be used in combination with white mineral oil) - AF, REG, < l50 ppm - In yeast from defoamer comp - 173.340; < 0.008% of wash water - Comp of defoaming agents in wash water for sliced potatoes - do; CTG, REG, GMP, on fruits & veg - 172.878; MISC, REG, GMP, Protective float on brine used in curing pickles - do;

GMP, Float-sealant on fermentation fluids in mfr of vinegar & wine - do; < 0.6% - In food as release agent, binder & lubricant in/on capsules & tabs containing food for sp diet use - do; < 0.02% - Dr fruits & veg as release agent in drying pans - do; < 0.95% - Frozen meat as hot melt coating - do; < 0.10% - Egg white solids as release agent in drying - do; < 0.15% - Bakery pdts as release agent & lubricant - do; < 0.15% - Yeast as release agent, binder & lubricant - do; < 0.2% - Release, sealing & polishing agent in confectionery - do; < 0.25% - Antidusting agent in sorbic acid for food use - do; < 0.3% - In molding starch used in mfr of confectionery - do; < 0.6% - Release agent, binder &/or lubricant in/on capsules or tabs containing concentrates of flavors, spices, condiments, & nutrients intended for addition to food, excluding confectionery; & in capsules & tabs containing foods for sp diet use - do; < 0.02% by wt - A dust control agent for wheat, corn, soybean, barley, rice, rye, oats, & sorghum - do; < 0.08% by wt – A dust control agent for rice; REG, < 10 ppm - In food as lubricant on food-processing equipment - 178.3570; FEED, REG, 0.06% - Of total ration of animal - 573.680; 3.0% - In mineral suppls - do; GMP, In feed grade biuret - do

Mixed Carbohydrase and Protease enzyme product - ENZ, GRAS, GMP - 184.1027

Modified Hop Extract – FLAV, REG, GMP – IN BEER 172.560

Molasses (extract) - ESO, GRAS - 182.20

Molecular sieve resins - MISC, REG, GMP, For final purification of partially delactosed whey - 173.40

Monensin, monensin sodium - FEED, REG, 0.05 ppm - As res in edible tissues of cattle - 556.420; 1.5 ppm - As res in muscle tissue of chicken & turkey - do; 3.0 ppm - As res in skin w/fat of chicken & turkey - do; 4.5 ppm - As res in liver of chicken - do; Uses in chicken & cattle feeds - 558.355, 558.1448b; Use as a medicated block for cattle - 520.1448a; Use in Liquid Feed for cattle - 558.355; VET, REG, Use in goat feed - 558.340; 0.05 ppm - As res in edible tissues of cattle & goats - 556.420

Monoammonium glutamate - MISC, GRAS - 182.1500

Monobutyl esters of polyethylene-polypropylene glycol produced by random condensation of a 1:1 mixture by weight of ethylene oxide & propylene oxide with butanol - BC, REG, GMP, Boiler water compound - 173.310

Monocalcium phosphate (calcium phosphate monobasic) - B&N, GRAS/FS, X-ref - calcium phosphate, monobasic - 182.1217, 182.5217, 182.6215, 182.8217; < 0.75 parts/100 parts of flour (Part 136, Bakery Pdts - 136.110, 136.115, 136.130, 136.160, 136.180); < 4.5 parts including sodium bicarbonate/100 parts of cereal pdt, Part 137 (137.180, 137.270); > 0.25% and < 0.75% phosphated flour; In Self-rising Cereal Flours or Meals - (Part 137 -

137.165, 137.175); In Fruit Butters, Jellies & Preserves, Part 150 (150.141; 150.161); < 0.1% wt of finished pdt - Part 155 (155.170, 155.190, 155.200), Cnd Vegs

Monochloracetic acid - PRES, BAN, Any amount in beverages & other foods will serve to adulterate them - 189.155

Monoester of alpha –hydro –omega –hydroxy –poly (oxyethylene)poly (oxypropylene) poly (oxyethylene) ((minimum 15 moles) blocked copolymer derived from low erucic acid rapeseed oil – Defoaming agent component used in processing beet sugar – 173.340

Monoethanolamine - MISC, REG, < 0.3 ppm in flume water - Used in flume water for washing sugar beets prior to slicing operation - 173.315

Monoglyceride citrate - MISC, REG, < 200 ppm, As a synergist & solubilizer for antioxidants in oils & fats - 172.832

Monoglycerides, distilled - VET, REG, For use in mastitis formulations for treating dairy animals - 526.820

Monoglycerides of fatty acids - STAB, REG, GMP, Used in mfr of stearyl monoglyceridyl citrate for shortenings - I72.755

Mono- & diglycerides of edible fats or oils, or edible fat forming acids - MISC, GRAS/FS - 184.1505; EMUL < 0.5% - 166.40, Oleomargarine; comb w/ monosodium phosphate derivatives < 0.5% - Part 163 (163.123, 163,130, 163.135, 163.140, 163.145, 163.150, 163.153, 163.155) Cacao Pdts; FS, < 20.0% of shortening ingredients - Part 136 (136.110, 136.115, 136.130, 136.160, 136.180), Bakery Pdts

Monoisopropyl citrate - SEQ, GRAS, GMP - 182.6511, X-ref - "Isopropyl Citrate"; EMUL Part 166 (166.40, 166.110) Margarine

Monopotassium glutamate - MISC, GRAS - 182.1516; NUTR/DS, REG - 172.320

Monopotassium phosphate (potassium phosphate, monobasic) - MISC, GRAS/FS, < 0.5% - In Frozen Eggs - Part 160.110

Monosodium glutamate - FLAV, GRAS/FS, GMP - 182.1; Part 155 (155.120, 155.130, 155.131, 155.170, 155.200, 155.201) - Cnd Vegs; 158.170 - Frozen peas; 161.190 - Cnd Tuna; Part 169 (169.115, 169.140, 169.150) Food Dressings; NUTR/DS, REG -172.320; In animal feeds - 582.156

Monosodium phosphate (sodium phosphate, monobasic) - GRAS/FS, GMP, X-ref - sodium phosphate (monobasic) & sodium phosphate (mono-, di-, and tribasic), MISC - 182.1778, DS - 182.5778, SEQ - 182.6085, 182.6778, NUTR - 182.8778; Part 133 (133.173, 133.174), Cheeses,

Various; Part 150 (150.141, 150.161), Art Sw Jellies, Jams & Preserves; < 0.5% - In frozen eggs - 160.110; Part 163 (163.123, 163.130, 163.135, 163.140, 163.145, 163.150, 163.153, 163.155), Chocolate Products

Monosodium phosphate derivatives of mono- & diglycerides of edible fats or oils, or edible fat-forming fatty acids - EMUL, GRAS, GMP - 184.1521

Morantel Tartrate - FEED/VET, REG, 1.2 ppm - As res in uncooked edible cattle muscle tissue - 556.425; 2.4 ppm - As res in cattle liver - do; 3.6 ppm - As res in cattle kidney - do; 4.8 ppm - As res in fat - do; 0.4 ppm - As res in milk - do; Use: As bolus - 520.1450; In cattle feed - 558.360; As sustained release triaminate cylinder sheet - 520.1450c Morpholine - CTG, REG, GMP, As the salt(s) of one or more fatty acids meeting 172.860 specs as comp of protective coatings applied to fresh fruits & veg - 172.235; BC, REG, 10 ppm in steam - Except in steam in contact w/milk or milk pdts - 173.310

Mullein flowers - FL/ADJ, REG, GMP, In alcoholic beverages only - 172.510

Musk (tonquin musk) - MISC, GRAS - 182.50

Mustard, brown or black - SP, GRAS - 182.10

Mustard, white or yellow - SP, GRAS - 182.10

Myclobutanil - FUNG, REG, Tolerances for Residues - 40 CFR 180.443

Myristic acid - CTG, REG, GMP - 172.210; NUTR, GMP - 172.860; AF used to process sugar beets and yeast - 173.340

Myristyl alcohol, synthetic - MISC, REG, GMP, See fatty alcohols, synthetic - 172.864

Myrj 45 (polyoxyethylene 8-stearate) - EMUL, ILL, (No petition filed) Use in foods unauthorized

Myrrh - FL/ADJ, REG, GMP, In conjunction w/flavors only - 172.510

Myrtle leaves - FL/ADJ, REG, GMP, In alcoholic beverages only - 172.510

N

Naphtha - SOLV, in color additive mixtures for shell eggs, w/o penetration of color to interior of shell - 73.1

Narasin - FEED, REG, Use: In broiler chicken feeds - 58.363

Naringin - ESO, GRAS - 182.20

NDGA - AOX, ILL, See Nordihydroguaiaretic acid - 189.165

Natamycin (pimaricin) - FUNG, REG, applied on cheese as an antimycotic not to exceed 20 milligrams per kilogram (20 ppm) in the finished product -172.155

Natural Flavoring Substances - see individual flavoring or go to 172.510 for complete list

Natural gas - x-ref combustion product gas - 173.350

Neomycin - VET, REG, 0.15 ppm neg res - As res in milk - 556.430: Use - 520.455; 0.25 ppm neg res - As res in edible tissues of calves - do; Use - 520.1484

Nequinate - FEED, REG, 0.1 ppm neg res - As res in uncooked edible tissue of chickens - 556.440; Use in chicken feeds - 558.365

Neroli, bigarade - ESO, GRAS - 182.20

Niacin - NUTR/DS, GRAS/FS - 182.5530, 184.1530; Part 137 (137.165, 137.185, 137.235, 137.260, 137.305, 137.350) Cereal Flours; Part 139 (139.115, 139.117, 139.122, 139.155, 139.165), Macaroni & Noodle Pdts; 136.115, Enriched Bread

Niacinamide - NUTR/DS, GRAS/FS - 182.5535, 184.1535; Part 137 (137.165, 137.185, 137.235, 137.260, 137.305, 137.350), Cereal Flours; Part 139 (139.115, 139.117, 139.122, 139.155, 139.165), Macaroni & Noodle Pdts; 136.115, Enriched Bread

Nicotinamide-ascorbic acid complex - DS, REG, In multi-vitamin prepns as source of ascorbic acid & nicotinamide - 172.315

Nicarbazin - FEED, REG, 4 ppm - As res in uncooked muscle, liver, skin, & kidney of chickens - 556.445; Use in chicken feeds - 558.366

Nickel - GRAS, GMP - 184.1537

Nisin preparation - MISC, GRAS - 184.1538; < 250 ppm - Antimicrobial in Cheese pdts, Part 133 (133.175., 133.176, 133.179, 133.180)

Nitapyrin - INSECT, REG, Tolerances for Residues - 40 CFR 180.350

Nitarsone - FEED, REG, 0.5 ppm as arsenic - As res in muscle meat & eggs of chicken - 556.60; Use: Feeds - 558.369

Nitrites (sodium and potassium) - X-ref sodium nitrite & potassium nitrite, PRES, PS, curing red meat & poultry pdts -181.34

Nitrofurazone - VET, REG, NOT PERMITTED FOR USE IN ANIMAL FEEDS - USE WITHDRAWN 8/23/91

Nitrogen - MISC, GRAS/FS - 184.1540; Part 169 (169.115, 169.140, 169.150), Dressings for Foods; Part 582.1540 - Animal Feeds

Nitrogen oxides - BL, FS, Part 137 (137.105, 137.155, 137.160, 137.165, 137.170, 137.175, 137.180, 137.185), Cereal Flours

3-Nitro-4-hydroxyphenylarsonic acid (Roxarsone) - FEED, REG, 0.5 ppm as arsenic - In muscle meat & eggs of chickens as res - 556.60; 2.0 ppm as arsenic - As res in edible by-products, turkeys, & swine - 556.60; 0.5 ppm as arsenic - As res in muscle tissue & by-products other than liver & kidney - 556.60; For feed uses see: 558.530, 558.55, 558.58, 558.76, 558.78, 558.128, 558.376, 558.450, 558.410, 558.680

Nitroimide w/Sulfanitran - FEED, REG, ZERO res for Nitroimide - As res in uncooked edible chicken tissue - 556.220; Use in chicken feeds - 558.376

Nitrosyl chloride - BL, FS, GMP, Part 137 (137.105, 137.155, 137.160, 137.165, 137.170, 137.175, 137.180, 137.185, 137.200, 137.205), Cereal Flours

Nitrous oxide - MISC, GRAS, Propellant for dairy & veg-fat toppings in pressurized containers - 184.1545

Nonanoic acid - SANI, REG - 178.1010

alpha-(p-Nonylphenyl)-omega-hydroxypoly (oxyethylene) - PEST, REG, GMP, Adjuvant for pesticide use - 172.710; SANI, REG, GMP, Adequate drainage

Nordihydroguaiaretic acid (NDGA) - AOX, ILL, Not legal for use in foods - 189.165

Norflurazon - HERB, REG, Tolerances for Residues - 40 CFR 40 CFR 180.356

Novobiocin - FEED/VET, REG, 0.1 ppm - In milk from dairy animals - 556.460; 1.0 ppm - In uncooked edible tissues of cattle, chickens, turkeys, & ducks - 556.060; Uses in chicken, turkey, & duck feeds - 558.415; 525.1590

Nutmeg - ESO/SP, GRAS - 182.10

Nystatin - FEED, REG, ZERO - In eggs of poultry & in uncooked edible tissues & by-products of swine & poultry from use in feed as res - 556.470; Use in chicken & turkey feeds - 558.430

O

Oak moss - FL/ADJ, REG, GMP, Thujone free Comp of flavors - 172.510

Oak, white, chips - FL/ADJ, REG, GMP, In conjunction w/flavors - 172.510

Oak, (English), wood - FL/ADJ, REG, GMP, In alcoholic beverages only - 172.510

Oat gum - STAB, GRAS, GMP, Part 135.30, Frozen Desserts; Part 133 (133.178, 133.179, 133.180), Cheese Pdts

Octadecylamine - BC, REG, < 3.0 ppm in steam - Excluding use of such steam in contact w/milk & milk pdts - 173.310

Octafluorocyclobutane - MISC, REG, GMP, Propellent for food pdts - 173.360

nOOctanoic (caprylic) acid - X-ref caprylic acid, MISC, GRAS 184.1025; < 0.013% baked pdts, < 0.04% cheeses, < 0.005% fats & oils, 0.016% snack foods, < 0.001% all other food categories - 182.1025; CTG, GMP, fresh citrus fruit, 172.210; MISC, REG, GMP, 172.860; part of aliphatic acid mixture < 1.0% lye peeling soln for fruits & vegs, 173.315; AF, REG, in processing beet sugar & yeast, 173.340; SANI, REG, 109-218 ppm - Comp of sanitizing solution - 178.1010; PRES, GRAS, GMP, in cheese wraps - 186.1025

1-Octenyl succinic anhydride - MISC, REG, < 3.0% alone or < 2.0% w/ < 2.0% aluminum sulfate - Modifier for food starch - 172.892; SANI - 178.178.1010

n-Octyl alcohol - AF, REG, GMP, Comp of microcapsules - 172.230

Octyl alcohol, synthetic - MISC, REG, GMP, See Fatty alcohols, synthetic - 172.864; SOLV, REG, extraction process for citric acid - 172.280

n-Octylbicycloheptane dicarboximide - FUM, REG, 10 ppm - In foods - 172.864

Octyldimethylamine and a mixture of n-carboxylic acids - SANI, REG - 178.1010

Octyl gallate - PRES, REG, < 0.0075% in margarine - 166.110

Oil of sassafras - FL/ADJ, BAN - Illegal for use in foods - 189.180

Oil of sassafras, safrole free - FL/ADJ, REG, GMP, Flavoring in food, See section 172.580 for specs

Oleandomycin - FEED, REG, 0.15 ppm - As res in edible tissues of chickens, turkeys & swine - 556.480; Uses - 558.435

Oleic acid - MISC, REG, GMP - In foods as a lubricant, binder, & defoaming agent & as comp in mfr of other "food grade" additives - 172.840, 172.860, 172.863; CTG, GMP, fresh citrus fruit, 172.210; MISC, REG, < 1.0 ppm in flume water - Used in flume water for washing sugar beets prior to slicing operation - 173.315; GRAS, GMP, substance migrating from cotton in dry food pkg - 182.70; GRAS, GMP, substance migrating to food from paper pdts - 182.90

Oleic acid derived from tall oil fatty acids - MISC, REG, GMP - As a comp in mfr of food-grade additives - 172.862; CTG, GMP, on fresh citrus fruit, 172.210; AF, GMP, in processing beet sugar & yeast - 173.340

Olestra - REG, May be used in place of fats and oils in prepackaged ready-to-eat savory snacks. In such foods, the additive may be used in place of fats and oils for frying or baking, in dough conditioners, in sprays, in filling ingredients, or in flavors - 172.867

Olibanum oil - FL/ADJ, REG, GMP, In conjunction w/flavors - 172.510

Onion - ESO, GRAS - 182.20

Opopanax - FL/ADJ, REG, GMP, In conjunction w/flavors - 172.510

Orange-bitter, flowers, peel - ESO, GRAS - 182.20

Orange-sweet, leaf, flower, peel - ESO, GRAS - 182.20

Oregano (origanum, Mexican oregano, Mexican sage, origan) - SP, GRAS - 182.10
Origanum - ESO, GRAS - 182.20

Ormetoprim (2,4-Diamino-5(6-methylveratryl)pyrimidine) - FEED, REG, 0.1 ppm - As res in edible tissues of chickens, ducks, turkeys, salmonids & catfish - 556.490; Use in animal feed w/sulfadimethoxine - 558.575

Orris root - FL/ADJ, REG, GMP, In conjunction w/flavors - 172.510

Oxamyl - PEST, REG, Tolerances for Residues - 40 CFR 180.303

Ox bile extract - EMUL, GRAS, GMP, < 0.002% cheese - 184.1560

Oxides of nitrogen - BL, FS, GMP, Part 137, Cereal Flours

Oxfendazol - VET, REG, Use: As suspension for cattle - 520.1630; 0.8 ppm - As res in cattle; liver (target tissue) - 556.495

Oxystearin - INH, REG, 0.125% comb wt of oil, plus the additive - In cottonseed & soybean cooking & salad oils - 172.818; INH, REG/FS, Part 169, Dressings for Foods; AF, REG, GMP, Comp of defoamer - 173.340

Oxytetracycline - FEED/VET, REG, 3 ppm - As res in uncooked kidneys of chickens & turkeys - 556.500; 1 ppm - In uncooked muscle, liver, fat & skin of chickens & turkeys as res - 556.500; 0.1 ppm neg res - In uncooked edible tis-

sues of salmonids, catfish, & lobsters as res - 556.500; 0.1 ppm neg res - In uncooked edible tissue of swine & beef cattle as res - 556.500; For feed uses, see: 558.376, 558.450, 558.515, Injection - 522.1660; For use in drinking water of chickens in combination with Carbomycin - 520.1660a; For use in tabs in cattle - 520.1660c; Use: As soluble powder - 520.1660d; PEST, REG, Tolerances for Residues - 40 CFR 180.337

Ozone - STERL, REG, GMP (< 0.4 mg/1l bottled water), Sterilizing bottled water - 184.1563 For use as an antimicrobial agent in the treatment, storage, and processing of foods, including meat and poultry – 173.368.

P

P-4000 (5-nitro-2-n-propoxyaniline) - NNS, ILL - Not legal in food - 189.175

Palmarosa - ESO, GRAS - 182.20

Palmitic acid - MISC, REG, GMP - In foods as a lubricant, binder, & defoaming agent & as comp in mfr of other "food grade" additives - 172.860; CTG, GMP, fresh citrus fruit, 172.210; AF, GMP, in the processing of foods - 173.340

Pansy - FL/ADJ, REG, GMP, In alcoholic beverages only - 172.510

D-Pantothenamide - NUTR, REG, GMP, In foods for sp diet use - 172.335

D-Panthothenyl alcohol - NUTR/DS, GRAS, GMP - 82.5580

Papain - MISC, GRAS/FS, GMP - 184.1585; 137.305 - Enriched Farina; Part 136 - Enriched Bread; Part 582.1585 - Animal feeds

Paprika - SP/ESO, GRAS - 182.10; color additive, GMP - 73.340

Paprika oleoresin - ESO, GRAS - 182.20; color additive, GMP -73.345

Paraffin wax (X-ref: Wax) - MISC, REG, Comp of chewing gum base - 172.615

Paraformaldehyde - PRES, REG, 2 ppm of formaldehyde in maple syrup - Used to control microbial or fungal growth in maple tree tapholes - CFR 40 182.4650

Paraquat - HERB, REG, Tolerances for Residues - 40 CFR 180.205

Parsley - SP/ESO, GRAS - 182.20

Passion flower - FL/ADJ, REG, GMP - In conjunction w/flavors - 172.510

Patchouly - FL/ADJ, REG, GMP, In conjunction w/flavors - 172.510

Peach kernel (persic oil) - NAT, SP/FL/ADJ, GRAS - 182.40

Peach leaves - FL/ADJ, REG, GMP, In alcoholic beverages only, < 25 ppm prussic acid in the flavor - 172.510

Peanut oil - GRAS, GMP, substance migrating from cotton in dried food pkg - 182.70

Peanut stearine - NAT, SP/FL/ADJ, GRAS - 182.40

Pectins (including pectin modified) - EMUL, STAB, GRAS, GMP - 184.1588; sodium methyl sulfate may be present in pectins < 0.1%, 173.385; Part 145, Cnd Fruit; Part 150, Fruit Butters, Jellies & Preserves

Pelargonic acid - MISC, REG, < 1.0% aliphatic acids - In peeling solution for fruits & vegs - 173.315

Pendimethalin - HERB, REG, Tolerances for Residues - 40 CFR 180.361

Penicillin - FEED/VET, REG, 0.05 ppm neg res - Res in uncooked edible tissue of cattle - 556.510; ZERO - Res in uncooked edible tissues of chickens, pheasants, quail, sheep & swine; In eggs & in milk or in processed food in which milk has been used - 556.510; 0.01 ppm - Res in uncooked edible tissues of turkeys - do; For feed uses, see: 558.55, 558.58, 558.62, 558.76, 558.78, 558.105, 558.274, 558.505; Other - 520.1660, 522.1662

Penicillium roquefortii - MISC, FS, Part 133 - Cheeses

Pennyroyal (American) - FL/ADJ, REG, GMP, In conjunction w/flavors - 172.510

Pennyroyal (European) - FL/ADJ, REG, GMP, In conjunction w/flavors - 172.510

Pentaerythritol ester of maleic anhydride modified wood rosin - CTG, REG, GMP, Coating on fresh citrus fruit - 172.210

Pentaerythritol ester of rosin - X-ref - Rosin

Pepper, black, white - SP/ESO, GRAS - 182.10, 182.20

Pepper, cayenne, red - SP, GRAS - 182.10

Peppermint - SP/ESO, GRAS - 182.10, 182.20

Pepsin - ENZ, < 0.1% by wt in Enriched Farina - 137.305

Peptones - NUTR/SUPPL, GRAS, GMP, Processing aid & surface acting agent - 184.1553

Peracetic acid - MISC, REG, Modifier for food starch, < 0.45% of active oxygen - 172.892; SANI, < 200 ppm - 178.1010

Perfluorohexane - MISC, REG, GMP, Mixture containing 1% perfluorohexane used to cool or freeze chickens - 173.342

Periodic acid - MISC, GMP, Fixing agent for the immobilization of enzyme preparations - 173.357

Peroxyacetic acid - MISC, REG, For washing fruits and vegetables that are not raw agricultural commodities at levels < 80 ppm in wash water - 173.315

Peroxyacids - REG, Antimicrobial agent on red meat carcasses with maximum concentration of 220 ppm as peroxyacetic acid and maximum concentration of hydrogen peroxide of 75 ppm. –173.370

Persic oil (see apricot/peach kernel oil) - NAT, SP/FL/ADJ, GRAS - 182.40

Peruvian balsam - ESO, GRAS - 182.20

Petigrain (citrus aurantium) lemon, mandarin, or tangerine - ESO, GRAS - 182.20

Petrolatum NF & USP - FEED, REG, 3.0% in mineral suppls or 0.06% in total ration - In animal feeds & mineral suppls to reduce dustiness & lubricant in pelleting, cubing or blocking feeds alone or comb/w white mineral oil - 573.720; CTG, REG, GMP, Coating for raw fruits & vegs - 172.880; AF, REG, in yeast & beet sugar - Comp of defoaming agent - 173.340; MISC, REG, < 0.2% - Release agent in confectionery - 172.880; < 0.15% - In bakery pdt as a release agent & lubricant, alone or comb/w white mineral oil - do; < 0.1% - In egg white solids from use as a release agent in drying pans - do; < 0.02% - In dr fruits & vegs from use as a release agent in drying pans - do

Petroleum hydrocarbons (Synthetic isoparaffinic) - MISC, REG, GMP, As ctg on shell eggs - 172.882; In froth-flotation cleaning of vegs - do; As a float on fermentation fluid as in mfr of vinegar, wine & pickle brine - do; As a comp of ctg of fruits & vegs - 172.882; AF, REG, Comp of defoaming agent in yeast & beet sugar - 173.340; SOLV, REG, GMP (< 0.47 ppm of citric acid) comp solv for extraction of citric acid from Aspergillus niger fermentation;

Petroleum hydrocarbons, odorless, light - AF, REG, GMP, As defoamer in processing beet sugar & yeast - 172.884, 173.340; MISC, REG, < 1.0 ppm - In modified hop extract of beer - 172.560; MISC, REG, GMP, As a float on fermentation fluids in mfr of vinegar & wine; In froth-floatation cleaning of vegs; As ctg on shell eggs - 172.884; In pest formulations - 172.884, 573.740

Petroleum naphtha - SOLV, REG, GMP, Ctg on fresh citrus - 172.210, 172.250

Petroleum wax - AF, REG, in beet sugar & yeast, 173.340; MISC, REG, GMP, In chewing gum base & in other foods - 172.615, 172.886; CTG, REG, GMP, Coating on cheese & fruits & vegs, 172.886; MISC, REG, < 50% of total wt of capsule & flavor - Comp of microcapsule for spice flavor for frozen pizza - 172.230, 172.886

Petroleum wax, synthetic - CTG, REG, GMP, On cheese & raw fruits & vegs - 172.888; MISC, REG, GMP, In chewing gum base - 172.615, 172.888; AF, REG, in beet sugar & yeast - Comp of defoaming agent - 173.340

Phenol-formaldehyde, cross-linked, tetraethylenepent-amine activated - Ion exchange resin for treatment of food or potable water - 173.25

Phenol-formaldehyde, cross-linked, triethylenete-tramine activated - Ion exchange resin for treatment of food or potable water - 173.25

Phenol-formaldehyde, cross-linked, triethylenete-tramine and tetraethylenepentamine activated - Ion exchange resin for treatment of food or potable water - 173.25

Phenol-formaldehyde, sulfite-modified, cross-linked - Ion exchange resin for treatment of food or potable water - 173.25

Phenylalanine, (L-form only) - NUTR/DS, REG, Food Additive Reg - 172.320

Phorate - PEST, REG, Tolerances for Residues - 40 CFR 180.206

Phosalone (S-(6-chloro-3-(mercapto-methyl)-2-benz oxazolinone) O,O-diethyl phosphorodithioate) - PEST, REG, Tolerances for Residues - 40 CFR 180.263

Phosphoric acid - MISC, GRAS/FS, GMP - 182.1073; 131.144, Acidified Skim Milk; Part 133 (133.123, 133.124, 133.125, 133.129, 133.147, 133.169, 133.170, 133.171, 133.173, 133.174, 133.178, 133.179, 133.180) Cheese; SANI, REG, 178.1010; Part 582.1073 - In animal feed practices

Phosphorus oxychloride - MISC, REG, < 0.1% w/ < 10% propylene oxide - In modifying food starch. Residual propylene chlorohydrin < 5 ppm - 172.892; < 0.1% or < 0.1% followed by either < 8% acetic anhydride or < 7.5% vinyl acetate - In modifying food starch, < 2.5% acetyl groups - 172.892

Pichia pastoris yeast - 573.750

Picloram - HERB, REG, Tolerances for Residues - 40 CFR 180.292

Pimenta oil, pimenta leaf - ESO, GRAS - 182.20

Pine, dwarf, needles & twigs - FL/ADJ, REG, GMP, In conjunction w/flavors - 172.510

Pine, scotch, needles & twigs - FL/ADJ, REG, GMP, In conjunction w/flavors - 172.510

Pine, white, bark - FL/ADJ, REG, GMP, In alcoholic beverages only - 172.510

Pine, white oil - FL/ADJ, REG, GMP, In conjunction w/flavors - 172.510

Piperonyl butoxide - FUM, REG, Tolerances for Residues - 40 CFR 180.127

Pipsissewa leaves - ESO, GRAS - 182.20

Poloxalene - FEED, REG, GMP, In molasses block & as feed additive in dry premixes to be fed to cattle for control of legume (alfalfa, clover) bloat - 558.464 & 520.1840; GMP, As liquified feed suppl - 558.465; < 0.32 oz/ton of feed - As a surfactant in flaking of feed grains - 573.760

Poly (Acrylic Acid Co-hypophosphorite) sodium salt - BC, REG, < 1.5 ppm - As a boiler water additive - 173.315

Polyacrylamide - MISC, REG, GMP, As a film former ctg < 0.2% acrylamide monomer in the imprinting of soft-shell gelatin capsules - 172.255; < 10 ppm & < 0.2% acrylamide monomer in wash water for fruits & vegs - 173.315

Polyacrylamide resin, modified - MISC, REG, < 5 ppm by wt of juice - Used as flocculent in the clarification of beet or cane sugar juice - 173.10

Poly(alkylmethacrylate) - MISC, REG, GMP, Adjuvant in production of petroleum wax - 172.886

Polydextrose - MISC, REG, GMP, As bulking agent, formulation aid, humectant, & texturizer in baked goods & baking mixes (fruit, custard, & pudding filled pies, cakes, cookies, & similar baked pdt only), chewing gums, confections, frostings & salad dressings, frozen dairy desserts & mixes, gelatins, puddings, fillings, hard & soft candy, film coating on single and multiple vitamin and mineral supplement tablets, where standards permit, pdts w/single serving ctg < 15 g polydextrose should have warning label for sensitive individuals to laxation effect - 172.841

Polyethylene - FEED, REG, 0.5 lb per head per day for 6 days - As roughage replacement in feedlot rations for cattle - 573.780

Polyethylene, mol. wt. 2,000 - 21,000 - MISC, REG, As constituent of chewing gum base - 172.615; Ion exchange resin material in mfr of grapefruit juice - 173.20

Polyethylene, oxidized - CTG, REG, GMP, On fresh citrus fruits, vegs & nuts - 172.260

Polyethylenimine reaction product with 1,2-dichloroethane - MISC, GRAS, GMP, Fixing agent in the mfr of fructose corn syrup. Fixing agent for the immobilization of glucoamylase enzyme preparations from Aspergillus niger for use in the manufacture of beer - 173.357.

Polyoxyethylene (600) dioleate - AF, REG, Defoamer agent comp in beet sugar & yeast - 173.340

Polyoxyethylene (600) monoricinoleate - AF, REG, Defoamer agent comp in beet sugar & yeast - 173.340

Polyoxyethylene (23) lauryl ether - Feed (Block), REG, Use: For bloat in cattle in block - 520.1846;

Polyethylene glycol - BC, REG, GMP, In boiler water - 173.310; AF, REG, GMP, Comp of defoaming agent - 173.340; CTG, REG, GMP, Ctg on fresh citrus fruits - 172.210

Polyethylene glycol (mean molecular weight 200 - 9,500) - MISC, REG, GMP, Ctg, binder, plasticizing agent, and/or lubricant in tabs used for food; Adjuvant in nonnutritive sweeteners, vitamin & mineral prepns; Ctg for sodium nitrite to inhibit hygroscopic properties - 172.820; ZERO - In milk - 172.820, 526.820

Polyethylene glycol (400) dioleate - EMUL, REG, < 10% by wt. of defoamer formulation - Processing beet sugar & yeast - 173.340

Polyethylene glycol (400) mono- & di- oleate - Feed, REG, 250 ppm in molasses - Used as a processing aid in the production of animal feeds when present as a result if its addition to molasses - 573.800

Polyglycerol esters of fatty acids - EMUL, REG, GMP, Used as emulsifiers in food or as cloud inhibitors in veg & salad oils where not precluded by standards - 172.854; 166.110 - Margarine, Part 169 (169.115, 169.140, 169.150) - Food Dressings

Polyisobutylene (minimum molecular weight 1,200-2,500) - MISC, REG, GMP, In chewing gum base - 172.615

Polyglycerol phthalate ester of coconut oil fatty acids - PEST, REG, GMP, Adjuvant for pesticide use - 172.710

Polymaleic acid and/or its sodium salts - BC, REG, < 1 ppm in boiler feed water - Boiler water additive - 173.310; Specific uses: Boiler water additives, use individually or together at not greater than 4 ppm in processing of beet or cane sugar juice or liquor process steam - 173.310, 173.45

Polyoxyethylene glycol (400) mono- & di- oleates - EMUL, REG, In milk replacer formulations for calves - 573.820

Polyoxyethylene (23) lauryl ether - FEED, REG, Use: In feed blocks for cattle - 520.1846

Polyoxyethylene (40) monostearate - AF, REG, Defoaming agent comp - 173.340

Polyoxyethylene-polyoxypropylene block polymers (avg molecular weight l900) - SANI, REG, GMP, Adequate drainage - 178.1010

Polyoxyethylene-polyoxypropylene block polymers (avg molecular weight 2000) - SANI, REG, GMP, Adequate drainage; May be used on glass containers for holding milk - 178.1010

Polyoxyethylene-polyoxypropylene block polymers (avg molecular weight 2800) - SANI, REG, < 80 ppm in soln - Adequate drainage - 178.1010

Polyoxyethylene (20) sorbitan monooleate - See Polysorbate 80 - 172.840

Polyoxyethylene (20) sorbitan monostearate - See Polysorbate 60 - 172.836

Polyoxyethylene (20) sorbitan tristearate - See Polysorbate 65 - 172.838

Polyoxypropylene glycol (Minimum molecular weight 1000) - BC, REG, GMP, In boiler water - 173.310

Polypropylene glycol (Molecular weight 1200-3000) - AF, REG, Defoaming agent comp used in beet sugar & yeast - 173.340

Polysorbate 60 (Polyoxyethylene (20) sorbitan monostearate) - EMUL, REG, < 0.40% alone or w/one or comb of sorbitan monostearate, Polysorbate 80, Polysorbate 65 - In whipped veg oil topping. Total amount any comb < 0.77% - 172.836; REG, < 0.46% alone or any w/sorbitan monostearate Polysorbate 65 - In cake mixes & cakes (dry wt basis). Total amt any comb < 0.66% - do; REG, < 0.5% of wt of finished pdts alone or in comb w/sorbitan monostearate - Part 163 (163.123, 163.130, 163.135, 163.140, 163.145, 163.150, 163.153, 163.155), Cocoa Pdts - do; REG, < 0.46% alone or any comb w/Sorbitan monostearate &/or Polysorbate 65 - In cake icing &/or cake filling containing shortening - do, Total amt any comb < 1.0% of finished wt; MISC, REG, <0.2% - To impart greater opacity to sugar-type confectionery coatings - do; EMUL, REG, < 0.3% - In non- standardized dressings - do; REG, < 1.0% alone or comb Polysorbate 80 - In shortening & edible oils intended for use in foods where standards permit - do; REG, < 0.40% alone or/w sorbitan monostearate or/w polysorbate 65 - In veg oil/water emulsion used as milk or cream substitute in beverage coffee - do; REG, < 4.5% by wt of nonalcoholic mix - As foaming agent in nonalcoholic beverages used in mixing - do; REG/FS, 0.5% by wt of flour alone or w/other emul - As a dough conditioner in yeast-leavened bakery pdts, 136.3 - do; EMUL, REG, GMP, Alone or w/sorbitan monostearate in formulations of white mineral oil &/or petroleum wax for ctgs on raw fruits & vegs - do; REG, 0.5% dry wt. basis - As dispersing agent in art sw gelatin desserts & mixes - do; REG, Total amt comb < 1.0%; < 0.05% in finished pdt - As emulsifier in chocolate flavored syrups - do; REG, As surfactant & wetting agent for natural & artificial colors in food; < 4.5% by wt of mix - In powdered soft drink mixes; < 0.5% by wt of mix - In sugar base gelatin dessert mixes; < 3.6% by wt. of mix - In art sw gelatin dessert mixes; < 0.5% by wt. of mix - In sugar based pudding mixes; < 0.5% by wt. of mix - In art sw pudding mixes - do; < 0.1% alone or w/one or comb of polysorbate 65 and/or polysorbate 80 – In ice cream, frozen sherbet aand non-standardized frozen desserts; REG, < 0.1% followed by either < 8% acetic anhydride or < 7.5% vinyl acetate - In modifying food starch < 2.5% acetyl groups - 172.892; AF, REG, GMP, Defoaming agent comp - 173.340; REG, diluent for color additive mixtures for drug use exempt from certification - 73.1001; FEED, REG, GMP alone or comb/ Sorbitan monostearate - In mineral premixes or diet suppl for animal feeds - 573.840

Polysorbate 65 (Polyoxyethylene (20) sorbitan tristearate) - EMUL, REG/FS, < 1.0% alone or w/Polysorbate 80 - Part 135, Frozen Desserts; Non-standardized Frozen Desserts - 172.838; REG, < 0.32% alone or any comb w/Polysorbate 60 &/or Sorbitan monostearate - In cake or cake mix on a dry wt basis - total amt any comb < 0.66% - do; REG, < 0.40% alone or w/one or comb of Sorbitan monostearate, Polysorbate 60, or Polysorbate 80 - In whipped edible oil topping - do; Total comb < 0.40%; REG, < 0.32% alone or any comb w/Polysorbate 60, Sorbitan monostearate - In cake icing or cake filling - do; Total amt any comb < 1.0% of finished wt; REG, 0.40% alone or w/sorbitan monostearate or w/Polysorbate 60 - In veg fat-water emulsion used as milk or cream substitute in beverage coffee - do; AF, REG, GMP, Defoaming agent compound - 173.340; REG, diluent for color additive mixtures for drug use exempt from certification - 73.1001

Polysorbate 80 (Polyoxyethylene (20) sorbitan monooleate) - EMUL, REG/FS, < 0.1% alone or with Polysorbate 65 - Part 135, Frozen Desserts - 172.840; AF, REG, < 4 ppm, Used as yeast defoaming agent - do; SDA, REG, < 500 ppm (0.05%) - In pickles & pickle products - do; SDA, REG, < 175 mg/day based on recommended daily dose - In vitamin-mineral prepns containing calcium caseinate w/o fat-soluble vitamins - do; < 300 mg/day - In fat-soluble vitamins in vitamin & vitamin-mineral prepns w/o calcium caseinate; < 475 mg/day - In vitamin-mineral prepns containing both calcium caseinate & fat-soluble vitamins; MISC, REG, < 10 ppm in finished sodium chloride - As a surfactant in pdtn of coarse crystal sodium chloride - do; EMUL, REG, < 360 mg/day - In sp diet foods - do; SDA, REG, < 30 ppm - For dill oil in cnd spiced green beans, Part 155, Cnd Vegs - do; EMUL, REG, < 1.0% alone or comb/ Polysorbate 60 - In shortening & edible oils - do; EMUL, REG, < 0.40% alone or comb/Sorbitan monostearate, Polysorbate 60, or Polysorbate 65 - In whipped veg oil topping - do; REG, < 0.0175% - In scald water for poultry defeathering followed by potable water rinse - do; SDA, REG, < 0.082% on dry wt basis - As dispersing agent in gelatin desserts & gelatin dessert mixes - do; REG, As an

adjuvant added to herbicide or plant-growth regulator dilutions prior to their application - do; AF, REG, < 0.008% by wt of finished pdt - In creaming mixture for cottage cheese & low fat cottage cheese as identified in 133.128 & 133.131 - do; REG, < 0.005% by wt of sauce - As surfactant & wetting agent for natural & art colors in barbecue sauce - do; REG, In milk replacer formula for calves - 573.860

Polysorbate 80 w/ carrageenan or carrageenan salts - MISC, REG, < 5% Polysorbate 80 - In carrageenan or its salts - 172.623; < 500 ppm Polysorbate 80 - In finished food containing additive - 172.623

Polyvinyl Acetate (molecular weight 2000 minimum) - MISC, REG, Comp of chewing gum base - 172.6l5; REG, diluent for color additive mixtures for drug use exempt from certification - 73.1

Polyvinylpolypyrrolidone - MISC, REG, Clarifying agent in beverages & vinegar to be removed with filtration - 173.50

Polyvinylpyrrolidone (avg molecular weight 40,000, except in beer) - MISC, REG, < 10 ppm (average molecular weight 360,000) - In beer from use as a clarifying agent - 173.55; < 40 ppm - In vinegar - do; REG, < 60 ppm - In wine from use as a clarifying agent - do; REG, GMP, As tableting adj in NNS & flavor, vitamin & mineral concentrates in tab form - do; MISC, REG, GMP, Stab, lodging agent & dispersant in NNS in conc liquid form or in vitamin & mineral concentrates in liquid form - do; ADJ, REG, GMP, As an adj w/ vinyl chloride, vinylidene chloride copolymer for ctg on fresh citrus fruit - 172.210; REG, diluent for color additive mixtures for drug use exempt from certification - 73.1, 73.1001

Poly(2-vinylpyridine-co-styrene) - FEED, CTG - Coating agent for nutrients for cattle - 573.870

Pomegranate - ESO, GRAS - 182.20

Poplar buds - FL/ADJ, REG, GMP, In alcoholic beverages only - 172.510

Poppy seed - SP, GRAS - 182.10

Pot marigold - SP, GRAS - 182.10

Pot marjoram - SP, GRAS - 182.10

Potassium acetate - B&N, FS - Unlisted GRAS

Potassium acid tartrate - B&N/MISC, GRAS, GMP - 184.1077; Part 150 (150.141, 150.161), Art Sw Jelly & Preserves; Part 582.1077 - In animal feeds

Potassium alginate - STAB, GRAS - Stabilizer & thickener, < 0.1% in confections & frostings, < 0.7% in gelatins & puddings, < 0.25% in processed fruits & fruit juices, < 0.01 % in all other food categories - 184.1610

Potassium alum - MISC, FS, Part 137, Flour; REG, used as comp of bleaching agent for dairy pdts in cheese prepn in Part 133 (133.102, 133.103, 133.104, 133.106, 133.111, 133.141, 133.165, 133.181, 133.195)

Potassium bicarbonate - B&N/MISC, GRAS/FS, GMP - 184.1613, Part 163 (163.110, 163.111 163.112, 163.114, 163.117), Cacao Pdts; Part 582.1613 - In animal feeds

Potassium bisulfite - PRES, GRAS/FS, GMP, Restrictions: Not in meats, foods recognized as source of Vitamin B1 , raw fruit & veg (incl fresh potatoes, i.e., not frozen, cnd or dehydrated) - served fresh - 182.3616

Potassium bromate - BL, FS, < 75 ppm added to whole wheat flour; 50 ppm in white flour - Part 137 (137.155, 137.205), Cereal Flours; Part 136 (136.110, 136.115, 136.130, 136.160, 136.180), Bakery Pdts; MISC, REG, < 75 ppm calc as bromine - In malt for pdtn of fermented malt beverages or distilled spirits - 172.730

Potassium bromide - SANI, REG, < 200 ppm available halogen - Adequate drainage - 178.1010; MISC, REG, For washing fruits & vegs - 173.315

Potassium caprate - MISC, REG, GMP - 172.863

Potassium caprylate - MISC, REG, GMP - 172.863

Potassium carbonate - B&N/MISC, GRAS/FS, GMP - 184.1619; Part 163, Cocoa Pdts; Used in treatment of modified hop extract - 172.560; BC, REG - 173.310; Part 582.1619 - In animal feeds - 184.1619

Potassium caseinate - MISC, FS, Part 135 (135.110, 135.140), Frozen Desserts

Potassium chloride - MISC, GRAS/FS - 184.1622; Part 150 (150.141, 150.161), Art Sw Jelly & Preserves, Added to margarine - 166.110; DS/NUTR, GRAS, GMP - 182.5622

Potassium citrate - MISC, GRAS/FS, GMP - 182.1625; SEQ, GRAS, GMP - 182.1625; Part 133 (133.169, 133.173, 133.179), Cheese; Part 150 (150.141, 150.161), Art Sw Jelly & Preserves; Part 582.1625 - In animal feeds

Potassium cyclamate - NNS, ILL, Removed from GRAS list 10-21-69 - 189.135

Potassium dichloroisocyanurate - SANI, REG, < 100 ppm available halogen - Adequate drainage - 178.1010

Potassium fumarate - REG, GMP, sp diet - 172.350

Potassium Gibberellate - REG, < 2 ppm as gibberellic acid in malting barley - 172.725

Potassium gluconate - MISC, FS, GMP

Potassium glycerophosphate - DS, GRAS, GMP - 182.5628; NUTR, GRAS, GMP - 182.8628

Potassium hydroxide - B&N/MISC, GRAS/FS - 184.1631; Part 163, Cacao Products; Part 582.1631 - In animal feeds

Potassium hypochlorite - SANI, REG, < 200 ppm available halogen as chlorine - Adequate drainage - 178.1010

Potassium iodate - BL/DS, GRAS/FS - 184.1635; < 0.0075% by wt flour - Part 136 (136.110, 136.115, 136.130, 136.160, 136.180), Bakery Pdts; Animal feed; Trace mineral in animal feeds - 582.80

Potassium iodide - NUTR, GRAS, < 0.01% - In table salt as source of dietary iodine - 184.1634; DS, REG, < 225 micrograms daily ingestion - For foods labeled w/o reference to age or physiological state - 172.375; < 45 micrograms daily ingestion for infants - For food when age or the cond of pregnancy or lactation are specified - 172.375; < 105 micrograms daily ingestion for < 4 yrs old; < 225 micrograms daily ingestion for adults & children 4+ yrs old; < 300 micrograms daily ingestion for pregnant or lactating women; Trace mineral in animal feeds - 582.80; SANI, REG, < 25 ppm iodine in soln - Adequate drainage - 178.1010

Potassium lactate - MISC, GRAS, GMP, used as flavor enhancer or adjuvant, humectant & pH control agent - 184.1639

Potassium laurate - MISC, REG, GMP - 172.863

Potassium metabisulfite - PRES, GRAS/FS, GMP, Restrictions: Not in meats, foods recognized as source of Vitamin B1 , raw fruit & veg (incl fresh potatoes, i.e., not frozen, cnd or dehydrated) - served fresh - 182.3617

Potassium N-methyldithiocarbamate - REG, 3.5 ppm in terms of wt of sugar cane being processed - Comp of bacteriostat in controlling microorganisms in cane sugar mills; 4.1 ppm in terms of wt of raw cane or beets - Comp of bacteriostat in controlling microorganisms in cane sugar & beet sugar mills - 173.320

Potassium myristate - MISC, REG, GMP - 172.863

Potassium nitrate - MISC, REG, < 200 ppm of finished roe Used as a curing agent in the processing of cod roe - 172.160; PRES, PS, source of nitrite used in pdtn of cured red meat & poultry pdts - 181.33

Potassium nitrite - PRES, PS, source of nitrite used in pdtn of cured red meat & poultry pdts - 181.34

Potassium oleate - MISC, REG, GMP - 172.863

Potassium palmitate - MISC, REG, GMP - 172.863

Potassium permanganate - BL, REG, < 50 ppm calc as manganese - used as bleaching agent in modified food starch - 172.892

Potassium persulfate - REG, GMP, Adj for coatings of fresh citrus - 172.210

Potassium phosphate (dipotassium phosphate) (dibasic) - SEQ, GRAS/FS, GMP - 182.6285; Part 133 (133.169, 133.173, 133.179), Process Cheeses

Potassium phosphate (monobasic) - REG, <0.5% by wt of frozen eggs as a color preservative - 160.110

Potassium salts of fatty acids - MISC, REG, GMP, In foods as binder, emulsifier, & anti-caking agent - 172.863

Potassium sorbate - PRES, GRAS/FS - 182.3640; < 0.3% as sorbic acid - Part 133 (133.123, 133.173, 133.179, 133.180, 133.188) Cheeses; FS, < 0.1% by wt - Part 150 (150.141, 150.161), Fruit Butter & Art Sw Jelly & Preserves; < 0.1% or 0.2% total in combination w/other pres, Margarine & Oleomargarine - 166.110; GRAS, substance migrating to food from paper & paperboard pdts - 182.90

Potassium stearate - MISC, REG, GMP, Specifications - 172.863; AF for beet sugar & yeast - 173.340; Comp of chewing gum - 172.615

Potassium sulfate - FL/ADJ, GRAS, GMP - 184.163

Potassium trichloroisocyanurate - SANI, REG, < 100 ppm avail halogen as chlorine - Adequate drainage - 178.1010

Potassium triphosphate - BC, REG, GMP - 173.310

Prednisolone - VET, REG, ZERO - In milk from dairy animals treated with mastitis formulations - 556.520

Prednisone - VET, REG, ZERO - In milk from dairy animals treated with mastitis formulations - 556.530

Prickly ash bark - ESO, GRAS - 182.20

Primisulfuron-methyl - REG, 0.02 ppm - As res in corn grain & milk - 40 CFR 180.452; 0.01 ppm - As res in eggs - do; 0.01 ppm - As res in meat, meat by-products & fat of cattle, goats, hogs, poultry & sheep & corn - do

Procaine penicillin - VET, REG, Used as injection in animals - 574.274b et al; 0.05 ppm - Res in uncooked edible tissues of cattle - 556.510; 0.01 ppm - Res in uncooked edible tissues of turkey - 556.510; ZERO - Res in uncooked edible tissues of chicken, pheasants, quail, swine, sheep, in eggs, in milk or any food processed with milk - 556.510

Profenofos - PEST, REG, Tolerances for Residues 40 CFR 180.404

Profluralin - HERB, REG, 0.3 ppm - As res in/on soybean hay - 40 CFR 180.348; 0.1 ppm - As res in/on cottonseed, pod vegs, sunflower seeds - do; 0.02 ppm - As res in/on eggs or milk, meat, fat & meat by-products of cattle, hogs, goats poultry & sheep - do

Progesterone - VET, REG, ZERO - No res above stated tolerances in uncooked edible tissues & by-products of lambs & steers - 556.540; Use as implant in combination with estradiol valerate - 522.1940 (**NOT TO BE USED IN VEAL CALVES**)

Proline (L form only) - NUTR/DS, REG, Food Additive Reg - 172.320

Propane - MISC, GRAS, GMP - 184.1655; Combustion product gas - 173.350

Propanil - HERB, REG, Tolerances for Residues - 40 CFR 180.272

Propanoic acid -SANI, REG - 178.1010

Propargite - PEST,REG, Tolerances for Residues - 40 CFR 180.259

Proparquite - PEST, REG, 80 ppm in dr apple pomace - In processed feeds as a result of application to growing crops as res - 40 CFR 186.5000; 40 ppm in dr citrus pulp & dr grape pulp

Propetamphos - PEST, REG, Use as spot/crack/crevice treatment (1 % max.) Tolerances for Residues - 40 CFR 180.541

Propionic acid - PRES, GRAS/FS, GMP - 184.1081; Part 133 (133.149, 133.195), Propionic acid produced by bacteria, Swiss & Gruyere Cheese

Propyl alcohol, normal - FEED, REG, Used in feeds as a source of metabolizable energy - 573.880

Propylene glycol - MISC, GRAS/FS - 184.1666; Part 169 (169.175, 169.176, 169.177, 169.178, 169.180, 169.181), Vanilla Extract; Carrier for enzyme modified soy protein; Part 582.1666 - In animal feeds

Propylene glycol alginate (Propylene glycol ester of alginic acid) - MISC, REG, stab < 0.5% by wt in frozen dairy desserts, emul/stab/or thickener < 0.5% by wt in baked goods, emul/stab/thickener < 0.9% by wt in cheeses, in - Part 135, Frozen Desserts; Part 166, Marg; REG, GMP, In processing foods - 172.858; FS, Part 133, Cheeses; Part 169, Dressings; MISC, REG, GMP, Adj for ctg fresh citrus fruit - 172.210

Propylene glycol mono- & di- esters of fats & fatty acids - EMUL, REG/FS, GMP - 172.856; Part 136 (136.110, 136.115, 136.130, 136.160, 136.180), Bakery Pdts; AF, REG, GMP, Defoamer agent compound - 173.340

Propylene oxide - MISC, REG, < 25% for treatment - In modifying food starch. Residual propylene chlorohydrin < 5 ppm - 172.892; FUM, REG, Tolerances for Residues - 40 CFR 180.491

Propyl gallate - AOX, GRAS, AOX content < 0.02% of fat or oil content incl essential oil content of food - 184.1660; Margarine - 166.110; REG, 0.1% alone or/BHA/BHT - Comp of chewing gum base - 172.615; Pressure-sensitive adhesives used as the food contact surface of labels &/or tapes applied to food - 175.125

Propylparaben (propyl-p-hydroxybenzoate) - PRES, GRAS/FS, GMP - 184.1670; < 0.1%, Part 150, 150.141, 150.161), Art Sw Jelly & Preserves; REG, 0.025%, In mastitis formulations - 526.820; REG, ZERO - In milk from dairy animals - 556.550

Protein concentrate, whole fish - DS, REG, GMP - 172.385

Protein, hydrolyzed - MISC, FS, Part 161.190(a), Cnd Tuna

Protein, vegetable, hydrolyzed - Cnd Vegs, Part 150 (155.120, 155.130, 155.170, 155.200)

Prussiate of soda, yellow (Na ferrocyanide decahydrate) - AC, REG, < 13 ppm calc as anhydrous Na ferrocyanide - Anticaking agent in salt - 172.490; AC/FEED, REG, 13 ppm - do; In salt for animal consumption - 573.1020

Psyllium seed husk - STAB, FS, 0.5% by wt - Part 135, Frozen Desserts

Pteroylglutamic acid (aka folic acid) - X-ref Folic acid, DS, REG, < 0.40 mg w/o ref to age or physiological state - As comp of dietary suppls, provided directions for use, when followed < tolerance - 172.345

Pyrantel tartrate - FEED/VET, REG, 10 ppm - In swine liver & kidney as res - 556.560; 1 ppm - In swine muscle as res - 556.560; Uses: In swine feeds - 558.485; Powder & Tabs - 520.2045

Pyrethrins - FUM, REG, Tolerances for Residues - 40 CFR 180.128

Pyridoxine hydrochloride - NUTR/DS, GRAS, GMP - 182.5676, 184.1676

Pyrophyllite (aluminum silicate monohydrate) - AC/MISC, REG, < 2.0% in complete animal feed - As sole anticaking aid, blending agent, pelleting aid, or carrier in animal feed - 573.900

Q

Quassia - FL/ADJ, REG, GMP, In conjunction w/flavors - 172.510

Quaternary ammonium chloride combination - PRES, REG, See Reg, In proc of sugar cane juice and in cane sugar mills - 172.165, 173.320

Quebracho bark - FL/ADJ, REG, GMP, In conjunction w/flavors - 172.510

Quillaia (soapbark) - FL/ADJ, REG, GMP, In conjunction w/flavors - 172.510

Quince seed - NAT, GRAS - 182.40

Quinine hydrochloride or sulfate - FLAV, REG, < 83 ppm as quinine - Flavoring agent in carbonated bevs - 172.575

Quizalofop ethyl - HERB, REG, USE: Tolerances for Residues - 40 CFR 180.441

R

Radiation and Radiation sources – Ionizing radiation for the treatment of food – REG gamma rays of the radionuclides cobalt-60 or cesium-137; electrons generated from machince sources at energies not to exceed 10 million electron volts; and x-rays generated frm machine sources at energies not to exceed 5 million electron volts.- 179.26 radiofrequency radiation including microwave – 179.30; ultraviolet radiation from low pressure mercury lamps at a wavelength of 253.7 nanometers (2,537 Angstroms). - 179.39; pulsed light when source is xenon flashlamps to emit broadband radiation ranging from 200-1,100 nanometers(nm) with pulse duration no longer than 2 milliseconds (msec). – 179.41.

Rapeseed oil, fully hydrogenated - STAB, GRAS, GMP, See REG, Use in peanut butter - 184.1555(a)

Rapeseed oil, fully hydrogenated, superglycerinated - EMUL, GRAS, GMP, See REG, Use in shortenings for cake mixes - 184.1555(b)

Rapeseed oil, low erucic acid - MISC, GRAS, GMP, See REG, Except in infant formula - 184.1555(c); May be declared on label as "Canola Oil"

Rapeseed oil, low erucic acid, partially hydrogenated - MISC, GRAS, GMP, See Reg, Except in infant formula - 184.1555(c)(2)

Red saunders (red sandalwood) - FL/ADJ, REG, GMP - In alc bevs only - 172.510

Regenerated cellulose - MISC, REG, See REG, As an ion-exchange resin - 173.25(a)(20)

Rennet (Rennin) - MISC, GRAS, Milk - Part 131; Cheese and Rel Cheese Prods - Part 133; In animal feeds - 582.1685; GRAS, GMP, See REG - 184.1685

Resin, from formaldehyde, acetone, or tetraethylene-pentamine - MISC, REG, See REG, As an ion-exchange resin - 173.25(a)(8)

Rhatany root - FL/ADJ, REG, GMP, In conjunction w/flavors - 172.510

Rhizopus oryzae - MISC, REG, Source of carbohydrase for prod of dextrose from starch - 173.130

Rhubarb, garden root (Rheum rhaponticum L) - FL/ADJ, REG, GMP, In alc bevs only - 172.510

Rhubarb root - FL/ADJ, REG, GMP, In conjunction w/flavors - 172.510

Riboflavin - NUTR/DS, GRAS/FS, Cereal Flours - Part 137; Alimentary Pastes - Part 139; Bakery Prods - Part 136; GRAS, GMP - 182.5695, 184.1695

Riboflavin-5-phosphate - NUTR/DS, GRAS, GMP - 182.5697, 184.1697

Rice bran wax - CTG/MISC, REG, < 50 m - Ctg for candy - 172.890; < 50 ppm - Ctg for fresh fruits & vegs -72.890; < 2.5% - In chewing gum as plasticizing material - 172.890, 172.615

Robenidine HCl - FEED, REG, 0.2 ppm - As residue in chicken fat & skin - 556.580; 0.1 ppm neg residue - In other edible tissue of chickens - 556.580; Use & other info - 558.515

Rose absolute (otto of roses, attar of roses) - ESO, GRAS - 182.20

Rose buds, flowers, fruit (hips), leaves - ESO, GRAS - 182.20

Rose geranium - ESO, GRAS - 182.20

Roselle - FL/ADJ, REG, GMP, In alc bevs only - 172.510

Rosemary - SP/ESO, GRAS - 182.10, 182.20

Rosidinha (rosadinha) - MISC, REG - 172.615

Rosin (colophony) - FL/ADJ, REG, GMP, In alc bevs only - 172.510

Rosin, gum, glycerol ester - MISC, REG, GMP, Softener for chewing gum - 172.615

Rosin, gum or wood, pentaerythritol ester, partially hydrogenated pentaerythritol ester, or partially hydrogenated glycerol ester - MISC, REG, GMP, Softener for chewing gum - 172.615

Rosin, methyl ester, partially hydrogenated - MISC, REG, GMP, Softener for chewing gum - 172.615; SY/FL - 172.515

Rosi, partial dimerized, calcium salt or partially (catalytically) hydrogenated - CTG, REG, GMP, Ctg on fresh citrus fruit - 172.210

Rosin, polymerized glycerol ester, partially hydrogenated glycerol ester, or partially dimerized glycerol ester - MISC, REG, Softener for chewing gum - 172.615 Rosin, tall oil, glycerol ester - MISC, REG, GMP, Softener for chewing gum - 172.615

Rosin, wood - CTG, REG, GMP, Ctg on fresh citrus fruit - 172.210

Rosin, wood, glycerol ester - MISC, REG, GMP, Softener for chewing gum - 172.615; MISC, REG - 172.735

Rosin, wood, pentaerythritol ester of maleic anhydride - CTG, REG, GMP, Ctg on fresh citrus fruit - 172.210

Roxarsone - FEED/VET, REG, See 3-nitro 4-hydroxy phenyl arsenic acid (Arsenic) for tolerances - 556.60; Use: In chicken & swine feeds - 558.530; In Drinking Water of chickens, turkeys, & swine - 520.2087, 520.2088

Rubber, butadiene-styrene - MISC, REG, Comp of chewing gum base - 172.615

Rubber (natural) smoked sheet and latex solids - MISC, REG, Comp of chewing gum base - 172.615

Rue - SP/ESO, GRAS, < 2 ppm - 184.1698

Rue, oil - FL/ADJ, GRAS, See REG - 184.1699

Rum - FLAV, FS, Cnd Fruits - Part 145

S

Saccharin (ammonicalcium, or sodium) - NNS, REG/ITEM, < 12 mg /fl oz - In bevs and fruit juice drinks & bases or mixes - 180.37; < 20 mg/teaspoonful of sugar sweetening equivalency - In sugar substitutes for cooking or table use - 180.37; < 30 mg/serving - In processed foods - 180.37; Part 145 - Cnd Fruits; Part 150 - Fruit Butters, Jellies, Pres, and Rel Prods

Saffron - SP/ESO, GRAS - 182.10, 182.20 - Not permitted in standardized mayonnaise (169.140) or salad dressing (169.150); Color additive - 73.500

Safrole & any oil containing safrole - ILL, No legal use in food 189.180

Safrole-free extract of sassafras - FLAV, REG, Flavoring in food - 172.580

Sage, Greek - ESO/SP, GRAS - 182.10, 182.20

Sage, Spanish - SP, GRAS - 182.20

St. John's bread - ESO, GRAS - 182.20

St. Johnswort leaves, flowers and caulis - FL/ADJ, REG, GMP - In alc bevs only, Hypericin-free alcohol distillate form only - 172.510

Salicylic acid - MISC, REG, Zero Tolerance - Residue in milk from dairy animals - 556.590; Use - Comp of mastitis formulations - 526.820

Salinomycin - FEED, REG, Use - In chicken feeds - 558.550

Salts of fatty acids - MISC, REG, GMP - 172.863

Sandalwood, white (yellow or East Indian), red - FL/ADJ, REG, GMP - In conjunction w/flavors - 172.510

Sandarac - FL/ADJ, REG, GMP, In alc bevs only - 172.510

Sanitizing solutions - SANI, REG, For use on food proc equipment followed by adequate draining. See individual compounds for limitations on uses and concentrations - 178.1010

Sarsaparilla - FL/ADJ, REG, GMP, Natural flavor - 172.510

Sassafras extract, safrole free - FLAV, REG, GMP - l72.580

Sassafras leaves - FLAV/ADJ, REG, GMP, Must be safrole free - 172.510

Savory, winter or summer - SP/ESO, GRAS - 182.10, 182.20

Schinus molle - ESO, GRAS - 182.20

Selenium as Sodium Selenite or Selenate - FEED, REG, < 0.1 ppm in complete feed - Uses: In complete feeds for chickens, swine, turkeys, sheep, beef cattle, dairy cattle & ducks - 573.920; < 0.3 ppm - In prestarter & starter rations for swine - 573.920

Senna, Alexandria - FL/ADJ, REG, GMP, In conjunction w/flavors - 172.510

Serine (L-form only) - NUTS/DS, REG - 172.320

Serpentaria (Virginia snakeroot) - FL/ADJ, REG, GMP, In alc bevs only - 172.510

Sesame - SP, GRAS - 182.10

Silica aerogel - AF, GRAS - 182.1711

Silicon dioxide - AC, REG, < 2.0% by wt of food - Used only in those foods where anticaking effect is demonstrated - 172.480; REG, < 2% by wt of feed - In feed & feed components as anticaking or grinding agent - 573.940 for use

limit; FS, < 1.0% by wt of finished food - In dried egg prods wi moisture < 5% by wt - 160.105, 160.185; STAB, REG, Stab for use in prod. of beer to be removed by filtration prior to final proc - 172.480; MISC, REG, GMP, As an absorbent for dl--tocopheryl acetate and pantothenyl alcohol in tableted foods for special dietary use - 172.480; REG, GMP, Comp of microcapsules for flavoring oils - 172.230; REG, GMP, Comp of defoaming agents - 173.340; GRAS, Migr to food from paper and paperboard prods - 182.90

Simaruba bark - FL/ADJ, REG, In alc bevs only - 172.510

Simazine - HERB, REG, Tolerances for Residues - 40 CFR 180.213

Sloe berries (blackthorn berries) - ESO, GRAS - 182.20

Smoke prepared by condensing or precipitating wood smoke - FLAV, FS, Past Proc Cheese - Part 133; Cnd Tuna - 161.190

Snakeroot, Canadian (wild ginger) - FL/ADJ, REG, GMP, In conjunction w/flavors - 172.510

Sodium acetate - B&N, GRAS/FS, Art Sw Fruit Jelly - 150.141, Art Sw Fruit Pres and Jams - 150.161; BC, REG, Comp of boiler water additive - 173.310; GRAS, GMP - 184.1721; GRAS, Migr from cotton and cotton fabrics used in dry food pkg - 182.70; In animal feeds - 582.121

Sodium acid phosphate - SEQ, GRAS, Cheeses and Rel Cheese Prods - Part 133; Froz Desserts - Part 135; GRAS, GMP - 182.6085

Sodium acid pyrophosphate - B&N, GRAS/FS, Cereal Flours - Part 137; EMUL, FS, Cheeses and Rel Cheese Prods - Part 133; INH, FS, < 0.5% finished food - Prevent struvite crystal formation in cnd tuna - 161.190(a); In animal feeds - 582.1087

Sodium alginate - STAB, GRAS/FS, Cheeses and Rel Prods - Part 133; Froz Desserts - Part 135; Art Sw Fruit Jelly - 150.141; Art Sw Fruit Pres and Jams - 150.161; GRAS - 184.1724; BC, REG, Comp of boiler water additive - 173.310

Sodium n-alkylbenzene sulfonate (alkyl group predominately C12 and C13 and not less than 95% C10 to C16) - MISC, REG, < 0.2% in wash water - Used in washing or to assist in lye peeling of fruits & vegs - 173.315

Sodium aluminate - BC, REG, Comp of boiler water additive - 173.310; GRAS, Migr to food from paper and paperboard prods - 182.90

Sodium aluminosilicate (sodium silicoaluminate) - AC, GRAS/FS, < 2%, Dried whole eggs and egg yolks - 160.105, 160.185; Grated Cheeses - 133.146; GRAS, < 2% - 182.2727

Sodium aluminum phosphate - MISC, GRAS/FS, Self-rising Flours & Meals - Part 137; EMUL, GRAS/FS, Cheeses, Various - Part 133; GRAS, GMP - 182.1781; In animal feeds - 582.1781

Sodium aluminum sulfate - MISC, GRAS/FS, Cereal Flours - Part 137

Sodium arsanilate - FEED, REG, See Arsenic

Sodium ascorbate - PRES, GRAS, GMP - 182.3731

Sodium benzoate GRAS/FS, < 0.1%, Fruit Pres & Art Sw Fruit Jelly & Pres - 150.141, 150.161; < 0.1%, Margarine - 166.110; Conc. Orange Juice - 146.152, 146.154; GRAS, GMP - 184.1733

Sodium bicarbonate - MISC, GRAS/FS, Cnd Peas - Part 155; Cnd Tomato Paste - 155.191; Cacao Prods - Part 163; Cereal Flours - Part 137; GRAS, GMP - 184.1736; MISC, REG, Used to treat sodium methyl sulfate - 173.385; SANI, REG - 178.1010(b)(41); In animal feeds - 582.1736

Sodium bisulfite - PRES, GRAS, Not in meats or foods recognized as source of Vit B1, etc., See REG - 182.3739; GRAS, FS, Cnd Shrimp - 161.173

Sodium borohydride - MISC, REG, < 310 ppm boron - Used as modifier for hop extract - 172.560

Sodium bromide - SANI, REG, < 200 ppm avail halogen - Adequate drainage - 178.1010

Sodium calcium aluminosilicate hydrated (sodium calcium silicoaluminate) - AC, GRAS, GMP, < 2% - 182.2729

Sodium carbonate - BC, REG, Boiler water additive - 173.310; B&N, GRAS/FS, Cacao Prods - Part 163; Cnd Vegs Part 155; In animal feeds - 582.1742; GRAS, GMP - 184.1742

Sodium carbonate w/sodium mono- & dimethyl naphthalene sulfonates - MISC, REG, For use in potable water systems - 172.824; MISC, < 0.2% in wash water - Used in washing or to assist in lye peeling of fruits and vegs - 173.315

Sodium carboxymethylcellulose (cellulose gum). The sodium salt of carboxymethylcellulose, not less than 99.5% on a dry weight basis - MISC, GRAS, GMP, With one or any mixture of two or more gums permitted - 182.1745; STAB, As optional ingredient in following standardized foods: Cheeses, Various - Part 133; Food Dress - Part 169; Art Sw Jelly & Fruit Jams - Part 150; Froz Desserts - Part 135

Sodium caseinate - MISC, GRAS/FS, Froz Desserts - 135.110, 135.140; Margarine - 166.110; GRAS, GMP - 182.1748; In animal feeds - 582.1748

Sodium chloride - GRAS/FS, Milk and Cream - Part 131; Cheeses and Rel Cheese Prods - Part 133; Cnd Fruits - Part 145; Cnd Vegs - Part 155; Veg Juices - Part 156; Froz Vegs -Part 158; Fish and Shellfish - Part 161; Cacao Prods - Part 163; Margarine - Part 166; Food Dress and Flavorings - Part 169; GRAS, GMP - 182.1; GRAS, Migr from cotton and cotton fabrics used in dry food pckg - 182.70; GRAS, Migr to food from paper and paperboard prods - 182.90

Sodium chlorite - MISC, REG, GMP, Modifier for food starch - 172.892

Sodium citrate - B&N/SEQ, GRAS/FS, Milk and Cream - Part 131; Cheeses and Rel Cheese Prods - Part 133; Art Sw Fruit Jelly, Jam, and Pres - 150.141, 150.161; GRAS, GMP - 182.1751, 182.6751; In animal feeds - 582.1751

Sodium cloxacillin - VET, REG, 0.01 ppm - As residues in milk - 556.165;

Sodium cyclamate - NNS, ILL - Removed from GRAS list 10-21-69 - 189.135

Sodium N-cyclohexyl-N-palmitoyl taurate - SANI, REG, Followed by adequate drainage - 178.1010(b)(40)

Sodium decylbenzenesulfonate - MISC, REG, GMP - Adjuvant for ctg on fresh citrus fruits - 172.210

Sodium diacetate - MISC, GRAS, GMP - 184.1754

Sodium dichloroisocyanurate - SANI, REG, < 100 ppm available halogen - Followed by adequate drainage - 178.1010

Sodium 2,2-dichloropropionate (Dalapon) - PEST, REG, 20 ppm (calc as acid) - In dehydrated citrus pulp for cattle feed from application to citrus during growing season - 40 CFR 186.1500

Sodium dimethyldithiocarbamate - PRES, REG, 3.0 ppm in raw cane - Comb wi Disodium ethylenebisdithiocarbamate for control of microorganisms in cane sugar mills - 173.320; 3.0 ppm in raw cane or sugar beets - Comb w/Disodium ethylene bisdithiocarbamate & ethylene diamine for control of micro organisms in cane sugar and beet sugar mills - 173.320; PEST, REG, Tolerances for Residues -40 CFR 180.152

Sodium dioctylsulfosuccinate - SANI, REG, GMP, Followed by adequate drainage - 178.1010

Sodium dodecylbenzenesulfonate - MISC, REG, < 0.2% in wash water - Surface active agent in commercial detergents used in washing fruits & vegs, or to assist in lye peeling these prods - 173.315

Sodium-2-ethyl-hexylsulfate - MISC, REG, < 0.2% in wash water - Used in washing or to assist in lye peeling of fruits & vegs - 173.315

Sodium ferrocyanide decahydrate - See Prussiate of soda

Sodium fluoride - NUTR, PD/ILL, GMP, X-ref - Fluorine containing compounds

Sodium glucoheptonate - BC, REG, < 1 ppm cyanide in compound - Boiler water additive - 173.310

Sodium gluconate - MISC, GRAS/FS, GMP - 182.6757

Sodium hexametaphosphate - BC, REG, GMP, Boiler water additive - 173.310; SEQ, GRAS/FS, Fruit Jellies - Part 150; Cheese - Part 133; Froz Desserts - Part 135; Food Dress - Part 169; GRAS, GMP - 182.6760; GRAS, Migr to food from paper and paperboard prods - 182.90

Sodium humate - BC, REG, GMP, Boiler water additive - 173.310

Sodium hydroxide - B&N, GRAS/FS, Cocoa Prods - Part 163; MISC, GRAS - 184.1763; BC, REG, GMP, Boiler water additive - 173.310; In animal feeds - 582.1763; MISC, REG, < 1% - In modifying food starch - 172.892; MISC - Used in manufacture of modified hop extract - 172.560; MISC - Used in manufacture of hydroxylated lecithin - 172.814

Sodium hypochlorite - MISC, REG, < 0.055 lb Cl per lb drystarch; 0.45% active O2 from H2O2; and < 25% propyleneoxide, or not to exceed 0.0082 lb Cl per lb of dry starch - In modifying food starch, residual propylene- chlorohydrin < 5 ppm - 172.892; REG, GMP, Used in washing or to assist in the lye peeling of fruits & vegs - 173.315; SANI, See REG, < 200 ppm available Cl - Followed by adequate drainage - 178.1010

Sodium hypophosphite - EMUL/STAB, GRAS, GMP - 184.1764

Sodium iodate - DS, GRAS, Animal feed; Source of Iodine - Trace Mineral - 582.80

Sodium iodide - DS, GRAS, Animal feed; Source of Iodine - Trace Mineral - 582.80; SANI, REG, < 25 ppm I in sln - Followed by adequate drainage - 178.1010

Sodium lactate - MISC, GRAS, GMP - 184.1768

Sodium laurate - MISC, REG, X-ref wi fatty acids, salts of - 172.863

Sodium lauryl sulfate - EMUL, REG, < 125 ppm (0.0125%) - In liquid & froz egg whites - 172.822; < 1,000 ppm (0.1%) - In egg white solids - 172.822; < 5,000 ppm (0.5%) wt of gelatin - Whipping agent in gelatin used in preparing marshmallows - 172.822; AF, REG, < 25 ppm in finished product - As a surfactant in fumaric acid-acidulated dry bev base & fruit juice drinks unless precluded by a food standard - 172.822; SDA, REG < 10 ppm - In the partition of high and low melting fractions of crude veg oils and ani-

mal fats provided partitioning is followed by a conventional refining process that includes alkali neutralization and deodorization of the fats and oils - 172.822; CTG, REG, GMP - For ctg on fresh citrus fruit - 172.210; SANI, REG, GMP - Followed by adequate drainage - 178.1010

Sodium lignosulfonate - BC, REG, GMP, Boiler water additive - 173.310

Sodium lignum sulfonate - FEED, REG, < 4% of finished pellets - As sole pelleting aid in animal feeds - 576.600

Sodium metabisulfite - PRES, GRAS, GMP, Not in meats or foods recognized as a source of Vit B1, etc., See REG - 182.3766; GRAS/FS, Fruit Jellies - Part 150; BC, REG, GMP, Boiler water additive - 173.310

Sodium metaphosphate - EMUL, GRAS/FS, Cheeses - Part 133; GRAS, GMP - 182.6769

Sodium metasilicate - BC, REG, GMP, Boiler water additive - 173.310; MISC, GRAS, GMP - 184.1769a

Sodium methyl sulfate - EMUL, REG, < 0.1% in pectin - As a proc residue in pectin - 173.385

Sodium mono- & di-methyl naphthalene sulfonates - MISC, REG, < 0.2% in wash water - Used in washing or to assist in lye peeling of fruits & vegs - 173.315; REG, < 250 ppm - In sodium carbonate for use in potable water systems - 172.824; AC, REG, < 0.1% - In sodium nitrite used in cured fish and meat - 172.824

Sodium myristate - MISC, REG, X-ref wi fatty acids, salts of - 172.863

Sodium nicotinate - ILL, Request for extension of statute and for filing of petition denied. Deceptive use in ground meat for color retention.

Sodium nitrate - PRES, REG, < 500 ppm - Alone or w/ sodium nitrite as a preservative and color fixative in smoked, cured salmon, shad, & sablefish, or in meat-curing preparations for home curing of meat & meat prods (including poultry & wild game) - 172.170; BC, REG, GMP, Boiler water additive -173.310; PS (by USDA) - As a source of nitrite, w/ or w/o sodium or potassium nitrite, in the prod of cured red meats and poultry - 181.33

Sodium nitrite - PRES, REG, < 200 ppm - Alone or with sodium nitrate as a preservative and color fixative in smoked, cured salmon, shad & sablefish; or in meat curing preparations for home curing of meat & meat prods - 172.175; REG, > 100 ppm to < 200 ppm - In loin muscle of smoked chub - 172.177; REG, < 10 ppm (0.001% sodium nitrite) - Alone as color fixative in smoked, cured tuna - 172.175; REG, < 20 ppm - In cnd pet food containing meat & fish and their by-prods - 573.700; PS (by USDA) - As a color fixative and preservative, wi or without sodium or potassium nitrate, in the curing of red meat and poultry - 181.34

Sodium 1-octanesulfonate - SANI, REG - Comp of sanitizing sln - > 156 to < 312 ppm, isopropyl alcohol may be added as an optional ingredient - Followed by adequate draining - 178.1010(b)(27); Comp of sanitizing sln - Sulfuric acid may be added as an optional ingredient - Followed by adequate draining - 178.1010

Sodium oleate - MISC, REG, X-ref wi fatty acids, salts of - 172.863

Sodium palmitate - MISC, REG, X-ref wi fatty acids, salts of - 172.863

Sodium pantothenate - MISC, GRAS, GMP - 182.5772

Sodium pectinate - MISC, GRAS - In animal feeds - 582.1775; EMUL/STAB, GRAS, GMP - 184.1588

Sodium phosphate (mono-, di-, and tribasic) - MISC, GRAS, GMP - 182.1778; SEQ, GRAS, GMP - 182.6778; DS/NUTR, GRAS, GMP - 182.5778, 182.8778; BC, REG, GMP, Boiler water additive - 173.310; GRAS/FS - Cheeses and Rel Cheese Prods - Part 133; Art Sw Fruit Jellies, Pres, and Jams - 150.141, 150.161

Sodium phosphate (monobasic) (monosodium phosphate) - PRES, GRAS/FS, < 0.5% - Froz Eggs - 160.110; Cacao Prods - Part 163

Sodium phosphate (dibasic) (disodium phosphate) - GRAS, GMP - 182.6290; GRAS/FS- Froz Deserts - Part 135; Enriched Farina - 137.305; Macaroni and Noodle Prods - Part 139;

Sodium polyacrylate-acrylamide resin - MISC, REG, < 2.5% wt of juice or liquor - In beet sugar or cane sugar juice to control organic and mineral scale - 173.5

Sodium polyacrylate - BC, REG, GMP, Boiler water additive - 173.310; MISC, REG, < 3.6 ppm of raw juice weight - Mineral scale inhibition in beet and cane sugar prod - 173.73

Sodium polymethacrylate - BC, REG, GMP, Boiler water additive - 173.310

Sodium potassium tartrate - MISC, GRAS/FS, Cheeses - Part 150; Art Sw Fruit Jellies, Pres, and Jams - 150.141, 150.161; MISC, GRAS, GMP - 184.1804; In animal feeds - 582.1804

Sodium propionate - PRES, GRAS/FS, GMP, Cheeses and Rel Cheese Prods - Part 133; Art Sw Fruit Jellies, Pres, and Jams -150.141, 150.161; Bakery Prods - Part 136; MISC, GRAS, GMP - 184.1784

Sodium pyrophosphate - SEQ, GRAS, GMP - 182.6787

Sodium saccharin - NNS, GRAS/INTERIM, See Saccharin - 180.37

Sodium salts of fatty acids - MISC, REG, GMP, Binder, emulsifier, and anticaking agent in food - 172.860, 172.863

Sodium sesquicarbonate - MISC, GRAS, GMP - 184.1792

Sodium silicate - BC, REG, GMP, Boiler water additive - 173.310;

Sodium silicoaluminate - AC, GRAS/FS, X-ref - Sodium aluminosilicate - Dried whole eggs and egg yolks - 160.105, 160.185

Sodium sorbate - PRES, GRAS/FS, < 0.3% by wt as sorbic acid - Cheeses and Rel Cheese Prods, alone or comb wi potassium sorbate or sorbic acid - Part 133; 0.1% by wt -Fruit Butter, Art Sw Fruit Jelly, Pres, and Jams - 150.110, 150.141, 150.161; < 0.2% in comb or < .1% - Margarine - 160.110; GRAS - Migr to food from paper and paperboard prods - 182.90

Sodium stearate MISC, REG, Comp of chewing gum base - 172.615; X-ref wi 172.863; STAB, PS, Migr from food pckg material - 181.29

Sodium stearoyl lactylate - REG, As follows unless precluded by Food Standards - 172.846; < 0.5% by weight of flour - As dough strengthener, emulsifier, or proc aid in baked prods, pancakes, waffles and prepared mixes of these; < 0.2% by weight of finished food - As surface active agent, emulsifier, or stabilizer in icings, fillings, puddings, toppings and prepared mixes of these; < 0.3% by weight of finished emulsion - As emulsifier or stabilizer in liquid and solid edible fat-water emulsion used as substitutes for milk and cream in coffee; < 0.5% of dry weight - As formulation aid, proc aid, or surface active agent in dehydrated potatoes; < 0.2% by weight - As emulsifier, stabilizer, or texturizer in snack dips and cheese and cheese product substitutes and imitations; < 0.25% by weight of finished food - As an emulsifier, stabilizer, or texturizer in sauces or gravies, prods containing same, and prepared mixes of same

Sodium stearyl fumarate - MISC, REG, < 1% by weight - As conditioning agent in dehydrated potatoes or in processed cereals for cooking unless food standards precludes such use - 172.826; REG, < 0.2% by weight of food - As a conditioning agent in starch thickened or flour-thickened foods - 172.826; STAB, REG, < 1% by weight of flour used - As stabilizing agent in non-yeast leavening bakery prods - 172.826; REG, < 0.5 part/100 part by weight of flour - As dough conditioner in yeast-leavened bakery prods - 172.826, Bakery Prods - Part 136

Sodium sulfachloropyrazine monohydrate - VET, REG, ZERO - Residues in edible tissues of chickens - 556.625; Use: Drinking water - 520.2184

Sodium sulfate - BC, REG, GMP, Boiler water additive - 173.310; MISC, REG, GMP, Comp of chewing gum base - 172.615

Sodium sulfide - MISC, REG, GMP, Comp of chewing gum base - 172.615

Sodium sulfite - BC, REG, GMP, Boiler water additive - 173.310; PRES, GRAS, GMP, Not in meats or foods recognized as source of Vit B1, etc., See REG - 182.3798

Sodium sulfo-acetate derivatives (mono- & di-glycerides) - EMUL, FS, < 0.5% - Margarine - 166.110

Sodium tartrate - MISC, GRAS/FS, Cheeses and Rel Cheese Prods - Part 133; Art Sw Fruit Jellies, Pres, and Jams - 150.141, 150.161; MISC, GRAS, GMP - 184.1801

Sodium tetrapyrophosphate - SEQ, GRAS/FS, X-ref wi tetrasodium pyrophosphate - 182.6789

Sodium thiosulfate - SEQ, GRAS, GMP, < 0.1% - In table salt - 184.1807; < 0.00005% - In alc bevs - 184.1807

Sodium p-toluenesulfonchloramide - SANI, REG, GMP - Followed by adequate drainage - 178.1010(b)(3)

Sodium trichloroisocyanurate - SANI, REG, < 100 ppm available Cl - Followed by adequate drainage - 178.1010

Sodium trimetaphosphate - MISC, REG, < 0.4% as phosphorus - Food starch modifier - 172.892

Sodium tripolyphosphate - BC, REG, GMP, Boiler water additive - 172.310; MISC, REG, < 0.4% as phosphorus - Food starch modifier - 172.892; SEQ, GRAS, GMP - 182.1810, 182.6810; GRAS, Migr from cotton and cotton fibers used in dry food pckg - 182.70; GRAS, Migr to food from paper and paperboard prods - 182.90; GRAS - In animal feeds - 582.1810

Sodium xylenesulfonate - SANI, REG, 31-62 ppm - Comp of sanitizing sln - 178.1010

Solvent Extraction Process for Citric Acid - MISC, REG - 173.280

Sorbic acid - PRES, GRAS/FS, < 0.2% - Cheeses and Cheese Rel Prods - Part 133; PRES, GRAS/FS, < 0.3% by weight as sorbic acid, alone or comb wi potassium or sodium sorbate -Cheeses and Rel Cheese Prods - Part 133; < 0.1% - Art Sw Fruit Jellies, Pres, and Jams - 150.141, 150.161; < 0.2% by wt Concentrated Orange Juice - 146.154; < 0.1% alone or < 0.2% in comb wi other preservatives - Margarine - 166.110; GRAS, GMP - 182.3089

Sorbitan monooleate - EMUL, REG, See REG, Use: In clarification of cane and beet sugar juice or liquor - 173.75

Sorbitan monostearate - EMUL, REG, < 0.4% alone or any comb of Polysorbate 60, 65, or 80 of the weight of finished whipped edible oil topping; > 0.4% in comb if Polysorbate 60 < 0.77% and Sorbitan monostearate < 0.27% of weight of finished whipped edible oil topping - In

whipped edible oil toppings - 172.842; REG, < 0.4% of weight of finished product - In veg oil/water emulsion used as a substitute for milk or cream in bev coffee; Used alone or comb wi Polysorbate 60 and/or 65 - 172.842; REG, < 0.61% - In cakes & cake mixes alone or comb wi < 0.46% Polysorbate 60 and/or < 0.32% Polysorbate 65 - Total amount any comb < 0.66% - 172.842; REG, < 1.0% by weight of finished product - In non-standardized confectionery ctg alone or comb wi < 0.5% Polysorbate 60, Total amount any comb < 1.0% - 172.842; REG, < 0.7% - In cake icing or filling containing shortening, alone or comb wi < 0.46% Polysorbate 60 and/or < 0.32% Polysorbate 65, Total amount any comb < 1.0% - 172.842; CTG, REG, GMP, Alone or wi Polysorbate 60 in formulations of white mineral oil and/or petroleum wax for ctgs on raw fruits & vegs - 172.842; AF, REG, GMP, Comp of defoaming agents - 173.340; FEED, REG, GMP, In mineral premixes & dietary supplies for animal feeds, alone or comb wi Polysorbate 60 - 573.960; MISC, REG, < 1% by weight of dry yeast - Used alone for rehydration aid in prod of active dry yeast - 172.842; FS, Cacao Prods - Part 163

Sorbitol - MISC, GRAS, GMP, See REG - 184.1835; GRAS,Migrate to food from paper and paperboard prods - 182.90

Soybean oil, hydrogenated - GRAS, Migr from cotton and cotton fabrics used in dry food pckg - 182.70

Soybean oil fatty acids, hydroxylated - AF, REG, GMP, Defoamer agent compound - 173.340

Soy protein, isolated - GRAS, Migr to food from paper and paperboard prods; GRAS/FS, Margarine - 166.110

Spearmint - SP/ESO, GRAS - 182.10, 182.20

Spectinomycin - VET, REG, 0.1 ppm (neg res) - In edible tissues of chickens as residue - 556.600; Use: Drinking water - 520.2123b; Injection - 522.2120

Sperm oil - CTG, REG, GMP, Adjuvant in ctgs on fresh citrus fruits - 172.210

Sperm oil, hydrogenated - MISC, REG, GMP, Release agent or lubricant in bakery pans - 173.275

Spike lavender - ESO, GRAS - 182.20

Spruce needles & twigs - FL/ADJ, REG, GMP, In conjunction w/flavors only - 172.510

Stannous chloride - PRES, GRAS/FS, < 15 ppm calc as tin - Cnd Asparagus in glass - 155.200; GRAS/FS, 15-20 ppm calc as tin - Cnd Asparagus in glass wi lids lined wi inert material -155.200; MISC, REG - < 20 ppm calc as tin - For color retention in glass-packed asparagus - 172.180; GRAS, GMP (< 0.0015% calc as tin) - 184.1845

Star anise - SP, GRAS - 182.10

Starch - SANI, REG - Comp, wi or without dextrin, of sanitizing sln - 178.1010

Starch, modified food - MISC, FS, GMP, Salad Dressing - 169.150; Vanilla powder - 169.179; Vanilla-vanillin powder - 169.182; REG, GMP, See REG for types of modified starch - 172.892

Starch, acid modified - GRAS, Migr to food from paper and paperboard prods - 182.90

Starch, pregelatinized - GRAS, Migr to food from paper and paperboard prods - 182.90; FEED, REG, 30 gm/twice daily - Use in water of newborn calves - 520.2155

Starch, unmodified - GRAS/FS, GMP, Cereal Flours and Rel Prods - Part 137; Salad Dressing - 169.150; Vanilla Powder -169.179; Vanilla-vanillin powder - 169.182; GRAS, Migr to food from paper and paperboard prods - 182.90

Starter Distillate - FL/ADJ, GRAS, GMP - 184.1848
Stearic acid - MISC, REG, GMP, Comp of chewing gum - 172.615; REG, X-ref wi fatty acids - 172.860; GRAS, GMP, 184.1090

Stearyl alcohol, synthetic - MISC, REG, GMP, X-ref wi fatty alcohols, synthetic - 172.864

Stearyl citrate - PRES, GRAS/FS, < 0.15% - Margarine - 166.110; GRAS, GMP, < 0.15% - 182.6851

Stearyl monoglyceridyl citrate - STAB, REG, GMP, In shortenings - 172.755

Stearoyl propylene glycol hydrogen succinate - See Succistearin

Sterculia gum (karaya gum) - MISC, GRAS - 184.1349

Storax, or styrax - FL/ADJ, REG, GMP, In conjunction w/flavors only - 172.510

Strawberry aldehyde (C-16 aldehyde) - SY/FL, GRAS, X-ref wi 3-Methyl-3-phenyl glycidic acid ethyl ester - 182.60

Streptomycin - FEED/VET, REG, ZERO - In edible tissues of chickens, turkeys, swine and in eggs as residue - 556.610; Feed use: 558.55; 558.58; 558.62; 558.274; 558.376; 558.430; 558.460; 558.530; Other; Dosage forms - 544.170, 544.173; Injection - 544.275; PEST,REG, Tolerances for Residues - 40 CFR 180.245

Styrene - MISC, REG, See REG - Ion-exchange membrane - 173.20; Ion-exchange resin - 173.25; SY/FL - 172.515

Styrene, polymeric compounds - MISC, REG, See REG - Ion-exchange resins - 173.25

Succinic acid - GRAS/FS - Acidified Skim Milk - 131.144; MISC, GRAS, GMP - 184.1091; In animal feeds - 582.1091

Succinic acid, 2,2-dimethylhydrazide - PLANT REGULATOR, REG, 135 ppm - In dried prunes resulting from application to the growing plums as residue - 193.410

Succinic anhydride - MISC, REG, GMP, Food starch modifier - 172.892

Succinylated gelatin - MISC, REG, < 15% - Comp of microcapsules for flavoring oils - 172.230

Succinylated monoglycerides - EMUL, REG, < 3.0% by weight - In liquid & plastic shortenings - 172.830; MISC, REG/FS, < 0.5% weight of flour - As a dough conditioner - alone or comb/w calcium stearyl-2-lactylate, lactylic stearate or sodium stearyl fumarate (See Part 136) - 172.830

Succistearin (stearoyl propylene glycol hydrogen succinate) - EMUL, REG, GMP, In or wi shortenings & edible oils used in cakes, cake mixes, fillings, icings, pastries, and toppings - 172.765

Sucralose - NUTRS, REG, GMP, Sweetening agent – 172.831

Sucrose - NUTRS, GRAS, GMP - 184.1854

Sucrose acetate isobutyrate (SAIB) - STAB, REG, Used as a stabilizer of emulsions of flavoring oils used in nonalcoholic beverages not to exceed 300 milligrams/kilogram of the finished beverage - 172.833

Sucrose fatty acid esters - REG, GMP, For use as emulsifier, texturizer, and component of fruit ctgs - in chewing gum, confections, frostings, surimi-based seafood products, coffee and tea beverages - See 172.859 for specifications

Sugar beet extract flavor base - FLAV, REG, GMP, In foods - 172.585

Sulfabromomethazine - VET, REG, 0.1 ppm - As residue in uncooked edible tissues of cattle - 556.620; In milk - do; Uses: As bolus - 520.2170

Sulfachloropyrazine - VET, REG, ZERO - Residue in uncooked edible chicken tissue - 556.625; Use: In drinking water of chickens - 520.2184

Sulfachlorpyridazine - VET, REG, 0.1 ppm - In uncooked edible tissue of calves & swine as residue - 556.630; Uses - 520.2200, 522.2200 (Oral Dosage Forms)

Sulfadimethoxine - VET/FEED, REG, 0.1 ppm - In uncooked edible tissues & by-prods of cattle, chickens, turkeys, and ducks as residue - 556.640; 0.01 ppm - In milk as residue - 556.640; Uses & other info - Drinking water, tablets, suspension - 520.2220: As injection - 522.2220

Sulfadimethoxine + Ormetoprim - FEED, REG, Sulfa 0.1 ppm neg residue - Residues in uncooked edible tissues of chickens, turkeys, cattle, ducks, salmonids and catfish - 556.640; Sulfa 0.01 ppm neg residue - Residue in milk - 556.640; Ormet 0.1 ppm neg residue - Residue in edible tissues of chickens, turkeys, ducks, salmonids and catfish - 556.490; Uses: Chicken, turkey, duck and fish (salmonids/catfish) feeds - 558.575

Sulfaethoxypyridazine - FEED/VET, REG, 0.1 ppm - Residue in edible tissues of cattle - 556.650; ZERO - Residues in milk and uncooked edible tissue of swine - 556.650; Use: Drinking water of cattle & swine & as tablets - 522.2240; Injection - 522.2240; Use: Feeds - 558.579

Sulfamerazine (N-[4 methyl-I2-pyrimidnyl] sulfanilamide) - FEED, REG, ZERO - In edible tissues of trout as residue - 556.660; Use if fish feed - 558.582

Sulfamethazine - VET, REG, Use: As tablet or bolus in cattle - 520.2260a; 0.1 ppm - As residue in uncooked edible tissues of cattle, swine, turkeys, chickens - 556.670

Sulfamethazine a) (w/chlortetracycline & penicillin) b) (w/tylosin) - VET/FEED, REG, 0.1 ppm - In uncooked edible tissues of chickens, turkeys, cattle & swine - 556.670; Use in swine feeds - 558.145 (CTC & Pen) and 558.630 (Tylosin); Use in dosage forms - 520.2260

Sulfamethazine sodium - VET, REG, 0.1 ppm - In uncooked edible tissue of chickens, turkeys, cattle & swine - 556.670; Use: In drinking water - 520.2661

Sulfanitran (Acetyl[p-nitrophenyl]sulfanilamide) (w/alklomide) - FEED/VET, REG, ZERO - Residue in edible tissues & by-prods of chickens - 556.680; Feed uses; 558.376; 558.530; 558.376; Other: Drinking water - 520.2320

Sulfaquinoxaline - FEED, REG, Use: Feed for chickens, turkeys, & rabbits - 558.586; Dosage forms: In drinking water for chickens, turkeys, & cattle - 520.2325a; In drench for cattle - 520.2325b

Sulfated butyl oleate - MISC, REG, < 2% by weight in aqueous emulsion - To dehydrate grapes to raisins - 172.270

Sulfathiazole (Combined w/Chlortetracycline and Penicillin) - FEED, REG, 0.1 ppm neg residue - In uncooked edible tissues of swine - 556.690; Uses in swine feeds - 558.155

Sulfiting agents - PRES, GRAS, GMP, X-ref wi individual sulfiting agents - 182.3616, 182.3637, 182.3739, 182.3766, 182.3798, 182.3862

Sulfomyxin (N-sulfomethylpolymyxin B-Sodium salt) - VET, REG, ZERO - In edible tissues of chickens & turkeys - 556.700; Use - 522.2340

Sulfonated lignin, primarily as calcium & sodium salts - SP/ADJ, REG, GMP, X-ref - Calcium lignosulfonate -

573.600; < 4% of finished pellets, of flake grain or fin feed - Pelleting aid, binding aid, of flake grain, source of metabolizable energy in finished feed; < 11% molasses - Surfactant in molasses used in feeds

Sulfonated 9-octadecanoic acid - SANI, REG, 156-312 ppm - Comp of sanitizing sln - Followed by adequate draining - 178.1010

Sulfonated oleic acid, Na salt - SANI, REG, GMP, Comp of sanitizing sln - Followed by adequate draining - 178.1010

Sulfur dioxide - PRES, GRAS/FS, Not in meats or in foods recognized as a source of Vitamin B1, etc. (See REG) - 182.3862; BL, REG, < 0.05% - Food starch modifier - 172.892; FUNG, REG, 10.0 ppm - As residues in/on grapes - 40 CFR 180.444

Sulfuric acid - MISC, GRAS, GMP - 184.1095; In animal feeds -582.1095; REG, GMP, Food starch modifier - 172.892; REG, Manufacture of modified hop extract - 172.560; REG, Manufacture of sodium methyl sulfate - 173.385; SANI, REG, GMP, Comp of sanitizing sln - Followed by adequate drainage - 178.1010

Synthetic fatty alcohols - MISC, REG, GMP, See Fatty Alcohols, synthetic - 172.864

Synthetic flavoring substances - SY/FL, REG, GMP, See 172.515 for listing and adjuvants

Synthetic glycerin - MISC, REG, GMP, In food - 172.866 forspecs

Synthetic isoparaffinic petroleum hydrocarbons - MISC, REG, GMP - 172.882

Synthetic paraffin & succinic derivatives - CTG, REG, GMP, Ctg on fresh citrus, muskmelons, and sweet potatoes - 172.275

T

Tagetes (marigold) oil - FL/ADJ, REG, GMP, As oil only - 172.510

Talc - GRAS - 182.2437 (magnesium silicate)

Tall oil rosin, glycerol ester of - MISC, REG, GMP, Softener for chewing gum - 172.615

Tallow alcohol, hydrogenated - AF, REG, GMP, Comp of defoaming agent - 173.340

Tallow, fatty acids - MISC, REG, GMP, In foods - 172.860 Tallow, hydrogenated, oxidized or sulfated - AF, REG, GMP, X-ref - Comp of defoaming agent - 173.340

Tamarind - ESO, GRAS - 182.20

Tangerine - ESO, GRAS - 182.20

Tannic acid - ESO, GRAS; NAT/FL/ADJ, GRAS, See REG, < .01% Baked Goods & Baking Mixes; < .015% - Alc bevs.; < .005% - Nonalc bevs.; < .04% - Froz dairy desserts & soft candy; 0.013% - Hard Candy; < 0.001% - Meat prods - 184.1097; REG, In rendered animal fat - See 9 CFR 318.7

Tannin (incl quebracho extract) - BC, REG, GMP, Boiler water additive - 173.310

Tansy - FL/ADJ, REG, GMP, In alc bevs only; Finished bev thujone free - 172.510

Tarragon - SP/ESO, GRAS - 182.10, 182.20

Tartaric acid - MISC, GRAS/FS; Art Sw Fruit Jellies, Pres, and Jams - 150.141, 150.161; Acidified Skim Milk - 131.144; GRAS, GMP - 184.1099; In animal feeds - 582.1099

Taurine - FEED, REG, <0.054% of the feed - Nutritional supplement in feed of growing chickens - 573.980

Tea - ESO, GRAS - 182.20

Technical white mineral oil - MISC, REG, < 3.0% - In mineral supplements for animals; < 0.06% - In total ration of feed or feed concentrates - 573.680. Specs - 172.878; 178.3620

Terpene resin (Beta-pinene polymer) - MISC, REG, < 0.07% of weight of capsule - Moisture barrier on soft gelatin capsules; < 7.0% of weight of powder - Moisture barrier on powders of ascorbic acid or its salts - 172.280

Terpene resin (synthetic polymers of -pinene, -pinene, and/or dipentene & natural polymers of -pinene) - MISC, REG, GMP, Comp of chewing gum bases - 172.615

Testosterone propionate - VET, REG, 1.3 ppb - As residues in liver of cattle (heifers) - 556.710; 1.9 ppb - As residues in kidney of cattle (heifers) - do; 2.6 ppb - As residues in fat of cattle (heifers) ; 0.64 ppb - As residues in muscle of cattle (heifers) - do

2,4,5,4'-Tetrachlorodiphenyl sulfone (Tetradifon or Tedion) - PEST, REG, Tolerances for Residues - 40 CFR 180.174

Tetracycline - VET, REG, 0.25 ppm - In uncooked tissues of calves, sheep, swine, chicken & turkeys - 556.720;

Tetraethylenepentamine crosslinked with epichlorohydrin - REG, Comp of ion-exchange resins - 173.25

-[p-(1,1,3,3-Tetramethylbutyl)phenyl]-omega-hydroxypoly (oxyethylene) - PEST, REG, GMP - Adjuvant for pesticide use - 172.710

Tetrasodium pyrophosphate - SEQ, GRAS/FS, Cheeses and Rel Cheese Prods - Part 133; Ice Cream - Part 135; BC, REG, Comp of boiler water additive - 173.310; MISC, REG, < 0.3 ppm in flume water - Used in flume water for washing sugar beets prior to slicing operation - 173.315

Tetrasodium ethylenediaminetetracetate - MISC, REG, < 0.1 ppm in flume water - Used in flume water for washing sugar beets prior to slicing operation - 173.315

TBHQ (tertiary butylhydroquinone) - AOX, REG, < 0.02% of fat or oil - Used alone or in comb wi BHA and/or BHT - Total antioxidants in food except standardized foods which do not list for such use - 172.185

THBP (2,4,5-trihydroxybutyrophenone) - AOX, REG, < 0.02% of fat or oil - Used alone or in comb wi other permitted antioxidants - Total antioxidants, in foods except standardized foods which do not list for such use - 172.190

Thiamine hydrochloride or mononitrate - NUTR/DS, GRAS/FS, Cereal Flours - Part 137; Macaroni/Noodle Prods - Part 139; Bakery Prods - Part 136; 184.1875/1878, 182.5875/5878

Thiabendazole - FEED/VET, REG, 0.1 ppm neg residue - Residue in edible tissues of cattle, goats, sheep and swine - 556.730; 0.05 ppm neg residue - Residue in milk - 556.730; Use: As dosage forms/block - 520.2380; As feed for cattle, goats, sheep, swine & pheasants - 558.615; FUNG, REG, Tolerances for Residues - 40 CFR 180.242

Thidiazuron - PEST, REG, Tolerances for Residues - 40 CFR 180.403

Thiodicarb - INSECT, REG, Tolerances for Residues - 40 CFR 180.407

Thiodipropionic acid - AOX, GRAS, GMP, < 0.02% of fat or oil - Total antioxidants in food - 182.3109; PS, AOX, Migr from food-pkg material (addition of < 0.005% to food) - 181.24

Thiophanate, methyl - FUNG, REG, Tolerances for Residues - 40 CFR 180.371

Thiourea - AOX, BAN, BANNED PRIOR TO FAA - USE ILLEGAL - 189.190

Thistle, blessed (holy thistle) - FL/ADJ, REG, GMP, In alc bevs only - 172.510

Threonine (L form only) - NUTR/DS, REG - 172.320

Thyme, White Thyme - SP/ESO, GRAS - 182.10, 182.20

Thyme, wild or creeping - SP/FLAV/ESO, GRAS - 182.10, 182.20

Thymol iodide - DS, GRAS, In animal feed as source of trace mineral - 582.80

Thymus capitatus (Spanish origanum) - FL/ADJ, REG, GMP, In conjunction w/flavors - 172.510

Tiamulin - FEED, REG, 0.4 ppm - Residue in swine liver - 556.738; Use: Drinking Water - 520.2455; Use: Medicated Feed - 558.600

Tocopherols - PRES, GRAS, GMP - 182.3890, 184.1890; DS/NUTR, GRAS, GMP - 182.5890, 182.8890

Tocopherol acetate - DS/NUTR, GRAS, GMP - 182.5892, 182.8892

Tolu, Balsam, extract ands gum - FL/ADJ, REG, GMP, In conjunction w/flavors - 172.510

Tonka extract - SY/FL, BAN - See "Coumarin" - 189.130

Torula yeast, dried (Candida utilis) - FLAV, REG, folic acid <0.04 mg/g yeast (approx 0.008 mg/g pteroyglutamic acid/g yeast) - In food, X-ref - Dried Yeasts - 172.896

Toxaphene (chlorinated camphene containing 67-69% chlorine) - PEST, REG, 6 ppm - In or on crude soybean oil from use on growing crop as residue - 40 CFR 193.450

Tragacanth (gum tragacanth) - STAB, GRAS/FS, Cheeses and Rel Cheese Prods - Part 133; Froz Desserts - Part 135; Food Dress and Flavorings - Part 169; Art Sw Fruit Jellies, Pres, and Jams - 150.141, 150.161; GRAS - 184.1351

Tralomethrin - INSECT, REG, Tolerances for Residues - 40 CFR 180.422

Trenbolone Acetate - VET, REG, 100 ppb - As residues in uncooked liver tissues of cattle - 556.739; 300 ppb - As residues in uncooked kidney tissues of cattle - do; 400 ppb - As residues in uncooked fat tissues of cattle - do; 500 ppb - As residues in uncooked muscle tissues of cattle - do; Use: As implant in cattle - 522.2476

Trenbolone Acetate & Estradiol - VET, REG, Use: As an implant in feedlot cattle (steers) - 522.2477; As residues in cattle - See 556.739 (Trenbolone Acetate) and 556.240 (Estradiol)

Triacetin (glyceryl triacetate or 1,2,3-propanetriol triacetate) - MISC, GRAS, GMP - 184.1901; FEED, REG, 6 ppm - In cottonseed hulls as residue - 40 CFR 186.5800

Tricalcium phosphate - MISC/DS, GRAS/FS, < 2% by wt - Vanilla Powder 169.179; Cereal Prods - Part 137

Tricalcium silicate - AC, GRAS, GMP, 2% - In table salt - 182.2906

Trichloroethylene - SOLV, REG, 25 ppm (0.0025%) - Decaffeinated ground coffee - 173.290; 10 ppm (0.001%) - Decaffeinated soluble (instant) coffee extract - 173.290; 30 ppm (0.003%) provided that if residues of other chlorinated

solvents are also present, total residues in spice oleoresins < 30 ppm (0.003%) - Spice oleoresins - 173.290

Trichloroisocyanuric acid - SANI, REG, < 100 ppm avail halogen - Followed by adequate drainage - 178.1010

Trichloromelamine - SANI, REG, GMP, See REG - Followed adequate drainage - 178.1010

N-Trichloromethyl mercapto-4-cyclohexene-1,2-dicarboximide - FUM, REG, See Captan

Triclopyr - FUNG, REG, 0.01 ppm - As residue in milk - 40 CFR 180.417; 0.05 ppm - As residue in meat, fat and meat by-prods of cattle, goats, hogs and sheep - do; 0.5 ppm - As residue in liver & kidneys of cattle, goats, hogs and sheep - do

Tricyclazole - FUNG, REG, 30 ppm - Residues in rice bran, rice hulls, and rice polishings

Triethanolamine - MISC, REG, < 2 ppm in flume water - Used in flume water for washing sugar beets prior to slicing operation - 173.315

Triethyl citrate - MISC, GRAS, 0.25% - In dried egg whites - 182.1911

Triethylenetetramine cross-linked with epichlorohydrin - REG, Comp of ion-exchange resins - 173.25

Triflouromethane sulfonic acid - CATALYST, REG, < 0.2% of the reaction mixture to catalyze the directed esterification, <0.2 ppm fluoride as residue in product - In prod of cocoa butter substitute - 173.395

Triflumizole - FUNG, REG, Tolerances for Residues - 40 CFR 180.476

Trifluoromethane sulfonic acid -MISC, REG -173.395

Triforine - FUNG, REG, Tolerances for Residues - 40 CFR 180.382

Trifuran - PEST, REG, 2 ppm - In peppermint & spearmint oil - 40 CFR 185.5900

2,4,5-Trihydroxybutyrophenone (THBP) - AOX, REG, < 0.02% of fat or oil - Total antioxidants, in foods except standardized foods which do not list for such use - 172.190

Trimethylamine - MISC, REG - 173.20

Trisodium nitrilotriacetate - BC, REG, < 5 ppm in boiler feedwater - Not for steam contacting milk or milk prods - 173.310

Trisodium phosphate - EMUL, GRAS/FS, < 3% by weight of cheese - Cheese - Part 133; MISC, FS, Art Sw Fruit Jellies, Pres, and Jams - 150.141, 150.161

Triticum (see dog grass) - ESO, GRAS - 182.20

Tryptophan (L-form only) - NUTR/DS, REG - l72.320

Tuberose - ESO, GRAS - 182.20

Turmeric - SP/ESO, GRAS, Not permitted in standardized mayonnaise (169.140) & salad dressing (169.150) - 182.20

Tunu - MISC, REG, Comp of chewing gum base - 172.615

Turpentine - FL/ADJ, REG, GMP, In conjunction w/flavors - 172.510

Tylosin - FEED/VET, REG, 0.05 ppm - Residue in milk - 556.740; 0.2 ppm - Residue in edible tissues of poultry, cattle & swine - do; Residues in eggs - do; Use: Drinking water - 520.2640; As Injection - 522.2640; For cattle, chicken, & swine feed uses see: 558.55; 558.58; 558.274; 558.625; 558.630; 558.680

Tylosin & Sulfamethazine - FEED, REG, 0.2 ppm - Use in swine feeds - 558.630; Residues (Tylosin) in edible tissue of swine - 556.740; 0.1 ppm - Residues (Sulfamethazine) in edible tissues of swine - 556.740

Tyrosine (L-form only) - NUTR/DS, REG - 172.320

U

Urea - GRAS, GMP, As formulation/fermentation aid in yeast -raised bakery prods, alc bevs, and gelatin prods - 184.1923

Urease enzyme from Lactobacillius fermentum - MISC, GRAS, To inhibit urethane formation in wine - 184.1924

V

Valerian rhizome & roots - FL/ADJ, REG, GMP, In conjunction w/flavors - 172.510

Valeric acid - MISC, REG, < 1% aliphatic acids - In lye peeling soln for fruits & vegs - 173.315

Valine (L-form only) - NUTR/DS, REG - 172.320

Vanilla - FLAV, GRAS/FS Cacao Prods - Part 163; Food Flavorings - Part 169; SP/ESO, GRAS - 182. 10, 182.20

Vanillin - SYN/FL, GRAS/FS - Cacao Prods - Part 163; Food Flavorings - Part 169; GRAS - 182.60; Migr to food from paper and paperboard prods - 182.90

Vegetable oils, brominated - FL/ADJ, INTERIM/REG, < 15 ppm - In fruit flavored bevs where not prohibited by Standards - 180.30

Veronica - FL/ADJ, REG, GMP, In alc bevs only - 172.510

Vervain, European - FL/ADJ, REG, GMP, In alc bevs only - 172.510

Verxite flakes - FEED, REG, < 1% - Anticaking or blending agent in ruminant feeds - 573.1000

Verxite granules (Exfoliated hydrobiotite) - FEED, REG, < 5% - Nonnutritive bulking agent in poultry feed - 573.1000; Anticaking, blending agent, pelleting aid, or non-nutritive carrier of nutrients in poultry, swine, & ruminant feed - do; < 1.5% - Anticaking, blending agent, etc. in dog food - 573.1000

Verxite grits - FEED, REG, < 1% - Partial roughage replaceent in ruminant feeds - 573.1000

Vetiver - FL/ADJ, REG, GMP, In alc bevs only - 172.510

Vinyl acetate - MISC, REG, Modifier for food starch - 172.892

Vinyl chloride-vinylidene chloride copolymer - CTG, REG, GMP, Comp of ctg on fresh citrus fruits - 172.210

Violet flowers & leaves - ESO, GRAS - 182.20

Violet leaves absolute - ESO, GRAS - 182.20

Violet, Swiss - FL/ADJ, REG, GMP, In conjunction w/flavors - 172.510

Virginiamycin - FEED, REG, 0.4 ppm - Residue in edible tissues, kidney, skin, & fat of swine - 556.750; 0.3 ppm - Residue in swine liver - 556.750; 0.1ppm - Residue in swine muscle - 556.750; Use in swine & chicken feeds - 558.635

Vitamin A - NUTR/DS, GRAS, GMP - 182.5930, 184.1930; GRAS/FS, Milk and Cream - Part 131; Cheeses and Rel Cheese Prods - Part 133; Mellorine - 135.130; Margarine - 166.110

Vitamin A acetate - NUTR/DS, GRAS, GMP - 182.5933, 184.1930

Vitamin A palmitate - NUTR/DS, GRAS, GMP - 182.5936, 184.1930

Vitamin B - NUTR/DS, GRAS

Vitamin B12 - NUTR/DS, GRAS, GMP - 182.5945, 184.1945

Vitamin C - See Ascorbic Acid

Vitamin D - NUTR/DS, GRAS, Nutrient supplement - 182.5950, 182.5953, 184.1950; > 350 IU/100 g, Cereal Prods - Part 137; 90 IU/100g, Macaroni and Noodle Prods - Part 139; 42 IU/100g, Milk - Part 131; 89 IU/100g - Milk prods

Volatile Fatty Acids: Isobutyric Acid, Isovaleric Acid, methylbutyric Acid, m-Valeric Acid (As calcium or ammonium salts) - ADD, REG, 48-54% as ammonia salts - Use in dairy cattle feeds as source of energy - 573.914; 58-72% as calcium salts

W

Walnut husks, leaves & green nuts - FL/ADJ, REG, GMP, In conjunction w/flavors - 172.510

Wax, paraffin (Fischer-Tropsch) - MISC, REG, GMP, Comp of chewing gum base - 172.615

Wax, paraffin - CTG, FS, Surface ctg for certain cheeses - Part 133

Wheat Starch - GRAS, Migr from cotton and cotton fabrics used in dry food pkg - 182.70

Wheat gluten, vital - GRAS, GMP - 184.1322

Whey, fermented, ammoniated, condensed - FA, REG, > 30% of dietary crude protein - Source of protein & nonprotein nitrogen for cattle - 573.450

Whey, reduced lactose whey, reduced minerals whey, whey protein concentrate - GRAS - 184.1979, 184.1979a-c; GRAS/FS, Froz Desserts - Part 135

White Mineral Oil – See Mineral Oil, White - 172.878

Whole fish protein concentrate - DS, REG, See REG, < 20 g/ day when consumed regularly by children up to 8 yrs of age - For household use only - package size < 1 lb net wt - 172.385; < 8 ppm total fluoride content of finished food - When used in manufactured food - 172.385

Wild Cherry bark - ESO, GRAS - 182.20

Wood rosin - CTG, REG, GMP, X-ref wi Rosin, wood, For fresh citrus fruits - 172.210

Woodruff, sweet - FL/ADJ, REG, GMP, In alc bevs only - 172.510

X

Xanthan gum - EMUL, REG, GMP, In foods which standards do not preclude use - 172.695; FS, Food Dress -Part 169; Cheeses and Rel Cheese Prods - Part 133; 0.25% max use level liquid feeds for ruminants - In animal feeds (stabilizer, thickener, suspending agent) - 573.1010; 0.1% in calf milk replacer (as fed)

Xylitol - MISC, REG, Amt used is not > that required to produce its intended effect - May be safely used in foods for special dietary uses - 172.395

Y

Yarrow - FL/ADJ, REG, GMP, In bevs only, finished bevs Thujone free - 172.510

Yeast (Bakers, Saccharomyces cerevisiae) - FS, Egg Prods - Part 160

Yeast, dried - DS, REG - In food provided total folic acid content < 0.04 mg/g of yeast - 172.896; NUTR, GRAS/FS, < 1.5% by wt of finished food - Enriched Corn Grits, Enriched Corn Meal - 137.235, 137.260; Macaroni and Noodle Prods - Part 139

Yeast, dried, inactive - FLAV, REG/FS, < 0.25 parts for each 100 parts by weight of flour used - Bakery Prods - Part 136; Macaroni and Noodle Prods - Part 139; DS, REG - See Yeast, dried - 172.896

Yeast, dried, irradiated - NUTR, GRAS/DS, Enriched Farina as source of Vitamin D - 137.305

Yeast extract (Bakers) - FL/ADJ, GRAS, < 5% in food, See Specs - 184.1983

Yeast, malt sprout extract - FL/ADJ, REG, GMP, As a flavor enhancer - 172.590

Yeast, torula, dried - DS, REG, GMP - In food provided total folic acid content < 0.04 mg/g of yeast - 172.896; X-Ref wi Torula Yeast

Yellow prussiate of soda (sodium ferrocyanide decahydrate) - See Prussiate of Soda, Yellow

Yerba santa - FL/ADJ, REG, GMP, In conjunction w/flavors - 172.510

Ylang-ylang - ESO, GRAS - 182.20

Yucca, Joshua-tree - FL/ADJ, REG, GMP, In conjunction w/flavors - 172.510

Yucca, Mohave - FL/ADJ, REG, GMP, In conjunction w/flavors - 172.510

Z

Zein, powder - GRAS, GMP - 184.1984

Zedoary - SP, GRAS - 182.10

Zedoary bark - ESO, GRAS - 182.20

Zeranol (Zearalanol) - VET, REG, ZERO - Residues in uncooked edible tissues of sheep - 556.760; 150 ppb - As residues in uncooked edible muscle tissue of cattle - 556.760; 300 ppb - As residues in uncooked liver of cattle - do; 450 ppb - As residues in uncooked kidney of cattle - do;

600 ppb - As residues in uncooked fat of cattle - do; Use as implant - 522.2680

Zinc (acetate, carbonate, chloride, oxide, sulfate) - NUTR, GRAS, As nutritional dietary supplement in animal feed - 582.80

Zinc bacitracin - FEED, REG, See Bacitracin

Zinc chloride - NUTR/DS, GRAS, GMP - 182.5985, 182.8985

Zinc gluconate - NUTR/DS, GRAS, GMP - 182.5988, 182.8988

Zinc methionine sulfate - NUTR, REG, Tablets - See 172.399 for specs

Zinc oxide - NUTR/DS, GRAS, GMP - 182.5991, 182.8991

Zinc stearate - NUTR/DS, GRAS, GMP, Free from chick edema factor - 182.5994, 182.8994

Zinc sulfate - NUTR/DS, GRAS, GMP - 182.5997, 182.8997; GRAS, Migr to food from paper and paperboard prods - 182.90

Zoalene - FEED, REG, 2 ppm - Residues in uncooked fat of chickens - 556.770; 3 ppm - Residues in uncooked muscle meat of chickens - do; 3 ppm - Residues in uncooked muscle meat & liver of turkeys - do; 6 ppm - Residues in uncooked liver & kidneys of chickens - do; Use in chicken & turkey feeds - 558.60; 558.62; 558.78; 558.128; 558.248; 558.274; 558.450; 558.530; 558.680

COLOR ADDITIVE STATUS LIST

Preface

This status list provides current information concerning color additives, and will enable you to determine the status and limitations of most color additives likely to be encountered in a food, drug, device, or cosmetic establishment.

To maintain concise form, this list is limited in many respects involving certification, regulations, labeling, etc. For specific details concerning these matters, please refer to the source documents, Code of Federal Regulations (CFR, Title 21, Parts 70 to 82) and to the Federal Food, Drug, and Cosmetic Act, as amended, Sections 601(e), 602(e), 706, and as it pertains to Sections 201(s)(3) and (t), 402(c), 403(m), 501(a), and 502(m).

Any color additives not included in this listing and found in the possession of manufacturers or processors where they may be used in foods, drugs, devices, or cosmetics should be referred to your district for consideration. Your Servicing Laboratory for color analysis is also a good reference source.

LAKES: Color additive lakes are provisionally listed under 21 CFR 81.1. Part 82 of 21 CFR explains how lakes may be manufactured and named and lists the color additives that may be used to manufacture lakes. All lakes are subject to certification.

Examples of nomenclature of lakes:

1.   The name of a lake is formed from the name of the color additive combined with the name of the basic radical and the word "Lake". For example, the name of the lake prepared by extending the aluminum salt of FD&C Blue No. 1 upon alumina would be FD&C Blue No. 1 - Aluminum Lake.

2.   If a lake is prepared by extending an FD&C color additive on a substratum other than alumina, the symbol "FD&C" will be replaced by "D&C". For example, the name of the lake prepared by extending the aluminum salt of FD&C Blue No. 1 upon a substratum other than alumina would be D&C Blue No. 1- Aluminum Lake.

NOTE: You are cautioned that this Exhibit is condensed and should be used for screening and guidance only. When you encounter situations involving possible violations of color additive regulations check the latest basic document as indicated in the second paragraph of this preface. Be certain of the complete status and report the facts. It is the district responsibility to instigate appropriate action, not yours. Do not advise firms to destroy stocks of possible suspect merchandise or institute recalls without district clearance.

LIST 1

Color Additives subject to certification and permanently listed (unless otherwise indicated) for FOOD DRUG and COSMETIC use.

(None of these colors may be used in products that are for use in the area of the eye, unless otherwise indicated).

FD&C Blue #1 - For food, drug and cosmetic use, including drugs and cosmetics for eye area - GMP - 74.101, 74.1101, 74.2101, 82.101 (Manganese dioxide now permitted in manufacturing process)

FD&C Blue #1 Aluminum Lake - For drug and cosmetic use in area of the eye - GMP

FD&C Blue #2 - For food and ingested drug use and for nylon surgical sutures (Limit £ 1% by wt of the suture) - GMP - 74.102, 74.1102, 82.102

FD&C Green #3 - For food, drug and cosmetic use - GMP -74.203, 74.1203, 74.2203, 82.203

FD&C Red #3 - For food and ingested drugs - GMP - 74.303, 74.1303. Lake use terminated 2-1-90; All cosmetic uses terminated 2-1-90.

FD&C Red #40 - For food, drug and cosmetic use, including drugs and cosmetics for eye area - GMP - 74.340, 74.1340, 74.2340

FD&C Red #40 Aluminum Lake - For drug and cosmetic eye area use - GMP

FD&C Yellow #5 - For food, drug and cosmetics, including drugs and cosmetics for eye area - GMP - 74.705, 74.1705, 74.2705, 82.705

FD&C Yellow #5 Aluminum Lake - For drug and cosmetic eye area use - GMP

FD&C Yellow #6 - For food, drug and cosmetics - GMP - 74.706, 74.1706, 74.2706, 82.706

FD&C Lakes (See Preface of this exhibit) - Provisionally listed. May be prepared from any of the above certified FD&C colors, except FD&C Red #3 - GMP - 81.1, 82.51

Citrus Red #2 - Permanently listed for use only in coloring of skins of mature oranges. Limit of 2 ppm calculated on basis of whole fruit weight - 74.302

Orange B - Permanently listed for use in coloring surfaces and casings of frankfurters or sausages. Limit £ 150 ppm by wt. of finished product - 74.250

The following colors, previously commonly used, are no longer authorized for use:
FD&C Green #1
FD&C Green #2
FD&C Red #1
FD&C Red #2 (Removed from list on 2-13-76)
FD&C Red #3 (Lakes removed from list for all uses on 2/1/90. Straight color removed from list for cosmetic and external drug use 2/1/90.)
FD&C Red #4 (Removed from list for ingested uses on 9-23-76)
FD&C Violet #1 (Removed from list on 4-10-73)

LIST 2

Color additives subject to certification and permanently listed (unless otherwise indicated) for <u>DRUG AND COSMETIC</u> use.
(None of these colors may be used in products that are for use in the area of the eye)

D&C Green #5 - For drugs generally and sutures (Limit £ 0.6% by wt of suture) - GMP - 74.1205, 74.2205, 82.1205

D&C Orange #5 - For mouthwashes and dentifrices that are ingested drugs (GMP) and for externally applied drugs, limit £ 5 mg per day; For mouthwashes and dentifrices that are ingested cosmetics and for external cosmetics, GMP; for lipsticks, limit £ 5% by wt of finished product - 74.1255, 74.2255, 82.1255

D&C Red #6 - For drugs (combined total of D&C Red No.6 & D&C Red No. 7 ≤ 5 mg per day); For cosmetics (GMP) - 74.1306, 74.2306, 82.1306

D&C Red #7 - For drugs (combined total of D&C Red No.6 & D&C Red No. 7 ≤ 5 mg per day); For cosmetics (GMP) - 74.1307, 74.2307, 82.1307

D&C Red #21 - For drugs generally and cosmetics - GMP - 74.1321, 74.2321, 82.1321

D&C Red #22 - For drugs generally and cosmetics - GMP - 74.1322, 74.2322, 82.1322

D&C Red #27 - For drugs generally and cosmetics - GMP - 74.1327, 74.2322, 82.1327

D&C Red #28 - For drugs generally and cosmetics - GMP - 74.1328, 74.2328, 82.1328

D&C Red #30 - For drugs generally and cosmetics - GMP - 74.1330, 74.2330

D&C Red #33 - For ingested drugs other than mouthwashes and dentifrices, limit ≤ 0.75 mg per day; for externally

applied drugs, mouthwashes and dentifrices, GMP; Cosmetics: lipsticks, limit ≤ 3% by wt of finished product; mouthwashes, dentifrices and externally applied cosmetics, GMP - 74.1333, 74.2333, 82.1333

D&C Red #36 - For ingested drugs other than mouthwashes and dentifrices, limit ≤ 1.7 mg per day (if taken continuously for < 1 year); ≤ 1.0 mg per day (if taken continuously for > 1 year); for externally applied drugs, GMP; Cosmetics: lipsticks, limit ≤ 3% by wt of finished product; externally applied cosmetics, GMP - 74.1336, 74.2336, 82.1336

D&C Yellow #10 - For drugs generally and cosmetics - GMP -74.1710, 74.2710, 82.1710

D&C Lakes (See Preface of this Exhibit) - Provisionally listed. May be prepared from any of the FD&C or D&C color additives listed in part 82

The following colors, previously commonly used, are no longer authorized for use:

D&C Black #1	D&C Orange #15	D&C Red #13
D&C Blue #6	D&C Orange #16	D&C Red #14
D&C Blue #7	D&C Orange #17	D&C Red #18
D&C Green #7	D&C #5	D&C Red #19
D&C Orange #3	D&C Red #8	D&C Red #24
D&C Orange #8	D&C Red #9	D&C Red #29
D&C Orange #14	D&C Red #10	D&C Red #35
D&C Red #11	D&C Red #37	D&C Red #12
D&C Red #38		

LIST 3

Color Additives subject to certification and permanently listed (unless otherwise indicated) for use in <u>EXTERNALLY APPLIED DRUGS & COSMETICS</u>.
(None of these colors may be used in products that are for use in the area of the eye)

D&C Brown #1 - GMP - 74.2151

FD&C Red #4 - For use only in externally applied drugs and cosmetics - GMP - 74.1304, 74.2304, 82.304

D&C Red #17 - GMP - 74.1317, 74.2317, 82.1317

D&C Red #31 - GMP - 74.1331, 74.2331, 82.1331

D&C Red #34 - GMP - 74.1334, 74.2334, 82.1334

D&C Red #39 - For use only in externally applied quaternary ammonium germicidal solutions (limit ≤ 0.1% by wt of the finished product) - 74.1339

D&C Violet #2 - GMP - 74.1602, 74.2602, 82.1602

Ext. D&C Violet #2 - For external cosmetics only - GMP - 74.2602a

D&C Blue #4 - GMP - 74.1104, 74.2104, 82.1104

D&C Green #6 - GMP - 74.1206, 74.2206, 82.1206

D&C Green #8 - Limit ≤ 0.01% by wt of finished drug or cosmetic - 74.1208, 74.2208

D&C Yellow #7 - GMP- 74.1707, 74.2707, 82.1707

Ext. D&C Yellow #7 - GMP - 74.1707a, 74.2707a, 82.2707a

D&C Yellow #8 - GMP - 74.1708, 74.2708, 82.1708

D&C Yellow #11 - GMP - 74.1711, 74.2711

D&C Orange #4 - GMP - 74.1254, 74.2254, 82.1254

D&C Orange #10 - GMP - 74.1260, 74.2260, 82.1260

D&C Orange #11 - GMP - 74.1261, 74.2261, 82.1261

Ext. D&C Lakes (See Preface of this Exhibit) - May be prepared from any of the above legal Ext. D&C colors - GMP -81.1, 82.2051

The following colors, previously commonly used, are no longer authorized for use:

Ext D&C Blue #1	Ext D&C Red #1
Ext D&C Red #11	Ext D&C Yellow #3
Ext D&C Blue #4	Ext D&C Red #2
Ext D&C Red #13	Ext D&C Yellow #5
Ext D&C Green #1	Ext D&C Red #3
Ext D&C Red #14	Ext D&C Yellow #6
Ext D&C Orange #1	Ext D&C Red #8
Ext D&C Red #15	Ext D&C Yellow #9
Ext D&C Orange #3	Ext D&C Red #10
Ext D&C Yellow #1	Ext D&C Yellow #10
Ext D&C Orange #4	

LIST 4

Color additives exempt from certification and permanently listed for FOOD use.

Algae Meal, dried - For use in chicken feed only. Ethoxyquin content ≤ 0.3% (Ethoxyquin content in final feed ≤ 150 ppm). 73.275

Annatto extract - GMP - 73.30

Astaxanthin - For use in salmonid fish feed only. Limit < 8 mg per kg of finished feed - 73.35

Beet juice - (as vegetable juice) - GMP - 73.260

Beet Powder (Dehydrated beets) - GMP - 73.40

Beta carotene - GMP - 73.95

Canthaxanthin - Limit: ≤ 30 mg/lb of solid or semisolid food or per pint of liquid food; may also be used in broiler chick-en feed at an amount ≤ 4.41 mg per kg (4 gm/ton) of complete feed - 73.75

Caramel - GMP - 73.85

Carmine - GMP - 73.100

Carrot oil - GMP - 73.300

Cochineal extract - GMP - 73.100

Corn Endosperm Oil - For use only in chicken feed - 73.315

Toasted partially defatted cooked cottonseed flour - GMP - 73.140

Ferrous Gluconate - To color ripe olives only - GMP - 73.160

Ferrous Lactate - To color ripe olives only - GMP - 73.165

Fruit juice - GMP - 73.250

Grape Color Extract - To color nonbeverage food - 73.169

Grape Skin Extract (enocianina) - To color still and carbonated drinks and ades, beverage bases and alcoholic beverages (in accordance with Parts 4 & 5 of 27 CFR) - 73.170

Haematococcus Algae Meal – For use in salmonid fish feed only. The quantity of astaxanthin in finished feed from haematococcus algae meal when used alone or in combination with other astaxanthin color additive sources listed in part 73, shall not exceed 80 mg per kg of finished feed – 73.185

Synthetic Iron Oxide - For coloring sausage casings and for cat & dog food. Limit: ≤ 0.1% by wt of finished food (humans) and 0.25% by wt of finished food for dogs and cats - 73.200

Paprika & Paprika oleoresin - GMP - 73.340; 73.345

Phaffla yeast – For use in salmonid fish feed only. The quantity of astaxanthin in finished feed from phaffla yeast when used alone or in combination with other astaxanthin color additive sources listed in part 73, shall not exceed 80 mg per kg of finished feed – 73.355

Riboflavin - GMP - 73.450

Saffron - GMP - 73.500

Tagetes Meal & Extract (Aztec Marigold) - For use in chicken feed only. Ethoxyquin content ≤ 0.3% (Ethoxyquin content in final feed ≤ 150 ppm) - 73.295

Titanium dioxide - Limit: ≤ 1.0% by wt of food - 73.575

Turmeric & Turmeric oleoresin - GMP - 73.600 & 73.615

Ultramarine Blue - To color salt for animal feed only; Limit: ≤ 0.5% by wt of salt - 73.50

Vegetable Juice - GMP - 73.260

Beta-Apo-8'-Caroteneal - Limit: ≤ 15 mg/lb of solid or semisolid food or per pint of liquid food - 73.90

The following colors, previously commonly used, are no longer authorized for use:

Alkanet (Alkane)	Ferrous sulfate
Calcium carbonate	Cudbear Logwood, chips & extract
Carbon black	Ferric chloride
Charcoal - NF XI	Safflower (American saffron)

LIST 5

Color additives exempt from certification and permanently listed for <u>DRUG</u> use.

Alumina - Drugs generally - GMP - 73.1010

Aluminum Powder - Externally applied drugs, including those for eye area use - GMP - 73.1645

Annatto Extract - Drugs generally, including those for eye area use - GMP - 73.1030

Bismuth oxychloride - Externally applied drugs only, including those for eye area - GMP - 73.1162

Bronze Powder - Externally applied drugs only, including those for eye area - GMP - 73.1646

Calcium carbonate - Drugs generally - GMP - 73.1070

Canthaxanthin - GMP - Ingested drugs only - 73.1075

Caramel - Drugs generally - GMP - 73.1085

Carmine - Drugs generally - GMP - 73.1100

Chlorophyllin, copper complex - To color dentrifices that are drugs only. Limit ≤ 0.1% - 73.1125

Cochineal extract - Drugs generally - GMP - 73.1100

Beta-carotene, natural and synthetic - Drugs generally, including those for eye area - GMP - 73.1095

Chromium hydroxide, green - Externally applied drugs, including those for eye area - GMP - 73.1326

Chromium oxides greens - Externally applied drugs, including those for eye area - GMP - 73.1327

Copper, metallic powder - Externally applied drugs, including those for eye area - GMP - 73.1647

Potassium sodium copper chlorophyllin (Chlorophyllin copper complex) - To color dentifrices that are drugs only. Limit ≤ 0.1% - 73.1125

Dihydroxyacetone - Externally applied drugs intended to impart a color to the human body - GMP - 73.1150

Ferric Ammonium ferrocyanide (Iron Blue) - Externally applied drugs, including those for eye area - GMP - 73.1298

Ferric Ferrocyanide (Iron Blue) - Externally applied drugs, including those eye area - GMP - 73.1299

Guanine (Pearl essence) - Externally applied drugs, including those eye area - GMP - 73.1329

Mica - To color dentifrices and externally applied drugs, including those for eye area - GMP - 73.1496

Pyrophyllite - Externally applied drugs - GMP - 73.1400

Synthetic iron oxide - Drugs generally. Limit for ingested drugs ≤ 5 mg elemental iron per day - 73.1200

Talc - Drugs generally - GMP - 73.1550

Titanium dioxide - Drugs generally, including those for eye area - GMP - 73.1575

Zinc oxide - Externally applied drugs, including those for eye area - GMP - 73.1991

The following colors, previously commonly used, are no longer authorized for use:

Bone Black	Charcoal NF XI
Chlorophyll copper complex	Ultramarine Blue
Fustic	

LIST 6

Color additives exempt from certification and permanently listed for <u>COSMETIC</u> use.

Aluminum Powder - Externally applied cosmetics, including those for eye area - GMP -73.2645

Annatto - Cosmetics generally, including those for eye area - GMP - 73.2030

Bismuth Citrate - For cosmetics intended to color hair on scalp only (Not for coloring eyelashes or eyebrows or other body hair). Limit ≤ 0.5% - 73.2110

Bismuth oxychloride - Cosmetics generally, including those for eye area - GMP - 73.2162

Bronze powder - Cosmetics generally, including those for eye area - GMP - 73.2646

Caramel - Cosmetics generally, including those for eye area -GMP - 73.2085

Carmine - Cosmetics generally, including those for eye area -GMP - 73.2087

Beta-carotene - Cosmetics generally, including those for eye area - GMP - 73.2095

Chromium hydroxide green - Externally applied cosmetics, including those for eye area - GMP - 73.2326

Chromium oxide greens - Externally applied cosmetics, including those for eye area - GMP -73.2327

Copper, metallic powder - Cosmetics generally, including those for eye area - GMP - 73.2647

Dihydroxyacetone - Externally applied cosmetics - GMP - 73.2150

Disodium EDTA-Copper - Cosmetic shampoos - GMP - 73.2120

Ferric ammonium ferrocyanide - Externally applied cosmetics, including those for eye area - GMP - 73.2298

Ferric ferrocyanide - Externally applied cosmetics, including those for eye area - GMP - 73.2299

Guanine (Pearl essence) - Cosmetics generally, including those for eye area - GMP - 73.2329

Guaiazulene (Azulene) - Externally applied cosmetics - GMP -73.2180

Henna - For coloring hair only, not for coloring eyelashes or eyebrows - 73.2190

Iron oxides - Cosmetics generally, including those for eye area - GMP - 73.2250

Lead Acetate - For coloring hair only, not for coloring mustaches, eyelashes, eyebrows or other body hair. Limit ≤0.6% (wt/v) - 73.2396

Luminescent zinc sulfide – Externally applied cosmetics (nail polish and facial) – 73.2995

Manganese Violet - Cosmetics generally, including those for eye area - GMP - 73.2775

Mica - Cosmetics generally, including those for eye area - GMP - 73.2496

Potassium sodium copper chlorophyllin (chlorophyllin copper complex) - For coloring cosmetic dentifrices. Limit ≤ 0.1%. May be used only in combination with the substances listed in 21 CFR 73.2125(b)(2) - 73.2125

Pyrophyllite - Externally applied cosmetics - GMP - 73.2400

Silver - For coloring fingernail polish. Limit ≤ 1% - 73.2500

Titanium dioxide - Cosmetics generally, including those for eye area - GMP - 73.2575

Ultramarines (Blue, Green, Pink, Red & Violet) - Externally applied cosmetics, including those for eye area - GMP - 73.2725

Zinc oxide - Cosmetics generally, including those for eye area - GMP - 73.2991

The following colors, previously commonly used, are no longer authorized for use:

4-Methyl-7-diethyl-aminocoumarin(MDAC)	
Alloxan	Cochineal
Bone Black	Fuller's Earth
Carbon Black (Channel Process)	
Carminic Acid	Graphite
Chlorophyll Copper Complex	
Cobaltous Aluminate (Cobalt Blue)	
Gloss White	Lithopone
Kieselguhr (Diatomite)	Sienna
Logwood (Gluewood, Campeche wood)	
Potassium Ferrocyanide	B-Methyl umbelliferone
Vermiculite	Umber
Zirconium oxide	Zirconium Silicate

LIST 7

Color Additives exempt from certification (unless otherwise indicated) and permanently listed for use in MEDICAL DEVICES

1,4-Bis[(2-hydroxyethyl)amino]-9,10-anthracenedione bis(2-propenoic)ester copolymers - For use in contact lenses - GMP - 73.3100

1,4-Bis[(2-methylphenyl)amino]9,10-anthracenedione - For use in contact lenses – GMP – 73.3105

1,4-Bis[4(2-methacryloxyethyl) phenylamino] 9,10-anthraquinone copolymers – For use in contact lenses – GMP – 73.3106

Carbazole violet - For use in contact lenses - GMP- 73.3107

Chlorophyllin-copper complex - For coloring polymethyl-meth-acrylate bone cement. Limit ≤ 0.003% by wt - 73.3110

Chromium-Cobalt-Aluminum oxide - For use in polyethylene surgical sutures. Limit ≤ 2% by wt - 73.1015

Chromium oxide greens - For use in contact lenses - GMP - 73.3111

C.I. Vat Orange 1 - For use in contact lenses – GMP – 73.3112

16,23-Dihydrodinaptho[2,3-a:2',3'-i]napth[2',3':6,7]indolo [2,3-c]carbazole-5,10,15,17,22,24-hexone - For use in contact lenses - GMP - 73.3117

N,N'-(9,10-Dihydro-9,10-dioxo-1,5-anthracenediyl) bis-benz-amide - For use in contact lenses - GMP - 73.3118

7,16-Dichloro-6,15-dihydro-5,9,14,18-anthrazinetetrone - For use in contact lenses - GMP - 73.3119

16,17-Dimethoxydinaptho[1,2,3-cd:3',2',1'-lm]perylene-5,10-dione - For use in contact lenses - GMP - 73.3120

4-[(2,4-dimethylphenyl)azo]-2,4-dihydro-5-methyl-2-phenyl -3H-pyrazol-3-one - For use in contact lenses - GMP - 73.3122

D&C Blue #6 - For use in surgical sutures. Subject to certification. Limits are in regulation - 74.3106

D&C Blue #9 - For use in surgical sutures. Subject to certification. Limit ≤ 2.5% by wt - 74.1109

D&C Green #5 - For sutures (Limit = 0.6% by wt of suture); For drugs and cosmetics generally, including drugs and cosmetics for eye area – GMP – 74.1205, 74.2205, 82.1205.

D&C Green #6 - For use in surgical sutures, haptics and contact lenses. Subject to certification. Limits are in regulation - 74.3206

D&C Red 17 - For use in contact lenses. Subject to certification - GMP - 74.3230

D&C Violet No. 2 - For use in absorbable sutures. Limits are in regulation. For use in polymethylmethacrylate intraocular lens haptics at a level < 0.2% by wt. For use in absorbable meniscal tacks made from poly(L-lactic acid) at a level < 0.15% by wt – 74.3602

2-[[2,5-Diethoxy-4-[(4-methylphenyl)thiol]phenyl]azo]-1,3,5- benzenetriol - For use in marking soft contact lenses with the letter R or L. Limit ≤ 0.11 microgram in a contact lens - 73.3115

6-Ethoxy-2-(6-ethoxy-3-oxobenzo[b]thien-2-(3H)-ylidene)benzo[b]thiophen-3-(2H)-one - For use in contact lenses - GMP -73.3123

[Phthalocyaninato(2-)] copper - For use in sutures (limit ≤ 0.5% by wt) and contact lenses (GMP). Subject to certification - 74.3045

Iron oxides - For use in contact lenses - GMP - 73.3125

Ferric Ammonium Citrate – For use in combination with pyrogallol for coloring plain or chromic catgut sutures. Limit FAC and pyrogallol ≤ 3% by wt - 73.1025

Logwood extract - for use in surgical sutures. Limit ≤ 1% by wt - 74.1410

Phthalocyanine green - For use in contact lenses - GMP - 73.3124

Poly(hydroxyethyl methacrylate)-dye copolymers - For use in contact lenses - GMP - 73.3121

The color additives are formed by reacting one or more of the following dyes with poly(hydroxyethyl methacrylate):
> Reactive Blue 21,
> Reactive Black 5,
> Reactive Yellow 15
> Reactive Orange 78
> Reactive Blue 19
> Reactive Blue 4
> C.I. Reactive Red 11
> C.I. Reactive Red 180
> C.I. Reactive Yellow 86
> C.I. Reactive Blue 163

Pyrogallol - For use in combination with ferric ammonium citrate for coloring plain or chromic catgut sutures. Limit FAC and pyrogallol ≤ 3% by wt - 73.1025

Titanium dioxide - For use in contact lenses – GMP – 73.3126

Vinyl alcohol/methyl methacrylate - dye reaction products - for use in contact lenses - GMP 73.3127

The color additives are formed by reacting one or more of the following dyes with vinyl alcohol/methyl methacrylate copolymers:
> C.I. Reactive Red 180
> C.I. Reactive Black 5
> C.I. Reactive Orange 78

21 CFR - SELECTED PARTS

PART 7, Subpart C - Recalls (Including Product Corrections) -Guidance on Policy, Procedures, and Industry Responsibilities

SOURCE: 43 FR 26218, June 16, 1978, unless otherwise noted.

7.40 Recall policy.

(a) Recall is an effective method of removing or correcting consumer products that are in violation of laws administered by the Food and Drug Administration. Recall is a voluntary action that takes place because manufacturers and distributors carry out their responsibility to protect the public health and well-being from products that present a risk of injury or gross deception or are otherwise defective. This section and 7.41 through 7.59 recognize the voluntary nature of recall by providing guidance so that responsible firms may effectively discharge their recall responsibilities. These sections also recognize that recall is an alternative to a Food and Drug Administration-initiated court action for removing or correcting violative, distributed products by setting forth specific recall procedures for the Food and Drug Administration to monitor recalls and assess the adequacy of a firm's efforts in recall.

(b) Recall may be undertaken voluntarily and at any time by manufacturers and distributors, or at the request of the Food and Drug Administration. A request by the Food and Drug Administration that a firm recall a product is reserved for urgent situations and is to be directed to the firm that has primary responsibility for the manufacture and marketing of the product that is to be recalled.

(c) Recall is generally more appropriate and affords better protection for consumers than seizure, when many lots of product have been widely distributed.
Seizure, multiple seizure, or other court action is indicated when a firm refuses to undertake a recall requested by the Food and Drug Administration, or where the agency has reason to believe that a recall would not be effective, determines that a recall is ineffective, or discovers that a violation is continuing.

[43CFR26218, June 16, 1978, as amended at 65 FR 56476, Sept. 19, 2000]

7.41 Health hazard evaluation and recall classification.

(a) An evaluation of the health hazard presented by a product being recalled or considered for recall will be conducted by an ad hoc committee of Food and Drug Administration scientists and will take into account, but need not be limited to, the following factors:

(1) Whether any disease or injuries have already occurred from the use of the product.

(2) Whether any existing conditions could contribute to a clinical situation that could expose humans or animals to a health hazard. Any conclusion shall be supported as completely as possible by scientific documentation and/or statements that the conclusion is the opinion of the individual(s) making the health hazard determination.

(3) Assessment of hazard to various segments of the population, e.g., children, surgical patients, pets, livestock, etc., who are expected to be exposed to the product being considered, with particular attention paid to the hazard to those individuals who may be at greatest risk.

(4) Assessment of the degree of seriousness of the health hazard to which the populations at risk would be exposed.

(5) Assessment of the likelihood of occurrence of the hazard.

(6) Assessment of the consequences (immediate or long-range) of occurrence of the hazard.

(b) On the basis of this determination, the Food and Drug Administration will assign the recall a classification, i.e., Class I, Class II, or Class III, to indicate the relative degree of health hazard of the product being recalled or considered for recall.

7.42 Recall strategy.

(a) General. (1) A recall strategy that takes into account the following factors will be developed by the agency for a Food and Drug Administration-requested recall and by the recalling firm for a firm-initiated recall to suit the individual circumstances of the particular recall:

(i) Results of health hazard evaluation.

(ii) Ease in identifying the product.

(iii) Degree to which the product's deficiency is obvious to the consumer or user.

iv) Degree to which the product remains unused in the market place.

(v) Continued availability of essential products.

(2) The Food and Drug Administration will review the adequacy of a proposed recall strategy developed by a recalling firm and recommend changes as appropriate. A recalling firm should conduct the recall in   accordance with an approved recall strategy but need not delay initiation of a recall pending review of its recall strategy.

(b) Elements of a recall strategy. A recall strategy will address the following elements regarding the conduct of the recall:

(1) *Depth of recall.* **Depending on the product's degree of hazard and extent of distribution, the recall strategy will specify the level in the distribution chain to which the recall is to extend, as follows:**

(i) Consumer or user level, which may vary with product, including any intermediate wholesale or retail level; or

(ii) Retail level, including any intermediate wholesale level; or

(iii) Wholesale level.

(2) *Public warning.* The purpose of a public warning is to alert the public that a product being recalled presents a serious hazard to health. It is reserved for urgent situations where other means for preventing use of the recalled product appear inadequate. The Food and Drug Administration in consultation with the recalling firm will ordinarily issue such publicity. The recalling firm that decides to issue its own public warning is requested to submit its proposed

public warning and plan for distribution of the warning for review and comment by the Food and Drug Administration. The recall strategy will specify whether a public warning is needed and whether it will issue as:

(i) General public warning through the general news media, either national or local as appropriate, or

(ii) Public warning through specialized news media, e.g., professional or trade press, or to specific segments of the population such as physicians, hospitals, etc.

(3) Effectiveness checks. The purpose of effectiveness checks is to verify that all consignees at the recall depth specified by the strategy have received notification about the recall and have taken appropriate action. The method for contacting consignees may be accomplished by personal visits, telephone calls, letters, or a combination thereof. A guide entitled "Method for Conducting Recall Effectiveness Checks" that describes the use of these different methods is available upon request from the Dockets Management Branch (HFA-305), Food and Drug Administration, rm. 1-23, 12420 Parklawn Dr., Rockville, MD 20857. The recalling firm will ordinarily be responsible for conducting effectiveness checks, but the Food and Drug Administration will assist in this task where necessary and appropriate. The recall strategy will specify the method(s) to be used for and the level of effectiveness checks that will be conducted, as follows:

(i) Level A - 100 percent of the total number of consignees to be contacted;

(ii) Level B - Some percentage of the total number of consignees to be contacted, which percentage is to be determined on a case-by-case basis, but is greater that 10 percent and less than 100 percent of the total number of consignees;

(iii) Level C - 10 percent of the total number of consignees to be contacted;

(iv) Level D - 2 percent of the total number of consignees to be contacted; or

(v) Level E - No effectiveness checks.

[43 FR 26218, June 16, 1978, as amended at 46 FR 8455, Jan. 27, 1981; 59 FR 14363, Mar. 28, 1994]

7.45 Food and Drug Administration - requested recall.

(a) The Commissioner of Food and Drugs or his designee under 5.20 of this chapter may request a firm to initiate a recall when the following determinations have been made:

(1) That a product that has been distributed presents a risk of illness or injury or gross consumer deception.

(2) That the firm has not initiated a recall of the product.

(3) That an agency action is necessary to protect the public health and welfare.

(b) The Commissioner or his designee will notify the firm of this determination and of the need to begin immediately a recall of the product. Such notification will be by letter or telegram to a responsible official of the firm, but may be preceded by oral communication or by a visit from an authorized representative of the local Food and Drug Administration district office, with formal, written confirma-

tion from the Commissioner or his designee afterward. The notification will specify the violation, the health hazard classification of the violative product, the recall strategy, and other appropriate instructions for conducting the recall.

(c) Upon receipt of a request to recall, the firm may be asked to provide the Food and Drug Administration any or all of the information listed in 7.46(a). The firm, upon agreeing to the recall request, may also provide other information relevant to the agency's determination of the need for the recall or how the recall should be conducted.

7.46   Firm-initiated recall.

(a) A firm may decide of its own volition and under any circumstances to remove or correct a distributed product. A firm that does so because it believes the product to be violative is requested to notify immediately the appropriate Food and Drug Administration district office listed in 5.115 of this chapter. Such removal or correction will be considered a recall only if the Food and Drug Administration regards the product as involving a violation that is subject to legal action, e.g., seizure. In such cases, the firm will be asked to provide the Food and Drug Administration the following information:

(1) Identity of the product involved.

(2) Reason for the removal or correction and the date and circumstances under which the product deficiency or possible deficiency was discovered.

(3) Evaluation of the risk associated with the deficiency or possible deficiency.

(4) Total amount of such products produced and/or the time span of the production.

(5) Total amount of such products estimated to be in distribution channels.

(6) Distribution information, including the number of direct accounts and, where necessary, the identity of the direct accounts.

(7) A copy of the firm's recall communication if any has issued, or a proposed communication if none has issued.

(8) Proposed strategy for conducting the recall.

(9) Name and telephone number of the firm official who should be contacted concerning the recall.

(b) The Food and Drug Administration will review the information submitted, advise the firm of the assigned recall classification, recommend any appropriate changes in the firm's strategy for the recall, and advise the firm that its recall will be placed in the weekly FDA Enforcement Report. Pending this review, the firm need not delay initiation of its product removal or correction.

(c) A firm may decide to recall a product when informed by the Food and Drug Administration that the agency has determined that the product in question violates the law, but the agency has not specifically requested a recall. The firm's action also is considered a firm-initiated recall and is subject to paragraphs (a) and (b) of this section.

(d) A firm that initiates a removal or correction of its product which the firm believes is a market withdrawal should consult with the appropriate Food and Drug Administration district office when the reason for the removal or correction is not obvious or clearly understood but where it is apparent, e.g., because of complaints or adverse reactions regarding the product, that the product is deficient in some respect. In such cases, the Food and Drug Administration will assist the firm in determining the exact nature of the problem.

7.49 Recall communications.

(a) *General.* A recalling firm is responsible for promptly notifying each of its affected direct accounts about the recall. The format, content, and extent of a recall communication should be commensurate with the hazard of the product being recalled and the strategy developed for that recall. In general terms, the purpose of a recall communication is to convey:

(1) That the product in question is subject to a recall.

(2) That further distribution or use of any remaining product should cease immediately.

(3) Where appropriate, that the direct account should in turn notify its customers who received the product about the recall.

(4) Instructions regarding what to do with the product.

(b) *Implementation.* A recall communication can be accomplished by telegrams, mailgrams, or first class letters conspicuously marked, preferably in bold red type, on the letter and the envelope: "DRUG   [or FOOD, BIOLOGIC, etc.] RECALL [or CORRECTION]".   The letter and the envelope should be also marked: "URGENT" for class I and class II recalls and, when appropriate, for class III recalls. Telephone calls or other personal contacts should ordinarily be confirmed by one of the above methods and/or documented in an appropriate manner.

(c) Contents. (1) A recall communication should be written in accordance with the following guidelines:

(i) Be brief and to the point;

(ii) Identify clearly the product, size, lot number(s), code(s) or serial number(s) and any other pertinent descriptive information to enable accurate and immediate identification of the product;

(iii) Explain concisely the reason for the recall and the hazard involved, if any;

(iv) Provide specific instructions on what should be done with respect to the recalled products; and

(v) Provide a ready means for the recipient of the communication to report to the recalling firm whether it has any of the product, e.g., by sending a postage-paid, self-addressed postcard or by allowing the recipient to place a collect call to the recalling firm.

(2) The recall communication should not contain irrelevant qualifications, promotional materials, or any other statement that may detract from the message. Where necessary, follow up communications should be sent to those who fail to respond to the initial recall communication.

(d) Responsibility of recipient. Consignees that receive a recall communication should immediately carry out the instructions set forth by the recalling firm and, where necessary, extend the recall to its consignees in accordance with paragraphs (b) and (c) of this section.

7.50   Public notification of recall.

The Food and Drug Administration will promptly make available to the public in the weekly FDA Enforcement

Report a descriptive listing of each new recall according to its classification, whether it was Food and Drug Administration-requested or firm-initiated, and the specific action being taken by the recalling firm. The Food and Drug Administration will intentionally delay public notification of recalls of certain drugs and devices where the agency determines that public notification may cause unnecessary and harmful anxiety in patients and that initial consultation between patients and their physicians is essential. The report will not include a firm's product removals or corrections which the agency determines to be market withdrawals or stock recoveries. The report, which also includes other Food and Drug Administration regulatory actions, e.g., seizures that were effected and injunctions and prosecutions that were filed, is available upon request from the Office of Public Affairs (HFI-1), Food and Drug Administration, 5600 Fishers Lane, Rockville, MD 20857.

7.53   Recall status reports.

(a) The recalling firm is requested to submit periodic recall status reports to the appropriate Food and Drug Administration district office so that the agency may assess the progress of the recall. The frequency of such reports will be determined by the relative urgency of the recall and will be specified by the Food and Drug Administration in each recall case; generally the reporting interval will be between 2 and 4 weeks.

(b) Unless otherwise specified or inappropriate in a given recall case, the recall status report should contain the following information:

(1) Number of consignees notified of the recall, and date and method of notification.

(2) Number of consignees responding to the recall communication and quantity of products on hand at the time it was received.

(3) Number of consignees that did not respond (if needed, the identity of non-responding consignees may be requested by the Food and Drug Administration).

(4) Number of products returned or corrected by each consignee contacted and the quantity of products accounted for.

(5) Number and results of effectiveness checks that were made.

(6) Estimated time frames for completion of the recall.

(c) Recall status reports are to be discontinued when the recall is terminated by the Food and Drug Administration.

7.55   Termination of a recall.

(a) A recall will be terminated when the Food and Drug Administration determines that all reasonable efforts have been made to remove or correct the product in accordance with the recall strategy, and when it is reasonable to assume that the product subject to the recall has been removed and proper disposition or correction has been made commensurate with the degree of hazard of the recalled product. Written notification that a recall is terminated will be issued by the appropriate Food and Drug Administration district office to the recalling firm.

(b) A recalling firm may request termination of its recall by submitting a written request to the appropriate Food and

Drug Administration district office stating that the recall is effective in accordance with the criteria set forth in paragraph (a) of this section, and by accompanying the request with the most current recall status report and a description of the disposition of the recalled product.

7.59 General industry guidance.

A recall can be disruptive of a firm's operation and business, but there are several steps a prudent firm can take in advance to minimize this disruptive effect. Notwithstanding similar specific requirements for certain products in other parts of this chapter, the following is provided by the Food and Drug Administration as guidance for a firm's consideration:

(a) Prepare and maintain a current written contingency plan for use in initiating and effecting a recall in accordance with 7.40 through 7.49, 7.53, and 7.55.

(b) Use sufficient coding of regulated products to make possible positive lot identification and to facilitate effective recall of all violative lots.

(c) Maintain such product distribution records as are necessary to facilitate location of products that are being recalled. Such records should be maintained for a period of time that exceeds the shelf life and expected use of the product and is at least the length of time specified in other applicable regulations concerning records retention.

PART 19 - STANDARDS OF CONDUCT AND CONFLICTS OF INTEREST

Subpart A - General Provisions

AUTHORITY: 21 U.S.C. 371. SOURCE: 42FR 15615; Mar 22, 1977 unless otherwise noted.

19.1 Scope.

This part governs the standards of conduct for, and establishes regulations to prevent conflicts of interest by, all Food and Drug Administration employees.

19.5 Reference to Department regulations.

(a) The provisions of 45 CFR part 73, establishing standards of conduct for all Department employees, are fully applicable to all Food and Drug Administration employees, except that such regulations shall be applicable to special government employees, i.e., consultants to the Food and Drug Administration, only to the extent stated in subpart L of 45 CFR part 73.

(b) The provisions of 45 CFR part 73a supplement the Department standards of conduct and apply only to Food and Drug Administration employees except special government employees.

19.6 Code of ethics for government service.

The following code of ethics, adopted by Congress on July 11, 1958, shall apply to all Food and Drug Administration employees:

CODE OF ETHICS FOR GOVERNMENT SERVICE

Any person in Government service should:

1. Put loyalty to the highest moral principles and to country above loyalty to persons, party, or Government department.

2. Uphold the Constitution, laws, and legal regulations of the United States and of all governments therein and never be a party to their evasion.

3. Give a full day's labor for a full day's pay; giving to the performance of his duties his earnest effort and best thought.

4. Seek to find and employ more efficient and economical ways of getting tasks accomplished.

5. Never discriminate unfairly by the dispensing of special favors or privileges to anyone, whether for remuneration or not; and never accept, for himself or his family, favors or benefits under circumstances which might be construed by reasonable persons as influencing the performance of his governmental duties.

6. Make no private promises of any kind binding upon the duties of office, since a Government employee has no private word which can be binding on public duty.

7. Engage in no business with the Government, either directly or indirectly, which is inconsistent with the conscientious performance of his governmental duties.

8. Never use any information coming to him confidentially in the performance of governmental duties as a means for making private profit.

9. Expose corruption wherever discovered.

10. Uphold these principles, ever conscious that public office is a public trust.

19.10 Food and Drug Administration Conflict of Interest Review Board.

(a) The Commissioner shall establish a permanent five-member Conflict of Interest Review Board, which shall review and make recommendations to the Commissioner on all specific or policy matters relating to conflicts of interest arising within the Food and Drug Administration that are forwarded to it by: (1) The Associate Commissioner for Management and Operations or (2) anyone who is the subject of an adverse determination by the Associate Commissioner for Management and Operations on any matter arising under the conflict of interest laws, except a determination of an apparent violation of law. The Director, Division of Ethics and Program Integrity, Office of Management and Operations, shall serve as executive secretary of the Review Board.

(b) It shall be the responsibility of every Food and Drug Administration employee with whom any specific or policy issue relating to conflicts of interest is raised, or who otherwise wishes to have any such matter resolved, to forward the matter to the Associate Commissioner for Management and Operations for resolution, except that reporting of apparent violations of law are governed by 19.21.

(c) All general policy relating to conflicts of interest shall be established in guidance pursuant to the provisions of

10.90(b) of this chapter and whenever feasible shall be incorporated in regulations in this subpart.

(d) All decisions relating to specific individuals shall be placed in a public file established for this purpose by the Freedom of Information Staff, e.g., a determination that a consultant may serve on an advisory committee with specific limitations or with public disclosure of stock holdings, except that such determination shall be written in a way that does not identify the individual in the following situations:

(1) A determination that an employee must dispose of prohibited financial interests or refrain from incompatible outside activities in accordance with established Department or agency regulations.

(2) A determination that a proposed consultant is not eligible for employment by the agency.

(3) A determination that public disclosure of any information would constitute an unwarranted invasion of personal privacy in violation of 20.63 of this chapter.

[42 FR 15615, Mar.22, 1977, as amended at 46 FR 8456, Jan. 27, 1981, 50 FR 52278, Dec. 23, 1985; 55 FR 1404, Jan. 16, 1990; 65 FR 56479, Sept. 19, 2000]

Subpart B - Reporting of Violations

19.21   Duty to report violations.

(a) The Office of Internal Affairs, Office of the Commissioner, is responsible for obtaining factual information for the Food and Drug Administration on any matter relating to allegations of misconduct, impropriety, conflict of interest, or other violations of Federal statutes by agency personnel.

(b) Any Food and Drug Administration employee who has factual information showing or who otherwise believes that any present or former Food and Drug Administration employee has violated or is violating any provision of this subpart or of 45 CFR parts 73 or 73a or of any statute listed in Appendix A to 45 CFR part 73 should report such information directly to the Office of Internal Affairs. Any such reports shall be in writing or shall with the assistance of the Office of Internal Affairs, be reduced to writing, and shall be promptly investigated.

(c) Any report pursuant to paragraph (b) of this section and any records relating to an investigation of such reports shall be maintained in strict confidence in the files of the Office of Internal Affairs, shall be exempt from public disclosure, and may be reviewed only by authorized Food and Drug Administration employees who are required to do so in the performance of their duties.

[42 FR 15615, Mar. 22, 1977, as amended at 46 FR 8456, Jan. 27, 1981; 50 FR 52278, Dec. 23, 1985; 60 FR 47478, Sept. 13, 1995]

Subpart C - Disqualification Conditions

19.45   Temporary disqualification of former employees.

Within 1 year after termination of employment with the Food and Drug Administration, no former Food and Drug Administration employee, including a special government employee, shall appear personally before the Food and Drug Administration or other federal agency or court as agent or attorney for any person other than the United States in connection with any proceeding or matter in which the United States is a party or has a direct and substantial interest and which was under his official responsibility at any time within one year preceding termination of such responsibility. The term official responsibility means the direct administrative or operating authority, whether intermediate or final, and either exercisable alone or with others, and either personally or through subordinates, to approve, disapprove, or otherwise direct government action.

19.55   Permanent disqualification of former employees.

No former Food and Drug Administration employee, including a special government employee, shall knowingly act as agent or attorney for anyone other than United States in connection with any judicial or other proceeding, application, request for a ruling or other determination, contract, claim, controversy, charge, accusation, or other particular matter involving a specific party or parties in which the United States is a party or has a direct and substantial interest and in which he participated personally and substantially through decision, approval, disapproval, recommendation, rendering of advice, investigation, or otherwise as a Food and Drug Administration employee.

PART 110-CURRENT GOOD MANUFACTURING PRACTICE IN MANUFACTURING, PACKING, OR HOLDING HUMAN FOOD

AUTHORITY: 21 U.S.C. 342, 371, 374; 42 U.S.C. 264. SOURCE: 51 FR 24475, June 19, 1986, unless otherwise noted

Subpart A - General Provisions

110.3   Definitions.

The definitions and interpretations of terms in section 201 of the Federal Food, Drug, and Cosmetic Act (the act) are applicable to such terms when used in this part. The following definitions shall also apply:

(a) Acid foods or acidified foods means foods that have an equilibrium pH of 4.6 or below.

(b) Adequate means that which is needed to accomplish the intended purpose in keeping with good public health practice.

(c) Batter means a semi-fluid substance, usually composed of flour and other ingredients, into which principal components of food are dipped or with which they are coated, or which may be used directly to form bakery foods.

(d) Blanching, except for tree nuts and peanuts, means a prepackaging heat treatment of foodstuffs for a sufficient time and at a sufficient temperature to partially or completely inactivate the naturally occurring enzymes and to effect other physical or biochemical changes in the food.

(e) Critical control point means a point in a food process where there is a high probability that improper control may cause, allow, or contribute to a hazard or to filth in the final food or decomposition of the final food.

(f) Food means food as defined in section 201(f) of the act and includes raw materials and ingredients.

(g) Food-contact surfaces are those surfaces that contact human food and those surfaces from which drainage onto the food or onto surfaces that contact the food ordinarily occurs during the normal course of operations. Food-contact surfaces includes utensils and food-contact surfaces of equipment.

(h) Lot means the food produced during a period of time indicated by a specific code.

(i) Microorganisms means yeasts, molds, bacteria, and viruses and includes, but is not limited to, species having public health significance. The term "undesirable microorganisms" includes those microorganisms that are of public health significance, that subject food to decomposition, that indicate that food is contaminated with filth, or that otherwise may cause food to be adulterated within the meaning of the act. Occasionally in these regulations, FDA used the adjective "microbial" instead of using an adjectival phrase containing the word microorganism.

(j) Pest refers to any objectionable animals or insects including, but not limited to, birds, rodents, flies, and larvae.

(k) Plant means the building or facility or parts thereof, used for or in connection with the manufacturing, packaging, labeling, or holding of human food.

(l) Quality control operation means a planned and systematic procedure for taking all actions necessary to prevent food from being adulterated within the meaning of the act.

(m) Rework means clean, unadulterated food that has been removed from processing for reasons other than insanitary conditions or that has been successfully reconditioned by reprocessing and that is suitable for use as food.

(n) Safe-moisture level is a level of moisture low enough to prevent the growth of undesirable microorganisms in the finished product under the intended conditions of manufacturing, storage, and distribution. The maximum safe moisture level for a food is based on its water activity (aW). An aW will be considered safe for a food if adequate data are available that demonstrate that the food at or below the given aW will not support the growth of undesirable microorganisms.

(o) Sanitize means to adequately treat food-contact surfaces by a process that is effective in destroying vegetative cells of microorganisms of public health significance, and in substantially reducing numbers of other undesirable microorganisms, but without adversely affecting the product or its safety for the consumer.

(p) Shall is used to state mandatory requirements.

(q) Should is used to state recommended or advisory procedures or identify recommended equipment.

(r) Water activity (aw) is a measure of the free moisture in a food and is the quotient of the water vapor pressure of the substance divided by the vapor pressure of pure water at the same temperature.

110.5   Current good manufacturing practice.

(a) The criteria and definitions in this part shall apply in determining whether a food is adulterated (1) within the meaning of section 402(a)(3) of the act in that the food has been manufactured section 402(a)(4) of the act in that the food has been prepared, packed, or held under insanitary conditions whereby it may have become contaminated with filth, or whereby it may have been rendered injurious to health. The criteria and definitions in this part also apply in determining whether a food is in violation of section 361 of the Public Health Service Act (42 U.S.C. 264).

(b) Food covered by specific current good manufacturing practice regulations also is subject to the requirements of those regulations.

110.10   Personnel.

The plant management shall take all reasonable measures and precautions to ensure the following:

(a) *Disease control.* Any person who, by medical examination or supervisory observation, is shown to have, or appears to have, an illness, open lesion, including boils, sores, or infected wounds, or any other abnormal source of microbial contamination by which there is a reasonable possibility of food, food-contact surfaces, or food-packaging materials becoming contaminated, shall be excluded from any operations which may be expected to result in such contamination until the condition is corrected. Personnel shall be instructed to report such health conditions to their supervisors.

(b) *Cleanliness.* All persons working in direct contact with food, food-contact surfaces, and food-packaging materials shall conform to hygienic practices while on duty to the extent necessary to protect against contamination of food. The methods for maintaining cleanliness include, but are not limited to:

(1) Wearing outer garments suitable to the operation in a manner that protects against the contamination of food, food-contact surfaces, or food-packaging materials.

(2) Maintaining adequate personal cleanliness.

(3) Washing hands thoroughly (and sanitizing if necessary to protect against contamination with undesirable microorganisms) in an adequate hand-washing facility before starting work, after each absence from the work station, and at any other time when the hands may have become soiled or contaminated.

(4) Removing all unsecured jewelry and other objects that might fall into food, equipment, or containers, and removing hand jewelry that cannot be adequately sanitized during periods in which food is manipulated by hand. If such hand jewelry cannot be removed, it may be covered by material which can be maintained in an intact, clean, and sanitary condition and which effectively protects against the contamination by these objects of the food, food-contact surfaces, or food-packaging materials.

(5) Maintaining gloves, if they are used in food handling, in an intact, clean, and sanitary condition. The gloves should be of an impermeable material.

(6) Wearing, where appropriate, in an effective manner, hair nets, headbands, caps, beard covers, or other effective hair restraints.

(7) Storing clothing or other personal belongings in areas other than where food is exposed or where equipment or utensils are washed.

(8) Confining the following to areas other than where

food may be exposed or where equipment or utensils are washed: eating food, chewing gum, drinking beverages, or using tobacco.

(9) Taking any other necessary precautions to protect against contamination of food, food-contact surfaces, or food-packaging materials with microorganisms or foreign substances including, but not limited to, perspiration, hair, cosmetics, tobacco, chemicals, and medicines applied to the skin.

(c) *Education and training.* Personnel responsible for identifying sanitation failures or food contamination should have a background of education or experience, or a combination thereof, to provide a level of competency necessary for production of clean and safe food. Food handlers and supervisors should receive appropriate training in proper food handling techniques and food-protection principles and should be informed of the danger of poor personal hygiene and insanitary practices.

(d) *Supervision.* Responsibility for assuring compliance by all personnel with all requirements of this part shall be clearly assigned to competent supervisory personnel.

[51 FR 24475, June 19, 1986, as amended at 54 FR 24892, June 12, 1989]

110.19   Exclusions.

(a) The following operations are not subject to this part: Establishments engaged solely in the harvesting, storage, or distribution of one or more "raw agricultural commodities," as defined in section 201(r) of the act, which are ordinarily cleaned, prepared, treated, or otherwise processed before being marketed to the consuming public.

(b) FDA, however, will issue special regulations if it is necessary to cover these excluded operations.

Subpart B - Buildings and Facilities

110.20   Plant and grounds.

(a) Grounds. The grounds about a food plant under the control of the operator shall be kept in a condition that will protect against the contamination of food. The methods for adequate maintenance of grounds include, but are not limited to:

(1) Properly storing equipment, removing litter and waste, and cutting weeds or grass within the immediate vicinity of the plant buildings or structures that may constitute an attractant, breeding place, or harborage for pests.

(2) Maintaining roads, yards, and parking lots so that they do not constitute a source of contamination in areas where food is exposed.

(3) Adequately draining areas that may contribute contamination to food by, foot-borne filth, or providing a breeding place for pests.

(4) Operating systems for waste treatment and disposal in an adequate manner so that they do not constitute a source of contamination in areas where food is exposed.

If the plant grounds are bordered by grounds not under the operator's control and not maintained in the manner described in paragraph (a) (1) through (3) of this section, care shall be exercised in the plant by inspection, extermi-

nation, or other means to exclude pests, dirt, and filth that may be a source of food contamination.

(b)   Plant construction and design. Plant buildings and structures shall be suitable in size, construction, and design to facilitate maintenance and sanitary operations for food-manufacturing purposes. The plant and facilities shall:

(1) Provide sufficient space for such placement of equipment and storage of materials as is necessary for the maintenance of sanitary operations and the production of safe food.

(2) Permit the taking of proper precautions to reduce the potential for contamination of food, food-contact surfaces, or food-packaging materials with microorganisms, chemicals, filth, or other extraneous material. The potential for contamination may be reduced by adequate food safety controls and operating practices or effective design, including the separation of operations in which contamination is likely to occur, by one or more of the following means: location, time, partition, air flow, enclosed systems, or other effective means.

(3) Permit the taking of proper precautions to protect food in outdoor bulk fermentation vessels by any effective means, including:

(i) Using protective coverings.

(ii) Controlling areas over and around the vessels to eliminate harborages for pests.

(iii) Checking on a regular basis for pests and pest infestation.

(iv) Skimming the fermentation vessels, as necessary.

(4) Be constructed in such a manner that floors, walls, and ceilings may be adequately cleaned and kept clean and kept in good repair; that drip or condensate from fixtures, ducts and pipes does not contaminate food, food-contact surfaces, or food-packaging materials; and that aisles or working spaces are provided between equipment and walls and are adequately unobstructed and of adequate width to permit employees to perform their duties and to protect against contaminating food or food-contact surfaces with clothing or personal contact.

(5) Provide adequate lighting in hand-washing areas, dressing and locker rooms, and toilet rooms and in all areas where food is examined, processed, or stored and where equipment or utensils are cleaned; and provide safety-type light bulbs, fixtures, skylights, or other glass suspended over exposed food in any step of preparation or otherwise protect against food contamination in case of glass breakage.

(6) Provide adequate ventilation or control equipment to minimize odors and vapors (including steam and noxious fumes) in areas where they may contaminate food; and locate and operate fans and other air-blowing equipment in a manner that minimizes the potential for contaminating food, food-packaging materials, and food-contact surfaces.

(7) Provide, where necessary, adequate screening or other protection against pests.

110.35   Sanitary operations.

(a) *General maintenance.* Buildings, fixtures, and other physical facilities of the plant shall be maintained in a sanitary condition and shall be kept in repair sufficient to prevent food from becoming adulterated within the meaning of the act. Cleaning and sanitizing of utensils and equipment shall be conducted in a manner that protects against contamination of food, food-contact surfaces, or food-packaging materials.

(b) *Substances used in cleaning and sanitizing; storage of toxic materials.* (1) Cleaning compounds and sanitizing agents used in cleaning and sanitizing procedures shall be free from undesirable microorganisms and shall be safe and adequate under the conditions of use. Compliance with this requirement may be verified by any effective means including purchase of these substances under a supplier's guarantee or certification, or examination of these substances for contamination. Only the following toxic materials may be used or stored in a plant where food is processed or exposed:

(i) Those required to maintain clean and sanitary conditions;

(ii) Those necessary for use in laboratory testing procedures;

(iii) Those necessary for plant and equipment maintenance and operation; and

(iv) Those necessary for use in the plant's operations.

(2) Toxic cleaning compounds, sanitizing agents, and pesticide chemicals shall be identified, held, and stored in a manner that protects against contamination of food, food-contact surfaces, or food-packaging materials. All relevant regulations promulgated by other Federal, State, and local government agencies for the application, use, or holding of these products should be followed.

(c) *Pest control.* No pests shall be allowed in any area of a food plant. Guard or guide dogs may be allowed in some areas of a plant if the presence of the dogs is unlikely to result in contamination of food, food-contact surfaces, or food-packaging materials. Effective measures shall be taken to exclude pests from the processing areas and to protect against the contamination of food on the premises by pests. The use of insecticides or rodenticides is permitted only under precautions and restrictions that will protect against the contamination of food, food-contact surfaces, and food-packaging materials.

(d) *Sanitation of food-contact surfaces.* All food-contact surfaces, including utensils and food-contact surfaces of equipment, shall be cleaned as frequently as necessary to protect against contamination of food.

(1) Food-contact surfaces used for manufacturing or holding low-moisture food shall be in a dry, sanitary condition at the time of use. When the surfaces are wet-cleaned, they shall, when necessary, be sanitized and thoroughly dried before subsequent use.

(2) In wet processing, when cleaning is necessary to protect against the introduction of microorganisms into food, all food-contact surfaces shall be cleaned and sanitized before use and after any interruption during which the food-contact surfaces may have become contaminated. Where equipment and utensils are used in a continuous production operation, the utensils and food-contact surfaces of the equipment shall be cleaned and sanitized as necessary.

(3) Non-food-contact surfaces of equipment used in the operation of food plants should be cleaned as frequently as

necessary to protect against contamination of food.

(4) Single-service articles (such as utensils intended for one-time use, paper cups, and paper towels) should be stored in appropriate containers and shall be handled, dispensed, used, and disposed of in a manner that protects against contamination of food or food-contact surfaces.

(5) Sanitizing agents shall be adequate and safe under conditions of use. Any facility, procedure, or machine is acceptable for cleaning and sanitizing equipment and utensils if it is established that the facility, procedure, or machine will routinely render equipment and utensils clean and provide adequate cleaning and sanitizing treatment.

(e) *Storage and handling of cleaned portable equipment and utensils.* Cleaned and sanitized portable equipment with food-contact surfaces and utensils should be stored in a location and manner that protects food-contact surfaces from contamination.

[51 FR 24475, June 19, 1986, as amended at 54 FR 24892, June 12, 1989]

110.37 Sanitary facilities and controls.

Each plant shall be equipped with adequate sanitary facilities and accommodations including, but not limited to:

(a) *Water supply.* The water supply shall be sufficient for the operations intended and shall be derived from an adequate source. Any water that contacts food or food-contact surfaces shall be safe and of adequate sanitary quality. Running water at a suitable temperature, and under pressure as needed, shall be provided in all areas where required for the processing of food, for the cleaning of equipment, utensils, and food-packaging materials, or for employee sanitary facilities.

(b) *Plumbing.* Plumbing shall be of adequate size and design and adequately installed and maintained to:

(1) Carry sufficient quantities of water to required locations throughout the plant.

(2) Properly convey sewage and liquid disposable waste from the plant.

(3) Avoid constituting a source of contamination to food, water supplies, equipment, or utensils or creating an unsanitary condition.

(4) Provide adequate floor drainage in all areas where floors are subject to flooding-type cleaning or where normal operations release or discharge water or other liquid waste on the floor.

(5) Provide that there is not backflow from, or cross-connection between, piping systems that discharge waste water or sewage and piping systems that carry water for food or food manufacturing.

(c) *Sewage disposal.* Sewage disposal shall be made into an adequate sewerage system or disposed of through other adequate means.

(d) *Toilet facilities.* Each plant shall provide its employees with adequate, readily accessible toilet facilities. Compliance with this requirement may be accomplished by:

(1) Maintaining the facilities in a sanitary condition.

(2) Keeping the facilities in good repair at all times.

(3) Providing self-closing doors.

(4) Providing doors that do not open into areas where

food is exposed to airborne contamination, except where alternate means have been taken to protect against such contamination (such as double doors or positive air-flow systems).

(e) *Hand-washing facilities.* Hand-washing facilities shall be adequate and convenient and be furnished with running water at a suitable temperature. Compliance with this requirement may be accomplished by providing:

(1) Hand-washing and, where appropriate, hand-sanitizing facilities at each location in the plant where good sanitary practices require employees to wash and/or sanitize their hands.

(2) Effective hand-cleaning and sanitizing preparations.

(3) Sanitary towel service or suitable drying devices.

(4) Devices or fixtures, such as water control valves, so designed and constructed to protect against recontamination of clean, sanitized hands.

(5) Readily understandable signs directing employees handling unprotected food, unprotected food-packaging materials, or food-contact surfaces to wash and, where appropriate, sanitize their hands before they start work, after each absence from post of duty, and when their hands may have become soiled or contaminated. These signs may be posted in the processing room(s) and in all other areas where employees may handle such food, materials, or surfaces.

(6) Refuse receptacles that are constructed and maintained in a manner that protects against contamination of food.

(f) *Rubbish and offal disposal.* Rubbish and any offal shall be so conveyed, stored, and disposed of as to minimize the development of odor, minimize the potential for the waste becoming an attractant and harborage or breeding place for pests, and protect against contamination of food, food-contact surfaces, water supplies, and ground surfaces.

Subpart C - Equipment

110.40   Equipment and utensils.

(a) All plant equipment and utensils shall be so designed and of such material and workmanship as to be adequately cleanable, and shall be properly maintained. The design, construction, and use of equipment and utensils shall preclude the adulteration of food with lubricants, fuel, metal fragments, contaminated water, or any other contaminants. All equipment should be so installed and maintained as to facilitate the cleaning of the equipment and of all adjacent spaces. Food-contact surfaces shall be corrosion-resistant when in contact with food. They shall be made of nontoxic materials and designed to withstand the action of food, and, if applicable, cleaning compounds and sanitizing agents. Food-contact surfaces shall be maintained to protect food from being contaminated by any source, including unlawful indirect food additives.

(b) Seams on food-contact surfaces shall be smoothly bonded or maintained so as to minimize accumulation of food particles, dirt, and organic matter and thus minimize the opportunity for growth of microorganisms.

(c) Equipment that is in the manufacturing or food-han-

dling area and that does not come into contact with food shall be so constructed that it can be kept in a clean condition.

(d) Holding, conveying, and manufacturing systems, including gravimetric, pneumatic, closed, and automated systems, shall be of a design and construction that enables them to be maintained
in an appropriate sanitary condition.

(e) Each freezer and cold storage compartment used to store and hold food capable of supporting growth of microorganisms shall be fitted with an indicating thermometer, temperature-measuring device, or temperature-recording device so installed as to show the temperature accurately within the compartment, and should be fitted with an automatic control for regulating temperature or with an automatic alarm system to indicate a significant temperature change in a manual operation.

(f) Instruments and controls used for measuring, regulating, or recording temperatures, pH, acidity, water activity, or other conditions that control or prevent the growth of undesirable microorganisms in food shall be accurate and adequately maintained, and adequate in number for their designated uses.

(g) Compressed air or other gases mechanically introduced into food or used to clean food-contact surfaces or equipment shall be treated in such a way that food is not contaminated with unlawful indirect food additives.

110.80   Processes and controls.

All operations in the receiving, inspecting, transporting, segregating, preparing, manufacturing, packaging, and storing of food shall be conducted in accordance with adequate sanitation principles. Appropriate quality control operations shall be employed to ensure that food is suitable for human consumption and that food-packaging materials are safe and suitable. Overall sanitation of the plant shall be under the supervision of one or more competent individuals assigned responsibility for this function. All reasonable precautions shall be taken to ensure that production procedures do not contribute contamination from any source. Chemical, microbial, or extraneous-material testing procedures shall be used where necessary to identify sanitation failures or possible food contamination. All food that has become contaminated to the extent that it is adulterated within the meaning of the act shall be rejected, or if permissible, treated or processed to eliminate the contamination.

(a) Raw materials and other ingredients. (1) Raw materials and other ingredients shall be inspected and segregated or otherwise handled as necessary to ascertain that they are clean and suitable for processing
into food and shall be stored under conditions that will protect against contamination and minimize deterioration. Raw materials shall be washed or cleaned as necessary to remove soil or other contamination. Water used for washing, rinsing, or conveying food shall be safe and of adequate sanitary quality. Water may be reused for washing, rinsing, or conveying food if it does not increase the level of contamination of the food. Containers and carriers of raw materials should be inspected on receipt to ensure that

their condition has not contributed to the contamination or deterioration of food.

(2) Raw materials and other ingredients shall either not contain
levels of microorganisms that may produce food poisoning or other disease in humans, or they shall be pasteurized or otherwise treated during manufacturing operations so that they no longer contain levels that would cause the product to be adulterated within the meaning of the act. Compliance with this requirement may be verified by any effective means, including purchasing raw materials and other ingredients under a
supplier's guarantee or certification.

(3) Raw materials and other ingredients susceptible to contamination with aflatoxin or other natural toxins shall comply with current Food and Drug Administration regulations, and action levels for poisonous or deleterious substances before these materials or ingredients are incorporated into finished food. Compliance with this requirement may be accomplished by purchasing raw materials and other ingredients under a supplier's guarantee or certification, or may be verified by analyzing these materials and ingredients for aflatoxins and other natural toxins.

(4) Raw materials, other ingredients, and rework susceptible to contamination with pests, undesirable microorganisms, or extraneous material shall comply with applicable Food and Drug Administration regulations, and defect action levels for natural or unavoidable defects if a manufacturer wishes to use the materials in manufacturing food. Compliance with this requirement may be verified by any effective means,
including purchasing the materials under a supplier's guarantee or certification, or examination of these materials for contamination.

(5) Raw materials, other ingredients, and rework shall be held in bulk, or in containers designed and constructed so as to protect against contamination and shall be held at such temperature and relative humidity and in such a manner as to prevent the food from becoming adulterated within the meaning of the act. Material scheduled for rework shall be identified as such.

(6) Frozen raw materials and other ingredients shall be kept frozen. If thawing is required prior to use, it shall be done in a manner that prevents the raw materials and other ingredients from becoming adulterated within the meaning of the act.

(7) Liquid or dry raw materials and other ingredients received and stored in bulk form shall be held in a manner that protects against contamination.

(b) Manufacturing operations. (1) Equipment and utensils and finished food containers shall be maintained in an acceptable condition through appropriate cleaning and sanitizing, as necessary. Insofar as necessary, equipment shall be taken apart for thorough cleaning.

(2) All food manufacturing, including packaging and storage, shall be conducted under such conditions and controls as are necessary to minimize the potential for the growth of microorganisms, or for the contamination of food. One way to comply with this requirement is
careful monitoring of physical factors such as time, temper-

ature, humidity, aW, pH, pressure, flow rate, and manufacturing operations such as freezing, dehydration, heat processing, acidification, and refrigeration to ensure that mechanical breakdowns, time delays, temperature fluctuations, and other factors do not contribute to the decomposition or contamination of food.

(3) Food that can support the rapid growth of undesirable microorganisms, particularly those of public health significance, shall be held in a manner that prevents the food from becoming adulterated within the meaning of the act. Compliance with this requirement may be accomplished by any effective means, including:

(i) Maintaining refrigerated foods at 45 deg.F (7.2 deg.C) or below as appropriate for the particular food involved.

(ii) Maintaining frozen foods in a frozen state.

(iii) Maintaining hot foods at 140 deg.F (60 deg.C) or above.

(iv) Heat treating acid or acidified foods to destroy mesophilic microorganisms when those foods are to be held in hermetically sealed containers at ambient temperatures.

(4) Measures such as sterilizing, irradiating, pasteurizing, freezing, refrigerating, controlling pH or controlling pH or controlling aW that are taken to destroy or prevent the growth of undesirable microorganisms, particularly those of public health significance, shall be adequate under the conditions of manufacture, handling, and distribution to prevent food from being adulterated within the meaning of the act.

(5) Work-in-process shall be handled in a manner that protects against contamination.

(6) Effective measures shall be taken to protect finished food from contamination by raw materials, other ingredients, or refuse. When raw materials, other ingredients, or refuse are unprotected, they shall not
be handled simultaneously in a receiving, loading, or shipping area if that handling could result in contaminated food. Food transported by conveyor shall be protected against contamination as necessary.

(7) Equipment, containers, and utensils used to convey, hold, or store raw materials, work-in-process, rework, or food shall be constructed, handled, and maintained during manufacturing or storage in a manner that protects against contamination.

(8) Effective measures shall be taken to protect against the inclusion of metal or other extraneous material in food. Compliance with this requirement may be accomplished by using sieves, traps, magnets,
electronic metal detectors, or other suitable effective means.

(9) Food, raw materials, and other ingredients that are adulterated within the meaning of the act shall be disposed of in a manner that protects against the contamination of other food. If the adulterated food is capable of being reconditioned, it shall be reconditioned using a method that has been proven to be effective or it shall be reexamined and found not to be adulterated within the meaning of the act before being incorporated into other food.

(10) Mechanical manufacturing steps such as washing, peeling, trimming, cutting, sorting and inspecting, mashing,

dewatering, cooling, shredding, extruding, drying, whipping, defatting, and forming shall be performed so as to protect food against contamination. Compliance with this requirement may be accomplished by providing adequate physical protection of food from contaminants that may drip, drain, or be drawn into the food. Protection may be provided by adequate cleaning and sanitizing of all food-contact surfaces, and by using time and temperature controls at and between each manufacturing step.

(11) Heat blanching, when required in the preparation of food, should be effected by heating the food to the required temperature, holding it at this temperature for the required time, and then either rapidly cooling the food or passing it to subsequent manufacturing
without delay. Thermophilic growth and contamination in blanchers should be minimized by the use of adequate operating temperatures and by periodic cleaning. Where the blanched food is washed prior to filling, water used shall be safe and of adequate sanitary quality.

(12) Batters, breading, sauces, gravies, dressings, and other similar preparations shall be treated or maintained in such a manner that they are protected against contamination. Compliance with this requirement may be accomplished by any effective means, including one or more of the following:

(i) Using ingredients free of contamination.

(ii) Employing adequate heat processes where applicable.

(iii) Using adequate time and temperature controls.

(iv) Providing adequate physical protection of components from contaminants that may drip, drain, or be drawn into them.

(v) Cooling to an adequate temperature during manufacturing.

(vi) Disposing of batters at appropriate intervals to protect against the growth of microorganisms.

(13) Filling, assembling, packaging, and other operations shall be performed in such a way that the food is protected against contamination. Compliance with this requirement may be accomplished by any effective means, including:

(i) Use of a quality control operation in which the critical control points are identified and controlled during manufacturing.

(ii) Adequate cleaning and sanitizing of all food-contact surfaces and food containers.

(iii) Using materials for food containers and food- packaging materials that are safe and suitable, as defined in Sec. 130.3(d) of this chapter.

(iv) Providing physical protection from contamination, particularly airborne contamination.

(v) Using sanitary handling procedures.

(14) Food such as, but not limited to, dry mixes, nuts, intermediate moisture food, and dehydrated food, that relies on the control of a<INF>w</INF> for preventing the growth of undesirable microorganisms shall be processed to and maintained at a safe moisture level.
Compliance with this requirement may be accomplished by any effective means, including employment of one or more of the following practices:

(i) Monitoring the aW of food.

(ii) Controlling the soluble solids-water ratio in finished food.

(iii) Protecting finished food from moisture pickup, by use of a moisture barrier or by other means, so that the aW of the food does not increase to an unsafe level.

(15) Food such as, but not limited to, acid and acidified food, that relies principally on the control of pH for preventing the growth of undesirable microorganisms shall be monitored and maintained at a pH of 4.6 or below. Compliance with this requirement may be accomplished by any effective means, including employment of one or more of the following practices:

(i) Monitoring the pH of raw materials, food in process, and finished food.

(ii) Controlling the amount of acid or acidified food added to low-acid food.

(16) When ice is used in contact with food, it shall be made from water that is safe and of adequate sanitary quality, and shall be used only if it has been manufactured in accordance with current good manufacturing practice as outlined in this part.

(17) Food-manufacturing areas and equipment used for manufacturing human food should not be used to manufacture nonhuman food-grade animal feed or inedible products, unless there is no reasonable possibility for the contamination of the human food.

[51 FR 24475, June 19, 1986, as amended at 65 FR 56479, Sept. 19, 2000]

110.93   Warehousing and distribution.

Storage and transportation of finished food shall be under conditions that will protect food against physical, chemical, and microbial contamination as well as against deterioration of the food and the container.

Subpart F-[Reserved]

Subpart G-Defect Action Levels

110.110   Natural or unavoidable defects in food for human use that present no health hazard.

(a) Some foods, even when produced under current good manufacturing practice, contain natural or unavoidable defects that at low levels are not hazardous to health. The Food and Drug Administration establishes maximum levels for these defects in foods produced under current good manufacturing practice and uses these levels in deciding whether to recommend regulatory action.

(b) Defect action levels are established for foods whenever it is necessary and feasible to do so. These levels are subject to change upon the development of new technology or the availability of new information.

(c) Compliance with defect action levels does not excuse violation of the requirement in section 402(a)(4) of the act that food not be prepared, packed, or held under unsanitary conditions or the requirements in this part that food manufacturers, distributors, and holders shall observe current good manufacturing practice.   Evidence indicating that such a violation exists causes the food to be adulterated within the meaning of the act, even though the amounts of natural or unavoidable defects are lower than the currently established defect action levels. The manufacturer, distributor, and holder of food shall at all times utilize quality control operations that reduce natural or unavoidable defects to the lowest level currently feasible.

(d) The mixing of a food containing defects above the current defect action level with another lot of food is not permitted and renders the final food adulterated within the meaning of the act, regardless of the defect level of the final food.

(e) A compilation of the current defect action levels for natural or unavoidable defects in food for human use that present no health hazard may be obtained upon request from the Industry Programs Branch (HFF 326), Center for Food Safety and Applied Nutrition, Food and Drug Administration, 200 C St. SW., Washington, DC 20204.

[51 FR 24475, June 19,1986, as amended at 61 CFR 14480, Apr. 2, 1996]

PART 210-CURRENT GOOD MANUFACTURING PRACTICE IN MANUFACTURING, PROCESSING, PACKING, OR HOLDING OF DRUGS; GENERAL

AUTHORITY: 21 U.S.C. 321, 351, 352, 355, 360b, 371, 374.
SOURCE: 43 FR 45076, Sept, 29, 1978, unless otherwise noted.

210.1 Status of current good manufacturing practice regulations.

(a) The regulations set forth in this part and in Parts 211 through 226 of this chapter contain the minimum current good manufacturing practice for methods to be used in, and the facilities or controls to be used for, the manufacture, processing, packing, or holding of a drug to assure that such drug meets the requirements of the act as to safety, and has the identity and strength and meets the quality and purity characteristics that it purports or is represented to possess.

(b) The failure to comply with any regulation set forth in this part and in Parts 211 through 226 of this chapter in the manufacture, processing, packing, or holding of a drug shall render such drug to be adulterated under section 501(a)(2)(B) of the act and such drug, as well as the person who is responsible for the failure to comply, shall be subject to regulatory action.

210.2 Applicability of current good manufacturing practice regulations.

(a) The regulations in this part and in Parts 211 through 226 of this chapter as they may pertain to a drug and in Parts 600 through 680 of this chapter as they may pertain to a biological product for human use, shall be considered to supplement, not supersede, each other, unless the regulations explicitly provide otherwise. In the event that it is impossible to comply with all applicable regulations in these parts, the regulations specifically applicable to the drug in question shall supersede the more general.

(b) If a person engages in only some operations subject to the regulations in this part and in Parts 211 through 226 and Parts 600 through 680 of this chapter, and not in others, that person need only comply with those regulations applicable to the operations in which he or she is engaged.

210.3 Definitions.

(a) The definitions and interpretations contained in section 201 of the act shall be applicable to such terms when used in this part and in Parts 211 through 226 of this chapter.

(b) The following definitions of terms apply to this part and to Parts 211 through 226 of this chapter.

(1) *Act* means the Federal Food, Drug, and Cosmetic Act, as amended (21 U.S.C. 301 et seq.).

(2) *Batch* means a specific quantity of a drug or other material that is intended to have uniform character and quality, within specified limits, and is produced according to a single manufacturing order during the same cycle of manufacture.

(3) *Component* means any ingredient intended for use in the manufacture of a drug product, including those that may not appear in such drug product.

(4) *Drug product* means a finished dosage form, for example, tablet, capsule, solution, etc., that contains an active drug ingredient generally, but not necessarily, in association with inactive ingredients. The term also includes a finished dosage form that does not contain an active ingredient but is intended to be used as a placebo.

(5) *Fiber* means any particulate contaminant with a length at least three times greater than its width.

(6) *Non-fiber-releasing filter* means any filter, which after any appropriate pre-treatment such as washing or flushing, will not release fibers into the component or drug product that is being filtered. All filters composed of asbestos are deemed to be fiber-releasing filters.

(7) *Active ingredient* means any component that is intended to furnish pharmacological activity or other direct effect in the diagnosis, cure, mitigation, treatment, or prevention of disease, or to affect the structure or any function of the body of man or other animals. The term includes those components that may undergo chemical change in the manufacture of the drug product and be present in the drug product in a modified form intended to furnish the specified activity or effect.

(8) *Inactive ingredient* means any component other than an active ingredient.

(9) *In-process material* means any material fabricated, compounded, blended, or derived by chemical reaction that is produced for, and used in, the preparation of the drug product.

(10) *Lot* means a batch, or a specific identified portion of a batch, having uniform character and quality within specified limits; or, in the case of a drug product produced by continuous process, it is a specific identified amount produced in a unit of time or quantity in a manner that assures its having uniform character and quality within specified limits.

(11) *Lot number, control number, or batch number* means any distinctive combination of letters, numbers, or symbols, or any combination of them, from which the complete history of the manufacture, processing, packing, holding, and

distribution of a batch or lot of drug product or other material can be determined.

(12) *Manufacture, processing, packing, or holding of a drug product* includes packaging and labeling operations, testing, and quality control of drug products.

(13) The term *medicated feed* means any Type B or Type C medicated feed as defined in 558.3 of this chapter. The feed contains one or more drugs as defined in section 201(g) of the act. The manufacture of medicated feeds is subject to the requirements of Part 225 of this chapter.

(14) The term *medicated premix* means a Type A medicated article as defined in 558.3 of this chapter. The article contains one or more drugs as defined in section 201(g) of the act. The manufacture of medicated premixes is subject to the requirements of Part 226 of this chapter.

(15) *Quality control unit* means any person or organizational element designated by the firm to be responsible for the duties relating to quality control.

(16) *Strength* means:

(i) The concentration of the drug substance (for example, weight/weight, weight/volume, or unit dose/volume basis), and/or

(ii) The potency, that is, the therapeutic activity of the drug product as indicated by appropriate laboratory tests or by adequately developed and controlled clinical data (expressed, for example, in terms of units by reference to a standard).

(17) *Theoretical yield* means the quantity that would be produced at any appropriate phase of manufacture, processing, or packing of a particular drug product, based upon the quantity of components to be used, in the absence of any loss or error in actual production.

(18) *Actual yield* means the quantity that is actually produced at any appropriate phase of manufacture, processing, or packing of a particular drug product.

(19) *Percentage of theoretical yield* means the ratio of the actual yield (at any appropriate phase of manufacture, processing, or packing of a particular drug product) to the theoretical yield (at the same phase), stated as a percentage.

(20) *Acceptance criteria* means the product specifications and acceptance/rejection criteria, such as acceptable quality level and unacceptable quality level, with an associated sampling plan, that are necessary for making a decision to accept or reject a lot or batch (or any other convenient subgroups of manufactured units).

(21) *Representative sample* means a sample that consists of a number of units that are drawn based on rational criteria such as random sampling and intended to assure that the sample accurately portrays the material being sampled.

(22) *Gang-printed labeling* means labeling derived from a sheet of material on which more than one item of labeling is printed.

[43 FR 45076, Sept. 29, 1978, as amended at 51 FR 7389, Mar. 3, 1986; 58 FR 41353, Aug. 3, 1993]

PART 211 - CURRENT GOOD MANUFACTURING PRACTICE FOR FINISHED PHARMACEUTICALS

AUTHORITY: 21 U.S.C. 321, 351, 352, 355, 360b, 371, 374.
SOURCE: 43 FR 45077, Sept. 29; 1978, unless otherwise noted.

Subpart A - General Provisions

211.1 Scope.
(a) The regulations in this part contain the minimum current good manufacturing practice for preparation of drug products for administration to humans or animals.

(b) The current good manufacturing practice regulations in this chapter, as they pertain to drug products, and in Parts 600 through 680 of this chapter, as they pertain to biological products for human use, shall be considered to supplement, not supersede, the regulations in this part unless the regulations explicitly provide otherwise. In the event it is impossible to comply with applicable regulations both in this part and in other parts of this chapter or in Parts 600 through 680 of this chapter, the regulation specifically supersede the regulation in this part.

(c) Pending consideration of a proposed exemption, published in the FEDERAL REGISTER of September 29, 1978, the requirements in this part shall not be enforced for OTC drug products if the products and all their ingredients are ordinarily marketed and consumed as human foods, and which products may also fall within the legal definition of drugs by virtue of their intended use. Therefore, until further notice, regulations under Part 110 of this chapter, and where applicable, Parts 113 to 129 of this chapter, shall be applied in determining whether these OTC drug products that are also foods are manufactured, processed, packed, or held under current good manufacturing practice.

[FR 45077, Sept. 29, 1978, as amended at 62 FR 66522, Dec. 19, 1997]

211.3 Definitions.
The definitions set forth in 210.3 of this chapter apply in this part.

Subpart B - Organization and Personnel

211.22 Responsibilities of quality control unit.
(a) There shall be a quality control unit that shall have the responsibility and authority to approve or reject all components, drug product containers, closures, in-process materials, packaging material, labeling, and drug products, and the authority to review production records to assure that no errors have occurred or, if errors have occurred, that they have been fully investigated. The quality control unit shall be responsible for approving or rejecting drug products manufactured, processed, packed, or held under contract by another company.

(b) Adequate laboratory facilities for the testing and approval (or rejection) of components, drug product containers, closures, packaging materials, in-process materials, and drug products shall be available to the quality control unit.

(c) The quality control unit shall have the responsibility for approving or rejecting all procedures or specifications impacting on the identity, strength, quality, and purity of the drug product.

(d) The responsibilities and procedures applicable to the quality control unit shall be in writing; such written procedures shall be followed.

211.25   Personnel qualifications.

(a) Each person engaged in the manufacture, processing, packing, or holding of a drug product shall have education, training, and experience, or any combination thereof, to enable that person to perform the assigned functions. Training shall be in the particular operations that the employee performs and in current good manufacturing practice (including the current good manufacturing practice regulations in this chapter and written procedures required by these regulations) as they relate to the employee's functions. Training in current good manufacturing practice shall be conducted by qualified individuals on a continuing basis and with sufficient frequency to assure that employees remain familiar with CGMP requirements applicable to them.

(b) Each person responsible for supervising the manufacture, processing, packing, or holding of a drug product shall have the education, training, and experience, or any combination thereof, to perform assigned functions in such a manner as to provide assurance that the drug product has the safety, identity, strength, quality, and purity that it purports or is represented to possess.

(c) There shall be an adequate number of qualified personnel to perform and supervise the manufacture, processing, packing, or holding of each drug product.

211.28   Personnel responsibilities.

(a) Personnel engaged in the manufacture, processing, packing, or holding of a drug product shall wear clean clothing appropriate for the duties they perform. Protective apparel, such as head, face, hand, and arm coverings, shall be worn as necessary to protect drug products from contamination.

(b) Personnel shall practice good sanitation and health habits.

(c) Only personnel authorized by supervisory personnel shall enter those areas of the buildings and facilities designated as limited-access areas.

(d) Any person shown at any time (either by medical examination or supervisory observation) to have an apparent illness or open lesions that may adversely affect the safety or quality of drug products shall be excluded from direct contact with components, drug product containers, closures, in-process materials, and drug products until the condition is corrected or determined by competent medical personnel not to jeopardize the safety or quality of drug products. All personnel shall be instructed to report to supervisory personnel any health conditions that may have an adverse effect on drug products.

211.34   Consultants.

Consultants advising on the manufacture, processing, packing, or holding of drug products shall have sufficient education, training, and experience, or any combination thereof, to advise on the subject for which they are retained. Records shall be maintained stating the name, address, and qualifications of any consultants and the type of service they provide.

Subpart C - Buildings and Facilities

211.42 Design and construction features.

(a) Any building or buildings used in the manufacture, processing, packing, or holding of a drug product shall be of suitable size, construction and location to facilitate cleaning, maintenance, and proper operations.

(b) Any such building shall have adequate space for the orderly placement of equipment and materials to prevent mixups between different components, drug product containers, closures, labeling, in-process materials, or drug products, and to prevent contamination. The flow of components, drug product containers, closures, labeling, in-process materials, and drug products through the building or buildings shall be designed to prevent contamination.

(c) Operations shall be performed within specifically defined areas of adequate size. There shall be separate or defined areas or such other control systems for the firm's operations as are necessary to prevent contamination or mixups during the course of the following procedures:

(1) Receipt, identification, storage, and withholding from use of components, drug product containers, closures, and labeling, pending the appropriate sampling, testing, or examination by the quality control unit before release for manufacturing or packaging;

(2) Holding rejected components, drug product containers, closures, and labeling before disposition;

(3) Storage of released components, drug product containers, closures, and labeling;

(4) Storage of in-process materials;

(5) Manufacturing and processing operations;

(6) Packaging and labeling operations;

(7) Quarantine storage before release of drug products;

(8) Storage of drug products after release;

(9) Control and laboratory operations;

(10) Aseptic processing, which includes as appropriate:

(i) Floors, walls, and ceilings of smooth, hard surfaces that are easily cleanable;

(ii) Temperature and humidity controls;

(iii) An air supply filtered through high-efficiency particulate air filters under positive pressure, regardless of whether flow is laminar or nonlaminar;

(iv) A system for monitoring environmental conditions;

(v) A system for cleaning and disinfecting the room and equipment to produce aseptic conditions;

(vi) A system for maintaining any equipment used to control the aseptic conditions.

(d) Operations relating to the manufacture, processing, and packing of penicillin shall be performed in facilities separate from those used for other drug products for human use.

[43 FR 45077, Sept. 29, 1978, as amended at 60 FR 4091, Jan. 20, 1995]

211.44   Lighting.

Adequate lighting shall be provided in all areas.

211.46   Ventilation, air filtration, air heating and cooling.

(a) Adequate ventilation shall be provided.

(b) Equipment for adequate control over air pressure, micro-organisms, dust, humidity, and temperature shall be provided when appropriate for the manufacture, processing, packing, or holding of a drug product.

(c) Air filtration systems, including pre-filters and particulate matter air filters, shall be used when appropriate on air supplies to production areas. If air is recirculated to production areas, measures shall be taken to control recirculation of dust from production. In areas where air contamination occurs during production, there shall be adequate exhaust systems or other systems adequate to control contaminants.

(d) Air-handling systems for the manufacture, processing, and packing of penicillin shall be completely separate from those for other drug products for human use.

211.48   Plumbing.

(a) Potable water shall be supplied under continuous positive pressure in a plumbing system free of defects that could contribute contamination to any drug product. Potable water shall meet the standards prescribed in the Environmental Protection Agency's Primary Drinking Water Regulations set forth in 40 CFR Part 141. Water not meeting such standards shall not be permitted in the potable water system.

(b) Drains shall be of adequate size and, where connected directly to a sewer, shall be provided with an air break or other mechanical device to prevent back-siphonage.

43 FR 45077, Sept. 29, 1978, as amended at 48 FR 11426, Mar. 18, 1983!

211.50   Sewage and refuse.

Sewage, trash, and other refuse in and from the building and immediate premises shall be disposed of in a safe and sanitary manner.

211.52   Washing and toilet facilities.

Adequate washing facilities shall be provided, including hot and cold water, soap or detergent, air driers or single-service towels, and clean toilet facilities easily accessible to working areas.

211.56   Sanitation.

(a) Any building used in the manufacture, processing, packing, or holding of a drug product shall be maintained in a clean and sanitary condition, Any such building shall be free of infestation by rodents, birds, insects, and other vermin (other than laboratory animals). Trash and organic waste matter shall be held and disposed of in a timely and sanitary manner.

(b) There shall be written procedures assigning responsibility for sanitation and describing in sufficient detail the cleaning schedules, methods, equipment, and materials to be used in cleaning the buildings and facilities; such written procedures shall be followed.

(c) There shall be written procedures for use of suitable rodenticides, insecticides, fungicides, fumigating agents, and cleaning and sanitizing agents. Such written procedures shall be designed to prevent the contamination of equipment, components, drug product containers, closures, packaging, labeling materials, or drug products and shall be followed. Rodenticides, insecticides, and fungicides shall not be used unless registered and used in accordance with the Federal Insecticide, Fungicide, and Rodenticide Act (7 U.S.C. 135).

(d) Sanitation procedures shall apply to work performed by contractors or temporary employees as well as work performed by full-time employees during the ordinary course of operations.

211.58   Maintenance.

Any building used in the manufacture, processing, packing, or holding of a drug product shall be maintained in a good state of repair.

Subpart D-Equipment

211.63   Equipment design, size, and location.

Equipment used in the manufacture, processing, packing, or holding of a drug product shall be of appropriate design, adequate size, and suitably located to facilitate operations for its intended use and for its cleaning and maintenance.

211.65   Equipment construction.

(a) Equipment shall be constructed so that surfaces that contact components, in-process materials, or drug products shall not be reactive, additive, or absorptive so as to alter the safety, identity, strength, quality, or purity of the drug product beyond the official or other established requirements.

(b) Any substances required for operation, such as lubricants or coolants, shall not come into contact with components, drug product containers, closures, in-process materials, or drug products so as to alter the safety, identity, strength, quality, or purity of the drug product beyond the official or other established requirements.

211.67 Equipment cleaning and maintenance.

(a) Equipment and utensils shall be cleaned, maintained, and sanitized at appropriate intervals to prevent malfunctions or contamination that would alter the safety, identity, strength, quality, or purity of the drug product beyond the official or other established requirements.

(b) Written procedures shall be established and followed for cleaning and maintenance of equipment, including utensils, used in the manufacture, processing, packing, or holding of a drug product. These procedures shall include, but are not necessarily limited to, the following:

(1) Assignment of responsibility for cleaning and maintaining equipment;

(2) Maintenance and cleaning schedules, including, where appropriate, sanitizing schedules;

(3) A description in sufficient detail of the methods, equipment, and materials used in cleaning and maintenance operations, and the methods of disassembling and reassembling equipment as necessary to assure proper cleaning and maintenance;

(4) Removal or obliteration of previous batch identification;

(5) Protection of clean equipment from contamination prior to use;

(6) Inspection of equipment for cleanliness immediately before use.

(c) Records shall be kept of maintenance, cleaning, sanitizing, and inspection as specified in 211.180 and 211.182.

211.68 Automatic, mechanical, and electronic equipment.

(a) Automatic, mechanical, or electronic equipment or other types of equipment, including computers, or related systems that will perform a function satisfactorily, may be used in the manufacture, processing, packing, and holding of a drug product. If such equipment is so used, it shall be routinely calibrated, inspected, or checked according to a written program designed to assure proper performance. Written records of those calibration checks and inspections shall be maintained.

(b) Appropriate controls shall be exercised over computer or related systems to assure that changes in master production and control records or other records are instituted only by authorized personnel. Input to and output from the computer or related system of formulas or other records or data shall be checked for accuracy. The degree and frequency of input/output verification shall be based on the complexity and reliability of the computer or related system. A backup file of data entered into the computer or related system shall be maintained except where certain data, such as calculations performed in connection with laboratory analysis, are eliminated by computerization or other automated processes. In such instances a written record of the program shall be maintained along with appropriate validation data. Hard copy or alternative systems, such as duplicates, tapes, or microfilm, designed to assure that backup data are exact and complete and that it is secure from alteration, inadvertent erasures, or loss shall be maintained.

[43 FR 45077, Sept. 29, 1978, as amended at 60 FR 4091, Jan. 20, 1995]

211.72 Filters.

Filters for liquid filtration used in the manufacture, processing, or packing of injectable drug products intended for human use shall not release fibers into such products. Fiber-releasing filters may not be used in the manufacture, processing, or packing of these injectable drug products unless it is not possible to manufacture such drug products without the use of such filters. If use of a fiber-releasing filter is necessary, an additional non-fiber-releasing filter of 0.22 micron maximum mean porosity (0.45 micron if the manufacturing conditions so dictate) shall subsequently be used to reduce the content of particles in the injectable drug product. Use of an asbestos-containing filter, with or without subsequent use of a specific non-fiber-releasing filter, is permissible only upon submission of proof to the appropriate bureau of the Food and Drug Administration that use of a non-fiber-releasing filter will, or is likely to, compromise the safety or effectiveness of the injectable drug product.

Subpart E - Control of Components and Drug Product Containers and Closures

211.80 General requirements.

(a) There shall be written procedures describing in sufficient detail the receipt, identification, storage, handling, sampling, testing, and approval or rejection of components and drug product containers and closures; such written procedures shall be followed.

(b) Components and drug product containers and closures shall at all times be handled and stored in a manner to prevent contamination.

(c) Bagged or boxed components of drug product containers, or closures shall be stored off the floor and suitably spaced to permit cleaning and inspection.

(d) Each container or grouping of containers for components or drug product containers, or closures shall be identified with a distinctive code for each lot in each shipment received. This code shall be used in recording the disposition of each lot. Each lot shall be appropriately identified as to its status (i.e., quarantined, approved, or rejected).

211.82 Receipt and storage of untested components, drug product containers, and closures.

(a) Upon receipt and before acceptance, each container or grouping of containers of components, drug product containers, and closures shall be examined visually for appropriate labeling as to contents, container damage or broken seals, and contamination.

(b) Components, drug product containers, and closures shall be stored under quarantine until they have been tested or examined, as appropriate, and released. Storage within the area shall conform to the requirements of 211.80.

211.84 Testing and approval or rejection of components, drug product containers, and closures.

(a) Each lot of components, drug product containers, and closures shall be withheld from use until the lot has been sampled, tested, or examined, as appropriate, and released for use by the quality control unit.

(b) Representative samples of each shipment of each lot shall be collected for testing or examination. The number of containers to be sampled, and the amount of material to be taken from each container, shall be based upon appropriate criteria such as statistical criteria for component variability, confidence levels, and degree of precision desired, the past quality history of the supplier, and the quantity needed for analysis and reserve where required by 211.170.

(c) Samples shall be collected in accordance with the following procedures:

(1) The containers of components selected shall be cleaned where necessary, by appropriate means.

(2) The containers shall be opened, sampled, and resealed in a manner designed to prevent contamination of their contents and contamination of other components, drug product containers, or closures.

(3) Sterile equipment and aseptic sampling techniques shall be used when necessary.

(4) If it is necessary to sample a component from the top, middle, and bottom of its container, such sample subdivisions shall not be composited for testing.

(5) Sample containers shall be identified so that the following information can be determined: name of the material sampled, the lot number, the container from which the sample was taken, the data on which the sample was taken, and the name of the person who collected the sample.

(6) Containers from which samples have been taken shall be marked to show that samples have been removed from them.

(d) Samples shall be examined and tested as follows:

(1) At least one test shall be conducted to verify the identity of each component of a drug product. Specific identity tests, if they exist, shall be used.

(2) Each component shall be tested for conformity with all appropriate written specifications for purity, strength, and quality. In lieu of such testing by the manufacturer, a report of analysis may be accepted from the supplier of a component, provided that at least one specific identity test is conducted on such component by the manufacturer, and provided that the manufacturer establishes the reliability of the supplier's analyses through appropriate validation of the supplier's test results at appropriate intervals.

(3) Containers and closures shall be tested for conformance with all appropriate written procedures. In lieu of such testing by the manufacturer, a certificate of testing may be accepted from the supplier, provided that at least a visual identification is conducted on such containers/closures by the manufacturer and provided that the manufacturer establishes the reliability of the supplier's test results through appropriate validation of the supplier's test results at appropriate intervals.

(4) When appropriate, components shall be microscopically examined.

(5) Each lot of a component, drug product container, or closure that is liable to contamination with filth, insect infestation, or other extraneous adulterant shall be examined against established specifications for such contamination.

(6) Each lot of a component, drug product container, or closure that is liable to microbiological contamination that is objectionable in view of its intended use shall be subjected to microbiological tests before use.

(e) Any lot of components, drug product containers, or closures that meets the appropriate written specifications of identity, strength, quality, and purity and related tests under paragraph (d) of this section may be approved and released for use. Any lot of such material that does not meet such specifications shall be rejected.

[43 FR 45077, Sept. 29, 1978, as amended at 63 FR 14356, Mar. 25, 1998]

211.86 Use of approved components, drug product containers, and closures.

Components, drug product containers, and closures approved for use shall be rotated so that the oldest approved stock is used first. Deviation from this requirement is permitted if such deviation is temporary and appropriate.

211.87 Retesting of approved components, drug product containers, and closures.

Components, drug product containers, and closures shall be retested or reexamined, as appropriate, for identity, strength, quality, and purity and approved or rejected by the quality control unit in accordance with 211.84 as necessary, e.g., after storage for long periods or after exposure to air, heat or other conditions that might adversely affect the component, drug product container, or closure.

211.89 Rejected components, drug product containers, and closures.

Rejected components, drug product containers, and closures shall be identified and controlled under a quarantine system designed to prevent their use in manufacturing or processing operations for which they are unsuitable.

211.94 Drug product containers and closures.

(a) Drug product containers and closures shall not be reactive, additive, or absorptive so as to alter the safety, identity, strength, quality, or purity of the drug beyond the official or established requirements.

(b) Container closure systems shall provide adequate protection against foreseeable external factors in storage and use that can cause deterioration or contamination of the drug product.

(c) Drug product containers and closures shall be clean and, where indicated by the nature of the drug, sterilized and processed to remove pyrogenic properties to assure that they are suitable for their intended use.

(d) Standards or specifications, methods of testing, and, where indicated, methods of cleaning, sterilizing, and processing to remove pyrogenic properties shall be written and followed for drug product containers and closures.

Subpart F-Production and Process Controls

211.100 Written procedures; deviations.

(a) There shall be written procedures for production and process control designed to assure that the drug products have the identity, strength, quality, and purity they purport or are represented to possess. Such procedures shall include all requirements in this subpart. These written procedures, including any changes, shall be drafted, reviewed, and approved by the appropriate organizational units and reviewed and approved by the quality control unit.

(b) Written production and process control procedures shall be followed in the execution of the various production and process control functions and shall be documented at the time of performance. Any deviation from the written procedures shall be recorded and justified.

211.101   Charge - in of components.

Written production and control procedures shall include the following, which are designed to assure that the drug products produced have the identity, strength, quality, and purity they purport or are represented to possess:

(a) The batch shall be formulated with the intent to provide not less than 100 percent of the labeled or established amount of active ingredient.

(b) Components for drug product manufacturing shall be weighed, measured, or subdivided as appropriate. If a component is removed from the original container to another, the new container shall be identified with the following information:

(1) Component name or item code;

(2) Receiving or control number;

(3) Weight or measure in new container;

(4) Batch for which component was dispensed, including its product name, strength, and lot number.

(c) Weighing, measuring, or subdividing operations for components shall be adequately supervised. Each container of component dispensed to manufacturing shall be examined by a second person to assure that:

(1) The component was released by the quality control unit;

(2) The weight or measure is correct as stated in the batch production records;

(3) The containers are properly identified.

(d) Each component shall be added to the batch by one person and verified by a second person.

211.103   Calculation of yield.

Actual yields and percentages of theoretical yield shall be determined at the conclusion of each appropriate phase of manufacturing, processing, packaging, or holding of the drug product. Such calculations shall be performed by one person and independently verified by a second person.

211.105   Equipment identification.

(a) All compounding and storage containers, processing lines, and major equipment used during the production of a batch of a drug product shall be properly identified at all times to indicate their contents and, when necessary, the phase of processing of the batch.

(b) Major equipment shall be identified by a distinctive identification number or code that shall be recorded in the batch production record to show the specific equipment used in the manufacture of each batch of a drug product. In cases where only one of a particular type of equipment exists in a manufacturing facility, the name of the equipment may be used in lieu of a distinctive identification number or code.

211.110   Sampling and testing of in-process materials and drug products.

(a) To assure batch uniformity and integrity of drug products, written procedures shall be established and followed

that describe the in-process controls, and tests, or examinations to be conducted on appropriate samples of in-process materials of each batch. Such control procedures shall be established to monitor the output and to validate the performance of those manufacturing processes that may be responsible for causing variability in the characteristics of in-process material and the drug product. Such control procedures shall include, but are not limited to, the following, where appropriate:

(1) Tablet or capsule weight variation;

(2) Disintegration time;

(3) Adequacy of mixing to assure uniformity and homogeneity;

(4) Dissolution time and rate;

(5) Clarity, completeness, or pH of solutions.

(b) Valid in-process specifications for such characteristics shall be consistent with drug product final specifications and shall be derived from previous acceptable process average and process variability estimates where possible and determined by the application of suitable statistical procedures where appropriate. Examination and testing of samples shall assure that the drug product and in-process material conform to specifications.

(c) In-process materials shall be tested for identity, strength, quality, and purity as appropriate, and approved or rejected by the quality control unit, during the production process, e.g., at commencement or completion of significant phases or after storage for long periods.

(d) Rejected in-process materials shall be identified and controlled under a quarantine system designed to prevent their use in manufacturing or processing operations for which they are unsuitable.

211.111 Time limitations on production.

When appropriate, time limits for the completion of each phase of production shall be established to assure the quality of the drug product. Deviation from established time limits may be acceptable if such deviation does not compromise the quality of the drug product. Such deviation shall be justified and documented.

211.113   Control of microbiological contamination.

(a) Appropriate written procedures, designed to prevent objectionable microorganisms in drug products not required to be sterile, shall be established and followed.

(b) Appropriate written procedures, designed to prevent microbiological contamination of drug products purporting to be sterile, shall be established and followed. Such procedures shall include validation of any sterilization process.

211.115   Reprocessing.

(a) Written procedures shall be established and followed prescribing a system for reprocessing batches that do not conform to standards or specifications and the steps to be taken to insure that the reprocessed batches will conform with all established standards, specifications, and characteristics.

(b) Reprocessing shall not be performed without the review and approval of the quality control unit.

Subpart G-Packaging and Labeling Control

211.122 Materials examination and usage criteria.

(a) There shall be written procedures describing in sufficient detail the receipt, identification, storage, handling, sampling, examination, and/or testing of labeling and packaging materials; such written procedures shall be followed. Labeling and packaging materials shall be representatively sampled, and examined or tested upon receipt and before use in packaging or labeling of a drug product.

(b) Any labeling or packaging materials meeting appropriate written specifications may be approved and released for use. Any labeling or packaging materials that do not meet such specifications shall be rejected to prevent their use in operations for which they are unsuitable.

(c) Records shall be maintained for each shipment received of each different labeling and packaging material indicating receipt, examination or testing, and whether accepted or rejected.

(d) Labels and other labeling materials for each different drug product, strength, dosage form, or quantity of contents shall be stored separately with suitable identification. Access to the storage area shall be limited to authorized personnel.

(e) Obsolete and outdated labels, labeling, and other packaging materials shall be destroyed.

(f) Use of gang-printed labeling for different drug products, or different strengths or net contents of the same drug product, is prohibited unless the labeling from gang-printed sheets is adequately differentiated by size, shape or color.

(g) If cut labeling is used, packaging and labeling operations shall include one of the following special control procedures:

(1) Dedication of labeling and packaging lines to each different strength of each different drug product;

(2) Use of appropriate electronic or electromechanical equipment to conduct a 100-percent examination for correct labeling during or after completion of finishing operations; or

(3) Use of visual inspection to conduct a 100-percent examination for correct labeling during or after completion of finishing operations for hand-applied labeling. Such examination shall be performed by one person and independently verified by a second person.

(h) Printing devices on, or associated with, manufacturing lines used to imprint labeling upon the drug product unit label or case shall be monitored to assure that all imprinting conforms to the print specified in the batch production record.

[43 FR 45077, Sept. 29, 1978, as amended at 58 FR 41353, Aug. 3, 1993]

211.125   Labeling issuance.

(a) Strict control shall be exercised over labeling issued for use in drug product labeling operations.

(b) Labeling materials issued for a batch shall be carefully examined for identity and conformity to the labeling specified in the master or batch production records.

(c) Procedures shall be utilized to reconcile the quantities of labeling issued, used, and returned, and shall require evaluation of discrepancies found between the quantity of drug product finished and the quantity of labeling issued when such discrepancies are outside narrow preset limits based on historical operating data. Such discrepancies shall be investigated in accordance with 211.192. Labeling reconciliation is waived for cut or roll a labeling if a 100-percent examination for correct labeling is performed in accordance with 211.122(g)(2).

(d) All excess labeling bearing lot or control numbers shall be destroyed.

(e) Returned labeling shall be maintained and stored in a manner to prevent mixups and provide proper identification.

(f) Procedures shall be written describing in sufficient detail the control procedures employed for the issuance of labeling; such written procedures shall be followed.

[43 FR 45077, Sept. 29, 1978, as amended at 58 FR 41354, Aug. 3, 1993]

211.130 Packaging and labeling operations.

There shall be written procedures designed to assure that correct labels, labeling, and packaging materials are used for drug products; such written procedures shall be followed. These procedures shall incorporate the following features:

(a) Prevention of mixups and cross-contamination by physical or spatial separation from operations on other drug products.

(b) Identification and handling of filled drug product containers that are set aside and held in unlabeled condition for future labeling operations to preclude mislabeling of individual containers, lots, or portions of lots. Identification need not be applied to each individual container but shall be sufficient to determine name, strength, quantity of contents, and lot or control number of each container.

(c) Identification of the drug product with a lot or control number that permits determination of the history of the manufacture and control of the batch.

(d) Examination of packaging and labeling materials for suitability and correctness before packaging operations, and documentation of such examination in the batch production record.

(e) Inspection of the packaging and labeling facilities immediately before use to assure that all drug products have been removed from previous operations. Inspection shall also be made to assure that packaging and labeling materials not suitable for subsequent operations have been removed. Results of inspection shall be documented in the batch production records.

[43 FR 45077, Sept. 29, 1978, as amended at 58 FR 41354, Aug. 3, 1993]

211.132 Tamper-evident packaging requirements for over-the-counter (OTC) human drug products.

(a) General. The Food and Drug Administration has the

authority under the Federal Food, Drug, and Cosmetic Act (the act) to establish a uniform national requirement for tamper-evident packaging of OTC drug products that will improve the security of OTC drug packaging and help assure the safety and effectiveness of OTC drug products. An OTC drug product (except a dermatological, dentifrice, insulin, or throat lozenge product) for retail sale that is not packaged in a tamper-resistant package or that is not properly labeled under this section is adulterated under section 501 of the act or misbranded under section 502 of the act, or both.

(b) Requirements for tamper-evident package. (1) Each manufacturer and packer who packages an OTC drug product (except a dermatological, dentifrice, insulin, or lozenge product) for retail sale shall package the product in a tamper-evident package, if this product is accessible to the public while held for sale. A tamper-evident package is one having one or more indicators or barriers to entry which, if breached or missing, can reasonably be expected to provide visible evidence to consumers that tampering has occurred. To reduce the likelihood of successful tampering and to increase the likelihood that consumers will discover if a product has been tampered with, the package is required to be distinctive by design or by the use of one or more indicators or barriers to entry that employ an identifying characteristic (e.g., a pattern, name, registered trademark, logo or picture). For purposes of this section, the term "distinctive by design" means the packaging cannot be duplicated with commonly available materials or through commonly available processes. A tamper evident package may involve an immediate-container and closure system or secondary-container or carton system or any combination of systems intended to provide visual indication of package integrity. The tamper-evident feature shall be designed to and shall remain intact when handled in a reasonable manner during manufacture, distribution and retail display.

(2) In addition to the tamper-evident packaging feature described in paragraph (b)(1) of this section, any two-piece, hard gelatin capsule, covered by this section must be sealed using an acceptable tamper-evident technology.

(c) Labeling. (1) In order to alert consumers to the specific tamper-evident feature(s) used, each retail package of an OTC drug product covered by this section (except ammonia inhalant in crushable glass ampules, containers of compressed medical oxygen, or aerosol products that depend upon the power of liquefied or compressed gas to expel the contents from the container) is required to bear a statement that:

(i) Identifies all tamper-evident feature(s) and any capsule sealing technologies used to comply with paragraph (b) of this section;

(ii) Is prominently placed on the package; and

(iii) Is so placed that it will be unaffected if the tamper-evident feature of the package is breached or missing.

(2) If the tamper-evident feature chosen to meet the requirements in paragraph (b) of this section uses an identifying characteristic, that characteristic is required to be referred to in the labeling statement. For example, the labeling statement on a bottle with a shrink band could say,

"For your protection, this bottle has an imprinted seal around the neck."

(d) Request for exemptions from packaging and labeling requirements. A manufacturer or packer may request an exemption from the packaging and labeling requirements of this section. A request for exemption is required to be submitted in the form of a citizen petition under 10.30 of this chapter and should be clearly identified on the envelope as a "Request for Exemption from the Tamper-Evident Packaging Rule". The petition is required to contain the following:

(1) The name of the drug product or, if the petition seeks an exemption for a drug class, the name of the drug class, and a list of products within that class.

(2) The reasons that the drug product's compliance with the tamper-evident packaging or labeling requirements of this section is unnecessary or can't be achieved.

(3) A description of alternative steps that are available, or that the petitioner has already taken, to reduce the likelihood that the product or drug class will be the subject of malicious adulteration.

(4) Other information justifying an exemption.

(e) OTC drug products subject to approved new drug applications. Holders of approved new drug applications for OTC drug products are required under 314.70 of this chapter to provide the agency with notification of changes in packaging and labeling to comply with the requirements of this section. Changes in packaging and labeling required by this regulation may be made before FDA approval, as provided under 314. 70 of this chapter. Manufacturing changes by which capsules are to be sealed require prior FDA approval under 314. 70(b) of this chapter.

(f) Poison Prevention Packaging Act of 1970. This section does not affect any requirements for "special packaging" as defined under 310.3(l) of this chapter and required under the Poison Prevention Packaging Act of 19707.

(Approved by the Office of Management and Budget under OMB control number 0910-0149)
[54 FR 5228, Feb. 2, 1989, as amended at 63 FR 59470, Nov. 4, 1998]

211.134   Drug product inspection.

(a) Packaged and labeled products shall be examined during finishing operations to provide assurance that containers and packages in the lot have the correct label.

(b) A representative sample of units shall be collected at the completion of finishing operations and shall be visually examined for correct labeling.

(c) Results of these examinations shall be recorded in the batch production or control records.

211.137   Expiration dating.

(a) To assure that a drug product meets applicable standards of identity, strength, quality, and purity at the time of use, it shall bear an expiration date determined by appropriate stability testing described in 211.166.

(b) Expiration dates shall be related to any storage conditions stated on the labeling, as determined by stability studies described in 211.166.

(c) If the drug product is to be reconstituted at the time of dispensing, its labeling shall bear expiration information for both the reconstituted and unreconstituted drug products.

(d) Expiration dates shall appear on labeling in accordance with the requirements of 201.17 of this chapter.

(e) Homeopathic drug products shall be exempt from the requirements of this section.

(f) Allergenic extracts that are labeled "No U.S. Standard of Potency" are exempt from the requirements of this section.

(g) New drug products for investigational use are exempt from the requirements of this section, provided that they meet appropriate standards or specifications as demonstrated by stability studies during their use in clinical investigations. Where new drug products for investigational use are to be reconstituted at the time of dispensing, their labeling shall bear expiration information for the reconstituted drug product.

(h) Pending consideration of a proposed exemption, published in the Federal Register of September 29, 1978, the requirements in this section shall not be enforced for human OTC drug products if their labeling does not bear dosage limitations and they are stable for at least 3 years as supported by appropriate stability data.

[43 FR 45077, Sept. 29, 1978, as amended at 46 FR 56412, Nov. 17, 1981; 60 FR 4091, Jan. 20, 1995]

Subpart H - Holding and Distribution

211.142 Warehousing procedures.

Written procedures describing the warehousing of drug products shall be established and followed. They shall include:

(a) Quarantine of drug products before release by the quality control unit.

(b) Storage of drug products under appropriate conditions of temperature, humidity, and light so that the identity, strength, quality, and purity of the drug products are not affected.

211.150 Distribution procedures.

Written procedures shall be established, and followed, describing the distribution of drug products. They shall include:

(a) A procedure whereby the oldest approved stock of a drug product is distributed first. Deviation from this requirement is permitted if such deviation is temporary and appropriate.

(b) A system by which the distribution of each lot of drug product can be readily determined to facilitate its recall if necessary.

Subpart I - Laboratory Controls

211.160 General requirements.

(a) The establishment of any specifications, standards, sampling plans, test procedures, or other laboratory control mechanisms required by this subpart, including any change in such specifications, standards, sampling plans, test pro-

cedures, or other laboratory control mechanisms, shall be drafted by the appropriate organizational unit and reviewed and approved by the quality control unit. The requirements in this subpart shall be followed and shall be documented at the time of performance. Any deviation from the written specifications, standards, sampling plans, test procedures, or other laboratory control mechanisms shall be recorded and justified.

(b) Laboratory controls shall include the establishment of scientifically sound and appropriate specifications, standards, sampling plans, and test procedures designed to assure that components, drug product containers, closures, in-process materials, labeling, and drug products conform to appropriate standards of identity, strength, quality, and purity. Laboratory controls shall include:

(1) Determination of conformance to appropriate written specifications for the acceptance of each lot within each shipment of components, drug product containers, closures, and labeling used in the manufacture, processing, packing, or holding of drug products. The specifications shall include a description of the sampling and testing procedures used. Samples shall be representative and adequately identified. Such procedures shall also require appropriate retesting of any component, drug product container, or closure that is subject to deterioration.

(2) Determination of conformance to written specifications and a description of sampling and testing procedures for in-process materials. Such samples shall be representative and properly identified.

(3) Determination of conformance to written descriptions of sampling procedures and appropriate specifications for drug products. Such samples shall be representative and properly identified.

(4) The calibration of instruments, apparatus, gauges, and recording devices at suitable intervals in accordance with an established written program containing specific directions, schedules, limits for accuracy and precision, and provisions for remedial action in the event accuracy and/or precision limits are not met. Instruments, apparatus, gauges, and recording devices not meeting established specifications shall not be used.

211.165 Testing and release for distribution.

(a) For each batch of drug product, there shall be appropriate laboratory determination of satisfactory conformance to final specifications for the drug product, including the identity and strength of each active ingredient, prior to release. Where sterility and/or pyrogen testing are conducted on specific batches of short-lived radiopharmaceuticals, such batches may be released prior to completion of sterility and/or pyrogen testing, provided such testing is completed as soon as possible.

(b) There shall be appropriate laboratory testing, as necessary, of each batch of drug product required to be free of objectionable microorganisms.

(c) Any sampling and testing plans shall be described in written procedures that shall include the method of sampling and the number of units per batch to be tested; such written procedure shall be followed.

(d) Acceptance criteria for the sampling and testing conducted by the quality control unit shall be adequate to assure that batches of drug products meet each appropriate specification and appropriate statistical quality control criteria as a condition for their approval and release. The statistical quality control criteria shall include appropriate acceptance levels and/or appropriate rejection levels.

(e) The accuracy, sensitivity, specificity, and reproducibility of test methods employed by the firm shall be established and documented. Such validation and documentation may be accomplished in accordance with 211.194(a)(2).

(f) Drug products failing to meet established standards or specifications and any other relevant quality control criteria shall be rejected. Reprocessing may be performed. Prior to acceptance and use, reprocessed material must meet appropriate standards, specifications, and any other relevant criteria.

211.166 Stability testing.

(a) There shall be a written testing program designed to assess the stability characteristics of drug products. The results of such stability testing shall be used in determining appropriate storage conditions and expiration dates. The written program shall be followed and shall include:

(1) Sample size and test intervals based on statistical criteria for each attribute examined to assure valid estimates of stability;

(2) Storage conditions for samples retained for testing;

(3) Reliable, meaningful, and specific test methods;

(4) Testing of the drug product in the same container-closure system as that in which the drug product is marketed;

(5) Testing of drug products for reconstitution at the time of dispensing (as directed in the labeling) as well as after they are reconstituted.

(b) An adequate number of batches of each drug product shall be tested to determine an appropriate expiration date and a record of such data shall be maintained. Accelerated studies, combined with basic stability information on the components, drug products, and container-closure system, may be used to support tentative expiration dates provided full shelf life studies are not available and are being conducted. Where data from accelerated studies are used to project a tentative expiration date that is beyond a date supported by actual shelf life studies, there must be stability studies conducted, including drug product testing at appropriate intervals, until the tentative expiration date is verified or the appropriate expiration date determined.

(c) For homeopathic drug products, the requirements of this section are as follows:

(1) There shall be a written assessment of stability based at least on testing or examination of the drug product for compatibility of the ingredients, and based on marketing experience with the drug product to indicate that there is no degradation of the product for the normal or expected period of use.

(2) Evaluation of stability shall be based on the same container-closure system in which the drug product is being marketed.

(d) Allergenic extracts that are labeled "No U.S. Standard of Potency" are exempt from the requirements of this section.

[43 FR 45077, Sept. 29, 1978, as amended at 46 FR 56412, Nov. 17, 1981]

211.167 Special testing requirements.

(a) For each batch of drug product purporting to be sterile and/or pyrogen-free, there shall be appropriate laboratory testing to determine conformance to such requirements. The test procedures shall be in writing and shall be followed.

(b) For each batch of ophthalmic ointment, there shall be appropriate testing to determine conformance to specifications regarding the presence of foreign particles and harsh or abrasive substances. The test procedures shall be in writing and shall be followed.

(c) For each batch of controlled-release dosage form, there shall be appropriate laboratory testing to determine conformance to the specifications for the rate of release of each active ingredient. The test procedures shall be in writing and shall be followed.

211.170 Reserve samples.

(a) An appropriately identified shipment of each active ingredient shall be retained. The reserve sample consists of at least twice the quantity necessary for all tests required to determine whether the active ingredient meets its established specifications, except for sterility and pyrogen testing. The retention time is as follows:

(1) For an active ingredient in a drug product other than those described in paragraphs (a) (2) and (3) of this section, the reserve sample shall be retained for 1 year after the expiration date of the last lot of the drug product containing the active ingredient.

(2) For an active ingredient in a radioactive drug product, except for non-radioactive reagent kits, the reserve sample shall be retained for:

(i) Three months after the expiration date of the last lot of the drug product containing the active ingredient if the expiration dating period of the drug product is 30 days or less; or

(ii) Six months after the expiration date of the last lot of the drug product containing the active ingredient if the expiration dating period of the drug product is more than 30 days.

(3) For an active ingredient in an OTC drug product that is exempt from bearing an expiration date under 211.137, the reserve sample shall be retained for 3 years after distribution of the last lot of the drug product containing the active ingredient.

(b) An appropriately identified reserve sample that is representative of each lot or batch of drug product shall be retained and stored under conditions consistent with product labeling. The reserve sample shall be stored in the same immediate container-closure system in which the drug product is marketed or in one that has essentially the same characteristics. The reserve sample consists of at least twice the quantity necessary to perform all the required tests, except those for sterility and pyrogens. Except for those for drug products described in paragraph (b)(2) of this section, reserve samples from representative sample lots or batches selected by acceptable statistical procedures shall be examined visually at least once a year for evidence of deterioration unless visual examination would affect the integrity of the reserve samples. Any evidence of reserve sample deterioration shall be investigated in accordance with 211.192. The results of the examination shall be recorded and maintained with other stability data on the drug product. Reserve samples of compressed medical gases need not be retained. The retention time is as follows:

(1) For a drug product other than those described in paragraphs (b) (2) and (3) of this section, the reserve sample shall be retained for 1 year after the expiration date of the drug product.

(2) For a radioactive drug product, except for non-radioactive reagent kits, the reserve sample shall be retained for:

(i) Three months after the expiration date of the drug product if the expiration dating period of the drug product is 30 days or less; or

(ii) Six months after the expiration date of the drug product if the expiration more than 30 days.

(3) For an OTC drug product that is exempt for bearing an expiration date under 211.137, the reserve sample must be retained for 3 years after the lot or batch of drug product is distributed.

[48 FR 13025, Mar. 29, 1983, as amended at 60 FR 4091, Jan 20, 1995]

211.173 Laboratory animals.

Animals used in testing components, in-process materials, or drug products for compliance with established specifications shall be maintained and controlled in a manner that assures their suitability for their intended use. They shall be identified, and adequate records shall be maintained showing the history of their use.

211.176 Penicillin contamination.

If a reasonable possibility exists that a non-penicillin drug product has been exposed to cross contamination with penicillin, the non-penicillin drug product shall be tested for the presence of penicillin. Such drug product shall not be marketed if detectable levels are found when tested according to procedures specified in `Procedures for Detecting and Measuring Penicillin Contamination in Drugs,' which is incorporated by reference. Copies are available from the Division of Research and Testing (HFD-470), Center for Drug Evaluation and Research, Food and Drug Administration, 200 C St. SW., Washington, DC 20204, or available for inspection at the Office of the Federal Register, 800 North Capitol Street, NW, Suite 800, Washington, DC 20408.

[43 FR 45077, Sept. 29, 1978, as amended at 47 FR 9396, Mar. 5, 1982; 50 FR 8996, Mar. 6, 1985; 55 FR 11577, Mar. 29, 1990]

Subpart J - Records and Reports

211.180 General requirements.

(a) Any production, control, or distribution record that is required to be maintained in compliance with this part and

is specifically associated with a batch of a drug product shall be retained for at least 1 year after the expiration date of the batch or, in the case of certain OTC drug products lacking expiration dating because they meet the criteria for exemption under 211.137, 3 years after distribution of the batch.

(b) Records shall be maintained for all components, drug product containers, closures, and labeling for at least 1 year after the expiration date or, in the case of certain OTC drug products lacking expiration dating because they meet the criteria for exemption under 211.137, 3 years after distribution of the last lot of drug product incorporating the component or using the container, closure, or labeling.

(c) All records required under this part, or copies of such records, shall be readily available for authorized inspection during the retention period at the establishment where the activities described in such records occurred. These records or copies thereof shall be subject to photocopying or other means of reproduction as part of such inspection. Records that can be immediately retrieved from another location by computer or other electronic means shall be considered as meeting the requirements of this paragraph.

(d) Records required under this part may be retained either as original records or as true copies such as photocopies, microfilm, microfiche, or other accurate reproductions of the original records. Where reduction techniques, such as microfilming, are used, suitable reader and photocopying equipment shall be readily available.

(e) Written records required by this part shall be maintained so that data therein can be used for evaluating, at least annually, the quality standards of each drug product to determine the need for changes in drug product specifications or manufacturing or control procedures. Written procedures shall be established and followed for such evaluations and shall include provisions for:

(1) A review of representative number of batches, whether approved or rejected, and, where applicable, records associated with the batch.

(2) A review of complaints, recalls, returned or salvaged drug products, and investigations conducted under 211.192 for each drug product.

(f) Procedures shall be established to assure that the responsible officials of the firm, if they are not personally involved in or immediately aware of such actions, are notified in writing of any investigations conducted under 211.198, 211.204, or 211.208 of these regulations, any recalls, reports of inspectional observations issued by the Food and Drug Administration, or any regulatory actions relating to good manufacturing practices brought by the Food and Drug Administration.

[43 FR 45077, Sept. 29, 1978, as amended at 60 FR 4091, Jan. 20, 1995]

211.182 Equipment cleaning and use log.

A written record of major equipment cleaning, maintenance (except routine maintenance such as lubrication and adjustments), and use shall be included in individual equipment logs that show the date, time, product, and lot number of each batch processed. If equipment is dedicated to manufacture of one product, then individual equipment logs are not required, provided that lots or batches of such product follow in numerical order and are manufactured in numerical sequence. In cases where dedicated equipment is employed, the records of cleaning, maintenance, and use shall be part of the batch record. The persons performing and double-checking the cleaning and maintenance shall date and sign or initial the log indicating that the work was performed. Entries in the log shall be in chronological order.

211.184 Component, drug product container, closure, and labeling records.

These records shall include the following:

(a) The identity and quantity of each shipment of each lot of components, drug product containers, closures, and labeling; the name of the supplier; the supplier's lot number(s) if known; the receiving code as specified in 211.80; and the date of receipt. The name and location of the prime manufacturer, if different from the supplier, shall be listed if known.

(b) The results of any test or examination performed (including those performed as required by 211.82(a), 211.84(d), or 211.122(a)) and the conclusions derived therefrom.

(c) An individual inventory record of each component, drug product container, and closure and, for each component, a reconciliation of the use of each lot of such component. The inventory record shall contain sufficient information to allow determination of any batch or lot of drug product associated with the use of each component, drug product container, and closure.

(d) Documentation of the examination and review of labels and labeling for conformity with established specifications in accord with 211.122(c) and 211.130(c).

(e) The disposition of rejected components, drug product containers, closure, and labeling.

211.186 Master production and control records.

(a) To assure uniformity from batch to batch, master production and control records for each drug product, including each batch size thereof, shall be prepared, dated, and signed (full signature, handwritten) by one person and independently checked, dated, and signed by a second person. The preparation of master production and control records shall be described in a written procedure and such written procedure shall be followed.

(b) Master production and control records shall include:

(1) The name and strength of the product and a description of the dosage form;

(2) The name and weight or measure of each active ingredient per dosage unit or per unit of weight or measure of the drug product, and a statement of the total weight or measure of any dosage unit;

(3) A complete list of components designated by names or codes sufficiently specific to indicate any special quality characteristic;

(4) An accurate statement of the weight or measure of each component, using the same weight system (metric, avoirdupois, or apothecary) for each component.

Reasonable variations may be permitted, however, in the amount of components necessary for the preparation in the dosage form, provided they are justified in the master production and control records;

(5) A statement concerning any calculated excess of component;

(6) A statement of theoretical weight or measure at appropriate phases of processing;

(7) A statement of theoretical yield, including the maximum and minimum percentages of theoretical yield beyond which investigation according to 211.192 is required;

(8) A description of the drug product containers, closures, and packaging materials, including a specimen or copy of each label and all other labeling signed and dated by the person or persons responsible for approval of such labeling;

(9) Complete manufacturing and control instructions, sampling and testing procedures, specifications, special notations, and precautions to be followed.

211.188 Batch production and control records.

Batch production and control records shall be prepared for each batch of drug product produced and shall include complete information relating to the production and control of each batch. These records shall include:

(a) An accurate reproduction of the appropriate master production or control record, checked for accuracy, dated, and signed;

(b) Documentation that each significant step in the manufacture, processing, packing, or holding of the batch was accomplished, including:

(1) Dates;

(2) Identity of individual major equipment and lines used;

(3) Specific identification of each batch of component or in-process material used;

(4) Weights and measures of components used in the course of processing;

(5) In-process and laboratory control results;

(6) Inspection of the packaging and labeling area before and after use;

(7) A statement of the actual yield and a statement of the percentage of theoretical yield at appropriate phases of processing;

(8) Complete labeling control records, including specimens or copies of all labeling used;

(9) Description of drug product containers and closures;

(10) Any sampling performed;

(11) Identification of the persons performing and directly supervising or checking each significant step in the operation;

(12) Any investigation made according to 211.192.

(13) Results of examinations made in accordance with 211.134.

211.192 Production record review.

All drug product production and control records, including those for packaging and labeling, shall be reviewed and approved by the quality control unit to determine compliance with all established, approved written procedures before a batch is released or distributed. Any unexplained discrepancy (including a percentage of theoretical yield exceeding the maximum or minimum percentages established in master production and control records) or the failure of a batch or any of its components to meet any of its specifications shall be thoroughly investigated, whether or not the batch has already been distributed. The investigation shall extend to other batches of the same drug product and other drug products that may have been associated with the specific failure or discrepancy. A written record of the investigation shall be made and shall include the conclusions and follow up.

211.194   Laboratory records.

(a) Laboratory records shall include complete data derived from all tests necessary to assure compliance with established specifications and standards, including examinations and assays, as follows:

(1) A description of the sample received for testing with identification of source (that is, location from where sample was obtained), quantity, lot number or other distinctive code, date sample was taken, and date sample was received for testing.

(2) A statement of each method used in the testing of the sample. The statement shall indicate the location of data that establish that the methods used in the testing of the sample meet proper standards of accuracy and reliability as applied to the product tested. (If the method employed is in the current revision of the United States Pharmacopoeia, National Formulary, Association of Official Analytical Chemists, Book of Methods**, or in other recognized standard references, or is detailed in an approved new drug application and the referenced method is not modified, a statement indicating the method and reference will suffice). The suitability of all testing methods used shall be verified under actual conditions of use.

[Footnote: **Copies may be obtained from: Association of Official Analytical Chemists, 2200 Wilson Blvd., Suite 400, Arlington, VA 22201 3301.]

(3) A statement of the weight or measure of sample used for each test, where appropriate.

(4) A complete record of all data secured in the course of each test, including all graphs, charts, and spectra from laboratory instrumentation, properly identified to show the specific component, drug product container, closure, in-process material, or drug product, and lot tested.

(5) A record of all calculations performed in connection with the test, including units of measure, conversion factors, and equivalency factors.

(6) A statement of the results of tests and how the results compare with established standards of identity, strength, quality, and purity for the component, drug product container, closure, in-process material, or drug product tested.

(7) The initials or signature of the person who performs each test and the date(s) the tests were performed.

(8) The initials or signature of a second person showing that the original records have been reviewed for accuracy, completeness, and compliance with established standards.

(b) Complete records shall be maintained of any modification of an established method employed in testing. Such records shall include the reason for the modification and data to verify that the modification produced results that are at least as accurate and reliable for the material being tested as the established method.

(c) Complete records shall be maintained of any testing and standardization of laboratory reference standards, reagents, and standard solutions.

(d) Complete records shall be maintained of the periodic calibration of laboratory instruments, apparatus, gauges, and recording devices required by 211.160(b)(4).

(e) Complete records shall be maintained of all stability testing performed in accordance with 211.166.

[43 FR 45077, Sept. 29, 1978, as amended at 55 FR 11577, Mar. 29, 1990; 65 FR 1889, APR 10,2000]

211.196   Distribution records.

Distribution records shall contain the name and strength of the product and description of the dosage form, name and address of the consignee, date and quantity shipped, and lot or control number of the drug product. For compressed medical gas products, distribution records are not required to contain lot or control numbers.

(Approved by the Office of Management and Budget under control number 0910 0139) [49 FR 9865, Mar. 16, 1984]

211.198   Complaint files.

(a) Written procedures describing the handling of all written and oral complaints regarding a drug product shall be established and followed. Such procedures shall include provisions for review by the quality control unit, of any complaint involving the possible failure of a drug product to meet any of its specifications and, for such drug products, a determination as to the need for an investigation in accordance with 211.192. Such procedures shall include provisions for review to determine whether the complaint represents a serious and unexpected adverse drug experience which is required to be reported to the Food and Drug Administration in accordance with 310.305 of this chapter.

(b) A written record of each complaint shall be maintained in a file designated for drug product complaints. The file regarding such drug product complaints shall be maintained at the establishment where the drug product involved was manufactured, processed, or packed, or such file may be maintained at another facility if the written records in such files are readily available for inspection at that other facility. Written records involving a drug product shall be maintained until at least 1 year after the expiration date of the drug product, or 1 year after the date that the complaint was received, whichever is longer. In the case of certain OTC drug products lacking expiration dating because they meet the criteria for exemption under 211.137, such written records shall be maintained for 3 years after distribution of the drug product.

(1) The written record shall include the following information, where known: the name and strength of the drug product, lot number, name of complainant, nature of complaint, and reply to complainant.

(2) Where an investigation under 211.192 is conducted, the written record shall include the findings of the investigation and follow up. The record or copy of the record of the investigation shall be maintained at the establishment where the investigation occurred in accordance with 211.180(c).

(3) Where an investigation under 211.192 is not conducted, the written record shall include the reason that an investigation was found not to be necessary and the name of the responsible person making such a determination.

[43 FR 45077, Sept. 29, 1978, as amended at 51 FR 24479, July 3, 1986]

Subpart K - Returned and Salvaged Drug Products

211.204 Returned drug products.

Returned drug products shall be identified as such and held. If the conditions under which returned drug products have been held, stored, or shipped before or during their return, or if the condition of the drug product, its container, carton, or labeling, as a result of storage or shipping, casts doubt on the safety, identity, strength, quality or purity of the drug product, the returned drug product shall be destroyed unless examination, testing, or other investigations prove the drug product meets appropriate standards of safety, identity, strength, quality, or purity. A drug product may be reprocessed provided the subsequent drug product meets appropriate standards, specifications, and characteristics. Records of returned drug products shall be maintained and shall include the name and label potency of the drug product dosage form, lot number (or control number or batch number), reason for the return, quantity returned, date of disposition, and ultimate disposition of the returned drug product. If the reason for a drug product being returned implicates associated batches, an appropriate investigation shall be conducted in accordance with the requirements of 211.192. Procedures for the holding, testing, and reprocessing of returned drug products shall be in writing and shall be followed.

211.208 Drug product salvaging.

Drug products that have been subjected to improper storage conditions including extremes in temperature, humidity, smoke, fumes, pressure, age, or radiation due to natural disasters, fires, accidents, or equipment failures shall not be salvaged and returned to the marketplace. Whenever there is a question whether drug products have been subjected to such conditions, salvaging operations may be conducted only if there is (a) evidence from laboratory tests and assays (including animal feeding studies where applicable) that the drug products meet all applicable standards of identity, strength, quality, and purity and (b) evidence from inspection of the premises that the drug products and their associated packaging were not subjected to improper storage conditions as a result of the disaster or accident. Organoleptic examinations shall be acceptable only as supplemental evidence that the drug products meet appropriate standards of identity, strength, quality,

and purity. Records including name, lot number, and disposition shall be maintained for drug products subject to this section.

PART 225 - CURRENT GOOD MANUFACTURING PRACTICE FOR MEDICATED FEEDS

AUTHORITY: 21 U.S.C. 351, 352 360b, 371, 374.
SOURCE: 41 FR 52618, Nov. 30, 1976, unless otherwise noted.

Subpart A-General Provisions

225.1 Current good manufacturing practice.

(a) Section 501(a)(2)(B) of the Federal Food, Drug, and Cosmetic Act provides that a drug (including a drug contained in a medicated feed) shall be deemed to be adulterated if the methods used in, or the facilities or controls used for, its manufacture, processing, packing, or holding do not conform to or are not operated or administered in conformity with current good manufacturing practice to assure that such drug meets the requirement of the act as to safety and has the identity and strength, and meets the quality and purity characteristics, which it purports or is represented to possess.

(b)(1) The provisions of this part set forth the criteria for determining whether the manufacture of a medicated feed is in compliance with current good manufacturing practice. These regulations shall apply to all types of facilities and equipment used in the production of medicated feeds, and they shall also govern those instances in which failure to adhere to the regulations has caused non-medicated feeds that are manufactured, processed, packed, or held to be adulterated. In such cases, the medicated feed shall be deemed to be adulterated within the meaning of section 501(a)(2)(B) of the act, and the non-medicated feed shall be deemed to be adulterated within the meaning of section 402(a)(2)(D) of the act.

(2) The regulations in 225.10 through 225.115 apply to facilities manufacturing one or more medicated feeds for which an approved medicated feed application is required. The regulations in 225.120 through 225.202 apply to facilities manufacturing solely medicated feeds for which an approved license is not required.

(c) In addition to the recordkeeping requirements in this part, Type B and Type C medicated feeds made from Type A articles or Type B feeds under approved NADA's and a medicated feed mill license are subject to the requirements of § 510.301 of this chapter.

[41 FR 52618, Nov. 30, 1976, as amended at 51 FR 7389, Mar. 3, 1986; 64 FR 63203, Nov. 19, 1999]]

225.10 Personnel.

(a) Qualified personnel and adequate personnel training and supervision are essential for the proper formulation, manufacture, and control of medicated feeds. Training and experience leads to proper use of equipment, maintenance of accurate records, and detection and prevention of possible deviations from current good manufacturing practices.

(b)(1) All employees involved in the manufacture of medicated feeds shall have an understanding of the manufacturing or control operation(s) which they perform, including the location and proper use of equipment.

(2) The manufacturer shall provide an on-going program of evaluation and supervision of employees in the manufacture of medicated feeds.

[41 FR 52618, Nov. 30, 1976, as amended at 42 FR 12426, Mar. 4, 1977]

Subpart B - Construction and Maintenance of Facilities and Equipment

225.20   Buildings.

(a) The location, design, construction, and physical size of the buildings and other production facilities are factors important to the manufacture of medicated feed. The features of facilities necessary for the proper manufacture of medicated feed include provision for ease of access to structures and equipment in need of routine maintenance; ease of cleaning of equipment and work areas; facilities to promote personnel hygiene; structural conditions for control and prevention of vermin and pest infestation; adequate space for the orderly receipt and storage of drugs and feed ingredients and the controlled flow of these materials through the processing and manufacturing operations; and the equipment for the accurate packaging and delivery of a medicated feed of specified labeling and composition.

(b) The construction and maintenance of buildings in which medicated feeds are manufactured, processed, packaged, labeled, or held shall conform to the following:

(1) The building grounds shall be adequately drained and routinely maintained so that they are reasonably free from litter, waste, refuse, uncut weeds or grass, standing water, and improperly stored equipment.

(2) The building(s) shall be maintained in a reasonably clean and orderly manner.

(3) The building(s) shall be of suitable construction to minimize access by rodents, birds, insects, and other pests.

(4) The buildings shall provide adequate space and lighting for the proper performance of the following medicated feed manufacturing operations:

(i) The receipt, control, and storage of components.

(ii) Component processing.

(iii) Medicated feed manufacturing.

(iv) Packaging and labeling.

(v) Storage of containers, packaging materials, labeling and finished products.

(vi) Routine maintenance of equipment.

225.30   Equipment.

(a) Equipment which is designed to perform its intended function and is properly installed and used is essential to the manufacture of medicated feeds. Such equipment permits production of feeds of uniform quality, facilitates cleaning, and minimizes spillage of drug components and finished product.

(b)(1) All equipment shall possess the capability to produce a medicated feed of intended potency, safety, and purity.

(2) All equipment shall be maintained in a reasonably clean and orderly manner.

(3) All equipment, including scales and liquid metering devices, shall be of suitable size, design, construction, precision, and accuracy for its intended purpose.

(4) All scales and metering devices shall be tested for accuracy upon installation and at least once a year thereafter, or more frequently as may be necessary to insure their accuracy.

(5) All equipment maintained as to prevent lubricants and coolants from becoming unsafe additives in feed components or medicated feed.

(6) All equipment shall be designed, constructed, installed and maintained so as to facilitate inspection and use of clean out procedure(s).

225.35   Use of work areas, equipment, and storage areas for other manufacturing and storage purpose.

(a) Many manufacturers of medicated feeds are also involved in the manufacture, storage, or handling of products which are not intended for animal feed use, such as fertilizers, herbicides, insecticides, fungicides, rodenticides, and other pesticides. Manufacturing, storage, or handling of non-feed and feed products in the same facilities may cause adulteration of feed products with toxic or otherwise unapproved feed additives.

(b) Work areas and equipment used for the manufacture or storage of medicated feeds or components thereof shall not be used for, and shall be physically separated from, work areas and equipment used for the manufacture of fertilizers, herbicides, insecticides, fungicides, rodenticides, and other pesticides unless such articles are approved drugs or approved food additives intended for use in the manufacture of medicated feed.

Subpart C-Product Quality Control

225.42   Components.

(a) A medicated feed, in addition to providing nutrients, is a vehicle for the administration of a drug, or drugs, to animals. To ensure proper safety and effectiveness, such medicated feeds must contain the labeled amounts of drugs. It is necessary that adequate procedures be established for the receipt, storage, and inventory control for all such drugs to aid in assuring their identity, strength, quality, and purity when incorporated into products.

(b) The receipt, storage, and inventory of drugs, including undiluted drug components, medicated premixes, and semi-processed (i.e., intermediate premixes, in plant premixes and concentrates) intermediate mixes containing drugs, which are used in the manufacture and processing of medicated feeds shall conform to the following:

(1) Incoming shipments of drugs shall be visually examined for identity and damage. Drugs which have been subjected to conditions which may have adversely affected their identity, strength, quality, or purity shall not be accepted for use.

(2) Packaged drugs in the storage areas shall be stored in their original closed containers.

(3) Bulk drugs shall be identified and stored in a manner

such that their identity, strength, quality, and purity will be maintained.

(4) Drugs in the mixing areas shall be properly identified, stored, handled, and controlled to maintain their integrity and identity. Sufficient space shall be provided for the location of each drug.

(5) A receipt record shall be prepared and maintained for each lot of drug received. The receipt record shall accurately indicate the identity and quantity of the drug, the name of the supplier, the supplier's lot number or an identifying number assigned by the feed manufacturer upon receipt which relates to the particular shipment, the date of receipt, the condition of the drug when received, and the return of any damaged drugs.

(6) A daily inventory record for each drug used shall be maintained and shall list by manufacturer's lot number or the feed manufacturer's shipment identification number at least the following information:

(i) The quantity of drug on hand at the beginning and end of the work day (the beginning amount being the same as the previous day's closing inventory if this amount has been established to be correct); the quantity shall be determined by weighing, counting, or measuring, as appropriate.

(ii) The amount of each drug used, sold, or otherwise disposed of.

(iii) The batches or production runs of medicated feed in which each drug was used.

(iv) When the drug is used in the preparation of a semi-processed intermediate mix intended for use in the manufacture of medicated feed, any additional information which may be required for the purpose of paragraph (b)(7) of this section.

(v) Action taken to reconcile any discrepancies in the daily inventory record.

(7) Drug inventory shall be maintained of each lot or shipment of drug by means of a daily comparison of the actual amount of drug used with the theoretical drug usage in terms of the semi-processed, intermediate and finished medicated feeds manufactured. Any significant discrepancy shall be investigated and corrective action taken. The medicated feed(s) remaining on the premises which are affected by this discrepancy shall be detained until the discrepancy is reconciled.

(8) All records required by this section shall be maintained on the premises for at least one year after complete use of a drug component of a specific lot number or feed manufacturer's shipment identification number.

225.58 Laboratory controls.

(a) The periodic assay of medicated feeds for drug components provides a measure of performance of the manufacturing process in manufacturing a uniform product of intended potency.

(b) The following assay requirements shall apply to medicated feeds:

(1) For feeds requiring approved Medicated Feed Applications (Form FDA 3448) for their manufacture and marketing, at least three representative samples of medicated feed containing each drug or drug combination used in the establishment shall be collected and assayed by approved official methods, at periodic intervals during the calendar year, unless otherwise specified in this chapter. At least one of these assays shall be performed on the first batch using the drug. If a medicated feed contains a combination of drugs, only one of the drugs need be subject to analysis each time, provided the one tested is different from the one(s) previously tested.

(2) Reserved

(c) The originals or copies of all results of assays, including those from State feed control officials and any other governmental agency, shall be maintained on the premises for a period of not less than 1 year after distribution of the medicated feed. The results of assays performed by State feed control officials may be considered toward fulfillment of the periodic assay requirements of this section.

(d) Where the results of assays indicate that the medicated feed is not in accord with label specifications or is not within permissible assay limits as specified in this chapter, investigation and corrective action shall be implemented and an original or copy of the record of such action maintained on the premises.

(e) Corrective action shall include provisions for discontinuing distribution where the medicated feed fails to meet the labeled drug potency. Distribution of subsequent production of the particular feed shall not begin until it has been determined that proper control procedures have been established.

[41 FR 52618, Nov. 30, 1976, as amended at 51 FR 7390, Mar. 3, 1986; 55 FR 11577, Mar. 29, 1990]

225.65 Equipment cleanout procedures.

(a) Adequate clean out procedures for all equipment used in the manufacture and distribution of medicated feeds are essential to maintain proper drug potency and avoid unsafe contamination of feeds with drugs. Such procedures may consist of cleaning by physical means, e.g., vacuuming, sweeping, washing, etc. Alternatively, flushing or sequencing or other equally effective techniques may be used whereby the equipment is cleaned either through use of a feed containing the same drug(s) or through use of drug free feedstuffs.

(b) All equipment, including that used for storage, processing, mixing, conveying, and distribution that comes in contact with the active drug component, feeds in process, or finished medicated feed shall be subject to all reasonable and effective procedures to prevent unsafe contamination of manufactured feed. The steps used to prevent unsafe contamination of feeds shall include one or more of the following, or other equally effective procedures:

(1) Such procedures shall, where appropriate, consist of physical means (vacuuming, sweeping, or washing), flushing, and/or sequential production of feeds.

(2) If flushing is utilized, the flush material shall be properly identified, stored, and used in a manner to prevent unsafe contamination of other feeds.

(3) If sequential production of medicated feeds is utilized, it shall be on a predetermined basis designed to prevent unsafe contamination of feeds with residual drugs.

Subpart D - Packaging and Labeling

225.80 Labeling.

(a) Appropriate labeling identifies the medicated feed, and provides the user with directions for use which, if adhered to, will assure that the article is safe and effective for its intended purposes.

(b)(1) Labels and labeling, including placards, shall be received, handled, and stored labeling mixups and assures that correct labeling is employed for the medicated feed.

(2) Labels and labeling, including placards, upon receipt from the printer shall be proofread against the Master Record File to verify their suitability and accuracy. The proofread label shall be dated, initialed by a responsible individual, and kept for 1 year after all the labels from that batch have been used.

(3) In those instances where medicated feeds are distributed in bulk, complete labeling shall accompany the shipment and be supplied to the consignee at the time of delivery. Such labeling may consist of a placard or other labels attached to the invoice or delivery ticket, or manufacturer's invoice that identifies the medicated feed and includes adequate information for the safe and effective use of the medicated feed.

(4) Label stock shall be reviewed periodically and discontinued labels shall be discarded.

Subpart E-Records and Reports

225.102 Master record file and production records.

(a) The Master Record File provides the complete procedure for manufacturing a specific product, setting forth the formulation, theoretical yield, manufacturing procedures, assay requirements, and labeling of batches or production runs. The production record(s) includes the complete history of a batch or production run. This record includes the amounts of drugs used, the amount of medicated feed manufactured, and provides a check for the daily inventory record of drug components.

(b) The Master Record File and production records shall comply with the following provisions:

(1) A Master Record File shall be prepared, checked, dated, and signed or initialed by a qualified person and shall be retained for not less than 1 year after production of the last batch or production run of medicated feed to which it pertains. The Master Record File or card shall include at least the following:

(i) The name of the medicated feed.

(ii) The name and weight percentage or measure of each drug or drug combination and each non-drug ingredient to be used in manufacturing a stated weight of the medicated feed.

(iii) A copy or description of the label or labeling that will accompany the medicated feed.

(iv) Manufacturing instructions or reference thereto that have been determined to yield a properly mixed medicated feed of the specified formula for each medicated feed produced on a batch or continuous operation basis, including mixing steps, mixing times and, in the case of medicated feeds produced by continuous production run, any additional manufacturing directions including, when indicated, the settings of equipment.

(v) Appropriate control directions or reference thereto, including the manner and frequency of collecting the required number of samples for specified laboratory assay.

(2) The original production record or copy thereof shall be prepared by qualified personnel for each batch or run of medicated feed produced and shall be retained on the premises for not less than 1 year. The production record shall include at least the following:

(i) Product identification, date of production, and a written endorsement in the form of a signature or initials by a responsible individual.

(ii) The quantity and name of drug components used.

(iii) The theoretical quantity of medicated feed to be produced.

(iv) The actual quantity of medicated feed produced. In those instances where the finished feed is stored in bulk and actual yield cannot be accurately determined, the firm shall estimate the quantity produced and provide the basis for such estimate in the Master Record File.

(3) In the case of a custom formula feed made to the specifications of a customer, the Master Record File and production records required by this section shall consist either of such records or of copies of the customer's purchase orders and the manufacturer's invoices bearing the information required by this section. When a custom order is received by telephone, the manufacturer shall prepare the required production records.

(4) Batch production records shall be checked by a responsible individual at the end of the working day in which the product was manufactured to determine whether all required production steps have been performed. If significant discrepancies are noted, an investigation shall be instituted immediately, and the production record shall describe the corrective action taken.

(5) Each batch or production run of medicated feed shall be identified with its own individual batch or production run number, code, date, or other suitable identification applied to the label, package, invoice or shipping document. This identification shall permit the tracing of the complete and accurate manufacturing history of the product by the manufacturer.

225.110 Distribution records.

(a) Distribution records permit the manufacturer to relate complaints to specific batches and/or production runs of medicated feed. This information may be helpful in instituting a recall.

(b) Distribution records for each shipment of a medicated feed shall comply with the following provisions:

(1) Each distribution record shall include the date of shipment, the name and address of purchaser, the quantity shipped, and the name of the medicated feed. A lot or control number, or date of manufacture or other suitable identification shall appear on the distribution record or the label issued with each shipment.

(2) The originals or copies of the distribution records shall be retained on the premises for not less than one year after the date of shipment of the medicated feed.

225.115   Complaint files.

(a) Complaints and reports of experiences of product defects relative to the drug's efficacy or safety may provide an indicator as to whether or not medicated feeds have been manufactured in conformity with current good manufacturing practices.   These complaints and experiences may reveal the existence of manufacturing problems not otherwise detected through the normal quality control procedures. Timely and appropriate follow-up action can serve to correct a problem and minimize future problems.

(b) The medicated feed manufacturer shall maintain on the premises a file which contains the following information:

(1) The original or copy of a record of each oral and written complaint received relating to the safety and effectiveness of the product produced. The record shall include the date of the complaint, the complainant's name and address, name and lot or control number or date of manufacture of the medicated feed involved, and the specific details of the complaint. This record shall also include all correspondence from the complainant and/or memoranda of conversations with the complainant, and a description of all investigations made by the manufacturer and of the method of disposition of the complaint.

(2) For medicated feeds whose manufacture require a feed mill license (Form FDA 3448) , records and reports of clinical and other experience with the drug shall be maintained and reported, under section 510.301 of this chapter.

[41 FR 52618, Nov. 30, 1976, as amended at 51 FR 7390, Mar. 3, 1986; 57 FR 6475, Feb. 25, 1992; 64 FR 63203, Nov.19,1999]

Subpart F - Facilities and Equipment

SOURCE: 51 FR 7390, Mar. 3, 1986, unless otherwise noted.

225.120   Buildings and grounds.

Buildings used for production of medicated feed shall provide adequate space for equipment, processing, and orderly receipt and storage of medicated feed. Areas shall include access for routine maintenance and cleaning of equipment. Buildings and grounds shall be constructed and maintained in a manner to minimize vermin and pest infestation.

225.130   Equipment.

Equipment shall be capable of producing a medicated feed of intended potency and purity, and shall be maintained in a reasonably clean and orderly manner. Scales and liquid metering devices shall be accurate and of suitable size, design, construction, precision, and accuracy for their intended purposes. All equipment shall be designed, constructed, installed, and maintained so as to facilitate inspection and use of clean out procedure(s).

225.135   Work and storage areas.

Work areas and equipment used for the production or storage of medicated feeds or components thereof shall not be used for, and shall be physically separated from, work areas and equipment used for the manufacture and storage

of fertilizers, herbicides, insecticides, fungicides, rodenticides, and other pesticides unless such articles are approved for use in the manufacture of animal feed.

Subpart G - Product Quality Assurance

SOURCE: 51 FR 7390, Mar. 3, 1986, unless otherwise noted.

225.142   Components.

Adequate procedures shall be established and maintained for the identification, storage, and inventory control (receipt and use) of all Type A medicated articles and Type B medicated feeds intended for use in the manufacture of medicated feeds to aid in assuring the identity, strength, quality, and purity of these drug sources. Packaged Type A medicated articles and Type B medicated feeds shall be stored in designated areas in their original closed containers. Bulk Type A medicated articles and bulk Type B medicated feeds shall be identified and stored in a manner such that their identity, strength, quality, and purity will be maintained. All Type A medicated articles and Type B medicated feeds shall be used in accordance with their labeled mixing directions.

225.158   Laboratory assays.

Where the results of laboratory assays of drug components, including assays by State feed control officials, indicate that the medicated feed is not in accord with the permissible limits specified in this chapter, investigation and corrective action shall be implemented immediately by the firm and such records shall be maintained on the premises for a period of 1 year.

225.165   Equipment clean out procedures.

Adequate procedures shall be established and used for all equipment used in the production and distribution of medicated feeds to avoid unsafe contamination of medicated and non-medicated feeds.

Subpart H - Labeling

225.180   Labeling.

Labels shall be received, handled, and stored in a manner that prevents label mixups and assures that the correct labels are used for the medicated feed. All deliveries of medicated feeds, whether bagged or in bulk, shall be adequately labeled to assure that the feed can be properly used.

[51 FR 7390, Mar. 3, 1986]

Subpart I - Records

225.202   Formula, production, and distribution records.

Records shall be maintained identifying the formulation, date of mixing, and if not for own use, date of shipment. The records shall be adequate to facilitate the recall of specific batches of medicated feed that have been distributed. Such records shall be retained on the premises for 1 year following the date of last distribution.

(Approved by the Office of Management and Budget under control number 0910- 0152) [51 FR 7390, Mar. 3, 1986]

226 - CURRENT GOOD MANUFACTURING PRACTICE FOR TYPE A MEDICATED ARTICLES

AUTHORITY: 21 U.S.C. 351, 352, 360b, 371, 374.
SOURCE: 40 FR 14031, Mar. 27, 1975, unless otherwise noted.
Editorial Note: Nomenclature change to Part 226 appears at 51 FR 7390, Mar. 3, 1986.

Subpart A - General Provisions

226.1 Current good manufacturing practice.

The criteria in 226.10 through 226.115, inclusive, shall apply in determining whether the methods used in, or the facilities and controls used for the manufacture, processing, packing, or holding of a Type A medicated article(s) conform to or are operated or administered in conformity with current good manufacturing practice to assure that a Type A medicated article(s) meets the requirements of the act as to safety, and has the identity and strength, and meets the quality and purity characteristics which it purports or is represented to possess, as required by section 501(a) (2)(B) of the act. The regulations in this Part 226 permit the use of precision, automatic, mechanical, or electronic equipment in the production of a Type A medicated article(s) when adequate inspection and checking procedures or other quality control procedures are used to assure proper performance.

226.10   Personnel.

The key personnel and any consultants involved in the manufacture and control of the Type A medicated article(s) shall have a background of appropriate education or appropriate experience or combination thereof for assuming responsibility to assure that the Type A medicated article(s) has the proper labeling and the safety, identity, strength, quality, and purity that it purports to possess.

Subpart B - Construction and Maintenance of Facilities and Equipment

226.20   Buildings.

Buildings in which Type A medicated article(s) are manufactured, processed, packaged, labeled, or held shall be maintained in a clear and orderly manner and shall be of suitable size, construction and location in relation to surroundings to facilitate maintenance and operation for their intended purpose. The building shall:

(a) Provide adequate space for the orderly placement of equipment and materials used in any of the following operations for which they are employed to minimize risk of mix-ups between different Type A medicated article(s), their components, packaging, or labeling:

(1) The receipt, sampling, control, and storage of components.

(2) Manufacturing and processing operations performed on the Type A medicated article(s).

(3) Packaging and labeling operations.

(4) Storage of containers, packaging materials, labeling, and finished products.

(5) Control laboratory operations.

(b) Provide adequate lighting and ventilation, and when necessary for the intended production or control purposes, adequate screening, dust and temperature controls, to avoid contamination of Type A medicated article(s), and to avoid other conditions unfavorable to the safety, identity, strength, quality, and purity of the raw materials and Type A medicated article(s) before, during, and after production.

(c) Provide for adequate washing, cleaning, toilet, and locker facilities.

Work areas and equipment used for the production of Type A medicated article(s) or for the storage of the components of Type A medicated article(s) shall not be used for the production, mixing or storage of finished or unfinished insecticides, fungicides, rodenticides, or other pesticides or their components unless such materials are recognized as approved drugs intended for use in animal feeds.

226.30   Equipment.

Equipment used for the manufacture, processing, packaging, bulk shipment, labeling, holding, or control of Type A medicated article(s) or their components shall be maintained in a clean and orderly manner and shall be of suitable design, size, construction, and location to facilitate maintenance and operation for its intended purpose. The equipment shall:

(a) Be so constructed that any surfaces that come into contact with Type A medicated article(s) are suitable, in that they are not reactive, additive, or absorptive to an extent that significantly affects the identity, strength, quality, or purity of the Type A medicated article(s) or its components.

(b) Be so constructed that any substance required for the operation of the equipment, such as lubricants, coolants, etc., may be employed without hazard of becoming an unsafe additive to the Type A medicated article(s).

(c) Be constructed to facilitate adjustment, cleaning, and maintenance, and to assure uniformity of production and reliability of control procedures and to assure the exclusion from Type A medicated article(s) of contamination, including cross-contamination from manufacturing operations.

(d) Be suitably grounded electrically to prevent lack of uniform mixing due to electrically charged particles.

(e) Be of suitable size and accuracy for use in any intended measuring, mixing, or weighing operations.

Subpart C - Product Quality Control

226.40   Production and control procedures.

Production and control procedures shall include all reasonable precautions, including the following, to assure that the Type A medicated article(s) produced have the identity, strength, quality, and purity they purport to possess:

(a) Each critical step in the process, such as the selection, weighing, and measuring of components; the addition of drug components during the process; weighing and measuring during various stages of the processing; and the determination of the finished yield, shall be performed by one or more competent, responsible individuals. If such are controlled by precision, automatic, mechanical, or electronic equipment, their proper performance shall be adequately checked by one or more competent, responsible individuals.

(b) All containers to be used for undiluted drugs, drug components, intermediate mixtures thereof, and Type A medicated article(s) shall be received, adequately identified, and properly stored and handled in a manner adequate to avoid mixups and contamination.

(c) Equipment, including dust-control and other equipment, such as that used for holding and returning recovered or flush-out materials back into production, shall be maintained and operated in a manner to avoid contamination of the Type A medicated article(s) and to insure the integrity of the finished product.

(d) Competent and responsible personnel shall check actual against theoretical yield of a batch of Type A medicated article(s), and, in the event of any significant discrepancies, key personnel shall prevent distribution of the batch in question and other associated batches of Type A medicated article(s) that may have been involved in a mixup with it.

(e) Adequate procedures for cleaning of those parts of storage, mixing conveying and other equipment coming in contact with the drug component of the Type A medicated article(s) shall be used to avoid contamination of Type A medicated article(s).

(f) If there is sequential production of batches of a Type A medicated article(s) containing the same drug component (or components) at the same or lower levels, there shall be sufficient safeguards to avoid any build up above the specified levels of the drug components in any of the batches of the Type A medicated article(s).

(g) Production and control procedures shall include provision for discontinuing distribution of any Type A medicated article(s) found by the assay procedures, or other controls performed to fail to conform to appropriate specifications. Distribution of subsequent production of such Type A medicated article(s) shall not begin until it has been determined that proper control procedures have been established.

226.42 Components.

(a) Drug components, including undiluted drugs and any intermediate mixes containing drugs used in the manufacture and processing of Type A medicated article(s), shall be received, examined or tested, stored, handled, and otherwise controlled in a manner to maintain the integrity and identification of such articles. Appropriate receipt and inventory records shall be maintained for 2 years, and such records shall show the origin of any drug components, the manufacturer's control number (if any), the dates and batches in which they were used, and the results of any testing of them.

(b) Non-drug components shall be stored and otherwise handled in a manner to avoid contamination, including cross-contamination from manufacturing operations.

226.58 Laboratory controls.

Laboratory controls shall include the establishment of adequate specifications and test procedures to assure that the drug components and the Type A medicated article(s) conform to appropriate standards of identity, strength, quality, and purity. Laboratory controls shall include:

(a) The establishment of master records containing appropriate specifications and a description of the test procedures used to check them for each kind of drug component used in the manufacture of Type A medicated article(s). This may consist of the manufacturer's or supplier's statement of specifications and methods of analyses.

(b) The establishment of specifications for Type A medicated article(s) and a description of necessary laboratory test procedures to check such specifications.

(c) Assays which shall be made of representative samples of finished Type A medicated article(s) in accordance with the following schedule:

(1) Each batch of a Type A medicated article(s) manufactured from an undiluted drug shall be assayed for its drug component(s).

(2) In the case of Type A medicated article(s) which are manufactured by dilution of Type A medicated article(s) assayed in accordance with paragraph (c)(1) of this section, each batch shall be assayed for its drug component(s) with the first five consecutive batches assaying within the limitations, followed thereafter by assay of representative samples of not less than 5 percent of all batches produced. When any batch does not assay within limitations, each batch should again be assayed until five consecutive batches are within limitations.

(d) A determination establishing that the drug components remain uniformly dispersed and stable in the Type A medicated article(s) under ordinary conditions of shipment, storage, and use. This may consist of a determination on a Type A medicated article(s) of substantially the same formula and characteristics. Suitable expiration dates shall appear on the labels of the Type A medicated article(s) to assure that the articles meet the appropriate standards of identity, strength, quality, and purity at the time of use.

(e) Adequate provision to check the reliability, accuracy, and precision of any laboratory test procedure used. The official methods in "Methods of Analysis of the Association of Official Analytical Chemists,"** methods described in an official compendium, and any method submitted as a part of a food additive petition or new-drug application that has been accepted by the Food and Drug Administration shall be regarded as meeting this provision.

[Footnote: **Copies may be obtained from: Association of Official Analytical Chemists, 2200 Wilson Blvd., Suite 400, Arlington, VA 22201 3301.]

(f) Provisions for the maintenance of the results of any assays, including dates and endorsement of analysts. Such records shall be retained in the possession of the manufacturer and shall be maintained for a period of at least 2 years after distribution by the manufacturer of the Type A medicated article(s) has been completed.

[40 FR 14031, Mar. 27, 1975, as amended at 55 FR 11577, Mar. 29, 1990 5; 55 FR 23703, June 12, 1990]

Subpart D-Packaging and Labeling

226.80   Packaging and labeling.

(a) Packaging and labeling operations shall be adequately controlled:

(1) To assure that only those Type A medicated article(s) that have met the specifications established in the master-formula records shall be distributed.

(2) To prevent mixups during the packaging and labeling operations.

(3) To assure that correct labeling is employed for each Type A medicated article(s).

(4) To identify Type A medicated article(s) with lot or control numbers that permit determination of the history of the manufacture and control of the batch of Type A medicated article(s).

(b) Packaging and labeling operations shall provide:

(1) For storage of labeling in a manner to avoid mixups.

(2) For careful checking of labeling for identity and conformity to the labeling specified in the batch-production records.

(3) For adequate control of the quantities of labeling issued for use with the Type A medicated article(s).

(c) Type A medicated article(s) shall be distributed in suitable containers to insure the safety, identity, strength, and quality of the finished product.

Subpart E - Records and Reports

226.102   Master-formula and batch-production records.

(a) For each Type A medicated article(s) master-formula records shall be prepared, endorsed, and dated by a competent and responsible individual and shall be independently checked, reconciled, endorsed, and dated by a second competent and responsible individual. The record shall include:

(1) The name of the Type A medicated article(s) and a specimen copy of its label.

(2) The weight or measure of each ingredient, adequately identified, to be used in manufacturing a stated weight of the Type A medicated article(s).

(3) A complete formula for each batch size, or of appropriate size in the case of continuous systems to be produced from the master-formula record, including a complete list of ingredients designated by names or codes sufficiently specific to indicate any special quality characteristics; an accurate statement of the weight or measure of each ingredient, except that reasonable variations may be permitted in the amount of ingredients necessary in the preparation of the Type A medicated article(s), provided that the variations are stated in the master formula; an appropriate statement concerning any calculated excess of an ingredient; and a statement of the theoretical yield.

(4) Manufacturing instructions for each type of Type A medicated article(s) produced on a batch or continuous operation basis, including mixing steps and mixing times that have been determined to yield an the case of Type A medicated article(s) produced by continuous production run, any additional manufacturing directions including, when indicated, the settings of equipment that have been determined to yield an adequately mixed Type A medicated article(s) of the specified formula.

(5) Control instructions, procedures, specifications, special notations, and precautions to be followed.

(b) A separate batch-production and control record shall be prepared for each batch or run of Type A medicated article(s) produced and shall be retained for at least 2 years after distribution by the manufacturer has been completed. The batch-production and control record shall include:

(1) Product identification, date of production, and endorsement by a competent and responsible individual.

(2) Records of each step in the manufacturing, packaging, labeling, and controlling of the batch, including dates, specific identification of drug components used, weights or measures of all components, laboratory-control results, mixing times, and the endorsements of the individual actively performing or the individual actively supervising or checking each step in the operation.

(3) A batch number that permits determination of all laboratory-control procedures and results on the batch and all lot or control numbers appearing on the labels of the Type A medicated article(s).

226.110   Distribution records.

Complete records shall be maintained for each shipment of Type A medicated article(s) in a manner that will facilitate the recall, diversion, or destruction of the Type A medicated article(s), if necessary. Such records shall be retained for at least 2 years after the date of the shipment by the manufacturer and shall include the name and address of the consignee, the date and quantity shipped, and the manufacturing dates, control numbers, or marks identifying the Type A medicated article(s) shipped.

226.115   Complaint files.

Records shall be maintained for a period of 2 years of all written or verbal complaints concerning the safety or efficacy of each Type A medicated article(s). Complaints shall be evaluated by competent and responsible personnel and, where indicated, appropriate action shall be taken. The record shall indicate the evaluation and the action.

PART 589 - SUBSTANCES PROHIBITED FROM USE IN ANIMAL FOOD OR FEED

AUTHORITY: 21 U.S.C. 321, 342, 343, 348, 371

Subpart A—General Provisions

589.1 Substances prohibited from use in animal food or feed.

(a) The substances listed in this part have been prohibited from use in animal food or feed by the Food and Drug Administration because of a determination that they present a potential risk to the public health or have not been shown by adequate scientific data to be safe for use in such food or feed. Use of any of these substances in violation of this part causes the animal food or feed involved to be adulterated and in violation of the Act.

(b) This part includes only a partial list of substances prohibited from use in animal food or feed; it is for easy reference purposes and is not a complete list of substances that may not lawfully be used in such animal food or feed. No substance may be used in animal food or feed unless it meets all applicable requirements of the Act.

(c) The Food and Drug Administration either on its own initiative or on behalf of any interested person who has submitted a petition, may publish a proposal to establish, amend, or repeal a regulation under this part on the basis of new scientific evaluation or information. Any such petition shall include an adequate scientific basis to support the petition, shall be the form set forth in Sec. 571.1 of this chapter, and will be published in the Federal Register for comment if it contains reasonable ground.

[45 FR 28319, Apr. 29, 1980]

Subpart B-Listing of Specific Substances Prohibited from Use in Animal Food or Feed

589.2000 Animal proteins prohibited in ruminant feed.

(a) *Definitions*—(1) Protein derived from mammalian tissues means any protein-containing portion of mammalian animals, excluding: Blood and blood products; gelatin; inspected meat products which have been cooked and offered for human food and further heat processed for feed (such as plate waste and used cellulosic food casings); milk products (milk and milk proteins); and any product whose only mammalian protein consists entirely of porcine or equine protein.

(2) *Renderer* means any firm or individual that processes slaughter byproducts, animals unfit for human consumption, or meat scraps. The term includes persons who collect such materials and subject them to minimal processing, or distribute them to firms other than renderers (as defined here) whose intended use for the products may include animal feed. The term includes renderers that also blend animal protein products.

(3) *Blender* means any firm or individual which obtains processed animal protein from more than one source or from more than one species, and subsequently mixes (blends) or redistributes an animal protein product.

(4) *Feed manufacturer* includes manufacturers of complete and intermediate feeds intended for animals, and includes on-farm in addition to off-farm feed manufacturing and mixing operations.

(5) *Nonmammalian protein* includes proteins from nonmammalian animals.

(6) *Distributor* includes persons who distribute or transport feeds or feed ingredients intended for animals.

(7) Ruminant includes any member of the order of animals which has a stomach with four chambers (rumen, reticulum, omasum, and abomasum) through which feed passes in digestion. The order includes, but is not limited to, cattle, buffalo, sheep, goats, deer, elk, and antelopes.

(b) *Food additive status.* The Food and Drug Administration has determined that protein derived from mammalian tissues for use in ruminant feed is a food additive subject to section 409 of the Federal Food, Drug, and Cosmetic Act (the act). The use or intended use in ruminant feed of any material that contains protein derived from mammalian tissues causes the feed to be adulterated and in violation of the act, unless it is the subject of an effective notice of claimed investigational exemption for a food additive under Sec. 570.17 of this chapter.

(c) *Requirements for renderers that are not included in paragraph (e) of this section.* (1) Renderers that manufacture products that contain or may contain protein derived from mammalian tissues and that are intended for use in animal feed shall take the following measures to ensure that materials identified in paragraph (b) of this section are not used in the feed of ruminants:

(i) Label the materials as follows: "Do not feed to cattle or other ruminants"; and

(ii) Maintain records sufficient to track the materials throughout their receipt, processing, and distribution, and make the copies available for inspection and copying by the Food and Drug Administration.

(2) Renderers described in paragraph (c)(1) of this section will be exempted from the requirements of paragraphs (c)(1)(i) and (c)(1)(ii) of this section if they:

(i) Use exclusively a manufacturing method that has been validated by the Food and Drug Administration to deactivate the agent that causes transmissible spongiform encephalopathy (TSE) and whose design has been made available to the public;

(ii) Use routinely a test method that has been validated by the Food and Drug Administration to detect the presence of the agent that causes TSE's and whose design has been made available to the public. Renderers whose products test positive for agents that cause TSE's must comply with paragraphs (c)(1)(i) and (c)(1)(ii) of this section. Records of the test results shall be made available for inspection by the Food and Drug Administration; or

(iii) Use exclusively a method for controlling the manufacturing process that minimizes the risk of the TSE agent entering the product and whose design has been made available to the public and validated by the Food and Drug Administration.

(3) Renderers described in paragraph (c)(1) of this section will be exempted from the requirements of paragraph (c)(1)(ii) of this section if they use a permanent method, approved by FDA, to make a mark indicating that the product contains or may contain protein derived from mammalian tissue. If the marking is by the use of an agent that cannot be detected on visual inspection, the renderer must use an agent whose presence can be detected by a method that has been validated by the Food and Drug Administration and whose design has been made available to the public.

(d) *Requirements for protein blenders, feed manufacturers, and distributors that are not included in paragraph (e) of this section.* (1) Protein blenders, feed manufacturers, and distributors that manufacture, blend, process, and distribute products that contain or may contain protein derived from mammalian tissues shall comply with paragraph (c)(1) of this section.

(2) Protein blenders, feed manufacturers, and distributors, shall be exempt from paragraphs (d)(1) of this section if they:

(i) Purchase animal products from renderers that certified compliance with paragraph (c)(2) of this section or purchase such materials from parties that certify that the materials were purchased from renderers that certified compliance with paragraph (c)(2) of this section; or

(ii) Comply with the requirements of paragraph (c)(2) of this section where appropriate.

(3) Protein blenders, feed manufacturers, and distributors, shall be exempt from paragraph (c)(1)(ii) of this section if they:

(i) Purchase animal protein products that are marked in accordance with paragraph (c)(3) of this section or purchase such materials from renderers that certified compliance with paragraph (c)(3) of this section, or purchase such materials from parties that certify that the materials were purchased from renderers that certified compliance with paragraph (c)(3) of this section; or

(ii) Comply with the requirements of paragraph (c)(3) of this section where appropriate.

(4) Pet food products that are sold or are intended for sale at retail and feeds for nonruminant laboratory animals are exempt from the labeling requirements in paragraphs (c) and (d) of this section. However, if the pet food products or feeds for nonruminant laboratory animals are sold or are intended for sale as distressed or salvage items, then such products shall be labeled in accordance with paragraph (c) or (d) of this section, as appropriate.

(5) Copies of certifications as described in paragraphs (d)(2) and (d)(3) of this section, shall be made available for inspection and copying by the Food and Drug Administration.

(e) *Requirements for persons that intend to separate mammalian and nonmammalian materials.* (1) Renderers, protein blenders, feed manufacturers, distributors, and others that manufacture, process, blend and distribute both products that contain or may contain protein derived from mammalian tissues or feeds containing such products, and protein products from other animal tissues or feeds containing such products, and that intend to keep those products separate shall:

(i) Comply with paragraphs (c)(1) or (d)(1) of this section as appropriate except that the labeling requirement shall apply only to products that contain or may contain protein derived from mammalian tissues or feeds containing such products;

(ii) In the case of a renderer, obtain nonmammalian or pure porcine or pure equine materials only from single-species slaughter facilities;

(iii) Provide for measures to avoid commingling or cross-contamination;

(A) Maintain separate equipment or facilities for the manufacture, processing, or blending of such materials; or
(B) Use clean-out procedures or other means adequate to prevent carry-over of products that contain or may contain protein derived from mammalian tissues into animal protein or feeds that may be used for ruminants; and

(iv) Maintain written procedures specifying the clean-out procedures or other means, and specifying the procedures

for separating products that contain or may contain protein derived from mammalian tissue from all other protein products from the time of receipt until the time of shipment.

(2) Renderers, blenders, feed manufacturers, and distributors will be exempted from applicable requirements of paragraph (e)(1) of this section, if they meet the criteria for exemption under paragraphs (c)(2) or (c)(3) of this section, and (d)(2) or (d)(3) of this section.

(f) *Requirements for establishments and individuals that are responsible for feeding ruminant animals.* Establishments and individuals that are responsible for feeding ruminant animals shall maintain copies of purchase invoices and labeling for all feeds containing animal protein products received, and make the copies available for inspection and copying by the Food and Drug Administration.

(g) *Adulteration and misbranding.* (1) Animal protein products, and feeds containing such products, that are not in compliance with paragraphs (c) through (f) of this section, excluding labeling requirements, will be deemed adulterated under section 402(a)(2)(C) or 402(a)(4) of the act. (2) Animal protein products, and feeds containing such products, that are not in compliance with the labeling requirements of paragraphs (c) through (f) of this section will be deemed misbranded under section 403(a)(1) or 403(f) of the act.

(h) *Inspection; records retention.* (1) Records that are to be made available for inspection and copying, as required by this section, shall be kept for a minimum of 1 year.

(2) Written procedures required by this section shall be made available for inspection and copying by the Food and Drug Administration.

[62 FR 30976, June 5, 1997] Effective Date Note: At 62 FR 30976, June 5, 1997, Sec. 589.2000 was added.

PART 606 - CURRENT GOOD MANUFACTURING PRACTICE FOR BLOOD AND BLOOD COMPONENTS

AUTHORITY: 21 U.S.C. 321, 331,351,352,355,360,360j, 371,374; 42 U.S.C. 216,262,263a,264. SOURCE: 40 FR 53532, Nov. 18, 1975, unless otherwise noted.

Subpart A - General Provisions

606.3   Definitions.

As used in this part:

(a) *Blood* means whole blood collected from a single donor and processed either for transfusion or further manufacturing.

(b) *Unit* means the volume of blood or one of its components in a suitable volume of anticoagulant obtained from a single collection of blood from one donor.

(c) *Component* means that part of a single-donor unit of blood separated by physical or mechanical means.

(d) *Plasma for further manufacturing* means that liquid portion of blood separated and used as material to prepare another product.

(e) *Plasmapheresis* means the procedure in which blood is removed from the donor, the plasma is separated from the formed elements and at least the red blood cells are returned to the donor. This process may be immediately repeated, once.

(f) *Plateletpheresis* means the procedure in which blood is removed from the donor, a platelet concentrate is separated, and the remaining formed elements and residual plasma are returned to the donor.

(g) *Leukapheresis* means the procedure in which blood is removed from the donor, a leukocyte concentrate is separated, and the remaining formed elements and residual plasma are returned to the donor.

(h) *Facilities* means any area used for the collection, processing, compatibility testing, storage or distribution of blood and blood components.

(i) *Processing* means any procedure employed after collection and before compatibility testing of blood and includes the identification of a unit of donor blood, the preparation of components from such unit of donor blood, serological testing, labeling and associated recordkeeping.

(j) *Compatibility testing* means the in vitro serological tests performed on donor and recipient blood samples to establish the serological matching of a donor's blood or blood components with that of a potential recipient.

(k) *Distributed* means:
(1) The blood or blood components have left the control of the licensed manufacturer, unlicensed registered blood establishment, or transfusion service; or
(2) The licensed manufacturer has provided Source Plasma or any other blood component for use in the manufacture of a licensed biological product.
(l) *Control* means having responsibility for maintaining the continued safety, purity, and potency of the product and for compliance with applicable product and establishment standards, and for compliance with current good manufacturing practices.

Subpart B - Organization and Personnel

606.20 Personnel.

(a) [Reserved]

(b) The personnel responsible for the collection, processing, compatibility testing, storage or distribution of blood or blood components shall be adequate in number, educational background, training and experience, including professional training as necessary, or combination thereof, to assure competent performance of their assigned functions, and to ensure that the final product has the safety, purity, potency, identity and effectiveness it purports or is represented to possess. All personnel shall have capabilities commensurate with their assigned functions, a thorough understanding of the procedures or control operations they perform, the necessary training or experience, and adequate information concerning the application of pertinent provisions of this part to their respective functions.

(c) Persons whose presence can adversely affect the safety and purity of the products shall be excluded from areas where the collection, processing, compatibility testing, storage or distribution of blood or blood components is conducted.

[40 FR 53532, Nov. 18, 1975, as amended at 49 FR 23833, June 8, 1984; 55 FR 11014, Mar. 26, 1990; 62 FR 53538, Oct.15, 1997]

606.40 Facilities.

Facilities shall be maintained in a clean and orderly manner, and shall be of suitable size, construction and location to facilitate adequate cleaning, maintenance and proper operations. The facilities shall:

(a) Provide adequate space for the following when applicable:

(1) Private and accurate examinations of individuals to determine their suitability as blood donors.

(2) The withdrawal of blood from donors with minimal risk of contamination, or exposure to activities and equipment unrelated to blood collection.

(3) The storage of blood or blood components pending completion of tests.

(4) The quarantine storage of blood or blood components in a designated location pending repetition of those tests that initially gave questionable serological results.

(5) The storage of finished products prior to distribution.

(6) The quarantine storage, handling and disposition of products and reagents not suitable for use.

(7) The orderly collection, processing, compatibility testing, storage and distribution of blood and blood components to prevent contamination.

(8) The adequate and proper performance of all steps in plasmapheresis, plateletpheresis and leukapheresis procedures

(9) The orderly conduction of all packaging, labeling and other finishing operations.

(b) Provide adequate lighting, ventilation and screening of open windows and doors.

(c) Provide adequate, clean, and convenient handwashing facilities for personnel, and adequate, clean, and convenient toilet facilities for donors and personnel. Drains shall be of adequate size and, where connected directly to a sewer, shall be equipped with traps to prevent back-siphonage.

(d) Provide for safe and sanitary disposal for the following:

(1) Trash and items used during the collection, processing and compatibility testing of blood and blood components.

(2) Blood and blood components not suitable for use or distribution.

Subpart D - Equipment

606.60 Equipment.

(a) Equipment used in the collection, processing, compatibility testing, storage and distribution of blood and blood components shall be maintained in a clean and orderly manner and located so as to facilitate cleaning and maintenance. The equipment shall be observed, standardized and calibrated on a regularly scheduled basis as prescribed in the Standard Operating Procedures Manual and shall perform in the manner for which it was designed so as to assure compliance with the official requirements prescribed in this chapter for blood and blood products.

(b) Equipment that shall be observed, standardized and calibrated with at least the following frequency, include but are not limited to:

Equipment	Performance check	Frequency	Frequency of Calibration
Temp. Recorder	Compare to thermometer	Daily	As necessary
Refrigerated Centrifuge	Check speed & temperature	Each day of use	As necessary.
Hematocrit Centrifuge	------------------------------	-------------------	Standardize before initial use, after repairs or adjustments, and annually. Timer every 3 months
General lab centrifuge	------------------------------	-------------------	Tachometer every 6 mo.
Automated blood-typing machine	Observe controls for correct results	Each day of use	
Hemoglobinometer	Standardize against cyanmethemoglobin standard	Each day of use	
Refractometer	Standardize against distilled water	Each day of use	
Blood container scale	Standardize against container of known weight	Each day of use	As necessary
Water Bath	Observe temperature	Each day of use	As necessary
Rh view box	Observed temperature	Each day of use	As necessary
Autoclave	Observe temperature	Each time of use	As necessary
Serologic rotators	Observe controls for correct results	Each day of use	Speed as necessary
Laboratory thermometers	------------------------------	-------------------	Before initial use.
Electronic thermometers	------------------------------	-------------------	Monthly
Vacuum blood agitator	Observe weight of the first container of blood filled for correct results	Each day of use	Standardize with container of known mass or volume before initial use, and after repairs or adjustments.

(c) Equipment employed in the sterilization of materials used in blood collection or for disposition of contaminated products shall be designed, maintained and utilized to ensure the destruction of contaminating microorganisms. The effectiveness of the sterilization procedure shall be no less than that achieved by an attained temperature of 121.5o C (251o F) maintained for 20 minutes by saturated steam or by an attained temperature of 170o C (338o F) maintained for 2 hours with dry heat.

[40 FR 53532, Nov. 18, 1975; 40 FR 55849, Dec. 2, 1975, as amended at 45 FR 9261, Feb 12, 1980; 57 FR 11263, Apr. 2, 1992; 57 FR 12862, Apr. 13, 1992]

606.65 Supplies and reagents.

All supplies and reagents used in the collection, processing, compatibility testing, storage and distribution of blood and blood components shall be stored in a safe, sanitary and orderly manner.

(a) All surfaces coming in contact with blood and blood components intended for transfusion shall be sterile, pyrogen-free, and shall not interact with the product in such a manner as to have an adverse effect upon the safety, purity, potency or effectiveness of the product. All final containers and closures for blood and blood components not intended for transfusion shall be clean and free of surface solids and other contaminants.

(b) Each blood collecting container and its satellite container(s), if any, shall be examined visually for damage or evidence of contamination prior to its use and immediately after filling. Such examination shall include inspection for breakage of seals, when indicated, and abnormal discoloration. Where any defect is observed, the container shall

not be used, or, if detected after filling, shall be properly discarded.

(c) Representative samples of each lot of the following reagents or solutions shall be tested on a regularly scheduled basis by methods described in the Standard Operating Procedures Manual to determine their capacity to perform as required:

Reagent or Solution	Frequency of "Testing"
Anti-human globulin	Each day of use
Blood grouping reagents	Each day of use
Lectins	Each day of use
Antibody screening and reverse grouping cells	Each day of use
Hepatitis test reagents	Each run
Syphilis serology reagents	Each run
Enzymes	Each day of use

(d) Supplies and reagents that do not bear an expiration date shall be stored in such a manner that the oldest is used first.

(e) Supplies and reagents shall be used in a manner consistent with instructions provided by the manufacturer.

(f) Items that are required to be sterile and come into contact with blood should be disposable whenever possible.

[40 FR 53532, Nov. 18, 1975, as amended at 59 FR 23636, May 6, 1994]

Subpart E - [Reserved]

Subpart F - Production and Process Controls

606.100 Standard operating procedures.

(a) In all instances, except clinical investigations, standard operating procedures shall comply with published additional standards in Part 640 of this chapter for the products being processed; except that, references in Part 640 relating to licenses, licensed establishments and submission of material or data to or approval by the Director, Center for Biologics Evaluation and Research, are not applicable to establishments not subject to licensure under section 351 of the Public Health Service Act.

(b) Written standard operating procedures shall be maintained and shall include all steps to be followed in the collection, processing, compatibility testing, storage and distribution of blood and blood components for homologous transfusion, autologous transfusion and further manufacturing purposes. Such procedures shall be available to the personnel for use in the areas where the procedures are performed, unless this is impractical. The written standard operating procedures shall include, but are not limited to, descriptions of the following, when applicable:

(1) Criteria used to determine donor suitability, including acceptable medical history criteria.

(2) Methods of performing donor qualifying tests and measurements, including minimum and maximum values for a test or procedure when a factor in determining acceptability.

(3) Solutions and methods used to prepare the site of phlebotomy to give maximum assurance of a sterile container of blood.

(4) Method of accurately relating the product(s) to the donor.

(5) Blood collection procedure, including in-process precautions taken to measure accurately the quantity of blood removed from the donor.

(6) Methods of component preparation, including any time restrictions for specific steps in processing.

(7) All tests and repeat tests performed on blood and blood components during processing, including testing for hepatitis B surface antigen as prescribed in 610.40 of this chapter.

(8) Pretransfusion testing, where applicable, including precautions to be taken to identify accurately the recipient blood samples and crossmatched donor units.

(9) Procedures for investigating adverse donor and recipient reactions.

(10) Storage temperatures and methods of controlling storage temperatures for all blood products and reagents as prescribed in 600.15 and 610.53 of this chapter.

(11) Length of expiration dates, if any, assigned for all final products as prescribed in 610.53 of this chapter.

(12) Criteria for determining whether returned blood is suitable for reissue.

(13) Procedures used for relating a unit of blood or blood component from the donor to its final disposition.

(14) Quality control procedures for supplies and reagents employed in blood collection, processing and pretransfusion testing.

(15) Schedules and procedures for equipment maintenance and calibration.

(16) Labeling procedures, including safeguards to avoid labeling mixups.

(17) Procedures of plasmapheresis, plateletpheresis, and leukapheresis, if performed, including precautions to be taken to ensure reinfusion of a donor's own cells.

(18) Procedure for preparing recovered (salvaged) plasma, if performed, including details of separation, pooling, labeling, storage and distribution.

(19) Procedures in accordance with 610.46 of this chapter to look at prior donations of Whole Blood, blood components, Source Plasma and Source Leukocytes from a donor who has donated blood and subsequently tests repeatedly reactive for antibody to human immunodeficiency virus (HIV) or otherwise is determined to be unsuitable when tested in accordance with 610.45 of this chapter. Procedures to quarantine in-house Whole Blood, blood components, Source Plasma and Source Leukocytes intended for further manufacture into injectable products that were obtained from such donors; procedures to notify consignees regarding the need to quarantine such products; procedures to determine the suitability for release of such products from quarantine; procedures to notify consignees of Whole Blood, blood components, Source Plasma and Source Leukocytes from such donors of the results of the antibody testing of such donors; and procedures in accordance with 610.47 of this chapter to notify attending physicians so that transfusion recipients are informed that they may have received Whole Blood and, blood components at increased risk for transmitting human immunodeficiency virus.

(20) Procedures for donor deferral as prescribed in 610.41 of this chapter; and procedures for donor notification and autologous donor referring physician notification, including procedures for the appropriate followup if the initial attempt at notification fails, as prescribed in 630.6 of this chapter.

(c) All records pertinent to the lot or unit maintained pursuant to these regulations shall be reviewed before the release or distribution of a lot or unit of final product. The review or portions of the review may be performed at appropriate periods during or after blood collecting, processing, compatibility testing and storing. A thorough investigation, including the conclusions and follow up, of any unexplained discrepancy or the failure of a lot or unit to meet any of its specifications shall be made and recorded.

(d) In addition to the requirements of this subpart and in conformity with this section, any facility may utilize current standard operating procedures such as the manuals of the following organizations, as long as such specific procedures are consistent with, and at least as stringent as, the requirements contained in this part.

(1) American Association of Blood Banks.

(2) American National Red Cross.

(3) Other organizations or individual blood banks, subject to approval by the Director, Center for Biologics Evaluation and Research.

[40 FR 53532, Nov. 18, 1975, as amended at 49 FR 23833, June 8, 1984; 55 FR 11013, Mar. 26, 1990; 61FR47422, Sept.9, 1996]]

606.110 Plateletpheresis, leukapheresis, and plasmapheresis.

(a) The use of plateletpheresis and leukapheresis procedures to obtain a product for a specific recipient may be at variance with the additional standards for specific products prescribed in this part provided that: (1) A physician has determined that the recipient must be transfused with the leukocytes or platelets from a specific donor, and (2) the procedure is performed under the supervision of a qualified licensed physician who is aware of the health status of the donor, and the physician has certified in writing that the donor's health permits plateletpheresis or leukapheresis.

(b) Plasmapheresis of donors who do not meet the donor requirements of 640.63, 640.64 and 640.65 of this chapter for the collection of plasma containing rare antibodies shall be permitted only with the prior approval of the Director, Center for Biologics Evaluation and Research.

[40 FR 53532, Nov. 18, 1975, as amended at 49 FR 23833, June 8, 1984; 55 FR 11013, Mar. 26, 1990]

Subpart G - Finished Product Control

606.120   Labeling, general requirements.

(a) Labeling operations shall be separated physically or spatially from other operations in a manner adequate to prevent mixups.

(b) The labeling operation shall include the following labeling controls:

(1) Labels shall be held upon receipt, pending review and proofing against an approved final copy, to ensure accuracy regarding identity, content, and conformity with the approved copy.

(2) Each type of label representing different products shall be stored and maintained in a manner to prevent mixups, and stocks of obsolete labels shall be destroyed.

(3) All necessary checks in labeling procedures shall be utilized to prevent errors in translating test results to container labels.

(c) All labeling shall be clear and legible.

[50 FR 35469, Aug. 30, 1985]

606.121   Container label.

(a) The container label requirements are designed to facilitate the use of a uniform container label for blood and blood components (except Source Plasma) by all blood establishments.

(b) The label provided by the collecting facility and the initial processing facility shall not be removed, altered, or obscured, except that the label may be altered to indicate the proper name and other information required to identify accurately the contents of a container after blood components have been prepared.

(c) The container label shall include the following information, as well as other specialized information as required in this section for specific products:

(1) The proper name of the product in a prominent position, and modifier(s), if appropriate.

(2) The name, address, registration number, and, if a licensed product, the license number of each manufacturer.

(3) The donor, pool, or lot number relating the unit to the donor.

(4) The expiration date, including the day, month, and year, and, if the dating period for the product is 72 hours or less, the hour of expiration.

(5) If the product is intended for transfusion, the appropriate donor classification statement, i.e., "paid donor" or "volunteer donor", in no less prominence than the proper name of the product.

(i) A paid donor is a person who receives monetary payment for a blood donation.

(ii) A volunteer donor is a person who does not receive monetary payment for a blood donation.

(iii) Benefits, such as time off from work, membership in blood assurance programs, and cancellation of nonreplacement fees that are not readily convertible to cash, do not constitute monetary payment within the meaning of this paragraph.

(6) For Whole Blood, Plasma, Platelets, and partial units of Red Blood Cells, the volume of the product, accurate to within 10 percent; or optionally for Platelets, the volume range within reasonable limits.

(7) The recommended storage temperature (in degrees Celsius).

(8) If the product is intended for transfusion, the statements:

(i) "Caution: Federal law prohibits dispensing without prescription."

(ii) "See circular of information for indications, contraindications, cautions, and methods of infusion."

(iii) "Properly identify intended recipient."

(9) The statement: "This product may transmit infectious agents."

(10) Where applicable, the name and volume of source material.

(11) The statement: "Caution: For Manufacturing Use Only", when applicable.

(12) If the product is intended for transfusion, the ABO and Rh groups of the donor shall be designated conspicuously. For Cryoprecipitated AHF, the Rh group may be omitted. The Rh group shall be designated as follows:

(i) If the test using Anti-D Blood Grouping Reagent is positive, the product shall be labeled: "Rh positive."

(ii) If the test using Anti-D Blood Grouping Reagent is negative but the test for Du is positive, the product shall be labeled: "Rh positive."

(iii) If the test using Anti-D Blood Grouping Reagent is negative and the test for Du is negative, the product shall be labeled: "Rh negative."

(13) The container label may bear encoded information in the form of machine-readable symbols approved for use by the Director, Center for Biologics Evaluation and Research (HFB 1).

(d) Except for recovered plasma intended for manufacturing use or as otherwise approved by the Director, Center for Biologics Evaluation and Research (HFB 1), the paper of the container label shall be white and print shall be solid black, with the following additional exceptions:

(1) The Rh blood group shall be printed as follows:

(i) Rh positive: Use black print on white background.

(ii) Rh negative: Use white print on black background.

(2) The proper name of the product, any appropriate modifier(s), the donor classification statement, and the statement "properly identify intended recipient" shall be printed in solid red or in solid black.

(3) The following color scheme may be used optionally for differentiating ABO Blood groups:

Blood Group	Color of label paper
O	Blue
A	Yellow
B	Pink
AB	White

(4) Ink colors used for the optional color coding system described in paragraph (d)(3) of this section shall be a visual match to specific color samples designated by the Director, Center for Biologics Evaluation and Research (HFB 1).

(5) Special labels, such as those described in paragraphs (h) and (i) of this section, may be color coded using the colors recommended in the guideline (see paragraph (a) of this section), or colors otherwise approved for use by the Director, Center for Biologics Evaluation and Research (HFB 1).

(e) Container label requirements for particular products or groups of products.

(1) Whole Blood labels shall include:

(i) The volume of anticoagulant.

(ii) The name of the applicable anticoagulant immediately preceding and of no less prominence than the proper name approved for use by the Director, Center for Biologics Evaluation and Research.

(iii) If tests for unexpected antibodies are positive, blood intended for transfusion shall be labeled: "Contains (name of antibody)."

(2) Except for frozen, deglycerolized, or washed Red Blood Cell products, red blood cell labels shall include:

(i) The volume and kind of Whole Blood, including the type of anticoagulant, from which the product was prepared.

(ii) If tests for unexpected antibodies are positive and the product is intended for transfusion, the statement: "Contains (name of antibody)."

(3) Labels for products with a dating period of 72 hours or less, including any product prepared in a system that may compromise sterility, shall bear the hour of expiration.

(4) If tests for unexpected antibodies are positive, Plasma intended for transfusion shall be labeled: "Contains (name of antibody)."

(5) Recovered plasma labels shall include:

(i) In lieu of an expiration date, the date of collection of the oldest material in the container.

(ii) The statement: "Caution: For Manufacturing Use Only"; or "Caution: For Use in Manufacturing Noninjectable Products Only", as applicable.

(iii) For recovered plasma not meeting the requirements for manufacture into licensable products, the statement:

"Not for Use in Products Subject to License Under Section 351 of the Public Health Service Act."

(f) Blood and blood components determined to be unsuitable for transfusion shall be prominently labeled: "NOT FOR TRANSFUSION", and the label shall state the reason the unit is considered unsuitable. The provision does not apply to recovered plasma labeled according to paragraph (e)(5) of this section.

(g) As required under 610.40 of this chapter, labels for blood and blood components that are reactive for Hepatitis B Surface Antigen, but that are intended for further manufacturing, shall state conspicuously that the material is reactive when tested for hepatitis B surface antigen and may transmit viral hepatitis or, as applicable, that blood was collected from a donor known to be reactive for hepatitis B surface antigen and is presumed to be infectious, although confirmatory hepatitis testing has not been done.

(h) The following additional information shall appear on the label for blood or blood components shipped in an emergency, prior to completion of required tests, in accordance with 640.2(f) of this chapter:

(1) The statement: "FOR EMERGENCY USE ONLY BY _____."

(2) Results of any tests prescribed under 610.40, 610.45, and 640.5 (a), (b), or (c) of this chapter completed before shipment.

(3) Indication of any tests prescribed under 610.40, 610.45, and 640.5 (a), (b) or (c) of this chapter and not completed before shipment.

(i) The following additional information shall appear on the label for Whole Blood or Red Blood Cells intended for autologous infusion:

(1) Information adequately identifying the patient, e.g., name, blood group, hospital, and identification number.

(2) Date of donation.

(3) The statement: "FOR AUTOLOGOUS USE ONLY."

(4) In place of the blood group label, each container of blood intended for autologous use and obtained from a donor who fails to meet any of the donor suitability requirements under 640.3 of this chapter or who is reactive in the hepatitis tests prescribed under 610.40 of this chapter shall be prominently and permanently labeled: "FOR AUTOLOGOUS USE ONLY."

(5) Units of blood originally intended for autologous use, except those labeled as prescribed under paragraph (i)(4) of this section, may be issued for homologous transfusion provided the container label complies with all applicable provisions of paragraphs (b) through (e) of this section. In such case, the special label required under paragraph (i) (1), (2), and (3) of this section shall be removed or otherwise obscured.

(j) A tie-tag attached to the container may be used for providing the information required by paragraph (e) (1)(iii), (2)(ii), and (4), (h), or (i)(1), (2), and (3) of this section.

[50 FR 35469, Aug. 30, 1985, as amended at 53 FR 116, Jan. 5, 1988; 55 FR 11014, Mar. 26, 1990; 57 FR 10814, Mar. 31, 1992; 59 FR 23636, May 6, 1994, 63 FR 16685, Apr. 6, 1998; 64 FR 45371, Aug. 19, 1999]

EFFECTIVE DATE NOTE: The information collection requirements contained in 606.121 will not become effective until OMB approval has been obtained. FDA will publish a notice of OMB approval in the FEDERAL REGISTER.

606.122   Instruction circular.

An instruction circular shall be available for distribution if the product is intended for transfusion. The instruction circular shall provide adequate directions for use, including the following information:

(a) Instructions to mix the product before use.

(b) Instructions to use a filter in the administration equipment.

(c) The statement "Do Not Add Medications" or an explanation concerning allowable additives.

(d) A description of the product, its source, and preparation, including the name and proportion of the anticoagulant used in collecting the Whole Blood from each product is prepared.

(e) Statements that the product was prepared from blood that was negative when tested for antibody to Human Immunodeficiency Virus (HIV) and nonreactive for hepatitis B surface antigen by FDA required tests and nonreactive when tested for syphilis by a serologic test for syphilis (STS).

(f) The statements: "Warning. The risk of transmitting infectious agents is present. Careful donor selection and available laboratory tests do not eliminate the hazard."

(g) The names of cryoprotective agents and other additives that may still be present in the product.

(h) The names and results of all tests performed when necessary for safe and effective use.

(i) The use of the product, indications, contraindications, side effects and hazards, dosage and administration recommendations.

(j) [Reserved]

(k) For Red Blood Cells, the instruction circular shall contain:

(1) Instructions to administer a suitable plasma volume expander if Red Blood Cells are substituted when Whole Blood is the indicated product.

(2) A warning not to add Lactated Ringer's Injection U.S.P. solution to Red Blood Cell products.

(l) For Platelets, the instruction circular shall contain:

(1) The approximate volume of plasma from which a sample unit of Platelets is prepared.

(2) Instructions to begin administration as soon as possible, but not more than 4 hours after entering the container.

(m) For Plasma, the instruction circular shall contain:

(1) A warning against further processing of the frozen product if there is evidence of breakage or thawing.

(2) Instructions to thaw the frozen product at a temperature between 30 and 37o C.

(3) When applicable, instructions to begin administration of the product within 6 hours after thawing.

(4) Instructions to administer to ABO-group-compatible recipients.

(5) A statement that this product has the same hepatitis risk as Whole Blood; other plasma volume expanders without this risk are available for treating hypovolemia.

(n) For Cryoprecipitated AHF, the instruction circular shall contain:

(1) A statement that the average potency is 80 or more International Units of antihemophilic factor.

(2) The statement: "Usually contains at least 150 milligrams of fibrinogen"; or, alternatively, the average fibrinogen level determined by assay of representative units.

(3) A warning against further processing of the product if there is evidence of breakage or thawing.

(4) Instructions to thaw the product for no more than 15 minutes at a temperature between 30 and 37o C.

(5) Instructions to store at room temperature after thawing and to begin administration as soon as possible but no more than 4 hours after entering the container or after pooling and within 6 hours after thawing.

(6) A statement that 0.9 percent Sodium Chloride Injection U.S.P. is the preferred diluent.

(7) Adequate instructions for pooling to ensure complete removal of all concentrated material from each container.

(8) The statement: "Good patient management requires monitoring treatment responses to Cryoprecipitated AHF transfusions with periodic plasma factor VIII or fibrinogen assays in hemophilia A and hypofibrinogenemic recipients, respectively."

[50 FR 35470, Aug. 30, 1985, as amended at 53 FR 116, Jan. 5, 1988; 64 FR 45371, Aug. 19, 1999]

EFFECTIVE DATE NOTE: The information collection requirements contained in 606.122 will not become effective until OMB approval has been obtained. FDA will publish a notice of OMB approval in the FEDERAL REGISTER.

Subpart H - Laboratory Controls

606.140   Laboratory controls.

Laboratory control procedures shall include:

(a) The establishment of scientifically sound and appropriate specifications, standards and test procedures to assure that blood and blood components are safe, pure, potent and effective.

(b) Adequate provisions for monitoring the reliability, accuracy, precision and performance of laboratory test procedures and instruments.

(c) Adequate identification and handling of all test samples so that they are accurately related to the specific unit of product being tested, or to its donor, or to the specific recipient, where applicable.

606.151   Compatibility testing.

Standard operating procedures for compatibility testing shall include the following:

(a) A method of collecting and identifying the blood samples of recipients to ensure positive identification.

(b) The use of fresh recipient serum samples less than 3-days old for all pretransfusion testing if the recipient has been pregnant or transfused within the previous 3 months.

(c) The testing of the donor's cell type with the recipient's serum type by a method that will demonstrate incompatibility.

(d) A provision that, if the unit of donor's blood has not been screened by a method that will demonstrate agglutinating, coating and hemolytic antibodies, the recipient's cells shall be tested with the donor's serum (minor crossmatch) by a method that will so demonstrate.

(e) Procedures to expedite transfusions in life-threatening emergencies. Records of all such incidents shall be maintained, including complete documentation justifying the emergency action, which shall be signed by a physician.

40 FR 53532, Nov. 18, 1975, as amended at 64 FR 45371, Aug. 19, 1999; 66 FR 1835, Jan 10, 2001]

Subpart I - Records and Reports

606.160 Records.

(a)(1) Records shall be maintained concurrently with the performance of each significant step in the collection, processing, compatibility testing, storage and distribution of each unit of blood and blood components so that all steps can be clearly traced. All records shall be legible and indelible, and shall identify the person performing the work, include dates of the various entries, show test results as well as the interpretation of the results, show the expiration date assigned to specific products, and be as detailed as necessary to provide a complete history of the work performed.

(2) Appropriate records shall be available from which to determine lot numbers of supplies and reagents used for specific lots or units of the final product.

(b) Records shall be maintained that include, but are not limited to, the following when applicable:

(1) Donor records:

(i) Donor selection, including medical interview and examination and where applicable, informed consent.

(ii) Permanent and temporary deferrals for health reasons including reason(s) for deferral.

(iii) Donor adverse reaction complaints and reports, including results of all investigations and follow up.

(iv) Therapeutic bleedings, including signed requests from attending physicians, the donor's disease and disposition of units.

(v) Immunization, including informed consent, identification of the antigen, dosage and route of administration.

(vi) Blood collection, including identification of the phlebotomist.

(vii) Records to relate the donor with the unit number of each previous donation from that donor.

(viii) Records of quarantine, notification, testing and disposition performed pursuant to 610.46 and 610.47 of this chapter.

(ix) Records of notification of donors deferred or determined not to be suitable for donation, including appropriate followup if the initial attempt at notification fails, performed under 630.6 of this chapter.

(x) The donor's address provided at the time of donation where the donor may be contacted within 8 weeks after donation.

(xi) Records of notification of the referring physician of a deferred autologous donor, including appropriate followup if the initial notification attempt fails, performed under 630.6 of this chapter.

(2) Processing records:

(i) Blood processing, including results and interpretation of all tests and retests.

(ii) Component preparation, including all relevant dates and times.

(iii) Separation and pooling of recovered plasma.

(iv) Centrifugation and pooling of source plasma.

(v) Labeling, including initials of person(s) performing the procedure.

(3) Storage and distribution records:

(i) Distribution and disposition, as appropriate, of blood and blood products.

(ii) Visual inspection of whole blood and red blood cells during storage and immediately before distribution.

(iii) Storage temperature, including initialed temperature recorder charts.

(iv) Reissue, including records of proper temperature maintenance.

(v) Emergency release of blood, including signature of requesting physician obtained before or after release.

(4) Compatibility test records:

(i) Results of all compatibility tests, including crossmatching, testing of patient samples, antibody screening and identification.

(ii) Results of confirmatory testing.

(5) Quality control records:

(i) Calibration and standardization of equipment.

(ii) Performance checks of equipment and reagents.

(iii) Periodic check on sterile technique.

(iv) Periodic tests of capacity of shipping containers to maintain proper temperature in transit.

(v) Proficiency test results.

(6) Transfusion reaction reports and complaints, including records of investigations and follow up.

(7) General records:

(i) Sterilization of supplies and reagents prepared within the facility, including date, time interval, temperature and mode.

(ii) Responsible personnel.

(iii) Errors and accidents.

(iv) Maintenance records for equipment and general physical plant.

(v) Supplies and reagents, including name of manufacturer or supplier, lot numbers, expiration date and date of receipt.

(vi) Disposition of rejected supplies and reagents used in the collection, processing and compatibility testing of blood and blood components.

(c) A donor number shall be assigned to each accepted donor, which relates the unit of blood collected to that donor, to his medical record, to any component or blood product from that donor's unit of blood, and to all records describing the history and ultimate disposition of these products.

(d) Records shall be retained for such interval beyond the expiration date for the blood or blood component as necessary to facilitate the reporting of any unfavorable clinical reactions. The retention period shall be no less than 5 years after the records of processing have been completed or 6 months after the latest expiration date for the individual product, whichever is a later date. When there is no expiration date, records shall be retained indefinitely.

(e) A record shall be available from which unsuitable donors may be identified so that products from such individuals will not be distributed.

[40 FR 53532, Nov.18, 1975, as amended at 61 FR 47422, Sept. 9, 1996; 64 FR 45371, Aug 19, 1999]

EFFECTIVE DATE NOTE: At 65 FR 66635, Nov 7, 2000, 606.160 was amended by revising paragraph (b)(7)(iii), effective May 7, 2000. At 66 FR 67477, Nov. 9, 2000, the effective date was corrected to read May 7, 2001. For the convenience of the user, the revised text is set forth as follows:

606.160 Records

*   *   *   *   *

(b) ***
(7) ***
(iii) Biological product deviations.

*   *   *   *   *

606.165   Distribution and receipt; procedures and records.

(a) Distribution and receipt procedures shall include a system by which the distribution or receipt of each unit can be readily determined to facilitate its recall, if necessary.

(b) Distribution records shall contain information to readily facilitate the identification of the name and address of the consignee, the date and quantity delivered, the lot number of the unit(s), the date of expiration or the date of collection, whichever is applicable, or for crossmatched blood and blood components, the name of the recipient.

(c) Receipt records shall contain the name and address of the collecting facility, date received, donor or lot number assigned by the collecting facility and the date of expiration or the date of collection, whichever is applicable.

606.170   Adverse reaction file.

(a) Records shall be maintained of any reports of complaints of adverse reactions regarding each unit of blood or blood product arising as a result of blood collection or transfusion. A thorough investigation of each reported adverse reaction shall be made. A written report of the investigation of adverse reactions, including conclusions and follow up, shall be prepared and maintained as part of the record for that lot or unit of final product by the collecting or transfusing facility. When it is determined that the product was at fault in causing a transfusion reaction, copies of all such written reports shall be forwarded to and maintained by the manufacturer or collecting facility.

(b) When a complication of blood collection or transfusion is confirmed to be fatal, the Director, Office of Compliance, Center for Biologics Evaluation and Research, shall be notified by telephone, facsimile, express mail, or electronically transmitted mail as soon as possible; a written report of the investigation shall be submitted to the Director, Office of Compliance, Center for Biologics Evaluation and Research, within 7 days after the fatality by the collecting facility in the event of a donor reaction, or by the facility that performed the compatibility tests in the event of a transfusion reaction.

(Information collection requirements approved by the Office of Management and Budget under control number 0910-0116). [40 FR 53532, Nov. 18, 1975, as amended at 49 FR 23833, June 8, 1984; 50 FR 35471, Aug. 30, 1985; 55 FR 11014, Mar. 26, 1990; 64 FR 45371, Aug. 19, 1999]

606.171 Reporting of product deviations by licensed manufacturers, unlicensed registered blood establishmkents, and transfusion services.

(a) Who must report under this section? You, a licensed manufacturer of blood and blood components, including Source Plasma; an unlicensed registered blood establishment; or a transfusion service who had control over the product when the deviation occurred, must report under this section. If you arrange for another person to perform a manufacturing, holding, or distribution step, while the product is in your control, that step is performed under your control. You must establish, maintain, and follow a procedure for receiving information from that person on all deviations, complaints, and adverse events concerning the affected product.

(b) What do I report under this section? You must report any event, and information relevant to the event, associated with the manufacturing, to include testing, processing, packing, labeling, or storage, or with the holding or distribution, of both licensed and unlicensed blood or blood components, including Source Plasma, if that event meets all the following criteria:

(1) Either:

(i) Represents a deviation from current good manufacturing practice, applicable regulations, applicable standards, or established specifications that may affect the safety, purity, or potency of that product; or

(ii) Represents an unexpected or unforeseeable event that may affect the safety, purity, or potency of that product; and

(2) Occurs in your facility or another facility under contract with you; and

(3) Involves distributed blood or blood components.

(c) When do I report under this section? You should report a biological product deviation as soon as possible but you must report at a date not to exceed 45-calendar days from the date you, your agent, or another person who performs a manufacturing, holding, or distribution step under your control, acquire information reasonably suggesting that a reportable event has occurred.

(d) How do I report under this section? You must report on Form FDA-3486.

(e) Where do I report under this section? You must send the completed Form FDA-3486 to the Director, Office of Compliance and Biologics Quality (HFM-600), 1401 Rockville Pike, Suite 200N, Rockville, MD 20852-1448, by either a paper or electronic filing:

(1) If you make a paper filing, you should identify on the envelope that a BPDR (biological product deviation report) is enclosed; or

(2) If you make an electronic filing, you may submit the completed Form FDA-3486 electronically through CBER's website at www.fda.gov/cber.

(f) How does this regulation affect other FDA regulations? This part supplements and does not supersede other provisions of the regulations in this chapter. All biological product deviations, whether or not they are required to be reported under this section, should be investigated in accordance with the applicable provisions of parts 211, 606, and 820 of this chapter.

[65 FR 66635, Nov. 7, 2000]

PART 803 - MEDICAL DEVICE REPORTING

AUTHORITY: 21 U.S.C. 352, 360, 360i, 360j, 371, 374. SOURCE: 60 FR 63597, Dec. 11, 1995, unless otherwise noted.

Subpart A - General Provisions

803.1 Scope

(a) This part establishes requirements for medical device reporting. Under this part, medical device user facilities, importers, and manufacturers, as defined in 803.3, must report deaths and serious injuries to which a device has or may have caused or contributed, must establish and maintain adverse event files, and must submit to FDA specified followup and summary reports. Medical device distributors, as defined in 803.3, are also required to maintain records of incidents (files). Furthermore, manufacturers and importers are also required to report certain device malfunctions. These reports will assist FDA in protecting the public health by helping to ensure that devices are not adulterated or misbranded and are safe and effective for their intended use.

(b) This part supplements and does not supersede other provisions of this subchapter, including the provisions of part 820 of this chapter.

(c) References in this part to regulatory sections of the Code of Federal Regulations are to Chapter I of title 21 unless otherwise noted.

[60 FR 63597, Dec 11, 1995, as amended at 62 FR 13306, Mar 20, 1997; 65 FR 4118, Jan. 26, 2000]

803.3 Definitions.

(a) *Act* means the Federal Food, Drug, and Cosmetic Act.

(b) *Ambulatory surgical facility (ASF)* means a distinct entity that operates for the primary purpose of furnishing same day outpatient surgical services to patients. An ASF may be either an independent entity (i.e., not a part of a provider of services or any other facility) or operated by another medical entity (e.g., under the common ownership, licensure or control of an entity). An ASF is subject to this regulation regardless of whether it is licensed by a Federal, State, municipal, or local government or regardless of whether it is accredited by a recognized accreditation organization. If an adverse event meets the criteria for reporting, the ASF must report that event regardless of the nature or location of the medical service provided by the ASF.

(c) *Become aware* means that an employee of the entity required to report has acquired information reasonably suggesting a reportable adverse event has occurred.

(1) Device user facilities are considered to have "become aware" when medical personnel, as defined in paragraph (s) of this section, who are employed by or otherwise formally affiliated with the facility, acquire such information about a reportable event.

(2) Manufacturers are considered to have become aware of an event when:

(i) Any employee becomes aware of a reportable event that is required to be reported within 30 days or that is required to be reported within 5 days under a written request from FDA under Sec. 803.53(b); and

(ii) Any employee, who is a person with management or supervisory responsibilities over persons with regulatory, scientific, or technical responsibilities, or a person whose duties relate to the collection and reporting of adverse events, becomes aware that a reportable MDR event or events, from any information, including any trend analysis, necessitate remedial action to prevent an unreasonable risk of substantial harm to the public health.

(3) Importers are considered to have become aware of an event when any employee becomes aware of a reportable event that is required to be reported by an importer within 30 days.

(d) *Caused or contributed* means that a death or serious injury was or may have been attributed to a medical device, or that a medical device was or may have been a factor in a death or serious injury, including events occurring as a result of:

(1)   Failure;
(2)   Malfunction;
(3)   Improper or inadequate design;
(4)   Manufacture;
(5)   Labeling; or
(6)   User error.

(e)(1) *Device family* means a group of one or more devices manufactured by or for the same manufacturer and having the same:

(i) Basic design and performance characteristics related to device safety and effectiveness,

(ii) Intended use and function, and

(iii) Device classification and product code.

(2) Devices that differ only in minor ways not related to safety or effectiveness can be considered to be in the same device family. Factors such as brand name and common name of the device and whether the devices were introduced into commercial distribution under the same 510(k) or premarket approval application (PMA), may be considered in grouping products into device families.

(f) *Device user* facility means a hospital, ambulatory surgical facility, nursing home, outpatient diagnostic facility, or outpatient treatment facility as defined in paragraphs (l), (b), (t), (u), and (v), respectively, of this section, which is not a "physician's office," as defined in paragraph (w) of this section. School nurse offices and employee health units are not device user facilities.

(g) *Distributor* means, for the purposes of this part, any person (other than the manufacturer or importer) who furthers the marketing of a device from the original place of manufacture to the person who makes final delivery or sale to the ultimate user, but who does not repackage or otherwise change the container, wrapper or labeling of the device or device package. One who repackages or otherwise changes the container, wrapper, or labeling, is a manufacturer under paragraph (o) of this section.

(h) [Reserved]

(i) *Expected life* of a device (required on the manufacturer's baseline report) means the time that a device is expected to remain functional after it is placed into use. Certain implanted devices have specified "end of life" (EOL) dates. Other devices are not labeled as to their respective EOL, but are expected to remain operational through maintenance, repair, upgrades, etc., for an estimated period of time.

(j) *FDA* means the Food and Drug Administration.

(k) *Five-day report* means a medical device report that must be submitted by a manufacturer to FDA pursuant to Sec. 803.53, on FDA Form 3500A or electronic equivalent as approved under Sec. 803.14, within 5 work days.

(l) *Hospital* means a distinct entity that operates for the primary purpose of providing diagnostic, therapeutic (medical, occupational, speech, physical, etc.), surgical and other patient services for specific and general medical conditions. Hospitals include general, chronic disease, rehabilitative, psychiatric, and other special-purpose facilities. A hospital may be either independent (e.g., not a part of a provider of services or any other facility) or may be operated by another medical entity (e.g., under the common ownership, licensure or control of another entity). A hospital is covered by this regulation regardless of whether it is licensed by a Federal, State, municipal or local government or whether it is accredited by a recognized accreditation organization. If an adverse event meets the criteria for reporting, the hospital must report that event regardless of the nature or location of the medical service provided by the hospital.

(m) *Importer* means, for the purposes of this part, any person who imports a device into the United States and who furthers the marketing of a device from the original place of manufacture to the person who makes final delivery or sale to the ultimate user, but who does not repackage or otherwise change the container, wrapper, or labeling of the device or device package. One who repackages or otherwise changes the container, wrapper, or labeling, is a manufacturer under paragraph (o) of this section.

(n) *Malfunction* means the failure of a device to meet its performance specifications or otherwise perform as intended. Performance specifications include all claims made in the labeling for the device. The intended performance of a device refers to the intended use for which the device is labeled or marketed, as defined in Sec. 801.4 of this chapter.

(o) *Manufacturer* means any person who manufactures, prepares, propagates, compounds, assembles, or processes a device by chemical, physical, biological, or other procedure. The term includes any person who:

(1) Repackages or otherwise changes the container, wrapper or labeling of a device in furtherance of the distribution of the device from the original place of manufacture;

(2) Initiates specifications for devices that are manufactured by a second party for subsequent distribution by the person initiating the specifications;

(3) Manufactures components or accessories which are devices that are ready to be used and are intended to be commercially distributed and intended to be used as is, or are processed by a licensed practitioner or other qualified person to meet the needs of a particular patient; or

(4) Is the U.S. agent of a foreign manufacturer.

(p) *Manufacturer or importer report number* means the number that uniquely identifies each individual adverse event report submitted by a manufacturer or importer. This number consists of three parts as follows:

(1) The FDA registration number for the manufacturing site of the reported device, or the registration number for the importer. (If the manufacturing site or the importer does not have a registration number, FDA will assign a temporary MDR reporting number until the site is officially registered. The manufacturer or importer will be informed of the temporary number.);

(2) The four-digit calendar year in which the report is submitted; and

(3) The five-digit sequence number of the reports submitted during the year, starting with 00001. (For example, the complete number will appear 1234567-1995-00001.)

(q) *MDR* means medical device report.

(r) *MDR reportable event (or reportable event)* means:

(1) An event about which user facilities become aware of information that reasonably suggests that a device has or may have caused or contributed to a death or serious injury; or

(2) An event about which manufacturers or importers have received or become aware of information that reasonably suggests that one of their marketed devices:

(i) May have caused or contributed to a death or serious injury; or (ii) Has malfunctioned and that the device or a similar device marketed by the manufacturer or importer would be likely to cause a death or serious injury if the malfunction were to recur.

(s) *Medical personnel*, as used in this part, means an individual who:

(1) Is licensed, registered, or certified by a State, territory, or other governing body, to administer health care;

(2) Has received a diploma or a degree in a professional or scientific discipline;

(3) Is an employee responsible for receiving medical complaints or adverse event reports; or

(4) Is a supervisor of such persons.

(t)(1) *Nursing home* means an independent entity (i.e., not a part of a provider of services or any other facility) or one operated by another medical entity (e.g., under the common ownership, licensure, or control of an entity) that operates for the primary purpose of providing:

(i) Skilled nursing care and related services for persons who require medical or nursing care;

(ii) Hospice care to the terminally ill; or

(iii) Services for the rehabilitation of the injured, disabled, or sick. (2) A nursing home is subject to this regulation regardless of whether it is licensed by a Federal, State, municipal, or local government or whether it is accredited by a recognized accreditation organization. If an adverse event meets the criteria for reporting, the nursing home must report that event regardless of the nature, or location of the medical service provided by the nursing home.

(u)(1) *Outpatient diagnostic facility* means a distinct entity that:

(i) Operates for the primary purpose of conducting medical diagnostic tests on patients;

(ii) Does not assume ongoing responsibility for patient care; and (iii) Provides its services for use by other medical personnel. (Examples include diagnostic radiography, mammography, ultrasonography, electrocardiography, magnetic resonance imaging, computerized axial tomography and in-vitro testing).

(2) An outpatient diagnostic facility may be either independent (i.e., not a part of a provider of services or any other facility) or operated by another medical entity (e.g., under the common ownership, licensure, or control of an entity). An outpatient diagnostic facility is covered by this regulation regardless of whether it is licensed by a Federal, State, municipal, or local government or whether it is accredited by a recognized accreditation organization. If an adverse event meets the criteria for reporting, the outpatient diagnostic facility must report that event regardless of the nature or location of the medical service provided by the outpatient diagnostic facility.

(v)(1) *Outpatient treatment facility* means a distinct entity that operates for the primary purpose of providing non-surgical therapeutic (medical, occupational, or physical) care on an outpatient basis or home health care setting. Outpatient treatment facilities include ambulance providers, rescue services, and home health care groups. Examples of services provided by outpatient treatment facilities include: Cardiac defibrillation, chemotherapy, radiotherapy, pain control, dialysis, speech or physical therapy, and treatment for substance abuse.

(2) An outpatient treatment facility may be either independent (i.e., not a part of a provider of services or any other facility) or operated by another medical entity (e.g., under the common ownership, licensure, or control of an entity). An outpatient treatment facility is covered by this regulation regardless of whether it is licensed by a Federal, State, municipal, or local government or whether it is accredited by a recognized accreditation organization. If an adverse event meets the criteria for reporting, the outpatient treatment facility must report that event regardless of the nature or location of the medical service provided by the outpatient treatment facility.

(w) *Patient of the facility* means any individual who is being diagnosed or treated and/or receiving medical care at or under the control or authority of the facility. For the purposes of this part, the definition encompasses employees of the facility or individuals affiliated with the facility, who in the course of their duties suffer a device-related death or serious injury that has or may have been caused or contributed to by a device used at the facility.

(x) *Physician's office* means a facility that operates as the office of a physician or other health care professional (e.g., dentist, chiropractor, optometrist, nurse practitioner, school nurse offices, school clinics, employee health clinics, or free-standing care units) for the primary purpose of examination, evaluation, and treatment or referral of patients. A physician's office may be independent, a group practice, or part of a Health Maintenance Organization.

(y) [Reserved]

(z) *Remedial action* means, for the purposes of this subpart, any action other than routine maintenance or servicing, of a device where such action is necessary to prevent recurrence of a reportable event. (aa) [Reserved] (bb)(1) Serious injury means an injury or illness that:

(i) Is life-threatening;

(ii) Results in permanent impairment of a body function or permanent damage to body structure; or

(iii) Necessitates medical or surgical intervention to preclude permanent impairment of a body function or permanent damage to a body structure.

(2) Permanent means, for purposes of this subpart, irreversible impairment or damage to a body structure or function, excluding trivial impairment or damage.

(cc) Shelf life, as required on the manufacturer's baseline report, means the maximum time a device will remain functional from the date of manufacture until it is used in patient care. Some devices have an expiration date on their labeling indicating the maximum time they can be stored before losing their ability to perform their intended function.

(dd) [Reserved]

(ee)(1) User facility report number means the number that uniquely identifies each report submitted by a user facility to manufacturers and FDA. This number consists of three parts as follows:

(i) The user facility's 10-digit Health Care Financing Administration (HCFA) number (if the HCFA number has fewer than 10 digits, fill the remaining spaces with zeros);

(ii) The four-digit calendar year in which the report is submitted; and

(iii) The four-digit sequence number of the reports submitted for the year, starting with 0001. (For example, a complete number will appear as follows: 1234560000-1995-0001.)

(2) If a facility has more than one HCFA number, it must select one that will be used for all of its MDR reports. If a facility has no HCFA number, it should use all zeros in the appropriate space in its initial report (e.g., 0000000000-1995-0001) and FDA will assign a number for future use. The number assigned will be used in FDA's record of that report and in any correspondence with the user facility. All zeros should be used subsequent to the first report if the user does not receive FDA's assigned number before the next report is submitted. If a facility has multiple sites, the primary site can report centrally and use one reporting number for all sites if the primary site provides the name, address and HCFA number for each respective site.

(ff) Work day means Monday through Friday, excluding Federal holidays.

[60 FR 63597, Dec. 11, 1995, as amended at 65 FR 4118, Jan. 26, 2000] Effective Date Note: At 61 FR 38347, July 23, 1996, in Sec. 803.3, paragraph (n)(4) was stayed indefinitely.

803.9 Public availability of reports.

(a) Any report, including any FDA record of a telephone report, submitted under this part is available for public disclosure in accordance with part 20 of this chapter.

(b) Before public disclosure of a report, FDA will delete from the report:

(1) Any information that constitutes trade secret or confidential commercial or financial information under Sec. 20.61 of this chapter;

(2) Any personal, medical, and similar information (including the serial number of implanted devices), which would constitute an invasion of personal privacy under Sec. 20.63 of this chapter. FDA will disclose to a patient who requests a report, all the information in the report concerning that patient, as provided in Sec. 20.61 of this chapter; and

(3) Any names and other identifying information of a third party voluntarily submitting an adverse event report.

(c) FDA may not disclose the identity of a device user facility which makes a report under this part except in connection with:

(1) An action brought to enforce section 301(q) of the act, including the failure or refusal to furnish material or information required by section 519 of the act;

(2) A communication to a manufacturer of a device which is the subject of a report required by a user facility under Sec. 803.30; or (3) A disclosure to employees of the Department of Health and Human Services, to the Department of Justice, or to the duly authorized committees and subcommittees of the Congress.

[60 FR 63597, Dec. 11, 1995, as amended at 65 FR 4119, Jan. 26, 2000]

803.10 General description of reports required from user facilities, importers, and manufacturers.

(a) *Device user facilities.* User facilities must submit the following reports, which are described more fully in subpart C of this part.

(1) User facilities must submit MDR reports of individual adverse events within 10 days after the user facility becomes aware of an MDR reportable event as described in Secs. 803.30 and 803.32.

(i) User facilities must submit reports of device-related deaths to FDA and to the manufacturer, if known.

(ii) User facilities must submit reports of device-related serious injuries to manufacturers, or to FDA, if the manufacturer is unknown.

(2) User facilities must submit annual reports as described in Sec. 803.33.

(b) *Device importers.* Importers must submit the following reports, which are described more fully in subpart D of this part.

(1) Importers must submit MDR reports of individual adverse events within 30 days after the importer becomes aware of an MDR reportable event as described in Secs. 803.40 and 803.42.

(i) Importers must submit reports of device-related deaths or serious injuries to FDA and to the manufacturer.

(ii) Importers must submit reports of malfunctions to the manufacturer.

(2) [Reserved]

(c) *Device manufacturers.* Manufacturers must submit the following reports as described more fully in subpart E of this part:

(1) MDR reports of individual adverse events within 30 days after the manufacturer becomes aware of a reportable death, serious injury, or malfunction as described in Secs. 803.50 and 803.52.

(2) MDR reports of individual adverse events within 5 days of:

(i) Becoming aware that a reportable MDR event requires remedial action to prevent an unreasonable risk of substantial harm to the public health or,

(ii) Becoming aware of an MDR reportable event for which FDA has made a written request, as described in Sec. 803.53.

(3) Annual baseline reports as described in Sec. 803.55.

(4) Supplemental reports if they obtain information that was not provided in an initial report as described in Sec. 803.56.

[60 FR 63597, Dec. 11, 1995, as amended at 65 FR 4119, Jan. 26, 2000; 66 FR 23157, May 8, 2001]

Sec. 803.11 Obtaining the forms.

User facilities and manufacturers must submit all reports of individual adverse events on FDA Form 3500A (MEDWATCH form) or in an electronic equivalent as approved under Sec. 803.14. This form and all other forms referenced in this section can also be obtained from the Consolidated Forms and Publications Office, Washington Commerce Center, 3222 Hubbard Rd., Landover, MD 20875; from the Food and Drug Administration, MEDWATCH (HF-2), 5600 Fishers Lane, Rockville, MD 20857, 301-827-7240; from the Division of Small Manufacturers Assistance, Office of Health and Industry Programs, Center for Devices and Radiological Health (HFZ-220), 1350 Piccard Dr. Rockville, MD 20850, FAX 301-443-8818; or from http://www.fda.gov/opacom/morechoices/fdaforms/cdrh.html on the Internet.

[65 FR 17136, Mar. 31, 2000]

Sec. 803.12 Where to submit reports.

(a) Any written report or additional information required under this part shall be submitted to: Food and Drug Administration, Center for Devices and Radiological Health, Medical Device Reporting, PO Box 3002, Rockville, MD 20847-3002.

(b) Each report and its envelope shall be specifically identified, e.g., "User Facility Report," "Annual Report," "Importer Report," "Manufacturer Report," "5-Day Report," "Baseline Report," etc.

(c) If an entity is confronted with a public health emergency, this can be brought to FDA's attention by contacting the FDA Emergency Operations Branch (HFC-162), Office of Regional Operations, at 301-443- 1240, and should be followed by the submission of a FAX report to 301- 443-3757.

(d) A voluntary telephone report may be submitted to, or information regarding voluntary reporting may be obtained from, the MEDWATCH hotline at 800-FDA-1088.

[60 FR 63597, Dec. 11, 1995, as amended at 65 FR 4119, Jan. 26, 2000]

803.13 English reporting requirement.

(a) All reports required in this part which are submitted in writing or electronic equivalent shall be submitted to FDA in English.

(b) All reports required in this part which are submitted on an electronic medium shall be submitted to FDA in a manner consistent with 803.14.

803.14 Electronic reporting.

(a) Any report required by this part may be submitted electronically with prior written consent from FDA. Such consent is revocable. Electronic report submissions include alternative reporting media (magnetic tape, disc, etc.) and computer-to-computer communication.

(b) Any electronic report meeting electronic reporting standards, guidance documents, or other procedures developed by the agency for MDR reporting will be deemed to have prior approval for use.

[60 FR 63597, Dec. 11, 1995, as amended at 65 FR 56480, Sept. 19, 2000]

803.15 Requests for additional information.

(a) FDA may determine that protection of the public health requires additional or clarifying information for medical device reports submitted to FDA under this part. In these instances, and in cases when the additional information is beyond the scope of FDA reporting forms or is not readily accessible, the agency will notify the reporting entity in writing of the additional information that is required.

(b) Any request under this section shall state the reason or purpose for which the information is being re-quested, specify the date that the information is to be submitted and clearly relate the request to a reported event. All verbal requests will be confirmed in writing by the agency.

803.16 Disclaimers.

A report or other information submitted by a reporting entity under this part, and any release by FDA of that report or information, does not necessarily reflect a conclusion by the party submitting the report or by FDA that the report or information constitutes an admission that the device, or the reporting entity or its employees, caused or contributed to the reportable event. The reporting entity need not admit and may deny that the report or information submitted under this part constitutes an admission that the device, the party submitting the report, or employees thereof, caused or contributed to a reportable event.

803.17 Written MDR procedures.

User facilities, importers, and manufacturers shall develop, maintain, and implement written MDR procedures for the following: (a) Internal systems that provide for:

(1) Timely and effective identification, communication, and evaluation of events that may be subject to medical device reporting requirements;

(2) A standardized review process/procedure for determining when an event meets the criteria for reporting under this part; and

(3) Timely transmission of complete medical device reports to FDA and/or manufacturers;

(b) Documentation and recordkeeping requirements for:

(1) Information that was evaluated to determine if an event was reportable;

(2) All medical device reports and information submitted to FDA and manufacturers;

(3) Any information that was evaluated for the purpose of preparing the submission of semiannual reports or certification; and

(4) Systems that ensure access to information that facilitates timely followup and inspection by FDA.

[60 FR 63597, Dec. 11, 1995, as amended at 65 FR 4119, Jan. 26, 2000]

803.18 Files and distributor records.

(a) User facilities, importers, and manufacturers shall establish and maintain MDR event files. All MDR event files shall be prominently identified as such and filed to facilitate timely access.

(b)(1) For purposes of this part, "MDR event files" are written or electronic files maintained by user facilities, importers, and manufacturers. MDR event files may incorporate references to other information, e.g., medical records, patient files, engineering reports, etc., in lieu of copying and maintaining duplicates in this file. MDR event files must contain:

(i) Information in the possession of the reporting entity or references to information related to the adverse event, including all documentation of the entity's deliberations and decision making processes used to determine if a device-related death, serious injury, or malfunction was or was not reportable under this part.

(ii) Copies of all MDR forms, as required by this part, and other information related to the event that was submitted to FDA and other entities (e.g., an importer, distributor, or manufacturer).

(2) User facilities, importers, and manufacturers shall permit any authorized FDA employee during all reasonable times to access, to copy, and to verify the records required by this part.

(c) User facilities shall retain an MDR event file relating to an adverse event for a period of 2 years from the date of the event. Manufacturers and importers shall retain an MDR event file relating to an adverse event for a period of 2 years from the date of the event or a period of time equivalent to the expected life of the device, whichever is greater. MDR event files must be maintained for the time periods described in this paragraph even if the device is no longer distributed.

(d)(1) A device distributor shall establish and maintain device complaint records containing any incident information, including any written, electronic, or oral communication, either received by or generated by the firm, that alleges deficiencies related to the identity (e.g., labeling), quality, durability, reliability, safety, effectiveness, or performance of a device. Information regarding the evaluation of the allegations, if any, shall also be maintained in the incident record. Device incident records shall be prominently identified as such and shall be filed by device, and may be maintained in written or electronic form. Files maintained in electronic form must be backed up.

(2) A device distributor shall retain copies of the records required to be maintained under this section for a period of 2 years from the date of inclusion of the record in the file or for a period of time equivalent to the expected life of the device, whichever is greater, even if the distributor has ceased to distribute the device that is the subject of the record.

(3) A device distributor shall maintain the device complaint files established under this section at the distributor's principal business establishment. A distributor that is also a manufacturer may maintain the file at the same location as the manufacturer maintains its complaint file under Secs. 820.180 and 820.198 of this chapter. A device distributor shall permit any authorized FDA employee, during all reasonable times, to have access to, and to copy and verify, the records required by this part.

(e) The manufacturer may maintain MDR event files as part of its complaint file, under Sec. 820.198 of this chapter, provided that such records are prominently identified as MDR reportable events. A report submitted under this subpart A shall not be considered to comply with this part unless the event has been evaluated in accordance with the requirements of Secs. 820.162 and 820.198 of this chapter. MDR files shall contain an explanation of why any information required by this part was not submitted or could not be obtained. The results of the evaluation of each event are to be documented and maintained in the manufacturer's MDR event file.

[60 FR 63597, Dec. 11, 1995, as amended at 65 FR 4119, Jan. 26, 2000]

803.19 Exemptions, variances, and alternative reporting requirements.

(a) The following persons are exempt from the reporting requirements under this part.

(1) An individual who is a licensed practitioner who prescribes or administers devices intended for use in humans and who manufactures or imports devices solely for use in diagnosing and treating persons with whom the practitioner has a "physician-patient" relationship.

(2) An individual who manufactures devices intended for use in humans solely for such person's use in research or teaching and not for sale, including any person who is subject to alternative reporting requirements under the investigational device exemption regulations, parts 812 and 813 of this chapter, which require reporting of all adverse device effects.

(3) Dental laboratories, or optical laboratories.

(b) Manufacturers, importers, or user facilities may request exemptions or variances from any or all of the reporting requirements in this part. The request shall be in writing and include information necessary to identify the firm and device, a complete statement of the request for exemption, variance, or alternative reporting, and an explanation why the request is justified.

(c) FDA may grant in writing, to a manufacturer, importer, or user facility, an exemption, variance, or alternative from, or to, any or all of the reporting requirements in this part and may change the frequency of reporting to quarterly, semiannually, annually, or other appropriate time period. These modifications may be initiated by a request as specified in this section, or at the discretion of FDA. When granting such modifications, FDA may impose other reporting requirements to ensure the protection of public health.

(d) FDA may revoke or modify in writing an exemption, variance, or alternative reporting requirements if FDA determines that protection of the public health justifies the modification or a return to the requirements as stated in this part.

(e) Firms granted a reporting modification by FDA shall provide any reports or information required by that approval. The conditions of the approval will replace and supersede the reporting requirement specified in this part until such time that FDA revokes or modifies the alternative reporting requirements in accordance with paragraph (d) of this section.

[60 FR 63597, Dec. 11, 1995, as amended at 61 FR 44615, Aug. 28, 1996; 65 FR 4119, Jan. 26, 2000; 65 FR 17136, Mar. 31, 2000]

Subpart B - Generally Applicable Requirements for Individual Adverse Event Reports

803.20 How to report.

(a) *Description of form.* There are two versions of the MEDWATCH form for individual reports of adverse events. FDA Form 3500 is available for use by health professionals and consumers for the submission of voluntary reports regarding FDA-regulated products. FDA Form 3500A is the mandatory reporting form to be used for submitting reports by user facilities and manufacturers of FDA-regulated products. The form has sections that must be completed by all reporters and other sections that must be completed only by the user facility, importer, or manufacturer.

(1) The front of FDA Form 3500A is to be filled out by all reporters. The front of the form requests information regarding the patient, the event, the device, and the "initial reporter" (i.e., the first person or entity that submitted the information to the user facility, manufacturer, or importer).

(2) The back part of the form contains sections to be completed by user facilities, importers, and manufacturers. User facilities must complete section F; device manufacturers must complete sections G and H. Manufacturers are not required to recopy information submitted to them on a Form 3500A unless the information is being copied onto an electronic medium. If the manufacturer corrects or supplies information missing from the other reporter's 3500A form, it should attach a copy of that form to the manufacturer's report form. If the information from the other reporter's 3500A form is complete and correct, the manufacturer can fill in the remaining information on the same form.

(b) *Reporting standards.* (1) User facilities are required to submit MDR reports to:

(i) The device manufacturer and to FDA within 10 days of becoming aware of information that reasonably suggests that a device has or may have caused or contributed to a death; or

(ii)The manufacturer within 10 days of becoming aware of information that reasonably suggests that a device has or may have caused or contributed to a serious injury. Such reports shall be submitted to FDA if the device manufacturer is not known.

(2) Importers are required to submit death and serious injury reports to FDA and the device manufacturer and submit malfunction reports to the manufacturer only:

(i) Within 30 days of becoming aware of information that reasonably suggests that a device has or may have caused or contributed to a death or serious injury.

(ii) Within 30 days of receiving information that a device marketed by the importer has malfunctioned and that such a device or a similar device marketed by the importer would be likely to cause or contribute to a death or serious injury if the malfunction were to recur.

(3) Manufacturers are required to submit MDR reports to FDA:

(i) Within 30 days of becoming aware of information that reasonably suggests that a device may have caused or contributed to a death or serious injury; or

(ii) Within 30 days of becoming aware of information that reasonably suggests a device has malfunctioned and that device or a similar device marketed by the manufacturer would be likely to cause a death or serious injury if the malfunction were to recur; or

(iii) Within 5 days if required by Sec. 803.53.

(c) *Information that reasonably suggests a reportable event occurred.* (1) Information that reasonably suggests that a device has or may have caused or contributed to an MDR reportable event (i.e., death, serious injury, and, for manufacturers, a malfunction that would be likely to cause or contribute to a death or serious injury if the malfunction were to recur) includes any information, such as professional, scientific or medical facts and observations or opinions, that would reasonably suggest that a device has caused or may have caused or contributed to a reportable event.

(2) Entities required to report under this part do not have to report adverse events for which there is information that would cause a person who is qualified to make a medical judgment (e.g., a physician, nurse, risk manager, or biomedical engineer) to reach a reasonable conclusion that a device did not cause or contribute to a death or serious injury, or that a malfunction would not be likely to cause or contribute to a death or serious injury if it were to recur. Information which leads the qualified person to determine that a device-related event is or is not reportable must be contained in the MDR event files, as described in Sec. 803.18.

[60 FR 63597, Dec. 11, 1995, as amended at 65 FR 4119, Jan. 26, 2000]

803.21 Reporting codes.

(a) FDA has developed a MEDWATCH Mandatory Reporting Form Coding Manual for use with medical device reports. This manual contains codes for hundreds of adverse events for use with FDA Form 3500A. The coding manual is available from the Division of Small Manufacturer Assistance, Center for Devices and Radiological Health, 1350 Piccard Dr., Rockville, MD 20850, FAX 301-443-8818.

(b) FDA may use additional coding of information on the reporting forms or modify the existing codes on an ad hoc or generic basis. In such cases, FDA will ensure that the new coding infor-mation is available to all reporters.

803.22 When not to file.

(a) Only one medical device report from the user facility, importer, or manufacturer is required under this part if the reporting entity becomes aware of information from multiple sources regarding the same patient and same event.

(b) A medical device report that would otherwise be required under this section is not required if:

(1) The user facility, importer, or manufacturer determines that the information received is erroneous in that a device-related adverse event did not occur. Documentation of such reports shall be retained in MDR files for time periods specified in Sec. 803.18.

(2) The manufacturer or importer determines that the device was manufactured or imported by another manufacturer or importer. Any reportable event information that is erroneously sent to a manufacturer or importer shall be forwarded to FDA, with a cover letter explaining that the device in question was not manufactured or imported by that firm.

[60 FR 63597, Dec. 11, 1995, as amended at 65 FR 4120, Jan. 26, 2000]

Subpart C - User Facility Reporting Requirements

803.30 Individual adverse event reports; user facilities.

(a) *Reporting standard.* A user facility shall submit the following reports to the manufacturer or to FDA, or both, as specified below:

(1) *Reports of death.* Whenever a user facility receives or otherwise becomes aware of information, from any source, that reasonably suggests that a device has or may have caused or contributed to the death of a patient of the facility, the facility shall as soon as practicable, but not later than 10 work days after becoming aware of the information, report the information required by 803.32 to FDA, on FDA Form 3500A, or an electronic equivalent as approved under 803.14, and if the identity of the manufacturer is known, to the device manufacturer.

(2) *Reports of serious injury.* Whenever a user facility receives or otherwise becomes aware of information, from any source, that reasonably suggests that a device has or may have caused or contributed to a serious injury to a patient of the facility, the facility shall, as soon as practicable but not later than 10 work days after becoming aware of the information, report the information required by 803.32,

on FDA Form 3500A or electronic equivalent, as approved under 803.14, to the manufacturer of the device. If the identity of the manufacturer is not known, the report shall be submitted to FDA.

(b) *Information that is reasonably known to user facilities.* User facilities must provide all information required in this subpart C that is reasonably known to them. Such information includes information found in documents in the possession of the user facility and any information that becomes available as a result of reasonable followup within the facility. A user facility is not required to evaluate or investigate the event by obtaining or evaluating information that is not reasonably known to it.

803.32. Individual adverse event report data elements.

User facility reports shall contain the following information. reasonably known to them as described in 803.30(b), which corresponds to the for-mat of FDA Form 3500A:

(a) Patient information (Block A) shall contain the following:

(1) Patient name or other identifier;

(2) Patient age at the time of event, or date of birth;

(3) Patient gender; and

(4) Patient weight.

(b) Adverse event or product problem (Block B) shall contain the following:

(1) Identification of adverse event or product problem;

(2) Outcomes attributed to the adverse event, e.g., death; or serious injury, that is:

(i) Life threatening injury or illness;

(ii) Disability resulting in permanent impairment of a body function or permanent damage to a body structure; or

(iii) Injury or illness that requires intervention to prevent permanent impairment of a body structure or function;

(3) Date of event;

(4) Date of report by the initial reporter;

(5) Description of event or problem, including a discussion of how the device was involved, nature of the problem, patient followup or required treatment, and any environmental conditions that may have influenced the event;

(6) Description of relevant tests including dates and laboratory data; and

(7) Description of other relevant his-tory including pre-existing medical conditions.

(c) Device information (Block D) shall contain the following:

(1) Brand name;

(2) Type of device;

(3) Manufacturer name and address;

(4) Operator of the device (health professional, patient, lay user, other);

(5) Expiration date;

(6) Model number, catalog number serial number, lot number, or other identifying number;

(7) Date of device implantation (month, day, year);

(8) Date of device explantation (month, day, year);

(9) Whether device was available for evaluation and whether device was returned to the manufacturer; if so, the date it was returned to the manufacturer; and

(10) Concomitant medical products and therapy dates. (Do not list products that were used to treat the event.)

(d) Initial reporter information (Block E) shall contain the following:

(1) Name, address, and telephone number of the reporter who initially provided information to the user facility, manufacturer, or distributor;

(2) Whether the initial reporter is a health professional;

(3) Occupation; and

(4) Whether initial reporter also sent a copy of the report to FDA, if known.

(e) User facility information (Block F) shall contain the following:

(1) Whether reporter is a user facility;

(2) User facility number;

(3) User facility address;

(4) Contact person;

(5) Contact person's telephone number;

(6) Date the user facility became aware of the event (month, day, year);

(7) Type of report (initial or followup; if followup, include report number of initial report);

(8) Date of the user facility report (month, day, year);

(9) Approximate age of device;

(10) Event problem codes—patient code and device code (refer to FDA "Coding Manual For Form 3500A");

(11) Whether a report was sent to FDA and the date it was sent (month, day, year);

(12) Location, where event occurred;

(13) Whether report was sent to the manufacturer and the date it was sent (month, day, year); and

(14) Manufacturer name and address; if available.

803.33 Annual reports.

(a) Each user facility shall submit to FDA an annual report on FDA Form 3419, or electronic equivalent as approved by FDA under Sec. 803.14. Annual reports shall be submitted by January 1 of each year. The annual report and envelope shall be clearly identified and submitted to FDA with information that includes:

(1) User facility's HCFA provider number used for medical device reports, or number assigned by FDA for reporting purposes in accordance with Sec. 803.3(ee);

(2) Reporting year;

(3) Facility's name and complete address;

(4) Total number of reports attached or summarized;

(5) Date of the annual report and the lowest and highest user facility report number of medical device reports submitted during the report period, e.g., 1234567890-1995-0001 through 1000;

(6) Name, position title, and complete address of the individual designated as the facility contact person responsible for reporting to FDA and whether that person is a new contact for that facility; and

(7) Information for each reportable event that occurred during the annual reporting period including:

(i) User facility report number;

(ii) Name and address of the device manufacturer;

(iii) Device brand name and common name;

(iv) Product model, catalog, serial and lot number;

(v) A brief description of the event reported to the manufacturer and/or FDA; and

(vi) Where the report was submitted, i.e., to FDA, manufacturer, distributor, importer, etc.

(b) In lieu of submitting the information in paragraph (a)(7) of this section, a user facility may submit a copy of FDA Form 3500A, or an electronic equivalent as approved under section 803.14, for each medical device report submitted to FDA and/or manufacturers by that facility during the reporting period.

(c) If no reports are submitted to either FDA or manufacturers during these time periods, no annual report is required.

[60 FR 63597, Dec. 11, 1995, as amended at 65 FR 4120, Jan. 26, 2000]

Subpart D - Importer Reporting Requirements

Source: 65 FR 4120, Jan. 26, 2000, unless otherwise noted

803.40 Individual adverse event reporting requirements; importers.

(a) An importer shall submit to FDA a report, and a copy of such report to the manufacturer, containing the information required by Sec. 803.42 on FDA form 3500A as soon as practicable, but not later than 30 days after the importer receives or otherwise becomes aware of information from any source, including user facilities, individuals, or medical or scientific literature, whether published or unpublished, that reasonably suggests that one of its marketed devices may have caused or contributed to a death or serious injury.

(b) An importer shall submit to the manufacturer a report containing information required by Sec. 803.42 on FDA form 3500A, as soon as practicable, but not later than 30 days after the importer receives or otherwise becomes aware of information from any source, including user facilities, individuals, or through the importer's own research, testing, evaluation, servicing, or maintenance of one of its devices, that one of the devices marketed by the importer has malfunctioned and that such device or a similar device marketed by the importer would be likely to cause or contribute to a death or serious injury if the malfunction were to recur.

803.42 Individual adverse event report data elements.

Individual medical device importer reports shall contain the following information, in so far as the information is known or should be known to the importer, as described in Sec. 803.40, which corresponds to the format of FDA Form 3500A:

(a) Patient information (Block A) shall contain the following:

(1) Patient name or other identifier;

(2) Patient age at the time of event, or date of birth;

(3) Patient gender; and

(4) Patient weight.

(b) Adverse event or product problem (Block B) shall contain the following:

(1) Adverse event or product problem;

(2) Outcomes attributed to the adverse event, that is:

(i) Death;

(ii) Life threatening injury or illness;

(iii) Disability resulting in permanent impairment of a body function or permanent damage to a body structure; or

(iv) Injury or illness that requires intervention to prevent permanent impairment of a body structure or function;

(3) Date of event;

(4) Date of report by the initial reporter;

(5) Description of the event or problem to include a discussion of how the device was involved, nature of the problem, patient followup or required treatment, and any environmental conditions that may have influenced the event;

(6) Description of relevant tests, including dates and laboratory data; and

(7) Other relevant patient history including preexisting medical conditions.

(c) Device information (Block D) shall contain the following:

(1) Brand name; (2) Type of device; (3) Manufacturer name and address; (4) Operator of the device (health professional, patient, lay user, other); (5) Expiration date; (6) Model number, catalog number, serial number, lot number or other identifying number; (7) Date of device implantation (month, day, year); (8) Date of device explantation (month, day, year); (9) Whether the device was available for evaluation, and whether the device was returned to the manufacturer, and if so, the date it was returned to the manufacturer; and (10) Concomitant medical products and therapy dates. (Do not list products that were used to treat the event.)

(d) Initial reporter information (Block E) shall contain the following: (1) Name, address, and phone number of the reporter who initially provided information to the user facility, manufacturer, or distributor; (2) Whether the initial reporter is a health professional; (3) Occupation; and (4) Whether the initial reporter also sent a copy of the report to FDA, if known.

(e) Importer information (Block F) shall contain the following: (1) Whether reporter is an importer; (2) Importer report number; (3) Importer address; (4) Contact person; (5) Contact person's telephone number; (6) Date the importer became aware of the event (month, day, year); (7) Type of report (initial or followup (if followup, include report number of initial report)); (8) Date of the importer report (month, day, year); (9) Approximate age of device; (10) Event problem codes—patient code and device code (refer to FDA "Coding Manual For Form 3500A"); (11) Whether a report was sent to FDA and the date it was sent (month, day, year); (12) Location, where event occurred; (13) Whether a report was sent to the manufacturer and the date it was sent (month, day, year); and (14) Manufacturer name and address; if available.

Subpart E - Manufacturer Reporting Requirements

803.50 Individual adverse event reports; manufacturers

(a) *Reporting standards.* Device manufacturers are required to report within 30 days whenever the manufacturer receives or otherwise becomes aware of information, from any source, that reasonably suggests that a device marketed by the manufacturer:

(1) May have caused or contributed to a death or serious injury; or

(2) Has malfunctioned and such device or similar device marketed by the manufacturer would be likely to cause or contribute to a death or serious injury, if the malfunction were to recur.

(b) *Information that is reasonably known to manufacturers.* (1) Manufacturers must provide all information required in this subpart E that is reasonably known to them. FDA considers the following information to be reasonably known to the manufacturer:

(i) Any information that can be obtained by contacting a user facility, distributor and/or other initial reporter;

(ii) Any information in a manufacturer's possession; or

(iii) Any information that can be obtained by analysis, testing or other evaluation of the device.

(2) Manufacturers are responsible for obtaining and providing FDA with information that is incomplete or missing from reports submitted by user facilities, distributors, and other initial reporters. Manufacturers are also responsible for conducting an investigation of each event, and evaluating the cause of the event. If a manufacturer cannot provide complete information on an MDR report, it must provide a statement explaining why such information was incomplete and the steps taken to obtain the information. Any required information not available at the time of the report, which is obtained after the initial filing, must be provided by the manufacturer in a sup-plemental report under 803.56.

803.52 Individual adverse event report data elements.

Individual medical device manufacturer reports shall contain the following information, known or reasonably known to them as described in 803.50(b), which corresponds to the format of FDA Form 3500A:

(a) Patient information (Block A) shall contain the following:

(1) Patient name or other identifier

(2) Patient age at the time of event, or date of birth;

(3) Patient gender; and

(4) Patient weight.

(b) Adverse event or product problem (Block B) shall contain the following:

(1) Adverse event or product problem

(2) Outcomes attributed to the adverse event, e.g., death; or serious injury, that is:

(i) Life threatening injury or illness;

(ii) Disability resulting in permanent impairment of a body function or permanent damage to a body structure, or

(iii) Injury or illness that requires intervention to prevent permanent impairment of a body structure or function;

(3) Date of event;

(4) Date of report by the initial reporter;

(5) Description of the event or problem to include a discussion of how the device was involved, nature of the problem, patient followup or required treatment, and any environmental conditions that may have influenced the event;

(6) Description of relevant tests, including dates and laboratory data, and

(7) Other relevant patient history including pre-existing medical conditions.

(c) Device information (Block D) shall contain the following:

(1) Brand name;

(2) Type of device

(3) Manufacturer name and address

(4) Operator of the device (health professional, patient, lay user, other);

(5) Expiration date;

(6) Model number, catalog number serial number, lot number or other identifying number;

(7) Date of device implantation (month, day, year);

(8) Date of device explantation (month, day, year);

(9) Whether the device was available for evaluation, and whether the device was returned to the manufacturer, and if so, the date it was returned to the manufacturer; and

(10) Concomitant medical products and therapy dates. (Do not list products that were used to treat the event.)

(d) Initial reporter information (Block E) shall contain the following:

(1) Name, address, and phone number of the reporter who initially provided information to the user facility, manufacturer, or distributor;

(2) Whether the initial reporter is a health professional;

(3) Occupation, and

(4) Whether the initial reporter also sent a copy of the report to FDA, if known.

(e) All manufacturers (Block G) shall contain the following:

(1) Contact office name and address and device manufacturing site;

(2) Telephone number;

(3) Report sources;

(4) Date received by manufacturer (month, day, year);

(5) Type of report being submitted (e.g., 5-day, initial, supplemental); and

(6) Manufacturer report number.

(f) Device manufacturers (Block H) shall contain the following:

(1) Type of reportable event (death serious injury, malfunction, etc.)

(2) Type of followup report, if appli-cable (e.g., correction, response to FDA request, etc.);

(3) If the device was returned to the manufacturer and evaluated by the manufacturer, a summary of the evaluation. If no evaluation was performed, provide an explanation why no evaluation was performed

(4) Device manufacture date (month, day, year);

(5) Was device labeled for single use;

(6) Evaluation codes (including event codes, method of evaluation, result and conclusion codes) (refer to FDA "Coding Manual for Form 3500A")

(7) Whether remedial action was taken and type

(8) Whether use of device was initial reuse, or unknown;

(9) Whether remedial action was reported as a removal or correction under section 519(f) of the act (list the correction/removal report number); and

(10) Additional manufacturer narrative; and/or

(11) Corrected data, including:

(i) Any information missing on the user facility report or distributor report, including missing event codes, or information corrected on such forms after manufacturer verification;

(ii) For each event code provided by the user facility under 803.32(d)(10) or a distributor, a statement of whether the type of the event represented by the code is addressed in the device labeling; and

(iii) If any required information was not provided, an explanation of why such information was not provided and the steps taken to obtain such information.

803.53 Five-day reports.

A manufacturer shall submit a 5-day report to FDA, on Form 3500A or electronic equivalent as approved by FDA under 803.14 within 5 workdays of:

(a) Becoming aware that a reportable MDR event or events, from any infor-mation, including any trend analysis, necessitates remedial action to prevent an unreasonable risk of substantial harm to the public health; or

(b) Becoming aware of an MDR reportable event for which FDA has made a written request for the submission of a 5-day report. When such a request is made, the manufacturer shall submit, without further requests, a 5-day report for all subsequent events of the same nature that involve substantially similar devices for the time period specified in the written request. The time period stated in the original written request can be extended by FDA if it is in the interest of the public health.

803.55 Baseline report.

(a) A manufacturer shall submit a baseline report on FDA Form 3417, or electronic equivalent as approved by FDA under 803.14 for a device when the device model is first reported under 803.50.

(b) Each baseline report shall be updated annually, on the anniversary month of the initial submission, after the initial baseline report is submitted. Changes to baseline information shall be reported in the manner described in 803.56 (i.e., include only the new, changed, or corrected information in the appropriate portion(s) of the report form). Baseline reports shall contain the following:

(1) Name, complete address, and registration number of the manufacturer's reporting site. If the reporting site is not registered, FDA will assign a temporary registration number until the reporting site officially registers. The manufacturer will be informed of the temporary registration number;

(2) FDA registration number of each site where the device is manufactured;

(3) Name, complete address, and telephone number of the individual who has been designated by the manufacturer as its MDR contact and date of the report. For foreign manufacturers, a confirmation that the individual submitting the report is the agent of the manufacturer designated under 803.58(a) is required;

(4) Product identification, including device family, brand name, generic name, model number, catalog number, product code and any other product identification number or designation;

(5) Identification of any device previously reported in a baseline report that is substantially similar (e.g., same device with a different model number, or same device except for cosmetic differences in color or shape) to the device being reported, including the identification of the previously reported device by model number, catalog number or other product identification, and the date of the baseline report for the previously reported device;

(6) Basis for marketing, including 510(k) premarket notification number or PMA number, if applicable, and whether the device is currently the subject of an approved post-market study under section 522 of the act;

(7) Date the device was initially marketed and, if applicable, the date on which the manufacturer ceased marketing the device;

(8) Shelf life, if applicable, and expected life of the device;

(9) The number of devices manufactured and distributed in the last 12 months and, an estimate of the number of devices in current use; and

(10) Brief description of any methods used to estimate the number of devices distributed and the method used to estimate the number of devices in current use. If this information was provided in a previous baseline report, in lieu of resubmitting the information, it may be referenced by providing the date and product identification for the previous baseline report.

EFFECTIVE DATE NOTE: At 61 FR 39869, July 31, 1996, in 803.55, paragraphs (b)(9) and (10) were stayed indefinitely.

803.56 Supplemental reports.

When a manufacturer obtains information required under this part that was not provided because it was not known or was not available when the initial report was submitted, the manufacturer shall submit to FDA the supplemental information within 1 month following receipt of such information. In supplemental reports, the manufacturer shall:

(a) Indicate on the form and the envelope, that the reporting form being submitted is a supplemental report. If the report being supplemented is an FDA Form 3500A report, the manufacturer must select, in Item H-2, the appropriate code for the type of supplemental information being submitted

(b) Provide the appropriate identification numbers of the report that will be updated with the supplemental information, e.g., original manufacturer report number and user facility report number, if applicable;

(c) For reports that cross reference previous reports, include only the new, changed, or corrected information in the appropriate portion(s) of the respective form(s).

803.58 Foreign Manufacturers

(a) Every foreign manufacturer whose devices are distributed in the United States shall designate a U.S. agent to be responsible for reporting in accordance with 807.40 of this chapter. The U.S. designated agent accepts responsibility for the duties that Such designation entails. Upon the effective date of this regulation, foreign manufacturers shall inform FDA, by letter, of the name and address of the U.S. agent designated under this section and 807.40 of this chapter, and shall update this information as necessary. Such updated information shall be submitted to FDA, within 5 days of a change in the designated agent information.

(b) U.S.-designated agents of foreign manufacturers are required to:

(1) Report to FDA in accordance with 803.50, 803.52, 803.53, 803.55, and 803.56;

(2) Conduct, or obtain from the foreign manufacturer the necessary information regarding, the investigation and evaluation of the event to comport with the requirements of 803.50;

(3) Forward MDR complaints to the foreign manufacturer and maintain documentation of this requirement;

(4) Maintain complaint files in accordance with 803.18; and

(5) Register, list, and submit premarket notifications in accordance with part 807 of this chapter.

EFFECTIVE DATE NOTE: At 61 FR 38347, July 23,1996, 803.58 was stayed indefinitely.

PART 820 - QUALITY SYSTEM REGULATION

AUTHORITY: 21 U.S.C. 351, 352, 360, 360c, 360d, 360e, 360h, 360j, 360l, 371, 374, 381, 383.
SOURCE: 61 FR 52654, Oct 7, 1996, unless otherwise noted.

Subpart A - General Provisions

820.1 Scope.

(a) *Applicability.* (1) Current good manufacturing practice (CGMP) requirements are set forth in this quality system regulation. The requirements in this part govern the methods used in, and the facilities and controls used for, the design, manufacture, packaging, labeling, storage, installation, and servicing of all finished devices intended for human use. The requirements in this part are intended to ensure that finished devices will be safe and effective and otherwise in compliance with the Federal Food, Drug, and Cosmetic Act (the act). This part establishes basic requirements applicable to manufacturers of finished medical devices. If a manufacturer engages in only some operations subject to the requirements in this part, and not in others, that manufacturer need only comply with those requirements applicable to the operations in which it is engaged. With respect to class I devices, design controls apply only to those devices listed in Sec. 820.30(a)(2). This regulation does not apply to manufacturers of components or parts of finished devices, but such manufacturers are encouraged to use appropriate provisions of this regulation as guidance. Manufacturers of human blood and blood components are not subject to this part, but are subject to part 606 of this chapter.

(2) The provisions of this part shall be applicable to any finished device as defined in this part, intended for human use, that is manufactured, imported, or offered for import in any State or Territory of the United States, the District of Columbia, or the Commonwealth of Puerto Rico.

(3) In this regulation the term "where appropriate" is used several times. When a requirement is qualified by "where appropriate," it is deemed to be "appropriate" unless the manufacturer can document justification otherwise. A requirement is "appropriate" if nonimplementation could reasonably be expected to result in the product not meeting its specified requirements or the manufacturer not being able to carry out any necessary corrective action.

(b) *Limitations.* The quality system regulation in this part supplements regulations in other parts of this chapter except where explicitly stated otherwise. In the event that it is impossible to comply with all applicable regulations, both in this part and in other parts of this chapter, the regulations specifically applicable to the device in question shall supersede any other generally applicable requirements.

(c) *Authority.* Part 820 is established and issued under authority of sections 501, 502, 510, 513, 514, 515, 518, 519, 520, 522, 701, 704, 801, 803 of the act (21 U.S.C. 351, 352, 360, 360c, 360d, 360e, 360h, 360i, 360j, 360l, 371, 374, 381, 383). The failure to comply with any applicable provision in this part renders a device adulterated under section 501(h) of the act. Such a device, as well as any person responsible for the failure to comply, is subject to regulatory action.

(d) *Foreign manufacturers.* If a manufacturer who offers devices for import into the United States refuses to permit or allow the completion of a Food and Drug Administration (FDA) inspection of the foreign facility for the purpose of determining compliance with this part, it shall appear for purposes of section 801(a) of the act, that the methods used in, and the facilities and controls used for, the design, manufacture, packaging, labeling, storage, installation, or servicing of any devices produced at such facility that are offered for import into the United States do not conform to the requirements of section 520(f) of the act and this part and that the devices manufactured at that facility are adulterated under section 501(h) of the act.

(e) *Exemptions or variances.* (1) Any person who wishes to petition for an exemption or variance from any device quality system requirement is subject to the requirements of section 520(f)(2) of the act. Petitions for an exemption or variance shall be submitted according to the procedures set forth in Sec. 10.30 of this chapter, the FDA's administrative procedures. Guidance is available from the Center for Devices and Radiological Health, Division of Small Manufacturers Assistance (HFZ-220), 1350 Piccard Dr., Rockville, MD 20850, U.S.A., telephone 1-800-638-2041 or 1-301-443-6597, FAX 301-443-8818.

(2) FDA may initiate and grant a variance from any device quality system requirement when the agency determines that such variance is in the best interest of the public health. Such variance will remain in effect only so long as there remains a public health need for the device and the device would not likely be made sufficiently available without the variance.

[61 FR 52654, Oct. 7, 1996, as amended at 65 FR 17136, Mar. 31, 2000; 65 FR 66636, Nov. 7, 2000]

820.3 Definitions.

(a) *Act* means the Federal Food, Drug, and Cosmetic Act, as amended (secs. 201-903, 52 Stat. 1040 et seq., as amended (21 U.S.C. 321-394)). All definitions in section 201 of the act shall apply to the regulations in this part.

(b) *Complaint* means any written, electronic, or oral communication that alleges deficiencies related to the identity, quality, durability, reliability, safety, effectiveness, or performance of a device after it is released for distribution.

(c) Component means any raw material, substance, piece, part, software, firmware, labeling, or assembly which is intended to be included as part of the finished, packaged, and labeled device.

(d) *Control number* means any distinctive symbols, such as a distinctive combination of letters or numbers, or both, from which the history of the manufacturing, packaging, labeling, and distribution of a unit, lot, or batch of finished devices can be determined.

(e) *Design history file (DHF)* means a compilation of records which describes the design history of a finished device.

(f) *Design input* means the physical and performance requirements of a device that are used as a basis for device design.

(g) *Design output* means the results of a design effort at each design phase and at the end of the total design effort. The finished design output is the basis for the device master record. The total finished design output consists of the device, its packaging and labeling, and the device master record.

(h) *Design review* means a documented, comprehensive, systematic examination of a design to evaluate the adequacy of the design requirements, to evaluate the capability of the design to meet these requirements, and to identify problems.

(i) *Device history record (DHR)* means a compilation of records containing the production history of a finished device.

(j) *Device master record (DMR)* means a compilation of records containing the procedures and specifications for a finished device.

(k) *Establish* means define, document (in writing or electronically), and implement.

(l) *Finished device* means any device or accessory to any device that is suitable for use or capable of functioning, whether or not it is packaged, labeled, or sterilized.

(m) *Lot or batch* means one or more components or finished devices that consist of a single type, model, class, size, composition, or software version that are manufactured under essentially the same conditions and that are intended to have uniform characteristics and quality within specified limits.

(n) *Management with executive responsibility* means those senior employees of a manufacturer who have the authority to establish or make changes to the manufacturer's quality policy and quality system.

(o) *Manufacturer* means any person who designs, manufactures, fabricates, assembles, or processes a finished device. Manufacturer includes but is not limited to those who perform the functions of contract sterilization, installation, relabeling, remanufacturing, repacking, or specifica-tion development, and U.S. designated agents of foreign entities performing these functions.

(p) *Manufacturing material* means any material or substance used in or used to facilitate the manufacturing process, a concomitant constituent, or a byproduct constituent produce during the manufacturing process, which is present in or on the finished device as a residue or impurity not by design or intent of the manufacturer.

(q) *Nonconformity* means the nonfulfillment of a specified requirement.

(r) *Product* means components, manufacturing materials, in-process devices, finished devices, and returned devices.

(s) *Quality* means the totality of features and characteristics that bear on the ability of a device to satisfy fitness-for-use, including safety and performance.

(t) *Quality audit* means a systematic, independent examination of a manufacturer's quality system that is performed at defined intervals and at sufficient frequency to determine whether both quality system activities and the results of such activities comply with quality system procedures, that these procedures are implemented effectively, and that these procedures are suitable to achieve quality system objectives.

(u) *Quality policy* means the overall intentions and direction of an organization with respect to quality, as established by management with executive responsibility.

(v) *Quality system* means the organizational structure, responsibilities, procedures, processes, and resources for implementing quality management.

(w) *Remanufacturer* means any person who processes, conditions, renovates, repackages, restores, or does any other act to a finished device that significantly changes the finished device's performance or safety specifications, or intended use.

(x) *Rework* means action taken on a nonconforming product so that it will fulfill the specified DMR requirements before it is released for distribution.

(y) *Specification* means any requirement with which a product, process, service, or other activity must conform.

(z) *Validation* means confirmation by examination and provision of objective evidence that the particular requirements for a specific intended use can be consistently fulfilled.

(1) Process validation means establishing by objective evidence that a process consistently produces a result or product meeting its predetermined specifications.

(2) Design validation means establishing by objective evidence that device specifications conform with user needs and intended use(s).

(aa) Verification means confirmation by examination and provision of objective evidence that specified requirements have been fulfilled.

820.5 Quality system.

Each manufacturer shall establish and maintain a quality system that is appropriate for the specific medical device(s) designed or manufactured, and that meets the requirements of this part.

Subpart B - Quality System Requirements

820.20 Management responsibility.

(a) *Quality policy*. Management with executive responsibility shall establish its policy and objectives for, and commitment to, quality. Management with executive responsibility shall ensure that the quality policy is understood, implemented, and maintained at all levels of the organization.

(b) *Organization*. Each manufacturer shall establish and maintain an adequate organizational structure to ensure that devices are designed and produced in accordance with the requirements of this part.

(1) Responsibility and authority. Each manufacturer shall establish the appropriate responsibility, authority, and interrelation of all personnel who manage, perform, and assess work affecting quality, and provide the independence and authority necessary to perform these tasks.

(2) Resources. Each manufacturer shall provide adequate resources, including the assignment of trained personnel, for management, performance of work, and assessment activities, including internal quality audits, to meet the requirements of this part.

(3) Management representative. Management with executive responsibility shall appoint, and document such appointment of, a member of management who, irrespective of other responsibilities, shall have established authority over and responsibility for:

(i) Ensuring that quality system requirements are effectively established and effectively maintained in accordance with this part; and

(ii) Reporting on the performance of the quality system to management with executive responsibility for review.

(c) *Management review*. Management with executive responsibility shall review the suitability and effectiveness of the quality system at defined intervals and with sufficient frequency according to established procedures to ensure that the quality system satisfies the requirements of this part and the manufacturer's established quality policy and objectives. The dates and results of quality system reviews shall be documented.

(d) *Quality planning*. Each manufacturer shall establish a quality plan which defines the quality practices, resources, and activities relevant to devices that are designed and manufactured. The manufacturer shall establish how the requirements for quality will be met.

(e) *Quality system procedures*. Each manufacturer shall establish quality system procedures and instructions. An outline of the structure of the documentation used in the quality system shall be established where appropriate.

820.22 Quality audit.

Each manufacturer shall establish procedures for quality audits and conduct such audits to assure that the quality system is in compliance with the established quality system requirements and to determine the effectiveness of the quality system. Quality audits shall be conducted by individuals who do not have direct responsibility for the matters being audited. Corrective action(s), including a reaudit of deficient matters, shall be taken when necessary. A report of the results of each quality audit, and reaudit(s) where taken, shall be made and such reports shall be reviewed by management having responsibility for the matters audited. The dates and results of quality audits and reaudits shall be documented.

820.25 Personnel.

(a) General. Each manufacturer shall have sufficient personnel with the necessary education, background, training, and experience to assure that all activities required by this part are correctly performed.

(b) Training. Each manufacturer shall establish procedures for identifying training needs and ensure that all personnel are trained to adequately perform their assigned responsibilities. Training shall be documented.

(1) As part of their training, personnel shall be made aware of device defects which may occur from the improper performance of their specific jobs.

(2) Personnel who perform verification and validation activities shall be made aware of defects and errors that may be encountered as part of their job functions.

Subpart C - Design Controls

820.30 Design controls.

(a) General. (1) Each manufacturer of any class III or class II device, and the class I devices listed in paragraph (a)(2) of this section, shall establish and maintain procedures to control the design of the device in order to ensure that specified design requirements are met.

(2) The following class I devices are subject to design controls:

(i) Devices automated with computer software; and

(ii) The devices listed in the following chart:

Section	Device
868.6810	Catheter, Tracheobronchial Suction
878.4460	Glove, Surgeon's
880.6760	Restraint, Protective
892.5650	System, Applicator, Radionuclide, Manual
892.5740	Source, Radionuclide Teletherapy

(b) *Design and development planning*. Each manufacturer shall establish and maintain plans that describe or reference the design and development activities and define responsibility for implementation. The plans shall identify and describe the interfaces with different groups or activities that provide, or result in, input to the design and development process. The plans shall be reviewed, updated, and approved as design and development evolves.

(c) *Design input*. Each manufacturer shall establish and maintain procedures to ensure that the design requirements relating to a device are appropriate and address the intended use of the device, including the needs of the user and patient. The procedures shall include a mechanism for addressing incomplete, ambiguous, or conflicting requirements. The design input requirements shall be documented and shall be reviewed and approved by a designated individual(s). The approval, including the date and signature of the individual(s) approving the requirements, shall be documented.

(d) *Design output*. Each manufacturer shall establish and maintain procedures for defining and documenting design output in terms that allow an adequate evaluation of conformance to design input requirements. Design output procedures shall contain or make reference to acceptance criteria and shall ensure that those design outputs that are essential for the proper functioning of the device are identified. Design output shall be documented, reviewed, and approved before release. The approval, including the date and signature of the individual(s) approving the output, shall be documented.

(e) *Design review*. Each manufacturer shall establish and maintain procedures to ensure that formal documented reviews of the design results are planned and conducted at appropriate stages of the device's design development. The procedures shall ensure that participants at each design review include representatives of all functions concerned with the design stage being reviewed and an individual(s) who does not have direct responsibility for the design stage being reviewed, as well as any specialists needed. The results of a design review, including identification of the design, the date, and the individual(s) performing the review, shall be documented in the design history file (the DHF).

(f) *Design verification*. Each manufacturer shall establish and maintain procedures for verifying the device design. Design verification shall confirm that the design output meets the design input requirements. The results of the design verification, including identification of the design, method(s), the date, and the individual(s) performing the verification, shall be documented in the DHF.

(g) *Design validation*. Each manufacturer shall establish and maintain procedures for validating the device design. Design validation shall be performed under defined operating conditions on initial production units, lots, or batches, or their equivalents. Design validation shall ensure that devices conform to defined user needs and intended uses and shall include testing of production units under actual or simulated use conditions. Design validation shall include software validation and risk analysis, where appropriate. The results of the design validation, including identification of the design, method(s), the date, and the individual(s) performing the validation, shall be documented in the DHF.

(h) *Design transfer*. Each manufacturer shall establish and maintain procedures to ensure that the device design is correctly translated into production specifications.

(i) *Design changes*. Each manufacturer shall establish and maintain procedures for the identification, documentation, validation or where appropriate verification, review, and approval of design changes before their implementation.

(j) *Design history file*. Each manufacturer shall establish and maintain a DHF for each type of device. The DHF shall contain or reference the records necessary to demonstrate that the design was developed in accordance with the approved design plan and the requirements of this part.

Subpart D - Document Controls

820.40 Document controls.

Each manufacturer shall establish and maintain procedures to control all documents that are required by this part. The procedures shall provide for the following:

(a) *Document approval and distribution*. Each manufacturer shall designate an individual(s) to review for adequacy and approve prior to issuance all documents established to meet the requirements of this part. The approval, including the date and signature of the individual(s) approving the document, shall be documented. Documents established to meet the requirements of this part shall be available at all locations for which they are designated, used, or otherwise necessary, and all obsolete documents shall be promptly removed from all points of use or otherwise prevented from unintended use.

(b) *Document changes*. Changes to documents shall be reviewed and approved by an individual(s) in the same function or organization that performed the original review and approval, unless specifically designated otherwise. Approved changes shall be communicated to the appropriate personnel in a timely manner. Each manufacturer shall maintain records of changes to documents. Change records shall include a description of the change, identification of the affected documents, the signature of the approving individual(s), the approval date, and when the change becomes effective.

Subpart E - Purchasing Controls

820.50 Purchasing controls.

Each manufacturer shall establish and maintain procedures to ensure that all purchased or otherwise received product and services conform to specified requirements.

(a) *Evaluation of suppliers, contractors, and consultants*. Each manufacturer shall establish and maintain the requirements, including quality requirements, that must be met by suppliers, contractors, and consultants. Each manufacturer shall:

(1) Evaluate and select potential suppliers, contractors, and consultants on the basis of their ability to meet specified requirements, including quality requirements. The evaluation shall be documented.

(2) Define the type and extent of control to be exercised over the product, services, suppliers, contractors, and consultants, based on the evaluation results.

(3) Establish and maintain records of acceptable suppliers, contractors, and consultants.

(b) *Purchasing data*. Each manufacturer shall establish and maintain data that clearly describe or reference the specified requirements, including quality requirements, for purchased or otherwise received product and services. Purchasing documents shall include, where possible, an agreement that the suppliers, contractors, and consultants agree to notify the manufacturer of changes in the product or service so that manufacturers may determine whether the changes may affect the quality of a finished device. Purchasing data shall be approved in accordance with 820.40.

Subpart F - Identification and Traceability

820.60 Identification.

Each manufacturer shall establish and maintain procedures for identifying product during all stages of receipt, production, distribution, and installation to prevent mixups.

820.65 Traceability.

Each manufacturer of a device that is intended for surgical implant into the body or to support or sustain life and whose failure to perform when properly used in accordance with instructions for use provided in the labeling can be reasonably expected to result in a significant injury to the user shall establish and maintain procedures for identifying with a control number each unit, lot, or batch of finished devices and where appropriate components. The procedures shall facilitate corrective action. Such identification shall be documented in the DHR.

Subpart G - Production and Process Controls

820.70 Production and process controls.

(a) *General.* Each manufacturer shall develop, conduct, control, and monitor production processes to ensure that a device conforms to its specifications. Where deviations from device specifications could occur as a result of the manufacturing process, the manufacturer shall establish and maintain process control procedures that describe any process controls necessary to ensure conformance to specifications. Where process controls are needed they shall include:

(1) Documented instructions, standard operating procedures (SOP's), and methods that define and control the manner of production;

(2) Monitoring and control of process parameters and component and device characteristics during production;

(3) Compliance with specified reference standards or codes;

(4) The approval of processes and process equipment; and

(5) Criteria for workmanship which shall be expressed in documented standards or by means of identified and approved representative samples.

(b) *Production and process changes.* Each manufacturer shall establish and maintain procedures for changes to a specification, method, process, or procedure. Such changes shall be verified or where appropriate validated according to 820.75, before implementation and these activities shall be documented. Changes shall be approved in accordance with 820.40.

(c) *Environmental control.* Where environmental conditions could reasonably be expected to have an adverse effect on product quality, the manufacturer shall establish and maintain procedures to adequately control these environmental conditions. Environmental control system(s) shall be periodically inspected to verify that the system, including necessary equipment, is adequate and functioning properly. These activities shall be documented and reviewed.

(d) *Personnel.* Each manufacturer shall establish and maintain requirements for the health, cleanliness, personal practices, and clothing of personnel if contact between such personnel and product or environment could reasonably be expected to have an adverse effect on product quality. The manufacturer shall ensure that maintenance and other personnel who are required to work temporarily under special environmental conditions are appropriately trained or supervised by a trained individual.

(e) *Contamination control.* Each manufacturer shall establish and maintain procedures to prevent contamination of equipment or product by substances that could reasonably be expected to have an adverse effect on product quality.

(f) *Buildings.* Buildings shall be of suitable design and contain sufficient space to perform necessary operations, prevent mixups, and assure orderly handling.

(g) *Equipment.* Each manufacturer shall ensure that all equipment used in the manufacturing process meets specified requirements and is appropriately designed, constructed, placed, and installed to facilitate maintenance, adjustment, cleaning, and use.

(1) Maintenance schedule. Each manufacturer shall establish and maintain schedules for the adjustment, cleaning, and other maintenance of equipment to ensure that manufacturing specifications are met. Maintenance activities, including the date and individual(s) performing the maintenance activities, shall be documented.

(2) Inspection. Each manufacturer shall conduct periodic inspections in accordance with established procedures to ensure adherence to applicable equipment maintenance schedules. The inspections, including the date and individual(s) conducting the inspections, shall be documented.

(3) Adjustment. Each manufacturer shall ensure that any inherent limitations or allowable tolerances are visibly posted on or near equipment requiring periodic adjustments or are readily available to personnel performing these adjustments.

(h) *Manufacturing material.* Where a manufacturing material could reasonably be expected to have an adverse effect on product quality, the manufacturer shall establish and maintain procedures for the use and removal of such manufacturing material to ensure that it is removed or limited to an amount that does not adversely affect the device's quality. The removal or reduction of such manufacturing material shall be documented.

(i) *Automated processes.* When computers or automated data processing systems are used as part of production or the quality system, the manufacturer shall validate computer software for its intended use according to an established protocol. All software changes shall be validated before approval and issuance. These validation activities and results shall be documented.

820.72 Inspection, measuring, and test equipment.

(a) *Control of inspection, measuring, and test equipment.* Each manufacturer shall ensure that all inspection, measuring, and test equipment, including mechanical, automated, or electronic inspection and test equipment, is suitable for its intended purposes and is capable of producing valid results.

Each manufacturer shall establish and maintain procedures to ensure that equipment is routinely calibrated, inspected, checked, and maintained. The procedures shall include provisions for handling, preservation, and storage of equipment, so that its accuracy and fitness for use are maintained. These activities shall be documented.

(b) *Calibration.* Calibration procedures shall include specific directions and limits for accuracy and precision. When accuracy and precision limits are not met, there shall be provisions for remedial action to reestablish the limits and to evaluate whether there was any adverse effect on the device's quality. These activities shall be documented.

(1) Calibration standards. Calibration standards used for inspection, measuring, and test equipment shall be traceable to national or international standards. If national or international standards are not practical or available, the manufacturer shall use an independent reproducible standard. If no applicable standard exists, the manufacturer shall establish and maintain an in-house standard.

(2) Calibration records. The equipment identification, calibration dates, the individual performing each calibration, and the next calibration date shall be documented. These records shall be displayed on or near each piece of equipment or shall be readily available to the personnel using such equipment and to the individuals responsible for calibrating the equipment.

820.75 Process validation.

(a) Where the results of a process cannot be fully verified by subsequent inspection and test, the process shall be validated with a high degree of assurance and approved according to established procedures. The validation activities and results, including the date and signature of the individual(s) approving the validation and where appropriate the major equipment validated, shall be documented.

(b) Each manufacturer shall establish and maintain procedures for monitoring and control of process parameters for validated processes to ensure that the specified requirements continue to be met.

(1) Each manufacturer shall ensure that validated processes are performed by qualified individual(s).

(2) For validated processes, the monitoring and control methods and data, the date performed, and, where appropriate, the individual(s) performing the process or the major equipment used shall be documented.

(c) When changes or process deviations occur, the manufacturer shall review and evaluate the process and perform revalidation where appropriate. These activities shall be documented.

Subpart H - Acceptance Activities

820.80 Receiving, in-process, and finished device acceptance.

(a) General. Each manufacturer shall establish and maintain procedures for acceptance activities. Acceptance activities include inspections, tests, or other verification activities.

(b) Receiving acceptance activities. Each manufacturer shall establish and maintain procedures for acceptance of incoming product. Incoming product shall be inspected, tested, or otherwise verified as conforming to specified requirements. Acceptance or rejection shall be documented.

(c) In-process acceptance activities. Each manufacturer shall establish and maintain acceptance procedures, where appropriate, to ensure that specified requirements for in-process product are met. Such procedures shall ensure that in-process product is controlled until the required inspection and tests or other verification activities have been completed, or necessary approvals are received, and are documented.

(d) Final acceptance activities. Each manufacturer shall establish and maintain procedures for finished device acceptance to ensure that each production run, lot, or batch of finished devices meets acceptance criteria. Finished devices shall be held in quarantine or otherwise adequately controlled until released. Finished devices shall not be released for distribution until:

(1) The activities required in the DMR are completed;

(2) The associated data and documentation is reviewed;

(3) the release is authorized by the signature of a designated individual(s); and

(4) the authorization is dated.

(e) Acceptance records. Each manufacturer shall document acceptance activities required by this part. These records shall include:

(1) The acceptance activities performed;

(2) the dates acceptance activities are performed;

(3) the results;

(4) the signature of the individual(s) conducting the acceptance activities; and

(5) where appropriate the equipment used. These records shall be part of the DHR.

820.86 Acceptance status.

Each manufacturer shall identify by suitable means the acceptance status of product, to indicate the conformance or nonconformance of product with acceptance criteria. The identification of acceptance status shall be maintained throughout manufacturing, packaging, labeling, installation, and servicing of the product to ensure that only product which has passed the required acceptance activities is distributed, used, or installed.

Subpart I - Nonconforming Product

820.90 Nonconforming product.

(a) *Control of nonconforming product.* Each manufacturer shall establish and maintain procedures to control product that does not conform to specified requirements. The procedures shall address the identification, documentation, evaluation, segregation, and disposition of nonconforming product. The evaluation of nonconformance shall include a determination of the need for an investigation and notification of the persons or organizations responsible for the nonconformance. The evaluation and any investigation shall be documented.

(b) *Nonconformity review and disposition.* (1) Each manufacturer shall establish and maintain procedures that define the responsibility for review and the authority for the disposition of nonconforming product. The procedures shall set forth the review and disposition process. Disposition of nonconforming product shall be documented. Documentation shall include the justification for use of nonconforming product and the signature of the individual(s) authorizing the use.

(2) Each manufacturer shall establish and maintain procedures for rework, to include retesting and reevaluation of the nonconforming product after rework, to ensure that the product meets its current approved specifications. Rework and reevaluation activities, including a determination of any adverse effect from the rework upon the product, shall be documented in the DHR.

Subpart J - Corrective and Preventive Action

820.100 Corrective and preventive action.

(a) Each manufacturer shall establish and maintain procedures for implementing corrective and preventive action. The procedures shall include requirements for:

(1) Analyzing processes, work operations, concessions, quality audit reports, quality records, service records, complaints, returned product, and other sources of quality data to identify existing and potential causes of nonconforming product, or other quality problems. Appropriate statistical methodology shall be employed where necessary to detect recurring quality problems;

(2) Investigating the cause of nonconformities relating to product, processes, and the quality system;

(3) Identifying the action(s) needed to correct and prevent recurrence of nonconforming product and other quality problems;

(4) Verifying or validating the corrective and preventive action to ensure that such action is effective and does not adversely affect the finished device;

(5) Implementing and recording changes in methods and procedures needed to correct and prevent identified quality problems;

(6) Ensuring that information related to quality problems or nonconforming product is disseminated to those directly responsible for assuring the quality of such product or the prevention of such problems; and

(7) Submitting relevant information on identified quality problems, as well as corrective and preventive actions, for management review.

(b) All activities required under this section, and their results, shall be documented.

Subpart K- Labeling and Packaging Control

820.120 Device labeling.

Each manufacturer shall establish and maintain procedures to control labeling activities.

(a) *Label integrity.* Labels shall be printed and applied so as to remain legible and affixed during the customary conditions of processing, storage, handling, distribution, and where appropriate use.

(b) *Labeling inspection.* Labeling shall not be released for storage or use until a designated individual(s) has examined the labeling for accuracy including, where applicable, the correct expiration date, control number, storage instructions, handling instructions, and any additional processing instructions. The release, including the date and signature of the individual(s) performing the examination, shall be documented in the DHR.

(c) *Labeling storage.* Each manufacturer shall store labeling in a manner that provides proper identification and is designed to prevent mixups.

(d) *Labeling operations.* Each manufacturer shall control labeling and packaging operations to prevent labeling mixups. The label and labeling used for each production unit, lot, or batch shall be documented in the DHR.

(e) Control number. Where a control number is required by 820.65, that control number shall be on or shall accompany the device through distribution.

820.130 Device packaging.

Each manufacturer shall ensure that device packaging and shipping containers are designed and constructed to protect the device from alteration or damage during the customary conditions of processing, storage, handling, and distribution.

Subpart L - Handling, Storage, Distribution, and Installation

820.140 Handling.

Each manufacturer shall establish and maintain procedures to ensure that mixups, damage, deterioration, contamination, or other adverse effects to product do not occur during handling.

820.150 Storage.

(a) Each manufacturer shall establish and maintain procedures for the control of storage areas and stock rooms for product to prevent mixups, damage, deterioration, contamination, or other adverse effects pending use or distribution and to ensure that no obsolete, rejected, or deteriorated product is used or distributed. When the quality of product deteriorates over time, it shall be stored in a manner to facilitate proper stock rotation, and its condition shall be assessed as appropriate.

(b) Each manufacturer shall establish and maintain procedures that describe the methods for authorizing receipt from and dispatch to storage areas and stock rooms.

820.160 Distribution.

(a) Each manufacturer shall establish and maintain procedures for control and distribution of finished devices to ensure that only those devices approved for release are distributed and that purchase orders are reviewed to ensure that ambiguities and errors are resolved before devices are released for distribution. Where a device's fitness for use or quality deteriorates over time, the procedures shall ensure that expired devices or devices deteriorated beyond acceptable fitness for use are not distributed.

(b) Each manufacturer shall maintain distribution records which include or refer to the location of:

(1) The name and address of the initial consignee;

(2) The identification and quantity of devices shipped;

(3) The date shipped; and

(4) Any control number(s) used.

820.170 Installation.

(a) Each manufacturer of a device requiring installation shall establish and maintain adequate installation and inspection instructions, and where appropriate test procedures. Instructions and procedures shall include directions for ensuring proper installation so that the device will perform as intended after installation. The manufacturer shall distribute the instructions and procedures with the device or otherwise make them available to the person(s) installing the device.

(b) The person installing the device shall ensure that the installation, inspection, and any required testing are performed in accordance with the manufacturer's instructions and procedures and shall document the inspection and any test results to demonstrate proper installation.

Subpart M - Records

820.180 General requirements

All records required by this part shall be maintained at the manufactur-ing establishment or other location that is reasonably accessible to respon-sible officials of the manufacturer and to employees of FDA designated to per-form inspections. Such records, includ-ing those not stored at the inspected establishment, shall be made readily available for review and copying by FDA employee(s). Such records shall be legible and shall be stored to minimize deterioration and to prevent loss. Those records stored in automated data processing systems shall be backed up.

(a) Confidentiality. Records deemed confidential by the manufacturer may be marked to aid FDA in determining whether information may be disclosed under the public information regula-tion in part 20 of this chapter.

(b) Record retention period. All records required by this part shall be retained for a period of time equivalent to the design and expected life of the device, but in no case less than 2 years from the date of release for commercial distribution by the manufacturer.

(c) Exceptions. This section does not apply to the reports required by 820.20(c) Management review, 820.22 Quality audits, and supplier audit reports used to meet the requirements of 820.50(a) Evaluation of suppliers, contractors, and consultants, but does apply to procedures established under these provisions. Upon request of a designated employee of FDA, an employee in management with executive responsibility shall certify in writing that the management reviews and quality audits required under this part, and supplier audits where applicable, have been performed and documented, the dates on which they were performed, and that any required corrective action has been undertaken.

820.181 Device master record.

Each manufacturer shall maintain device master records (DMR's). Each manufacturer shall ensure that each DMR is prepared and approved in accordance with 820.40. The DMR for each type of device shall include, or refer to the

location of, the following information:

(a) Device specifications including appropriate drawings, composition, formulation, component specifications, and software specifications;

(b) Production process specifications including the appropriate equipment specifications, production methods, production procedures, and production environment specifications;

(c) Quality assurance procedures and specifications including acceptance criteria and the quality assurance equipment to be used;

(d) Packaging and labeling specifications, including methods and processes used; and

(e) Installation, maintenance, and servicing procedures and methods.

820.184 Device history record.

Each manufacturer shall maintain device history records (DHR's). Each manufacturer shall establish and main-tain procedures to ensure that DHR's for each batch, lot, or unit are main-tained to demonstrate that the device is manufactured in accordance with the DMR and the requirements of this part. The DHR shall include or refer to the location of, the following information:

(a) The dates of manufacture;

(b) The quantity manufactured;

(c) The quantity released for dis-tribution;

(d) The acceptance records which demonstrate the device is manufactured in accordance with the DMR;

(e) The primary identification label and labeling used for each production unit; and

(f) Any device identification(s) and control number(s) used.

820.186 Quality system record.

Each manufacturer shall maintain a quality system record (QSR). The QSR shall include, or refer to the location of, procedures and the documentation of activities required by this part that are not specific to a particular type of device(s), including, but not limited to, the records required by 820.20. Each manufacturer shall ensure that the QSR is prepared and approved in accordance with 820.40.

820.198 Complaint files.

(a) Each manufacturer shall maintain complaint files. Each manufac-turer shall establish and maintain procedures for receiving, reviewing, and evaluating complaints by a formally designated unit. Such procedures shall ensure that:

(1) All complaints are processed in a uniform and timely manner;

(2) Oral complaints are documented upon receipt; and

(3) Complaints are evaluated to determine whether the complaint represents an event which is required to be reported to FDA under part 803 or 804 of this chapter, Medical Device Reporting.

(b) Each manufacturer shall review and evaluate all complaints to determine whether an investigation is necessary. When no investigation is made, the manufacturer shall maintain a record that includes the reason no investigation was made and the name of the individual responsible for the deci-sion not to investigate.

(c) Any complaint involving the possible failure of a device, labeling, or packaging to meet any of its specifications shall be reviewed, evaluated, and investigated, unless such investigation has already been performed for a similar complaint and another investigation is not necessary.

(d) Any complaint that represents an event which must be reported to FDA under part 803 or 804 of this chapter shall be promptly reviewed, evaluated, and investigated by a designated individual(s) and shall be maintained in a separate portion of the complaint flies or otherwise clearly identified. In addition to the information required by 820.198(e), records of investigation under this paragraph shall include a determination of:

(1) Whether the device failed to meet specifications;

(2) Whether the device was being used for treatment or diagnosis; and

(3) The relationship, if any, of the device to the reported incident or adverse event.

(e) When an investigation is made under this section, a record of the investigation shall be maintained by the formally designated unit identified in paragraph (a) of this section. The record of investigation shall include:

(1) The name of the device;

(2) The date the complaint was received;

(3) Any device identification(s) and control number(s) used

(4) The name, address, and phone number of the complainant;

(5) The nature and details of the complaint;

(6) The dates and results of the investigation;

(7) Any corrective action taken; and

(8) Any reply to the complainant.

(f) When the manufacturer's formally designated complaint unit is located at a site separate from the manufacturing establishment, the investigated complaint(s) and the record(s) of investigation shall be reasonably accessible to the manufacturing establishment.

(g) If a manufacturer's formally designated complaint unit is located out-side of the United States, records required by this section shall be reasonably accessible in the United States at either:

(1) A location in the United States where the manufacturer's records are regularly kept; or

(2) The location of the initial distributor.

Subpart N — Servicing

820.200 Servicing.

(a) Where servicing is a specified re-quirement, each manufacturer shall establish and maintain instructions and procedures for performing and verifying that the servicing meets the specified requirements.

(b) Each manufacturer shall analyze service reports with appropriate statistical methodology in accordance with 820.100.

(c) Each manufacturer who receives a service report that represents an event which must be reported to FDA under part 803 or 804 of this chapter shall automatically consider the report a complaint and shall process it in accordance with the requirements of 820.198.

(d) Service reports shall be documented and shall include:

(1) The name of the device serviced;

(2) Any device identification(s) and control number(s) used;

(3) The date of service;

(4) The individual(s) servicing the device;

(5) The service performed; and

(6) The test and inspection data.

Subpart O — Statistical Techniques

820.250 Statistical techniques.

(a) Where appropriate, each manufacturer shall establish and maintain procedures for identifying valid statistical techniques required for establishing, controlling, and verifying the acceptability of process capability and product characteristics.

(b) Sampling plans, when used, shall be written and based on a valid statistical rationale. Each manufacturer shall establish and maintain procedures to ensure that sampling methods are adequate for their intended use and to ensure that when changes occur the sampling plans are reviewed. These activities shall be documented.

PRINCIPAL STORED GRAIN INSECTS

For safe and effective use of insecticides, always identify the problem correctly.

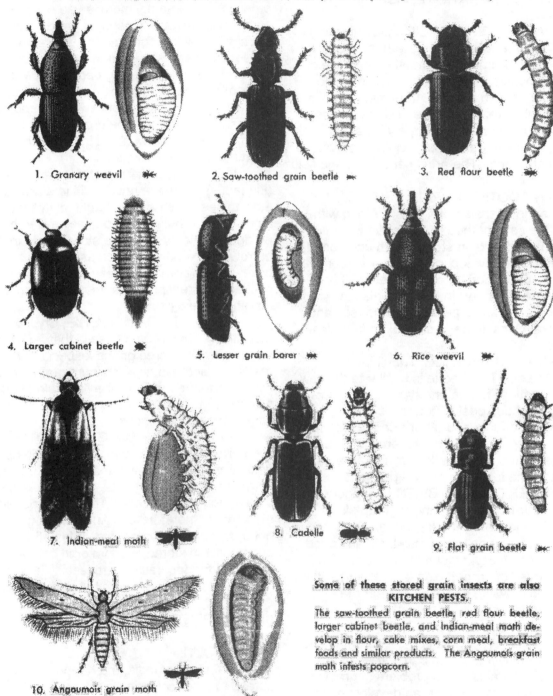

1. Granary weevil
2. Saw-toothed grain beetle
3. Red flour beetle
4. Larger cabinet beetle
5. Lesser grain borer
6. Rice weevil
7. Indian-meal moth
8. Cadelle
9. Flat grain beetle
10. Angoumois grain moth

Some of these stored grain insects are also KITCHEN PESTS.

The saw-toothed grain beetle, red flour beetle, larger cabinet beetle, and Indian-meal moth develop in flour, cake mixes, corn meal, breakfast foods and similar products. The Angoumois grain moth infests popcorn.

Prepared by Extension Entomologists of the North Central States in cooperation with the Federal Extension Service, U. S. Department of Agriculture

FACT SHEET ON PRINCIPAL STORED GRAIN INSECTS

THE INFORMATION OUTLINED BELOW IS REPRINTED WITH PERMISSION, AND ADAPTED FROM PUBLICATION E-80, APRIL, 1967, DEPARTMENT OF ENTOMOLOGY, COOPERATIVE EXTENSION SERVICE, PURDUE UNIVERSITY, LAFAYETTE, INDIANA 47907.

1. GRANARY WEEVIL, Sitophilus granarius (Linnaeus). This true weevil, along with the closely related rice weevil, is among the most destructive of all stored grain insects. The larvae develop inside kernels of whole grain in storage, thus making an infestation difficult to remove in the milling process. Therefore, the granary weevil is largely a pest of stored wheat, corn and barley, especially in elevators, mills and bulk storages. The adult cannot fly, and field infestations do not occur.

2. SAW-TOOTHED GRAIN BEETLE, Oryzaephilus surinamensis (Linnaeus). Along with flour beetles, the saw-toothed grain beetle is one of the most common insects in stored grain and cereal products. The larvae develop in flour, cereal products and many other dried foods, For this reason, it is a common pest not only in grain bins, but also in elevators, mills, processing plants, warehouses and kitchens. In grain bins, it feeds on broken kernels and grain residues.

3. RED FLOUR BEETLE, Tribolium castaneum (Herbst). This beetle is similar to the saw-toothed grain beetle in habits and types of products infested. It is a serious pest in flour mills and wherever cereal products and other dried foods are processed or stored. Like the confused flour beetle (not pictured), the red flour beetle may impart a bad odor that affects the taste of infested products.

4. LARGER CABINET BEETLE, Trogoderma inclusum (LeConte). Representing a group also referred to as Trogoderma, the larger cabinet beetle is a scavenger that feeds on cereal products and dried animal matter. The fuzzy, slow-moving larvae - similar to the larvae of carpet, hide and larder beetles - are often found crawling about on or near the products they infest.

5. LESSER GRAIN BORER, Rhyzopertha dominica (Fahricius). This pest is most common and destructive in warm climates but can spread to any area in transported grain. It is a problem of grain only and not cereal products. The larvae develop inside the kernels of whole grain. The adults also damage grain by boring into the kernels and leaving them covered with powder from the chewed material.

6. RICE WEEVIL, Sitophilus oryzae (Linnaeus). The rice weevil is similar to the granary weevil in both appearance and habits. The name is misleading, however, since it infests other grains besides rice. Adults can fly and, in warm climates, can cause widespread damage to corn, wheat and other grains before harvest.

7. INDIAN-MEAL MOTH, Plodia interpunctella (Hubner). Common to both stored grain and cereal products, Indian-meal moth larvae cause damage in corn meal, packaged foods, bagged grain and grain in storage. Attack is confined to surface layers of stored shelled corn and small grains. In the case of stored ear corn, however, feeding occurs anywhere, since the moths crawl among the ears to lay their eggs. Larval feeding is characterized by a webbing of the material infested. The mature larvae then often leave the material and crawl about in homes or buildings in search of a place to pupate.

8. CADELLE, Tenebroides mauritanicus (Linnaeus). Both the adult and larva are large and easy to see. Both stages feed mainly on the germ of stored grains, but may also attack milled cereal products. The larvae leave stored grain in the fall and burrow into woodwork, such as wooden bins or boxcars, to hibernate. They may also burrow into packaged cereal products, thus providing an entrance for other cereal pests.

9. FLAT GRAIN BEETLE, Cryptolestes pusillus (Schonherr). This is a tiny beetle that feeds primarily on the germ of stored grains, especially wheat. It is readily attracted to high-moisture grain. In fact, under high moisture conditions, the flat grain beetle may also develop in many cereal products, but it is not a common pest in kitchens.

10. ANGOUMOIS GRAIN MOTH, Sitotroga cerealella (Olivier). This is a common and destructive pest of crib ear corn. It also infests stored shelled corn and other small grains, but attack is confined to the surface layer of grain. The larvae develop within the kernels; therefore, the Angoumois grain moth is not a pest of cereal products. Infestations in homes often occur in stored popcorn or in colored ears of corn kept for decoration purposes. The moth resembles the clothes moth but does not shun light.

KHAPRA BEETLE

BACKGROUND

A native of India, the Khapra Beetle has spread to other countries in Asia, Africa, Europe, & North America. While it thrives best in warm climates, there is evidence that the beetle can survive cold winter months in heated warehouses and grain storage tanks. The beetle is a sluggish insect. It cannot fly and is spread entirely by shipping & trade. The problem of preventing the insect's spread is compounded by its ability to survive for several years without food & by its habit of hiding in cracks, crevices, and even behind paint scales. Left uncontrolled, they can make the surface of a grain bin come literally alive with millions of wiggling larvae eating their way down to the bottom.

HOSTS

In addition to the obvious grain and stored product hosts, the beetle turns up in a variety of locations that would not be obvious food sources for the pest. It is often found in the ears & seams of burlap bags & wrappers, in baled crepe rubber, automobiles, steel wire, books, corrugated boxes (glue), bags of bolts, & even soiled linen & priceless oil paintings. It is frequently intercepted on obvious food products such as rice and peanuts as well as dried animal skins. Such infestations result from storage of the products in infested warehouses, by transportation in infested carriers or from re-use of sacks that previously contained products infested by the Khapra Beetle.

DETECTION

Except for some attempts to develop traps and lures for the Khapra Beetle, the only sure inspection is visual. Certainly this is a meticulous chore because of the tiny size of the Khapra Beetle.

High risk areas first checked include:
1. cracks in flooring & walls
2. behind loose paint
3. along pallets
4. seams of burlap bags
5. any low light areas & dark crevices
6. trash from cleaning devices

Low risk areas for inspection include:
1. well-lighted areas or areas where sun-light penetrates
2. areas which are moist or where debris are covered by mold

Vacuum cleaners are now being used by inspectors to assist the inspection process to draw larvae & cast skins out of cracks & crevices. Filters are changed between inspection locations.

LIFE CYCLE AND DESCRIPTION

The tell-tale signs of a Khapra Beetle infestation are the larvae & their cast skins. The larvae are yellowish or reddish brown. Clothed with long barbed brown hairs, the larva has a tuft of longer hairs which gives it the typical carper beetle larva look. Adults are brown to blackish in color with indistinct red-brown markings on the wing covers. Hairy on top, they may have a slick appearance when hairs are rubbed off. Mature larvae and adult females are about 1/8 inch long; males are somewhat smaller. They pass through 5-9 moults during this stage, resulting in numerous cast skins. Adults are short-lived, persisting for a few days at temperatures over 100°F, or for perhaps several months or even years, at temperatures below 50°F. Adult activity is little noticed except at dusk, while remnants are seldom found as they are cleaned up by larvae. Mating occurs almost immediately following adult emergence, and egg deposition follows in from 1 to 6 days. Eggs are laid loosely among the host material infested. Hatching follows from 1 week to 2 weeks after deposition. Two types of larvae, short or long cycle, may develop. Under optimum conditions, the larval stage may be completed in less than a month, whereas under crowded, starving or cold conditions, long cycle larvae may hide out in large numbers in building crevices and may persist from several months to 3 years without food.

TREATMENT

Fumigation using methyl bromide is the treatment of choice. Because the pest secrets itself in cracks & crevices of the building it is in, in addition to the contents, the whole building must be treated. Typically, the building is covered tightly with tarpaulins and fumigant is pumped in at the approved rate of 6 to 9 pounds per 1,000 cu. ft. The process takes several hours depending on the size of the building, and strict safety precautions are taken.

MISCELLANEOUS FACTS

1. Last Khapra Beetle significant incident: 1978, single infested warehouse in Linden, NJ.
2. Last infestation found and eradicated: 1966.
3. Domestic quarantine revoked: September 2, 1972
4. Original find in U.S.: grain warehouse at Alpaugh, CA, November, 1973.
5. Infestations subsequently found and eradicated in Arizona, California, New Mexico, Texas, & Mexico.
6. Report suspected Khapra beetle infestations to State or Federal plant pest control inspectors. Collect samples in vials of alcohol. Submit samples of unsuspected Khapra Beetles to your District lab or mail to:

U.S. Department of Agriculture
Plant Protection & Quarantine Program
Federal Building
Hyattsville, Maryland 20782

LIFE CYCLES OF SELECTED STORAGE INSECTS

*These figures are approximate, and depend on food and environmental factors.

Insect	Number Eggs laid by female	Length of egg stage (days)	Length larval or nymphal stage (days)	Days of Total Development	Length of Adult Life
Coleoptera					
Cigarette/drug store	100	12-17	36-200	60-240	2-6 weeks
Cadelle	1000	7-10	60-400	85-400	1-2 years
Dermestids	100-200	7-14	30-700+	50-800+	2-4 weeks
Flat grain	100-400	3-4	20-80	40-90	1-12 months
Granery/Rice Maize	50-400	3-5	10-30	25-50	4-8 months
Tribolium	350-400	4-12	20-100	30-120	to 3 years
Sawtooth/ Merchant	20-285	3-5	14-50	20-70	6 months to 3 years
Lepidoptera (moths)					
Angoumois	40-389	7-14	25-100	35-150	2-15 days
Almond/Raisin/ Tobacco	20-400	3-4	20-60	35-60	2-26 days
Indian Meal	100-300	3-4	21-120	45-150	2-25 days
Mediterranean	100-400	3-9	22-120	30-150	9-14 days
Diptera (flies)					
Housefly	200-1000	1-3	3-60	6-65	19-50 days
Drosophila	400-900	1-2	3-8	7-12	2-5 months
Orthoptera Cockroaches	100-1000	35-100	30-500	65-600	up to 2.5 years

PERPETUAL JULIAN CALENDAR
For NON-LEAP YEARS*

	JAN	FEB	MAR	APR	MAY	JUN	JUL	AUG	SEP	OCT	NOV	DEC	
1	1	32	60	91	121	152	182	213	244	274	305	335	1
2	2	33	61	92	122	153	183	214	245	275	306	336	2
3	3	34	62	93	123	154	184	215	246	276	307	337	3
4	4	35	63	94	124	155	185	216	247	277	308	338	4
5	5	36	64	95	125	156	186	217	248	278	309	339	5
6	6	37	65	96	126	157	187	218	249	279	310	340	6
7	7	38	66	97	127	158	188	219	250	280	311	341	7
8	8	39	67	98	128	159	189	220	251	281	312	342	8
9	9	40	68	99	129	160	190	221	252	282	313	343	9
10	10	41	69	100	130	161	191	222	253	283	314	344	10
11	11	42	70	101	131	162	192	223	254	284	315	345	11
12	12	43	71	102	132	163	193	224	255	285	316	346	12
13	13	44	72	103	133	164	194	225	256	286	317	347	13
14	14	45	73	104	134	165	195	226	257	287	318	348	14
15	15	46	74	105	135	166	196	227	258	288	319	349	15
16	16	47	75	106	136	167	197	228	259	289	320	350	16
17	17	48	76	107	137	168	198	229	260	290	321	351	17
18	18	49	77	108	138	169	199	230	261	291	322	352	18
19	19	50	78	109	139	170	200	231	262	292	323	353	19
20	20	51	79	110	140	171	201	232	263	293	324	354	20
21	21	52	80	111	141	172	202	233	264	294	325	355	21
22	22	53	81	112	142	173	203	234	265	295	326	356	22
23	23	54	82	113	143	174	204	235	266	296	327	357	23
24	24	55	83	114	144	175	205	236	267	297	328	358	24
25	25	56	84	115	145	176	206	237	268	298	329	359	25
26	26	57	85	116	146	177	207	238	269	299	330	360	26
27	27	58	86	117	147	178	208	239	270	300	331	361	27
28	28	59	87	118	148	179	209	240	271	301	332	362	28
29	29		88	119	149	180	210	241	272	302	333	363	29
30	30		89	120	150	181	211	242	273	303	334	364	30
31	31		90		151		212	243		304		365	31

*A leap year is any year whose number is exactly divisible by 4, except century years, which are leap years only if exactly divisible by 400.

Leap years from 1960 to 2000:

1960	1964	1968	1972
1976	1980	1984	1988
1992	1996	2000	

The Julian Calendar for Leap years is provided by adding 1 to all values starting with March 1, in the above table; and by assigning 60 to February 29.

BLOOD VALUES
Blood Chemistry - Normal Values

B – Whole Blood   P – Plasma   S – Serum

Constituent	Material	Mg./100 cc. (mg. %) (or as noted)
Electrolytes		
Calcium	S	9 - 11 (4.5-5.5 mEq./l.)
Chloride	S	350 - 390 (100-110 mEq./l.)
Chloride as NaCl	P	580 - 630 (99-106 mEq./l.)
Magnesium	S	1.8 - 3.6 (1.5-3.0 mEq./l.)
Phosphorus:		
Children	S	4 - 6.5 (2.3-3.8 mEq./l.)
Adults	S	3 - 4.5 (1.8-2.3 mEq./l.)
Potassium	S	18 - 22 (3.5-5.5 mEq./l.)
Sodium	S	310 - 340 (135-147 mEq./l.)
Enzymes		
Amylase	P, S	70 - 200 units (Somogyi)
Cholinesterase	S	0.5 - 1.5 pH units
Lipase.	S	0.2 - 1.5 units/cc. (N/20 NaOH)
Phosphatase, acid	S	0.5 - 3.5 units (King - Armstrong)
Phosphatase, alkaline:		
Children	S	5 - 14 units (Bodansky)
		15 - 20 units (King - Armstrong)
Adults	S	2 - 4.5 units (Bodansky)
Transaminase		4 - 13 units (King - Armstrong)
Glutamic oxalacetic (SGOT)	S	up to 40 units
Pyruvic (SGPT)	S	up to 30 units
Steroids		
17-Hydroxycorticosteroids:		
Males	P	13 ± 6 mcg./100 ml.
Females	P	15 ± 6 mcg./100 ml.
17-Ketosteroids	P	60 mcg./100 ml.
Vitamins		
Ascorbic acid	P	0.4 - 1.0
Nicotinic acid	P	0.1 - 0.3
Riboflavin	B	35 - 45 mcg./100 cc.
Thiamine	S	3.5 - 4.2 mcg./100 cc.
Vitamin A	S	40 - 60 mcg./100 cc.
Vitamin B	P	0.8 - 1.2
Other		
Albumin.	S	3.5 - 5.5 Gm./100 cc.
Carbon Dioxide (combining power)	S	56 - 65 Vol. % (25-30 mEq./l.)
Carotenoids	S	100 - 300 int. units/100 cc.
Cholesterol, total	S	110 - 300
Cholesterol, free	S	40 - 50
Cholesterol, esterfied.	S	75 - 210
Creatine	B	3 - 7
Creatinine	B	1 - 2
Fibrinogen	P	150 - 300
Globulin	S	1.5 - 3.4 Gm./100 cc.
Glucose	B	80 - 120
Glutamine	P, S	0 - 2
Iodide, Protein-bound	S	4 - 8 mcg./100 cc.
Iron	P	50 - 180 mcg./100 cc.
Iron-binding capacity	S	300 - 360 mcg./100 cc.
Lactic acid	B	6 - 20
Non-protein Nitrogen	B,S	25 - 40
Proteins, total	P,S	6.3 - 8.0 Gm./100 cc.
Pyruvic acid.	B	0.7 - 1.2
Urea	B	20 - 40
Urea nitrogen	B,S	10 - 20
Uric acid	S	2 - 4

BLOOD VALUES
Normal Blood

HEMATOCRIT	Men: 45% (38-54%) Women: 40% (36-47%)	**HEMOGLOBIN**	Men: 14 - 18 Gm.% Women: 12 - 16 Gm.% Children: 12 - 14 Gm.% Newborn: 14.5 -24.5 Gm.%*

Blood Counts	per cu. mm.	%
Erythrocytes		
Men	$5.0 (4.5 - 6.0) \times 10^4$	
Women.	$4.5 (4.3 - 5.5) \times 10^4$	
Reticulocytes.		0 - 1%
Leukocytes, total		100%
Myelocytes.	5,000 - 10,000	0%
Juvenile neutrophiles.	0	0 - 1%
Band neutrophiles	0 - 100	0 - 5%
Segmented neutrophiles . . .	0 - 500	40 - 60%
Lymphocytes	2,500 - 6,000	20 - 40%
Eosinophiles	1,000 - 4,000	1 - 3%
Basophiles	50 - 300	0 - 1%
Monocytes	0 - 100	4 - 8%
Platelets	200 - 800 200,000 - 500,000	

RBC Measurements	
Diameters	5.5 - 8.8 microns (Newborn: 8.6*)
Mean Corpuscular	
Volume	80 - 94 cu. microns (Newborn: 106*)
Mean Corpuscular Hb	27 - 32 micro-micrograms
Mean Corpuscular Hb	(Newborn: 38*)
Conc.	33 - 38%
Color, Saturation and Volume	
Indices, each:	*1*

Miscellaneous	
Bleeding time	1 - 3 minutes (Duke) 2 - 4 minutes (Ivy)
Circulation time, arm to tongue (sodium dehydrocholate). . .	9 - 16 seconds
Clot retraction time	2 - 4 hours
Coagulation time (venous). . .	6 - 10 minutes (Lee & White) 10 - 30 minutes (Howell)
Fragility, erythorocyte (hemolysis)	0.44 - 0.35% NaCl
Prothrombin time.	10 - 20 seconds (Quick)
Sedimentation rate:	
Men.	0 - 9 mm. per hour (Wintrobe)
Women	0 - 20 mm. per hour (Wintrobe)

*Values for newborn are shown only where they may differ significantly from those of older children and adults.

CONVERSION FACTORS

TEMPERATURE: If F and C denote readings on the Fahrenheit and centigrade standard scales, respectively, for the same, then

$$C = 5/9*(F - 32) \qquad F = (9/5)*C + 32$$

Some common reference points are:

0°C = 32°F, 22°C = 71.6°F, 37°C = 98.6°F, and 100°C = 212°F.

CONVERSION TABLE FOR MEDICATED FEEDS:

1 Pound = 453.6 Grams
1 Gram = 0.0022 Pounds
1 Gram = 1,000 Milligrams
1 Gram = 1,000,000 Micrograms
1 Kilogram = 1,000 Grams
1 Kilogram = 2.205 Pounds
1 Milligram = 0.001 Grams

1 Milligram = 1,000 Micrograms
1 Microgram = 0.001 Milligrams
1 Milicrogram Per Gram = 1 Part Per Million
1 Part Per Million (PPM) = 0.454 Mg/Lb.
1 Part Per Million (PPm) = 0.907 Grams Per Ton

HOUSEHOLD MEASURES:
1 teaspoon (tsp) = 5cc = 1 fl dram
1 dessertspoon = 8cc = 2 fl drams
1 tablespoon (tbsp) = 15cc = 1/2 fl ounce
1 teacup = 120cc = 4 fl ounces
1 tumbler = 240cc = 8 fl ounces = 1/2 pint
8 pints = 4 quarts = 1 gallon = 128 fluid ounces

CONVERSION TABLES

To convert From	To	Multiply By	To convert From	To	Multiply By
Length			Length		
mm	Inches	.03937	inches	mm	25.40
Inches	.3937	inches	cm		**2.540**
meters	Inches	39.37	inches	meters	.0254
meters	Feet	3.281	feet	meters	.3048
meters	Yards	1.0936	feet	km	.0003048
km	Feet	3230.8	yards	meters	.9144
km	Yards	1093.6	yards	km	.0009144
km	Miles	.6214	miles	km	1.609
Area			Area		
sq mm	sq inches	.00155	sq inches	sq mm	645.2
sq cm	sq inches	.155	sq inches	sq cm	6.452
sq meters	sq feet	10.764	sq feet	sq meters	.09290
sq meters	sq yards	1.196	sq yards	sq meters	.8361
sq km	sq miles	.3861	sq miles	sq km	2.590
hectares	Acres	2.471	acres	hectares	.4047
Volume			Volume		
cu cm	cu inches	.06102	cu inches	cu cm	16.387
cu cm	fl ounces	.03381	cu inches	liters	.01639
cu meters	cu feet	35.314	cu feet	cu meters	.02832
cu meters	cu yards	1.308	cu feet	liters	28.317
cu meters	US gal	264.2	cu yards	cu meters	.7646
liters	cu inches	61.023	fl ounces	cu cu	29.57
liters	cu feet	.03531	US gal	cu meters	.003785
liters	US gal	.2642	US gal	liters	3.785
Weight			Weight		
grams	Grains	15.432	grains	grams	.0648
grams	Ounces*	.0353	ounces*	grams	28.350
kg	Ounces*	35.27	ounces*	kg	.02335
kg	Pounds	2.2046	pounds*	kg	.4536
kg	US tons	.001102	pounds*	metric tons	.000454
kg	long tons	.000984	US tons	kg	907.2
metric tons	Pounds	2204.6	US tons	metric tons	.9072
metric tons	US tons	1.1023	long tons	kg	1016.
metric tons	long tons	.9842	long tons	metric tons	1.0160
Unit Weight			Unit Weight		
gr/sq cm	lb/sq in	.01422	lb/ft	kg/m	1.4881
gr/cu cm	lb/cu in	.0361	lb/sq in	gr/sq cm	70.31
kg/sq cm	lb/sq in	14.22	lb/sq in	kg/sq cm	.07031
kg/cu m	lb/cu ft	.0624	lb/cu in	gr/cu cm	27.68
kg/m	lb/ft	.6720	lb/cu ft	kg/cu m	16.018

CONVERSION TABLES (cont.)

To convert From	To	Multiply By	To convert From	To	Multiply By
Unit Volume			Unit Volume		
liters/min	US gpm	.2642	US gpm	liters/min	3.785
liters/min	Cfm	.03531	US gpm	liters/hr	237.1
liters/hr	US gpm	.0044	US gpm	cu m/hr	.2371
cu m/min	Cfm	35.314	cfm	liters/min	26.317
cu m/hr	Cfm	.5886	cfm	cu m/min	.02832
cu m/hr	US gpm	4.4028	cfm	cu m/hr	1.6992
Power			Power		
watts	ft-lb/sec	.7376	ft-lb/sec	watts	1.365
watts	Hp	.00134	hp	watts	745.7
kw	Hp	1.3410	hp	kw	.7457
cheval-vap	Hp	.9863	hp	cheval-vap	1.0139
Heat			Heat		
gr-cal	Btu	.003969	Btu	gr-cal	252.
kg/cal	Btu	3.9693	Btu	kg/cal	.252
kg-cal/kg	Btu/lb	1.800	Btu/lb	kg-cal/kg	.5556
gr-cal/sq cm	Btu/sq ft	3.687	Btu/ sq ft	gr-cal/sq cm	.2713
kg-cal/cu m	Btu/cu ft	.1124	Btu/cu ft	kg-cal/cu m	8.899
Work/Energy			Work/Energy		
joule	ft-lb	.7376	ft-lb	joule	1.356
meter-kg	ft-lb	7.2330	ft-lb	meter-kg	.1383
gr-cal	ft-lb	3.067	ft-lb	gr-cal	.3239
kg-cal	ft-lb	3067	ft-lb	kg-cal	.0003239
hp-hr	ft-lb	1,980,000	ft-lb	hp-hr	5.051×10
kwhr	ft-lb	2,650,000	ft-lb	kwhr	3.766×10
Btu	ft-lb	778.	ft-lb	Btu	.0012856

*---------- pounds and ounces

Food and Drug Administration Field Offices

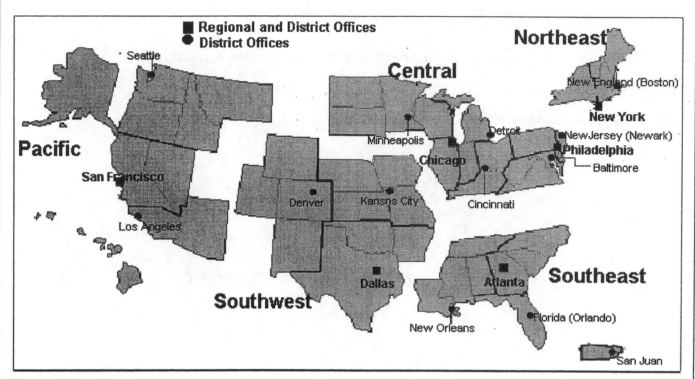

■ Regional and District Offices
● District Offices

Alaska is in the Seattle District
Hawaii, Guam and American Somoa are in the San Francisco District
Puerto Rico (San Juan District) is in the Southeast Region
The U.S. Virgin Islands are in the San Juan District

Directions: To file a request for change in the IOM, complete the top portion of this form, down to and including "Attachments: Yes or No". E-mail your request to IOM@ORA.FDA.GOV or send it to Alan Gion FDA/Division of Field Investigations (DFI) (HFC-130), 5600 Fishers Lane, Room 13-64, Rockville, Maryland 20857

IOM CHANGE REQUEST

ICR No._____(HQ assigned)   Date ___/___/___

IOM Subchapter _____(or Foreword, Contents, Exhibits, Appendix, Index)

Originator_____District/HQ_____ Phone_____

Reason for Change Request (Define in Detail)

Solution Recommended (If known)   Priority - Urgent / High / Routine

Attachments: Yes or No _____

(For HQ use only)

Concurred Yes or No Signature_____Date ___/___/___

Comment

Assigned To   _____Priority - Urgent / High/Routine

IOM Change Notice (ICN) No. _____Date ___/___/___

Solution to Problem

Concurred/Signature _____Date ___/___/___
===

Form No.   Rev. 03   Approved by   RPM   Date 04/2000

INDEX

A

D

G

H

I

J

L

M

MACARONI, 147, 253, 448, 476-477, 479, 485, 499, 503, 505-506

MACHINERY, 19, 137, 224, 252, 255-256, 472, 475

MANUFACTURING CODES, 157, 262, 270-271, 280-282

MARSHAL, U.S., 234, 332, 335-336, 382

MEDICAL DEVICE REPORT
  distinguishing from consumer complaint, 383

MEDICAL DEVICE REPORTING, 231, 266, 329, 345, 362, 382, 440, 450, 557, 558, 560-561, 565, 575

MEDICAL DEVICES, 35, 42-45, 50, 81, 91, 97-98, 105, 107, 109, 120-121, 137, 148, 164, 219, 225, 231, 266-268, 273, 277, 280, 331, 342, 344-346, 359, 361, 363, 382, 384-385, 391-392, 435-436, 440-441, 443, 446-447, 450, 512, 568
  IDE, 37-38, 42, 44, 270, 281, 329, 343
  PMA, 42, 44, 225-226, 266-267, 269-270, 274, 281, 344, 361-362, 440-441, 557, 567

METHYL BROMIDE, 13, 475, 483

MILK, 17, 48, 50-51, 56, 58-59, 63, 67, 73, 91, 95-96, 109-111, 119-122, 141, 143, 238-239, 258, 277, 310, 329, 331, 337, 341, 349-350, 359, 361, 380, 390, 437, 448, 451, 458-462, 465-468, 470-472, 474, 477-483, 485-486, 488-491, 493-494, 496-497, 499-506, 547
  cultured milk products, 258
  dry milk, 95-96, 119-121, 258, 349
  dry milk plants, 95
  milk act,, 310, 331, 451
  milk safety, 48, 51, 239, 258, 350, 437
  pasteurized, 51, 331, 349, 523

MIRANDA
  miranda warning, 334

MOU, 50, 91-102, 105-112, 119-122, 150, 258, 272, 274-275, 345

N

NARCOTICS, 91, 100, 135

NATIONAL INSTITUTE OF DRUG ABUSE (NIDA), 91, 99

NEW ANIMAL DRUG APPLICATION, 85, 277, 318, 329, 347, 444

NOTICE OF INSPECTION, 103, 105, 128, 130, 134, 150, 218, 220, 223, 227-228, 233-235, 244, 250, 256, 258, 271, 279, 330, 333, 360, 364

O

OASIS, 24, 51, 86, 163, 222, 309, 312-315, 319

OFFICE OF REGULATORY AFFAIRS, 11, 34, 48, 398, 434, 445

OFFICIAL CREDENTIALS, BADGE, 1, 19
  CSO limits, 11, 24, 108, 330

OFFICIAL SAMPLES, 6, 105, 128, 130-133, 136, 240, 257, 276, 341, 395

ORGANOLEPTIC EXAMINATION, 148, 231, 254, 317, 335

OSHA, 11-12, 16, 91, 100, 105-106, 272, 382

OUT OF BUSINESS, 364, 399

P

PACKAGING, 47, 146, 159-160, 162-164, 166, 218, 231, 253-254, 264, 310, 317, 331, 348, 361, 390, 395-396, 439, 441-442, 451-452, 454, 456, 470, 519, 522-524, 526-528, 531-533, 537, 539-540, 542, 544, 546, 549, 568-569, 573-576
  package identification, 129, 162

PER DIEM, 1, 5, 315, 336

PERSONAL SAFETY, 234, 236, 386

PESTICIDES, 15, 47, 64, 95-96, 106, 109-111, 121, 164, 219, 224, 231, 252, 255, 274-276, 309, 317, 341, 376, 437, 457, 463, 540, 543-544

PHOSPHINE, 13, 458

PHOTOGRAPHS, 4, 129, 133, 142, 144-145, 153, 155, 158-159, 218, 233, 240-242, 251-252, 255-256, 270, 280-282, 336, 373, 381, 391, 396

POULTRY PRODUCTS, 93-94, 96, 108, 257, 329, 331, 334, 338, 375, 387, 389
  Poultry Products Inspection Act, 93-94, 257, 329, 334, 338, 387

PRESS, 1, 18, 92, 224, 231, 236, 240, 343, 360, 381, 433, 515

PROCESS FILING, 329, 341, 347-348

PROFESSIONAL STATURE, 1, 20

PROMOTION, 50, 153, 219, 244, 257, 260, 264, 270-271, 277, 281-283, 392, 459

PROSECUTION, 128, 131, 149-150, 228, 235, 279, 319, 329, 332-333, 337, 374, 394

PROTECTION, 1, 3-4, 12-13, 16-17, 19, 22, 43, 50, 91-92, 97, 102-106, 108-109, 111-122, 159, 218, 235, 252, 254-255, 275, 315, 332, 336-337, 375, 386, 389, 395, 448, 454, 514, 520, 524, 528-530, 533, 561-562

PROTECTIVE EQUIPMENT, 1, 11-13, 15

PUBLIC HEALTH SERVICE (PHS), 331

PUBLIC HEALTH SERVICE ACT, 50, 234-235, 271, 310, 331, 345-346, 519, 551, 553

PUBLICITY, 18, 364, 514

Q

QUALITY
  quality assurance, 36, 39, 51, 92, 97-99, 105, 133, 157, 218-219, 223, 226, 231, 233, 244, 264-265, 267, 269, 272, 278, 435, 543, 575
  quality audit, 219, 267, 569-570, 574
  quality control, 44, 120, 218, 233, 252, 254, 264, 330, 337, 345, 360-361, 364, 444, 448, 519, 522, 524-527, 529-531, 534-535, 537-538, 540, 543-544, 551, 555

R

RADIATION, 14, 16, 35, 43, 67, 98, 100, 109, 114, 117,

119, 162, 220, 265, 267, 310, 318-319, 329-331, 335, 345, 387, 391, 451, 479, 494, 539
ionizing radiation, 16, 451, 494
RAW MATERIALS INSPECTION, 16, 20, 132-133, 145-146, 149, 218, 240, 244, 251-256, 259-260, 263-264, 283, 337, 396, 519, 522-524, 544
RECALL
audit checks, 23, 359-360, 364-365
RECALL AUDIT CHECK, 364-365
RECALLS, 96-97, 110, 128, 140, 225, 265-266, 270-272, 281-282, 331, 337, 359-361, 363-365, 435, 508, 514, 516, 536
RECONDITIONING, 128, 133, 136, 155, 309, 311, 314-315, 329, 332, 335-337, 341, 361, 365, 370, 386, 389-391
RECORDINGS, 25, 218, 224, 236, 241-243
video, 241-242, 264, 434
RECORDS, 7, 11, 17, 21, 23-24, 26, 92, 96-97, 99, 106, 108-109, 128-132, 135-136, 139, 148-152, 154-156, 158-159, 162-163, 218-222, 226-228, 230-231, 233, 236, 240-248, 250, 254, 257, 261, 263-265, 267-272, 276, 280, 283, 309-310, 316, 318, 330-332, 343-345, 348-349, 360-361, 370, 373-374, 376, 378-384, 389, 391, 397-399, 438, 446-448, 451, 517-518, 526-527, 529, 531-533, 536-539, 541-543, 545-548, 551, 555-557, 561-562, 569, 571, 573-576
electronic, 18-19, 24-25, 35, 37, 42, 44, 100, 102, 109, 119, 154, 158, 164, 218-220, 230, 237, 242, 245-248, 264-265, 270, 278, 281-283, 311-313, 316, 318-319, 330-331, 335, 343, 345, 361, 363, 398, 434-436, 441, 446-448, 451, 523, 529, 532, 536, 544-545, 556-558, 560-565, 567, 569, 572
identifying originals, 245
listing, 6, 44, 80, 89, 94, 109, 112, 119, 145-146, 152, 163, 218-219, 225, 232, 235, 247-248, 250, 253, 257, 259-260, 262, 264, 266-267, 270, 272-273, 276, 282, 310, 313, 316-318, 329, 342-343, 345-348, 391, 399, 433-434, 440-441, 445, 448-452, 502, 508, 516
non-FDA documents, 218, 222
records obtained, 132, 149, 218, 244-245
review, 15, 21, 25, 34, 36-41, 43-44, 46-48, 100, 106, 122, 136, 148, 154, 158, 160, 164, 218, 224-226, 229, 231-232, 235-236, 243-245, 248-250, 254, 256-268, 270, 272, 276-278, 281, 309, 312-314, 316-319, 333, 342-345, 360-361, 373, 377-378, 380-384, 386, 389, 392, 395, 397-399, 433, 440, 446, 448, 454, 459, 462, 514-515, 517, 526, 531, 536-538, 551-552, 561, 569-571, 573-575
sample records, 128, 149, 159
written demand for records, 220, 250
RECRUITING, 1, 18
REFERENCES MATERIALS, 271, 433
REFUSAL, 21, 24, 128, 134, 150, 152, 218, 220, 227, 233-236, 253, 262, 272, 281, 309-311, 313-316, 438, 560
to Permit Sampling, 128, 134, 141, 233
REGISTRATION/LISTING, 219, 260, 273, 316, 345
REGULATORY NOTES, 1, 5, 25-26, 139, 142, 241-242, 245

REGULATORY SAMPLE, 341
RELABELING, 279, 309, 314-315, 329, 332, 335, 370, 389, 569
RENTAL, 1-3, 6
REPORTING, 1-2, 4-5, 9, 11, 18, 20, 24-25, 36, 48, 79, 98, 101, 105, 129, 153, 219, 222-223, 230-232, 236, 249, 257, 259, 261-266, 274-275, 278-281, 318, 329, 331, 336-337, 341, 345, 359, 361-362, 365, 370-373, 375, 378-385, 391-394, 398-399, 440-445, 450, 516-518, 555-567, 570, 575
REPROCESSING, 263, 390, 440, 519, 531, 535, 539
RESEARCH, 9, 16, 34-40, 42-43, 45-50, 54, 69, 72, 91, 97, 105-107, 120, 163-164, 221, 261, 268, 318, 329, 342, 345-346, 359, 370, 381, 383, 385, 392-394, 441, 446, 449, 451, 536, 551-553, 556, 562, 565
RESERVE SAMPLES, 397, 535-536
RESPONSIBLE OFFICIALS, 536
RODENTS, 17, 143, 160, 239-240, 254-256, 378, 437, 519, 528, 540

S

SAFETY, 1, 3-4, 11-16, 21-22, 34, 36-51, 53, 69-71, 74, 91, 94-98, 100-103, 105-109, 112, 120-122, 139, 141, 146, 150, 160, 162-164, 220-222, 224, 234-236, 238-239, 250, 254, 258, 265, 267, 269, 272, 277-278, 310, 329-331, 336, 338, 344-345, 347-348, 350, 359-360, 365, 379, 383, 385-386, 435, 437-443, 445, 454-455, 519-520, 525, 527-530, 533, 539-540, 543-544, 546, 549-550, 556-557, 562, 569
ethylene oxide, 13, 15, 265, 467, 469, 471, 473, 484
ethylene oxide, 13, 15, 265, 467, 469, 471, 473, 484
from blood borne pathogens, 272
from contagious animal disease, 239
guidelines, 6, 37, 39, 43, 46-47, 51, 93-95, 108, 160, 219, 229, 260, 272-273, 433, 437, 439, 441, 444, 448-449, 516
material safety data sheets, 13, 160, 224, 238
material safety data sheets, 13, 160, 224, 238
personal safety, 234, 236, 386
personal safety, 234, 236, 386
safety hazards, 15, 437
vaccination against viral infection, 16
SALMONELLA SURVEILLANCE PROGRAM, 96
SAMPLE INTEGRITY
and the common carrier, 133, 159, 161, 165
SAMPLE SCHEDULE, 129, 138, 142, 145, 195-217, 254, 276, 317, 319, 376, 378, 390
canned foods, 146, 220, 317, 391
colors, 34, 46-47, 163, 253-254, 276, 348-349, 384-385, 436, 448, 491, 508-512, 553
drugs, 15, 34-35, 38-41, 45, 50, 64, 75, 81, 95-100, 105-111, 113-120, 122, 128, 132, 135, 148, 150, 157, 163-166, 219, 221, 225-226, 231-233, 239, 252-253, 259-262, 271-273, 277-278, 280, 309-310, 315, 317-318, 329-331, 337, 342, 344, 346-347, 359, 365, 370, 380-381, 384-387, 396, 398, 433, 435-436, 439, 441-445, 447-453, 458, 508-509, 511, 513, 515-516, 525-526, 536, 540-542,